Lecture Notes in Artificial Intelligence 2475
Subseries of Lecture Notes in Computer Science
Edited by J. G. Carbonell and J. Siekmann

Lecture Notes in Computer Science
Edited by G. Goos, J. Hartmanis, and J. van Leeuwen

Springer
*Berlin
Heidelberg
New York
Hong Kong
London
Milan
Paris
Tokyo*

James J. Alpigini   James F. Peters
Andrzej Skowron   Ning Zhong (Eds.)

Rough Sets and Current Trends in Computing

Third International Conference, RSCTC 2002
Malvern, PA, USA, October 14-16, 2002
Proceedings

Springer

Series Editors

Jaime G. Carbonell, Carnegie Mellon University, Pittsburgh, PA, USA
Jörg Siekmann, University of Saarland, Saarbrücken, Germany

Volume Editors

James J. Alpigini
Penn State Great Valley School of Professional Graduate Studies
30 East Swedesford Road, Malvern, PA 19355, USA
E-mail: jja7@psu.edu

James F. Peters
University of Manitoba, Department of Electrical and Computer Engineering
Winnipeg, MB R3T 5V6, Canada
E-mail: jfpeters@ee.umanitoba.ca

Andrzej Skowron
Warsaw University, Institute of Mathematics
Banacha 2, 02-097 Warsaw, Poland
E-mail: skowron@mimuw.edu.pl

Ning Zhong
Maebashi Institute of Technology
Department of Systems and Information Engineering
460-1 Kamisadori-Cho, Maebashi-City 371-0816, Japan
E-mail: zhong@maebashi-it.ac.jp

Cataloging-in-Publication Data applied for

Die Deutsche Bibliothek - CIP-Einheitsaufnahme

Rough sets and current trends in computing : third international conference ;
proceedings / RSCTC 2002, Malvern, PA, USA, October 14 - 16, 2002.
James J. Alpigini ... (ed.). - Berlin ; Heidelberg ; New York ; Hong Kong ;
London ; Milan ; Paris ; Tokyo : Springer, 2002
  (Lecture notes in computer science ; Vol. 2475 : Lecture notes in
artificial intelligence)
  ISBN 3-540-44274-X

CR Subject Classification (1998): I.2, F.4.1, F.1, I.5.1, I.4, H.2.8

ISSN 0302-9743
ISBN 3-540-44274-X Springer-Verlag Berlin Heidelberg New York

This work is subject to copyright. All rights are reserved, whether the whole or part of the material is
concerned, specifically the rights of translation, reprinting, re-use of illustrations, recitation, broadcasting,
reproduction on microfilms or in any other way, and storage in data banks. Duplication of this publication
or parts thereof is permitted only under the provisions of the German Copyright Law of September 9, 1965,
in its current version, and permission for use must always be obtained from Springer-Verlag. Violations are
liable for prosecution under the German Copyright Law.

Springer-Verlag Berlin Heidelberg New York,
a member of BertelsmannSpringer Science+Business Media GmbH

http://www.springer.de

© Springer-Verlag Berlin Heidelberg 2002
Printed in Germany

Typesetting: Camera-ready by author, data conversion by PTP-Berlin, Stefan Sossna e.K.
Printed on acid-free paper   SPIN: 10871364   06/3142   5 4 3 2 1 0

Preface

This volume contains the papers selected for presentation at the Third International Conference on Rough Sets and Current Trends in Computing (RSCTC 2002) held at Penn State Great Valley, Malvern, Pennsylvania, U.S.A., 14–16 October 2002. Rough set theory and its applications constitute a branch of soft computing that has exhibited a significant growth rate during recent years. RSCTC 2002 provided a forum for exchanging ideas among many researchers in the rough set community and in various areas of soft computing and served as a stimulus for mutual understanding and cooperation. In recent years, there have been a number of advances in rough set theory and applications. Hence, we have witnessed a growing number of international workshops on rough sets and their applications. In addition, it should be observed that one of the beauties of rough sets and the rough set philosophy is that it tends to complement and reinforce research in many traditional research areas and applications. This is the main reason that many international conferences are now including rough sets into the list of topics.

It is our great pleasure to dedicate this volume to Professor Zdzislaw Pawlak, who created rough set theory over twenty years ago. The growth of rough set theory and applications owes a great deal to Professor Pawlak's vibrant enthusiasm and wit as well as his great generosity towards others, especially in encouraging and advising beginners in rough sets. The depth, breadth, and richness of current rough set research are directly traceable to Professor Pawlak's inventiveness and the richness of his many insights and ideas concerning data mining, machine learning, logic, and mathematics. The computational features of rough sets are also giving rise to new forms of neurocomputing based on rough sets and to a family known as rough processors for digital computers. We would also like to congratulate Professor Pawlak, who received an honorary doctorate (Doctor Honoris Causa) from Poznań Polytechnic University, Poznań, Poland on 10 April 2002.

We wish to express our gratitude to Professors Zdzislaw Pawlak and Lotfi A. Zadeh, who accepted our invitation to serve as honorary chairs and to present keynote papers for this conference. We also wish to thank Professors J. Komorowski, T.Y. Lin, D.W. Russell, R. Slowiński, and I.B. Türksen for accepting our invitation to be plenary speakers at RSCTC 2002.

The papers contributed to this volume reflect advances in rough sets as well as complementary research efforts in the following areas:

- Rough set foundations
- Rough sets and fuzzy sets
- Rough neurocomputing
- Rough sets and probabilistic reasoning
- Rough set methods

- Rough set applications in biology, classification, dynamical systems, image processing, medical diagnosis, musicology, neurology, pattern recognition, robotics and robotic control systems, signal analysis, software engineering, and web mining
- Computing with words and granular computing
- Machine learning and pattern recognition
- Data mining

We wish to express our thanks to the members of the Advisory Board: N. Cercone, J. Grzymała-Busse, T.Y. Lin, A. Nakamura, S.K. Pal, L. Polkowski, R. Slowiński, H. Tanaka, S. Tsumoto, Y.Y. Yao, and W. Ziarko for their contribution to the scientific program of this conference. We also wish to thank the local committee for their help in organizing this conference: P. McFadden, C. Neill, K. Patel, F. Ramsey, and S.S. Slish.

The accepted papers that appear in this volume were selected from over 100 submitted draft papers. These papers were divided into regular communications (each allotted 8 pages) and short communications (each allotted 4 pages) on the basis of reviewer evaluations. Most papers received three or more reviews. The reviewing process itself rested with the RSCTC 2002 Program Chairs, members of the RSCTC 2002 Advisory Board, and the following members of the Program Committee: P. Apostoli, M. Beynon, H.D. Burkhard, G. Cattaneo, J.S. Deogun, P. Doherty, D. Dubois, I. Duentsch, S. Greco, X. Hu, M. Inuiguchi, J. Järvinen, J. Komorowski, B. Kostek, J. Koronacki, M. Kryszkiewicz, C.-J. Liau, P. Lingras, B. Matarazzo, E. Menasalvas, Z. Michalewicz, R. Michalski, N. Michinori, S. Miyamoto, M. Moshkov, T. Murai, H.S. Nguyen, E. Orłowska, W. Pedrycz, M. Quafafou, S. Ramanna, Z. Raś, J. Stefanowski, J. Stepaniuk, Z. Suraj, A. Szałas, M. Szczuka, A. Wakulicz-Deja, G. Wang.

We also would like to acknowledge help in reviewing from P. Balbiani, J. Bazan, K. Dembczynski, D. Niwiński, G. Góra, Y. Kawahara, R. Latkowski, J. Małuszyński, H. Midelfart, J.M. Peña, A. Radzikowska, D. Ślęzak, P. Synak, S. Wilk, A. Wojna, J. Wróblewski, M. Zawadowski.

Special thanks are also extended to Marcin Szczuka, Jakub Wróblewski, and Dominik Ślęzak for their help in typesetting and preparing the RSCTC 2002 proceedings.

Our special thanks go to all individuals who submitted valuable papers for the RSCTC 2002 conference and to all conference participants.

We also wish to express our thanks to Alfred Hofmann at Springer-Verlag for his support and cooperation.

October 2002

James Alpigini
James F. Peters
Andrzej Skowron
Ning Zhong

RSCTC 2002 Conference Committee

Honorary Chairs: Zdzisław Pawlak, Lotfi A. Zadeh
Conference Chair: James Alpigini
Program Chairs: James F. Peters, Andrzej Skowron, Ning Zhong

Advisory Board

Nick Cercone
Jerzy Grzymała-Busse
Tsau Young Lin
Akira Nakamura

Sankar K. Pal
Lech Polkowski
Roman Slowiński
Hideo Tanaka

Shusaku Tsumoto
Yiyu Yao
Wojciech Ziarko

Local Committee

Patty McFadden
Colin Neill

Kalpesh Patel
Fred Ramsey

Sally Sue Slish

Program Committee

Peter Apostoli
Ali Arsanjani
Malcolm Beynon
Hans Dieter Burkhard
Mihir Kr. Chakraborty
Liu Chunnian
Andrzej Czyżewski
Jitender S. Deogun
Patrick Doherty
Dieder Dubois
Ivo Duentsch
Maria C. Fernandez
Fernando Gomide
Salvatore Greco
Xiaohua Hu
Masahiro Inuiguchi
Jouni Järvinen
Janusz Kacprzyk
Daijin Kim
Jan Komorowski

Bożena Kostek
Jacek Koronacki
Marzena Kryszkiewicz
Churn-Jung Liau
Pawan Lingras
Jiming Liu
Qing Liu
Solomon Marcus
Benedetto Matarazzo
Ernestina Menasalvas
Zbigniew Michalewicz
Ryszard Michalski
Nakata Michinori
Sadaaki Miyamoto
Mikhail Moshkov
Tetsuya Murai
Nguyen Hung Son
Ewa Orłowska
Witold Pedrycz
Mohamed Quafafou

Sheela Ramanna
Zbigniew W. Raś
Ron Shapira
Jerzy Stefanowski
Jarosław Stepaniuk
Zbigniew Suraj
Roman Świniarski
Andrzej Szałas
Marcin Szczuka
Francis E.H. Tay
Helmut Thiele
Mihaela Ulieru
Alicja Wakulicz-Deja
Guoyin Wang
Anita Wasilewska
Michael Wong
Xindong Wu
Hussein Zedan

Table of Contents

Keynote Papers

In Pursuit of Patterns in Data Reasoning from Data
– The Rough Set Way 1
    Zdzisław Pawlak

Toward a Theory of Hierarchical Definability (THD)
(Causality Is Undefinable) 10
    Lotfi A. Zadeh

Plenary Papers

Modelling Biological Phenomena with Rough Sets 13
    Jan Komorowski

Database Mining on Derived Attributes
(Granular and Rough Computing Approach) 14
    Tsau Young Lin

A Proposed Evolutionary, Self-Organizing Automaton for the
Control of Dynamic Systems 33
    David W. Russell

Rough Set Analysis of Preference-Ordered Data....................... 44
    Roman Słowiński, Salvatore Greco, Benedetto Matarazzo

Fuzzy Sets, Multi-valued Mappings, and Rough Sets................... 60
    I.B. Türksen

Foundations and Methods I

Investigating the Choice of l and u Values in the Extended Variable
Precision Rough Sets Model 61
    Malcolm J. Beynon

A Quantitative Analysis of Preclusivity vs. Similarity Based
Rough Approximations 69
    Gianpiero Cattaneo, Davide Ciucci

Heyting Wajsberg Algebras as an Abstract Environment Linking
Fuzzy and Rough Sets 77
    Gianpiero Cattaneo, Davide Ciucci

Dominance-Based Rough Set Approach Using Possibility and
Necessity Measures 85
    Salvatore Greco, Masahiro Inuiguchi, Roman Słowiński

Generalized Decision Algorithms, Rough Inference Rules,
and Flow Graphs 93
    Salvatore Greco, Zdzisław Pawlak, Roman Słowiński

Generalized Rough Sets and Rule Extraction 105
    Masahiro Inuiguchi, Tetsuzo Tanino

Towards a Mereological System for Direct Products and
Relations 113
    Ryszard Janicki

On the Structure of Rough Approximations 123
    Jouni Järvinen

Modification of Weights of Conflict Profile's Elements and
Dependencies of Attributes in Consensus Model 131
    Radoslaw Katarzyniak, Ngoc Thanh Nguyen

Reasoning about Information Granules Based on Rough Logic 139
    Qing Liu, S.L. Jiang

Foundations and Methods II

A Rough Set Framework for Learning in a Directed Acyclic Graph 144
    Herman Midelfart, Jan Komorowski

On Compressible Information Systems 156
    Mikhail Moshkov

Functional Dependencies in Relational Expressions Based on Or-Sets ... 161
    Michinori Nakata, Tetsuya Murai

On Asymptotic Properties of Rough–Set–Theoretic Approximations.
Fractal Dimension, Exact Sets, and Rough Inclusion in Potentially
Infinite Information Systems 167
    Lech Polkowski

About Tolerance and Similarity Relations in Information Systems ... 175
    J.A. Pomykała

Rough Sets, Guarded Command Language, and Decision Rules 183
    Frederick V. Ramsey, James J. Alpigini

Collaborative Query Processing in DKS Controlled by Reducts 189
    Zbigniew W. Raś, Agnieszka Dardzińska

A New Method for Determining of Extensions and Restrictions of
Information Systems 197
    Wojciech Rząsa, Zbigniew Suraj

A Logic Programming Framework for Rough Sets 205
    Aida Vitória, Jan Małuszyński

Attribute Core of Decision Table 213
    G.Y. Wang

Foundations and Methods III

Signal Analysis Using Rough Integrals 218
    Maciej Borkowski

How Much Privacy? — A System to Safe Guard Personal Privacy
while Releasing Databases 226
    Yi-Ting Chiang, Yu-Cheng Chiang, Tsan-sheng Hsu,
    Churn-Jung Liau, Da-Wei Wang

Rough Clustering: An Alternative to Find Meaningful Clusters by
Using the Reducts from a Dataset 234
    Hércules Antonio do Prado, Paulo Martins Engel, Homero Chaib Filho

Concept Learning with Approximation: Rough Version Spaces 239
    Vincent Dubois, Mohamed Quafafou

Variable Consistency Monotonic Decision Trees 247
    Silvio Giove, Salvatore Greco, Benedetto Matarazzo,
    Roman Słowiński

Importance and Interaction of Conditions in Decision Rules 255
    Salvatore Greco, Benedetto Matarazzo, Roman Słowiński,
    Jerzy Stefanowski

Time Complexity of Rough Clustering: GAs versus K-Means 263
    Pawan Lingras, Y.Y. Yao

Induction of Decision Rules and Classification in the Valued
Tolerance Approach 271
    Jerzy Stefanowski, Alexis Tsoukiàs

Time Series Model Mining with Similarity-Based Neuro-fuzzy
Networks and Genetic Algorithms: A Parallel Implementation 279
    Julio J. Valdés, Gabriel Mateescu

Granular and Neuro Computing

Closeness of Performance Map Information Granules: A Rough Set
Approach 289
    James J. Alpigini

Granular Computing on Binary Relations (Analysis of Conflict
and Chinese Wall Security Policy)...................................... 296
    Tsau Young Lin

Measures of Inclusion and Closeness of Information Granules:
A Rough Set Approach 300
    James F. Peters, Andrzej Skowron, Zbigniew Suraj, Maciej Borkowski,
    Wojciech Rząsa

Rough Neurocomputing: A Survey of Basic Models
of Neurocomputation 308
    James F. Peters, Marcin S. Szczuka

Rough Neurocomputing Based on Hierarchical Classifiers 316
    Andrzej Skowron, Jarosław Stepaniuk, James F. Peters

Using Granular Objects in Multi-source Data Fusion 324
    Ronald R. Yager

Induction of Classification Rules by Granular Computing 331
    J.T. Yao, Y.Y. Yao

Probabilistic Reasoning

Acquisition Methods for Contextual Weak Independence 339
    C.J. Butz, M.J. Sanscartier

A Method for Detecting Context-Specific Independence in
Conditional Probability Tables.. 344
    C.J. Butz, M.J. Sanscartier

Properties of Weak Conditional Independence 349
    C.J. Butz, M.J. Sanscartier

A Proposal of Probability of Rough Event Based on Probability of
Fuzzy Event... 357
    Rolly Intan, Masao Mukaidono

Approximate Bayesian Network Classifiers 365
    Dominik Ślęzak, Jakub Wróblewski

Accuracy and Coverage in Rough Set Rule Induction 373
    Shusaku Tsumoto

Statistical Test for Rough Set Approximation Based on Fisher's
Exact Test 381
   Shusaku Tsumoto

Triangulation of Bayesian Networks: A Relational Database
Perspective.. 389
   S.K.M. Wong, D. Wu, C.J. Butz

Data Mining, Machine Learning, and Pattern Recognition

A New Version of Rough Set Exploration System 397
   Jan G. Bazan, Marcin S. Szczuka, Jakub Wróblewski

Local Attribute Value Grouping for Lazy Rule Induction 405
   Grzegorz Góra, Arkadiusz Wojna

Incomplete Data Decomposition for Classification 413
   Rafał Latkowski

Extension of Relational Management Systems with Data Mining
Capabilities 421
   *Juan F. Martinez, Anita Wasilewska, Michael Hadjimichael,
   Covadonga Fernandez, Ernestina Menasalvas*

Reducing Number of Decision Rules by Joining 425
   Michał Mikołajczyk

Scalable Classification Method Based on Rough Sets 433
   Hung Son Nguyen

Parallel Data Mining Experimentation Using Flexible Configurations 441
   *José M. Peña, F. Javier Crespo, Ernestina Menasalvas,
   Victor Robles*

An Optimization of Apriori Algorithm through the Usage of
Parallel I/O and Hints... 449
   *María S. Pérez, Ramón A. Pons, Félix García, Jesús Carretero,
   María L. Córdoba*

Patterns in Information Maps 453
   Andrzej Skowron, Piotr Synak

Discernibility Matrix Approach to Exception Analysis 461
   Min Zhao, Jue Wang

Gastric Cancer Data Mining with Ordered Information 467
   Ning Zhong, Ju-Zhen Dong, Y.Y. Yao, Setsuo Ohsuga

Web Mining

A Granular Approach for Analyzing the Degree of Affability
of a Web Site... 479
    Esther Hochsztain, Socorro Millán, Ernestina Menasalvas

Comparison of Classification Methods for Customer Attrition Analysis.... 487
    Xiaohua Hu

User Profile Model: A View from Artificial Intelligence................... 493
    Yuefeng Li, Y.Y. Yao

Mining the Client's Life Cycle Behaviour in the Web 497
    Oscar Marban, Javier Segovia, Juan J. Cuadrado, Cesar Montes

PagePrompter: An Intelligent Web Agent Created Using Data Mining
Techniques 506
    Y.Y. Yao, H.J. Hamilton, Xuewei Wang

VPRSM Approach to WEB Searching 514
    Wojciech Ziarko, Xue Fei

Applications I

Rough Set Approach to the Survival Analysis........................... 522
    Jan Bazan, Antoni Osmólski, Andrzej Skowron, Dominik Ślęzak,
    Marcin Szczuka, Jakub Wróblewski

The Identification of Low-Paying Workplaces: An Analysis Using
the Variable Precision Rough Sets Model................................ 530
    Malcolm J. Beynon

A Search for the Best Data Mining Method to Predict Melanoma 538
    Jerzy W. Grzymała-Busse, Zdzisław S. Hippe

Towards the Classification of Musical Works: A Rough Set Approach 546
    Monika P. Hippe

Segmentation of Medical Images Based on Approximations in Rough
Set Theory 554
    Shoji Hirano, Shusaku Tsumoto

Adaptive Robust Estimation for Filtering Motion Vectors 564
    Seok-Woo Jang, Essam A. El-Kwae, Hyung-Il Choi

Rough Set Feature Selection and Diagnostic Rule Generation for
Industrial Applications 568
    Seungkoo Lee, Nicholas Propes, Guangfan Zhang, Yongshen Zhao,
    George Vachtsevanos

Applications II

λ-Connected Approximations for Rough Sets 572
  Li Chen

Adaptive Classifier Construction: An Approach to Handwritten
Digit Recognition 578
  Tuan Trung Nguyen

The Application of Support Diagnose in Mitochondrial
Encephalomyopathies... 586
  Piotr Paszek, Alicja Wakulicz-Deja

Obstacle Classification by a Line-Crawling Robot: A Rough
Neurocomputing Approach 594
  James F. Peters, T.C. Ahn, Maciej Borkowski

Rough Neural Network for Software Change Prediction 602
  Sheela Ramanna

Handling Spatial Uncertainty in Binary Images: A Rough Set Based
Approach 610
  D. Sinha, P. Laplante

Evolutionary Algorithms and Rough Sets-Based Hybrid Approach to
Classificatory Decomposition of Cortical Evoked Potentials 621
  *Tomasz G. Smolinski, Grzegorz M. Boratyn, Mariofanna Milanova,
  Jacek M. Zurada, Andrzej Wrobel*

Rough Mereological Localization and Navigation 629
  Adam Szmigielski

Author Index 639

In Pursuit of Patterns in Data Reasoning from Data – The Rough Set Way

Zdzisław Pawlak

Institute of Theoretical and Applied Informatics, Polish Academy of Sciences,
ul. Bałtycka 5, 44 100 Gliwice, Poland
zpw@ii.pw.edu.pl

Abstract. This paper concerns some aspects of rough set based data analysis. In particular rough set look on Bayes' formula leads to new methodology of reasoning from data and shows interesting relationship between Bayes' theorem, rough sets and flow graphs. Three methods of flow graphs application in drawing conclusions from data are presented and examined.

MOTTO:
"It is a capital mistake to theorise before one has data"
Sherlock Holmes
In: A Scandal in Bohemia

1 Introduction

No doubt that the most famous contribution to reasoning from data should be attributed to the renowned Mr. Sherlock Holmes, whose mastery of using data in reasoning has been well known world wide for over hundred years.

More seriously, reasoning from data is the domain of inductive reasoning, which uses data about sample of larger reality as a starting point of inference – in contrast to deductive reasoning, where axioms expressing some universal truths are used as a departure point of reasoning.

In the rough set approach granular structure of data imposed by the indiscernibility relation is used do discover patterns in data. In rough set theory patterns in data can be characterized by means of approximations, or equivalently by decision rules induced by the data. With every decision rule in a decision table three coefficients are associated: the *strength*, the *certainty* and the *coverage factors* of the rule. It is shown that these coefficients satisfy Bayes' theorem and the total probability theorem. This enables us to use Bayes' theorem to discover patterns in data in a different way from that offered by standard Bayesian inference technique employed in statistical reasoning, without referring to prior and posterior probabilities, inherently associated with Bayesian inference methodology. Besides, a new form of Bayes' theorem is introduced, based on the strength of decision rules, which simplifies essentially computations.

Furthermore, it is shown that the decision rules define a relation between condition and decision granules, which can be represented by a flow graph. The certainty and coverage factors determine a "flow of information" in the graph, ruled by the total probability theorem and Bayes' theorem, which shows clearly the relationship between condition and decision granules determined by the decision table. This leads to a new class of flow networks, unlike to that introduced by Ford and Fulkerson [1]. The introduced flow graphs may have many applications not necessarily associated with decision tables, but this requires further study.

The decision structure of a decision table can be represented in a "decision space", which is Euclidean space, in which dimensions of the space are determined by decision granules, points in the space are condition granules and coordinates of the points are strengths of the corresponding rules. Distance in the decision space between condition granules allows to determine how "distant" are decision makers in view of their decisions. This idea can be viewed as a generalization of the indiscernibility matrix [7], basic tool to find reducts in information systems. Besides, the decision space gives a clear insight in the decision structure imposed by the decision table.

A simple tutorial example is used to illustrate the basis ideas discussed in the paper.

2 Basic Concepts

In this section we recall basic concepts of rough set theory [4,5,6,7].

An *information system* is a pair $S = (U, A)$, where U and A, are non-empty finite sets called the *universe*, and the set of *attributes*, respectively such that $a : U \rightarrow V_a$, where V_a, is the set of all values of a called the *domain* of a. Any subset B of A determines a binary relation $I(B)$ on U, which will be called an *indiscernibility relation*, and defined as follows: $(x, y) \in I(B)$ if and only if $a(x) = a(y)$ for every $a \in A$, where $a(x)$ denotes the value of attribute a for element x. Obviously $I(B)$ is an equivalence relation. The family of all equivalence classes of $I(B)$, i.e., a partition determined by B, will be denoted by $U/I(B)$, or simply by U/B; an equivalence class of $I(B)$, i.e., block of the partition U/B, containing x will be denoted by $B(x)$ and called *B-granule* induced by x.

If (x, y) belongs to $I(B)$ we will say that x and y are *B-indiscernible* (*indiscernible with respect to B*). Equivalence classes of the relation $I(B)$ (or blocks of the partition U/B) are referred to as *B-elementary* sets or *B-granules*.

If we distinguish in the information system two disjoint classes of attributes, called *condition* and *decision attributes*, respectively, then the system will be called a *decision table* and will be denoted by $S = (U, C, D)$, where C and D are disjoint sets of condition and decision attributes, respectively and $C \cup D = A$.

$C(x)$ and $D(x)$ will be referred to as the condition granule and the decision granule induced by x, respectively.

An example of a decision table is shown in Table 1.

Table 1. An example of decision table

Fact no.	Driving conditions			Consequence	N
	weather	road	time	accident	
1	misty	icy	day	yes	80
2	foggy	icy	night	yes	140
3	misty	not icy	night	yes	40
4	sunny	icy	day	no	500
5	foggy	icy	night	no	20
6	misty	not icy	night	no	200

In the table, 6 facts concerning 980 cases of driving a car in various driving conditions are presented. In the table columns labeled *weather*, *road* and *time*, called *condition attributes*, represent driving conditions. The column labeled by *accident*, called *decision attribute*, contains information whether an accident has occurred or not. N denotes the number of analogous cases.

3 Decision Rules

Each row of the decision table determines a decision rule, e.g., row 1 determines the following decision rule *"if weather is misty and road is icy and time is day then accident occurred"* in 80 cases.

Let $S = (U, C, D)$ be a decision table. Every $x \in U$ determines a sequence $c_1(x), \ldots, c_n(x), d_1(x), \ldots, d_m(x)$ where $\{c_1, \ldots, c_n\} = C$ and $\{d_1, \ldots, d_m\} = D$.

The sequence will be called a *decision rule induced by* x (in S) and denoted by $c_1(x), \ldots, c_n(x) \rightarrow d_1(x), \ldots, d_m(x)$ or in short $C \rightarrow_x D$.

The number $supp_x(C, D) = |C(x) \cap D(x)|$ will be called a support of the decision rule $C \rightarrow_x D$ and the number

$$\sigma_x(C, D) = \frac{supp_x(C, D)}{|U|},$$

will be referred to as the *strength* of the decision rule $C \rightarrow_x D$, where $|X|$ denotes the cardinality of X.

With every decision rule $C \rightarrow_x D$ we associate a *certainty factor* of the decision rule, denoted $cer_x(C, D)$ and defined as follows:

$$cer_x(C, D) = \frac{|C(x) \cap D(x)|}{|C(x)|} = \frac{\sigma_x(C, D)}{\pi(C(x))},$$

where $C(x) \neq \emptyset$ and $\pi(C(x))$.

The certainty factor may be interpreted as conditional probability that y belongs to $D(x)$ given y belongs to $C(x)$, symbolically $\pi_x(D|C)$, i.e., $cer_x(C, D) = \pi_x(D|C)$.

If $cer_x(C,D) = 1$, then $C \to_x D$ will be called a *certain decision rule*; if $0 < cer_x(C,D) < 1$ the decision rule will be referred to as an *uncertain decision rule*.

Besides, we will also use a *coverage factor* (see [8]) of the decision rule, denoted $cov_x(C,D)$ defined as

$$cov_x(C,D) = \frac{|C(x) \cap D(x)|}{|D(x)|} = \frac{\sigma_x(C,D)}{\pi(D(x))},$$

where $D(x) \neq \emptyset$ and $\pi(D(x)) = \frac{|D(x)|}{|U|}$. Similarly

$$cov_x(C,D) = \pi_x(C|D).$$

If $C \to_x D$ is a decision rule then $D \to_x C$ will be called an *inverse decision rule*. The inverse decision rules can be used to give *explanations (reasons)* for a decision.

In Table 2 the *strength, certainty* and *coverage factors* for Table 1 are given.

Table 2. Characterization of decision rules

fact no.	Strength	Certainty	Coverage
1	0.082	1.000	0.308
2	0.143	0.877	0.538
3	0.041	1.167	0.154
4	0.510	1.000	0.695
5	0.020	0.123	0.027
6	0.204	0.833	0.278

4 Properties of Decision Rules

Decision rules have important probabilistic properties which are discussed next [2,3].

Let $C \to_x D$ be a decision rule. Then the following properties are valid:

$$\sum_{y \in C(x)} cer_y(C,D) = 1 \qquad (1)$$

$$\sum_{y \in D(x)} cov_y(C,D) = 1 \qquad (2)$$

$$\pi(D(x)) = \sum_{y \in C(x)} cer_y(C,D) \cdot \pi(C(x)) = \qquad (3)$$

$$= \sum_{y \in C(x)} \sigma_y(C,D)$$

$$\pi\left(C\left(x\right)\right) = \sum_{y \in D(x)} cov_y\left(C, D\right) \cdot \pi\left(D\left(y\right)\right) = \tag{4}$$

$$= \sum_{y \in D(x)} \sigma_y\left(C, D\right)$$

$$cer_x\left(C, D\right) = \frac{cov_x\left(C, D\right) \cdot \pi\left(D\left(x\right)\right)}{\pi\left(C\left(x\right)\right)} = \tag{5}$$

$$= \frac{\sigma_x\left(C, D\right)}{\pi\left(C\left(x\right)\right)}$$

$$cov_x\left(C, D\right) = \frac{cer_x\left(C, D\right) \cdot \pi\left(D\left(x\right)\right)}{\pi\left(D\left(x\right)\right)} = \tag{6}$$

$$= \frac{\sigma_x\left(C, D\right)}{\pi\left(D\left(x\right)\right)}$$

That is, any decision table, satisfies (1)–(6). Observe that (3) and (4) refer to the well known *total probability theorem*, whereas (5) and (6) refer to *Bayes' theorem*.

Thus in order to compute the certainty and coverage factors of decision rules according to formula (5) and (6) it is enough to know the strength (support) of all decision rules only.

Formulas (5) and (6) can be rewritten as

$$cer_x\left(C, D\right) = cov_x\left(C, D\right) \cdot \gamma_x\left(C, D\right) \tag{7}$$

$$cov_x\left(C, D\right) = cer_x\left(C, D\right) \cdot \gamma_x^{-1}\left(C, D\right) \tag{8}$$

where $\gamma_x(C, D) = \frac{|D(x)|}{|C(x)|} = \frac{cer_x(C,D)}{cov_x(C,D)}$

Let us observe that

$$cov_x\left(C, D\right) \cdot \pi\left(D\left(x\right)\right) = \sigma_x\left(C, D\right) \tag{9}$$

$$cer_x\left(C, D\right) \cdot \pi\left(C\left(x\right)\right) = \sigma_x\left(C, D\right) \tag{10}$$

5   Granularity of Data and Flow Graphs

With every decision table we associate a *flow graph*, i.e., a directed acyclic graph defined as follows: to every decision rule $C \rightarrow_x D$ we assign a *directed branch* x connecting the *input node* $C(x)$ and the *output node* $D(x)$. Strength of the decision rule represents a *throughflow* of the corresponding branch. The throughflow of the graph is governed by formulas (1),...,(6).

Classification of objects in this representation boils down to finding the maximal output flow in the flow graph, whereas explanation of decisions is connected with the maximal input flow associated with the given decision.

A flow graph for decision table shown in Table 1 is given in Figure 1.

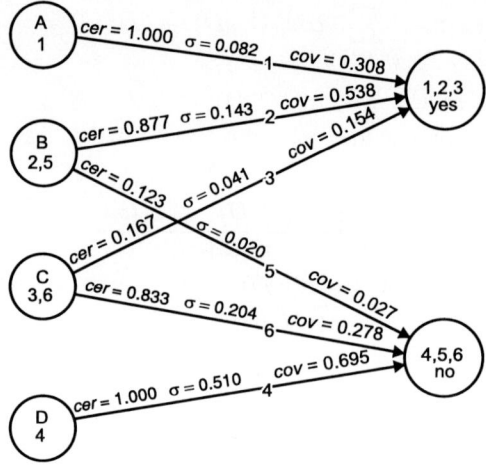

Fig. 1. Flow graph

6 Decision Space

With every decision table having one n-valued decision attribute we can associate n-dimensional Euclidean space, where decision granules determine n axis of the space and condition granules determine points of the space. Strengths of decision rules are to be understood as coordinates of corresponding granules.

Distance $\delta(x, y)$ between granules x and y in the n-dimensional decision space is defined as

$$\delta(x, y) = \sqrt{\sum_{i=1}^{n}(x_i - y_j)^2}$$

where $x = (x_1, \ldots, x_n)$ and $y = (y_1, \ldots, y_n)$ are vectors of strengths of corresponding decision rules.

A decision space for Table 1 is given in Figure 2.

Distances between granules A, B, C and D are shown in Table 3.

Table 3. Distance matrix

	A	B	C	D
A				
B	0.064			
C	0.208	0.210		
D	0.517	0.510	0.309	

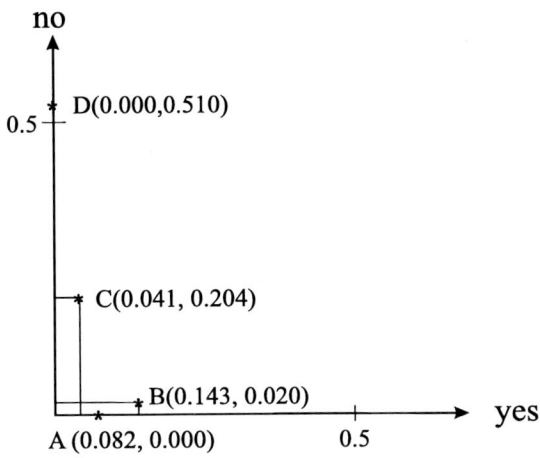

Fig. 2. Decision space

7 Flow Diagrams, Another Approach

Flow diagrams can be also employed without referring to decision tables, but using other kind of information about the problem we are interested in. We will consider here two cases. In the first case, called in the classical flow network terminology *supply-demand* problem [1], we are given demand of some commodities and we want to find supply of components necessary to produce the commodities. The second case, which will be considered here, is in some sense inverse.

For the sake of simplicity we will explain the problem by means of a simple example for paint demand in a car factory.

Suppose that cars are painted into two colors Y_1 and Y_2 and that these colors can be obtained by mixing three paints X_1, X_2 and X_3 in the following proportions:

- Y_1 contains 20% of X_1, 70% of X_2 and 10% of X_3,
- Y_2 contains 30% of $X1$, 50% of X_2 and 20% of X_3.

We have to find demand of each paint and their distribution among colors Y_1 and Y_2.

Employing terminology introduced in previous sections we can represent our problem by means of flow graph shown in Figure 3. Thus in order to solve our task first we have to compute strength of each decision rule using formula (9). Next applying formula (4) to each X_i we obtain demand of each paint. Finally, employing formula (5) we get the distribution of each paint among colors of cars.

The final result is presented in Figure 4.

For the sake of simplicity we will use the same numerical data to illustrate the inverse problem. Suppose we want to know distribution of votes of three disjoint group X_1, X_2 and X_3 of voters among two political parties Y_1 and Y_2 assuming now that we are given data, as shown in Figure 5.

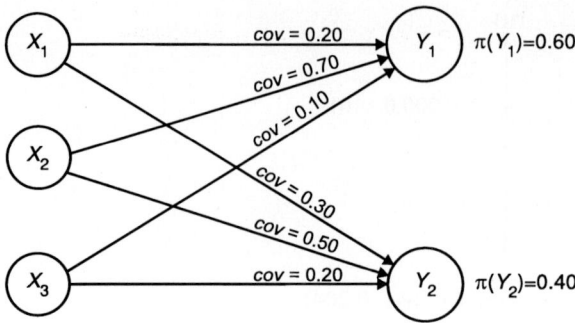

Fig. 3. Supply – demand

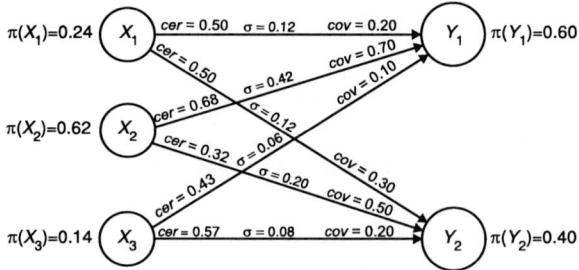

Fig. 4. Final results

That is the group X_1 consists of 24% of voters, X_2 - 62% and X_3 - 14%. Votes distribution among parties is as follows:

- group X_1 gave 50% of its votes for each party,
- group X_2 gave 68% of votes for party Y_1 and 32% for party Y_2,
- group X_3 gave 43% votes for party Y_1 and 57% votes for party Y_2.

Proceeding in the inverse order as in the previous example we get the final results shown in Figure 4.

That is, first we apply formula (10) and compute strength of each decision rule. Having done this we use formula (6) and compute coverage factors of each decision rule. Next applying formula (3) we obtain the final results, i.e., party Y_1 obtained 60% votes, whereas party Y_2 obtained 40% votes. Votes distribution for each party is as follows:

- party Y_1 obtained 20% votes from group X_1, 70% from group X_2 and 10% from group X_3,
- party Y_2 obtained 30% votes from group X_1, 50% from group X_2 and 20% from group X_3.

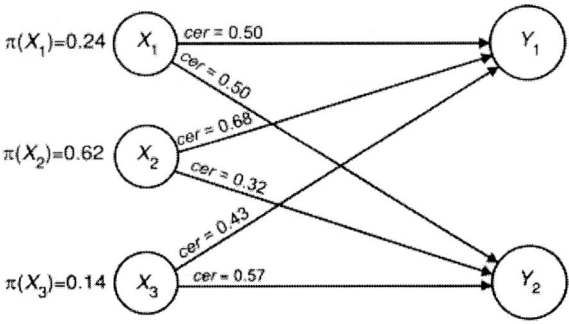

Fig. 5. Inverse problem

8 Conclusions

Decision tables display interesting probabilistic features, i.e., the obey the total probability theorem and Bayes' theorem. This gives rise to a new perspective on Bayesian inference methodology, leads to new algorithms and new areas of applications.

Furthermore, representation of decision tables by flow graphs and decision spaces gives new insight into the data analysis processes.

References

1. Ford, L.R., Fulkerson, D.R.: Flows in Networks, Princeton University Press, Princeton. New Jersey
2. Pawlak, Z.: Theorize with Data using Rough Sets (to appear)
3. Pawlak, Z.: Rough Sets, Decision Algorithms and Bayes' Theorem. European Journal of Operational Research 136 (2002) 181–189
4. Polkowski, L., Skowron, A., (eds.).: Rough Set and Current Trends in Computing. Lecture Notes in Artificiale Intelligence 1424, Springer (1998)
5. Polkowski, L., Skowron, A. (eds.).: Rough Sets in Knowledge Discovery. Vol. 1-2, Physica Verlag, Springer (1998)
6. Polkowski, L., Tsumoto, S., Lin, T.Y., (eds.).: Rough Set Methods and applications – New Developments in Knowledge Discovery in Information Systems. Springer (to appear)
7. Skowron, A., Rauszer, C.: The discernibility matrices and functions in information systems, in: Słowiński (ed.), Intelligent Decision Support, – Handbook of Applications and Advances in Rough Set Theory, Kluwer Academic Publishers, Dordrech (1992) 311–362
8. Tsumoto, S., Tanaka, H.: Discovery of Functional Components of Proteins Based on PRIMEROSE and Domain Knowledge Hierarchy. Proceedings of the Workshop on Rough Sets and Soft Computing (RSSC-94), 1994: Lin, T.Y., and Wildberger, A.M. (eds.) Soft Computing, SCS (1995) 280–285

Toward a Theory of Hierarchical Definability (THD)
Causality Is Undefinable

Lotfi A. Zadeh

Professor in the Graduate School and Director
Berkeley Initiative in Soft Computing (BISC)
Computer Science Division, Department of EECS
University of California, Berkeley

Summary

Attempts to formulate mathematically precise definitions of basic concepts such as causality, randomness and probability have a long history. The concept of hierarchical definability that is outlined in the following suggests that such definitions may not exist. Furthermore, it suggests that existing definitions of many basic concepts, among them those of linearity stability, statistical independence and Pareto-optimality, may be in need of reformulation.

In essence, definability is concerned with whether and how a concept, X, can be defined in a way that lends itself to mathematical analysis and computation. In mathematics, though not in logic, definability of mathematical concepts is taken for granted. But as we move further into the age of machine intelligence and automated reasoning, the issue of definability is certain to grow in importance and visibility, raising basic questions that are not easy to resolve.

To be more specific, let X be the concept of, say, a summary, and assume that I am instructing a machine to generate a summary of a given article or a book. To execute my instruction, the machine must be provided with a definition of what is meant by a summary. It is somewhat paradoxical that we have summarization programs that can summarize, albeit in a narrowly prescribed sense, without being able to formulate a general definition of summarization. The same applies to the concepts of causality, randomness and probability. Indeed, it may be argued that these and many other basic concepts cannot be defined within the conceptual framework of classical logic and set theory.

The point of departure in our approach to definability is the assumption that definability has a hierarchical structure. Furthermore, it is understood that a definition ought to be unambiguous, precise, operational, general and co-extensive with the concept which it defines.

In THD, a definition of X is represented as a quadruple (X, L, C, D), where L is the language in which X is defined; C is the context; and D is the definition. The context, C, delimits the class of instances to which D applies, that is, C defines the domain of D. For example, if X is the concept of volume, D may not apply to a croissant or a tree.

The language, L, is assumed to be a member of hierarchy represented as (NL, BL, F, F.G, PNL). In this hierarchy, NL is a natural language-a language which is in predominant use as a definition language in social sciences and law; and BL is the binary-logic-based mathematical language used in all existing scientific theories. Informally, a concept, X, is BL-definable if it is a crisp concept, e.g., a prime number, a linear system or a Gaussian distribution. F is a mathematical language based on fuzzy logic and F.G is an extension of F in which variables and relations are allowed to have granular structure. The last member of the hierarchy is PNL-Precisiated Natural Language. PNL is a maximally-expressive language which subsumes BL, F and F.G. In particular, the language of fuzzy if-then rules is a sublanguage of PNL.

X is a fuzzy concept if its denotation, D(X), is a fuzzy set in its universe of discourse. A fuzzy concept is associated with a membership function that assigns to each point, u, in the universe of discourse of X, the degree to which u is a member of D(X). Alternatively, a fuzzy concept may be defined algorithmically in terms of other fuzzy concepts. Examples of fuzzy concepts are: small number, strong evidence and similarity. It should be noted that many concepts associated with fuzzy sets are crisp concepts. An example is the concept of a convex fuzzy set. Most fuzzy concepts are context-dependent.

The next level in the hierarchy is that of F.G-definability, with G standing for granular, and F.G denoting the conjunction of fuzzy and granular. Informally, in the case of a concept which is F.G-granular, the values of attributes are granulated, with a granule being a clump of values that are drawn together by indistinguishability, similarity, proximity, or functionality. F.G-granularity reflects the bounded ability of the human mind to resolve detail and store information. An example of an F.G-granular concept that is traditionally defined as a crisp concept, is that of statistical independence. This is a case of misdefinition–a definition that is applied to instances for which the concept is not defined, e.g., fuzzy events. In particular, a common misdefinition is to treat a concept as if it were BL-definable, whereas in fact it is not. In THD, the concept of context serves to differentiate between "defined" and "definability."

The next level is that of PNL-definability. Basically, PNL consists of propositions drawn from a natural language that can be precisiated through translation into what is called precisiation language. An example of a proposition in PNL is: It is very unlikely that there will be a significant increase in the price of oil in the near future.

In the case of PNL, the precisiation language is the Generalized Constraint Language (GCL). A generic generalized constraint is represented as Z isr R, where Z is the constrained variable, R is the constraining relation and r is a discrete-valued indexing variable whose values define the ways in which R constrains Z. The principal types of constraints are: possibilistic (r = blank); veristic (r = v); probabilistic (r = p); random set (r = rs); usuality (r = u); fuzzy graph (r = fg); and Pawlak set (r = ps). The rationale for constructing a large variety of constraints is that conventional crisp constraints are incapable of representing the meaning of propositions expressed in a natural language–most of which are intrinsically imprecise–in a form that lends itself to computation.

The elements of GCL are composite generalized constraints that are formed from generic generalized constraints by combination, modification and qualification. An example of a generalized constraint in GCL is ((Z isp R) and (Z, Y) is S) is unlikely.

By construction, the Generalized Constraint Language is maximally expressive. What this implies is that PNL is the largest subset of a natural language that admits precisiation. Informally, this implication serves as a basis for the conclusion that if a concept, X, cannot be defined in terms of PNL, then, in effect, it is undefinable or, synonymously, amorphic.

In this perspective, the highest level of definability hierarchy, which is the level above PNL-definability, is that of undefinability or amorphicity. A canonical example of an amorphic concept is that of causality. More specifically, is it not possible to construct a general definition of causality such that given any two events A and B and the question, "Did A cause B?", the question could be answered based on the definition. Equivalently, given any definition of causality, it will always be possible to construct examples to which the definition would not apply or yield counterintuitive results. In general, definitions of causality are non-operational because of infeasibility of conducting controlled experiments.

In dealing with an amorphic concept, X, what is possible–and what we generally do–is to restrict the domain of applicability of X to instances for which X is definable. For example, in the case of the concept of a summary, which is an amorphic concept, we could restrict the length, type, and other attributes of what we want to summarize. In this sense, an amorphic concept may be partially definable or, p-definable, for short. The concept of p-definability applies to all levels of the definability hierarchy.

The use of PNL as a definition language opens the door to definition of concepts of the form "approximate X," e.g., approximate linearity, approximate stability and, most importantly, approximate theorem. What we do not want to do is to use a BL-based language to define "approximate X," since such BL-based definitions may lead to counterintuitive conclusions. The theory of hierarchical definability is not a theory in the traditional spirit. The definitions are informal and conclusions are not theorems. Nonetheless, it serves a significant purpose by raising significant questions about a basic issue–the issue of definability of concepts that lie at the center of scientific theories.

Modelling Biological Phenomena with Rough Sets

Jan Komorowski

The Linnaeus Centre for Bioinformatics
Uppsala University and Swedish University of Agricultural Sciences

Summary

Biology is going through a dramatic change of its research paradigm. For the past 400 years biology was done without any significant involvement of mathematics. The first serious use of mathematics in biology was effected by genetics and its theories of Mendelian inheritance. Eventually, a solid analytical foundation was created for evolutionary biology. These developments are in a strong contrast to physics, which was very early forced to apply methods of mathematics in order to understand and model physical phenomena.

The foremost reason for mathematization of biology are the enormous amounts of data that become available through a variety of genome projects and through the so-called high-throughput techniques such as, for instance, microarray technologies that allow genome-wide studies of gene expressions in living cells or organisms. We also note that biological knowledge in itself is rather often example-based and only exceptionally expressed in concise mathematical terms such as equations. Furthermore, there exist huge repositories of informal or qualitative biological background knowledge often expressed in scientific articles or books, not to mention molecular or genomic databases.

Given the amount of data, it appears that standard mathematical methods are not sufficient and new developments are needed. In our research on gene expressions, we found that approximate methods of rough sets suit particularly well the goal of modelling biological systems. In certain cases, we are able to perform approximate modelling and to represent some background knowledge achieving rather much more than traditional methods seem to have done.

In my talk I shall present a selection of our recent developments in the area of Computational Functional Genomics. The approach is based on Pawlak's information system and Boolean reasoning as in standard rough sets. It is interesting to notice that through our research we may be contributing to the establishment of Qualitative Biology, a relative of Qualitative Physics; it should be, however, noted that in the present stage of knowledge of biology such an approach is well justified.

It is possible that the introduction of approximate methods to biology may help biology find new research methodologies fitting present and future demands. It is already clear that biology provides significant challenges to computer science. Answering these challenges confirms Stanislaw Ulam's statement on the relationship between biology and computer science.

Database Mining on Derived Attributes
Granular and Rough Computing Approach

Tsau Young ("T.Y.") Lin

Department of Mathematics and Computer Science
San Jose State University, San Jose, California 95192
tylin@cs.sjsu.edu

Abstract. Selecting a desirable set of attributes is essential in data mining. In this paper, we develop the notion of universal model, on which a complete set of all possible derived attributes can be generated. Then, for any data mining task, the relation can select desirable attributes by interpreting them from the universal model. The development of the universal model is based on the relation lattice, which was initiated by T. T. Lee around 1983. However, we define the lattice differently. The relation lattice theory, as rough sets, is based on the partitions induced by attributes.

Keywords: Data mining, derived attribute, attribute(feature) transformation, lattice, partition

1 Introduction

Let us quote from [21], "In AI, one often uses knowledge representations to describe an unknown universe by known features. So the selected features are often suitable for knowledge discovery. However in database, the attributes are often selected for totally different purposes; they are selected primary for record keeping. So the existing attributes might not be suitable for data mining". We need to generate new attributes, called derived attribute, from the given ones; see motivational example in Section 8. In this paper, we refine the construction of derived attributes and formalize the notion of data mining on derived attributes.

1.1 Main Idea

1 A sub-tuple is a patterns, such as association rules, if the frequency of occurrences is above certain threshold.

Based on this notion of patterns, we observe

2 Isomorphic relations have isomorphic patterns; roughly two relations are isomorphic, if one can be transformed to the other by re-labeling the attribute values.

So patterns are properties of the whole isomorphic class, not an individual relation. To profit from this observation, we construct a canonical model for each isomorphic class.

3 A canonical model is a mathematical relation, where an attribute is an equivalence relation and an attribute value is an equivalence class; no equivalence class is assigned a label (meaningful to human). The equivalence relation is called the formal attribute, and its equivalence classes the formal attribute values.

4 The patterns of any relation in the isomorphic class are isomorphic to the patterns of the canonical model.

So all patterns based on the given attributes can be generated from the canonical model. However, as the example in Section 8 shows some patterns are invisible in the given attributes. So we construct a universal model for each canonical model.

5 A universal model is a mathematical relation that contains the complete set of all formal attributes derived from the canonical model.

6 Data mining on a sub-relation of the universal model is called data mining on formal derived attributes.

7 A background knowledge is (1) a subset of formal attributes in the universal model, and (2) an interpretation for each formal attribute. By an interpretation we mean each formal attribute value (equivalence class) is assigned a label (meaningful to human).

1.2 Some Basics

Let us set up some notations and some basic notions. The center of our objects of study are bag relations (we allow repeated rows [41]), to be more emphatics, bag relation instances. A bag relation (an instance) is a knowledge representation of a set of real world entities, called the universe, by tuples of elementary concepts, that represent some properties, characteristics or attributes of entities.

Formally, let V be the universe. Let $A = \{A^1, A^2, \ldots, A^n\}$ be a set of attributes, and their attribute domains be $C = \{C^1, C^2, \ldots, C^n\}$. We may write $C^j = Dom(A^j)$, and $C = Dom(A)$, where, by abuse of notation, $C = C^1 \times \ldots \times C^n$. Each C^j is a set of elementary concepts (attribute vaues). Technically, they are the so-called semantics primitives [8]. Mathematically a bag relation is, then, a map $K : V \longrightarrow C$.

We can view an attribute as a map $A^j : V \longrightarrow C^j$ (a single column knowledge representation) which is the composition of K and a projection $C \longrightarrow C^j$. A map induces a partition (see Appendix), so each A^j induces a partition on V, denoted by Q^j. We let Q denote such a collection. In [23,14,16], we have regarded attributes and their values as names of equivalence relations and their classes.

Now we can turn around and regard a bag relation $K : V \longrightarrow C$ as a multiple column knowledge representation, namely, a product of the attributes, that is, $K = A^1 \wedge, \ldots \wedge A^n$; we have taken such a view in [20,22]. If we use the information table format (see below), the product is the join (a relational operator) over the entity column. Essentially K determines and is determined by the attributes A:

- The essential ingredients of a bag relation are the universe, the attributes and, elementary concepts(attribute domains). So we write a bag relation as a tripe, $K = (V, A, C)$.

In traditional database theory, the image of the knowledge representation K is called the relation. The "independent variable V" plays no explicit role. For data mining, it is more convenient to have independent variables in the formulation. So in this paper, we prefer to use the graph $(v, K(v))$ of the map K; it is called the information table in rough set community. Throughout the whole paper K may mean the map, the image, or the graph, by abuse of language.

Two measures, called the support and confidence, are used in mining association rules. In this paper, we will be interested in the patterns that may not be in the forms of rules. So the main measure is the support. For definitive, we assert

- an item is an attribute value,
- a q-itemset is a sub-tuple of length q, and
- a large q-itemset is a high frequency q-pattern or simply a pattern.

This paper is a continuation of previous efforts on the systematic studies on attribute transformations [21], [17], [18]. Our approach is based on rough and granular computing, including T. T. Lee's lattice theory; see [14], [20], [22], [23], [27], [26].

2 Two Views of Derived Attributes

An attribute is often called a feature, especially in AI; many authors use them interchangeably. Traditionally, an attribute is a representation of property, characteristic, and etc.; see e.g., [34,35]. In other words, it represents a human perception about the data. However, we note that in a given relation instance(in database language, an extension), the data itself cannot fully reflect such a human perception. For example, an extension function dependency in a given table (data view) cannot imposes an intension function dependency on the relation scheme (human view). Therefore in data mining, we should and will take the data view, not human view. In other words, the notion of attributes is defined by the given instance of data, not what human perceived.

In this section, we give an example showing that many very distinct attributes (in the traditional view) are actually isomorphic from the view of data (Section 4). In other words, by taking the traditional view, there are chances that we spend a great deal of computing power in mining two appeared to be distinct relations that are actually isomorphic to each other. This paper presents a methodology to ensure that such waste will not happen.

2.1 A Numerical Example

To understand the nature of data mining on derived attributes, let us examine a simple example. Table 1 is a numerical information table of 9 points in the Euclidean 3-space; see Section 8 about numerical tables. The first column is the names of the points, the second columns and etc are X-, Y- and Z-coordinates (for simplicity, we consider points with integer coordinates)

Table 1. 9 points with coordinate in Euclidean 3-space

Point	X	Y	Z
P_1	200	0	0
P_2	100	0	0
P_3	173	100	1
P_4	87	50	1
P_5	44	25	1
P_6	141	141	2
P_7	71	71	2
P_8	36	36	2
P_9	0	200	3

Table 2. 9 points with coordinate in various axes; they rotate radians, 0.2, 0.3, 0.53(=30°), 0.79(=45°)

point	Z	X	Y	X20	Y20	X30	Y30	X52	Y52	X79	Y79
P_1	0	200	0	196	−40	191	−59	174	−99	141	−142
P_2	0	100	0	98	−20	96	−30	87	−50	70	−71
P_3	1	173	100	189	64	195	44	200	0	193	−53
P_4	1	87	50	95	32	98	22	100	0	97	−27
P_5	1	44	25	48	16	49	11	51	0	49	−14
P_6	2	141	141	166	110	176	93	192	52	199	0
P_7	2	71	71	84	55	89	47	97	26	100	0
P_8	2	36	36	42	28	45	24	49	13	51	0
P_9	3	0	200	40	196	59	191	99	174	142	141

2.2 Table of Derived Attributes

Next, let us consider a transformation that rotates around Z-axis. Table 2 expands Table 1 by including new X- and Y- coordinates of various degrees of rotations. The suffixes, 20, 30, 52, and 79, represent the new coordinate axes (attribute names) that rotate 0.20, 0.30 and etc radians. Each new axis is a new derived attribute. Table 2 indicates, from traditional view, that there are at least as many new attributes as rotations. Several questions arise:

1. Are all these attributes distinct? (from data mining point of view)
2. Could we find the *complete* set of all derived attributes?
3. Should we do data mining algorithm on all of them?

We will answer the first and second one in next few sections. For third question, from scientific point of view, we should consider all, however, from practical application point of view, we may only want to select some only. We proposal a notion of background knowledge to handle such situation.

Now, we take the data view and consider the isomorphism (Section 4.1) and find that in Table 2,

$$X \cong X20 \cong X30 \cong X52 \cong X79 \cong Y20 \cong Y30;$$

where $\cong$ means isomorphic. So by dropping the isomorphic attributes, Table 2 is reduced to Table 3.

Table 3. Isomorphic attributes are removed

point	Z	X	Y	Y52	Y79
P_1	1	200	0	−99	−142
P_2	1	100	0	−50	−71
P_3	1	173	100	0	−53
P_4	1	87	50	0	−27
P_5	1	44	25	0	−14
P_6	2	141	141	52	0
P_7	2	71	71	26	0
P_8	2	36	36	13	0
P_9	3	0	200	174	141

The association rules in Table 3 are Z=1,Y52=0; Z=2,Y79=0(support $\geq$ 3) and we can generate all association rules in Table 2 by Theorem 4.4.

3 Derived Attributes – Features Extraction and Construction

The goal of this section is to understand the derived attributes from data mining prospect.

3.1 New Attributes and Attribute Transformations

In this section, we will examine how a new attribute is generated from the given attributes. Let B be a subset of A and assume there is a function g defined on $Dom(B) = Dom(B^1) \times \ldots \times Dom(B^k)$. We collect all function values and call it D. In the mapping notations, we have a map $g : Dom(B) \longrightarrow D$, and call it an attribute transformation. Since attributes are maps, we have the composition:

$$g \circ B : V \longrightarrow Dom(B) \longrightarrow D$$

Definition 3.1.1
1. The map $g \circ B : V \longrightarrow D$ is called a derived attribute (since it is derived from the given ones) and denoted by $Y = g \circ B$. We write $D = Dom(Y)$.
2. By joining K and Y, we have a new relation K':

$$K' = K \wedge Y = A^1 \wedge \ldots \wedge A^n \wedge Y : V \longrightarrow Dom(A^1) \times \ldots \times Dom(A^n) \times Dom(Y)$$

3. Such an attribute transformation is denoted by $Y = g(B^1, B^1, \ldots, B^k)$.

Table 4. An Attribute Transformation in Table K

B^1	B^2	$\ldots$	B^k	Y
b_1^1	b_1^2	$\ldots$	b_1^k	$y_1 = f(b_1^1, b_1^2, \ldots, b_1^k)$
b_2^1	b_2^2	$\ldots$	b_2^k	$y_2 = f(b_2^1, b_2^2, \ldots, b_2^k)$
b_3^1	b_3^2	$\ldots$	b_3^k	$y_3 = f(b_3^1, b_3^2, \ldots, b_3^k)$
		$\ldots$		$\ldots$
b_i^1	b_i^2		b_i^k	$y_i = f(b_i^1, b_i^2, \ldots, b_i^k)$
		$\ldots$		

3.2 Derived Attributes and Extension Function Dependency

The goal of this section is to relate the derived attributes with classical database concepts. Let Y and $B = \{B^1, B^2, \ldots, B^k\}$ be an element and a subset of A respectively. Then,

Proposition 3.2. Y is a derived attribute of B iff Y is extension functionally depended (EFD) on B.

By definition, the occurrence of an EFD means there is an attribute transformation $f : Dom(B^1) \times \ldots Dom(B^k) \longrightarrow Dom(Y)$ such that $f(B(v)) = Y(v)$, $\forall\ v \in V$. By definition, $Y = f(B^1, B^1, \ldots, B^k)$. Q.E.D.

Table 4 illustrates the notion of EFD and attribute transformations.

3.3 Traditional Feature Extractions and Constructions

Feature extractions and constructions are much harder to describe in the traditional view; feature represents human view. It is much harder to create one view from the others. We will take the data view. Let us re-phrase some assertions (in traditional view) from [33],

1. ("All new constructed features are defined in terms of original features, ..") Taking the data view, this assertion implies the new constructed feature is a function of old features; see appendix for the notion of functions.
2. "Feature extraction is a process that extracts a set of new features from the original features through some functional mapping." So a new extracted feature is a function (functional mapping) of old features.

Let $A = \{A^1, \ldots A^n\}$ be the attributes *before* the extractions or constructions, and $A^{n+1} \ldots A^{n+m}$ be the *new* attributes. From the analysis above, the new attributes (features) are functions of old ones, we have

$$f : Dom(A^1) \times \ldots \times Dom(A^n)) \longrightarrow Dom(A^{n+k}).$$

From the analysis on Section 3.2, 3.1, A^{n+k} is a derived attribute of A. We summarize the analysis in:

Proposition 3.4. The attributes constructed from traditional feature extractions or constructions are derived attributes (in data view).

3.4 Derived Attributes in the Canonical Model

This section appears before the notion of canonical model is introduced, so we need some forward references. From Proposition 5.2., K is isomorphic to the canonical model C_K. So there is a corresponding Table 4 in the canonical model. In other words, there is a map,

$$V/B_E^1 \times \ldots \times V/B_E^k = V/(B_E^1 \cap \ldots \cap B_E^k) \longrightarrow V/Y_E$$

This map between quotient sets implies a refinements in the partitions; that is, Y_E is a coarsening of $B_E = B^1 \cap \ldots \cap B^k$. So we have the following:

Proposition 3.5. Y is a derived attribute of B, iff Y_E is a coarsening of $B_E = B^1 \cap \ldots B^k$, where $Y \in A$ and $B \subseteq A$

4 Patterns of Isomorphic Relations

Intuitively, by re-labeling a relation, we will not get a new relation, but a copy of the old one; so are the patterns. This section formalizes such an intuition.

4.1 Isomorphisms of Attributes and Relations

Given a map, its inverse images forms a partition (see Appendix), so each attribute A^j induces an equivalence relation Q^j on V; we write $Q = \{Q^1, Q^2, \ldots, Q^n\}$. Their quotient sets are V/Q^j and $V/Q = Q^1 \times \ldots \times Q^n = V/(Q^1 \cap \ldots \cap Q^n)$. These notations are fixed through out the whole paper.

Definition 4.1. Attributes A^i and A^j are isomorphic iff there is a one-to-one and onto map, $s : Dom(A^i) \longrightarrow Dom(A^j)$ such that $A^j(v) = s(A^i(v))\ \forall\ v \in V$. The map s is called an isomorphism.

Intuitively, two columns are isomorphic iff one column turns into another one by properly renaming its attribute values.

Definition 4.2. Let $K = (V, A)$ and $H = (V, B)$ be two information tables, where $A = \{A^1, A^2, \ldots A^n\}$ and $B = \{B^1, B^2, \ldots B^m\}$. Then, K and H are said to be isomorphic if every A^i is isomorphic to some B^j, and vice versa. It is a strict isomorphism, if K and H have the same degree (number of attributes).

This isomorphism is reflexive, symmetric, and transitive, so it classifies all relations into equivalence classes; we call them isomorphic classes.

Definition 4.3. H is a simplified information table of K, if H is isomorphic to K and only has non-isomorphic attributes.

Theorem 4.4. Let H be the simplified information table of K. Then the patterns (large itemsets) of K can be obtained from those of H by elementary operations that will be defined below.

Corollary 4.5. (Strict) Isomorphic Relations have strict isomorphic patterns.

To prove the Theorem, we will set up a lemma, in which we assume there are two isomorphic attributes B and B' in K, that is, degree K - degree H =1. Let $s : Dom(B) \longrightarrow Dom(B')$ be the isomorphism and $b' = s(b)$. Let H be the new table in which B' has been removed.

Lemma 4.6. The patterns of K can be generated from those of H by elementary operations, namely,

1. If b is a large itemset in H, then b' and (b, b') are large in K.
2. If (a. ., b, c. . .) is a large itemset in H, then (a. . , b', c. . .) and (a. . , b, b', c,. . .) are large in K.
3. These are the only large itemsets in K.

The validity of this lemma is rather straightforward; and it provides the critical inductive step for Theorem; we ill skip the proof and only give the illustration.

Convention 4.7. From now on all relations (information tables) are assumed to have non-isomorphic attributes only; that is, all relations are simplified relations. Therefore every isomorphism is a strict isomorphism.

Table 5. Right-hand-side Table H is simplified from Left-hand-side Table K by removing $RANK$

Left hand side Table K					Right hand side Table H			
V	(S#	STATUS	RANK	CITY)	V	(S#	STATUS	CITY)
$v_1 \longrightarrow$	$(S_1$	$TWENTY$	$SECOND$	$C_1)$	$v_1 \longrightarrow$	$(S_1$	$TWENTY$	$C_1)$
$v_2 \longrightarrow$	$(S_2$	TEN	$THIRD$	$C_2)$	$v_2 \longrightarrow$	$(S_2$	TEN	$C_2)$
$v_3 \longrightarrow$	$(S_3$	TEN	$THIRD$	$C_2)$	$v_3 \longrightarrow$	$(S_3$	TEN	$C_2)$
$v_4 \longrightarrow$	$(S_4$	TEN	$THIRD$	$C_2)$	$v_4 \longrightarrow$	$(S_4$	TEN	$C_2)$
$v_5 \longrightarrow$	$(S_5$	TEN	$THIRD$	$C_2)$	$v_5 \longrightarrow$	$(S_5$	TEN	$C_2)$
$v_6 \longrightarrow$	$(S_6$	TEN	$THIRD$	$C_2)$	$v_6 \longrightarrow$	$(S_6$	TEN	$C_2)$
$v_7 \longrightarrow$	$(S_7$	$TWENTY$	$SECOND$	$C_3)$	$v_7 \longrightarrow$	$(S_7$	$TWENTY$	$C_3)$
$v_8 \longrightarrow$	$(S_8$	$THIRTY$	$FIRST$	$C_3)$	$v_8 \longrightarrow$	$(S_8$	$THIRTY$	$C_3)$
$v_9 \longrightarrow$	$(S_9$	$THIRTY$	$FIRST$	$C_3)$	$v_9 \longrightarrow$	$(S_9$	$THIRTY$	$C_3)$

4.2 An Example

We will illustrate the idea by Table 6. The right-hand-side table K has two isomorphic attributes, $STATUS$ and $RANK$. By removing the attribute $RANK$, we get the right-hand-side table H. Let us assume we require the *support* ≤ 4. It is easy to see that in H (left-hand-side table):

1. the 1-itemsets, TEN, and C_2, are large,
2. the 2-itemset, (TEN, C_2), is large

By elementary operations, we can generate the patterns (large itemsets) of K as follows:

1. the 1-itemsets, TEN, C_2 and THIRD, are large
2. the 2-itemsets, (TEN, THIRD) and (C_2, THIRD), are large
3. the 3-itemset, (TEN, C_2, THIRD), is large

It is obvious that searching K is more expensive than H. To find the patterns on K, we will find patterns on H, then generate the answer by elementary operations.

5 Canonical Models and Interpretations

In this section, we construct the canonical model per isomorphic class, and reduce a data mining task(on the given attributes) into

1. Searching formal patterns in the canonical model; we have shown it to be very efficient [31].
2. An interpretation of formal patterns; it is merely a re-labeling of the formal patterns. Observe that we have assumed all relations have distinct attributes (non-isomorphic); otherwise, we use Theorem 4.4.

5.1 Examining a Single Attribute

First we state a simple observation ([22], pp. 25):

Proposition 5.1. Each attribute $A^j : V \longrightarrow C^j = Dom(A^j)$ can be factored into the natural projection and interpretation:

Natural projection: $Q^j : V \longrightarrow V/Q^j : v \longrightarrow [v]$.
Interpretation: $NAME^j : V/Q^j \longrightarrow C^j = Dom(A^j) : [v] \rightarrow NAME^j([v])$.

where

1. The interpretation induces an isomorphism from V/Q^j to C^j, where C^j is the set of symbols representing elementary concepts; these symbols are the so called semantics primitives of K [8]. The interpretation assigns each granule (equivalence class) a symbol (an attribute value) in C^j; we can regard the symbol as a meaningful name of the granule.
2. The interpretation actually also assigns each Q^j a meaningful name A^j; so the notation $NAME : Q^j \longrightarrow A^j$ includes this additional semantics.
3. The natural projection and the induced partition determine each other, we use Q^j to denote the partition as well as the natural projection. We use Q to denote the collection.
4. The natural projection Q^j can be regarded as a single column representation of V into the quotient set, hence,
   a) Q^j is a formal attribute and $Dom(Q^j) = V/Q^j$; in the spirit of [20], they are canonical attribute and canonical domain.
   b) Each granule(equivalence class), as an element of V/Q^j, is a formal attribute value; it was regarded as the canonical name of the granule.

5.2 Full Table

The bag relation K is a product of maps, $K = A^1 \wedge \ldots \wedge A^n$; the product is, in fact, the join operation over the entity column, if each A^j is represented as an information table [20]. So from previous proposition we have,

Proposition 5.2. The bag relation $K = A^1 \wedge \ldots \wedge A^n$ can be factored, i.e., $K = C_K \circ NAME$, where

1. $C_K = Q^1 \wedge \ldots Q^n : V \longrightarrow V/Q^1 \times \ldots V/Q^n = V/(Q^1 \cap \ldots Q^n)$ is the natural projection (an onto map); we abbreviate the last term by V/Q.
2. $NAME = \prod_j NAME^j : \prod_j V/Q^j \longrightarrow \prod_j C^j = Dom(A^j)$ is the interpretation (an isomorphism); as in Section 5.1, we use $NAME : Q \longrightarrow A$ to denote the additional semantics.

In the spirit of Section 1.2, we give several remarks:

1. The notation C_K could mean (by abuse of language)
   (1') the natural projection $Q^1 \wedge \ldots Q^n$ which is a formal knowledge representation,

(2') the image $V/Q = V/Q^1 \times \ldots Q^n = V/(Q^1 \cap \ldots V/Q^n)$ which is a formal relation, or

(3') the graph $\{(v, [v]_{Q^1} \times \ldots [v]_{Q^n}) \mid v \in V\}$ which is a formal information table.

2. The essential ingredients of C_K are the trip $(V, Q, C = V/Q)$, which will be abbreviated to (V, Q).
3. The pair (V, Q) is a very simple kind of models in logic [6], in which the relational structure is a finite set of equivalence relations.
4. Some history: Pawlak calls (V, Q) a knowledge base and an approximation space if Q is a singleton [36]; however, since knowledge base often has different meaning, we do not use it. We simply refer to it as the canonical model; see next.

Table 6. The canonical model C_K at left-hand-side is mapped to K at right-hand-side (by convention K is assumed to be the simplified H)

	Canonical Model C_K				Information Table H		
V	$(Q^0$	Q^2	$Q^3)$		$(S\#$	$STATUS$	$CITY)$
v_1	$(\{v_1\}$	$\{v_1, v_7\}$	$\{v_1\})$		$(S_1$	$TWENTY$	$C_1)$
v_2	$(\{v_2\}$	$\{v_2,v_3,v_4,v_5,v_6\}$	$\{v_2,v_3,v_4,v_5,v_6\})$		$(S_2$	TEN	$C_2)$
v_3	$(\{v_3\}$	$\{v_2,v_3,v_4,v_5,v_6\}$	$\{v_2,v_3,v_4,v_5,v_6\})$	NAME	$(S_3$	TEN	$C_2)$
$v_4 \longrightarrow$	$(\{v_4\}$	$\{v_2,v_3,v_4,v_5,v_6\}$	$\{v_2,v_3,v_4,v_5,v_6\})$	$\longrightarrow$	$(S_4$	TEN	$C_2)$
v_5	$(\{v_5\}$	$\{v_2,v_3,v_4,v_5,v_6\}$	$\{v_2,v_3,v_4,v_5,v_6\})$		$(S_5$	TEN	$C_2)$
v_6	$(\{v_6\}$	$\{v_2,v_3,v_4,v_5,v_6\}$	$\{v_2,v_3,v_4,v_5,v_6\})$		$(S_6$	TEN	$C_2)$
v_7	$(\{v_7\}$	$\{v_1, v_7\}$	$\{v_7, v_8, v_9\})$		$(S_7$	$TWENTY$	$C_3)$
v_8	$(\{v_8\}$	$\{v_8, v_9\}$	$\{v_7, v_8, v_9\})$		$(S_8$	$THIRTY$	$C_3)$
v_9	$(\{v_9\}$	$\{v_8, v_9\}$	$\{v_7, v_8, v_9\})$		$(S_9$	$THIRTY$	$C_3)$

Definition 5.3. The natural projection $C_K : V \longrightarrow Q^1 \times, \ldots, \times Q^n$ is the canonical model of K. It is a formal knowledge representation in the sense C_K represents entities by tulpes of formal attribute values; The equivalence relation Q^j's are the formal attributes and their granules (equivalence classes) are the formal attribute values.

Table 6 illustrates how K is factored into the pair.

The Corollary in Section 4 implies the following:
Theorem 5.4. Patterns of C_K is isomorphic (via interpretation) to the patterns in K.

So to find all patterns of K, we only need to find the patterns on C_K, then generate the patterns of K via Theorem 4.4. Previously, we have shown that finding patterns (large itemsets) in C_K [31] is extremely fast. Therefore, it is beneficial to view a bag relation as a pair:

Definition 5.4. A bag relation is a pair that consists of the canonical model and an interpretation, in notation, $K{=}(C_K, \text{NAME})$, where $NAME : Q \longrightarrow A$ maps the Q^j to A^j and its equivalence classes to attribute values.

6 Universal Model and Feature Completion

The primary goal of this section is to construct the complete set of formal attributes of the canonical model.

6.1 The Relation Lattice – Non Standard Rough Set Theory

The power set 2^A of attributes forms a lattice (Boolean algebra), where meet and join operations are the set theoretical union and intersection respectively; please notice the twist from the common intuition. Let $\Delta(V)$ be the set of all partitions of V (equivalence relations); $\Delta(V)$ forms a lattice, where meet is the intersection of equivalence relations and join is the "union;" the "union," denoted by $\cup_j Q^j$, is the smallest coarsening of all $Q^j, j = 1, 2, \ldots$ Lee calls $\Delta(V)$ the partition lattice. At the beginning of Section 4, we observe that an attribute induces a partition, or more generally, any subset of A does the same [37,9]. We use Q^j to denote the partition induced by A^j. Recall the convention, all attributes are non-isomorphic attributes. Hence all equivalence relations are distinct; see the Convention at Section 4. Next proposition is due to Lee:

Proposition 6.1.1. There is a map

$$\theta : 2^A \longrightarrow \Delta(V),$$

that respects the meet, but not the join, operations. Lee called the image, $Im\theta$, the relation lattice and observe that

1. The join in $Im\theta$ is different from that of $\Delta(V)$.
2. So $Im\theta$ is a subset, but not a sublattice, of $\Delta(V)$.

Such an embedding is an unnatural one, but Lee focused his efforts on it; he established many connections between database concepts and lattice theory. However, we will, instead, take a natural embedding

Definition 6.1.1. The smallest lattice generated by $Im\theta$, by abuse of language, is called the (Lin's) relation lattice, denoted by L(Q).

This definition will not cause confusing, since we will not use Lee's notion all all. The difference between $L(Q)$ and $Im\theta$ is that former contains all the join of distinct attributes.

6.2 Completing the Relation Lattice

Definition 6.1. The smallest lattice, denoted by $L^*(Q)$, containing all coarsening of L(Q) is called the complete relation lattice.

Main Theorem 6.2. $L^*(Q)$ is the set of all derived formal attributes of the canonical model.

Proof: (1) Let $P \in L^*(Q)$, that is, P is an equivalence relation coarser than some $Q^{j_1} \cap ... \cap Q^{j_k}$. Our first task is to prove it is a derived attribute. The coarsening implies a map on their respective quotient sets,

$$g : V/Q^{j_1} \times V/Q^{j_2} ... V/Q^{j_k} = V/(Q^{j_1} \cap Q^{j_2} ... Q^{j_k}) \longrightarrow V/P$$

In terms of relational notations, that is

$$g : Dom(Q^{j_1}) \times ... \times Dom(Q^{j_k}) \longrightarrow Dom(P)$$

Using the notations of functional dependency, we have (equivalence relations are formal attributes in the canonical model)

$$P = g(Q^{j_1}, Q^{j_2}..., Q^{j_k})$$

So g, as a map between attributes, is an attribute transformation. Hence P is a derived attribute.

(2) Let P be a derived attribute of C_K. That is, there is an attribute transformation

$$Dom(Q^{j_1}) \times ... \times Dom(Q^{j_k})) \longrightarrow Dom(P)$$

As C_K is the canonical model, it can be re-expressed in terms of quotient sets,

$$f : V/Q^{j_1} \times ... \times V/Q^{j_k} \longrightarrow V/P$$

Observe that $V/Q^{j_1} \times ... \times V/Q^{j_k} = V/(Q^{j_1} \cap ... \cap Q^{j_k})$, so the existence of f implies that P is coarser than $Q^{j_1} \cap ... \cap Q^{j_k}$. By definition P is an element in $L^*(Q)$. Q.E.D

Corollary 6.3. $L^*(Q)$ is finite. This follows from the fact $\Delta(V)$ is finite.

The pair $U_K = (V, L^*(Q))$ defines a formal bag relation $V \longrightarrow \prod_{P \in L^*(Q)} V/P$. Its formal attributes are all the partitions in $L^*(Q)$, which contains all possible derived formal attributes of $K = (V, Q)$, by the theorem.

Definition 6.4. The pair $U_K = (V, L^*(Q))$ is the completion of $C_K = (V, Q)$ and is called the universal model of K.

6.3 Data Mining with Background Knowledge

In *Definition* 5.4, we write a bag relation as a pair K=(C_K, NAME), where NAME can be viewed as the given knowledge about the bag relation. If in addition there is a given concept hierarchy (Section 9), that is, an extension of E_NAME is defined on a subset of $L^*(Q)$. This additional information is called background knowledge, formally.

Definition 6.5. E_NAME is called a background knowledge, if E_NAME is an extension of NAME, that is, it is defined on $E(Q)$ and equal to NAME on Q, where $Q \subseteq E(Q) \subseteq L^*(Q)$.

Definition 6.6. Data mining with this additional background knowledge on E(Q) is called data mining on derived attributes. We use triple to denote the additional back ground knowledge $(U_K, E(Q), L^*(Q))$

Note that the given relation could be expressed as (K, NAME)=$(U_K$, Q, NAME).

7 Conclusions

The simple observation that isomorphic relations have isomorphic patterns has a strong impact on the meaning of high frequency patterns. Isomorphism is a syntactic notion; it is highly probable that two isomorphic relations have totally different semantics. The patterns mined for one particular application may contain patterns for other applications. Therefore the observation may imply that some additional structures may be needed to capture deeper application semantics. Some authors, including us, have begun to explore this area [30,19,20,22, 28,25,27], [12], [32].

We hope the readers are convinced that data mining on derived attributes are very important, but quite difficult. Though we have shown that the possible derived attributes are finite (from traditional view of features, conceivably it may be infinite), but the best possible bound of all derived attributes is very large; it is the Bell number B_n [3], where n is the number of equivalence classes in the $\bigcap Q^j$; further research is necessary. In the mean time, we set up a framework of background knowledge to cope with the big number.

8 Appendix – Invisible Patterns

In this section we give a numerical example to illustrate the given set of attribute is inadequate. A numerical tuple can be interpreted as a coordinate of a point in Euclidean space. The attribute $\{A_1, A_2, ..., A_n\}$ are the coordinate system $\{X_1, X_2, ..., X_n\}$ of an Euclidean space. A numerical tuple is the coordinate $x = (x_1, x_2, ..., x_n)$ of a point p_x. One should note that p_x is a geometric object, but x is, merely a coordinate, not a geometric entity.

Table 7 consists of two tables. The right side table has

one association rule of length 2: $(X_3, 2.0)$

However the left hand side table has no association rules,

the only association rule disappears.

A moment of reflection, one should realize that since the association rule is a real world phenomenon (a geometric fact), the same information should be still carried in left hand side table. The question

How can this "invisible" association rule be mined?

This phenomenon reflects the fact that the given set of attributes is inadequate; we need derived attributes.

Though our discussions have focused on numerical attributes, the same arguments are valid for symbolic data. We have not used symbolic data, because the complex mathematics may obscure the issues.

Table 7. Left-hand-side Table: segments in(X,Y)-coordinates; Right-hand-side Table: segments in polar coordinates

Segment#	Begin_point	Horizontal	Vertical	Segment#	Begin_point	Length	Direction
S_0	X_1	6	0	S_0	X_1	6.0	0
S_1	X_2	$3\sqrt{3}$	3	S_1	X_2	6.0	60
S_2	X_3	0	2	S_2	X_3	2.0	90
S_3	X_3	-1	$\sqrt{3}$	S_3	X_3	2.0	120
S_4	X_3	$-\sqrt{2}$	$\sqrt{2}$	S_4	X_3	2.0	135
S_5	X_3	$-\sqrt{3}$	1	S_5	X_3	2.0	150
S_6	X_3	-2	0	S_6	X_3	2.0	180
S_7	X_3	$-\sqrt{3}$	-1	S_7	X_3	2.0	210
S_8	X_3	$-\sqrt{2}$	$-\sqrt{2}$	S_8	X_3	2.0	225
S_9	X_3	$-\sqrt{3}$	-1	S_9	X_3	2.0	240

9 Appendix – Attribute-Oriented Generalization and Concept Hierarchies

Attribute-oriented generalization (AOG) is a technique to summarize information using concepts which are higher level than the original data. In AOG [2], the input consists of a table of tuples retrieved by a database query, and a set of concept hierarchies. Attribute values of tuples are generalized by replacing them with concepts higher up in the concept hierarchy for that attribute. This process decreases the number of tuples, yielding more general statements about the relation. The goal of this section is to show that the concept hierarchy is a nested sequence of named equivalence relations on attribute values Let us examine the concept hierarchy in a fixed attribute, say B.

1. A level-0 node(leaf) $L_j^0 = NAME(C_j^0)$ is a name (level-0 base concept) of an attribute value C_j^0.
   Each leaf has a unique parent. By grouping those leaves that have the same parent (a level-1 node) into granules (equivalence classes), we get an equivalence relation R^0.
2. A level-1 node $L_h^1 = NAME(C_h^1)$ is a name (level-1 base concept) of an R^0-granule C_h^1 of level-0 base concepts.
   Again, each level-1 base concept has a unique parent. By grouping these base concepts that have the same parent (a level-1 node) into granules, we get R^1, an equivalence relation on level-1 base concepts.

3. A level-2 node $L_i^2 = NAME(C_i^2)$ is a name (level-2 base concept) of R^1-granules of level-1 base concepts L_i^1.
   A level-2 base concept is a name of names. The equivalence relation R^1 (on the level-1 base concepts) induces an equivalence relation F^1 on the attribute values (leaves): A R^1-granule consists of $L_i^1 = NAME(C_i^1)$. So if we take the union of C_i^1 's we get an equivalence class of leaves.
4. In general, a level-n node $L_k^n = NAME(C_k^n)$ is a name (level-n base concept) of $R^{(n-1)}$-granule of level-(n-1) base concepts $L_k^{(n-1)}$.

A level-n ($n \geq 2$) base concept is a name of names of names ... The equivalence relation $R^{(n-1)}$ (on the level-(n-1) base concepts) induces an equivalence relation $F^{(n-1)}$ on the attribute values (leaves). Note that F^j is a coarsening of F^i, if $i < j$.

Definition Two concept hierarchies are equivalent, if there is a one to one, onto and order preserving map between the nodes of two concept hierarchies.

Proposition A concept hierarchy induces a nested sequence of named partitions (equivalence relations) $F^j, j = 1, 2, \ldots$, on the attribute values (leaves) of the given attribute.

Such a nested sequence of named or labeled partition is called a background knowledge.

10 Appendix – Functions and Maps

Function and map are synonym. A map, $F : X \longrightarrow Y$, is a single valued function or more precisely, an association that assigns each element x of the domain X a unique value in the range Y, written as $y = F(x)$. In general, not every y can be so written, the collection of all such y. The set $F(X) = \{F(x) \mid x \in X\}$ is called the image of F, and denoted by imF We write $F^{-1}(y) = \{x \mid y = f(x)\}$ and call it inverse image of y under f. The collection of all such inverse images, $\{F^{-1}(y) \mid y \in Y\}$, forms a partition on X; hence an equivalence relation and a quotient set. We say the map F is onto if every y can be written as y = F(x). A map is on-to-one, if there is only one x that maps to $y = F(x)$, that is, $F(x) = F(x')$ implies $x = x'$.

Each map F can be factored through the quotient set, that is,
$$F(x) = EM \bullet NP(x) = EM(NP(x)),$$
where NP(x) is the natural projection that map each x to the equivalence class [x] containing x; it is onto. EM is the embedding that maps [x] to y; note that y=F(x), so $[x] = F^{-1}(y)$; it is one-to-one. If F is onto, then EM is also onto. In this paper, EM has been called naming map. Finally, we conclude this section with a general comment. A function is often confused with "formula," a function is not necessary expressible by a "formula."

References

1. R. Agrawal, T. Imielinski, and A. Swami, "Mining Association Rules Between Sets of Items in Large Databases," in Proceeding of ACM-SIGMOD international Conference on Management of Data, pp. 207–216, Washington, DC, June, 1993
2. G. Birkhoff and S. MacLane, A Survey of Modern Algebra, Macmillan, 1977
3. Richard A. Brualdi, Introductory Combinatorics, Prentice Hall, 1992.
4. Y.D. Cai, N. Cercone, and J. Han. Attribute-oriented induction in relational databases. In Knowledge Discovery in Databases, pages 213–228. AAAI/MIT Press, Cambridge, MA, 1991.
5. C. J. Date, C. DATE, An Introduction to Database Systems, 7th ed., Addison-Wesley, 2000.
6. Herbert B, Enderton, A mathematical Introduction to logic, Academic Press, 1972.
7. Fayad, U. M., Piatetsky-Sjapiro, G. Smyth, P. ¿From Data Mining to Knowledge Discovery: An overview. In Fayard, Piatetsky-Sjapiro, Smyth, and Uthurusamy eds., Knowledge Discovery in Databases, AAAI/MIT Press, 1996.
8. A. Barr and E.A. Feigenbaum, The handbook of Artificial Intelligence, Willam Kaufmann 1981
9. T. T. Lee, "Algebraic Theory of Relational Databases," The Bell System Technical Journal Vol 62, No 10, December, 1983, pp.3159–3204
10. T. Y. Lin, "Issues in Data Mining," in:the Proceeding of 26th IEEE Internaational Conference on Computer Software and Applications, Oxford, UK, Aug 26–29, 2002.
11. T. Y. Lin "Feature Completion," Communication of IICM (Institute of Information and Computing Machinery, Taiwan) Vol 5, No. 2, May 2002, pp. 57–62. This is the proceeding for the workshop "Toward the Foundation on Data Mining" in PAKDD2002, May 6, 2002.
12. Ng, R., Lakshmanan, L.V.S., Han, J. and Pang, A. Exploratory mining and pruning optimizations of constrained associations rules, *Proceedings of 1998 ACM-SIGMOD Conference on Management of Data*, 13–24, 1998.
13. T. Y. Lin, Y. Y. Yao, and E. Louie, "Value Added Association Rules, " 6th Pacific-Asia Conference, Taipei, Taiwan, May 6-8, 2002, pp. 328–333, Lecture Notes on Artificial Intelligent series 2336
14. T. Y. Lin "The Lattice Structure of Database and Mining Multiple Level Rules." Presented in the Workshop on Data Mining and E-organizations, COMPSAC 2001, Chicago, Oct 8–12, 2001; due to some clerical error, the paper was presented, but the text was not in the Proceeding; however, the exact copy appear SPIE conference; see next
15. T. Y. Lin "Feature Transformations and Structure of Attributes" In: Data Mining and Knowledge Discovery: Theory, Tools, and Technology IV, Proceeding of SPIE's aeroSence, Orlando, FL. April 1–4, 2002, pp. 1–8; a reprint of [14]
16. T. Y. Lin "Data Model for Data Mining" In: Data Mining and Knowledge Discovery: Theory, Tools, and Technology IV, Proceeding of SPIE's aeroSence, Orlando, FL. April 1–4, 2002 , pp. 138–145.
17. T. Y. Lin "Attributes Transformations for Data Mining: Theoretical Explorations," International Journal of Intelligent Systems, to appear
18. T. Y. Lin and J. Tremba "Attribute Transformations for Data Mining II: Applications to Economic and Stock Market Data," International Journal of Intelligent Systems, to appear

19. T. Y. Lin, "Association Rules in Semantically Rich Relations: Granular Computing Approach" JSAI International Workshop on Rough Set Theory and Granular Computing May 20–25, 2001. The Post Proceeding is in Lecture note in AI 2253, Springer-Verlag, 2001, pp. 380–384.
20. T. Y. Lin, "Data Mining and Machine Oriented Modeling: A Granular Computing Approach," Journal of Applied Intelligence, Kluwer, Vol. 13, No 2, September/October,2000, pp.113-124.
21. T. Y. Lin, "Attribute Transformations on Numerical Databases," Lecture Notes in Artificial Intelligence 1805, Terano, Liu, Chen (eds), PAKDD2000, Kyoto, Japan, April 18–20, 2000, 181–192.
22. T. Y. Lin, "Data Mining: Granular Computing Approach." In: Methodologies for Knowledge Discovery and Data Mining, Lecture Notes in Artificial Intelligence 1574, Third Pacific-Asia Conference, Beijing, April 26–28, 1999, 24–33.
23. T. Y. Lin, "Granular Computing on Binary Relations I: Data Mining and Neighborhood Systems." In: Rough Sets In Knowledge Discovery, A. Skoworn and L. Polkowski (eds), Springer-Verlag, 1998, 107–121.
24. T. Y. Lin " Discovering Patterns in Numerical Sequences Using Rough set Theory," In: Proceeding of the Third World Multi-conferences on Systemics, Cybernatics, and Informatics, Vol 5, Computer Science and Engineering, Orlando, Florida, July 31-Aug 4, 1999
25. "Frameworks for Mining Binary Relations in Data." In: Rough sets and Current Trends in Computing, Lecture Notes on Artificial Intelligence 1424, A. Skoworn and L. Polkowski (eds), Springer-Verlag, 1998, 387–393.
26. T. Y. Lin, "Rough Set Theory in Very Large Databases," Symposium on Modeling, Analysis and Simulation, CESA'96 IMACS Multi Conference (Computational Engineering in Systems Applications), Lille, France, July 9–12, 1996, Vol. 2 of 2, 936–941.
27. T. Y. Lin and M. Hadjimichael, "Non-Classificatory Generalization in Data Mining," in Proceedings of the Fourth International Workshop on Rough Sets, Fuzzy Sets, and Machine Discovery, November 6-8, Tokyo, Japan, 1996, 404–411.
28. T. Y. Lin, and Y.Y. Yao "Mining Soft Rules Using Rough Sets and Neighborhoods," Symposium on Modeling, Analysis and Simulation, CESA'96 IMACS Multiconference (Computational Engineering in Systems Applications), Lille, France, July 9-12, 1996, Vol. 2 of 2, pp. 1095–1100.
29. T.Y. Lin, Eric Louie, "Modeling the Real World for Data Mining: Granular Computing Approach" Joint 9th IFSA World Congress and 20th NAFIPS Conference, July 25–28, Vancouver, Canada, 2001
30. E. Louie,T. Y. Lin, "Semantics Oriented Association Rules," In: 2002 World Congress of Computational Intelligence, Honolulu, Hawaii, May 12-17, 2002, 956–961 (paper # 5702)
31. E. Louie and T. Y. Lin, "Finding Association Rules using Fast Bit Computation: Machine-Oriented Modeling," in: Foundations of Intelligent Systems, Z. Ras and S. Ohsuga (eds), Lecture Notes in Artificial Intelligence 1932, Springer-Verlag, 2000, pp. 486–494. (12th International symposium on methodologies for Intelligent Systems, Charlotte, NC, Oct 11–14, 2000)
32. Lu, S. Hu. H. and Li, F. Mininh weighted association rules, *Intelligent data analysis*, **5**, 211–225, 2001.
33. Hiroshi Motoda and Huan Liu "Feature Selection, Extraction and Construction," Communication of IICM (Institute of Information and Computing Machinery, Taiwan) Vol 5, No. 2, May 2002, pp. 67–72. This is the proceeding for the workshop "Toward the Foundation on Data Mining" in PAKDD2002, May 6, 2002.

34. H. Liu and H. Motoda, "Feature Transformation and Subset Selection," IEEE Intelligent Systems, Vol. 13, No. 2, March/April, pp.26–28 (1998)
35. H. Liu and H. Motoda (eds), Feature Extraction, Construction and Selection - A Data Mining Perspective, Kluwer Academic Publishers (1998).
36. Z. Pawlak, Rough sets. Theoretical Aspects of Reasoning about Data, Kluwer Academic Publishers, 1991
37. Z. Pawlak, Rough sets. International Journal of Information and Computer Science **11**, 1982, pp. 341–356.
38. R. Ng, L. V. S. Lakshmanan, J. Han and A. Pang, " Exploratory Mining and Pruning Optimizations of Constrained Associations Rules", Proc. of 1998 ACM-SIGMOD Conf. on Management of Data, Seattle, Washington, June 1998, pp. 13–24.
39. Pei, J. Han, and L. V. S. Lakshmanan, "Mining Frequent Itemsets with Convertible Constraints", Proc. 2001 Int. Conf. on Data Engineering (ICDE'01), Heidelberg, Germany, April 2001.
40. J. Pei and J. Han, "Can We Push More Constraints into Frequent Pattern Mining?", Proc. Sixth ACM SIGKDD International Conference on Knowledge Discovery and Data Mining (KDD'2000), Boston, MA, August 2000.
41. J. Ullman and J. Windom, A First Course in Database Systems, Prentice Hall, 1997.

A Proposed Evolutionary, Self-Organizing Automaton for the Control of Dynamic Systems

David W. Russell

Penn State Great Valley
Malvern, PA 19355, USA
drussell@psu.edu

Abstract. BOXES is a well known methodology that learns to perform control maneuvers for dynamic systems with only cursory a priori knowledge of the mathematics of the system model. A limiting factor in the BOXES algorithm has always been the assignment of appropriate boundaries to subdivide each state variable into regions. In addition to suggesting a method of alleviating this weakness, the paper shows that the accumulated statistical data in near neighboring states may be a powerful agent in accelerating learning, and may eventually provide a possible evolution to self-organization. A heuristic process is postulated that may allow strong areas of knowledge in the system domain to create larger cellular structures, while causing the more delicate, uncertain, or untested regions to take on a finer granularity. The paper theorizes that these *untrainable* states may contain valuable and sufficient information about the location of switching surfaces. The paper concludes with some future research questions.

1 Introduction

The modeling and control of poorly-defined, non-linear, real-time dynamic systems has always been classically problematic, and mathematically approximate at best. An awareness of the paucity of linearized models of real systems has caused researchers to turn to artificial intelligence (AI) for a possible source of solutions. The attractiveness of systems that utilize genetic algorithms, fuzzy logic, and neural networks, and their collected ability to tolerate uncertainty needs hardly to be mentioned. Perhaps the strongest feature that AI-based paradigms offer is their ability to adapt both parametrically and structurally.

When the configuration of a system is made to alter from within, directed by some performance heuristic, it is said to self-organizing. The recognition and admiration of the rapidity and agility of the human problem-solving cognitive process has always been seen as a possible metaphor for the (optimal) solution of "wicked" [1] control problems that are difficult for even the usual AI-based systems to control. Because in these systems, there is always a very real possibility that a significant variable may have been omitted from the model or some unexpected unstable or chaotic behavior may be exhibited during prolonged operation of the system. For example, as the components of a real-world system wear so the surfaces of controllability (presuming they exist) migrate nomadically inside the system domain. To adapt to the new problem is often temporally prohibitive or systemically impossible while the system is on-line.

One fairly well known group of AI-based controllers utilizes a *signature-table* [2] mechanism in which to contain decision intelligence, and requires only that the state variables be normalized and that the boundaries dividing each state variable into regions be known. The mathematical model of the dynamics of the system does not feature in the structure of the controller, which learns using a statistical inference procedure that is based on performance criteria only. The basic premise is that the system space can be divided into many (non-equal) regions of operation and that each region can be uniquely identified. Each region, or cell, owns a decision value that can only be altered at the end of the current sequence. It is in this respect that control problems can adopt the similitude of a board game. For example in chess, there is always an end-result or end-of-game event, namely win, draw or loss. What is often ignored is the heuristic import in a flawed game. For example when an opponent, realizing the hopelessness of the situation, retires without playing out the game; or an illegal move or move sequence is made; or more drastically, that the game board is physically moved or even dropped, so destroying that instance of the game. The chess-game metaphor can be easily adapted to partially fit real-world systems. For example, in a dynamic system, the unavoidable end-game incident may be a timeout or programmed interrupt, and the flawed game occurring because of a component failure or critical fault.

2 The Simple Boxes Signature Table Controller

The BOXES methodology [3] is an example (and precursor) of a signature-table controller. Seminal work [4] on the control of a real inverted pendulum – in the form of a "pole and cart" – was performed in Liverpool. The problem is still a popular topic of study [5]. Stated simply, a motorized trolley is made to move in such a way as to balance a freely hinged pole; the control task is to keep the pole from falling while also keeping the trolley, which may skid, on a finite track. This is not to be confused with the relatively simple swing-up pole balancing systems that are readily available and a favorite in student laboratories. The non-trivial solution to the pole and cart problem is to make the pole swing with steady bounded motion that is forced by moving the cart back and forth along a track. The switching surface has been shown [6] to lie between clearly defined bi-polar regions. A Pontriagin analysis [7] of the system model confirms that optimal control is achievable using a *bang-bang* schema, which means that the optimal solution is contained in a sequence of binary (LEFT or RIGHT) control decisions within the state space control region. The control task is simply to provide the motorized cart with the correct sequence of LEFT and RIGHT directives. The system is deemed to fail if any state variable (see below) falls outside of pre-set boundaries, in which case, the BOXES algorithm re-computes its control matrix and restarts another run.

To implement a BOXES-type controller for the trolley and pole system, certain rules are therefore enforceable, which include:

- The motor on the trolley is to be digitally switched between full LEFT or full RIGHT only
- The system will usually fail or be terminated by a timeout after a long run
- Learning is to be effected only after the system fails or the run is aborted
- The initial control matrix is randomly seeded with LEFT and RIGHT decisions
- Failure is defined by any state-variable going out of range
- Reasonable initial conditions of the state variables are to be randomly generated

On-line, real time control can be imposed on the system by the following:
- Real-time signal processing of state variables
- Computing the current state region identification integer, m, based solely on the sampled values of the state variables
- Indexing the signature-table control matrix, Φ, to obtain a control value, $u=\Phi[m]$, where Φ exists only as a set of +1 and -1 values, representing the demand for LEFT or RIGHT motion
- Returning u as the closed-loop control decision to the system
- Enforcing the decision using a rapid reversal motor (e.g. printed armature)
- Sampling the state variables at a sufficiently rapid rate

2.1 Overall Performance Metric

In order to evaluate the efficacy of control, it is commonplace to monitor the progression of *system merit* over many training runs. The basic merit of the system, for a trolley and pole, is an average of run time-to-failure weighted by a *forgetfulness factor*, δk. This factor downgrades early experience and eliminates skewing due to the random initial control matrix. Equations (1)-(3) show how merit may be defined:

$$global\_life = global\_life * \delta k + T_f \qquad (1)$$

$$global\_use = global\_use * \delta k + 1 \qquad (2)$$

$$system\_merit = global\_life / global\_use \qquad (3)$$

where
 $global\_life$ = weighted average run-time, T_f = the last run time-to-failure
 $global\_use$ = weighted experience, δk = forgetfulness factor (usually ~0.99)

As the system learns to perform the task (of balancing the pole), the value of *system merit* should increase, in which case contributing cells ($\Phi[m]$) should be rewarded. Conversely, if the last run produced a shorter than average performance, those cells that contributed to the decisions must be penalized.

2.2 The Importance of State Boundaries

It is obvious that the location and number of boundaries for each of the state variables attached to the BOXES system is of paramount importance. Russell [8] in a critique of the BOXES method observes that these boundary values present a "potential flaw in the methodology." It is the thesis of this paper that within this "flaw" may lay a novel mechanism for self-organization. To simplify the process, all **N** state variables are normalized before entering the state allocation algorithm. It is assumed here that an a priori knowledge of the maximum and minimum value for each variable is available. Equation (4) shows the process that transforms $var_i(t)$ into V_i its normalized value.

$$V_i = (Vmax_i - var_i(t)) / (Vmax_i - Vmin_i) \qquad (4)$$

where

$var_i(t)$ = current sampled value of the i-th. state variable
$Vmax_i$ = maximum value of the i-th. state variable
$Vmin_i$ = minimum value of the i-th. state variable

If each state variable (V_i) is sub-dividable into N_{bi} zones as shown in Figure 1, then it is a simple algorithmic process to assign individual "zone numbers" ($\mathbf{Z_1}$ to $\mathbf{Z_N}$) for each normalized state variable (all $V_i(t) \in 0..1$).

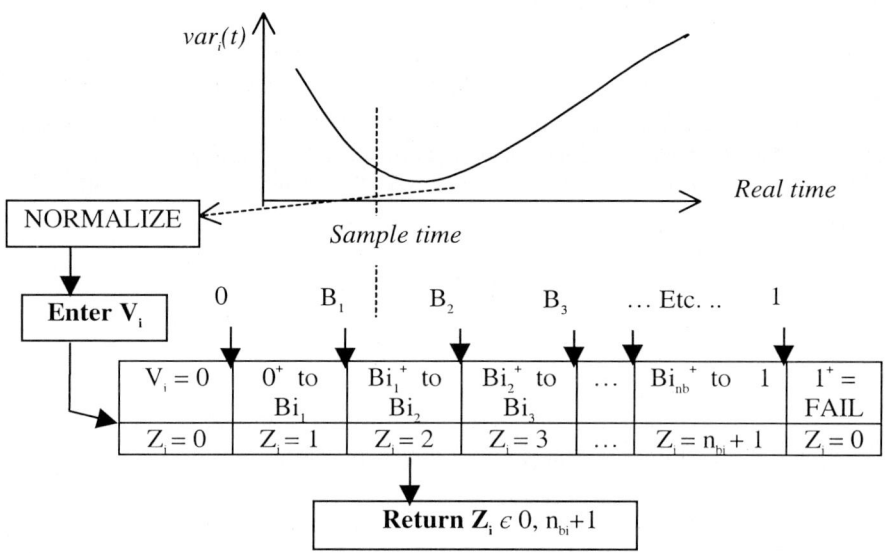

Fig. 1. Assignment of State Variable Zone Number, $\mathbf{Z_i}$

2.3 Unique State Number Allocation

In the BOXES method, the set of zone integers $\{Z_1...Z_n\}$ defines the system at any time within a given sample period. If the number of boundaries for each variable is contained in the set $\{Nb_1...Nb_n\}$, simple integer arithmetic yields a unique state number **m** for any given set of zones as seen in Equation 5.

$$m = Z_1 + \Sigma_{k=2..N} (\Pi_{i=1..k-1}(Nb_i).(Z_k-1))) \tag{5}$$

2.3.1 A Numerical Example. In the classic work by Michie and Chambers [3], for a trolley and pole system, the state variables x (the trolley position) and θ (the pole angle) were divided into five regions (i.e. $Nb_1=Nb_3=5$), whereas dx/dt (the trolley velocity) and dθ/dt (the pole velocity) were divided into three (i.e. $Nb_2=Nb_4=3$). Applying end values for each zone, Equation (5) above for four state variables (N = 4), yields:

for $\{Z_1..Z_4\} = \{1,1,1,1\}$, m=1 + (5*0+5*3*0+ 5*3*5*0) = 1
for $\{Z_1..Z_4\} = \{5,3,5,3\}$, m =5+ (5*2+5*3*4+5*3*5*2) = 225

This means that the control matrix would have 225 elements (5*3*5*3), which was the indeed the case. If the value of any variable strays outside of the posted minimum or maximum values, the system is deemed to have failed, and the value m=0 returned.

2.4 Run-Time Data

As the system functions, data is collected by the BOXES algorithm. This may be a count of the number of times any particular state (or "box") is entered, or a summation of the amount of time that the system populated any given state. In practice, these data items are determined by the required learning task. If the idea is to balance a pole for extended periods of time, it should not be surprising that the time the system dwells within any given cell would be important. If the primary learning task is to eliminate bounce [9], then data related to divergence from some datum line etc. would be more appropriate. In any event, data is accumulated for each entered state only, which implies that all states are not going to be entered during any specific run, and as such are non-contributors to the control this time. If the initial conditions of all variables are always set to be random, yet rational, values the system will be forced into exploring its operational domain.

2.5 Statistical Database Update

At the end of each learning run the system merit is recomputed according to Equations (1)–(3) above, and reflects the current overall performance or skill level of the system. To effect learning, the BOXES post-processing algorithm must now update the statistical database for each cell by merging the data accumulated during the previous run with statistics stored from all previous runs. Because the decision context is binary (e.g. LEFT/RIGHT) two sets of statistics must be kept for each value of **m**, one for either value.
If the heuristic calls for a count of entries into a state, the data elements (for the i-th. cell) would be *left_count$_i$* and *right_count$_i$*. If the time spent populating that cell was

selected as another statistical parameter, the data elements would be *left_life*$_i$ and *right_life*$_i$. If the prior run had used the i-th cell n_i times and spent *tim*$_i$ (time units) in that cell, and if it was currently supplying LEFT as its knowledge element, Equations (6)-(9) show how the statistics would be updated.

$$left\_count_i = left\_count_i * \delta k + n_i \quad (6)$$

$$right\_count_i = right\_count_i * \delta k \quad (7)$$

$$left\_life_i = left\_life_i * \delta k + tim_i \quad (8)$$

$$right\_life_i = right\_life_i * \delta k \quad (9)$$

In the case of the trolley and pole system, sometimes the *time to fail* is used instead of *tim*$_i$. Aging both phyla is appropriate in order that past data is uniformly rated as less significant (i.e. forgotten).

2.6 Decision Strength Determination

Once the statistical database has been updated to include the current run, and a new overall system merit identified, the BOXES algorithm assigns statistical strengths for both control decisions. Equations (10)–(12) are typical of this calculation, again shown for the i-th. cell.

$$dla = C_0 + C_1 * merit \quad (10)$$

$$left\_strength_i = \frac{[left\_life_i + K*dla])}{[left\_count_i + K]} \quad (11)$$

$$right\_strength_i = \frac{[right\_life_i + K*dla]}{[right\_count_i + K]} \quad (12)$$

where
    C_0 = learning coefficient,   dla = desired level of achievement
    C_1 = learning coefficient,   K = desired learning rate

In the learning phase, the decision matrix, $\Phi[i]$, for each cell is updated based on the value of the statistical strengths of each decision using:

```
Repeat
        If left_strength (i) > right_strength (i)
   then Φ[i] = "LEFT"
        If right_strength (i) > left_strength (i)
   then Φ[i] = "RIGHT"
for all "i" cells
```

Figure 2 is a stylization of typical learning runs for the original BOXES algorithm that was connected to the physical system compared with human performance on the Liverpool rig and random decisions and are based on actual data.

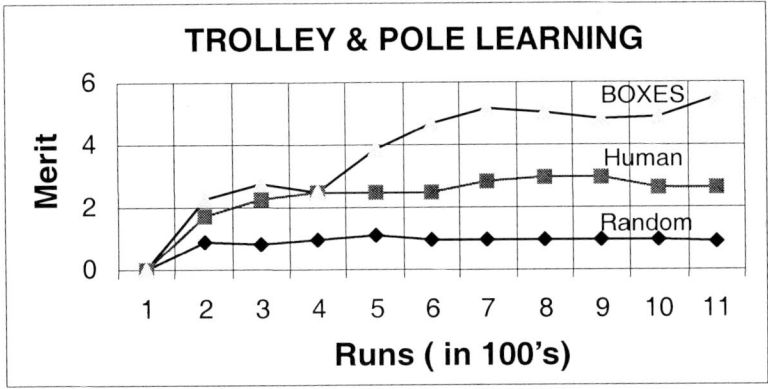

Fig. 2. Comparison of the BOXES Algorithm to a Human Operator and Random Decisions

3 Further Use of the Statistical Data

In subsequent studies [10], the author discovered that the performance of the learning algorithm could be much improved by the addition of advisor logic into the decision matrix update procedure. Two advisor schemas were tested, namely, winner-takes-all voting and statistical strength aggregation.

3.1 Winner-Takes-All Voting

Basically, before a control decision ($u = \Phi[m]$) is returned to the trolley's actuator, the advisor system identifies a set of neighboring matrix cells (ADV{1..na}) and inspects the decision each would have returned had it been the state of choice. This is straightforward to implant into the standard algorithm, provided the edges of state space are handled correctly. The "advice" from each state was weighted (w_j) according to its proximity in the control domain to the selected, actual cell. Recalling that the matrix values of are usually ± 1 to represent LEFT/RIGHT motion, the weighted control decisions contribute their vote by algebraic summation (see Equation (13).) If a net negative result ensued, a LEFT decision would be returned, regardless of the cell's true value, and vice versa if positive.

$$u = \text{SIGN}[\ \Phi[m] + \Sigma_{j \in ADV\{1..na\}}\ w_j * \Phi[j]\ ] \tag{13}$$

where
ADV = the set of "na" advisor state number, na = # of advisors proximate to cell-m
w_j = *value weighting factor for each advisor, u = control decision (+1 or −1)*

3.2 Statistical Strength Aggregation

A second, more computationally intensive, method performed a similar scan of all possible advisor states, but instead of returning a simple "vote", an aggregation of the decision strengths of the selected advisors was used to offer advice to the true cell. The following pseudocode describes the process more exactly for the selected cell "m".

```
if Φ[m] = "L" then
            strength_m = left_strength_m
      else
            strength_m = right_stength_m
endif
advice=0
for each advisor, j ∈ ADV{1..na}
   if φ[j] = "L" then
         advice=advice+left_strength_j* w_j* φ[j]
      else
         advice=advice+right_strength_j* w_j* φ[j]]
   endif
next advisor
```

If the cumulative value of the *advice* outweighs the natural strength (*strength_m*), the advisor aggregate decision is made to prevail – and the control value (u) is assigned the value of SIGN(*advice*)*1. If the advice is considered weak, the natural stored value (*φ[m]*) is asserted. In both cases, during the post-processing phase, the advisor cells are statistically rewarded or penalized based on their contribution to the change in system merit. In this manner, the advisors were made actually "accountable" for their influence on the native cell value. This was seen as necessary in order to respect the strength of mature cells and to incidentally add a secondary heuristic to the learning process as the advisor learns from the advisee.

Figure 3 at the next page shows the effect of using an accountable advisor scheme within the BOXES methodology. It clearly shows that delaying the advisor algorithm until the signature table had experience caused a better growth in system merit.

4 Self Organization

The location of advisors for any selected cell is relatively simple to compute and importance weightings are assigned by the proximity of the advisor to the cell and its strength. Ideally, the whole signature table could be considered as a grand advisor, with weaker and weaker weights the further the advisor cell is from the selected cell. The set of advisor states and their control knowledge (*Φ[j]*, $strength_i$ and weight (w_j)) contains spatial and decisional information about the region around any cell. Because the statistics for each advisor are also available, it was demonstrated any cell can use this peripheral knowledge in correcting its own value when selected and contributing to other cells itself by acting in an advisory capacity.

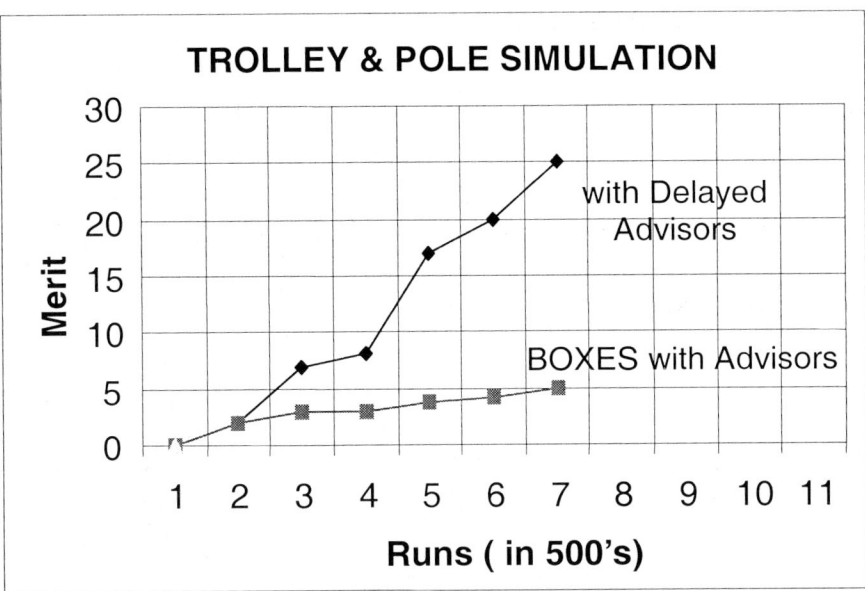

Fig. 3. Comparison of the BOXES Algorithm with Accountable Advisors-delayed advisor data is shown for when advising is suspended for the first 1500 runs allowing the algorithm to gain experience

When the goal is purely to return a *more intelligent* control value, advising is enough. However, an interesting evolution of this paradigm is that there may be a greater advantage in locating *self-similar* cells inside the advisor set. By self-similar, it is meant that these proximate cells agree in decision value and relative strengths with the currently selected cell. When such occurrences exist, the internal structure of the BOXES method could then be reorganized by removing the common cell boundary. Conversely, if a cell is stranded in a cluster of uncertainty, the process can be reversed forcing the system to divide the state space into finer cell structures. In this latter case, each fragment would be initialized with the current parent cell strengths and statistics. Both cases would be extremely problematic for the BOXES algorithm, because the intrinsic knowledge of the cells is keyed from a unique cell number that is computed from the number of regions that exist by virtue of the boundary data in each variable.

A better scheme may be to move a cell's boundary value towards a neighboring boundary in proportion to the neighboring cell strengths, thus retaining the original number of regions. In this way, a cell can grow in response to strong performance and shrink if the system performance deteriorates over time. Figure 4 shows how a weak zone could be compressed by strong conflicting neighbors. The inner configuration of the BOXES cellular structure is therefore evolving and self-organizing. The research is indicating that after several compressions a zone may become very small and be untrainable, which would seem to indicate the proximity of a switching surface.

Post –processing: Initial Condition

Initial Configu-Ration	0^+ to Bi_1 $Z_i=1$	Bi_1^+ to Bi_2 $Z_i=2$	Bi_2^+ to Bi_3 $Z_i=3$	Zone $_K$	Bi_{nb}^+ to 1 $Z_i=n_{hi}+1$	
	STRONG RIGHT	WEAK LEFT	MEDIUM RIGHT	WEAK LEFT	STRONG LEFT	FAIL
	→		→	←→	←	

Post –processing: Compression in zone "K"

Initial Configu-ration	0^+ to Bi_1 $Z_i=1$	Bi_1^+ to Bi_2 $Z_i=2$	Bi_2^+ to Bi_3 $Z_i=3$	K	Bi_{nb}^+ to 1 $Z_i=n_{hi}+1$	
	STRONG RIGHT	WEAK LEFT	MEDIUM-STRONG RIGHT		VERY STRONG LEFT	FAIL
	→		→	←→	←	

On Further Post –processing: Is zone "K" on the Switching Curve?

Initial Configu-ration	0^+ to Bi_1 $Z_i=1$	Bi_1^+ to Bi_2 $Z_i=2$	Bi_2^+ to Bi_3 $Z_i=3$	Bi_{nb}^+ to 1 $Z_i=n_{hi}+1$	
	STRONG RIGHT	WEAK LEFT	VERY STRONG RIGHT	VERY STRONG LEFT	FAIL
	→		→	←	

Fig. 4. Evolution of Cellular Boundaries to Discover Switching Surfaces

5 Conclusions and Future Research

The paper has demonstrated how the BOXES controller, which is of the "black-box" signature table variety, can be extended to reduce dependency on the decision contained in any unique state. Advising causes the controller to scan near neighbor states before returning a control value. Because the method by which the state variables are segmented into zones is largely intuitive, the notion of self-organization enables the system to alter the physical dimensions of the hypercubes that make up the cell structure that define the problem domain. On reflection, this morphological process attacks the uncertainty associated with the location of cell boundaries, which is a major flaw in the BOXES paradigm. Another benefit, and the focus of future research, may be that the method should alter the cell size rather than alter the number of cells, so that the small zones, which indicate a possible switching surface, can be identified. The stable zones will become larger as is expected in a bang-bang control system such is desired for the forced trolley and pole. As the system matures, it should be possible, even in an ill-defined system, to estimate the location of these difficult control surfaces simply by an inspection of the generated thin boundary locations in the state space.

The self-organizing implementation of the BOXES method is intriguing in that it possibly may contain a connection to the human adaptive cognitive process by which learning and certainty of persuasion occur. Most models of the brain have difficulty with the explanation of how humans differentiate between "knowing for sure" and "believing." For example, the accumulation of experience in some familiar area may reduce the cognitive effort to produce an action plan or "pattern" for a similar task, which in turn may well both hinder or enhance the ability to solve previously unknown problems. Humphrey [11] discussed the recovery of some level of sight in patients suffering from blind-sightedness that had been caused by damage to the visual cortex. His observation was that there seemed to be "... a residual capacity for vision of which (the subject) was unaware."

Future research will explore the possibility of a connection between the popular metaphor of cellular synaptic connectivity to an ideology of self-organizing and regenerative neural regions such as observed in the advanced BOXES algorithm.

References

1. Blum, B.I. 1996. *Beyond Programming: to a New Era of Design,* 132–134. New York: Oxford University Press
2. Canudas de Wit, C. A. 1988. *Adaptive Control for Partially-known Systems*, 99ff. Amsterdam: Elsevier
3. Michie, D. and Chambers, R.A. 1968. BOXES--an Experiment in Adaptive Control. *Machine Intelligence II,* 137–152. London: Oliver & Boyd
4. Russell, D.W., Rees S.J. and Boyes, J.A. 1977. A Micro-system for Control by Automata in Real-Life Situations. *Proc. Conf. on Information Sciences and Systems.* Johns Hopkins University, Baltimore. 226–230
5. Widjaja M. and Yurkovich, S. 1995 Intelligent Control for Swing Up and Balancing of an Inverted Pendulum System. *Proc. 4th. IEEE Conference on Control Applications*, Albany New York. 534–542.
6. Russell, D.W. and Rees, S.J. 1975. System Control—a Case Study of a Statistical Learning Automaton. *Progress in Cybernetics Systems Research* 2:114–120, New York: Hemisphere Publishing Co.
7. Rees, S.J. PhD Thesis. Liverpool Polytechnic, 1977
8. Russell, D. W., 1993. A Critical Assessment of the BOXES Paradigm. *J. Applied Artificial Intelligence* 7(4): 383–395
9. Russell, D. W. 1991. Further Studies in AI-Augmented Process Control using the BOXES Methodology. *Proc. 3rd. IFAC Int. Workshop on Artificial Intelligence in Real-Time Systems:AIRTC'91.* September 23-25, Sonoma, CA. Pergammon Press
10. Russell, D.W., 1995. Advisor Logic. *Control Engineering Practice* 3(7): 977–984 July, Oxford: Pergammon Press.
11. Humphrey, N. 1992. *A History of the Mind,* 82–91. New York: Simon & Schuster

Rough Set Analysis of Preference-Ordered Data

Roman Słowiński[1], Salvatore Greco[2], and Benedetto Matarazzo[2]

[1] Institute of Computing Science, Poznan University of Technology,
Piotrowo 3a, 60-965 Poznan, Poland
slowinsk@sol.put.poznan.pl
[2] Faculty of Economics, University of Catania,
Corso Italia, 55, 95129 Catania, Italy
{salgreco,matarazz}@mbox.unict.it

Abstract. The paper is devoted to knowledge discovery from data, taking into account prior knowledge about preference semantics in patterns to be discovered. The data concern a set of situations (objects, states, examples) described by a set of attributes (properties, features, characteristics). The attributes are, in general, divided into condition and decision attributes, corresponding to input and output of a situation. The situations are partitioned by decision attributes into decision classes. A pattern discovered from the data has a symbolic form of decision rule or decision tree. In many practical problems, some condition attributes are defined on preference-ordered scales and the decision classes are also preference-ordered. The known methods of knowledge discovery ignore, unfortunately, this preference information, taking thus a risk of drawing wrong patterns. To deal with preference-ordered data we propose to use a new approach called Dominance-based Rough Set Approach (DRSA). Given a set of situations described by at least one condition attribute with preference-ordered scale and partitioned into preference-ordered classes, the new rough set approach is able to approximate this partition by means of dominance relations. The rough approximation of this partition is a starting point for induction of *"if..., then..."* decision rules. The syntax of these rules is adapted to represent preference orders. The DRSA analyses only facts present in data and possible inconsistencies are identified. It preserves the concept of granular computing, however, the granules are dominance cones in evaluation space, and not bounded sets. It is also concordant with the paradigm of computing with words, as it exploits ordinal, and not necessarily cardinal, character of data.

1 How Prior Knowledge Influences Knowledge Discovery?

Discovering knowledge from data means being able to find concise classification patterns that agree with *situations* described by the data. They are useful for explanation of data and for prediction of future situations in such applications as technical diagnostics, performance evaluation or risk assessment. The situations are described by a set of *attributes*, called also properties, features, characteristics, etc. The attributes may be either on *condition* or *decision* side of the description, corresponding to input or output of a situation. The situations may be objects, states, examples, etc. It will be convenient to call them *objects* in this paper.

The data set in which classification patterns are searched for is called *learning sample*. Learning of patterns from this sample assumes certain *prior knowledge* that may include the following items:

(i) domains of attributes, i.e. sets of values that an attribute may take while being meaningful for user's perception,

(ii) division of attributes into condition and decision attributes, restricting the range of patterns to functional relations between condition and decision attributes,

(iii) preference order in domains of some attributes and semantic correlation between pairs of these attributes, requiring the patterns to observe the dominance principle.

In fact, item (i) is usually taken into account in knowledge discovery. With this prior knowledge only, one can discover patterns called *association rules* [1], showing strong relationships between values of some attributes, without fixing which attributes will be on the condition and which ones on the decision side in all rules.

If item (i) is combined with item (ii) in prior knowledge, then one can consider a partition of the learning sample into decision classes defined by decision attributes. The patterns to be discovered have then the form of *decision trees* or *decision rules* representing functional relations between condition and decision attributes. These patterns are typically discovered by machine learning and data mining methods [19]. As there is a direct correspondence between decision tree and rules, we will concentrate further our attention on decision rules.

As item (iii) is crucial for this paper, let us explain it in more detail. Consider an example of data set concerning pupils' achievements in a high school. Suppose that among attributes describing the pupils there are results in *mathematics* (*Math*) and *physics* (*Ph*), and a *general achievement* (*GA*). The domains of these attributes are composed of three values: *bad*, *medium* and *good*. This information constitutes item (i) of prior knowledge. The preference order of the attribute values is obvious: *good* is better than *medium* and *bad*, and *medium* is better than *bad*. It is known, moreover, that *Math* is semantically correlated with *GA*, as well as *Ph* with *GA*. This is, precisely, item (iii) of prior knowledge. Attributes with preference-ordered domains are called *criteria* in decision theory. We will use the name of *regular attributes* for those attributes whose domains are not preference-ordered. *Semantic correlation between two criteria* means that an improvement on one criterion should not worsen evaluation on the second criterion. In our example, improvement of a pupil's score in *Math* or *Ph*, with other attribute values unchanged, should not worsen pupil's general achievement *GA*, but rather improve it.

What classification patterns can be drawn from the pupils' data set? If prior knowledge includes items (i) and (iii) only, then association rules can be induced; if item (ii) is known in addition to (i) and (iii), then decision rules can be induced. The next question is: how item (iii) influences association rules and decision rules? It has been specified above that item (iii) requires the patterns to observe the dominance principle. The dominance principle (called also Pareto principle) should be observed by (association and decision) rules having at least one pair of semantically correlated criteria spanned over condition and decision part. Each rule is characterized by *condition profile* and *decision profile*, corresponding to vectors of threshold values of attributes in condition and decision part of the rule, respectively. We say that one profile *dominates* another if they both involve the same attributes and the criteria values of the first profile are not worse than criteria values of the second profile, while the values of regular attributes in both profiles are indiscernible.

The *dominance principle* requires the following: consider two rules, r and s, involving the same regular attributes and criteria, such that each criterion used in the condition part is semantically correlated with at least one criterion present in the decision part of these rules; if condition profile of rule r dominates condition profile of rule s, then the decision profile of rule r should also dominate decision profile of rule s.

Suppose that two rules induced from the pupils' data set relate *Math* and *Ph* on the condition side, with *GA* on the decision side:

rule #1: if *Math=medium* and *Ph=medium*, then *GA=good*,

rule #2: if *Math=good* and *Ph=medium*, then *GA=medium*,

The two rules do not observe the dominance principle because the condition profile of rule #2 dominates the condition profile of rule #1, while the decision profile of rule #2 is dominated by the decision profile of rule #1. Thus, in the sense of the dominance principle the two rules are inconsistent, that is they are wrong.

One could say that the above rules are true because they are supported by examples of pupils from the learning sample, but this would mean that the examples are also inconsistent. The *inconsistency* may come from many sources, e.g.:

- missing attributes (regular ones or criteria) in the description of objects; maybe the data set does not include such attribute as *opinion of pupil's tutor* (OT) expressed only verbally during assessment of pupil's GA by school teachers' council,
- unstable preferences of decision makers; maybe the members of school teachers' council changed their view on influence of *Math* on *GA* during the assessment.

Handling these inconsistencies is of crucial importance for knowledge discovery. They cannot be simply considered as noise or error to be eliminated from data, or amalgamated with consistent data by some averaging operators, but they should be identified and presented as uncertain patterns.

If item (iii) would be ignored in prior knowledge, then the handling of above mentioned inconsistencies would be impossible. Indeed, there would be nothing wrong in rules #1 and #2: they are supported by different examples discerned by considered attributes.

It has been acknowledged by many authors that *rough set theory* provides excellent framework for dealing with inconsistency in knowledge discovery [18, 20, 21, 22, 24, 27, 29, 30]. The paradigm of rough set theory is that of *granular computing*, because the main concept of the theory – rough approximation of a set – is build up of blocks of objects indiscernible by a given set of attributes, called *granules of knowledge*. In space of regular attributes, the granules are bounded sets. Decision rules induced from rough approximation of a classification are also build up of such granules. While taking into account prior knowledge of type (i) and (ii), the rough approximation and the inherent rule induction ignore, however, prior knowledge of type (iii). In consequence, the resulting decision rules may be inconsistent with the dominance principle.

The authors have proposed an extension of the granular computing paradigm that permits taking into account prior knowledge of type (iii), in addition to either (i) only [17], or (i) and (ii) together [5, 6, 10, 13, 15, 26]. Combination of the new granules with the idea of rough approximation makes the, so-called, *Dominance-based Rough Set Approach* (DRSA).

In the following sections we present the concept of granules permitting to handle prior knowledge of type (iii), then we briefly sketch DRSA and its main extensions; as sets of decision rules resulting from DRSA can be seen as preference models in multicriteria decision problems, we briefly comment this issue; application of the new paradigm of granular computing to induction of association rules is also mentioned before conclusions.

2 How Prior Knowledge about Preference Order in Data Influences the Granular Computing?

In other words, how should be defined the granule of knowledge in the attribute space in order to take into account prior knowledge about preference order in data when searching for rules?

As it is usual in knowledge discovery methods, information about objects is represented in a *data table*, in which rows are labelled by *objects* and contain the values of attributes for each corresponding object, whereas columns are labelled by *attributes* and contain the values of each corresponding attribute for the objects.

Let U denote a finite set of objects (universe) and Q a finite set of attributes divided into set C of *condition attributes* and set D of *decision attributes*; $C \cap D = \emptyset$. Let also $X_C = \prod_{q=1}^{|C|} X_q$ and $X_D = \prod_{q=1}^{|D|} X_q$ be attribute spaces corresponding to sets of condition and decision attributes, respectively. Elements of X_C and X_D can be interpreted as possible evaluation of objects on attributes from set $C=\{1,\ldots,|C|\}$ and from set $D=\{1,\ldots,|D|\}$, respectively. Therefore, X_q

is the set of possible evaluations of considered objects with respect to attribute q. Value of object x on attribute $q \in Q$ is denoted by x_q. Objects x and y are indiscernible by $P \subseteq C$ if $x_q = y_q$ for all $q \in P$ and, analogously, objects x and y are indiscernible by $R \subseteq D$ if $x_q = y_q$ for all $q \in R$. Sets of indiscernible objects are equivalence classes of the corresponding indiscernibility relation I_P or I_R. Moreover, $I_P(x)$ and $I_R(x)$ denote equivalence classes including object x. I_D makes a partition of U into a finite number of decision classes $\boldsymbol{Cl}=\{Cl_t, t \in T\}$, $T=\{1,...,n\}$. Each $x \in U$ belongs to one and only one class $Cl_t \in \boldsymbol{Cl}$.

The above definitions take into account prior knowledge of type (i) and (ii) only. In this case, the **granules of knowledge are bounded sets** in X_P and X_R ($P \subseteq C$ and $R \subseteq D$), defined by partitions of U induced by indiscernibility relations I_P and I_R, respectively. Then, classification patterns to be discovered are functions representing granules $I_R(x)$ by granules $I_P(x)$ in condition attribute space X_P, for any $P \subseteq C$ and any $x \in U$.

If prior knowledge includes item (iii) in addition to (i) and (ii), then indiscernibility relation is unable to produce granules in X_C and X_D taking into account the preference order. To do so, it has to be substituted by dominance relation in X_P and X_R ($P \subseteq C$ and $R \subseteq D$). Suppose, for simplicity, that all condition attributes in C and all decision attributes in D are criteria, and that C and D are semantically correlated.

Let $\succeq_q$ be a *weak preference relation* on U (often called outranking) representing a preference on the set of objects with respect to criterion $q \in \{C \cup D\}$; $x_q \succeq_q y_q$ means "x_q is at least as good as y_q with respect to criterion q". On the one hand, we say that x *dominates* y with respect to $P \subseteq C$ (shortly, x *P-dominates* y) in condition attribute space X_P (denotation xD_Py) if $x_q \succeq_q y_q$ for all $q \in P$. Assuming, without loss of generality, that the domains of criteria are numerical, i.e. $X_q \subseteq \boldsymbol{R}$ for any $q \in C$, and that they are ordered such that preference increases with the value, one can say that xD_Py is equivalent to: $x_q \geq y_q$ for all $q \in P$, $P \subseteq C$. Observe that for each $x \in X_P$, xD_Px, i.e. P-dominance is reflexive. On the other hand, analogical definition holds in decision attribute space X_R (denotation xD_Ry), $R \subseteq D$.

The dominance relations xD_Py and xD_Ry ($P \subseteq C$ and $R \subseteq D$) are directional statements where x is a subject and y is a referent.

If $x \in X_P$ is the referent, then one can define a set of objects $y \in X_P$ dominating x, called *P-dominating set*, $D_P^+(x)=\{y \in U: yD_Px\}$.

If $x \in X_P$ is the subject, then one can define a set of objects $y \in X_P$ dominated by x, called *P-dominated set*, $D_P^-(x)=\{y \in U: xD_Py\}$.

P-dominating sets $D_P^+(x)$ and P-dominated sets $D_P^-(x)$ correspond to *positive* and *negative dominance cones* in X_P, with the origin x.

As to decision attribute space X_R, $R \subseteq D$, the R-dominance relation permits to define sets:

$$Cl_R^{\geq x}=\{y \in U: yD_Rx\}, \quad Cl_R^{\leq x}=\{y \in U: xD_Ry\}.$$

$Cl_{t_q}=\{x \in X_D: x_q = t_q\}$ is a decision class with respect to $q \in D$. $Cl_R^{\geq x}$ is called *upward union* of classes, and $Cl_R^{\leq x}$, *downward union* of classes. If $x \in$

$Cl_R^{\geq x}$, then x belongs to class Cl_{t_q}, $x_q = t_q$, or better on each decision attribute $q \in R$; if $x \in Cl_R^{\leq x}$, then x belongs to class Cl_{t_q}, $x_q = t_q$, or worse on each decision attribute $q \in R$. The downward and upward unions of classes correspond to *positive* and *negative dominance cones* in X_R, respectively.

In this case, the **granules of knowledge are open sets** in X_P and X_R defined by dominance cones $D_P^+(x)$, $D_P^-(x)$ $(P \subseteq C)$ and $Cl_R^{\geq x}$, $Cl_R^{\leq x}$ $(R \subseteq D)$, respectively. Then, classification patterns to be discovered are functions representing granules $Cl_R^{\geq x}$, $Cl_R^{\leq x}$ by granules $D_P^+(x)$, $D_P^-(x)$, respectively, in condition attribute space X_P, for any $P \subseteq C$ and $R \subseteq D$ and any $x \in X_P$.

In both cases above, the functions are sets of decision rules.

3 Dominance-Based Rough Set Approach (DRSA)

3.1 Granular Computing with Dominance Cones

Suppose, for simplicity, that set D of decision attributes is a singleton, $D=\{d\}$. Decision attribute d makes a partition of U into a finite number of classes **Cl**=$\{Cl_t, t \in T\}$, $T=\{1,...,n\}$. Each $x \in U$ belongs to one and only one class $Cl_t \in$ **Cl**. The upward and downward unions of classes boil down, respectively, to:

$$Cl_t^{\geq} = \bigcup_{s \geq t} Cl_s, \quad Cl_t^{\leq} = \bigcup_{s \leq t} Cl_s, \quad t=1,...,n.$$

Notice that for $t=2,...,n$ we have $Cl_n^{\leq} = U - Cl_{t-1}^{\leq}$, i.e. all the objects not belonging to class Cl_t or better, belong to class Cl_{t-1} or worse.

Let us explain how the rough set concept has been generalized to DRSA in order to enable granular computing with dominance cones (for more details, see [5, 6, 10, 13, 26]).

Given a set of criteria $P \subseteq C$, the inclusion of an object $x \in U$ to the upward union of classes $Cl_t^{\geq}$, $t=2,\ldots,n$, creates an *inconsistency in the sense of dominance principle* if one of the following conditions holds:

- x belongs to class Cl_t or better but it is P-dominated by an object y belonging to a class worse than Cl_t, i.e. $x \in Cl_t^{\geq}$ but $D_P^+(x) \cap Cl_{t-1}^{\leq} \neq \emptyset$,
- x belongs to a worse class than Cl_t but it P-dominates an object y belonging to class Cl_t or better, i.e. $x \notin Cl_t^{\geq}$ but $D_P^-(x) \cap Cl_t^{\geq} \neq \emptyset$.

If, given a set of criteria $P \subseteq C$, the inclusion of $x \in U$ to $Cl_t^{\geq}$, $t=2,\ldots,n$, creates an inconsistency in the sense of dominance principle, we say that x belongs to $Cl_t^{\geq}$ *with some ambiguity*. Thus, x belongs to $Cl_t^{\geq}$ *without any ambiguity* with respect to $P \subseteq C$, if $x \in Cl_t^{\geq}$ and there is no inconsistency in the sense of dominance principle. This means that all objects P-dominating x belong to $Cl_t^{\geq}$, i.e. $D_P^+(x) \subseteq Cl_t^{\geq}$. Geometrically, this corresponds to inclusion of the complete set of objects contained in the positive dominance cone originating in x, in the positive dominance cone $Cl_t^{\geq}$ originating in Cl_t.

Furthermore, x *possibly belongs to* $Cl_t^{\geq}$ with respect to $P \subseteq C$ if one of the following conditions holds:

1. according to decision attribute d, x belongs to $Cl_t^\geq$,
2. according to decision attribute d, x does not belong to $Cl_t^\geq$ but it is inconsistent in the sense of dominance principle with an object y belonging to $Cl_t^\geq$.

In terms of ambiguity, x possibly belongs to $Cl_t^\geq$ with respect to $P \subseteq C$, if x belongs to $Cl_t^\geq$ with or without any ambiguity. Due to reflexivity of the dominance relation D_P, conditions 1) and 2) can be summarized as follows: x possibly belongs to class Cl_t or better, with respect to $P \subseteq C$, if among the objects P-dominated by x there is an object y belonging to class Cl_t or better, i.e. $D_P^-(x) \cap Cl_t^\geq \neq \emptyset$. Geometrically, this corresponds to non-empty intersection of the set of objects contained in the negative dominance cone originating in x, with the positive dominance cone $Cl_t^\geq$ originating in Cl_t.

For $P \subseteq C$, the set of all objects belonging to $Cl_t^\geq$ without any ambiguity constitutes the *P-lower approximation* of $Cl_t^\geq$, denoted by $\underline{P}\,Cl_t^\geq$, and the set of all objects that possibly belong to $Cl_t^\geq$ constitutes the *P-upper approximation* of $Cl_t^\geq$, denoted by $\overline{P}(Cl_t^\geq)$:

$$\underline{P}(Cl_t^\geq) = \{x \in U: D_P^+(x) \subseteq Cl_t^\geq\}, \quad \overline{P}(Cl_t^\geq) = \{x \in U: D_P^-(x) \cap Cl_t^\geq \neq \emptyset\},$$
for $t=1,\ldots,n$.

Analogously, one can define *P-lower approximation* and *P-upper approximation* of $Cl_t^\leq$ as follows:

$$\underline{P}(Cl_t^\leq) = \{x \in U: D_P^-(x) \subseteq Cl_t^\leq\}, \quad \overline{P}(Cl_t^\leq) = \{x \in U: D_P^+(x) \cap Cl_t^\leq \neq \emptyset\},$$
for $t=1,\ldots,n$.

All the objects belonging to $Cl_t^\geq$ and $Cl_t^\leq$ with some ambiguity constitute the *P-boundary* of $Cl_t^\geq$ and $Cl_t^\leq$, denoted by $Bn_P(Cl_t^\geq)$ and $Bn_P(Cl_t^\leq)$, respectively. They can be represented in terms of upper and lower approximations as follows:

$$Bn_P(Cl_t^\geq) = \overline{P}(Cl_t^\geq) - \underline{P}(Cl_t^\geq), \quad Bn_P(Cl_t^\leq) = \overline{P}(Cl_t^\leq) - \underline{P}(Cl_t^\leq),$$
for $t=1,\ldots,n$.

P–lower and P–upper approximations of unions of classes $Cl_t^\geq$ and $Cl_t^\leq$ have an important property of *complementarity*. It says that if object x belongs without any ambiguity to class Cl_t or better, it is impossible that it could belong to class Cl_{t-1} or worse, i.e. $\underline{P}(Cl_t^\geq) = U - \overline{P}(Cl_{t-1}^\leq)$, $t=2,\ldots,n$. Due to complementarity property, $Bn_P(Cl_t^\geq) = Bn_P(Cl_{t-1}^\leq)$, for $t=2,\ldots,n$, which means that if x belongs with ambiguity to class Cl_t or better, it also belongs with ambiguity to class Cl_{t-1} or worse.

From the knowledge discovery point of view, P-lower approximations of unions of classes represent *certain knowledge* provided by criteria from $P \subseteq C$, while P-upper approximations represent *possible knowledge* and the P-boundaries contain *doubtful knowledge*.

The above definition of rough approximations are based on a strict application of the dominance principle. However, when defining non-ambiguous objects, it is reasonable to accept a limited proportion of negative examples, particularly for large data tables. Such extended version of DRSA is called Variable-Consistency DRSA model (VC-DRSA) [16].

For every $P \subseteq C$, the objects being consistent in the sense of dominance principle with all upward and downward unions of classes are *P-correctly classified*. For every $P \subseteq C$, the *quality of approximation of classification* **Cl** by set of criteria P is defined as the ratio between the number of P-correctly classified objects and the number of all the objects in the data sample set. Since the objects P−correctly classified are those ones that do not belong to any P-boundary of unions $Cl_t^{\geq}$ and $Cl_t^{\leq}$, $t=1,...,n$, the quality of approximation of classification **Cl** by set of criteria P, can be written as

$$\gamma_P(\mathbf{Cl}) = = \frac{\left|\left(U - \left(\bigcup_{t \in T} Bn_P\left(Cl_t^{\geq}\right)\right)\right)\right|}{|U|}.$$

$\gamma_P(\mathbf{Cl})$ can be seen as a measure of the quality of knowledge that can be extracted from the data table, where P is the set of criteria and **Cl** is the considered classification.

Each minimal subset $P \subseteq C$ such that $\gamma_P(\mathbf{Cl}) = \gamma_C(\mathbf{Cl})$ is called a *reduct* of **Cl** and is denoted by RED_{Cl}. Let us remark that a data sample set can have more than one reduct. The intersection of all reducts is called the *core* and is denoted by $CORE_{Cl}$. Criteria from $CORE_{Cl}$ cannot be removed from the data sample set without deteriorating the knowledge to be discovered. This means that in set C there are three categories of criteria:

1) *indispensable* criteria included in the core,
2) *exchangeable* criteria included in some reducts but not in the core,
3) *redundant* criteria being neither indispensable nor exchangeable, thus not included in any reduct.

3.2 Induction of Decision Rules

The dominance-based rough approximations of upward and downward unions of classes can serve to induce a generalized description of objects contained in the data table in terms of "*if..., then...*" decision rules. For a given upward or downward union of classes, $Cl_t^{\geq}$ or $Cl_s^{\leq}$, the decision rules induced under a hypothesis that objects belonging to $\underline{P}(Cl_t^{\geq})$ or $\underline{P}(Cl_s^{\leq})$ are *positive* and all the others *negative*, suggest an assignment to "class Cl_t or better", or to "class Cl_s or worse", respectively. On the other hand, the decision rules induced under a hypothesis that objects belonging to the intersection $\overline{P}(Cl_s^{\leq}) \cap \overline{P}(Cl_t^{\geq})$ are *positive* and all the others *negative*, are suggesting an assignment to some classes between Cl_s and Cl_t ($s<t$).

In case of preference-ordered data it is meaningful to consider the following five types of decision rules:

1. *certain* $D_\geq$-*decision rules*, providing lower profile descriptions for objects belonging to $Cl_t^\geq$ without ambiguity: *if* $x_{q1} \succeq_{q1} r_{q1}$ *and* $x_{q2} \succeq_{q2} r_{q2}$ *and* ... $x_{qp} \succeq_{qp} r_{qp}$, *then* $x \in Cl_t^\geq$, where for each $w_q, z_q \in X_q$, "$w_q \succeq_q z_q$" means "w_q is <u>at least</u> as good as z_q",

2. *possible* $D_\geq$-*decision rules*, providing lower profile descriptions for objects belonging to $Cl_t^\geq$ with or without any ambiguity: *if* $x_{q1} \succeq_{q1} r_{q1}$ *and* $x_{q2} \succeq_{q2} r_{q2}$ *and* ... $x_{qp} \succeq_{qp} r_{qp}$, *then* x possibly belongs to $Cl_t^\geq$,

3. *certain* $D_\leq$-*decision rules*, providing upper profile descriptions for objects belonging to $Cl_t^\leq$ without ambiguity: *if* $x_{q1} \preceq_{q1} r_{q1}$ *and* $x_{q2} \preceq_{q2} r_{q2}$ *and* ... $x_{qp} \preceq_{qp} r_{qp}$, *then* $x \in Cl_t^\leq$, where for each $w_q, z_q \in X_q$, "$w_q \preceq_q z_q$" means "w_q is <u>at most</u> as good as z_q",

4. *possible* $D_\leq$-*decision rules*, providing upper profile descriptions for objects belonging to $Cl_t^\leq$ with or without any ambiguity: *if* $x_{q1} \preceq_{q1} r_{q1}$ *and* $x_{q2} \preceq_{q2} r_{q2}$ *and* ... $x_{qp} \preceq_{qp} r_{qp}$, *then* x possibly belongs to $Cl_t^\leq$,

5. *approximate* $D_{\geq\leq}$-*decision rules*, providing simultaneously lower and upper profile descriptions for objects belonging to $Cl_s \cup Cl_{s+1} \cup ... \cup Cl_t$ without possibility of discerning to which class: *if* $x_{q1} \succeq_{q1} r_{q1}$ *and*... $x_{qk} \succeq_{qk} r_{qk}$ *and* $x_{qk+1} \preceq_{qk+1} r_{qk+1}$ *and* ... $x_{qp} \preceq_{qp} r_{qp}$, *then* $x \in Cl_s \cup Cl_{s+1} \cup ... \cup Cl_t$.

In the left hand side of a $D_{\geq\leq}$-decision rule we can have "$x_q \succeq_q r_q$" and "$x_q \preceq_q r'_q$", where $r_q \leq r'_q$, for the same $q \in C$. Moreover, if $r_q = r'_q$, the two conditions boil down to "$x_q \sim_q r_q$", where for each $w_q, z_q \in X_q$, "$w_q \sim_q z_q$" means "w_q is indifferent to z_q".

Since a decision rule is an implication, by a *minimal* rule we understand such an implication that there is no other implication with the left hand side (LHS) of at least the same weakness (in other words, rule using a subset of elementary conditions or/and weaker elementary conditions) and the right hand side (RHS) of at least the same strength (in other words, a $D_\geq$- or a $D_\leq$-decision rule assigning objects to the same union or sub-union of classes, or a $D_{\geq\leq}$-decision rule assigning objects to the same or larger set of classes).

The rules of type 1) and 3) represent certain knowledge extracted from the data table, while the rules of type 2), 4) represent possible knowledge, and rules of type 5) represent doubtful knowledge.

The rules of type 1) and 3) are *exact*, if they do not cover negative examples, and they are *probabilistic*, otherwise. In the latter case, each rule is characterized by a confidence ratio, representing the probability that an object matching LHS of the rule matches also its RHS. Probabilistic rules are concordant with the VC-DRSA model mentioned above.

Let us comment application of decision rules to the objects described by criteria from C. When applying $D_\geq$-decision rules to object x, it is possible that x either matches LHS of at least one decision rule or does not match LHS of any decision rule. In the case of at least one matching, it is reasonable to conclude that x belongs to class Cl_t, being the lowest class of the upward union $Cl_t^\geq$

resulting from intersection of all RHS of rules covering x. Precisely, if x matches LHS of rules $\rho_1, \rho_2,\ldots,\rho_m$, having RHS $x \in Cl_{t1}^{\geq}$, $x \in Cl_{t2}^{\geq},\ldots$, $x \in Cl_{tm}^{\geq}$, then x is assigned to class Cl_t, where $t=\max\{t1,t2,\ldots,tm\}$. In the case of no matching, it is concluded that x belongs to Cl_1, i.e. to the worst class, since no rule with RHS suggesting a better classification of x is covering this object.

Analogously, when applying $D_{\leq}$-decision rules to object x, it is concluded that x belongs either to class Cl_z, being the highest class of the downward union $Cl_t^{\leq}$ resulting from intersection of all RHS of rules covering x, or to class Cl_n, i.e. to the best class, when x is not covered by any rule. Precisely, if x matches the LHS of rules $\rho_1, \rho_2,\ldots,\rho_m$, having RHS $x \in Cl_{t1}^{\leq}$, $x \in Cl_{t2}^{\leq},\ldots$, $x \in Cl_{tm}^{\leq}$, then x is assigned to class Cl_t, where $t=\min\{t1,t2,\ldots,tm\}$. In the case of no matching, it is concluded that x belongs to the best class Cl_n because no rule with RHS suggesting a worse classification of x is covering this object.

Finally, when applying $D_{\geq\leq}$-decision rules to object x, it is concluded that x belongs to the union of all classes suggested in RHS of rules covering x.

A set of decision rules is *complete* if it is able to cover all objects from the data table in such a way that consistent objects are re-classified to their original classes and inconsistent objects are classified to clusters of classes referring to this inconsistency. We call *minimal* each set of decision rules that is complete and non-redundant, i.e. exclusion of any rule from this set makes it non-complete.

One of three induction strategies can be adopted to obtain a set of decision rules [28]:

- generation of a *minimal* description, i.e. a minimal set of rules,
- generation of an *exhaustive* description, i.e. all rules for a given data table,
- generation of a *characteristic* description, i.e. a set of rules covering relatively many objects each, however, all together not necessarily all objects from U.

Let us observe that the syntax of decision rules induced from rough approximations defined using dominance cones, consistently use this type of granules. Each condition profile defines a dominance cone in X_C, and each decision profile defines a dominance cone in X_D – in both cases, the cone is positive for $D_{\geq}$-rules and negative for $D_{\leq}$-rules.

Let also remark that dominance cones corresponding to condition profiles can originate in any point of X_C, without risk of being too specific. Thus, contrary to traditional granular computing, the condition attribute space X_C need not to be discretized.

To conclude the description of DRSA, let us mention that the dominance-based rough approximations can also serve to induce decision trees representing knowledge discovered from preference-ordered data [3].

4 Extensions of DRSA Dealing with Preference-Ordered Data

4.1 Rough Approximation of Preference Relations and Decision Rule Preference Model

It is natural that people make decisions and then search for rules that justify their choices. The rules make evidence of decision policy and can be used for both explanation of past decisions and recommendation of future decisions. The set of rules representing decision policy of a decision maker (DM) is called *preference model*. It is a necessary component of decision support systems for multicriteria choice and ranking problems. Classically, it has been a utility function or a binary relation – its construction requires some *preference information* from the DM, like substitution ratios among criteria, importance weights, or indifference, preference and veto thresholds [23]. Acquisition of this preference information from the DM is not easy and, moreover, the resulting preference model is not intelligible for the DM. In this situation, the preference model in terms of decision rules induced from *decision examples* provided by the DM has two advantages over the classical models: (i) it is intelligible and speaks the language of the DM, (ii) the preference information comes from observation of DM's decisions.

There is, however, a problem with inconsistency often present in the set of decision examples. Rather than correct or ignore these inconsistencies, we propose to take them into account in the preference model construction using the *rough set* concept.

We have extended DRSA in order to approximate comprehensive preference relations in multicriteria choice and ranking problems [5, 6, 10]. In particular, DRSA has been adapted to analysis of, so-called, pairwise comparison tables (PCT), where each row corresponds to a pair of objects described by binary relations on particular criteria and by a comprehensive preference relation, e.g. the outranking relation.

Using DRSA to the analysis of the PCT, we obtain rough approximation of the outranking relation by dominance relation. Decision rules derived from rough approximations may then be applied to a new set of objects concerned by the choice or ranking problem. As a result, one obtains a four-valued outranking relation on this set. In order to obtain a recommendation, it is advisable to use an exploitation procedure based on the net flow score of the objects.

The preference model in terms of decision rules has several advantages over the classical models:

- the decision rules do not convert ordinal information into numeric one but keep the ordinal character of input data due to the syntax proposed; in this sense, DRSA is concordant with the paradigm of computing with words which are hardly convertible to numerical scales,
- heterogeneous information (qualitative and quantitative, ordered and non-ordered) and scales of preference (ordinal, cardinal) can be processed within

the DRSA, while classical methods consider only quantitative ordered evaluations with rare exceptions,
- the decision rule preference model resulting from the DRSA can represent even inconsistent preferences.

We proved the equivalence of preference representation by a general non-additive and non-transitive utility function and by *"if..., then..."* decision rules [12, 14]. Moreover, some well known multicriteria aggregation procedures (lexicographic aggregation, majority aggregation, ELECTRE I and TACTIC) were represented in terms of the decision rule model; in these cases the decision rules decompose the synthetic aggregation formula used by these procedures; the rules involve partial profiles defined for subsets of criteria plus a dominance relation on these profiles and pairs of actions. Such decomposition makes the preference model more understandable for the decision maker.

If the comprehensive outranking relation is a complete preorder, i.e. it is strongly complete (for all objects x,y, x outranks y or y outranks x) and transitive, it can be represented by a utility function. We proved that a utility function is equivalent to a set of certain decision rules, either $D_{\leq}$-*decision rules* or $D_{\geq}$-*decision rules*. We proved, moreover, that the Sugeno integral, considered to be the most general form of the 'max-min' ordinal utility function, can be represented by a set of certain decision rules having a very specific syntax (single graded decision rules). The capacity of representation of preferences by set of decision rule is thus far more general than the Sugeno integral [25].

4.2 Missing Values of Attributes and Criteria

In practical applications, the data table is often not complete because some data are missing. To deal with this case, we proposed in [8] an extension of the rough set methodology to the analysis of incomplete data tables. The extension concerns both the classical rough set approach (CRSA) based on the use of indiscernibility relations and the DRSA.

The relations of indiscernibility or dominance between two objects are considered as directional statements where a subject is compared to a referent object. We require that the referent object has no missing data. The two extended rough set approaches boil down to the original approaches when there are no missing data. The rules induced from the newly defined rough approximations defined are either exact or probabilistic, depending whether they are supported by consistent objects or not. The way of handling the missing values in the proposed approach seems faithful with respect to available data because the decision rules are robust in the sense of being grounded on objects existing in the data set and not on hypothetical objects created by putting some possible values instead of the missing ones.

4.3 Fuzzy Set Extension of DRSA

In [9] and in [4], we extended and characterized DRSA by using *fuzzy dominance* and *similarity relations* considered jointly. We proved that our extension of the rough approximation into the fuzzy context maintains the same desirable properties of the crisp rough approximation of decision classes. In this generalization, we distinguished all possible cases where either approximating granules in X_C (dominance cones in X_C) are fuzzy, or approximated granules in X_D (preference-ordered decision classes) are fuzzy, or both these granules are fuzzy.

4.4 DRSA for Decisions under Risk

In [11] we opened a new avenue for applications of the rough set concept to analysis of preference-ordered data. We considered the classical problem of decision under risk extending DRSA by using *stochastic dominance*. We considered the case of traditional additive probability distribution over the set of states of the world, however, the model is rich enough to handle non-additive probability distributions and even qualitative ordinal distributions. The rough set approach gives a representation of DM's preferences under risk in terms of *"if..., then..."* decision rules induced from rough approximations of sets of exemplary decisions (preference ordered classification of acts described in terms of outcomes in uncertain states of the world).

4.5 Hierarchical Structure of Attributes and Criteria

In many real life situations, the process of decision-making is decomposable into sub-problems; this decomposition may either follow from a, naturally, hierarchical structure of the evaluation, or from a need of simplification of a complex decision problem. These situations are referred to call *Hierarchical Decision Problems*. The hierarchical structure of a problem has the form of a *tree* whose *nodes* are attributes and criteria describing objects. In [2], we are considering hierarchical decision problems where the decision is made in finite number of steps due to hierarchical structure of regular attributes and criteria. We propose a methodology based on decision rule preference model induced from examples of hierarchical decisions made by the decision maker on a reference set of objects. To deal with inconsistencies appearing in decision examples we adapt the rough set approach to the hierarchical classification problems (HCP). In HCP, the main difficulty consists in *propagation* of inconsistencies along the tree, i.e. taking into account at each node of the tree the inconsistent information coming from lower level nodes. In the proposed methodology, the inconsistencies are propagated from the bottom to the top of the tree in the form of *subsets* of possible attribute values. In the case of hierarchical criteria, these subsets are *intervals* of possible criterion values. Subsets of possible values may also appear in leafs of the tree, i.e. in evaluations of objects by the lowest-level attribute and criteria. To deal with multiple values of attributes for object description the classical rough set approach and DRSA have been adapted adequately.

5 Induction of Association Rules with Prior Knowledge of Type (i) and (iii)

Problems of discovering association rules in preference-ordered data sets have been considered in [17]. Such data are typically related to economic issues, like finance or marketing. We introduced a specific form of association rules involving criteria. Discovering such rules requires new concepts: semantic correlation of criteria, inconsistency of objects with respect to the dominance robust items, credibility index. Properties of these rules concerning their generality and interdependencies were studied in view of constructing an algorithm for mining such rules. The algorithm is an extension of the algorithm proposed in [1]. The approach can be combined with methods handling missing or imprecise values of attributes and criteria.

In case of association rules induced with prior knowledge of type (i) and (iii), the rules have the same syntax as in case of prior knowledge of type (i), (ii) and (iii), however, there is a joint attribute space X_Q and the granules corresponding to condition and decision profiles are defined in disjoint sub-spaces of X_Q.

6 Conclusions

Knowledge discovery from preference-ordered data differs from usual knowledge discovery since the former involves preference orders in domains of attributes and in the set of decision classes. This requires that a knowledge discovery method applied to preference-ordered data respects the dominance principle. As this is not the case for the well-known methods of data mining and knowledge discovery, they are not able to discover all relevant knowledge contained in the analysed data sample and, even worse, they may yield unreasonable discoveries, because inconsistent with the dominance principle. These deficiencies are repaired in DRSA based on the concept of rough approximations consistent with the dominance principle. DRSA permits, moreover, to apply rough set approach to some new fields, like multicriteria decision making and decision under uncertainty. Multiple extensions proposed for DRSA make of this approach a useful tool for practical applications.

Acknowledgement. The first author wishes to acknowledge financial support from the State Committee for Scientific Research, KBN research grant no. 8T11F 006 19, and from the Foundation for Polish Science, subsidy no. 11/2001. The research of the two other authors has been supported by the Italian Ministry of Education, University and Scientific Research (MIUR).

References

1. Agrawal, R., Mannila, H., Srikant, R., Toivinen, H., Verkamo, I.: "Fast discovery of association rules". [In]: U.M.Fayyad et al. (eds.), *Advances in Knowledge Discovery and Data Mining.* AAAI Press, 1996, pp. 307–328

2. Dembczynski, K., Greco, S., Slowinski, R.: "Methodology of rough-set-based classification and sorting with hierarchical structure of attributes and criteria". *Control & Cybernetics* 31 (2002) (to appear)
3. Giove, S., Greco, S., Matarazzo, B. and Slowinski, R.: "Variable consistency monotonic decision trees". [In]: *Proceedings RSCTC'2002*, (in this volume)
4. Greco, S., Inuiguchi, M., Slowinski, R.: "Dominance-based rough set approach using possibility and necessity measures". [In]: *Proceedings RSCTC'2002*, (in this volume)
5. Greco, S., Matarazzo, B., Slowinski, R.: "A new rough set approach to evaluation of bankruptcy risk". [In]: C.Zopounidis (ed.), *Operational Tools in the Management of Financial Risk*. Kluwer Academic Publishers, Boston, 1998, pp. 121–136
6. Greco, S., Matarazzo, B., Slowinski, R.: "The use of rough sets and fuzzy sets in MCDM". Chapter 14 [in]: T.Gal, T.Stewart, T.Hanne (eds.), *Advances in Multiple Criteria Decision Making*. Kluwer Academic Publishers, Boston, 1999, pp. 14.1–14.59
7. Greco, S., Matarazzo, B., Slowinski, R.: "Rough approximation of preference relation by dominance relations". *European Journal of Operational Research*, 117 (1999) 63–83
8. Greco, S., Matarazzo, B., Slowinski, R.: "Dealing with missing data in rough set analysis of multi-attribute and multi-criteria decision problems". [In]: S.H.Zanakis, G.Doukidis and C.Zopounidis (eds.), *Decision Making: Recent Developments and Worldwide Applications*. Kluwer Academic Publishers, Boston, 2000, pp. 295–316
9. Greco, S., Matarazzo, B., Slowinski, R.: "Fuzzy extension of the rough set approach to multicriteria and multiattribute sorting". [In]: J. Fodor, B. De Baets and P. Perny (eds.), *Preferences and Decisions under Incomplete Knowledge*, Physica-Verlag, Heidelberg, 2000, pp.131–151
10. Greco, S., Matarazzo, B., Slowinski, R.: "Rough sets theory for multicriteria decision analysis". *European Journal of Operational Research* 129, 1 (2001) 1–47
11. Greco, S., Matarazzo, B., Slowinski, R.: "Rough set approach to decisions under risk". [In]: W.Ziarko, Y.Yao (eds.): *Rough Sets and Current Trends in Computing*, LNAI 2005, Springer-Verlag, Berlin, 2001, pp. 160–169
12. Greco, S., Matarazzo, B., Slowinski, R.: "Conjoint measurement and rough set approach for multicriteria sorting problems in presence of ordinal criteria". [In]: A.Colorni, M.Paruccini, B.Roy (eds.), *A-MCD-A: Aide Multi Critère à la Décision – Multiple Criteria Decision Aiding*, European Commission Report EUR 19808 EN, Joint Research Centre, Ispra, 2001, pp. 117–144
13. Greco, S., Matarazzo, B., Slowinski, R.: "Rough sets methodology for sorting problems in presence of multiple attributes and criteria". *European J. of Operational Research* 138, 2 (2002) 247–259
14. Greco, S., Matarazzo, B., Slowinski, R.: "Preference representation by means of conjoint measurement and decision rule model". [In]: D.Bouyssou, E.Jacquet-Lagrèze, P.Perny, R.Slowinski, D.Vanderpooten, Ph.Vincke (eds.), *Aiding Decisions with Multiple Criteria – Essays in Honor of Bernard Roy*. Kluwer Academic Publishers, Boston, 2002, pp. 263–313
15. Greco, S., Matarazzo, B., Slowinski R.: "Multicriteria classification by dominance-based rough set approach", Chapter 16.1.9 [in]: W.Kloesgen, J.Zytkow (eds.), *Handbook of Data Mining and Knowledge Discovery*, Oxford University Press, New York, 2002 (to appear)

16. Greco, S., Matarazzo, B., Slowinski, R., Stefanowski, J.: "Variable consistency model of dominance-based rough set approach". [In]: W.Ziarko, Y.Yao: *Rough Sets and Current Trends in Computing*, LNAI 2005, Springer-Verlag, Berlin, 2001, pp. 170-181
17. Greco, S., Matarazzo, B., Slowinski, R., Stefanowski, J.: "Mining association rules in preference-ordered data". Proc. 13th Int. Symposium on Methodologies for Intelligent Systems (ISMIS). Lyon, June 26–29, 2002, Springer Verlag, Berlin, 2002 (to appear)
18. Grzymala-Busse, J.W., Zou, X.: "Classification strategies using certain and possible rules". [In]: L.Polkowski, A.Skowron (eds.), *Rough Sets and Current Trends in Computing*. LNAI 1424, Springer-Verlag, Berlin, 1998, pp. 37–44
19. Michalski, R., Bratko, I., Kubat, M. (eds.): *Machine Learning and Data Mining*. John Wiley & Sons, Chichester, 1998
20. Pawlak, Z.: "*Rough Sets. Theoretical Aspects of Reasoning about Data*". Kluwer Academic Publishers, Dordrecht, 1991
21. Pawlak, Z., Grzymala-Busse, J.W., Slowinski, R., Ziarko, W.: "Rough sets". *Communications of the ACM* 38, 11 (1995) 89–95
22. Polkowski, L., Skowron, A.: "Calculi of granules based on rough set theory: approximate distributed synthesis and granular semantics for computing with words". [In]: N.Zhong, A.Skowron, S.Ohsuga (eds.), *New Directions in Rough sets, data Mining, and Soft-Granular Computing*. LNAI 1711, Springer-Verlag, Berlin, 1999, pp. 20–28
23. Roy, B.: "*Méthodologie Multicritère d'Aide à la Décision*". Economica, Paris, 1985
24. Slowinski, R. (ed.): "*Intelligent Decision Support. Handbook of Applications and Advances of the Rough Sets Theory*". Kluwer Academic Publishers, Boston, 1992.
25. Slowinski, R., Greco, S., Matarazzo, B.: "Axiomatization of utility, outranking and decision-rule preference models for multiple-criteria classification problems under partial inconsistency with the dominance principle". *Control & Cybernetics* 31 (2002) (to appear)
26. Slowinski, R., Stefanowski, J., Greco, S., Matarazzo, B.: "Rough sets based processing of inconsistent information in decision analysis". *Control & Cybernetics* 29, 1 (2000) 379–404
27. Slowinski, R., Zopounidis, C.: "Application of the rough set approach to evaluation of bankruptcy risk". *Intelligent Systems in Accounting, Finance and Management* 4 (1995) 27-41
28. Stefanowski J.: "On rough set based approaches to induction of decision rules". In Polkowski L., Skowron A. (eds.), *Rough Sets in Data Mining and Knowledge Discovery*, Physica-Verlag, vol.1, Heidelberg, 1998, pp. 500–529
29. Ziarko, W.: "Rough sets as a methodology for data mining". [In]: L.Polkowski, A.Skowron (eds.), *Rough Sets in Knowledge Discovery*. Vol. 1, Physica-Verlag, Heidelberg, 1998, pp. 554–576
30. Ziarko, W., Shan, N.: "KDD-R, a comprehensive system for knowledge discovery in databases using rough sets". [In]: Lin, T.Y, Wildberg, A.M., (eds.), *Soft Computing: Rough Sets, Fuzzy Logic, Neural Networks, Uncertainty Management, Knowledge Discovery*, Simulation Council Inc., San Diego, 1995, pp. 93–96

Fuzzy Sets, Multi-valued Mappings, and Rough Sets

I.B. Türksen

Intelligent Fuzzy Systems Laboratory
Department of Mechanical and Industrial Engineering
University of Toronto, Canada

Summary

It is shown that there is a natural transformation of Dempster's multi-valued mapping and Pawlak's rough sets and vice-versa. Furthermore, Dempster's schema is modified and restricted by Turksen in a particular manner to generate interval-valued Type 2 fuzzy sets. This is named Dempster-Turksen schema.

In particular, upper set formula of Dempster is modified to be a containment as opposed to the non-empty intersection. As well, instead of considering the set of all sets in the power set, they are restricted only to a well known class of information granules. Furthermore, the target sets for the "AND" linguistic combinations of any two or more sets are taken to be the usual conjunctive information granules. These information granules identify the lower set of "AND" combinations. All information granules that totally contain the target set form the set of information granules which are intersected to identify the upper set of "AND" combinations.

The target sets for the "OR" linguistic combinations of any two or more sets are taken to be the usual disjunctive information granules. These information granules identify the upper set of the "OR" combinations. All information granules that are totally contained in the target set form the set of information granules that are disjuncted to identify the lower set of "OR" combinations. The lower sets of all combinations that are constructed by both "AND" and "OR" linguistic connectives are formed by disjunction of all information granules that are totally contained in the target set, while the upper sets are formed by conjunction of all information granules that totally contain the target set.

It is found that the upper sets are equivalent to the Fuzzy Conjunctive Canonical Forms, FCCF, and the lower sets are equivalent to the Fuzzy Disjunctive Canonical Forms, FDCF. As well, the nature of this construction schema establishes the fact that FDCF is contained in FCCF in general.

This containment argument carries over to t-norm and t-conorm space since they are monotonic operators over sets. Finally, Dempster-Turksen schema shows in general that the combinations of two or more linguistic values that are identified by Type 1 memberships generate an interval-valued Type 2 fuzzy sets which are specified by FDCF and FCCF formulas.

Investigating the Choice of l and u Values in the Extended Variable Precision Rough Sets Model

Malcolm J. Beynon

Cardiff Business School, Cardiff University,
Colum Drive, Cardiff, CF10 3EU, Wales, UK
BeynonMJ@cardiff.ac.uk

Abstract. The extended variable precision rough sets model incorporating asymmetric bounds is a generalisation of the original rough set theory. This paper introduces the (l, u)-quality graph, which elucidates the associated level of quality of classification (QoC), based on the choice of l and u values. A number of summary measures and lines are defined which pass over the domain of the (l, u)-quality graph. The defined lines are used to identify a choice of l and u values, based on retaining the underlying level of QoC from the whole (l, u)-quality graph.

1 Introduction

The Variable Precision Rough Sets Model (VPRS$_\beta$) [5] was a development on the original Rough Set theory (RST) [4] as a tool for the classification of objects, which allowed a level of missclassification (based on a β threshold) in the subsequent classification. This was further extended by [3], which allowed asymmetric bounds l and u to be used, defined VPRS$_{l,u}$. The inclusion of the asymmetric bounds l and u in VPRS$_{l,u}$ added a further *a priori* consideration, with the two values (l and u) required to be chosen before the subsequent analysis (construction of a set of decision rules). The selection of appropriate l and u values was investigated by [6, 7].

In this paper, the effect of the l and u values on the associated level of quality of classification ((l, u)-QoC) of the objects is further elucidated. More specifically, the notion of a '(l, u)-quality graph' is introduced which elicits a representation of the different levels of (l, u)-QoC inherent, for different combinations of the l and u values. These include certain defined lines which are utilised in the choice of l and u based on retaining the underlying (l, u)-QoC in the problem under analysis.

2 Brief Description of Extended VPRS

Central to RST and its associated techniques is the information system (decision table). The decision table is made up of a set objects (U) each characterized by a set of categorical condition attributes (C) and classified by a set of categorical decision attributes (D). VPRS$_{l,u}$ extends RST (and VPRS$_\beta$), allowing probabilistic information on object classification by utilising two control parameters, defined lower (l) and upper (u) limits respectively, constrained by $0 \leq l < u \leq 1$.

From C and D, certain equivalence classes $E(C)$ and $E(D)$ are constructed, then with $Z \subseteq U$ and $P \subseteq C$ three approximation regions are defined. Firstly the u-positive and l-negative regions:

$$POS_u(Z) = \bigcup \{X_i \in E(P) : \Pr(Z/X_i) \geq u\},$$
$$NEG_l(Z) = \bigcup \{X_i \in E(P) : \Pr(Z/X_i) \leq l\},$$

where in each region $\Pr(Z/X_i)$ is a conditional probability estimate of Z given X_i. The $POS_u(Z)$ and $NEG_l(Z)$ regions represent the acceptability of the membership of $E(P)$ as being likely or unlikely to belong to Z respectively (subject to l and u). Where there is no acceptable likeliness, then the $E(P)$ is a member of the (l, u)-boundary region, defined by

$$BNR_{l,u}(Z) = \bigcup \{X_i \in E(P) : l < \Pr(Z/X_i) < u\}.$$

That is, $E(P) \subseteq BNR_{l,u}(Z)$ cannot be classified to Z or the compliment of Z with an acceptable error rate. When considering the whole decision table, the existence of a nonempty $BNR_{l,u}$ region implies a number of objects are not given a classification. This enables the definition of the (l, u)-quality of classification ((l, u)-QoC) or $\gamma^{l,u}(P, D)$ - $P \subseteq C$, and for $Z \subseteq U$ is given by

$$\gamma^{l,u}(P,D) = 1 - \frac{\operatorname{card}(BNR_{l,u}(Z))}{\operatorname{card}(U)}.$$

That is, $\gamma^{l,u}(P, D)$ represents the proportion of the objects that are given a classification from the decision table, again based on the l and u bounds.

3 Description of (l, u)-Quality Graph

In this section, the (l, u)-quality graph is introduced as a representation of the level of the associated (l, u)-QoC, for different values of l and u. In Fig. 1a) the general (l, u)-quality graph is illustrated, which encompasses the full domains of the l and u values ($0 \leq l < u \leq 1$). A point in the (l, u)-quality graph is denoted by (l, u), the example case $l = 0.6$ and $u = 0.7$ is also shown (considered in [3]).

Within the (l, u)-quality graph, the domain of the original RST is defined only by the point (0, 1). Similarly for VPRS$_\beta$ its domain is defined by the dashed line from ($1 - u$, u) to (0, 1), with $0.5 < u = \beta \leq 1$. Also defined (for use later) is the line (0, 0) to (1, 1), which is considered the v-axis here, hence $0 \leq v \leq \sqrt{2}$.

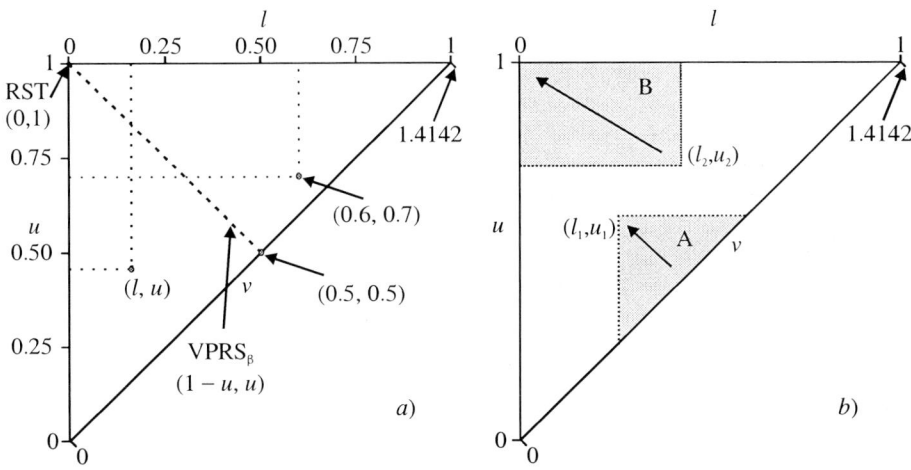

Fig. 1. *a*) General (l, u)-quality graph and *b*) Restrictions on l and u values

With respect to VPRS$_{l,u}$ in [3], propositions 6.1 (generalised to $l \geq l_1$ and $u \leq u_1$ then $\gamma^{l,u}(P,D) \geq \gamma^{l_1,u_1}(P,D)$) and 6.2 (generalised to $l \leq l_2$ and $u \geq u_2$ then $\gamma^{l,u}(P,D) \leq \gamma^{l_2,u_2}(P,D)$) inferred certain restrictions were put on the l and u values which related to their effect on the (l, u)-QoC for a set of objects. Within the (l, u)-quality graph, the shaded regions in Fig. 1*b*) show the sub-domains of (l, u) around (l_1, u_1) and (l_2, u_2) which relate to propositions 6.1 (region A) and 6.2 (region B) respectively. Also the general direction the level of (l, u)-QoC decreases is shown in each shaded region. That is, the level of (l, u)-QoC decreases (discontinuously) from the v-axis towards the point (0, 1) (except when (l, u)-QoC = 1 for all l and u).

To further elucidate the (l, u)-quality graph the example problem (decision table) presented in [3, Table 1] is further exposited. This problem related to finishing mill data, with two condition attributes C = {Width, Gauge} = {c_1, c_2}. It follows the associated (l, u)-quality graph is given in Fig. 2.

In Fig. 2, for regions of the (l, u)-quality graph, different levels of (l, u)-QoC exist. These regions of $\gamma^{l,u}(C,D)$ are separated by boundary lines, i.e. vertical l_i (i = 1, .., n_l) and horizontal u_i (i = 1, .., n_u) boundary lines, where n_l and n_u are the respective number of these lines (indeed $n_l = n_u$). As for VPRS$_\beta$ in [1, 2], in VPRS$_{l,u}$ the (l, u)-quality graph can be used to elucidate the levels of $\gamma^{l,u}(C,D)$ on subsets of the condition attributes ($P \subseteq C$), see Fig. 3.

The (l, u)-quality graphs in Fig. 3 show regions of different levels of $\gamma^{l,u}(P,D)$ (P = {c_1} or P = {c_2}) for choices of l and u values (separated by dotted boundary lines). In these graphs (Fig. 3), the shaded areas identify regions in the (l, u)-quality graphs which have the same level of (l, u)-QoC as for the whole set of condition attributes P = C (in Fig. 2).

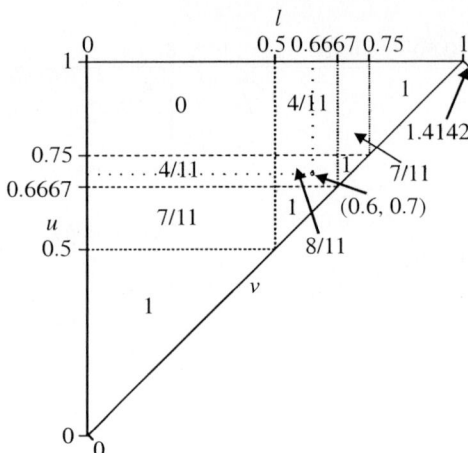

Fig. 2. (l, u)-quality graph for the finishing mill data set using $C = \{c_1, c_2\}$.

For $P = \{c_2\}$, the complete (l, u)-quality graph is shaded, indicating any combination of l and u with $P = \{c_2\}$ would give the same level of (l, u)-QoC with $P = C$. For $P = \{c_1\}$, there are shaded and non-shaded regions of the (l, u)-quality graph, hence there are choices of l and u such that the level of (l, u)-QoC associated with $P = \{c_1\}$ would be different to that for $P = C$.

A direct consequence of the (l, u)-quality graph is the proportion of area (defined $PoA(\cdot)$) of the (l, u)-quality graph which is shaded, hence $0 \leq PoA(P) \leq 1$ ($P \subset C$). The (l, u)-quality graphs for $P = \{c_1\}$ and $P = \{c_2\}$ given in Fig. 3 have PoA values, $PoA(\{c_1\}) = 0.5890$ and $PoA(\{c_2\}) = 1$. In general the larger the value of $PoA(P)$, the more similar $P \subset C$ to C with respect to the range of (l, u)-QoC.

A further result is the area-weighted mean (l, u)-QoC value, defined $\gamma_{AW}^{l,u}(P, D)$, associated with the (l, u)-quality graph. That is, each level of (l, u)-QoC in the graph is weighted by its associated proportion of the area of the graph. For this example, when $P = C$, $\gamma_{AW}^{l,u}(C, D) = 0.5606$. Similar values can be calculated for $P \subset C$, i.e. $\gamma_{AW}^{l,u}(\{c_1\}, D) = 0.5372$ and $\gamma_{AW}^{l,u}(\{c_2\}, D) = 0.5606$.

The (l, u)-discernibility of a subset of objects X was also considered in [3], i.e. if X is (l, u)-discernible then its (l, u)-boundary region is empty. For a choice of l and u then (l, u)-discernible is when $\gamma^{l,u}(P, D) = 1$. Analogous to the $PoA(\cdot)$ measure, we can calculate the proportion of (l, u)-discernibility, defined $PoD(\cdot)$. For the finishing mill example $PoD(C) = 0.3472$, $PoD(\{c_1\}) = 0.5372$ and $PoD(\{c_2\}) = 0.3472$.

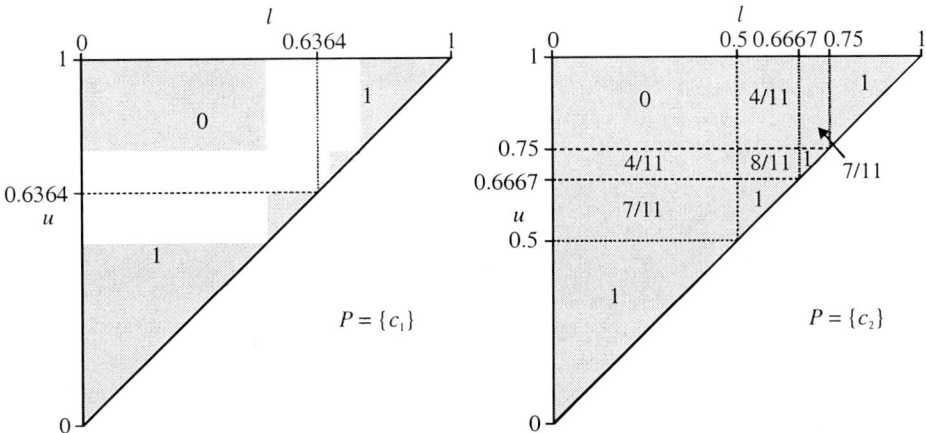

Fig. 3. (l, u)-quality graphs based on $P = \{c_1\}$ and $P = \{c_2\}$ sets of condition attributes

4 (l, u) Weighted Lines

From section 3 the (l, u)-quality graph transforms the choice of l and u to identifying a point in the domain of the (l, u)-quality graph. Before further elucidation is given on the choice of l and u (see section 5), a number of straight lines which pass across the domain of the (l, u)-quality graph are defined, see Fig. 4.

A factor also introduced in this section for each line and analogous to the $\gamma_{AW}^{l,u}(P,D)$ value for the whole (l, u)-quality graph is their line-weighted mean (l, u)-QoC. That is, different areas of the (l, u)-quality graph have different levels of (l, u)-QoC, and a single line may pass over a number of regions with different levels of (l, u)-QoC. These are then summed together using a weight which is the proportion of the line actually within the region of each level of (l, u)-QoC.

The first line is the v-Parallel line (P_z) and is parallel to the v-axis, defined by its proportional distance z from the v-axis to (0, 1), hence $0 < z \leq 1$, see Fig. 4a). The two end points of the P_z line are given by $l_z = 1 - z$ and $u_z = z$. The coordinates along the boundary lines crossed by P_z are sorted into ascending order based on their distance from $(0, u_z)$ and represented by $(l_{z,i}, u_{z,i})$ $i = 1, .., n_z$, also defined $p_{z,i}^S$ $i = 1, .., n_z$. The associated distances between each set of cross points are defined $p_{z,i} = p_{z,i}^S - p_{z,i-1}^S$ $i = 1, .., n_z$ with $(l_{z,0}, u_{z,0}) = (0, u_z)$ and $(l_{z,n_z}, u_{z,n_z}) = (l_z, 1)$. It follows, the line-weighted mean QoC value (defined $\gamma_{P_z,z}^{l,u}(P,D)$) is given by

$$\gamma_{P_z,z}^{l,u}(P,D) = \frac{1}{\sqrt{2}(1-z)} \sum_{i=1}^{n_z} p_{z,i} \gamma^{\frac{1}{2}(l_{z,i-1}+l_{z,i}),\frac{1}{2}(u_{z,i-1}+u_{z,i})}(P,D).$$

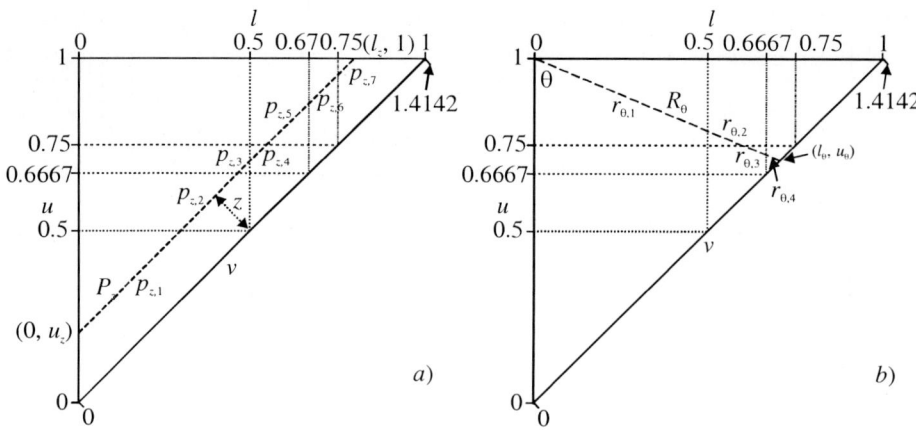

Fig. 4. The *v*-Parallel (P_z) and θ-Radial lines (R_θ) in the (l, u)-quality graph.

The domain of the θ-Radial line (R_θ) shown in Fig. 4b) is a line from the point (0, 1) to where it touches the *v*-axis, defined (l_θ, u_θ). The value θ represents the angle between the θ-Radial line and the *u*-axis, hence $0 \leq \theta \leq \pi/2$, with $l_\theta = u_\theta = \dfrac{\sin \vartheta}{\sin \vartheta + \cos \vartheta}$. The list of sorted boundary line cross points are defined $(l_{\theta,i}, u_{\theta,i})$ $i =$ 1, .., n_θ, where $(l_{\theta,0}, u_{\theta,0}) = (0, 1)$ and $(l_{\theta,n_\theta}, u_{\theta,n_\theta}) = (l_\theta, u_\theta)$. Each separate distance $r_{\theta,i} = r^S_{\theta,i} - r^S_{\theta,i-1}$ $i = 1, .., n_\theta$, where $r^S_{\theta,i}$ are the distances of the cross points $(l_{\theta,i}, u_{\theta,i})$ from (0, 1). The θ-Radial line-weighted mean (l, u)-QoC value, defined $\gamma^{l,u}_{R_\theta,\vartheta}(P,D)$ is given by

$$\gamma^{l,u}_{R_\theta,\vartheta}(P,D) = \frac{\sin \vartheta + \cos \vartheta}{\sin 3\pi/4} \sum_{i=1}^{n_\theta} r_{\theta,i} \gamma^{\frac{1}{2}(l_{\theta,i-1}+l_{\theta,i}), \frac{1}{2}(u_{\theta,i-1}+u_{\theta,i})}(P,D).$$

5 Identifying a Choice of *l* and *u* Values

In this section the lines defined in section 4 are employed to enable an understandable (automated) choice of the required *l* and *u* values, utilised later. Moreover, the specific lines found are based on their associated line-weighted mean (l, u)-QoC values. For the small example considered previously, Fig. 5a) reports the values of the defined lines $\gamma^{l,u}_{P_z,z}(C,D)$ and $\gamma^{l,u}_{R_\theta,\vartheta}(C,D)$ over their respective domains.

The specific lines are then defined such that their line-weighted mean (l, u)-QoC measures have the same values as $\gamma^{l,u}_{AW}(C,D)$. In the example $\gamma^{l,u}_{AW}(P,D) = 0.5606$, and Fig. 5a) identifies the values $z = 0.3239$ and $\theta = 0.2504$ such that the respective line-weighted mean (l, u)-QoC values ($\gamma^{l,u}_{P_v,z}(C,D)$ and $\gamma^{l,u}_{R_\theta,\vartheta}(C,D)$) also equal 0.5606. In Fig. 5b), these specific v-Parallel and θ-Radial lines (using $z = 0.3239$ and $\theta = 0.2504$) are drawn in the (l, u)-quality graph. Their point of intersection (l_c, u_c) is shown to be when $l_c = 0.1174$ and $u_c = 0.4413$.

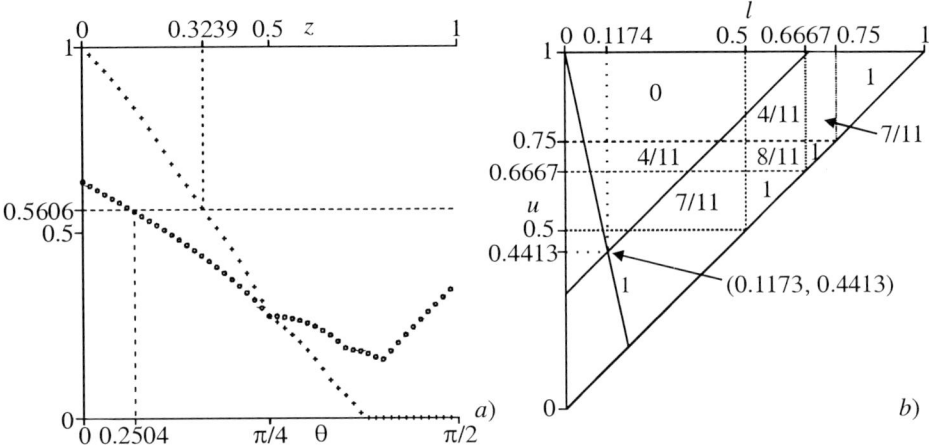

Fig. 5. a) Values of v-Parallel and θ-Radial lines and b) cross point on (l, u)-quality graph

While the specific values of l and u are important, it is the region of $\gamma^{l,u}(P,D)$ it lies within, which is of more relevance. That is, anywhere in the region including the point (0.1174, 0.4413) will have the same set of objects given a classification (this is slightly redundant here since for $l_c = 0.1174$ and $u_c = 0.4413$, $\gamma^{l,u}(P,D) = 1$, so all objects given a classification).

6 Conclusion

This paper has further investigated the extended Variable Precision Rough Sets Model. The notion of a (l, u)-quality graph is introduced, which elucidates the varying levels of (l, u)-QoC for choices of the l and u values. It is found, regions of the (l, u)-quality graph exist within which the level of (l, u)-QoC is the same. The (l, u)-quality graph is shown to further allow a number of related measures to be constructed. The proportion of area (*PoA*) measure allows any subset of the condition attributes to be given a measure of similarity to the whole set of condition attributes. That is, based on the proportion of the (l, u)-quality graph for which they have the same level of (l, u)-QoC as the whole set of condition attributes.

Two straight lines are also defined, namely v-Parallel and θ-Radial lines, which pass over the (l, u)-quality graph, representing a subset of the l and u values. Certain line-weighted mean (l, u)-QoC measures are defined for each of the lines. When these measures are constrained to be equal to the related $\gamma_{AW}^{l,u}(P,D)$ measure, specific lines are identified. Through this equating of the area and line-weighted mean (l, u)-QoC measures a choice of l and u is identified. These lines do need to be fully interpreted. For example the v-Parallel line defined by the z value. The z value restricts the inter-distances between the l and u values. To illustrate, $z = 0$, then $l = u$ (zero inter-distance), also $z = 0.75$ then line of points from $(0, 0.75)$ to $(0.25, 1)$ always with a distance of 0.75 between l and u.

A full investigation to incorporate the results in this paper within a criteria for the effective choice of l and u values is still required. Indeed, it is stressed a variety of other lines can also be identified, all of which need also to be fully interpreted to find the optimal choice of lines etc. The related measures defined (as well as others) also need to be considered further on their optimal utilisation. It is hoped, future utilisation of these results in real world applications will elucidate their impact on the associated choice of the l and u values.

References

1. Beynon, M.: An Investigation of β-reduct Selection within the Variable Precision Rough Sets Model. In: The Second International Conference on Rough Sets and Current Trends in Computing, Lecture Notes in Artificial Intelligence Series, Springer-Verlag (2000) 114–122
2. Beynon, M.: Reducts within the Variable Precision Rough Set Model. A Further Investigation. European Journal of Operational Research 134 (2001) 592–605
3. Katzberg, J.D. Ziarko, W.: Variable precision extension of rough sets. Fundamenta Informaticae 27 (1996), 155–168
4. Pawlak, Z.: Rough Sets. International Journal of Information and Computer Sciences 11 (1982) 341–356
5. Ziarko, W.: Analysis of uncertain information in the framework of variable precision rough sets. Foundations of Computing and Decision Sciences 18 (1993) 381–396
6. Ziarko, W.: Decision making with probabilistic decision tables. In: Zhong, N., Skowron, A., Ohsuga, S. (eds.): New Directions in Rough Sets, Data Mining, and Granular-Soft Computing. Proceedings 7th International Workshop, RSFDGrC'99, Yamaguchi Japan (1999) 463–471
7. Ziarko, W.: Probabilistic Decision Tables in the Variable Precision Rough Set Model. Computational Intelligence 17 (2001) 593–603

A Quantitative Analysis of Preclusivity vs. Similarity Based Rough Approximations*

Gianpiero Cattaneo and Davide Ciucci

Dipartimento Di Informatica, Sistemistica e Comunicazione
Università di Milano – Bicocca
Via Bicocca degli Arcimboldi 8, I–20126 Milano (Italia)
{cattang,ciucci}@disco.unimib.it

Abstract. In the context of generalized rough sets, it is possible to introduce in an Information System two different rough approximations.These are induced, respectively, by a Similarity and a Preclusivity relation ([3,4]). It is possible to show that the last one is always better than the first one. Here, we present a quantitative analysis of the relative performances of the two different approximations. The most important conclusion is that preclusive and similar approximation consistently differ when there is a low quality of approximation.

Keywords: Preclusivity spaces, rough approximations, asymmetric accuracy measure.

1 Preclusivity Approximation Spaces

Let us first consider a non empty set U, which intuitively represents a given *universe of discourse* (we will shortly say a *universe*). Needless to say, the choice of the universe will depend on the intended application. The relationship among individuals of our universe can be described by a binary relation $\mathcal{R}$. A classification and logical–algebraic characterization of such binary relations can be found in literature (for an overview see [11]). Generally, the different relations are divided in two groups:*indistinguishability* and *distinguishability* relations.

In our analysis, we are dealing with a *tolerance* (or *similarity*) relation, i.e., a reflexive and symmetric relation, and its opposite, a *preclusivity* relation, i.e., an irreflexive and symmetric relation. From the intuitive point of view, two individuals are similar when they have an "indistinguishable role" with respect to the intended application, even if they are not equivalent. On the other side, they are preclusive if they have a distinguishable role, even if they are not totally different. As showed in [4], both relations give rise to a rough approximation, with the preclusive always better than the similarity one. In the present paper we give a quantitative measure of such a better behavior.

First, we define the environment we are working in.

---

* This work has been supported by MIUR\COFIN project "Formal Languages and Automata: Theory and Application".

Definition 1.1. *A* similarity space *is a structure* $\mathcal{S} = \langle X, \mathcal{R} \rangle$, *where* X *(called the* universe *of the space) is a non empty set, while* $\mathcal{R}$ *(called the* similarity relation *of the space) is a reflexive and symmetric relation, defined on* X.

Given a similarity space $\langle X, \mathcal{R} \rangle$, the similarity class generated by the element $x \in X$ is defined as: $S(x) := \{y \in X : x\mathcal{R}y\}$. Moreover, a rough approximation of a set $A \subseteq X$ can be given, as usual, by the following lower approximation, $\mathbf{L}_\mathcal{R}$, and upper approximation, $\mathbf{U}_\mathcal{R}$:

$$\mathbf{L}_\mathcal{R}(A) := \{x \in X : S(x) \subseteq A\} \quad \mathbf{U}_\mathcal{R}(A) := \{x \in X : S(x) \cap A \neq \emptyset\}. \qquad (1)$$

Definition 1.2. *A* preclusivity space *is a structure* $\mathcal{S} = \langle X, \# \rangle$, *where* X *(called the* universe *of the space) is a non empty set, while* $\#$ *(called the* preclusivity relation *of the space) is an irreflexive and symmetric relation, defined on* X.

Needless to stress, any similarity space determines a corresponding preclusivity space, and vice versa.

Suppose, now, a preclusivity space $\langle X, \# \rangle$ and consider the complete Boolean algebra based on the power set of X: $\langle \mathcal{P}(X), \cap, \cup, {}^c, \emptyset, X \rangle$. The preclusivity relation $\#$ permits us to define a further complementation $^\#$ on $\mathcal{P}(X)$:

$$\forall H \in \mathcal{P}(X) : H^\# := \{x \in X : \forall y \in H (x \# y)\}.$$

In other words, $H^\#$ contains all and only the elements of X that are distinguishable from all the elements of H. We will call the operation $^\#$, induced by the preclusivity relation $\#$, a *preclusive complement*. Whenever $x \in H^\#$ we will also write: $x \# H$ and we will say that x is *preclusive* to the set H. Further, we will say that two subsets H and K of X are *mutually preclusive* ($H \# K$) iff all the elements of H are preclusive to K, and all the elements of K are preclusive to H.

We remark that, in the context of modal analysis of rough approximation spaces, the operator $^\#$ is a *sufficiency* operator ([7]).

Now, we define Information Systems which generate in a canonical way a preclusivity space.

Definition 1.3. *An* Information System *is a structure* $\mathcal{K} = \langle X, Att(X), val(X), F \rangle$, *where the* universe X *is a non empty set of* objects; $Att(X)$ *is a non empty set of* attributes, *which assume values for the objects belonging to the set* X; $val(X)$ *is the set of all* possible values *that can be observed for an attribute* a *from* $Att(X)$ *in the case of an object* x *from* X; F *(called the* information map*) is a function* $F : X \times Att(X) \to val(X)$ *which associates to any pair, consisting of an object* $x \in X$ *and of an attribute* $a \in Att(X)$, *the value* $F(x, a) \in val(X)$ *assumed by* a *for the object* x.

The simplest similarity relation on an Information System is the Pawlak's one: $x\mathcal{R}y$ iff $\forall a \in Att(X) \; F(x,a) = F(y,a)$. Obviously the corresponding preclusive relation is: $x \# y$ iff $\forall a \in Att(X) \; F(x,a) \neq F(y,a)$.

2 Quasi BZ Distributive Lattice and Rough Approximations

Definition 2.1. *A system* $(A, \wedge, \vee, \sim, \neg, 0, 1)$ *is a* quasi Brouwer Zadeh (BZ) distributive lattice *if the following conditions hold:*

(1) A is a distributive lattice with respect to the join and the meet operations $\vee, \wedge$ whose induced partial ordering relation is $a \leq b$ iff $a = a \wedge b$ (equivalently, iff $b = a \vee b$). A is bounded by the least element $0 := \neg 1$ and the greatest element 1.

(2) The unary operation $\neg : A \mapsto A$ is a Kleene *(or* Zadeh*) orthocomplementation. In other words: $\neg(\neg x) = x$, $\neg(x \vee y) = \neg x \wedge \neg y$, $x \wedge \neg x \leq y \vee \neg y$.*

(3) The unary operation $\sim : A \mapsto A$ is a Brouwer *orthocomplementation. In other words: $x \wedge \sim\sim x = x$, $\sim (x \vee y) = \sim x \wedge \sim y$, $x \wedge \sim x = 0$.*

(4) The two orthocomplementations are linked by the interconnection rule: $\sim x \leq \neg x$.

In the framework of quasi-BZ posets, one can naturally define the *anti-Brouwer complement* $\flat : \forall a \in \Sigma : \flat a := \neg \sim \neg a$. Using the two negations $\sim, \flat$ one can define a rough approximation space $\langle A, \mathbf{L}, \mathbf{U} \rangle$ where $\mathbf{L} : A \to A$ and $\mathbf{U} : A \to A$ are defined as $\mathbf{L}(a) := \flat\flat a$ and $\mathbf{U}(a) := \sim\sim a$. These approximation maps satisfy the axioms of *abstract approximation space* ([4]). So, they are the best approximation of an element $a \in A$ from the bottom (resp., top) by inner (resp., outer) definable elements. This does not hold for the operators of necessity, $\nu(a) := \neg \sim a$, and possibility $\mu(a) := \sim \neg a$. In fact, in general, they do not satisfy the axiom $\nu(\nu(a)) = \nu(a)$ (resp., $\mu(\mu(a)) = \mu(a)$). As a consequence, we have that the following chain holds: $\nu(a) \leq \mathbf{L}(a) \leq a \leq \mathbf{U}(a) \leq \mu(a)$.

Let us now go back to the complete Boolean algebra based on the power set of X (the support of a preclusivity space). We can enrich our algebra by adding the new operation $^\#$. One can easily show that the resulting structure is a quasi-BZ distributive lattice.

Theorem 2.1. *Let $S = \langle X, \# \rangle$ be a preclusivity space and let $\langle \mathcal{P}(X), \cap, \cup, ^c, \emptyset, X \rangle$ be the complete Boolean algebra based on the power set of X. Consider the structure: $\mathcal{S} = \langle \mathcal{P}(X), \cap, \cup, ^\#, ^c, \emptyset, X \rangle$, where $\forall H \in \mathcal{P}(X) : H^\# := \{x \in X : x \# H\}$. Such a structure is a quasi-BZ distributive lattice.*

Above we showed that any quasi-BZ distributive lattice determines a rough approximation space. As a consequence, by Theorem 2.1, we immediately obtain that any preclusivity space $\langle X, \# \rangle$ determines a rough approximation space $\langle \mathcal{P}(X), \mathbf{L}_\#, \mathbf{U}_\# \rangle$, where $\forall H \in \mathcal{P}(X): \mathbf{L}_\#(H) = H^{\flat\flat}$, $\mathbf{U}_\#(H) = H^{\#\#}$. Let us stress, in particular, the validity of the following chain of inclusions, for any $H \in \mathcal{P}(X)$:

$$H^{c\#} \subseteq H^{\flat\flat} \subseteq H \subseteq H^{\#\#} \subseteq H^{\#c}. \tag{2}$$

Consider the quasi-BZ distributive lattice determined by a preclusivity space $\langle X, \# \rangle$ and let $\langle X, \mathcal{R} \rangle$ be the similarity space associated to our preclusivity space. One can easily prove that $\nu(H) = H^{c\#}$ and $\mu(H) = H^{\#c}$ turn out to be exactly the similar approximations defined by Equation (1).

We remark that the only Similarity Space where $H^{c\#} = H^{bb}$ and $H^{\#\#} = H^{\#c}$, is the one generated by an equivalence relation. So, in the context of Pawlak rough sets theory, we have that the two approximations collapse in the same classical one.

Moreover, Equation (2) says that Preclusive approximations are always better than the corresponding Similar ones. However, this result does not say how much they differ. So, we first present some tolerance relation and then measure the performances of the two approximations on some test case.

3 Tolerance Relations

In this section, we present four similarity (tolerance) relations which has been used to compute rough approximations in our tests.

Let us first consider incomplete information systems. In this context a natural tolerance relation, introduced by Kryszkiewicz in [10], is that two objects are similar if they have same values for all known attributes. In a more formal way: let $D \subseteq Att(X)$, then $\forall x, y \in X, x\mathcal{R}_D y$ iff

$$\forall a_i \in D \quad F(x, a_i) = F(y, a_i) \quad \text{or} \quad F(x, a_i) = * \quad \text{or} \quad F(y, a_i) = * \quad . \quad \text{(T1)}$$

where the symbol $*$ represents an *unknown (null) value*. The peculiarity of this relation is that it does not require to set any parameter, but it only relies on the information contained in the dataset.

A typical example of function which is symmetric and not transitive is a distance measure. So, if we can introduce such a function in an information system we could say that two objects are similar if their distance is less than a value ϵ, which can be fixed or dependent on some other parameter. Given a numeric valued attribute $a \in Att(X)$, a way to define a metric is:

$$d_a(x, y) := \frac{|F(x, a) - F(y, a)|}{max\{F(x, a) : x \in X\} - min\{F(x, a) : x \in X\}} \quad \text{(T2)}$$

In presence of two or more attributes, we can introduce an overall distance: $d_D(x, y) := \sum_{a \in D} \omega_a d_a(x, y)$ where ω_a are weights such that $\sum \omega_a = 1$. A common choice is $\omega_a = 1/|D|$. So, $x\mathcal{R}_{(D,\epsilon)} y$ iff $d_D(x, y) \leq \epsilon$.

When dealing with nominal (categorical) attributes a suitable choice is to use the Value Difference Metric ([13,14]), i.e., a distance between values v, v' of an attribute $a \in Att(X)$ which can be used as a metric between two objects having values v, v'. The definition of such a metric is:

$$vdm_a(y, z) := \frac{1}{c(d)} \sum_{i=1}^{c(d)} \left(\frac{|X_y \cap X_i|}{|X_y|} - \frac{|X_z \cap X_i|}{|X_z|} \right)^2 \quad . \quad \text{(T3)}$$

where a is a given attribute, d is a decision attribute, $c(d)$ the number of decision classes and $X_y := \{x \in X : a(x) = a(y)\}$, $X_i := \{x \in X : d(x) = i\}$.

So, a tolerance relation can be defined, for a single attribute, as $x\mathcal{R}_{(a,\epsilon_a)}y$ iff $vdm_a(x,y) \leq \epsilon_a$, and, for a set of attributes, as $x\mathcal{R}_{(D,\underline{\epsilon})}y$ iff $\forall a \in D \quad x\mathcal{R}_{a,\epsilon_a}y$. In our tests, we set $\epsilon_a = \epsilon$, i.e., the parameter ϵ was fixed equal for all the attributes.

The last relation considered is a generalization of the classical indiscernibility relation (sometimes called "weak indiscernibility", [5,11]) In Pawlak rough set theory we say that two objects are equivalent if for all selected attributes they have same values. If we relax this requirement we can say that two objects are similar if they have same values for some attribute.

Let $D \subseteq Att(X)$. We say that x is similar to y with respect to D and ϵ, where $\epsilon \in [0,1]$, and write $x\mathcal{R}_{D,\epsilon}y$, iff

$$\frac{|\{a_i \in D : F(a_i,x) = F(a_i,y)\}|}{|D|} \geq \epsilon. \tag{T4}$$

This relation says that two objects are similar if they have at least $\epsilon|D|$ attributes with the same value.

4 Results

In order to evaluate the performance of an approximation we use the following accuracy measure:

$$AM(H) = \frac{|\mathbf{L}(H)|}{|H|}. \tag{3}$$

This measure has the advantage that it does not depend on the approximation of H^c ([6]). On the contrary, Pawlak accuracy measure $\frac{|\mathbf{L}(H)|}{|\mathbf{U}(H)|}$ ([9]), relies also on H^c, in fact, $|\mathbf{U}(H)| = |X| - |\mathbf{L}(H^c)|$. So, in measuring the accuracy of an approximation we use the couple: $(AM(H), AM(H^c))$, remarking that $AM(H^c) = \frac{|X - \mathbf{U}(H)|}{|H|}$.

To evaluate the relative performance of preclusive approximation with respect to the similarity one, we simply compute the ratio of the respective accuracy measures:

$$AMR(H) := \frac{AM_p(H)}{AM_s(H)} = \frac{|\mathbf{L}_\#(H)|}{|\mathbf{L}_\mathcal{R}(H)|}.$$

$$AMR(H^c) := \frac{AM_p(H^c)}{AM_s(H^c)} = \frac{|\mathbf{L}_\#(H^c)|}{|\mathbf{L}_\mathcal{R}(H^c)|} = \frac{|X - \mathbf{U}_\#(H)|}{|X - \mathbf{U}_\mathcal{R}(H)|}.$$

Thus, the two relative accuracy measures give us a degree of how the knowledge about a set H is greater in using the preclusive relation instead of the corresponding similarity one.

To have an analysis as objective as possible, we measured the above quantities on different datasets and using the similarity (preclusive) relations of previous section with several values of parameters. Once fixed dataset, relation and possible parameters, the algorithm followed is:

1. Repeat 1000 times:
   – Choose randomly a set of attributes A and a set of objects H;
   – Compute $AM_p(H), AM_s(H), AM_p(H^c), AM_s(H^c)$;
   – Increase a counter c_l (resp., c_u) if $|\mathbf{L}_\#(H)| \neq |\mathbf{L}_\mathcal{R}(H)|$ (resp., $|\mathbf{U}_\#(H)| \neq |\mathbf{U}_\mathcal{R}(H)|$).
2. Compute the average of $AM_p(H)$, $AM_s(H)$, $AM_p(H^c)$, $AM_s(H^c)$, $AMR(H)$, $AMR(H^c)$, and the percentage of cases where preclusive and similar approximation differ, i.e., $c_l/10$, $c_u/10$.

When reporting the results (tables 1, 2) for each pair dataset–relation it is showed: the value of ϵ used (when required); c_m, that is the mean of c_l and c_p (we choose not to report them separately because in all cases they were similar); the average of $AMR(H)$ and $AMR(H^c)$; the average of $AM_p(H)$ and $AM_p(H^c)$.

Let us first consider the performances obtained with relation $T1$. The results are reported in Table 1. As can be seen, preclusive and tolerance analysis are very close, except in the case of VOTES dataset. This exception is due to the peculiarity of the dataset, where each attribute is either 0 or 1. This feature leads to a high probability that two objects are similar and consequently to a "weak" classification. The bad classification is also confirmed by the absolute performances.

Table 1. T1 performances.

Dataset	Relation	c_m (%)	$AMR(H)$	$AMR(H^c)$	$AM_p(H)$	$AM_p(H^c)$
ANNEAL	$T1$	38.0	1.011	1.020	0.297	0.197
AUDIOLOGY	$T1$	23.7	1.010	1.032	0.444	0.270
HEPATITIS	$T1$	56.2	1.029	1.033	0.616	0.363
VOTES	$T1$	30.9	1.225	1.189	0.068	0.077

Table 2. Differences between H and H^c relative performances for low absolute performances ($AM_p(H) \simeq 0.030$).

Dataset	Relation	ϵ	c_m (%)	$AMR(H)$	$AMR(H^c)$	$AM_p(H)$	$AM_p(H^c)$
GLASS	$T2$	0.15	43.4	1.653	2.621	0.030	0.046
IONOSPHERE	$T2$	0.3	50.9	2.146	3.601	0.030	0.017
IRIS	$T2$	0.11	36.1	3.031	2.486	0.034	0.077
IRIS	$T3$	0.004	30.5	1.921	1.520	0.032	0.079
LUNG	$T3$	0.15	9.4	1.430	2.352	0.036	0.038

Indeed, it is a general result that "weaker" classifications lead to better relative performances. In fact, in considering all the other relations and datasets, one has that relative and absolute performances are inversely proportional. Thus,

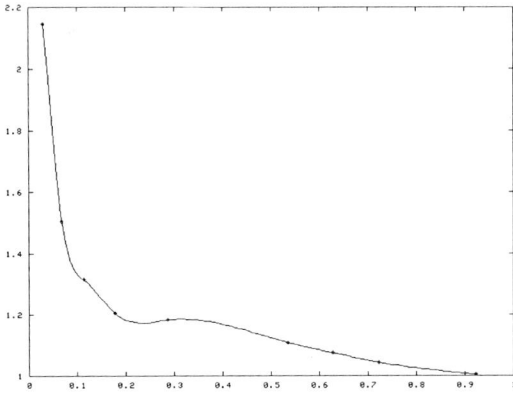

Fig. 1. $AMR(H)$ wrt $AM(H)$, IONOSPHERE dataset,$T2$, $\epsilon \in [0.01, 0.4]$.

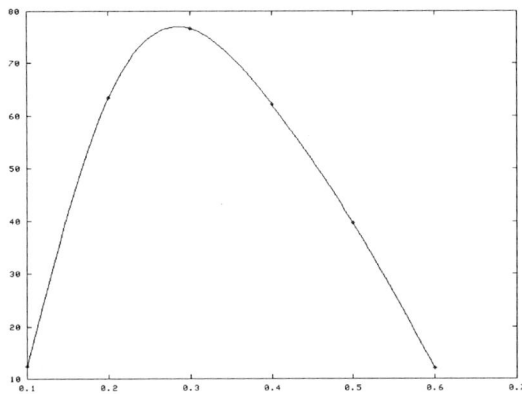

Fig. 2. Relation between ϵ and c_m, FLAG dataset, $T4$.

even if preclusive approximations are always better than similar ones, the best relative performances are obtained in the case one can only have a poor classification. In figure 1, as an example, it is drawn the relation between $AMR(H)$ and $AM(H)$ in the case of IONOSPHERE dataset and relation $(T2)$.

However, the great value in relative performances could regard a small number of cases. In fact, another result, common to all datasets and relations, is the "parabolic" dependency of c_m on ϵ. In figure 2, it is drawn, as an example, the relation of c_m and ϵ in the case of FLAGS dataset, with tolerance relation $(T4)$. Low values of c_m for "low" (where low is relative to the dataset and relation considered) values of ϵ can be explained by the few possibilities of approximation in the case of low ϵ: only very close elements can be considered similar. The fact that also with "high" values of ϵ one have low values of c_m is due to the poor quality of approximation. In fact, in such a case it often happens that $\mathbf{L}_\mathcal{R}(H) = \mathbf{L}_\#(H) = \emptyset$ and $\mathbf{U}_\mathcal{R}(H) = \mathbf{U}_\#(H) = X$.

As to the diversity of H and H^c approximations, we encountered meaningful differences between $AMR(H)$ and $AMR(H^c)$ only for low quality of approximations, i.e., for low values of $AM(H)$ and $AM(H^c)$. In such a case (see table 2) the relative approximations differs and, depending on the dataset considered, one is much higher than the other. So, mainly in presence of a bad approximation, it is worthwhile to consider also the approximation of H^c.

Acknowledgments. All tests presented in the paper were done using a modified version of Rough Set Library ([8], ftp://ftp.ii.pw.edu.pl/pub/Rough) on datasets from UCI repository of machine learning databases ([1]).

References

[1] Blake , C. Merz, C.: UCI repository of machine learning databases (1998) http://www.ics.uci.edu/~mlearn/MLRepository.html.

[2] Cattaneo, G. Nisticò, G.: Brouwer-Zadeh posets and three valued Lukasiewicz posets. Fuzzy Sets Syst. **33** (1989) 165–190

[3] Cattaneo, G.: Generalized rough sets (preclusivity fuzzy-intuitionistic (BZ) lattices). Studia Logica **58** (1997) 47–77

[4] Cattaneo, G.: Abstract approximation spaces for rough theories. In Polkowski, L., Skowron, A., eds.: Rough Sets in Knowledge Discovery 1: Methodology and Applications. Physica–Verlag, Heidelberg (1998) 59–98

[5] Düntsch, I., Gediga, G.: Logical and algebraic techniques for rough set data analysis. In Polkowski, L., Tsumoto, S., Lin, T.-Y., eds.: Rough Set Methods and Applications. Physica–Verlag, Heidelberg (2000) 521–544

[6] Gediga, G. Düntsch, I.: Rough approximation quality revisited. Artificial Intelligence **132** (2001) 219–234

[7] Düntsch, I., Orlowska, E.: Beyond modalities: Sufficiency and mixed algebras. In Orlowska, E., Szalas, A., eds.: Relational Methods for Computer Science Applications. Physica–Verlag, Heidelberg (2001) 277–299

[8] Gawryś, M., Sienkiewicz. J.: RSL – the rough set library, version 2.0. Technical Report 27, Institute of Computer Science, University of Technology, Warsaw (1994)

[9] Komorowski, J., Pawlak, Z., Polkowski, L., Skowron, A.: Rough sets: A tutorial. In Pal, S. Skowron, A., eds.: Rough Fuzzy Hybridization: A New Trend in Decision Making. Springer–Verlag, Singapore (1999) 3–98

[10] Kryszkiewicz, M.: Rough set approach to incomplete information systems. Information Sciences **112** (1998) 39–49

[11] Orlowska, E.: Introduction: What you always wanted to know about rough sets. In [12] 1–20

[12] Orlowska, E., ed.: Incomplete Information: Rough Set Analysis. Physica–Verlag, Heidelberg (1998)

[13] Stepaniuk, J.: Approximation spaces in extensions of rough sets theory. In Polkowski, L., Skowron, A., eds.: Rough Sets and Current Trends in Computing, First International Conference, RSCTC'98 (Warsaw, Poland). Volume 1424 of Lecture Notes in Computer Science, Berlin, Springer (1998) 290–297

[14] J. Stepaniuk. Optimizations of rough set model. Fundamenta Informaticae **36** (1998) 265–283

Heyting Wajsberg Algebras as an Abstract Environment Linking Fuzzy and Rough Sets*

Gianpiero Cattaneo and Davide Ciucci

Dipartimento Di Informatica, Sistemistica e Comunicazione
Università di Milano – Bicocca
Via Bicocca degli Arcimboldi 8, I–20126 Milano (Italia)
{cattang,ciucci}@disco.unimib.it

Abstract. Heyting Wajsberg (HW) algebras are introduced as algebraic models of a logic equipped with two implication connectives, the Heyting one linked to the intuitionistic logic and the Wajsberg one linked to the Łukasiewicz approach to many–valued logic. On the basis of an HW algebra it is possible to obtain a de Morgan Brouwer–Zadeh (BZ) distributive lattice with respect to the partial order induced from the Łukasiewicz implication. Modal-like operators are also defined generating a rough approximation space. It is shown that standard Pawlak approach to rough sets is a model of this structure.

Keywords: Heyting algebra, Wajsberg algebra, fuzzy sets, rough approximation space, rough sets.

1 Real Unit Interval

In Sections 1 and 2, we discuss two examples which give us some hint to introduce the structure of Heyting Wajsberg (HW) algebras. This structure results to be a good environment to link fuzzy sets and rough sets. In fact, by a suitable definition of the operators, both the collection of fuzzy sets and the collection of rough sets can be naturally equipped with a structure satisfying HW axioms.

As a first example, let us consider the real unit interval endowed with *continuous t-norms*, i.e., continuous mappings $\mathbf{t} : [0,1] \times [0,1] \mapsto [0,1]$ fulfilling the following properties for all $a, b, c \in [0,1]$:

(a) $a\mathbf{t}b = b\mathbf{t}a$ (commutativity)
(b) $(a\mathbf{t}b)\mathbf{t}c = a\mathbf{t}(b\mathbf{t}c)$ (associativity)
(c) $a \leq b$ implies $a\mathbf{t}c \leq b\mathbf{t}c$ (monotonicity)
(d) $a\mathbf{t}1 = 1\mathbf{t}a = a$

Two important examples of continuous t-norm are Łukasiewicz and Gödel t-norm, defined respectively as: $a \odot b := \max\{0, a+b-1\}$ and $a \wedge b := \min\{a,b\}$.

---

* This work has been supported by MIUR\COFIN project "Formal Languages and Automata: Theory and Application".

A *continuous t-conorm* is a continuous mapping $s : [0,1] \times [0,1] \mapsto [0,1]$ fulfilling properties $(a), (b), (c)$ and the boundary condition $as0 = 0sa = a$ for all $a \in [0,1]$. The *standard complementation* function is defined for all $a \in [0,1]$ as $\mathbf{N}(a) = 1 - a$. Now, given a t-norm $\mathbf{t}$, it is possible to introduce the *dual* t-conorm s_t as the mapping $as_t b = \mathbf{N}(\mathbf{N}(a)\mathbf{t}\mathbf{N}(b))$. Lukasiewicz and Gödel t-conorm are respectively $a \oplus b := \min\{1, a+b\}$ and $a \vee b := \max\{a, b\}$. The *implication* or *quasi-inverse* operation induced by a t-norm $\mathbf{t}$ (called also t-implication) is the map $\rightarrow_\mathbf{t} : [0,1] \times [0,1] \mapsto [0,1]$ defined for arbitrary $a, b \in [0,1]$ as: $a \rightarrow_\mathbf{t} b := \sup\{c \in [0,1] : a\mathbf{t}c \leq b\}$. Lukasiewicz and Gödel t-norms induce the following two implications:

$$a \rightarrow_L b := \min\{1, 1 - a + b\} \qquad a \rightarrow_G b := \begin{cases} 1 & \text{if } a \leq b \\ b & \text{if } a > b \end{cases}.$$

Any t-implication operation satisfies the *implication* (or *adjointness*) condition: $c \leq (a \rightarrow_\mathbf{t} b)$ iff $a\mathbf{t}c \leq b$ which, in the particular case of $c = 1$ assumes the form $a \rightarrow_\mathbf{t} b = 1$ iff $a \leq b$.

Let $\mathbf{t}$ be a t-norm with associated implication operation $\rightarrow_\mathbf{t}$. The *negation* induced from $\mathbf{t}$ is the unary operation $\neg_\mathbf{t} : [0,1] \mapsto [0,1]$ defined as: $\neg_\mathbf{t} a := a \rightarrow_\mathbf{t} 0 = \sup\{c \in [0,1] : a\mathbf{t}c = 0\}$. The negation induced by Lukasiewicz and Gödel t-norms are respectively: $\neg a := a \rightarrow_L 0 = 1 - a = \mathbf{N}(a)$ and $\sim a := a \rightarrow_G 0 = 1$ if $a = 0$, 0 otherwise.

Finally, thanks to a suitable composition of the two negations one can define the necessity (ν) and the possibility (μ) operators in the following way: $\nu(a) := \sim \neg a = 1$ if $a = 1$, 0 otherwise; $\mu(a) := \neg \sim a = 0$ if $a = 0$, 1 otherwise, and a third kind of negation: $\flat a := \sim \neg \sim a = 0$ if $a = 1$, 1 otherwise.

2 Fuzzy Sets

The operators introduced in the previous example (the real unit interval $[0,1]$) can be defined in an analogous way also in a fuzzy sets environment. Let us consider the collection $[0,1]^X$ of all *generalized characteristic functionals* (or *fuzzy sets*) on the *universe* X defined as $[0,1]$–valued functions on X, i.e., $f : X \mapsto [0,1]$. This set contains the characteristic functionals χ_Δ of the subsets Δ of X, s.t. $\chi_\Delta(x) = 1$, if $x \in \Delta$; $\chi_\Delta(x) = 0$, otherwise (equivalently, $\{0,1\}$–valued functions on X).

In this context, the operations corresponding to the norms and conorms on $[0,1]$ are defined as:
$(f_1 \odot f_2)(x) := \max\{0, f_1(x) + f_2(x) - 1\}$, $(f_1 \wedge f_2)(x) := \min\{f_1(x), f_2(x)\}$
$(f_1 \oplus f_2)(x) := \min\{1, f_1(x) + f_2(x)\}$, $(f_1 \vee f_2)(x) := \max\{f_1(x), f_2(x)\}$.

Let us remark that $\wedge, \vee$ are lattice operators whose induced partial order is the usual pointwise ordering: $\forall f_1, f_2 \in [0,1]^X$, $f_1 \leq f_2$ iff for all $x \in X$, $f_1(x) \leq f_2(x)$.

Analogously, the operations corresponding to the Łukasiewicz and the Gödel implications are respectively: $(f_1 \rightarrow_L f_2)(x) := \min\{1, 1 - f_1(x) + f_2(x)\}$ and

$$(f_1 \rightarrow_G f_2)(x) := \begin{cases} 1 & f_1(x) \leq f_2(x) \\ f_2(x) & \text{otherwise} \end{cases}.$$

Also in this case two negation operators can be induced by these implications. In fact, by setting $\underline{0}(x) := 0$ for all x, we can define $(f \to_L \underline{0})(x) := \neg f(x) = 1 - f(x)$ and $(f \to_G \underline{0})(x) := \sim f(x) = 1$ if $f(x) = 0$, 0 otherwise.

For any fuzzy set $f \in [0,1]^X$ one can single out some peculiar subsets of the universe X: the *certainly-yes* (also the *necessity*) domain of f: $\Delta_1(f) := \{x \in X : f(x) = 1\}$; the *certainly-no* (also the *impossibility*) domain of f: $\Delta_0(f) := \{x \in X : f(x) = 0\}$; the *possibility* domain of f: $\Delta_p(f) := \{x \in X : f(x) \neq 0\} = (\Delta_0(f))^c$; the *contingency* domain of f: $\Delta_c(f) := \{x \in X : f(x) \neq 1\} = (\Delta_1(f))^c$.

The necessity of a fuzzy set f is defined as $\nu(f) := \sim \neg f$ which turns out to be the characteristic functional of the certainly-yes domain of f: $\nu(f) = \chi_{\Delta_1(f)}$ (where $\nu(f)(x) = 1$, if $f(x) = 1$; $\nu(f)(x) = 0$, otherwise). The possibility of a fuzzy set f is defined as $\mu(f) := \neg \sim f$ which is $\mu(f) = \chi_{\Delta_p(f)}$ (where $\mu(f)(x) = 1$ if $f(x) \neq 0$; $\mu(f)(x) = 0$, otherwise). Hence the impossibility operator is given by the characteristic functional of the certainly-no domain of f, and it turns out to be the negation $\sim$: $\neg \mu(f) = \chi_{\Delta_0(f)} = \sim f$. Moreover, one has $\flat(f) = \sim \neg \sim f = \chi_{(\Delta_1(f))^c}$.

3 HW Algebras

Now, we introduce an algebraic structure which admits as models both the unit interval and the collection of fuzzy sets, once endowed with the mappings described in the previous sections. Basic aspect of the algebra is the use of two different implications, a Lukasiewicz and an intuitionistic one, as the only primitive operators. Moreover, it is shown that rough approximation spaces can be introduced in such a structure.

Definition 3.1. *A system* $\mathbf{A} = (A, \to_L, \to_G, 0)$ *is a* Heyting Wajsberg *(HW) algebra if A is a non empty set, $0 \in A$, $\to_L, \to_G$ are binary operators, such that, once defined* $\neg a := a \to_L 0$, $\sim a := a \to_G 0$, $1 := \neg 0$, $a \wedge b := \neg((\neg a \to_L \neg b) \to_L \neg b)$, $a \vee b := (a \to_L b) \to_L b$ *the followings are satisfied:*

(HW1) $a \to_G a = 1$
(HW2) $(a \to_G b) \wedge b = b$
(HW3) $a \to_G (b \wedge c) = (a \to_G b) \wedge (a \to_G c)$
(HW4) $a \wedge (a \to_G b) = a \wedge b$
(HW5) $(a \vee b) \to_G c = (a \to_G c) \wedge (b \to_G c)$
(HW6) $1 \to_L a = a$
(HW7) $a \to_L (b \to_L c) = \neg(a \to_L c) \to_L \neg b$
(HW8) $(a \to_G b) \vee (b \to_G a) = 1$
(HW9) $(a \to_G b) \to_L (a \to_L b) = 1$

In any HW algebra we can define a partial order relation as follows:

$$a \leq b \quad \text{iff} \quad a \to_L b = 1 \quad . \tag{1}$$

Theorem 3.1. *Let $\mathbf{A}$ be a HW algebra. Once defined the order relation as in (1), the following equivalences hold:* $a \leq b$ *iff* $a \wedge b = a$ *iff* $a \to_G b = 1$.

Theorem 3.2. *Let* **A** *be a HW algebra. Then* $(A, \rightarrow_L, 1)$ *is a Wajsberg (W) algebra according to [13,14], i.e.,* **A** *satisfies the following axioms:*

(W1) $1 \rightarrow_L a = a$
(W2) $(a \rightarrow_L b) \rightarrow_L ((b \rightarrow_L c) \rightarrow_L (a \rightarrow_L c)) = 1$
(W3) $(a \rightarrow_L b) \rightarrow_L b = (b \rightarrow_L a) \rightarrow_L a$
(W4) $(\neg a \rightarrow_L \neg b) \rightarrow_L (b \rightarrow_L a) = 1$

Let us note that the structure of W algebra induces a distributive lattice with respect to the partial order formally defined as in (1). In this lattice one can define the unary operator $\neg a := a \rightarrow_L 0$ which turns out to be a Kleene (or Zadeh) orthocomplementation. In other words the following hold:

(K1) $\neg(\neg a) = a$
(K2) $\neg(a \vee b) = \neg a \wedge \neg b$
(K3) $a \wedge \neg a \leq b \vee \neg b$.

Under condition $(K1)$, the *de Morgan* law $(K2)$ is equivalent both to the dual de Morgan law "$\neg(a \wedge b) = \neg a \vee \neg b$" and to the Kleene *contraposition* law "$a \leq b$ implies $\neg b \leq \neg a$". In general neither the *non-contradiction* law "$\forall a : a \wedge \neg a = 0$" nor the *excluded-middle* law "$\forall a : a \vee \neg a = 1$" hold, also if for some element e (for instance 0, 1) it may happen that $e \wedge \neg e = 0$ and $e \vee \neg e = 1$.

Theorem 3.3. *Let* **A** *be a HW algebra. Then by defining* $\wedge$ *and* $\vee$ *as in Definition (3.1),* $\leq$ *as in (1), we have that* $(A, \rightarrow_G, \wedge, \vee, \neg)$ *is a linear symmetric Heyting algebra according to [9], i.e.,* **A** *satisfies the following properties (adopting the original Monteiro enumeration):*

(A1) $a \rightarrow_G a = b \rightarrow_G b$
(A2) $(a \rightarrow_G b) \wedge b = b$
(A3) $a \rightarrow_G (b \wedge c) = (a \rightarrow_G b) \wedge (a \rightarrow_G c)$
(A4) $a \wedge (a \rightarrow_G b) = a \wedge b$
(A5) $(a \vee b) \rightarrow_G c = (a \rightarrow_G c) \wedge (b \rightarrow_G c)$
(A6) $\neg(\neg a) = a$
(A7) $\neg(a \wedge b) = \neg a \vee \neg b$
(K) $a \wedge \neg a \leq b \vee \neg b$
(L) $(a \rightarrow_G b) \vee (b \rightarrow_G a) = 1$

In particular, the unary operation $\sim a = a \rightarrow_G 0$ is a Brouwer orthocomplementation. In other words:

(B1) $a \wedge \sim\sim a = a$
(B2) $\sim(a \wedge b) = \sim a \vee \sim b$
(B3) $a \wedge \sim a = 0$

As to the Brouwer negation, we have that under condition $(B1)$ (also written as a weak form of double negation law: $\forall a : a \leq \sim\sim a$) the de Morgan law $(B2)$ is only equivalent to the Brouwer contraposition law "$a \leq b$ implies $\sim b \leq \sim a$". In general, the dual de Morgan law of Brouwer negation $\sim(a \vee b) = \sim a \wedge \sim b$ is not equivalent to the previous two conditions. The intuitionistic *non-contradiction* law (B3) is verified by Brouwer negation, but the excluded middle law "$\forall a : a \vee \sim a = 1$" is not required to hold. Note that it may happen that for some element f (for instance $0, 1$) $f = \sim\sim f$.

Proposition 3.1. *Both $\langle [0,1], \to_L, \to_G, 0 \rangle$ and $\langle [0,1]^X, \to_L, \to_G, \mathbf{0} \rangle$, once defined the operators respectively as in Sections 1 and 2, satisfy HW axioms.*

4 Rough Approximations

In this section the relationship between the two orthocomplementation, $\neg$ and $\sim$, is investigated.

Theorem 4.1. *Let $\mathbf{A}$ be a HW algebra. Then $(A, \wedge, \vee, \neg, \sim, 1)$ is a $BZ^{(dM)}$ distributive lattice according to [4]. In other words: A is a distributive lattice with a Kleene orthocomplementation, $\neg : A \mapsto A$, a Brouwer orthocomplementation, $\sim : A \mapsto A$ linked by the interconnection rule $\neg \sim a = \sim\sim a$ and satisfying the dual de Morgan law of Brouwer negation, $\sim (a \vee b) = \sim a \wedge \sim b$.*

Let us recall that a third kind of complement, called *anti-intuitionistic orthocomplementation*, can be defined in any BZ lattice as the unary operation $\flat : A \mapsto A$, $\flat a := \neg \sim \neg a$.

4.1 Modal Operators from $\mathbf{BZ}^{(dM)}$ Distributive Lattices

Definition 4.1. *For any element a of a $BZ^{(dM)}$ distributive lattice $\mathbf{A}$, the necessity of a is defined as $\nu(a) := \sim \neg a = \flat\flat a$, and the possibility as $\mu(a) := \neg\nu(\neg a) = \neg \sim a = \sim\sim a$.*

As a consequence, one obtains: $\sim a = \nu(\neg a) = \neg \mu(a)$ and $\flat a = \neg\nu(a) = \mu(\neg a)$. On this basis, similarly to the modal interpretation of intuitionistic logic, the Brouwer complement $\sim$ is the negation of possibility or *impossibility*. Analogously, the anti-Brouwer complement $\flat$ is the negation of necessity or *contingency*. Our modal operations ν and μ turn out to have an S_5-like behavior based on a Kleene lattice instead of a Boolean one, as expressed by the following proposition.

Proposition 4.1. *In any $BZ^{(dM)}$ distributive lattice the following conditions hold:*

(1) $\nu(a) \leq a \leq \mu(a)$. In other words: necessity implies actuality and actuality implies possibility (a characteristic principle of the modal system T, see [1]).
(2) $\nu(\nu(a)) = \nu(a)$, $\mu(\mu(a)) = \mu(a)$. Necessity of necessity is equal to necessity; similarly for possibility (a characteristic S_4-principle, see [1]).
(3) $a \leq \nu(\mu(a))$. Actuality implies necessity of possibility (a characteristic B-principle, see [1]).
(4) $\mu(a) = \nu(\mu(a))$, $\nu(a) = \mu(\nu(a))$. Possibility is equal to the necessity of possibility; whereas necessity is equal to the possibility of necessity (a characteristic S_5-principle, see [1]).

4.2 Rough Approximation Spaces in BZ Lattices

As stated in Theorem 4.1 in general the following order chain $\nu(a) \leq a \leq \mu(a)$ holds. Clearly, this is a fuzzy situation. In a crisp environment, we would have no difference among necessity, actuality and possibility, i.e., we are interested to those elements for which $e = \mu(e)$ (equivalently, $e = \nu(e)$). This leads one to define the substructure of all *sharp* (exact, crisp) elements A_e: $A_e := \{e \in A : \mu(e) = e\} = \{e \in A : \nu(e) = e\}$.

Let us stress that this is not the only way to define sharp elements. In fact, since in general $a \wedge \neg a \neq 0$ (equivalently, $a \vee \neg a \neq 1$) it is possible to consider as *Kleene sharp (K-sharp)* the elements which satisfy the non contradiction (or equivalently the excluded middle) law with respect to the Kleene negation. Alternatively, considering the Brouwer negation we have that the *weak double negation* law holds ($\forall a \in A, a \leq \sim\sim a$) but not the double negation law. So we can introduce a further definition of *Brouwer sharp* (B-sharp) elements as those element for which $e = \sim\sim e$. However, inside the structure of $BZ^{(dM)}$ distributive lattice all these notions of sharpness coincide: an element is sharp iff it is K-sharp iff it is B-sharp. Moreover, in A_e the three negations collapse in a unique standard negation ($\forall e \in A_e : \neg e = \sim e = \flat e$) and $(A_e, \wedge, \vee, \neg)$ turns out to be a Boolean lattice (algebra).

Thus, the modal operators ν and μ can be used to have a rough approximation of any element $a \in A$ by sharp definable elements. In fact, $\nu(a)$ (resp., $\mu(a)$) turns out to be the best approximation from the bottom (resp., top) of a by sharp elements. To be precise, for any element $a \in A$ the following hold: $\nu(a)$ and $\mu(a)$ are sharp (i.e., $\nu(a) \in A_e$, $\mu(a) \in A_e$), $\nu(a)$ (resp., $\mu(a)$) is an *inner* (resp., *outer*) approximation of a: $\nu(a) \leq a \leq \mu(a)$, $\nu(a)$ (resp., $\mu(a)$) is the best inner (resp., outer) approximation of a by sharp elements (let $e \in A_e$ be such that $e \leq a$ (resp., $a \leq e$), then $e \leq \nu(a)$ (resp., $\mu(a) \leq e$)).

Definition 4.2. *Given a $BZ^{(dM)}$ distributive lattice* **A** *the induced rough approximation space is the structure $\langle A, A_e, \nu, \mu \rangle$ consisting of the set A of all approximable elements, the set A_e of all definable (or sharp) elements, and the inner (resp., outer) approximation map $\nu : A \to A_e$ (resp., $\mu : A \to A_e$).*
For any element $a \in A$, its rough approximation is defined as the pair of sharp elements: $r(a) := \langle \nu(a), \mu(a) \rangle$ [with $\nu(a) \leq a \leq \mu(a)$].

Clearly, sharp elements are characterized by the property that they coincide with their rough approximation: $e \in A_e$ iff $r(e) = \langle e, e \rangle$.

Equivalently, it is possible to identify the rough approximation of a with the *necessity – impossibility* pair: $r_{BZ}(a) := \langle \nu(a), \neg \mu(a) \rangle = \langle \nu(a), \sim a \rangle$. We, now, show that it is possible to give the structure of an HW algebra at the space of all couples *necessity – impossibility* pair (sometimes called interior – exterior). For the sake of simplicity let us set $a_i = \nu(a)$ and $a_e = \neg \mu(a)$ and let us denote by $\mathbb{A}$ the collection of all such pairs for a running on A. The following theorem holds:

Theorem 4.2. *The structure* $(\mathbb{A}, \to_L, \to_G, \mathbf{0})$, *where* $\to_L, \to_G$ *and* $\mathbf{0}$ *are defined as* $\langle a_i, a_e \rangle \to_L \langle b_i, b_e \rangle := \langle (\neg a_i \wedge \neg b_e) \vee a_e \vee b_i, a_i \wedge b_e \rangle$, $\langle a_i, a_e \rangle \to_G \langle b_i, b_e \rangle := \langle (\neg a_i \wedge \neg b_e) \vee a_e \vee b_i, \neg a_e \wedge b_e \rangle$, $\mathbf{0} := \langle 0, 1 \rangle$ *is a HW algebra.*

In particular, $\neg \langle a_i, a_e \rangle = \langle a_e, a_i \rangle$ and $\sim \langle a_i, a_e \rangle = \langle a_e, \neg a_e \rangle$. Thus, the necessity and possibility operators (in this case denoted by $\square$ and $\lozenge$ respectively) are $\square(\langle a_i, a_e \rangle) = \langle a_i, \neg a_i \rangle = r_{BZ}(a_i)$, and $\lozenge(\langle a_i, a_e \rangle) = \langle \neg a_e, a_e \rangle = r_{BZ}(a_e)$. As to the lattice operations we have that $\langle a_i, a_e \rangle \wedge \langle b_i, b_e \rangle = \langle a_i \wedge b_i, a_e \vee b_e \rangle$ and $\langle a_i, a_e \rangle \vee \langle b_i, b_e \rangle = \langle a_i \vee b_i, a_e \wedge b_e \rangle$. Note that the induced partial ordering is $\langle a_i, a_e \rangle \leq \langle b_i, b_e \rangle$ iff $a_i \leq b_i$ and $b_e \leq a_e$.

In the next section this theorem will be applied to Information Systems showing that also Pawlak rough sets are a model of HW algebras.

5 Rough Approximation Spaces from Information Systems

An *Information System* is a structure $\mathcal{K} = \langle X, Att(X), val(X), F \rangle$, where X (called the *universe*) is a non empty set of *objects* (*situations, entities, states*); $Att(X)$ is a non empty set of *attributes*, which assume values for the objects belonging to the set X; $val(X)$ is the set of all *possible values* that can be observed for an attribute a from $Att(X)$ in the case of an object x from X; F (called the *information map*) is a function $F : X \times Att(X) \to val(X)$ which associates to any pair, consisting of an object $x \in X$ and of an attribute $a \in Att(X)$, the value $F(x, a) \in val(X)$ assumed by a for the object x.

The *indiscernibility* relation that may hold between the objects under investigation represents the mathematical basis for the rough set approach. Suppose an information system $\mathcal{K} = \langle X, Att(X), val(X), F \rangle$, and let $\mathcal{A}$ be any family of attributes (a convenient subset of $Att(X)$). Then, $\mathcal{A}$ determines a binary relation $I_{\mathcal{A}}$ on the set of objects X, called the *indiscernibility relation* generated by $\mathcal{A}$, and defined as follows: $x \, I_{\mathcal{A}} \, y$ if and only if $\forall a \in \mathcal{A} : F(x, a) = F(y, a)$. In other words, two objects x and y are $I_{\mathcal{A}}$-indiscernible iff they have same values for *all* the attributes belonging to the family $\mathcal{A}$. Trivially, the *discernibility* generated by $\mathcal{A}$ is $x \#_{\mathcal{A}} y$ iff $\exists a \in \mathcal{A} : F(x, a) \neq F(y, a)$.

$I_{\mathcal{A}}$ turns out to be an *equivalence relation* whose equivalence classes are $M_{\mathcal{A}}(x) := \{y \in X : x \, I_{\mathcal{A}} \, y\}$, i.e., $M_{\mathcal{A}}(x)$ consists of all the objects $y \in X$ that share with x the same value for all the attributes belonging to $\mathcal{A}$. In other words: $\forall a \in \mathcal{A} : F(y, a) = F(x, a)$. We will denote by $\pi_{\mathcal{A}}(X)$ the collection of all such equivalence classes, and by $\mathcal{P}_{\mathcal{A}}(X)$ the collection of all subsets of X which are union of elements from $\pi_{\mathcal{A}}(X)$, plus the empty set.

Proposition 5.1. *Let $\mathcal{K}$ be an Information System and $\mathcal{A}$ a set of attributes, then the structure* $\langle \mathcal{P}, \cap, \cup, {}^c, \#_{\mathcal{A}}, \emptyset, X \rangle$ *where* $\forall H \in \mathcal{P}(X) : H^{\#_{\mathcal{A}}} := \{x \in X : \forall y \in H, x \#_{\mathcal{A}} y\}$ *is a BZ distributive complete lattice.*

Moreover, a rough approximation as given in Definition 4.2 corresponds to the classical inner and exterior approximation maps: $\nu(H) = H_i := \cup \{M_i \in \pi_{\mathcal{A}}(X) :$

$M_i \subseteq H\}$ and $\mu(H) = H_e := \cup\{M_j \in \pi_\mathcal{A}(X) : M_j \cap H = \emptyset\}$. A rough set is then defined as the mapping $r_{BZ} : \mathcal{P}(X) \to \mathcal{P}_\mathcal{A}(X) \times \mathcal{P}_\mathcal{A}(X)$, $r_{BZ}(H) := \langle H_i, H_e \rangle$. Let us denote by $RS_\mathcal{A}(\mathcal{K})$ the collection of all rough sets based on the Information System $\mathcal{K}$ with respect to the attributes collection $\mathcal{A}$. Then, Theorem 4.2 says that the structure $\langle RS_\mathcal{A}(\mathcal{K}), \to_L, \to_G, \mathbf{0} \rangle$ is a HW algebra once defined $\mathbf{0} := \langle \emptyset, X \rangle$ and the implication operators:

$$\langle H_i, H_e \rangle \to_L \langle K_i, K_e \rangle := \langle (H_i^c \cap K_e^c) \cup (H_e \cup K_i), H_i \cap K_e \rangle$$
$$\langle H_i, H_e \rangle \to_G \langle K_i, K_e \rangle := \langle (H_i^c \cap K_e^c) \cup (H_e \cup K_i), H_e^c \cap K_e \rangle$$

The constant unit element is defined as $\mathbf{1} = \langle X, \emptyset \rangle$ and derived complementations are: $\neg \langle H_i, H_e \rangle = \langle H_e, H_i \rangle$, $\sim \langle H_i, H_e \rangle = \langle H_e, H_e^c \rangle$ and $\flat \langle H_i, H_e \rangle = \langle H_i, H_i^c \rangle$. The lattice operations are: $\langle H_i, H_e \rangle \vee \langle K_i, K_e \rangle := \langle H_i \cup K_i, H_e \cap K_e \rangle$ and $\langle H_i, H_e \rangle \wedge \langle K_i, K_e \rangle := \langle H_i \cap K_i, H_e \cup K_e \rangle$. Finally, the modal operators are defined as : $\Box(\langle H_i, H_e \rangle) = \langle H_i, H_i^c \rangle = r_{BZ}(H_i)$ and $\Diamond(\langle H_i, H_e \rangle) = \langle H_e^c, H_e \rangle = r_{BZ}(H_e)$.

References

[1] Chellas, B.F..: Modal Logic, An Introduction. Cambridge University Press, Cambridge (1988)
[2] Cattaneo, G. Ciucci, D.: BZW algebras for an abstract approach to roughness and fuzziness. Accepted to IPMU 2002 (2002)
[3] Cattaneo, G., Dalla Chiara, M.L., Giuntini, R.: Some algebraic structures for many-valued logics. Tatra Mountains Mathematical Publication **15** (1998) 173–196
[4] Cattaneo, G., Giuntini, R., Pilla, R.: $BZMV^{dM}$ and Stonian MV algebras (applications to fuzzy sets and rough approximations). Fuzzy Sets Syst. **108** (1999) 201–222
[5] Cattaneo, G., Nisticò, G.: Brouwer-Zadeh posets and three valued Łukasiewicz posets. Fuzzy Sets Syst. **33** (1989) 165–190
[6] Chang, C.C.: Algebraic analysis of many valued logics. Trans. Amer. Math. Soc. **88** (1958) 467–490
[7] Hájek, P.: Metamathematics of Fuzzy Logic. Kluwer, Dordrecht (1998)
[8] Klement, E. P., Mesiar, R., Pap, E.: Triangular Norms. Kluwer Academic, Dordrecht (2000)
[9] Monteiro, A.A..: Sur les algèbres de Heyting symétriques. Portugaliae Mathematica **39** (1980) 1–237
[10] Pagliani, P.: Rough set theory and logic–algebraic structures. In Orlowska, E., ed.: Incomplete Information: Rough Set Analysis. Physica–Verlag, Heidelberg (1998) 109–190
[11] Rasiowa, H. Sikorski, R.: The Mathematics of Metamathematics. Third edn. Polish Scientific Publishers, Warsaw (1970)
[12] Rescher, N.: Many-valued logic. Mc Graw-Hill, New York (1969)
[13] Surma S.: Logical Works. Polish Academy of Sciences, Wroclaw (1977)
[14] Turunen, E.: Mathematics Behind Fuzzy Logic. Physica–Verlag, Heidelberg (1999)

Dominance-Based Rough Set Approach Using Possibility and Necessity Measures

Salvatore Greco[1], Masahiro Inuiguchi[2], and Roman Słowiński[3]

[1] Faculty of Economics, University of Catania,
Corso Italia, 55, 95129 Catania, Italy,
salgreco@unict.it
[2] Graduate School of Engineering, Osaka University,
Suita, Osaka 565-0871, Japan,
inuiguti@eie.eng.osaka-u.ac.jp
[3] Institute of Computing Science, Poznan University of Technology,
60-965 Poznan, Poland,
slowinsk@sol.put.poznan.pl

Abstract. Dominance-based rough set approach is an extension of the basic rough set approach proposed by Pawlak, to multicriteria classification problems. In this paper, the dominance-based rough set approach is considered in the context of vague information on preferences and decision classes. The vagueness is handled by possibility and necessity measures defined using modifiers of fuzzy sets. Due to this way of handling the vagueness, the lower and upper approximations of preference-ordered decision classes are fuzzy sets whose membership functions are necessity and possibility measures, respectively.

1 Introduction

The rough set theory has been proposed by Z. Pawlak [8,9] to deal with inconsistency problems following from information granulation. It operates on an information table composed of a set U of objects (actions) described by a set Q of attributes. Its basic notions are: indiscernibility relation on U, lower and upper approximation of a subset or a partition of U, dependence and reduction of attributes from Q, and decision rules derived from lower approximations and boundaries of subsets identified with decision classes. The original rough set idea has proved to be particularly useful in the analysis of multiattribute classification problems; however, it was failing when attributes whose domains are preference-ordered (criteria) had to be taken into account. In order to deal with problems of multicriteria decision making (MCDM), like sorting, choice or ranking, a number of methodological changes to the original rough set theory were necessary [3]. The main change is the substitution of the indiscernibility relation by a dominance relation (crisp or fuzzy), which permits approximation of ordered sets in multicriteria sorting. In this paper we propose a fuzzy extension of the rough approximation by dominance relation based on the concepts of necessity and possibility. In particular, we are considering a special definition of necessity and possibility measures introduced in [6,7]. For an alternative fuzzy extension of rough approximation by dominance relation see [3,4,5]. The paper is organized as follows. Section two illustrates the motivations for approximation by dominance relations. Section three recalls necessity and possibility measures. Section four presents basic idea of rough approximation by fuzzy dominance. Conclusions are grouped in the last section.

2   Rough Approximation by Dominance Relations

As pointed out by Greco, Matarazzo and Słowiński [2] the original rough set approach cannot extract all the essential knowledge contained in the decision table of multicriteria sorting problems, i.e. problems of assigning a set of actions described by a set of criteria to one of pre-defined and preference-ordered classes. Notwithstanding, in many real problems it is important to consider the ordinal properties of the considered criteria. For example, in bankruptcy risk evaluation, if the debt index (total debt/total activity) of firm A has a modest value, while the same index of firm B has a significant value, then, within the rough set approach, the two firms are merely discernible, but no preference is given to one of them with reference to the attribute "debt ratio". In reality, from the point of view of the bankruptcy risk evaluation, it would be advisable to consider firm A better than firm B, and not simply different (discernible). Therefore, the attribute "debt ratio" is a criterion. Consideration of criteria in rough set approximation can be made by replacing indiscernibility or similarity relation by the dominance relation, which is a very natural concept within multicriteria decision making.

On the basis of these considerations, Greco, Matarazzo and Słowiński [1,2,3] have proposed a new rough set approach to multicriteria sorting problems based on dominance relation.

3   Possibility and Necessity Measures

Possibility and necessity measures are defined by

$$\Pi(B|A) = \sup_x C(\mu_A(x), \mu_B(x)), \qquad N(B|A) = \inf_x I(\mu_A(x), \mu_B(x)),$$

where A and B are fuzzy sets with membership functions μ_A and μ_B. C and $I : [0,1] \times [0,1] \to [0,1]$ are conjunction and implication functions such that

C1) $C(0,0) = C(0,1) = C(1,0) = 0$ and $C(1,1) = 1$,
I1) $I(0,0) = I(0,1) = I(1,1) = 1$ and $I(1,0) = 0$.

In the following we use also a negation function $neg : [0,1] \to [0,1]$, such that $neg(0) = 1$, $neg(neg(a)) = a$ and neg is a non-increasing function.

We often use monotonic conjunction and implication functions C and I which satisfy

Table 1. An example of Q_h^i, $i = 1, 2$, m_h and M_h

Modifier	0	$\to$	h	$\to$	1
Q_h^1	most weakly	more or less	normally	very	most strongly
Q_h^2	most weakly	more or less	normally	very	most strongly
m_h	most strongly	very	normally	more or less	most weakly
M_h	most weakly	more or less	normally	very	most strongly

C2) $C(a,b) \leq C(c,d)$ if $a \leq c$ and $b \leq d$,
I2) $I(a,b) \leq I(c,d)$ if $a \geq c$ and $c \leq d$.

If C and I satisfies C2) and I2) then we have the following properties, respectively:

$\Pi(B_1|A_1) \leq \Pi(B_2|A_2)$ and $N(B_1|A_2) \leq N(B_2|A_1)$ if $A_1 \subseteq A_2$ and $B_1 \subseteq B_2$.

Since there exist many conjunction and implication functions, we have also many possibility and necessity measures. Thus we have a question, how we select possibility and necessity measures. To answer this question, in [6,7] the level cut conditioning approach has been proposed. In this approach, we can specify possibility and necessity measures based on the following equivalences:

$$\Pi(B|A) \leq h \text{ if and only if } Q_h^1(A) \subseteq \left(Q_h^2(B)\right)^c, \qquad (1)$$

$$N(B|A) \geq h \text{ if and only if } m_h(A) \subseteq M_h(B), \qquad (2)$$

where A^c is the complement fuzzy set of A and inclusion relation $A \subseteq B$ is defined by $\mu_A \leq \mu_B$. Q_h^i, $i = 1, 2$, m_h and M_h are modifiers vary with a parameter $h \in (0,1)$. An example of Q_h^i, $i = 1, 2$, m_h and M_h is given in Table 1. As h becomes large, condition $Q_h^1(A) \subseteq \left(Q_h^2(B)\right)^c$ becomes weak while condition $m_h(A) \subseteq M_h(B)$ becomes strong. In the case of Table 1, the first equivalence implies that if (most weakly A) $\subseteq$ (most weakly B)^c then $\Pi(B|A) = 0$, but if (most strongly A) $\not\subseteq$ (most strongly B)^c then $\Pi(B|A) = 1$. Similarly, the second equivalence implies that if (most weakly A) $\subseteq$ (most strongly B) then $N(B|A) = 1$, but if (most strongly A) $\not\subseteq$ (most weakly B) then $N(B|A) = 0$.

In order to treat the equivalences above mathematically, $Q_h^i(A)$, $i = 1, 2$, $m_h(A)$ and $M_h(A)$ are defined by the following membership functions:

$\mu_{Q_h^i(A)}(x) = g_i^Q(\mu_A(x), h)$, $i = 1, 2$,
$\mu_{m_h(A)}(x) = g^m(\mu_A(x), h)$ and $\mu_{M_h(A)}(x) = g^M(\mu_A(x), h)$.

From the properties of modifiers Q_h^i, m_h and M_h, modifier functions g_i^Q, g^m and g^M should satisfy the following requirements:

q1) $g_i^Q(a, \cdot)$ is lower semi-continuous for all $a \in [0,1]$,
q2) $g_i^Q(1, h) = 1$ and $g_i^Q(0, h) = 0$ for all $h < 1$,
q3) $g_i^Q(a, 1) = 0$ for all $a \in [0,1]$,
q4) $g_i^Q(a, \cdot)$ is non-increasing for all $a \in [0,1]$,
q5) $g_i^Q(\cdot, h)$ is non-decreasing for all $h \in [0,1]$,
q6) $g_i^Q(a, 0) > 0$ for all $a \in (0,1)$,

g1) $g^m(a,\cdot)$ and $g^M(a,\cdot)$ are lower and upper semi-continuous for all $a \in [0,1]$, respectively,
g2) $g^m(1,h) = g^M(1,h) = 1$ and $g^m(0,h) = g^M(0,h) = 0$ for all $h > 0$,
g3) $g^m(a,0) = 0$ and $g^M(a,0) = 1$ for all $a \in [0,1]$,
g4) $g^m(a,\cdot)$ is non-decreasing and $g^M(a,\cdot)$ is non-increasing for all $a \in [0,1]$,
g5) $g^m(\cdot,h)$ and $g^M(\cdot,h)$ are non-decreasing for all $h \in [0,1]$,
g6) $g^m(a,1) > 0$ and $g^M(a,1) < 1$ for all $a \in (0,1)$.

Requirements q1) and g1) are technical conditions so that possibility and necessity measures which satisfy (1) and (2) exist. Other requirements are naturally established. From Table 1, transitions of Q_h^i ($i = 1,2$) and M_h which respectively correspond to g_i^Q ($i = 1,2$) and g^M are similar but they are different as in technical conditions q1) and g1) and in boundary conditions q3), q6), g3) and g6).

Given modifier functions g_i^Q ($i = 1,2$), g^m and g^M, it is shown that possibility and necessity measures are obtained as (see [6,7])

$$\Pi^L(B|A) = \inf_h \{h \in [0,1] \mid Q_h^1(A) \subseteq (Q_h^2(B))^c\} = \sup_x C^L(\mu_A(x), \mu_B(x)),$$

$$N^L(B|A) = \sup_h \{h \in [0,1] \mid m_h(A) \subseteq M_h(B)\} = \inf_x I^L(\mu_A(x), \mu_B(x)),$$

where conjunction function C^L and implication function I^L are defined by

$$C^L(a,b) = \inf_h \{h \in [0,1] \mid g_1^Q(a,h) \leq neg(g_2^Q(b,h))\},$$

$$I^L(a,b) = \sup_h \{h \in [0,1] \mid g^m(a,h) \leq g^M(b,h)\}.$$

Conjunction and implication functions C^L and I^L satisfy C2) and I2), respectively. It is shown that many famous conjunction functions and implication functions are obtained from modifier functions g_i^Q (i=1,2), g^m and g^M (see [7]). Properties of C^L and I^L are investigated in [6,7].

4 Approximations by Means of Fuzzy Dominance Relations

Let us remember that formally, by an *information table* we understand the 4-tuple $S = \langle U, Q, V, f \rangle$, where U is a finite set of objects, Q is a finite set of attributes, $V = \bigcup_{q \in Q} V_q$ and V_q is a domain of the attribute q, and $f : U \times Q \to V$ is a total function such that $f(x,q) \in V_q$ for every $q \in Q$, $x \in U$, called an *information function* (cf. [9]).

Furthermore an information table can be seen as *decision table* assuming that the set of attributes $Q = K \cup D$ and $K \cap D = \emptyset$, where set K contains so-called *condition attributes*, and D, *decision attributes*. In the dominance-based rough set approach we are considering attributes with preference-ordered domains – such attributes are called *criteria*.

In this section we refine the concept of dominance-based rough approximation recalled in section 2, by introducing gradedness through the use of fuzzy sets.

In the following we shall use the concepts of T-norm T and T-conorm T^* defined as follows: $T : [0,1] \times [0,1] \to [0,1]$ such that for each $a, b, c, d \in [0,1]$, $T(a,b) \geq T(c,d)$ when $a \geq c$ and $b \geq d$, $T(a,1) = a$, $T(a,b) = T(b,a)$ and $T(a,T(b,c)) = T(T(a,b),c)$; $T^* : [0,1] \times [0,1] \to [0,1]$ such that for each $a, b, c, d \in [0,1]$, $T^*(a,b) \geq T^*(c,d)$ when $a \geq c$ and $b \geq d$, $T^*(a,0) = a$, $T^*(a,b) = T^*(b,a)$ and $T^*(a,T^*(b,c)) = T^*(T^*(a,b),c)$.

Let S_q be a fuzzy outranking relation on U with respect to criterion $q \in K$, i.e. $S_q : U \times U \to [0,1]$, such that $S_q(x,y)$ represents the credibility of the proposition "x is at least as good as y with respect to criterion q". It is natural to consider S_q as a fuzzy partial T-preorder, i.e. reflexive (for each $x \in U$, $S_q(x,x) = 1$) and T-transitive (for each $x, y, z \in U$, $T(S_q(x,y), S_q(y,z)) \leq S_q(x,z)$). Fuzzy outranking relation S_q can be build from another fuzzy complete T-preorder defined on domain V_q of criterion $q \in K$, i.e. $S_{V_q} : V_q \times V_q \to [0,1]$ such that $S_q(x,y) = S_{V_q}(f(x,q), f(y,q))$.

Using the fuzzy outranking relations S_q, $q \in K$, a fuzzy dominance relation on U (denotation $D_P(x,y)$) can be defined for each $P \subseteq K$ as follows:

$$D_P(x,y) = \underset{q \in P}{T} S_q(x,y).$$

Given $(x,y) \in U \times U$, $D_P(x,y)$ represents the credibility of the proposition "x outranks y on each criterion q from P". Let us remark that from the reflexivity of fuzzy outranking S_q, $q \in K$, we have that for each $x \in U$ $D_P(x,x) = 1$, i.e. also D_P is reflexive.

Since the fuzzy outranking relations S_q are supposed to be partial T-preorders, then also the fuzzy dominance relation D_P is a partial T-preorder.

Furthermore, let $\boldsymbol{Cl} = \{Cl_t, t \in H\}$, $H = \{1, ..., n\}$, be a set of fuzzy classes in U, such that for each $x \in U$, $Cl_t(x)$ represents the membership function of x to Cl_t. We suppose that the classes of $\boldsymbol{Cl}$ are ordered according to increasing preference, i.e. that for each $r, s \in H$, such that $r > s$, the elements of Cl_r have a better comprehensive evaluation than the elements of Cl_s. For example, in a problem of bankruptcy risk evaluation, Cl_1 is the set of unacceptable risk firms, Cl_2 is a set of high risk firms, Cl_3 is a set of medium risk firms, and so on.

On the basis of the membership functions of the fuzzy class Cl_t, we can define fuzzy membership functions of two merged fuzzy sets:

1) the upward merged fuzzy set $Cl_t^{\geq}$, whose membership function $Cl_t^{\geq}(x)$ represents the credibility of the proposition "x is at least as good as the objects in Cl_t",

$$Cl_t^{\geq}(x) = \begin{cases} 1 & \text{if } \exists s \in H : Cl_s(x) > 0 \text{ and } s > t \\ Cl_t(x) & \text{otherwise,} \end{cases}$$

2) the downward merged fuzzy set $Cl_t^{\leq}$, whose membership function $Cl_t^{\leq}(x)$ represents the credibility of the proposition "x is at most as good as the objects in Cl_t",

$$Cl_t^{\leq}(x) = \begin{cases} 1 & \text{if } \exists s \in H : Cl_s(x) > 0 \text{ and } s < t \\ Cl_t(x) & \text{otherwise.} \end{cases}$$

We say that the credibility of the statement "x belongs without ambiguity to $Cl_t^{\geq}$" is equal to the degree of necessity of the statement "all objects $y \in U$ dominating x belong to $Cl_t^{\geq}$". Furthermore, we say that the credibility of the statement "x possibly belongs to $Cl_t^{\geq}$" is equal to the degree of possibility of the statement "some object $y \in U$ dominated by x belongs to $Cl_t^{\geq}$". Analogous statements can be formulated for inclusion of x in $Cl_t^{\leq}$.

Therefore, the P-lower and the P-upper approximations of $Cl_t^{\geq}$ with respect to $P \subseteq K$ are fuzzy sets in U, whose membership functions (denotation $\underline{P}[Cl_t^{\geq}(x)]$ and $\overline{P}[Cl_t^{\geq}(x)]$, respectively) are defined as:

$$\underline{P}[Cl_t^{\geq}(x)] = N(Cl_t^{\geq}|D_p^+(x)) = \inf_{y \in U} I(D_p(y,x), Cl_t^{\geq}(y)),$$

$$\overline{P}[Cl_t^{\geq}(x)] = \Pi(Cl_t^{\geq}|D_p^-(x)) = \sup_{y \in U} C(D_p(x,y), Cl_t^{\geq}(y)),$$

where $D_p^+(x)$ is a fuzzy set of objects $y \in U$ dominating x with respect to $P \subseteq K$ and $D_p^-(x)$ is a fuzzy set of objects $y \in U$ dominated by x with respect to $P \subseteq K$. The membership functions of $D_p^+(x)$ and $D_p^-(x)$ are defined as follows:

$$\mu(y, D_p^+(x)) = D_p(y,x), \qquad \mu(y, D_p^-(x)) = D_p(x,y).$$

The P-lower and P-upper approximations of $Cl_t^{\leq}$ with respect to $P \subseteq K$ (denotation $\underline{P}[Cl_t^{\leq}(x)]$ and $\overline{P}[Cl_t^{\leq}(x)]$) can be defined, analogously, as:

$$\underline{P}[Cl_t^{\leq}(x)] = N(Cl_t^{\leq}|D_p^-(x)) = \inf_{y \in U} I(D_p(x,y), Cl_t^{\leq}(y)),$$

$$\overline{P}[Cl_t^{\leq}(x)] = \Pi(Cl_t^{\leq}|D_p^+(x)) = \sup_{y \in U} C(D_p(y,x), Cl_t^{\leq}(y)),$$

The following theorem states that the basic properties of rough set theory hold for the above definitions of lower and upper approximations subject to some conditions on modifiers used in definitions of possibility and necessity measures.

Theorem 1. *The following results hold:*

1) $\underline{P}[Cl_t^{\geq}(x)] \leq Cl_t^{\geq}(x)$ and $\underline{P}[Cl_t^{\leq}(x)] \leq Cl_t^{\leq}(x)$, for each $x \in U$ and for each $t \in H$ if necessity measure N is defined using implication function I such that $I(1,a) = a$, for all $a \in [0,1]$; moreover, if necessity measure N is defined using modifiers g^m and g^M, then it must satisfy the following property for $g^M: g^M(a,h) < 1$ if and only if $h > a$.

2) $Cl_t^{\geq}(x) \leq \overline{P}[Cl_t^{\geq}(x)]$ and $Cl_t^{\leq}(x) \leq \overline{P}[Cl_t^{\leq}(x)]$, for each $x \in U$ and for each $t \in H$ if possibility measure Π is defined using conjunction function C such that $C(1,a) = a$, for all $a \in [0,1]$; moreover, if possibility measure Π is defined using modifiers g_1^Q and g_2^Q, then it must satisfy the following property for $g_2^Q: g_2^Q(a,h) > 0$ if and only if $h < a$.

3) If $neg(Cl_t^{\geq}(x)) = Cl_{t-1}^{\leq}(x)$ for each $x \in U$, i.e. $(Cl_t^{\geq})^c = Cl_{t-1}^{\leq}$, for $t = 2, ..., n$, and $N(B|A) = neg(\Pi(B^c|A))$ for all fuzzy sets $A, B \subseteq U$, then the following properties hold:

   3.1) $\underline{P}[Cl_t^{\geq}(x)] = neg(\overline{P}[Cl_{t-1}^{\leq}(x)])$, $t = 2, \ldots, n$,
   3.2) $\underline{P}[Cl_t^{\leq}(x)] = neg(\overline{P}[Cl_{t+1}^{\geq}(x)])$, $t = 1, \ldots, n-1$,
   3.3) $\overline{P}[Cl_t^{\geq}(x)] = neg(\underline{P}[Cl_{t-1}^{\leq}(x)])$, $t = 2, \ldots, n$,
   3.4) $\overline{P}[Cl_t^{\leq}(x)] = neg(\underline{P}[Cl_{t+1}^{\geq}(x)])$, $t = 1, \ldots, n-1$.

   Moreover, if necessity measure N is defined using modifiers g^m and g^M, and possibility measure Π is defined using modifiers g_1^Q and g_2^Q, then the following equivalence is sufficient for properties 3.1) to 3.4): $g^m(a,h) \leq g^M(b,h) \Leftrightarrow g_1^Q(a, neg(h)) \leq neg(g_2^Q(neg(b), neg(h)))$ for all $a, b \in [0,1]$.

4) Given $R \subseteq P$, if implication function I used in necessity measure N satisfies the condition $I(a,c) \leq I(b,c)$ for each $a \geq b$, then for each $x \in U$ and for each $t \in H$,

   4.1) $\underline{P}[Cl_t^{\geq}(x)] \geq \underline{R}[Cl_t^{\geq}(x)]$, 4.2) $\underline{P}[Cl_t^{\leq}(x)] \geq \underline{R}[Cl_t^{\leq}(x)]$.

   Moreover, if necessity measure N is defined using modifiers g^m and g^M, then properties 4.1), 4.2) are always satisfied.

5) Given $R \subseteq P$, if conjunction function C used in possibility measure Π satisfies the condition $C(a,c) \geq C(b,c)$ for each $a \geq b$, then for each $x \in U$ and for each $t \in H$,

   5.1) $\overline{P}[Cl_t^{\geq}(x)] \leq \overline{R}[Cl_t^{\geq}(x)]$, 5.2) $\overline{P}[Cl_t^{\leq}(x)] \geq \overline{R}[Cl_t^{\leq}(x)]$.

   Moreover, if possibility measure Π is defined using modifiers g_1^Q and g_2^Q, then properties 5.1), 5.2) are always satisfied.

Results 1) to 5) of Theorem 1 can be read as the fuzzy counterparts of the following results well known within the classical rough set approach: 1) states that $Cl_t^{\geq}$ and $Cl_t^{\leq}$ include their P-lower approximations, 2) states that $Cl_t^{\geq}$ and $Cl_t^{\leq}$ are included in their P-upper approximations, 3) (complementarity property) states that the P-lower (P-upper) approximation of $Cl_t^{\geq}$ is the complement of the P-upper (P-lower) approximation of its complementary set $Cl_{t-1}^{\leq}$ (analogous property holds for $Cl_t^{\leq}$), 4) and 5) state that, using greater sets of criteria, it is possible to obtain more accurate approximations of $Cl_t^{\geq}$ and $Cl_t^{\leq}$: thus, while in the crisp case the lower approximation becomes greater (more precisely, not smaller) and the upper approximation becomes smaller (not greater), in the fuzzy case the membership of the lower approximation increases (it does not decrease) and the membership of the upper approximation decreases (it does not increase) if passing from set A of criteria to set B of criteria such that $B \supseteq A$.

Given the rough approximations of fuzzy decision classes being merged according to the preference order, one is able to induce certain and possible decision rules from these approximations. Each certain rule is characterized by a necessity degree, and each possible rule, by a possibility degree, corresponding to rule credibility.

5 Conclusion

We introduced fuzzy rough approximation using fuzzy dominance to deal with multicriteria sorting problems. We proved that our extension of rough approximation maintains the same desirable properties of classical rough set approximation within fuzzy set context. The fuzzy dominance relation can be applied to the pairwise comparison table (PCT) [5] in order to deal with choice and ranking multicriteria problems.

Acknowledgement. The first author wishes to acknowledge financial support from the Italian Ministry of Education, University and Scientific Research (MIUR). The research of the third author has been supported by the State Committee for Scientific Research (KBN), research grant no. 8T11F 006 19, and by the Foundation for Polish Science, subsidy no. 11/2001.

References

1. Greco, S., B. Matarazzo and R. Słowiński. "Rough Approximation of Preference Relation by Dominance Relations". *ICS Research Report* 16/96, Warsaw University of Technology, 1996 and *European Journal of Operational Research*, vol.117, pp. 63–83, 1999
2. Greco, S., B. Matarazzo and R. Słowiński. "A new rough set approach t evaluation of bankruptcy risk". In: C. Zopounidis (ed.): *Operational Tools in the Management of Financial Risk*. Kluwer Academic Publishers, Dordrecht, Boston, pp. 121–136, 1998.
3. Greco, S., B. Matarazzo and R. Słowiński. "The use of rough sets and fuzzy sets in MCDM". In: T. Gal, T. Hanne and T. Stewart (eds.): *Advances in Multiple Criteria Decision Making*. Kluwer Academic Publishers, Dordrecht, Boston, chapter 14, pp. 14.1–14.59, 1999.
4. Greco, S., B. Matarazzo and R. Słowiński. "A fuzzy extension of the rough set approach to multicriteria and multiattribute sorting". In J. Fodor, B. De Baets and P. Perny (eds.): *Preferences and Decisions under Incomplete Information*, Physica-Verlag, Heidelberg, 2000, pp. 131–154.
5. Greco, S., B. Matarazzo and R. Słowiński. "Fuzzy dominance-based rough set approach" In F. Masulli, R. Parenti, G. Pasi (eds), *Advances in Fuzzy Systems and Intelligent Technologies*, Shaker Publishing Maastricht (NL), 2000, pp. 56–66.
6. Inuiguchi, M., S. Greco, R. Słowiński and T. Tanino. "Possibility and necessity measure specification using modifiers for decision making under fuzziness". *Fuzzy Sets and Systems*, to appear
7. Inuiguchi, M. and T. Tanino. "Necessity measures and parametric inclusion relations of fuzzy sets". *Fundamenta Informaticae*, vol.42, pp. 279–302, 2000.
8. Pawlak, Z. "Rough sets". *International Journal of Information & Computer Sciences*, vol. 11, pp. 341–356. 1982.
9. Pawlak, Z. *Rough Sets. Theoretical Aspects of Reasoning about Data*. Kluwer Academic Publishers, Dordrecht, 1991.

Generalized Decision Algorithms, Rough Inference Rules, and Flow Graphs

Salvatore Greco[1], Zdzisław Pawlak[2], and Roman Słowiński[3]

[1] Faculty of Economics, University of Catania,
Corso Italia, 55, 95129 Catania, Italy
salgreco@mbox.unict.it
[2] Institute of Theoretical and Applied Informatics, Polish Academy of Sciences,
Baltycka 5, 44-100 Gliwice, Poland
zpw@ii.pw.edu.pl
[3] Institute of Computing Science, Poznan University of Technology,
Piotrowo 3a, 60-965 Poznan, Poland
slowinsk@sol.put.poznan.pl

Abstract. Some probabilistic properties of decision algorithms composed of *"if..., then..."* decision rules are considered. With every decision rule three probabilities are associated: the *strength*, the *certainty* and the *coverage* factors of the rule. It has been shown previously that the certainty and the coverage factors are linked by Bayes' theorem. Bayes' theorem has also been presented in a simple form employing the strength of decision rules. In this paper, we relax some conditions on the decision algorithm, in particular, a condition on mutual exclusion of decision rules, and show that the former properties still hold. We also show how the total probability theorem is related with *modus ponens* and *modus tollens* inference rules when decision rules are true in some degree of the certainty factor. Moreover, we show that under the relaxed condition, with every decision algorithm a flow graph can be associated, giving a useful interpretation of decision algorithms.

1 Introduction

We are considering some probabilistic properties of decision algorithms being finite sets of *"if..., then..."* decision rules. The rules are induced from a data table where a finite set of objects is described by a finite set of condition and decision attributes. With every decision rule three probabilities are associated: the *strength*, the *certainty* and the *coverage* factors of the rule. Pawlak (2002a) has shown that the certainty and the coverage factors are linked by Bayes' theorem. Moreover, Bayes' theorem in the proposed setting can be presented in a simple form employing the strength of decision rules. These properties have been derived under specific conditions imposed on decision rules, in particular, a mutual exclusion (or independence) condition. In this paper we relax these conditions and show that the former properties still hold. We also show how the total probability theorem is related with *modus ponens* and *modus tollens* inference rules when decision rules are true in degree of the certainty factor and the decision algorithm satisfies the relaxed conditions.

Moreover, we show that under the relaxed conditions, with every decision algorithm a flow graph can be associated. The through-flow in the graph is related to above-mentioned probabilities and is ruled by the total probability theorem and Bayes' theorem. The flow graph satisfies the usual properties of network flows, i.e. conservation of flow in each node and in the whole network. Simple tutorial examples illustrate the interest of the flow graph for practical interpretation of decision algorithms.

2 Decision Rules and Decision Algorithms

Let S = (U, A) be an information system, where U and A are finite, non-empty sets called the *universe* and the set of *attributes*, respectively. If in the set A two disjoint classes of attributes, called *condition* and *decision attributes*, are distinguished, then the system is called a *decision table* and is denoted by S = (U, C, D), where C and D are sets of condition and decision attributes, respectively. With every subset of attributes, one can associate a formal language of formulas **L** defined in a standard way and called the *decision language*. Formulas for a subset B⊆A are build up from attribute-value pairs (a, v), where a∈B and v∈V_a (set V_a is domain of a), by means of logical connectives ∧ (*and*), ∨ (*or*), ¬ (*not*). We assume that the set of all formula sets in **L** is partitioned into two classes, called *condition* and *decision formulas*, involving condition and decision attributes, respectively.

A *decision rule* induced from S and expressed in **L** is an implication $\Phi \to \Psi$, read "*if* Φ, *then* Ψ", where Φ and Ψ are condition and decision formulas in **L**, respectively.

Let $||\Phi||$ denote the set of all objects from universe U, having the property Φ in S.

If $\Phi \to \Psi$ is a decision rule, then $supp_S(\Phi,\Psi) = \text{card}(||\Phi \wedge \Psi||)$ will be called the *support* of the decision rule and $\sigma_S(\Phi,\Psi) = \frac{supp_S(\Phi,\Psi)}{\text{card}(U)}$ will be referred to as the *strength* of the decision rule.

With every decision rule $\Phi \to \Psi$ we associate a *certainty factor* $cer_S(\Phi,\Psi) = \frac{supp_S(\Phi,\Psi)}{\text{card}(||\Phi||)}$ and a *coverage factor* $cov_S(\Phi,\Psi) = \frac{supp_S(\Phi,\Psi)}{\text{card}(||\Psi||)}$.

If $cer_S(\Phi,\Psi)=1$, then the decision rule $\Phi \to \Psi$ will be called *certain*, otherwise the decision rule will be referred to as *uncertain*.

A set of decision rules covering all objects of the universe U creates a *decision algorithm* in S. Pawlak (2002a) points out that every decision algorithm associated with S displays well-known probabilistic properties, in particular it satisfies the total probability theorem and Bayes' theorem. As a decision algorithm can also be interpreted in terms of the rough set concept, these properties give a new look on Bayes' theorem from the rough set perspective. In consequence, one can draw conclusions from data without referring to prior and posterior probabilities, inherently associated with Bayesian reasoning. The revealed relationship can be used to invert decision rules, i.e., giving reasons (explanations) for decisions, which is useful in decision analysis.

The relationship revealed by Pawlak (2002a) uses, however, some restrictive assumptions that we want to relax in the present study.

3 Some Properties of Decision Algorithms

Pawlak (2002a) defines the decision algorithm as a set of decision rules $Dec_S(\Phi,\Psi) = \{\Phi_i \to \Psi_i\}_{i=1,...,m}$, m≥2, associated with a decision table S = (U, C, D), satisfying the following conditions:

1. *Mutual exclusion (independence)*:
   for every $\Phi_i \to \Psi_i$ and $\Phi_j \to \Psi_j \in Dec_S(\Phi,\Psi)$, $\Phi_i = \Phi_j$ or $||\Phi_i \wedge \Phi_j|| = \emptyset$, and $\Psi_i = \Psi_j$ or $||\Psi_i \wedge \Psi_j|| = \emptyset$,

2. *Admissibility*: $supp_S(\Phi,\Psi) \neq \emptyset$ for any $\Phi \to \Psi \in Dec_S(\Phi,\Psi)$,

3. *Covering*: $\bigcup_{i=1}^{m} ||\Phi_i||=U$ and $\bigcup_{i=1}^{m} ||\Psi_i||=U$.

Under these conditions, the following properties of decision algorithms hold:

$$\sum_{\Psi' \in D(\Phi)} cer_S(\Phi,\Psi') = \sum_{\Psi' \in D(\Phi)} \frac{card(||\Phi \wedge \Psi'||)}{card(||\Phi||)} = 1, \quad (1)$$

$$\sum_{\Phi' \in C(\Psi)} cov_S(\Phi',\Psi) = \sum_{\Phi' \in C(\Psi)} \frac{card(||\Phi' \wedge \Psi||)}{card(||\Psi||)} = 1, \quad (2)$$

$$\pi_S(\Psi) = \sum_{\Phi' \in C(\Psi)} cer_S(\Phi',\Psi)\pi_S(\Phi') = \sum_{\Phi' \in C(\Psi)} \sigma_S(\Phi',\Psi), \quad (3)$$

$$\pi_S(\Phi) = \sum_{\Psi' \in D(\Phi)} cov_S(\Phi,\Psi')\pi_S(\Psi') = \sum_{\Psi' \in D(\Phi)} \sigma_S(\Phi,\Psi'), \quad (4)$$

$$cer_S(\Phi,\Psi) = \sigma_S(\Phi,\Psi)/\pi_S(\Phi), \quad (5)$$

$$cov_S(\Phi,\Psi) = \sigma_S(\Phi,\Psi)/\pi_S(\Psi) \quad , \quad (6)$$

where $\pi_S(\Phi) = \frac{card(||\Phi||)}{card(U)}$, $\pi_S(\Psi) = \frac{card(||\Psi||)}{card(U)}$, while D($\Phi$) = {$\Psi$: $\Phi \to \Psi \in Dec_S(\Phi,\Psi)$} and C($\Psi$) = {$\Phi$: $\Phi \to \Psi \in Dec_S(\Phi,\Psi)$} denote the set of all decisions of Φ and the set of all conditions of Ψ in $Dec_S(\Phi,\Psi)$, respectively.

It can be observed that (3) and (4) refer to the total probability theorem, whereas (5) and (6) refer to Bayes' theorem, without using prior and posterior probabilities. In other words, if we know the ratio of Φ_S in Ψ, thanks to Bayes' theorem we can compute the ratio of Ψ_S in Φ.

We want to generalize formulae (1)–(6) to the case where condition 1) on mutual exclusion (independence) of the decision rules in the decision algorithm is not satisfied. This relaxation means that there may exist at least two decision rules $\Phi' \to \Psi'$ and $\Phi'' \to \Psi'' \in Dec(\Phi, \Psi)$ such that $||\Phi' \wedge \Phi''|| \neq \emptyset$ or $||\Psi' \wedge \Psi''|| \neq \emptyset$.

We claim that if the independence condition does not hold with respect to decisions (i.e. if there exist at least two decisions ψ' and ψ'' such that $||\psi' \wedge \psi''|| \neq \emptyset$), formula (1) becomes:

$$\sum_{\Psi' \in D(\Phi)} cer_S(\Phi, \Psi') - \sum_{\Psi', \Psi'' \in D(\Phi)} cer_S(\Phi, \Psi' \wedge \Psi'') +$$
$$+ \sum_{\Psi', \Psi'', \Psi''' \in D(\Phi)} cer_S(\Phi, \Psi' \wedge \Psi'' \wedge \Psi''') + ... =$$
$$= \sum_{\Psi' \in D(\Phi)} \frac{\text{card}(||\Phi \wedge \Psi'||)}{\text{card}(||\Phi||)} - \sum_{\Psi'', \Psi' \in D(\Phi)} \frac{\text{card}(||\Phi \wedge \Psi' \wedge \Psi''||)}{\text{card}(||\Phi||)} +$$
$$+ \sum_{\Psi''', \Psi'', \Psi' \in D(\Phi)} \frac{\text{card}(||\Phi \wedge \Psi' \wedge \Psi'' \wedge \Psi'''||)}{\text{card}(||\Phi||)} ... = 1. \tag{1'}$$

Analogously, if independence condition does not hold with respect to conditions (i.e. if there exist at least two conditions Φ' and Φ'' such that $||\Phi' \wedge \Phi''|| \neq \emptyset$), formula (2) becomes:

$$\sum_{\Phi' \in C(\Psi)} cov_S(\Phi', \Psi) - \sum_{\Phi', \Phi'' \in C(\Psi)} cov_S(\Phi' \wedge \Phi'', \Psi) +$$
$$+ \sum_{\Phi', \Phi'', \Phi''' \in C(\Psi)} cov_S(\Phi' \wedge \Phi'' \wedge \Phi''', \Psi) ... =$$
$$= \sum_{\Phi' \in C(\Psi)} \frac{\text{card}(||\Phi' \wedge \Psi||)}{\text{card}(||\Psi||)} - \sum_{\Phi', \Phi'' \in C(\Psi)} \frac{\text{card}(||\Phi' \wedge \Phi'' \wedge \Psi||)}{\text{card}(||\Psi||)} +$$
$$+ \sum_{\Phi', \Phi'', \Phi''' \in C(\Psi)} \frac{\text{card}(||\Phi' \wedge \Phi'' \wedge \Phi''' \wedge \Psi||)}{\text{card}(||\Psi||)} ... = 1 \tag{2'}$$

Similar transformation can be performed on formula (3):

$$\pi_S(\Psi) = \sum_{\Phi' \in C(\Psi)} cer_S(\Phi', \Psi)\pi_S(\Phi') - \sum_{\Phi', \Phi'' \in C(\Psi)} cer_S(\Phi' \wedge \Phi'', \Psi)\pi_S(\Phi' \wedge \Phi'') +$$
$$+ \sum_{\Phi', \Phi'', \Phi''' \in C(\Psi)} cer_S(\Phi' \wedge \Phi'' \wedge \Phi''', \Psi)\pi_S(\Phi' \wedge \Phi'' \wedge \Phi''') ... =$$
$$= \sum_{\Phi' \in C(\Psi)} \sigma_S(\Phi', \Psi) - \sum_{\Phi', \Phi'' \in C(\Psi)} \sigma_S(\Phi' \wedge \Phi'', \Psi) +$$
$$+ \sum_{\Phi', \Phi'', \Phi''' \in C(\Psi)} \sigma_S(\Phi' \wedge \Phi'' \wedge \Phi''', \Psi)... \tag{3'}$$

and on formula (4)

$$\pi_S(\Phi) = \sum_{\Psi' \in D(\Phi)} cov_S(\Phi, \Psi')\pi_S(\Psi') - \sum_{\Psi', \Psi'' \in D(\Phi)} cov_S(\Phi, \Psi' \wedge \Psi'')\pi_S(\Psi' \wedge \Psi'') +$$
$$+ \sum_{\Psi', \Psi'' \in D(\Phi)} cov_S(\Phi, \Psi' \wedge \Psi'' \wedge \Psi''')\pi_S(\Psi' \wedge \Psi'' \wedge \Psi''') ... =$$
$$= \sum_{\Psi' \in D(\Phi)} \sigma_S(\Phi, \Psi') - \sum_{\Psi', \Psi'' \in D(\Phi)} \sigma_S(\Phi, \Psi' \wedge \Psi'') +$$
$$+ \sum_{\Psi', \Psi'', \Psi''' \in D(\Phi)} \sigma_S(\Phi, \Psi' \wedge \Psi'' \wedge \Psi''') + ... \tag{4'}$$

4 Total Probability Theorems and Rough Inference Rules

Remark that formulae (3') and (4') referring to total probability theorems are closely related with *modus ponens* (MP) and *modus tollens* (MT) inference rules in some specific way.

Classically, MP has the following form:

if	$\Phi \to \psi$	is true
and	Φ	is true
then	ψ	is true

If we replace truth values by corresponding probabilities, we can generalize the inference rule as *rough modus ponens* (RMP):

if	$\Phi \to \psi$	is true with probability $cer_S(\Phi,\psi)$
and	Φ	is true with probability $\pi_S(\Phi)$
then	ψ	is true with probability $\pi_S(\Psi)$ given by (3').

RMP enables us to calculate the probability of conclusion ψ of a decision rule $\Phi \to \psi$ in terms of strengths of all decision rules in the form $\Phi' \to \psi$, $\Phi' \wedge \Phi'' \to \psi$, $\Phi' \wedge \Phi'' \wedge \Phi''' \to \psi$ and so on. In comparison with the *rough modus ponens* of Pawlak (2002a), the above RMP handles a set of rules suggesting the same decision and such that the intersection of supports of their condition parts can be non-empty.

Classically, MT has the following form:

if	$\Phi \to \psi$	is true
and	$\neg\psi$	is true
then	$\neg\Phi$	is true

If we replace truth values by corresponding probabilities, we can generalize the inference rule as *rough modus tollens* (RMT):

if	$\Phi \to \psi$	is true with probability $cer_S(\Phi,\psi)$
and	ψ	is true with probability $\pi_S(\psi)$
then	Φ	is true with probability $\pi_S(\Phi)$ given by (4').

RMT enables us to calculate the probability of condition Φ of a decision rule $\Phi \to \psi$ in terms of strengths of all decision rules in the form $\Phi \to \psi'$, $\Phi \to \psi' \wedge \psi''$, $\Phi \to \psi' \wedge \psi'' \wedge \psi'''$ and so on. Again, in comparison with the *rough modus tollens* of Pawlak (2002a), the above RMT handles a set of rules having the same condition and such that the intersection of supports of their decision parts can be non-empty.

5 Decision Algorithms and Flow Graphs

Pawlak (2002b, 2002c) has shown recently that a decision algorithm (decision table) can be represented by a flow graph in which the flow is ruled by the total probability theorem and by the Bayes' theorem. The graph is acyclic, directed and connected; there are two layers of nodes – input nodes, corresponding to particular conditions of decision rules, and output nodes, corresponding to decisions of particular decision rules. To every decision rule $\Phi \to \psi$ there is assigned an arc connecting the input node Φ and the output node ψ. Strength of the decision rule represents the through-flow of the corresponding arc. The through-flow of the graph is governed by formulas (1)-(6) that can be considered as flow conservation equations. In particular, formula (3) states that the outflow of the output node amounts to the sum of its inflows, whereas formula (4) says that the sum of outflows of the input node equals to its inflow. Moreover, formulas (5) and (6) reveal how through-flow in the flow graph is distributed between its inputs and outputs.

In this section we propose an interpretation of the decision table in terms of the flow graph when the independence condition does not hold.

The generalized flow graph will be explained using two simple examples inspired by Berthold and Hand (1999) and Pawlak (2002b).

Table 1. Statistical summary of a sample of cases

Fact	T_1	T_2	D	Number of cases
1	-	-	-	9320
2	-	-	+	200
3	+	-	-	150
4	+	-	+	20
5	-	+	-	5
6	-	+	+	140
7	+	+	-	5
8	+	+	+	300

Example 1. Consider two physician's diagnostic tests T_1 and T_2, for presence of disease D. Table 1 presents the results of the tests and the presence or absence of the disease on a sample of 10140 cases (660 with and 9480 without disease D). Table 1 represents decision table S.

One can induce from Table 1 a set of decision rules relating results of the tests with the presence of disease D. The rules are presented in Table 2 using the following notation: 1 means positive and -1 means negative result of the corresponding test, and 0 means that the corresponding test is not considered. For example, rule #2 can be read as: "in 97.8% of cases in which test T_2 is positive, disease D is present". Analogously, rule #5 can be read as: "in 11.8% of cases in which test T_1 is positive and test T_2 is negative, disease D is present".

As the ratio of the number of cases with disease D to the total number of cases in the sample is 0.065, there is also a "default" rule #0 having the following interpretation: "without considering any test, in 6.5% of cases disease D is present". Another decision rule is also interesting for interpretation in terms of flow graph:

Rule #6: "in 74.2% of cases in which test T_1 or test T_2 is positive, disease D is present" (coverage=0.697, support=460, strength=.045).

Table 2. Decision rules concluding the presence of disease D, induced from Table 1

Rule	T_1	T_2	D	Certainty factor	Coverage	Support	Strength
Rule #1	1	0	+	.674	.485	320	.032
Rule #2	0	1	+	.978	.667	440	.043
Rule #3	1	1	+	.983	.454	300	.030
Rule #4	1	-1	+	.118	.061	20	.002
Rule #5	-1	1	+	.966	.212	140	.014

The flow graph corresponding to decision algorithm composed of the six decision rules is presented in Figure 1. The graph is composed of three input nodes, corresponding to performed tests (T_1 alone, T_2 alone, T_1 and T_2 together) and of one output node corresponding to the presence of disease D. The input and the output nodes have circular shapes in the flow graph, while the rectangular boxes on the arcs include information on the through-flow of the arcs. Let us remark that the through-flows of the arcs in Figure 1 represent the strength of the corresponding decision rules. In other words, the flow graph can be seen as a decomposition of the output flow, equal to probability $\pi_S(D) = \frac{\text{card}(\|D\|)}{\text{card}(U)}$ of disease D in S, into subsets of patients supporting particular decision rules. This decomposition is as follows.

The flow leaving node T_1 and entering node D is equal to the strength of Rule #1:

$$\sigma(\#1) = \sigma(T_1, D) = \frac{\text{card}(\|T_1 \wedge D\|)}{\text{card}(U)}.$$

It represents the contribution to $\pi_S(D)$ of a subset of patients having positive result of test T_1 (with no regard to test T_2 that may give positive or negative result). Analogously, the flow leaving node T_2 and entering node D is equal to the strength of Rule #2:

$$\sigma(\#2) = \sigma(T_2, D) = \frac{\text{card}(\|T_2 \wedge D\|)}{\text{card}(U)}.$$

It represents the contribution to $\pi_S(D)$ of a subset of patients having positive result of test T_2 (with no regard to test T_1 that may give positive or negative result).

Since the subset of patients having simultaneously positive result of T_1 and T_2 is included in both $\sigma(\#1)$ and $\sigma(\#2)$, to obtain $\pi_S(D)$ its contribution must be subtracted from the sum of $\sigma(\#1)$ and $\sigma(\#2)$. The subtraction is represented by the flow leaving node D and entering node (T_1,T_2), having strength of Rule #3:

$$\sigma(\#3) = \sigma(T_1 \wedge T_2, D) = \frac{\text{card}(\|T_1 \wedge T_2 \wedge D\|)}{\text{card}(U)},$$

It represents the contribution to $\pi_S(D)$ of a subset of patients having simultaneously positive result of T_1 and T_2.

Thus, the algebraic sum $\sigma(\#1)+\sigma(\#2)-\sigma(\#3)$ is equal to the probability $\pi_S(D)$ corresponding to the output flow. Remark that the output flow is equal to the strength of the most general decision rule in S, i.e. Rule #6:

$$\sigma(\#6) = \sigma(T_1 \vee T_2, D) = \frac{\text{card}(\|T_1 \vee T_2 \wedge D\|)}{\text{card}(U)}.$$

The output flow is returned to the input nodes of the graph, giving another decomposition of the probability $\pi_S(D)$. In fact, the output flow is split among:

- the input node T_1, in amount equal to the strength of Rule #4:
  $$\sigma(\#4) = \sigma(T_1 \wedge \neg T_2, D) = \frac{\text{card}(\|T_1 \wedge \neg T_2 \wedge D\|)}{\text{card}(U)};$$
  it represents the contribution to $\pi_S(D)$ of a subset of patients having positive result of T_1 and negative result of T_2;

- the input node T_2, in amount equal to the strength of Rule #5:
  $$\sigma(\#5) = \sigma(\neg T_1 \wedge T_2, D) = \frac{\text{card}(\|\neg T_1 \wedge T_2 \wedge D\|)}{\text{card}(U)};$$
  it represents the contribution to $\pi_S(D)$ of a subset of patients having negative result of T_1 and positive result of T_2;

- the input node (T_1, T_2), in amount equal to the strength of Rule #3, representing the contribution to $\pi_S(D)$ of a subset of patients having simultaneously positive result of T_1 and T_2.

The balance of flows in the input node T_1 can be interpreted as follows. The contribution to $\pi_S(D)$ of a subset of patients with positive result of T_1 and negative result of T_2 is equal to the difference between flow $\sigma(\#1)$ from node T_1 to node D, representing the contribution to $\pi_S(D)$ of a subset of patients with positive result of T_1, and flow $\sigma(\#3)$ from node (T_1, T_2) to node D, representing the contribution to $\pi_S(D)$ of a subset of patients having simultaneously positive result of T_1 and T_2. This follows from the observation that $\|T_1\| - \|T_1 \wedge T_2\| = \|T_1 \wedge \neg T_2\|$.

Analogously, the contribution to $\pi_S(D)$ of a subset of patients with positive result of T_2 and negative result of T_1 is equal to the difference between flow $\sigma(\#2)$ from node T_2 to node D, representing the contribution to $\pi_S(D)$ of a subset of patients with positive result of T_2, and flow $\sigma(\#3)$ from node (T_1, T_2) to node D, representing the contribution to $\pi_S(D)$ of a subset of patients having simultaneously positive result of T_1 and T_2. This follows from the observation that $\|T_2\| - \|T_1 \wedge T_2\| = \|\neg T_1 \wedge T_2\|$.

The flow graphs representing the coverage and the support of the rules have the same structure and the through-flows of the arcs are proportional to those in Figure 1. Indeed, given rule $\Phi \to \Psi$, coverage $cov(\Phi, \Psi)$ and support $supp(\Phi, \Psi)$ can be calculated from the strength by a linear transformation:

$$cov(\Phi, \Psi) = \sigma(\Phi, \Psi) \pi_S(\Psi) \text{ and } supp(\Phi, \Psi) = \sigma(\Phi, \Psi) \text{card}(U).$$

Let us remark that the graph presented in Figure 1 satisfies two important properties of the flow graphs: (i) at each node of the flow graph there is a zero algebraic sum of the inflow and the outflow; (ii) the sum of flows entering the input nodes is equal to the sum of flows leaving the output node.

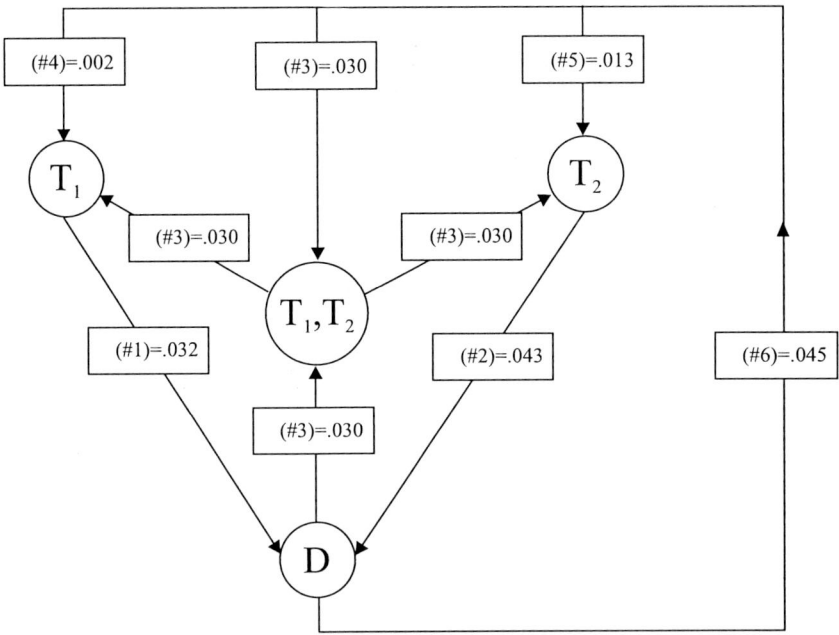

Fig. 1. The flow graph of the decision algorithm representing a decomposition of the output flow, equal to probability $\pi_S(D)$, in terms of the strength of particular decision rules.

Example 2. While in Example 1 we considered strength, coverage and support of decision rules, the present example underlines the interest of the flow graph in representation of the certainty factor.

Consider one physician's diagnostic test T, for presence of two diseases D_1 and D_2. Table 3 presents the results of the test and the presence or absence of the diseases on a sample of 3850 cases (all with positive result of test T). Table 3 represents decision table S.

Table 3. Statistical summary of a sample of cases

Fact	T	D_1	D_2	Number of cases
1	+	-	-	200
2	+	+	-	400
3	+	-	+	250
4	+	+	+	3000

One can induce from Table 3 a set of decision rules relating results of the test with the presence or absence of disease D_1 and/or D_2. The rules are presented in Table 4 using the following notation: 1 means presence and -1 means absence of the corresponding disease, and 0 means that the corresponding disease is not considered. For example, rule #1 can be read as: "in 88.3% of cases in which the result of test T is positive, disease D_1 is present". Analogously, rule #5 can be read as: "in 6.5% of cases in which the result of test T is positive, disease D_1 is present while disease D_2 is absent".

Table 4. Decision rules

Rule	T	D_1	D_2	Certainty factor
Rule #1	+	1	0	.883
Rule #2	+	0	1	.844
Rule #3	+	1	1	.779
Rule #4	+	-1	1	.104
Rule #5	+	1	-1	.065

Another decision rule is also interesting for interpretation in terms of flow graph:

Rule #6: "in 94.8% of cases in which test T is positive, one of the diseases is present".

The flow graph corresponding to decision algorithm composed of the six decision rules is presented in Figure 2. The graph is composed of one input node, corresponding to test T, and of three output nodes corresponding to the presence of diseases (D_1 alone, D_2 alone, and D_1 and D_2 together). The input and the output nodes have again circular shapes in the flow graph, while the rectangular boxes on the arcs include information on the through-flow of the arcs. Let us remark that the through-flows of the arcs in Figure 2 represent the certainty factors of the corresponding decision rules. In other words, the flow graph can be seen as a decomposition of the input flow, equal to certainty factor of the most general decision rule in S, i.e. Rule #6. This decomposition is as follows.

The input flow equal to certainty of Rule #6,

$$cer_S(\#6) = cer_S(\text{T}, D_1 \vee D_2) = \frac{\text{card}(\|T \wedge (D_1 \vee D_2)\|)}{\text{card}(\|T\|)}$$

is a sum of output flows corresponding to certainties of Rule #3, Rule #4 and Rule #5, respectively, i.e.

$$cer_S(\text{T}, D_1 \vee D_2) = cer_S(\text{T}, D_1 \wedge D_2) + cer_S(\text{T}, D_1 \wedge \neg D_2) + cer_S(\text{T}, \neg D_1 \wedge D_2).$$

This is based on the observation that $\|T \wedge (D_1 \vee D_2)\| = \|T \wedge D_1 \wedge D_2\| \cup \|T \wedge D_1 \wedge \neg D_2\| \cup \|T \wedge \neg D_1 \wedge D_2\|$.

The graph shows also another decomposition of the input flow and, therefore, of the certainty of Rule #6. This new decomposition is as follows.

The input flow, equal to certainty of Rule #6, is a sum of flows leaving node D, i.e. certainties of Rule #1 and Rule #2, minus flows entering node D, i.e. certainty of Rule #3:

$$cer_S(\text{T}, D_1 \vee D_2) = cer_S(\text{T}, D_1) + cer_S(\text{T}, D_2) - cer_S(\text{T}, D_1 \wedge D_2).$$

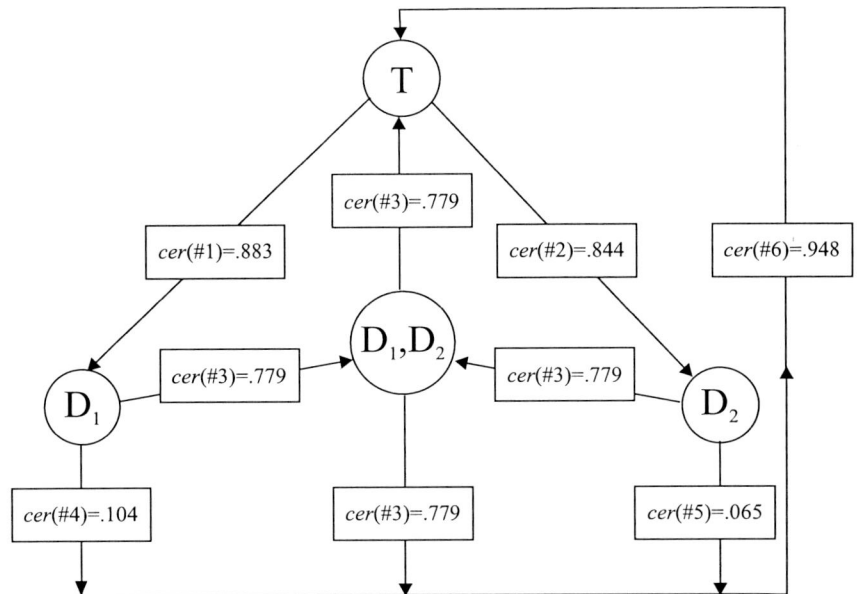

Fig. 2. The flow graph of the decision algorithm representing a decomposition of the input flow in terms of the certainty factor of particular decision rules.

This is based on the observation that $||T\wedge(D_1\vee D_2)||=(||T\wedge D_1||\cup||T\wedge D_2||) - ||T\wedge\neg D_1\wedge D_2||$.

Moreover, in the output node D_1, the certainty factor of Rule #4:

$$cer_S(\#4) = cer_S(T, D_1 \wedge \neg D_2) = \frac{\text{card}(||T\wedge D_1\wedge\neg D_2||)}{\text{card}(||T||)}$$

is equal to the difference between flow

$$cer_S(\#1) = cer_S(T, D_1) = \frac{\text{card}(||T\wedge D_1||)}{\text{card}(||T||)},$$

leaving node T and entering node D_1 (Rule #1), and flow

$$cer_S(\#3) = cer_S(T, D_1\wedge D_2) = \frac{\text{card}(||T\wedge D_1\wedge D_2||)}{\text{card}(||T||)},$$

leaving node D_1 and entering node (D_1, D_2) (Rule #3). This is based on the observation that $||T\wedge D_1|| - ||T\wedge D_1\wedge D_2|| = ||T\wedge D_1 \wedge \neg D_2||$.

Analogously, in the output node D_2, the certainty factor of Rule #5:

$$cer_S(\#5) = cer_S(T, \neg D_1\wedge D_2) = \frac{\text{card}(||T\wedge\neg D_1\wedge D_2||)}{\text{card}(||T||)}$$

is equal to the difference between flow

$$cer_S(\#2) = cer_S(T, D_2) = \frac{\text{card}(||T\wedge D_2||)}{\text{card}(||T||)},$$

leaving node T and entering node D_2 (Rule #2), and flow

$$cer_S(\#3) = \frac{\text{card}(\|T \wedge D_1 \wedge D_2\|)}{\text{card}(\|T\|)},$$

leaving node D$_1$ and entering in node (D$_1$,D$_2$) (Rule #3). This is based on the observation that $\|T \wedge D_2\| - \|T \wedge D_1 \wedge D_2\| = \|T \wedge \neg D_1 \wedge D_2\|$.

Finally, let us remark that the flow graph presented in Figure 2 also satisfies the properties 1) and 2) of the flow graph from Figure 1.

6   Conclusions

This paper shows some interesting probabilistic features of decision rules inferred from data tables. It extends some previous results in this field by relaxing the assumption of mutual exclusion (independence) of decision rules. Due to some interesting theoretical developments, this relaxation enables interpretation of decision rules encountered in real-life applications where the independence property of a decision algorithm is often violated.

The interpretation of the probabilistic features in terms of flow graphs gives an interesting representation of the relations between the strength, support, coverage and certainty of decision rules induced from one data table. This permits the user to have a deeper comprehension of the fundamental relations in the data.

Acknowledgement. The first author wishes to acknowledge financial support from Italian Ministry of Education, University and Scientific Research (MIUR) The research of the third author has been supported by the State Committee for Scientific Research (KBN), research grant no. 8T11F 006 19, and by the Foundation for Polish Science, subsidy no. 11/2001.

References

Berthold, M., Hand, D. J.: *Intelligent data analysis, an introduction.* Springer-Verlag, Berlin, Heidelberg, New York (1999)

Pawlak, Z.: *Rough Sets - Theoretical Aspects of Reasoning about Data.* Kluwer Academic Publishers, Boston Dordrecht, London (1991)

Pawlak, Z.: Rough sets, decision algorithm and Bayes' theorem. *European Journal of Operational Research* 136 (2002a) pp. 181–189

Pawlak, Z.: *Bayes' Theorem – the Rough Sets Perspective.* Working paper, Warsaw (2002b)

Pawlak, Z.: *Decision Algorithms, Bayes' Theorem and Flow Graph.* Working paper, Warsaw (2002c)

Generalized Rough Sets and Rule Extraction

Masahiro Inuiguchi and Tetsuzo Tanino

Department of Electronics and Information Systems
Graduate School of Engineering, Osaka University
2-1, Yamada-Oka, Suita, Osaka 565-0871, Japan
{inuiguti,tanino}@eie.eng.osaka-u.ac.jp
http://vanilla.eie.eng.osaka-u.ac.jp

Abstract. In this paper, we discuss two extensions of rough sets and the rule extraction based on the rough sets. We introduce two interpretations of rough sets, i.e., rough sets for distinction and rough sets for approximation. Based on those different interpretations, we generalize rough sets in two different ways. The if-then rules extracted based on each generalized rough set are discussed. Based on a decision matrix, a method to extract all minimal rules from a given information table is proposed in each case. The difference of extracted rules between two generalized rough sets and the correspondence between definitions of rough sets and extracted rules are shown. Finally a simple example is given.

1 Introduction

Rough sets [2] are useful in applications to data mining, knowledge discovery, conflict analysis, and so on. Rough set methodology has been developed mainly under equivalence relations which are often called indiscernibility relations. Recently there are various extensions of rough sets under generalized settings [1][4]. Most of those generalizations are based on more or less mathematical correspondence to modality logic, topology and so on. Interpretations of mathematical definitions are required for proper applications to real world problems. Until now, two interpretations, i.e., rough sets as distinction among positive, negative and boundary regions and rough sets as approximation by means of elementary sets, are proposed [1]. However, the rule extraction based on the extended rough sets has not been considerably discussed.

In this paper, we introduce two interpretations of rough sets and define two kinds of rough sets based on the interpretations. For rough sets for distinction, we assume that there is a relation which intuitively implies that all elements in the relation with an element x are in a set X when x is known as a member of X. Using the relation, lower and upper approximations which compose a rough set are defined. On the other hand, for rough sets for approximation, we assume a family of subsets of the universe is given. We approximate a set X internally by a union of elementary sets and externally by an intersection of the complements of elementary sets. We show that those two rough sets coincide when the given relation satisfies reflexivity and transitivity. Then we discuss the rule extraction from an information table based on both generalized rough sets. We emphasize the correspondence between definitions of rough sets and types of extracted if-then rules. Methods for extracting all if-then rules from an information table are discussed. A simple example is given to show the difference of the extracted if-then rules between the two kinds of extended rough sets.

2 Traditional Rough Sets

2.1 Definitions and Properties

Let R be an equivalence relation in the finite universe U, i.e., $R \subseteq U^2$. In rough set literature, R is referred to as an indiscernibility relation and a pair (U, R) is called an approximation space. By the equivalence relation R, U can be partitioned into a collection of equivalence classes or elementary sets, $U|R = \{E_1, E_2, \ldots, E_n\}$. Define $R(x) = \{y \in U \mid (y, x) \in R\}$. Then we have $x \in E_i$ if and only if $E_i = R(x)$. Note that $U|R = \{R(x) \mid x \in U\}$.

Let X be a subset of U. Using $R(x)$, a rough set of X is defined by a pair of the following lower and upper approximations;

$$R_*(X) = \{x \in U \mid R(x) \subseteq X\} = \bigcup \{E_i \mid E_i \subseteq X, \ i = 1, 2, \ldots, n\}, \qquad (1)$$

$$R^*(X) = \bigcup \{R(x) \mid x \in X\} = U - \bigcup \{E_i \mid E_i \subseteq U - X, \ i = 1, 2, \ldots, n\}. \qquad (2)$$

Let us interpret $R(x)$ as a set of elements we intuitively identify as members of X from the fact $x \in X$. Then, from the first expression of $R_*(X)$ in (1), $R_*(X)$ is interpreted as a set of elements which are consistent with the intuition that $R(x) \subseteq X$ if $x \in X$. Under the same interpretation of $R(x)$, $R^*(X)$ is interpreted as a set of elements which can be intuitively inferred as members of X from the first expression of $R^*(X)$ in (2). In other words, $R_*(X)$ and $R^*(X)$ show positive (consistent) and possible members of X. Moreover, $R^*(X) - R_*(X)$ and $U - R^*(X)$ show ambiguous (boundary) and negative members of X. In this way, a rough set classifies elements of U into three classes, i.e., positive, negative and boundary sets.

On the other hand, from the second expression of $R_*(X)$ in (1), $R_*(X)$ is the best approximation of X by means of the union of elementary sets E_i such that $R_*(X) \subseteq X$. Similarly, from the second expression of $R^*(X)$ in (2), $R^*(X)$ is the complement of $R_*(U-X)$. Since $R_*(U-X)$ is the best approximation of $U-X$ by means of the union of elementary sets E_i such that $R_*(U-X) \subseteq U-X$, $R^*(X)$ is the best approximation of X by means of the intersection of the complementary elementary sets $U - E_i$ such that $R^*(X) \supseteq X$.

We introduced only two kinds of expressions of lower and upper approximations but there are other many expressions [1][4]. The interpretation of rough sets depends on the expression of lower and upper approximations. Thus we may have more interpretations by adopting the other expressions. However two interpretations described above seem appropriate for applications of rough sets.

2.2 Rough Set Analysis of an Information Table

Rough sets are frequently applied to the analysis of information tables. The information table is a 4-tuple $\mathcal{I} = \langle U, AT, V, \rho \rangle$, where U is a finite set of objects, AT is a finite set of attributes, $V = \bigcup_{a \in AT} V_a$ and V_a is a domain of the attribute a, and $\rho : U \times AT \to V$ is a total function such that $\rho(x, a) \in V_a$ for every $a \in AT$, $x \in U$, called information function.

When AT is partitioned into a condition attribute set C and a decision attribute set D, the information table is called a decision table. Decision attributes $d \in D$ are distinguished attributes whose values are usually difficult or expensive to obtain but worthwhile to know. On the other hand, condition attributes $c \in C$ are attributes which may be related to decision attributes and whose values are relatively easy or inexpensive to obtain. Thus, it is worthwhile describing decision attribute values by condition attribute values. D is a singleton in many applications and so we assume in what follows, i.e., $D = \{d\}$.

For a given attribute set $A \subseteq AT$, we have indiscernibility relation defined by $I_A = \{(x, y) \mid \rho(x, q) = \rho(y, q), \forall q \in A\}$. Obviously, I_A is an equivalence relation. Decision attribute d induces a partition $U|I_D = \mathcal{P}_D = \{D_1, D_2, \ldots, D_m\}$. For any $A \subseteq C$, we have a family of lower approximations, $A_*(\mathcal{P}_D) = \{A_*(D_1), A_*(D_2), \ldots, A_*(D_m)\}$, where for convenience, notation $A_*(X)$ is used instead of $I_{A*}(X)$. D_i is called a decision class.

In rough set approaches, we discuss minimally required conditional attributes without deterioration of the quality of approximation and minimal conditions for an object to be a member of a decision class. For the former discussion, all minimal subsets $A \subseteq C$ such that $A_*(\mathcal{P}_D) = C_*(\mathcal{P}_D)$ are called relative reducts, or simply, reducts of the information table. Such reducts show minimally required conditional attributes. Many approaches [2] have been proposed to calculate all reducts. For the latter discussion, minimal conditions for each decision class are calculated. By performing this calculation for every decision class, we obtain all consistent if-then rules to classify objects into decision classes. For this calculation, a method proposed by Shan and Ziarko [3] is one of the most useful methods. In the real world problems, it is difficult to have the decision table includes all possible objects. Assuming that the obtained decision table include all patterns of decision, the obtained if-then rules is used even for objects not listed in the given decision table.

3 Generalization of Rough Sets

3.1 Distinction among Positive, Negative, and Boundary Elements

Suppose that a set $X \subseteq U$ is given and that a nonempty relation P in U^2 is equipped with X such that if $x \in X$ then for any y satisfying $(y, x) \in P$, we intuitively regard it as a member of X. Let $P(x) = \{y \mid (y, x) \in P\}$. If we have $P(x) \subseteq X$ for $x \in X$ then the fact $x \in X$ is consistent with the intuition and $x \in X$ is positively confirmed. On the other hand, $y \in P(x)$ with $x \in X$ is intuitively identified as a member of X. Namely, such y is a possible member of X. Hence, we define lower and upper approximations by

$$P_*(X) = \{x \mid P(x) \subseteq X\}, \tag{3}$$
$$P^*(X) = X \cup \bigcup \{P(x) \mid x \in X\}. \tag{4}$$

Since we do not assume the reflexivity of P, we take a union with X in (4). Under the interpretation of rough sets as distinction among positive, negative and boundary regions, we may find the other definitions in [1].

Using lower and upper approximations, U is divided into three categories, i.e., positive region $P_*(X)$, negative region $U - P^*(X)$ and boundary region $P^*(X) - P_*(X)$.

3.2 Approximations by Means of Elementary Sets

In interpretation of rough sets as approximations of sets by means of elementary sets, we can assume a general setting, i.e., a case when a family $\mathcal{F} = \{F_1, F_2, \ldots, F_n\}$ is given. When a relation P is given, for example, we may obtain a family as $\mathcal{P} = \{P(x_1), P(x_2), \ldots, P(x_u)\}$. Under a family $\mathcal{F}$, we should consider lower and upper approximations defined by

$$\mathcal{F}_*(X) = \bigcup\{F_i \mid F_i \subseteq X, \ i = 1, 2, \ldots, n\}, \tag{5}$$
$$\mathcal{F}^*(X) = U - \bigcup\{F_i \mid F_i \subseteq U - X, \ i = 1, 2, \ldots, n\}. \tag{6}$$

Those are extensions of the second expressions of (1) and (2), respectively.

In a special case, the two kinds of rough sets coincide. This is shown in the following theorem.

Theorem 1. *Let P be a reflexive and transitive relation and let us define $\mathcal{F} = \{P(x_1), P(x_2), \ldots, P(x_u)\}$. Then for any $X \in U$, we have*

$$P_*(X) = \mathcal{F}_*(X), \quad P^*(X) = \mathcal{F}^*(X). \tag{7}$$

4 Rule Extraction

4.1 Rule Extraction Based on Positive Regions

Let us discuss rule extraction based on rough sets for distinction. Consider a decision table $\mathcal{I} = \langle U, C \cup \{d\}, V, \rho \rangle$. By decision attribute value $\rho(x, d)$, we assume that we can group objects into several classes D_i, $i = 1, 2, \ldots, m$. D_i, $i = 1, 2, \ldots, m$ do not necessary form a partition but a cover. Namely, $D_i \cap D_j = \emptyset$ does not always hold but $\bigcup_{i=1,2,\ldots,m} D_i = U$. Without loss of generality, we assume that $\forall x_j \in U$, $\exists D_i$; $I_C(x_j) \subseteq D_i$ since otherwise, we can define a new decision class D^{new} by $D^{\text{new}} = \bigcup\{D_k \mid x \in I_C(x_j), x \in D_k\}$. Corresponding to D_i, $i = 1, 2, \ldots, m$, we assume that there is a relation $P_c \in V_c^2$ is given to each

condition attribute $c \in C$ so that if $x \in D_i$ and $(y,x) \in P_c$ then we intuitively conclude $y \in D_i$ from the viewpoint of attribute c. For each $A \subseteq C$, we define a relation,
$$P_A = \{(x,y) \mid (\rho(x,c), \rho(y,c)) \in P_c, \; \forall c \in A\}. \tag{8}$$

$\Delta(\boldsymbol{a}, \boldsymbol{v})$ denotes a condition '$\rho(x, a_1) = v_1$ and $\cdots$ and $\rho(x, a_p) = v_p$' where $\boldsymbol{a} = (a_1, a_2, \ldots, a_p)$, $a_i \in C$, $i = 1, 2, \ldots, p$, $a_i \neq a_j$ for $i \neq j$, $\boldsymbol{v} = (v_1, v_2, \ldots, v_p)$, $v_i \in V_{a_i}$, $i = 1, 2, \ldots, p$ and $p \leq \mathrm{Card}(C)$.

Let $\Delta(\boldsymbol{a}, \boldsymbol{v})$ and $\Delta(\bar{\boldsymbol{a}}, \bar{\boldsymbol{v}})$ be two conditions such that $\boldsymbol{a} = (a_1, a_2, \ldots, a_p)$, $\boldsymbol{v} = (v_1, v_2, \ldots, v_p)$, $\bar{\boldsymbol{a}} = (\bar{a}_1, \bar{a}_2, \ldots, \bar{a}_q)$ and $\bar{\boldsymbol{v}} = (\bar{v}_1, \bar{v}_2, \ldots, \bar{v}_q)$. It is said that $\Delta(\boldsymbol{a}, \boldsymbol{v})$ is smaller than $\Delta(\bar{\boldsymbol{a}}, \bar{\boldsymbol{v}})$ if and only if, for every $i \in \{1, 2, \ldots, p\}$, there exists $j \in \{1, 2, \ldots, q\}$ such that $a_i = \bar{a}_j$ and $v_i = \bar{v}_j$. Let $X(\Delta(\boldsymbol{a}, \boldsymbol{v})) \subseteq U$ be a set whose members satisfy the condition $\Delta(\boldsymbol{a}, \boldsymbol{v})$.

For each class D_i and for each $A \subseteq C$, we have a lower approximation of D_i as $P_{A*}(D_i)$. Enumerating all minimal conditions $\Delta(\boldsymbol{a}, \boldsymbol{v})$ such that $\emptyset \neq X(\Delta(\boldsymbol{a}, \boldsymbol{v})) \subseteq P_{A(\boldsymbol{a})*}(D_i)$, we can obtain minimal conditions for an object to be a positive (consistent) member of D_i, where $A(\boldsymbol{a})$ is a set of all attributes composing $\boldsymbol{a}$, i.e., $A(\boldsymbol{a}) = \{a_1, a_2, \ldots, a_p\}$. For a given minimal condition $\Delta(\boldsymbol{a}, \boldsymbol{v})$ of a class D_i, the corresponding if-then rule is obtained as follows:

if $\rho(x, a_1) = v_1$ and $\cdots$ and $\rho(x, a_p) = v_p$ then $x \in D_i$.

This type of if-then rule is called an identity if-then rule (for short, id-rule). Note that, for any id-rule, there exists $x_j \in D_i \subseteq U$ such that $\rho(x_j, a_k) = v_k$, $k = 1, 2, \ldots, p$.

If P_A is transitive, the following if-then rule is derived from an id-rule.

if $(\rho(x, a_1), v_1) \in P_{a_1}$ and $\cdots$ and $(\rho(x, a_p), v_p) \in P_{a_p}$ then $x \in D_i$.

This type of if-then rule is called a relational if-then rule (for short, P-rule). Consider the following id- and P-rules with the same conclusion part:

id-rule: if $\rho(x, a_1) = v_1^j$ and $\cdots$ and $\rho(x, a_p) = v_p^j$ then $x \in D_i$,
P-rule: if $(\rho(x, a_1), v_1^k) \in P_{a_1}$ and $\cdots$ and $(\rho(x, a_q), v_q^k) \in P_{a_q}$ then $x \in D_i$.

Let us assume $p \geq q$. If $(v_1^j, v_1^k) \in P_{a_1}$ and $\cdots$ and $(v_q^j, v_q^k) \in P_{a_q}$ then the id-rule is a special case of the P-rule. Therefore, the id-rule can be omitted. Especially, if P satisfies the reflexivity, all id-rules are omitted.

For extracting all decision rules, we can utilize the decision matrix [3]. We extract all minimal rules having a common conclusion part, $x \in D_k$. To do this, we partition the index set $\{1, 2, \ldots, n\}$ into two subsets $K^+ = \{i \mid x_i \in D_k\}$ and $K^- = \{i \mid x_i \notin D_k\}$. The decision matrix $M(\mathcal{I}) = (M_{ij})$ is defined by

$$M_{ij} = \{(a, \rho(x_i, a)) \mid (\rho(x_j, a), \rho(x_i, a)) \notin P_a\}, \; i \in K^+, \; j \in K^-. \tag{9}$$

Let $Id((a, v))$ be a statement '$\rho(x, a) = v$' and $Q((a, v))$ a statement '$(\rho(x, a), v) \in P_a$'. Then the condition parts of all minimal decision rules with respect to D_k are obtained as conjunctive terms in the disjunctive normal form of the following logical function:

$$B_k = \begin{cases} \bigvee_{i \in K^+} \bigwedge_{j \in K^-} \bigvee Id(M_{ij}), & \text{if P is not transitive,} \\ \left(\bigvee_{i \in K^+} \bigwedge_{j \in K^-} \bigvee Id(M_{ij})\right) \vee \left(\bigvee_{i \in K^+} \bigwedge_{j \in K^-} \bigvee Q(M_{ij})\right), \\ & \text{if P is transitive.} \end{cases} \quad (10)$$

Under the interpretation of rough sets as distinction among positive, negative and boundary elements, the extracted if-then rules are conservative since the conditions are given for consistent elements of classes. Thus this approach can be regarded as a passive and safety-oriented approach.

4.2 Rule Extraction Based on Lower Approximations

Let us discuss rule extraction based on rough sets for approximation. Consider a decision table $\mathcal{I} = \langle U, C \cup \{d\}, V, \rho \rangle$ such that a relation $P_c \in V_c^2$ is given to each condition attribute $c \in C$. We assume that V_c is finite. For a given attribute set $A = \{a_1, a_2, \ldots, a_p\}$, we consider a cover. We may construct many covers with respect to A. We use a family $\mathcal{P}_A = \{Z_A(v^1), Z_A(v^2), \ldots, Z_A(v^w)\}$ obtained from relations P_{a_j}, $j = 1, 2, \ldots, p$, where $w = \text{Card}(|V_{a_1} \times \cdots \times V_{a_p}|)$, $v^j = (v_1^j, v_2^j, \cdots, v_p^j)$, $j = 1, 2, \ldots, w$ are all possible combinations of attribute values of A and $Z_A(v^j) = \{x \in U \mid (\rho(x, a_i), v_i^j) \in P_{a_i}, i = 1, 2, \ldots, p\}$. By decision attribute value $\rho(x, d)$, we assume that we can group objects into several classes D_i, $i = 1, 2, \ldots, m$ which form a cover. Thus, we have lower approximations $\mathcal{P}_{A*}(D_i)$, $i = 1, 2, \ldots, m$.

Corresponding to the lower approximations $\mathcal{P}_{A*}(D_i)$, $i = 1, 2, \ldots, m$, we can extract if-then rules. Let $\tilde{\Delta}(\boldsymbol{a}, \boldsymbol{v})$ be a condition '$(\rho(x, a_1), v_1) \in P_{a_1}$ and $\cdots$ and $(\rho(x, a_p), v_p) \in P_{a_p}$' where $\boldsymbol{a} = (a_1, a_2, \ldots, a_p)$, $a_i \in C$, $i = 1, 2, \ldots, p$, $a_i \neq a_j$ for $i \neq j$, $\boldsymbol{v} = (v_1, v_2, \ldots, v_p)$, $v_i \in V_{a_i}$, $i = 1, 2, \ldots, p$ and $p \leq \text{Card}(C)$.

Let $\tilde{\Delta}(\boldsymbol{a}, \boldsymbol{v})$ and $\tilde{\Delta}(\bar{\boldsymbol{a}}, \bar{\boldsymbol{v}})$ be two conditions such that $\boldsymbol{a} = (a_1, \ldots, a_p)$, $\boldsymbol{v} = (v_1, \ldots, v_p)$, $\bar{\boldsymbol{a}} = (\bar{a}_1, \ldots, \bar{a}_q)$ and $\bar{\boldsymbol{v}} = (\bar{v}_1, \ldots, \bar{v}_q)$. It is said that $\tilde{\Delta}(\boldsymbol{a}, \boldsymbol{v})$ is smaller than $\tilde{\Delta}(\bar{\boldsymbol{a}}, \bar{\boldsymbol{v}})$ if and only if $\tilde{\Delta}(\bar{\boldsymbol{a}}, \bar{\boldsymbol{v}})$ implies $\tilde{\Delta}(\boldsymbol{a}, \boldsymbol{v})$. Of course, if, for every $i \in \{1, 2, \ldots, p\}$, there exists $j \in \{1, 2, \ldots, q\}$ such that $a_i = \bar{a}_j$ and $v_i = \bar{v}_j$, then $\tilde{\Delta}(\boldsymbol{a}, \boldsymbol{v})$ is smaller than $\tilde{\Delta}(\bar{\boldsymbol{a}}, \bar{\boldsymbol{v}})$ as in Subsection 4.1. Moreover, when $p \leq q$ and $a_i = \bar{a}_i$, $i = 1, 2, \ldots, q$, $\tilde{\Delta}(\boldsymbol{a}, \boldsymbol{v})$ is smaller than $\tilde{\Delta}(\bar{\boldsymbol{a}}, \bar{\boldsymbol{v}})$ if $(\rho(x, a_i), \bar{v}_i) \in P_{a_i}$ implies $(\rho(x, a_i), v_i) \in P_{a_i}$ for $i \in \{1, 2, \ldots, q\}$. Let $X(\tilde{\Delta}(\boldsymbol{a}, \boldsymbol{v}))$ be a set composed of elements of U which satisfies the condition $\tilde{\Delta}(\boldsymbol{a}, \boldsymbol{v})$.

For each decision class D_i and for each $A \subseteq C$, we have a lower approximation of D_i as $\mathcal{P}_{A*}(D_i)$. Enumerating all minimal conditions $\tilde{\Delta}(\boldsymbol{a}, \boldsymbol{v})$ such that $\emptyset \neq X(\tilde{\Delta}(\boldsymbol{a}, \boldsymbol{v})) \subseteq \mathcal{P}_{A(\boldsymbol{a})*}(D_i)$, or equivalently, $\emptyset \neq X(\tilde{\Delta}(\boldsymbol{a}, \boldsymbol{v})) \subseteq D_i$, we can obtain minimal conditions for an object to be a member of D_i. For a given minimal condition $\tilde{\Delta}(\boldsymbol{a}, \boldsymbol{v})$ of a decision class D_i, the corresponding if-then rule is obtained as follows:

if $(\rho(x, a_1), v_1) \in P_{a_1}$ and $\cdots$ and $(\rho(x, a_p), v_p) \in P_{a_p}$ then $x \in D_i$.

For extracting all decision rules, the decision matrix [3] is useful. We extract all minimal rules having a common conclusion part, $x \in D_k$. To do this, we partition the index set $\{1, 2, \ldots, n\}$ into two subsets $K^+ = \{i \mid x_i \in D_k\}$ and $K^- = \{i \mid x_i \notin D_k\}$. The decision matrix $\tilde{M}(\mathcal{I}) = (\tilde{M}_{ij})$ is defined by

$$\tilde{M}_{ij} = \{(a, v) \mid (\rho(x_j, a), \rho(x_i, a)) \notin P_a,\ (\rho(x_i, a), v) \in P_a,\ (\rho(x_j, a), v) \notin P_a\}, \\ i \in K^+,\ j \in K^-. \tag{11}$$

Then the condition parts of all minimal decision rules with respect to D_k are obtained as conjunctive terms in the disjunctive normal form of the following logical function:

$$\tilde{B}_k = \bigvee_{i \in K^+} \bigwedge_{j \in K^-} \bigvee Q(\tilde{M}_{ij}). \tag{12}$$

Under the interpretation of rough sets as approximations by means of elementary sets, the extracted if-then rules are expansive since the rules are fired for objects only having similar properties specified in the conditions. However, it tends to come into conflict among rules. Thus this approach can be regarded as a risk accepting but active and applicativity-oriented approach.

4.3 Comparison and Correspondence between Definitions and Rules

The extracted if-then rules based on two rough sets are different. While extracted if-then rules are for reasoning about positive members of decision classes in rough sets for distinction, they are for reasoning about members of decision classes in rough sets for approximation. The former body of if-then rules is obtained by covering positive members, but the latter body of if-then rules is obtained by excluding negative members. Therefore, the former is easier to conclude unknown than the latter and the latter often concludes some decisions. On the contrary, the latter is easier to have confliction between rules than the former.

Moreover, in the case of rough sets for distinction, we need a special relation P which should be associated with the decision classes D_i such that if $x \in D_i$ and $(y, x) \in P$ then we intuitively conclude $y \in D_i$. Rough sets for approximation do not require such a special relation but a relation to group objects. In this sense, rough sets for approximation would be more applicable in many situations.

Finally, we emphasize the correspondence between the definitions of lower approximations and types of extracted if-then rules. The correspondence is shown

Table 1. Correspondence between definition of rough sets and extracted if-then rules

rough sets for	definition of l-approx.	extracted body of if-then rules
distinction	$\{x \in U \mid P(x) \subseteq X\}$	if $\rho(x, a_1) = v_1$ and $\cdots$ and $\rho(x, a_p) = v_p$ then $x \in D_i$
approximation	$\bigcup\{F_i \in \mathcal{F} \mid F_i \subseteq X\}$	if $(\rho(x, a_1), v_1) \in P_{a_1}$ and $\cdots$ and $(\rho(x, a_p), v_p) \in P_{a_p}$ then $x \in D_i$

Table 2. Survivability of alpinists with respect to foods and tools

	foods	tools	survivability
Alp1	$\{a\}$	$\{A,B\}$	low
Alp2	$\{a,b,c\}$	$\{A,B\}$	high
Alp3	$\{a,b\}$	$\{A\}$	low
Alp4	$\{b\}$	$\{A\}$	low
Alp5	$\{a,b\}$	$\{A,B\}$	high

in Table 1. In rough sets for distinction, x corresponds to '$\rho(x,a_1) = v_1$ and $\cdots$ and $\rho(x,a_p) = v_p$' which characterizes the object x. On the other hand, F_i corresponds to '$(\rho(x,a_1),v_1) \in P_{a_1}$ and $\cdots$ and $(\rho(x,a_p),v_p) \in P_{a_p}$' which characterizes the members of F_i.

5 A Simple Example

Consider an alpinist problem. There are three packages a, b and c of foods and two packages A and B of tools. When an alpinist climbs a mountain, he/she should carry foods and tools in order to be back safely. Assume the survivability Sur is determined by foods Fo and tools To packed in his/her knapsack and a set of data is given as in Table 2. Discarding the weight, we think that the more foods and tools, the higher the survivability is. In this sense, we consider an inclusion relation $\supseteq$ for both attributes Fo and To. Since the inclusion relation satisfies the reflexivity and transitivity, rough sets for both distinction and approximation coincide.

Let us extract rules concluding $Sur =$ 'high'. Based on rough sets for distinction, following rules are extracted:

if $Fo \supseteq \{a,b,c\}$ then $Sur =$ 'high', and
if $Fo \supseteq \{a,b\}$ and $To \supseteq \{A,B\}$ then $Sur =$ 'high'.

On the other hand, based on rough sets for approximation, we obtain

if $Fo \supseteq \{c\}$ then $Sur =$ 'high', and
if $Fo \supseteq \{b\}$ and $To \supseteq \{B\}$ then $Sur =$ 'high'.

As shown in this example, even if rough sets coincide each other, the extracted if-then rules are different.

References

1. Inuiguchi, M., Tanino, T.: On rough sets under generalized equivalence relations. *Bulletin of International Rough Set Society* **5**(1/2) (2001) 167–171
2. Pawlak, Z.: *Rough Sets: Theoretical Aspects of Reasoning About Data*, Boston, MA, Kluwer Academic Publishers (1991)
3. Shan, N., Ziarko, W.: Data-based acquisition and incremental modification of classification rules. *Computational Intelligence* **11** (1995) 357–370
4. Słowiński, R., Vanderpooten, D.: A generalized definition of rough approximations based on similarity. *IEEE Transactions on Data and Knowledge Engineering* **12**(2) (2000) 331–336

Towards a Mereological System for Direct Products and Relations[*]

Ryszard Janicki

Department of Computing and Software,
McMaster University,
Hamilton, ON, L8S 4K1 Canada,
janicki@mcmaster.ca

Abstract. An algebraic model for a "part of" relation proposed in [13] is applied to direct product and relations. The basic properties are proven.

1 Introduction

One of the concepts that is frequently used in computer science, on various level of abstractions, is the concept of being a "part of". The concepts "whole" and "part of" abound in human experience but their fully adequate conceptualization has yet eluded our most able thinkers. Attempts to formalize the concept of "part of" go back to S. Leśniewski (1916-1937,[22]), and H. Leonard, N. Goodman (1930-1950,[7]), however they have never become very popular from the application view point. Leśniewski's systems are different from the standard set theory based on Zermello-Freankl axioms [17], which makes their straightforward application quite difficult[1]. Leonard and Goodman Calculus of Individuals was defined in terms of the standard set theory, but it was too much influenced by "spacial reasoning" (see [7]), and as a result of this it is too rigid for many applications. It resembles theories based on the concept of a lattice, but many posets defined by "part of" like relations that may occur in practice are not lattices.

The basic difference between the approach of [13] and the models mentioned above is that it *does not* start with an axiomatic definition of a "part of" relation. It is assumed that the complex objects can be built from the more primitive ones by using "constructor" operations, and the less complex objects can be derived from the more complex ones by using "destructor" operations. A mereological system is a kind of an abstract algebra, and the relation "part of" can be derived from the set of "constructor" and "destructor" operations.

Main motivation for this work was provided by an attempt to define a formal semantics for *tabular expressions* [9,10,14]. Tabular expressions (Parnas et al. [1, 15,18]) are means to represent the complex relations that are used to specify and

---

[*] Partially supported by NSERC of Canada.
[1] A very recent application of Leśniewski's ideas to approximate reasoning can be found in [20,21].

It was first developed in work for the U.S. Navy and applied to the A-7E aircraft [2]. The ideas were picked up by Grumman, the U.S. Air Force, Bell Laboratories and many others. The tabular notation have also been applied in Canada by Ontario Hydro in Darlington Nuclear Plant (see [15,18,19]). However a formal semantics of tabular expressions has only recently been developed [9,10,14]. When software engineers discuss a specification using *tabular expressions*, the statements like "this is *a part of* a bigger relation", "this relation is composed of the following *parts*", etc., can be heard very often.

From the mathematical viewpoint tabular expressions are means to specify formally complex heterogenous relations [14]. One of the biggest advantages of tabular expression technique is the ability to define a relation R that describes the properties of the system specified, as an easy to understand composition[2] of the relations R_α, $\alpha \in I$, where R_α is a *part of* R. The problem is that the standard algebra of relations lacks the formal concept of being a *part of*. The concept of subset is not enough, for instance if $A \subseteq B$ and $D = B \times C$, then A is not a subset of D, but according to standard intuition it is a *part of D*.

A concept of "part of" for relations was proposed in [10], used in [14] and its properties were first analysed in [11]. The approach of [11] does not take into account "elementary components" from which the other elements are built. A simple solution to this problem was first proposed in [12] and then fully explored in [13]. This paper can be treated as a direct continuation of [11,13], but for the sake of self-completness all the major results of [11,13] will be stated.

We assume that the reader is familiar with the basic concepts of abstract and relational algebras, set and lattice theory ([3,17]). The following notation will be used. For every set A, ub A (lb A) denote the set of all *upper bounds* (*lower bounds*) of A, for every poset $(X, \preceq)$, $\top$ denotes the top of X(if exists), $\bot$ denotes the bottom of X (if exists). The set of all *minimal* (*maximal*) elements of A will be denoted by min A (max A). For every set A, inf A denotes the greatest lower bound (infimum) of A, sup A denotes the least upper bound (supremum) of A.

2 Grids and Mereological Systems

In this section we comprise major results of [13] and the first part of [11]. Since posets generated by "part of" relations are not lattices in many cases, the concept of a *grid*, an extension of a lattice, was introduced and analysed.

The set min A (max A) is *complete* iff $\forall x \in A.\ \exists a \in \min A.\ a \preceq x$ ($\forall x \in A.\ \exists a \in \max A.\ x \preceq a$). Let cmin $A = \min A$ (cmax $A = \max A$) if min A is complete (max A is complete), and undefined otherwise.

For every set $A \subseteq X$, we define cminub$A$ = cmin ub$A$, cmaxlb$A$ = cmax lb$A$. For every $k \geq 0$, we define cminub $^k A$ as: cminub $^0 A = A$ and cminub $^{k+1} A =$ cminub (cminub $^k A$), and similarly for cmaxlb$^k A$. Note that for every $a \in X$, we

---

[2] The word "composition" here means "the act of putting together" (*Oxford English Dictionary*, 1990), not "the" composition of relations that is usually denoted by ";" or "∘" ([3,17]. In this sense "∪" is a composition.

have: $\mathrm{ub}\{a\} = \mathrm{lb}\{a\} = \mathrm{cmin}\{a\} = \mathrm{cmax}\{a\} = \mathrm{cminub}\{a\} = \mathrm{cmaxlb}\{a\} = \{a\}$, and $\sup\{a\} = \inf\{a\} = a$.

Lemma 1. *For every $A \subseteq X$, $(|\mathrm{cminub}\,^j A| = 1 \Rightarrow |\mathrm{cminub}\,^{j+1} A| = 1)$ and $(|\mathrm{cmaxlb}\,^j A| = 1 \Rightarrow |\mathrm{cmaxlb}\,^{j+1} A| = 1)$.* ∎

For every $A \subseteq X$, let $d_t(A)$ $(d_b(A))$, *degree of the top of A (degree of the bottom of A)*, be the smallest k such that $|\mathrm{cminub}\,^k A| = 1$ $(|\mathrm{cmaxlb}\,^k A| = 1)$.

For every $A \subseteq X$, top A, the top of A, is defined as
$$\mathrm{top}\,A = a \iff \{a\} = \mathrm{cminub}\,^{d_t(A)} A.$$
Similarly, bot A, the bottom of A, is defined as
$$\mathrm{bot}\,A = a \iff \{a\} = \mathrm{cmaxlb}\,^{d_b(A)} A.$$
Of course it may happen that neither top A, nor bot A exists.

We will write $a = \mathrm{top}\,^k A$ $(a = \mathrm{bot}\,^k A)$ if $a = \mathrm{top}\,A$ and $d_t(A) = k$ $(a = \mathrm{bot}\,A$ and $d_b(A) = k)$.

Lemma 2. *If $\sup A$ exists then $\sup A = \mathrm{top}\,^1 A$, and if $\inf A$ exists then $\inf A = \mathrm{bot}\,^1 A$.* ∎

A poset $(X, \preceq)$ is called a **grid** if for each $a, b \in X$, top $\{a,b\}$ and bot $\{a,b\}$ exist. A poset $(X, \preceq)$ is called a **grid of degree** (k,n) if it is a grid and for every finite $A \subseteq X$, $d_t(A) \leq k$, $d_b(A) \leq n$. A grid $(X, \preceq)$ is *regular* iff $\forall A \subseteq X. \forall B \subseteq A.$ top $B \preceq$ top A and bot $A \preceq$ bot B.

Corollary 1. *A lattice is a grid of degree $(1,1)$.* ∎

Figure 1(a) illustrates the concepts introduced above.

A grid is called *infimum complete* (*supremum complete*) iff for every $A \subseteq X$, bot A (top A) do exist. Immediately from the definitions we conclude that if top X exists than top $X = \sup X = \top$, and dually, if bot X exists, then bot $X = \inf X = \bot$. A grid is *complete* if it is infimum complete and supremum complete.

Let $a, b \in X$, and let $A \subseteq X$. We define: $a \sqcup b = \mathrm{top}\,\{a,b\}, a \sqcap b = \mathrm{bot}\,\{a,b\}$. Unfortunately it might happen that $a \sqcup (b \sqcup c) \neq (a \sqcup b) \sqcup c$, or $a \sqcap (b \sqcap c) \neq (a \sqcap b) \sqcap c$, as in the example in Figure 1(b).

Let $(X, \preceq)$ be an infimum complete grid. The minimal elements of $X \setminus \{\bot\}$ are called *atoms*. Let $\mathrm{atoms}_\preceq(X)$ denote the set of all atoms of $(X, \preceq)$.

The grids from Figures 1(a) and 1(b) are not atomistic whilst the grid from Figure 1(c) is atomistic.

Let $(X, \preceq)$ be an infimum complete grid, and let η be the following total function $\eta : X \setminus \{\bot\} \to 2^{\mathrm{atoms}_\preceq(X)}$, such that for each $x \in X$,
$$\eta(x) = \{a \mid a \in \mathrm{atoms}_\preceq(X) \wedge a \preceq x\}.$$
For every $A \subseteq X$, let $\eta(A) = \bigcup_{a \in A} \eta(a)$, $X\downarrow_A^\eta = \{x \mid x \in X \wedge \eta(x) \subseteq \eta(A)\}$, $\sqsubseteq\downarrow_A^\eta = \{(x,y) \mid x \sqsubseteq y \wedge x, y \in A\}$.

The following convention will be used: $\overline{\mathrm{ub}}\,A$ denotes the set of all upper bounds of A in $(X\downarrow_A^\eta, \sqsubseteq\downarrow_A^\eta)$, $\overline{\mathrm{top}}\,A$ denotes the top of A in $(X\downarrow_A^\eta, \sqsubseteq\downarrow_A^\eta)$, $a\overline{\sqcup}b = \overline{\mathrm{top}}\,\{a,b\}$, $a\overline{\sqcap}b = \overline{\mathrm{bot}}\,\{a,b\}$, etc.

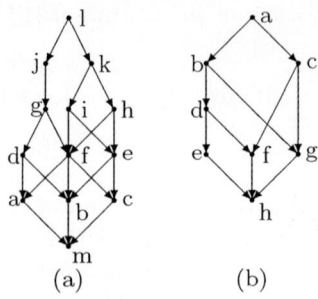

Fig. 1. (a) The poset is a *grid of degree* $(3,3)$ and for example: $g = \text{top}^2\{a,b\}$, $k = \text{top}^3\{b,c\}$, cminub $\{b,c\} = \{e,f\}$, cminub $^2\{b,c\} =$ cminub $\{e,f\} = \{i,h\}$, cminub $^3\{b,c\} =$ cminub $^2\{e,f\} =$ cminub $\{i,h\} = \{k\}$, cminub $\{a,b\} = \{d,f\}$, cminub $^2\{a,b\} =$ cminub $\{d,f\} = \{g\}$. The grid is not regular since top $\{a,b,c\} = f \preceq g = \text{top}\{a,b\}$.
(b) The poset is a *grid of degree* $(2,2)$. We have $e \sqcup f = d$, $d \sqcup g = b$, so $(e \sqcup f) \sqcup g = b$, but $f \sqcup g = a$, $e \sqcup a = a$, so $e \sqcup (f \sqcup g) = a$, i.e. $(e \sqcup f) \sqcup g \neq e \sqcup (f \sqcup g)$. Note that top $^2\{e,f,g\} = b$. By reversing arrows the same example works for "$\sqcap$".

For every set of functions $\mathcal{F}$, and every set A, let $A^{\mathcal{F}}$ denote the smallest set containing A and closed under $\mathcal{F}$.

How can we built complex object from the more primitive ones? Usually we assume to have a set of *elementary* objects, that are considered to be "atomic", and two sets of (partial) operations, *constructors*, transform less complex objects into more complex, and *destructors*, that transforms more complex object into less complex. Also there should be some relationship between the operators and the "part of" relation.

By a *mereological system* we mean a tuple
$$MS = (X, E, \bot, \Theta, \Delta, \eta),$$
where:

- X is a set of *elements*,
- $E \subseteq X$ is a set of *elementary* elements,
- $\bot \in X \setminus E$ is an *empty* element,
- Θ is the set of *constructors*, each $\theta \in \Theta$ is a partial function $\theta : X^k \to X$,
- Δ is the set of *destructors*, each $\delta \in \Delta$ is a partial function $\delta : X^k \to X$,
- $\eta : X \setminus \{\bot\} \to 2^E$ is a total function interpreted as the *elementary elements assignment* function.

and the folowing conditions are satisfied:

1. $E^{\Theta \cup \Delta} = X$,
2. $E^{\Delta} \subseteq E \cup \{\bot\}$,
3. $\forall e \in E.\ \eta(e) = \{e\}$,
   $\forall \theta \in \Theta.\ \eta(\theta(a_1,\ldots,a_k)) = \eta(a_1) \cup \ldots \cup \eta(a_k)$,
   $\forall \delta \in \Delta.\ \eta(\delta(a_1,\ldots,a_k)) \subseteq \eta(a_1)$.

4. For every $A \subseteq X$, $(X\downarrow_A^\eta, \sqsubseteq\downarrow_A^\eta)$ is an infimum complete grid, where: $\sqsubseteq = \dot{\sqsubseteq}^*$ and $\dot{\sqsubseteq}$ is defined as follows

$$a\dot{\sqsubseteq}b \iff (\exists \theta \in \Theta. \exists a_1, ..., a_k \in X. \exists i \in \{1, ..., k\}. a = a_i \land b = \theta(a_1, ..., a_k))$$
$$\lor \; (\exists \delta \in \Delta. \exists b_2, ..., b_k \in X. a = \delta(b, b_2, ..., b_k)).$$

The condition (1) says that that each object is either elementary, or it can be constructed from the elementary objects by the using constructors and destructors. The condition (2) states that the elements of E cannot be decomposed any further. The condition (3) described naturally desired properties of the η function. The relation SQ defined in the condition (4) is interpreted as a "part of" generated by MS. The condition (4) defines the relationship between "part of" and "constructors/destructors".

Lemma 3. 1. $\forall x \in X. \eta(x) = \{a \mid a \in E \land a \sqsubseteq x\}$.
2. $\forall A \subseteq X.$ sup $A = \overline{\text{sup}} \, A$, inf $A = \overline{\text{inf}} \, A$, $\overline{\text{top}} \, A \sqsubseteq$ top A, bot $A \sqsubseteq \overline{\text{bot}} \, A$ ∎

A mereological system $MS = (X, E, \bot, \Theta, \Delta, \eta)$ is *constructive* if $E^\Theta = X \setminus \{\bot\}$, and it is *complete* if for every $A \subseteq X$, $(X \downarrow_A, \sqsubseteq \downarrow_A)$ is complete.

Corollary 2. *If MS is constructive then the mapping η is entirely defined by the elements of Θ, so MS can be defined as a tuple $(X, E, \bot, \Theta, \Delta)$.* ∎

For every mereological system $MS = (X, E, \Theta, \Delta, \eta)$, (X, E) is called a *domain* of MS. Let $\mathcal{MS}$ be a family of mereological systems with a common domain. We will say that a mereological system MS_U is *universal* for $\mathcal{MS}$ if for every $MS \in \mathcal{MS}$, $a \sqsubseteq_{MS} b \Rightarrow a \sqsubseteq_{MS_U} b$.

Example 1. For every set A, let $\hat{A} = \{\{a\} \mid a \in A\}$ is the set of all singletons generated by A, i.e. if $A = \{a, b\}$, then $\hat{A} = \{\{a\}, \{b\}\}$.
Let $E = \hat{D}_1 \cup \hat{D}_2$, where $D_1 = \{a, b\}$, $D_2 = \{1, 2\}$, $\bot = \emptyset$, $\Theta = \{\cup, \dot{\times}\}$, where $\dot{\times}$ (a restricted Cartesian Product) is defined as: $A \dot{\times} B = \{(x, y) \mid x \in A \subseteq D_1 \land y \in B \subseteq D_2\}$, $\Delta = \{\pi_1, \pi_2, \setminus\}$, where π_i is a projection of sets on the ith coordinate, formally defined as $\pi_i : 2^{D_i} \cup 2^{D_1 \times D_2}$ with $\pi_i(A) = A$ if $A \subseteq D_i$ and $\pi_1(A) = \{x \mid (x, y) \in A\}$, $\pi_2(A) = \{y \mid (x, y) \in A\}$ if $A \subseteq D_1 \times D_2$. Let $X = 2^{D_1} \cup 2^{D_2} \cup 2^{D_1 \times D_2}$, and let η satisfies: $\eta(A) = \hat{A}$ if $A \subseteq D_1 \cup D_2$, and $\eta(A) = \{\{x\} \mid (x, y) \in A\} \cup \{\{y\} \mid (x, y) \in A\}$ if $A \subseteq D_1 \times D_2$.
Note that in this case we have $X \setminus \{\emptyset\} = E^{\{\cup, \dot{\times}\}}$. For instance: $\{(a, 1), (b, 2)\} = \{a\}\dot{\times}\{1\} \cup \{b\}\dot{\times}\{2\}$.
Define $\sqsubseteq$ as follows: $A \sqsubseteq B \iff A \subseteq B \lor A \subseteq \pi_i(B), i = 1, 2$.
One can show by inspection that $(X, E, \bot, \Theta, \Delta, \eta)$ is a *constructive*, and *complete mereological system*, and for every $A \subseteq X$, $(X_A, \sqsubseteq_A)$ is a complete grid of degree (2,2) with sup $X = \top = D_1 \times D_2$. As Figure 2 shows, the poset $(X, \sqsubseteq)$ is not a lattice. This example is a special case of a more general result that will be discussed in the next section.

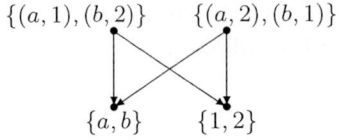

Fig. 2. Part of the poset from the Example 1 illustrating that this poset is not a lattice.

3 Mereological Systems for Direct Products and Relations

For simplicity we restrict our discussion to Direct Products, and next show briefly how the results can be extended to Heterogenious Relations.

Let T be a universal set of indexes and let $\{D_t \mid t \in T\}$ be an appropriate set of domains. We assume also that the set T is *finite*. From the viewpoint of applications in Software Engineering this is not a restriction at all ([1,14]).

For every $I \subseteq T$, let $D_I = \prod_{i \in I} D_i$, where $\prod_{i \in I}$ is a *Direct Product* over I. For example if $I = \{2, 5, 9\}$, then $D_I = \prod_{i \in I} D_i = D_2 \times D_5 \times D_9$. In other words, the set D_I is the set of all functions $f : I \to \bigcup_{i \in I} D_i$ such that $\forall i \in I.\ f(i) \in D_i$. Usually, in particular for concrete cases, such functions are represented as vectors. For instance $f : \{2,5,9\} \to D_2 \cup D_5 \cup D_9$ with $f(2) = a_2$, $f(5) = a_5$, $f(9) = a_9$ is represented as a vector $(a_2, a_5, a_9) \in D_2 \times D_5 \times D_9$. However for theoretical reasoning the functional representation is more convenient. For every function $f : X \to Y$, and every $Z \subseteq X$, the symbol $f|_Z$ will denote the restriction of f to Z. For every function f, $\mathrm{dom}\, f$ will denote the domain of f. We will also assume that $D_i \cap D_j = \emptyset$ if $i \neq j$. This assumption allows us to identify every element of $a \in D_i$ with the function $f_a : \{i\} \to D_i$ where $f_a(i) = a$, which makes the notation more consistent and less ambiguous. We do not lose any generality here, moreover, in practical applications each D_i has a different interpretation anyway (for instance: input current, output current; Amperes in both cases but different meaning).

For every D_I, $I \subseteq T$, let $\mathcal{X}_I = \bigcup_{J \subseteq I} 2^{D_J}$. Also let $\mathcal{E} = \bigcup_{i \in T} \hat{D}_i$. Clearly $\mathcal{E} \subseteq \mathcal{X}_T$. Note also that for every $A \in \mathcal{X}_T$ and for every $f, g \in A$ we have $\mathrm{dom}\, f = \mathrm{dom}\, g$.

For every $A \in \mathcal{X}$, let $\tau(A) \subseteq T$, the *index set* of A, be defined as follows: $I = \tau(A) \iff A \subseteq D_I$. In other words, $f \in A \Rightarrow \mathrm{dom}\, f = \tau(A)$. We assume that $\tau(\emptyset) = \emptyset$. For instance if $A \subseteq D_2 \times D_5 \times D_7$ then $\tau(A) = \{2, 5, 7\}$. For every $A \in \mathcal{X}$ and every $K \subseteq T$, let $A|_K = \{f|_{K \cap \tau(A)} \mid f \in A\}$ if $K \cap \tau(A) \neq \emptyset$, and $A|_K = \emptyset$ if $K \cap \tau(A) = \emptyset$. Clearly $A|_K \subseteq D_{K \cap \tau(A)}$. We will write $A|_i$ instead of $A|_{\{i\}}$ for all $i \in T$.

By a *mereological system for direct products* we mean any mereological system with the domain $(\mathcal{X}_T, \mathcal{E})$. There can be many of them, dependently on the sets Θ and Δ. In this section we show the property of a *potential candidate for the universal mereological system for direct products*.

For every $I \subseteq T$, let $\pi_I : \mathcal{X}_T \to \mathcal{X}_I$, be mapping defined by: $\pi_I(A) = A|_I$. Every such a mapping is called a *projection*.

Define $\Theta_T = \{\cup\} \cup \{\prod_{i \in I} \mid I \subseteq T\}$, $\Delta_T = \{\backslash\} \cup \{\pi_I \mid I \subseteq T\}$, and let $\eta_T : \mathcal{X}_T \to 2^{\mathcal{E}}$ be defined as follows: for every $A \in \mathcal{X}_T$ $\eta_T(A) = \bigcup_{i \in \tau(A)} \hat{A}|_i$. For example: $\eta_T(\{(a,1), (b,2)\}) = \{\{a\}, \{b\}\} \cup \{\{1\}, \{2\}\} = \{\{a\}, \{b\}, \{1\}, \{2\}\}$.

Consider the tuple $(\mathcal{X}_T, \mathcal{E}, \Theta_T, \Delta_T, \eta_T)$. Let $\sqsubseteq_T \subseteq \mathcal{X}_T \times \mathcal{X}_T$ be a relation defined by the condition (4) of the definition of a mereological system.

Lemma 4. 1. $(\mathcal{X}_T, \sqsubseteq_T)$ is a bounded poset with $\top = D_T$, $\bot = \emptyset$.
2. $\forall \mathcal{A} \subseteq \mathcal{X}_T$. $\overline{\text{top}}\,{}^2 \mathcal{A} = \bigcup_{A \in \overline{\text{cmin ub}}\,\mathcal{A}} A$ and $\overline{\text{bot}}\,{}^2 \mathcal{A} = \bigcap_{A \in \overline{\text{cmax lb}}\,\mathcal{A}} A|_J$, where $J = \bigcap_{A \in \overline{\text{cmax lb}}\,\mathcal{A}} \tau(A)$.
3. For every $\mathcal{A} \subseteq_T$, the tuple $((\mathcal{X}_T) \downarrow_{\mathcal{A}}, (\sqsubseteq_T) \downarrow_{\mathcal{A}})$ is a grid of degree $(2,2)$.

Proof. (Sketch of (2), (1) and (3) are rather straightforward) The proof is based on the ideas of the proof of Theorem 4 in [11]. First we prove that $\overline{\text{top}}\,{}^2 \mathcal{A} = \sup \overline{\text{cmin ub}}\,\mathcal{A}$ exists. Let $C \subseteq \overline{\text{ub}}\,\mathcal{A}$ be a chain. We can show that $\inf C$ exists and $\inf C \in \overline{\text{ub}}\,\mathcal{A}$. Hence by (a dual version) of Kuratowski-Zorn Lemma ([17]) we have that $\overline{\min \text{ub}}\,\mathcal{A}$ exists and for every $A \in \overline{\text{ub}}\,\mathcal{A}$ there is $B \in \overline{\min \text{ub}}\,\mathcal{A}$ such that $B \sqsubseteq A$. In other words $\overline{\text{cmin ub}}\,\mathcal{A}$ exists. Next we prove that $\sup \overline{\text{cmin ub}}\,\mathcal{A} = \bigcup_{A \in \overline{\text{cmin ub}}\,\mathcal{A}} A$. Hence $\overline{\text{top}}\,{}^2 \mathcal{A}$ exists and $\overline{\text{top}}\,{}^2 \mathcal{A} = \bigcup_{A \in \overline{\min \text{ub}}\,\mathcal{A}} A$,. For $\overline{\text{bot}}\,{}^2 \mathcal{A}$ we proceed similarly. ∎

From Lemma 4 we can derive the following important result.

Theorem 1. *The 5-tuple $(\mathcal{X}_T, \mathcal{E}, \Theta_T, \Delta_T, \eta_T)$ is a complete and constructive mereological system.* ∎

Proposition 1. 1. For every $I \subseteq T$, $\mathcal{X}_I = \{A \mid A \sqsubseteq_I D_I\}$.
2. For every $A, B \in \mathcal{X}_T$, $A \sqsubseteq_T B \iff \tau(A) \subseteq \tau(B) \land A \subseteq B|_{\tau(A)}$.
3. $\text{atoms}_{\sqsubseteq_T}(\mathcal{X}_T) = \mathcal{E}$. ∎

The formula from Proposition 1(2) was used as a *definition* in [10,11,14].

The fundamental principle behind a successful Tabular Expressions ([9, 15]) specification technique is that most of relations may be described as $R = \bigcirc_{i \in I} R_i$, where $\bigcirc$ is an operation, or composition of operations, each R_i is easy to specify. A variety of operations was introduced and discussed (see [1,10, 11,14,6]). We will not discuss most of them due to lack of space. We will discuss only two operations denoted by $\uplus$ and $\otimes$. We shall show that the operator $\uplus$ corresponds to $\sqcup$, and that $\uplus$ could be defined in terms of more intuitive $\otimes$, where $\otimes$ corresponds to the well known join operator of Codd's relational data-base model [4].

Let $A, B \in \mathcal{X}_T$ and let $K = \tau(A) \cup \tau(B)$, $J = \tau(A) \cap \tau(B)$. We define the operations "$\uplus$", and "$\otimes$ as follows.
$A \uplus B = \{f \mid \text{dom } f = K \land ((f|_{\tau(A)} \in A \land f|_{\tau(B) \setminus \tau(A)} \in B|_{\tau(B) \setminus \tau(A)}) \lor$
$\qquad\qquad\qquad ((f|_{\tau(B)} \in B \land f|_{\tau(A) \setminus \tau(B)} \in A|_{\tau(A) \setminus \tau(B)}))\}$,
$A \otimes B = \{f \mid \text{dom } f = K \land (f|_{\tau(A)} \in A \land f|_{\tau(B)} \in B)\}$.

Let $A \subseteq D|_{\{1,3,5\}}$, $B \subseteq D|_{\{1,2,4\}}$. Then
$A \uplus B = \{(x_1, x_2, x_3, x_4, x_5) \mid ((x_1, x_3, x_5) \in A \land (x_2, x_4) \in B|_{\{2,4\}}) \lor$
$((x_1, x_2, x_4) \in B \land (x_3, x_5) \in A|_{\{3,5\}})\}$,
$A \otimes B = \{(x_1, x_2, x_3, x_4, x_5) \mid (x_1, x_3, x_5) \in A \land (x_1, x_2, x_4) \in B\}$.

Let I be some index set, and let $\mathcal{A} = \{A_i \mid A_i \in \mathcal{P}_\sqsubseteq(D_T) \land i \in I\}$, $K = \bigcup_{i \in I} \tau(A_i)$, $J = \bigcap_{i \in I} \tau(A_i)$. Let $\mathrm{Comp}_i \mathcal{A}$ be the set of all the *components*[3] of K that are NOT contained in A_i.

For example if $I = \{1, 2\}$, $\tau(A_1) \setminus \tau(A_2) \neq \emptyset$ and $\tau(A_2) \setminus \tau(A_1) \neq \emptyset$ then there are three components of K generated by $\tau(A_1)$ and $\tau(A_2)$, namely $\tau(A_1) \cap \tau(A_2)$t, $\tau(A_1) \setminus \tau(A_2)$, and $\tau(A_2) \setminus \tau(A_1)$, so $\mathrm{Comp}_1\{A_1, A_2\} = \{\tau(A_2) \setminus \tau(A_1)\}$, and $\mathrm{Comp}_2\{A_1, A_2\} = \{\tau(A_1) \setminus \tau(A_2)\}$.

We define the operations "$\biguplus_{i \in I}$" as:
$\biguplus_{i \in I} A_i = \{f \mid \mathrm{dom}\, f = K \land \exists i \in I.\ (f|_{\tau(A)} \in A \land \forall C \in \mathrm{Comp}_i \mathcal{A}.\ f|_C \in \bigcup_{j \neq i} A_j|_C)\}$.

Lemma 5 ([11]). $A \uplus B = (A \otimes B|_{\tau(B) \setminus \tau(A)}) \cup (B \otimes A|_{\tau(A) \setminus \tau(B)})$. ∎

We may now formulate the second main result of this section.

Theorem 2. 1. $A \uplus B = A \sqcup B = \overline{\mathrm{top}}^2 \{A, B\}$,
2. $\biguplus_{i \in I} A_i = \bigsqcup_{i \in I} A_i = \overline{\mathrm{top}}^2 \{A_i \mid i \in I\}$

Proof. (Sketch of (1)) The case (1) is a special case of (2) but it is more intuitive one. The proof of (2) is very similar. The idea of the proof is similar to the proof of Theorem 7 in [11]. Let $\mathcal{A} \subseteq \mathcal{X}_T$. It is obviously true if $\tau(A) = \tau(B)$, since in such a case $A \uplus B = A \cup B = \sup\{A, B\} = \overline{\mathrm{top}}^1\{A, B\}$. Assume that $\tau(A) \neq \tau(B)$. Let $f \in A$ and let $\phi \in B$. We define the function $f^\phi : \tau(A) \cup \tau(B) \to \bigcup_{i \in \tau(A) \cup \tau(B)} D_i$ in the following way:

$$f^\phi(i) = \begin{cases} f(i) & \text{if } i \in \tau(A) \\ \phi(i) & \text{if } i \in \tau(B) \setminus \tau(A) \end{cases}$$

For every $\phi \in B$, let $A^\phi = \{f^\phi \mid f \in A\}$. Similarly, for every $g \in B$, and every $\psi \in A$, we define the function $g^\psi : \tau(A) \cup \tau(B) \to \bigcup_{i \in \tau(A) \cup \tau(B)} D_i$ in the following way:

$$g^\psi(i) = \begin{cases} g(i) & \text{if } i \in \tau(B) \\ \psi(i) & \text{if } i \in \tau(A) \setminus \tau(B) \end{cases}$$

For every $\psi \in$, let $B^\psi = \{g^\psi \mid g \in B\}$. Note that $A^\phi \cup B^\psi \subseteq \prod_{i \in \tau(A) \cup \tau(B)} D_i$.

Obviously, every $A^\phi \cup B^\psi \in \overline{\mathrm{ub}}\,(A \uplus B)$. Let $C \in \overline{\mathrm{ub}}\,(A \uplus B)$. If $\tau(C) \neq \tau(A) \cup \tau(B)$, then from the definition of $\sqsubseteq$ we have $\neg(C \sqsubseteq A^\phi \cup B^\psi)$, for all ϕ and ψ. Assume that $\tau(C) = \tau(A) \cup \tau(B)$, and that $C \sqsubseteq A^\phi \cup B^\psi$ for some ϕ and ψ. Since $\tau(C) = \tau(A) \cup \tau(B)$, then this is equivalent to $C \subseteq A^\phi \cup B^\psi$. Let $f \in A^\phi \cup B^\psi$ and $f \notin C$. Assume that $f \in A^\phi$ and $f \notin C$. This means that for every

---
[3] Let X be a set, $X_i \subseteq X$ for all $i \in I$. Define $X_i^0 = X_i$ and $X_i^1 = X \setminus X_i$. A nonempty set $A = \bigcap_{i \in I} X_i^{k_i}$, where $k_i = 0, 1$, is called a *component* of X generated by the sets X_i, $i \in I$. The components are disjoint and cover the entire set X (see [17]).

$g \in C$, there exists $i \in \tau(A) \cup \tau(B)$ such that $g(i) \neq \phi(i)$. But this contradicts the assumption $C \subseteq A^\phi \cup B^\psi$. Similarly if $f \in B^\psi$. Hence $\overline{\min}\ \overline{\text{ub}}\ \{A, B\} = \{A^\phi \cup B^\psi \mid \phi \in B \wedge \psi \in A\}$. It can be proven that $\overline{\min}\ \overline{\text{ub}}\ \{A, B\}$ is complete, so $\overline{\min}\ \overline{\text{ub}}\{A,B\} = \overline{\text{cmin}}\ \overline{\text{ub}}\{A,B\}$. Since $\tau(A^\phi \cup B^\psi) = \tau(A \uplus B) = \tau(A) \cup \tau(B)$, then $\sup \overline{\text{cmin}}\ \text{ub}\,\{A, B\} = \bigcup_{\phi \in B \,\wedge\, \psi \in A}(A^\phi \cup B^\psi)$. But $\bigcup_{\phi \in B \,\wedge\, \psi \in A}(A^\phi \cup B^\psi) = A \uplus B$ just from the definition of "$\uplus$", so we have proven that $A \uplus B = A \sqcup B = \overline{\text{top}}\,^2\{A, B\}$. ∎

Unfortunately, it may happen that $A \uplus (B \uplus C) \neq (A \uplus B) \uplus C$. Consider $T = \{1, 2\}$ and $D_T = \{a, b\} \times \{1, 2\}$ and $A = \{a\}$, $B = \{1\}$ and $C = \{(b, 2)\}$. We have $A \uplus (B \uplus C) = \{a\} \uplus (\{1\} \uplus \{(b, 2)\}) = \{a\} \uplus \{(b,1), (b,2)\} = \{(a, 1), (a, 2), (b, 1), (b, 2)\}$, while $(A \uplus B) \uplus C = (\{a\} \uplus \{1\}) \uplus \{(b, 2)\} = \{(a, 1)\} \uplus \{(b, 2)\} = \{(a, 1), (b, 2)\}$.

We do not have any operational definition of "⊓", in the style of "$\uplus$", and the properties of "⊓" seem to occasionally be counterintuitive. Consider again $D_T = \{a, b\} \times \{1, 2\}$. One may prove that $\{(a,1), (b,1), (b,2)\} \sqcap \{(a,2), (b,1), (b,2)\} = \{b\}$, NOT equal to $\{(b,1), (b,2)\}$, as one might expect.

We now show how the results stated above can be extended to heterogenous relations. Let $T_{\text{left}} \subseteq T$ and $T_{\text{right}} \subseteq T$ be universal set of indexes satisfying $T_{\text{left}} \cap T_{\text{right}} = \emptyset$ and $T_{\text{left}} \cup T_{\text{right}} = T$, where T is our universal and finite set of indexes. Consider the product $D_T = \prod_{i \in T} D_i$. It could also be interpreted as: $D_T = D_{T_{\text{left}}} \times D_{T_{\text{right}}}$. A set $R \sqsubseteq D_T = D_{T_{\text{left}}} \times D_{T_{\text{right}}}$ is called a *relation* iff $\tau(R) \cap T_{\text{left}} \neq \emptyset$ and $\tau(R) \cap T_{\text{right}} \neq \emptyset$. If R is a relation than $R \subseteq D_{\tau(R) \cap T_{\text{left}}} \times D_{\tau(R) \cap T_{\text{right}}}$ which is a standard definition of a relation over product domains ([3, 14]). The set $D_{\tau(R) \cap T_{\text{left}}}$ is a *domain* of R, and the set $D_{\tau(R) \cap T_{\text{right}}}$ is a *co-domain* of R. Define $\mathcal{R}_{T_{\text{right}}}^{T_{\text{left}}} = \{R \mid R \sqsubseteq D_T \wedge \tau(R) \cap T_{\text{left}} \neq \emptyset \wedge \tau(R) \cap T_{\text{right}} \neq \emptyset\} \cup \{\emptyset\}$. It can be proven (more or less in the style of [11]) that all the results that hold for $\mathcal{X}_T$ also hold for $\mathcal{R}_{T_{\text{right}}}^{T_{\text{left}}}$.

Some properties of "$\sqsubseteq$", and "⊗ in the framework of tabular expressions but from the viewpoint of relational and cylindric algebras were analysed in [6,14].

4 Final Comment

The approach presented above could also be applied to the relational database theory as there is a relationship between the operations considered in this paper and considered in [10,11,14] and the cylindric operations for relational databases as defined in [5,8].

In this paper we discussed only one mereological system for direct products (and consequently for heterogenous relations), a potential candidate for being universal. The approach allows us to create a variety of mereological systems, dependently on our needs. A family of possible operations is discussed in [11, 14]. Recently the relation $\sqsubseteq$ from section 4 was applied to define and to detect formality discrepancy between two Requirements Scenarios [16].

References

1. R. Abraham, Evaluating Generalized Tabular Expressions in Software Documentation, CRL Report 346, McMaster University, Hamilton, Ontario, Canada, 1997. Available at http://www.crl.mcmaster.ca/SERG/serg.publications.html
2. T. A. Alspaugh, S. R. Faulk, K. Heninger-Britton, R. A. Parker, D. L. Parnas, J. E. Shore, Software Requirements for the A-7E Aircraft, NRL Memoramdum Report 3876, Naval Research Lab., Washington, DC, 1992.
3. C. Brink, W. Kahl, G. Schmidt (eds.), *Relational Methods in Computer Science*, Springer 1997.
4. E. F. Codd, A relational model of data for large shared data banks, *Comm. of the ACM*, 13 (1970) 377–388.
5. I. Düntsh, S. Mikulás, Cylindric structures and dependencies in data bases, *Theoretical Computer Science*, 269,1,2 (2001), 451–468.
6. J. Desharnais, R. Khédri, A. Mili, Towards a Uniform Relational Semantics for Tabular Expressions, Proc. RELMICS 98, Warsaw 1998.
7. N. Goodman, *The Structure of Appearance*, 3rd edition, D. Reidel, 1977
8. T. Imielinski, W. Lipski, The relational model of data and cylindric algebras, *Journal of Computer and System Sciences*, 28 (1984), 80–102.
9. R. Janicki, Towards a Formal Semantics of Parnas Tables, *17th International Conference on Software Engineering (ICSE'95)*, IEEE Computer Society, Seattle, WA, 1995, 231–240.
10. R. Janicki, On Formal Semantics of Tabular Expressions, CRL Report 355, McMaster University, Hamilton, Ontario, Canada 1997. Available at http://www.crl.mcmaster.ca/SERG/serg.publications.html
11. R. Janicki, Remarks on Mereology of Direct Products and Relations, in J. Desharnais (ed.), *Relational Methods in Computer Science*, Methodos Publ. 2002, to appear, early version at http://www.crl.mcmaster.ca/SERG/serg.publications.html
12. R. Janicki, Y. Zhang, A Simplistic Mereological System for Relations, *Proc. of Int. Workshop on Computational Models of Scientific Reasoning and Applications CMSRA'02*, Las Vegas, USA, 2002.
13. R. Janicki, On a Mereological System for Relational Software Specifications, Proceedings of MFCS'02 (Mathematical Foundations of Computer Science), *Lecture Notes in Computer Science*, to appear.
14. R. Janicki, R. Khédri, On a Formal Semantics of Tabular Expressions, *Science of Computer Programming*, 39 (2001) 189–214.
15. R. Janicki, D. L. Parnas, J. Zucker, Tabular Representations in Relational Documents, in [3].
16. R. Khédri, Requirements Scenarios Formalization Technique: n Versions Towards One Good Version, Proc. of RELMICS'01, Genova 2001.
17. K. Kuratowski, A. Mostowski, *Set Theory*, North Holland, 1976.
18. D. L. Parnas, Tabular representations of relations, CRL Report 260, McMaster University, Hamilton, Ontario, Canada 1992.
19. D. L. Parnas, J. Madey, Functional Documentation for Computer System Egineering, *Science of Computer Programming*, 24, 1 (1995), 41–61.
20. L. Polkowski, On Connection Synthesis via Rough Mereology, *Fundamenta Informaticae*, 46 (2001) 83-96.
21. L. Polkowski, A. Skowron, Rough Mereology; A New Paradigm for Approximate Reasoning, *Journal of Approximate Reasoning*, 15, 4 (1997), 316–333.
22. J. T. J. Strzednicki, V. F. Rickey (eds.), *Leśniewski's Systems*, Kluwer Academic, 1984.

On the Structure of Rough Approximations
(Extended Abstract)

Jouni Järvinen

Turku Centre for Computer Science (TUCS)
Lemminkäisenkatu 14 A, FIN-20520 Turku, Finland
jjarvine@cs.utu.fi

Abstract. We study rough approximations based on indiscernibility relations which are not necessarily reflexive, symmetric or transitive. For this, we define in a lattice-theoretical setting two maps which mimic the rough approximation operators and note that this setting is suitable also for other operators based on binary relations. Properties of the ordered sets of the upper and the lower approximations of the elements of an atomic Boolean lattice are studied.

1 Introduction

The basic ideas of rough set theory introduced by Pawlak [12] deal with situations in which the objects of a certain universe can be identified only within the limits determined by the knowledge represented by a given indiscernibility relation.

Usually indiscernibility relations are supposed to be equivalences. In this work we do not restrict the properties of an indiscernibility relation. Namely, as we will see, it can be argued that neither reflexivity, symmetry nor transitivity are necessary properties of indiscernibility relations.

We start our study by defining formally the upper and the lower approximations determined by an indiscernibility relation $\approx$ on U. For any $x \in U$, we denote

$$[x]_\approx = \{y \in U \mid x \approx y\}.$$

Thus, $[x]_\approx$ consists of the elements which cannot be discerned from x. For any subset X of U, let

(1.1) $\qquad X^\blacktriangledown = \{x \in U \mid [x]_\approx \subseteq X\}$ and
(1.2) $\qquad X^\blacktriangle = \{x \in U \mid X \cap [x]_\approx \neq \emptyset\}$.

The sets $X^\blacktriangledown$ and $X^\blacktriangle$ are called the *lower* and the *upper approximation* of X, respectively. The set $B(X) = X^\blacktriangle - X^\blacktriangledown$ is the *boundary* of X.

The above definitions mean that $x \in X^\blacktriangle$ if there is an element in X to which x is $\approx$-related. Similarly, $x \in X^\blacktriangledown$ if all the elements to which x is $\approx$-related are in X. Furthermore, $x \in B(X)$ if both in X and outside X there are elements to which x is $\approx$-related.

Two sets X and Y are said to be *equivalent*, denoted by $X \equiv Y$, if $X^\blacktriangledown = Y^\blacktriangledown$ and $X^\blacktriangle = Y^\blacktriangle$. The equivalence classes of $\equiv$ are called *rough sets*. It seems that there is no natural representative for a rough set. However, this problem can be easily avoided by using Iwiński's [4] approach to rough sets based on the fact that each rough set S is uniquely determined by the pair $(X^\blacktriangledown, X^\blacktriangle)$, where X is any member of S. Now there is a natural order relation on the set of all rough sets defined by

$$(X^\blacktriangledown, X^\blacktriangle) \leq (Y^\blacktriangledown, Y^\blacktriangle) \iff X^\blacktriangledown \subseteq Y^\blacktriangledown \text{ and } X^\blacktriangle \subseteq Y^\blacktriangle.$$

For an arbitrary binary relation we can give the following definition.

Definition 1. A binary relation $\approx$ on a nonempty set U is said to be

(a) *reflexive*, if $x \approx x$ for all $x \in U$;
(b) *symmetric*, if $x \approx y$ implies $y \approx x$ for all $x, y \in U$;
(c) *transitive*, if $x \approx y$ and $y \approx z$ imply $x \approx z$ for all $x, y, z \in U$;
(d) a *quasi-ordering*, if it is reflexive and transitive;
(e) a *tolerance relation*, if it is reflexive and symmetric;
(f) an *equivalence relation*, if it is reflexive, symmetric, and transitive.

It is commonly assumed that indiscernibility relations are equivalences. However, in the literature one can find studies in which rough approximation operators are determined by tolerances (see e.g. [6]). Note also that Kortelainen [9] has studied so-called compositional modifiers based on quasi-orderings, which are quite similar to operators (1.1) and (1.2).

Next we will argue that there exist indiscernibility relations which are not reflexive, symmetric, or transitive.

Reflexivity. It may seem reasonable to assume that every object is indiscernible from itself. But in some occasions this is not true, since it is possible that our information is so imprecise. For example, we may discern persons by comparing photographs taken of them. But it may happen that we are unable to recognize that a same person appears in two different photographs.

Symmetry. Usually it is supposed that indiscernibility relations are symmetric, which means that if we cannot discern x from y, then we cannot discern y from x either. But indiscernibility relations may be directional. For example, if a person x speaks English and Finnish, and a person y speaks English, Finnish and German, then x cannot discern y from himself by the property "knowledge of languages" since y can communicate with x in any languages that x speaks. On the other hand, y can discern x from himself by asking a simple question in German, for example.

Transitivity. Transitivity is the least obvious of the three properties usually associated with indiscernibility relations. For example, if we define an indiscernibility relation on a set of human beings in such a way that two person are indiscernible with respect to the property "age" if their time of birth differs by less than two hours. Then there may exist three persons x, y, and z, such that x is born an hour before y and y is born $1\frac{1}{2}$ hours before z. Hence, x is indiscernible from y and y is indiscernible from z, but x and z are not indiscernible.

This work is structured as follows. The next section is devoted to basic notations and general conventions concerning ordered sets. In Section 3 we introduce generalizations of lower and upper approximations in a lattice-theoretical setting and study their properties. Note that the proofs of our results and some examples can be found in [7].

2 Preliminaries

We assume that the reader is familiar with the usual lattice-theoretical notation and conventions, which can be found in [1,2], for example.

First we recall some definitions concerning properties of maps. Let $\mathcal{P} = (P, \leq)$ be an ordered set. A map $f \colon P \to P$ is said to be *extensive*, if $x \leq f(x)$ for all $x \in P$. The map f is *order-preserving* if $x \leq y$ implies $f(x) \leq f(y)$. Moreover, f is *idempotent* if $f(f(x)) = f(x)$ for all $x \in P$.

A map $c \colon P \to P$ is said to be a *closure operator* on $\mathcal{P}$, if c is extensive, order-preserving, and idempotent. An element $x \in P$ is *c-closed* if $c(x) = x$. Furthermore, if $i \colon P \to P$ is a closure operator on $\mathcal{P}^{\partial} = (P, \geq)$, then i is an *interior operator* on $\mathcal{P}$.

Let $\mathcal{P} = (P, \leq)$ and $\mathcal{Q} = (Q, \leq)$ be ordered sets. A map $f \colon P \to Q$ is an *order-embedding*, if for any $a, b \in P$, $a \leq b$ in $\mathcal{P}$ if and only if $f(a) \leq f(b)$ in $\mathcal{Q}$. Note that an order-embedding is always an injection. An order-embedding f onto Q is called an *order-isomorphism* between $\mathcal{P}$ and $\mathcal{Q}$. When there exists an order-isomorphism between $\mathcal{P}$ and $\mathcal{Q}$, we say that $\mathcal{P}$ and $\mathcal{Q}$ are *order-isomorphic* and write $\mathcal{P} \cong \mathcal{Q}$. If $(P, \leq)$ and $(Q, \geq)$ are order-isomorphic, then $\mathcal{P}$ and $\mathcal{Q}$ are said to be *dually order-isomorphic*.

Next we define dual Galois connections. It is known [6] that the pair of maps which assigns to every set its upper and lower approximations forms a dual Galois connection when the corresponding indiscernibility relation is symmetric. In the next section we will show that an analogous result holds also in our generalized setting.

Definition 2. Let $\mathcal{P} = (P, \leq)$ be an ordered set. A pair $(\blacktriangleright, \blacktriangleleft)$ of maps $\blacktriangleright \colon P \to P$ and $\blacktriangleleft \colon P \to P$ (which we refer to as the *right map* and the *left map*, respectively) is called a *dual Galois connection* on $\mathcal{P}$ if $\blacktriangleright$ and $\blacktriangleleft$ are order-preserving and $p^{\blacktriangleleft\blacktriangleright} \leq p \leq p^{\blacktriangleright\blacktriangleleft}$ for all $p \in P$.

The following proposition presents some basic properties of dual Galois connections, which follow from the properties of Galois connections (see [2], for example).

Proposition 3. *Let $(\blacktriangleright, \blacktriangleleft)$ be a dual Galois connection on a complete lattice $\mathcal{P}$.*

(a) *For all $p \in P$, $p^{\blacktriangleright\blacktriangleleft\blacktriangleright} = p^{\blacktriangleright}$ and $p^{\blacktriangleleft\blacktriangleright\blacktriangleleft} = p^{\blacktriangleleft}$.*
(b) *The map $c \colon P \to P$, $p \mapsto p^{\blacktriangleright\blacktriangleleft}$ is a closure operator on $\mathcal{P}$ and the map $k \colon P \to P$, $p \mapsto p^{\blacktriangleleft\blacktriangleright}$ is an interior operator on $\mathcal{P}$.*
(c) *If c and k are the mappings defined in (b), then restricted to the sets of c-closed elements P_c and k-closed elements P_k, respectively, $\blacktriangleright$ and $\blacktriangleleft$ yield a pair $\blacktriangleright \colon P_c \to P_k$, $\blacktriangleleft \colon P_k \to P_c$ of mutually inverse order-isomorphisms between the complete lattices $(P_c, \leq)$ and $(P_k, \leq)$.*

Next we introduce the notion of the dual of a map. Recall that Boolean lattices are bounded distributive lattices with a complementation operation.

Definition 4. Let $\mathcal{B} = (B, \leq)$ be a Boolean lattice. Two maps $f \colon B \to B$ and $g \colon B \to B$ are the *duals* of each other if

$$f(x') = g(x)' \text{ and } g(x') = f(x)'$$

for all $x \in B$.

The next lemma shows that the dual of a closure operator is an interior operator (see [11], for example)

Lemma 5. *Let $\mathcal{B} = (B, \leq)$ be a Boolean lattice and let $f\colon B \to B$ be a closure operator on $\mathcal{B}$. If $g\colon B \to B$ is the dual of f, then g is an interior operator on $\mathcal{B}$.*

We end this section by introducing atomic lattices. Let $(P, \leq)$ be an ordered set and $x, y \in P$. We say that *x is covered by y* (or that *y covers x*), and write $x \prec y$, if $x < y$ and there is no element z in P with $x < z < y$.

Definition 6. Let $\mathcal{L} = (L, \leq)$ be a lattice with a least element 0. Then $a \in L$ is called an *atom* if $0 \prec a$. The set of atoms of $\mathcal{L}$ is denoted by $\mathcal{A}(\mathcal{L})$. The lattice $\mathcal{L}$ is *atomic* if every element x of L is the supremum of the atoms below it, that is, $x = \bigvee \{a \in \mathcal{A}(\mathcal{L}) \mid a \leq x\}$.

3 Generalizations of Approximations

In this section we study properties of approximations in a more general setting of complete atomic Boolean lattices. We begin with the following definition.

Definition 7. Let $\mathcal{B} = (B, \leq)$ be a complete atomic Boolean lattice. We say that a map $\varphi \colon \mathcal{A}(\mathcal{B}) \to B$ is

(a) *extensive*, if $x \leq \varphi(x)$ for all $x \in \mathcal{A}(\mathcal{B})$;
(b) *symmetric*, if $x \leq \varphi(y)$ implies $y \leq \varphi(x)$ for all $x, y \in \mathcal{A}(\mathcal{B})$;
(c) *closed*, if $y \leq \varphi(x)$ implies $\varphi(y) \leq \varphi(x)$ for all $x, y \in \mathcal{A}(\mathcal{B})$.

Let $\approx$ be a binary relation on a set U. The ordered set $(\wp(U), \subseteq)$ is a complete atomic Boolean lattice. Since the atoms $\{x\}$ ($x \in U$) of $(\wp(U), \subseteq)$ can be identified with the elements of U, the map
$$(3.1) \qquad \varphi \colon U \to \wp(U), x \mapsto [x]_\approx$$
may be considered to be of the form $\varphi \colon \mathcal{A}(\mathcal{B}) \to B$, where $\mathcal{B} = (B, \leq)$ is $(\wp(U), \subseteq)$. The following observations are obvious:

(a) $\approx$ is reflexive $\iff \varphi$ is extensive;
(b) $\approx$ is symmetric $\iff \varphi$ is symmetric;
(c) $\approx$ is transitive $\iff \varphi$ is closed.

Next we introduce the generalizations of lower and upper approximations.

Definition 8. Let $\mathcal{B} = (B, \leq)$ be a complete atomic Boolean lattice and let $\varphi \colon \mathcal{A}(\mathcal{B}) \to B$ be any map. For any element $x \in B$, let

$$(3.2) \qquad x^{\blacktriangledown} = \bigvee \{a \in \mathcal{A}(\mathcal{B}) \mid \varphi(a) \leq x\},$$

$$(3.3) \qquad x^{\blacktriangle} = \bigvee \{a \in \mathcal{A}(\mathcal{B}) \mid \varphi(a) \wedge x \neq 0\}.$$

The elements $x^{\blacktriangledown}$ and $x^{\blacktriangle}$ are the *lower* and the *upper approximation of x* with respect to φ, respectively. Two elements x and y are *equivalent* if they have the same upper and the same lower approximations. The resulting equivalence classes are called *rough sets*.

It is clear that if φ is a map defined in (3.1), then the functions of Definition 8 coincide with the operators (1.1) and (1.2).

The end of this work is devoted to the study of the operators (3.2) and (3.3) in cases when the map φ is extensive, symmetric, or closed. However, we begin by assuming that φ is arbitrary and present some obvious properties of the maps $^\blacktriangledown\colon B \to B$ and $^\blacktriangle\colon B \to B$.

Lemma 9. *Let $\mathcal{B} = (B, \leq)$ be a complete atomic Boolean lattice and let $\varphi\colon \mathcal{A}(\mathcal{B}) \to B$ be any map.*

(a) $0^\blacktriangle = 0$ *and* $1^\blacktriangledown = 1$;
(b) $x \leq y$ *implies* $x^\blacktriangledown \leq y^\blacktriangledown$ *and* $x^\blacktriangle \leq y^\blacktriangle$.

Note that Lemma 9(b) means that the maps $^\blacktriangledown$ and $^\blacktriangle$ are order-preserving. For all $S \subseteq B$, we denote $S^\blacktriangledown = \{x^\blacktriangledown \mid x \in S\}$ and $S^\blacktriangle = \{x^\blacktriangle \mid x \in S\}$.

Recall that for a semilattice $\mathcal{P} = (P, \circ)$, an equivalence Θ on P is a *congruence* on $\mathcal{P}$ if $x_1 \Theta x_2$ and $y_1 \Theta y_2$ imply $x_1 \circ y_1 \Theta x_2 \circ x_2$, for all $x_1, x_2, y_1, y_2 \in P$.

Proposition 10. *Let $\mathcal{B} = (B, \leq)$ be a complete atomic Boolean lattice and let $\varphi\colon \mathcal{A}(\mathcal{B}) \to B$ be any map.*

(a) *The maps $^\blacktriangle\colon B \to B$ and $^\blacktriangledown\colon B \to B$ are mutually dual.*
(b) *For all $S \subseteq B$, $\bigvee S^\blacktriangle = (\bigvee S)^\blacktriangle$.*
(c) *For all $S \subseteq B$, $\bigwedge S^\blacktriangledown = (\bigwedge S)^\blacktriangledown$.*
(d) *$(B^\blacktriangle, \leq)$ is a complete lattice; 0 is the least element and $1^\blacktriangle$ is the greatest element of $(B^\blacktriangle, \leq)$.*
(e) *$(B^\blacktriangledown, \leq)$ is a complete lattice; $0^\blacktriangledown$ is the least element and 1 is the greatest element of $(B^\blacktriangledown, \leq)$.*
(f) *The kernel $\Theta_\blacktriangledown = \{(x,y) \mid x^\blacktriangledown = y^\blacktriangledown\}$ of the map $^\blacktriangledown\colon B \to B$ is a congruence on the semilattice $(B, \wedge)$ such that the $\Theta_\blacktriangledown$-class of any x has a least element.*
(g) *The kernel $\Theta_\blacktriangle = \{(x,y) \mid x^\blacktriangle = y^\blacktriangle\}$ of the map $^\blacktriangle\colon B \to B$ is a congruence on the semilattice $(B, \vee)$ such that the $\Theta_\blacktriangle$-class of any x has a greatest element.*

Let us denote by $c_\blacktriangle(x)$ the greatest element in the $\Theta_\blacktriangle$-class of any $x \in B$. It is easy to see that the map $x \mapsto c_\blacktriangle(x)$ is a closure operator on $\mathcal{B}$. Similarly, if we denote by $c_\blacktriangledown(x)$ the least element of the $\Theta_\blacktriangledown$-class of x, then the map $x \mapsto c_\blacktriangledown(x)$ is an interior operator on $\mathcal{B}$ (see [5] for details).

Remark 11. In [10] Lemmon introduced the term modal algebra. A structure $(B, \vee, \wedge, ', 0, 1, \mu)$ is a *modal algebra* if

(a) $(B, \vee, \wedge, ', 0, 1)$ is a Boolean algebra and
(b) $\mu\colon B \to B$ is a function such that $\mu(x \vee y) = \mu(x) \vee \mu(y)$ for all $x, y \in B$.

Furthermore, a modal algebra is *normal* if $\mu(0) = 0$. It is clear by Lemma 9 and Proposition 10 that $(B, \vee, \wedge, ', 0, 1, ^\blacktriangle)$ is a normal modal algebra in the sense of [10]. Note also that already in [8] Jónsson and Tarski studied Boolean algebras with normal and "completely additive" operators.

By our next lemma $(B^\blacktriangle, \leq)$ and $(B^\blacktriangledown, \leq)$ are dually order-isomorphic.

Lemma 12. $(B^\blacktriangle, \leq) \cong (B^\blacktriangledown, \geq)$.

Next we study the properties of approximations more closely in cases when the corresponding map $\varphi\colon \mathcal{A}(\mathcal{B}) \to B$ is extensive, symmetric, or closed.

Extensiveness

In this short subsection we study the functions $^{\blacktriangle}\colon B \to B$ and $^{\blacktriangledown}\colon B \to B$ defined by an extensive mapping φ. We show that $(B^{\blacktriangledown}, \leq)$ and $(B^{\blacktriangle}, \leq)$ are bounded by 0 and 1. Furthermore, each element of B is proved to be between its approximations.

Proposition 13. *Let $\mathcal{B} = (B, \leq)$ be a complete atomic Boolean lattice and let $\varphi\colon \mathcal{A}(\mathcal{B}) \to B$ be an extensive map. Then*

(a) $0^{\blacktriangle} = 0^{\blacktriangledown} = 0$ and $1^{\blacktriangle} = 1^{\blacktriangledown} = 1$;
(b) $x^{\blacktriangledown} \leq x \leq x^{\blacktriangle}$ for all $x \in B$.

Symmetry

Here we assume that φ is symmetric. First we show that the pair $(^{\blacktriangle}, ^{\blacktriangledown})$ is a dual Galois connection.

Proposition 14. *Let $\mathcal{B} = (B, \leq)$ be a complete atomic Boolean lattice and let $\varphi\colon \mathcal{A}(\mathcal{B}) \to B$ be a symmetric map. Then $(^{\blacktriangle}, ^{\blacktriangledown})$ is a dual Galois connection on $\mathcal{B}$.*

By the previous proposition, the pair $(^{\blacktriangle}, ^{\blacktriangledown})$ is a dual Galois connection whenever the map φ is symmetric. This means that these maps have the properties of Proposition 3. In particular, the map $x \mapsto x^{\blacktriangle\blacktriangledown}$ is a closure operator and the map $x \mapsto x^{\blacktriangledown\blacktriangle}$ is an interior operator. Let us denote $B_g = \{x^{\blacktriangle\blacktriangledown} \mid x \in B\}$ and $B_l = \{x^{\blacktriangledown\blacktriangle} \mid x \in B\}$

Proposition 15. *Let $\mathcal{B} = (B, \leq)$ be a complete atomic Boolean lattice and let $\varphi\colon \mathcal{A}(\mathcal{B}) \to B$ be a symmetric map. Then*

(a) $a^{\blacktriangle} = \varphi(a)$ for all $a \in \mathcal{A}(\mathcal{B})$;
(b) $x^{\blacktriangle} = \bigvee \{\varphi(a) \mid a \in \mathcal{A}(\mathcal{B}) \text{ and } a \leq x\}$ for every $x \in B$;
(c) $B_g = B^{\blacktriangledown}$ and $B_l = B^{\blacktriangle}$;
(d) $(B^{\blacktriangle}, \leq) \cong (B^{\blacktriangledown}, \leq)$.

We denoted by $c_{\blacktriangle}(x)$ the greatest element in the $\Theta_{\blacktriangle}$-class of x. Similarly, $c_{\blacktriangledown}(x)$ denotes the least element in the x's $\Theta_{\blacktriangledown}$-class. We can now write the following corollary.

Corollary 16. *Let $\mathcal{B} = (B, \leq)$ be a complete atomic Boolean lattice and let $\varphi\colon \mathcal{A}(\mathcal{B}) \to B$ be a symmetric map. Then*

(a) $c_{\blacktriangle}(x) = x^{\blacktriangle\blacktriangledown}$ for all $x \in B$,
(b) $c_{\blacktriangledown}(x) = x^{\blacktriangledown\blacktriangle}$ for all $x \in B$,
(c) $(B^{\blacktriangledown}, \leq)$ is dually isomorphic with itself, and
(d) $(B^{\blacktriangle}, \leq)$ is dually isomorphic with itself.

Note that we have now showed that

$$\{x^{\blacktriangle\blacktriangledown} \mid x \in B\} = \{c_{\blacktriangle}(x) \mid x \in B\} = \{x^{\blacktriangledown} \mid x \in B\}$$

and

$$\{x^{\blacktriangledown\blacktriangle} \mid x \in B\} = \{c_{\blacktriangledown}(x) \mid x \in B\} = \{x^{\blacktriangle} \mid x \in B\}.$$

Closedness

We end this work by studying the case in which φ is closed. First we present the following observation.

Lemma 17. *Let $\mathcal{B} = (B, \leq)$ be a complete atomic Boolean lattice and let $\varphi\colon \mathcal{A}(\mathcal{B}) \to B$ be a closed map. Then for all $x \in B$,*

(a) $x^{\blacktriangle\blacktriangle} \leq x^{\blacktriangle}$;
(b) $x^{\blacktriangledown} \leq x^{\blacktriangledown\blacktriangledown}$.

By Lemmas 9 and 17 and Proposition 13 we can write our next proposition.

Proposition 18. *Let $\mathcal{B} = (B, \leq)$ be a complete atomic Boolean lattice and let $\varphi\colon \mathcal{A}(\mathcal{B}) \to B$ be an extensive and closed map.*

(a) *The map $^{\blacktriangle}\colon B \to B$ is a closure operator.*
(b) *The map $^{\blacktriangledown}\colon B \to B$ is an interior operator.*
(c) *$(B^{\blacktriangledown}, \leq)$ and $(B^{\blacktriangle}, \leq)$ are sublattices of $(B, \leq)$.*

It is known that every sublattice of a distributive lattice is distribute (see [2], for example). Therefore, we can write the following corollary.

Corollary 19. *Let $\mathcal{B} = (B, \leq)$ be a complete atomic Boolean lattice. If $\varphi\colon \mathcal{A}(\mathcal{B}) \to B$ is extensive and closed map, then $(B^{\blacktriangledown}, \leq)$ and $(B^{\blacktriangle}, \leq)$ are distributive.*

Note that it is known that if $\varphi\colon \mathcal{A}(\mathcal{B}) \to B$ is extensive and symmetric, then $(B^{\blacktriangledown}, \leq)$ and $(B^{\blacktriangle}, \leq)$ are not necessarily distributive (see [5] for an example).

Lemma 20. *Let $\mathcal{B} = (B, \leq)$ be a complete atomic Boolean lattice and let $\varphi\colon \mathcal{A}(\mathcal{B}) \to B$ be extensive, symmetric, and closed. Then for all $x \in B$,*

$$x^{\blacktriangledown\blacktriangle} = x^{\blacktriangledown} \text{ and } x^{\blacktriangle\blacktriangledown} = x^{\blacktriangle}.$$

By Lemma 20 it is clear that if $\varphi\colon \mathcal{A}(\mathcal{B}) \to B$ is an extensive, symmetric, and closed map, then $B^{\blacktriangledown} = \{x^{\blacktriangledown} \mid x \in B\}$ equals $B^{\blacktriangle} = \{x^{\blacktriangle} \mid x \in B\}$. For simplicity, let us denote $\mathcal{E} = B^{\blacktriangledown} = B^{\blacktriangle}$.

Proposition 21. *Let $\mathcal{B} = (B, \leq)$ be a complete atomic Boolean lattice and let $\varphi\colon \mathcal{A}(\mathcal{B}) \to B$ be an extensive, symmetric, and closed map. The ordered set $(\mathcal{E}, \leq)$ is a complete atomic Boolean sublattice of $\mathcal{B}$.*

Remark 22. We have proved that if $\varphi\colon \mathcal{A}(\mathcal{B}) \to B$ is extensive, symmetric, and closed, then $(\mathcal{E}, \leq)$ is a complete atomic Boolean sublattice of $\mathcal{B}$. Furthermore, $\{a^{\blacktriangle} \mid a \in \mathcal{A}(\mathcal{B})\}$ is the set of atoms of $(\mathcal{E}, \leq)$.

Now we may present a result similar to Theorem 2 of Gehrke and Walker [3]. We state that the pointwise ordered set of all rough sets $\{(x^{\blacktriangledown}, x^{\blacktriangle}) \mid x \in B\}$ is order-isomorphic to $2^I \times 3^J$, where $I = \{a^{\blacktriangle} \mid a \in \mathcal{A}(\mathcal{B}) \text{ and } \varphi(a) = a\}$ and $J = \{a^{\blacktriangle} \mid a \in \mathcal{A}(\mathcal{B}) \text{ and } \varphi(a) \neq a\}$.

We end this paper with the following result which follows from Proposition 21.

Proposition 23. *Let $\mathcal{B} = (B, \leq)$ be a complete atomic Boolean lattice. If $\varphi\colon \mathcal{A}(\mathcal{B}) \to B$ is symmetric and closed, then $(B^{\blacktriangle}, \leq)$ and $(B^{\blacktriangledown}, \leq)$ are complete atomic Boolean lattices.*

Acknowledgements. Many thanks are due to Magnus Steinby for the careful reading of the manuscript and for his valuable comments and suggestions. An anonymous referee is also gratefully acknowledged for pointing out the connection to modal algebras.

References

1. G. Birkhoff, *Lattice Theory, 3rd ed.*, Colloquium Publications **XXV** (American Mathematical Society, Providence, R. I., 1967).
2. B. A. Davey, H. A. Priestley, *Introduction to Lattices and Order* (Cambridge University Press, Cambridge, 1990).
3. M. Gehrke, E. Walker, On the Structure of Rough Sets, *Bulletin of the Polish Academy of Sciences, Mathematics* **40** (1992) 235–245.
4. T. B. Iwiński, Algebraic Approach to Rough Sets, *Bulletin of the Polish Academy of Sciences, Mathematics* **35** (1987) 673–683.
5. J. Järvinen, *Knowledge Representation and Rough Sets*, TUCS Dissertations **14** (Turku Centre for Computer Science, Turku, 1999).
6. J. Järvinen, Approximations and Rough Sets Based on Tolerances, in: W. Ziarko, Y. Yao (eds.), *Proceedings of The Second International Conference on Rough Sets and Current Trends in Computing (RSCTC 2000)*, Lecture Notes in Artificial Intelligence **2005** (Springer, Berlin, 2001) 182-189.
7. J. Järvinen, On the Structure of Rough Approximations, *TUCS Technical Report* **447** (Turku Centre for Computer Science, Turku, 2002)
   http://www.tucs.fi/Research/Series/techreports/
8. B. Jónsson, A. Tarski, Boolean Algebras with Operators. Part I, *American Journal of Mathematics* **73** (1951) 891–939.
9. J. Kortelainen, *A Topological Approach to Fuzzy Sets*, Ph.D. Dissertation, Lappeenranta University of Technology, Acta Universitatis Lappeenrantaensis **90** (1999).
10. E. J. Lemmon, Algebraic Semantics for Modal Logics. Part I, *Journal of Symbolic Logic* **31** (1966) 46–65.
11. J. C. C. McKinsey, A. Tarski, The Algebra of Topology, *Annals of Mathematics* **45** (1944) 141–191.
12. Z. Pawlak, Rough Sets, *International Journal of Computer and Information Sciences* **5** (1982) 341–356.

Modification of Weights of Conflict Profile's Elements and Dependencies of Attributes in Consensus Model*

Radoslaw Katarzyniak and Ngoc Thanh Nguyen

Wroclaw University of Technology, Poland
katarzyniak@ists.pwr.wroc.pl; thanh@pwr.wroc.pl

Abstract. The consensus model presented in this paper refers to Pawlak's conflict model and serves to determining consensus as the solution of a conflict situation. In this paper we consider two problems. The first of them refers to the modification of the weights of profile's elements in purpose to determine a "good" consensus. The second problem concerns the dependencies of attributes representing the content of conflicts, which cause that one may not treat the attributes independently in consensus determining. We show that using some kind of distance functions may enable to determine mine consensus in the same way when the attributes are independent from each other.

1 Introduction

For a conflict one can distinguish the following three components: *conflict body*, *conflict subject* and *conflict content*. In his model [8] Pawlak proposes to represent a conflict by means of an information table, in which the following components are distinguished: a set of agents (the conflict body); a set of contentious issues (the conflict subject) and a set of tuples (the conflict content) presenting the opinions of the agents on these issues. The agents and issues are related with one another in some social or political contexts. Each agent has 3 possibilities (elementary values) for describing his opinions: (+) – yes, (−) – no and (0) – neutral. Thus a conflict takes place if there exist at least two agents whose opinions referring to an issue are different. Levels of conflicts are considered in work [3].

Consensus models seem to be useful in conflict solving. The oldest consensus model was worked out by such authors as Condorcet, Arrow, Kemeny [1]. This model serves to solve such conflicts in which the content may be represented by orders or rankings. Models of Barthelemy and Janowitz [2] enable to solve such conflicts for which the structures of the conflict contents are n-trees, semilattices, partitions etc. A consensus problem may also be solved by Boolean reasoning [9]. All these consensus models are not suitable for conflicts modeled by Pawlak, because they can include only one-attribute conflicts, while Pawlak's conflicts are multi-attribute.

---

* The authors would like to thank Professor Andrzej Skowron for his helpful remarks.

In works [5],[7] the authors presents a consensus model, in which multi-attribute conflicts may be represented. Furthermore, in this model attributes are multi-valued, what means that for representing an opinion of an agent on some issue one may use not only one elementary value (such as +, −, or 0) but a set of elementary values. Some details of this model are given in Section 2. Section 3 presents the criterion for so called *susceptibility* to consensus for a conflict profile, which should assess if given profile, as the set of opinions of agents on some issue, is susceptible to consensus. In other words, owing to this criterion one should get to know if the agents could achieve a (good) compromise or not. The main subject of this paper is included in sections 4 and 5. In these sections we present some solutions for two problems: The first of them concerns a situation when a conflict profile (whose element weights are equal to 1), is not susceptible to consensus and the way for modifying the weights such that the new profile is susceptible to consensus. The second problem refers to the way for determining consensus in such situations when some attribute representing the conflict content is dependent from another.

2 The Consensus Model

The consensus model has been discussed in detail in work [5], here we present only some its elements needed for further considerations. We assume that some real world is commonly considered by several agents that are placed in different sites of a distributed system. The interest of the agents consists of events which occur (or have to occur) in the world. The task of the agents is based on determining the values of attributes describing the events. If some agents consider the same event then they may generate different descriptions for this event. Thus we say that a conflict takes place. For representing potential conflicts we use a finite set $\boldsymbol{A}$ of attributes and a set $\boldsymbol{V}$ of attribute elementary values, where $\boldsymbol{V} = \bigcup_{a \in A} V_a$ (V_a is the domain of attribute a). Let $\prod(V_a)$ denote the set of subsets of set V_a and $\prod(V_B) = \bigcup_{b \in B} \prod(V_b)$. Let $B \subseteq A$, a tuple r_B of type B is a function $r_B : B \to \prod(V_B)$ where $r_B(b) \subseteq V_b$ for each $b \in B$. Empty tuple is denoted by symbol ϕ. The set of all tuples of type B is denoted by $TYPE(B)$. The consensus system is defined as a triple $Consensus\_Sys = (\boldsymbol{A}, \boldsymbol{X}, \boldsymbol{P})$, where: $\boldsymbol{A}$ is a finite; $\boldsymbol{P}$ is set of attributes, which includes a special attribute $Agent$; values of attribute a are subsets of V_a; values of attribute $Agent$ are singletons which identify the agents; $\boldsymbol{X} = \{\prod(V_a) : a \in \boldsymbol{A}\}$ is a finite set of consensus carriers; $\boldsymbol{P}$ is a finite set of relations on carriers from $\boldsymbol{X}$, each relation $P \in \boldsymbol{P}$ is of some type T_P (for $T_P \subseteq \boldsymbol{A}$ and $Agent \in T_P$). Relations belonging to set $\boldsymbol{P}$ are classified into groups in such way that each of them includes relations representing similar events. For identifying relations belonging to the same group we use symbols "+" and "−" as the upper index to the group name. For example, if R is the name of a group, then relation R^+ is called the positive relation (contains positive knowledge) and R^- is the negative relation (contains negative knowledge).

The structures of the consensus carriers are defined by means of a distance function between tuples of the same type. This function can be defined on the basis of one of distance functions δ^P and ρ^P between sets of elementary values [5]. These functions are defined as follows: Function δ measures the distance between 2 sets X and Y ($X, Y \subseteq V_a$) as the minimal costs of the operation which transforms set X into set Y; the distance measured by function ρ is equal to the sum of shares of elements from V_a in this distance. Functions δ and ρ are called propositional (denoted by δ^P and ρ^P respectively) if the condition $(X \div Y \supseteq X' \div Y') \Rightarrow (\kappa(X,Y) \geq \kappa(X',Y'))$ is satisfied for any $X, X', Y, Y' \subseteq V_a$ and $\kappa \in \{\rho, \delta\}$. The distance $\partial(r, r')$ between 2 tuples r and r' of type A is equal to the number $\frac{1}{card(A)} \sum_{a \in A} \kappa(r_a, r'_a)$ where $\kappa \in \{\rho^P, \delta^P\}$.

A consensus is considered within a conflict situation, which is defined as a pair $\langle \{P^+, P^-\}, A \to B \rangle$ where $A, B \subseteq \mathbf{A}$, $A \cap B = \emptyset$ and $r_A \neq \phi$ holds for any tuple $r \in P^+ \cup P^-$. The first element of a conflict situation (i.e. set of relations $\{P^+, P^-\}$) includes the domain from which consensus should be chosen, and the second element (i.e. relationship $A \to B$) presents the subjects of consensus and the content of consensus, such that for a subject e there should be assigned only one tuple of type B. A conflict situation yields a set $Subject(s)$ of conflict subjects which are represented by tuples of type A. For each subject e two conflict profiles, i.e. $profile(e)^+$ and $profile(e)^-$, as relations of $TYPE(\{Agent\} \cup B)$ should be determined. Profile $profile(e)^+$ contains the positive opinions of the agents on the subject e, while profile $profile(e)^-$ contains agents' negative opinions on this subject.

Definition 1. *Consensus on a subject $e \in Subject(s)$ is a pair $(C(s,e)^+, C(s,e)^-)$ of 2 tuples of type $A \cup B$ which fulfill the following conditions:*

a) $C(s,e)^+_A = C(s,e)^-_A = e$ and $C(s,e)^+_B \cap C(s,e)^-_B = \phi$,
b) *The sums* $\sum_{r \in profile(e)^+} \partial \left(r_B, C(s,e)^+_B \right)$ *and* $\sum_{r \in profile(e)^-} \partial \left(r_B, C(s,e)^-_B \right)$ *are minimal.*

Any tuples $C(s,e)^+$ and $C(s,e)^-$ satisfying the conditions of Definition 1 are called consensuses of profiles $profile(e)^+$ and $profile(e)^-$ respectively.

3 Susceptibility to Consensus

In this section we present a problem referring to susceptibility to consensus for conflict profiles. For given situation $s = \langle \{P^+, P^-\}, A \to B \rangle$ it is often possible to determine consensus. The question is: Is the chosen consensus good enough and can it be acceptable as the solution of given conflict situation? In other words, is the conflict situation susceptible to (good) consensus? We will consider the susceptibility to consensus for conflict profiles. The notion of susceptibility to consensus has been presented and justified among others in work [6]. Below we mention the definition.

Let $X \in \{profile(e)^+_B, profile(e)^-_B\}$ for $e \in Subject(s)$, $U = TYPE(B)$, $card(X) = n$, $\hat{\partial}(X) = \frac{\sum\limits_{x,y \in X} \partial(x,y)}{n(n+1)}$, $\hat{\partial}(x, X) = \frac{\sum\limits_{y \in X} \partial(x,y)}{n}$, $\hat{\partial}_{min}(X) = \min\limits_{x \in U} \hat{\partial}(x, X)$.

Definition 2. *Profile X is susceptible to consensus if $\hat{\partial}(X) \geq \hat{\partial}_{min}(X)$.*

4 Modification of Profile' Elements Weights

If a profile is not susceptible to consensus, the following problem should be generated: How to modify the elements of the profile so that the new profile is susceptible to consensus? We should notice that the interference with the content of the profile elements is rather impossible because of their integrity. We propose to introduce the weights of these elements, which represent the degrees (or participation) of the profile elements in the determination of consensus. This approach may be useful in such practical applications, in which agents may not achieve the compromise (consensus) because of too large differences of their opinions on some subject. In such cases one of the possible solutions is relied on assigning the agents their priorities which can be represented by the weights. By modification of the priorities one may determine a profile susceptible to consensus, that is the agents can now achieve the compromise. Such approach can find applications, for example in reconciling inconsistency of agent knowledge states [4], or creating intelligent user interfaces [11].

We assume that the profile elements represent the opinions of the conflict participants; each of these opinions belongs to one participant and each participant can give only one opinion. We assume a weight function which for each participant assigns a real number belonging to interval $[0, 1]$. Thus we have the function $f : X \to [0, 1]$. Let us consider the following consensus choice postulate O_1^f, in which the weight function is taken into account:

$$(x \text{ is a consensus for } X) \Rightarrow \left(\sum_{y \in X} f(y)\delta(x, y) = \min_{z \in U} f(y)\delta(z, y) \right).$$

A consensus function which satisfies the above postulate is for example the function c_1^f defined as follows:

$$c_1^f(X) = \left\{ x \in U : \sum_{y \in X} f(y)\delta(x, y) = \min_{z \in U} \sum_{y \in X} f(y)\delta(z, y) \right\},$$

which is the modification of Kemeny function known in consensus theory. The values evaluating the susceptibility to consensus are defined as follows:

$$\hat{\delta}(X) = \frac{\sum_{x,y \in X} \delta(x,y)f(y)}{k(k+1)}, \hat{\delta}_x(X) = \frac{\sum_{y \in X} \delta(x,y)f(y)}{k} \text{ and } \hat{\delta}_{min}(X) = \min_{x \in U} \hat{\delta}_x(X).$$

Let us consider the following problem: *Assume that profile X is not susceptible to consensus in the sense of function c_1, how to construct function f such that profile X is susceptible to consensus in the sense of function c_1^f?*

A simple answer for the above question may be the following: $f(x) = 0$ for any $x \in X$, because the equality $\hat{\delta}(X) = \hat{\delta}_{min}(X) = 0$ should follow. Unfortunately, this answer is not satisfactory, because in this case each element of U may be a consensus. We are interested in the minimal modification of function f (at the beginning, $f(x) = 1$ for any $x \in X$) to achieve the susceptibility of profile X, that is to achieve the inequality $\hat{\delta}(X) \geq \hat{\delta}_{min}(X)$. The following theorem presents the possibility of weight modification for achieving consensus susceptibility [7].

Theorem 1. *If profile X is not susceptible to consensus for the weights equal to 1, then there always exists a weight function f such that $f(x) > 0$ for any $x \in X$, for which profile X is susceptible to consensus using function c_1^f.*

We present now an algorithm, which for a profile unsusceptible to consensus modifies minimally the values of function f (at the beginning they are equal to 1) so that X becomes susceptible to consensus in the sense of function c_1^f.

The idea of this algorithm relies on the following steps: at the first, we count the consensus according to function c_1, next we determine sets X' and X'' on the basis of the proof of *Theorem 1*. Having these sets we can minimally modify the values of function f, so that the inequality $\hat{\delta}(X) \geq \hat{\delta}_{min}(X)$ takes place.

Algorithm 1. Modification of function f.
Input: Profile X unsusceptible to consensus in the sense of function c_1 and $card(X) = k$.
Result: New values of function f, for which profile is susceptible to consensus.
BEGIN

1. Calculate $z \in U$ such that $\sum_{y \in X} \delta(z, y) = \min_{x \in U} \sum_{y \in X} \delta(x, y)$.
2. Divide set X into disjoined sets X' and X'' for each $y' \in X'$ and $y'' \in X''$ the inequalities $\alpha(y') - \delta(z, y') \leq 0$ and $\alpha(y'') - \delta(z, y'') > 0$ follow respectively, where $\alpha(y) = \frac{\sum_{x \in X} \delta(x,y)}{k+1}$.
3. For $y \in X'$ set $f(y)$ such that $f(y) > 0$ and the following inequality becomes true $\sum_{y \in X''} [\alpha(y) - \delta(z, y)] \geq \sum_{y \in X'} f(y) [\alpha(y) - \delta(z, y)]$.
4. For $y \in X''$ set $f(y) = 1$.

END.

5 Dependencies of Attributes in Determining Consensus

In *Definition 1* the most important is condition *b)* which requires the tuples $C(s,e)_B^+$ and $C(s,e)_B^-$ to be determined in such way thus the sums

$$\sum_{r \in profile(e)^+} \partial(r_B, C(s,e)_B^+) \quad \text{and} \quad \sum_{r \in profile(e)^-} \partial(r_B, C(s,e)_B^-)$$

are minimal respectively. These tuples can be calculated in the following way: For each attribute $b \in B$ one can determine sets $C(s,e)_b^+$ and $C(s,e)_b^-$, which minimize sums

$$\sum_{r \in profile(e)^+} \partial(r_b, C(s,e)_b^+) \quad \text{and} \quad \sum_{r \in profile(e)^-} \partial(r_b, C(s,e)_b^-)$$

respectively. Such way is an effective one, but it is correct only if the attributes from set B are independent. In this section we consider consensus choice assuming that some attributes from set B are dependent. The definition of attribute dependence given below is consistent with those given in the information system model [10]:

Definition 3. *Attribute b is dependent from attribute a if and only if there exists a function $f_b^a : V_a \to V_b$ such that in any consensus system (A, X, P) for each relation $P \in \mathbf{P}$ of type T_P and $a, b \in T_P$ the formula $(\forall r \in P)\left(r_b = \bigcup_{x \in r_a} \{f_b^a(x)\}\right)$ is true.*

The dependency of attribute b from attribute a means that in the real word if for some object the value of a is known then the value of b is also known. Instead of $\bigcup_{x \in Y} \{f_b^a(x)\}$ we will write $f_b^a(Y)$.

Consider now a conflict situation $s = \langle \{P^+, P^-\}, A \to B\rangle$, in which attribute b is dependent from attribute a where $a, b \in B$. Let $profile(e)^+$ be the positive profile for given conflict subject $e \in Subject(s)$. The problem relies on determining consensus for this profile. We can solve this problem using two approaches:

1. Notice that $profile(e)^+$ is a relation of type $B \cup \{Agent\}$. The dependency of attribute b from attribute a implies that there exists a function from set $TYPE(B \cup \{Agent\})$ to set $TYPE(B \cup \{Agent\}\setminus\{b\})$ such that for each profile $profile(e)^+$ one can assign exactly one set $profile'(e)^+ = \{r_{B \cup \{Agent\}\setminus\{b\}} : r \in profile(e)^+\}$.
   Set $profile'(e)^+$ can be treated as a profile for subject e in the following conflict situation $s' = \langle \{P^+, P^-\}, A \to B\setminus\{b\}\rangle$.
   Notice that the difference between profiles $profile(e)^+$ and $profile'(e)^+$ relies only on the lack of attribute b and its values in profile $profile(e)^+$. Thus one can expect that the consensus $C(s, e)^+$ for profile $profile(e)^+$ can be determined from the consensus $C(s, e)'^+$ for profile $profile(e)'^+$ after adding to tuple $C(s, e)'^+$ attribute b and its value which is equal to $f_b^a(C(s, e)_a'^+)$. In the similar way one can determine the consensus for profile $profile(e)^-$.
2. In the second approach attributes a and b are treated equivalently. That means they take the same partition in consensus determining for profiles $profile(e)^+$ and $profile(e)^-$.

The consensus for profiles $profile(e)^+$ and $profile(e)^-$ are defined as follows:

Definition 4. *The consensus for subject $e \in Subject(s)$ in situation $s = \langle \{P^+, P^-\}, A \to B\rangle$ is a pair of tuples $(C(s, e)^+, C(s, e)^-)$ of type $A \cup B$, which satisfy the following conditions:*

a) $C(s, e)_A^+ = C(s, e)_A^- = e$ and $C(s, e)_B^+ \cap C(s, e)_B^- = \phi$,
b) $C(s, e)_b^+ = f_b^a(C(s, e)_a^+)$ and $C(s, e)_b^- = f_b^a(C(s, e)_a^-)$,
c) The sums $\sum_{r \in profile(e)^+} \partial(r_B, C(s, e)_B^+)$ and $\sum_{r \in profile(e)^-} \partial(r_B, C(s, e)_B^-)$ are minimal.

We are interested in these cases when conditions *b)* and *c)* of *Definition 4* can be satisfied simultaneously. The question is: Is it true that if set $C(s,e)_a^+$ is a consensus for profile $profile(e)_a^+$ (as the projection of profile $profile(e)^+$ on attribute a) then set $f_b^a(C(s,e)_a^+)$ will be a consensus for profile $profile(e)_b^+$ (as the projection of profile $profile(e)^+$ on attribute)? It is possible to prove the following theorem [7]:

Theorem 2. *With using distance function ρ^P or δ^P if a set $C(s,e)_a^+$ is a consensus for profile $profile(e)_a^+$ then there exists a set $C(s,e)_b^+$ being a consensus for profile $profile(e)_b^+$ such that $f_b^a(C(s,e)_a^+) \subseteq C(s,e)_b^+$.*

A similar theorem may be formulated and proved for consensuses of profiles $profile_a^-$ and $profile(e)_b^-$.

Example 1. Let profiles $profile(e)_a^+$ and $profile(e)_b^+$ and function f be the following:

$profile(e)_a^+$	$profile(e)_b^+$
a_1, a_3	b_2
a_2, a_3	b_1, b_2
a_1, a_4	b_1, b_2
a_1, a_4, a_5	b_1, b_2

Function $f_b^a : V_a \to V_b$	
a_1	b_2
a_2	b_1
a_3	b_2
a_4	b_1
a_5	b_1

The consensus for profile $profile(e)_a^+$ is the set $\{a_1, a_3\}$ and the consensus for profile $profile(e)_b^+$ is the set $\{b_1, b_2\}$. Notice that $f_b^a(\{a_1, a_3\}) = \{b_2\} \subseteq \{b_1, b_2\}$.

The following example shows that using other distance functions than ρ^P and δ^P can cause the inconsistency of consensuses for $profile(e)_a^+$ and $profile(e)_b^+$ in the sense that if an element x belongs to the consensus of $profile(e)_a^+$ then $f_b^a(x)$ does not have to belong to the consensus of $profile(e)_b^+$.

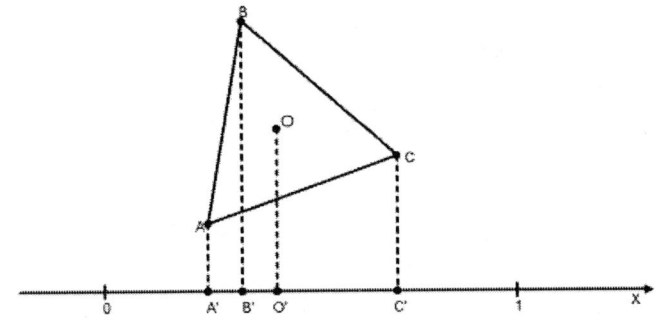

Fig. 1. Profile $profile(e)_a^+$ and function f_b^a

Example 2. Let profile $profile(e)_a^+$ consist of 3 points (A,B and C) on the plane creating an equilateral triangle (*see Figure 1*). The location of this triangle is such that any of its sides is not parallel to axis X. The function f_b^a assigns for each point of the triangle a point on axis X being its projection on X. These points (A', B' and C') create profile $profile(e)_b^+$.

Let the distances between these points be measured by the Euclidean distance function. It is easy to note that the consensus of profile $profile(e)_a^+$ is the center of gravity of triangle ABC, while the consensus of profile $profile(e)_b^+$ is point B', but not point $f_b^a(O)$, i.e. O'.

6 Conclusions

In this work we present solution of two problems arising in the consensus model, which refer to the modification of profile' elements weights for achieving the susceptibility to consensus and the influence of attribute dependencies on consensus calculation. The future works should concern working out of algorithms for determining consensus for conflict profiles with attribute dependencies, and investigation of the influence of other kinds of distance functions on consensus.

References

1. Arrow, K.J.: Social Choice and Individual Values. Wiley New York (1963)
2. Barthelemy, J.P., Janowitz, M.F.: A Formal Theory of Consensus. SIAM J. Discrete Math. **4** (1991) 305–322
3. Deja, R., Slezak, S.: Rough Set Theory in Conflict Analysis. Bulletin of International Rough Set Society 5 (1/2) (2001) 225–230
4. Katarzyniak, K., Nguyen, N.T.:Reconciling Inconsistent Profiles of Agents' Knowledge States in Distributed Multiagent Systems Using Consensus Methods. System Science **26** (2001) 93-119
5. Nguyen, N.T.: Consensus System for Solving Conflicts in Distributed Systems. To appear in Information Sciences – An International Journal
6. Nguyen, N.T.: Conflict Profiles' Susceptibility to Consensus in Consensus Systems. Bulletin of International Rough Set Society 5 (1/2) (2001) 217–224
7. Nguyen, N.T.: Methods for Consensus Choice and their Applications in Conflict Resolving in Distributed Systems. Wroclaw University of Technology Press (2002), (in Polish)
8. Pawlak, Z.: An Inquiry into Anatomy of Conflicts. Information Sciences **108** (1998) 65–78
9. Pawlak, Z., Skowron, A.: A Rough Set Approach to Decision Rules Generation. Reports of Institute of Computer Science, Warsaw University of Technology (1993)
10. Skowron, A., Rauszer, C.: The Discernibility Matrices and Functions in Information Sytems. In: E. Słowiński (ed.): Intelligent Decision Support, Handbook of Applications and Advances of the Rough Sets Theory, Kluwer Academic Publishers (1992) 331–362
11. Sobecki, J.: One Suits All - Is It Possible to Build a Single Interface Appropriate for All Users? In: Proc. of the 23rd Int. Sci. School ISAT. PWr Press Wroclaw (2001) 125–131

Reasoning about Information Granules Based on Rough Logic

Qing Liu and S.L. Jiang

Department of Computer Science
NanChang University, NanChang 330029, China

Abstract This paper presents an approach to reasoning about information granules based on a form of rough logic with formulas and constructed granules that are interpreted in the context of rough set theory. Rough logic is defined over a given information system IS=(U,A). The propositions (or predicates) of this logic are logical formulas defined by attributes in IS. The semantics of such propositions is defined in the context of subsets of the universe U.

Keywords. Granular computing, information granules, rough logic, rough sets

1 Introduction

This paper presents an approach to reasoning about granules of information using rough logic defined over a given information system IS=(U,A) and rough set theory [2,3,4,5,6,7]. Based on rough set approach [2,3,7], a logical formula can be transformed into what is known as a granule-formula (or G-formula). The truth-value of a G-formula can be a value in [0, 1], and, hence, has the flavor of the multivalued logic introduced by Łukasiewicz [8]. The contribution of this paper is the introduction to an approach to reasoning about information granules based on what is known as rough logic.

2 Rough Logic

Based on the results from [1,2,3,4], let RL_{IS} denote a logic defined in the context of an information system IS=(U,A). The logic is considered rough because it is defined in the context of rough set theory [2].

2.1 Syntax

S1 Let Ξ, Ω denote constant atomic (indecomposable) formulas [2] and let (Ξ, $\varnothing$), (Ω, U) denote "elementary" granules called G-atoms, where $\varnothing$ and U denote the empty set and universe, respectively. A G-atom gives the meaning or explanation of a constant atomic formula.

Remark. Ξ and Ω are interpreted to be false or closeness false and true or closeness true, respectively. Because there is possibility of an atomic formula denoting a rough (or closeness) value, so Ξ and Ω can assume the values $\bot$ (false) and T (true) from classical logic as well as rough values. A more detailed explanation of this idea is given in [2]. Let $\bot_R$, T_R denote closeness $\bot$ (e.g., $\bot_R$ equal to a truth value in (0, 1), where 0 denotes $\bot$ and 1 denotes T) and closeness true.

S2. Let $R_B(x,y) \in RL_{IS}$ denote predicate written relative to a binary relation on elements $x,y \in X \subseteq U$ and attribute subset $B \subseteq A$ on IS. Let $m(R)$ denote the meaning of R. Then formulate a G-atom by writing $(R, m(R))$.

Remark. Let Ind_B denote the indiscernibility relation from rough set theory and let $B \subseteq A$ in IS=(U,A). Then many possible G-atoms can be constructed. For example, if B={a}, then $m(Ind_B) = \{(x,y) \in U \times U \mid a(x)=a(y)=v \in V_a\}$, where V_a is a set of values of attribute $a \in A$, and $(Ind_B, m(Ind_B))$ is a G-atom. If, for example again, B={a,b}, then $m(R)=\{(x,y) \in U \times U \mid a(x)=a(y)=v_1 \in V_a \wedge b(x)=b(y)=v_2 \in V_b\}$.

S3. Let a_v be an atomic formula that denotes the value $v \in V_a$ of attribute $a \in A$. Then formulate the G-atom $(a_v, m(a_v))$, where $m(a_v)$ specifies the meaning of a_v.

S4. Let φ, ψ denote formulas in RL_{IS}. Let $L \bullet$ denote the lower approximation of formula $\bullet$ in the sense that $L \bullet$ expresses certain knowledge about $\bullet$. Then formulate a granule-formula (G-formula) by writing $(\varphi, m(\varphi))$, $(\sim\varphi, m(\sim\varphi))$, $(\varphi \vee \psi, m((\varphi \vee \psi))$, $(\varphi \wedge \psi, m(\varphi \wedge \psi))$, $((\forall x)(\varphi(x)), m(((\forall x)(\varphi(x))))$, $(L\varphi, m(L\varphi))$ using the boolean operators $\vee$ (or), $\wedge$ (and) and quantification $\forall$ (all) as well as approximation operator L.

Remark. Let $m(\varphi)$ denote a set of such objects in the universe U that satisfy formula φ in RL_{IS}. Let $\mid\approx$ denote *roughly satisfies*. That is, $m(\varphi)=\{x \in U \mid x \mid\approx \varphi\}$. Further, $m(L\varphi)$ may be written as $L(m(\varphi))$ to denote the lower approximation of $m(\varphi)$. The semantics of $L\varphi$ is also defined in [2].

2.2 Axioms and Rules

Let $\mid\sim$ denote rough derivability relation in the sense that the truth value of a roughly derivable formula is in the interval [0,1]. The symbol $\mid\sim$ is used instead of the usual $\mid\!-$ from classical logic derivations of formulas in rough logic, which are interpreted in both logic and rough set theory. Let $\mid\sim A$, $\mid\sim \varphi \rightarrow \psi$ denote that formula A is roughly derivable and φ implies ψ, respectively. The formula $(\bullet) \subseteq (\bullet')$ represents the fact that knowledge expressed by $(\bullet)$ is in some sense included in $(\bullet')$. For example, if the structure of the G-formula $(\varphi, m(\varphi))$ satisfies $(\varphi, m(\varphi)) \subseteq (\psi, m(\psi))$, it signifies that $\varphi \rightarrow \psi$ is derivable (or roughly derivable), namely $\varphi \rightarrow \psi$ is true or roughly (close to) true and the truth-value set of $(\varphi, m(\varphi))$ is included in $(\psi, m(\psi))$, which is also derivable (or roughly derivable).

GA1 There is a G-axiom for each axiom in the calculus of classical logic.
GA2 If $\mid\sim L(\varphi \rightarrow \psi) \rightarrow (L\varphi \rightarrow L\psi)$ is an axiom in RL_{IS}, then
$\mid\sim L(\varphi, m(\varphi)) \subseteq L(\psi, m(\psi)) \rightarrow (L\varphi, m(L\varphi)) \subseteq (L\varphi, m(L\varphi))$ is a G-axiom.

Remark. In this paper, notation $L \bullet$ is used to denote operation on a formula, whereas $L(\bullet)$ denotes operation on a set. A detailed explanation of this idea is given in [2].
GA3 If $\mid\!- L\varphi \rightarrow \varphi$ is an axiom in RL_{IS}, then $\mid\sim L(\varphi, m(\varphi)) \subseteq (\varphi, m(\varphi))$ is a G-axiom.

2.3 Notation

Let $(\bullet)$, $(\bullet')$ denote G-formulas, represented by $(\bullet_F, m(\bullet_F))$ and $(\bullet'_F, m(\bullet'_F))$. Formula $(\bullet) \cap (\bullet')$ should express that some portion of knowledge related to $(\bullet)$ is in some sense in common with knowledge related to $(\bullet')$. Formula $(\bullet) \cup (\bullet')$ should express knowledge related to $(\bullet)$, $(\bullet')$ or both $(\bullet)$ and $(\bullet')$.

Remark. Let $(\bullet)$ and $(\bullet')$ denote G-formulas, represented as above. Then one can consider the following operators:

$$(\bullet) \otimes (\bullet') = (\bullet_F \wedge \bullet'_F, m(\bullet_F) \cap m(\bullet'_F))$$
$$(\bullet) \oplus (\bullet') = (\bullet_F \vee \bullet'_F, m(\bullet_F) \cup m(\bullet'_F))$$

2.4 Semantics

Semantics of a formula from RL_{IS} is defined by means of notions of a model and joint valuation. Hence satisfiability of a G-formula is corresponded with the meaning set of the formula being non-empty. If the domain of a formula in the logic is undefinable, then satisfiability of the formula can be analyzed by the rough lower and upper approximations. Let the model of satisfiability of a formula $\varphi \in RL_{IS}$ be a five tuple M = (U, A, T_{IruR}, m, R), where U is a set of entities; A is a set of attributes; T_{IruR} is a symbol of joint valuation; m and R are defined as before [1,7].

3 Granules and Granular Computing

G-formulas $(\varphi, m(\varphi))$ are logical combinations of G-atoms. If $m(\varphi) = \emptyset$, then φ evaluates to false in IS. If $m(\varphi) = U$, then φ evaluates to true in IS. In addition, if $\emptyset \subset m(\varphi) \subseteq U$, then φ is thought to be satisfiable in IS.

Let $T_{IruR}(\varphi) = Card(m(\varphi))/Card(U)$ denote rough interpretation of formula φ, i.e. degree, to which φ is in some sense close to the universe of IS [7]. If $T_{IruR}(\varphi) \in (0.5, 1)$, then φ is said to be roughly true in IS. If $T_{IruR}(\varphi) \in (0, 0.5)$, then φ is said to be roughly false in IS. If $T_{IruR}(\varphi) = 0.5$, then φ is said to be undecidable in IS.

For any $\varphi \in RL_{IS}$ and $B \subseteq A$, $(B_*\varphi, B_*(m(\varphi)))$ and $(B^*\varphi, B^*(m(\varphi)))$ are called lower and upper approximation of G-formula $(\varphi, m(\varphi))$, respectively. The following lists the granular computing corresponding with rough logical formula $\varphi \in RL_{IS}$.

Proposition 3.1. Let $\varphi, \psi \in RL_{IS}$. We can write:

1. $(\sim\varphi, m(\sim\varphi)) = (\sim\varphi, U - m(\varphi))$
2. $(\varphi \vee \psi, m(\varphi \vee \psi)) = (\varphi, m(\varphi)) \cup (\psi, m(\psi))$
3. $(\varphi \wedge \psi, m(\varphi \wedge \psi)) = (\varphi, m(\varphi)) \cap (\psi, m(\psi))$
4. $((\forall x)\varphi(x), m(\varphi)) = (\varphi(e_1) \wedge \ldots \wedge \varphi(e_n), m(\varphi(e_1) \wedge \ldots \wedge \varphi(e_n))) =$
   $(\varphi(e_1), m(\varphi)) \cap \ldots \cap (\varphi(e_n), m(\varphi))$
5. $(L\varphi, m(L\varphi)) = (L\varphi, L(m(\varphi)))$ with respect to $m(\varphi)$

Proposition 3.2. Let $\varphi, \psi \in RL_{IS}$. Then:

$$\mid\sim (\varphi, m(\varphi)) \to (\psi, m(\psi)) \text{ iff } \mid\sim \varphi \to \psi \text{ and } \mid\sim m(\varphi) \subseteq m(\psi)$$

4 Logical Reasoning Based on Granular Computing

This section briefly introduces a framework for logical reasoning based on granular computing. The set theoretical operations $-$, $\cup$ and $\cap$ on semantic parts of G-formulas correspond to the operations on φ defined by propositional connectives $\sim$, $\vee$ and $\wedge$ in logic. Let $|\approx_{IS} \varphi$ denote that φ is satisfied relative to IS.

Definition 4.1. Let $\varphi, \psi \in RL_{IS}$. The logical operations on φ, ψ with respect to $\sim$, $\vee$ and $\wedge$ are defined by the set operations on $(\varphi, m(\varphi))$ and $(\psi, m(\psi))$ with respect to $-$, $\cup$ and $\cap$, respectively.

1. $|\approx_{IS} \sim\varphi$ iff $|\approx_{IS} (U - (\varphi, m(\varphi))) \neq \emptyset$
2. $|\approx_{IS} \varphi \vee \psi$ iff $|\approx_{IS} ((\varphi, m(\varphi)) \cup (\psi, m(\psi))) \neq \emptyset$
3. $|\approx_{IS} \varphi \wedge \psi$ iff $|\approx_{IS} ((\varphi, m(\varphi)) \cap (\psi, m(\psi))) \neq \emptyset$

Definition 4.2. Let $\varphi \in RL_{IS}$. We call $(\varphi, m(\varphi))$ a ground G-formula, if there is not free individual variable in φ.

Theorem 4.1. G-formula $(\varphi, m(\varphi))$ corresponding to any $\varphi \in RL_{IS}$ can be transformed to the equivalent G-clause form $(C_1, m(C_1)) \cap ... \cap (C_n, m(C_n))$, where each $(C_i, m(C_i))$ is an elementary granule of the form $(a_v, m(a_v))$, $(a_v, B_*(a_v))$, $(a_v, B^*(a_v))$ or its complement or a union of such granules.

Definition 4.3. Let C_1 and C_2 be two ground G-clauses called granules, where

C_1: $(C_1', m(C_1')) \cup (a_v, m(a_v))$
C_2: $(C_2', m(C_2')) \cup (b_w, m(b_w))$
$m(a_v)$ is complementary to $m(b_w)$

Then the resolvent of C_1 and C_2, denoted by $GR(C_1, C_2)$, is defined as follows:

C_1: $(C_1', m(C_1')) \cup (a_v, m(a_v))$
C_2: $(C_2', m(C_2')) \cup (b_w, m(b_w))$
C: $(C_1', m(C_1')) \cup (C_2', m(C_2'))$

Remark. The above can be also extended onto roughly complementary granules, as well as their lower and upper approximations.

Example 4.1 Let IS=(U,A) be an information system as the following table shows:

U	A	A	B	C	d	e
1		5	4	0	1	0
2		3	4	0	2	1
3		3	4	0	2	2
4		0	2	0	1	2
5		3	2	1	2	2
6		5	2	1	1	0

One can construct a system of rough logic from the table (see [1,2,3,4]), using RL_{IS} language. Let us consider formula (1) from RL_{IS}

$$\varphi(a_5, b_2, b_4, c_0, \sim e_0) = (a_5 \vee b_4) \wedge b_2 \wedge (c_0 \vee \sim e_0) \qquad (1)$$

which can be rewritten as shown in (2)

$G\text{-}\varphi(a_5, b_2, b_4, c_0, \sim e_0) =$

$$((a_5, m(a_5)) \cup (b_4, m(b_4))) \cap (b_2, m(b_2)) \cap ((c_0, m(c_0)) \cup (\sim e_0, m(\sim e_0))) \quad (2)$$

From Theorem 4.1 (2) is in G-clause form, where each intersection item is a G-clause. The ground G-clause form of G-φ is given in (3).

G-$\varphi(a_5, b_2, b_4, c_0, \sim e_0)$ =

$$((a_5,\{1,6\}) \cup (b_4,\{1,2,3\})) \cap (b_2,\{4,5,6\}) \cap ((c_0,\{1,2,3,4\}) \cup (\sim e_0,\{2,3,4,5\})) \quad (3)$$

where each intersection item is a ground G-clause. $(a_5,\{1,6\})$ and $(\sim e_0,\{2,3,4,5\})$ is a complement ground literal pair [1,7]. So, the resolvent of C_1: $(a_5,\{1,6\}) \cup (b_4,\{1,2,3\})$ and C_2: $(c_0,\{1,2,3,4\}) \cup (\sim e_0,\{2,3,4,5\})$, GR($C_1,C_2$) make it possible to write

C_1: $(a_5,\{1,6\}) \cup (b_4,\{1,2,3\})$

$\underline{C_2: (c_0,\{1,2,3,4\}) \cup (\sim e_0,\{2,3,4,5\})}$

C: $(b_4,\{1,2,3\}) \cup (c_0,\{1,2,3,4\})$

Hence, from (3), we have $((b_4,\{1,2,3\}) \cup (c_0,\{1,2,3,4\})) \cap (b_2,\{4,5,6\})$.

Theorem 2 Let Δ be a set of G-clauses. If there is a deduction of G-resolution of G-clause C from Δ, then Δ logically implies C.

5 Conclusion

In the paper, an approach to reasoning about information granules using a form of rough logic. Granules of information are viewed in the context of information systems and rough set theory. Rough logic makes it possible to construct structures that facilitate reasoning about granules of information where there is some uncertainty concerning the truth or falsity of assertions about these granules.

This logic is also called a granular logic, because a combination of general logical connectives and rough set theory can be used in G-formulas. Further research will cover the soundness theorem and the completeness theorem of G-resolution (by refutation), and the approximate reasoning based on granular computing.

Acknowledgements. This study is supported by the State Natural Science Fund (#60173054).

References

1. Q. Liu, The OI-Resolution of Operator Rough Logic, LNAI 1424, Springer, June 22-26, 1998, 432–435.
2. T.Y. Lin, Q. Liu, First-Order Rough Logic I: Approximate Reasoning via Rough Sets, Fundamenta Informaticae, Vol.27, No.2-3, Aug.1996, 137–154.
3. Q. Liu, S.H. Liu, F. Zheng, Rough Logic and Its Applications in Data Mining Journal of Software (in Chinese), Vol.12, No.3, 2001, 3, 415–419.
4. Q. Liu, Granular Language and Its Deductive Reasoning, Communications of IICM, Vol.5, No.2, Taiwan, 63–66.
5. A. Skowron, Toward Intelligent Systems: Calculi of Information Granules, Proceedings of International Workshop on Rough Set Theory and Granular Computing (RSTGrC-2001).
6. A. Skowron, J. Stepaniuk, Extracting Patterns Using Information Granules, In: [5], 135–142.
7. Q. Liu, Rough Sets and Rough Reasoning (in Chinese), Academic Pub., Beijing, 2001.
8. J. Lukasiewicz, On Three-Valued Logic, Ruch Filozoficzny 5, 1920. In: L. Borkowski (Ed.), Jan Lukasiewicz Selected Works, Amsterdam, North-Holland, 1970, 87–89.

A Rough Set Framework for Learning in a Directed Acyclic Graph

Herman Midelfart and Jan Komorowski

Department of Computer and Information Science
Norwegian University of Science And Technology
N-7491 Trondheim, Norway
{herman,janko}@idi.ntnu.no

Abstract. Prediction of gene function from expression profiles introduces a new learning problem where the decision classes associated with the objects (i.e., genes) are organized in a directed acyclic graph (DAG). Standard learning methods such a Rough Sets assume that these classes are unrelated, and cannot handle this problem properly. To this end, we introduce an extended rough set framework with several new operators. We show how these operators can be used in an new learning algorithm.

1 Introduction

The objective of supervised learning is to find a function that maps an object to one of several classes based on some observed attributes of the object. A supervised learning algorithm takes a set of objects with known classes as training data and finds a function that fits the data. The discovered function can later on be used to classify objects with unknown class. The classes are usually assumed to be discrete and unordered.

In real-life problems, however, this assumption does not always hold. Classification of genes from gene expression profiles is one particular example. Molecular biologists have identified genes in various organisms through sequence projects, but have little knowledge of their function, i.e., the objective of a gene in the cell. However, Eisen et al. [3] measured gene expression profiles with cDNA microarray technology [11] and found, using hierarchical clustering [12], that genes with similar expression profiles tend to participate in the same biological process. Studies on predicting gene function from microarray data were later conducted by Brown et al. [1] using support vector machines, and more recently by Hvidsten et al. [6] using Rough Sets [10]. In both studies a set of classes was selected and a classifier was trained and evaluated for each class.

Still, the categories typically used by biologists for characterizing function are structurally related. One example is the Gene Ontology [2], in which the classes form a directed acyclic graph (DAG). Support vector machine and Rough Set Theory (RST) do not take such structures into account. In a previous paper [9], we therefore developed a new algorithm for learning in an ontology. However, some aspects of this approach were not developed formally. In particular, the operators used for approximating the classes and dividing the genes into a positive

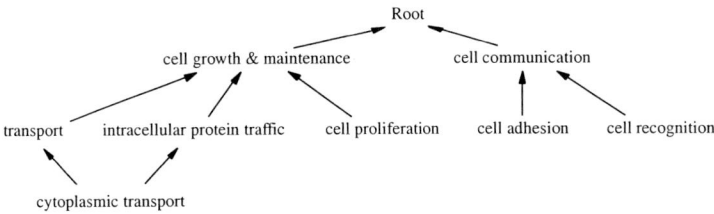

Fig. 1. A small part of the Gene Ontology

and negative set for learning were informal. In this paper, we introduce an extension to RST and present several new operators for approximating classes in an ontology. We show how these operators can be used in the algorithm developed in [9].

The structure of the paper is as follows. The issue of learning in an ontology is discussed in more detail. Extensions to RST in form of a DAG-decision system and new operators are presented next. The learning algorithm is described. We close the paper with conclusions and a discussion of future research. We assume that the reader is familiar with RST, and RST notation follows Komorowski et al. [7].

2 Classification in an Ontology

The classes in our learning problem are organized in an ontology, which provides a controlled vocabulary for describing the function of genes. A part of this ontology is shown in Fig. 1, and as the figure reveals the ontology forms a DAG. Our task in this regard is to predict the function from experimental microarray data. Each microarray measures the expression level of every gene and defines a conditional attribute in our data. The genes correspond to objects (in RST). Each gene is annotated with one or more classes from the ontology, and an object is made for each class that a gene has.

It may not be apparent that learning in a DAG poses a special problem that cannot be handled by an ordinary learning algorithm with a flat set of classes. Take for instance the classes "cytoplasmic transport" and "transport" in Fig. 1. These are related, but if we ignore the ontology and use a standard algorithm, it will try to discriminate the classes. This would result in very specific rules for these (and other classes) and make the algorithm sensitive to noise.

We may try to reduce the problem by using only the leaf classes as a set of unordered classes. However, the existing biological knowledge about the function of genes has a strongly varying level of detail, and the genes are as likely to be annotated with non-leaf classes as with leaf classes. The non-leaf annotations would be lost if only the leaf classes were used. Alternatively, we could select the most general classes, which contain genes (e.g., "cell growth & maintenance" and "cell adhesion") and move the annotations from the subclasses to these classes. However, the detail of the annotations would be lost in this case.

Thus, the problem cannot be reduced without some loss. All classes and the structure should be taken into account when learning in a DAG. Still, the annotations may be spread throughout the whole ontology so that each class may hold for very few objects. Finding genuine distinguishing properties in the expression profiles of the gene may therefore be hard, and this may result in rules with poor performance. So it may be necessary to move the annotations either upwards or downwards in the ontology in order to collect more annotations in a single class. Moving genes downwards is preferable since more detailed predictions are gained, but this process is also more difficult. A decision must be made regarding the subclass to which an annotation should be moved. This class is obviously unknown, and must be predicted. The number of classes also increases as one moves downwards in the ontology. Annotations from a smaller number of classes will have to be spread over a larger of number classes, and the number of objects in each class may still be very sparse. At the same time more classes must be separated with the same available information (i.e., the expression profiles). Hence, moving annotations downwards may be insufficient to obtain acceptable precision, and it may not be possible to have both detail and precision. Details may therefore have to be sacrificed in order to get satisfactory results. However, no more details should be given away than what is absolutely necessary.

The algorithm presented in Sec. 4 attempts this by learning a set of rules for each class in the ontology and by using objects both from the class and its subclass. At the same time it avoids discriminating these objects from the objects in the superclasses. A prediction scheme that prefers more detailed predictions is constructed. Still, it is necessary to handle the uncertainty about the data just as in ordinary learning problems. Approximations of the classes are needed. However, RST assumes that the decision classes constitute a flat set. The upper and lower approximation cannot be used directly on this problem. An extended RST framework is thus required.

3 Extensions to Rough Set Theory

3.1 DAG-Decision Systems

In order to represent the ontology, in a formal manner, we introduce a DAG-decision system $\mathcal{A} = \langle U, A, d, \succcurlyeq \rangle$ where

- U is a non-empty finite set of (observable) objects, called the universe.
- A is a set of conditional attributes describing the objects. Each attribute $a \in A$ is a function $a : U \to V_a$ where V_a is a set of values that an object may take for a.
- d is the decision attribute, which is not in A. It is a function $d : U \to V_d$ where V_d is a set of classes.
- $\succcurlyeq$ is a partial order on the classes in V_d where $p \succcurlyeq r$ denotes that p is *more general than* r $(p, r \in V_d)$.

Notice that the partial order $\succcurlyeq$ corresponds to a DAG. If $E \subseteq V_d \times V_d$ is the set of edges in the DAG, $\succcurlyeq$ can be defined as (1) $p \succcurlyeq p$ for all $p \in V_d$ and (2) for all $p, r \in V_d$, $p \succcurlyeq r$, if there is a $q \in V_d$ such that $p \succcurlyeq q$ and $\langle q, r \rangle \in E$.

p is *strictly more general* that q, denoted $p \succ q$, if $p \succcurlyeq q$ and $p \neq q$. In this case, we say that p is a *superclass* q and q is a *subclass* of p. $p \approx q$ denotes that p and q are *related* classes where one is a superclass of the other (or $p = q$), i.e., $p \succcurlyeq q$ or $q \succcurlyeq p$. If $p \not\approx q$, we say that they are *unrelated*. Notice that $\approx$ is reflexive and symmetric, but not transitive. The set of paths between a and b ($a \succ b$), is $Paths(a,b) = \{\{a, c_1, \ldots, c_n, b\} \mid a \succ c_1 \succ \ldots \succ c_n \succ b\}$.

Furthermore, a *leaf* class c is defined as class that has no subclasses (i.e., $\forall d \in V_d : c \not\succ d$). A *non-leaf* class c has at least one subclass (i.e., $\exists d \in V_d : c \succ d$), and a *root* class has no superclasses (i.e., $\forall d \in V_d : d \not\succ c$). The DAG is *rooted* if it has a unique root class. The DAG is a *tree* if it is rooted and for each class c all superclasses of c are related ($\forall a, b, c \in V_d \; a \succcurlyeq c \wedge b \succcurlyeq c \rightarrow a \approx b$). Given a set $C \subseteq V_d$ of classes, the complement classes of C is $\sim C = \{e \in V_d \mid \forall c \in C \; e \not\approx c\}$.

3.2 Unknown Set Membership

In set theory, the membership of all objects in the universe is assumed to be known. An object y is either a member of a set X or it is not. This is also the starting point in RST, but here an elementary set may belong to both X and the complement $-X$ in which case the membership is inconsistent. Hence, RST distinguishes between three different ways a element can be related to a set: *in*, *not in*, and *inconsistent*.

However, we may also recognize a fourth category; it may be *unknown* whether an object belongs to a set or not. This situation arises in the DAG as shown in Fig. 2 for class c. The objects of the superclasses a and *root* may belong to c or some of the classes that are unrelated to c, i.e., b_1, b_2, and b_3. However, we do not know which class. The membership of these objects are with other words unknown wrt. c. Notice, however, that we assume that *each object of a class must belong to at least one of the subclasses*.

We deal with this problem by adopting the rough set strategy of finding a lower and an upper boundary of the set of objects belonging to c. The lower boundary K_c consists basically of the objects in c and the subclasses of c since the objects of these subclasses are also members of c. The upper boundary P_c contains in addition the objects of the superclasses of c whose membership is unknown. We could define these sets as:

$$K_c = \{x \in U \mid c \succcurlyeq d(x)\} \text{ and } P_c = \{x \in U \mid c \approx d(x)\}$$

For a set of class $C \subseteq V_d$, these boundaries could be defined as the union of the corresponding boundaries of each class, i.e., $P_C = \bigcup_{c \in C} P_c$ and $K_C = \bigcup_{c \in C} K_c = \{x \in U \mid \exists c \in C \; c \succcurlyeq d(x)\}$. However, the definitions are complicated for several reason.

Firstly, we would like K_C to be complementary to $P_{\sim C}$ (i.e., $K_C = U - P_{\sim C}$) and P_C complementary to $K_{\sim C}$ (i.e., $P_C = U - K_{\sim C}$). However, $K_C = U - P_{\sim C}$

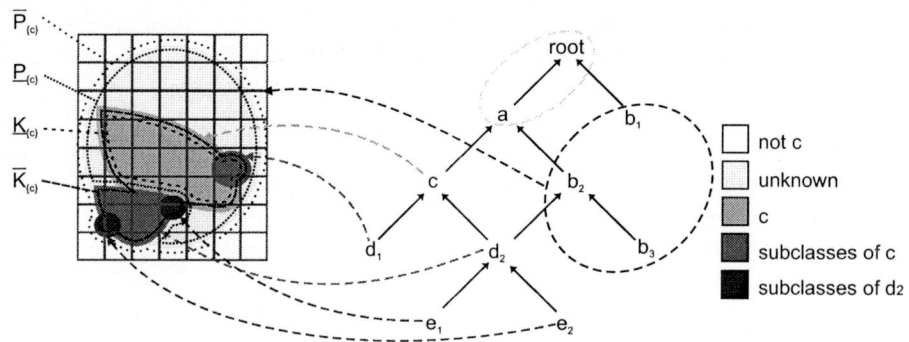

Fig. 2. Discernibility of the class c

does not hold unfortunately. Assume for example that $C = \{d_1, d_2\}$ in Fig. 2. Then K_C consists of the objects in d_1, d_2, e_1, and e_2. $\sim C = \{b_1, b_3\}$, and $P_{\sim C}$ consists of the objects in $root$, a, b_1, b_2, and b_3. The objects in c however do not occur in either set. The reason is that c has no other immediate subclasses than d_1 and d_2 — all of its subclasses are related to C. Its objects are therefore not included in $P_{\sim C}$. Moreover, $c \notin C$ such that its objects are not in K_C either. Notice that this issue also occurs in a tree and is not specific to a DAG.

We may correct this problem by changing the definition of either K_C or $P_{\sim C}$. Defining $P_{\sim C}$ so that the objects in c are included would be counterintuitive, however. c is not a superclass of any class in $\sim C$, and its objects are not potential members of these classes. On the other hand, the objects of c must belong to either d_1 or d_2. Thus we *know* that the objects of c belong to C since C includes both classes. Hence, K_C should include objects from a class *if all of its subclasses are related to C*. More formally, object x should be in K_C if x satisfies

$$\forall e \in V_d \; d(x) \succcurlyeq e \rightarrow \exists c \in C \; e \approx c \qquad \text{(Cond. 1)}$$

As the following proposition states any object that satisfies $\exists c \in C \; c \succcurlyeq d(x)$ also satisfies Cond. 1. Hence, we may replace it in the definition of K_C with Cond. 1.

Proposition 1. *Given an object $x \in U$, $(\exists c \in C \; c \succcurlyeq d(x))$ implies $(\forall e \in V_d \; d(x) \succcurlyeq e \rightarrow \exists c \in C \; e \approx c)$*[1].

Secondly, a class may have several immediate superclasses in a DAG. This means that its objects may be included in the (lower and upper) boundaries of both a set C and its complement $\sim C$. For example, if $C = \{c\}$ (in Fig. 2), we have $\sim C = \{b_1, b_2, b_3\}$. The classes d_2, e_1, and e_2 are then subclasses of some class in both C and $\sim C$, and their objects will consequently be in K_C, $K_{\sim C}$, P_C, and $P_{\sim C}$. The DAG introduces in this way a new type of inconsistency. For this reason, we introduce a lower and an upper approximation of K_C and P_C. The

---

[1] The proofs are omitted due to lack of space and will be included in a longer journal version of this paper.

upper approximations contain all objects from the subclasses of the classes in C as before. The lower approximations on the other hand do not contain objects from subclasses, which introduce this type of inconsistency.

The situation occurs when a subclass of a class in C also has another superclass in $\sim C$ (which is not related to any class in C). Hence, the objects of a class should only be included in the lower approximations if *all superclasses are related to a class in C*. Formally, object x should be included if

$$\forall e \in V_d \ e \succ d(x) \to \exists c \in C \ e \approx c \qquad \text{(Cond. 2)}$$

This results in the following boundaries:

1. $\underline{K}_C = \{x \in U \mid \text{Cond. 1 and 2}\} = \{x \in U \mid \forall e \in V_d \ d(x) \approx e \to \exists c \in C \ e \approx c\}$
2. $\overline{K}_C = \{x \in U \mid \text{Cond. 1}\} \quad\quad = \{x \in U \mid \forall e \in V_d \ d(x) \succ e \to \exists c \in C \ e \approx c\}$
3. $\underline{P}_C = \{x \in U \mid (\exists c \in C \ c \approx d(x)) \text{ and Cond. 2}\}$
   $= \{x \in U \mid (\exists c \in C \ c \approx d(x)) \text{ and } (\forall e \in V_d \ e \succ d(x) \to \exists c \in C \ e \approx c)\}$
4. $\overline{P}_C = \{x \in U \mid \exists c \in C \ c \approx d(x)\}$

Notice that only $\overline{K}_{C \cup D} \supseteq \overline{K}_C \cup \overline{K}_D$ holds. This is true for $\underline{K}_C$ and $\underline{P}_C$ as well. The complements of the sets are related as shown in the following lemmas.

Lemma 1.

1. $\underline{K}_{\sim C} = U - \overline{P}_C$
2. $\overline{K}_{\sim C} = U - \underline{P}_C$
3. $\underline{P}_{\sim C} = U - \overline{K}_C$
4. $\overline{P}_{\sim C} = U - \underline{K}_C$

Lemma 2.

1. $\underline{K}_{\sim(\sim C)} = \underline{K}_C$
2. $\overline{K}_{\sim(\sim C)} = \overline{K}_C$
3. $\underline{P}_{\sim(\sim C)} = \underline{P}_C$
4. $\overline{P}_{\sim(\sim C)} = \overline{P}_C$

The upper and lower approximations of K_C and P_C are only necessary if the DAG is not a tree. If it is a tree, there cannot be any conflict with regard to the membership of the objects in the subclasses, and the difference between the upper and lower approximations vanishes.

Proposition 2. *If the DAG forms a tree, $\overline{K}_C = \underline{K}_C$ and $\overline{P}_C = \underline{P}_C$.*

3.3 Operators

The sets $\underline{K}_C$, $\overline{K}_C$, $\underline{P}_C$, and $\overline{P}_C$ solve only the part of the problem that is related to the DAG. They do not consider the uncertainty (due to noise), which is handled by the standard Rough Set approximations, and they may be inconsistent in terms of the elementary sets partitioned by the indiscernibility relation on the conditional attributes. Hence, we may use the standard rough set lower and upper approximation of these sets ($B \subseteq A$):

$$\underline{B}_X(C) = \{x \in U \mid [x]_B \subseteq X_C\} \text{ and } \overline{B}_X(C) = \{x \in U \mid [x]_B \cap X_C \neq \emptyset\}$$

and create two operators for each of $\underline{K}$, $\overline{K}$, $\underline{P}$, and $\overline{P}$ by replacing X with the corresponding set. Notice that each operator has a dual which is complementary for the complement classes, i.e., $X_C = U - Y_{\sim C}$ and $X_{\sim C} = U - Y_C$ for operators X and Y (denoted as $X \leftrightarrow Y$). We have following duals: $\underline{B}_K \leftrightarrow \overline{B}_{\overline{P}}$, $\overline{B}_K \leftrightarrow \underline{B}_{\overline{P}}$, $\underline{B}_{\overline{K}} \leftrightarrow \overline{B}_{\underline{P}}$, and $\overline{B}_{\overline{K}} \leftrightarrow \underline{B}_{\underline{P}}$.

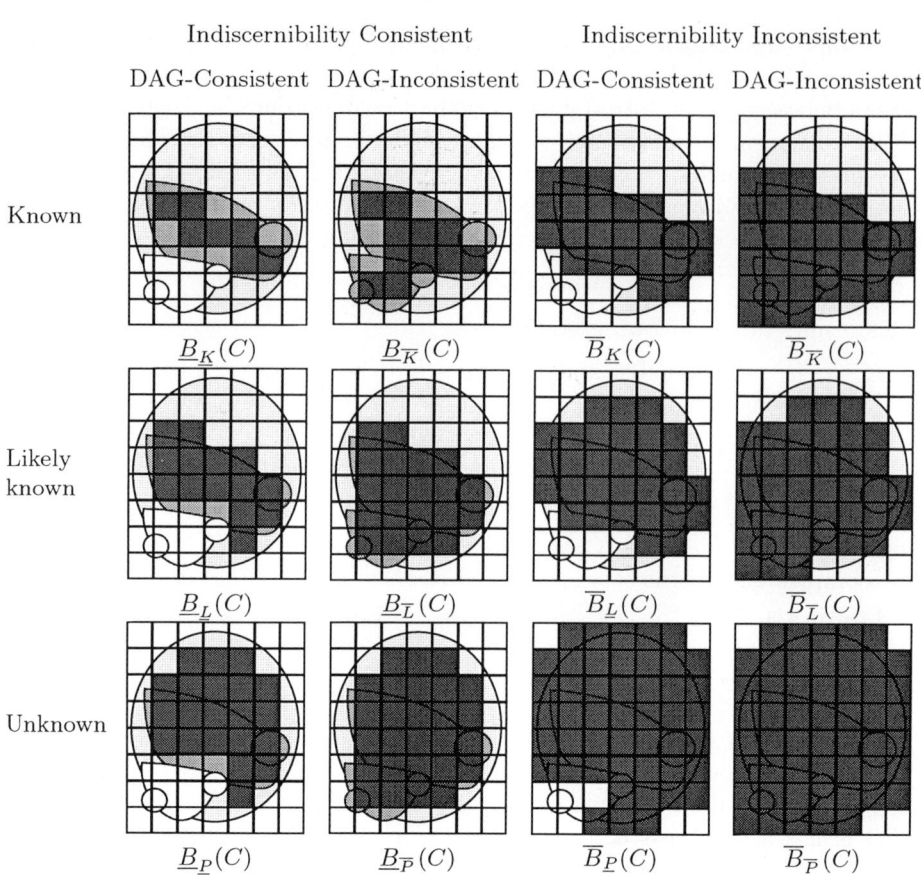

Fig. 3. An illustration of the operators on the DAG in Fig. 2 where $C = \{c\}$. The unknown region is displayed as light gray, the region corresponding to c and its subclasses is shown as medium gray, and the negative region is white. The region covered by each operator is dark gray.

These operators are illustrated in Fig. 3. The lower approximations $\underline{B}_K(C)$ and $\underline{B}_{\overline{K}}(C)$ are very conservative. In particular, they do not cover the elementary sets where at least some of the objects are known (wrt. C) and the remaining ones are unknown. If we assume that the unknown objects in these sets belong to the complement classes, we will introduce new inconsistencies since some of these objects are already known to belong c. If all objects in these sets belong to c on the other hand, no such inconsistencies will occur. Hence, the unknown objects in these elementary sets most likely belong to c since this would lead to the fewest number of inconsistencies. We call these elementary sets for *C-likely-known* sets.

The upper approximations $\overline{B}_K(C)$ and $\overline{B}_{\overline{K}}(C)$ cover the C-likely-known sets, but they cover also the inconsistent elementary set where some objects are known to belong to $\sim C$. Their corresponding upper approximations $\underline{B}_{\overline{P}}(C)$ and $\underline{B}_P(C)$

cover the C-likely-known sets as well, but cover in addition completely unknown elementary sets, i.e., sets consisting of only unknown objects. The intersection of $\overline{B}_{\overline{K}}(C)$ and $\underline{B}_{\overline{P}}(C)$ on the other hand (and similarly for $\overline{B}_K(C)$ and $\underline{B}_P(C)$) contains only sets where all objects are either known or unknown and at least some objects are known. Hence, C-likely-known sets may be added to $\underline{B}_K(C)$ and $\underline{B}_{\overline{K}}(C)$ by using combination of these operators. This motivates us to define another set of operators:

$$\underline{B}_L(C) = \underline{B}_P(C) \cap \overline{B}_K(C) = \{x \in U \mid [x]_B \subseteq \underline{P}_C \text{ and } [x]_B \cap \underline{K}_C \neq \emptyset\}$$
$$\underline{B}_{\overline{L}}(C) = \underline{B}_{\overline{P}}(C) \cap \overline{B}_{\overline{K}}(C) = \{x \in U \mid [x]_B \subseteq \overline{P}_C \text{ and } [x]_B \cap \overline{K}_C \neq \emptyset\}$$
$$\overline{B}_L(C) = \underline{B}_P(C) \cup \overline{B}_K(C) = \{x \in U \mid [x]_B \subseteq \underline{P}_C \text{ or } [x]_B \cap \underline{K}_C \neq \emptyset\}$$
$$\overline{B}_{\overline{L}}(C) = \underline{B}_{\overline{P}}(C) \cup \overline{B}_{\overline{K}}(C) = \{x \in U \mid [x]_B \subseteq \overline{P}_C \text{ or } [x]_B \cap \overline{K}_C \neq \emptyset\}$$

Notice that $\overline{B}_L(C)$ and $\overline{B}_{\overline{L}}(C)$ contain the same elementary sets as $\overline{B}_P(C)$ and $\overline{B}_{\overline{P}}(C)$ except for the $(\sim C)$-likely-known sets, which is not included. $\underline{B}_L(C)$ and $\underline{B}_{\overline{L}}(C)$ are complementary to $\overline{B}_{\overline{L}}(C)$ and $\overline{B}_L(C)$ as shown by this theorem.

Theorem 1. 1. $\underline{B}_L(\sim C) = U - \overline{B}_{\overline{L}}(C)$ 3. $\overline{B}_L(\sim C) = U - \underline{B}_{\overline{L}}(C)$
2. $\underline{B}_{\overline{L}}(\sim C) = U - \overline{B}_L(C)$ 4. $\overline{B}_{\overline{L}}(\sim C) = U - \underline{B}_L(C)$

4 A Learning Algorithm

Our learning algorithm finds a set of rules for each class in the ontology except for the root. When a class c is learned, the objects are divided into a positive set $\mathcal{P}$ containing the objects that should be covered by the rules for c and a negative set $\mathcal{N}$ containing the genes that should not be covered.

The definition of $\mathcal{P}$ and $\mathcal{N}$ is crucial since these sets control the type of rules made by the algorithm. In our case, these sets should fulfill several requirements. Firstly, the rules learned for class c should not discriminate the objects of c from the objects in the classes related to c as argued in Sec. 2. Hence, $\mathcal{N}$ should not contain objects that belong to c-related classes and are not $\sim\{c\}$-likely-known. Secondly, the scarcity of the available data for each class may also result in very specific rules. This may be compensated by extending $\mathcal{P}$ to include all known and likely-known objects (wrt. c) and not only object annotated with c. Thirdly, a gene may have several annotations and we want to predict all of them. We need therefore to find possible rules (as in [5]), which cover the upper approximation.

The first and third conditions are fulfilled if $\mathcal{N} = U - \overline{A}_{\overline{L}}(\{c\}) = \underline{A}_L(\sim\{c\})$. The second and third may be satisfied by setting $\mathcal{P}$ to either $\overline{A}_{\overline{K}}(\{c\})$ or $\overline{A}_{\overline{L}}(\{c\})$. The difference between these is that $\overline{A}_{\overline{L}}(\{c\})$ also contains elementary sets that are completely unknown wrt. c. However, these sets will also be covered by any siblings of c (i.e., the unrelated classes that have same immediate superclass as c) if $\mathcal{P} = \overline{A}_{\overline{L}}(\{c\})$. They will also be covered by the superclasses c even if $\mathcal{P} = \overline{A}_{\overline{K}}(\{c\})$. Nothing is gained by including these sets in $\mathcal{P}$. We therefore

Algorithm 1 The learning part
Input: A rooted DAG-decision system $\langle U, A, d, \succcurlyeq \rangle$ and an accuracy threshold α.
Output: A set of rules RS.
   $RS = \emptyset$
   for all $c \in C - \{Root\}$ **do**
      $\mathcal{P} = \overline{A_{\overline{K}}}(\{c\})$, $\mathcal{N} = \underline{A_L}(\sim\{c\})$, and $R = \{Inf_A(x) \mid x \in \mathcal{P}\}$
      while two antecedent in R can be merged into r and $acc(r, \mathcal{P}, \mathcal{N}) \geq \alpha$ **do**
         select the two most similar $r_1, r_2 \in R$, i.e., those with the least $dist(r_1, r_2)$
         create $r = merge(r_1, r_2)$
         remove r_1, r_2 from R and add r
      end while
      $RS = RS \cup \left\{ (\bigwedge_{s \in I} s) \rightarrow \langle d, c \rangle \mid I \in R \right\}$
   end for
   return RS

---

choose $\overline{A_{\overline{K}}}(\{c\})$ as $\mathcal{P}$. Notice that this means that we do not set an absolute restriction on the coverage of the rules, but set a lower $\overline{A_{\overline{K}}}(\{c\})$ and upper limit $\overline{A_{\overline{L}}}(\{c\})$. The rules created for c could consequently cover completely unknown elementary sets, but in this case they are included because this results in the simplest and most accurate rules with respect to $\overline{A_{\overline{K}}}(\{c\})$ and $\underline{A_L}(\sim\{c\})$ (since $\mathcal{N} = U - \overline{A_{\overline{L}}}(\{c\})$). The rules of c and its siblings may, of course, cover the same completely unknown elementary sets, but a completely unknown set will typically be covered by the rules of only one class.

The learning algorithm is shown in detail in Alg. 1. After $\mathcal{P}$ and $\mathcal{N}$ have been estimated, the rules are found by bottom-up searching the hypothesis space consisting of conjunctions of attribute-value pairs. A most specific antecedent, which is the information vector, is created for each object in the positive set. The two most similar antecedents are then merged into a more general antecedent by dropping dissimilar attribute-value pairs using: $merge(r_1, r_2) = \{\langle a, v \rangle \mid \langle a, v \rangle \in r_1, \langle a, v \rangle \in r_2\}$. The similarity of the antecedents is measured by: $dist(r_1, r_2) = |\{a \mid \langle a, v_1 \rangle \in r_1, \langle a, v_2 \rangle \in r_2, v_1 \neq v_2\}|$. The generalization process is repeated as long as there are some antecedents that may be merged and the resulting antecedent r has accuracy above a given threshold α. The accuracy is defined as $acc(\beta, P, N) = |\beta_P|/(|\beta_P| + |\beta_N|)$ where $\beta_U = \{x \in U \mid \forall \langle a, v \rangle \in \beta : a(x) = v\}$.

Since the rules of each class cover all known objects, an object will be covered by the rules of its originally assigned class and any of the superclasses. Consequently, all of these classes will be predicted for the object, and we will get many redundant predictions. We resolve this issue with a voting scheme where a class inherits votes from its superclasses, and the most detailed classes are preferred.

This scheme is shown in Alg. 2. Each class with a rule that covers the object in question receives one initial vote. It obtains an additional vote for each class that occurs on the path to the root and has an initial vote. If there are several paths to the root (cf. DAG), the highest vote among the paths is chosen. If a class has a subclass with an initial vote, the subclass is preferred, and the class is given no votes. The votes are normalized, and the classes having a normalized

Algorithm 2 The prediction part

Input: An object x, a set of rules RS, a DAG $\langle V_d, E \rangle$, and a threshold t.
Output: A set P of class predictions for x.

for all $c \in V_d$ do
$\quad u_c = \begin{cases} 1 \text{ if there is a rule in } RS \text{ covering } x \text{ and predicting } c \text{ and } c \neq Root \\ 0 \text{ otherwise} \end{cases}$
end for
for all $c \in V_d$ do
$\quad$ if $u_c = 1$ and there is no d such that $c \succ d$ and $u_d = 1$ then
$\quad\quad votes_c = \max_{P \in Paths(Root, c)} \sum_{d \in P} u_d$
$\quad$ else
$\quad\quad votes_c = 0$
$\quad$ end if
end for
$P = \{c \mid \frac{vote_c}{Norm} > t\}$ where $Norm = \sum_{c \in C} votes_c$
return P

vote higher than a given threshold are returned as the predicted classes. Notice that this method reduces the risk of making an incorrect prediction. A correct prediction will typically receive votes from all of the superclasses and will get a high normalized vote, while an incorrect prediction will not receive votes from the superclasses, and will get a low normalized vote that is filtered out.

5 Conclusions and Future Research

The task of predicting gene function from expression profiles requires new learning algorithms. The classes are organized in a DAG and the algorithm must take the ordering of the classes into account. We have presented a new rough set framework, which captures the DAG and new operators for approximating a class in this structure. The utility of these operators have been demonstrated in a new learning algorithm. This algorithm have previously been tested with good results [9]. The operators used in that work were not formally developed. However, they were quite similar, although not identical. In terms of the operators presented here, positive and negative set was $\mathcal{P} = \overline{K}_{\{c\}}$ and $\mathcal{N} = \underline{K}_{\sim\{c\}} \cap \underline{B}_P(\sim\{c\})$. Hence, some of the objects in the inconsistent and $\{c\}$-likely-known elementary sets where not considered. The reader is referred to this paper for further details. Implementation and experimental evaluation of the new operators will be done in the near future.

There are some related approaches. The Dominance-Based Rough Set Approach (e.g. [4]) considers also an ordering of the classes. However, the ordering relation is in this case is a linear ordering (or at least a total preorder). Any two classes are therefore related since the relation is total. A class c may not have two or more unrelated subclasses. Hence, the membership of the objects of c is not unknown wrt. a subclass. This unknown-property simple does not occur. Moreover, the inconsistency introduced by the DAG does not arise either. The concept of unknown objects may occur in other settings however. Małuszyński and Vitoria [8] present an RST framework for Prolog with unknown objects. However, they develop a Rough Datalog language and define its semantics, and do not develop operators for unknown objects.

Several extensions to this work are possible. Other learning algorithms could be used with our framework. The search could, for example, be done in a top-down fashion as in LEM2 [5]. The objects in the superclasses could also be utilized more than in our current framework where the membership of these objects is assumed unknown. We may assume that objects in a superclass belong to the subclass with most similar objects and divide the objects into a positive and a negative set accordingly. Proximity based operators relaxing our current operators could be developed for this purpose. This relaxation could be similar to the one made by the variable precision rough set model [13] to the original rough set operators. However, in this case a similarity measures such as $dist(r_1, r_2)$ would have to be used rather than the degree of mismatch between elementary sets and the set of objects in a class.

Acknowledgment. Jan Komorowski was supported by The Wallenberg Foundation and The Swedish Foundation for Strategic Research.

References

1. M. P. S. Brown, W. N. Grundy, D. Lin, N. Cristianini, C. W. Sugnet, T. S. Furey, M. Ares, Jr., and D. Haussler. Knowledge-based analysis of microarray gene expression data by using support vector machines. *PNAS*, 97(1):262–267, 2000.
2. The Gene Ontology Consortium. Gene ontology: tool for the unification of biology. *Nature Genetics*, 25(1):25–29, 2000.
3. M. B. Eisen, P. T. Spellman, P. O. Brown, and D. Botstein. Cluster analysis and display of genome-wide expression patterns. *PNAS*, 95(25):14863–14868, 1998.
4. S. Greco, B. Matarazzo, and R. Słowiński. A new rough set approach to multi-criteria and multiattribute classification. In *Proc. of the 1st Intl. Conf. on Rough Sets and Current Trends in Computing*, LNAI 1424, pp. 60–67. Springer-Verlag, 1998.
5. J. W. Grzymala-Busse. LERS – A system for learning from examples based on rough sets. In *Intelligent decision support: Handbook of Applications and Advances of Rough Sets Theory*, pp. 3–18. Kluwer Academic Publishers, 1992.
6. T. R. Hvidsten, J. Komorowski, A. K. Sandvik, and A. Lægreid. Predicting gene function from gene expressions and ontologies. In *Proceedings of the Pacific Symposium on Biocomputing 6 (PSB-2001)*, pp. 299–310. World Scientific Press, 2001.
7. J. Komorowski, Z. Pawlak, L. Polkowski, and A. Skowron. A rough set perspective on data and knowledge. In *Rough Fuzzy Hybridization*, pp. 107–121. Springer-Verlag, 1999.
8. J. Małuszyński and A. Vitoria. Towards rough datalog: embedding rough sets in prolog. To appear in *Rough-Neuro Computing*, AI series. Springer-Verlag, 2002.
9. H. Midelfart, A. Lægreid, and J. Komorowski. Classification of gene expression data in an ontology. In *Proceedings of Second Symposium on Medical Data Analysis (ISMDA-2001)*, LNCS 2199, pp. 186–194. Springer-Verlag, 2001.

10. Z. Pawlak. *Rough Sets: Theoretical Aspects of Reasoning about Data*. Kluwer Academic Publishers, 1991.
11. M. Schena, D. Shalon, R. Davis, and P. Brown. Quantitative monitoring of gene expression patterns with a complementary DNA microarray. *Science*, 270:467–470, 1995.
12. R. Sokal and C. Mitchener. A statistical method for evaluation systematic relationships. *University of Kansas Science Bulletin*, 38:1409–1438, 1958.
13. W. Ziarko. Variable precision rough set model. *Journal of Computer and System Sciences*, 46:39–59, 1993.

On Compressible Information Systems

Mikhail Moshkov

Faculty of Computing Mathematics and
Cybernetics of Nizhny Novgorod State University
23, Gagarina Av., Nizhny Novgorod, 603950, Russia
moshkov@unn.ac.ru

Abstract. In the paper infinite information systems are investigated which are used in pattern recognition, discrete optimization, and computational geometry. An information system is called compressible relatively to a weight function if for each problem with enough big weight (total weight of attributes in problem description) there exists a decision tree which solves this problem and which weighted depth is less than the problem weight. In the paper all pairs of information systems and weight functions are described such that the information system is compressible relatively to the weight function.

1 Introduction

An information system [6, 7] consists of a set A and attributes defined on this set. We consider only information systems with infinite set of attributes. A weight function assigns a weight to each attribute. This weight characterizes the complexity of attribute value computation.

The notion of a problem over information system defines as follows. We take finite number of attributes. These attributes divide the set A into classes (for each class values of the attributes are constant on elements from the class). These classes are numbered such that different classes can have the same number. For a given element a from A it is required to recognize the number of a class which contains a. Problems from various areas of applications can be represented in such form. The weight of a problem is the total weight of attributes from the problem description.

As algorithms for problem solving we consider decision trees which use attributes from the information system. As time complexity measure we consider weighted depth of decision trees. It is clear that for each problem there exists trivial decision tree which solves this problem and which weighted depth is equal to the problem weight.

The information system is called compressible relatively to the considered weight function if for each problem with enough big weight there exists a decision tree which solves this problem and which weighted depth is less than the problem weight.

The information systems which are compressible relatively to the weight function which is equal identically to 1 were investigated in [3, 4, 5]. Here we consider information systems which are compressible relatively to an arbitrary weight function. Also we investigate the behavior of Shannon type function which characterizes the growth in the worst case of minimal weighted depth of decision trees with the growth of problem weight.

Long proofs based on methods of test theory [1, 2] and rough set theory [6, 7] are omitted.

2 Basic Notions

Let A be a nonempty set, B be a finite nonempty set of integers with at least two elements, and F be a nonempty set of functions from A to B. Functions from F will be called *attributes* and the triple $U = (A, B, F)$ will be called *an information system*. If F is a finite set then U is called *a finite* information system. If F is an infinite set then U is called *an infinite* information system. Later on we will consider only infinite information systems.

A function $\psi : F \to \mathbf{N}$ will be called a *weight function* for U. Here $\mathbf{N}$ is the set of natural numbers. We denote by h the weight function for which $h(f) = 1$ for any $f \in F$.

We will consider problems over the information system U. *A problem over U* is an arbitrary $(n+1)$-tuple $z = (\nu, f_1, \ldots, f_n)$ where $\nu : B^n \to \mathbf{Z}$, $\mathbf{Z}$ is the set of integers, and $f_1, \ldots, f_n \in F$. The number $\psi(z) = \sum_{i=1}^{n} \psi(f_i)$ will be called *the weight* of the problem z. Note that $h(z) = n$. The problem z may be interpreted as a problem of searching for the value $z(a) = \nu(f_1(a), \ldots, f_n(a))$ for an arbitrary $a \in A$. Different problems of pattern recognition, discrete optimization, fault diagnosis and computational geometry can be represented in such form. We denote by $P(U)$ the set of problems over U.

As algorithms for problem solving we will consider decision trees. *A decision tree over U* is a marked finite tree with the root in which each terminal node is assigned a number from $\mathbf{Z}$; each node which is not terminal (such nodes are called *working*) is assigned an attribute from F; each edge is assigned an element from B, and edges starting in a working node are assigned pairwise different elements.

Let Γ be a decision tree over U. A *complete path* ξ in Γ is an arbitrary path from the root to a terminal node. Now we define a number $\psi(\xi)$ and a subset $\mathcal{A}(\xi)$ of the set A associated with ξ. If there are no working nodes in ξ then $\psi(\xi) = 0$ and $\mathcal{A}(\xi) = A$. Let $\xi = v_1, d_1, \ldots, v_m, d_m, v_{m+1}$ where $m > 0$, v_1 is the root, v_{m+1} is a terminal node, and v_i is the initial and v_{i+1} is the terminal node of the edge d_i for $i = 1, \ldots, m$. Let the attribute f_i be assigned to the node v_i and δ_i be the element from B assigned to the edge d_i, $i = 1, \ldots, m$. Then $\psi(\xi) = \sum_{i=1}^{m} \psi(f_i)$ and $\mathcal{A}(\xi) = \{a : a \in A, f_1(a) = \delta_1, \ldots, f_m(a) = \delta_m\}$. The number $\psi(\xi)$ will be called *the weight* of the complete path ξ. Note that $h(\xi)$ is the length of the path ξ.

We will say that a decision tree Γ over U solves a problem z over U if for each $a \in A$ there exists a complete path ξ in Γ such that $a \in \mathcal{A}(\xi)$, and the terminal node of the path ξ is assigned the number $z(a)$.

As time complexity measure we will consider *the weighted depth* $\psi(\Gamma)$ of Γ which is the maximal weight of a complete path in the tree. The number $h(\Gamma)$ will be called *the depth* of a decision tree Γ.

For a problem $z \in P(U)$ we denote by $\psi_U(z)$ the minimal weighted depth of a decision tree over U which solves the problem z. For any $n \in \mathbf{N}$ let

$$\psi_U(n) = \max\{\psi_U(z) : z \in P(U), \psi(z) \le n\}.$$

It is clear that $\psi_U(n) \le n$ for any n. The information system U will be called ψ-compressible if there exists n_0 such that for any $n \ge n_0$ the inequality $\psi_U(n) < n$ holds.

3 h-Compressible Information Systems

At first we consider h-compressible information systems. Let $U = (A, B, F)$ be an infinite information system.

We will say that the information system U has *infinite independence dimension* (or, in short, *infinite I-dimension*) if the following condition holds: for each $t \in \mathbf{N}$ there exist attributes $f_1, \ldots, f_t \in F$ and two-element subsets $B_1, \ldots, B_t$ of the set B such that for arbitrary $\delta_1 \in B_1, \ldots, \delta_t \in B_t$ the system of equations

$$\{f_1(x) = \delta_1, \ldots, f_t(x) = \delta_t\} \tag{1}$$

is compatible (has solution) on the set A. If the considered condition does not hold then we will say that the information system U has *finite I-dimension*.

Now we consider the condition of decomposition for the information system U. Let $t \in \mathbf{N}$. A nonempty subset D of the set A will be called (t, U)-set if D coincides with the set of solutions on A of a system of the kind (1), where $f_1, \ldots, f_t \in F$ and $\delta_1, \ldots, \delta_t \in B$.

We will say that the information system U satisfies *the condition of decomposition* if there exist numbers $m, p \in \mathbf{N}$ such that every $(m+1, U)$-set is a union of p sets each of which is (m, U)-set.

The following theorem from [5] describes all h-compressible infinite information systems.

Theorem 1. *Let U be an infinite information system. Then the system U is h-compressible iff it has finite I-dimension and satisfies the condition of decomposition. If U is h-compressible then $h_U(n) = \Omega(\log n)$ and $h_U(n) = O((\log n)^{1+\varepsilon})$ for any $\varepsilon > 0$.*

Consider an example from [5].

Example 1. Let $m, t \in \mathbf{N}$. We denote by $Pol(m)$ the set of all polynomials which have integer coefficients and depend on variables $x_1, \ldots, x_m$. We denote by $Pol(m, t)$ the set of all polynomials from $Pol(m)$ such that the degree of each polynomial is at most t. We define information systems $U(m)$ and $U(m, t)$ as follows: $U(m) = (\mathbf{R}^m, E, F(m))$ and $U(m, t) = (\mathbf{R}^m, E, F(m, t))$ where $\mathbf{R}$

is the set of real numbers, $E = \{-1, 0, +1\}$, $F(m) = \{\text{sign}(p) : p \in Pol(m)\}$ and $F(m,t) = \{\text{sign}(p) : p \in Pol(m,t)\}$. One can prove that $U(m)$ has infinite I-dimension, but $U(m,t)$ has finite I-dimension and satisfies the condition of decomposition.

4 ψ-Compressible Information Systems

Now we consider ψ-compressible information systems. Let $U = (A, B, F)$ be an infinite information system and ψ be a weight function for U.

For $p \in \mathbf{N}$ denote $F(\psi, p) = \{f : f \in F, \psi(f) \leq p\}$. We will say that U is *two-layer* information system if there exists $p \in \mathbf{N}$ such that the system $(A, B, F(\psi, p))$ is h-compressible and for any attribute $f \in F \setminus F(\psi, p)$ there exists a decision tree Γ with attributes from $F(\psi, p)$ which computes the attribute f and for which $\psi(\Gamma) < \psi(f)$. If U is a two-layer system and p is the minimal number for which the considered conditions hold then the system U will be called (ψ, p)-*two-layer* system.

Let U be (ψ, p)-two-layer system. Denote $F' = F \setminus F(\psi, p)$. For any $f \in F'$ denote by $\psi_U(f)$ minimal weighted depth of a decision tree with attributes from $F(\psi, p)$ which computes f. Define a function $H_{U,\psi} : \mathbf{N} \to \mathbf{N} \cup \{0\}$. If $F' = \emptyset$ then $H_{U,\psi} \equiv 0$. Let $F' \neq \emptyset$ and $q = \min\{\psi(f) : f \in F'\}$. Let $n \in \mathbf{N}$. If $n < q$ then $H_{U,\psi}(n) = 0$. Let $n \geq q$. Then

$$H_{U,\psi}(n) = \max\{\psi_U(f) : f \in F', \psi(f) \leq n\}.$$

Denote $k = |B|$. Define a function $Q_{U,\psi} : \mathbf{N} \to \mathbf{N} \cup \{0\}$ as follows:

$$Q_{U,\psi}(n) = \max(H_{U,\psi}(n), \log_k n - \log_k p).$$

Theorem 2. *Let U be an infinite information system and ψ be a weight function for U. Then the system U is ψ-compressible iff it is a two-layer system. If U is ψ-compressible then $\psi_U(n) = \Omega(Q_{U,\psi}(n))$ and $\psi_U(n) = O(Q_{U,\psi}(n)^{1+\varepsilon})$ for any $\varepsilon > 0$.*

The following theorem from [3] (see also [4]) describes possible behavior of the function $\psi_U(n)$ for ψ-compressible information system U.

Theorem 3. *Let $\varphi : \mathbf{N} \cup \{0\} \to \mathbf{N} \cup \{0\}$ be a non-decreasing function such that $\lfloor \log_2 n \rfloor + 2 \leq \varphi(n) \leq n - 3$ for $n \geq 7$. Then there exist an infinite information system U and a weight function ψ for U such that $\varphi(n) \leq \psi_U(n) \leq \varphi(n) + 2$ for $n \geq 7$.*

5 Conclusion

In the paper all pairs of information systems and weight functions are described such that the information system is compressible relatively to the weight function. This result may be useful for the choice of information systems and weight functions for investigation of problems of pattern recognition, discrete optimization, and computational geometry.

Acknowledgments. The author would like to thank the referees for useful comments and suggestions.

This work was partially supported by Russian Foundation for Basic Research (project 02-01-00543).

References

1. Chegis, I.A., Yablonskii, S.V.: Logical methods of electric circuit control. Trudy MIAN SSSR **51** (1958) 270–360 (in Russian)
2. Moshkov, M.Ju.: Conditional tests. Problemy Kybernetiki **40**. Edited by S.V. Yablonskii. Nauka Publishers, Moscow (1983) 131–170 (in Russian)
3. Moshkov, M.Ju.: Decision Trees. Theory and Applications. Nizhny Novgorod University Publishers, Nizhny Novgorod (1994) (in Russian)
4. Moshkov, M.Ju.: Unimprovable upper bounds on time complexity of decision trees. Fundamenta Informaticae **31**(2) (1997) 157–184
5. Moshkov, M.Ju.: Classification of infinite information systems. Proceedings of the Second Internationsl Conference on Rough Sets and Current Trends in Computing (RSCTC'2000), Banff, Canada, October 16-19, 2000. Edited by W. Ziarko and Yiyu Yao (2000) 167–171
6. Pawlak, Z.: Rough Sets – Theoretical Aspects of Reasoning about Data. Kluwer Academic Publishers, Dordrecht, Boston, London (1991)
7. Skowron, A., Rauszer, C.: The discernibility matrices and functions in information systems. Intelligent Decision Support. Handbook of Applications and Advances of the Rough Set Theory. Edited by R. Slowinski. Kluwer Academic Publishers, Dordrecht, Boston, London (1992) 331–362

Functional Dependencies in Relational Expressions Based on Or-Sets

Michinori Nakata[1] and Tetsuya Murai[2]

[1] Faculty of Management and Information Science,
Josai International University,
1, Gumyo, Togane, Chiba 283-8555, Japan
`nakata@jiu.ac.jp`
[2] Division of Systems and Information Engineering,
Graduate School of Engineering, Hokkaido University,
Kita 13, Nishi 8, Kita-ku, Sapporo 060-8628, Japan
`murahiko@main.eng.hokudai.ac.jp`

Abstract. Partial functional dependencies, functional dependencies accompanied by a factor, are examined in a relational database based on or-sets. The partial functional dependencies are dealt with under tuples having their belongingness degree to a relation. Whether a functional dependency accompanied by a factor holds in a relation is determined by comparing the factor with to what degree the relation satisfies the functional dependency. Inference rules, similar to Armstrong's axioms in the conventional relational databases, are obtained. Thus, we can discover another functional dependencies related with a partial functional dependency by using the inference rules.

1 Introduction

Rough sets are widely used in the field of data mining[2,10]. In particular, rough sets are suitable to extract cause-effect relationships from databases. Discovered rules expressing cause-effect relationships have the form of partial functional dependencies, functional dependencies accompanied by a factor expressing the degree of dependency[1,5,9].

Imperfect information is ubiquitous in the real world[6]. When we extract rules from realistic databases, we are faced on handling databases containing imperfect information. It is necessary to investigate properties of partial functional dependencies in order to use the discovered partial functional dependencies in realistic databases. Thus, partial functional dependencies are examined in the framework of databases handling imperfect information by using or-sets in this paper.

We deal with discovered functional dependencies under the following viewpoints. First, a compatibility degree of a tuple with a functional dependency is not a binary value[8]. Second, the rules containing functional dependencies should be dealt with under tuples having their belongingness degree to a relation[4]. Under considering these points, we deal with partial functional dependencies in an extended relational model based on or-sets. In particular, we focus on inference rules in this paper.

2 Relational Databases Based on Or-Sets

2.1 Framework

Rough sets, introduced by Pawlak[7], capture indiscernibility. The indiscernibility is much related with incompleteness of information[3]. Representing the incompleteness by or-sets means handling a kind of indiscernibility.

Definition 2.1.1
The value $t[A_j]$ of an attribute A_j in a tuple t is represented by an or-set where every element is included in a domain D_j.

When an attribute value $t[A_j]$ is expressed by an or-set with plural elements, we cannot discern which element of the set is the actual value of the attribute value. Elements of an or-set are not distinguishable, but absolutely equivalent in having the same probability of being the actual value. Thus, the elements in an or-set create an equivalence relation for the attribute value. This is equivalence in the attribute level.

In addition to the above extension, we introduce a supplementary attribute, as is done by some authors in data models handling a kind of imperfect information[11].

Definition 2.1.2
A relation r is an extended set of tuple values with their supplementary attribute value $t[\mu] > 0$, where $t[\mu]$ denotes with what degree a tuple value $t[\mathcal{A}]$ belongs to the relation r; namely, $r = \{(t[\mathcal{A}], t[\mu]) \mid t[\mu] > 0\}$.

Definition 2.1.3
A supplementary attribute value of a tuple that exists in a relation is equal to a compatibility degree of its tuple value with the imposed restrictions on the relation.

The imposed restrictions come from integrity constraints, query processing, and update processing. This means that the supplementary attribute values are ones calculated under restrictions. Consequently, any supplementary attribute value is an inevitable product created from allowing an or-set with plural elements as an attribute value.

2.2 Restrictions and Supplementary Attribute Values

Each restriction is expressed by elementary restrictions and logical operators. An elementary restriction is "A_i *is* m" or "$A_i \theta A_j$," where m is a predicate that is expressed by a set contained in a domain D_i and θ is one of arithmetic comparators: $<, \leq, =, >,$ and $\geq$. When a restriction c is "$A_i \theta A_j$,"

$$Com(c \mid t[\mathcal{A}]) = \sum_{x \in t[A_i], y \in t[A_j]} \mu_\theta(x,y) / |t[A_i]| \times |t[A_j]|,$$

where $\mu_\theta(x,y)$ is a binary relation that expresses an arithmetic comparator θ. If this is the only one restriction imposed on a relation r, a supplementary attribute value $t[\mu]$ of a tuple t is equal to $Com(c \mid t[\mathcal{A}])$.

Logical operators are $not(\neg), and(\wedge)$ and $or(\vee)$. For negated restriction $\neg c$,

$$Com(\neg c \mid t[\mathcal{A}]) = 1 - Com(c \mid t[\mathcal{A}]).$$

For conjunction and disjunction of two elementary restrictions c_1 and c_2,

$$Com(c_1 \wedge c_2 \mid t[\mathcal{A}]) = Com(c_1 \mid t[\mathcal{A}]) \times Com(c_2 \mid t[\mathcal{A}]),$$
$$Com(c_1 \vee c_2 \mid t[\mathcal{A}]) = 1 - (1 - Com(c_1 \mid t[\mathcal{A}])) \times (1 - Com(c_2 \mid t[\mathcal{A}])),$$

where the two restrictions c_1 and c_2 are noninteractive.

2.3 Satisfaction Degrees with Rules

When we have a rule for a relation, we calculate to what extent each tuple, belonging with a supplementary attribute value to the relation, satisfies the rule.

Definition 2.3.1
A satisfaction degree $D(c|t)$ of a tuple t with a rule c is:

$$D(c|t) = \begin{cases} 1 & \text{if } t[\mu] \leq Com(c \mid t[\mathcal{A}]) \\ Com(c \mid t[\mathcal{A}]) & \text{otherwise,} \end{cases}$$

It is said that a rule c holds in a tuple t, if $D(c|t) = 1$; namely, $Com(c \mid t[\mathcal{A}]) \geq t[\mu]$. To what degree a tuple satisfies a rule should be distinguished from the fact that its tuple value has a compatibility degree with that rule. Both are linked by the above definition.

Definition 2.3.2
A satisfaction degree $D(c|r)$ of a relation r with a rule c is:

$$D(c|r) = \sum_t D(c|t)/|r|,$$

where $|r|$ is the number of tuples that consist of the relation r.

It is said that a rule c holds in a relation r, if $D(c|r) = 1$; namely, if $\forall t$ $Com(c \mid t[\mathcal{A}]) \geq t[\mu]$. $0 < D(c|r) < 1$ means that the rule partially holds. When the attribute values are precise in a relation, there are tuples that absolutely satisfy the restriction at the rate of $D(c|r)$ in the relation. Note that $D(c|r)$ coincides with the degree of dependency, when c is a body of a partial functional dependency discovered by using rough sets under no imprecise attribute values.

2.4 Satisfaction Degrees with Rules Accompanied by a Factor

Discovered rules, which are obtained by data mining on the basis of rough sets, are usually accompanied by a factor expressing approximation quality. This factor denotes the number ratio of tuples that satisfy the body of the discovered rule, when the attribute values are precise. Each discovered rule is expressed by the form c_α where c is a body and α is a factor contained in $(0, 1]$.

Definition 2.4.1
A satisfaction degree of a relation r with a rule c_α is:

$$D(c_\alpha|r) = \begin{cases} 1 & if\ \alpha \leq D(c|r) \\ D(c|r)\ otherwise. \end{cases}$$

It is said that a rule c_α holds in a relation, if $D(c_\alpha|r) = 1$.

Theorem 2.4.2
When a satisfaction degree $D(c|r)$ is obtained for a rule c in a relation r, a rule c_α holds in the relation, where $\alpha = D(c|r)$.

Theorem 2.4.3
If a rule accompanied by a factor holds in a relation, any rule accompanied by a lower one than the factor also holds in that relation.

3 Functional Dependencies

We apply data mining to the relation by using approaches based on rough sets. Cause-effect relationships are obtained in the form of functional dependencies accompanied by a factor, which are called partial functional dependencies[9]. It is valuable to obtain inference rules, because by using inference rules we can discover another functional dependency.

3.1 Formulation of Functional Dependencies

When Y is functionally dependent on X in a relational database, this is expressed by $X \to Y$.

Definition 3.1.1
The requirement of a functional dependency $X \to Y$ in a relation r is that, for every pair of tuples (t_i, t_j), if $t_i[X] = t_j[X]$, then $t_i[Y] = t_j[Y]$.

A functional dependency can be considered as an implication statement[8]. We use $X \to Y = \neg X \vee Y$ according to Vassiliou[8]. This is equal to $1 - X + X \times Y$, when $X \cap Y = \emptyset$, which corresponds to using Reichenbach implication. Under Reichenbach implication, a functional dependency $f = X \to Y$ holds, when

$X = 0$ or $Y = 1$; namely, values of X are absolutely not equal or those of Y are absolutely equal.

Every functional dependency f_α is dealt with as merely a rule. Thus, we can use all the expressions in the previous section by replacing c by f. A compatibility degree of a tuple value $t_i[\mathcal{A}]$ with a body f of a functional dependency must be calculated for all pairs of that tuple value and others.

$$Com(f|t_i[\mathcal{A}]) = \wedge_{j \neq i} Com(f|t_i[\mathcal{A}], t_j[\mathcal{A}]),$$

where $Com(f|t_i[\mathcal{A}], t_j[\mathcal{A}])$ is a compatibility degree of a pair $(t_i[\mathcal{A}], t_j[\mathcal{A}])$ of tuple values with the body f of f_α. Under $f = X \rightarrow Y = \neg X \vee Y$,

$$Com(f|t_i[\mathcal{A}], t_j[\mathcal{A}]) = 1 - X_{ij} + X_{ij} \times Y_{ij},$$

where

$$X_{ij} = Com(= |t_i[X], t_j[X]|), \quad Y_{ij} = Com(= |t_i[Y], t_j[Y]|).$$

When X and Y are a single attribute,

$$Com(= |t_i[X], t_j[X]|) = |t_i[X] \cap t_j[X]|/|t_i[X]| \times |t_j[X]|.$$

3.2 Inference Rules of Functional Dependencies

When a set of functional dependencies holds in a relation, functional dependencies not contained in that set may also hold. Inference rules are the rules that derive implicit functional dependencies from given ones.

Theorem 3.2.1
The following inference rules are sound:[1]
WA1. Reflexivity
  If $Y \subseteq X$, then $X \rightarrow Y|_1$.
WA2. Augmentation
  If $X \rightarrow Y|_\alpha$, then $ZX \rightarrow ZY|_\alpha$.
WA3. Transitivity
  If $X \rightarrow Y|_{\alpha_1}$ and $Y \rightarrow Z|_{\alpha_2}$, then $X \rightarrow Z|_\alpha$, where $\alpha = \alpha_1 + \alpha_2 - 1$.

Among inference rules for functional dependencies we do not include the rule that functional dependencies with the same body as and with a lower factor than a functional dependency can be derived from that functional dependency. Such a rule is valid for any rule and is not characteristic of functional dependencies in our framework, as is shown in theorem 2.4.3. By using the inference rules, we can discover another functional dependency related with a partial functional dependency in the relational database based on or-sets.

---
[1] Novotný and Pawlak address some inference rules when the attribute values are precise[5].

4 Conclusions

Partial functional dependencies, functional dependencies accompanied by a factor, have been examined in a relational database based on or-sets. The partial functional dependencies are discovered from data mining by using rough sets. When a partial functional dependency is used, a compatibility degree with the partial functional dependency is calculated for every tuple under tuples having their belongingness degree to a relation. Whether a functional dependency accompanied by a factor holds in a relation is determined by comparing the factor with to what degree the relation satisfies the body of the functional dependency

We have examined what inference rules are valid. Obtained inference rules are similar to Armstrong's axioms in the conventional relational databases. Thus, we can discover another functional dependency related with a partial functional dependency by using the inference rules in the relational database based on or-sets.

Acknowledgment. This research has been partially supported by the Grant-in-Aid for Scientific Research (B) and (C), Japan Society for the Promotion of Science, No. 14380171 and No.13680475, respectively.

References

1. Gediga, G. and Düntsch, I. [2001] Rough Approximation Quality Revisited, Artificial Intelligence, **132**, 219–234.
2. Lin, T. Y. and Cercone, N., eds. [1997] Rough Sets and Data Mining: Analysis for Imprecise Data, Kluwer Academic Publishers 1997.
3. Lipski, W. [1979]On Semantics Issues Connected with Incomplete Information Databases. ACM Transactions on Database Systems, **4**:3, 262–296.
4. Nakata, M. [2000] On Inference Rules of Dependencies in Fuzzy Relational Data Models: Functional Dependencies, in *Knowledge Management in Fuzzy Databases*, Eds., O. Pons, M. A. Vila, and J. Kacprzyk, Physica Verlag, pp. 36–66.
5. Novotný, M. and Pawlak, Z. [1988] Partial Dependencies of Attributes, Bulletin of the Polish Academy of Sciences, **36**(7-8), 453–458.
6. Parsons, S. [1996] Current Approaches to Handling Imperfect Information in Data and Knowledge Bases, IEEE Transactions on Knowledge and Data Engineering, **8**:3, 353–372.
7. Pawlak, Z. [1991] Rough Sets: Theoretical Aspects of Reasoning about Data, Kluwer Academic Publishers 1991.
8. Vassiliou, Y. [1980]Functional Dependencies and Incomplete Information, in Proceedings of the 6th VLDB Conference, pp. 260–269.
9. Ziarko, W. [1991]The Discovery, Analysis, and Representation of Data Dependencies in Databases, in: Knowledge Discovery in Databases, Eds., G. Piatetsky and W. J. Frawley, AAAI Press/ The MIT Press 1991, pp. 195–209.
10. Ziarko, W. P., ed. [1994] Rough Sets, Fuzzy Sets and Knowledge Discovery, Springer 1994.
11. Zimányi, E. [1997]Query Evaluation in Probabilistic Relational Databases, Theoretical Computer Science, **171**, 179–220.

On Asymptotic Properties of Rough–Set–Theoretic Approximations. Fractal Dimension, Exact Sets, and Rough Inclusion in Potentially Infinite Information Systems

Lech Polkowski

Polish–Japanese Institute of Information Technology
Koszykowa 86, 02-008 Warsaw, Poland
and
Department of Mathematics and Computer Science
University of Warmia and Mazury
Zolnierska 14, Olsztyn 10 670, Poland
polkow@pjwstk.edu.pl

Abstract. We look at asymptotic properties of rough set approximations exploiting them to three–fold purpose viz. to introduce a counterpart of fractal dimension in abstract information systems, to define the notion of an exact set in infinite information system to the result that so defined exact sets form a compact metric Boolean algebra of sets, and to introduce rough inclusion measures for rough mereology for infinitary concepts.

Keywords: Fractals, the Minkowski dimension, information systems, rough sets, $\mathcal{A}$–dimension

1 Introduction

The notions: an exact set, a rough set are among basic notions in Rough Set Theory [10]. They are usually defined in the setting of a finite information system i.e. an information system having finite numbers of objects as well as attributes.

In theoretical studies e.g. of topological properties of rough sets [14], one has to trespass this limitation and to consider information systems with potentially unbound number of attributes. In such setting, the notions of rough and exact sets may be defined in terms of topological operators of interior and closure with respect to an appropriate topology [14] following the ideas from the finite case cf. e.g. [11], where it is noticed that in the finite case rough–set–theoretic operators of lower and upper approximation are identical with the interior, respectively, closure operators in topology induced by equivalence classes of the indiscernibility relation.

Extensions of finite information systems are also desirable from application point of view in the area of Knowledge Discovery and Data Mining, when demands of e.g. mass collaboration and/or huge experimental data e.g. in genomic studies [2], [15] call for need of working with large data tables so the sound theoretical generalization of these cases is an information system with the number of attributes not bound in advance by a fixed integer i.e. an information system with countably but infinitely many attributes. In large information systems, a need arises for parameter–free qualitative measures of complexity of concepts involved cf. e.g. applications for the Vapnik–Czervonenkis dimension [1].We study here in the theoretical setting of infinite information system a proposal to apply fractal dimensions suitably modified as measures of concept complexity.

In the finite case, exact sets form a field of sets $\mathcal{E}$ cf. e.g. [11]. Clearly, from topological point of view $\mathcal{E}$ is a compact metric space under the discrete metric on equivalence classes of the indiscernibility relation.

The question poses itself, whether it is possible to define exact sets in the setting of an infinite information system in such a way that the space of exact sets $\mathcal{E}_\infty$ will be a compact metric space and a field of sets as well.

We study in this note a way to define exact and rough sets which stems from the rough–set notion of an approximation. We apply to this end the notion of a fractal dimension adopted to the case of an information system i.e. rid of the geometric content and underlying metric characterization.

We introduce notions of the lower and the upper fractal dimensions and we define exact sets as those sets for which the two dimensions coincide; otherwise, we declare the set as rough.

It turns out that exact sets defined in this way extend the classical notion of an exact set and as in the classical finite case they form a field of sets. From topological point of view, exact sets form a compact metric space under the metric D defined originally for topological rough sets [14] and extended here over topological exact sets as well.

We also introduce measures of rough inclusion based on asymptotic behavior of approximations. We apply these measures to introduce infinitary counterparts of partial dependence.

We first give a short account on rough sets, fractals, and metrics on rough sets as preliminaries.

1.1 Rough Set Theory: A Nutshell Account

Rough sets arise in an attempt at formalization of the notion of uncertain knowledge [10], [13]. In this paradigm, knowledge is represented in the form of an *information system*. An information system consists of a non–empty set U of objects described by means of *attributes (features, properties)* collected in a set A. The pair $\mathcal{A} = (U, A)$ is an *information system*, called also a *data table*. For an object $x \in U$ and an attribute $a \in A$ we denote by the symbol $a(x)$ the *value* of a on x. Thus, any attribute a is formally a function $a : U \to V_a$ from the set U into the *value set* of a. We admit here for generality's sake the case when the set U may be infinite and the set A of attributes may consist of countably many attributes a_n where $n = 1, 2, ...$

Each attribute a_n induces the $\{a_n\}$–indiscernibility relation IND_{a_n} on the set U defined as follows

$$xIND_{a_n}y \Leftrightarrow a_n(x) = a_n(y) \qquad (1)$$

which is an equivalence relation and thus it partitions the set U into classes $[x]_{a_n}$; we denote by the symbol $\mathcal{P}_n$ the resulting partition. We may assume that $\mathcal{P}_{n+1} \subseteq \mathcal{P}_n$ for each n (if not, we may define new attributes by letting $a'_n = a_1 \wedge ... \wedge a_n$ for each n where the $\wedge$ sign means generally an operator producing a collective attribute from a given set of attributes).

A subset (*concept*) $T \subseteq U$ is n–*exact* in case it is a union of a family of classes of Ind_{a_n} i.e.

$$T = \bigcup\{[x]_{a_n} : x \in T\} \qquad (2)$$

Otherwise, T is said to be n–*rough*.

Rough sets are approximated by exact sets:

$$\begin{aligned}\underline{a_n}T &= \bigcup\{[x]_{a_n} : [x]_{a_n} \subseteq T\} \\ \overline{a_n}T &= \bigcup\{[x]_{a_n} : [x]_{a_n} \cap T \neq \emptyset\}\end{aligned} \qquad (3)$$

The set $\underline{a_n}T$ is the *lower a_n–approximation* of T and the set $\overline{a_n}T$ is the *upper a_n–approximation* of T.

Then clearly, a set T is n–exact if and only if $\underline{a_n}T = \overline{a_n}T$. Moreover, it follows by definition that n–exact sets form a field of sets.

It was observed [11] that approximations to T may be given a topological interpretation viz. taking as a base for open sets the collection $\mathcal{P}_n$ (meaning that a set is open if and only if it is the union of a sub–family of $\mathcal{P}_n$) defines a topology Π_n on the set U and we have

$$\begin{aligned}\underline{a_n}T &= Int_{\Pi_n}T \\ \overline{a_n}T &= Cl_{\Pi_n}T\end{aligned} \qquad (4)$$

for each T where Int_{Π_n}, Cl_{Π_n} are operators of resp. *interior, closure* with respect to Π_n, see also [14].

Following this idea, one may consider the family $\mathcal{P} = \bigcup_n \mathcal{P}_n$ of all equivalence classes of all relations Ind_{a_n} and one may introduce a topology Π_A on the set U by taking as an open base for this topology the family $\mathcal{P}$. Thus $T \in \Pi_A$ if and only if $T = \bigcup \mathcal{P}'$ for some $\mathcal{P}' \subseteq \mathcal{P}$. In this way, we define a taxonomy of sets in U: they may be divided into three classes: sets which are Π_n–exact for every n, sets which are Π_A–exact and sets which are Π_A–rough (for a detailed study of topologies on rough sets see [14]).

1.2 Fractal Dimensions

Objects called now "fractals" have been investigated since 1920's [3], [5] yet the renewed interest in them goes back to 1970's in connection with studies of chaotic behavior, irregular non–smooth sets, dynamic systems, information compression and computer graphics [8].

For our purposes, the *Minkowski dimension* (*box dimension*) is a valuable guiding notion. For a bounded set $T \subseteq E^n$ (i.e. $diam(T) < \infty$), and $\delta > 0$, we denote by $n_\delta(T)$ the least number of n–cubes of diameter less than δ that cover T. Then we may consider the fraction $\frac{-log n_\delta(T)}{log \delta}$ and we may evaluate its limit.

When the limit $lim_{\delta \to 0} \frac{-log n_\delta(T)}{log \delta}$ exists, it is called the *Minkowski dimension* of the set T and it is denoted $dim_{\mathcal{M}}(T)$.

An advantage of the Minkowski dimension is that families of δ–cubes in its dimension may be selected in many ways, one among them is to consider a δ–grid of cubes of side length δ on E^n and to count the number $N_\delta(T)$ of those among them which intersect T; then we have cf. [4]: if the limit $lim_{\delta \to 0} \frac{-log N_\delta(T)}{log \delta}$ exists, then it is equal to $dim_{\mathcal{M}}(T)$.

1.3 Metrics on Rough Sets

Given a Π_A–rough set X, we may observe that it may be represented as a pair (Q, T) of Π_A–closed sets Q, T where $Q = Cl_{\Pi_A} X$, $T = U \setminus Int_{\Pi_A} X$. We have the following cf. [14]:

Proposition 1. *A pair (Q, T) of Π_A–closed subsets in U satisfies conditions $Q = Cl_{\Pi_A} X, T = U \setminus Int_{\Pi_A} X$ with a rough set $X \subseteq U$ if and only if Q, T satisfy the following conditions*

$$\begin{aligned}&(i) \ U = Q \cup T \\ &(ii) \ Q \cap T \neq \emptyset \\ &(iii) \ Q \cap T \text{ contains no } x \text{ with } \{x\} \ \Pi_A - open\end{aligned} \quad (5)$$

We consider an information system $\mathcal{A} = (U, A)$ as introduced above with $A = \{a_n : n = 1, 2, ...\}$. We assume from now on that
(Fin) for each $a \in A$, the value set V_a is finite.
For $n = 1, 2, ...$, we define a function $d_n : U \times U \to \mathbf{R}^+$:

$$(RSM) \ d_n(x, y) = \begin{cases} 1 & in \ case \ [x]_n \neq [y]_n \\ 0, & otherwise \end{cases} \quad (6)$$

This done, we define a function $d : U \times U \to \mathbf{R}^+$ as follows

$$d(x, y) = \sum_n 10^{-n} \cdot d_n(x, y) \quad (7)$$

Then d is a pseudo–metric on U. Now we introduce a metric d_H into the family $\mathcal{C}(U)$ of closed subsets of U in the topology Π_A. For $K, L \in \mathcal{C}(U)$, we let

$$(HPM) \ d_H(K, L) = max\{max_{x \in K} dist(x, L), max_{y \in L} dist(y, K)\} \quad (8)$$

(recall that $dist(x, L) = min\{d(x, z) : z \in L\}$ is the *distance* of x to the set L). The standard proof shows that d_H is a metric on $\mathcal{C}$ cf. [6].

Now, for any pair $(Q_1, T_1), (Q_2, T_2)$ of rough sets, we let

$$D((Q_1, T_1), (Q_2, T_2)) = max\{d_H(Q_1, Q_2), d_H(T_1, T_2)\} \qquad (9)$$

Then D is a metric on rough sets cf. [14].

Let us observe that any Π_A–exact set X may be represented in similar manner as a pair (Q, T) of Π_A–closed sets where $U = Q \cup T$ but $Q \cap T = \emptyset$. Nevertheless, the metric D may be as well defined for those pairs.

2 Fractal Dimension dim_A

For an information system $\mathcal{A} = (U, A)$ with the countable set $A = \{a_n : n = 1, 2, ...\}$ of attributes such that $IND_{a_{n+1}} \subseteq IND_{a_n}$ for $n = 1, 2, ...$, we will define the notion of an $\mathcal{A}$–dimension, denoted dim_A.

We assume (Fin) and additionally
(1) the number of equivalence classes of Ind_{a_1} is k_1;
(2) each class of IND_{a_n} ramifies into k_{n+1} classes of $IND_{a_{n+1}}$.

Thus the number of equivalence classes of the relation IND_{a_n} is $m_n = \prod_{i=1}^{n} k_i$. We will say that the information system $\mathcal{A}$ is of type $\kappa = (k_i)_i$. Although these assumptions impose some regularity conditions on the information system, yet they may be satisfied by subdividing classes if necessary.

We denote by the symbol $eq_n(X)$ the number of equivalence classes of IND_{a_n} contained in X.

For a bounded set $T \subseteq U$, we let

$$(FDU) \; \overline{dim_A}(T) = lim_{n \to \infty} \frac{log \prod_{i=1}^{n} eq_n(\overline{a_n}T)}{log \prod_{i=1}^{n} m_i} \qquad (10)$$

where m_i has been defined as the number of classes of Ind_{a_i}.
Similarly, we let

$$(FDL) \; \underline{dim_A}(T) = lim_{n \to \infty} \frac{log \prod_{i=1}^{n} eq_n(\underline{a_n}T)}{log \prod_{i=1}^{n} m_i} \qquad (11)$$

with the additional agreement that $\underline{dim_A}(T) = 0$ in case $eq_n(\underline{a_n}T) = 0$ for some n.

In case $\underline{dim_A}(T) = \overline{dim_A}(T)$ we denote the common value with the symbol $dim_A(T)$ and call it the $\mathcal{A}$–dimension of T.

We say that T is $\mathcal{A}$–exact in this case.

Let us collect here basic properties of dim_A which are parallel to respective properties of the Minkowski (box) dimension.

Proposition 2. 1. $dim_A(Z) \leq dim_A(T)$ whenever $Z \subseteq T$
2. $dim_A(Z) = dim_A(Cl_{\Pi_A} Z)$

Proof. Indeed, (1) follows by the very definition of dim_A. (2) follows from the fact that closure does not change parameters l_i, k_i.

We demonstrate the continuity property of the function dim_A.

Proposition 3. *Assume that $\mathcal{A}$ is of type κ with $k_i \geq 2$ for infinitely many i, a sequence $(T_n)_n$ of sets is convergent in the metric D to a set T and $\underline{dim}_{\mathcal{A}}(T_n)$, $\overline{dim}_{\mathcal{A}}(T_n)$ exist for each n.*
Then
$$\begin{aligned} lim_{n \to \infty} \underline{dim}_{\mathcal{A}}(T_n) &= \underline{dim}_{\mathcal{A}}(T) \\ lim_{n \to \infty} \overline{dim}_{\mathcal{A}}(T_n) &= \overline{dim}_{\mathcal{A}}(T) \end{aligned} \qquad (12)$$

Proof. We give a proof for the upper dimension; assume $\varepsilon > 0$. There exists $n(\varepsilon)$ with the property that $D(T_n, T) < \varepsilon$ for $n > n(\varepsilon)$ hence for a natural number $M(\varepsilon)$ we have
$$\overline{a_m}T_n = \overline{a_m}T \qquad (13)$$
for each $m \leq M(\varepsilon)$ and $n > n(\varepsilon)$. Clearly, $n(\varepsilon), M(\varepsilon) \to \infty$ as $\varepsilon \to 0$.
For $n > n(\varepsilon)$ we thus have

$$lim_{n \to \infty} \overline{dim}_{\mathcal{A}}(T_n) = lim_{n \to \infty} lim_{j \to \infty} \frac{\log \prod_{i=1}^{j} l_i^{(n)}}{\log \prod_{i=1}^{j} m_i} = $$
$$lim_{j \to \infty}[lim_{n \to \infty} \frac{\log \prod_{i=1}^{j} l_i^{(n)}}{\log \prod_{i=1}^{j} m_i}] = lim_{j \to \infty}[\frac{\log \prod_{i=1}^{j} l_i}{\log \prod_{i=1}^{j} m_i}] = \overline{dim}_{\mathcal{A}}(T) \qquad (14)$$

where $l_i^{(n)}, l_i$ stand for $eq_i(\overline{a_i}T_n)$, $eq_i(\overline{a_i}T)$ respectively.

Corollary 1. *$dim_{\mathcal{A}}$ is continuous with respect to the metric D.*

Corollary 2. $\overline{dim}_{\mathcal{A}}(T \cup W) \leq max\{\overline{dim}_{\mathcal{A}}T, \overline{dim}_{\mathcal{A}}W\}$

Indeed, the proof goes similarly to the proof of Proposition 3.

3 $\mathcal{A}$–Exact Sets

Let us record basic properties of those sets.

Proposition 4. 1. *every $\Pi_{\mathcal{A}}$-exact set is $\mathcal{A}$-exact;*
2. *the union $T \cup W$ of $\mathcal{A}$-exact sets is $\mathcal{A}$-exact;*
3. *the complement $U \setminus T$ to an $\mathcal{A}$-exact set T is $\mathcal{A}$-exact;*
4. *the limit of a sequence $(T_n)_n$ of a convergent in the metric D sequence of $\mathcal{A}$-exact sets is an $\mathcal{A}$-exact set;*
5. *$\mathcal{A}$-exact sets form a compact metric space under the metric D.*

Proof. Claim (1) follows from Claim (2). Indeed, in case of Claim (1), we use compactness of topology Π on U due to (Fin) cf. [14]. As exact sets are closed–open they are compact, hence they are unions of finitely many basic sets of the form $(v_1, .., v_n) = \{x : a(x) = v_i, i \leq n\}$. Each of these sets is clearly $\mathcal{A}$-exact hence the result follows by Claim (2). To prove Claim (2), we resort to definition. We assume that sets T, W are $\mathcal{A}$-exact. By $k_{i,X}$ resp. $l_{i,X}$ we denote $eq_i(\overline{a_i}X)$, resp. $eq_i(\underline{a_i}X)$.

Clearly, $k_{i,T\cup W} \leq k_{i,T} + k_{i,W} \leq 2max\{k_{i,T}, k_{i,W}\}$ and $max\{l_{i,T}, l_{i,W}\} \leq l_{i,T\cup W}$. Thus,

$$lim_{j\to\infty} \frac{log\Pi_{i=1}^j l_{i,T\cup W}}{log\Pi_{i=1}^j m_i} \leq \qquad (15)$$
$$lim_{j\to\infty} \frac{log\Pi_{i=1}^j k_{i,T\cup W}}{log\Pi_{i=1}^j m_i}$$

and both are bounded by

$$max\{lim_{j\to\infty} \frac{log\Pi_{i=1}^j l_{i,T}}{log\Pi_{i=1}^j m_i}, lim_{j\to\infty} \frac{log\Pi_{i=1}^j l_{i,W}}{log\Pi_{i=1}^j m_i}\} \qquad (16)$$

from below and

$$lim_{j\to\infty} \frac{log\Pi_{i=1}^j 2max\{k_{i,T}, k_{i,W}\}}{log\Pi_{i=1}^j m_i} \qquad (17)$$

from above which implies directly that $T\cup W$ is $\mathcal{A}$-exact once T,W are such.

Claim (3) follows obviously, as the complement turns upper dimension into lower and vice versa: $l_{i,T} = k_{i,U\setminus T}$ and $l_{i,U\setminus T} = k_{i,T}$. Claim (4) is a consequence of Proposition 1 and Claim (5) follows from Claim (4), as it is easy to see that under (Fin) any sequence of pairs $((Q_n, T_n))_n$ with $Q_n \cup T_n = U$ for each n either contains an infinite subsequence $((Q_{n_k}, T_{n_k}))_k$ of rough sets and this subsequence converges in D to a rough set by compactness of the space of rough sets proved in [14], or it contains an infinite sequence $((Q_{n_k}, T_{n_k}))_k$ of exact sets which by the assumption (Fin) as may be easily seen contains a subsequence eventually constant hence converging with respect to D to an exact set. Thus the space $\mathcal{ER}$ of pairs (Q,T) with $Q\cup T = U$ is compact under D and Claim(4) implies that the space $\mathcal{E}_\infty$ of $\mathcal{A}$-exact sets is a closed subspace of the space $\mathcal{ER}$ hence it is compact.

Corollary 3. *$\mathcal{A}$-exact sets form a field of sets*

Proof. Indeed, by Proposition 4, 2, 3, we have for $\mathcal{A}$-exact sets T,W that $T\cap W = U \setminus [(U\setminus T) \cup (U\setminus W)]$ is $\mathcal{A}$-exact.

4 Rough Mereology and Dependencies on Infinitary Concepts

Given concepts $X, Y \subseteq U$, we let $\mu(X,Y) = r$ if $lim_{n\to\infty} \frac{eq_n(X\cup U\setminus Y)}{eq_n(U)} = r$. Then

Proposition 5. *1. $\mu(X,X) = 1$ 2. $\mu(X,Y) = 1 \Rightarrow \forall Z.[(\mu(Z,Y) \geq \mu(Z,X)$ 3. $\mu(X,Y) = r \wedge \mu(Y,Z) = s \Rightarrow \mu(X,Z) \geq \otimes(r,s)$ where $\otimes(x,y) = max\{0, r+s-1\}$ is the Łukasiewicz tensor product.*

Proof. 1. is obvious. For 2., given $\varepsilon > 0$, there is $n(\varepsilon)$ such that if $n > n(\varepsilon)$ then (i) $eq_n(X\cup U\setminus Y) \geq (1-\varepsilon)\cdot eq_n(U)$ hence (ii) $eq_n[(U\setminus X)\cap(U\setminus Y)] \leq \varepsilon\cdot eq_n(U)$. From the identity $(Z\cup U\setminus X)\cap(Z\cup U\setminus Y) = (Z\cup U\setminus X)\cup(U\setminus X)\cap(U\setminus Y)$

and (ii) we get passing to the limit (so $\varepsilon \to 0$) that $\mu(Z,Y) \geq \mu(Z,X)$. For 3., by the identity $(X \cup U \setminus Y) \cap (Y \cup U \setminus Z) \subseteq (X \cup U \setminus Z)$, we get that $eq_n(U) - eq_n(X \cup U \setminus Z) \leq eq_n(U) - eq_n(X \cup U \setminus Y) + eq_n(U) - eq_n(Y \cup U \setminus Z)$ whence dividing by $eq_n(U)$ and passing to the limit, we get that $\mu(X,Z) \geq \mu(X,Y) + \mu(Y,Z) - 1$.

The measure μ satisfies basic postulates for *rough inclusion*. We may define a generalized notion of partial dependence for infinite concepts X, Y as $X \mapsto_r Y$ if $\mu(X,Y) = r$. Then by Proposition 5, 3., we have the deduction rule: $\frac{X \mapsto_r Y, Y \mapsto_s Z}{X \mapsto_{\otimes(r,s)} Z}$ which extends the result known for dependencies among attributes in the finite case cf.[9].

Acknowledgement. This work has been supported by the Grant No. 8T11C 024 17 from the State Committee for Scientific Research (KBN) of the Republic of Poland.

References

1. N. Agarwal, Applications of Generalized Support Vector Machines to Predictive Modelling, in: [7], invited talk.
2. R. B. Altman, K3: Challenges for Knowledge Discovery in Biology, in: [7], keynote talk.
3. C.Carathéodory, Über das lineare Mass von Punktmenge eine Verallgemeinerung des Längenbegriffs, Nach. Gesell. Wiss. Göttingen, 1914, pp. 406–426.
4. K. J. Falconer, Fractal Geometry. Mathematical Foundations and Applications, Wiley and Sons, 1990.
5. F.Hausdorff, Dimension und ausseres Mass, Math.Annalen, 79, 1919, pp. 157–179.
6. F. Hausdorff, Mengenlehre, Leipzig, 1914.
7. KDD–2001, 7th ACMSIGKDD Intern. Conf. on Knowledge Discovery and Data Mining, San Francisco, August 26–29, 2001; www.acm.org/sigkdd/
8. B. Mandelbrot, Les Objects Fractals: Forme, Hasard et Dimension, Flammarion, Paris, 1975.
9. M. Novotný and Z. Pawlak, Partial dependency of attributes, Bull. Polish Acad. Sci. Math., 36 (1988), 453–458.
10. Z. Pawlak, Rough Sets. Theoretical Aspects of Reasoning about Data, Kluwer, Dordrecht, 1991.
11. Z. Pawlak, Rough sets, algebraic and topological approach, Int. J. Inform. Comp. Sciences, 11(1982), pp. 341–366.
12. L.Polkowski, On fractal dimension in information systems. Toward exact sets in infinite information systems, Fundamenta Informaticae, 50(3–4) (2002), in print.
13. L. Polkowski, S. Tsumoto, and T. Y. Lin, (eds.), Rough Set Methods and Applications. New Developments in Knowledge Discovery in Information Systems, Physica Verlag/Springer Verlag, Heidelberg, 2000.
14. L. Polkowski, Mathematical morphology of rough sets, Bull. Polish Acad. Sci. Math., 41, 1993, pp. 241–273.
15. R. Ramakrishnan, Mass collaboration and Data Mining, in: [7], keynote talk.

About Tolerance and Similarity Relations in Information Systems

J.A. Pomykała

Manager Academy, Society for Trade Initiatives
ul. Kawęczyńska, Warsaw, Poland
pomykala_andrzej@mac.edu.pl

Abstract. The tolerance and similarity relations in information systems are considered. Some properties and connections are shown and the relation to the dependency of attributes in relational databases is developed. In particular a new definition of similarity dependency of attributes is formulated.

Keywords. Information system, dependency of attributes, similarity relation

1 Introduction

The notion of information systems formulated by Pawlak and developed by him and co-workers (see eg. Orłowska [10], Skowron [21], Dűntsch and Gediga [4], Vakarelov [24]) and Słowiński [22] is now a well developed branch of data analysis formalisms. It is strongly related (but different) to relational database theory on the one hand and to the fuzzy sets theory on the other.

In this paper we propose new notion of similarity of systems and we formulate some properties of attribute dependency, expressed in the language of weak and strong similarity relations $\operatorname{sim}(X)$ and $\operatorname{Sim}(X)$, respectively. This note can be seen as a step toward the solution of the open problem formulated in Orłowska [10]. Some results in this paper were presented in the proceedings of the Sixth International Workshop of Relational Methods in Computer Science, the Netherlands, October 2001.

2 Information Systems

We recall again that the aim of this paper is twofold: first give a broad motivation for studying similarity of systems and similarity relations (or equivalently tolerance relations) in geometry, and logic, and second give a new definition of dependency of attributes in RDB (relational database) and IST (information systems theory).

Any collection of data specified as a structure (O, A, V, f) *such that O is a nonempty set of objects, A is a nonempty set of attributes, V is a nonempty*

set of values and f is a function of $O \times A$ into $2^{V \setminus \{\emptyset\}}$, is referred to as an *information system*.

In this paper we assume that with every attribute $a \in A$ is related a tolerance relation (i.e. reflexive and symmetric relation) $\tau(a)$. In most cases this relation shall be defined in the following way. Let $a \in A$ and $B \subseteq A$:

$$\text{Sim}(a)xy \quad \text{iff} \quad f(x,a) \cap f(y,a) \neq \emptyset$$
$$\text{sim}(a)xy = \text{Sim}(a)xy,$$
$$\text{Sim}(B)xy \quad \text{iff} \quad \forall b \in B \ \text{Sim}(b)xy$$
$$\text{sim}(B)xy \quad \text{iff} \quad \exists b \in B \ \text{sim}(b)xy.$$

$\text{Sim}(B)$ is called (strong) similarity relation and $\text{sim}(B)$ is called weak similarity with respect to the set of attributes $B \subseteq A$.

The set $\{f(x,a) : a \in A\}$ shall be called an information about the object x, in short a record of x or a row determined by x. We shall say that two records determined by x, y are strongly τ-similar iff $\forall a \in A \ f(x,a)\tau(a)f(y,a)$. We will also consider the case when the above notion is restricted to a set $B \subseteq A$ i.e. two records $\{f(x,a) : a \in B\}$ and $\{f(y,b) : b \in B\}$ are similar with respect to the set $B \subseteq A$ iff

$$\forall b \in B \ f(x,b)\tau(b)f(y,b).$$

We shall say that two objects (records) x, y are weakly τ-similar if for some attribute $a \in A$, values $f(x,a)$, $f(y,a)$ are similar with respect to $\tau(a)$.

In symbols: $\exists b \in B f(x,b)\tau(b)f(y,b)$. We denote strong relation by $\tau(B^\wedge)$ and weak one by $\tau(B^\vee)$, respectively.

We can express special kind of similarity of records by formulating the proper query in the system. It is however strongly determined by the possibilities of a given RDB system. By analogy to indiscernibility matrices (see Skowron, Rauszer [21]) we propose to use similarity matrices. We begin with the definition:

the set of attributes $Y \subseteq A$ depends on the set $X \subseteq A$ with respect to the similarity relation Sim *if and only if*

$$\text{Sim}(X) \subseteq \text{Sim}(Y).$$

We shall write in symbols

$$X \xrightarrow{S} Y \quad \text{or} \quad X \xrightarrow{\text{Sim}} Y.$$

In the same way we can define dependency of attributes with respect to weak similarity relation sim:

$$X \xrightarrow{s} Y \quad \text{iff} \quad \text{sim}(X) \leq \text{sim}(Y)$$

(here $\leq$ is the usual inclusion relation between binary relations).

In other words, $X \xrightarrow{S} Y$ if strong similarity of objects with respect to the set of attributes X implies strong similarity of objects with respect to the set of attributes Y.

Let me recall now Armstrong axioms for functional dependency (Let me recall that XY abbreviates $X \cup Y$.):

B1 If $Y \subseteq X \subseteq A$ then $X \to Y$.
B2 If $X \to Y$ and $Z \subseteq A$ then $XZ \to YZ$.
B3 If $X \to Y \to Z$ then $X \to Z$.

The axioms hold for strong similarity relation Sim. They hold in some other classes of strong relations also, cf. MacCaull [8].
Remark: for weak similarity we have just the opposite:

$$\text{if } Y \subseteq X \subseteq A \text{ then } Y \xrightarrow{\text{sim}} X.$$

■

Also for weak similarity relation the axioms B2, B3 holds easily.
Let me finally introduce the mixed similarity dependency:

$$X \xrightarrow{Ss} Y \text{ iff } \text{Sim}(X) \leq \text{sim}(Y) \text{ and}$$
$$X \xrightarrow{sS} Y \text{ iff } \text{sim}(X) \leq \text{Sim}(Y).$$

$X \xrightarrow{Ss} Y$ if for all objects $x, y \in O$ strong similarity of x, y with respect to the set of attributes X implies weak similarity of x, y with respect to the set Y. ■

3 Tolerance Relation

"Any model of perception must take account of the fact that we cannot distinguish between points that are sufficiently close" (Zeeman [25]). Similar statement was formulated for choice behaviour by Luce. In consequence the notions of tolerance, threshold, just noticable difference has been formulated. We can say that the above notions of similarity and <u>tolerance</u>, threshold, <u>just noticable difference</u> have the same physical and philosophical foundation and the same role to play.
If we substitute closeness for identity then we can define <u>tolerance geometry</u>. In the approach of Roberts it is important to "Study finite sets and axioms necessary and sufficient for isomorphism (or homomorphism) into certain kinds of spaces" [20].
Now let me define several relations considered in information systems:

a) $x\tau y$ iff $|x - y| < \varepsilon$,
b) $x\tau y$ iff $\rho(x, y) < \varepsilon$, here ρ is a distance function,
c) $(x_1 \ldots x_n) \tau (y_1 \ldots y_n)$ iff $\exists_{i,j}(|x_i - y_j| < \varepsilon$,
d) Assume that $x \in O_1$, $y \in O_2$, $(O_1 A_1 V_1 f_1)$, $(O_2 A_2 V_2 f_2)$ are information systems and we define:

$$x \tau y \text{ iff } \exists_{a_1, a_2} \ f(x, a_1) \cap f(y, a_2) \neq \emptyset$$

and

$$x \tau (B_1, B_2) y \text{ iff } \exists b_1 \in B_1, \ b_2 \in B_2,$$
$$f(x, b_1) \cap f(y, b_2) \neq \emptyset.$$

e) Assume that $\tau_1\ \tau_2\ \tau_3\ \ldots\ \tau_n$ are tolerances on U, we define the relation τ^n

$$x\tau^n y \text{ iff } (\exists x_1 \ldots x_n\ x_1 = x\ x_n = y$$
$$\&\ \forall_i\ x_i \tau_i\ x_{i+1}).$$

We say that τ^n is generated by $\tau_1 \ldots \tau_n$. It is clear that for a wide class of nontrivial tolerance relations there is n_0 s.t. for all $n > n_0$ we cannot say reasonably that objects x, y related by τ^n are similar. In other words there is a threshold of similarity for a given information system.

4 Similarity of Systems

The basic notion which expresses similarity of systems or algebras is the notion of homomorphism. We propose here slightly different notion, relating similarity of systems to the similarity structures which can be defined in (or on) the system.

Example: Similarity structure on information system.

By similarity structure on the system (O, A, V, f) we mean the following structure:

$$(B, C, D, \ldots, T)\Big(\text{Sim}(B), \text{Sim}(C) \ldots\Big)\Big(U_1^B \ldots U_{B(i)}^B\Big)$$
$$\Big(U_1^C \ldots U_{C(i)}^C\Big) \ldots \Big(U_1^T \ldots U_{T(i)}^T\Big)$$

where $B, C, D, \ldots, T$ are subsets of A, $\text{Sim}(B), \ldots$ are similarity relations,

$$\Big(U_1^B \ldots U_{B(i)}^B\Big) \ldots \Big(U_1^T \ldots U_{T(i)}^T\Big)$$

are partitions of the universe of objects O, satisfying conditions:

$$\forall_{E \in \{B,C,D,\ldots,T\}} \forall_{x,y \in U_i^E}\ \text{Sim}(E)xy$$

and

$$\forall x \in U_i^E,\ y \in U_j^E \text{ for } i \neq j$$
$$\text{non}\quad (x\,\text{Sim}(E)y).$$

Of course the above definition can be formulated also for weak similarity relations $\text{sim}(B), \ldots$ or other kind of tolerances related to attributes. The proposed notion of similarity of information systems can be especially useful in case when we have fixed set of objects O and dynamically changing sets A, V, f. In other words we can compare fixed set of objects from a different perspectives (in this case expressed by sets A, V and functions f) (cf. [17], [18]).

Approximation space

By approximation space in general sense we shall understand the family of operators on subsets of a given universe. The operators are usually called lower and upper approximation operators. They can be defined using equivalence relations, partitions, covers, tolerances etc., or can be given analytically in a fixed cartesian space. This definition is broad enough to cover many operators which are useful in many areas of applications eg.: in geometry, medicine, logic, algebra etc. Let us mention that one of the first strong papers analysing the role of operators based on the relations is the Tarski-Jonnson paper [23].

Notation: $\mathbb{E}$ is a family of subsets of the universe O. For every $X \subset 0$

$$\mathbb{E}(X) = \mathbb{E}^1(X) = \bigcup \{E \in \mathbb{E} : E \cap X \neq \emptyset\}$$
$$\mathbb{E}^w(X) = \underbrace{\left(\mathbb{E}^1(\ldots \mathbb{E}^1(X))\ldots\right)}_{w-\text{times}}$$

$\mathbb{E}^n(X)$ is denoted also $u\mathbb{E}^n(X)$ and is called n-th upper approximation of X using $\mathbb{E}$. Analogously, $l\mathbb{E}^n = -\mathbb{E}^n(-X)$ is called n-th lower approximation by $\mathbb{E}$ of the set X.

Let us assume that notions of pixel, neighbour $N_i(p)$ from computer graphics are known and that $\mathbb{E}$ is defined in one of the following ways:

a) $\mathbb{E}$ is a family of all pairs of 2-neighbour pixels,
b) $\mathbb{E}$ is a family of all triples quadriples, n-tuples etc. of 3-neighbour pixels (4, n etc.),
c) $\mathbb{E}$ is a family of all pairs of 2-neighbour pixels in a horizontal position,
d) $\mathbb{E}$ is a family of all pairs of 2-neighbour pixels in a vertical position,
e) $\mathbb{E}$ is a family of all patterns of some finite number of pixels defined by a simple geometric rules.

Then we can apply approximation operations to computer graphics. ∎

5 Independency with Respect to Similarity

Let rel $: P(A) \to P(\mathbb{O} \times \mathbb{O})$ be arbitrary function satisfying the condition: (see Pomykała [16]) for every subset $B \subseteq A$

$$\begin{aligned} \text{rel}(B) &= \bigcap\{\text{rel}(\{b\}) : b \in B\} \\ \text{rel}(\emptyset) &= \mathbb{O} \times \mathbb{O} \end{aligned} \tag{1}$$

Let $X \subseteq A$. We say that X is rel-independent iff for every set $X' \subset X$ it holds $\text{rel}(X') \neq \text{rel}(X)$. Otherwise we say that X is rel-dependent. We say that $X' \subseteq X$ is rel-reduct of X iff $\text{rel}(X') = \text{rel}(X)$ and X' is independent.

The set of all reducts of any subset $B \subseteq A$ will be denoted by Redrel (B). The set of all reducts of A will be denoted by Redrel. The set of independent subsets of A shall be denoted by Indrel. Assume $X \subseteq A$. An element $x \in X$ is called rel-dispensable in X if $\text{rel}(X) = \text{rel}(X - \{x\})$. Otherwise x is called rel-indispensable. The core of X is the following set (see [9]):

$$\text{Core}(X) = \{x \in X : x \text{ is rel-indispensable in } X\}.$$

Let $X \subseteq A$. We shall say that the set X is Sim-independent iff for every set $X' \subsetneq X$ it holds $\text{Sim}(X') \neq \text{Sim}(X)$. Otherwise we say that X is dependent with respect to similarity relation Sim. We will say that $X' \subseteq X$ is a reduct of X with respect to similarity Sim iff $\text{Sim}(X') = \text{Sim}(X)$ and X' is Sim-independent. In other words X' is minimal generating set for X with respect to the relation Sim.

Lemma: $X \subseteq A$ is Sim-independent iff for every $p \in X$

$$\text{Sim}(X) \neq \text{Sim}(X - \{p\}).$$

An attribute $x \in X \subseteq A$ is called *dispensable* in X with respect to similarity relation Sim if

$$\text{Sim}(X) = \text{Sim}(X - \{x\}).$$

Otherwise x is called Sim *indispensable*. By a Sim-core of X we shall mean the following set (cf. Ind-core in [9]):

$$\text{Core}^{\text{Sim}}(X) = \{x \in X : x \text{ is Sim-indispensable in } X\}$$

We shall formulate this result for similarity relation Sim:

Theorem: *For every $X \subseteq A$*

$$\text{Core}^{\text{Sim}}(X) = \bigcap \{Q : Q \text{ is a reduct of } X$$
$$\text{with respect to strong similarity Sim.}\}$$

The theorem is not true for the weak similarity sim. It holds dual form of it. For every $X \subseteq A$ we have the family of Sim-independent subsets of X, the family of maximal Sim-independent subsets of X and the family of attributes X_0 s.t. $X_0 = \{x \in X : \text{Sim}(x) = \text{Sim}(\emptyset)\}$. By convention $\text{Sim}(\emptyset) = \mathbb{O} \times \mathbb{O}$. The lemma below shows the connection between these families:

Lemma: *For every $X \subseteq A$, A finite, it holds:*

(a) $X = X_0 \cup \bigcup \{X' \subseteq X : X' \text{ is a Sim-independent}\}$,
(b) $X = X_0 \cup \bigcup \{X' \subseteq X : X' \text{ is a maximal Sim-independent subset of } X\}$.

Let $X \subseteq A$. If $X' \subseteq X$ is a maximal rel-independent subset of X, then it is called rel-subreduct of X. If moreover $\text{rel}(X') \neq \text{rel}(X)$ then X' is called the proper subreduct.

We denote the set of all rel-subreducts by $\text{Subr}(X)$. Let $X \subseteq A$. The set $X_0 = \{x \in X : \text{rel}(X) = \text{rel}(\emptyset)\}$ will be called null-part of X.

Theorem: *If $X' \in \text{Subr } X - \text{Redrel } X$ then for every $z \in X - X'$ there exists $Z \subseteq X' \cup \{z\}$ such that*

$$\bigcap \{\text{rel}(x) : x \in X' \cup \{z\} - Z\} \subseteq \bigcap \{\text{rel}(x) : x \in Z\}.$$

The weak similarity relation satisfies the conditions

1) $\text{sim}(B) = \bigcup \{\text{sim}(b) : b \in B\}$,
2) $\text{sim}(\emptyset) = \emptyset$.

Therefore in some properties below we can use arbitrary relation rel satisfying 1), 2). First we state some definitions:
Let $X \subseteq A$. We say that X is sim-*independent iff for every* $X' \not\subseteq X$ *it holds* sim $X' \neq$ sim X. If sim $X =$ sim A then X is a generating set for A.

Still another formulation is the following: X' is called sim-reduct of X iff sim $X' =$ sim X and X' is independent with respect to the relation sim. An attribute $x \in X$ is called sim-dispensable in X if $\text{sim}\,(X) = \text{sim}\,(X - \{x\})$, i.e. it holds $\text{sim}\,(x) \subseteq \bigcup\{\text{sim}\,(b) : b \in X - \{x\}\}$.

Otherwise x will be called indispensable for X w.r.t. sim-relation.

Finally we define

$$\text{Core}^{\text{sim}}\,X = \{x \in X : x \text{ is sim-indispensable in } X\}.$$

By duality some properties of $\text{Core}^{\text{sim}}\,X$ can be obtained from $\text{Core}^{\text{Sim}}\,X$.

Example: Let $O = \{o_1, \ldots, o_{n+1}\}$, $A = \{a_1, \ldots, a_m\}$ and let the system will be given by the following table:

	a_1	a_2	a_3	...	a_i	...	a_{n-1}	a_n
o_1	1	1	1		1		1	1
o_2	1	1	1		1		1	1
o_3	1	1	1		1		1	1
$\vdots$	$\vdots$	$\vdots$	0	$\vdots$	$\vdots$		$\vdots$	$\vdots$
o_i	0	0	1		1		1	1
$\vdots$	$\vdots$	$\vdots$	$\vdots$		0	$\vdots$	$\vdots$	$\frac{1}{2}\frac{2}{3}\ldots$
o_{n-1}	0	0	0		0		1	$n-i-2$
o_n	0	0	0		0		0	$n-i-1$
o_{n+1}	0	0	0		0		0	$n-i$

It is easy to notice that for $\text{rel}\,(A) = \text{Ind}\,(A)$ it holds:

$$\text{Redrel}\,(A) = \{\{a_1, \ldots, a_i, a_n\}\} \text{ and}$$
$$\text{Subr}\,(A) = \{\{a_1, \ldots, a_{n-1}\}, \{a_1, \ldots, a_i, a_n\}\}.$$

Therefore the problem of finding reducts and subreducts of a given information system may force us to examine the subsets of A of arbitrary cardinality. In other words sometimes we have to investigate almost all subsets of the set of attributes.

References

1. W.W. Armstrong, *Dependency structures of data base relationships*, Information Processing 74. Schek, Saltor, Ramos, Alonso (Eds.).
2. I. Chajda, B. Zelinka, *Tolerance relation on lattices*, Casopis pro pestovani matematiky, roc. 99 (1974), Praha.
3. E.F. Codd, *A Relational Model of Data for Large Shared Data Banks*, Communications of the ACM, vol. 13, No 6, June 1970.
4. I. Dűntsch, G. Gediga, *Rough set data analysis*.
5. R. Fagin, *Multivalued Dependencies and a New Normal Form for Relational Databases*, ACM Trans. on Database Systems, Sept. 1977, vol. 2, No 3.
6. T.B. Iwiński, *Algebraic approach to rough sets*, Bull. Pol. Ac. Math. 35, 1987.
7. T.T. Lee, *An Algebraic Theory of Relational Databases*, The Bell System Technical Journal vol. 62, No. 10, December 1983.
8. W. MacCaull, *A proof System for Dependencies for Information Relations*, Fundamenta Informaticae, vol. 42, No 1, April 2000.
9. M. Nowotny, Z. Pawlak, *Independence of attributes*, Bull. Pol. Ac. Math. 36, 1988.
10. E. Orłowska, (ed.), *Incomplete Information: Rough Set Analysis*, Physica-Verlag 2000.
11. K. Otsuka and T. Togawa, *A model of cortical neural network structure*, 20th Int. Conf. of IEEE, vol. 20, No 4, 1998.
12. Z. Pawlak, *Information Systems*, Theoret. Found., Inf. Systems 3 (1981).
13. Z. Pawlak, *Rough classification*, Int. J. Man-Machine Studies 20 (1984).
14. J.A. Pomykała, *Approximation Operations in Approximation Space*, Bull. Pol. Ac. Math. vol. 35, No. 9–10, 1987.
15. J.A. Pomykała, *A remark about the paper of H. Rasiowa and W. Marek*, Bull. Pol. Ac. Math., vol. 36, No. 7–8, 1988.
16. J.A. Pomykała, *Approximation, Similarity and Rough Constructions*, ILLC Prepublication Series for Computation and Complexity Theory CT-93-07, University of Amsterdam.
17. J.A. Pomykała, *On similarity based approximation of information*, Demonstratio Mathematica, vol. XXVII, No. 3–4, 1994, 663–671.
18. J.A. Pomykała, J. M. Pomykała *On regularity of hypergraph sequences*, Demonstratio Mathematica, vol. XXVII, No. 3–4, 1994, 651–662.
19. C.M. Rauszer, *Algebraic Properties of Functional Dependencies*, Bull. Pol. Ac. Sc., vol. 33, No 9–10, 1985.
20. F.S. Roberts, *Tolerance Geometry*, JSL, vol. XIV, No 1, January 1973.
21. A. Skowron, C. Rauszer, *The Discernibility matrices and functions in Information Systems*, (in [22]).
22. R. Słowiński (ed.), *Intelligent Decision Support*, Handbook of Applications and Advances of the Rough Set Theory, Kluwer, 1991.
23. A. Tarski, B. Jonsson, *Boolean Algebras with Operators*, American Journal of Mathematics, vol. 74, 1952.
24. D. Vakarelov, *Modal logics for knowledge representation systems*, TCS 90, Elsevier (1991), 433–456.
25. E.C. Zeeman, *The Topology of the Brain and Visual Perception*, in M. K. FORT, J. R. Ed., Prentice Hall, 1962.
26. W. Żakowski, *Approximations in the space* (U, π), Demonstratio Math. 16 (1983).

Rough Sets, Guarded Command Language, and Decision Rules

Frederick V. Ramsey[1] and James J. Alpigini[2]

[1] Software Technology Research Laboratory
De Montfort University
Leicester LE1 9BH, UK
`Frederick.Ramsey@students.dmu.ac.uk`
[2] Assistant Professor, Systems Engineering
Penn State Great Valley School of Graduate Professional Studies
Malvern, PA 19355, USA
`jja7@psu.edu`

Abstract. The rough set approach is a mathematical tool for dealing with imprecision, uncertainty, and vagueness in data. Guarded command languages provide logical approaches for representing constrained non-determinacy in an otherwise deterministic system without incorporating probabilistic elements. Although from dramatically different functional and mathematical origins, both approaches attempt to resolve observed or anticipated discontinuities between specific pre- and post-condition states of a given information system. This paper investigates the use of a guarded command language in the generation of rough data from explicit decision rules, and in the extraction of implicit decision rules from rough experimental data. Based on these findings, rough sets and guarded command languages appear to be compatible and complementary in their approaches to imprecision and uncertainty. As the association between rough sets and guarded command language represents a new and heretofore untested research direction, possible research alternatives are suggested.

1 Introduction

The rough set approach employs mathematical constructs to deal with imprecision, uncertainty, and vagueness in data. Within a given information system, rough sets can be used to describe and resolve inconsistencies relative to specific values of a reduced set of condition attributes and the corresponding decisions. With rough set techniques, implicit decision rules can be extracted and presented, which reflect the imprecision, uncertainty, and vagueness of the original data. Guarded command languages are logical and systematic approaches for representing constrained non-determinacy into an otherwise deterministic system. A guarded command language approach allows the incorporation of imprecision, uncertainty, and vagueness into the output states of explicit systems without incorporating probabilistic elements. This paper investigates the use of a guarded command language in the generation of rough data from explicit decision rules, and in the analysis and extraction of implicit decision rules from rough experimental data.

2 Rough Sets and Guarded Command Language

Rough set theory, introduced by Pawlak [1,2], is a mathematical approach to deal with imprecision, uncertainty, and vagueness in data. Rough set theory offers a systematic approach to the conceptualization of decision systems and the derivation of rules that are useful in approximate reasoning. The mathematical basis for rough set rules and the application of rough sets to decision systems is described in Peters et. al [3].

Dijkstra [4,5] introduced the logical concept of a 'guarded command' that allows operational non-determinacy with respect to the final system state based on, and subject to, the current initial state of a given system. This construct allows for the selection of a final system state from a set of multiple possible system states, any of which could be triggered based on the same initial system state. When the system is executed repetitively, different final states may result from the same initial state. A guarded command set is defined as a series of multiple guarded commands. Each guarded command is composed of a tuple of a Boolean expression and an associated statement list. The Boolean expression is sometimes referred to as the 'guarding head' or 'guard,' in that the statements associated with that Boolean expression can be executed only if that Boolean expression evaluates true. Using the if...fi form, the guarded command construct takes the following form:

```
if  <Boolean expression> → <statement list>
[]  <Boolean expression> → <statement list>
[]  ...
[]  <Boolean expression> → <statement list>
fi
```

where the 'bar' symbol [] represents a separator between otherwise unordered alternatives. As many guarded commands as necessary are allowed to satisfy all pre-condition system states.

During the execution of this construct, all Boolean expressions are first evaluated. If none of the Boolean expressions evaluate true, then the construct terminates, and no actions are taken. If one or more of the Boolean expressions, or guards, evaluate true, then one and only one of the true guards is chosen non-deterministically and only the statement list associated with that true guard is executed. Thus, with overlapping guards, i.e., multiple guards that can be true at the same time, non-determinacy can be achieved. In its purest form, selection of the true guard for execution from among multiple true guards must be random. Adding a probabilistic approach to the selection and execution of a single true guard from among multiple true guards forms the basis of *probabilistic* guarded command language (*pGCL*) [6,7].

3 Generating Rough Data from an Explicit Rule

A rough set can be readily generated using a simple rule and a guarded command set. Consider the following simple employee service award rule based on years of service for employees with one to four years of service.

1. If worker has one year of service, worker receives Award A.
2. If worker has two years of service, worker receives Award B.
3. If worker has three years of service, worker may choose Award B or C.
4. If worker has four years of service, worker may choose Award B, C, or D.

This simple rule can be expressed in the form of guarded command language:

$$\begin{aligned}
&\text{if } \text{YearsService} = 1 \rightarrow \text{Award} = A \\
&[] \text{ YearsService} \geq 2 \rightarrow \text{Award} = B \\
&[] \text{ YearsService} \geq 3 \rightarrow \text{Award} = C \\
&[] \text{ YearsService} = 4 \rightarrow \text{Award} = D \\
&\text{fi}
\end{aligned}$$

When data from the service award program are reviewed using rough set techniques, the award distribution will be rough with respect to years of service. Barring any data noise resulting from administrative errors, the decision concepts of Award = A and Award = D are uniquely associated with the attributes YearsService = 1 and YearsService = 4, respectively. These decision concepts are crisp based on the attribute YearsService. However, Awards B and C are rough with respect to the attribute YearsService. Workers with three years of service may have chosen Award B or C, and workers with four years of service may have chosen Award B, C, or D. Therefore, decision concepts represented by Awards B or C are rough based on the attribute YearsService.

This example demonstrates how a rough data set can result from a simple explicit rule that incorporates only one attribute and a small element of non-determinacy. Real world systems operating under explicit decision rules with multiple attributes and some aspect of non-determinacy associated with one or more of those attributes can result in notably rough output data.

4 Analyzing Rough Data and Expressing Rough Rules

The guarded command language concept can be applied to the analysis and expression of rough rules derived from observational data. Consider the inconsistent information presented in Table 1.

This minimal reduct is inconsistent because the same sets of attribute values result in different and conflicting decision concepts. For example, Cases e5 and e7 are described by the same attribute conditions – no headache and high temperature. However, Case e5 exhibited no flu, whereas Case e7 exhibited flu. Cases e6 and e8 are also inconsistent. Again, both are described by the same attribute conditions, in this case, no headache and very high temperature. However, Case e6 exhibited flu, whereas Case e8 exhibited no flu. These data are considered rough with respect to the decision concept flu, as different instances with the same attribute conditions may or may not exhibit flu.

Table 1. Minimal reduct from flu example presented in [8]

Case	Attribute Headache	Attribute Temperature	Decision Flu
e1	yes	normal	no
e2	yes	high	yes
e3	yes	very high	yes
e4	no	normal	no
e5	no	high	no
e6	no	very high	yes
e7	no	high	yes
e8	no	very high	no

For the decision concept of flu {e2, e3, e6, e7}, the lower and upper approximations can be defined. The lower approximation, the greatest definable set of people with the flu, is the set {e2, e3}. Within this set, the attribute conditions resulting in flu are consistent, but this set does not include all instances of the decision concept flu. Cases e6 and e7 are not captured by this lower approximation. The upper approximation, the least definable set of people with the flu, is the set {e2, e3, e5, e6, e7, e8}. This set captures all cases of the flu, i.e., cases e2, e3, e6, and e7, but also captures the two inconsistent cases, e5 and e8, which are not flu. These two inconsistent cases cannot be excluded or otherwise differentiated using only the two attributes of headache and temperature. The boundary region between the lower and upper approximations is the set {e5, e6, e7, e8}. The uncertainty associated with these data stem from this boundary region as these elements cannot be classified with certainty as members of the decision concept of flu. This pair of lower and upper approximations form a rough set with respect to the decision concept of flu, as the decision concept of flu cannot be crisply defined using only the two attributes of headache and temperature. With respect to decision rules, [8] presents the following possibly valid rules induced from the upper approximation: (Headache, no) → (Flu, no); (Temperature, normal) → (Flu, no); (Temperature, high) → (Flu, yes); and (Temperature, very high) → (Flu, yes).

Using the if...fi form of guarded command language, this system and all post-condition system states can be described as follows:

```
if  Ache = yes ∧ Temp = norm → Flu = no
[]  Ache = yes ∧ Temp = high → Flu = yes
[]  Ache = yes ∧ Temp = very → Flu = yes
[]  Ache = no  ∧ Temp = norm → Flu = no
[]  Ache = no  ∧ Temp = high → Flu = no
[]  Ache = no  ∧ Temp = very → Flu = yes
[]  Ache = no  ∧ Temp = high → Flu = yes
[]  Ache = no  ∧ Temp = very → Flu = no
fi
```

On execution, all pre-condition states described in the original data will result in the corresponding post-condition state of flu or no flu, consistent with the original data. With each execution of this guarded command set, flu may or may not be indicated, depending on the input data regarding the pre-condition state and the guard that is selected at random in the event of multiple guards being satisfied. Thus, the inconsistency of the original data is preserved by the non-determinacy of the guarded command language approach. Given random selection from multiple guards that may be satisfied by the input data, the results generated by this guarded command set will have the same accuracy measure relative to the upper and lower approximations of the original data.

This guarded language approach facilitates evaluating the completeness of the entire rule with regard to possible pre-condition states, i.e., that the guards are well defined in all states. Reordering and condensing the above guarded command set results in the following logically equivalent guarded command set. The obvious tautologies are preserved for reader clarity regarding the demonstration of all possible pre-condition states of the two decision attributes.

if (Ache = yes ∨ Ache = no) ∧ Temp = norm → Flu = no
[] (Ache = yes ∨ Ache = no) ∧ (Temp = high ∨ Temp = very) → Flu = yes
[] Ache = no ∧ (Temp = high ∨ Temp = very ∨ Temp = norm)
    → Flu = no
fi

In this reduced form, it is clear that all possible input or pre-condition data states are addressed by the rule, and that the guards are well-defined in all states. Thus, this guarded command set can be used with the confidence that this rule would terminate properly, i.e., not fail due to an undefined input state.

Finally, eliminating the embedded tautologies leaves a guarded command set that corresponds with the previously presented possible rule set induced from the upper approximation of the rough set.

if Temp = norm → Flu = no
[] Temp = high ∨ Temp = very → Flu = yes
[] Ache = no → Flu = no
fi

The programmatic use of this reduced guarded command set would not result in the same accuracy relative to the upper and lower approximations of the original data due to the reduction in the number of overlapping guards. To achieve the same degree of uncertainty represented in the original data set, a probabilistic operator would have to be used during execution to make the selection of a single true guard from amongst multiple true guards.

5 Discussion and Concluding Remarks

With respect to decision rules, rough sets and guarded command language are both ways of analyzing, representing, and re-creating the apparent inconsistencies in the observed or anticipated performance of certain information systems.

Whereas data inconsistency is an *a posteriori* or reverse-looking view, and nondeterminacy is an *a priori* or forward-looking view, both can be seen as different representations of the same concept – an observed or anticipated discontinuity between specific pre- and post-condition states of a given information system. Although they stem from dramatically different functional and mathematical origins, rough sets and guarded command language appear to be compatible and complementary in their approaches to imprecision and uncertainty.

A literature review yielded no references or previous research describing rough set approaches in terms of guarded command languages or the associated weakest pre-condition predicate transformer. Therefore, numerous possible research directions exist. Various implementations of guarded command language and the associated weakest pre-condition predicate transformer offer complete and well-formed semantics for rule transformation that may facilitate the formal analysis of implicit rules extracted through rough set techniques. Guarded command language may provide a meaningful framework for the organization and analysis of concurrency rules derived using rough set approaches. Guarded command language approaches may provide a logical and systematic methodology for representing and analyzing possible pre-condition/post-condition implications and/or causalities relative to the imprecision, uncertainty, and vagueness identified through rough set analysis. Finally, guarded command languages are a convenient and well-documented framework for the programmatic implementation of implicit rules recovered using rough set techniques.

References

1. Pawlak Z.: Rough Sets. International Journal of Computer and Information Science. Vol. 11 (1982) 341–356
2. Pawlak, Z.: Rough Sets: Theoretical Aspects of Reasoning About Data. Kluwer Academic Publishers, Boston, MA (1991)
3. Peters, J.F., Skowron, A., Suraj, Z., Pedrycz, W., Ramanna, S.: Approximate Real-Time Decision-Making: Concepts and Rough Fuzzy Petri Net Models. International Journal of Intelligent Systems 14/8 (1999) 805–839
4. Dijkstra, E.W.: Guarded Commands, Nondeterminacy and the Formal Derivation of Programs. Communications of the ACM, Vol. 18 (1975) 453–457
5. Dijkstra, E.W.: A Discipline of Programming. Prentice Hall International, Englewoood Clifts, NJ (1976)
6. He, J., Seidel, K., McIver, A.: Probabilistic Models for the Guarded Command Language. Science of Computer Programming, Vol. 28 (1997) 171–192
7. Morgan, C., McIver, A.: pGCL: Formal Reasoning for Random Algorithms. South African Computer Journal, Vol. 22 (1999) 14–27
8. Pawlak Z., Grzymala-Busse J., Slowinski R., Ziarko, W.: Rough Sets. Communications of the ACM, Vol. 38 (1995) 88–95

Collaborative Query Processing in DKS Controlled by Reducts

Zbigniew W. Raś[1,2] and Agnieszka Dardzińska[3]

[1] University of North Carolina, Department of Computer Science
Charlotte, N.C. 28223, USA
ras@uncc.edu
[2] Polish Academy of Sciences, Institute of Computer Science
Ordona 21, 01-237 Warsaw, Poland
[3] Bialystok University of Technology, Department of Mathematics
Wiejska 45 A, 15-351 Bialystok, Poland
adardzin@uncc.edu

Abstract. Traditional query processing provides exact answers to queries. In this paper, we introduce, so called, non-local queries which allow us to use attributes outside the local domain. Definitions of these attributes, if only exist, can be extracted from databases at other sites. Before, these definitions can be locally applied, problems related to their different semantics have to be resolved first. Rough-ontology is one of the possible tools which can be used here quite successfully to tackle the problem. We introduce a tree-resolution for a non-local query which helps us to identify all steps which should be followed to replace a non-local query by a semantically similar local one.

1 Introduction

In the common experience of data miners, each new database acquired for the purpose of data mining is a source of recurring problems with data. Some attributes are not understood, some others seem to be understood in principle, but some of their values seem strange, out of range or missing. Overcoming problems of this sort is among the prominent consumers of research effort at the stage typically called data preprocessing.

We must treat those problems carefully, as serious misconceptions will result when the users of data and knowledge understand them differently from providers and as knowledge derived from problematic data may be misleading.

A seemingly different problem is created by attributes, whose values are codes, such as disease or treatment code, occupation code, or customer category. They are nominal attributes with large numbers of values. Such attributes do not lead to useful generalizations because they have very many values and must be treated as nominal, whereas they hide plenty of information. When we ask how those values were encoded, we can find their definitions in terms of attributes which are much more conducive to data analysis and knowledge discovery. With the use of its definition, one coded attribute can be typically replaced by several attributes, each with a small numbers of values and clear meaning. For instance, a code for broken bone indicates the broken bone, the location, the type of fracture, and several other properties.

The problems experienced in mining a single database multiply when we try combining data and knowledge from many databases. When we combine relational tables, for instance, we want to avoid JOIN on attributes the values of which are only superficially equal. We must carefully compare attributes which occur under same names and verify compatibility of their values. Ontologies and operational definitions can be instrumental in those comparisons.

Despite problems, when multiple databases are available, new sources of knowledge are enabled. Operational definitions (see [Ras] [8]) can not only explain meaning of attributes in one database but can be used to bring meaning to attributes in other databases. Operational definitions can be even more useful in creating a shared semantics for distributed databases.

In many fields, such as medical, manufacturing, banking, military and educational, similar databases are kept at many sites. Each database stores information about local events and uses attributes suitable for locally collected information, but since the local situations are similar, the majority of attributes are compatible among databases. Yet, an attribute may be missing in one database, while it occurs in many others. For instance, different but equivalent tests that measure a common medical condition may be applied in different hospitals. A doctor who researches effectiveness of a particular treatment may find it difficult to compare the treatment in several hospitals, because they use different tests and because one test replaces another over the course of time. But if the relations between values of different tests can be discovered from data or found in medical references, many attributes acquire a shared meaning and many datasets can be used together. As the meaning can be expanded from data to knowledge, the shared semantics can be used to combine knowledge coming from many sources ([3], [4], [5], [6], [7], [8]).

In this paper, we show how operational definitions (see [Ras] [8]) can be constructed in an efficient way. We search first for sequences of definitions at server sites and next apply them to transfer a user query to a form which is manageable by a client site. To handle differences in semantics, if any, rough-ontologies can also be used.

2 Distributed Information Systems

In this section, we recall definitions of an information system and a distributed knowledge system. Also, we introduce the notion of local and global queries.

By an *information system* we mean $S = (X, A, V)$, where X is a finite set of objects, A is a finite set of attributes, and $V = \bigcup\{V_a : a \in A\}$ is a set of their values. We assume that:

- V_a, V_b are disjoint for any $a, b \in A$ such that $a \neq b$,

- $a : X \longrightarrow 2^{V_a} - \{\emptyset\}$ is a function for every $a \in A$.

By a *distributed information system* we mean a pair $DS = (\{S_i\}_{i \in I}, L)$ where:
- I is a set of sites.
- $S_i = (X_i, A_i, V_i)$ is an information system for any $i \in I$,
- L is a symmetric, binary relation on the set I.

Let $S_j = (X_j, A_j, V_j)$ for any $j \in I$. In the remainder of this paper we assume that $V_j = \bigcup \{V_{ja} : a \in A_j\}$.

From now on, in this section, we use A to denote the set of all attributes in DS, $A = \bigcup \{A_j : j \in I\}$. Also, by V we mean $\bigcup \{V_j : j \in I\}$.

Before introducing the notion of a knowledgebase, we begin with a definition of $s(i)$-terms and their standard interpretation M_i in $DS = (\{S_j\}_{j \in I}, L)$, where $S_j = (X_j, A_j, V_j)$ and $V_j = \bigcup\{V_{ja} : a \in A_j\}$, for any $j \in I$.

By a set of $s(i)$-terms (also called a set of local queries for site i) we mean a least set T_i such that:

- **0, 1** $\in T_i$,
- $w \in T_i$ for any $w \in V_i$,
- if $t_1, t_2 \in T_i$, then $(t_1 + t_2), (t_1 * t_2), \sim t_1 \in T_i$.

Definition of DS-terms (also called a set of global queries) is quite similar (we only replace T_i by $\bigcup \{T_i : i \in I\}$ in the definition above).

We say that:
- $s(i)$-term t is *primitive* if it has the form $\prod \{w : w \in U_i\}$ for any $U_i \subseteq V_i$,
- $s(i)$-term is in *disjunctive normal form* (DNF) if $t = \sum \{t_j : j \in J\}$ where each t_j is primitive.

Similar definitions can be given for DS-terms.

The expression:

select $*$ from $Flights$
where $airline$ = "$Delta$"
and $departure\_time$ = "$morning$"
and $departure\_airport$ = "$Charlotte$"
and $aircraft$ = "$Boeing$"

is an example of a non-local query (DS-term) in a database

$Flights(airline, departure\_time, arrival\_time,$
$departure\_airport, arrival\_airport)$.

Semantics of $s(i)$-terms is seen as the standard interpretation M_i in a distributed information system $DS = (\{S_j\}_{j \in I}, L)$. It is defined as follows:

- $M_i(\mathbf{0}) = \emptyset$, $M_i(\mathbf{1}) = X_i$
- $M_i(w) = \{x \in X_i : w \in a(x)\}$ for any $w \in V_{ia}$,
- if t_1, t_2 are s(i)-terms, then
  $M_i(t_1 + t_2) = M_i(t_1) \cup M_i(t_2)$,
  $M_i(t_1 * t_2) = M_i(t_1) \cap M_i(t_2)$,
  $M_i(\sim t_1) = X_i - M_i(t_1)$.

Now, we are ready to introduce the notion of (k,i)-rules, for any $i \in I$. We use them to build a knowledgebase at site $i \in I$.

By (k,i)-rule in $DS = (\{S_j\}_{j \in I}, L)$, $k, i \in I$, we mean a triple (c, t, s) such that:

- $c \in V_k - V_i$,
- t, s are $s(k)$-terms in DNF and they both belong to $T_k \cap T_i$,
- $M_k(t) \subseteq M_k(c) \subseteq M_k(t+s)$.

Any (k,i)-rule (c,t,s) in DS can be seen as a definition of c which is extracted from S_k and can be used in S_i.

For any (k,i)-rule (c,t,s) in $DS = (\{S_j\}_{j \in I}, L)$, we say that:

- $(t \rightarrow c)$ is a k-certain rule in DS,
- $(t + s \rightarrow c)$ is a k-possible rule in DS.

Now, we are ready to define a knowledgebase D_{ki}. Its elements are called definitions of values of attributes from $V_k - V_i$ in terms of values of attributes from $V_k \cap V_i$.

Namely, D_{ki} is defined as a set of (k,i)-rules such that:
if $(c, t, s) \in D_{ki}$ and the equation $t_1 =_\sim (t + s)$ is true in M_k, then $(\sim c, t1, s) \in D_{ki}$.

The idea here is to add definition of $\sim c$ to D_{ki} if a definition of c is already in D_{ki}. It will allow us to approximate (learn) concept c from both sites, if needed.

By a knowledgebase for site i, denoted by D_i, we mean any subset of $\bigcup\{D_{ki} : (k,i) \in L\}$. If definitions can not be extracted at a remote site, partial definitions (c, t) corresponding to $(t \rightarrow c)$, if available, can be extracted and stored in a knowledgebase at a client site.

By Distributed Knowledge System (DKS) we mean $DS = (\{(S_i, D_i)\}_{i \in I}, L)$ where $(\{S_i\}_{i \in I}, L)$ is a distributed information system, $D_i = \bigcup\{D_{ki} : (k,i) \in L\}$ is a knowledgebase for $i \in I$.

In [Ras/Dardzinska] [6] we gave an example of DKS and its query answering system that handles global queries.

Also, in [Ras/Dardzinska] [6], we stated that the set of semantics $\{M_i\}_{i \in I}$ representing all involved sites in processing query q is a partially ordered set. If it preserves monotonicity property for + and $*$, then $M_{min} = \bigcap \{M_i\}_{i \in I}$ (the greatest lower bound) and $M_{max} = \bigcup \{M_i\}_{i \in I}$ (the least upper bound) can be taken as two common semantics for processing query q. The pair $[M_{min}, M_{max}]$ can be seen as a rough-semantics.

3 Query Answering Based on Reducts

In this section we recall the notion of a reduct (see [Pawlak] [2]) and show how a query can be processed by a distributed knowledge system.

Let us assume that $S = (X, A, V)$, is an information system and $V = \bigcup \{V_a : a \in A\}$. Let $B \subset A$. We say that $x, y \in X$ are indiscernible by B, denoted $[x \approx_B y]$, if $(\forall a \in B)[a(x) = a(y)]$.

Now, assume that both B_1, B_2 are subsets of A. We say that B_1 depends on B_2 if $\approx_{B_2} \subset \approx_{B_1}$. Also, we say that B_1 is a covering of B_2 if B_2 depends on B_1 and B_1 is minimal.

By a reduct of A in S (for simplicity reason we say A-reduct of S) we mean any covering of A.

Example. Assume the following scenario (see Figure 1):

- $S_1 = (X_1, \{c, d, e, g\}, V_1)$, $S_2 = (X_2, \{a, b, c, d, f\}, V_2)$, $S_3 = (X_3, \{b, e, g, h\}, V_3)$ are information systems,
- User submits a query $q = q(c, e, f)$ to the query answering system QAS associated with system S_1,
- Systems S_1, S_2, S_3 are parts of DKS.

Attribute f is non-local for a system S_1 so the query answering system associated with S_1 has to contact other sites of DKS requesting a definition of f in terms of $\{d, c, e, g\}$. Such a request is denoted by $<f : d, c, e, g>$. Assume that system S_2 is contacted. The definition of f, extracted from S_2, involves only attributes $\{d, c, e, g\} \cap \{a, b, c, d, f\} = \{c, d\}$. There are three f-reducts (coverings of f) in S_2. They are: $\{a, b\}, \{a, c\}, \{b, c\}$. The optimal f-reduct is the one which has minimal number of elements outside $\{c, d\}$. Assume that $\{b, c\}$ is chosen as an optimal f-reduct in S_2.

Then, the query answering system of S_2 will contact other sites of DKS requesting definition of b (which is non-local for S_1) in terms of attributes $\{d, c, e, g\}$. If definition of b is found, then it is sent to QAS of the site 1. Also, the definition of f in terms of attributes $\{b, c\}$ will be extracted from S_2 and send to S_1. Figure 1 shows all the steps needed to resolve query $q = q(c, e, f)$. This steps can be represented as a sequence of equations $q = q(c, e, f) = q(c, e, f(b, c)) = q(c, e, f(b(e), c))$. Also, a tree called "tree-resolution for q", represented by Figure 2, gives an alternative representation of that process. Definition of q is called "operational".

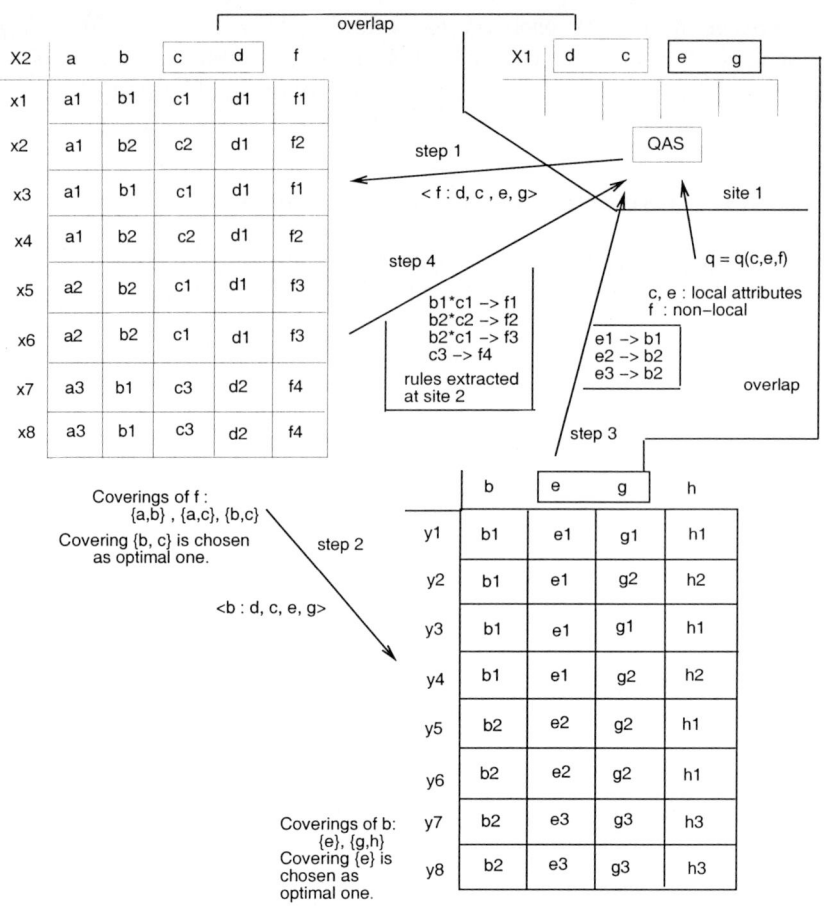

Fig. 1. Process of resolving a query by QAS in DKS

To present more general scenario, let us assume that query $q = q(A_1)$ is submitted to the information system $S = S(A)$ which is a part of DKS and $a_1 \in A_1 - A$. Since attribute a_1 is non-local for S, QAS for the system S sends a system query $[a_1(A)]_?$ to all remote sites $S(B)$ in DKS satisfying the property $a_1 \in B$ and $A \cap B \neq \emptyset$. System query $[a_1(A)]_?$ should be read "find description of attribute a_1 in terms of attributes from A at minimum one of the remote sites for $S(A)$". Now, assuming that $S(B)$ is such a remote site, all a_1-reducts in $S(B)$ are computed. For all a_1-reducts R included in A, our procedure stops and the system query $[a_1(A)]_?$ will be replaced by a term $[a_1(R)]_{S(B)}$. This term should be read "description of a_1 in terms of attributes from R can be discovered in $S(B)$". For any other a_1-reduct A_2 and $a_2 \in A_2 - A$, system $S(B)$ will send a system query $[a_1(A_2)]_{S(B)}, [a_2(A)]_?$ to all other remote sites. This system query should be read "find description of a_2 in terms of A which is needed to find description of a_1 in terms of A in $S(B)$. Assuming that $S(C)$ is one of the remote

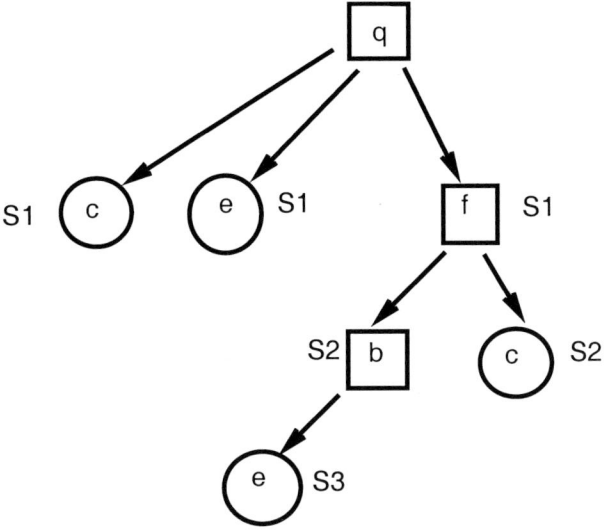

Fig. 2. Tree-resolution for q

sites which can provide us with this kind of help, we compute all a_2-reducts in $S(C)$. For each a_2-reduct R included in A, our procedure stops and the system query $[a_1(A_2)]_{S(B)}, [a_2(A)]_?$ is replaced by a term $[a_1(A_2)]_{S(B)}, [a_2(R)]_{S(C)}$. For all other a_2-reducts A_3 and $a_3 \in A_3 - A$, system $S(C)$ sends a system query $[a_1(A_2)]_{S(B)}, [a_2(A_3)]_{S(C)}, [a_3(A)]_?$ to all other remote sites. This process will continue untill a reduct which is included in A is found. Such a system query is called successful. Clearly, each set in the sequence $A_i - A, ..., A_2 - A, A_1 - A$ may contain more than one attribute. This means that many system queries $[a_1(A_2)]_{S(B)}, [a_2(A_3)]_{S(C)}, [a_3(A)]_?$ can be formed. Some of them will be successful and some will fail. If one of the attributes is repeated in a system query, this query fails and the same can not be used in the process of constructing operational definition of a_1. Each system query which is successful can be used to construct a disjunct of the local term approximating query q.

4 Conclusion

Any non-local query, submitted to one of the sites of DKS, generates a collection of system queries represented by sequences of attributes. For instance, query $[a_1(A_2)]_{S(B)}, [a_2(A_3)]_{S(C)}, [a_3(A)]_?$ is represented by a sequence of attributes (a_1, a_2, a_3). Only sequences with non-repeated attributes (no loops) are used in the final process of query resolution. All these sequences are used to find local approximation of the initial query. More sequences we have, more objects can be identified as the answer to the initial query. Also, it should be added that each such a sequence generates its own query processing steps based on its own rough-ontology (see [Ras/Dardzinska] [6]).

References

1. Mizoguchi, R., "Ontological engineering: foundation of the next generation knowledge processing", in *Proceedings of Web Intelligence: Research and Development*, LNCS/LNAI, Springer-Verlag, No. 2198, 2001, 44–57
2. Pawlak, Z., "Rough classification", in *International Journal of Man-Machine Studies*, Vol. 20, 1984, 469–483
3. Prodromidis, A.L. & Stolfo, S., "Mining databases with different schemas: Integrating incompatible classifiers", in *Proceedings of The Fourth Intern. Conf. onn Knowledge Discovery and Data Mining*, AAAI Press, 1998, 314–318
4. Ras, Z., "Dictionaries in a distributed knowledge-based system", in *Concurrent Engineering: Research and Applications, Conference Proceedings*, Pittsburgh, Penn., Concurrent Technologies Corporation, 1994, 383–390
5. Ras, Z., "Query answering based on distributed knowledge mining", in *Intelligent Agent Technology, Research and Development*, Proceedings of IAT'01 (Eds. N. Zhong, J. Lin, S. Ohsuga, J. Bradshaw), World Scientific, 2001, 17–27
6. Ras, Z., Dardzinska, A., "Handling semantic inconsistencies in query answering based on distributed knowledge mining", in *Foundations of Intelligent Systems*, Proceedings of ISMIS'02 Symposium, Lyon, France, LNCS/LNAI, No. 2366, Springer-Verlag, 2002, 69–77
7. Ras, Z., Żytkow, J., "Mining for attribute definitions in a distributed two-layered DB system", *Journal of Intelligent Information Systems*, Kluwer, Vol. 14, No. 2/3, 2000, 115–130
8. Ras, Z., Żytkow, J.,"Discovery of equations to augment the shared operational semantics in distributed autonomous BD System", in *PAKDD'99 Proceedings*, LNCS/LNAI, No. 1574, Springer-Verlag, 1999, 453-463

A New Method for Determining of Extensions and Restrictions of Information Systems

Wojciech Rząsa[1] and Zbigniew Suraj[2]

[1] Institute of Mathematics,
University of Rzeszow,
Rejtana 16A, 35-310 Rzeszow, Poland
`wrzasa@univ.rzeszow.pl`
[2] Chair of Computer Science Foundations,
University of Information Technology and Management,
H. Sucharskiego 2, 35-225 Rzeszow, Poland
`zsuraj@wenus.wsiz.rzeszow.pl`

Abstract. The aim of the paper is presentation of some results that concern consistent extensions and consistent restrictions of information systems and decision systems. It is possible to determine them on the base of knowledge contained in rules generated from a given information (decision) system. The paper presents a way of consistent extensions and consistent restrictions determining, different from the one mentioned above. The paper contains also the definitions of notions of strict consistent extension (restriction) system and a necessary and sufficient condition for the existence of them for information (decision) system.

1 Introduction

Suraj in [2], [3] presents problems from domain of concurrency which may be formulated by rough set theory notions and may be solved finding consistent extensions of a given information or decision system. The problems are among others: discovering concurrent data models from experimental tables, re-engineering problem for cooperative information systems, the real time decision making problem and the control design problem for discrete event system. This paper presents further results that concern consistent extensions (restrictions). In particular in section 2 there are proofs of two propositions inserted in [3] and a corollary of the propositions. There are also algorithms of maximal consistent extension and minimal consistent restriction finding for information and decision systems, different from the algorithms proposed in [3]. In section 3 notions of strict consistent extension and restriction are considered. Although many notions of the rough set theory is used in the paper, most of them are fundamental or very common so their definitions are passed over. If the need arises the reader is referred to [1], [2], [3]. However, we define a special kind of reduct, namely the reduct related to fixed object and attribute, that is crucial in some places of the paper. This notion may be occur in two forms. For information system $S = (U, A)$ and fixed object $u \in U$ and attribute $a \in A$, a class of minimal sets of attributes

$X \subseteq A - \{a\}$ (with respect to inclusion) such that $\forall u' \in U - \{u\}[(u',u) \notin IND(\{a\}) \wedge (u',u) \notin IND(A - \{a\}) \Rightarrow (u',u) \notin IND(X)]$ is denoted in the paper as $u, \sim a, U - RR$ in contradistinction to a class of reducts $u, a, U - RR$, which is a class of minimal sets of attributes $Y \subseteq A - \{a\}$ such that $\forall u' \in U - \{u\}[(u',u) \in IND(\{a\}) \wedge (u',u) \notin IND(A - \{a\}) \Rightarrow (u',u) \notin IND(Y)]$. A set of all rules true in S [2] is denoted in the paper by $RUL(S)$ whilst set of minimal rules that are the rules true in S with minimal left hand sides [2] is denoted by $OPT(S)$. It may be determined as described in [2].

2 Consistent Extensions and Restrictions

2.1 Consistent Extensions of Information Systems

Let $S = (U, A)$ and $S' = (U', A')$ be information systems. The information system S' is called a consistent extension of system S if and only if the following conditions are satisfied:

1. $U \subseteq U'$;
2. $card(A) = card(A')$;
3. $\forall a \in A \exists a' \in A'[V_{a'} = V_a \wedge a'(u) = a(u)$ for all $u \in U]$;
4. $RUL(S) \subseteq RUL(S')$.

Below, sets A and A' are marked by the same letter A, so consequently $S' = (U', A)$ is written instead of $S' = (U', A')$. If $U' \neq U$ then S' is called a nontrivial consistent extension of system S. Set $EXT(S)$ of all consistent extensions of a given information system S may be ordered by relation '$\leqslant$', defined as follows: $\forall S'_1 = (U'_1, A), S'_2 = (U'_2, A) \in EXT(S)[S'_1 \leqslant S'_2$ if and only if $U'_1 \subseteq U'_2]$. Maximal elements in the set $EXT(S)$ ordered by $\leqslant$ are called maximal consistent extensions of system S. If S' is a consistent extension of S then S is called a consistent restriction of S'. A set of all consistent restrictions of a given information system S is denoted by $RES(S)$. If we order set $RES(S)$ in the same way as set $EXT(S)$ was ordered, then every minimal element of such ordered set $RES(S)$ is called a minimal consistent restriction of system S.

Proposition 1. *[3] There exists exactly one maximal consistent extension for every information system $S = (U, A)$.*

Proof. $EXT(S)$ is nonempty for every S because $S \in EXT(S)$ and obviously $EXT(S)$ is finite for every S. Thus, there are maximal elements in the set $EXT(S)$, ordered as above. Let us assume that there are at least two maximal elements $S'_1 = (U'_1, A), S'_2 = (U'_2, A)$ and let $u'_1 \in U'_1$ but $u'_1 \notin U'_2$. $RUL(S) \subseteq RUL(S'_1)$ and moreover for any $R \in RUL(S)$ such that: $R := a_{i_1} = v_{i_1} \wedge \ldots \wedge a_{i_n} = v_{i_n} \Rightarrow a_p = v_p$ implication $a_{i_1} = a_{i_1}(u') \wedge \ldots \wedge a_{i_n} = a_{i_n}(u') \Rightarrow a_p = a_p(u')$ is identical with R or its predecessor differs from predecessor of R. Therefore, $RUL(S) \subseteq RUL(S''_2)$, where $S''_2 = (U'_2 \cup \{u'_1\}, A)$ and that is contradiction with maximal character of S'_2. $\square$

Suraj in [3] describes algorithms of finding maximal consistent extensions for arbitrary information system S with use of the set $OPT(S)$. However, the problem of $OPT(S)$ generating is NP-hard (cf. [4]). Moreover, the set $OPT(S)$ is unique for every information system S. Therefore, it seems natural to try to miss the step of $OPT(S)$ generating in the process of maximal consistent extensions finding. It is also useful to check, not in a very complex way, whether there exists non-trivial consistent extension. Now, we will prove, proposed in [3], necessary condition of the fact.

Proposition 2. *[3] If $S = (U, A)$ has non-trivial consistent extension S', then for at least two attributes $a_1, a_2 \in A$ $card(V_{a_1}) > 2$ and $card(V_{a_2}) > 2$.*

First we will prove the following lemma.

Lemma 1. *If information system $S = (U, A)$ has non-trivial consistent extension S', then for at least one attribute $a \in A$ $card(V_a) > 2$.*

Proof (of Lemma). Let the information system $S = (U, A)$ ($card(A) = k$) have a consistent extension $S' = (U', A)$. Then, for every $u' \in U'$, such that $v(u') = (a_1(u'), \ldots, a_k(u'))$ the following conditions are satisfied:

1. $\forall i \leqslant k \exists u \in U [a_i(u') = a_i(u)]$;
2. $RUL(S) \subseteq RUL(S'')$, where $S'' = (U \cup \{u'\})$.

Moreover, let

3. $\forall a_i \in A [card(V_{a_i}) \leqslant 2]$.

We will show that conditions 1. - 3. imply existence of only a trivial consistent extension for a given information system S. The rule of mathematical induction is used to show, that for satisfied conditions 1. - 3. every object $u' \in U'$ is indiscernible from some object $u \in U$ with respect to all k attributes. Condition 1 shows that for any $u' \in U'$ there is object $u \in U$ such that $a_i(u) = a_i(u')$ for arbitrary $i \leqslant k$. Now, let $u \in U$ be such object that $a_{i_1}(u) = a_{i_1}(u') \wedge \ldots \wedge a_{i_n}(u) = a_{i_n}(u')$ for some $a_{i_1}, \ldots, a_{i_n} \in A$. If $a_{i_{n+1}}(u) = a_{i_{n+1}}(u')$ for some $a_{i_{n+1}} \in A$ different from $a_{i_1}, \ldots, a_{i_n}$ then it is the end of the proof. So, let $a_{i_{n+1}}(u) \neq a_{i_{n+1}}(u')$ for every $a_{i_{n+1}}$ different from $a_{i_1}, \ldots, a_{i_n}$. If condition 2 is satisfied then it is impossible that the rule $a_{i_1} = a_{i_1}(u) \wedge \ldots \wedge a_{i_n} = a_{i_n}(u) \Rightarrow a_{i_{n+1}} = a_{i_{n+1}}(u)$ is true in system S. That means there is object $w \in U$, such that $a_{i_1}(u) = a_{i_1}(w) \wedge \ldots \wedge a_{i_n}(u) = a_{i_n}(w) \wedge a_{i_{n+1}}(u) \neq a_{i_{n+1}}(w)$. Taking into account condition 3 and the fact that $a_{i_{n+1}}(u) \neq a_{i_{n+1}}(u')$ it is easy to prove that $a_{i_{n+1}}(u') = a_{i_{n+1}}(w)$. The rule of mathematical induction ends the proof of lemma. □

Proof (of Proposition 2). Let $u' \in U'$ and $v(u') = (a_1(u'), a_2(u'), \ldots, a_k(u'))$. Conditions 1. - 2. from the lemma are satisfied and let the following condition 3' be true:

3'. Exactly one attribute $a \in A$ has more than 2 values.

In the same way as above it may be shown, that if some object $u \in U$ is indiscernible from u' with respect to n ($n < k$) attributes, including a ($card(V_a) > 2$), then there is also object $w \in U$ indiscernible from u' with the use of $n+1$ attributes, $n < k$. □

Corollary 1. *If for $S = (U, A)$ there exists non-trivial consistent extension $S' = (U', A')$ and $B = \{a \in A \mid \text{for no more than one attribute } card(V_a) > 2\}$, then $\forall u' \in U' - U \exists u \in U[(u, u') \in IND(B)]$.*

Table 1.

$U \setminus A$	a	b	c
u_1	0	2	1
u_2	1	0	1
u_3	1	1	0
u_4	1	1	2

Information system S presented in Table 1 satisfies necessary condition for existence of non-trivial, consistent extension. None of objects u such that $v(u) = (0, 0, *)$ or $v(u) = (0, 1, *)$ or $v(u) = (1, 2, *)$ or $v(u) = (0, *, 0)$ or $v(u) = (0, *, 2)$ belongs to consistent extension of system S.

The following proposition gives necessary and sufficient condition for existence of non-trivial consistent extension of a given information system.

Proposition 3. *An information system $S' = (U', A)$ is a consistent extension of system $S = (U, A)$ if and only if $\forall u \in U, u' \in U', a \in A[(u', u) \notin IND(\{a\}) \Rightarrow u, \sim a, U - RR = u, \sim a, U \cup \{u'\} - RR]$.*

Proof. Validity of sufficient condition is implied by correctness of algorithm of set $OPT(S)$ generating. Now, let us check whether the necessary condition is true. So, let $u, \sim a, U - RR \neq u, \sim a, U \cup \{u'\} - RR$ for some $u \in U, u' \in U'$ and $a \in A$ such that $(u', u) \notin IND(\{a\})$. Obviously, every element of the set $u, \sim a, U - RR$ is a subset of some element from the set $u, \sim a, U \cup \{u'\} - RR$. Let $R \in u, \sim a, U - RR$ be a proper subset of $R' \in u, \sim a, U - \{u'\} - RR$. It means that the rule, for which predecessor is created from R and which is true in S, is not true in S'. This implies that $OPT(S)$ is not a subset of $OPT(S')$ and S' is not a consistent extension of S. □

Below, the algorithm of maximal consistent extension generation for a given information system is presented. This algorithm is based on propositions presented above and misses the stage of the set $OPT(S)$ generating.

Algorithm 1
Input: Information system $S = (U, A)$, $card(A) = k$.
Output: Maximal consistent extension of S.

Step 1. Verify, whether there are at least two attributes $a_i, a_j \in A$, such that $card(V_{a_i}) > 2$ and $card(V_{a_j}) > 2$; if not – go to *Step 10*.

Step 2. From among objects u', such that $v(u') \in V_{a_1} \times \ldots \times V_{a_k}$, throw away all belonging to U.

Step 3. Test, whether there exist such attributes $a \in A$ that $card(V_a) \leqslant 2$; if not – go to *Step* 5.

Step 4. Throw away all objects that do not satisfy corollary concerning necessary condition for existence of non-trivial consistent extension.

Step 5. Create a discernibility matrix for information system S.

Step 6. Complete matrix made in *Step* 5 with a column corresponding to object u' which has not been thrown away, yet. If there is no such object – go to *Step* 10.

Step 7. For the first cell in added column do the following operation: check whether for every attribute from the cell there exists a cell in the same row of the discernibility matrix such that includes considered attribute and which is a subset of the cell from added column. If for some attribute such cell is not found, break the comparison, otherwise repeat the same operation with next cells of the added column. If all cells have been checked, then break the comparison and go to the *Step* 8; otherwise go to *Step* 9.

Step 8. $U := U \cup \{u'\}$.

Step 9. Delete added column, throw away considered object and go back to *Step* 6.

Step 10. Write $S = (U, A)$.

The meaning of the *Step* 7 is as follows: it tests whether $u, \sim a, U - RR = u, \sim a, U \cup \{u'\} - RR$ without those reducts' generating; there is only used the fact that $X \cap Y = X$ if and only if $X \subseteq Y$. X is a symbol of $u, \sim a, U - RR$ and Y denotes $u, \sim a, U \cup \{u'\} - RR$.

Unfortunately, it may happen that not too many objects will be reduced in *Step* 4 or the step will not be made at all. Then, a sequence of *Steps* 6-9 will be repeated $\prod_{p=1}^{k} card(V_{a_p}) - card(U)$ times, in spite of possibility that there is no non-trivial consistent extension for a given information system. Thus, the algorithm is useful rather for systems with considerable number of attributes with no more than 2 values, or when the number $\prod_{p=1}^{k} card(V_{a_p}) - card(U)$ is not too large. If a given system is little, and $\prod_{p=1}^{k} card(V_{a_p}) - card(U)$ is large, then the algorithm with $OPT(S)$ generation may be more efficient.

Algorithm for finding of maximal consistent extension of decision systems is similar to `Algorithm 1`. The difference results two facts: necessary condition for existence of non-trivial extension formulated for information systems is not true for decision systems (see Table 2). Moreover, verifications or comparisons made in the case of information systems for all attributes focus on decision attribute only in decision systems. Thus algorithm for determining of consistent extension of decision system is a sequence of the following steps from `Algorithm 1`: *Step* 2, *Step* 4 - *Step* 10 with simplified *Step* 7.

2.2 Consistent Restrictions of Information Systems

A dual problem for finding maximal consistent extension of a given information system is a problem of minimal consistent restriction determining. This is not a

Table 2.

$U \setminus A$	a	b	c	d
u_1	0	1	1	0
u_2	0	1	0	1
u_3	1	0	1	0
u_4	1	0	0	1
u'	0	0	1	0
u''	0	0	0	1

rule that there exists exactly one minimal consistent restriction for any information system. For information system given by Table 3, two minimal consistent restrictions exist. Those are as follows: the system without object u_6 or without object u_7. Yet, the system without u_6 and u_7 is not a minimal consistent restriction of a given system.

Table 3.

$U \setminus A$	a	b
u_1	1	1
u_2	0	0
u_3	0	2
u_4	2	0
u_5	3	2
u_6	1	0
u_7	1	2

Necessary condition for existence of non-trivial consistent restriction for a given information system is analogous to condition of non-trivial extensions.

Proposition 4. *If $S = (U, A)$ has non-trivial consistent restriction then for at least two attributes $a_1, a_2 \in A$ $card(V_{a_1}) > 2$ and $card(V_{a_2}) > 2$.*

Proof. If Proposition 4 is not true, then S is not a non-trivial consistent extension of any information system. In consequence, there is not any non-trivial consistent restriction of S. □

Both, the corollary for Proposition 4 and the necessary and sufficient condition for existence of non-trivial consistent restriction are also analogous to the corresponding propositions of consistent extensions so proofs of correctness of them as like correctness of `Algorithm 2` that is based on those theorems are omitted.

Corollary 2. *If $S' = (U', A)$ is non-trivial consistent restriction of $S = (U, A)$ and $B = \{a \in A \mid$ for no more than one attribute $card(V_a) > 2\}$, then $\forall u' \in U' - U \exists u \in U[(u, u') \in IND(B)]$.*

Proposition 5. *An information system* $S = (U, A)$ *is a consistent restriction of system* $S' = (U', A)$ *if and only if* $\forall u \in U, u' \in U', a \in A[(u, u') \notin IND(\{a\}) \Rightarrow u, \sim a, U - RR = u, \sim a, U \cup \{u'\} - RR]$.

The following algorithm of minimal restriction determining is based on the above propositions.

Algorithm 2
Input: Information system $S = (U, A)$.
Output: Minimal consistent restriction of S.

Step 1. Check, whether there are at least two attributes $a_i, a_j \in A$, such that $card(V_{a_i}) > 2$ and $card(V_{a_j}) > 2$; if not – go to *Step* 7.
Step 2. Determine set U' of objects belonging to U and indiscernible with some objects from U with the use of every set B from corollary.
Step 3. Create a discernibility matrix for information system $S = (U, A)$.
Step 4. Choose arbitrary object u from set U'; if the set is empty – go to *Step* 7.
Step 5. For object chosen in *Step* 4 check, whether it belongs to consistent extension of system $S' = (U - \{u\}, A)$; if yes, then $U := U - \{u\}$ and modify discernibility matrix by reducing a row and a column corresponding to object u.
Step 6. Throw away object u from set U' and come back to *Step* 4.
Step 7. Write system $S = (U, A)$.

When *Steps* 1 -2 are missed and set U' in *Step* 4 is replaced by U, then algorithm for minimal restriction of decision system determinig is received.

3 Strict Consistent Extensions and Restrictions

Now, let us consider a special kind of consistent extensions or restriction of information (decision) system. If a system S' is a consistent extension of system S and $RUL(S') = RUL(S)$, then system S' is called a strict consistent extension of system S and respectively S is called a strict consistent restriction of S'. The following proposition expresses necessary and sufficient condition for existence of a strict consistent extension S' of system S:

Proposition 6. *System* $S' = (U', A)$ *is a strict consistent extension of system* $S = (U, A)$ *if and only if* S' *is consistent extension of* S *and*

$$\forall u' \in U' - U, a \in A[u', a, U \cup \{u'\} - RR \cap u', \sim a, U' - RR = \emptyset].$$

Proof. It is enough to prove that the second condition of proposition 6 is equivalent with $RUL(S') \subseteq RUL(S)$. Let us put attention on arbitrary object $u' \in U' - U$ and attribute $a \in A$ and let $X = \{a_{i_1}, \ldots, a_{i_n}\}$ ($a \notin X$) be an element of $u', a, U \cup \{u'\} - RR \cap u', \sim a, U' - RR$. $X \in u', \sim a, U' - RR$ implies that object u' is discernible from all objects $u \in U' - \{u'\}$ such that $(u, u') \notin IND(\{a\})$ with the use of reduct X and rule $a_{i_1} = a_{i_1}(u') \wedge \ldots \wedge a_{i_n} = a_{i_n}(u') \Rightarrow a = a(u')$ is true in system S'. $X \in u', a, U \cup \{u'\} - RR$ means that rule $a_{i_1} = a_{i_1}(u') \wedge \ldots \wedge a_{i_n} = a_{i_n}(u') \Rightarrow a = a(u')$ is not true in system S. That is equivalent to $RUL(S') \not\subseteq RUL(S)$. □

Proposition 6 is true for decision systems if expression '$\forall a \in A$' is replaced with 'decision attribute'. Moreover, set of reducts $u', \sim a, U' - RR$ that appears in the proposition means the impossibility of checking one after another whether objects $u' \notin U$ belong to strict consistent extension. Table 2 presents decision system with its strict consistent extension, but system S with universum $U = (u_1, u_2, u_3, u_4)$ extended with only one object from among u', u'' is not strict consistent extension of S because objects u' and u'' added one by one 'bring in' rule $a = 0 \wedge b = 0 \Rightarrow d = 0$ or rule $a = 0 \wedge b = 0 \Rightarrow d = 1$, respectively.

4 Conclusions

In the paper the new results concerning the extensions and restrictions of information systems have been presented. The results involve necessary and sufficient conditions together with the proofs for existence of extensions (restrictions) of information systems. Moreover, new algorithms for determining of extensions (restrictions) without the set of minimal rules generating have been proposed. It is still a challenge to pass more efficient algorithm of consistent extensions (restrictions) generating for large information systems, for instance by finding stronger necessary condition of existing non-trivial extensions (restrictions) of an information system. Actually algorithms proposed in the paper are implemented to execute some experiments using real life data. It will make possible to compare efficiency of the algorithms described in the paper and those ones described in [3].

Acknowledgment. This work was partially supported by the grant #8 T11C 025 19 from the State Committee for Scientific Research (KBN) in Poland.

References

1. Pawlak, Z.: Rough sets: Theoretical Aspects of Reasoning About Data, Boston, MA, Kluwer Academic Publishers, 1991
2. Suraj, Z.: Rough Set Methods for the Synthesis and Analysis of Concurrent Processes, in: Studies in Fuzziness and Soft Computing, Rough Set Methods and Applications. New Developments in Knowledge Discovery in Information Systems, L. Polkowski, S. Tsumoto, T.Y. Lin (Eds.), Physica-Verlag,Heidelberg, 2000, 379-488
3. Suraj, Z.: Some Remarks on Extensions and Restrictions of Information Systems. Proceedings of the Second International Conference on Rough Sets and Current Trends in Computing (RSCTC'2000), Banff, Canada, October 16-19, 2000, 172–179
4. Wegener, I.: The complexity of Boolean Functions, Wiley and B.G. Teubner Stuttgart 1987

A Logic Programming Framework for Rough Sets

Aida Vitória[1] and Jan Małuszyński[2]

[1] Dept. of Science and Technology, Linköping University,
S 601 74 Norrköping, Sweden
aidvi@itn.liu.se
[2] Dept. of Computer and Information Science,
Linköping University, S 581 83 Linköping, Sweden
janma@ida.liu.se

Abstract. We propose a framework for defining and reasoning about rough sets based on *definite extended logic* programs. Moreover, we introduce a rough-set-specific query language. Several motivating examples are also presented. Thus, we establish a link between rough set theory and logic programming that makes possible transfer of expertise between these fields and combination of the techniques originating from both fields.

1 Introduction

The main aim of this paper is to show how rough sets can be defined and combined by means of logic programs.

The formalism of *rough sets* [1] makes it possible to represent and handle uncertain information. Rough sets have been a subject of intensive research mainly focused on theoretical studies of algebraic and logical properties (like [2]) and applications (e.g. [3]).

Viewing rows of a decision table, with a binary decision attribute, as datalog facts gives a basis for extending rough sets to Rough Datalog. In our previous work [4], we proposed such an extension. With rough datalog it is possible to define rough sets not only explicitly as collections of facts (as the decision tables do) but also implicitly by rules. The fixpoint semantics of rough datalog links the predicates of a program to rough relations. However, the intuition of a rule as a definition of a rough set is quite complex, since the same rule has to define both the positive and the negative examples of the defined rough set. Moreover, compilation of datalog rules to Prolog, described in [4], may cause explosion of the number of Prolog clauses necessary to deal with negative examples.

In this paper, we propose a simplified approach based on the concept of *definite extended logic program* [5] (DXL programs). As mentioned above, decision tables for rough sets include explicit negative information. This information can be expressed in DXL programs by using *explicit negation*. Thus, DXL programs are well suited to represent rough sets. The semantics of DXL determines then the rough sets specified by a given program. DXL programs can be easily implemented and queried in pure Prolog. However, DXL is not expressive enough for stating rough-set-specific queries. For example, in DXL it is not possible to query lower approximations of the defined rough sets. To achieve this we propose to extend DXL with a query language tailored to rough sets.

2 Preliminaries

2.1 Rough Sets

Intuitively, to define a rough set S, we will specify those elements of the universe which may belong to S and those which may not belong to S. Some elements may fall in both categories. They constitute the conflicting *boundary* cases. It is often assumed that the union of both categories covers the universe. It should be stressed that we do not make this assumption: for some elements of the universe the membership information concerning S may be missing. As this subset may be empty, our framework is more general.

As usual, we assume that the universe consists of objects associated with attributes and different objects with same attribute values are indiscernible (cf. [6]). An attribute a can be seen as a partial function $a : U \to V_a$, where U is a universe of objects and V_a is called the *value domain* of a. In this paper we deal only with classes of indiscernible objects, represented by tuples of attribute values and, therefore, we adopt the following definition.

Definition 1. *A rough set (or rough relation) S is a pair (S^+, S^-) such that $S^+, S^- \subseteq V_{a_1} \times \cdots \times V_{a_n}$, for some non empty set of attributes $\{a_1, \cdots, a_n\}$.*

The indiscernibility classes S^+ (to be called the *upper approximation* or the *positive information* of S) include all elements which (are known to) belong to S. Similarly, the classes S^- (to be called the *negative information*) include all elements known not to belong to S. The *lower approximation* of S defined as $(S^+ - S^-)$ includes only the non conflicting elements that belong to S. The *rough complement* of a rough set $S = (S^+, S^-)$ is the rough set $\neg S = (S^-, S^+)$.

Rough sets are commonly represented by decision tables [1] (see Example 1).

2.2 Logic Programs

This section introduces (a subset of) *definite programs*, the basic class of logic programs. In the sequel, we will extend them to define rough sets. For a more general introduction to logic programming see, e.g [7].

Definite programs are constructed over the alphabet including *variables* (denoted by identifiers starting with a capital letter), *function symbols* and *predicate symbols*. In this paper we restrict function symbols to constants. This is sufficient for representing rough sets defined by decision tables.

Definition 2. *An atom is an expression of the form $p(t_1, \ldots, t_m)$, where p is an m-ary predicate symbol and $t_1, \ldots, t_m$ are variables or constants.*

Definition 3. *A definite clause is a formula of the form* $h :\!\!- b_1, \ldots, b_n.$, *where* $n \geq 0$ *and* $h, b_1, \ldots, b_n$ *are atoms. If* $n = 0$ *the symbol* $:\!\!-$ *is omitted. Such clauses are called* facts *in contrast to the clauses with* $n > 0$*, which are called* rules*. A* definite program $\mathcal{P}$ *is a finite set of definite clauses.*

A definite clause $h :\!\!- b_1, \ldots, b_n.$ can be seen as an alternative notation for the formula of first order predicate logic $\forall \boldsymbol{X}(b_1 \wedge \ldots \wedge b_n \rightarrow h)$, where $\boldsymbol{X}$ represents all variables in the formula. The antecedent of a fact is *true*. Hence, a definite program represents a conjunction of logical formulas.

The set of all atoms whose predicate symbols appear in $\mathcal{P}$ and whose arguments are constants occurring in $\mathcal{P}$ is called the *Herbrand base* of $\mathcal{P}$, denoted as $\mathcal{H}_{\mathcal{P}}^B$. By a *ground instance* of a clause $C \in \mathcal{P}$, we mean a clause C' obtained by replacing each occurrence of every variable X in C by a constant c occurring in $\mathcal{P}$. We denote by $g(\mathcal{P})$ the set of all ground instances of the clauses of $\mathcal{P}$.

Definition 4. *A* Herbrand interpretation $\mathcal{I}$ *for a definite program* $\mathcal{P}$ *is a subset of the Herbrand base for* $\mathcal{P}$*. Moreover,* $\mathcal{I}$ satisfies *an atom* a *iff* $a \in \mathcal{I}$*. A Herbrand interpretation* $\mathcal{I}$ *is a* model *of* $\mathcal{P}$ *iff for every* $h :\!\!- b_1, \ldots, b_n \in g(\mathcal{P})$ *either* $h \in \mathcal{I}$ *or some* $b_i \notin \mathcal{I}$ *($1 \leq i \leq n$).*

Intuitively, a Herbrand interpretation $\mathcal{I}$ is a 2-valued interpretation that assigns to each ground atom a either *true*, if $a \in \mathcal{I}$, or *false*, if $a \notin \mathcal{I}$. It is a model if $\mathcal{P}$ seen as logical formula is true in $\mathcal{I}$.

Proposition 1. *[7] For every definite program* $\mathcal{P}$ *there exists the least (w.r.t. set inclusion) Herbrand model* $M_{\mathcal{P}}$*. Moreover,* $M_{\mathcal{P}}$ *captures the semantics of* $\mathcal{P}$*.*

Clearly, the least model associates a relation with each predicate of a definite program. Thus, a definite program can be seen as a definition of a family of relations.

A logic program $\mathcal{P}$ is used to query its least Herbrand model $M_{\mathcal{P}}$. Syntactically, a *query* $\mathcal{Q}$ is a sequence (interpreted as conjunction) of atoms, possibly including variables. The *SLD-resolution* technique (see e.g. [7]) makes it possible to check whether all atoms of a ground query are in $M_{\mathcal{P}}$. For a non-ground query, it finds instances of the query such that all atoms belong to $M_{\mathcal{P}}$.

In practice, Prolog [8] is also able to deduce negative information by using the *negation-as-failure*, i.e. any atom that can be finitely proved not to belong to the semantics of the program is considered to be false. Using negation-as-failure, it is possible to include negated atoms in the queries and in the bodies of clauses.

3 Definite Extended Logic Programs and Rough Relations

This section recalls the concept of definite extended logic program [5] and relates it to rough relations.

Definition 5. *A* literal *L is an expression of the form* a *or* $\neg a$, *where* a *is an atom (recall Definition 2). They are called* positive *and* negative *literals, respectively.*

Definition 6. *A* definite extended clause *is a formula of the form*

$$H :- B_1, \ldots, B_n.$$

where H and each B_i ($0 \leq i \leq n$) is a literal. A definite extended logic program *(DXL for short) $\mathcal{P}$ is a finite set of definite extended clauses.*

Note that negative literals can occur both in the head and in the body of a definite extended clause. The intention is to define explicitly not only a set of atomic formulae, as in the case of definite programs, but also a set of negated atomic formulae, thus providing explicitly negative information.

We extend to DXL programs all the notational conventions of Section 2.2

We now sketch the semantics of DXL programs that associates with each predicate symbol p occurring in a DXL program $\mathcal{P}$ a rough relation P. Informally, P corresponds to a pair of sets consisting of positive literals of the form $p(\ldots)$ (defining the positive information of P) and negative literals of the form $\neg p(\ldots)$ (defining the negative information of P).

Lower case-letters are used for predicate symbols (e.g. p, q, ft) and the same sequence of characters, in slanted style and starting with capital letter, are used for the denoted rough relation (e.g. P, Q, Ft). If $A = \{a1, a2, \cdots\}$ is a set of atoms then we denote by $\neg A$ the set of negative literals $\{\neg a1, \neg a2, \cdots\}$.

Definition 7. *Let $\mathcal{P}$ be a DXL program. A* Herbrand interpretation *$\mathcal{I}$ for $\mathcal{P}$ is a subset of $\mathcal{H}_{\mathcal{P}}^B \cup \neg \mathcal{H}_{\mathcal{P}}^B$. Moreover, an interpretation $\mathcal{I}$* satisfies *a literal L iff $L \in \mathcal{I}$.*

In contrast to the notion of interpretation for definite programs, if a literal $L \notin \mathcal{I}$ then its truth value is *undefined*. Thus, a definite program is not a DXL program. Notice also that $\mathcal{I}$ may include both an atom and its negation.

The notion of satisfiability can be extended to clauses. An interpretation $\mathcal{I}$ *satisfies* a ground clause $H :- B_1, \ldots, B_n$. *iff* either $H \in \mathcal{I}$ or $\{B_1, \cdots, B_n\} \not\subseteq \mathcal{I}$.

Definition 8. *An interpretation $\mathcal{I}$ is a* model *of a DXL program $\mathcal{P}$ iff $\mathcal{I}$ satisfies each clause of $g(\mathcal{P})$.*

The set $\mathcal{H}_{\mathcal{P}}^B \cup \neg \mathcal{H}_{\mathcal{P}}^B$ is a model of any DXL program $\mathcal{P}$ and several models of $\mathcal{P}$ may exist. Moreover, it is easy to prove that the intersection of all models of $\mathcal{P}$ is also a model, called the *least Herbrand model* of $\mathcal{P}$.

Definition 9. *The* semantics $M_{\mathcal{P}}$ *of a DXL program $\mathcal{P}$ is the least Herbrand model of $\mathcal{P}$. Moreover, each predicate symbol p with arity n, occurring in $\mathcal{P}$, denotes the rough relation*

$$P = (\{(c_1, \ldots, c_n) \,|\, p(c_1, \ldots, c_n) \in M_{\mathcal{P}}\}, \{(c_1, \ldots, c_n) \,|\, \neg p(c_1, \ldots, c_n) \in M_{\mathcal{P}}\}) \,.$$

We now illustrate introduced concepts by a simple example.

Example 1. Consider the rough relations *Flu* and *Patient* specified by the decision tables below. Intuitively, in the first table, the symptom attributes are used to decide whether a patient has flu. The second table contains records of people who visited a doctor. Its decision attribute shows whether a person has to be treated for some disease, and, therefore, is considered as a patient. All the decisions, may be made independently by more than one expert, are recorded.

temp	cough	headache	flu
normal	no	no	no
subfev	no	yes	no
subfev	no	yes	yes
high	yes	no	no
high	yes	no	yes
high	yes	yes	yes

id	sex	temp	cough	headache	patient
1	m	normal	no	no	no
2	m	subfev	no	yes	yes
3	f	subfev	no	yes	no
3	f	subfev	no	yes	yes
4	m	high	yes	yes	yes

Assume that someone is qualified for flu treatment if he/she might be a patient, who may have flu according to the first decision table. It is also reasonable to assume that people not treated for flu are those not qualified as patients or those qualified as patients who may not have flu. To express this intuition, we can define a new rough relation *Ft*.

All the information described previously can easily be represented by a DXL program. Moreover, it will be possible to query it. For example, it would be interesting to know who are the people possibly qualified for flu treatment.

The following clauses would be part of our DXL program, representing the rough relation *Ft* and the rough relations specified by the decisions tables above.

ft(Id,Sex) :- patient(Id,Sex,Fev,C,Ha), flu(Fev,C,Ha).
¬ft(Id,Sex) :- ¬patient(Id,Sex,Fev,C,Ha).
¬ft(Id,Sex) :- patient(Id,Sex,Fev,C,Ha), ¬flu(Fev,C,Ha).

¬flu(normal,no,no).   ¬patient(1,m,normal,no,no).
¬flu(subfev,no,yes).   patient(2,m,subfev,no,yes).
flu(subfev,no,yes).   ¬patient(3,f,subfev,no,yes).
⋮   ⋮

The rule with head ft(Id,Sex) captures the positive information about the new rough relation *Ft*, while the rules with head ¬ft(Id,Sex) express the negative information.

4 A Query Language for Rough Relations

Although DXL programs have a simple semantics and can be easily implemented in Prolog [5], their language is not expressive enough for stating rough-set-specific queries. For instance, it is not possible to refer to the lower approximation of a rough relation in DXL. Therefore, we propose a richer query language tailored to rough relations.

Definition 10. *A rough query $\mathcal{Q}$ is a pair $(Q, \mathcal{P})$, where $\mathcal{P}$ is a DXL program and Q is defined by the following abstract syntax rule*

$$Q \longrightarrow a \mid \neg a \mid \underline{a} \mid \underline{\neg a} \mid \overline{a} \mid a? \ ,$$

where a is an atom.

Informally, with a rough query $(r(c_1, c_2), \mathcal{P})$ $((\neg r(c_1, c_2), \mathcal{P}))$, we want to know whether the tuple (c_1, c_2) belongs to the upper approximation of the rough relation R ($\neg R$), defined in program $\mathcal{P}$. Instead, the query $(\underline{r}(c_1, c_2), \mathcal{P})$ $((\underline{\neg r}(c_1, c_2), \mathcal{P}))$ can be thought as "does the tuple (c_1, c_2) belong to the lower approximation of R ($\neg R$)?". The query $(\overline{r}(c_1, c_2), \mathcal{P})$ represents our interest in knowing if (c_1, c_2) belongs to the boundary region of R or not.

A query like $(r(c_1, c_2)?, \mathcal{P})$ asks what program $\mathcal{P}$ knows about the tuple (c_1, c_2) w.r.t. rough relation R. There are four possible answers: there is no information at all, i.e. it is not possible to conclude that (c_1, c_2) is a positive nor a negative example of R; (c_1, c_2) is both a positive and a negative example of R (i.e. belongs to the boundary of R); (c_1, c_2) is only a positive example of R (i.e. belongs to the lower approximation of R); (c_1, c_2) is only a negative example of R (i.e. belongs to the lower approximation of $\neg R$) .

If the atom occurring in a query is not ground then, as answer, we may get a list of examples. For instance, the query $(r(X, Y), \mathcal{P})$ requests a list of positive examples of R. For a query like $(r(X, Y)?, \mathcal{P})$, we get as answer three lists: the members of the lower approximation of R, the members of the lower approximation of $\neg R$, and the members of the boundary of R.

Example 2. Consider the DXL program $\mathcal{P}$ of example 1 and the following queries.

- *Which man might be qualified for flu treatment?*
  The corresponding rough query is $(\mathtt{ft(Id,m)}, \mathcal{P})$ and the answer is
  $\{\mathtt{Id = 2, Id = 4}\}$.
- *Who is definitely not qualified for flu treatment?*
  The corresponding rough query is $(\underline{\neg\mathtt{ft}}(\mathtt{Id,S}), \mathcal{P})$ and the answer is
  $\{\mathtt{(Id = 1, S = m)}\}$.
- *What do we know about the female patient 3 w.r.t. to flu treatment?*
  The corresponding rough query is $(\mathtt{ft(3,f)}?, \mathcal{P})$ and the answer is that *the patient might be qualified for flu treatment* (i.e. the tuple $(\mathtt{3,f})$ belongs to the boundary of Ft).

An answering algorithm can be built by compiling DXL programs and rough queries, to definite programs [5] and to queries to such definite programs, respectively. The compilation of rough queries may introduce negation-as-failure in the queries. For more details about an answering algorithm, see [9].

5 Extending Rough Relations

In this section, we discuss how Prolog built-ins such as arithmetic, negation--as-failure, etc. could be used in this context. We illustrate our ideas by some examples.

Arithmetic. An arithmetic constraint has the form

$$\langle arithmetic\ term\rangle \otimes \langle arithmetic\ term\rangle,$$

where $\otimes$ is a predefined arithmetic predicate. There is a finite number of predefined arithmetic predicates, such as equality, inequality, disequality, etc. with a predefined interpretation on a domain of numbers (floating point numbers or integers). Assume now that we allow for placing an arithmetic constraint in the body of a DXL program. This makes it possible to define rough relations with infinite number of elements.

Example 3. The following program defines an infinite binary rough relation.

```
r(X,Y):- X<Y, X+2>Y, X>0.
¬r(X,Y):- X^2 + Y^2 < 4.
```

Its positive information includes pairs of positive numbers which can be geometrically represented as points between two parallel lines. Its negative information can be depicted as the circle of radius 2 centered at $(0,0)$.

Definitions of infinite rough relations may be used for stating hypotheses which are expected to generalize results of experiments. Given a (finite) n-ary rough relation e based on the experimental results and a possibly infinite relation h describing the hypothesis, both defined in a DXL program $\mathcal{P}$ using arithmetic constraints, we may use the definitions to check how well the hypothesis conforms to the experimental data. For instance, the examples obtained by the query

$$(\underline{e}(X1,\ldots,Xn), \underline{\neg h}(X1,\ldots,Xn), \mathcal{P})$$

indicate the (certainly) positive outcomes of the experiment which are classified by the hypothesis as (certainly) negative.

Lower approximations. The next example, inspired by an example from [5], motivates usefulness of allowing them in DXL clause bodies.

Example 4. A relation *Train* has two arguments (attributes) representing time and location, respectively. Two sensors automatically detect presence/absence of approaching train at a crossing, producing facts like `train(12:50,Montijo).` automatically added to the knowledge base. A malfunction of a sensor may result in the contradictory fact `¬train(12:50,Montijo).` being added, too. Crossing is allowed if for sure no train approaches. This can be described by the following rule involving lower approximation in the body.

```
cross(X,Y)  :- ¬train(X,Y).
```

6 Conclusions

We have shown that DXL programs can be used as definitions of rough sets (catering for the combination of decision tables) and in that way we established a formal link between rough sets and logic programming. Lower approximations of the defined rough sets cannot be queried within DXL. Therefore, we proposed an extended query language.

This paper opens the possibility for transfer of techniques between logic programming and rough sets and for generalizations of both formalisms. For example, we have shown how Prolog arithmetic can be used to define rough relations. Transfer of rough set techniques to DXL programs is also possible.

While unrestricted combination of negation-as-failure and explicit negation in DXL requires more complex semantics, a disciplined use of lower approximations in the bodies not involving recursion, needs only a restricted use of negation-as-failure hidden from the user and semantics of such extension would still be quite simple and intuitive. An open question is whether such unrestricted combination is really needed.

As a next step, we plan implementation of a system based on the ideas of this paper and integrating it with existing rough sets software, like Rosetta [10].

References

1. Pawlak, Z.: Rough sets. Theoretical Aspects of Reasoning about Data. Kluwer Academic Publishers, Dordrecht (1991)
2. Pagliani, P.: Rough set theory and logic-algebraic structures. In Incomplete Information. Rough Set Analysis. Springer Physica-Verlag (1998)
3. Pawlak, Z., Slowinski, K., Slowinski. R.: Rough classification of patients after highly selective vagotomy for duodenal ulcer. International Journal of Man-Machine Studies (1998) 413–433
4. Małuszyński, J., Vitória, A.: Towards rough datalog: Embedding rough sets in Prolog. In Pal, S. K., Polkowski, L., eds.: Rough-Neuro Computing, AI, (Springer-Verlag) To appear.
5. Damásio,C. V., Pereira, L.M.: A survey of paraconsistent semantics for logic programs. In Gabbay, D. M., Smets, Ph., eds.: Handbook of Defeasible Reasoning and Uncertainty Management Systems. Volume 2, Kluwer Academic Publishers (1998) 241–320
6. Komorowski, J., Pawlak, Z., Polkowski, L., Skowron, A.: Rough sets: A tutorial. In: Rough Fuzzy Hybridization. A New Trend in Decision-Making. Springer-Verlag (1999)
7. Lloyd, J.W.: Foundations of Logic Programming. Springer-Verlag (1987)
8. Deransart, P., Ed-Bali, A., Cervoni, L.: Prolog: The Standard Reference Manual. Springer-Verlag (1996)
9. Małuszyński, J., Vitória, A.: Defining rough sets by extended logic programs. In: Paraconsistent Computational Logic Workshop (PCL'02). (2002) To appear.
10. Øhrn, A., Komorowski, J.: ROSETTA: A rough set toolkit for analysis of data. In: Proc. of Third International Joint Conference on Information Sciences, Fifth International Workshop on Rough Sets and Soft Computing (RSSC'97). Volume 3, Durham, NC, USA (1997) 403–407

Attribute Core of Decision Table

G.Y. Wang

Institute of Computer Science and Technology
Chongqing University of Posts and Telecommunications
Chongqing, 400065, P. R. China
`wanggy@cqupt.edu.cn`

Abstract. Attribute core of a decision table is often the start point and key of many information reduction procedures. In this paper, we will study the problem of calculating the attribute core of a decision table. We find some errors in some former results by Hu and Ye [1, 2]. Both definitions of attribute core in the algebra view and information view are studied and their difference is discovered. An algorithm for calculating the attribute core of a decision table in the information view and a systemic method for calculating the attribute core of a decision table in different cases are developed.

1 Introduction

Rough set theory has been applied in such fields as machine learning, data mining, etc., successfully since Professor Z. Pawlak developed it in 1982. Reduction of decision table is one of the key problems of rough set theory. The attribute core of a decision table is always the start point of information reduction. In this paper, we will study the problem of calculating the attribute core of a decision table. There are some theory results on this problem by Hu [1] and Ye [2]. Unfortunately, there are some errors in these results. We will study these problems and develop some new theory and algorithm through examining the difference between the algebra view and information view of rough set.

2 Problem in Calculating Attribute Core of a Decision Table

Hu developed a method to calculate the attribute core of a decision table based on Skowron's discernibility matrix [1].

Def. 1. For a set of attributes $B \subseteq C$ in a decision table $S=(U, C \cup D, V, f)$, the discernibility matrix can be defined by $C_D(B)=\{C_D(i,j)\}_{n \times n}$, $1 \leq i,j \leq n=|U/\text{Ind}(B)|$, where

$$C_D(i, j) = \begin{cases} \{a \in B \mid a(O_i) \neq a(O_j), O_i \in U, O_j \in U\} & d(O_i) \neq d(O_j) \\ 0 & d(O_i) = d(O_j) \end{cases},$$

for $i,j=1,2,\ldots,n$.

Hu drew the following conclusion in [1]: $|C_D(i,j)|=1$ if and only if the attribute in it belongs to $\text{CORE}_D(C)$. This conclusion is used in many later documents.

Ye proved Hu's conclusion might not be true under some conditions by giving a counterexample. He developed an improved method to calculate the attribute core through improving the definition of discernibility matrix in the following way.

Def. 2. For a set of attributes $B\subseteq C$ in a decision table $S=(U, C\cup D, V, f)$, the discernibility matrix can be defined by $C'_D(B)=\{C'_D(i,j)\}_{n\times n}, 1\le i,j\le n=|U/\text{Ind}(B)|$, where

$$C'_D(i,j) = \begin{cases} C_D(i,j) & , \min\{|D(x_i)|,|D(x_j)|\}=1 \\ & , else \end{cases}$$

for $i,j=1,2,\ldots,n$, $|D(x_i)|=|\{d_y|y\in [x_i]_C\}|$.

In [2], Ye drew another conclusion: $|C'_D(i,j)|=1$ if and only if the attribute in it belongs to $\text{CORE}_D(C)$.

Unfortunately, Ye did not find the real reason leading to the error of Hu's conclusion and method, the inconsistency in the decision table. The methods for calculating the attribute core of a decision table in [1] and [2] are not complete.

3   Information View of Rough Set

For the convenience of later illustration, we discuss some basic concepts about the information view of rough set at first [3].

Def. 3. Given an information system $S=(U, C\cup D, V, f)$, and a partition of U with classes X_i, $1\le i\le n$. The entropy of attributes B is defined as

$$H(B) = -\sum_{i=1}^{n} p(X_i)\log(p(X_i))$$

, where, $p(X_i)=|X_i|/|U|$.

Def. 4. Given an information system $S=(U, C\cup D, V, f)$, the conditional entropy of D ($U/\text{Ind}(D)=\{Y_1,Y_2,\ldots,Y_m\}$) given $B\subseteq C$ ($U/\text{Ind}(B)=\{X_1,X_2,\ldots,X_n\}$) is

$$H(D|B) = -\sum_{i=1}^{n} p(X_i)\sum_{j=1}^{m} p(Y_j|X_i)\log(p(Y_j|X_i))$$

, where $p(Y_j|X_i)=|Y_j\cap X_i|/|X_i|$, $1\le i\le n$, $1\le j\le m$.

The following 3 theorems can be proved easily.

Theorem 1. Given a relatively consistent decision table $S=(U, C\cup D, V, f)$, an attribute $r\in C$ is relatively reducible if and only if $H(D|C)=H(D|C-\{r\})$.

Theorem 2. Given a relatively consistent decision table $S=(U, C\cup D, V, f)$, the attribute set C is relatively independent if and only if $H(D|C)\ne H(D|C-\{r\})$ for all $r\in C$.

Theorem 3. Given a relatively consistent decision table $S=(U, C\cup D, V, f)$, attribute set $B\subseteq C$ is a relatively reduct of condition attribute set C if and only if $H(D|B)=H(D|C)$, and the attribute set B is relatively independent.

From the above 3 theorems we can find that the definition of reduct of a relatively consistent decision table in the information view is equivalent to its definition in the algebra view. Unfortunately, it will be different for a relatively inconsistent decision table. Now, let's have a look at the definitions of reduct and attribute core for a relatively inconsistent decision table in the information view.

Def. 5. Given a decision table $S=(U, C\cup D, V, f)$, attribute set $B\subseteq C$ is a relatively reduct of condition attribute set C if and only if

(1) $H(D|B)=H(D|C)$, and
(2) $H(\{d\}|B)\ne H(\{d\}|B-\{r\})$ for any attribute $r\in B$.

Def. 6. $\text{CORE}_Q(P)=\cap \text{RED}_Q(P)$ is called the Q-core of attribute set P.

4   Calculating the Attribute Core of a Decision Table

In the algebra view, it will depend on whether the lower approximation of all decision classes of a decision table will be changed after deleting an attribute to decide whether it is reducible. That is, whether the consistent part of a decision table is changed is the determinant condition for calculating its reducts.

According to Def. , in the information view, it will depend on whether the conditional entropy will be changed after deleting an attribute to decide whether it is reducible. The conditional entropy of the consistent part of a decision table is 0. All conditional entropy of a decision table is courted by its inconsistent part. That is, a condition attribute should be reducible if the probability distribution of the whole decision table will not be changed after deleting the condition attribute.

Now, let's have a look at the 2 examples presented by Ye in [2].

Eg. 1.   A decision table is shown in Table 1. $C=\{c_1, c_2, c_3\}$ is the condition attribute set, $D=\{d\}$ is the decision attribute set.

Attribute cores of Table 1 generated by Hu's method (CORE$_1$), Ye's method (CORE$_2$), algebra view (CORE$_3$) and information view (CORE$_4$) are as followings.
$CORE_{1D}(C)=\{c_1, c_2\}$, $CORE_{2D}(C)=\{c_2\}$,
$CORE_{3D}(C)=\{c_2\}$, $CORE_{4D}(C)=\{c_2\}$.

Table 1. Decision Table 1

	c_1	c_2	c_3	d
x_1	1	0	1	1
x_2	1	0	1	0
x_3	0	0	1	1
x_4	0	0	1	0
x_5	1	1	1	1

In this example, the result of Hu's method is different from the algebra view. Ye found the error of Hu's method from this example.

Eg. 2.   Table 2 is generated through deleting the first line (x_1) of Table 1. Then,
$CORE_{1D}(C)=\{c_1, c_2\}$, $CORE_{2D}(C)=\{c_1, c_2\}$,
$CORE_{3D}(C)=\{c_1, c_2\}$, $CORE_{4D}(C)=\{c_1, c_2\}$.

Table 2. Decision Table 2

	c_1	c_2	c_3	d
x_2	1	0	1	0
x_3	0	0	1	1
x_4	0	0	1	0
x_5	1	1	1	1

The result generated by Hu's method is the same as the result generated by the algebra view although there is still inconsistent data in Table 2. Based on this example, Ye said that the reason leading to the error of Hu's method is not the inconsistent data in a decision table [2].

Eg. 3.   Let's consider what will happen by inserting another line (x'_3) into Table 1. Table 3 is generated through inserting another line (x'_3) into Table 1. Then,
$CORE_{1D}(C)=\{c_1, c_2\}$, $CORE_{2D}(C)=\{c_2\}$,
$CORE_{3D}(C)=\{c_2\}$, $CORE_{4D}(C)=\{c_1, c_2\}$.

Table 3. Decision Table 3

	c_1	c_2	c_3	d
x_1	1	0	1	1
x_2	1	0	1	0
x'_3	1	0	1	2
x_3	0	0	1	1
x_4	0	0	1	0
x_5	1	1	1	1

From this example we can find that the attribute core in the algebra view may be different from the information view.

Through analyzing the two definitions of reduct we can find that the definition of reduct of a decision table in the algebra view guarantees the indiscernibility relation of the consistent part of the decision table will not be changed, while its definition in the information view guarantees the indiscernibility relation of the whole decision table will not be changed. Thus, the definition of reduct in the information view is complete. We can draw the following conclusions.

- The two definitions of reduct of a consistent decision table are equivalent. Hu's method is correct and Ye's method is not necessary in this case.

- The definition of reduct of an inconsistent decision table in the algebra view is included in its definition in the information view. The result of Ye's method is the attribute core in the algebra view only, while Hu's method may not be correct in this case. The result of Hu's method may be neither the attribute core in the algebra view nor the attribute core in the information view.

The reason leading to the difference between the result generated by Hu's method and the attribute core in the information view is all condition attributes with two different values for a pair of objects with different decisions are used to discern these two objects in Hu's method. However, the difference on a condition attribute of any two objects with different decisions can be ignored if the condition probability of these two objects will not be changed after deleting the condition attribute.

Based on all the above analysis, the following conclusions can be drown.
- In an inconsistent decision table: $CORE_2=CORE_3 \subseteq CORE_4 \subseteq CORE_1$,
- In a consistent decision table: $CORE_1=CORE_2=CORE_3=CORE_4$.

The attribute core of an inconsistent decision table in the information view can be calculated using the following theorem and algorithm.

Theorem 4. Given a decision table $S=(U, C \cup D, V, f)$, where $D=\{d\}$, attribute $r \in C$ is a core attribute if and only if $H(\{d\}|C) < H(\{d\}|C-\{r\})$.

In order to prove this theorem, Lemma 1 in [3] should be used.

Lemma 1. Given a decision table $S=(U, C \cup D, V, f)$, $A_1=\{X_1,X_2,\ldots,X_n\}$ is a partition of U induced by some equivalence relation, $A_2=\{X_1,\ldots,X_{i-1},X_{i+1},\ldots,X_{j-1},X_{j+1},\ldots,X_n,X_i \cup X_j\}$ is another partition generated through combining equivalence blocks X_i and X_j to $X_i \cup X_j$, and

$$H(D|A_1) = -\sum_{i=1}^{n} p(X_i) \sum_{j=1}^{m} p(Y_j|X_i) \log(p(Y_j|X_i)),$$

$$H(D|A_2) = H(D|A_1) - p(X_i \cup X_j) \sum_{k=1}^{m} p(Y_k|X_i \cup X_j) \log(p(Y_k|X_i \cup X_j))$$
$$+ p(X_i) \sum_{k=1}^{m} p(Y_k|X_i) \log(p(Y_k|X_i)) + p(X_j) \sum_{k=1}^{m} p(Y_k|X_j) \log(p(Y_k|X_j)),$$

then $H(D|A_2) \geq H(D|A_1)$.

Let's prove Theorem 4 then.

Proof.

($\Leftarrow$) If $H(\{d\}|C) < H(\{d\}|C-\{r\})$, then any sub-set of $C-\{r\}$ can't be a reduct of C according to Lemma 1. That is, any attribute sub-set not including attribute r can't be a reduct of C. It means that r is included in every reduct of C. Thus, r is a core attribute.

($\Rightarrow$) According to Lemma 1 we know $H(\{d\}|C) \leq H(\{d\}|C-\{r\})$.

Let's prove $H(\{d\}|C)=H(\{d\}|C-\{r\})$ can not hold using reduction to absurdity.

Suppose $H(\{d\}|C)=H(\{d\}|C-\{r\})$ at first. Thus, there must be an attribute set Q ($Q \subseteq C-\{r\}$) that is a reduct of C. We know r is a core attribute by conditions. So, $r \in Q$ according to the definition of reduct and core. It conflicts with $Q \subseteq C-\{r\}$. Thus, $H(\{d\}|C) \neq H(\{d\}|C-\{r\})$. So, $H(\{d\}|C) < H(\{d\}|C-\{r\})$. □

We developed the following algorithm to calculate the attribute core of a decision table in the information view based on Theorem 4.

ALGORITHM for finding the attribute core of a decision table in the information view:
  Input: A decision table $S=(U, R, V, f)$.
  Output: The attribute core of S in the information view, $CORE_D(C)$.
  Step 1. $CORE_D(C)=\phi$.
  Step 2.   For each condition attribute r in C, do
          If $H(\{d\}|C) < H(\{d\}|C-\{r\})$, then $CORE_D(C)=CORE_D(C)\cup\{r\}$.
  Step 3.   Stop.

The result of the above algorithm is the attribute core of the input decision table in the information view. We can calculate the attribute core of a decision table with different methods in different cases in the following way.
- If the decision table is consistent, both the method of Hu and the algorithm of this paper can be used.
- If the decision table is inconsistent, the method of Ye can be used to calculate its attribute core in the algebra view, while the algorithm of this paper can be used to calculate its attribute core in the information view.

5 Conclusion

Calculation of the attribute core of a decision table is one of the key problems in information reduction. There are some errors in former results about attribute core due to the inconsistency of a decision table. In this paper, we find the difference between the definitions of attribute core of a decision table in the information view and algebra view, point out the reason leading to the error of Hu's method, and develop an algorithm to calculate the attribute core of a decision table in the information view, and a systemic method to calculate the attribute core in different cases.

Acknowledgements. This paper is partially supported by National Science Foundation of China (No.69803014), National Climb Program of China, Foundation for University Key Teacher by the State Education Ministry of China (No.GG-520-10617-1001), Scientific Research Foundation for the Returned Overseas Chinese Scholars by the State Education Ministry of China, and Application Science Foundation of Chongqing.

References

1. Hu X., Cercone N.: Learning in Relational Databases: a Rough Set Approach. Computational Intelligence, 2 (1995) 323–337
2. Ye D. Y., Chen Z. J.: A New Discernibility Matrix and the Computation of a Core. ACTA Electronica Sinica, to appear
3. Wang G. Y.: Algebra View and Information View of Rough Sets Theory, in Data Mining and Knowledge Discovery: Theory, Tools, and Technology III, Belur V. Dasarathy, Editor, Proceedings of SPIE Vol. 4384 (2001) 200–07

Signal Analysis Using Rough Integrals

Maciej Borkowski

Department of Electrical and Computer Engineering, University of Manitoba
Winnipeg, Manitoba, Canada R3T 5V6
maciey@ee.umanitoba.ca

Abstract. This paper presents an approach to the use of rough integrals in signal analysis. For each set of sample sensor signal values, the average accuracy of set approximation is computed using a rough integral. In rough set theory, set approximation is carried out in non-empty, finite universes of objects. In this article, by contrast, set approximation is carried out inside non-empty, uncountable sets (universes) of points. This study is motivated by an interest in classifying sample values for various types of sensors. One result of this study has been the introduction of discrete integrals based on rough set theory. The rough integrals used in this article have practical implications, since these integrals serve as an aid in sensor reduction and in pattern recognition in analyzing segments of continuous signals. In the context of sensor reduction, rough integrals provide a basis for determining the relevance of sensors over a particular sampling period. In the context of pattern recognition, rough integrals can be useful in doing such things as classifying radar weather data, vehicular traffic patterns, robot navigation and waveforms of power system faults. A sample application of the rough integral in estimating the accuracy of set approximation of a sensor signal is given. The contribution of this article is an approach to measuring the relevance and accuracy of approximation of sample sensor signal values based on rough set methods.

Keywords: Approximation, pattern recognition, rough integral, rough sets, sensor, signal analysis.

1 Introduction

This paper presents an approach to approximating sensor signals using various forms of the discrete rough integral [4]-[5]. The basic idea is to integrate a set approximation functional with respect to a rough measure. The rough integral itself serves an set approximation aggregation operator inasmuch as it aggregates the cumulative effect of set approximation relative to approximation parameters affecting the granularity of sensor measurements. The discrete rough integral computes what is known as an elementary information granule. This granule contains a single value, namely, an ordered weighted average. The weighting derives from a rough measure defined in the context of an indistinguishability relation.

The contribution of this article is an approach to measuring the relevance and accuracy of approximation of sample sensor signal values based on rough set methods [2]-[6], [8], [10], [12]-[15]. Traditional rough set methods are based on set approximation, partition of each finite universes using an indiscernibility relation, attribute reduction, decision-rule derivation, and many useful measures such as approximation accuracy and rough inclusion [2]. In the context of sensor signals, set approximation is carried in the context of partitions of a set of points (on the line) using what is known as an indistinguishability relation, rough inclusion, approximation accuracy, and sensor fusion. This research is part of a Manitoba Hydro project devoted to the design of sensor signal classification systems useful in robotic inspection and maintenance of power system equipment (e.g., towers, insulators, and conductors).

2 Indistinguishability and Set Approximation

This section introduces the basis for the approximation and measurement of sets of uncountable sets of points (reals). Let $IS = (U, A)$ be an infinite information system where U is a non-empty subset of the reals $\Re$ and A is a non-empty, finite set of attributes, where $a : U \to V_a$ and $V_a \subseteq \Re$ for every $a \in A$, so that $\Re \supseteq V = \bigcup_{a \in A} V_a$. Let $a(x) \geqslant 0$, $\delta > 0$, $x \in \Re$ (set of reals) and let $\lfloor a(x)/\delta \rfloor$ denote the greatest integer less than or equal to $a(x)/\delta$ ("floor" of a(x)/δ). The parameter δ serves as a "neighborhood" size on real-valued intervals. Reals within the same subinterval bounded by $k\delta$ and $(k+1)\delta$ are considered indistinguishable. For each $B \subseteq A$, there is associated an equivalence relation

$$\mathrm{Ing}_{A,\delta}(B) = \{\, (x, x') \in \Re^2 \mid \forall a \in B.\, \lfloor \mathrm{a(x)}/\delta \rfloor = \lfloor \mathrm{a(x')}/\delta \rfloor \,\}$$

Proposition 1. $\mathrm{Ing}_{A,\delta}(B)$ is an equivalence relation.

The notation $[x]_B^\delta$ denotes equivalence classes of $\mathrm{Ing}_{A,\delta}(B)$. Further, partition $U/\mathrm{Ing}_{A,\delta}(B)$ denotes the family of all equivalence classes of relation $\mathrm{Ing}_{A,\delta}(B)$ on U. For $X \subseteq U$, the set X can be approximated only from information contained in B by constructing a B-lower and a B-upper approximation denoted by $\underline{B}X$ and $\overline{B}X$, respectively, where $\underline{B}X = \{x \mid [x]_B^\delta \subseteq X\}$ and $\overline{B}X = \{x \mid [x]_B^\delta \cap X \neq \emptyset\}$. In cases where instead of using x we use sensor reading y. we create equivalence class consisting from all points for which sensor readings are 'close' to y and define $[y]_B^\delta = [x]_B^\delta$ for x such that $a(x) = y$.

2.1 Rough Measure

In this section, a measure based on rough set theory [2] and classical measure theory [1] is introduced.

Definition 1. Let $IS = (U, A)$ be an information system with non-empty set U and non-empty set of attributes A. Further, let $B \subseteq A$ and let $[y]_B^\delta$ be an equivalence class of any sensor reading $y \in \Re$. Let ρ be a measure of a set

$X \in \wp(U)$, where $\wp(U)$ is a class (set of all subsets of U). Then for any $X \in \wp(U)$ the *rough membership set function (rmf)* $\mu_y^{B,\delta} : \wp(U) \to [0,1]$ is defined as follows:

$$\mu_y^{B,\delta}(X) = \frac{\rho\left(X \cap [y]_B^\delta\right)}{\rho\left([y]_B^\delta\right)} \tag{1}$$

If $\rho([y]_B^\delta)=0$, then of course $\rho(X \cap [y]_B^\delta) = 0$ and in this situation we consider symbol $\frac{0}{0}$ to be equal to 0.

Example 1. The ρ in the rmf can be interpreted as follows:

$$\mu_y^{B,\delta}(X) = \frac{\rho\left(X \cap [y]_B^\delta\right)}{\rho\left([y]_B^\delta\right)} = \frac{\int_{X \cap [y]_B^\delta} 1\, dx}{\int_{[y]_B^\delta} 1\, dx} \tag{2}$$

Proposition 2. The rmf $\mu_y^{B,\delta}$ in (1) is additive on U.

Proof. Let $X, Y \subset U$, and $X \cap Y = \emptyset$. From definition (1) we know that ρ is a measure. Therefore, ρ must be additive. Thus we have

$$\mu_y^{B,\delta}(X \cup Y) = \frac{\rho\left((X \cup Y) \cap [y]_B^\delta\right)}{\rho\left([y]_B^\delta\right)} = \frac{\rho\left((X \cap [y]_B^\delta) \cup (Y \cap [y]_B^\delta)\right)}{\rho\left([y]_B^\delta\right)} =$$

$$\frac{\rho\left(X \cap [y]_B^\delta\right)}{\rho\left([y]_B^\delta\right)} + \frac{\rho\left(Y \cap [y]_B^\delta\right)}{\rho\left([y]_B^\delta\right)} = \mu_y^{B,\delta}(X) + \mu_y^{B,\delta}(Y) \qquad \blacksquare$$

Example 2. The integral in (2) is evaluated relative to subintervals over which sensors $a \in B$ are defined (i.e., subintervals wherein sensor measurements have been recorded). Consider, for example, a sampling of a real-valued signal in Fig. 1 from a sensor. From a 24 second signal we are able to measure every odd 0.8 sec. period. Our target value is $y=0.5$ with tolerance $\delta=0.1$. Therefore, $X = \bigcup_{k=0}^{14} [1 + 1.6k, 1.8 + 1.6k]$ and then construct $[y]_B^{0.1}\big|_{y=0.5}$ as follows.

$$[y]_B^{0.1}\big|_{y=0.5} = [1.32, 1.8] \cup [3.42, 3.72] \cup \cdots \cup [23.32, 23.74] \cup [24.56, 25]$$

Hence,

$$X \cap [y]_B^{0.1}\big|_{y=0.5} = [1.32, 1.8] \cup [11.22, 11.36] \cup \cdots \cup [22.33, 22.6] \cup [23.4, 23.74]$$

Then the rough membership function value can be computed as follows.

$$\mu_{0.5}^{B,0.1}(X) = \frac{\int_{X \cap [y]_B^{0.1}|_{y=0.5}} 1\, dx}{\int_{[y]_B^{0.1}|_{y=0.5}} 1\, dx} =$$

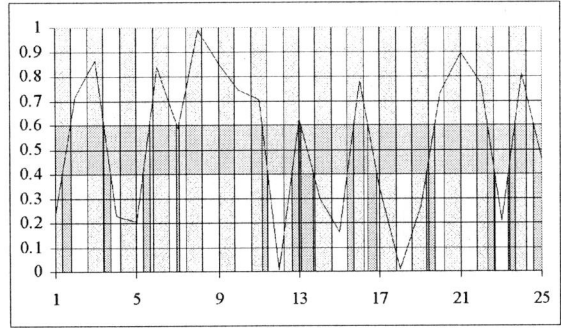

Fig. 1. Sampling of real-valued signal

$$\frac{1.8 - 1.32 + 11.36 - 11.22 + \ldots + 23.74 - 23.4}{1.8 - 1.32 + 3.72 - 3.42 + \ldots + 25 - 24.56} = \frac{1.96}{4.43} = 0.44$$

3 Discrete Rough Integral

The discrete rough integral was introduced in [4]. In the earlier study of rough integrals, only rough measures define relative to finite sets were considered. In this paper, the discrete rough integral is defined relative the measure of uncountable sets.

Definition 2. Discrete Rough Integral. Let ρ_y for $y = a(x)$ and $x \in U$ be a *rough measure* on the δ-indistinguishability space $(X, \wp(X), U/\mathrm{Ing}_{A,\delta}(B))$ relative to $U/\mathrm{Ing}_{A,\delta}(B)$ and y, and let $f: X \to \Re^+$ be a function such that $f(x_{(1)}) \leqslant \ldots \leqslant f(x_{(n)})$ (monotonic non-decreasing), $X_{(i)} := \{x_{(i)}, \ldots, x_{(n)}\}$, and $f(x_{(0)}) = 0$, where $\bullet_{(i)}$ is a permuted index. Then the discrete rough integral of f with respect to rough measure ρ_y is defined in the following way.

$$\int_X f \, d\rho = \sum_{i=1}^{n} \left[\left(f\left(x_{(i)}\right) - f\left(x_{(i-1)}\right) \right) \rho_u \left(X_{(i)} \right) \right]$$

It has been shown that the discrete rough integral computes an ordered weighted average [5]. This integral value can be useful in evaluating the relevance of sensors, if we enforce the criterion that the integral of a sensor must have a value greater than (or less than) some pre-set threshold.

Example 3. [**Average Accuracy Discrete Rough Integral**]. Let X be a set of points on a line. In addition, assume that X contains subintervals $\{X_1, \ldots, X_n\}$, i.e., $X_i \in X$, $i = 1, \ldots, n$. Further, for an information system $IS = (U, A)$ where U is a set of points and A is a set of attributes, let $X \subseteq U$ and let $B \subseteq A$. Assume that the $\mathrm{card}(\underline{B}X_0)/\mathrm{card}(\overline{B}X_0) = 0$. Define the set function $f : \wp(X) \to [0, 1]$ such that

$$f(X_i) = \frac{|\underline{B}X_i|}{|\overline{B}X_i|}, X_i \in X$$

Then the ordering $f(X_{(1)}) \leqslant \ldots \leqslant f(X_{(n)})$ uses the rule that $f(X_{(i)}) \leqslant f(X_{(i+1)})$ if

$$\frac{|\underline{B}X_{(i)}|}{|\overline{B}X_{(i)}|} \leqslant \frac{|\underline{B}X_{(i+1)}|}{|\overline{B}X_{(i+1)}|}$$

where $\bullet_{(i)}$ is a permuted index. From Def. 2, we can formulate a rough integral based on the accuracy of the approximation of the subintervals relative to a set of points of interest that is represented by $[y]_B^\delta$. This integral measures the average accuracy of a succession of rough sets.

$$\int_{E_{ac}} f(X) \, d\mu_y^{B,\delta} = \sum_{i=1}^{n} \left[\frac{|\underline{B}X_{(i)}|}{|\overline{B}X_{(i)}|} - \frac{|\underline{B}X_{(i-1)}|}{|\overline{B}X_{(i-1)}|} \right] \mu_y^{B,\delta} \left(X_{(i)} \right)$$

Example 4. Consider the information system $IS = (U, A)$ where U is a set of points on a line and A is a set of sensors. Then divide $X \subseteq U$ into n equal intervals of length $\operatorname{card}(X)/n$. Let $B = \{g\} \subseteq A$ where the model of the sensor g is defined as follows:

$$g : \wp(X) \to \Re \text{ such that } g(x) = 0.2 * \sin(x) + 2 * \sin(x/20)$$

$$f(X_i) = \frac{|\underline{B}X_i|}{|\overline{B}X_i|}, \, X_i \in X, \, B = \{g\}$$

where $x \in [0, 10]$. A plot of this sensor over $[0, 10]$ is shown in Fig. 2. Next consider the interval [6,8]. This interval contains all analog signal values of $g(x)$ such that $0.596 < g(x) < 0.998$. We want to consider the process of sampling an analog signal. Consider analog (continuous) signal $g(x)$ as defined above. Standard analog-to-digital conversion consists of three steps [11].

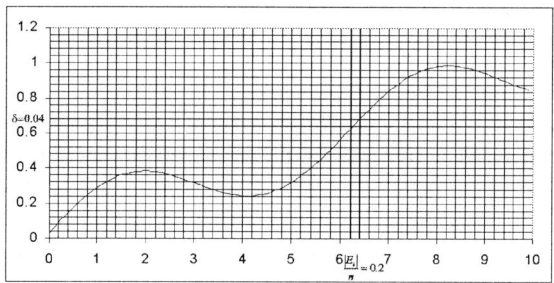

Fig. 2. Sampling-quantization grid

1. **Sampling.** Sampling consists in the conversion of a continuous-time signal into discrete-time signal obtained by taking "samples" of the continuous-time signal at discrete-time instants.

2. **Quantization**. Quantization entails the conversion of discrete-time continuous-values signal into a discrete-time, discrete-valued (digital) signal.
3. **Coding**. Coding consists in representing each discrete value $g_q(x)$ by a b-bit binary sequence.

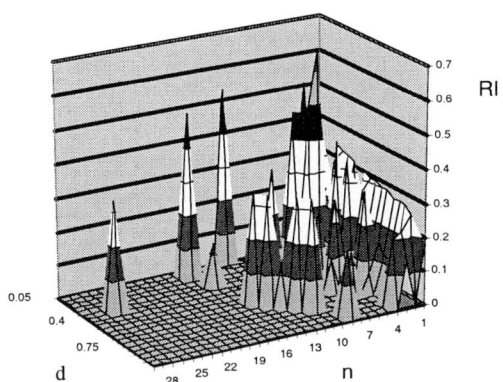

Fig. 3. Accuracy of Approximation RI Values

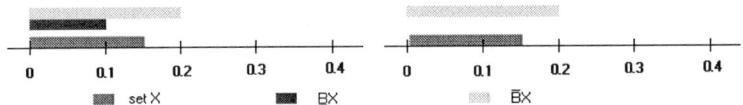

Fig. 4. Sample Approximations

We are interested in steps 1 and 2. Notice that parameter n corresponds to the sampling frequency. The larger n is, the more X_i sets we have, and (probably) the more precisely we can describe a function $g(x)$. On the other hand, δ is used with respect to sensor values. Therefore, it can be seen as a quantization parameter (see Fig. 2).

The accuracy of approximation rough integral $RI_{\delta,n}$ is parameterized relative to δ and n. The "ice-cream" cone plot in Fig. 3 shows rough integral values where $n \in [1,30]$ and $\delta \in (0,1)$ with step 0.05.

Each cone in Fig. 3 is constructed from a succession of accuracy of approximations over a succession of subintervals of the sample signal. The height of each cone is a measure of the ordered weighted average of the accuracy of approximation. Next consider $\delta = 0.1$ and $X_{(i)}$ is a subset of $\Re$ (set of reals). For the sake of simplicity, assume we are interested only in calculating $f(X_{(1)})$ and $X_{(1)} = [0, 0.15]$. On the left side of Fig. 4 we see this case. It is easy to calculate that

$$f(X_{(1)}) = f([0, 0.15)] = \frac{\underline{B}X_{(1)}}{\overline{B}X_{(1)}} = \frac{0.1}{0.2} = 0.5$$

Now, shift the set $X_{(1)}$ by 0.001. This case is shown on the right side of Fig. 4 where X'$_{(1)}$=[0.001,0.151]. We see that the lower approximation is just an empty set. Therefore, $f(X'_{(1)}) = 0$. It is clear, that instead of number 0.001, we can use any small number greater then zero. Therefore, the RI would have at this point a discontinuity (i.e., even the smallest change of set $X_{(1)}$ would be followed by a sudden change of the rough integral). After we go further from zero, there are no such discontinuities.

The same pattern would take place in every point being multiple of δ. Thus RI has two interesting properties, when considering its value with respect to shift of its argument X. It is discontinuous and periodic with a period δ.

The information contained in the plot in Fig. 3 would be useful in a training a sensor signal classification system. That is, the choice of a rough integral useful in classifying a particular form of sensor signal reduces to appropriate selection of δ and n parameters. There are many questions connected with these examples that merit further study (e.g., discontinuities, choices of δ and n) but consideration of answers to these questions is outside the scope of this paper. In other words, the form of rough integral introduced in this article can be calibrated in the context of a particular signal classification problem.

4 Conclusion

An approach to measuring the average accuracy of approximations of sensor signals using rough integration has been presented. This study is motivated by an interest in classifying sample signal values for various types of sensors. A byproduct of this study has been the introduction of a family of discrete rough integrals based on rough set theory. The discrete rough integral used in this article has practical implications, since these integrals serve as an aid in approximate reasoning and in pattern recognition relative to segments of continuous signals. The rough measure used in this article makes it possible to compare the degree of overlap between uncountable sets. This measure is fundamental in the definition of the discrete rough integral. The discrete approximation accuracy integral introduced in this article is new, and illustrates how one might evaluate set approximations for a succession of segments of a sensor signal. There are quite a number of practical applications of rough integrals (e.g., sensor fusion, tuning sensors in data acquisition systems or in the design of sensor signal classification systems for various forms of autonomous robots).

Acknowledgements. The research of Maciej Borkowski has been supported by a grant from Manitoba Hydro and partially by Natural Sciences and Engineering Research Council of Canada (NSERC) research grant 185986. The author also wishes to gratefully acknowledge the help and support of Dr. James Peters, University of Manitoba, Canada.

References

1. P.R. Halmos, Measure Theory. London: D. Van Nostrand Co., Inc., 1950.
2. Z. Pawlak, Rough Sets: Theoretical Aspects of Reasoning About Data. Boston, MA, Kluwer Academic Publishers, 1991.
3. Z. Pawlak, A. Skowron, Rough membership functions. In: R. Yager, M. Fedrizzi, J. Kacprzyk (Eds.), Advances in the Dempster-Shafer Theory of Evidence, NY, John Wiley & Sons, 1994, 251–271.
4. Z. Pawlak, J.F. Peters, A. Skowron, Z. Suraj, S. Ramanna, M. Borkowski, Rough measures: Theory and Applications. In: S. Hirano, M. Inuiguchi, S. Tsumoto (Eds.), Rough Set Theory and Granular Computing, Bulletin of the International Rough Set Society, vol. 5, no. 1 / 2, 2001, 177–184.
5. Z. Pawlak, J.F. Peters, A. Skowron, Z. Suraj, S. Ramanna, M. Borkowski, Rough measures, rough integrals, and sensor fusion. In: S. Hirano, M. Inuiguchi, S. Tsumoto (Eds.), *Rough Sets and Granular Computing*. Berlin: Physica Verlag [to appear].
6. J.F.Peters, W. Pedrycz, Computational Intelligence. In: J.G. Webster (Ed.), *Encyclopedia of Electrical and Electronic Engineering* 22 vols. NY: John Wiley & Sons, Inc., 1999.
7. J.F. Peters, S. Ramanna, M. Borkowski, A. Skowron, Approximate sensor fusion in a navigation agent. In: N. Zhong, J. Liu, S. Ohsuga and J. Bradshaw (Eds.), Intelligent agent technology: Research and development. Singapore: World Scientific Publishing, 2001, 500–504.
8. J.F. Peters, A. Skowron, J. Stepaniuk, Rough granules in spatial reasoning. In: Proc. Joint 9th International Fuzzy Systems Association (IFSA) World Congress and 20th North American Fuzzy Information Processing Society (NAFIPS) Int. Conf., Vancouver, British Columbia, Canada, 25-28 June 2001, 1355–1361.
9. J.F. Peters, S. Ramanna, M. Borkowski, A. Skowron, Z. Suraj, Sensor, filter and fusion models with rough Petri nets, *Fundamenta Informaticae*, vol. 34, 2001, 1–19.
10. J.F. Peters, A. Skowron, A rough set approach to knowledge discovery, *International Journal of Intelligent Systems*, 2002 [to appear].
11. J.G.Proakis, D.G.Manolakis, Digital Signal Processing. Upper Saddle River, New Jersey: Prentice-Hall, 07458, 1996.
12. A. Skowron, J. Stepaniuk, J.F. Peters, Extracting patterns using information granules. In: S. Hirano, M. Inuiguchi, S. Tsumoto (Eds.), *Proc. of Int. Workshop on Rough Set Theory and Granular Computing* (RSTGC'01), Matsue, Shimane, Japan, 20-22 May 2001, 135–142.
13. A. Skowron, R.W. Swiniarski, Information granulation and pattern recognition. In S. Pal, L. Polkowski, A. Skowron (Eds.), Rough-Neuro Computing. Berlin: Physica-Verlag, 2002, 636–670.
14. A. Skowron, J. Stepaniuk, J.F. Peters, Towards discovery of relevant patterns from parameterized schemes of information granule construction. In: S. Hirano, M. Inuiguchi, S. Tsumoto (Eds.), *Rough Sets and Granular Computing*. Berlin: Physica Verlag [to appear].
15. A. Skowron, J. Stepaniuk, J.F. Peters, Hierarchy of information granules. In: L. Czala (Ed.), *Proc. of the Workshop on Concurrency, Specification and Programming*, Oct. 2001, Warsaw, Poland, 254–268.

How Much Privacy? — A System to Safe Guard Personal Privacy while Releasing Databases

Yi-Ting Chiang[1], Yu-Cheng Chiang[2], Tsan-sheng Hsu[1], Churn-Jung Liau[1], and Da-Wei Wang[1]

[1] Institute of Information Science,
Academia Sinica, Taipei, Taiwan
{ytc,tshsu,liaucj,wdw}@iis.sinica.edu.tw
[2] Institute for Information Industry, Taipei, Taiwan

Abstract. We propose two models to quantitatively measure the degree of privacy invasion based on the granular computing methodology. The total cost model measures the privacy invasion in light of the effort needed for an investigator to find individual's private information. The average benefit model measures the privacy invasion in light of the benefit an investigator gets when his investigation improves the assessment of individuals private information. These two models can remedy the inadequacy of the deterministic formulation of privacy proposed in [4]. These two measurements have been implemented in CellSecu 2.0, and a more relaxed generalization procedure, called external generalization, has also been implemented.

1 Introduction

The question to publish a database while preserving confidentiality is an old problem. The Social Security Administration (SSA) in the USA employs the "bin size" as the measurement of the "anonymity" [2]. Two recent systems, Datafly [17] and μ-argus [14], also use bin size as the anonymity measurement. A bin corresponds to an information granule in granular computing[20] and is usually defined as an equivalence class of individuals with some common attribute values. The sizes of granules then have significant effect on the protection of privacy.

By anonymity we mean that no one can identify certain records belonging to any specific individual, while data confidentiality refers to the condition that a person cannot identify the value of certain fields belonging to any specific individual. If the meaning of "identify" is the same for anonymity and confidentiality, then it can be deduced that data confidentiality implies anonymity. However, in some cases we do want more fine-grained privacy protection, namely data confidentiality. Data confidentiality can be defined in epistemic logic[7], a mathematical framework to reason about the meaning of "knowing". A formal framework for data confidentiality was reported in [13]. CellSecu[4] is a web based prototype system based on the framework mentioned above. The system is based on a deterministic view on privacy, and introduces a confidentiality criteria called "non uniqueness". It uses generalization mechanisms proposed in

Datafly to enhance the confidentiality when the data set does not satisfy the confidentiality criteria. This paper reports on the effort to improve CellSecu. Specifically, two new measurements of confidentiality with intuitive explanation are developed, one more generalization mechanism called "external" generalization is designed and many engineering efforts have improved the performance to make the new system CellSecu2.0 acceptable in practice. As depicted in Figure 1 we envision that Cellsecu 2.0 can serve as a gate-keeper such that users can freely query the data center. All the answers approved by Cellsecu 2.0 preserve the data confidentiality according to a rigorously defined criteria.

The rest of the paper is organized as follows. In Section 2 we give a brief review of previous works on database confidentiality. In Section 3 we present the system architecture of Cellsecu 2.0. In Section 4 quantitative measurements of privacy breach are presented. The external generalization mechanism is introduced in Section 5. We conclude with some future research directions in Section 6.

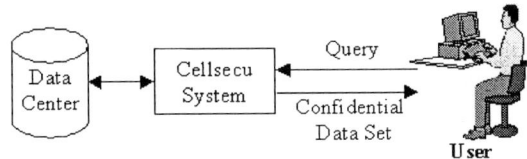

Fig. 1. Cellsecu 2.0 system as a gate-keeper.

2 Related Work

Statistical database inference has been a subject for intensive research for three decades starting with a study by Hoffman and Miller [12]. A statistical database is a database system that enables its users to retrieve only aggregate statistics (e.g., sample mean and count) for a subset of the entities represented in the database. Many data collecting agents face the dilemma that, on the one hand, such database systems are expected to satisfy user requests of aggregate statistics related to non-confidential and confidential attributes. On the other hand, the system should be secure enough to guard against the user's ability to infer any confidential information related to a specific individual represented in the database. Readers are referred to [1] for a survey on the statistical database system security problem before 1989.

The *inference* problem, the problem that users can deduce classified information from unclassified information, is defined in [18]. Garvey et al.[8,9] defined three inference channels, namely the deductive inference channel, the abductive inference channel and the probabilistic inference channel. The problem that users can aggregate lower level security information to form data with higher security levels than that of the forming elements, is called the *aggregation* problem. Denning et al.[6,19] identified two kinds of aggregation, namely *attribute association* and *size-based record association*. Attribute association is also called "data association" and size-based association is called "cardinal association" [11,15]. We are facing the same problems in spirit, but different in the sense that our goal is to publish the data set itself, instead of the statistical data, e.g., sum or average of certain fields. However, techniques such as query restriction approaches, data perturbation methods, and output-perturbation methods can be helpful in our study.

Datafly [17] and μ-argus [14] are two systems which tackle exactly the same problem as we do. In 1996, the European Union funded an effort to develop specialized software for disclosing data such that the identity of any individual contained in the released data cannot be recognized. Statistics Netherlands has produced a program named μ-argus. The Datafly system, developed in MIT by Dr. Sweeney in 1997, was written in Symantec C version 7.1 and Oracle's pro *C pre-compiler version 1.4. Both systems make decisions based on the bin sizes, generalize values within fields as needed, and remove extreme outlier information from the released data. The μ-argus system blanks out the outlier values at the cell-level with the cell-suppression process. The Datafly system uses generalization as the primary mechanism to enhance anonymity.

3 System Architecture and Methods

We focus on relational databases. For each data table, the fields are partitioned into the following three sets — Identifying (ID) Fields, Easily-Known (EK) fields and Unknown (U) fields. ID fields, e.g. social security number, are those that can be used to uniquely identify an individual. EK fields, e.g., the height and eye color of an individual, are those that can easily be found by observation or other sources. Using a combination of several EK fields, it may be plausible to uniquely identify an individual. U fields, e.g. the test result of a certain disease, are those we want to protect.

The link mode and the query mode are two ways for users to query the database. In *link* mode, the user already has some data from other sources and wants to link with the data center to get more fields. The *query* mode allows the user to query the database with SQL queries. The overall architecture of the system Cellsecu 2.0 is shown in Figure 2. When a query is submitted to the data center, the data center first produces the original query results by issuing queries to the corresponding databases. The filter process then removes all the ID fields to form the filtered query-set. The confidentiality test module then tests the confidential condition. If the filtered query-set does not meet the confidentiality requirements, it will be processed by the "generalization" module to reduce the specificity of data in the EK fields to produce a confidential query-set. The generalization mechanism usually increases the size of each information granule defined by the values of EK fields. The audit center records the user identity as well as the result of the confidentiality test. The admin configuration allows the data center privacy officer to set the sensitivity of each field, to partition the fields into three sets, to decide the confidentiality conditions, and to set the generalization parameters.

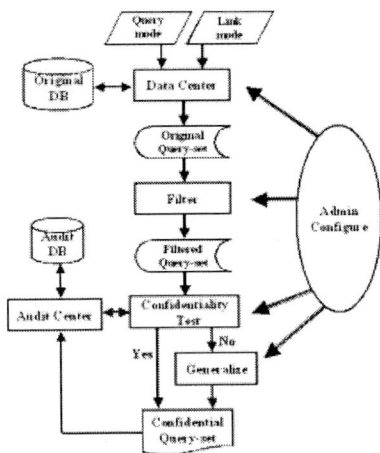

Fig. 2. System architecture.

4 Measuring the Privacy Breach

A deterministic view of privacy breach is taken in [4]. A privacy breach occurs only when the data recipient can definitely deduce some private information. However, consider the case that the data recipient changes his assessment on a specific individual's test result from "it is 1 with probability 0.1" to "it is 1 with probability 0.9". In many situations we might be inclined to conclude that a certain amount of individual privacy has been leaked. However, in the deterministic formulation, the increase in this probability is not considered. We propose two quantitative measurement models: the total cost model and the average benefit model to remedy the problem.

4.1 Total Cost Model

The bin(or granule) size is used to measure the anonymity of a data set. Intuitively, the larger the bin size, the harder to find some attribute of one specific individual in that bin. However, there is no quantitative model to measure the anonymities of different sizes of bins. Consider A and B, two bins each of 100 records. Consider a binary attribute. For that attribute assume that there are 50 records in A with value 1, and there are only 10 records in B with value 1. Intuitively we would consider bin B as being more revealing. However, the bin size concept cannot capture this intuition. We give a simple quantitative measurement of the anonymity intuitively captured by the concept of bin size. Consider N balls, numbered and colored with either black or white, in a box. To determine the color of each ball, one has to take the balls out of the box one by one. However, if we know the number of white balls and black balls, then we might not have to pick up all the balls to know the color of each ball. Each record in a bin can be considered as a ball in the box and the color of the ball corresponds to the value of the unknown field in that record. The cost of picking up a ball out of the box corresponds with the investigating cost to determine the value of some record. Let $E(m,n)$ denote the expected average cost to find the color of every ball, providing that the number of white and black balls are known to be respectively m and n in advance. It can be shown that $E(m,n) = \frac{mn}{m+1} + \frac{mn}{n+1}$. If the ratio of black and white balls is fixed, $E(m,n)$ increases while the number of balls increases. This gives an intuitive explanation why larger bins seem to be more confidential. Figure 3 is a plot of $E(m,n)$ by fixing $n = 100$ and where m vary from 1 to 100.

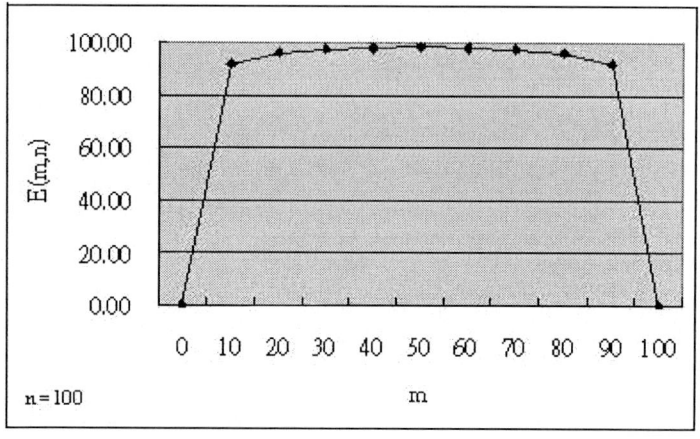

Fig. 3. E(m,100)

4.2 Average Benefit Model

Consider a data set that contains a bin where 99 percent of the records in that bin has the same value for one specific attribute. It is tempting to conclude that this is a situation where personal privacy can be in danger. However, if this distribution is not far from the distribution of the whole database, it seems pointless to consider above mentioned data set as a threat to personal privacy. Therefore, it is important to consider the original distribution of values of attributes in the database. The sensitivity of data is also an important aspect regarding personal privacy. For example, to let someone know the result of an HIV test is considered a more serious privacy violation than to let someone know the test result for blood type. Moreover, for the same attribute, revealing one value might be a more serious violation of personal privacy than the other. For example, knowing someone tested HIV negative is almost harmless to that individual, while knowing someone test positive can be costly to that individual. Below we propose an information theoretical approach to measure the syntactic information gain after receiving the data set and we also incorporate the idea of data sensitivity into the formulation. Let p_0 and p_1 denote the percentage of records with value 0 and 1 respectively. Let p'_0, p'_1 denote the percentage of records with value 0 and 1 in the specific bin. Let c_0, c_1 be two non-negative numbers, representing the sensitivity of the attribute being 0 or 1. The average benefit of receiving such a bin, denoted by $C(p_0, p_1, p'_0, p'_1)$, is defined as the follows:

$$C(p_0, p_1, p'_0, p'_1, c_0, c_1) = \begin{cases} c_0 \cdot \left(\dfrac{\log \frac{1}{p_0} - \log \frac{1}{p'_0}}{\log \frac{1}{p_0}} \right) & \text{if } 0 < p_0 \leq p'_0 \\ c_1 \cdot \left(\dfrac{\log \frac{1}{p_1} - \log \frac{1}{p'_1}}{\log \frac{1}{p_1}} \right) & \text{if } p'_0 \leq p_0 \end{cases}$$

Since $p_0 + p_1 = 1$ and $p'_0 + p'_1 = 1$ the function actually needs only four parameters, p_1, p'_1, c_0, c_1. In figure 4, we note that the average benefit is 0 when $p'_1 = p_1$, it reaches 30 and 10 when p'_1 is 1 and 0 respectively in the case of $p_1 = 0.5$. The case of $p_1 = 0.9$ illustrates the situation that 90 percent of records in the data set have value 1. The case of $p_1 = 0.01$ illustrates a situation very similar to the HIV test, only a very small percentage of records have value 1 and the sensitivity of value 1 and 0 are very different.

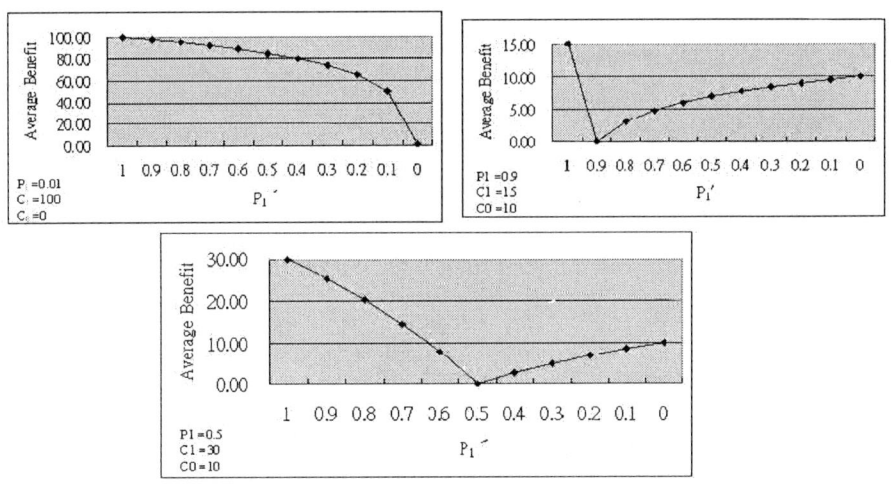

Fig. 4. Distribution of average benefit when $p_1 = 0.01, 0.5, 0.9$.

5 External Generalization

In CellSecu 2.0, the total cost and average benefit of a data set to be released will be calculated. If the data set does not pass the privacy criteria, i.e., the total cost and average benefit are greater than the threshold preset by the administrator, then the generalization module will be invoked to generalize some easily known fields as described in [3,17]. In [3] the generalization process performs on the resulting data set. In other words, the number of records in the resulting data set never increases. Here we propose another generalization process, called *enteral generalization*. In the external generalization process, when an easily known field, say height, gets generalized, our system will go back to query the database system with the now more relaxed criteria. For example, the original query contains a condition that the height should be in between 172 to 177 cm, if the resulting data set is considered unsafe for release then the external generalization process will generalize the criteria to a more relax condition, for example the height should be in between 170 to 180 cm. By allowing external generalization, we can increase the chance that the data set can pass the privacy check and still provide the user some useful information.

6 Conclusion

Two quantitative privacy measurements have been proposed. It is our hope that these measurements can capture people's intuition about privacy well enough so that the CellSecu system can really serve as a gate keeper. Our preliminary performance evaluation shows that the system can be used in the real environment.

To gauge the quality of the generalized data set is an important and interesting question. We believe both theoretical study and experimental works are needed to evaluate the impact of Cellsecu on the quality of research outcomes based on generalized data sets. Last we want to point out that technology alone cannot resolve the complicated issue regarding publishing data for the benefit of the population and protecting individual confidentiality. However, our system can provide some clarification on the boundary between data sets which are unlikely to cause violation of personal confidentiality, and those which are. We believe that privacy policy and privacy protection legislation, together with strong technological protection, can make sharing data, yet preserving confidentiality, plausible.

References

1. Adam, N.R. and Wortmann, J.C., Security-control methods for statistical databases: A comparative study. *ACM Computing Surveys*, Vol. 21, No. 4, December 1989.
2. Alexander, L. and Jabine, T., Access to social security microdata files for research and statistical purposes. *Social Security Bulletin*, (41) No. 8, 1978.
3. Chiang, Y.-C., *Protecting privacy in public database* (in Chinese), Master's thesis, Graduate Institute of Information Management, National Taiwan University, 2000.

4. Chiang, Y.-C. and Hsu, T.-s. and Kuo, S. and Wang, D.-W., Preserving confidentially when sharing medical data. In *Proceedings Asia Pacific Medical Informatics Conference (APAMI-MIC)*, 2000.
5. Chellas, B.F., *Modal Logic*. Cambridge, U.K.: Cambridge University Press, 1980.
6. Denning, D.E. and Akl, S.G. and Heckman, M. and Lunt, T.F. and Morgenstern, M. and Neumann, P.G. and Schell, R. R., Views for multilevel database security. *In IEEE Transactions on Software Engineering*, Vol.13, No.2, pp.129–140, February 1987.
7. Fagin, R. and Halpern, J.Y. and Moses, Y. and Vardi, M.Y., *Reasoning about knowledge* MIT Press 1995.
8. Ford, W.R. and O'Keefe, J. and Thuraisingham, M.B., *Database Inference Controller: An Overview*. Technical Report MTR 10963 Vol. 1. The MITRE Corporation. August 1990.
9. Garvey, T.D. and Lunt, T.F. and Quin, X. and Stickel, M.E. *Inference Channel Detection and Elimination in Knowledge-Based Systems*. Final Report ECU 2528, SRI International, October 1994.
10. Halpern, J.K. and Tuttle, M.R., Knowledge, probability, and adversaries. *Journal of the ACM* 40(4), 917-962, 1993.
11. Hinke, T.H., Inference aggregation detection in database management systems. In *Proceedings of the IEEE Symposium on Research in Security and Privacy*, pp.96–106, April 1988.
12. Hoffman, L.J. and Miller, W.F., Getting a personal dossier from a Statistical data bank. *Datamation*, vol. 16, No.5, pp.74–74, May 1970.
13. Hsu, T.-s. and Liau, C.-J and Wang, D.-W., A logical model for privacy protection. *In Proceedings of Information Security Conference (ISC)*, Springer-Verlag LNCS# 2200, pp.110–124, 2001.
14. Hundepool, A. and Willenborg, L., μ and τ-argus: software for statistical disclosure control. In *Procceedings of the Third International Seminar on Statistical Confidentiality*, Bled, 1996.
15. Jajodia, S., Aggregation and inference problems in multilevel secure systems. In *Proceedings of the 5th Rome Laboratory Database Security Workshop*, 1992.
16. Krasucki, P. and Parikh, R. and Ndjatou, G. Probabilistic knowledge and probabilistic common knowledge(preliminary report). In Ras, Z. W. and Zemankova, M. and Emrich, M.L. editors, *Methodologies for Intelligent Systems*, vol 5, pp.1–8. Elsevier Science Publishing Co., Inc., The Hague, 1990.
17. Sweeney, L., *Guaranteeing Anonymity When Sharing Medical Data, the Datafly System*. MIT A.I. Working Paper No. AIWP-WP334. May 1997.
18. Morgenstern, M., Controlling logical inference in multilevel database systems. In *Proceedings of the IEEE Symposium on Security and Privacy*, pp.245–255, April 1988.
19. Palley, M.A., Security of statistical databases compromise through attribute correlational modeling. In *Proceedings of IEEE Conference on Data Engineering*, pp.67–74, 1986.
20. Yao Y.Y. and Liau C.J., A generalized decision logic language for granular computing. In *Proceedings of the 11th IEEE International Conference on Fuzzy Systems*, IEEE Press, 2002.

Rough Clustering: An Alternative to Find Meaningful Clusters by Using the Reducts from a Dataset

Hércules Antonio do Prado[1,3], Paulo Martins Engel[2], and Homero Chaib Filho[1,3]

[1] Brazilian Agricultural Research Corporation
Center for Agricultural Research on Savannah,
Caixa Postal 08.223 - CEP 70770-000
Planaltina, DF, Brasil
{hercules,homero}@cpac.embrapa.br
[2] Federal University of Rio Grande do Sul
Instituto de Informática
Caixa Postal 15.064 - CEP 91.501-970
Porto Alegre, RS, Brasil
engel@inf.ufrgs.br
[3] Catholic University of Brasília
Graduate Program in Management of Knowledge and Information Technology
CEP: 70.790-160
Brasília, DF, Brasil
{hercules,homero}@ucb.br

Abstract. Rough Sets Theory has been applied to build classifiers by exploring symbolic relations in data. Indiscernibility relations combined with the *concept* notion, and the application of set operations, lead to knowledge discovery in an elegant and intuitive way. In this paper we argue that the indiscernibility relation has a strong appeal to be applied in clustering since itself is a sort of natural clustering in the n-dimensional space of attributes. We explore this fact to build a clustering scheme that discovers straight structures for clusters in the sub-dimensional space of the attributes. As the usual clustering process is a kind of search for concepts, the scheme here proposed provides a better description of such clusters allowing the analyst to figure out what cluster has meaning to be considered as a concept. The basic idea is to find reducts in a set of objects and apply them to any clustering procedure able to cope with discrete data. We apply the approach to a toy example of animal taxonomy in order to show its functionality.

1 Introduction and Motivation

Knowledge discovery from unlabeled data comprises the identification of "natural groups" and analysis of these groups in order to interpret their meaning. According to Wrobel [1], a concept is "a generalized description of sets of objects". In this sense, Easterlin and Langley [2] analyze the concept formation process in three steps: (a) Consider a set of objects descriptions; (b) Find sets of objects that can be grouped together, and (c) Find intensional description of these sets of objects. Unfortunately, usual clustering algorithms just generate extensional (i.e., what objects are members of each cluster) descriptions of groups. Intensional descriptions (i.e., what are the main characteristics of each cluster) are not issued. The work of Agrawal *et al.* [3] is an exception to this rule, that reinforce the necessity for clustering algorithms to generate intensional descriptions. Rough Sets Theory (RST) is a mathematical approach, proposed by Z. Pawlak ([4], [5] and [6]) in the early eighties, to cope with data analysis in the presence of imprecision, vagueness, and uncertainty. Its intuitive appeal comes from the notions of *information systems* - referring to a relation in a database - and the relation of *indiscernibility* between elements of a set; both posed as important concepts of the theory. The theory departs from a set of objects of interest and information characterizing them. A subset of these objects is said to be *indiscernible* or *similar* if they are characterized by the same information. RST also allows the expression of certainty - as belief and plausibility - on both a mathematical and an intuitive basis. Some basics on the related concepts are described below. An *Information system* is a pair $\mathbf{A} = (U, A)$ where U is a non-empty, *finite* set called the universe and A is a non-empty, finite set of *attributes*, where $a : U \to V_a$ for $a \in A$, being V_a called the *value set* of attribute a. Elements of U are called *objects*. Every information system $\mathbf{A} = (U, A)$ and a non-empty set $B \subseteq A$ define a *B-information function* by $Inf_B(u) = (a_i(u) : a_i \in B)$. An *indiscernibility relation IND(B)* for any $B \subseteq A$ is definided by $IND(B) = \{(u,u') \in U \times U : Inf_B(u) = Inf_B(u')\}$. The lower approximation $L_B(X)$ and the upper approximation $U_B(X)$ for any subset $X \subseteq U$ are defined, as illustrated by Figure 1, by the equations:

$$L_B(X) = x \in U : [x]_B \subseteq X \text{ and } U_B(X) = x \in U : [x]_B \cap X \neq \varnothing$$

A particular notion of interest for us is the *reduct*, that emerge from sets of indiscernible objects under particular relations. Intuitively, reducts defines sets of objects that share the same values in specific attributes, uniquely associated to a decision attribute. For our aiming, we restrict the notion of reduct to be minimal sets of objects sharing the same values in specific attributes, without concerning to any decision attribute, since we have no decision attributes in clustering procedures. Our motivation for this work comes from the notion of indiscernibility that we consider very attractive, since each indiscernible relation is also a sort of cluster. In addition we have not seen research focussed in applying RST to clustering.

2 Proposed Approach

Our approach departs from the reducts found in an information system $\mathbf{A}=(U, A)$ by any reduct generation algorithm (e.g., the Expansion Algorithm presented in [7]), applying them to any clustering algorithm that accept discrete values as input. For the clustering process, each input record contains the attributes and values that uniquely define the reducts $RED_i(\mathbf{A})$, $i=1,2,...,n$, and the relative frequency f_i defined by the fraction $s(RED_i(\mathbf{A}))/s(U)$, in which $s(RED_i(\mathbf{A}))$ is the amount of objects covered by $RED_i(\mathbf{A})$ and $s(U)$ the amount of objects in U. To illustrate, lets disregard the core set X from Figure 1 and simulate a clustering process. Each reduct is identified by two numbers, the first one meaning the region (1: *POSITIVE(X)*, 2: *BOUND(X)* and 3: *NEGATIVE(X)*) and the second one a sequence number inside each region. These reducts, after applying the clustering process with, say, two centroids, would appear like in Figure 2. In order to avoid considering inexpressive reducts, we take only those with $f_i > t$, where t is an arbitrary threshold. Also, the number of attribute-values admitted for each reduct is limited to a quantity q that express the independent variables that will be used to explain a certain cluster. The shaded reducts refers to those with a stronger connection to the respective centroids (S_1 or S_2).

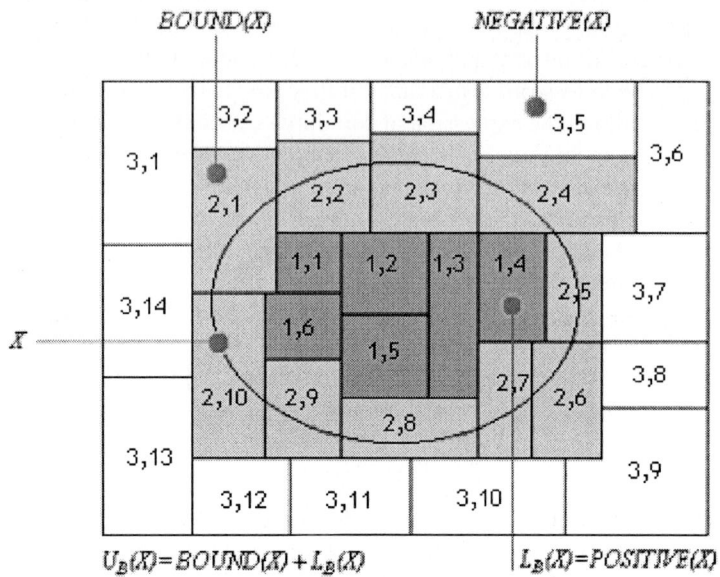

Fig. 1. Partitions of U

3 Example of Application: The Animal Taxonomy Problem

In this section we explore an application of the proposed approach to the Biology domain. We take the animal taxonomy problem, for which we build the reducts with $f_i \geq 0,2$ and $q = 3$, and apply, as clustering algorithm, an ART1 model [8]. ART1 algorithm proceeds, in general steps, as follows: (a) the first input is selected to be the first cluster; (b) each next input is compared with each existing cluster; the nearest cluster where the distance to the input is less than a threshold is chosen to cluster the input. Otherwise, the input defines a new cluster and proceeds with the new examples.

The training set contains information concerning to 8 animals that we know, a priori, to belong to the classes of amphibians and mammals, according to the phylogenetic characterizations existing in Biology. The classes, however, are not informed. It is expected that some near-real grouping come up from the process. The attributes *metabolism*, *cover* (wet skin or hair), *dentition*, *reproduction*, and *number of feet* were chosen to describe the objects. The tuples in the training set are: {(Frog, ectothermic, wet skin, superior, oviparous, 4), (Toad, ectothermic, wet skin, no, oviparous, 4), (Elephant, endothermic, hair, complete, viviparous, 4), (Dog, endothermic, hair, complete, viviparous, 4),

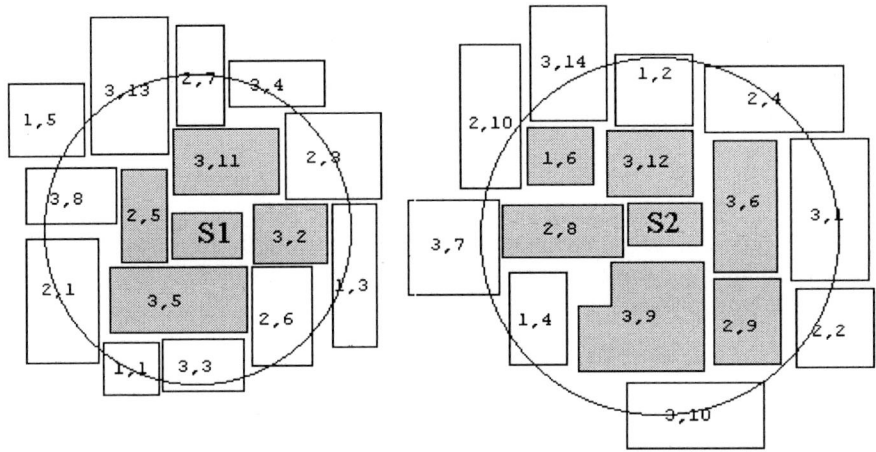

Fig. 2. Generated clusters

Table 1. Results from the clustering process

Reducts	Groups	Rules extracted from the cluster prototypes
1	0	If *ectothermic* and *wet skin* and *oviparous* then *group 0*
2	0	If *ectothermic* and *wet skin* and *has 4 feet* then *group 0*
3	0	If *ectothermic* and *oviparous* and *has 4 feet* then group 0
4	0	If *wet skin* and *oviparous* and *has 4 feet* then group 0
5	1	If *endothermic* and *has hair* and *dentition complete* then *group 1*
6	0	If *endothermic* and *has hair* and *viviparous* them *group 0* (*)
7	0	If *endothermic* and *has hair* and has *4 feet* then *group 0* (*)
8	1	If *endothermic* and *dentition complete* and *viviparous* then *group 1*
9	1	If *endothermic* and *dentition complete* and *4 feet* then *group 1*
10	0	If *endothermic* and *viviparous* and *4 feet* then *group 0* (*)
11	1	If *has hair* and *dentition complete* and *viviparous* then *group 1*
12	1	If *has hair* and *dentition complete* and *4 feet* then *group 1*
13	0	If *has hair* and *viviparous* and *4 feet* then *group 0* (*)
14	1	If *dentition complete* and *viviparous* and *4 feet* then *group 1*

(Cat, endothermic, hair, complete, viviparous, 4), (Rabbit, endothermic, hair, complete, viviparous, 4), (Jaguar, endothermic, hair, complete, viviparous, 4), (Whale, endothermic, hair, the youngest, viviparous, 0)}. Taking the threshold $f_i \geq 0,2$ and, for the sake of simplicity, the amount of attributes $q = 3$, the following reducts are found: {(#1, ectothermic, wet skin, -, oviparous, -, 0.25), (#2, ectothermic, wet skin, -, -, 4, 0.25), (#3, ectothermic, -, -, oviparous, 4, 0.25), (#4, - ,wet skin, -, oviparous, 4, 0.25), (#5, endothermic, hair, complete, -, -, 0.63), (#6, endothermic, hair, -, viviparous, -, 0.75), (#7, endothermic, hair, -, -, 4, 0.63), (#8, endothermic, -, complete, viviparous, -, 0.63), (#9, endothermic, -, complete, -, 4, 0.63), (#10, endothermic, -, -, viviparous, 4, 0.63), (#11, -, hair, complete, viviparous, -, 0.63), (#12, -, hair, complete,-, 4, 0.63), (#13, -, hair, -, viviparous, 4, 0.63), (#14, -, -, complete, viviparous, 4, 0.63)}. Each element in the set above contains the variables: *# reduct, metab, cover, dentition, reprod, feet, and f_i*. This set are then applied to the ART1 model with the vigilance parameter ρ (a similarity metric) set to 0, 2. The results issued by ART1 are shown in the columns 1 and 2 of Table 1. Notice that every reduct related to amphibians are grouped together, representing a good result. On the other hand, although the wrong association of 4 cases in the mammals group, the final result can be seen as a good approximation to the real situation.

From the reducts belonging to each cluster we can extract the intensional descriptions shown in column 3 of Table 1. The lines marked with (*) are those wrongly grouped.

4 Conclusions and Future Work

In this work we present some preliminary results in exploring the use of reducts from a data set to find clusters with some intensional descriptions, beyond the usual extensional ones. Reducts were explored as kinds of clusters that were later grouped in major clusters by an ART1 model. Considering that we have constrained the reducts for a specific size, more research is required to decide how to cope with any size reducts. On the other hand, ART1 has an important drawback, generating results that are dependent on the input order. This problem points out to the necessity of further experiments using other clustering algorithms.

References

1. Wrobel, S.: Concept Formation and Knowledge Revision. Dordrecht, The Netherlands: Kluwer, 1994. 240pp.
2. Easterlin, J. D., Langley, P., A Framework for Concept Formation. In: Seventh Annual Conference of the Cognitive Science Society, Irvine, CA, 1985.
3. Agrawal, R., Gehrke, J., Gunopulos, D., Raghavan P. Automatic Subspace Clustering of High Dimensional Data for Data Mining Applications, *Proc. of SIGMOD*, Seattle, Washington, June 1998.
4. Pawlak, *Rough Sets: Theoretical Aspects of Reasoning About Data*, Boston, MA, Kluwer Academic Publishers, 1991.
5. Yao, Y. Y., Wong, S. K. M. and Lin, T. Y. A Review of Rough Set Models. In: LYN, T. Y; Cercone. N. (Eds.). Rough Sets and Data Mining: Analysis of Imprecise Data, Kluwer Academic Pub. 1997.
6. Komorowski, J., Pawlak, Z., Polkowski, Skowron, A. Rough sets: A tutorial. In: S. K. Pal, A. Skowron (Ed.). Rough Fuzzy Hybridization: A new Trend in Decision-Making. Berlin: Springer-Verlag, 1999, 3–98.
7. Starzyk, J., Nelson, D. E. and Sturtz, K. Reduct Generation in Information Systems. Bulletin of International Rough Set Society, 3(1/2): 19–22, 1999.
8. Carpenter, G.; Grossberg, S. Neural Dynamics of Category Learning and Recognition: Attention, Memory, Consolidation, and Amnesia. In: Davis J. L. (Ed.). Brain structure, learning, and memory. AAAS Symposia Series, Boulder, CO: Westview Press, 1988, 233–287

Concept Learning with Approximation: Rough Version Spaces

Vincent Dubois and Mohamed Quafafou

IRIN, Université de Nantes, France

Abstract. The concept learning problem is a general framework for learning concept consistent with available data. Version Spaces theory and methods are build in this framework. However, it is not designated to handle noisy (possibly inconsistent) data. In this paper, we use rough set theory to improve this framework. Firstly, we introduce a rough consistency. Secondly, we define an approximative concept learning problem. Thirdly, we present a Rough Version Space theory and related methods to address the approximative concept learning problem. Using a didactic example, we put these methods into use. An overview of possible extension of this work concludes this article.

Keywords. Approximation, Concept Learning, Rough Sets, Version spaces

1 Introduction

The concept learning problem is a well-known and fruitful framework, as numerous developments in the Version Space field attests, but is ill-suited to real-word, inconsistent data. This come from the harsh consistency property it is build upon: either a concept is consistent with the data, either it is not. We alleviate this problem by using rough set theory to soften the consistency requirement. As a consequence, newly defined approximative concept learning framework and in particular Rough Version Space can handle inconsistent data, as shown in our example.

This paper is organized as follow: section 2 introduces the Concept Learning Task and version spaces and their properties. Section 3 presents an approximative version of concepts developed in section 2. Section 4 proposes algorithms and methods to handle the approximative concept learning problem. Section 5 puts them in action on a didactic example. Section 6 concludes this paper.

2 Concept Learning

2.1 Notations

We note $^\mathsf{C}A$ the complementary of A in the space it is defined. We note segment $[A, B]$ the set of all element x such that $A \subset x \subset B$. If $f : A \mapsto B$, and $C \subset A$, we note $f(C) = \{c \in B | \exists a \in C, f(a) = c\}$.

We note I the set of all instances. The set 2^I of all concepts is denoted C. Let L_I and L_C denotes language on I and C. The function $R_I : L_I \mapsto I$ (resp. $R_C : L_C \mapsto C$) maps a instance (resp. a concept) representation to the instance (resp. a concept) it represents. R_C and R_I are not necessarily injective nor surjective, i.e. some concept or instances may have many or no representation in the chosen language.

Definition 1. *A concept $c \in C$ is said to* cover *an instance $i \in I$ iff $i \in c$. This definition extends to the language by the following way:* $\forall i \in L_I, \forall c \in L_C, c$ cover $i \Leftrightarrow R_I(i) \in R_C(c)$

Definition 2. *A concept c is said to be* consistent *with a set of positive instances P and a set of negative instances iff $P \subset c$ and $c \cap N = \emptyset$*

Definition 3. *The* concept class of representable concept *is the set of all concepts having a representation in the concept language and is defined by* $C_{R_C} = R_C(L_C)$

2.2 Version Spaces

Mitchell [1] introduced the theoretical framework of versions spaces. He defines Version Space as the set of all concepts in L_C that are consistent with the sets of positive and negative examples P and N.

$$VS_{L_C}(P, N) = \{c \in L_C | R_C(c) \subset R_I(P), R_C(c) \cap R_I(N) = \emptyset\} \quad (1)$$
$$= R_C^{-1}([R_I(P), {}^{\complement}R_I(N)]) \quad (2)$$

Mitchell proposes to represent version spaces by the mean of their boundaries. Both the Candidate Elimination algorithm and the Description Identification [2] Algorithms use maximally specific and maximally general concepts sets (resp. S and G) to represent the version space, and effectively compute them. The main flaw of this approach is the size of these boundaries. Haussler [3] has pointed out that the boundary size may grow exponentially in the number of examples. Thus, alternative representations have been proposed for the versions spaces.

Hirsh proposes to replace the set of maximally general concept G by the list of negative examples [4], and later to replace both S and G by the list of examples [5]. He also highlighted properties of intersecting version space: the intersection of two version spaces is the version space built by using $P_1 \cup P_2$ and $N_1 \cup N_2$ as positive and negative example sets. Another approach is to keep only one element of each boundary set, together with backtrack information [6]. This prevent exponential growth of the boundary set at reasonable computational cost. In order to address inconsistency problem, M. Sebag proposes to compute [7] simple version spaces (one positive example and all negative consistent ones) for each positive example and perform a vote among them.

3 Approximation and Version Spaces

Rough Set Theory (RST) efficiently deals with sets approximation [8]. Given a relation $\sim$ on C, it defines the dual operators H and L on 2^C such that $H(A) = \{a \in S / \exists b \in A, a \sim b\}$ and $L(A) = \{a \in S / \forall b, a \sim b \Rightarrow b \in A\}$ These operator were initially defined by Pawlak, with an equivalence relation $\sim$. However, requiring an equivalence relation is a strong constraint, and it has been relaxed, the definition of H and L being applied on any relation. Of course, many of the original RST properties are lost (see [9] for correspondence between $\sim$ properties and H and L ones).

3.1 Rough Consistency

Definition 4. *A concept $c \in C$ (resp. $\in L_C$) is said to be roughly consistent with positive and negative example sets P, N iff c (resp. $R_C(c)$) is similar to a concept consistent with P, N.*

Proposition 1. *A concept c roughly consistent with the example sets $(P_1 \cup N_1, P_2 \cup N_2)$ is necessarily roughly consistent with (P_1, N_1) and roughly consistent with (P_2, N_2). The converse proposition does not necessarily holds.*

Proof. $\exists c'$ consistent with $(P_1 \cup N_1, P_2 \cup N_2)$ such that $c \sim c'$. c' is consistent with both (P_1, N_1) and (P_2, N_2). Thus c is roughly consistent with both. The converse is not necessarily true because the concept consistent with (P_1, N_1) and (P_2, N_2) is not necessarily the same.

Definition 5. *We call a partition of the set of example (P, N) a strategy and note it Pa. The family of positives and negatives examples are noted $(P_{Pa})_i$ and $(N_{Pa})_i$ respectively. Whenever there is no ambiguity about Pa, it is omitted.*

We now express the approximative concept learning problem:
Given:
- a language L_I of instance representation and a language L_C of concept representation;
- a relation $cover \subset L_I \times L_c$
- a similarity relation $\sim$ on concepts $\subset C \times C$
- a set of positive example $P \subset L_I$ and a set of negative example $N \subset L_I$
- a strategy Pa based on (P, N)

Find: a concept $c \in L_C$ such that $R_C(c)$ is roughly consistent with each (P_i, N_i).

The approximative learning problem definition introduces two new element: the similarity relation and the strategy. The relation defines how to perform approximation. The strategy defines which examples are to be processed simultaneously.

Proposition 2. *Let us consider two different approximative concept learning problem (ACLP and ACLP′) that are alike in respect to all parameters except the strategy (Pa and Pa′). If the strategy Pa′ is finer than the strategy Pa, then every solution to ACLP is a solution to ACLP′.*

Proof. This comes from proposition 1: if a concept is consistent with a set of examples, it is consistent with any of its subset. Each (P'_i, N'_i) in Pa' is a subset of some P_j, N_j in Pa. Thus, any concept roughly consistent with each P_j, N_j is also roughly consistent with each (P'_i, N'_i). As L_C is the same, the proposition holds.

3.2 RVS Definition

Definition 6. *Given an instance space I, an instance language L_I and its representation function R_I, a concept language L_C and its representation function R_C, a similarity relation $\sim$ on concepts and the associated approximation operator H and L, a set of positive examples P, a set of negatives examples N, a partition Pa of (P, N), the rough version spaces $RVS_H(Pa)$ is defined by:*

$$RVS_H(Pa) = \bigcap_i R_C^{-1}(H([R_I(P_i), {}^CR_I(N_i)])) \qquad (3)$$

Although H and L are dual operator, RVS_H and RVS_L do not share the same properties. We will show that RVS_H is the most important and useful in this pair. This work is focused on RVS_H, given its nice properties in handling inconsistency.

Proposition 3. *$RVS_H(Pa)$ is exactly the set of all solutions to the approximate concept learning problem*

Proof. Using H definition, we expand $H([R_I(P_i), {}^CR_I(N_i)])$: $\{c \in C / \exists c' \in [R_I(P_i), {}^CR_I(N_i)], c \sim c'\}$, i.e. the set of all concepts similar to any concept consistent with (P_i, N_i). It holds that $R_C^{-1}(H([R_I(P_i), {}^CR_I(N_i)]))$ is the set of all concept in L_C that are roughly consistent with (P_i, N_i). Hence, the set of concepts in L_C that is consistent with all (P_i, N_i) is the intersection of these set, $RVS_H(Pa)$.

We now define a notation for rough version space in the particular case where the strategy is a singleton.

Definition 7. *We call simple RVS a RVS defined using a strategy $Pa = \{(P, N)\}$ that is singleton. It is convenient to note it by the following way:*

$$RVS_H(P, N) = RVS_H(\{(P, N)\}) = R_C^{-1}(H([R_I(P), {}^CR_I(N)])) \qquad (4)$$

Property 1. *Any RVS can be expressed by using only simple RVS: $RVS_H(Pa) = \bigcap_i RVS_H(P_i, N_i)$*

Most result can be established on simple RVS and generalized to any RVS by using this fundamental property.

Property 2. *Hirsh property on intersection does not hold with simple RVS. $RVS_H(P_1 \cup P_2, N_1 \cup N_2) \subset RVS_H(P_1, N_1) \cap RVS_H(P_2, N_2)$, and equality does not hold in general.*

Proof. Using property 3, we translate directly property 1 in RVS terms.

Property 3. If we use the equality relation to build our upper operator (i.e. identity operator Id), we get: $VS_{L_C}(P,N) = RVS_{Id}(P,N)$

Any classical VS is particular case of a simple RVS.

3.3 Properties

The main bias in version space is the language. Only representable concept can be learn trough version space. Rough Version Spaces add a new bias to the language: the upper approximation operator H.

Definition 8. *The induced concept class C_H associated with the upper approximation operator H is defined by $C_H = H(C)$*

Property 4. The induced concept class C_H is directly related to the relation $\sim$:

$$C_H = \{c | \exists c' \in C, c \sim c'\} \tag{5}$$

This property is useful when creating a relation with a given induced concept class. It is also possible to restrict $\sim$ on $C_{R_C} \times C$. We get $C_H \subset C_{R_C}$ without changing $RVS_H(Pa)$.

Proposition 4. *If Pa is finer than Pa', then $RVS_H(Pa') \subset RVS_H(Pa)$*

Proof. As $RVS_H(Pa)$ is the set of all solution to the approximate concept learning, this proposition is a direct application of proposition 2.

Proposition 5. *If $\sim$ restriction on $C_{R_C} \times C$ is reflexive, then*

$$VS_{L_C}(P,N) \subset RVS_H(P,N) \subset RVS_H(Pa) \tag{6}$$

Proof. First part: Let c be a concept in $VS_{L_C}(P,N)$. By definition of VS, $R_C(c) \in [R_I(P), {}^\complement R_I(N)]$ and $R_C(c) \in C_{R_C}$. Thus, $R_C(c) \sim R_C(c)$ and $R_C(c) \in H([R_I(P), {}^\complement R_I(N)])$. It proves that $c \in RVS_H(P,N)$. The second part is the previous proposition.

4 Algorithms and Implementation

The method proposed to deal with inconsistency when using RVS is to search a strategy Pa such that $RVS(Pa)$ does not collapse. The algorithm is the following : starting with the partition $Pa = \{(P,N)\}$, we refine it by dividing its larger part in two until $RVS(Pa)$ does not collapse. This ensures that if there exists Pa such that $RVS(Pa)$ does not collapse, then we will find one.

Computing RVS extensively is not affordable, except on toy problems. Thus, we propose to find a bounding segment to the simple $RVS(P,N)$.

Proposition 6. *Given positive and negative example sets P, N, we search for P', N' such that:*

$$P' = \{x \in L_I | \forall c \in RVS_H(P,N), c \text{ cover } x\} \tag{7}$$
$$N' = \{x \in L_I | \forall c \in RVS_H(P,N), \neg c \text{ cover } x\} \tag{8}$$

We have the following VS bound for $RVS_H(P,N)$

$$RVS_H(P,N) \subset VS_{L_C}(P', N') \tag{9}$$

Proof. Any concept c in $RVS_H(P,N)$ cover all example in P' and no example in N', and is in L_C. Therefore, c is in $VS_{L_C}(P', N')$

Property 5. *If $\sim$ restriction on C_{R_C} is reflexive, then:*

$$VS_{L_C}(P,N) \subset RVS_H(P,N) \subset VS_{L_C}(P', N') \tag{10}$$

Corollary 1. *If $\sim$ restriction on C_{R_C} is reflexive, then $N' \subset N$ and $P' \subset P$.*

Proof. The previous property gives $VS_{L_C}(P,N) \subset VS_{L_C}(P', N')$. Equivalently, $(P', N') \subset (P, N)$: the more example, the smaller the VS.

Computing P' and N' may be a hard task if H is only known extensively. However, we expect that in case where H is defined using logic proposition, figuring out P' and N' is affordable (it is possible do define H to fit our needs). If any representable concept is similar to itself, then the corollary hold. In this case, we only need to test each example.

4.1 RVS Approximation Combination

RVS can be approximated by using simple RVS approximation and Hirsh property on VS intersection:

$$RVS_H(Pa) \subset VS_{L_C}(\bigcup_i P'_i, \bigcup_i N'_i) \tag{11}$$

Using this property, we approximate RVS by using only classical VS tools. VS use and computation is a well known problem, and any results on VS apply here.

4.2 Refining RVS Approximation

The RVS approximation by VS may be considered as a sufficient result: it allows concept learning in case where VS collapsed by using VS as a tool. but it may be interesting to give a glimpse at the "real" RVS. As RVS set is not a segment (in fact, it is not a convex set), it can only be bounded by a pair of boundary sets S and G, not fully described. The previous approximation provides such bounds, namely the approximation VS bounds, but there is no guarantee that any element in S or G is actually in RVS. So the idea is to refine these bound by using each simple RVS in turn until it collapse or an element in RVS is found.

Table 1. Positive and negative examples

P/N							P'/N'
P_1	sun	warm	normal	strong	warm	same	P'_1
P_1	sun	warm	high	strong	warm	same	P'_1
P_1	sun	warm	high	strong	cool	change	P'_1
P_1	sun	warm	normal	strong	cool	change	P'_1
P_1	rain	cold	normal	weak	warm	same	
P_2	sun	warm	normal	weak	warm	same	
P_2	sun	cold	normal	strong	warm	same	
N_1	rain	cold	high	strong	warm	change	N'_1
N_1	rain	cold	normal	strong	warm	same	N'_1
N_1	rain	cold	normal	weak	cool	change	N'_1
N_1	rain	cold	normal	weak	cool	same	N'_1
N_1	sun	cold	normal	weak	warm	same	N'_1
N_1	rain	warm	normal	weak	cool	same	N'_1
N_2	rain	cold	high	weak	cool	same	N'_2
N_2	rain	cold	high	strong	warm	change	N'_2
N_2	rain	cold	normal	strong	cool	same	
N_2	sun	cold	normal	strong	warm	change	

5 RVS by Hand

This example is strongly inspired by Mitchell EnjoySport's one in [10]. It explains the extend if empty algorithm on data for a case where $RVS_H(P, N)$ collapse, and show how it is possible to find a successful strategy. $L_I = (sun, rain) \times (warm, cold) \times (normal, high)$
$\times (strong, weak) \times (warm, cool) \times (same, change)$

$L_C = (sun, rain, \star) \times (warm, cold, \star) \times (normal, high, \star)$
$\times (strong, weak, \star) \times (warm, cool, \star) \times (same, change, \star) \cup \{\emptyset\}$

Examples are given in table 5 ($N = N_1 \cup N_2$ and $P = P_1 \cup P_2$) $H(A) = \{a \in C_{R_C} / \exists a' \in A, |a \Delta a'| \leq 1\}$

This states that approximately valid concepts are defined by the following properties: They are representable and they classify all examples as some valid concept, except at most one.

Remarks that $c \in C_{R_C} \Rightarrow c \in [c]$, so $\sim$ is reflexive on C_{R_C}. Hence, we have $P' \subset P$ and $N' \subset N$ (Corollary 1).

If p is in P but not in P', it means that it exists $c \in H([P, {}^{\complement}N])$ such that $p \not\in c$, i.e. $c \in C_{R_C} \cap [P - \{p\}, {}^{\complement}N - \{p\}]$. This state that $VS_{L_C}(P - \{p\}, N \cup \{p\})$ does not collapse. Conversely, if it does not collapse, p is not in P'. We find dual property for N and N'. By using this on P, N, we have that $P' = P$ and $N = N'$, and then $RVS_H(P, N) = VS_H(P, N) = \emptyset$. Thus, we need another strategy. Let us try $Pa = \{(P_1, N_1), (P_2, N_2)\}$.

By using collapse tests, we get P'_1, P'_2 and N'_1, N'_2 given in table 5. Using these result and the approximation property of RVS, we found that: $RVS_H(Pa) \leq VS_{L_C}(P'_1 \cup P'_2, N'_1 \cup N'_2)$.

We search S and G bounding set for $VS_{L_C}(P_1' \cup P_2', N_1' \cup N_2')$: $S = \{(sun, warm, \star, strong, \star, \star)\}$

$G = \{(sun, warm, \star, \star, \star, \star), (\star, warm, \star, strong, \star, \star), (sun, \star, \star, strong, \star, \star)\}$

Actually, $VS = S \cup G$. Let us now search a concept in $RVS_H(Pa)$. The concept in S is not valid according for $RVS_H(P_2, S_2)$. The first concept in G is the only one valid.

So we have $RVS_H(Pa) = \{(sun, warm, \star, \star, \star, \star)\}$.

If it had been empty, we would have try to refine our strategy. Obviously, if each example is isolated, we get a non empty RVS ($\emptyset$ is in this RVS). We are sure to always find a valid strategy.

6 Conclusion

In this paper, we have proposed an approximative extension of the classical consistency property by using rough set theory. This allowed us to build an approximative concept learning framework, and an improved Version Space, namely the Rough Version Space. Taking advantage of some useful properties of this Rough Version Space, we proposed some general methods and algorithms to compute this Rough Version Space. These have been applied on an example where classical version space would have collapsed, and our methods give a meaningful result.

As previously stated here, methods and algorithms proposed are generic. It is possible to take advantage of particular approximation operator to develop more efficient specific approach to handle RVS.

References

1. Mitchell, T.M.: Version Spaces: An approach to Concept Learning. PhD thesis, Stanford University (1978)
2. Mellish, C.: The description identification problem. Artificial Intelligence **52** (1991) 151–167
3. Haussler, D.: Quantifying inductive bias: AI learning algorithms and valiant's learning framework. Artificial Intelligence **36** (1988) 177–221
4. Hirsh, H.: Polynomial-time learning with version spaces. In : National Conference on Artificial Intelligence (1992) 117–122
5. Hirsh, H., Mishra, N., Pitt, L.: Version spaces without boundary sets. In: AAAI/IAAI. (1997) 491–496
6. Sablon, G., De Raedt, L., Bruynooghe, L.: Iterative versionspaces. Artificial Intelligence **69** (1994) 393–409
7. Sebag, M.: Delaying the choice of bias: A disjunctive version space approach. In: International Conference on Machine Learning.(1996) 444–452
8. Pawlak, Z.: Rough Sets: Theorical Aspects of Reasoning About Data. Kluwer Academic Publishers, Dordrecht, Netherlands. (1991)
9. Yao, Y.Y.: Constructive and algebraic approaches for generalized rough set models. (In: Bulletin of International Rough Set Society)
10. Mitchell, T.M.. Machine Learning. McGraw-Hill. (1997)

Variable Consistency Monotonic Decision Trees

Silvio Giove[1], Salvatore Greco[2], Benedetto Matarazzo[2], and Roman Słowiński[3]

[1] Department of Applied Mathematics, University Ca' Foscari of Venice,
Dorsoduro n. 3825/E – 30125 Venice, Italy
sgiove@unive.it
[2] Faculty of Economics, University of Catania,
Corso Italia, 55, 95129 – Catania, Italy
{salgreco,matarazz}@unict.it;
[3] Institute of Computing Science, Poznan University of Technology,
Piotrowo 3a, 60-965 Poznan, Poland
slowinski@sol.put.poznan.pl

Abstract. We introduce the concept of variable-consistency monotonic decision tree induced from preference-ordered data concerning a multi-criteria sorting (classification) problem. Given the data in form of an information table including some sorting examples, we propose to induce a decision tree using an inductive learning algorithm. The decision tree can be considered as a preference model of a decision maker who supplied the sorting examples. Moreover, a partial violation of the dominance principle is admitted and controlled by an index called consistency level. The monotonic decision trees with variable consistency can be applied to a wide range of possible applications, for instance, financial rating, bank creditworthiness, medical diagnosis, and the like.

1 Introduction

We are considering a classification problem in the presence of multiple criteria, called multi-criteria sorting problem. Such a problem consists in the assignment of objects (actions) to some pre-defined and preference-ordered decision classes. In the specialized literature, this problem was approached using different preference models, like utility functions or outranking relations (see, e.g., [3]). In this paper, we propose to use a specific decision tree as a preference model. It is inferred from preferential information provided by a decision maker in the form of sorting examples, i.e. exemplary assignments of some reference objects to the decision classes. The specific decision tree is inferred using an inductive machine learning method (see, e.g., [12]). Differently from the usual decision trees induced from data, our decision tree uses a syntax of the type *if* $x_i \geq r$, then $x \in Cl_t^\geq$, in *at least* $p\%$ of the cases, where $Cl_t^\geq$ represents the upward union of classes, that is the union of all the classes dominating Cl_t. The obtained decision tree is thus monotonic (see [1],[2],[9],[10]) because it satisfies the dominance principle. It requires that objects having not-worse evaluation with respect to a set of considered criteria than a referent object cannot be assigned to a worse class than the referent object. Although the dominance principle is commonly approved, a strict observation of this principle in knowledge discovery may prevent discovering strong patterns in data. For this reason, a variable-consistency decision tree is used, admitting a partial data inconsistency, managed by means of a relaxation of the strict dominance principle. Depending on the choice of the tree structure, three different trees can be built-up, namely single class, progressively ordered, or all-class decision trees. A single class tree is computed such as to assign each object to an upward or a downward union of classes with respect to a required class. In a progressively ordered decision tree, the upward unions of classes to which an object has to be assigned are considered progressively, according to ascending order of classes. Finally, in a full range tree, all possible unions of classes are considered in each stage of tree construction.

2 Variable-Consistency Dominance-Based Rough Set Approach (VC-DRSA)

Let us consider a finite set of objects described by a finite set of attributes. For algorithmic reasons, information about objects is presented in the form of an *information table*. The rows of the table are labeled by *objects*, whereas columns are labeled by *attributes* and entries of the table are *attribute-values*. Formally, by an information table we understand the 4-tuple $S = <U, Q, V, f>$, where U is a finite set of objects, Q is a finite set of *attributes*, $V = \bigcup_{q \in Q} V_q$ is a domain of attribute q, and and $f : U \times Q \to V$ is a total function such that $f(x, q) \in V_q$ for every $q \in Q$, $x \in U$, called an information function [8]. The set Q is, in general, divided into set C of *condition attributes* and set D of *decision attributes*. Assuming that all condition attributes $q \in C$ are criteria, let $\succeq_q$ be a weak preference relation on U with respect to criterion q such that $x \succeq_q y$ means "x is at least as good as y with respect to criterion q". We suppose that $\succeq_q$ is a total preorder, i.e. a strongly complete and transitive binary relation, defined on U on the basis of evaluations $f(.,q)$. More precisely, if $\forall x, y \in U$ $f(x,q) \leq f(y,q) \Leftrightarrow x \succeq_q y$, then criterion q has an increasing scale of evaluation, while if $\forall x, y \in U$ $f(y,q) \leq f(x,q) \Leftrightarrow x \succeq_q y$ then criterion q has a decreasing scale of evaluation. Furthermore, assuming that the set of decision attributes D (usually a singleton d) makes a partition of U into a finite number of decision classes, let $\mathbf{Cl} = \{Cl_t, t \in T\}$, $T = \{1, ..., n\}$, be a set of these classes such that each $x \in U$ belongs to one and only one class $Cl_t \in \mathbf{Cl}$. We suppose that the classes are preference-ordered, i.e. $\forall r, s \in T$, such that $r > s$, the objects from Cl_r are preferred to the objects from Cl_s. The above assumptions are typical for consideration of a *multiple-criteria sorting problem*. In order to express decision classes in terms of evaluations by a set of criteria $P \subseteq C$, one can use the Rough Set concept proposed by [8] and further extended by [5], [7] to Dominance-Based Rough Set Approach (DRSA) in view of handling preference-ordered data. The key idea of rough sets is approximation of one knowledge by another knowledge. In classical rough set approach (CRSA), the knowledge approximated is a partition of U into classes generated by a set of decision attributes; the knowledge used for approximation is a partition of U into elementary sets of objects that are indiscernible by a set of condition attributes. These elementary sets are seen as *granules of knowledge* used for approximation. In DRSA, where condition attributes are criteria and classes are preference-ordered, the knowledge approximated is a collection of upward and downward unions of classes and the *granules of knowledge* are sets of objects defined using a dominance relation instead of the indiscernibility relation. This is the main difference between CRSA and DRSA. The sets to be approximated in DRSA, i.e. upward and downward unions of classes, are defined, respectively, as:

$$Cl_t^{\geq} = \cup_{s \geq t} Cl_s, \quad Cl_t^{\leq} = \cup_{s \leq t} Cl_s, \quad t = 1,..,n. \tag{1}$$

The statement $x \in Cl_t^{\geq}$ means x belongs *at least* to class Cl_t, while $x \in Cl_t^{\leq}$ means x belongs *at most* to class Cl_t. Let us remark that $Cl_1^{\geq} = Cl_n^{\leq} = U$, $Cl_n^{\geq} = Cl_n$ and $Cl_1^{\leq} = Cl_1$. Furthermore, for $t = 2,...,n$ we have:

$$Cl_{t-1}^{\leq} = U - Cl_t^{\geq}, \quad Cl_t^{\geq} = U - Cl_{t-1}^{\leq} \tag{2}$$

Let us define now the dominance relation. We say that x *dominates* y with respect to $P \subseteq C$, denoted by xD_Py, if $x \succeq_q y$, $\forall q \in P$. Given $P \subseteq C$ and $x \in U$, the *granules of knowledge* used for approximation in DRSA are: a set of objects dominating x, called P-*dominating set*, $D_P^+(x) = \{y \in U : yD_Px\}$, and a set of objects dominated by x, called P-*dominated set*, $D_P^-(x) = \{y \in U : xD_Py\}$. For any $P \subseteq C$ we say that the rough membership of $x \in U$ to $Cl_t^{\geq}$, denotation $\mu_P(x, Cl_t^{\geq})$, is equal to the percentage of all objects $y \in U$ dominating x with respect to P which also belong to $Cl_t^{\geq}$, i.e.

$$\mu_P(x, Cl_t^{\geq}) = \frac{card(D_P^+(x) \cap Cl_t^{\geq})}{card(D_P^+(x))} \tag{3}$$

Analogously, for any $P \subseteq C$ we say that the rough membership of $x \in U$ to $Cl_t^{\leq}$, denotation $\mu_P(x, Cl_t^{\leq})$, is equal to the percentage of all objects $y \in U$ dominated by x with respect to P which also belong to $Cl_t^{\leq}$, i.e.

$$\mu_P(x, Cl_t^{\leq}) = \frac{card(D_P^-(x) \cap Cl_t^{\leq})}{card(D_P^-(x))} \tag{4}$$

If $P = C$, we denote the above rough membership simply by $\mu(x, Cl_t^{\geq})$ and $\mu(x, Cl_t^{\leq})$ respectively. The rough membership information can serve to build-up lower approximations of upward or downward unions of decision classes. In variable-consistency DRSA (VC-DRSA), proposed by [6], $\forall P \subseteq C$, the P-lower approximation of $Cl_t^{\geq}$ is composed of all objects $x \in U$, whose $\mu_P(x, Cl_t^{\leq}) \geq l$ where $l \in (0,1]$. The level l is called *consistency level* because it controls the degree of consistency between objects qualified as belonging to without any ambiguity. In other words, if $l < 1$, then $(1-l) * 100\%$ of all objects $y \in U$

dominating x with respect to P do not belong to $Cl_t^{\geq}$ and thus contradict the inclusion of x in $Cl_t^{\geq}$. Analogously, $\forall P \subseteq C$, the P-lower approximation of $Cl_t^{\leq}$ is composed of all objects $x \in U$, whose $\mu_P(x, Cl_t^{\leq}) \geq l$ where $l \in (0,1]$.

VC-DRSA permits to relax the dominance principle to some extent. This is worthwhile because in practical applications, when data sets are large, some objects inconsistent with the dominance principle may decrease the cardinality of lower approximations to such an extent that it is impossible to discover strong patterns in the data. When inconsistency is allowed in some tolerable degree, the knowledge discovered from data is usually more expressive, with stronger and more synthetic conclusions.

3 Variable Consistency Monotonic Decision Trees

3.1 Architecture of Decision Trees

The tree consists of a number of nodes, including one root and a number of leafs, connected by directed paths from the root, through intermediate nodes, to the leafs. Each node at a given level of the tree corresponds to a subset of universe U submitted to a test. The root corresponds to U. Depending on result of the test, the subset is divided into two disjoint subsets (two nodes at subsequent level of the tree) composed of objects that passed or did not pass the test, respectively. In our case, the tests have the following formulations: $f(x,q) \geq r$? if criterion q has an increasing scale of evaluation or $f(x,q) \leq r$? if criterion q has a decreasing scale of evaluation. For the sake of simplicity in the following we shall consider only increasing scales of evaluation. In each test node the branching proceeds as follows. If object x passes the test $f(x,q) \geq r$? then it is assigned to one or more *upward* unions of classes with some credibility; the subset of objects that passed the test is represented by a node branching on the right side. If object x did not pass the test, it is assigned to one or more *downward* unions of classes with some credibility; this subset of object is represented by a node branching on the left side. Thus, a test node is branched into two assignment nodes called right-branching node and left-branching node. One can see that the above procedure gives a univariate binary decision tree. The tree is univariate because each division is based on information concerning one attribute only. The tree is binary because in each test node a set of objects is divided in two subsets. The tree can have elements of two types: *type 1* and *type 2*. A basic element of *type 1* considers only one t, $t = 2, ..., n$, and it is as follows:
- if object x passes the test "$f(x,q) \geq r$?", then it is assigned to upward union Cl_t with credibility $p\%$,
- if object x does not pass the test "$f(x,q) \geq r$?", i.e. "$f(x,q) \leq r$", then it is assigned to downward union $Cl_t^{\leq}$ with credibility $q\%$.

A basic element of *type 2* considers all $t = 2, ..., n$ and it is as follows:
- if object x passes the test "$f(x,q) \geq r$?", then it is assigned to upward union $Cl_t^{\geq}$ with credibility $p_t\%$, $t = 2, ..., n$,
- if object x does not pass the test "$f(x,q) \geq r$?", i.e. "$f(x,q) \leq r$", then it is

assigned to downward union $Cl_{t-1}^{\leq}$ with credibility $q_{t-1}\%$, $t = 1, ..., n-1$.
Using basic elements of type 1 and of type 2, three different architectures of decision tree can be defined:

- *single class decision tree*: in this decision tree, basic elements of type 1 are used and in each of them the same upward and downward unions, $Cl_t^{\geq}$ and $Cl_{t-1}^{\leq}$, are considered for a single $t \in T$;
- *progressively ordered decision tree*: in this decision tree, basic elements of type 1 are used but the upward and downward unions are changing progressively; in the root, $Cl_2^{\geq}$ and $Cl_1^{\leq}$ are considered; when credibility $p_2\%$ concerning $Cl_2^{\geq}$ reaches its maximum value (100%, in the case where no inconsistencies exist in S), $Cl_3^{\geq}$ and $Cl_2^{\leq}$ are considered next, and so on, until $Cl_n^{\geq}$ and $Cl_{n-1}^{\leq}$;
- *full range tree*: in this decision tree, basic elements of type 2 are used only.

Remark that basic elements of both types include a test node and two assignment nodes giving information about credibility of assignment of the objects that passed or did not pass the test to the considered unions of decision classes. In all kinds of decision trees defined above, each assignment node, different from a leaf, is connected by an outgoing arc to a new test node inheriting the subset of objects considered in this assignment node. Of course, information given by one of above decision trees can always be transformed into information specific for another decision tree.

3.2 A Procedure for Building Variable Consistency Decision Trees

A procedure to induce a decision tree from a data set must contain the following elements: 1) a branching rule, defining the test for dividing a set of objects in each node; 2) an assignment rule; 3) a variable consistency stopping rule, determining when to stop the branching. The branching rule is based on the following ratio

$$\rho(q, r, t) = \frac{card(x \in N : f(x, q) \geq r, x \in Cl_t^{\geq})}{card(N)} \qquad (5)$$

where:
- N is a set of objects in the considered test node,
- $r \in V_q$ such that $\exists w \in N$ for which $f(w, q) = r$,
- $t \in T$.

The use of ratio $rho(q, r, t)$ depends on the kind of decision tree being induced:
- in a single class decision tree, $t \in T$ is fixed in all the tree: for example, if the tree concerns assignment of objects to $Cl_3^{\geq}$, then $t = 3$;
- in a progressively ordered decision tree, $t \in T$ is changing according to the upward union of classes considered in the corresponding node: in the root and, possibly, few subsequent nodes, $t = 2$, then $t = 3$, and so on, until $t = n$;
- in a full range decision tree, all possible values of $t \in T$ are considered in each node.

In each test node, from among all possible triples (q, r, t) one has to select the triple $(q*, r*, t*)$ maximizing the ratio $rho(q, r, t)$. The selected triple determines the test in the corresponding node. The assignment rule is quite obvious. The upward unions of classes $Cl_t^\geq$, $t = 2, ..., n$, are considered in the right-branching assignment nodes, while the downward unions of classes $Cl_s^\leq$, $s = 1, ..., n-1$, are considered in the left-branching nodes. In the assignment nodes, the relative frequency of objects belonging to $Cl_t^\geq$ or to $Cl_s^\leq$ is considered. The credibility p_t of assigning objects of node η to $Cl_t^\geq$, $t = 2, ..., n$, is set equal to the relative frequency of objects belonging to $Cl_s^\leq$ in node η, defined as

$$F(Cl_t^\geq, \eta) = \frac{card(x \in N(\eta) : x \in Cl_t^\geq)}{card(N(\eta))} \qquad (6)$$

where $N(\eta)$ is the set of objects in the considered node η.
Analogously, the credibility q_s of assigning objects of node η to $Cl_s^\leq$, $s = 1, ..., n-1$, is set equal to the relative frequency of objects belonging to $Cl_s^\leq$ in node η, defined as:

$$F(Cl_s^\leq, \eta) = \frac{card(x \in N(\eta) : x \in Cl_s^\leq)}{card(N(\eta))} \qquad (7)$$

Therefore,
- in a single class decision tree, concerning $Cl_t^\geq$, $t = 2, ..., n$, the right-branching nodes include information about relative frequency $F(Cl_t^\geq, \eta)$, while the left-branching nodes include information $F(Cl_{t-1}^\leq, \eta)$,
- in a progressively ordered decision tree, the frequencies concerning the upward and the downward unions of classes are considered locally; more precisely, in the first nodes, where the assignment concerns $Cl_2^\geq$, in the right-branching nodes there are frequencies $F(Cl_2^\geq, \eta)$, while in the left-branching nodes there are frequencies $F(Cl_1^\leq, \eta)$; in the following nodes, when the considered upward union of classes is $Cl_3^\geq$, in the right-branching nodes there are frequencies $F(Cl_3^\geq, \eta)$, while in the left-branching nodes there are frequencies $F(Cl_2^\leq, \eta)$; and so on, until $Cl_n^\geq$ and $Cl_{n-1}^\leq$;
- in a full range decision tree, each right-branching node includes frequencies concerning each upward union of classes $Cl_t^\geq$, $t = 2, ..., n$, while each left-branching node includes frequencies concerning each downward union of classes $Cl_s^\leq$, $s = 1, ..., n-1$.

The stopping rule is based on the concept of rough membership and variable consistency presented in section 2. Let us consider a test node η and an assignment node λ branching from η. If the branching should continue from node λ then the objects belonging to $N(\lambda)$ would be submitted to a new test, according to the best selected triple $(q*, r*, t*)$; in this way, the following test node is inheriting subset $N(\lambda)$ from its predecessor (assignment node λ) and the branching leads to partition of $N(\lambda)$ in two subsets considered in the next two assignment nodes. Clearly, the objects in $N(\lambda)$ satisfy all the tests on the backward path from node η, up the tree, until the root. The subset of criteria from C selected in all test nodes on this backward path is denoted by P.

The branching continues from a right-branching node λ if the following two conditions are satisfied simultaneously:

1) $card(N(\lambda)) > 1$
2) $F(Cl_t^{\geq}, \lambda) < l$, where $l \leq \mu_P(x, Cl_t^{\geq})$, $t \in T$,
$l \in (0, 1]$ being an acceptable consistency level. Analogously, the branching continues from a left-branching node λ if the following two conditions are satisfied simultaneously:
1) $card(N(\lambda)) > 1$
2) $F(Cl_s^{\leq}, \lambda) < l$, where $l \leq \mu_P(x, Cl_s^{\leq})$, $s \in T$,
In particular
- in a single class decision tree, concerning $Cl_t^{\geq}$ for some $t \in T$, a right-branching node λ is to be branched further if $card(N(\lambda)) > 1$ and $F(Cl_t^{\geq}, \lambda) < l$, for some chosen $l \leq \mu_P(x, Cl_t^{\geq})$; analogously, a left-branching node ρ is to be branched further if $card(N(\rho)) > 1$ and $F(Cl_{t-1}^{\leq}, \rho) < l$ for some chosen $l \leq \mu_P(x, Cl_s^{\leq})$;
- in a progressively ordered decision tree, the stopping rule concerns progressively $Cl_2^{\geq}$ and $Cl_1^{\leq}$, then $Cl_3^{\geq}$ and $Cl_2^{\leq}$, and so on, until $Cl_n^{\geq}$ and $Cl_{n-1}^{\leq}$; the stopping rule for each right- or left- branching node is the same as in the single class decision tree for the corresponding $t \in T$; switching from the branching into $Cl_t^{\geq}$ and $Cl_{t-1}^{\leq}$ to $Cl_{t+1}^{\geq}$ and $Cl_t^{\leq}$ takes place when the first branching is stopped; the switching continues down the tree until the branching into $Cl_n^{\geq}$ and $Cl_{n-1}^{\leq}$ is stopped;
- in a full range decision tree, a right-branching node λ is to be branched further if $card(N(\lambda)) > 1$ and $F(Cl_t^{\geq}, \lambda) < l$, for some chosen $l \leq \mu_P(x, Cl_t^{\geq})$ and at least one $t \in \{2, ..., n\}$; analogously, a left-branching node ρ is to be branched further if $card(N(\rho)) > 1$ and $F(Cl_{t-1}^{\leq}, \rho) < l$ for some chosen $l \leq \mu_P(x, Cl_s^{\leq})$ and at least one $s \in \{1, ..., n-1\}$.

4 Conclusions

In this paper, we introduced the concept of variable-consistency monotonic decision tree induced from preference-ordered data in view of solving a multi-criteria sorting problem. Even if both inductive learning approaches and statistical methods can support a multi-attribute classification [4] they are not able to deal with preference-ordered data encountered in multi-criteria sorting problems. We proposed a particular type of tests, assigning objects to upward ("at least") or downward ("at most") unions of decision classes, thus obtaining a monotonic decision tree. Let us remark that this method is able to define a set of hierarchical rules and, unlike other approaches, it requires no particular hypotheses on the considered data set. For instance, it can work even when the popular *Choquet* integral approach [11] fails. In fact, it is easy to verify that in some cases the *Choquet* integral requires the preferential independence, while our approach does not. The monotonic decision trees with variable consistency can be applied to a wide range of possible applications, for instance, financial rating, bank creditworthiness, medical diagnosis, and the like. As a future research item, we will explore the algorithm generalization to incomplete decision tables.

Acknowledgment. The research of the first three authors has been supported by the Italian Ministry of Education, University and Scientific Research (*MIUR*). The fourth author wishes to acknowledge financial support from State Committee for Scientific Research (KBN), research grant no. 8T11F 006 19, and from the Foundation for Polish Science, subsidy no. 11/2001.

References

1. BIOCH J.C., POPOVA V., Bankruptcy prediction with rough sets, *Technical Report, Dept. of Computer Science*, 121, 1996, 421–464.
2. BIOCH J.C., POPOVA V., Rough sets and ordinal classification, *ERIM Research Report in Management, ERS-2001-11-LIS, Erasmus University Rotterdam*, ERS-2001-11-LIS 121, 2001.
3. BOUYSSOU D., JACQUET-LAGREZE E., PERNY P., SLOWINSKI R., VANDERPOOTEN D., VINCKE PH (EDS.), Aiding decisions with multiple criteria - Essays in honor of Bernard Roy,*Kluwer Academic Publishers, Boston*, 2002.
4. ELLARD C., ET AL., Programme Elysée: presentation et application, *Revue Metra*, 1967, 503–520.
5. GRECO S., MATARAZZO B.,SLOWINSKI R., The use of rough sets and fuzzy sets in MCDM, *Chapter 14 in: T. Gal, T. Stewart and T. Hanne (eds.), Advances in Multicriteria Decision Making*, Kluwer Academic Publishers, Dordrecht, 1999, 14.1–14.59.
6. GRECO S., MATARAZZO B., SLOWINSKI R., STEFANOWSKI J., Variable consistency model of dominance-based rough set approach, *in: W.Ziarko, Y.Yao: Rough Sets and Current Trends in Computing, Lecture Notes in Artificial Intelligence,*, Springer-Verlag, Berlin, 2005, 2001, 170–181.
7. GRECO S., MATARAZZO B., SLOWINSKI R., Rough sets methodology for sorting problems in presence of multiple attributes and criteria, *European Journal of Operational Research*, 138, 2002, 247–259.
8. PAWLAK, Z., Rough Sets. Theoretical Aspects of Reasoning about Data, *Kluwer Academic Publishers*, Dordrecht, 1991.
9. POTHARST R., BIOCH J.C., Monotone decision trees, *Intelligent data analysis*, 4(2), 2000, 97–112.
10. POTHARST R., BIOCH J.C., VAN DORDREGT R., Quasi-Monotone decision trees for ordinal classification, *Technical Report, eur-few-cs-98-01*, Dept. of Computer Science, Erasmus University Rotterdam, 1997.
11. MUROFUSHI T., SUGENO M., An interpretation of fuzzy measures and the Choquet integral as an integral with respect to a fuzzy measures, *Fuzzy Sets and Systems*, 29, 1989, 201–227.
12. QUINLAN J.R., Induction of decision trees, *Machine Learning*, 1, 1986, 81-106.

Importance and Interaction of Conditions in Decision Rules

Salvatore Greco[1], Benedetto Matarazzo[1], Roman Słowiński[2], and Jerzy Stefanowski[2]

[1] Faculty of Economics, University of Catania, Corso Italia 55, 95129 Catania, Italy
{salgreco, mataraz}@vm.unict.it
[2] Institute of Computing Science, Poznan University of Technology,
3A Piotrowo Street, 60-965 Poznan, Poland,
slowinsk@sol.put.poznan.pl; Jerzy.Stefanowski@cs.put.poznan.pl

Abstract. Knowledge discovered from data tables is often presented in terms of "if...then..." decision rules. With each rule a confidence measure is associated. We present a method for measuring importance of each single condition or interactions among groups of conditions in the "if" part of the rules. The methodology is based on some indices introduced in literature to analyze fuzzy measures.

1 Introduction

We are interested in evaluation of *"if...then..."* decision rules discovered from data. Various quantitative measures have been already proposed, each of them capturing different characteristics of rules. For instance, Yao and Zhong presented in [12] a systematic review including, e.g. generality, support, confidence, quality, mutual support of implication or rule interestingness. Many of these measures are derived by analysing relationship between parts (condition and decision) of the rule and the data set from which the rule is discovered. However, the relationship concerns complete set of conditions in the *"if"* part of the rule. An interesting, although more difficult, issue is to evaluate the importance of each single condition or even interactions among the set of condition in this *"if"* part of the rule. The interest is at least twofold: (1) in the phase of selection of the "best" decision rule; (2) in the phase of application of the decision rule.

In the first phase, if a condition part of a rule contains a single condition with very low importance, we can remove this unimportant condition. Analogously, if the condition part of a rule contains two conditions with a negative interaction, i.e. giving redundant information, we can substitute this rule with another rule obtained from the first one by removing one of these two conditions. In the application phase, the knowledge on the different importance of conditions in a decision rule, can give an order for their progressive verification. The most important condition should be verified first and the less important conditions after it. Moreover, the presence of conditions interacting positively, i.e. giving complementary information, can suggest to verify these conditions simultaneously. Analogously, the presence of conditions interacting negatively, i.e. giving redundant information, can suggest to verify first only one of these conditions and then, if necessary, to verify the other condition.

In this paper, we introduce a new method for evaluating the importance of single conditions, subsets of conditions and their interaction, which is based on special *set functions* introduced in literature to analyze *fuzzy measures*. Originally, they were applied to the game theory [10], then they were adopted to analyse conjoint importance of criteria in multicriteria decision problems [2,4]. These fuzzy measures have been already considered by Greco, Matarazzo and Slowinski within rough set theory to study the relative value of information supplied by different attributes to the quality of approximation of classification [5,6]. The importance and the interactions of elementary conditions in decision rules are evaluated on the basis of the contribution that an elementary condition gives to a *confidence* of a decision rule. The confidence was chosen, as it is one of the most important indices of decision rules. Moreover, a decision rule is a logical implication and confidence measures the credibility of this implication.

The paper is organized as follows. In the next section, we remind representation of decision rules and the confidence measure. Section 3 presents fuzzy measures and their alternative representations. In Section 4, basic relationship of fuzzy measures and decision rules is discussed. In section 5, we illustrate on an example the usefulness of applying these measures to some decision rules. Final section presents the conclusions.

2 Evaluation of Decision Rules Induced from Examples

Learning examples are represented in a form of *decision table* $DT =(U, A \cup \{d\})$, where U is a set of examples (objects), A is a set of condition attributes describing examples and $d \notin A$ is a decision attribute that partitions examples into a set of decision classes $\{K_j : j =1,...,k\}$. We assume that decision rule r describing class K_j is represented in the following form: *if Φ then Ψ*, where $\Phi = \Phi_1 \wedge \Phi_2 \wedge \ldots \wedge \Phi_m$ is a *condition part* of the rule and Ψ is a *decision part* of the rule indicating that an example should be assigned to class K_j. The *elementary condition* Φ_i of the rule r is a test on a value of a given attribute, e.g. defined as a simple checking if an attribute value is equal to a chosen constant. Alternatively decision rules are represented as a statement $\Phi \rightarrow \Psi$.

Measures evaluating rules are defined using the set-theoretic interpretation [12]. Let $m(\Phi)$ denote the set of objects of U satisfying conditions in Φ and $m(\Psi)$ is a set of objects satisfying Ψ. The confidence of the rule r is defined as:

$$Conf(r) = \frac{|m(\Phi) \cap m(\Psi)|}{|m(\Phi)|}$$

where $|\cdot|$ denotes the cardinality of a set. The range of this measure is $[0,1]$, and shows the degree to which Φ implies Ψ. If $Conf(r) = \alpha$, then $(100 \cdot \alpha)\%$ of objects satisfying Φ also satisfy Ψ. It may be interpreted as a conditional probability that a randomly selected object satisfying Φ also satisfies Ψ. This is a standard measure used to evaluate the discovered rules, e.g. association rules. The literature review shows that other authors often report its use. However, they give different names for this measure, e.g. *certainty factor, accuracy, strength, discrimination measure*; for more extensive discussion, see e.g. [8,11,12].

3 Main Concepts Related to Analysis of Set Functions

Let $X = \{1,2,...,n\}$ be a finite set, whose elements could be players in a game, criteria in a multicriteria decision problem, attributes in an information table, etc., and let $P(X)$ denote the power set of X, i.e. the set of all subsets of X. In the following we consider a set function $\mu: P(X) \to [0,1]$. Function $\mu(\cdot)$ is a *fuzzy measure (capacity)* on X if satisfies the following axioms: (1) $\mu(\emptyset) = 0, \mu(X) = 1$, (2) $A \subseteq B$ implies $\mu(A) \leq \mu(B)$, for all $A, B \in P(X)$.

According to Grabisch[4] only the monotonicity is inherent to fuzzy measures. This permits to skip condition 1) from a general definition of fuzzy measures. In fact, in the following we consider set functions, which do not satisfy both condition 1) and 2). We call these set functions non-monotonic fuzzy measures. We prefer to speak of non-monotonic fuzzy measures rather than simple set functions to remember the context in which the indices recalled below were introduced.

Within game theory, the function $\mu(A)$ is called *characteristic function* and represents the payoff obtained by the coalition $A \subseteq X$ in a cooperative game [1, 10]; in a multicriteria decision problem, $\mu(A)$ can be interpreted as the *conjoint importance* of the criteria from $A \subseteq X$ [3]. Some indices have been introduced in game theory as specific solutions of cooperative games. The most important are the Shapley value and the Banzhaf value. The Shapley value for every $i \in X$ is defined by

$$\phi_S(i) = \sum_{K \subseteq X - \{i\}} \frac{(n-|K|-1)!|K|!}{n!} [\mu(K \cup \{i\}) - \mu(K)].$$

The Banzhaf value [1] for every $i \in X$ is defined by

$$\phi_B(i) = \frac{1}{2^{n-1}} \sum_{K \subseteq X - \{i\}} [\mu(K \cup \{i\}) - \mu(K)].$$

The Shapley value and the Banzhaf value can be interpreted as a kind of a *weighted average contribution* of element i alone in all coalitions. Let us remind that in the case of $\phi_S(i)$ the value of $\mu(X)$ is shared among the elements of X, i.e. $\sum_{i=1}^{n} \phi_S(i) = 1$, while an analogous property does not hold for $\phi_B(i)$. The Shapley and the Banzhaf indices have also been proposed to represent the average importance of particular criteria within multicriteria decision analysis when fuzzy measures are used to model the conjoint importance of criteria.

In addition to the indices concerning particular criteria, other indices have been proposed to measure the *interaction between pairs of criteria*. Interaction indices have been proposed by Murofushi and Soneda [7] with respect to Shapley value and by Roubens [9] with respect to Banzhaf value.

The Murofushi-Soneda interaction index for elements $i, j \in X$ is defined by

$$I_{MS}(i,j) = \sum_{K \subseteq X-\{i,j\}} \frac{(n-|K|-2)!|K|!}{(n-1)!} [\mu(K \cup \{i,j\}) - \mu(K \cup \{i\}) - \mu(K \cup \{j\}) + \mu(K)].$$

The Roubens interaction index for elements $i, j \in X$ is defined by

$$I_R(i,j) = \frac{1}{2^{n-2}} \sum_{K \subseteq X-\{i,j\}} [\mu(K \cup \{i,j\}) - \mu(K \cup \{i\}) - \mu(K \cup \{j\}) + \mu(K)].$$

The interaction indices $I_{MS}(i,j)$ and $I_R(i,j)$ can be interpreted as a kind of an average added value resulting from putting i and j together in all coalitions. The following cases can happen:

$I_{MS}(i,j) > 0$ $(I_R(i,j) > 0)$: i and j are complementary,
$I_{MS}(i,j) < 0$ $(I_R(i,j) < 0)$: i and j are substitutive,
$I_{MS}(i,j) = 0$ $(I_R(i,j) = 0)$: i and j are independent.

The definition of *interaction indices* can be extended from non-ordered pairs $i, j \in X$ to any subset $A \subseteq X, A \neq \emptyset$. Extensions of interaction indices in this sense have been proposed by Grabisch [3] and Roubens [9], with respect to Shapley value and Banzhaf value, respectively.

The Shapley interaction index of elements from $A \subseteq X$ is defined by

$$I_S(A) = \sum_{K \subseteq X-A} \frac{(n-|K|-|A|)!|K|!}{(n-|A|+1)!} \sum_{L \subseteq A} (-1)^{|A|-|L|} \mu(K \cup L).$$

The Banzhaf interaction index of elements from $A \subseteq X$ is defined by

$$I_B(A) = \frac{1}{2^{n-|A|}} \sum_{K \subseteq X-A} \sum_{L \subseteq A} (-1)^{|A|-|L|} \mu(K \cup L).$$

In addition to the interaction indices, another concept useful for the interpretation of the fuzzy measures is the Möbius representation of μ, i.e. the set function m: $P(X) \to R$ defined by

$$m(A) = \sum_{B \subseteq A} (-1)^{|A-B|} \mu(B)$$

for any $A \subseteq X$. Within the theory of evidence, $m(A)$ is interpreted as basic probability assignment.

The relations between fuzzy measure μ, interaction indices I_S and I_B and Möbius representation m have been extensively studied in [3,4,9]. In the following sections, we will alternatively call the interaction indices and the Möbius representation by the name *set indices*. Let us remind that the set indices defined above are also valid for non-monotonic fuzzy measures [2].

4 Analysis of Confidence of Decision Rules Using Set Indices

Interaction indices I_S and I_B and Möbius representation can be used to study the relative contribution of each elementary condition Φ_i of a rule $(\Phi_1 \wedge \Phi_2 \wedge \ldots \wedge \Phi_m) \to \Psi$ to the confidence measure of this rule. Let us consider two rules r_1: $(\Phi_1 \wedge \Phi_2 \wedge \ldots \wedge \Phi_m) \to \Psi$ and r_2: $(\Phi_{j1} \wedge \Phi_{j2} \wedge \ldots \wedge \Phi_{jk}) \to \Psi$. If $(\Phi_{j1}, \Phi_{j2}, \ldots, \Phi_{jk}) \subseteq (\Phi_1, \Phi_2, \ldots, \Phi_m)$, rule r_2 is defined as a rule included in rule r_1.

Given a decision rule $r: (\Phi_1 \wedge \Phi_2 \wedge \ldots \wedge \Phi_m) \to \Psi$, in the following, we consider a set function $\mu(r) : P(\{\Phi_1, \Phi_2, \ldots, \Phi_m\}) \to [0,1]$, such that for each $(\Phi_{j1}, \Phi_{j2}, \ldots, \Phi_{jk}) \subseteq (\Phi_1, \Phi_2, \ldots, \Phi_m)$ with $(\Phi_{j1}, \Phi_{j2}, \ldots, \Phi_{jk}) \neq \emptyset$, we get:

$$\mu(r)(\{(\Phi_{j1}, \Phi_{j2}, \ldots, \Phi_{jk})\}) = \text{conf}[(\Phi_{j1} \wedge \Phi_{j2} \wedge \ldots \wedge \Phi_{jk}) \to \Psi] \text{ and}$$

$$\mu(r)(\emptyset) = \frac{|m(\psi)|}{|U|}.$$

Considering the decision rule $(\Phi_1 \wedge \Phi_2 \wedge \ldots \wedge \Phi_m) \to \Psi$ and the set function $\mu(r)$ defined above we conclude that:
1) the Shapley index $\phi_S(i)$ and the Banzhaf index $\phi_B(i)$ can be interpreted as measures of the contribution of elementary condition Φ_i, $i = 1, \ldots, n$, to the confidence of the considered rule,
2) the Murofushi-Soneda interaction index $I_{MS}(i,j)$ and Roubens interaction index $I_R(i,j)$ can be interpreted as the average joint share of the non-ordered pair of conditions Φ_i, Φ_j, $i,j = 1, \ldots, m, i \neq j$, in the confidence of all decision rules $(\Phi_{h1} \wedge \Phi_{h2} \wedge \ldots \wedge \Phi_{hg}) \to \Psi$ such that $(\Phi_{h1}, \Phi_{h2}, \ldots, \Phi_{hg}) \subset (\Phi_1, \Phi_2, \ldots, \Phi_m)$ and $(\Phi_{h1}, \Phi_{h2}, \ldots, \Phi_{hg}) \cap \{\Phi_i, \Phi_j\} = \emptyset$,
3) the Shapley interaction index $I_S(\{\Phi_{h1}, \Phi_{h2}, \ldots, \Phi_{hg}\})$ and the Banzhaf interaction index $I_B(\{\Phi_{h1}, \Phi_{h2}, \ldots, \Phi_{hg}\})$ can be interpreted as the average joint share of the subset of conditions attributes $\{\Phi_{h1}, \Phi_{h2}, \ldots, \Phi_{hg}\} \subset \{\Phi_1, \Phi_2, \ldots, \Phi_m\}$ in the confidence of all decision rules $(\Phi_{k1} \wedge \Phi_{k2} \wedge \ldots \wedge \Phi_{kf}) \to \Psi$ such that $(\Phi_{h1}, \Phi_{h2}, \ldots, \Phi_{hg}) \cap (\Phi_{k1}, \Phi_{k2}, \ldots, \Phi_{kf}) = \emptyset$,
4) the Möbius representation $m(\{\Phi_{h1}, \Phi_{h2}, \ldots, \Phi_{hg}\})$ of μ can be interpreted as the joint share of the subset of conditions $\{\Phi_{h1}, \Phi_{h2}, \ldots, \Phi_{hg}\} \subset \{\Phi_1, \Phi_2, \ldots, \Phi_m\}$ in the confidence of rule r.

All these indices can be useful to analyse the informational dependence among the considered conditions and to choose the set of decision rules having the greatest value of information. For example, let us suppose that in the decision rule $r : (\Phi_1 \wedge \Phi_2 \wedge \ldots \wedge \Phi_m) \to \Psi$ there is a strong dependence between conditions $\Phi_i, \Phi_j, i,j \in \{1, \ldots, m\}, i \neq j$. This dependence is indicated by a negative value of the interaction indices. In this case, in the set of decision rules, we can substitute rule r with a new rule r': $(\Phi_1 \wedge \Phi_2 \wedge \ldots \Phi_{i-1} \wedge \Phi_{i+1} \wedge \ldots \wedge \Phi_{j-1} \wedge \Phi_{j+1} \wedge \ldots \wedge \Phi_m) \to \Psi$ obtained from rule r after removing conditions Φ_i, Φ_j.

5 Example of Using Set Indices

Let us use the simple example to illustrate how the set indices can be applied to analyze decision rules. Suppose that in one hospital the patients suspected to have disease δ are submitted to three medical tests: α, β, γ. Table 1 presents the statistical results of the test related to the presence or absence of the disease ("+" means positive result of the tests and presence of the disease, while "–" means negative result of the test and absence of the disease). The last column of the table shows the number of the patients with given combination of tests and disease.

Table 1. Data table with statistical data on medical tests: α, β, γ and disease δ

α	β	γ	δ	No. of patients
−	−	−	−	300
−	−	−	+	20
+	−	−	−	40
+	−	−	+	850
−	+	−	−	10
−	+	−	+	350
+	+	−	−	500
+	+	−	+	250
−	−	+	−	50
−	−	+	+	150
+	−	+	−	150
+	−	+	+	500
−	+	+	−	150
−	+	+	+	300
+	+	+	−	30
+	+	+	+	3000

On the basis of the data in Table 1 the following set of decision rules relating results of test with presence of disease can be inferred:

Rule #1: *if* $(\alpha=+)$ *then* $(\delta=+)$ with confidence 86.5% (i.e. "in the 86.5% of the case in which test α is positive, the disease δ is present"),

Rule #2: *if* $(\beta=+)$ *then* $(\delta=+)$ with confidence 85% (i.e. "in the 85.0% of the case in which test β is positive, disease δ is present "),

Rule #3: *if* $(\alpha=+)$ and $(\beta=+)$ *then* $(\delta=+)$ with confidence 86% (i.e. "in the 86% of the case in which tests α and β are positive, disease δ is present "),

Rule #4: *if* $(\gamma=+)$ *then* $(\delta=+)$ with confidence 91.2 % (i.e. "in the 91.2% of the case in which test γ is positive, disease δ is present "),

Rule #5: *if* $(\alpha=+)$ and $(\gamma=+)$ *then* $(\delta=+)$ with confidence 95.1% (i.e. "in the 95.1% of the case in which tests α and γ are positive, disease δ is present "),

Rule #6: *if* $(\beta=+)$ and $(\gamma=+)$ *then* $(\delta=+)$ with confidence 94.8% (i.e. "in the 94.8% of the case in which tests β and γ are positive, disease δ is present "),

Rule #7: *if* $(\alpha=+)$ and $(\beta=+)$ and $(\gamma=+)$ *then* $(\delta=+)$ with confidence 99.1% (i.e. "in the 99.1% of the case in which tests α, β and γ are positive, disease δ is present ").

We can also consider "default" **rule #0** having the following interpretation: "without consideration of any test, in 81.5% of cases disease δ is present".

For these 8 rules we calculated set indices defined in the previous sections. They are presented in Table 2.

The problem we are considering is the following: what is the share of the result of each test or of combination of tests in the confidence of each rule? In the following we shall consider rule #7. Last three columns of Table 2 present

Table 2. Set indices for induced decision rules

rule	α	β	γ	Confidence	Möbius	Shapley	Banzhaf
Rule #0				.815	0	0	0
Rule #1	+			.865	.050	.039	0.058
Rule #2		+		.850	.035	.030	0.049
Rule #3	+	+		.860	-.039	-.018	-.018
Rule #4			+	.912	.097	.107	.103
Rule #5	+		+	.951	-.018	.010	.011
Rule #6		+	+	.948	.001	.022	.023
Rule #7	+	+	+	.991	.042	.042	.042

the analysis of the contribution of different tests to confidence of presence of disease using rule #7. These results can be interpreted as follows:

1. the Möbius representation gives a measure of joint share of the corresponding subset of conditions (tests) in the confidence of the rule; the negative value for subset $\{\alpha,\gamma\}$ and $\{\alpha,\beta\}$ should be read as a measure of information redundancy of the two conditions;
2. the Shapley index corresponding to a single condition can be interpreted as a measure of importance of the corresponding test and its share in the confidence of the rule, while the Shapley index corresponding to groups of conditions can be interpreted as measures of redundancy (in case of negative value) or complementarity (in case of positive value) of the information relative to corresponding tests. One can notice a relative great importance of test γ and a relative redundancy of tests α and β;
3. the values of Banzhaf index are quite similar to the values of Shapley index. This enforces the conclusions in point 2).

Let us remark that the observations at point 2) can be very interesting when applying the decision rules. A relatively great importance of test γ and the relative redundancy of tests α and β can suggest the doctors to give an order of priority to the tests: the patients can be submitted first to test γ and after to tests α and β. Moreover, when the patient is positive to test γ and to either α or β, some therapies can be started due to relative high confidence of the diagnosis. In this case, tests α and β give similar (redundant) information, as shown by Shapley index relative to pair $\{\alpha, \beta\}$.

6 Conclusions

We presented a method for evaluation an importance of each single condition or interactions among group of conditions in the "*if*" part of decision rules, which is based on some indices introduced in literature to analyze fuzzy measures. This can be useful both in interpretation of the decision rules and in selection of a set of the most interesting decision rules. Although these indices require additional calculations of several coefficients for rules included in the analyzed rule, they provide valuable information on contribution of single elementary conditions and/or subsets of conditions to confidence of the analyzed decision rule. Such detailed information cannot be simply obtained by analyzing confidence measures of rules only.

Acknowledgement. The research of the first two authors has been supported by the Italian Ministry of University and Scientific Research (MURST) and two other authors by State Committee for Scientific Research, KBN research grant no. 8 T11C 006 19.

References

1. Banzhaf, J. F., Weighted voting doesn't work: A mathematical analysis, *Rutgers Law Review*, 19, 1965, 317–343.
2. Chateaneuf A., Jaffray, J., Some charactrtizations of Lower Probabilities and other Monotone Capacities through the use of Möbius Inversion, *Mathematical Social Science*, 17, 1989, 263–283
3. Grabisch M., The application of fuzzy integrals in muliticriteria decision making, *European Journal of Operational Research*, 89, 1996, 445–456.
4. Grabisch M., k-order additive discrete fuzzy measures and their representation, *Fuzzy Sets and Systems*, 89, 1997, 445–456.
5. Greco S., Matarazzo B., Slowinski R., Fuzzy measures as a technique for rough set analysis, in *Proc. 6th European Congress on Intelligent Techniques & Soft Computing (EUFIT'98)*, Aachen, September 7-10, 1998, 99–103.
6. Greco S., Matarazzo B., Slowinski R., The use of rough sets and fuzzy sets in MCDM, in T. Gal, T. Hanne and T. Stewart (eds.), *Advances in Multiple Criteria Decision Making*. Kluwer Academic Publishers, 1999, 14.1–14.59.
7. Murofushi T., Soneda S., Techniques for reading fuzzy measures (iii): interaction index, in *Proc. 9th Fuzzy Systems Symposium*, Sapporo, May 1993, 693–696, in Japanese.
8. Pawlak Z., Rough sets and decision algorithms, in Ziarko W., Yao Y.Y. (eds.), *Proc. 2nd Int. Conf. on Rough Sets and Current Trends in Computing*, Banff, October 16-19, 2000, 1–16.
9. Roubens, M., *Interaction between criteria through the use of fuzzy measures*, Report 96.007, Institut de Mathématique, Université de Liège, 1996.
10. Shapley L. S., A value for n-person games, in H. W. Kuhn, A. W. Tucker (eds.), *Contributions to the Theory of Games II*, Princeton University Press, Princeton, 1953, 307–317.
11. Stefanowski J., On rough set based approaches to induction of decision rules, in Polkowski L., Skowron A. (eds.), *Rough sets in knowledge discovery, vol 1. Methodology and applications*, Physica-Verlag, Heidelberg, 1998, 500–529.
12. Yao Y.Y., Zhong N., An analysis of quantitative measures associated with rules, in *Proceedings of the Third Pacific-Asia Conference on Knowledge Discovery and Data Mining*, LNAI 1574, Springer, 1999, 479–488.

Time Complexity of Rough Clustering: GAs versus K-Means

Pawan Lingras[1] and Y.Y. Yao[2]

[1] Saint Mary's University
Halifax, Nova Scotia, B3H 3C3, Canada.
Pawan.Lingras@StMarys.CA
[2] University of Regina
Regina, Saskatchewan, S4S 0A2, Canada.
yyao@cs.uregina.ca

Abstract. Typical clustering operations in data mining involve finding natural groupings of resources or users. Conventional clusters have crisp boundaries, i.e. each object belongs to only one cluster. The clusters and associations in data mining do not necessarily have crisp boundaries. An object may belong to more than one cluster. Researchers have studied the possibility of using fuzzy sets in data mining clustering applications. Recently, two different methodologies based on properties of rough sets were proposed for developing interval representations of clusters. One approach is based on Genetic Algorithms, and the other is an adaptation of K-means algorithm. Both the approaches have been successful in generating intervals of clusters. The efficiency of the clustering algorithm is an important issue when dealing with a large dataset. This paper provides comparison of the time complexity of the two rough clustering algorithms.

1 Introduction

The clustering in data mining faces several additional challenges [2]. The clusters tend to have fuzzy boundaries. Instead of an object precisely belonging to a cluster, it may be assigned a degree of fuzzy membership to one or more clusters. There is a likelihood that an object may be a candidate for more than one cluster. Joshi and Krishnapuram [2] argued that clustering operation in web mining involves modeling an unknown number of overlapping sets. They proposed the use of fuzzy clustering for grouping web users. Similar arguments can be extended to clustering in data mining in general.

Any classification scheme can be represented as a partition of a given set of objects. Objects in each equivalence class of the partition are assumed to be identical or similar. In data mining, it is not possible to provide an exact representation of each class in the partition [2]. Rough sets [6] enable us to represent such classes using upper and lower bounds. Lingras [3] described how a rough set theoretic classification scheme can be represented using a rough set genome. In subesquent publication [5], a modification of K-means approach was proposed to create intervals of clusters based on rough set theory.

Both GAs and K-means approaches were used for grouping web users. The web site that was used for the experimentation catered to first year computing science students. The students used the web site for downloading classnotes and lab assignments; downloading, submitting and viewing class assignments; checking their current marks; as well as for accessing the discussion board. The web site logged as many as 30,000 entries during a busy week. Over 16 week period under study, the number of entries in the web log was more than 360,000. The web site was accessed from a variety of locations. Only some of the web accesses were identifiable by the student ID. Therefore, instead of analyzing individual students, it was decided to analyze each visit.

A first year course consists of a wide variety of student behaviour. It will be interesting to study the behaviour pattern of the students over several weeks. For the initial analysis, it was hypothesized that there are three types of visitors: studious, crammers, and workers. Studious visitors download notes from the site regularly. Crammers download all the notes before an exam. Workers come to the site to finish assigned work such as lab and class assignments. Generally, the boundaries of these classes will not be precise.

Both the approaches were successful in creating meaningful intervals of clusters. However, there was a significant difference between the computational time requirements. The GAs based approach was feasible for grouping 1264 web visitors who downloaded at least one set of classnotes during two weeks around the midterm examination. However, it couldn't be used for 8442 visitors who downloaded at least one set of classnotes for the entire duration of course. This paper presents detailed analysis of time requirements for various datasets for the GAs as well as the modified K-means algorithm.

2   Rough Set Genome and Its Evaluation

This section describes the notion of a rough set genome. Due to space limitations, certain familiarity with genetic algorithms and rough sets [1] is assumed.

A rough set genome represents the entire clustering scheme. Let $U = \{u_1, u_2, \ldots, u_n\}$ be the set of objects that are to be partitioned into k classes given by: $U/P = \{X_1, X_2, \ldots, X_k\}$.

The rough set genome consists of n genes, one gene per object. The gene for an object is a string of bits that describes which lower and upper approximations the object belongs to. Properties of rough sets provide certain restrictions on the memberships. An object $u_p \in U$ can belong to the lower approximation of at most one class X_i. If an object belongs to the lower approximation of X_i then it also belongs to the upper approximation of X_i. If an object does not belong to the lower approximation of any X_i, then it belongs to the upper approximation of at least two (possibly more) X_i.

Based on these observations the string for a gene can be partitioned into two parts, *lower* and *upper*. Both lower and upper parts of the string consist of k bits each. The ith bit in lower/upper string tells whether the object is in the lower/upper approximation of X_i.

If $u_p \in \underline{A}(X_i)$, then based on properties of rough sets, $u_p \in \overline{A}(X_i)$. Therefore, the ith bit in both the lower and upper strings will be turned on. Based on properties of rough sets, all the other bits must be turned off.

If u_p is not in any of the lower approximations, then according to properties of rough sets, it must be in two or more upper approximations of $X_i, 1 \leq i \leq m$, and the corresponding i^{th} bits in the upper string will be turned on. Lingras [3] provides a detailed discussion on the encoding of rough set genomes.

A genetic algorithm package makes it possible to describe a set of valid gene values or alleles. All the standard genetic operations only create genomes that have valid values. Therefore, the conventional genetic operations can be used with rough set genomes in such a package.

The quality of a conventional clustering scheme is determined using the within-group-error $\triangle$ given by:

$$\triangle = \sum_{i=1}^{m} \sum_{u_h, u_p \in X_i} d(u_h, u_p), \qquad (1)$$

where u_h and u_p are objects from the same class X_i. The function d provides the distance between two objects. The exact form of the d function depends on the application and representation of the objects. The distance $d(\mathbf{v}, \mathbf{x})$ in this study is given by:

$$d(\mathbf{v}, \mathbf{x}) = \frac{\sum_{j=1}^{m}(v_j - x_j)^2}{m} \qquad (2)$$

For a rough set classification scheme, the exact values of classes $X_i \in U/P$ are not known. Given two objects $u_h, u_p \in U$ we have three distinct possibilities:

1. Both u_h and u_p are in the same lower approximation $\underline{A}(X_i)$.
2. Object u_h is in a lower approximation $\underline{A}(X_i)$ and u_p is in the corresponding upper approximation $\overline{A}(X_i)$, and case 1 is not applicable.
3. Both u_h and u_p are in the same upper approximation $\overline{A}(X_i)$, and cases 1 and 2 are not applicable.

For these possibilities, one can define three corresponding types of within-group-errors, $\triangle_1, \triangle_2$, and $\triangle_3$ as:

$$\triangle_1 = \sum_{i=1}^{m} \sum_{u_h, u_p \in \underline{A}(X_i)} d(u_h, u_p),$$

$$\triangle_2 = \sum_{i=1}^{m} \sum_{u_h \in \underline{A}(X_i), u_p \in \overline{A}(X_i); u_p \notin \underline{A}(X_i)} d(u_h, u_p),$$

$$\triangle_3 = \sum_{i=1}^{m} \sum_{u_h, u_p \in \overline{A}(X_i); u_h, u_p \notin \underline{A}(X_i)} d(u_h, u_p).$$

The total error of rough set classification will then be a weighted sum of these errors:

$$\Delta_{total} = w_1 \times \Delta_1 + w_2 \times \Delta_2 + w_3 \times \Delta_3. \quad (3)$$

Since Δ_1 corresponds to situations where both objects definitely belong to the same class, the weight w_1 should have the highest value. On the other hand, Δ_3 corresponds to the situation where both objects may or may not belong to the same class. Hence, w_3 should have the lowest value. In other words, $w_1 > w_2 > w_3$. There are many possible ways of developing an error measure for rough set clustering. The measure Δ_{total} is perhaps one of the simplest possibilities. More sophisticated alternatives may be used for different applications.

If we used genetic algorithms to minimize Δ_{total}, the genetic algorithms would try to classify all the objects in upper approximations by taking advantage of the fact that $w_3 < w_1$. This may not necessarily be the best classification scheme. We want the rough set classification to be as precise as possible. Therefore, a precision measure needs to be used in conjunction with Δ_{total} for evaluating the quality of a rough set genome. A possible *precision* measure can be defined following Pawlak [6] as:

$$\frac{\text{Number of objects in lower approximations}}{\text{Total number of objects}} \quad (4)$$

The objective of the genetic algorithms is to maximize the quantity:

$$objective = p \times precision + \frac{e}{\Delta_{total}}, \quad (5)$$

where p and e are additional parameters. The parameter p describes the importance of the precision measure in determining the quality of a rough set genome. Higher values of p will result in smaller boundary regions. Similarly, e indicates the importance of within-group-errors relative to the size of the boundary regions. It should perhaps be noted here that it was necessary to add five new parameters $w_1, w_2, w_3, p,$ and e for the rough set theoretic evolutionary clustering. The values of these parameters need to be adjusted based on the application, similar to other genetic algorithm parameters. Lingras [3,4] describes how these parameters were chosen for highway classification and web visitors clustering.

3 Adaptation of K-Means to Rough Set Theory

K-means clustering is a process of finding centroids for all clusters, and assigning objects to each cluster based on their distances from the centroids. This process is done iteratively until stable centroid values are found. Incorporating rough sets into K-means clustering requires the addition of the concept of lower and upper bounds. Calculations of the centroids of clusters need to be modified to include the effects of lower as well as upper bounds. The modified centroid calculations for rough sets is then given by:

$$x_j = \begin{cases} w_{lower} \times \dfrac{\sum_{v \in \underline{A}(\mathbf{x})} v_j}{|\underline{A}(\mathbf{x})|} + w_{upper} \times \dfrac{\sum_{v \in (\overline{A}(\mathbf{x}) - \underline{A}(\mathbf{x}))} v_j}{|\overline{A}(\mathbf{x}) - \underline{A}(\mathbf{x})|} & \text{if } \overline{A}(\mathbf{x}) - \underline{A}(\mathbf{x}) \neq \emptyset \\ w_{lower} \times \dfrac{\sum_{v \in \underline{A}(\mathbf{x})} v_j}{|\underline{A}(\mathbf{x})|} & \text{otherwise} \end{cases},$$

(6)

where $1 \leq j \leq m$. The parameters w_{lower} and w_{upper} correspond to the relative importance of lower and upper bounds. It can be shown that eq. 6 is a generalization of K-means equation for calculating centroids [5]. If the upper bound of each cluster were equal to its lower bound, the clusters will be conventional clusters. Therefore, the boundary region $\overline{A}(\mathbf{x}) - \underline{A}(\mathbf{x})$ will be empty, and the second term in the equation will be ignored. Thus, eq. 6 will reduce to conventional K-means calculations [5].

The next step in the modification of the K-means algorithms for rough sets is to design criteria to determine whether an object belongs to the upper or lower bound of a cluster. For each object vector, $\mathbf{v}$, let $d(\mathbf{v}, \mathbf{x}_i)$ be the distance between itself and the centroid of cluster X_i. The differences $d(\mathbf{v}, \mathbf{x}_i) - d(\mathbf{v}, \mathbf{x}_j)$, $1 \leq i, j \leq k$, were used to determine the membership of $\mathbf{v}$ as follows.

1. If $d(\mathbf{v}, \mathbf{x}_i)$ is the minimum for $1 \leq i \leq k$, and $d(\mathbf{v}, \mathbf{x}_i) - d(\mathbf{v}, \mathbf{x}_j) \leq threshold$, for any pair (i, j), then $\mathbf{v} \in \overline{A}(\mathbf{x}_i)$ and $\mathbf{v} \in \overline{A}(\mathbf{x}_j)$. Furthermore, $\mathbf{v}$ is not part of any lower bound.
2. Otherwise, $\mathbf{v} \in \underline{A}(\mathbf{x}_i)$ such that $d(\mathbf{v}, \mathbf{x}_i)$ is the minimum for $1 \leq i \leq k$. In addition, by properties of rough sets, $\mathbf{v} \in \overline{A}(\mathbf{x}_i)$.

The rough K-means algorithm, described above, depends on three parameters w_{lower}, w_{upper}, and $threshold$. Experimentation with various values of the parameters is necessary to develop a reasonable rough set clustering. Lingras and West [5] sections describe the design and results of such an experiment.

4 Time Requirements of the Two Rough Clustering Techniques

The time requirements for the two clustering methods can be analyzed using the common instruction that will have to be executed in either method. Typically, such instruction will also be the most frequently executed step. Both the methods must make calls to the distance function $d(\mathbf{u}, \mathbf{v})$. Assuming that the dimensions of the vector are constant at m, the function $d(\mathbf{u}, \mathbf{v})$ requires constant time. The number of calls made to the distance function will determine the order of computational time requirement of each method. The time requirement for the rough clustering based on GAs depends on the sizes of upper and lower bounds of clusters. For each generation, there are many different clustering schemes given by the population at that generation. Let pop be the population size at each generation and gen be the number of generations. The time requirement for each chromosome c in the population will be the one required to calculate within-group error for each cluster:

$$time_c = \sum_{i=1}^{k} O\left(|\underline{A}(cluster_i)|^2 + |\overline{A}(cluster_i)|^2\right). \tag{7}$$

For the entire population, the time requirement will be:

$$time_{pop} = \sum_{c=1}^{pop} time_c = \sum_{c=1}^{pop}\sum_{i=1}^{k} O\left(|\underline{A}(cluster_i)|^2 + |\overline{A}(cluster_i)|^2\right). \tag{8}$$

Summing it up for all the generations, the time requirement will be:

$$time_{GA} = \sum_{g=1}^{gen} time_{pop} = \sum_{g=1}^{gen}\sum_{c=1}^{pop} time_c \tag{9}$$

$$= \sum_{g=1}^{gen}\sum_{c=1}^{pop}\sum_{i=1}^{k} O\left(|\underline{A}(cluster_i)|^2 + |\overline{A}(cluster_i)|^2\right). \tag{10}$$

The time requirement will depend on the size of the upper and lower bounds of the clusters. In the worst case, all the upper bounds of the clusters will be of uniform size of n, and all the lower bounds will be empty. Therefore, the time requirement will be:

$$time_{GA} = \sum_{g=1}^{gen} time_{pop} = \sum_{g=1}^{gen}\sum_{c=1}^{pop} time_c \tag{11}$$

$$= \sum_{g=1}^{gen}\sum_{c=1}^{pop}\sum_{i=1}^{k} O\left(|\underline{A}(cluster_i)|^2 + |\overline{A}(cluster_i)|^2\right) \tag{12}$$

$$= \sum_{g=1}^{gen}\sum_{c=1}^{pop}\sum_{i=1}^{k} O\left(0 + n^2\right) \tag{13}$$

$$= \sum_{g=1}^{gen}\sum_{c=1}^{pop}\sum_{i=1}^{k} O\left(n^2\right) \tag{14}$$

$$= \sum_{g=1}^{gen}\sum_{c=1}^{pop} O\left(k \times n^2\right) \tag{15}$$

$$= \sum_{g=1}^{gen} O\left(pop \times k \times n^2\right) \tag{16}$$

$$= O\left(gen \times pop \times k \times n^2\right) \tag{17}$$

The time requirement of $O\left(gen \times pop \times k \times n^2\right)$ is acceptable for small values of n such as 100-500. Such was the case for the highway sections used in [3]. The clustering of 350 highway sections with number of generation of 1000 and population size of 100 would result in approximately 36 billion calls to the distance function. The clustering was done in a few minutes on a 1.2GHz Linux computer.

Lingras [4] applied the rough GAs clustering on data obtained from the web access logs of the introductory first year course in computing science at Saint Mary's University.

It was hoped that the students could be clustered into studious, crammer, and worker classes based on the number of web accesses, types of documents downloaded, and time of day.

The web visits were identified based on their IP address. This also made sure that the user privacy was protected. The data was restricted to two weeks around the midterm examination. These two weeks logged 54528 entries. The data preparation identified a total of 3243 visits. The visitors that did not download any notes clearly fall in the worker category. Therefore, the clustering was restricted to those 1264 visits, which downloaded at least one classnotes file. The lower and upper bounds of the clusters were meaningful. The clustering process took close to an hour on the 1.2GHz Linux computer. The computational time seemed to make sense because 1000 generations with population size of 100 would require approximately 480 billion calls to the distance function. However, when the clustering was applied to the sixteen week period, the dataset was larger than the initial experiment. The approach could not be easily extended to the longer period of sixteen weeks.

Lingras and West [5] used all 361,609 entries from the web log over the sixteen week period. There were a total of 22,996 visits. The visits that didn't download any classnotes were treated as workers. The clustering was applied to the remaining 8,442 visits. With 100 chromosomes evolving for 1000 generation would have resulted in approximately 21 trillion calls to the distance function. Therefore, the rough set based K-means clustering was developed. The clustering process took only a few minutes. This experimental results can be easily confirmed by studying the theoretical time complexity of the algorithm.

The time requirement for K-means method is considerably smaller. It depends on the number of iterations required for the centroid vectors to stabilize. For each iteration, n objects are compared with k clusters, leading to $n \times k$ calls to the distance function. For the complete execution of K-means method, the time requirement is $O(iter \times k \times n)$, where $iter$ corresponds to the number of iterations. The clustering of 8,442 visits into upper and lower bounds of three clusters required less than 100 iterations. The number of calls to distance function with 100 iterations would have been 2 million. This is several orders smaller than expected 21 trillion calls with the GAs approach. Recent experiments with over 100,000 supermarket customers also shows that the modified K-means may be a feasible approach for creating intervals of clusters for large datasets, which are typical in data mining.

5 Summary and Conclusions

The clusters in data mining do not necessarily have precise boundaries. This paper discusses the time complexity of two approaches for obtaining intervals of clusters. Both the approaches use properties of rough sets. The clustering in one approach was achieved by evolving rough set genomes. The other approach used a modified K-means algorithm. The genetic algorithms based approach requires $O\left(gen \times pop \times k \times n^2\right)$ calls to the distance function, where gen is the number generations, pop is the population size, k is the number of clusters, and n is the number of objects. The K-means algorithm requires $O\left(iter \times k \times n\right)$ calls to the distance function, where $iter$ is the number of iterations required to get stable centroid values.

GAs based approach was feasible for grouping 350 highway sections, and 1264 web visits around midterm for a course. However, it was found infeasible for grouping all the 8442 visits that downloaded at least a classnotes file in the course. K-means approach requires significantly smaller computational time. It has been successful in creating interval of clusters of not only 8000+ web visitors, but also approximately 100,000 supermarket customers.

References

1. J.H. Holland: Adaptation in Natural and Artificial Systems. University of Michigan Press Ann Arbor (1975)
2. A. Joshi and R. Krishnapuram: Robust Fuzzy Clustering Methods to Support Web Mining. Proceedings of the workshop on Data Mining and Knowledge Discovery, SIGMOD '98, Seattle (1998) 15/1–15/8 .
3. P. Lingras: Unsupervised Rough Set Classification using GAs. Journal Of Intelligent Information Systems, Vol. 16:3 (2001) 215–228
4. P. Lingras: Rough set clustering for web mining. To appear in Proceedings of 2002 IEEE International Conference on Fuzzy Systems (2002)
5. P. Lingras and C. West: Interval Set Clustering of Web Users with Rough K-means. submitted to the Journal of Intelligent Information Systems
6. Z. Pawlak: Rough classification. International Journal of Man-Machine Studies, Vol. 20, (1984) 469–483
7. A. Skowron and J. Stepaniuk: Information granules in distributed environment. In Zhong, N. Skowron, A. Ohsuga, S. (eds.): New Directions in Rough Sets, Data Mining, and Granular-Soft Computing, Lecture notes in Artificial Intelligence, Vol. 1711. Springer-Verlag, Tokyo (1999) 357–365
8. Y.Y. Yao, X. Li, T.Y. Lin, and Q. Liu: Representation and Classification of Rough Set Models. Proceeding of Third International Workshop on Rough Sets and Soft Computing, San Jose, California (1994) 630–637

Induction of Decision Rules and Classification in the Valued Tolerance Approach

Jerzy Stefanowski[1] and Alexis Tsoukiàs[2]

[1] Institute of Computing Science
Poznań University of Technology, 60-965, Poznań, Poland
Jerzy.Stefanowski@cs.put.poznan.pl
[2] LAMSADE - CNRS, Université Paris Dauphine
75775 Paris Cedex 16, France
tsoukias@lamsade.dauphine.fr

Abstract. The problem of uncertain and/or incomplete information in information tables is addressed in the paper, mainly as far as the induction of classification rules is concerned. Two rule induction algorithms are introduced, discussed and tested on a number of benchmark data sets. Moreover, two different strategies for classifying objects on the basis of induced rules are introduced.

1 Introduction

Inducing decision rules from data sets, representing sets of learning examples described by attributes, is one of the main tasks in knowledge discovery. Most of the known algorithms find rules by inductive generalisation of learning examples descriptions [2,4]. A key issue in all such approaches is the comparison of descriptions of examples represented in a form of attribute-values vectors. Intuitively, we have to compare descriptions of examples among them in order to establish their "similarity". We also have to compare descriptions of new objects (unseen in the learning phase) to the condition parts of induced decision rules, if these rules are used for classification aims. When such attribute-value vectors are compared, it is not always the case that a crisp relation between two descriptions can be established. This is due either to the presence of incomplete descriptions or to the presence of uncertainty, imprecision and any other source of ambiguity within the descriptions. For this purpose we developed, the so called, "*valued tolerance approach*", which consists in adopting a precise version of valued similarity when multidimensional objects are compared [5,6,7].

Typical rule induction algorithms are based on the exploitation of crisp comparisons. In order to be able to induce rules from examples using the valued tolerance approach we need new specific procedures. Therefore, we present two different algorithms for rule induction using the valued tolerance approach. The first algorithm finds the set of all rules that can be induced from a given set of examples. The second algorithm constructs the minimal set of rules, i.e. covering the set of examples by a smallest number of rules.

The aim of this paper is experimental. Firstly, we compare on several data sets these two algorithms. A second experiment is then conducted, where we compare two different strategies for classifying new objects on the basis of rule sets induced by these algorithms. The difference between these strategies concerns the type of information used in order to classify any new object. Moreover, we examine the use of different uncertainty aggregation operators.

The paper is organised as follows. In section 2, a brief reminder of the approach based on the valued tolerance relation is given. In section 3, we introduce two different algorithms for rule induction using this approach. In section 4, we discuss various strategies that can be applied to classify new objects on the basis of induced rules. Section 5 presents the results of the computational experiments. Discussion of these results and conclusions are presented in the final section.

2 Basic Concepts of Valued Tolerance Approach

An *information table* is composed of a set of objects U described by a set of attributes A. If objects are classfied by one distinguished attribute $\{d\} \notin A$, called a *decision attribute*, we can define a *decision table* $DT = (U, A \cup \{d\})$. The decision attribute d partitions set U into decision classes denoted as $\Phi, \Psi, \ldots$. In the valued tolerance approach we assume: $\exists\ R_B(x, y) : U \times U \mapsto [0, 1]$, R_B representing a valued tolerance relation among the objects from U, established using the attributes $B \subseteq A$. R_B, which is also a fuzzy set, satisfies two properties: (1) reflexivity: $\forall x\ R_B(x, x) = 1$; (2) symmetry: $\forall x, y\ R_B(x, y) = R_B(y, x)$. We are not going to discuss in this paper how R_B is computed (for more details see [7]). We consider R_B as established.

Following rough sets theory [3] and its extension in the valued tolerance case [5,6,7], given a set of objects $Z \subset U$, we define as *lower approximability* of a class Φ by Z, the degree by which all objects in Z, and all objects (more or less) similar to them, are (more or less) similar to the elements in Φ. In other words, we "measure" the degree by which set Z approximates set Φ using for "similarity" the valued tolerance R_B. More formally: $\mu_{\Phi_B}(Z) = T_{z \in Z}(T_{x \in \Theta_B(z)}(I(R_B(z, x), \hat{x})))$, $\mu_{\Phi^B}(Z) = T_{z \in Z}(S_{x \in \Theta_B(z)}(T(R_B(z, x), \hat{x})))$, where: $\mu_{\Phi_B}(Z)$ is the degree for set Z to be a B-lower approximation of Φ; $\mu_{\Phi^B}(Z)$ is the degree for set Z to be a B-upper approximation of Φ; $\Theta_B(z)$ is the tolerance class of element z; T, S, I are functions representing the usual logical operators and satisfying the De Morgan law. $R_B(z, x)$ is the membership degree of x in the tolerance class of z (at the same time it is the valued tolerance relation between x and z for attribute set B); $\hat{x}$ is the membership degree of element x in the set Φ ($\hat{x} \in \{0, 1\}$).

Decision rules are represented as: $\rho_i =_{def} \wedge_{c_j \in B} (c_j(x) = v) \to (d = \phi)$; where $B \subseteq A$, v is the value of condition attribute $c_j \in B$, ϕ is the value of decision attribute d. In the valued tolerance approach a special *credibility degree* is associated with each rule ρ_i. We shortly remind how this degree is calculated [5]. The valued tolerance relation $s_B(x, \rho_i)$ is used in order to indicate that example x "supports" rule ρ_i, or in other words that, x is similar to some extend to the condition part of rule ρ_i on attributes B. We denote as $S(\rho_i) = \{x$:

$s_B(x, \rho_i) > 0\}$ and as $\Phi = \{x : d(x) = \phi\}$. A credibility degree for rule ρ_i is calculated as $\mu(\rho_i) = T_{x \in S(\rho_i)}(I(s_B(x, \rho_i), T_{y \in \Theta_B(x)}(I(\mu_{\Theta_B(x)}(y), \mu_\Phi(y)))))$, where: $\mu_{\Theta_B(x)}(y) = R_B(x, y)$ and $\mu_\Phi(y) \in \{0, 1\}$. We quote the following result from [6]:

Proposition 1. *Consider a rule ρ_i classifying objects to a set $\Phi \subset U$ under a set of attributes B. If T, S, I satisfy the De Morgan law and R_B is a valued tolerance, the credibility $\mu(\rho_i)$ of the rule is upper bounded by the lower approximability of set Φ by the element x_k whose description (under attributes B) coincides with the condition part of the rule.*

The proof was presented in [6]. One should observe that: - the concept of rule credibility allows to fix an acceptance threshold, let's say λ, which may avoid the generation of unsafe rules; - proposition 2 allows to consider as candidates for rule generation only the examples having a sufficient high lower approximability - not smaller than λ. This reduces the rule generation cost.

3 Algorithms of Rule Induction

The rough sets based rule induction algorithms can be divided into two main categories [2,4]. The first group is focused on inducing the complete set of *all rules* in the given syntax, which can be generated from the examples. The other group of algorithms is focused on *minimal set of rules*, i.e. covering the learning examples using the minimum number of rules. Inducing all rules is characterised by exponential time complexity in the worst case, while minimal sets of rules are usually generated in a heuristic way. Following this categorisation, we also present two different algorithms for rule induction using valued tolerance.

Let us suppose that the credibility threshold for the induced rules is fixed at λ. In both algorithms descriptions of objects, being completely defined by attribute-value pairs, are considered as conjunctions of elementary conditions which can be used to create condition parts of rules. According to Proposition 1 an object x is a candidate for creating a rule indicating class Φ_i if: (1) its lower approximability $\mu_\Phi(x) \geq \lambda$ (computed for completely defined attributes, where Φ is the decision class which object x belongs to); (2) the credibility of the rule using as condition part its description is also $\mu(\rho_x) \geq \lambda$. Other objects could be skipped, as they will not lead to rules with sufficient credibility.

3.1 Algorithm Inducing All Rules

The algorithm is based on looking for all possible reduced descriptions of candidate objects from the decision table, which lead to rules with credibility $\mu(\rho_x) \geq \lambda$. The general schema of the algorithm is presented below.

    Procedure *Allrules*(DT: decision table; var $\mathcal{R}$: set of rules);
    begin $\mathcal{R} \leftarrow \emptyset$
       for $i = 1$ **to** n **do begin**{ n – number of objects in DT }
          $x \leftarrow$ *read_i_the_object*(DT);
          if not(*exist_rule*($\mathcal{R}, x$)) **then begin**

$\mu_\Phi(x) \leftarrow compute\_lower\_approximation(\Phi, x)$; { Φ decision class of x }
if $\mu_\Phi(x) \geq \lambda$ **then** { Apply Proposition 1 }
  if $\mu(\rho_x) \geq \lambda$ **then begin**{ ρ_x decision rule created using x }
    $RT \leftarrow Create\_Tree\_reducts(\Phi, x)$; {find all reduced forms of ρ_x}
    $\mathcal{R} \leftarrow \mathcal{R} \cup RT$ **end**
  end
end
end

Function *Create Tree Reducts* checks possible reductions of the condition part by dropping elementary conditions. Starting from one description of a candidate object, a "tree" of all admissible reduced condition parts is constructed, where each path should fulfill sufficient rule credibility and cannot be a conjunction of conditions already used in other condition parts. The induced rules are stored in a special structure and function *Exist rule* checks whether a description of object x is equal to, or is a subset of, already induced rules. The objects in decision table DT are sorted from ones having the most complete description, so "longer" candidate objects are checked the first.

3.2 Algorithm Inducing Minimal Set of Rules

This algorithm induces in a heuristic way the smallest number of rules covering all such objects from the decision table that approximate decision classes with degree $\mu_\Phi(x) \geq \lambda$. By objects covered by the rule we understand the objects, which are described by the same values of attributes as used in the condition part (non zero valued tolerance relation). The main idea of *MinimalCover* algorithm is inspired by techniques of linear dropping conditions used in the *LEM1* algorithm [2]. In this form of dropping, the list of all elementary conditions in the rule ρ_x is scanned from the left to the right with attempt to drop any of $(c_j = v)$ conditions, while checking whether the simplified rule does not decrease rule credibility below threshold λ - see function *Dropcondition*. In this technique, only one reduced form of a condition part is found. The order in the list of condition is determined by function *determine order conditions* on the basis of increasing number of positive examples covered by an elementary condition. So, first these conditions are dropped, which cover the smallest number of examples belonging to the decision class indicated by the rule.

Procedure *MinimalCover*(DT: decision table; **var** $\mathcal{R}$: set of rules);
begin $\mathcal{R} \leftarrow \emptyset$
  for $i = 1$ **to** n **do begin**
    $x \leftarrow read\_i\_the\_object(DT)$;
    $\mu_\Phi(x) \leftarrow compute\_lower\_approximation(\Phi, x)$;
    if $\mu_\Phi(x) \geq \lambda$ **then**
      if $\mu(\rho_x) \geq \lambda$ **then begin**{ ρ_x decision rule created using x }
        $determine\_order\_conditions(x, condx)$;
        $r \leftarrow \rho_x$;
        for $j = 1$ **to** $|condx|$ **do begin**{ perform linear dropping of }
          $\rho_y \leftarrow dropcondition(j, r)$; { conditions from ρ_x }

```
            if μ(ρ_y) ≥ λ then r ← ρ_y; end
         R ← R ∪ r;   remove from DT objects x covered by r; end
   end
end.
```

4 Strategies for Classifying New Objects

Induced decision rules are the basis for classifying new or testing objects. The classification problem is to assign such objects to a decision class on the basis of their similarity/tolerance to the condition part of rules. There are two sources of uncertainty in this problem. First, the new object will be similar to a certain degree to the condition part of a given rule (due to the valued tolerance relation). Second, the rule itself has a credibility (classification is not completely sure any more). In general, the new object will be more or less similar to more than one decision rule and such rules may indicate different decision classes (with a different membership degree). In order to make a precise decision to which class the new object belongs we consider two kinds of information: (1) rule credibility and similarity/tolerance of the new object to its condition part; (2) number of objects supporting the rule, i.e. learning examples similar to condition part of the rule and belonging to the decision class indicated by the rule. The following two classification strategies are thus proposed:

Strategy A: 1. For each decision rule ρ_i in the set of induced rules, the tolerance of new object z to its condition part, $R_B(z, \rho_i)$, is calculated (where B is a set of attributes used in the condition part of ρ_i).
2. Then, the tolerance of the object z to the condition part of the rule, is aggregated with the credibility of the rule: $\mu_{\rho_i}(z) = T(R_B(z, \rho_i), \mu(\rho_i))$.
3. The membership degree of object z to decision class Φ_i is calculated on the basis of all rules $R(\Phi_i)$ - indicating Φ_i and having $\mu_{\rho_i}(z) > 0$: as $\mu_{\Phi_i}(z) = S_{\rho_i \in R(\Phi_i)}(\mu_{\rho_i}(z))$. Choose the class with the maximum membership degree.
4. If a tie occurs (the same membership for different classes), take into account information about the relative supports of rules denoted as $Supp(\rho_i)$ (it is a ratio of the number of objects supporting the rule to the total number of examples from the given decision class). For each competitive class Φ_i and its rules $R(\Phi_i)$ calculate the aggregated support as $Supp_{\Phi_i}(z) = S_{\rho_i \in R(\Phi_i)}(Supp(\rho_i))$. The object z is classified as being a member of class Φ_i with highest $Supp_{\Phi_i}(z)$.

Strategy B 1. As in strategy A.
2. As in strategy A, but $\mu_{\rho_i}(z) = T(R_B(z, \rho_i), \mu(\rho_i), Supp(\rho_i))$.
3. As in strategy A.

Practically the two strategies differ in that the first uses a lexicographic procedure in order to consider the support of a rule, while the second uses this information directly in the membership degree. A question arising at this point is the influence on the final result of the choice of the family of T, S, I operators. In this paper we consider three particular cases of T-norms:
– the min T-norm: $T(\alpha, \beta) = \min(\alpha, \beta), S(\alpha, \beta) = \max(\alpha, \beta)$;
– the product T-norm: $T(\alpha, \beta) = \alpha \cdot \beta, S(\alpha, \beta) = \alpha + \beta - \alpha \cdot \beta$;
– the Lukasiewicz T-norm: $T(\alpha, \beta) = \max(\alpha + \beta - 1, 0), S(\alpha, \beta) = \min(\alpha + \beta, 1)$;

5 Experiments

In the first part of the experiment we wanted to compare both algorithms inducing all rules and minimal cover on several data sets taking into account the following criteria: number of rules and classification accuracy. Classification accuracy was estimated by performing 10 fold cross-validation technique. We also analysed the influence of changing the number of attributes and the number of examples in data sets on the performance of both algorithms.

Table 1. The number of rules induced by both compared algorithms from Mushroom data (first number) and obtained classification accuracy [in %] for both algorithms (second number)

No. of objects	Algorithm	Number of attributes					
		5	7	9	11	15	21
50	Allrules	46/68	133/82	327/82	618/84	2713/90	10499/82
	MinCover	17/64	18/74	13/76	12/76	9/84	9/84
100	Allrules	69/63	206/84	482/86	1275/90	6787/86	–
	MinCover	27/57	26/72	29/75	22/80	19/83	–
250	Allrules	87/71	306/80	873/90	2895/91	18283/96	–
	MinCover	47/67	56/75	51/81	44/82	30/92	–
500	Allrules	72/51	350/80	1109/91	4875/93	–	–
	MinCover	47/48	79/77	86/86	83/85	–	–
1000	Allrules	80/51	396/80	1138/91	6596/95	–	–
	MinCover	27/48	120/77	131/86	133/87	–	–
4000	Allrules	13/8	160/36	1052/75	–	–	–
	MinCover	13/8	88/35	193/74	–	–	–
8124	Allrules	8/2	92/17	–	–	–	–
	MinCover	8/2	50/17	–	–	–	–

We used 5 real life data sets of different size and characteristics, which are coming from Machine Learning Database, University of California at Irvine [1]. The *Breast Cancer* and *Credit* data sets, which originally contained continuous-valued attributes, were discretised by means of the minimal class entropy method. Data sets contained the following ratio of missing values: *Breast cancer* - 6.14 [%], *Credit* - 2.1 [%], *Bridge* - 5.4 [%], *Hungarian* - 25.9 [%]. Moreover, the last *Mushroom* data set was artificially changed to obtain series of data sets with different number of attributes and objects. Originally, it contained 8124 objects described by 21 attributes and classified into two categories. From this data set we randomly sampled subsets containing 5, 7, 9 and 15 attributes. Then, in order to obtain data sets diversified by number of objects, we randomly created samples of data sets containing 50, 100, 250, 500, 1000 and 4000 objects. Since we wanted all such subsets of examples to contain a certain degree of missing values, we randomly introduced missing values into each data in these series (finally each data contained 20% missing values). As computational costs were high for the *All rules* algorithm, we decided to skip some combinations of highest number of attributes and highest number of objects. All computations for *Mushroom* data sets were performed with fixed threshold value of accepted rule credibility $\lambda = 0.75$. Results are summarised in the Table 1. To classify objects, we used strategy B (it gives higher accuracy).

Table 2. Classification accuracies [in %] obtained by using different classification strategies and different representations of aggregation operators; decision rules were induced by *All rules* algorithm

Data set	Strategy A			Strategy B
	min T-norm	product T-norm	Lukasiewicz T-norm	
Breast	61.56	66.93	66.79	71.26
Credit	57.53	59	63.95	65.55
Bridges	44.84	48.05	47.53	50.64
Hungarian	72.91	74.23	75.25	76.46

In the second part of the experiment we wanted to check the influence of using the two classification strategies, A and B, on the value of classification accuracy. Moreover, we wanted to examine the influence of choosing different representations of aggregation operators. We considered three particular cases presented in Section 4, i.e. the min T-norm, the product T-norm and the Lukasiewicz T-norm. These experiments were performed using the four data sets *Breast Cancer*, *Credit Approval*, *Bridges*, *Hungarian* and with credibility threshold $\lambda = 0.9$. The first observation was that the choice of classification strategies and T operators had no significant influence in the case of the minimal cover algorithm. On the other hand, we observed such an influence when the algorithm inducing all rules was used. Thus, we summarise the experimental results for this case in Table 2.

6 Conclusions

Two algorithms for inducing classification rules from "uncertain" information tables were presented. We consider as "uncertain" the case where comparing any two objects we obtain a valued similarity (objects are more or less similar) and the induced rules are associated a credibility degree. These two algorithms, the first inducing all rules, the second a minimal set, have been tested on a number of benchmark data sets. The experimental results clearly shows that the *All rules* algorithm induces higher number of rules than *Minimal cover*. Moreover, the number of rules induced by *Minimal cover* is relatively stable, while another algorithm induces larger and larger sets of rules with increasing number of attributes. The increase of the number of objects has smaller influence on the number of rules than increasing number of attributes. The computational time is much higher for *All rules* algorithm and it exponentially grows with increasing the number of attributes. Classification accuracy is higher for decision rules generated by *All rules* algorithm. The accuracies for both algorithms usually grow with increasing number of attributes. However, the difference of accuracies between algorithms decreases with the increase of the number of objects. To sum up, both algorithms induce sets of rules having different properties. Their choice should depend on data characteristics, interest of the user and its resources.

Comparing the results of using classification strategies, first we observed that their choice had an influence on the classification accuracy only in the case of using *All rules* algorithm. For *Minimal Cover* the differences of accuracies were not significant. The results presented in Table 2 showed that better classification accuracy was obtained by using strategy B. The aggregation of similarity, credibility and rule support degrees in a lexicographic order was less efficient. The analysis of choosing particular representation of T norms to aggregate the considered degrees showed that higher classification accuracies were obtained by using either product or Łukasiesiewicz T-norms.

Acknowledgement. The research of the first author has been supported by KBN research grant no. 8 T11C 006 19.

References

1. Blake, C.L., Merz, C.J., UCI Repository of machine learning databases [http://www.ics.uci.edu/~mlearn/MLRepository.html]. Irvine, CA: University of California, Department of Information and Computer Science, 1998.
2. Grzymala-Busse J. W. LERS - A system for learning from examples based on rough sets, in Słowiński R. (ed.), *Intelligent Decision Support. Handbook of Applications and Advances of the Rough Sets Theory*, Kluwer Academic Publishers, 1992, 3–18.
3. Pawlak Z., *Rough sets. Theoretical aspects of reasoning about data.* Kluwer Acad. Publs., Dordrecht, 1991.
4. Stefanowski J., On rough set based approaches to induction of decision rules, in Polkowski L., Skowron A. (eds.), *Rough Sets in Data Mining and Knowledge Discovery*, Physica-Verlag, 1998, 500–530.
5. Stefanowski J., Tsoukiàs A., On the extension of rough sets under incomplete information, in N. Zhong, A. Skowron, S. Ohsuga, (eds.), New Directions in Rough Sets, Data Mining and Granular-Soft Computing, Springer Verlag, LNAI 1711, Berlin, 1999, 73–81.
6. Stefanowski J., Tsoukiàs A., Valued tolerance and decision rules, in W.Ziarko, Y.Yao (eds.), *Rough Sets and Current Trends in Computing*, Springer Verlag, LNAI 2005, Berlin, 2001, 212–219.
7. Stefanowski J., Tsoukiàs A., Incomplete information tables and rough classification. *Computational Intelligence*, 2001, vol. 17, 545–566.

Time Series Model Mining with Similarity-Based Neuro-fuzzy Networks and Genetic Algorithms: A Parallel Implementation

Julio J. Valdés[1] and Gabriel Mateescu[2]

[1] National Research Council of Canada
Institute for Information Technology
1200 Montreal Road, Ottawa ON K1A 0R6, Canada
julio.valdes@nrc.ca
[2] National Research Council of Canada
Information Management Services Branch
100 Sussex Drive, Ottawa ON K1A 0R6, Canada
gabriel.mateescu@nrc.ca

Abstract. This paper presents a parallel implementation of a hybrid data mining technique for multivariate heterogeneous time varying processes based on a combination of neuro-fuzzy techniques and genetic algorithms. The purpose is to discover patterns of dependency in general multivariate time-varying systems, and to construct a suitable representation for the function expressing those dependencies. The patterns of dependency are represented by multivariate, non-linear, autoregressive models. Given a set of time series, the models relate future values of one target series with past values of all such series, including itself. The model space is explored with a genetic algorithm, whereas the functional approximation is constructed with a similarity based neuro-fuzzy heterogeneous network. This approach allows rapid prototyping of interesting interdependencies, especially in poorly known complex multivariate processes. This method contains a high degree of parallelism at different levels of granularity, which can be exploited when designing distributed implementations, such as workcrew computation in a master-slave paradigm. In the present paper, a first implementation at the highest granularity level is presented. The implementation was tested for performance and portability in different homogeneous and heterogeneous Beowulf clusters with satisfactory results. An application example with a known time series problem is presented.

1 Introduction

Multivariate time-varying processes are common in a wide variety of important domains like medicine, economics, industry, communications, environmental sciences, etc. Developments in sensor and communication technology enable the simultaneous monitoring and recording of large sets of variables quickly, therefore generating large sets of data. Processes of this kind are usually described by sets of variables, sometimes of heterogeneous nature. Some are numeric, others are non-numeric, for example, describing discrete state transitions. In real world situations, it is practically impossible to record all variables at all time frames, which leads to incomplete information. In practice, the degree of accuracy associated with the observed variables is irregular, resulting in data sets with different kinds and degrees of imprecision. All of these problems severely limit the applicability of most classical methods. Many techniques have been developed for time series prediction from a variety of conceptual approaches ([3], [6]), but the problem of finding models of internal dependencies has received much less attention. However, in real world multivariate processes, the patterns of internal dependencies are usually unknown and their discovery is crucial in order to understand and predict them. In the present approach, the space of possible models of a given kind is explored with genetic algorithms and their quality evaluated by constructing a similarity-based neuro-fuzzy network representing a functional approximation for a prediction operator. This approach to model mining is compute-intensive, but it is well suited for supercomputers and distributed computing systems. In the parallel implementation of this soft-computing approach to model discovery, several hierarchical levels can be identified, all involving intrinsically parallel operations. Therefore, a variety of implementations exploiting different degrees of granularity in the evolutionary algorithm and in the neuro-fuzzy network is possible. Here, following a parsimonious principle, the highest level is chosen for a first parallel implementation: that of population evaluation within a genetic algorithm.

2 Problem Formulation

The pattern of mutual dependencies is an essential element of this methodology. The purpose is to explore multivariate time series data for plausible dependency models expressing the relationship between future values of a previously selected series (the target), with past values of itself and other time series. Some of the variables composing the process may be numeric (ratio or interval scales), and some qualitative (ordinal or nominal scales). Also, they might contain missing values. Many different families of functional models describing the dependency of future values of a target series on the previous values can be considered, and the classical linear models AR, MA, ARMA and ARIMA [3], have been extensively studied. The choice of the functional family will influence the overall result. The methodology proposed here does not require a particular model. Because the generalized nonlinear AR model expressed by relation (1) is a simple model which makes the presentation easier to follow, we use this basic model:

$$S_T(t) = F \begin{pmatrix} S_1(t-\tau_{1,1}), S_1(t-\tau_{1,2}), \cdots, S_1(t-\tau_{1,p_1}), \\ S_2(t-\tau_{2,1}), S_2(t-\tau_{2,2}), \cdots, S_2(t-\tau_{2,p_2}), \\ \cdots \\ S_n(t-\tau_{n,1}), S_n(t-\tau_{n,2}), \cdots, S_n(t-\tau_{n,p_n}) \end{pmatrix} \quad (1)$$

where $S_T(t)$ is the target signal at time t, S_i is the i-th time series, n is the total number of signals, p_i is the number of time lag terms from signal i influencing $S_T(t)$, $\tau_{i,k}$ is the k-th lag term corresponding to signal i ($k \in [1, p_i]$), and F is the unknown function describing the process.

The goal is the simultaneous determination of: *i)* the number of required lags for each series, *ii)* the sets of particular lags within each series carrying dependency information, and *iii)* the prediction function, in some optimal sense. The size of the space of possible models is immense (even for only a few series and a limited number of time lags), and the lack of assumptions about the prediction function makes the set of candidates unlimited. A natural requirement on function F is the minimization of a suitable prediction error and the idea is to find a reasonably small subset with the best models in the above mentioned sense.

2.1 A Soft Computing Model Mining Strategy

A soft computing approach to the model mining problem can be: *i)* exploration of the model space with evolutionary algorithms, and *ii)* representation of the unknown function with a neural network (or a fuzzy system). The use of a neural network allows a flexible, robust and accurate predictor function approximator operator. Feed-forward networks and radial basis functions are typical choices. However, the use of these classical network paradigms might be difficult or even prohibitive, since for each candidate model in the search process, a network of the corresponding type has to be constructed and trained. Issues like chosing the number of neurons in the hidden layer, mixing of numeric and non-numeric information (discussed above), and working with imprecise values add even more complexity. Moreover, in general, these networks require long and unpredictable training times. The proposed method uses a heterogeneous neuron model [9], [10]. It considers a neuron as a general mapping from a heterogeneous multidimensional space composed by cartesian products of the so called extended sets, to another heterogeneous space. These are formed by the union of real, ordinal, nominal, fuzzy sets, or others (e.g. graphs), with the missing value (e.g. for the reals $\hat{\mathcal{R}} = \mathcal{R} \cup \{\chi\}$, where χ is the missing value). Their cartesian product forms the heterogeneous space, which in the present case, is given by $\hat{\mathcal{H}}^n = \hat{\mathcal{R}}^{n_r} \times \hat{\mathcal{O}}^{n_o} \times \hat{\mathcal{N}}^{n_n} \times \hat{\mathcal{F}}^{n_f}$. In the *h-neuron*, the inputs, and the weights, are elements of the n-dimensional heterogeneous input space. Among the many kinds of possible mappings, the one using a similarity function [4] as the aggregation function and the identity mapping as the activation function is used here. Its image is the real interval [0,1] and gives the degree of similarity between the input pattern and neuron weights. See Fig-2.1 (left).

The h-neuron can be used in conjunction with the classical (dot product as aggregation and sigmoid or hyperbolic tangent as activation), forming hybrid network architectures. They have general function approximation properties [1], and are trained with evolutionary algorithms in the case of heterogeneous inputs and missing values due to lack of continuity in the variable's space. The hybrid network used here has a hidden layer of h-neurons and an output layer of classical neurons. In the special case of predicting a single real-valued target time series, the architecture is shown in Fig-2.1 (right).

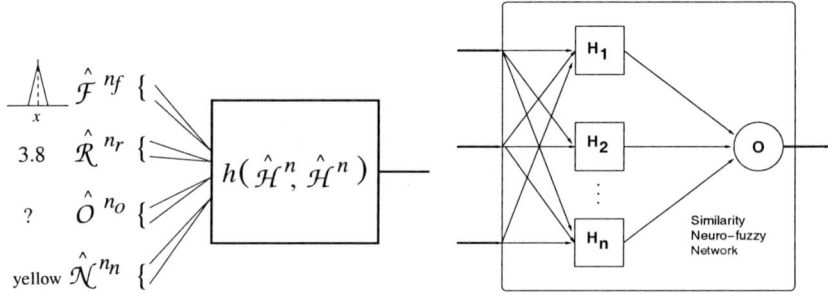

Fig. 1. Left: A heterogeneous neuron. Right: A hybrid neuro-fuzzy network.

This network works like a *k-best* interpolator algorithm: Each neuron in the hidden layer computes its similarity with the input vector and the k-best responses are retained (k is a pre-set number of h-neurons to select). Using as activation a linear function with a single coefficient equal to the inverse of the sum of the k-similarities coming from the hidden layer, the output is given by (2).

$$output = (1/\Theta) \sum_{i \in \mathcal{K}} h_i W_i, \qquad \Theta = \sum_{i \in \mathcal{K}} h_i \qquad (2)$$

where $\mathcal{K}$ is the set of k-best h-neurons of the hidden layer and h_i is the similarity value of the i-best h-neuron w.r.t the input vector. These similarities represent the fuzzy memberships of the input vector to the set classes defined by the neurons in the hidden layer. Thus, (2) represents a fuzzy estimate for the predicted value. Assuming that a similarity function $\mathcal{S}$ has been chosen and that the target is a single time series, this *case-based* neuro-fuzzy network is built and trained as follows: Define a similarity threshold $T \in [0, 1]$ and extract the subset $\mathcal{L}$ of the set of input patterns Ω ($\mathcal{L} \subseteq \Omega$) such that for every input pattern $x \in \Omega$, there exist a $l \in \mathcal{L}$ such that $\mathcal{S}(x, l) \geq T$. Several algorithms for extracting subsets with this property can be constructed in a single cycle through the input pattern set (note that if $T = 1$, the hidden layer becomes the whole training set). The hidden layer is constructed by using the elements of $\mathcal{L}$ as h-neurons. While the output layer is built by using the corresponding target outputs as the weights of the neuron(s). This training procedure is very fast and allows construction and testing of many hybrid neuro-fuzzy networks in a short time. Different sets of individual lags selected from each time series will define different training sets, and therefore, different hybrid neuro-fuzzy networks. This one-to-one correspondence between dependency models and neuro-fuzzy networks, makes the search in the model space equivalent to the search in the space of networks. Thus, given a model describing the dependencies and a set of time series, a hybrid network can be constructed according to the outlined procedure, and tested for its prediction error on a segment of the target series not used for training (building) the network. The Root Mean Squared (RMS) error is a typical goodness of fit measure and is the one used here. For each model the quality indicator is given by the prediction error on the test set of its equivalent similarity-based neuro-fuzzy network (the prediction function). The search for *optimal* models can be made with an evolutionary algorithm minimizing the prediction error measure. Genetic Algorithms and Evolution Strategies are typical for this task and many problem representations are possible. Genetic algorithms were used with a simple model coding given by binary chromosomes of length equal to the sum of the maximal number of lags considered for each of the time series (the *time window depth*). Within each chromosome segment corresponding to a given series, the non-zero values will indicate which time lags should be included in the model, as shown in Fig-2.1.

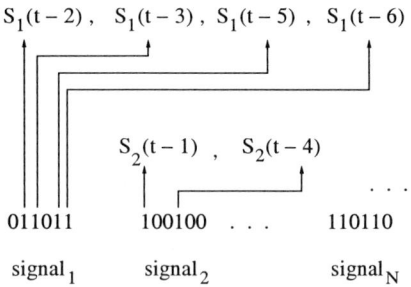

Fig. 2. Chromosome decodification.

The system architecture is illustared in Fig-2.1. The series are divided into training and test sets. A model is obtained from a binary chromosome by decodification. With the model and the series, a hybrid neuro-fuzzy network is built and trained, representing a prediction function. It is applied to the test set and a prediction error is obtained, which is used by the genetic algorithm internal operators. Models with smaller errors are the fittest.

At the end of the evolutionary process, the best model(s) are obtained and if the test errors are acceptable, they represent meaningful dependencies within the multivariate process. Evolutionary algorithms can't guarantee the global optimum, thus, the models found can be seen only as plausible descriptors of important relationships present in the data set. Other neural networks based on the same model may have better approximation capabilities. In this sense, the proposed scheme should be seen as giving a *coarse* prediction operator. The advantage is the speed with which hundreds of thousands of models can be explored and tested (not possible with other neural networks). Once the best models are found, more powerful function approximators can be obtained with other types of neural networks, fuzzy systems, or other techniques. This method depends

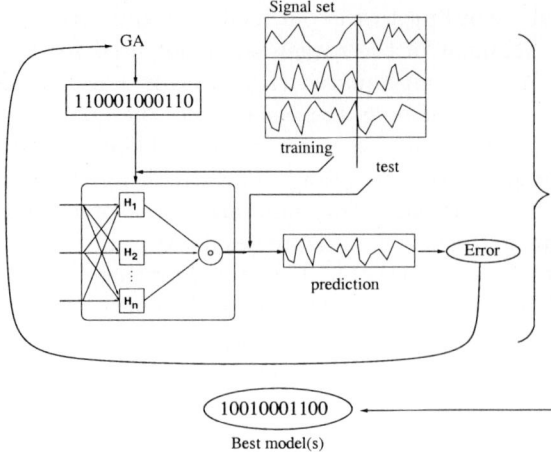

Fig. 3. System architecture.

on different parameters which must be defined in advance (the similarity function, the similarity threshold, etc). In order to account for an optimal selection of these parameters, meta-evolutionary paradigms like the one outlined in Fig-4 are relevant. The outermost genetic structure explores the space of problem parameters.

3 Parallel Implementation

The hybrid nature of the soft-computing method described in the previous section allows several different approaches for constructing parallel and distributed computer implementations. Hierarchically, several levels can be distinguished: the evolutionary algorithm (the genetic algorithm in this case) operates on a least squared type functional containing a neuro-fuzzy network. In turn, inside the network there are neuron layers, which themselves involve the work of individual neurons (h-neurons and classical). Finally, inside each neuron, a similarity function is evaluated on the input and the weight vector in a componentwise operation (e.g. a correlation, a distance metric, or other function). All of these are typical cases of the workcrew computation paradigm at different levels of *granularity*. Clearly, a completely parallel algorithm could be ultimately constructed by parallelizing all levels traversing the entire hierarchy. This approach however, will impose a big amount of communication overhead between the physical computation elements, especially in the case of Beowulf clusters (the most affordable supercomputer platform). Following the principle of parsimony, the implementation was done at the highest granularity level in the genetic algorithm, namely at the population evaluation level (clearly, other operations can be parallelized within the other steps of the genetic algorithm like selection, etc.). The classical

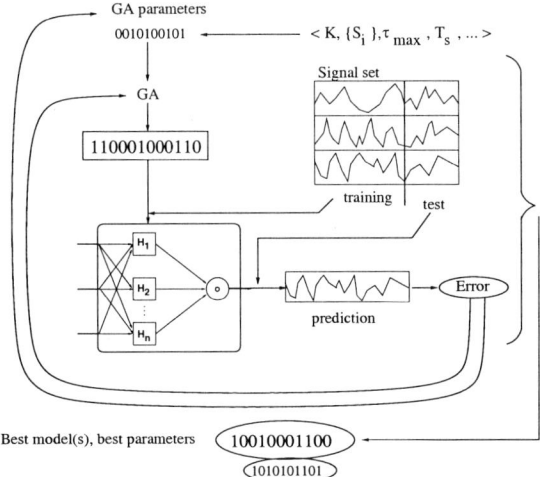

Fig. 4. Meta-genetic algorithm architecture. The outermost genetic structure explores the space of problem parameters and the inner process finds the best model(s) for a given set of them.

type of genetic algorithm chosen (with binary chromosomes, simple crossover and mutation, etc) makes the population initialization and evaluation steps a natural first choice. The evaluation of a population involves the parallel evaluation of all its individuals (models) which can be done in parallel. At this level, there is a high degree of parallelism. A master-slave computation structure is employed, where the master initializes and controls the overall process, collecting the partial results, and the slaves construct the neuro-fuzzy network based on the decoded chromosome, and evaluate it on the time series. In our implementation, the workload is managed dynamically, so that the load is well balanced in a heterogeneous cluster environment. The communication overhead was reduced by replicating the data set on all the machines in the cluster. Thus, the master program is relieved from sending a copy of the entire data set to each slave program each time a model has to be evaluated. Messages sent to the slaves are binary chromosomes, while messages received back by the master contain only a single floating point number with the RMS error associated with the chromosome (model).

The Parallel Virtual Machine PVM [5] message passing system (version 3.4) has been used, with GaLib 2.4 [12] as the general genetic algorithm library. The same source code corresponding to the previously described parallel implementation was compiled with the g++ compiler in two different distributed environments, both being Beowulf clusters running Red Hat Linux 7.2 and connected with an EtherFast-100 ethernet switch (Linksys):

- a two-node cluster (ht-cluster), with a Pentium III processor (1000 MHz, 512 MB RAM), and an AMD Athlon processor (750 Mhz, 256 MB RAM).

– a 4 CPU homogeneous cluster (HG-cluster), with two dual Xeon processor (2 GHz, 1 GB RAM) DELL Workstations.

Both clusters were benchmarked with an off-the-shelf Poisson solver giving the following results: (i) ht-cluster: 68.59 MFlops for Pentium III, 111.58 MGlops for Athlon, 180.17 MFlops total; (ii) HG-cluster: 218.5 MFlops/CPU, 874 MFlops total.

3.1 Example

The parallel implementation was tested using the Sunspot prediction one dimensional problem [7]. This univariate process describes the American relative sunspot numbers (mean number of sunspots for the corresponding months in the period 1/1945 – 12/1994), from AAVSO - Solar Division [12]. It contains 600 observations, and in this case, the first 400 were used as training and the remaining 200 for testing. A maximum time lag of 30 years was pre-set, defining a search space size of 2^{30} models.

No preprocessing was applied to the time series. This is not the usual way to analyze time series data, but by eliminating additional effects, the properties of the proposed procedure in terms of approximation capacity and robustness are better exposed. The similarity function used was $\mathcal{S} = (1/(1+d))$, where d is a normalized euclidean distance. The number of responsive h-neurons in the hidden layer was set to $k = 7$, and the similarity threshold for the h-neurons was $T = 1$. No attempt to optimize these parameters was made, but meta-algorithms can be used for this purpose.

The experiments have been conducted with the following set of genetic algorithm parameters: number of generations = 2, population size = 100, mutation probability = 0.01, crossover probability = 0.9. Single point crossover and single bit mutation were used as genetic operators with roulette selection and elitism being allowed.

The performance of the two clusters w.r.t the parallel algorithm is illustrated in table 1.

As an illustration of the effectiveness of the method, a run with 2000 generations and 50 individuals per population was made. The best model found contained 10 time lags, namely: (t-1), (t-2), (t-4), (t-10), (t-12), (t-14), (t-16), (t-20), (t-28), (t-29). Its RMS prediction error in the test set was 20.45, and the real and predicted values are shown in Fig 5.

4 Conclusions

Time series model mining using evolutionary algorithms and similarity-based neuro-fuzzy networks with h-neurons is flexible, robust and fast. Its parallel implementation runs well on inexpensive Beowulf clusters, making intensive data mining in time series affordable. This method is appropriate for the exploratory stages in the study of multivariate time varying processes for quickly finding

Table 1. ht-cluster and HG-cluster performance

No. slaves	No. CPUs	Time(secs) Time(secs)	Ratio (2 CPU/ 1 CPU)	Time(secs) Time(secs)	Ratio (4 CPU/ 2 CPU)
1	2	117	0.991	60	1
	4	116		60	
2	2	120	0.642	60	0.45
	4	77		27	
3	2	116	0.689	61	0.377
	4	80		23	
4	2	120	0.658	60	0.467
	4	79		28	
5	2	116	0.672	60	0.45
	4	78		27	

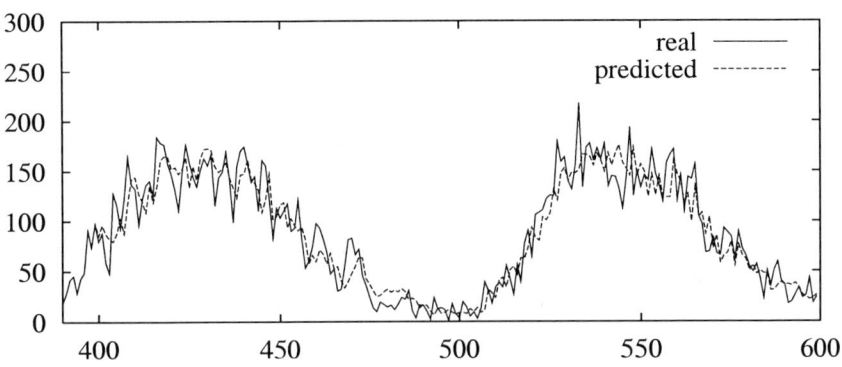

Fig. 5. Comparison of the real and predicted values for sunspot data (test set).

plausible dependency models and hidden interactions between time dependent heterogeneous sets of variables, possibly with missing data. The dependency structure is approximated or narrowed down to a manageable set of plausible models. These models can be used by other methods such as neural networks or non-soft-computing approaches for constructing more accurate prediction operators.

Many parallel implementations of this methodology are possible. Among many elements to be considered are: deeper granularity in the parallelization, use of other chromosome schemes for model representation, variations in the type of genetic algorithm used (steady state, mixed populations, different crossover, mutation and selection operators, etc.), use of other kinds of evolutionary algorithms (evolution strategies, ant colony methods, etc.), variations in the neuro-fuzzy paradigm (kind of h-neuron used, its parameters, the network architecture, etc), the sizes of the training and test set, the maximum exploration time-depth window. These considerations make meta-evolutionary algorithms an attractive approach, introducing a higher hierarchical level of granularity. Furthermore, the intrinsic parallelism of the algorithms allows for efficient parallel implementations. The results presented are promising but should be considered preliminary. Further experiments, research and comparisons with other approaches are required.

Acknowledgments. The authors are very grateful to Alan Barton and Robert Orchard from the Integrated Reasoning Group, Institute for Information Technology, National Research Council of Canada. A. Barton made insightful comments and suggestions, while R. Orchard gave his big understanding and support for this project.

References

1. Belanche, Ll.: Heterogeneous neural networks: Theory and applications. PhD Thesis, Department of Languages and Informatic Systems, Polytechnic University of Catalonia, Barcelona, Spain, July, (2000)
2. Birx, D., Pipenberg, S.: Chaotic oscillators and complex mapping feedforward networks for signal detection in noisy environment. Int. Joint Conf. On Neural Networks (1992)
3. Box, G., Jenkins, G.: Time Series Analysis, Forecasting and Control. Holden-Day. (1976)
4. Chandon, J.L., Pinson, S.: Analyse Typologique. Théorie et Applications. Masson, Paris, (1981)
5. Gueist, A., et.al.: PVM. Parallel Virtual Machine. Users Guide and Tutorial for Networked Parallel Computing. MIT Press 02142, (1994)
6. Lapedes, A., Farber, R.: Nonlinear signal processing using neural networks: prediction and system modeling. Tech. Rep. LA-UR-87-2662, Los Alamos National Laboratory, NM, (1987)
7. Masters, T.: Neural, Novel & Hybrid Algorithms for Time Series Prediction. John Wiley & Sons, (1995)
8. Specht, D.: Probabilistic Neural Networks, Neural Networks **3**. (1990), 109–118
9. Valdés, J.J., García, R.: A model for heterogeneous neurons and its use in configuring neural networks for classification problems. Proc. IWANN'97, Int. Conf. On Artificial and Natural Neural Networks. Lecture Notes in Computer Science **1240**, Springer Verlag, (1997), 237–246
10. Valdés, J.J., Belanche, Ll., Alquézar, R.: Fuzzy heterogeneous neurons for imprecise classification problems. Int. Jour. Of Intelligent Systems, **15** (3), (2000), 265–276.
11. Valdés, J.J.: Similarity-based Neuro-Fuzzy Networks and Genetic Algorithms in Time Series Models Discovery. NRC/ERB-1093, 9 pp. NRC 44919. (2002)
12. Wall, T.: GaLib: A C++ Library of Genetic Algorith Components. Mechanical Engineering Dept. MIT (http://lancet.mit.edu/ga/), (1996)
13. Zadeh, L.: The role of soft computing and fuzzy logic in the conception, design and deployment of intelligent systems. Proc. Sixth Int IEEE Int. Conf. On Fuzzy Systems, Barcelona, July 1–5, (1997)

Closeness of Performance Map Information Granules: A Rough Set Approach

James J. Alpigini

Penn State Great Valley School of Graduate Professional Studies
30 East Swedesford Road, Malvern, PA 19355, USA
jja7@psu.edu

Abstract. This article introduces a rough set approach to measuring of information granules derived from performance maps. A performance map employs intuitive color-coding to visualize the behavior of system dynamics resulting from variations in system parameters. The resulting image is developed algorithmically via digital computation. With only moderate à priori knowledge, mathematical analysis of a performance map provides an immediate wealth of information. This study is motivated by an interest in measuring the separation between "islands" (collections of pixels with the same color) representing normal (e.g., black pixels) and potentially chaotic (e.g., red pixels) system behavior. A performance map island or sector is identified with groupings of cells in a mesh resulting from the partition of a performance map into equivalence classes. The information granules considered in this paper are associated with a feature set in an information system. The contribution of this article is the application of a measures of granule closeness based on an indistinguishability relation that partitions performance maps intervals into subintervals (equivalence classes). Such partitions are useful in measuring closeness of map cells containing color-coded pixels used to visualize dynamical system behavior.

Keywords. Closeness, indistinguishability, information granule, measure, performance map, rough sets.

1 Introduction

This article introduces an approach to measures of a particular class of information granules based on rough set theory [1], namely, granules derived from performance maps [7]-[9]. A performance map is an adaptation of the Julia set method that makes it possible to visualize control and other dynamic systems [9]. Such a map produces colored pixels that reflect the dynamic performance of the system across intervals of system parameters. Such a technique addresses the problem of visualizing automatically the state values of some system as its parameters are varied. Julia sets are fractals with shapes that are generated by iteration of simple complex mappings [12]. The term fractal was introduced by Mandelbrot in 1982 to denote sets with fractured structure. This article suggests a solution to the problem of measuring the separation between clusters of pixels representing normal and potentially chaotic system behavior.

The study of information granule construction and measurement is extensive (see, e.g., [2]-[5], [10]). This paper is limited to a consideration of measure of closeness of a particular class of information granules (collections of pixels in a performance map). Such a measure can be calibrated. A parameter δ in the definition of the relation Ing makes it possible to adjust the coarseness or "granularity" of a partition of the subinterval of reals (universe) over which sensor signals are classified. This parameter provides a basis for training an approximate reasoning system relative to particular forms of sensor signal samples. Hence, such a measure has been used in the design of neurons in rough neural networks (see, e.g., [6]). Measurement of information granules has been motivated by recent studies of sensor signals [2], [10]. The contribution of this article is the application of a measure of closeness of information granules in the context of clusters of similar pixels in performance maps.

This paper is organized as follows. Section 2 presents gives an overview of performance maps. Section 3 briefly presents a parameterized indistinguishability relation and proposes an approach to measurements of closeness of information granules contained in performance maps.

2 Performance Maps

The performance map technique is ultimately derived from the familiar Julia set that is used to visualize the dynamics of iterative chaotic formulae [9]. By visualizing automatically, the state values of a system as a pair of its parameters are varied, the method produces a color-coded *performance map*, PM, which reflects the dynamic performance of the system across intervals of system parameters. A PM is generated via digital computation using rules appropriate to the system for which dynamic behavior is being visualized. The generation of a PM begins with a pixel mapping and color scheme selection. The pixel mapping for a PM reflects the problem domain, e.g., a pair of system parameters. Intervals of system parameters, say parameters a and b, are mapped to a computer screen that represents the parameter plane of the system. Consider, for example, the system initially investigated by Rubio et al [11] and modified to include both parameters and a sinusoidal driving force (see Fig. 1) where $r(t) = \sin(\omega \cdot t)$, and $x(t)=$ computed output, $a, b, c, \omega=$ parameters. The system exhibits parametrically dependent chaotic motion for both non-zero initial conditions without external perturbation ($r(t) = 0$), and also when using the sinusoidal driving function. Such aperiodic unstable oscillations in a state value can be well detected with a fire/nofire performance rule by triggering on the numerical first difference, while simple magnitude tests may be sufficient to detect undesired state values. The parameters of the system are (a,b,c,ω) with pixel mapping performed for intervals of any two of the four parameters while holding the remaining parameters constant. With the performance rule established, the system is then exercised for each pixel, using a common set of initial conditions, and the pixels are colored according to the result of the rule test.

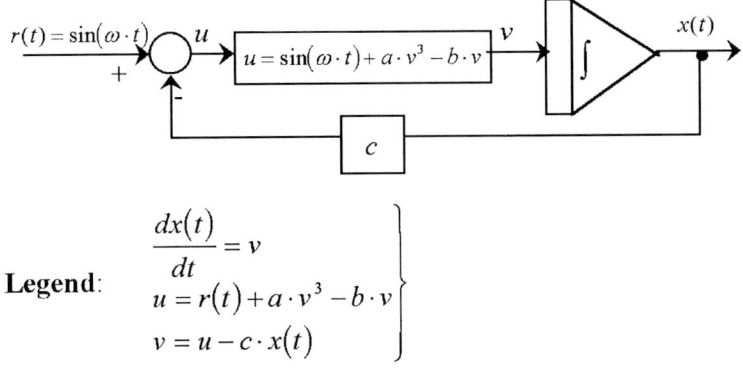

Fig. 1. Block diagram of nonlinear system

The color codes employed for a performance map are arbitrary. For each pixel, i.e. set of parameter values, the system is integrated numerically for a fixed time period, using a common set of initial conditions. The pixel is then colored based on evaluation of the dynamic behavior of the system using intuitively selected *performance rules*. A "fire/nofire" type rule will *fire* if a programmed *trigger* condition such as the onset of chaotic motion is satisfied during a dynamical system simulation. A sample performance map of a nonlinear system is shown in Fig. 3. The map is generated for intervals of parameters a and b, while holding parameters c and ω constant. The color black is assigned if no chaotic motion is detected. The color white is assigned at the onset of instability, and other colors are assigned to reflect the relative time, with respect to the maximum number of integration steps, with which a performance rule fired.

3 Indistinguishability and Set Approximation

A straightforward extension of the traditional indiscernibility relation [1] in partitioning of uncountable sets (reals) is given in this section (see, e.g., [10]). That is, consider a universe that is a subset of the reals, where traditional set approximation and measurement can be carried out relative to partitions of the universe into equivalence classes. This partition is accomplished using what we call an indistinguishability relation.

3.1 Indistinguishability Relation

To begin, let $S = (U, A)$ be an information system where U is a non-empty set and A is a non-empty, finite set of attributes, where $a : U \to V_a$ and $V_a \subseteq \Re$ for

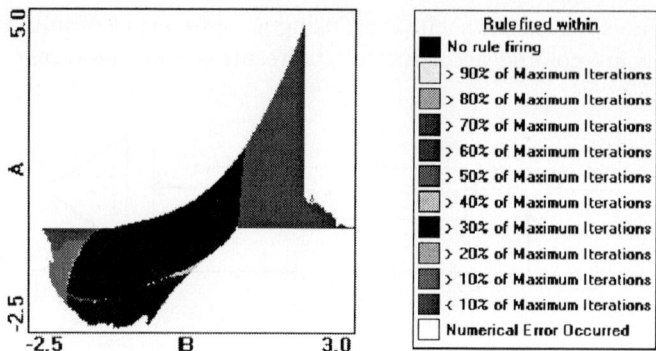

Fig. 2. Performance map

every $a \in A$, so that $\Re \supseteq V = \bigcup_{a \in A} V_a$. Let $a(x) \geqslant 0$, $\delta > 0$ and let $\lfloor a(x)/\delta \rfloor$ denotes the greatest integer less than or equal to $a(x)/\delta$ ("floor" of a(x)/δ). Reals representing sensor measurements within the same subinterval bounded by $k\delta$ and $(k+1)\delta$ for integer k are considered δ-indistinguishable.

Definition 1. For each $B \subseteq A$, there is associated an equivalence relation $\mathrm{Ing}_{A,\delta}(B)$ defined in (1).

$$\mathrm{Ing}_{A,\delta}(B) = \{(x,x') \in \Re^2 \,|\, \forall a \in B. \lfloor a(x)/\delta \rfloor = \lfloor a(x')/\delta \rfloor\} \quad (1)$$

$\mathrm{Ing}_{A,\delta} B \cup \mathit{Id}$ is an equivalence relation. A subscript Id denotes a set consisting of the identity sensor $id(x) = x$. The identity sensor id has been introduced to avoid the situation where there is more then one stimuli for which a sensor takes the same value. The notation $[x]^{\delta}_{B \cup Id}$ denotes equivalence classes of $\mathrm{Ing}_{A,\delta}$ $(B \cup \mathit{Id})$. Further, partition $U/\,\mathrm{Ing}_{A,\delta}(B \cup \mathit{Id})$ denotes the family of all equivalence classes of relation $\mathrm{Ing}_{A,\delta}$ $(B \cup \mathit{Id})$ on U. For $X \subseteq U$, the set X can be approximated only from information contained in B by constructing a B-lower and a B-upper approximation denoted by $\underline{B}X$ and $\overline{B}X$, respectively. The B-lower approximation of X is the set $\underline{B}X = \{x \,|\, [x]^{\delta}_{B \cup Id} \subseteq X\}$ and the B-upper approximation of X is the set $\overline{B}X = \{x \,|\, [x]^{\delta}_{B \cup Id} \cap X \neq \emptyset\}$. In cases where we need to reason about a sensor reading y instead of stimulus x, we introduce an equivalence class consisting of all points for which sensor readings are 'close' to y and define $[y]^{\delta}_{B \cup Id} = [x]^{\delta}_{B \cup Id}$ for x such that $a(x) = y$.

$$[y']^{0.1}_{\{a\} \cup Id} = \{x' \in U \,|\, \lfloor x'/0.1 \rfloor = \lfloor x/0.1 \rfloor \wedge \lfloor y'/0.1 \rfloor = \lfloor a(x')/0.1 \rfloor\}$$

Assume $\lfloor y'/0.1 \rfloor \in [n \cdot 0.1, (n+1) \cdot 0.1)$ and $\lfloor x/0.1 \rfloor \in [m \cdot 0.1, (m+1) \cdot 0.1)$, for some m, n, and obtain (2).

$$[y']^{0.1}_{\{a\} \cup Id} = \{x' \in U \,|\, \lfloor x'/0.1 \rfloor = m \wedge \lfloor y'/0.1 \rfloor = n\} \quad (2)$$

For simplicity, let N_n denote the interval $[n \cdot 0.1, (n+1) \cdot 0.1)$, let M_m denote the interval $[m \cdot 0.1, (m+1) \cdot 0.1)$. In addition, let $E_{n,m}$ denote the equivalence class given in (2), where n, m denote integers. In the following sections, we write $[y]_B^\delta$ instead of $[y]_{B \cup Id}^\delta$ because we consider only sensor values relative to partitions of the universe using $Ing_{A,\delta}(B)$. The partition of U that results from an application of the δ-indistinguishability relation is called a δ-mesh.

Example 1. An example of a δ-mesh superimposed on a time graph exhibiting the behavior of a non-linear system is shown in Fig. 3. Consider, next, a mesh superimposed on a time graph limited to a plot of parameters x and v, where a = 0.2, b = 2, c = 0.2, w = 1, x_0 = -1.75, v_0 = -0.78, u_0 = 1. For such an information system and its partition $U/Ing_{A,\delta}(B)$, let $d(E_{n1,m1}, E_{n2,m2}) = max \{|n_1 - n_2|, |m_1 - m_2|\}$ (distance metric). The distance between two equivalence classes containing values of parameter v where high oscillation begins (i.e., $E_{2,2}$ and $E_{5,-2}$) as shown in Fig. 4 (this illustrates measurement of closeness of clusters of parameter values).

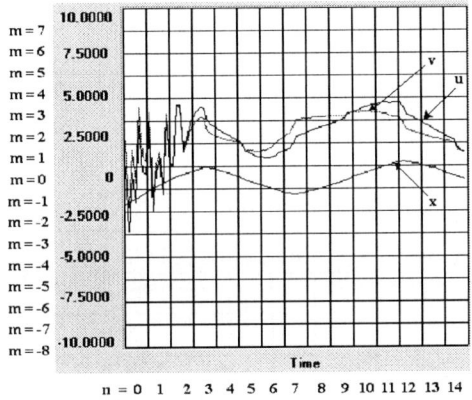

Fig. 3. Sample δ-mesh

Example 2. An example of a δ-mesh superimposed on a performance map exhibiting the behavior of a non-linear system is shown in Fig. 5. Figure 5 shows how the maximum metric measures distance. For example, $d(E_{2,0}, E_{5,3})=\max\{|5-2|,|3-0|\}=3$ between equivalence classes $E_{2,0}$ and $E_{5,3}$ may be of interest in cases where measurement of the separation between clusters of sample sensor values is important (e.g., separation of cells in a mesh covering a control system performance map that contains "islands" of system response values, some normal and some verging on chaotic behavior as in [7]). The mesh in 5 suggests the following measurement problems that can yield useful information for the designer of a dynamical system.

1. Distances between "no-fire" and "fire" cells. The measurements are "rough" (not crisp) because they are made relative to δ-indistinguishability classes.
2. Identify clusters of points (pixels) representing "no-fire" and "fire" conditions.

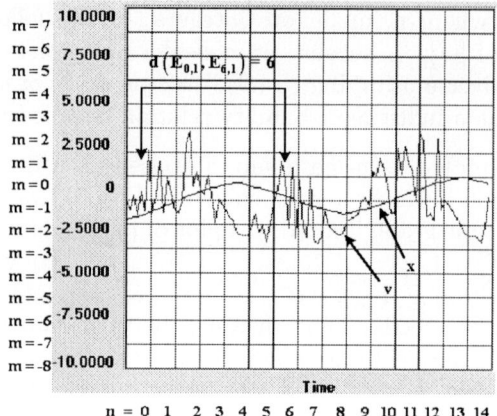

Fig. 4. Separation between oscillation granules

The interesting clusters would start in mesh cells with black (see examples in Fig. 5) bordering on cells containing red.

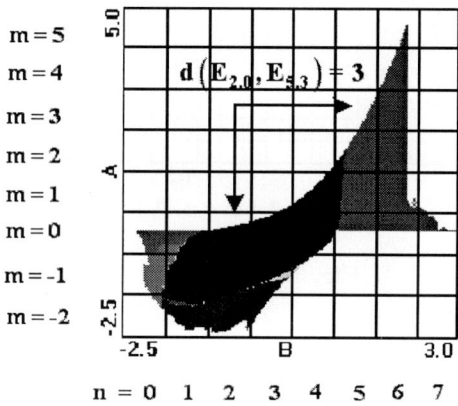

Fig. 5. Distance between PM mesh cells

4 Conclusion

An approach to measurements of closeness of information granules contained in performance maps and time graphs exhibiting the behavior of dynamical systems have been presented in this paper. The indistinguishability relation Ing has been used to identify elements that are considered "indistinguishable" from each other because the elements belong to the same subinterval of reals. The partition of a universe using Ing results in a mesh of cells (called a δ-mesh), where each cell of the mesh represents an equivalence class. The configuration of cells in a δ-mesh yields a useful granule measure for performance maps as well as time graphs. That is, a measure of closeness of a pair of information granules contained in cells of the δ-mesh results from determining the number of cells separating members of the pair using a distance metric. In future work, an algorithm for finding an appropriate δ used to construct a δ-mesh for performance map cells will be investigated. The selection of δ is important in finding clusters of related (same color) pixels in a performance map.

References

1. Z. Pawlak, *Rough Sets: Theoretical Aspects of Reasoning About Data*, Boston, MA, Kluwer Academic Publishers, 1991.
2. J.F. Peters, A. Skowron, Z. Suraj, W. Rzasa, M. Borkowski, Clustering: A rough set approach to constructing information granules. In: Z. Suraj (Ed.), Soft Computing and Distributed Processing (SCDP'02), Rzeszów, Poland, 24–25 June 2002 [to appear].
3. A. Skowron, Toward intelligent systems: Calculi of information granules. In: S. Hirano, M. Inuiguchi, S. Tsumoto (Eds.), Bulletin of the International Rough Set Society, vol. 5, no. 1 / 2, 2001, 9–30.
4. A. Skowron, J. Stepaniuk, J.F. Peters, Extracting patterns using information granules. In: S. Hirano, M. Inuiguchi, S. Tsumoto (Eds.), Bulletin of the International Rough Set Society, vol. 5, no. 1 / 2, 2001, 135-142.
5. A. Skowron, J. Stepaniuk, J.F. Peters, Hierarchy of information granules. In: H.D. Burkhard, L. Czaja, H.S. Nguyen, P. Starke (Eds.), *Proc. of the Workshop on Concurrency, Specification and Programming*, Oct. 2001, Warsaw, Poland , 254–268.
6. J.F. Peters, T.C. Ahn, M. Borkowski, V. Degtyaryov, S. Ramanna, Line-crawling robot navigation: A rough neurocomputing approach. In: D. Maravall, D. Zhou (Eds.), Fusion of Soft Computing and Hard Computing Techniques for Autonomous Robotic Systems. Studies in Fuzziness and Soft Computing, J. Kacprzyk (Ed.). Berlin: Physica-Verlag, 2002 [to appear].
7. J.J. Alpigini, J.F. Peters, Dynamic visualization with rough performance maps. In: W.Ziarko, Y.Yao (Eds.), Rough Sets and Current Trends in Computing, Lectures Notes in Artificial Intelligence 2005. Berlin: Springer-Verlag, 2001, 90–97.
8. J.J. Alpigini, The evaluation and visualization of system performance in chaotic dynamical systems. *Information Sciences*, Volume 127 (3-4), 2000, 173–192.
9. J.J. Alpigini, A Paradigm for the Visualization of Dynamic System Performance Using Methodologies Derived from Chaos Theory, Ph.D. Thesis, University of Wales, Swansea, UK, 1999.
10. J.F. Peters, A. Skowron, Z. Suraj, M. Borkowski, W. Rzasa, Measures of closeness and inclusion of information granules: A rough set approach. In: RSCTC'02 [to appear].
11. F.R. Rubio, J. Aracil, E.F. Camacho, Chaotic Motion in an Adaptive Control System, *International Journal of Control*, vol. 42 (2), 1985, 353–360.
12. G. Julia, Memoire sur l'iteration des fonctions rationnelles. J. de Math., vol. 8, 1918, 47–245.

Granular Computing on Binary Relations
Analysis of Conflict and Chinese Wall Security Policy

Tsau Young ("T.Y.") Lin

Department of Mathematics and Computer Science
San Jose State University, San Jose, California 95192
tylin@cs.sjsu.edu

Abstract. In this paper, a study of the granular computing on binary relations is presented. The result is applied to the analysis of conflict of interests relation(CIR) and the Chinese wall security policy (CWSP).

Keywords: Chinese wall security policy, binary relation, conflict of interests

1 Introduction

Granular computing [8] has been proved to be a powerful methodology. In this paper, we focus on binary relations, and apply it to computer security.

In 1989 IEEE Symposium on Security and Privacy, Brewer and Nash proposed a very intriguing security model, called the Chinese Wall Security Policy (CWSP) [1]. The essential idea was based on their formal analysis on the conflict of interests classes; unfortunately, they oversimplified the situation by erroneously assuming a granulation were a partition of data. Later in the same year, we re-presented their idea in terms of granulation, not partition. The resulting model was called an aggressive Chinese wall security policy model (ACWSP) [2]. The expected crisp-ness and sharp-ness on the locations of Chinese walls, contributed from the partitioning of data, is no longer presented. In practice, we do need to Chinese wall (an impenetrable fire wall) to perform a correct separation of data. In [4], we fuzzify the boundary so there are rooms for errors.

In [3], we observe that granular and rough computing appear in pair. In other words, each granule has a center, and the collection of all these centers forms a partition. Based on this phenomena, in this paper, we show that some crisp-ness and sharp-ness ACWSP can be captured.

Totally from different context, Pawlak, in his best paper award acceptance speech at 1998 JCIS, outlined an approach to conflict analysis [5,6]. His goals are different from the security community; however the methodologies do overlap: Three values, "conflict, alliance and neutrality," considered by Pawlak are similar to two relations, CIR and IAR ("conflict of interests" and "in ally with" relations) considered in ACWSP.

2 Granular Computing on Binary Relations

A binary relation is a subset, $R \subseteq V \times V$. For each object $p \in V$, we associate a set $N_p = \{v \in V \mid p \, R \, v\}$, called a binary neighborhood. If the binary relation is an equivalence relation, then N_p is the equivalence class containing p. In stead of using a binary relation, we can define neighborhoods directly, that is, we can consider a map, $B : V \longrightarrow 2^V$, called binary granulation. The collection of the images $B(p)$ is called a binary neighborhood system. It is easy to check that binary relation (BR), binary neighborhood system(BNS) or binary granulation(BG) are equivalent.

2.1 The Induced Rough Computing

In this section, we will recall some result from [3]: Given a map $g : V \longrightarrow W$, one can consider the collection, $\{g^{-1}(w) \mid w \in W\}$, of all inverse image of w under g. The collection forms a partition on V. Since a binary granulation (BG, BR, BNS) is a map, we have a partition, called the induced partition (equivalence relation) of B, and denoted by E_B. The equivalence class, $[p]_{E_B} = B^{-1}(B_p)$, is called the *center* of B_p (we will drop the subscript, if no confusing may occur). It is immediate that the center $[p]$ consists of all those points that have (are mapped to) the same set $B_p \subseteq V$.

In [7], Polkowski, Skowron, and Zytkow investigated rough sets theory of symmetric binary relations; They also found an equivalence relation. However, the method is rather complicated; it is unclear at this point how our result is related to theirs.

3 Symmetric Binary Granulation

Let us recall some definitions. A binary relation B is *anti-reflexive*, if B is non-empty and no pair (v, v) is in B. That is, $B \cap \Delta = \emptyset$, where $\Delta = \{(v,v) \mid v \in V\}$ is called diagonal set. A binary relation B is *anti-transitive*, if B is non-empty and if (u, v) belongs to B implies that for all w either (u, w) or (w, v) belongs to B. The set complement, $B' = V \times V \sim B$, is called the complement binary relation (CBR) of B.

Proposition 1. E_B is a refinement of symmetric B, that is, each B-binary neighborhood is a union of E_B-equivalence classes.

Proof: Let B_p be a binary neighborhood and x a point in it. Assume y is E_B-equivalent to x. By definition, $B_x = B_y$. Since B is symmetric $x \in B_p$ implies $p \in B_x = B_y$, and hence $y \in B_p$. Since y is arbitrary, so $[x] \subseteq B_p$, that is B_p contains the equivalence class $[x]$ of its member x. QED

Mathematically this proposition is the best possible; we skip the example.

Proposition 2. If B is symmetric, anti-reflexive and anti-symmetric, then B' is an equivalence relation.

Proof: B is anti-reflexive, B' is reflexive. Assume (u,w) and (w,v) are in B', that is, (u,w) and (w,v) do not belong to B, then by anti-transitive, (u,v) does not belong to B either (that is, $(u,v) \in B'$); QED

Proposition 3. If B is symmetric, anti-reflexive and anti-transitive, then B' is E_B.

Proof: Let B_v be the binary neighborhood of v. We *claim*: $B' \subseteq E_B$.

To show the claim, first, we need to prove $B_v \subseteq B_u$, if $(u,v) \in B'$. Let $p \in B_v$, that is, $(v,p) \in B$. By anti-transitive and symmetry, $(u,p) \in B$ (otherwise, $(u,v) \in B$; which is absurd). That is, $p \in B_u$, and hence $B_v \subseteq B_u$. Bt reversing the role of u and v; we get $B_u \subseteq B_v$. This conclude that $B' \subseteq E_B$.

To prove the reverse inclusion, note that $(u,v) \in E_B$ implies $B_u = B_v$. Let $p \in B_u(= B_v)$, that is, both (u,p) and (p,v) belong to B. By anti-transitivity and symmetric, (u,v) belongs to B'. So we have $E_B \subseteq B'$. QED

4 The Axioms on the Conflict Interests Relations (CIR)

Though Brewer and Nash's intuitive idea was an attracting one, their model made an erroneously assumption that CIR were as equivalence relation. ACWSP) was based on CIR-1, -2, and -3 axioms (see below). In this paper, a new observation is added; the data can be partitioned by induced equivalence relation.

For convenience of readers, we recall and modify some of our earlier analysis: Let O be a set of objects; an object is a dataset of a company. We observed that, $CIR \subseteq O \times O$ as a binary relation, satisfies the following properties.

CIR-1: CIR is symmetric.
CIR-2: CIR is anti-reflexive.
CIR-3: CIR is anti-transitive.
CIR-4: The granulation of CIR and partition of E_{CIR} are compatible; see Proposition 1.
CIR-5 (IAR): The complement of CIR, "in ally with"-relation (IAR), is an equivalence relation and equal to E_{CIR}; see Proposition 3.

We only need CIR-1 to CIR-3, CIR-4 and -5 are added for helpful hints. It should be clear CIR-2 is necessary; a company cannot conflict to itself. If company A is in conflicts with B, B is certainly in conflicts with A, so CIR-1 is valid.

To see CIR-3, let $O = \{USA, UK, USSR\}$ be a set of three countries. Let CIR be "in cold war with". If the relation "in cold war with" were transitive, then the following two statements, (1) USA is in cold war with USSR. (2) USSR is in cold war with UK, would imply that (3) USA is in cold war with UK. Obviously, this is absurd. In fact this argument is applicable to any country; In other words, (2) and (3) cannot be both true for any country (that replaces UK). So we have anti-transitivity for CIR.

In [2], we placed the Chinese walls on the boundary of a CIR-neighborhood, this new axiom, CIR-4, implies that that such a boundary is actually on the boundary of some unions of E_{CIR}-equivalence classes. In terms of Pawlk's approach, CIR is the subset taking the value "conflict." IAR is the subset that takes values alliance or neutrality.

5 A New View of Chinese Wall Security Policy

The phenomena that granular and rough computing appear in pairs gives a new insight into ACWSP; Chinese walls are precise located on some boundaries of E_{CIR}-partition. Once a agent S_i has accessed an object O_j, the only other objects O_k accessible by S_i is inside the allied dataset of O_j which is exactly the outside of CIR_{O_j}. We rephrase the main result from [2] and [1].

THEOREM. The flow of unsanitized information is confined to its allied dataset; sanitized information may, however, flow freely through the system.

6 Conclusions

The intuitive idea behind Brewer and Nash theory is a correct idea for commercial security, in particular eCommerce. In [4], we fuzzify the ACWSP model making it more susceptible to uncertainty. In this paper, we use the observation that to each granular computing, there is an induced rough computing (See Section 2.1) to strength the ACWSP model. That is, the Chinese walls are always siting on a crisp boundary.

References

1. David D. C. Brewer and Michael J. Nash: "The Chinese Wall Security Policy" IEEE Symposium on Security and Privacy, Oakland, May, 1988, pp. 206–214,
2. T. Y. Lin, "Chinese Wall Security Policy–An Aggressive Model", Proceedings of the Fifth Aerospace Computer Security Application Conference, December 4–8, 1989, pp 286–293.
3. T. Y. Lin "Granular Computing on Binary Relations I: Data Mining and Neighborhood Systems." In: Rough Sets In Knowledge Discovery, A. Skoworn and L. Polkowski (eds), Physica-Verlag, 1998, 107–121
4. T. Y. Lin "Chinese Wall Security Model and Conflict Analysis," the 24th IEEE Computer Society International Computer Software and Applications Conference (Compsac2000) Taipei, Taiwan, Oct 25–27, 2000
5. Z. Pawlak, "On Conflicts," Int J. of Man-Machine Studies, 21 pp. 127–134, 1984
6. Z. Pawlak, Analysis of Conflicts, Joint Conference of Information Science, Research Triangle Park, North Carolina, March 1-5, 1997, 350–352.
7. Polkowski, L., Skowron, A., and Zytkow, J., (1995), Tolerance based rough sets. In: T.Y. Lin and A. Wildberger (eds.), Soft Computing: Rough Sets, Fuzzy Logic Neural Networks, Uncertainty Management, Knowledge Discovery, Simulation Councils, Inc. San Diego CA, 1995, 55–58.
8. Lotfi A. Zadeh "Some Reflections on Information Granulation and its Centrality in Granular Computing, Computing with Words, the Computational Theory of Perceptions and Precisiated Natural Language," In: Data Mining, Rough Sets and Granular Computing, T. Y. Lin, Y. Y. Yao, L. Zadeh (eds), Physica-Verlag, 2002.

Measures of Inclusion and Closeness of Information Granules: A Rough Set Approach

James F. Peters[1], Andrzej Skowron[2], Zbigniew Suraj[3], Maciej Borkowski[1], and Wojciech Rząsa[4]

[1] Department of Electrical and Computer Engineering, University of Manitoba
Winnipeg, Manitoba R3T 5V6 Canada,
jfpeters@ee.umanitoba.ca
[2] Institute of Mathematics, Warsaw University,
Banacha 2, 02-097 Warsaw, Poland,
skowron@mimuw.edu.pl
[3] Univ. of Information Technology and Management
H. Sucharskiego 2, 35-225 Rzeszów, Poland,
zsuraj@wenus.wsiz.rzeszow.pl
[4] Institute of Mathematics, Rzeszów University
Rejtana 16A 35-310 Rzeszów, Poland,
wrzasa@univ.rzeszow.pl

Abstract. This article introduces an approach to measures of information granules based on rough set theory. The information granules considered in this paper are partially ordered multisets of sample sensor signal values, where it is possible for such granules to contain duplicates of the same values obtained in different moments of time. Such granules are also associated with a feature set in an information system. Information granules considered in this paper are collections of sample values derived from sensors that are modelled as continuous real-valued functions representing analog devices such as proximity (e.g., ultrasonic) sensors. The idea of sampling sensor signals is fundamental, since granule approximations and granule measures are defined relative to non-empty temporally ordered multisets of sample signal values. The contribution of this article is the introduction of measures of granule inclusion and closeness based on an indistinguishability relation that partitions real-valued universes into subintervals (equivalence classes). Such partitions are useful in measuring closeness and inclusion of granules containing sample signal values. The measures introduced in this article lead to the discovery of clusters of sample signal values.

Keywords: Closeness, inclusion, indistinguishability, information granule, measure, rough sets, sensor.

1 Introduction

This article introduces an approach to measures of a particular class of information granules based on rough set theory. Informally, a granule is a multiset (or bag) [19]-[20] of real-world objects that are somehow indistinguishable (e.g., water samples taken from the same source at approximately the same time), or similar (e.g., Chopin concerts), or which have the same functionality (e.g., unmanned helicopters). A multiset is a set where duplicates are counted. Examples of measures of granules are inclusion, closeness, size and enclosure. This paper is limited to a consideration of measures of inclusion based on a straightforward extension of classical rough membership functions [2], and the introduction of a measure of closeness of information granules. Measurement of sensor-based information granules have been motivated by recent studies of sensor signals [3], [5]-[6]. In this article, the term *sensor signal* is a non-empty, finite, discrete multiset of sample (either continuous or continuous) sensor signal values. Sample signal values are collected in temporally ordered multisets (repetitions of the same signal value are counted). In this article, classification of sensor signals is carried out using new forms of set approximation derived from classical rough set theory [1]-[2], [4]. This is made possible by introducing a number of additions to the basic building blocks of rough set theory, namely, (i) parameterized indistinguishability equivalence relation Ing defined relative to elements of an uncountable set, (ii) lower and upper approximation of information granules relative to a partition of an interval of the reals, and (iii) parameterized rough membership set function. A fundamental step in such a classification is a measure of the degree of overlap between a granule of sample sensor signal values and a target granule (collection ideal signal values for an application). Such a measure can be calibrated. A parameter δ in the definition of the relation Ing makes it possible to adjust the courseness or "granularity" of a partition of the subinterval of reals (universe) over which sensor signals are classified. Hence, such a measure has been used in the design of neurons in rough neural networks (see, e.g., [11]).

Granule approximation in this paper is cast in the context of infinite rather than finite universes. This study is motivated by the need to approximate and classify a number of different forms of uncountable sets (e.g., analog sensor signals such as speech, electrocardiograms, electroencephalograms). This is important in the context of parameterized approximation spaces used in designing intelligent systems [10], [12]-[15], [16]-[17], especially [12].

This paper is organized as follows. Section 2 presents introduces the parameterized indistinguishability relation and approximation of sets. This section also introduces a new form of rough membership set function. A natural extension of these ideas is the introduction of a rough measure space. Measurement of rough inclusion of granules is considered in Section 3.

2 Indistinguishability and Set Approximation

2.1 Indistinguishability Relation

To begin, let $S = (U, A)$ be an infinite information system where U is a non-empty set and A is a non-empty, finite set of attributes, where $a : U \to V_a$ and $V_a \subseteq \Re$ for every $a \in A$, so that $\Re \supseteq V = \bigcup_{a \in A} V_a$. Let $a(x) \geq 0$, $\delta > 0$ and let $\lfloor a(x)/\delta \rfloor$ denotes the greatest integer less than or equal to $a(x)/\delta$ ("floor" of a(x)/δ) whilst $\lceil a(x)/\delta \rceil$ denotes the least integer bigger than or equal to $a(x)/\delta$ ("ceiling" of $a(x)/\delta$) for attribute a. If $a(x) < 0$, then $\lfloor a(x)/\delta \rfloor = -\lceil |a(x)|/\delta \rceil$, where $|\bullet|$ denotes the absolute value of $\bullet$. The parameter δ serves as a means of computing a "neighborhood" size on real-valued intervals. Reals representing sensor measurements within the same subinterval bounded by $k\delta$ and $(k+1)\delta$ for integer k are considered δ-indistinguishable.

Definition 1. For each $B \subseteq A$, there is associated an equivalence relation $\text{Ing}_{A,\delta}(B)$ defined in (1).

$$\text{Ing}_{A,\delta}(B) = \{(x,x') \in \Re^2 \,|\, \forall a \in B.\, \lfloor a(x)/\delta \rfloor = \lfloor a(x')/\delta \rfloor\} \quad (1)$$

If $(x,x') \in \text{Ing}_{A,\delta}(B)$, we say that objects x and x' are indistinguishable from each other relative to attributes from B. A subscript Id denotes a set consisting of the identity sensor $id(x) = x$. The identity sensor id has been introduced to avoid the situation where there is more then one stimuli for which a sensor takes the same value (see example in the next section).

From (1), we can write $\text{Ing}_{A,\delta}(B)$ as in (2).

$$\text{Ing}_{A,\delta}(B \cup Id) = \{(x,x') \in \Re^2 \,|\, \lfloor x/\delta \rfloor = \lfloor x'/\delta \rfloor \,\wedge\, \forall a \in B.\, \lfloor a(x)/\delta \rfloor = \lfloor a(x')/\delta \rfloor\} \quad (2)$$

Proposition 1. $\text{Ing}_{A,\delta}(B \cup Id)$ is an equivalence relation.

The notation $[x]^\delta_{B \cup Id}$ denotes equivalence classes of $\text{Ing}_{A,\delta}(B \cup Id)$. Further, partition $U/\text{Ing}_{A,\delta}(B \cup Id)$ denotes the family of all equivalence classes of relation $\text{Ing}_{A,\delta}(B \cup Id)$ on U. For $X \subseteq U$, the set X can be approximated only from information contained in B by constructing a B-lower and a B-upper approximation denoted by $\underline{B}X$ and $\overline{B}X$, respectively. The B-lower approximation of X is the set $\underline{B}X = \{x \,|\, [x]^\delta_{B \cup Id} \subseteq X\}$ and the B-upper approximation of X is the set $\overline{B}X = \{x \,|\, [x]^\delta_{B \cup Id} \cap X \neq \emptyset\}$.

In cases where we need to reason about a sensor reading y instead of stimulus x, we introduce an equivalence class consisting of all points for which sensor readings are 'close' to y and define $[y]^\delta_{B \cup Id} = [x]^\delta_{B \cup Id}$ for x such that $a(x) = y$.

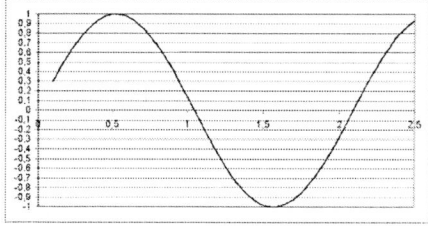

Fig. 1a. Sample Sensor Signal

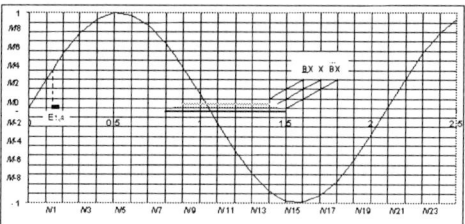

Fig. 1b. Sample approximations plus $E_{1,4}$ for $\delta = 0.1$

2.2 Sample Set Approximation

In this section, we want to consider a sample approximation of sensor stimuli relative to a set of points from a universe (subset of the reals). Consider the following continuous information system $S = (U, A)$, where U is a set of points in a subinterval $[0, 2.5)$, and A is a set of sensors, e.g., $\{a \mid a_k(x) = \sin(kx)$ for $x \in [0, 2.5), k \in Z^+$ (positive integers)$\}$.

Let parameter δ be set to 0.1 and let set $X = [0.85, 1.45]$. We want to consider $B \subset A$ such that $B = \{a_3(x) = \sin(3x)$ for $x \in [0, 2.5)\}$ (see Fig. 1a). A depiction of the upper and lower approximations of X is shown in Fig. 1b. To construct lower approximation, we need to find all δ-indistinguishability classes for $\delta = 0.1$ (sample δ-value). To elaborate using $id(x) = x$, the δ-indistinguishability relation $\text{Ing}_{A,\delta}(B \cup Id)$ in (2) can be instantiated with a specific set B and choice of δ. That is, consider $y' = a(x')$ for some $x' \in U$ (sample universe) and $\delta = 0.1$, and then consider

$$[y']_{\{a\} \cup Id}^{0.1} = \{x' \in U \mid \lfloor x'/0.1 \rfloor = \lfloor x/0.1 \rfloor \wedge \lfloor y'/0.1 \rfloor = \lfloor a(x')/0.1 \rfloor\}$$

Assume $\lfloor y'/0.1 \rfloor \in [n \cdot 0.1, (n+1) \cdot 0.1)$ and $\lfloor x/0.1 \rfloor \in [m \cdot 0.1, (m+1) \cdot 0.1)$, for some m, n, and obtain (3).

$$[y']_{\{a\} \cup Id}^{0.1} = \{x' \in U \mid \lfloor x'/0.1 \rfloor = m \wedge \lfloor y'/0.1 \rfloor = n\} \quad (3)$$

For simplicity, let N_n denote the interval $[n \cdot 0.1, (n+1) \cdot 0.1)$, let M_m denote the interval $[m \cdot 0.1, (m+1) \cdot 0.1)$. In addition, let $E_{n,m}$ denote the equivalence class given in (3), where n, m denote integers. For $y = 0.45$ $a(0.155) = \sin(0.466) = 0.45$ ($0.45 \in N_4, 0.155 \in M_1$) so that $0.155 \in E_{1,4}$ (see Fig. 2). But also $a(0.891) = 0.45$ and $a(2.249) = 0.45$, so $0.891 \in E_{8,4}$ and $2.249 \in E_{22,4}$. For example $E_{1,4} = [0.137, 0.174)$, $E_{1,5} = [0.174, 0.2)$ and $E_{1,6} = \emptyset$ (empty set). $\underline{B}X = \bigcup_{n=0}^{24} \bigcup_{m=-1}^{10} E_{n,m}$ where $E_{n,m} \subseteq X$. Then the 0.1-lower approximation of X is $\underline{B}X = [0.9, 1.4)$. Similarly, we can find upper approximation of X to be $\overline{B}X = [0.8, 1.5)$. In the following sections, we write $[y]_B^\delta$ instead of $[y]_{B \cup Id}^\delta$ because we consider only sensor values relative to partitions of the universe using $\text{Ing}_{A,\delta}(B)$.

2.3 Rough Membership Set Function

In this section, a set function form of the traditional rough membership function is presented

Definition 2. Let $S = (U, A)$ be an information system with non-empty set U and non-empty set of attributes A. Further, let $B \subseteq A$ and let $[y]_B^\delta$ be an equivalence class of any sensor reading $y \in \Re$. Let ρ be a measure of a set $X \in \wp(U)$, where $\wp(U)$ is a class (set of all subsets of U). Then for any $X \in \wp(U)$ the *rough membership set function (rmf)* $\mu_y^{B,\delta} : \wp(U) \to [0,1]$ is defined in (4).

$$\mu_y^{B,\delta}(X) = \frac{\rho\left(X \cap [y]_B^\delta\right)}{\rho\left([y]_B^\delta\right)} \quad (4)$$

If $\rho([y]_B^\delta)=0$, then of course $\rho(X \cap [y]_B^\delta) = 0$ and in this situation we consider symbol $\frac{0}{0}$ to be equal to 0.

A form of rough membership set function for non-empty, finite sets was introduced in [3]. Definition 2 is slightly different from the classical definition where the argument of the rough membership function is an object x and the set X is fixed [2].

2.4 Rough Measures

In what follows, a distance metric is introduced that will make it possible to measure the closeness of information granules. Recall that a function $d: X \times X \to \Re$ is called a metric on a set X if and only if for any $x, y, z \in X$ the function d satisfies the following three conditions: (i) $d(x, y) = 0$ if and only if $x = y$; (ii) $d(x, y) = d(x, y)$; (iii) $d(x, y) + d(y, z) \geq d(x, z)$.

Proposition 2. Let $S = (U, A)$ be an information system and let $\rho(Y)$ be defined as $\int_{x \subseteq Y} 1 dx$. The function $\mu_{B,y}^\delta : \wp(U) \to \Re$ in (5) is measure of a set $X \subseteq U$.

$$\mu_{B,y}^\delta(X) = \sum_{[y']_B^\delta \subseteq \overline{B}X} \frac{\rho(X \cap [y']_B^\delta)}{(d([y']_B^\delta, [y]_B^\delta) + 1) \cdot \rho([y']_B^\delta)} \quad (5)$$

where $d(\bullet)$ denotes a metric on the partition $U/\text{Ing}_{A,\delta}(B)$ of U defined by equivalence relation $\text{Ing}_{A,\delta}(B)$. The formula (5) may be written as shown in (6)

$$\mu_{B,y}^\delta(X) = \frac{\rho(X \cap [y]_B^\delta)}{\rho([y]_B^\delta)} + \sum_{\substack{[y']_B^\delta \subseteq \overline{B}X \\ [y']_B^\delta \neq [y]_B^\delta}} \frac{\rho(X \cap [y']_B^\delta)}{\rho([y']_B^\delta)} \cdot \frac{1}{d([y']_B^\delta, [y]_B^\delta) + 1} \quad (6)$$

It is clearly seen that $\mu_{B,y}^\delta$ defined in (6) is measure (4) completed with a sum of analogous measures for the remaining equivalence classes weighted by the reverse of distance (plus one) between distinct class $[y]_B^\delta$ and the remaining equivalence classes. The ratio $1/d([y']_B^\delta, [y]_B^\delta) + 1$ serves as a weight of the sum in (6). Thanks to the number 1 in the denominator of this weight, it is possible to include measure (4) as a term in the sum in (6). To obtain values in the interval $[0, 1]$ for the measure (5), the normalization coefficient $\alpha(y)$ in (7) is introduced.

$$\alpha(y) = \frac{1}{\sum_{[y']_B^\delta \subseteq \overline{B}X} \frac{1}{d([y']_B^\delta, [y]_B^\delta)+1}} \quad (7)$$

As a result, the following proposition holds.

Proposition 3. Let $S = (U, A)$ be an information system and let $\rho(Y)$ be defined as $\int_{x \subseteq Y} 1 dx$. If d is a metric defined on the set $U/\text{Ing}_{A,\delta}(B)$ and $\alpha(y)$ is as in formula (7), then function $\mu_{B,y}^\delta : \wp(U) \to [0, 1]$ such that

$$\mu^{\delta}_{B,y}(X) = \alpha(y) \cdot \sum_{[y']^{\delta}_B \subseteq \overline{B}X} \frac{\rho(X \cap [y']^{\delta}_B)}{(d([y']^{\delta}_B, [y]^{\delta}_B) + 1) \cdot \rho([y']^{\delta}_B)} \tag{8}$$

is a measure on the set $\wp(U)$.

Consider the sample universe $U = [0, 0.4) \times [0, 0.3)$, a finite sample $X \subset U$ as shown in Fig. 2. The equivalence relation $\mathrm{Ing}_{A,\delta}(B)$ partitions this sample universe as it is shown on Figure 2. Let us assume that each equivalence class consists of just 8 points. Every equivalence class (also called a mesh cell) is numbered by a pair of indices $E_{n,m}$. Notice that two sensor values are approximately equal in $E_{0,0}$, and are not considered duplicates. In addition, sensor values in $E_{0,0}$ are time-ordered with the relation $\leqslant_{\mathrm{before}}$. For example, assume that $a(x(t))$ occurs before $a(x(t'))$. Then we write $a(x(t)) \leqslant_{\mathrm{before}} a(x(t'))$. In effect, $E_{0,0}$ and every other cell in the mesh in Fig. 2 constitutes a temporally ordered multiset. For such an information system and its partition $U/\mathrm{Ing}_{A,\delta}(B)$, a well-known maximum metric is chosen, $d(E_{n1,m1}, E_{n2,m2}) = \max\{\,|\,n_1 - n_2\,|,\,|\,m_1 - m_2\,|\,\}$. Finding equivalence class with the biggest measure of X in sense of (5) leads to choice of $E_{0,0}$ while applying measure (8) gives as result class $E_{3,1}$. If we are interested in finding single equivalence class with the bigger (or least) degree of overlapping with set X, then measure (4) should be chosen, but when we want to find a group of 'neighbour' (in sense of "close") equivalence classes that overlap with X in the biggest (least) degree, then measure (8) is suggested. Figure 2

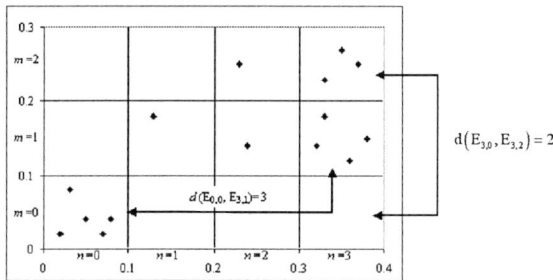

Fig. 2. Sample Distance Measurements in a δ-mesh

shows how the maximum metric measures distance. For example, $d(E_{3,0}, E_{3,2}) = \max\{\,|\,3\text{-}3\,|,\,|\,2\text{-}0\,|\,\} = 2$ between equivalence classes $E_{3,0}$ and $E_{3,2}$ may be of interest in cases where measurement of the separation between clusters (i.e., multiset that is the union of sensor values in a mesh cell and in neighboring cells) of sample sensor values is important (e.g., separation of cells in a mesh covering a control system performance map that contains "islands" of system response values, some normal and some verging on chaotic behavior as in [21], [22]).

3 Conclusion

Measures of inclusion and closeness of information granules have been introduced in the context of rough set theory. The partition of a universe using Ing results in a mesh of cells (called a δ-mesh), where each cell of the mesh represents an equivalence class. The configuration of cells in a δ-mesh yields a useful granule measure. That is, a measure of closeness of a pair of information granules contained in cells of the δ-mesh results from determining the number of cells separating members of the pair using a distance metric. Using a combination of the distance metric and a form of thresholding on the search space in a δ-mesh, the first of a family of algorithms for finding clusters of sensor values has been introduced. For simplicity, this algorithm has been restricted to δ-meshes covering a finite number of sample values for a single sensor. In future work, this algorithm will be extended to find clusters of sample values for more than one sensor. In addition, a calibration algorithm for finding an appropriate δ used to construct a δ-mesh will be introduced in further work on the problem of discovering clusters (granules) of sample sensor values.

Acknowledgements. The research of James Peters has been supported by the Natural Sciences and Engineering Research Council of Canada (NSERC) research grant 185986 and grants from Manitoba Hydro, and University of Information Technology and Management, Rzeszów, Poland. The research of Maciej Borkowski has been supported by a grant from Manitoba Hydro. The research of Andrzej Skowron and Zbigniew Suraj has been supported by grant 8 T11C 025 19 from the State Committee for Scientific Research (KBN). Moreover, the research of Andrzej Skowron has been supported by a grant from the Wallenberg Foundation.

References

1. Z. Pawlak, *Rough Sets: Theoretical Aspects of Reasoning About Data*, Boston, MA, Kluwer Academic Publishers, 1991.
2. Z. Pawlak, A. Skowron, Rough membership functions. In: R. Yager, M. Fedrizzi, J. Kacprzyk (Eds.), *Advances in the Dempster-Shafer Theory of Evidence*, NY, John Wiley & Sons, 1994, 251–271.
3. Z. Pawlak, J.F. Peters, A. Skowron, Z. Suraj, S. Ramanna, M. Borkowski, Rough measures: Theory and Applications. In: S. Hirano, M. Inuiguchi, S. Tsumoto (Eds.), Bulletin of the International Rough Set Society, vol. 5, no. 1 / 2, 2001, 177–184.
4. Z. Pawlak, On rough derivatives, rough integrals, and rough differential equations. ICS Research Report 41/95, Institute of Computer Science, Nowowiejska 15/19, 00-665 Warsaw, Poland, 1995.
5. J.F. Peters, V. Degtyaryov, M. Borkowski, S. Ramanna, Line-crawling robot navigation: Rough neurocomputing approach. In: C. Zhou, D. Maravall, D. Ruan, Fusion of Soft Computing and Hard Computing for Autonomous Robotic Systems. Berlin: Physica-Verlag, 2002 [to appear].

6. J.F. Peters, S. Ramanna, A. Skowron, J. Stepaniuk, Z. Suraj, M. Borkowski, Sensor fusion: A rough granular approach. In: *Proc. Joint 9th International Fuzzy Systems Association (IFSA) World Congress and 20th North American Fuzzy Information Processing Society (NAFIPS) Int. Conf.*, Vancouver, British Columbia, Canada, 25-28 June 2001, 1367–1372.
7. J.F. Peters, S. Ramanna, L. Han, The Choquet integral in a rough software cost estimation system. In: M. Grabisch, T. Murofushi, M. Sugeno (Eds.), *Fuzzy Measures and Integrals: Theory and Applications.* (Springer-Verlag, Heidelberg, Germany, 2000) 392–414.
8. J.F. Peters, S. Ramanna, M. Borkowski, A. Skowron: Approximate sensor fusion in a navigation agent, in: N. Zhong, J. Liu, S. Ohsuga and J. Bradshaw (Eds.), Intelligent agent technology: Research and development. Singapore: World Scientific Publishing, 2001, 500–504.
9. J.F. Peters, S. Ramanna, A. Skowron, M. Borkowski: Wireless agent guidance of remote mobile robots: Rough integral approach to sensor signal analysis. In: N. Zhong, Y.Y. Yao, J. Liu, S. Ohsuga (Eds.), Web Intelligence, Lecture Notes in Artificial Intelligence 2198. Berlin: Springer-Verlag, 2001, 413–422.
10. L. Polkowski, A. Skowron, Towards adaptive calculus of granules. In: Proc. of the Sixth Int. Conf. on Fuzzy Systems (FUZZ-IEEE'98), Anchorage, Alaska, 4-9 May 1998, 111–116.
11. S.K. Pal, L. Polkowski, A. Skowron, Rough-neuro computing: Technologies in Computing with Words. Berlin: Physica-Verlag, 2002 [to appear].
12. A. Skowron, Toward intelligent systems: Calculi of information granules. In: S. Hirano, M. Inuiguchi, S. Tsumoto (Eds.), Bulletin of the International Rough Set Society, vol. 5, no. 1 / 2, 2001, 9–30.
13. A. Skowron, J. Stepaniuk, S. Tsumoto, Information granules for spatial reasoning, Bulletin of the International Rough Set Society, vol. 3, no. 4, 1999, 147–154.
14. A. Skowron, J. Stepaniuk, Constructive information granules. In: Proc. of the 15th IMACS World Congress on Scientific Computation, Modelling and Applied Mathematics, Berlin, Germany, 24-29 August 1997. Artificial Intelligence and Computer Science 4, 1997, 625-630.
15. A. Skowron, J. Stepaniuk, J.F. Peters, Extracting patterns using information granules. In: S. Hirano, M. Inuiguchi, S. Tsumoto (Eds.), Bulletin of the International Rough Set Society, vol. 5, no. 1 / 2, 2001, 135–142.
16. A. Skowron, J. Stepaniuk, Information granules and approximation spaces. In: Proc. of the 7th Int. Conf. on Information Processing and Management of Uncertainty in Knowledge-based Systems, Paris, France, 6-10 July 1998, 1354–1361.
17. A. Skowron, J. Stepaniuk, J.F. Peters, Hierarchy of information granules. In: H.D. Burkhard, L. Czaja, H.S. Nguyen, P. Starke (Eds.), *Proc. of the Workshop on Concurrency, Specification and Programming*, Oct. 2001,Warsaw,Poland, 254–268.
18. P.R. Halmos, Measure Theory. London: D. Van Nostrand Co., Inc., 1950.
19. R. R. Yager, On the theory of bags, Intern. J. General Systems, 13 (1986), 23–37.
20. A. Syropoulos, Mathematics of multisets, in Pre-proceedings of the Workshop on Multiset Processing, Curtea de Arges, Romania, 2000 (C.S. Calude, M.J. Dinneen, Gh. Paun, eds.), CDMTCS Res. Report 140, Auckland Univ., 2000, 286–295.
21. J.J. Alpigini, J.F. Peters, Dynamic visualization with rough performance maps. In: W.Ziarko, Y.Yao (Eds.), RSCTC'00, Lectures Notes in Artificial Intelligence 2005. Berlin: Springer-Verlag, 2001, 90–97.
22. J.J. Alpigini, Measures of closeness of performance map information granules: A rough set approach. In: RSCTC'02 [submitted].

Rough Neurocomputing: A Survey of Basic Models of Neurocomputation

James F. Peters[1] and Marcin S. Szczuka[2]

[1] Department of Electrical and Computer Engineering,
University of Manitoba, Winnipeg, Manitoba R3T 5V6, Canada
jfpeters@ee.umanitoba.ca
[2] Institute of Mathematics, Warsaw University
Banacha 2, 02-097, Warsaw, Poland
szczuka@mimuw.edu.pl

Abstract. This article presents a survey of models of rough neurocomputing that have their roots in rough set theory. Historically, rough neurocomputing has three main threads: training set production, calculus of granules, and interval analysis. This form of neurocomputing gains its inspiration from the work of Pawlak on rough set philosophy as a basis for machine learning and from work on data mining and pattern recognition by Swiniarski and others in the early 1990s. This work has led to a variety of new rough neurocomputing computational models that are briefly presented in this article. The contribution of this article is a survey of representative approaches to rough neurocomputing.

Keywords. Information granule, mereology, neural network, rough sets.

1 Introduction

The hint that rough set theory provides a good basis for neurocomputing can be found in a discussion about machine learning by Zdzisław Pawlak in 1991 [1]. Studies of neural networks in the context of rough sets [4,5] and granular computing [6] are extensive. The first comprehensive, encyclopedic presentation of rough neurocomputing theory and numerous case studies appears in [5]. Other good sources of intensive studies of rough neurocomputing appear in [4,5].

Rough neurocomputing has three main threads: training set production, calculus of granules, and interval analysis. The first thread of rough neurocomputing, namely, rough set philosophy focuses on inductive learning and the production of training sets using knowledge reduction algorithms. This first thread has a strong presence in current rough neurocomputing research, and leads to a rough set approach to preprocessing that provides input to various forms of neural networks (see, e.g., [6]). The second thread in rough neurocomputing has two main components: information granule construction in distributed systems of agents and local parameterized approximation spaces (see, e.g., [6]). A formal treatment of the hierarchy of relations of being a part in a degree (also known as approximate rough mereology) was introduced by Polkowski and Skowron in the mid- and late-1990s [9]. Approximate rough mereology provides a basis for an agent-based, adaptive calculus of granules. This calculus serves as a guide in designing rough neurocomputing systems. A number of touchstones of rough neurocomputing have emerged from efforts to establish the foundations for granular computing: cooperating agent, granule, granule measures (e.g., inclusion, closeness), and approximation space parameter calibration. The notion of a cooperating agent in a distributed system of agents provides a model for a neuron. Information granulation and granule approximation define two principal activities of a neuron. Included in the toolbox of an agent (neuron) are measures of granule inclusion and closeness of granules. Agents (neurons) acquire knowledge by granulating (fusing) and approximating sensor inputs and input (granules) from other agents. The second component of the granular form of rough neurocomputing is a new approach to training agents (neurons). In this new paradigm, training a network of agents (neurons) is defined by algorithms for adjusting parameters in the parameter space of each agent instead of vectors of weights commonly used in conventional neural networks. That is, parameters accessible to rough neurons replace the usual scalar weights on (strengths-of-) connections between neurons. Hence, learning in a rough neural network is defined relative to local parameter adjustments. In sum, the granule construction paradigm provides a model for approximate reasoning by systems of communicating agents. The third thread in rough neurocomputing stems from the introduction of a rough set approach to interval analysis by Banerjee, Lingras, Mitra and Pal in the latter part of the 1990s (see, e.g., [4,5,8]).

Practical applications of rough neurocomputing have recently been found in predicting urban highway traffic volume, speech analysis, classifying the waveforms of power system faults, signal analysis, assessing software quality, control of autonomous vehicles, line-crawling robot navigation, EEG analysis, and handwriting recognition (see, e.g., [4,5,7,8]). In its most general form, rough neurocomputing provides a basis for granular computing. A rough mereological approach to rough neural network springs from an interest in knowledge synthesized (induced) from successive granule approximations performed by neurons [6].

This article is organized as follows. A rough set approach to preprocessing in the preparation of inputs to various forms of neural networks is presented in Section 1. An overview of a granular approach to rough neurocomputing is presented in Section 3. A number of different forms of neurons are briefly described in Section 4. The architectures of hybrid forms of neural networks are briefly described in Section 5.

2 Preprocessing with Rough Sets

Rough sets provide symbolic representation of data and the representation of knowledge in terms of attributes, information tables, semantic decision rules, rough measures of inclusion and closeness of information granules, and so on. By contrast, traditional neural networks in their basic form do not consider the detailed meaning of knowledge gained in the process of model construction and learning. Rather, the focus until recently has been on polynomial approximation in neural computing. In what follows it is assumed that the reader is familiar with the fundamentals of rough set theory [1] and with basic concepts in neurocomputing. This section considers how one can incorporate both approaches (rough sets and neural computing) in a combined system.

Rough set methods make it possible to reduce the size of a dataset by removing some of the attributes while preserving the partitioning of the universe of an information system into equivalence classes. We may consider the possibility of reducing the dataset during preprocessing and then performing construction and learning by a neural network. Let $DT = (U, A, \{d\})$, where U is a finite, non-empty set of objects (universe), A is a set of condition attributes such that for $a \in A$, $X \subseteq U$, $a : X \to V_a$ (value set), and d is a decision attribute. Recall that the indiscernibility relation IND is an equivalence relation such that

$$IND_{DT}(B) = \{(x, x') \in U^2 | \ \forall_{a \in B \subseteq A} a(x) = a(x')\}$$

Further, a reduct is minimal set of attributes $B \subseteq A$ such that $IND_{DT}(B) = IND_{DT}(A)$, i.e., B preserves the indiscernibility relation [8]. A high-level description of the basic steps in a rough set approach to preprocessing is given in the following algorithm.

Algorithm [Rough Set Approach to Preprocessing]

Input Decision table $DT = (U, A, \{d\})$, where U is a finite, non-empty set of objects (universe), A is a set of condition attributes such that for $a \in A$, $X \subseteq U$, $a : X \to V_a$ (value set), and d is a decision attribute.
Output Reduced table $DT_{reduced}$, calibrated neural network NN
Step 1 Using A, find set of possibly shortest reducts.
Step 2 Reduce DT using some reduct or union of several reducts to create reduced table $DT_{reduced}$, i.e., remove from DT attributes not belonging to the union of selected reducts.
Step 3 Construct a neural network NN over $DT_{reduced}$
Step 4 Calibrate NN from Step 3
Step 5 Repeat Steps 3-4 until sufficient classification accuracy is achieved.
Step 6 Repeat Steps 2-5 until sufficient quality is obtained, then STOP

This algorithm has proven to be very effective for some datasets. Two constraints should be considered in a rough set approach to preprocessing. First, finding a minimal reduct is NP-hard. Hence, it is helpful to use different approximating techniques to find a set of reducts. Second, real-valued attributes can have a very large set of possible values. The solution to this problem is to attempt to reduce the size of an attribute value set.

3 Granular Neural Network Architecture

In this section, the fulfillment of an ontology of approximate reason in a neural network stems from a consideration of granular computing in the context of parameterized approximation spaces as a realization of an adaptive granule calculus [9]. This realization is made possible by the introduction of a parameterized approximation space in the design of a reasoning system for an agent. A step towards the realization of an adaptive granule calculus in a rough neurocomputing scheme is described in this section and is based on [6]. In a scheme for information granule construction in a distributed system of cooperating agents, weights are defined by approximation spaces. In effect, each agent (neuron) in such a scheme controls a local parameterized approximation space.

Definition 1. *Parameterized Approximation Space. A parameterized approximation space is a system* $AS_{\#,\$} = (U, I_\#, R, \nu_\$)$ *where* $\#, \$$ *denote vectors of parameters, U is a non-empty set of objects and*

- $I_\# : U \to \mathcal{P}(U)$ *is an uncertainty function, where* $\mathcal{P}(U)$ *denotes the powerset of U.*
- $\nu_\$: \mathcal{P}(U) \times \mathcal{P}(U) \to [0,1]$ *denotes rough inclusion*

The uncertainty function defines for every object $x \in U$ a set of similarly described objects. A constructive definition of an uncertainty function can be based on the assumption that some metrics (distances) are given on attribute values. The family R describes a set of patterns (e.g., representing the sets described by the left hand sides of decision rules). A set $X \subseteq U$ is definable on $AS_{\#,\$}$ if it is a union of some values of the uncertainty function. The rough inclusion function $\nu_\$$ defines the value of inclusion between two subsets of U. Using rough inclusion, the neighborhood $I_\#(x)$ can usually be defined as a collection of close objects. It should also be noted that for some problems it is convenient to define an uncertainty set function of the form $I_\# : \mathcal{P}(U) \to \mathcal{P}(U)$. This form of uncertainty function works well in signal analysis, where we want to consider a domain over sets of sample signal values.

For a parameterized approximation space $AS_{\#,\$}$ and any subset $X \subseteq U$, the lower and upper approximations of X in U are defined as follows.

$LOW(AS_{\#,\$}, X) = \{x \in U : \nu_\$(I_\#(x), X) = 1\}$ [lower approximation]

$UPP(AS_{\#,\$}, X) = \{x \in U : \nu_\$(I_\#(x), X) > 0\}$ [upper approximation]

Using rough inclusion, the neighborhood $I_\#(x)$ can usually be defined as a collection of close objects. Sets of objects that are collections of objects from a data table are examples of information granules. A parameterized approximation space can be treated as an analogy to a neural network weight. The parameters of an approximation space should be learned to induce the relevant information granules.

4 Rough Neurons

The term *rough neuron* was introduced in 1996 by Lingras [8]. In its original form, a rough neuron was defined relative to upper and lower bounds and inputs were assessed relative to boundary values. Hence this form of neuron might also be called a boundary value neuron. This form of rough neuron has been used in predicting urban high traffic volumes [4]. More recent work considers rough neural networks (rNNs) with neurons that construct rough sets and output the degree of accuracy of an approximation [5]. This has led to the introduction of approximation neurons [5] and their application in classifying electrical power system faults, signal analysis, and in assessing software quality (see, e.g., [4,5]). More recent work on rough measures [3] has led to improved designs of approximation neurons (see, e.g, [5]). An information granulation model of a rough neuron was introduced by Skowron and Stepaniuk in the late 1990s (see, e.g., exposition in [5]). This model of a rough neuron is inspired by the notion of a cooperating agent (neuron) that constructs granules, perceives by measuring values of available attributes, granule inclusion, granule closeness, and by granule approximation, learns by adjusting parameters in its local parameter space, and shares its knowledge with other agents (neurons). A rough-fuzzy multilayer perceptron (MLP) useful in knowledge encoding and classification was introduced in 1998 by Banerjee, Mitra and Pal (see, e.g., [4]). The study of various forms of rough neurons is part of a growing number of papers on neural networks based on rough sets.

4.1 Interval-Based Rough Neuron

An interval-based rough neuron was introduced in 1996 [8]. A brief introduction to this form of rough neuron is given in this section. Rough neurons are defined in the context of rough patterns. Objects such as a fault signal or daily weather can described by a finite set of features (e.g., amplitude, type-of-waveform, high frequency component, rain fall, temperature) characterizing each object. The description of an object is an n-dimensional vector, where n is the number of features used to characterize an object. A pattern is class of objects based on the values of some features of objects belonging to a class. Let x be a feature variable in the description of an object. Further, let $\overline{x}, \underline{x}$ represent upper and lower bounds of x. In a rough pattern, the value of each feature variable x is specified with $\overline{x}, \underline{x}$ (called rough values). Rough values are useful in representing an interval or set of values for a feature, where only the upper and lower bounds are considered relevant in a computation. This form of rough neuron can be used to process intervals in a neural network.

Let $r, \underline{r}, \overline{r}$ denote a rough neuron, lower neuron and upper neuron, respectively. A rough neuron is a pair $(\underline{r}, \overline{r})$ with three types of connections: i/o connections to $\underline{r}$, i/o connections to $\overline{r}$, and connections between $\underline{r}$ and $\overline{r}$. In effect, a rough neuron stores the upper and lower bounds of input values for a feature and uses these bounds in its computations. Let in_i, out_j, w_{ij} denote input from neuron i, output from neuron j, and strength of connection between neurons i and j, respectively. The input to an upper, lower or conventional neuron i is calculated as a weighted sum as in 1.

$$in_i = \sum_{j=1}^{n} w_{ij} out_j \quad \text{(neuron } j \text{ is connected to neuron } i\text{)} \tag{1}$$

The subscript $i = \underline{r}$ for input to a lower neuron, and $i = \overline{r}$ for input to an upper neuron. Let t be a transfer function used to evaluate the input to an upper {lower} neuron. Then the output of an upper {lower} neuron is computed as in (2) and (3), respectively.

$$out_{\overline{r}} = \max(t(in_{\overline{r}}), t(in_{\underline{r}})) \tag{2}$$

$$out_{\underline{r}} = \min(t(in_{\overline{r}}), t(in_{\underline{r}})) \tag{3}$$

The output of the rough neuron will be computed in form (4).

$$rough\ neuron\ output = \frac{out_{\overline{r}} - out_{\underline{r}}}{average(out_{\overline{r}}, out_{\underline{r}})} \tag{4}$$

4.2 Approximation Neurons

This section considers the design of rough neural networks containing neurons that perform set approximations and measure rough inclusion, and hence this form of network is called an approximation neural network (aNN). This section is limited to a brief description of one type of neuron in an aNN, namely, approximation neurons (aNs). The architecture of aNs is described in detail in [5]. Preliminary computations in an aN are carried out with a layer of aNs, which construct rough sets and where the output of each aN is a measurement of rough inclusion. Let B, F, $(newObj \cup F)_{B_{approx}}$, $[f]_B$ denote set of attributes, finite set of neuron inputs (this is an archival set representing past stimuli, a form of memory accessible to a neuron), non-empty finite set of new neural stimuli, set approximation, and equivalence class containing measurements derived from known objects, respectively. Further, the output of aN i.e. the degree of overlap between $(newObj \cup F)_{B_{approx}}$ and $[u]_B$ is measured using (5).

$$\mu_u^B(newObj \cup F_{B_{approx}}) = \frac{\text{Card}(\ [u]_B \cap (newObj \cup F)_{B_{approx}})}{\text{Card}(\ [u]_B)} \tag{5}$$

Other forms of rough neurons are described in [[4,5].

5 Hybrid Neural Networks

A number of hybrid neural networks with architectural designs based on rough set theory and more traditional neural structures have been proposed: rough-fuzzy MLP, evolutionary rough-fuzzy MLP, interval-based rough-fuzzy networks, interval-based fuzzy-rough networks, and approximation rough-fuzzy networks (see, e.g., [4,5]). It should also be mentioned that it is common to use rough set theory as a basis for preprocessing inputs to a neural network . In this section, one form of hybrid network is briefly described: a rough-fuzzy multi-layer perceptron neural network. The Rough-fuzzy MLP (Multi Layer Perceptron) was developed for pattern classification. This form of MLP combines both rough sets and fuzzy sets with neural networks for building an efficient connectionist system. In this hybridization, fuzzy sets help in handling linguistic input information and ambiguity in output decision, while rough sets extract the domain knowledge for determining the network parameters. The first step in the design of a rough-fuzzy MLP is establish a basis for working with real-valued attribute tables of fuzzy membership values. The traditional model of a discernibility matrix is replaced by (6).

$$c_{ij} = \{a \in B | |a(x_i) - a(x_i)| > Th\} \quad (6)$$

for $i, j = 1, ..., n_k$, where Th is an adaptive threshold. Let a_1, a_2 correspond to two membership functions (attributes) with a_2 being steeper as compared to a_1. It is observed that $r_1 > r_2$. This results in an implicit adaptivity of Th while computing c_{ij} in the discernibility matrix directly from the real-valued attributes. Here lies the novelty of the proposed method. Moreover, this type of thresholding also enables the discernibility matrix to contain all the representative points/clusters present in a class. This is particularly useful in modeling multi-modal class distributions.

6 Concluding Remarks

Various approaches to rough neurocomputing have been presented in this article. A scheme for designing rough neural networks based on an adaptive calculus of granules for distributed systems of cooperating agents has been presented. This scheme is defined in context of an approximate rough mereology, granule construction and granule approximation algorithms, measures of granule inclusion and closeness, and local parameterized approximation spaces. Adaptivity is also a feature of this scheme where agents can change local parameters in response to changing signals from other agents and from the environment.

Acknowledgements. The research of James Peters has been supported by the Natural Sciences and Engineering Research Council of Canada (NSERC) research grant 185986, a grant from Manitoba Hydro, research support from the University of Information Technology and Management, Rzeszów, Poland. The work of Marcin Szczuka has been supported by grant 8T11C02519 from State Committee for Scientific Research and by the Wallenberg Foundation in frame of the WITAS project.

References

1. Z. Pawlak, Rough Sets: Theoretical Aspects of Reasoning About Data. Boston, MA, Kluwer Academic Publishers, 1991.

2. Z. Pawlak, A. Skowron, Rough membership functions. In: R. Yager, M. Fedrizzi, J. Kacprzyk (Eds.), Advances in the Dempster-Shafer Theory of Evidence, NY, John Wiley & Sons, 1994, 251–271.
3. Z. Pawlak, J.F. Peters, A. Skowron, Z. Suraj, S. Ramanna, M. Borkowski, Rough measures: Theory and Applications. In: S. Hirano, M. Inuiguchi, S. Tsumoto (Eds.), Rough Set Theory and Granular Computing, Bulletin of the International Rough Set Society, vol. 5, no. 1 / 2, 2001, 177–184.
4. S.K. Pal, W. Pedrycz, A. Skowron, R. Swiniarski (Guest Eds.), Neurocomputing: An International Journal, vol. 36, Feb. 2001.
5. S.K. Pal, L. Polkowski, A. Skowron (Eds.), Rough-Neuro Computing: Techniques for Computing with Words. Berlin: Springer-Verlag, 2002.
6. A. Skowron, Toward intelligent systems: Calculi of information granules. In: S. Hirano, M. Inuiguchi, S. Tsumoto (Eds.), Bulletin of the International Rough Set Society, vol. 5, no. 1 / 2, 2001, 9–30.
7. M. S. Szczuka, Rough sets and artificial neural networks. In: L. Polkowski, A. Skowron (Eds.), Rough Sets in Knowledge Discovery 2: Applications, Cases Studies and Software Systems. Berlin: Physica Verlag, 1998, 449–470.
8. P.J. Lingras, Rough neural networks. In: Proc. of the 6th Int. Conf. on Information Processing and Management of Uncertainty in Knowledge-based Systems (IPMU'96), Granada, Spain, 1996, 1445–1450.
9. L. Polkowski, A. Skowron, Towards adaptive calculus of granules. In: Proc. of the Sixth Int. Conf. on Fuzzy Systems (FUZZ-IEEE'98), Anchorage, Alaska, 4-9 May 1998, 111–116.

Rough Neurocomputing Based on Hierarchical Classifiers

Andrzej Skowron[1], Jarosław Stepaniuk[2], and James F. Peters[3]

[1] Institute of Mathematics
Warsaw University
Banacha 2, 02-097 Warsaw, Poland
skowron@mimuw.edu.pl
[2] Department of Computer Science
Białystok University of Technology
Wiejska 45a, 15-351 Białystok, Poland
jstepan@ii.pb.bialystok.pl
[3] Department of Electrical and Computer Engineering
University of Manitoba
Winnipeg, Manitoba R3T 5V6, Canada
jfpeters@ee.umanitoba.ca

Abstract. In the paper we discuss parameterized approximation spaces relevant for rough neurocomputing. We propose to use standards defined by classifiers in approximate reasoning. In particular, such standards are used for extraction rules of approximate reasoning (called productions) from data and next for deriving approximate reasoning schemes.

1 Introduction

Information sources provide us with granules of information that must be transformed, analyzed and built into structures that support problem-solving. Lotfi A. Zadeh has recently pointed out the need to develop a new research branch called Computing with Words (see, e.g., [13,14,15]). One way to achieve Computing with Words is through rough neurocomputing (see, e.g., [3,4,9,10]) based on granular computing (GC) (see, e.g., [10]) and on rough neural networks performing computations on information granules rather than on vectors of real numbers (i.e., weights). GC is based on information granule calculi [7]. One of the main goals of information granule calculi is to develop algorithmic methods for construction of complex information granules from elementary ones by means of available operations and inclusion (closeness) measures. These constructions can also be interpreted as approximate reasoning schemes (AR-schemes, for short) (see, e.g., [6,8,10]). Such schemes in distributed environments can be extended by adding interfaces created by approximation spaces. They make it possible to induce approximations of concepts (or information about relations among them) exchanged between agents. In the paper, we introduce parameterized approximation spaces as one of the basic concepts of the rough neurocomputing paradigm. Moreover, we propose to use patterns defined by classifier approximations as standards in approximate reasoning. Such standards are next used for extraction from data rules of approximate reasoning, called productions. AR-schemes can be derived using productions (see, e.g. [3,4,10]).

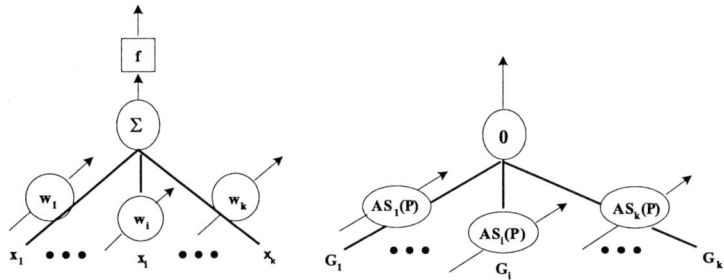

Fig. 1. Classical neuron and rough neuron

A parameterized approximation space can be treated as an analogy to a neural network weight (see Fig. 1). In Fig. 1, $w_1, \cdots, w_k, \Sigma, f$ denote weights, aggregation operator, and activation function of a classical neuron, respectively, while $AS_1(P), \cdots, AS_k(P)$ denote parameterized approximations spaces where agents process input granules $G_1, \cdots, G_k$ and O denotes an operation (usually parameterized) that produces the output of a granular network. The parameters P of approximation spaces should be learned to induce the relevant information granules.

2 Information Granule Systems and Parameterized Approximation Spaces

In this section, we present a basic notion for our approach, i.e., information granule system. Any information granule system is any tuple

$$S = (G, R, Sem) \tag{1}$$

where

1. G is a finite set of parameterized constructs (e.g., formulas) called information granules;
2. R is a finite (parameterized) relational structure;
3. Sem is a semantics of G in R.

For any information granule system two more components are fixed:

1. A finite set H of granule inclusion degrees with a partial order relation $<$ which defines on H a structure used to compare the inclusion degrees; we assume that H consists of the lowest degree 0 and the largest degree 1;

2. A binary relation $\nu_p \subseteq G \times G$ to be a part to a degree at least $p \in H$ between information granules from G, called *rough inclusion*. (Instead of $\nu_p(g,g')$ we also write $\nu(g,g') \geq p$.)

Components of an information granules system are parameterized. This means that we deal with parameterized formulas and a parameterized relational system. The parameters are tuned to make it possible to construct finally relevant information granules, i.e., granules satisfying a given specification or/ and some optimization criteria.

There are two kinds of computations on information granules. These are computations on information granule systems and computations on information granules in such systems, respectively. The purpose of the first type of computation is the relevant information granule systems defining parameterized approximation spaces for concept approximations used on different levels of target information granule constructions and the purpose of the second types of computation is to construct information granules over such information granule systems to obtain target information granules, e.g., satisfying a given specification (at least to a satisfactory degree).

Examples of complex granules are tolerance granules created by means of similarity (tolerance) relation between elementary granules, decision rules, sets of decision rules, sets of decision rules with guards, information systems or decision tables (see, e.g., [8], [11], [10]). The most interesting class of information granules are information granules approximating concepts specified in natural language by means of experimental data tables and background knowledge.

One can consider as an example of the set H of granule inclusion degrees the set of binary sequences of a fixed length with the relation ν to be a part defined by the lexicographical order. This degree structure can be used to measure the inclusion degree between granule sequences or to measure the matching degree between granules representing classified objects and granules describing the left hand sides of decision rules in simple classifiers (see, e.g., [9]). However, one can consider more complex degree granules by taking as degree of inclusion of granule g_1 in granule g_2 the granule being a collection of common parts of these two granules g_1 and g_2.

New information granules can be defined by means of operations performed on already constructed information granules. Examples of such operations are set theoretical operations (defined by propositional connectives). However, there are other operations widely used in machine learning or pattern recognition [2] for construction of classifiers. These are the *Match* and *Conflict_res* operations [9]. We will discuss such operations in the following section. It is worthwhile mentioning yet another important class of operations, namely, operations defined by data tables called decision tables [11]. From these decision tables, decision rules specifying operations can be induced. More complex operations on information granules are so called transducers [1]. They have been introduced to use background knowledge (not necessarily in the form of data tables) in construction of new granules. One can consider theories or their clusters as information granules. Reasoning schemes in natural language define the most important class of operations on information granules to be investigated. One of the basic problems for such operations and schemes of reasoning is how to approximate them by available information granules, e.g., constructed from sensor measurements.

In an information granule system, the relation ν_p to be a part to a degree at least p has a special role. It satisfies some additional natural axioms and additionally some axioms of mereology [7]. It can be shown that the rough mereological approach built on the basis of the relation to be a part to a degree generalizes the rough set and fuzzy set approaches. Moreover, such relations can be used to define other basic concepts like closeness of information granules, their semantics, indiscernibility and discernibility of objects, information granule approximation and approximation spaces, perception structure of information granules as well as the notion of ontology approximation. One can observe that the relation to be a part to a degree can be used to define operations on information granules corresponding to generalization of already defined information granules. For details the reader is referred to [4].

Let us finally note that new information granule systems can be defined using already constructed information granule systems. This leads to a hierarchy of information granule systems.

3 Classifiers as Information Granules

An important class of information granules create classifiers. The classifier construction from data table $DT = (U, A, d)$ can be described as follows:

1. First, one can construct granules G_j corresponding to each particular decision $j = 1, \ldots, r$ by taking a collection $\{g_{ij} : i = 1, \ldots, k_j\}$ of left hand sides of decision rules for a given decision.
2. Let E be a set of elementary granules (e.g., defined by conjunction of descriptors) over $IS = (U, A)$. We can now consider a granule denoted by

$$Match(e, G_1, \ldots, G_r)$$

   for any elementary granules $e \in E$ described by a collection of coefficients ε_{ij} where $\varepsilon_{ij} = 1$ if the set of objects defined by e in IS is included in the meaning of g_{ij} in IS, i.e., $Sem_{IS}(e) \subseteq Sem_{IS}(g_{ij})$; and 0, otherwise. Hence, the coefficient ε_{ij} is equal to 1 if and only if the granule e matches in IS the granule g_{ij}.
3. Let us now denote by $Conflict\_res$ an operation (resolving conflict between decision rules recognizing elementary granules) defined on granules of the form $Match(e, G_1, \ldots, G_r)$ with values in the set of possible decisions $1, \ldots, r$. Hence,

$$Conflict\_res(Match(e, G_1, \ldots, G_r))$$

is equal to the decision predicted by the classifier

$$Conflict\_res(Match(\bullet, G_1, \ldots, G_r))$$

on the input granule e.

Hence, classifiers are special cases of information granules. Parameters to be tuned are voting strategies, matching strategies of objects against rules as well as other parameters like closeness of granules in the target granule.

The classifier construction is illustrated in Fig. 2 where three sets of decision rules are presented for the decision values $1, 2, 3$, respectively. Hence, we have $r = 3$. In figure to omit too many indices we write α_i instead of g_{i1}, β_i instead of g_{i2}, and γ_i instead of g_{i3}, respectively. Moreover, $\varepsilon_1, \varepsilon_2, \varepsilon_3$, denote $\varepsilon_{1,1}, \varepsilon_{2,1}, \varepsilon_{3,1}$; $\varepsilon_4, \varepsilon_5, \varepsilon_6, \varepsilon_7$ denote $\varepsilon_{1,2}, \varepsilon_{2,2}, \varepsilon_{3,2}, \varepsilon_{4,2}$; and $\varepsilon_8, \varepsilon_9$ denote $\varepsilon_{1,3}, \varepsilon_{2,3}$, respectively.

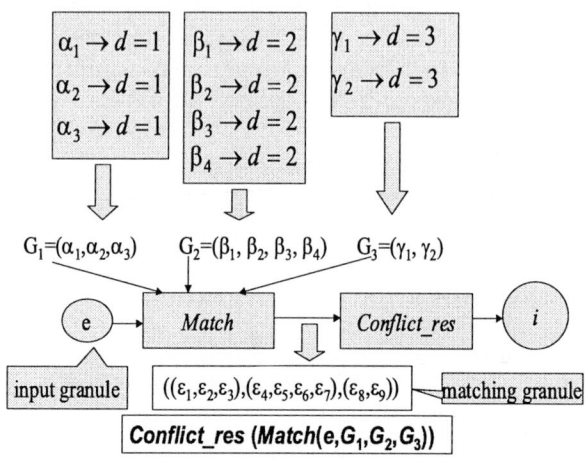

Fig. 2. Classifiers as Information Granules

The reader can now easily describe more complex classifiers by means of information granules. For example, one can consider soft instead of crisp inclusion between elementary information granules representing classified objects and the left hand sides of decision rules or soft matching between recognized objects and left hand sides of decision rules.

4 Approximation Spaces in Rough Neurocomputing

In this section we would like to look more deeply on the structure of approximation spaces in the framework of information granule systems.

Such information granule systems are satisfying some conditions related to their information granules, relational structure as well as semantics. These conditions are the following ones:

1. Semantics consists of two parts, namely relational structure R and its extension R^*.

2. Different types of information granules can be identified: (i) object granules (denoted by x), (ii) neighborhood granules (denoted by n with subscripts), (iii) pattern granules (denoted by pat), and (iv) decision class granules (denoted by c).
3. There are decision class granules $c_1, \cdots, c_r$ with semantics in R^* defined by a partition of object granules into r decision classes. However, only the restrictions of these collections to the object granules from R are given.
4. For any object granule x there is a uniquely defined neighborhood granule n_x.
5. For any class granule c there is constructed a collection granule $\{(pat, p) : \nu_p^R(pat, c)\}$ of pattern granules labeled by maximal degrees to which pat is included in c (in R).
6. For any neighborhood granule n_x there is distinguished a collection granule $\{(pat, p) : \nu_p^R(n_x, pat)\}$ of pattern granules labeled by maximal degrees to which n_x is at least included in pat (in R).
7. There is a class of $Classifier$ functions transforming collection granules (corresponding to a given object x) described in two previous steps into the power-set of $\{1, \cdots, r\}$. One can assume object granules to be the only arguments of $Classifier$ functions if other arguments are fixed.

The classification problem is to find a $Classifier$ function defining a partition of object granules in R^* as close as possible to the partition defined by decision classes.

Any such $Classifier$ defines the lower and the upper approximations of family of decision classes c_i over $i \in I$ where I is a non-empty subset of $\{1, \cdots, r\}$ by

$$\underline{Classifier}(\{c_i\}_{i \in I}) = \{x \in \bigcup_{i \in I} c_i : \emptyset \neq Classifier(x) \subseteq I\}$$

$$\overline{Classifier}(\{c_i\}_{i \in I}) = \{x \in U^* : Classifier(x) \cap I \neq \emptyset\}.$$

The positive region of $Classifier$ is defined by

$$POS(Classifier) = \underline{Classifier}(\{c_1\}) \cup \cdots \cup \underline{Classifier}(\{c_r\}).$$

The closeness of the partition defined by the constructed $Classifier$ and the partition in R^* defined by decision classes can be measured, e.g., using ratio of the positive region size of $Classifier$ to the size of the object universe. The quality of $Classifier$ can be defined taking, as usual, only into account objects from $U^* - U$:

$$quality(Classifier) = \frac{card(POS(Classifier) \cap (U^* - U))}{card((U^* - U))}.$$

One can consider neural networks as a special case of the above classifiers.

Approximation spaces have many parameters to be tuned to construct the approximation of granules of high quality.

5 Standards, Productions, and AR-Schemes

AR-schemes have been proposed as schemes of approximate reasoning in rough neurocomputing (see, e.g., [4,6,9,10]). The main idea is that the deviation of objects from some distinguished information granules, called standards or prototypes, can be controlled in appropriately tuned approximate reasoning. Several possible standard types can be chosen. Some of them are discussed in the literature (see, e.g., [12]). We propose to use standards defined by classifiers. Such standards correspond to lower approximations of decision classes or (definable parts of) boundary regions between them.

Rules for approximate reasoning, called productions, are extracted from data (for details see [4,9,10]). Any production has some premisses and conclusion. In the considered case each premiss and each conclusion consists of a pair ($classifier, standard$). This idea in hybridization with rough-fuzzy information granules (see, e.g., [10]) seems to be especially interesting. The main reasons are:

- standards are values of classifiers defining approximations of cut differences and boundary regions between cuts [10],
- there is a natural order on such standards defined by classifiers.

We assume productions satisfy a *monotonicity* property. To explain this property, let us consider a production with two premisses:

if $(C_1, stand_1)$ and $(C_2, stand_2)$ then $(C, stand)$

In this production, classifiers C_1, C_2, C are labelled by standards $stand_1$, $stand_2$, $stand$. The intended meaning of such a production is that if input patterns characterizing a given object are classified at least by C_1 and C_2 to $stand_1$ and $stand_2$, then the composition of such patterns characterizing the object is classified to at least $stand$ by the classifier C.

From productions extracted from data, it is possible to derive productions robust with respect to deviations of premisses and from such productions AR-schemes (see, e.g., [9,10]).

6 Conclusion

Parameterized Approximation Spaces Are Basic constructs in the rough neurocomputing paradigm. They can be treated as target information granule systems. Such systems are making possible to perform efficient searches for relevant information granules for concepts approximations. The concept of approximation known from rough set theory [5] has been modified to capture approximate reasoning aspects. We have proposed to use in rough neurocomputing standards defined by classifiers. Such standards can next be used in the process of extracting of productions from data and for deriving AR-schemes.

Acknowledgements. The research of Andrzej Skowron and Jarosław Stepaniuk has been supported by the State Committee for Scientific Research of the Republic of Poland (KBN) research grants 8 T11C 025 19, 8 T11C 003 23. Moreover, the research of Andrzej Skowron has been partially supported by the Wallenberg Foundation grant. The research of James Peters has been supported by the Natural Sciences and Engineering Research Council of Canada (NSERC) research grant 185986.

References

1. Doherty, P., Łukaszewicz, W., Skowron, A., Szałas, A.: *Combining rough and crisp knowledge in deductive databases.* (to appear in [4])
2. Mitchell, T.M.: *Machine Learning.* Mc Graw-Hill, Portland (1997)
3. Pal, S.K., Pedrycz, W., Skowron, A., Swiniarski, R. (Eds.): Rough-Neuro Computing. *Neurocomputing: An International Journal* (special issue) **36** (2001)
4. Pal, S.K., Polkowski, L., Skowron, A. (Eds.): *Rough-Neuro Computing: Techniques for Computing with Words.* Springer-Verlag, Berlin (2002) (to appear).
5. Pawlak, Z.: *Rough Sets–Theoretical Aspects of Reasoning about Data.* Kluwer Academic Publishers, Dordrecht (1991)
6. Peters, J.F., Skowron, A., Stepaniuk, J., Ramanna, S.: Towards an ontology of approximate reason. *Fundamenta Informaticae*, **51**(1-2) (2002) (to appear)
7. Polkowski, L., Skowron, A.: Rough mereology: a new paradigm for approximate reasoning. *International J. Approximate Reasoning* **15**(4) (1996) 333–365
8. Polkowski, L., Skowron, A.: Towards adaptive calculus of granules. In [16] (1999) 201–227
9. Polkowski, L., Skowron, A.: Rough-neuro computing. *Lecture Notes in Artificial Intelligence* **2005**, Springer-Verlag, Berlin (2002) 57–64
10. Skowron, A.: Toward intelligent systems: Calculi of information granules. *Bulletin of the International Rough Set Society* **5**(1-2) (2001) 9–30
11. Skowron, A., Stepaniuk, J.: Information granules: Towards foundations of granular computing. *International Journal of Intelligent Systems* **16**(1) (2001) 57–86
12. Skowron, A., Stepaniuk, J.: Information Granules and Rough-Neuro Computing. (to appear in [4])
13. Zadeh, L.A.: Fuzzy logic = computing with words. *IEEE Trans. on Fuzzy Systems* **4** (1996) 103–111
14. Zadeh, L.A.: Toward a theory of fuzzy information granulation and its certainty in human reasoning and fuzzy logic. *Fuzzy Sets and Systems* **90** (1997) 111–127
15. Zadeh, L.A.: A new direction in AI: Toward a computational theory of perceptions. *AI Magazine* **22**(1) (2001) 73–84
16. Zadeh, L.A., Kacprzyk, J. (Eds.): *Computing with Words in Information/Intelligent Systems* **1–2**. Physica-Verlag, Heidelberg (1999)

Using Granular Objects in Multi-source Data Fusion

Ronald R. Yager

Machine Intelligence Institute, Iona College
New Rochelle, NY 10801
ryager@iona.edu

Abstract. We focus on the problem of fusing data from multiple sources. A framework based on a calculation of the support from each of the sources for a proposed fused value is introduced. A number of features are provided on which to base the support; among these are ideas of compatibility and reasonableness. After considering the case where the fused value must be a point, we turn to the case in which we allow granules (subsets) as fused values.

Keywords. Fusion, granular objects, proximity relationship, knowledge of reasonableness

1 Multi-source Data Fusion

At a meta level multi-source data fusion is a process in which the individual information sources, the source S_i must agree on a solution that is acceptable to each of them, a solution compatible with the data they each have provided. Let V be an attribute variable whose value lies in the set X. Assume a collection $S_1, S_2, ..., S_q$ of information sources. Each source provides a value a_i. The problem here is to fuse these pieces of data to obtain a fused value $\tilde{a} \in X$ appropriate for the user's requirements. We denote this as $\tilde{a} = \text{Agg}(a_1, ..., a_n)$. The issue becomes that of obtaining the process Agg that fuses these pieces of data. One obvious requirement of such an aggregation process is idempotency.

Let **a** be a proposed solution. Each source can be seen as "voting" whether to support this solution. Let $\text{Sup}_i(\mathbf{a})$ denote the support (vote) of source i for solution **a**. Combining these we obtain the overall support for **a**. We let $\text{Sup}(\mathbf{a}) = F(\text{Sup}_1(\mathbf{a}), \text{Sup}_2(\mathbf{a}), ..., \text{Sup}_q(\mathbf{a}))$ be the total support for **a**. F is the function that combines the support from each of the sources. The fused value is then obtained as the value $\tilde{a} \in X$ that maximizes $\text{Sup}(\mathbf{a})$. Thus $\tilde{a}$ is such that $\text{Sup}(\tilde{a}) = \text{Max}_{\mathbf{a} \in X}[\text{Sup}(\mathbf{a})]$.

Let us consider the function F. One property associated with F is that the more support from the individual sources the more overall support for **a**. Formally if **a** and **b** are two values and if $\text{Sup}_i(\mathbf{a}) \geqslant \text{Sup}_i(\mathbf{b})$ for all i then $\text{Sup}(\mathbf{a}) \geqslant \text{Sup}(\mathbf{b})$. This requires that F be a monotonic function, $F(x_1, x_2, ..., x_q) \geqslant F(y_1, y_2, ..., y_q)$ if $x_i \geqslant y_i$ for all i.

Another property desired of F is a symmetry with respect to the arguments, the indexing of the arguments should not affect the answer. This symmetry implies a more expansive situation with respect to monotonicity. Assume $t_1, ..., t_q$ and $\hat{t}_1, ..., \hat{t}_q$ are two sets of arguments of F, $\text{Sup}_i(a) = t_i$ and $\text{Sup}_i(\hat{a})=\hat{t}_i$. Let perm indicate a permutation of the arguments, where $perm(i)$ is the index of the ith element under the permutation. Then if there exists some permutation such that $t_i \geqslant \hat{t}_{perm(i)}$ for all i we get $F(t_1, ..., t_q) \geqslant F(\hat{t}_1, ..., \hat{t}_q)$.

In addition to the symmetry and monotonicity we have implicitly made an assumption of the pointwiseness of F, the determination of $\text{Sup}(a)$ depends only on a it is independent of any of other possible solutions. This property imposes the condition of indifference to irrelevant alternatives a requirement that plays a central role in two fundamental works on opinion aggregation Arrow's impossibility theorem [1] and Nash's bargaining problem [2]. Specifically this condition assures us that the addition or removal of possible solutions does not affect the relationship between other solutions, if $\text{Sup}(x) \geqslant \text{Sup}(y)$ then this will not change if we add or remove elements in the space X.

Another property we want to associate with F is related to the idea of self-identity [3]. Assume that we have a data set $<a_1, ..., a_q>$ and we find that $\tilde{a}$ is the best solution. Assume now that we are provided with an additional piece of data a_{q+1} such that $a_{q+1} = \tilde{a}$, the new data suggests $\tilde{a}$ as its value. Then clearly $\tilde{a}$ should still be the best solution.

In [4] we show that using an F having these properties leads to a mean like aggregation operator, the fused value is bounded by the data set.

So far we assumed a very general formulation for F. If we consider the situation in which the individual support functions provide numeric values, for example numbers in the unit interval, one form for F that meets our required conditions is the sum $F(x_1, x_2, ...x_q) = \sum_{i=1}^{q} x_i$.

In the preceding we have described a process for determining the fused value of a data collection $<a_1, ..., a_q>$ to consist of the following.
1 For any $x \in X$ obtain $\text{Sup}_i(x)$, **2** Obtain $\text{Sup}(x) = F(\text{Sup}_i(x), .., \text{Sup}_q(x))$ **3** Select as fused value $\tilde{a}$ such that $\text{Sup}(\tilde{a}) = \text{Max}_{x \in X}[\text{Sup}(x)]$.

2 Formulation of Source Support

The formulation of $\text{Sup}_i(a)$ depends upon a number of aspects. One is the compatibility of the proposed solution a with the value provided by the source, a_i. Here we mean to capture some measure of the lack of conflict (compatibility) between the data provided and the proposed solution. We indicate this as $\text{Comp}(a, a_i)$. This of compatibility should be based upon some context dependent relationship on the space X.

The concept of a **proximity relationship** [5] is useful in formalizing this idea of compatibility. A proximity relationship on X is a mapping $\text{Prox}: X \times X \to 1$ with properties: **1.** $\text{Prox}(x, x) = 1$ and **2.** $\text{Prox}(y, x) = \text{Prox}(x, y)$. Intuitively $\text{Prox}(x, y)$ is a measure of degree to which the values x and y are close and non-conflicting with respect to context in which the user is seeking the value of V. The concept of metric or distance is related in an inverse way to the concept of proximity. A closely related and stronger concept is Zadeh's similarity relationship [6]. A similarity relationship is a proximity relationship having the additional property of transitivity it provides a generalization of the concept of equivalence relationships. In the following we assume our compatibility relationship, Comp(a, a_i), is based on a proximity relationship.

We emphasize that the determination of this relationship is a context dependent highly empirical process very sensitive to the user's perceptions of the situation. In environments in which V is numeric scale then the basis of a proximity relationship is the often the difference $|x - y|$. However the mapping of $|x - y|$ into Prox(x, y) may be highly non-linear. For attributes assuming non-numeric values a relationship of proximity is based on relevant features associated with the elements in the variables universe. Here we can envision a variable having multiple appropriate proximity relationships. As an example let V be the country in which John was born, its domain X is the collection of all the countries of the world. Let us see what types of proximity relationship can be introduced on X in this context. One can consider the continent in which a country lies as the basis of a proximity relationship, this would actually generate an equivalence relationship. More generally, the physical distance between countries can be the basis of a proximity relationship. The spelling of the country's name can be the basis of a proximity relationship. The primary language spoken in a country can be the basis of a proximity relationship. We can even envision notable topographic or geographic features as the basis of proximity relationships. Thus many different proximity relationships may occur. The important point here is that the association of a proximity relationship over the domain over a variable can be seen as a very creative activity. The choice of proximity relationship can play a significant role in the resolution of conflicting information.

Another factor in the formulation of Sup_i is the credibility of the source. The more credible the source the more influence it has in the fusion process. We shall assume each source has a credibility weight w_i lying in the unit interval.

If a source with credibility w_i inputs a data value a_i then its support for the fused value **a** is $Sup_i(a) = g(w_i, Comp(a, a_i)) = w_i\ Comp(a, a_i)$.

3 Including Knowledge about Reasonableness

Another factor that must be considered in the determination of the fused value is any information we may have about the attribute of interest in addition to the data provided by the sources. This can be seen as a kind of situational knowledge. For example, when searching for the age of Osaka Bin Laden, if one of the sources report that he is eighty years old we would consider this information unreasonable, this conflicts with what we know to be reasonable. In this case our action is clear: we discount this observation. As this illustrates situational knowledge often reflects itself to some restriction on the reasonableness of values for V. We shall refer to this available information as knowledge of **reasonableness**.

Knowledge about reasonableness affects the fusion process in at least two ways. First it will interact with the data provided by the sources. The influence of a source currently providing an unreasonable input value should be diminished, its importance in the current fusion process is reduced. Secondly a mechanism need be included in the fusion process to block unreasonable values from being provided as the fused value.

A complete discussion of the issues related to the representation and inclusion of knowledge of reasonableness data fusion is complex and beyond our immediate aim. In many ways the issue of reasonableness goes to the very heart of intelligence. We leave a general discussion of this concept to some future work. Here we shall focus on the representation of some very specific type of knowledge.

Knowledge about the reasonableness of values of a variable of interest can be either pointed or diffuse. By pointed we mean information specifically about the object while diffuse information is about objects of a class in which our object of interest lies. Generally pointed information has a possibilistic nature while diffuse information has a probabilistic nature. Here we consider the situation in which our information about reasonableness is pointed and is captured by a fuzzy subset, a mapping $R: X \to [0, 1]$ and thus has a possibilistic nature. Here for any $x \in X$, $R(x)$ indicates the reasonableness (or possibility) that x is a solution of variable of interest. For example, if our interest is to obtain somebody's age and before soliciting data from external sources we know that the person is *young* then we can capture this information with R and thus constrain the values that are reasonable.

Let us see how we can include this information into our data fusion process. Assume the data provided by source i is denoted a_i and w_i is the credibility assigned to source i. In the fusion process the importance weight, u_i, assigned to the data a_i should be a function of the credibility of the source, w_i and the reasonableness of its data, $R(a_i)$. An unreasonable value, whatever the credibility of the source, should not be given much consideration in the fusion process. Using the product to implement the "anding" we obtain $u_i = R(a_i) w_i$ as the importance weight assigned to the data coming from this source. Thus here we have modified the influence of a source to reflect both its 'historical' credibility, w_i, and the reasonableness of the current data it is providing.

The support provided from source i for solution **a**, $Sup_i(a)$, should depend on the importance weight u_i assigned to data supplied by source i and the compatibility of **a** with the data, $Comp(a, a_i)$. In addition, we must also include information about the reasonableness of the proposed solution **a**. Specifically for a solution **a** to be able to get support from any source i, in addition to it being compatible with the sources data a_i, it should be compatible with what we consider to be reasonable, $Comp(a, R)$. Here we let $Comp_i(a) = Comp(a, a_i) Comp(a, R)$. Since $Comp(a, R) = R(a)$ we have $Comp_i(a) = Comp(a, a_i) R(a)$. Including this we get $Sup_i(a) = g(u_i, Comp_i(a)) = u_i\, Comp_i(a) = R(a_i)\, w_i\, Comp(a, a_i)\, R(a)$.
Combining this with our use of summation for F we get

$$F(a) = \sum_{i=1}^{q} R(a_i) \; w_i \; \text{Comp}(a, a_i) \quad R(a) = R(a) \sum_{i=1}^{q} R(a_i) \; w_i \; \text{Comp}(a, a_i).$$

Finding the value of **a** that maximizes this gives us a solution to our multi-sensor data fusion problem.

4 Granular Objects as Fused Value

We now look at the situation in which we allow our fused value to be some subset of X. The use of subsets as our fused value is an example of what Zadeh [7] calls granulation.

Assume V can take its value in X. Let our data be the collection a_i for i = 1 to q. Let A be any subset of X. Using the approach introduced in the preceding we define the support for A as the fused value

$$\text{Sup}(A) = F(\text{Sup}_1(A), \text{Sup}_2(A), ..., \text{Sup}_q(A)) = \sum_{i=1}^{q} \text{Sup}_i(A)$$

We select as our fused value the subset A having largest value for Sup.

Here $\text{Sup}_i(A)$, the support for A from source i, is the maximal support source i gives any element in A, $\text{Sup}_i(A) = \text{Max}_{y \in A}[\text{Sup}_i(y)]$. If A is a fuzzy subset we can express this as $\text{Sup}_i(A) = \text{Max}_{y \in X}[A(y) \; \text{Sup}_i(y)]$. Since $\text{Sup}_i(y) = R(a_i) \; w_i \; \text{Comp}(y, a_i) \; R(y)$ we get

$$\text{Sup}_i(A) = R(a_i) \; w_i \; \text{Max}_{y \in X}[A(y) \; \text{Comp}(y, a_i) \; R(y)]$$

Usually when we allow subsets as the fused value there are some constraints on which granules we can use. However first, we consider the situation in which we have no explicitly stated restriction on which subsets we can use as the fused value. For simplicity we neglect reasonableness, $R(x) = 1$ for all x. Let B be the subset of all the data, $B = \{a_1, ..., a_q\}$. Here $\text{Sup}_i(B) = w_i \; \text{Max}_{y \in B}[\text{Comp}(y, a_i)]$ and since $a_i \in B$ then $\text{Max}_{y \in B}[\text{Comp}(y, a_i)] = 1$ for all i. From this we see for any subset A of X, $\text{Sup}_i(B) \geqslant \text{Sup}_i(A)$ hence $\text{Sup}(B) \geqslant \text{Sup}(A)$. Thus if we have no restrictions on which subsets we can use the best solution is always the subset consisting of all the input data values. This however may not be the case when we introduce considerations of reasonableness.

We now turn to the case in which there is some constraints on the subsets allowed as the fused value. Sometimes these constraints are explicit, other times they may implicit. A number of methods are available for introducing meaningful constraints. One approach is to supply the system with a collection of subsets of X from which it must select the fused value. We call this the case of **user supplied vocabulary**. If $A = \{A_1, ..., A_m\}$ is the vocabulary we select as our fused value the subset $A^* \in A$ such that $\text{Sup}(A^*) = \text{Max}_j[\text{Sup}(A_j)]$. Use can be made of fuzzy set theory and Zadeh's idea of computing with words [8] to provide a mechanism for representing linguistic concepts in terms of sets. An example is one in which the A_j are a collection of fuzzy subsets, corresponding to linguistic terms related to the variable V. For example if V is age then these could be terms like *old, young, middle age*.

A more general approach to restricting the granules available as outputs of the fusion process is to use a measure, $\mu : 2^X \to [0, 1]$ to indicate our constraints. Here for any subset of A of X, $\mu(A)$ indicates the degree to which it is acceptable to the user to provide A as the fused value. We denote this measure as the **C**lient **A**cceptability **M**easure (CAM).

With the availability of a CAM we proceed as follows. We calculate support for A by source i as $\text{Sup}_i(A) = \mu(A) \text{Max}_y[A(y) \text{Sup}_i(y)]$ where $\text{Sup}_i(y) = (R(a_i) w_i \text{Comp}(y, a_i) R(y))$.

With these CAM's we are trying to reflect some constraints implied by how a client will use the fused value. Often these constraints reflect some operational need or cognitive limitation of the user. We now describe two attributes associated with a subset that can be used to help in the expression of these constraints within a CAM.

Genenerally when we allow subsets as fused values we prefer them to contain elements that are consistent (similar) rather then a collection of diverse values. To capture this feature of granularization we can make use of the proximity relationship. Specifically some indication of **internal compatibility** of the elements in A can be used to convey this preference in the CAM μ. We suggest using as the internal compatibility of the subset A I-Comp(A) = $\underset{x,y \in A}{Min}[\text{Comp}(x, y)]$, the smallest compatibility of any two elements in A. Thus I-Comp can be used to help in the formulation of μ to aid in capturing this notion of consistency. In the most basic application of this we can define $\mu(A)$ = I-Comp(A). We note that if $A \subset D$ then I–Comp(A) $\geq$ I–Comp(D). If A is a singleton set, A = {x}, since Comp(x, x) = 1 for all x then I–Comp(A) = 1.

Above we implicitly assumed that A was a crisp set when A is fuzzy we can define I-Comp(A) = $\underset{x,y \in X}{Min}[(\overline{A}(x) \wedge \overline{A}(y)) \vee \text{Comp}(x, y)]$ where $\overline{A}(x) = 1 - A(x)$. Other more sophisticated definitions of the notion of internal compatibility of a set be can be obtained with the use of soft computing technologies such as fuzzy modeling [9].

Another characteristic of a subset useful in determining its appropriateness as a fused value is its size. This has to do with the fact that generally the fewer the number of elements in a subset the more informative and useful it is as a fused value. Thus the second feature of a subset that can be used in the formulation of the CAM is the cardinality of a subset. This observation is reflected in the general feature that $\mu(A) \geq \mu(D)$ if $A \subset D$. A related property is that any subset consisting of a singleton should be completely acceptable, $\mu(\{x\}) = 1$.

Here we shall not pursue this connection between the definition of a CAM and subset cardinality but only indicate that considerable use can be made of Zadeh's idea of computing with words to relate information about the cardinality of a set A and its value $\mu(A)$. For example we can capture a users desire that the fusion granule contain "only a few" elements. Here we can represent "only a few" as a fuzzy subset Q of non-negative numbers. Then for any A we obtain $\mu(A) = Q(\text{Card } A)$.

The specification of a user supplied vocabulary can made with a CAM μ in which all words in the vocabulary have $\mu(A) = 1$ and all those not in the vocabulary have $\mu(A) = 0$. In some situations we may describe our desired fused sets using both a user supplied vocabulary as well as criteria based on I-Comp(A) and/or the cardinality of A. An example of this is the case where we require that our fused subsets be **intervals**. We recall that A is an interval if there exists some if x and $z \in X$ such that $A = \{y \mid x \leqslant y \leqslant z\}$. In this case we may also associate with each interval a value $\mu_2(A)$ which depends on I-Comp(A) and a value $\mu_3(A)$ which depends on Q(Card A). Then we use $\mu(A) = \mu_1(A) \wedge \mu_2(A) \wedge \mu_3(A)$ where $\mu_1(A) = 1$ if A is an interval and $\mu_1(A) = 0$ if A is not an interval.

References

1. Arrow, K. J., Social Choice and Individual Values, John Wiley & Sons: New York, 1951.
2. Nash, J. F., "The bargaining problem," Econometrica 18, 155-162, 1950.
3. Yager, R. R. and Rybalov, A., "Noncommutative self-identity aggregation," Fuzzy Sets and Systems 85, 73-82, 1997.
4. Yager, R. R., "A framework for multi-source data fusion," Technical Report# MII-2214 Machine Intelligence Institute, Iona College, New Rochelle, NY, 2002.
5. Kaufmann, A., Introduction to the Theory of Fuzzy Subsets: Volume I, Academic Press: New York, 1975.
6. Zadeh, L. A., "Similarity relations and fuzzy orderings," Information Sciences 3, 177-200, 1971.
7. Zadeh, L. A., "Toward a theory of fuzzy information granulation and its centrality in human reasoning and fuzzy logic," Fuzzy Sets and Systems 90, 111-127, 1997.
8. Zadeh, L. A., "Fuzzy logic = computing with words," IEEE Transactions on Fuzzy Systems 4, 103-111, 1996.
9. Yager, R. R. and Filev, D. P., Essentials of Fuzzy Modeling and Control, John Wiley: New York, 1994.

Induction of Classification Rules by Granular Computing

J.T. Yao and Y.Y. Yao

Department of Computer Science, University of Regina
Regina, Saskatchewan, Canada S4S 0A2
{jtyao,yyao}@cs.uregina.ca

Abstract. A granular computing model is used for learning classification rules by considering the two basic issues: concept formation and concept relationships identification. A classification rule induction method is proposed. Instead of focusing on the selection of a suitable partition, i.e., a family of granules defined by values of an attribute, in each step, we concentrate on the selection of a single granule. This leads to finding a covering of the universe, which is more general than partition based methods. For the design of granule selection heuristics, several measures on granules are suggested.

1 Introduction

Classification deals with grouping or clustering of objects based on certain criteria. It is one of the basic learning tasks and is related to concept formation and concept relationship identification. While concept formation involves the construction of classes and description of classes, concept relationship identification involves the connections between classes. These two related issues can be studied formally in a framework that combines formal concept analysis and granular computing (GrC) [9].

There are two aspects of a concept, the intension and extension of the concept [3,8]. In the granular computing model for knowledge discovery, data mining, and classification, a set of objects are represented using an information table [5, 9]. The intension of a concept is expressed by a formula of the language, while the extension of a concept is represented as the set of objects satisfying the formula. This formulation enables us to study formal concepts in a logic setting in terms of intensions and also in a set-theoretic setting in terms of extensions.

Classification rules obtained from a supervized classification problem capture the relationships between classes defined by a set of attributes and the expert class. In many classical top-down induction methods such as ID3 [6], one attribute is selected in each step [4]. The selected attribute induces a partition that is more informative about the expert classes than other attributes. There are several problems with such attribute centered strategies. Although the selected partition as a whole may be more informative, each equivalence class may not be more informative than equivalence classes produced by another attribute.

Attribute centered strategy may introduce unnecessary attributes in classification rules [2]. In order to resolve such problems, granule centered strategies can be used, in which one granule is defined by an attribute-value pair. An example of granule centered strategies is the PRISM learning algorithm [1,2].

There has been very little attention paid to granule centered strategies. Based on the granular computing model, we provide a formal and more systematic study of granule centered strategies for the induction of classification rules.

2 A Granular Computing Model

This section presents an overview of the granular computing model [9,11].

2.1 Information Tables

An information table can be formulated as a tuple:

$$S = (U, At, \mathcal{L}, \{V_a \mid a \in At\}, \{I_a \mid a \in At\}),$$

where U is a finite nonempty set of objects, At is a finite nonempty set of attributes, $\mathcal{L}$ is a language defined using attributes in At, V_a is a nonempty set of values for a $\in At$, and $I_a : U \to V_a$ is an information function. An information table represents all available information and knowledge [5]. In the language $\mathcal{L}$, an atomic formula is given by $a = v$, where $a \in At$ and $v \in V_a$. Formulas can be formed by logical negation, conjunction and disjunction. If a formula ϕ is satisfied by an object x, we write $x \models_S \phi$ or in short $x \models \phi$ if S is understood[9]. If ϕ is a formula, the set $m_S(\phi)$ defined by: $m_S(\phi) = \{x \in U \mid x \models \phi\}$, is called the meaning of ϕ in S. If S is understood, we simply write $m(\phi)$. The meaning of a formula ϕ is the set of all objects having the property expressed by the formula ϕ. A connection between formulas of $\mathcal{L}$ and subsets of U is thus established. With the introduction of language $\mathcal{L}$, we have a formal description of concepts. A concept definable in an information table is a pair $(\phi, m(\phi))$, where $\phi \in \mathcal{L}$. More specifically, ϕ is a description of $m(\phi)$ in S, the intension of concept $(\phi, m(\phi))$, and $m(\phi)$ is the set of objects satisfying ϕ, the extension of concept $(\phi, m(\phi))$. An example information table is given by Table 1, which is adopted from Quinlan [6].

Granulation of a universe involves dividing the universe into subsets or grouping individual objects into clusters. A granule is a subset of the universe. A family of granules that contains every object in the universe is called a granulation of the universe. Partitions and coverings are two simple and commonly used granulations of universe. A partition consists of disjoint subsets of the universe, and a covering consists of possibly overlap subsets. Partitions are a special type of coverings.

Definition 1. *A partition of a finite universe U is a collection of non-empty, and pairwise disjoint subsets of U whose union is U. Each subset in a partition is also called a block or an equivalence granule.*

Table 1. An information table

Object	height	hair	eyes	class
o_1	short	blond	blue	+
o_2	short	blond	brown	-
o_3	tall	red	blue	+
o_4	tall	dark	blue	-
o_5	tall	dark	blue	-
o_6	tall	blond	blue	+
o_7	tall	dark	brown	-
o_8	short	blond	brown	-

Definition 2. *A covering of a finite universe U is a collection of non-empty subsets of U whose union is U. A covering τ of U is said to be a non-redundant covering if any collection of subsets of U derived by deleting one or more granules from τ is not covering.*

By using the language $\mathcal{L}$, we can construct various granules. For an atomic formula $a = v$, we obtain a granule $m(a = v)$. If $m(\phi)$ and $m(\psi)$ are granules corresponding to formulas ϕ and ψ, we obtain granules $m(\phi) \cap m(\psi) = m(\phi \wedge \psi)$ and $m(\phi) \cup m(\psi) = m(\phi \vee \psi)$. In an information table, we are only interested in granules, partitions and coverings that can be described by the language $\mathcal{L}$.

Definition 3. *A subset $X \subseteq U$ is called a definable granule in an information table S if there exists a formula ϕ such that $m(\phi) = X$. A subset $X \subseteq U$ is a conjunctively definable granule in an information table S if there exists a formula ϕ such that ϕ is a conjunction of atomic formulas and $m(\phi) = X$.*

Definition 4. *A partition π is called a conjunctively definable partition if every equivalence class of π is a conjunctively definable granule. A covering τ is called a conjunctively definable covering if every granule of τ is a conjunctively definable granule.*

One can obtain a finer partition by further dividing equivalence classes of a partition. Similarly, one can obtain a finer covering by further decomposing a granule of a covering. This naturally defines a refinement order on the set of all partitions $\Pi(U)$ and the set of all covering $\mathcal{T}(U)$.

Definition 5. *A partition π_1 is refinement of another partition π_2, or equivalently, π_2 is a coarsening of π_1, denoted by $\pi_1 \preceq \pi_2$, if every block of π_1 is contained in some block of π_2. A covering τ_1 is refinement of another covering τ_2, or equivalently, τ_2 is a coarsening of τ_1, denoted by $\tau_1 \preceq \tau_2$, if every granule of τ_1 is contained in some granule of τ_2.*

Since a partition is also a covering, we use the same symbol to denote the refinement relation on partitions and refinement relation on covering. For a covering τ and a partition π, if $\tau \preceq \pi$, we say that τ is a refinement of π. Based on the refinement relation, we can construct multi-level granulations of the universe.

2.2 Measures Associated with Granules

We introduce and review three types of quantitative measures associated with granules, measures of a single granule, measures of relationships between a pair of granules [9,10], and measures of relationships between a granule and a family of granules, as well as a pair of family of granules.

The measure of a single granule $m(\phi)$ of a formula ϕ is the *generality* $G(\phi) = |m(\phi)|/|U|$ which indicates the relative size of the granule $m(\phi)$. Given two formulas ϕ and ψ, we introduce a symbol $\Rightarrow$ to connect ϕ and ψ in the form of $\phi \Rightarrow \psi$. The strength of $\phi \Rightarrow \psi$ can be quantified by two related measures [7,9]. The *confidence* or *absolute support* of ψ provided by ϕ is $AS(\phi \Rightarrow \psi) = |m(\phi \wedge \psi)|/|m(\phi)| = |m(\phi) \cap m(\psi)|/|m(\phi)|$. The *coverage* ψ provided by ϕ is the quantity $CV(\phi \Rightarrow \psi) = |m(\phi \wedge \psi)|/|m(\psi)| = |m(\phi) \cap m(\psi)|/|m(\psi)|$.

Consider now a family of formulas $\Psi = \{\psi_1, \ldots, \psi_n\}$ which induces a partition $\pi(\Psi) = \{m(\psi_1), \ldots, m(\psi_n)\}$ of the universe. Let $\phi \Rightarrow \Psi$ denote the inference relation between ϕ and Ψ. In this case, we obtain the following probability distribution in terms of $\phi \Rightarrow \psi_i$'s:

$$P(\Psi \mid \phi) = \left(P(\psi_1 \mid \phi) = \frac{|m(\phi) \cap m(\psi_1)|}{|m(\phi)|}, \ldots, P(\psi_n \mid \phi) = \frac{|m(\phi) \cap m(\psi_n)|}{|m(\phi)|} \right).$$

The conditional entropy $H(\Psi \mid \phi)$ defined by:

$$H(\Psi \mid \phi) = -\sum_{i=1}^{n} P(\psi_i \mid \phi) \log P(\psi_i \mid \phi), \qquad (1)$$

provides a measure that is inversely related to the strength of the inference $\phi \Rightarrow \Psi$. Suppose another family of formulas $\Phi = \{\phi_1, \ldots, \phi_m\}$ define a partition $\pi(\Phi) = \{m(\phi_1), \ldots, m(\phi_m)\}$. The same symbol $\Rightarrow$ is also used to connect two families of formulas that define two partitions of the universe, namely, $\Phi \Rightarrow \Psi$. The strength of this connection can be measured by the conditional entropy:

$$H(\Psi \mid \Phi) = \sum_{j=1}^{m} P(\phi_j) H(\Psi \mid \phi_j) = -\sum_{j=1}^{m} \sum_{i=1}^{n} P(\psi_i \wedge \phi_j) \log P(\psi_i \mid \phi_j), \qquad (2)$$

where $P(\phi_j) = G(\phi_j)$. In fact, this is a most commonly used measure for selecting attribute in the construction of decision tree for classification [6].

The measures discussed so far quantified two levels of relationships, i.e., granule level and granulation level. As we will show in the following section, by focusing on different levels, one may obtain different methods for the induction of classification rules.

3 Induction of Classification Rules by Searching Granules

This section first clearly defines the consistent classification problem and then suggests a granule based rule induction method based on the measures discussed in the last section.

3.1 Consistent Classification Problems

In supervised classification, each object is associated with a unique and predefined class label. Objects are divided into disjoint classes which form a partition of the universe. Suppose an information table is used to describe a set of objects. Without loss of generality, we assume that there is a unique attribute **class** taking class labels as its value. The set of attributes is expressed as $At = F \cup \{\textbf{class}\}$, where F is the set of attributes used to describe the objects. The goal is to find classification rules of the form, $\phi \Longrightarrow \textbf{class} = c_i$, where ϕ is a formula over F and c_i is a class label.

Let $\pi_{\textbf{class}} \in \Pi(U)$ denote the partition induced by the attribute **class**. An information table with a set of attributes $At = F \cup \{\textbf{class}\}$ is said to provide a consistent classification if all objects with the same description over F have the same class label, namely, if $I_F(x) = I_F(y)$, then $I_{\textbf{class}}(x) = I_{\textbf{class}}(y)$.

For a subset $A \subseteq At$, it defines a partition π_A of the universe [5]. The consistent classification problem can be formally defined [11].

Definition 6. *An information table with a set of attributes $At = F \cup \{\textbf{class}\}$ is a consistent classification problem if and only if $\pi_F \preceq \pi_{\textbf{class}}$.*

For the induction of classification rules, the partition π_F is not very interesting. In fact, one is interested in finding a subset of attributes from F that also produces the correct classification. It can be easily verified that a problem is a consistent classification problem if and only if there exists a conjunctively definable partition π such that $\pi \preceq \pi_{\textbf{class}}$. Likewise, the problem is a consistent classification problem if and only if there exists a non-redundant conjunctively definable covering τ such that $\tau \preceq \pi_{\textbf{class}}$. This leads to different kinds of solutions to the classification problem.

Definition 7. *A partition solution to a consistent classification problem is a conjunctively definable partition π such that $\pi \preceq \pi_{\textbf{class}}$. A covering solution to a consistent classification problem is a conjunctively definable covering τ such that $\tau \preceq \pi_{\textbf{class}}$.*

Let X denote a granule in a partition or a covering of the universe, and let $des(X)$ denote its description using language $\mathcal{L}$. If $X \subseteq m(\textbf{class} = c_i)$, we can construct a classification rule: $des(X) \Rightarrow \textbf{class} = c_i$. For a partition or a covering, we can construct a family of classification rules. The main difference between a partition solution and a covering solution is that an object is only classified by one rule in a partition based solution, while an object may be classified by more than one rule in a covering based solution.

Consider the consistent classification problem of Table 1. We have the partition by **class**, a conjunctively defined partition π, and a conjunctively non-redundant covering τ:

$$\pi_{\textbf{class}}: \quad \{\{o_1, o_3, o_6\}, \{o_2, o_4, o_5, o_7, o_8\}\},$$
$$\pi: \quad \{\{o_1, o_6\}, \{o_2, o_8\}, \{o_3\}, \{o_4, o_5, o_7\}\},$$
$$\tau: \quad \{\{o_1, o_6\}, \{o_2, o_7, o_8\}, \{o_3\}, \{o_4, o_5, o_7\}\}.$$

Clearly, $\pi \preceq \pi_{\mathbf{class}}$ and $\tau \preceq \pi_{\mathbf{class}}$. A set of classification rules of π may include rules such as "**hair** = blond $\wedge$ **eyes** = blue $\Longrightarrow$ **class** = +".

3.2 Construction of a Granule Network

The top-down construction of a decision tree for classification searches for a partition solution to a classification problem. The induction process can be briefly described as follows. Based on a measure of connection between two partitions such as $H(\Psi \mid \Phi)$, one selects an attribute to divide the universe into a partition [6]. If an equivalence class is not a subset of a user defined class, it is further divided by using another attribute. The process continues until one finds a decision tree that correctly classifies all objects. Each node of the decision tree is labelled by an attribute, and each branch is labelled by a value of the parent attribute.

When we search a covering solution, we can not immediately use a decision tree to represent the results. We modify the decision tree method and introduce the concept of granule network. In a granule network, each node is labelled by a subset of objects. The arc leading from a larger granule to a smaller granule is labelled by an atomic formula. In addition, the smaller granule is obtained by selecting those objects of the larger granule that satisfy the atomic formula. The family of the smallest granules thus forms a conjunctively definable covering of the universe.

Atomic formulas define *basic* granules, which serve as the basis for the granule network. The pair $(a = v, m(a = v))$ is called a basic concept. Each node in the granule network is a conjunction of some basic granules, and thus a conjunctively definable granule. The granule network for a classification problem can constructed by a top-down search of granules. Figure 1 outline an algorithm for the construction of a granule network.

The two importance issues of the algorithm is the evaluation of the fitness of each basic concept and the modification of existing partial granule network. The algorithm is basically a heuristic search algorithm. The measures discussed in the last section can be used to define different fitness functions. This will be topics of our future research. In the rest of this section, we will use an example to illustrate the basic ideas.

Table 2 summarizes the measures of basic concepts with respect to the partition $\pi_{\mathbf{class}}$. There are three granules which are subset of one of class values, i.e., $\{o_3\} \subseteq (\mathbf{class} = +)$, $\{o_4, o_5, o_7\} \subseteq (\mathbf{class} = -)$ and $\{o_2, o_7, o_8\} \subseteq (\mathbf{class} = -)$. The values of entropy of these granules are the minimum, i.e., 0. The generality of last two granules are among the highest, so they are chosen first. One of possible orders of selection of these granules is $m(\mathbf{hair} = \text{dark})$, $m(\mathbf{eyes} = \text{brown})$ and then $m(\mathbf{hair} = \text{red})$. These three granules cannot cover the universe, i.e., they are not a covering solution to the classification problem. We will further analyze on other granules in order to find a set of granules that cover the whole universe. With the consideration of non-redundant covering, if adding candidate covering granule cannot form a non-redundant covering, we will not choose this granule even if other measure are in favor of this granule. If many

(1) **Construct** the family of basic concept with respect to atomic formulas:
$$BC(U) = \{(a = v, m(a = v)) \mid a \in F, v \in V_a\}.$$

(2) **Set** the unused basic concepts to the set of basic concepts:
$$UBC(U) = BC(U).$$

(3) **Set** the granule network to $GN = (\{U\}, \emptyset)$, which is a graph consists of only one node and no arc.

(4) **While** the set of smallest granules in GN is not a covering solution of the classification problem **do** the following:

  (4.1) **Compute** the fitness of each unused basic concept.
  (4.2) **Select** the basic concept $C = (a = v, m(a = v))$ with maximum value of fitness.
  (4.3) **Set** $UBC(U) = UBC(U) - \{C\}$.
  (4.4) **Modify** the granule network GN by adding new nodes which are the intersection of $m(a = v)$ and the original nodes of GN; **connect** the new nodes by arcs labelled by $a = v$.

Fig. 1. An Algorithm for constructing a granule network

Table 2. Basic granules and their measures

Formula	Granule	Generality	Confidence +	Confidence -	Coverage +	Coverage -	Entropy
height = short	$\{o_1, o_2, o_8\}$	3/8	1/3	2/3	1/3	2/5	0.92
height = tall	$\{o_3, o_4, o_5, o_6, o_7\}$	5/8	2/5	3/5	2/3	3/5	0.97
hair = blond	$\{o_1, o_2, o_6, o_8\}$	4/8	2/4	2/4	2/3	2/5	1.00
hair = red	$\{o_3\}$	1/8	1/1	0/1	1/3	0/5	0.00
hair = dark	$\{o_4, o_5, o_7\}$	3/8	0/3	3/3	0/3	3/5	0.00
eyes = blue	$\{o_1, o_3, o_4, o_5, o_6\}$	5/8	3/5	2/5	3/3	2/5	0.97
eyes = brown	$\{o_2, o_7, o_8\}$	3/8	0/3	3/3	0/3	3/5	0.00

objets in a candidate granule are already in granule network, this granule will not be chosen. Granule $m(\mathbf{hair} = \mathrm{blond})$ is considered the most suitable granule in this example and thus will be chosen. Now we have a covering $\tau = \{\{o_4, o_5, o_7\}, \{o_2, o_7, o_8\}, \{o_3\}, \{o_1, o_2, o_6, o_8\}\}$ which covers the universe. Obliviously, the objects in $m(\mathbf{hair} = \mathrm{blond})$ are not belong to the same class, therefore a further granulation to this granule will be conducted in order to find smaller definable granules. Considering the generality and non-redundant covering, granule $m(\mathbf{hair} = \mathrm{blond} \wedge \mathbf{eyes} = \mathrm{blue}) = \{o_1, o_6\}$ became the most suitable granule of a covering solution.

4 Conclusion

A consistent classification problem can be modelled as a search for a partition or a covering defined by a set of attribute values. In this paper, we apply a granular computing model for solving classification problems. The notion of granule network is used to represent the classification knowledge. The set of the smallest granules in the granule network forms a covering of the universe. Although the classification rules may have overlaps with each other, they may be shorter than the rules obtained from classical decision tree methods. This stem from the fact that at each step, only the most suitable granule defined by an attribute-value pair is selected, instead of a partition.

The main contribution of the paper is the formal development of the granule centered strategy for classification. As future research, we will study various heuristics defined using the measures suggested in this paper, the evaluation of the proposed algorithm using real world data sets.

References

1. Bramer, M.A.,"Automatic induction of classification rules from examples using N-PRISM", *Research and Development in Intelligent Systems XVI*, Springer-Verlag, pp.99–121, 2000.
2. Cendrowska, J., "PRISM: an algorithm for inducing modular rules", *International Journal of Man-Machine Studies*, **27**, 349–370, 1987.
3. Demri, S. and Orlowska, E., "Logical analysis of indiscernibility", in: *Incomplete Information: Rough Set Analysis*, Orlowska, E. (Ed.), Physica-Verlag, Heidelberg, pp.347–380, 1998.
4. Ganascia, J.-G., "TDIS: an algebraic formalization", *Proceedings of IJCAI 1993*, pp.1008–1015, 1993.
5. Pawlak, Z. *Rough Sets: Theoretical Aspects of Reasoning about Data*, Kluwer Academic Publishers, Dordrecht, 1991.
6. Quinlan, J.R. "Learning efficient classification procedures and their application to chess end-games", in: *Machine Learning: An Artificial Intelligence Approach*, Vol. 1, Michalski, J.S. et al.(Eds.), Morgan Kaufmann, pp.463–482, 1983.
7. Tsumoto, S., "Modelling medical diagnostic rules based on rough sets", *Rough Sets and Current Trends in Computing, Lecture Notes in Artificial Intelligence, 1424*, Springer-Verlag, Berlin, pp.475–482, 1998.
8. Wille, R., "Concept lattices and conceptual knowledge systems", *Computers Mathematics with Applications*, **23**, 493–515, 1992.
9. Yao, Y.Y, "On Modeling data mining with granular computing", *Proceedings of COMPSAC 2001*, pp.638–643, 2001.
10. Yao, Y.Y. and Zhong, N. An analysis of quantitative measures associated with rules, *Proceedings of PAKDD'99*, pp.479–488, 1999.
11. Yao, Y.Y. and Yao, J. T., "Granular computing as a basis for consistent classification problems", *Proceedings of PAKDD'02 Workshop on Toward the Foundation of Data Mining*, pp.101–106, 2002.
12. Zadeh, L.A., "Towards a theory of fuzzy information granulation and its centrality in human reasoning and fuzzy logic", *Fuzzy Sets and Systems*, **19**, 111–127, 1997.

Acquisition Methods for Contextual Weak Independence

C.J. Butz and M.J. Sanscartier

Department of Computer Science, University of Regina,
Regina, Canada, S4S 0A2,
{butz,sanscarm}@cs.uregina.ca

Abstract. Although *contextual weak independence* (CWI) has shown promise in leading to more efficient probabilistic inference, no investigation has examined how CWIs can be obtained. In this paper, we suggest and analyze two methods for obtaining this kind of independence.

1 Introduction

Probabilistic reasoning would not be feasible without making some kind of independency assumptions. By making *conditional independence* (CI) assumptions, *Bayesian networks* have become an established framework for uncertainty management. More recently, focus has shifted somewhat from *non-contextual* independencies such as CI to *contextual* independencies such as *contextual weak independence* (CWI) [3] and *context-specific independence* (CSI) [1]. Although more efficient probabilistic inference can be achieved in a CWI approach using independencies that would go unnoticed in a CSI approach [2], *no* study has ever investigated how CWIs can be obtained.

In this paper, we suggest two methods for obtaining contextual weak independencies. The first approach is to directly obtain the independencies from a human expert. In the case when no expert is available, the second approach we propose is to detect the CWIs from data. This investigation, by giving one method to obtain CWIs from an expert and another for obtaining CWIs from data, complements the work in [2] on more efficient inference using CWIs.

This paper is organized as follows. Section 2 introduces *contextual weak independence* (CWI). In Section 3, we give a method for obtaining CWIs from an expert. In Section 4, we propose a method for detecting CWIs in a given CPT. The conclusion is presented in Section 5.

2 Contextual Weak Independence

Consider the *conditional probability table* (CPT) $p(D|A, B)$ in Fig. 1 (i). It can be verified that variables D and B are *not* conditionally independent given A. The notion of *context-specific independence* (CSI) allows for the case when the independence holds in a particular context of A. It can be verified that variables

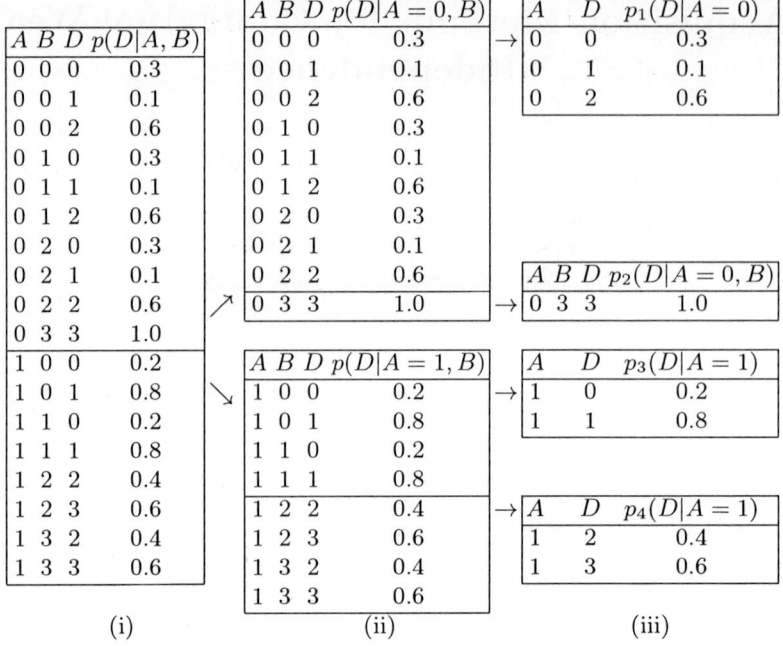

Fig. 1. Unlike CI and CSI, the notion of CWI can simplify the CPT $p(D|A,B)$.

D and B are *not* conditionally independent in the context $A = 0$, nor in context $A = 1$. The important point is that CI and CSI *fail* to simplify $p(D|A,B)$.

Let U be a finite set of variables and V_X be the frame of $X \subseteq U$. Let X, Y, Z, C be pairwise disjoint subsets of U and $c \in V_C$. We say Y and Z are *weakly independent* [3] given X in context $C = c$, if both of the following two conditions are satisfied: (i) there exists a maximal disjoint compatibility class $\pi = \{t_i, \ldots, t_j\}$ in the relation $\theta(X, Y, C = c) \circ \theta(X, Z, C = c)$, and (ii) given any $x \in V_X^\pi$, $y \in V_Y^\pi$, then for all $z \in V_Z^\pi$,

$$p(y \mid x, z, c) = p(y \mid x, c), \text{ whenever } p(x, z, c) > 0,$$

where $\theta(W)$ denotes the equivalence relation induced by the set W of variables, $\circ$ denotes the composition operator, and V_W^π denotes the set of values for W appearing in π.

Example 1. Let us partition the CPT $p(D|A,B)$ in Fig. 1 (i) into the four blocks shown in Fig. 1 (ii). In three of these blocks, variables D and B are conditionally independent given A. Hence, variable B can be dropped as shown in Fig. 1 (iii). For simplicity, $p_{B \in \{0,1,2\}}(D|A=0)$, $p(D|A=0, B=3)$, $p_{B \in \{0,1\}}(D|A=1)$, and $p_{B \in \{2,3\}}(D|A=1)$, are written as $p_1(D|A=0)$, $p_2(D|A=0,B)$, $p_3(D|A=1)$, and $p_4(D|A=1)$, respectively.

In practice, the four *partial functions* $p_1(D|A = 0)$, $p_2(D|A = 0, B)$, $p_3(D|A = 1)$, and $p_4(D|A = 1)$ will be stored in place of the single CPT $p(D|A, B)$. Unfortunately, the *union product* operator $\odot$ in [4] for combining partial functions is not sufficient for CWI, since

$$p(D|A, B) \neq p_1(D|A = 0) \odot p_2(D|A = 0, B) \odot p_3(D|A = 1) \odot p_4(D|A = 1).$$

By $\oplus$, we denote the *weak join* operator defined as:

$$p(y,x) \oplus q(x,z) = \begin{cases} p(y,x) \cdot q(x,z) & \text{if both } p(y,x) \text{ and } q(x,z) \text{ are defined} \\ p(y,x) & \text{if } p(y,x) \text{ is defined and } q(x,z) \text{ is undefined} \\ q(x,z) & \text{if } p(y,x) \text{ is undefined and } q(x,z) \text{ is defined} \\ 0.0 & \text{if } p(y,x) \text{ and } q(x,z) \text{ are inconsistent} \\ \text{undefined} & \text{if both } p(y,x) \text{ and } q(x,z) \text{ are undefined.} \end{cases}$$

We leave it to the reader to verify that:

$$p(D|A, B) = p_1(D|A = 0) \oplus p_2(D|A = 0, B) \oplus p_3(D|A = 1) \oplus p_4(D|A = 1).$$

The important point in this section is that CWI together with the weak join operator $\oplus$ allow the given CPT $p(D|A, B)$ to be faithfully represented by four *smaller* distributions. Such a CWI representation can lead to more efficient inference than with CI and CSI [2]. Thereby, it is useful to study ways to obtain the CWIs holding in a problem domain.

3 Specification of CWIs by a Human Expert

Instead of viewing a CPT as a table, here we view a CPT as a tree structure, called a *CPT-tree* [1]. The CPT-tree representation is advantageous since it makes it particularly easy to elicit probabilities from a human expert. The *label* of a path in a CPT-tree is defined as the value of the nodes on that path. By (A, B, X) we denote a directed edge from variable A to variable B in the CPT-tree with label X.

Example 2. A human expert could specify the CPT-tree in Fig. 2 representing the CPT $p(D|A, B)$ in Fig. 1.

Algorithm 1 transforms a single CPT into several *partial* CPTs based on the CWIs in the CPT-tree given by a human expert.

Algorithm 1 DECOMPOSE CPT
Input: an expert specified CPT-tree defining a single CPT $p(A|X)$
Output: the *partial* CPTs faithfully representing $p(A|X)$
1. Block the CPT according to the levels in the CPT-tree.
2. For any edge (A, B, X) where X is non-singleton,
    Remove A from the corresponding block.

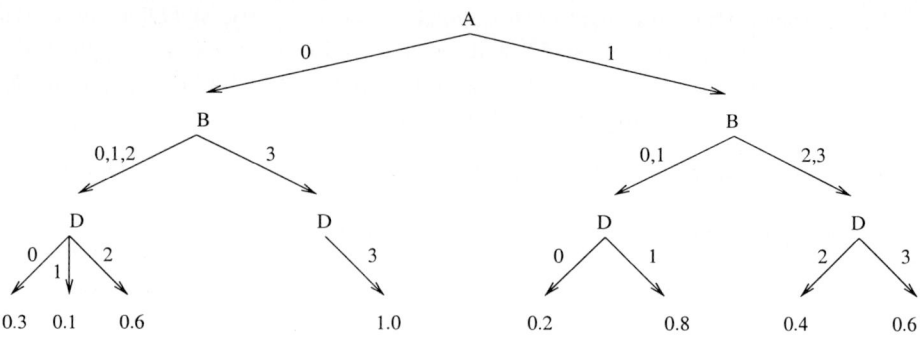

Fig. 2. The CPT-tree given by a human expert representing $p(D|A,B)$ in Fig. 1.

Example 3. The given expert specified CPT-tree in Fig. 2 defines the CPT $p(D|A,B)$ in Fig. 1 (i). By step (1) of Algorithm 1, the CPT-tree indicates the following four blocks:

$$Block\ \#1:\quad A \in \{0\}, B \in \{0,1,2\}, D \in \{0,1,2\},$$
$$Block\ \#2:\quad A \in \{0\}, B \in \{3\}, D \in \{3\},$$
$$Block\ \#3:\quad A \in \{1\}, B \in \{0,1\}, D \in \{0,1\},$$
$$Block\ \#4:\quad A \in \{1\}, B \in \{2,3\}, D \in \{2,3\}.$$

By step (2) of Algorithm 1, variable B can be deleted from the first, third, and fourth partial CPTs. Observe that this indicates the presence of CWIs, for instance, $p_1(D|A=0,B) = p_1(D|A=0)$.

4 Detecting CWIs in a Conditional Probability Table

In this section, we propose a method for detecting contextual weak independencies from a CPT. Such a method is useful when no human expert is available.

As it may be difficult to determine CWIs directly from a CPT, a given CPT can be represented as a CPT-tree. For example, given the CPT $p(D|A,B)$ in Fig. 1 (i), one *initial* CPT-tree is shown in Fig. 3. Algorithm 2 *refines* an initial CPT-tree so that Algorithm 1 can be applied.

Algorithm 2 REFINE CPT-TREE
Input: an *initial* CPT-tree for a given CPT
Output: the *refined* CPT-tree obtained by removing all vacuous edges
If some children of a node A are identical, then combine these children into one node by augmenting the labels of the combined edges.

Example 4. Consider the initial CPT-tree in Fig. 3. When $A = 0$, node B has identical children, namely, the three children with edge labels 0, 1, and 2. Hence,

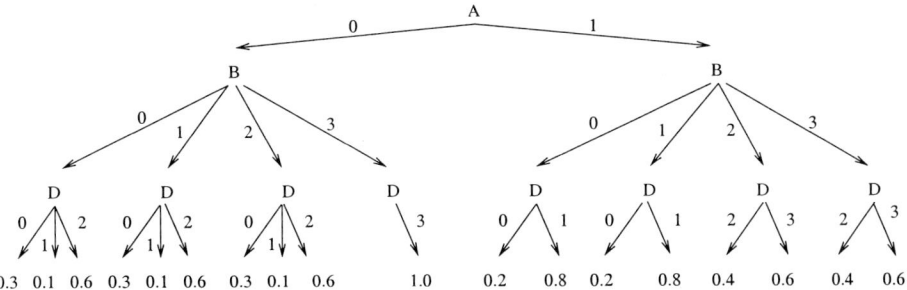

Fig. 3. One initial CPT-tree defined by the CPT $p(D|A,B)$ in Fig. 1.

these three edges can be combined into a single edge with label $0, 1, 2$. Moreover, when $A = 1$, node B has identical children for its values 0 and 1. Hence, these edges are grouped together. Similarly, for when $A = 1$ and $B \in \{2, 3\}$. The *refined* CPT-tree after these deletions is shown in Fig. 2.

The important point is that CWIs can be obtained from a CPT. From a given CPT, we can construct an *initial* CPT-tree. Algorithm 2 can then be applied to *refine* the tree. Finally Algorithm 1 can be applied to decompose the given CPT into the smaller *partial* CPTs based on detected CWIs.

5 Conclusion

We have suggested a method (Algorithm 1) for obtaining CWIs from a human expert and another (Algorithm 2) for the situation when no expert is available. Acquiring CWIs is quite important since probabilistic inference using CWIs can be more efficient than inference using CIs and CSIs [2].

References

1. Boutilier, C., Friedman, N., Goldszmidt, M., Koller, D.: Context-specific independence in Bayesian networks, *Twelfth Conference on Uncertainty in Artificial Intelligence*, 115–123, 1996.
2. Butz, C.J., Sanscartier, M.J.: On the role of contextual weak independence in probabilistic inference, *Fifteenth Canadian Conference on Uncertainty in Artificial Intelligence*, (to appear) 2002.
3. Wong, S.K.M., Butz, C.J.: Contextual weak independence in Bayesian networks. In *Fifteenth Conference on Uncertainty in Artificial Intelligence*, 670–679, 1999.
4. Zhang, N., Poole, D.: On the role of context-specific independence in probabilistic inference, *Sixteenth Int. Joint Conf. on Artificial Intelligence*, 1288–1293, 1999.

A Method for Detecting Context-Specific Independence in Conditional Probability Tables

C.J. Butz and M.J. Sanscartier

Department of Computer Science, University of Regina,
Regina, Canada, S4S 0A2,
{butz,sanscarm}@cs.uregina.ca

Abstract. Context-specific independence is useful as it can lead to improved inference in Bayesian networks. In this paper, we present a method for detecting this kind of independence from data and emphasize why such an algorithm is needed.

1 Introduction

Based upon the notions of *conditional probability tables* (CPTs) and *probabilistic conditional independence* [3], the *Bayesian network* [2] is an elegant and formal framework for probabilistic reasoning. More recently, the Bayesian community has become interested in *contextual* independencies such as *context-specific independence* (CSI) [1]. Contextual independencies are useful since they may lead to more efficient probabilistic inference [4]. However, the *acquisition* of contextual independencies has not received as much attention. In [1], *CPT-trees* were introduced to help a human expert specify a CPT. A graphical method, which we call *csi-detection*, was provided to read CSIs from a CPT-tree [1].

In some situations, however, no human expert is available. In addition, we explicitly demonstrate that the csi-detection may *fail* to detect valid CSIs holding in the CPT-tree constructed directly from a given CPT. Thus, a method for detecting CSIs from data is needed. In this paper, we suggest a procedure (Algorithm 1) for detecting CSIs in a given CPT.

This paper is organized as follows. Section 2 introduces *context-specific independence*. In Section 3, we review a method for obtaining CSIs from an expert. In Section 4, we propose a method for detecting CSIs in a given CPT. The conclusion is presented in Section 5.

2 Context-Specific Independence

Let p be a *joint probability distribution* (jpd) [3] over a set U of variables and X, Y, Z be subsets of U. We say Y and Z are *conditionally independent* given X, if given any $x \in V_X$, $y \in V_Y$, then for all $z \in V_Z$,

$$p(y \mid x, z) \quad = \quad p(y \mid x), \quad \text{whenever } p(x, z) > 0. \tag{1}$$

Consider a Bayesian network with directed edges $\{(A,C), (A,D), (A,E), (B,D), (C,E), (D,E)\}$. Based on the *conditional independence* (CI) assumptions encoded in this network, the jpd $p(A,B,C,D,E)$ can be factorized as

$$p(A,B,C,D,E) \;=\; p(A) \cdot p(B) \cdot p(C|A) \cdot p(D|A,B) \cdot p(E|A,C,D), \quad (2)$$

where $p(D|A,B)$ and $p(E|A,C,D)$ are shown in Fig. 1. The marginal $p(A,B,C,E)$ can be computed from Eq. (2) as follows: (i) compute the product $p(D|A,B) \cdot p(E|A,C,D)$; (ii) marginalize out variable D from this product; and (iii) multiply the resulting distribution with $p(A) \cdot p(B) \cdot p(C|A)$.

A B D	$p(D|A,B)$	A C D E	$p(E|A,C,D)$
0 0 0	0.3	0 0 0 0	0.1
0 0 1	0.7	0 0 0 1	0.9
0 1 0	0.3	0 0 1 0	0.1
0 1 1	0.7	0 0 1 1	0.9
1 0 0	0.6	0 1 0 0	0.8
1 0 1	0.4	0 1 0 1	0.2
1 1 0	0.8	0 1 1 0	0.8
1 1 1	0.2	0 1 1 1	0.2
		1 0 0 0	0.6
		1 0 0 1	0.4
		1 0 1 0	0.3
		1 0 1 1	0.7
		1 1 0 0	0.6
		1 1 0 1	0.4
		1 1 1 0	0.3
		1 1 1 1	0.7

Fig. 1. The CPTs $p(D|A,B)$ and $p(E|A,C,D)$ in Eq. (2).

In some situations, however, the conditional independence may only hold for certain *specific* values in V_X, called *context-specific independence* (CSI) [1]. Let X, Y, Z, C be pairwise disjoint subsets of U and $c \in V_C$. We say Y and Z are *conditionally independent* given X in *context* $C = c$, if

$$p(y \mid x, z, c) = p(y \mid x, c), \quad \text{whenever } p(x, z, c) > 0.$$

For example, consider again the CPT $p(D|A,B)$ redrawn in Fig. 2 (i). Although variables D and B are *not* conditionally independent given A, it can be seen in Fig. 2 (ii,iii) that D and B are independent in context $A = 0$. Similarly, for the CPT $p(E|A,C,D)$, variables E and D are independent given C in context $A = 0$, while variables E and C are independent given D in context $A = 1$.

The CPTs $p(D|A,B)$ and $p(E|A,C,D)$ can then be rewritten as

$$p(D|A,B) \;=\; p(D|A=0) \odot p(D|A=1, B), \quad (3)$$

and

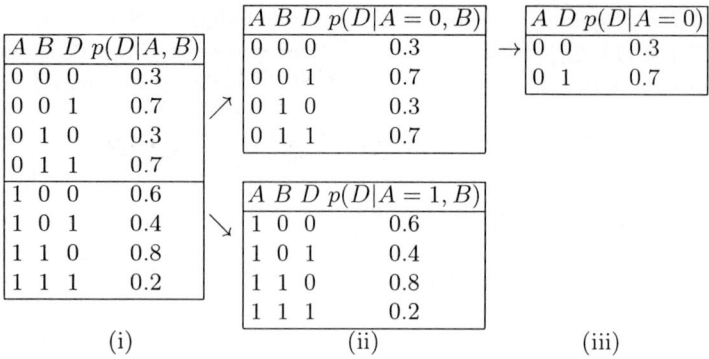

Fig. 2. Variables D and B are conditionally independent in context $A = 0$.

$$p(E|A,C,D) \;=\; p(E|A=0,C) \odot p(E|A=1,D), \qquad (4)$$

where $\odot$ is the *union product* operator [4]. By substituting Eqs. (3) and (4) into Eq. (2), the factorization of the jpd $p(A,B,C,D,E)$ using CSI is

$$\begin{aligned} p(A,B,C,D,E) \;=\;& p(A) \cdot p(B) \cdot p(C|A) \odot p(D|A=0) \odot p(D|A=1,B) \\ & \odot\, p(E|A=0,C) \odot p(E|A=1,D). \end{aligned} \qquad (5)$$

Computing $p(A,B,C,E)$ from Eq. (5) requires 16 fewer multiplications and 8 fewer additions compared to the respective number of computations needed to compute $p(A,B,C,E)$ from the CI factorization in Eq. (2).

3 Specification of CSIs by a Human Expert

Instead of viewing a CPT as a table, here we view a CPT as a tree structure, called a *CPT-tree* [1]. The CPT-tree representation is advantageous since it makes it particularly easy to elicit probabilities from a human expert. A second advantage of CPT-trees is that they allow a simple graphical method, which we call *csi-detection*, for detecting CSIs [1]. We describe csi-detection as follows.

Given a CPT-tree for a variable A and its parent set π_A, i.e., a CPT-tree for the CPT $p(A|\pi_A)$. The *label* of a path is defined as the value of the nodes on that path. A path is *consistent* with a context $C = c$ iff the labeling of the path is consistent with the assignment of the values in c. Given the CPT-tree depicting $p(Y|X,Z,C)$, we say that variable Y is independent of variable Z given X in the specific context $C = c$, if Z does not appear on any path consistent with $C = c$.

Example 1. A human expert could specify the the CPT-tree in Fig. 3 representing the CPT $p(E|A,C,D)$ in Fig. 1. Consider the context $A = 0$. Since variable D does not appear on any path consistent with $A = 0$, we say that variables E and D are independent given C in context $A = 0$. It can be verified that variables E and C are independent given D in context $A = 1$.

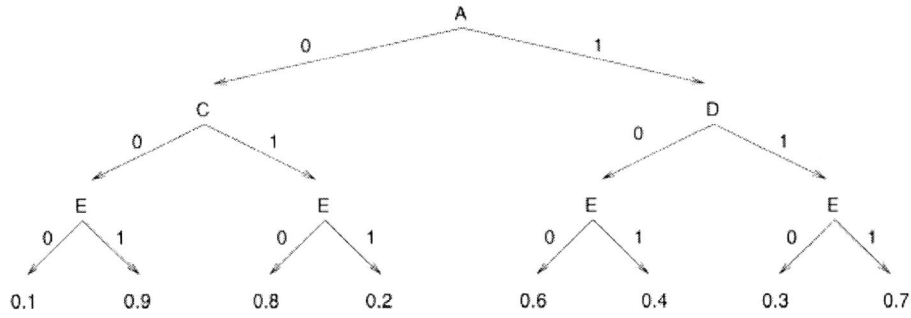

Fig. 3. The CPT-tree given by a human expert representing $p(E|A,C,D)$ in Fig. 1.

4 Detecting CSIs in a Conditional Probability Table

In this section, we propose a method for detecting context-specific independencies from a CPT. We begin by showing why this approach is needed.

In many situations, no human expert is available and one must rely solely on data. Moreover, the csi-detection method presented in the last section may *not* work on the CPT-tree built directly from a given CPT.

Example 2. Suppose there is no human expert available. The *initial* CPT-tree in Fig. 4 is obtained directly from the CPT in Fig. 1. Although variables E and D are independent given C in context $A = 0$, while variables E and C are independent given D in context $A = 1$, the csi-detection method does *not* detect any CSIs holding in this initial CPT-tree.

The problem here is that the csi-detection method is based on missing arcs in the CPT-tree. Thus, we suggest the following algorithm to remove the vacuous arcs in the initial CPT-tree constructed directly from a given CPT.

Algorithm 1 REFINED CPT-TREE
Input: an *initial* CPT-tree for a given CPT
Output: the *refined* CPT-tree obtained by removing all vacuous arcs
1. If all children of a node A are identical, then replace A by one of its offspring.
2. Delete all other children of node A.

Example 3. Consider again the initial CPT-tree in Fig. 4. When $A = 0$ and $C = 0$, node D has identical children. Hence, node D can be replaced with node E. Similarly, for when $A = 0$ and $C = 1$. Moreover, when $A = 1$, node C has identical children. Node C can then be replaced by node D. The *refined* CPT-tree after these deletions is shown in Fig. 3.

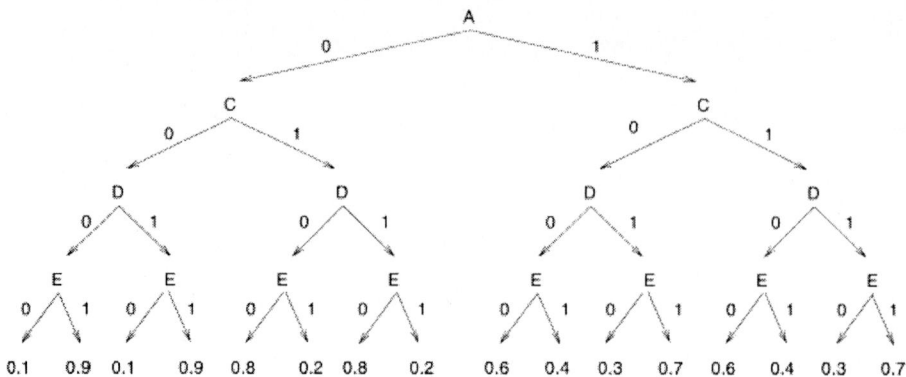

Fig. 4. The *initial* CPT-tree for the given CPT $p(E|A,C,D)$ in Fig. 1.

5 Conclusion

Contextual independencies such as *context-specific independence* (CSI) [1] are important, since they can lead to more efficient inference [4]. Previous work has suggested using *CPT-trees* and *csi-detection* to elicit CSIs from an expert [1]. In some situations, however, no human expert is available. Moreover, Example 2 explicitly demonstrates that the csi-detection may *fail* to detect valid CSIs holding in the CPT-tree constructed directly from a given CPT. Thus, a method for detecting CSIs from data is needed. In this paper, we proposed Algorithm 1 for detecting CSIs in a given CPT.

References

1. Boutilier, C., Friedman, N., Goldszmidt, M., Koller, D.: Context-specific independence in Bayesian networks, *Twelfth Conference on Uncertainty in Artificial Intelligence*, 115–123, 1996.
2. Pearl, J.: *Probabilistic Reasoning in Intelligent Systems: Networks of Plausible Inference*. Morgan Kaufmann Publishers, 1988.
3. Wong, S.K.M., Butz, C.J., Wu, D.: On the implication problem for probabilistic conditional independency. *IEEE Transactions on Systems, Man, and Cybernetics*, Vol. 30, Part A, No. 6, 785–805, 2000.
4. Zhang, N., Poole, D.: On the role of context-specific independence in probabilistic inference, *Sixteenth International Joint Conference on Artificial Intelligence*, 1288–1293, 1999.

Properties of Weak Conditional Independence

C.J. Butz and M.J. Sanscartier

Department of Computer Science, University of Regina,
Regina, Canada, S4S 0A2,
{butz,sanscarm}@cs.uregina.ca

Abstract. *Object-oriented Bayesian networks* (OOBNs) facilitate the design of large Bayesian networks by allowing Bayesian networks to be nested inside of one another. *Weak conditional independence* has been shown to be a necessary and sufficient condition for ensuring consistency in OOBNs. Since weak conditional independence plays such an important role in OOBNs, in this paper we establish two useful results relating weak conditional independence with *weak multivalued dependency* in relational databases. The first result strengthens a previous result relating conditional independence and multivalued dependency. The second result takes a step towards showing that the complete axiomatization for weak multivalued dependency is also *complete* for full weak conditional independence.

1 Introduction

Recently, *object-oriented Bayesian networks* (OOBNs) [2] were introduced to facilitate the construction of large *Bayesian networks* [4,8]. In this framework, each variable may be itself a Bayesian network, that is, OOBNs allow the value of a variable to be itself a distribution. To ensure that an OOBN defines a *unique* coarsened distribution, certain conditional independence assumptions were made in [2]. However, we will explicitly demonstrate here that conditional independence is *not* a necessary condition for ensuring consistency. *Weak conditional independence* was introduced in [6] and shown to be a necessary and sufficient condition for ensuring a unique coarsened distribution.

Since weak conditional independence plays such an important role in OOBNs, in this paper we establish two useful results relating weak conditional independence with *weak multivalued dependency* [1] in relational databases. The first result strengthens a previous result by Malvestuto [3] and Wong [5] relating conditional independence and multivalued dependency. The second result takes a step towards showing that the complete axiomatization for weak multivalued dependency [1] is also *complete* for full weak conditional independence.

This paper is organized as follows. Section 2 briefly outlines OOBNs and introduces the inconsistency problem. In Section 3, we review weak conditional independence. The relationship between weak conditional independence and weak multivalued dependency is studied in Section 4. The conclusion is presented in Section 5.

2 Object-Oriented Bayesian Networks

Consider a finite set $U = \{A_1, A_2, \ldots, A_n\}$ of discrete random variables, where each variable $A \in U$ takes on values from a finite domain V_A. We may use capital letters, such as A, B, C, for variable names and lowercase letters a, b, c to denote specific values taken by those variables. Sets of variables will be denoted by capital letters such as X, Y, Z, and assignments of values to the variables in these sets (called configurations or tuples) will be denoted by lowercase letters x, y, z. We use V_X in the obvious way.

Let p be a *joint probability distribution* (jpd) [4] over the variables in U and X, Y, Z be subsets of U. We say Y and Z are *conditionally independent* given X, denoted $\mathbf{I}(Y, X, Z)$, if given any $x \in V_X$, $y \in V_Y$, then for all $z \in V_Z$,

$$p(y \mid x, z) = p(y \mid x), \quad \text{whenever } p(x, z) > 0. \tag{1}$$

A *Bayesian network* [4] is a *directed acyclic graph* (DAG) together with a corresponding set of conditional probability tables. The DAG graphically encodes conditional independencies assumed to hold in the problem domain. For example, based on the conditional independencies encoded in the Bayesian network in Fig. 1, the jpd $p(A, B, C, D, E)$ can be factorized as

$$p(A, B, C, D, E) = p(A) \cdot p(B) \cdot p(C|A) \cdot p(D|A, B) \cdot p(E|A, C, D).$$

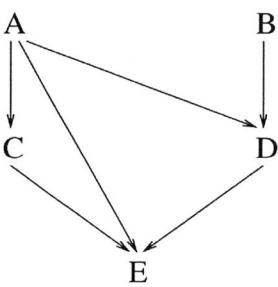

Fig. 1. A Bayesian network on variables $U = \{A, B, C, D, E\}$.

We now turn our attention to *granular* probabilistic networks [2]. We use the term granular to mean the ability to *coarsen* and *refine* parts of a probabilistic network.

Example 1. Consider the Bayesian network for a car accident [2] as shown in Fig. 2. One can *refine* the node *Car* to reveal the internal structure as shown in Fig. 3, where the rest of the network is not illustrated due to space limitations.

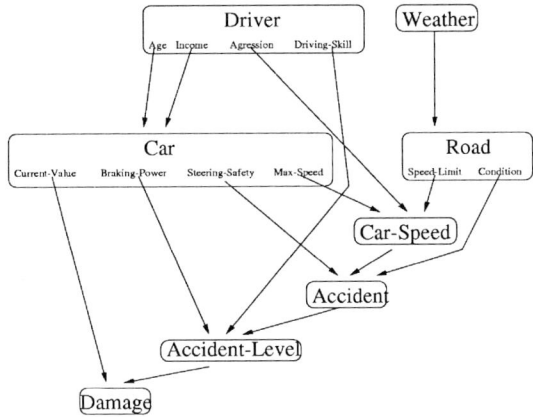

Fig. 2. A Bayesian network for a car accident.

The *nest* operator [6], denoted ϕ, is used to *coarsen* a distribution $\mathbf{r}(XY)$. Intuitively, $\phi_{B=Y}(\mathbf{r})$ groups together the set Y of variables into a single variable B by forming a nested distribution given the same value for X.

Example 2. Consider $\mathbf{r}(ABC)$ in Fig. 4 (left). Coarsened distributions $\phi_{D=A}(\mathbf{r})$ (middle) and $\phi_{E=C}(\phi_{D=A}(\mathbf{r}))$ (right).

The main problem is that the nest operator does not necessarily commute.

Example 3. Recall $\mathbf{r}(ABC)$ in Fig. 4. It can be verified that $\phi_{D=A}(\phi_{E=C}(\mathbf{r})) \neq \phi_{E=C}(\phi_{D=A}(\mathbf{r}))$.

In order to ensure that the nest operator commutes, i.e.,

$$\phi_{A=Y}(\phi_{B=Z}(\mathbf{r})) = \phi_{B=Z}(\phi_{A=Y}(\mathbf{r})), \qquad (2)$$

assumptions must be made on the original joint distribution $\mathbf{r}$. Koller and Pfeffer [2] established that if the distribution $\mathbf{r}(YXZ)$ satisfies the conditional independence $\mathbf{I}(Y, X, Z)$, then Equation (2) holds. In other words, if Y and Z are conditionally independent given X, then $\phi_{A=Y}(\phi_{B=Z}(\mathbf{r})) = \phi_{B=Z}(\phi_{A=Y}(\mathbf{r}))$. The next example, however, explicitly demonstrates that conditional independence is *not* a necessary condition to ensure a unique coarsened distribution.

Example 4. The joint probability distribution $\mathbf{r}(ABC)$ in Fig. 5 (left) does *not* satisfy $\mathbf{I}(A, B, C)$, i.e., variables A and C are *not* conditionally independent given B. Nevertheless, it is still the case that $\phi_{D=A}(\phi_{E=C}(\mathbf{r}))$ in Fig. 5 (middle) is equal to $\phi_{E=C}(\phi_{D=A}(\mathbf{r}))$ in Fig. 5 (right).

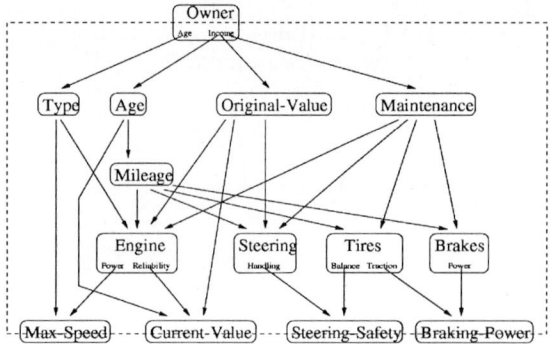

Fig. 3. Refining the Bayesian network in Fig. 2 to reveal the internal structure of the variable Car.

A	B	C	p(ABC)
0	0	0	0.4
1	0	0	0.4
1	0	1	0.2

D	B	C	p(DBC)
	A	p(A)	
	0	0.5	
	1	0.5	
0	0		0.8

	A	p(A)
	1	1.0
0	1		0.2

D	B	E	p(DBE)
	A	p(A)	C	p(C)	
	0	0.5	0	1.0	
	1	0.5			
0	0				0.8

	A	p(A)	C	p(C)
	1	1.0	1	1.0
1	1				0.2

Fig. 4. A joint distribution $\mathbf{r}(ABC)$ (left). Coarsened distributions $\phi_{D=A}(\mathbf{r})$ (middle) and $\phi_{E=C}(\phi_{D=A}(\mathbf{r}))$ (right).

3 Weak Conditional Independence

As pointed out in [6], when introducing nested distributions one steps outside the realm of conditional independence and into the realm of *weak conditional independence*. In the following definition of weak conditional independence, $\circ$ denotes the usual *composition* of relations, while $\theta(X)$ denotes the *equivalence relation* (partition) of $\mathbf{r}(XYZ)$ induced by the set X of variables [6].

We say variables Y and Z are *weakly independent* given X in $\mathbf{r}(XYZ)$, denoted $\mathbf{W}(Y,X,Z)$, if the following two conditions hold: (i) $\theta(XY) \circ \theta(XZ) = \theta(XZ) \circ \theta(XY)$, and (ii) for every equivalence class π in $\theta(XY) \circ \theta(XZ)$, the distribution $\mathbf{r}_\pi(XYZ)$ satisfies $\mathbf{I}(Y,X,Z)$, where $\mathbf{r}_\pi(XYZ)$ is defined as: $\mathbf{r}_\pi(XYZ) = \{\ t\ |\ t \in \mathbf{r}$ and $t \in \pi\ \}$. Condition (i) says that $\theta(XY) \circ \theta(XZ)$ is an *equivalence relation*. Condition (ii) says that each equivalence class satisfies $\mathbf{I}(Y,X,Z)$.

Example 5. Let us verify that $\mathbf{r}(ABC)$ in Fig. 5 satisfies $\mathbf{W}(A,B,C)$. By definition, $\theta(AB) = \{\ [t_1,t_2],\ [t_3,t_4],\ [t_5]\ \}$ and $\theta(BC) = \{\ [t_1,t_3],\ [t_2,t_4],\ [t_5]\ \}$. Condition (i) is satisfied since

A	B	C	p(ABC)
0	0	0	0.225
0	0	1	0.375
1	0	0	0.075
1	0	1	0.125
2	0	2	0.200

D	B	E	p(BDE)
A p(A) 0 0.75 1 0.25	0	C p(C) 0 0.375 1 0.625	0.8
A p(A) 2 1.0	0	C p(C) 2 1.0	0.2

D	B	E	p(BDE)
A p(A) 0 0.75 1 0.25	0	C p(C) 0 0.375 1 0.625	0.8
A p(A) 2 1.0	0	C p(C) 2 1.0	0.2

Fig. 5. Distribution $\mathbf{r}(ABC)$ does not satisfy $\mathbf{I}(A,B,C)$, yet $\phi_{D=A}(\phi_{E=C}(\mathbf{r}))$ (middle) is equal to $\phi_{E=C}(\phi_{D=A}(\mathbf{r}))$ (right).

$$\theta(AB) \circ \theta(BC) = \{ \pi_1 = [t_1, t_2, t_3, t_4],\ \pi_2 = [t_5] \} = \theta(BC) \circ \theta(AB).$$

It can be verified that the (horizontal) distribution $\mathbf{r}_{\pi_1}(ABC) = \{t_1, t_2, t_3, t_4\}$ satisfies $\mathbf{I}(A, B, C)$. Since $\mathbf{r}_{\pi_2}(ABC) = \{t_5\}$ also satisfies $\mathbf{I}(A, B, C)$, by definition, $\mathbf{r}(ABC)$ satisfies $\mathbf{W}(A, B, C)$.

Weak conditional independence is very important in OOBNs, since it has been shown [6] that a distribution $\mathbf{r}(XYZ)$ satisfies $\mathbf{W}(Y, X, Z)$ if and only if $\phi_{A=Y}(\phi_{B=Z}(\mathbf{r})) = \phi_{B=Z}(\phi_{A=Y}(\mathbf{r}))$.

4 Properties of Weak Conditional Independence

In this section, we establish two properties of weak conditional independence in its relationship to *weak multivalued dependency* [1] in relational databases.

Before discussing weak conditional independence $\mathbf{W}(Y, X, Z)$ and weak multivalued dependency $W(Y, X, Z)$, let us first recall one result by Malvestuto [3] and Wong [5] relating conditional independence $\mathbf{I}(Y, X, Z)$ with *multivalued dependency* $I(Y, X, Z)$ in relational databases.

Theorem 1. [3,5] *Let $r(XYZ)$ be a relation with n tuples. Let $\mathbf{r}(XYZ)$ be the uniform joint distribution corresponding to $r(XYZ)$, i.e., the probability value of each tuple in $\mathbf{r}(XYZ)$ is $1/n$. Then $r(XYZ)$ satisfies the multivalued dependency $I(Y, X, Z)$ iff $\mathbf{r}(XYZ)$ satisfies the conditional independence $\mathbf{I}(Y, X, Z)$.*

Since conditional independence is a special case of weak conditional independence and multivalued dependency is a special case of weak multivalued dependency, Theorem 1 is strengthened as follows.

Theorem 2. *Let $r(XYZ)$ be a relation with n tuples. Let $\mathbf{r}(XYZ)$ be the uniform joint distribution corresponding to $r(XYZ)$, i.e., the probability value of each tuple in $\mathbf{r}(XYZ)$ is $1/n$. Then $r(XYZ)$ satisfies the weak multivalued dependency $W(Y, X, Z)$ iff $\mathbf{r}(XYZ)$ satisfies the weak conditional independence $\mathbf{W}(Y, X, Z)$.*

Proof: ($\Rightarrow$) Suppose relation $r(XYZ)$ satisfies $\mathbf{W}(Y, X, Z)$. From an equivalent definition of weak multivalued dependency [7], $\theta(XY) \circ \theta(XZ) = \theta(XZ) \circ \theta(XY)$. This implies that every equivalence class $\pi = \{t_1, t_2, \ldots, t_k\}$ in the equivalence relation $\theta(XY) \circ \theta(XZ)$ satisfies $I(Y, X, Z)$. Since $\mathbf{r}(XYZ)$ is a uniform distribution, the probabilistic distribution $\mathbf{r}_\pi(XYZ) = \{\, t \mid t \in \mathbf{r}(XYZ) \text{ and } t \in \pi \,\}$, is also a *constant* distribution. Since $\pi = \{t_1, t_2, \ldots, t_k\}$ satisfies $I(Y, X, Z)$, by Theorem 1, the constant distribution $\mathbf{r}_\pi(XYZ)$ satisfies $\mathbf{I}(Y, X, Z)$. This observation holds for every equivalence class in $\theta(XY) \circ \theta(XZ)$. Since $\theta(XY) \circ \theta(XZ) = \theta(XZ) \circ \theta(XY)$ and every equivalence class satisfies $\mathbf{I}(Y, X, Z)$, by definition, the uniform distribution $\mathbf{r}(XYZ)$ satisfies $\mathbf{W}(Y, X, Z)$.

($\Leftarrow$) Suppose the uniform distribution $\mathbf{r}(XYZ)$ satisfies $\mathbf{W}(Y, X, Z)$. By definition, $\theta(XY) \circ \theta(XZ) = \theta(XZ) \circ \theta(XY)$ and every equivalence class in $\theta(XY) \circ \theta(XZ)$ satisfies $\mathbf{I}(Y, X, Z)$. By the former, $r(XYZ)$ satisfies $W(Y, X, Z)$. $\square$

Corollary 1. *In non-uniform distributions, weak multivalued dependency is a necessary but not a sufficient condition for weak conditional independence.*

Theorem 2 says that a traditional relation $r(XYZ)$ satisfies $W(Y, X, Z)$ if and only if the uniform probabilistic distribution $\mathbf{r}(XYZ)$ satisfies $\mathbf{W}(Y, X, Z)$.

Example 6. The traditional relation $r(ABC)$ in Fig. 6 satisfies the weak multivalued dependency $W(A, B, C)$. By Theorem 2, the corresponding *uniform* distribution $\mathbf{r}(ABC)$ must satisfy the weak conditional independence $\mathbf{W}(A, B, C)$.

A B C	A B C	p(ABC)
0 0 0	0 0 0	0.2
0 0 1	0 0 1	0.2
1 0 0	1 0 0	0.2
1 0 1	1 0 1	0.2
2 0 2	2 0 2	0.2

Fig. 6. A traditional relation $r(ABC)$ and the corresponding the *uniform* distribution.

Our last objective in this exposition strives toward a complete axiomatization for the class of *full* weak conditional independence. Given $R = ABCD$, the weak independence $\mathbf{W}(A, B, CD)$ is called *full*, while $\mathbf{W}(A, B, C)$ is *embedded* since $ABC \subset R$. One approach would be to develop a set of axioms and establish completeness. Similar to [9], the approach we take here is to draw a one-to-one correspondence between weak conditional independence and weak multivalued dependency in relational databases.

The class of weak multivalued dependency has a *complete* axiomatization [1] consisting of four inference axioms (W1)-(W4). If we could establish that the *logical implication* [9], denoted $\models$, of (the numeric) weak conditional independence is exactly the same as that of (the non-numeric) weak multivalued dependency, then the complete axiomatization for weak multivalued dependency would also *complete* for full weak conditional independence. Hence, let the corresponding inferences axioms (**W1**) – (**W4**) for weak conditional independence be defined by replacing each occurrence of $W(Y, X, Z)$ in (W1)-(W4) by $\mathbf{W}(Y, X, Z)$.

Theorem 3. Given the *complete* axiomatization (W1)-(W4) for the weak multivalued dependency class. If the corresponding axioms (**W1**)-(**W4**) for the weak conditional independence class are *sound* [9], then

$$\mathbf{C} \models \mathbf{c} \iff C \models c,$$

where $\mathbf{C}$ is a set of weak conditional independencies, the corresponding set of weak multivalued dependencies is $C = \{W(Y, X, Z) \mid \mathbf{W}(Y, X, Z) \in \mathbf{C}\}$, and c is the weak multivalued dependency corresponding to a full weak conditional independence $\mathbf{c}$.

Proof: ($\Rightarrow$) Suppose $\mathbf{C} \models \mathbf{c}$. We will prove the claim by contradiction. That is, suppose that $C \not\models c$. By definition, there exists a relation $r(R)$ such that $r(R)$ satisfies all of the weak multivalued dependencies in C, but $r(R)$ does not satisfy the weak multivalued dependency c. Let k denote the number of tuples in $r(R)$. We construct a distribution $\mathbf{r}(R)$ from $r(R)$ by appending the attribute A_p. For each of the k tuples in $\mathbf{r}(R)$, set $\mathbf{t}(A_p) = 1/k$. Thus, $\mathbf{r}(R)$ represents a *uniform* distribution. In the uniform case, by Theorem 2, $\mathbf{r}(R)$ satisfies $\mathbf{C}$ if and only if $r(R)$ satisfies C. Again using the uniform case, $\mathbf{r}(R)$ does not satisfy $\mathbf{c}$ since $r(R)$ does not satisfy c. By definition, $\mathbf{C}$ does not logically imply $\mathbf{c}$, namely, $\mathbf{C} \not\models \mathbf{c}$. A contradiction to the initial assumption that $\mathbf{C} \models \mathbf{c}$. Therefore, $C \models c$.

($\Leftarrow$) Let $C \models c$. Since (W1)-(W4) are *complete*, $C \models c$ implies that there exists a derivation sequence s of the weak multivalued dependency c by applying the weak multivalued dependency axioms to the weak multivalued dependencies in C. That c can be derived from C is written $C \vdash c$. On the other hand, each weak multivalued dependency axiom has a corresponding weak conditional independence axiom. This means there exists a derivation sequence $\mathbf{s}$ of the weak conditional independence $\mathbf{c}$ using the weak conditional independence axioms (**W1**)-(**W4**) on the weak conditional independencies in $\mathbf{C}$, which parallels the derivation sequence s of the weak multivalued dependency c. That is, $\mathbf{C} \vdash \mathbf{c}$. Since the weak conditional independence axioms are assumed to be sound, $\mathbf{C} \vdash \mathbf{c}$ implies that $\mathbf{C} \models \mathbf{c}$. $\square$

5 Conclusion

Since *weak conditional independence* is a necessary and sufficient condition for the nest operator to commute [6], we established useful results relating weak conditional independence to weak multivalued dependency in relational databases.

Theorem 2 strengthens a previous result by Malvestuto [3] and Wong [5] relating conditional independence and multivalued dependency. The other result (Theorem 4) shows that the complete axiomatization for weak multivalued dependency [1] is also *complete* for full weak conditional independence, provided that the corresponding weak conditional independence inference axioms are sound.

References

1. Fischer, P., Van Gucht, D.: Weak multivalued dependencies, *Proceedings of the Third ACM SIGACT-SIGMOD Symposium on the Principles of Database Systems*, 266–274, 1984.
2. Koller, D.,Pfeffer, A.: Object-oriented Bayesian networks. In *Thirteenth Conference on Uncertainty in Artificial Intelligence*, 302–313, 1997.
3. Malvestuto, F.: A unique formal system for binary decompositions of database relations, probability distributions and graphs. *Information Sciences*, 59:21–52, 1992.
4. Pearl, J.: *Probabilistic Reasoning in Intelligent Systems: Networks of Plausible Inference*. Morgan Kaufmann Publishers, 1988.
5. Wong, S.K.M.: An extended relational data model for probabilistic reasoning. *Journal of Intelligent Information Systems*, 9:181–202, 1997.
6. Wong, S.K.M., Butz, C.J.: Contextual weak independence in Bayesian networks. In *Fifteenth Conference on Uncertainty in Artificial Intelligence*, 670–679, 1999.
7. Wong, S.K.M., Butz, C.J.: A comparative study of noncontextual and contextual dependencies. In *12th International Symposium on Methodologies for Intelligent Systems*, 247-255, 2000.
8. Wong, S.K.M., Butz, C.J.: Constructing the dependency structure of a multi-agent probabilistic network. *IEEE Transactions on Knowledge and Data Engineering*, Vol. 13, No. 3, 395–415, 2001.
9. Wong, S.K.M., Butz, C.J., Wu, D.: On the implication problem for probabilistic conditional independency. *IEEE Transactions on Systems, Man, and Cybernetics*, Vol. 30, Part A, No. 6, 785–805, 2000.

A Proposal of Probability of Rough Event Based on Probability of Fuzzy Event

Rolly Intan[1,2] and Masao Mukaidono[1]

[1] Meiji University, Kawasaki-shi, Kanagawa-ken, Japan
[2] Petra Christian University, Surabaya, Indonesia 60236

Abstract. Probability and fuzziness are different measures for dealing with different uncertainties in which they be able to be combined and considered as a complementary tool. In this paper, the relationship between probability and fuzziness are discussed based on the process of perception. In probability, set theory is used to provide a language for modeling and describing random experiments. Here, as a generalization of crisp set, fuzzy set is used to model fuzzy event as defined by Zadeh. Similarly, rough set can be also used to represent rough event in terms of probability measure. Special attention will be given to conditional probability of fuzzy event as well as conditional probability of rough event. Their several combinations of formulation and properties are defined.

1 Introduction

Since the appearance of the first article on fuzzy sets proposed by zadeh in 1965, the relationship between probability and fuzziness in representing uncertainty has been an object of debate among many people. The main problem is whether or not probability theory by itself is sufficient for dealing with uncertainty. This question has been discussed at length in many papers such as written by Nguyen 1977 [5], Kosko 1990 [4], Zadeh 1968 [9], 1995 [10], and so on.

In this paper, again we try to simply understand the relationship between probability and fuzziness using the process of perception performed by human being. In the process of perception, subject (human, computer, robot, etc) tries to recognize and describe a given object (anything such as human, plant, animal, event, condition, etc). To perform perception successfully, subject needs adequate knowledge. On the other hand, object needs a clear definition. However, human (as subject) does not know what happen in the future and also has limited knowledge. In other words, human is not omniscient being. In this case, subject is in a non-deterministic situation in performing a perception. On the other hand, mostly objects (shape, feel, mentality, etc) cannot usually be defined clearly. Therefore, the process of perception turns into uncertainty.

To summarize the relation between subject and object in the process of perception, there are four possible situations as follows.

(a) If subject has sufficient knowledge and object has clear definition, it comes to be a *certainty*.

(b) If subject has sufficient knowledge and object has unclear definition, it comes to be *fuzziness*. In general, fuzziness, called deterministic uncertainty, may happen in the situation when one is subjectively able to determine or describe a given object, although somehow the object does not have a certain or clear definition. For example, a man describes a woman as a *pretty* woman. Obviously definition of a pretty woman is unclear, uncertain and subjective. The man however is convinced of what he describes as a pretty woman.

(c) If subject does not have sufficient knowledge and object has clear definition, it comes to be *randomness*. Randomness is usually called non-deterministic uncertainty because subject cannot determine or describe a given object even though the object has clear definition. Here, probability exists for measuring a random experiment. For example, in throwing a dice, even though there are six definable and certain possibilities of outcome, one however cannot assure the outcome of dice. Still another example, because of his limited knowledge, for instance, one cannot assure to choose a certain answer in a multiple choice problem in which there are 4 possible answers, but only one answer is correct.

(d) If subject does not have sufficient knowledge and object has unclear definition, it comes to be a *probability of fuzzy event* [9]. In this situation, both probability and fuzziness are combined. For example, how to predict the ill-defined event: *"Tomorrow will be a warm day"*. Talking about tomorrow means talking about the future in which subject cannot determine what happen in the future. The situation should be dealt by probability. However, *warm* is an ill-defined event (called fuzzy event). Therefore, it comes to be a *probability of fuzzy event*.

From these four situations, it is obviously seen that probability and fuzziness work in different areas of uncertainty and that probability theory by itself is not sufficient for especially dealing with ill-defined event. Instead, probability and fuzziness must be regarded as a complementary tool.

In probability, set theory is used to provide a language for modeling and describing random experiments. In (classical) set theory, subsets of the sample space of an experiment are reffered to as *crisp events*. Fuzzy set theory, proposed by Zadeh in 1965, is considered as a generalization of (classical) set theory in which fuzzy set is to represent deterministic uncertainty by a class or classes which do not possess sharply defined boundaries [8]. By fuzzy set, an ill-defined event, called fuzzy event, can be described in the presence of probability theory providing *probability of fuzzy event* [9] in which fuzzy event might be regarded as a generalization of crisp event. Conditional probability as an important property in probability theory for inference rule can be extended to conditional probability of fuzzy event. In the situation of uniform probability distribution, conditional probability of fuzzy event can be simplified to be what we call *fuzzy conditional probability relation* as proposed in [1,2] for dealing with similarity of two fuzzy labels (sets).

Similarly, rough set theory generalizes classical set theory by studying sets with imprecise boundaries. A rough set [6], characterized by a pair of lower and upper approximations, may be viewed as an approximate representation of a given crisp set in terms of two subsets derived from a partition on the universe [3, 7]. By rough set theory, we propose a rough event representing two approximate events, namely lower and upper approximate events, in the presence of probability theory providing *probability of rough event*. Therefore, rough event might be considered as approximation of a given crisp event. Moreover, probability of rough event gives semantic formulation of interval probability. Formulation of interval probability is useful in order to represent the worst and the best case in decision making process. In this paper, special attention will be given to conditional probability of rough event providing several combinations of formulation and properties.

2 Probability of Fuzzy Event

Probability theory is based on the paradigm of a random experiment; that is, an experiment whose outcome cannot be predicted with certainty, before the experiment is run. In other word, as discussed in the previous section, probability is based on that subject has no sufficient knowledge in certainly predicting (determining) outcome of an experiment. In probability, set theory is used to provide a language for modeling and describing random experiments. The sample space of a random experiment corresponds to universal set. In (classical) set theory, subsets of the sample space of an experiment are refferred to as *crisp events*.

In order to represent an ill-defined event, crisp event must be generalized to *fuzzy event* in which fuzzy set is used to represent fuzzy event. Formally, probability of fuzzy event is defined as the following [9]:

Definition 1. *Let $(U, \mathcal{F}, P)$ be a probability space in which U is the sample space, $\mathcal{F}$ is sigma algebra of events and P is a probability measure over U. Then, a fuzzy event $A \in \mathcal{F}$ is a fuzzy set A on U whose membership function, $\mu_A : U \to [0, 1]$. The probability of fuzzy event A is defined by:*
– *continuous sample space:* – *discrete sample space:*

$$P(A) = \int_U \mu_A(u) dP = \int_U \mu_A(u) p(u) du, \qquad P(A) = \sum_U \mu_A(u) p(u),$$

where $p(u)$ is probability distribution function of element $u \in U$.

For example, given a sentence "John ate *a few* eggs for breakfast" in which we do not know exactly how many eggs John ate for breakfast. Instead, arbitrarily given probability distribution function of "John ate $u \in U$ egg(s) for breakfast" as shown in Table 1. "a few" is a fuzzy label that also means a fuzzy event as arbitrarily given by the following fuzzy set: $\mu_{a few} = \{1/1, 0.6/2, 0.2/3\}$, where $\mu_{a few}(2) = 0.6$. By Definition 1, probability of "John ate a few eggs for breakfast", denoted by $P(a\ few)$, is calculated as:

$$P(a\ few) = 1 \times 0.33 + 0.6 \times 0.27 + 0.2 \times 0.2 = 0.532.$$

There are several basic concepts relating to fuzzy sets. For A and B are two fuzzy sets on U [8],

Table 1. Probability Distribution of u

u	1	2	3	4	5	6	$\cdots$
$p(u)$	0.33	0.27	0.2	0.13	0.07	0	$\cdots$

Equality: $A = B \iff \mu_A(u) = \mu_B(u), \forall u$,
Containment: $A \subset B \iff \mu_A(u) \leq \mu_B(u), \forall u$,
Complement: $B = \neg A \iff \mu_B(u) = 1 - \mu_A(u), \forall u$,
Union: $\mu_{A \cup B}(u) = \max[\mu_A(u), \mu_B(u)]$,
Intersection: $\mu_{A \cap B}(u) = \min[\mu_A(u), \mu_B(u)]$,
Product: $\mu_{AB}(u) = \mu_A(u)\mu_B(u)$,
Sum: $\mu_{A \oplus B}(u) = \mu_A(u) + \mu_B(u) - \mu_A(u)\mu_B(u)$.

Obviously, it can be proved that probability of fuzzy event satisfies some properties: for A and B are two fuzzy sets on U,

(1) $A \subset B \implies P(A) \leq P(B)$, (4) $P(A \cup \neg A) \leq 1$,
(2) $P(A \cup B) = P(A) + P(B) - P(A \cap B)$, (5) $P(A \cap \neg A) \geq 0$.
(3) $P(A \oplus B) = P(A) + P(B) - P(AB)$,

(1), (2) and (3) show that probability of fuzzy event satisfies monotonicity and additivity axiom of union as well as sum operation, respectively. However, it does not satisfy law of excluded middle and law of non-contradiction as shown in (4) and (5).

We turn next to notion of conditional probability of fuzzy events. Conditional Probability of an event is the probability of the event occurring given that another event has already occurred. The relationship between conditional and unconditional probability satisfies the following equation:

$$P(A|B) = P(A \cap B)/P(B),$$

where suppose B is an event such that $P(B) \neq 0$.
In discrete sample space, conditional probability of fuzzy event migh be defined as follow: for A and B are two fuzzy sets on U,

$$P(A|B) = \frac{\sum_u \min\{\mu_A(u), \mu_B(u)\}p(u)}{\sum_u \mu_B(u)p(u)}, \quad \forall u \in U,$$

where $\sum_u \mu_B(u)p(u) > 0$. Some properties are satisfied in conditional probability of fuzzy event: for A and B be two fuzzy sets on U,

(1) Normalization: $P(A|B) + P(\neg A|B) \geq 1$,
(2) Total Probability; If $\{B_k | k \in \mathbb{N}_n\}$ are crisp, pairwise disjoint and exhaustive events, i.e., $P(B_i \cap B_j) = 0$ for $i \neq j$ and $\bigcup B_k = U$, then:

$$P(A) = \sum_k P(B_k)P(A|B_k).$$

(3) Bayes Theorem: $P(A|B) = [P(B|A) \times P(A)]/P(B)$.

Also, the relationship between A and B in conditional probability of fuzzy event can be represented into three conditions:

(a) positive correlation:
$P(A|B) > P(A) \Leftrightarrow P(B|A) > P(B) \Leftrightarrow P(A \cap B) > P(A) \times P(B)$,
(b) negative correlation:
$P(A|B) < P(A) \Leftrightarrow P(B|A) < P(B) \Leftrightarrow P(A \cap B) < P(A) \times P(B)$,
(c) independent correlation:
$P(A|B) = P(A) \Leftrightarrow P(B|A) = P(B) \Leftrightarrow P(A \cap B) = P(A) \times P(B)$.

In uniform distribution, probability distribution function, $p(u) = 1/|U|$, is regarded as a constant variable. Therefore, conditional probability of fuzzy event A given B is defined more simply without $p(u)$ by:

$$P(A|B) = \frac{\sum_u \min\{\mu_A(u), \mu_B(u)\}}{\sum_u \mu_B(u)}, \forall u \in U.$$

In [1,2], we used the formula to calculate degree of similarity relationship between two fuzzy labels (sets) and called it *fuzzy conditional probability relation*.

3 Probability of Rough Event

Rough set is another generalization of crisp set by studying sets with imprecise boundary. A rough set, characterized by a pair of lower and upper approximations, may be viewed as an approximate representation of a given crisp set in terms of two subsets derived from a partition on the universe [3,7]. The concept of rough sets can be defined precisely as follows. Let U denotes a finite and non-empty universe, and let R be an equivalence relation on U. The equivalence relation R induces a partition of the universe. The partition is also referred to as the quotient set and is denoted by U/R. Suppose $[u]_R$ is the equivalence class in U/R that contains $u \in U$. A rough set approximation of a subset $A \subseteq U$ is a pair of lower and upper approximations. The lower approximation,

$$\underline{A} = \{u \in U \mid [u]_R \subseteq A\} = \bigcup \{[u]_R \in U/R \mid [u]_R \subseteq A\},$$

is the union of all equivalence classes in U/R that are contained in A. The upper approximation,

$$\overline{A} = \{u \in U \mid [u]_R \cap A \neq \emptyset\}, = \bigcup \{[u]_R \in U/R \mid [u]_R \cap A \neq \emptyset\},$$

is the union of all equivalence classes in U/R that overlap with A. Similarly, by rough set, a rough event can be described into two approximate events, namely lower and upper approximate events. Rough event might be considered as approximation and generalization of a given crisp event. Probability of rough event is then defined as follows.

Definition 2. Let $(U, \mathcal{F}, P)$ be a probability space in which U is the sample space, $\mathcal{F}$ is sigma algebra of events and P is a probability measure over U. Then, a rough event of $A = [\underline{A}, \overline{A}] \in \mathcal{F}^2$ is a pair of lower and upper approximation of $A \subseteq U$. The probability of rough event A is defined by an interval probability $[P(\underline{A}), P(\overline{A})]$, where $P(\underline{A})$ and $P(\overline{A})$ are lower and upper probabilities, respectively.

– lower probability:
$$P(\underline{A}) = \sum_{\{u \in U \mid [u]_R \subseteq A\}} p(u) = \sum_{\bigcup\{[u]_R \in U/R \mid [u]_R \subseteq A\}} P([u]_R),$$

– upper probability:
$$P(\overline{A}) = \sum_{\{u \in U \mid [u]_R \cap A \neq \emptyset\}} p(u), = \sum_{\bigcup\{[u]_R \in U/R \mid [u]_R \cap A \neq \emptyset\}} P([u]_R),$$

where $p(u)$ is probability distribution function of element $u \in U$.

The definition shows that probability of rough event gives semantic formulation of interval probability. By combining with other set-theoretic operators such as $\neg, \cup$ and $\cap$, we have the following results:

(1) $P(\underline{A}) \leq P(A) \leq P(\overline{A})$,
(2) $A \subseteq B \Leftrightarrow [P(\underline{A}) \leq P(\underline{B}), P(\overline{A} \leq P(\overline{B})]$,
(3) $P(\neg \underline{A}) = 1 - P(\overline{A})$, $P(\neg \overline{A}) = 1 - P(\underline{A})$,
(4) $P(\underline{\neg A}) = P(\neg \overline{A})$, $P(\overline{\neg A}) = P(\neg \underline{A})$,
(5) $P(\underline{U}) = P(U) = P(\overline{U}) = 1$, $P(\underline{\emptyset}) = P(\emptyset) = P(\overline{\emptyset}) = 0$,
(6) $P(\underline{A \cap B}) = P(\underline{A} \cap \underline{B})$, $P(\overline{A \cap B}) \leq P(\overline{A} \cap \overline{B})$,
(7) $P(\underline{A \cup B}) \geq P(\underline{A}) + P(\underline{B}) - P(\underline{A \cap B})$,
(8) $P(\overline{A \cup B}) \leq P(\overline{A}) + P(\overline{B}) - P(\overline{A \cap B})$,
(9) $P(A) \leq P((\overline{A}))$, $P(A) \geq P((\underline{A}))$,
(10) $P(\underline{\underline{A}}) = P(\underline{A})$, $P(\overline{\overline{A}}) = P(\overline{A})$,
(11) $P(\underline{A} \cup \neg \underline{A}) \leq 1$, $P(\overline{A} \cup \neg \overline{A}) \geq 1$,
(11) $P(\underline{A} \cap \neg \underline{A}) = 0$, $P(\overline{A} \cap \neg \overline{A}) \geq 0$.

Conditional probability of rough event migh be considered in the following four combination of formulation: For $A, B \subseteq U$, conditional probability of A given B is defined by,

$$(1)\ P(\underline{A}|\underline{B}) = \frac{P(\underline{A} \cap \underline{B})}{P(\underline{B})}, \quad (2)\ P(\underline{A}|\overline{B}) = \frac{P(\underline{A} \cap \overline{B})}{P(\overline{B})},$$

$$(3)\ P(\overline{A}|\underline{B}) = \frac{P(\overline{A} \cap \underline{B})}{P(\underline{B})}, \quad (4)\ P(\overline{A}|\overline{B}) = \frac{P(\overline{A} \cap \overline{B})}{P(\overline{B})}.$$

Some relations are given by:

$$P(\underline{A} \cap \underline{B}) \leq P(\overline{A} \cap \underline{B}) \Rightarrow P(\underline{A}|\underline{B}) \leq P(\overline{A}|\underline{B}),$$
$$P(\underline{A} \cap \overline{B}) \leq P(\overline{A} \cap \overline{B}) \Rightarrow P(\underline{A}|\overline{B}) \leq P(\overline{A}|\overline{B}).$$

Similary, they also satisfy some properties:

(1) Normalization:

(i) $P(\underline{A}|\underline{B}) + P(\neg \underline{A}|\underline{B}) \leq 1$, (ii) $P(\underline{A}|\overline{B}) + P(\neg \underline{A}|\overline{B}) \leq 1$,
(iii) $P(\overline{A}|\underline{B}) + P(\neg \overline{A}|\underline{B}) \geq 1$, (iv) $P(\overline{A}|\overline{B}) + P(\neg \overline{A}|\overline{B}) \geq 1$.

(2) Total Probability; If $\{B_k | k \in \mathbb{N}_n\}$ are crisp, pairwise disjoint and exhaustive events, i.e., $P(B_i \cap B_j) = 0$ for $i \neq j$ and $\bigcup B_k = U$, then:

(i) $P(\underline{A}) \geq \sum_k P(\underline{B_k}) P(\underline{A}|\underline{B_k})$, (ii) $P(\underline{A}) \leq \sum_k P(\overline{B_k}) P(\underline{A}|\overline{B_k})$,

(iii) $P(\overline{A}) \geq \sum_k P(\underline{B_k}) P(\overline{A}|\underline{B_k})$, (iv) $P(\overline{A}) \leq \sum_k P(\overline{B_k}) P(\overline{A}|\overline{B_k})$.

Note: $\{B_k | k \in \mathbb{N}_n\}$ might be different from U/R.

(3) Bayes Theorem:

(i) $P(\underline{A}|\underline{B}) = \dfrac{P(\underline{B}|\underline{A}) P(\underline{A})}{P(\underline{B})}$, (ii) $P(\underline{A}|\overline{B}) = \dfrac{P(\overline{B}|\underline{A}) P(\underline{A})}{P(\overline{B})}$,

(iii) $(\overline{A}|\underline{B}) = \dfrac{P(\underline{B}|\overline{A}) P(\overline{A})}{P(\underline{B})}$, (iv) $P(\overline{A}|\overline{B}) = \dfrac{P(\overline{B}|\overline{A}) P(\overline{A})}{P(\overline{B})}$.

Other considerable formulations of conditional probability of rough event are the following: For $A, B \subseteq U$, conditional probability of A given B can be also defined by,

(1) $P_1(A|B) = \dfrac{P(\underline{A} \cap \underline{B})}{P(\underline{B})}$, (2) $P_2(A|B) = \dfrac{P(\underline{A} \cap \underline{B})}{P(\overline{B})}$,

(3) $P_3(A|B) = \dfrac{P(\overline{A} \cap \overline{B})}{P(\underline{B})}$, (4) $P_4(A|B) = \dfrac{P(\overline{A} \cap \overline{B})}{P(\overline{B})}$.

Also some relations concerning the above formulations are given by:

- $P_2(A|B) \leq P_1(A|B) \leq P_3(A|B)$,
- $P_4(A|B) \leq P_3(A|B)$,
- $P_2(A|B) \leq P_4(A|B)$,
- $P(\overline{A} \cap B) = P(\underline{A} \cap B) \Rightarrow P_1(A|B) = P(\underline{A}|\underline{B})$.

They satisfy some properties of conditional probability:

(1) Normalization:

(i) $P_1(A|B) + P_1(\neg A|B) \leq 1$, (ii) $P_2(A|B) + P_2(\neg A|B) \leq 1$,
(iii) $P_3(A|B) + P_3(\neg A|B) \geq 1$, (iv) $P_4(A|B) + P_4(\neg A|B) \geq 1$.

(2) Total Probability; If $\{B_k | k \in \mathbb{N}_n\}$ are crisp, pairwise disjoint and exhaustive events, i.e., $P(B_i \cap B_j) = 0$ for $i \neq j$ and $\bigcup B_k = U$, then:

(i) $P(\underline{A}) \geq \sum_k P(\underline{B_k}) P_1(A|B_k)$, (ii) $P(\underline{A}) \geq \sum_k P(\overline{B_k}) P_2(A|B_k)$,

(iii) $P(\overline{A}) \leq \sum_k P(\underline{B_k}) P_3(A|B_k)$, (iv) $P(\overline{A}) \leq \sum_k P(\overline{B_k}) P_4(A|B_k)$.

Note: $\{B_k | k \in \mathbb{N}_n\}$ might be different from U/R.

(3) Bayes Theorem:

$$(i)\ P_1(A|B) = \frac{P_1(B|A)P(\underline{A})}{P(\underline{B})}, \quad (ii)\ P_2(A|B) = \frac{P_2(B|A)P(\underline{A})}{P(\overline{B})},$$

$$(iii)\ P_3(A|B) = \frac{P_3(B|A)P(\overline{A})}{P(\underline{B})}, \quad (iv)\ P_4(A|B) = \frac{P_4(B|A)P(\overline{A})}{P(\overline{B})}.$$

4 Conclusion

The relationship between probability and fuzziness was simply discussed based on the process of perception. Probability and fuzziness work in different areas of uncertainty; hence probability theory by itself is not sufficient for dealing with uncertainty in the real-world application. Instead, probability and fuzziness must be regarded as a complementary tool providing probability of fuzzy event in which fuzzy event was represented by fuzzy set. Fuzzy event was considered as a generalization of crisp event as well as fuzzy set generalizes crisp set. Similarly, rough set, as another generalization of crisp set, was used to represent rough event. Probability of rough event was proposed. Conditional probability of fuzzy event as well as rough event and their some properties were examined.

References

1. Intan, R., Mukaidono, M., 'Conditional Probability Relations in Fuzzy Relational Database ', *Proceedings of RSCTC'00, LNAI 2005, Springer & Verlag*, (2000), pp.251–260.
2. Intan, R., Mukaidono, M.,Yao, Y.Y., 'Generalization of Rough Sets with α-coverings of the Universe Induced by Conditional Probability Relations', *Proceedings of International Workshop on Rough Sets and Granular Computing, LNAI 2253, Springer & Verlag*, (2001), pp. 311 -315.
3. Klir, G.J., Yuan, B., *Fuzzy Sets and Fuzzy Logic: Theory and Applications*,(Prentice Hall, New Jersey, 1995).
4. Kosko, B., 'Fuzziness VS. Probability', *International Journal of General Systems*, Vol 17, pp. 211–240.
5. Nguyen, H. T., 'On Fuzziness and Linguistic Probabilities', *Journal of Mathematical Analysis and Applications, 61*, pp. 658–671.
6. Pawlak, Z. (1982) Rough sets, *International Journal Computation & Information Science*, **11**, pp. 341–356.
7. Yao, Y.Y. (1996) Two views of the theory of rough sets in finite universe, *International Journal of Approximate Reasoning 15*, pp. 291–317.
8. Zadeh, L.A., 'Fuzzy Sets and Systems', *International Journal of General Systems*, Vol 17, (1990), pp. 129–138.
9. Zadeh, L.A., 'Probability Measures of Fuzzy Events', *Journal of Mathematical Analysis and Applications, Vol 23*, (1968), pp. 421–427.
10. Zadeh, L.A., 'Discussion: Probability Theory and Fuzzy Logic Are Complementary Rather Than Competitive', *Technometrics, Vol 37, No.3*, (1995), pp. 271–276.

Approximate Bayesian Network Classifiers

Dominik Ślęzak and Jakub Wróblewski

Polish-Japanese Institute of Information Technology
Koszykowa 86, 02-008 Warsaw, Poland
{slezak,jakubw}@pjwstk.edu.pl

Abstract. Bayesian network (BN) is a directed acyclic graph encoding probabilistic independence statements between variables. BN with decision attribute as a root can be applied to classification of new cases, by synthesis of conditional probabilities propagated along the edges. We consider approximate BNs, which almost keep entropy of a decision table. They have usually less edges than classical BNs. They enable to model and extend the well-known Naive Bayes approach. Experiments show that classifiers based on approximate BNs can be very efficient.

1 Introduction

Bayesian network (BN) is a directed acyclic graph (DAG) designed to encode knowledge about probabilistic conditional independence (PCI) statements between considered variables, within a given probabilistic space [6]. Its expressive power increases while removing the edges, unless it causes a loss of control of exactness of derivable PCI-statements. When mining real-life data, one needs less accurate, approximate criteria of independence. We base such an approximation on the information measure of entropy [4], by letting a reasonably small increase of its quantity during the edge reduction. It leads to approximate BNs corresponding to approximate PCI-statements, introduced in [7].

BN can model the flow of information in decision tables, while reasoning about new cases. Necessary probabilities can be calculated directly from training data, by substituting the foregoing decision values in a loop. One can maximize the product of such probabilities and choose the most probable decision value. This is, actually, an example of the bayesian reasoning approach (cf. [2]).

We analyze how the strategies of choosing the approximation threshold and searching for corresponding approximate BNs can influence the new case classification results. We extract optimal DAGs from data in a very basic way, just to provide a material for simulations. Development of more sophisticated methods is a direction for further research. Some algorithms for learning approximate BNs are proposed in [8]. Various other approaches to extraction of classical BNs (cf. [3]) are worth generalizing onto the approximate case as well.

Although BN-related framework can be regarded as purely probabilistic, let us stress its relationship to the rough set theory [5], by means of correspondence between fundamental notions, like e.g. these of decision reduct and Markov boundary (cf. [7]), as well as between optimization problems concerning extraction of approximate BNs and rough-set-based models from data (cf. [8]).

2 Probabilities in Information Systems

Following [5], we represent data as information systems – tuples $\mathbb{A} = (U, A)$. Each attribute $a \in A$ is identified with function $a : U \to V_a$, for V_a denoting the set of all possible values on a. Let us assume ordering $A = \langle a_1, \ldots, a_n \rangle$. For any $B \subseteq A$, consider B-information function, which labels objects $u \in U$ with vectors $\langle a_{i_1}(u), \ldots, a_{i_m}(u) \rangle$, where values of $a_{i_j} \in B$, $j = 1, \ldots, m$, occur due to the ordering on A. We denote this function by $B : U \to V_B^U$, where $V_B^U = \{B(u) : u \in U\}$ is the set of all vectors of values on B occurring in $\mathbb{A}$.

Classification problems concern distinguished decisions to be predicted under information provided over conditional attributes. For this purpose, one represents data as a decision table $\mathbb{A} = (U, A \cup \{d\})$, $d \notin A$. One can use various classification methodologies, provided, e.g., by statistical calculus [2]. Occurrence of $v_d \in V_d$ conditioned by $w_B \in V_B^U$, can be expressed as probability

$$P_\mathbb{A}(v_d/w_B) = |\{u \in U : B(u) = w_B \wedge d(u) = v_d\}| / |\{u \in U : B(u) = w_B\}| \quad (1)$$

For a given $\alpha \in [0, 1]$, we say that α-inexact decision rule $(B = w_B) \Rightarrow_\alpha (d = v_d)$ is satisfied iff $P_\mathbb{A}(v_d/w_B) \geq \alpha$, i.e., iff for at least $\alpha \cdot 100\%$ of objects $u \in U$ such that $B(u) = w_B$ we have also $d(u) = v_d$. The strength of the rule is provided by prior probability $P_\mathbb{A}(w_B) = |\{u \in U : B(u) = w_B\}| / |U|$. It corresponds to the chance that an object $u \in U$ will satisfy the rule's left side. One can consider such probabilities not only for the case of a distinguished decision attribute at the right side of a rule. In case of bayesian approaches to the new case classification one uses probabilistic rules with decision features involved in their left sides.

3 Probabilistic Decision Reducts

Each pair $(B, u) \in \mathcal{P}(A) \times U$ generates approximate decision rule pointing at the $d(u)$-th decision class. It is described by means of the following parameters:

Definition 1. *Let $\mathbb{A} = (U, A \cup \{d\})$, $B \subseteq A$ and $u \in U$ be given. By the accuracy and support coefficients for (B, u) we mean, respectively, quantities*

$$\mu_{d/B}(u) = P_\mathbb{A}(d(u)/B(u)) \qquad \mu_B(u) = P_\mathbb{A}(B(u)) \quad (2)$$

In the context of the above coefficients, the rough-set-based principle of reduction of redundant information [5] corresponds to the following notion:

Definition 2. *Let $\mathbb{A} = (U, A \cup \{d\})$ be given. $B \subseteq A$ μ-preserves d iff*

$$\forall_{u \in U} \left[\mu_{d/B}(u) = \mu_{d/A}(u) \right] \quad (3)$$

B is a μ-decision reduct iff it satisfies (3) and none of its proper subsets does it.

Property (3) is an example of a probabilistic conditional independence (PCI) statement. Usually, PCI is defined over subsets of variables considered within a discrete product probabilistic space, over all possible configurations of vectors of values. Since we deal with probabilistic distributions derived directly from information systems, let us focus on the following, equivalent [7] definition:

Definition 3. Let $\mathbb{A} = (U, A)$ and $X, Y, Z \subseteq A$ be given. We say that Y makes X conditionally independent from Z iff

$$\forall_{u \in U} P_\mathbb{A}(X(u)/Y(u)) = P_\mathbb{A}(X(u)/(Y \cup Z)(u)) \tag{4}$$

Corollary 1. Let $\mathbb{A} = (U, A \cup \{d\})$ and $B \subseteq A$ be given. B is a μ-decision reduct iff it is a Markov boundary of d within A, i.e., it is an irreducible subset, which makes d probabilistically independent from the rest of A.

4 Entropy-Based Approximations

Each $B \subseteq A$ induces in $\mathbb{A} = (U, A \cup \{d\})$ the bunch of inexact decision rules $B = B(u) \Rightarrow_{\mu_{d/B}(u)} d = d(u)$ for particular objects $u \in U$. One can measure the quality of B in terms of both accuracy and support of such rules.

Definition 4. Let $\mathbb{A} = (U, A \cup \{d\})$ and $B \subseteq A$ be given. We put

$$G_\mathbb{A}(B) = \sqrt[|U|]{\Pi_{u \in U} \mu_B(u)} \qquad G_\mathbb{A}(d/B) = \sqrt[|U|]{\Pi_{u \in U} \mu_{d/B}(u)} \tag{5}$$

$G_\mathbb{A}$ corresponds to the measure of information entropy adapted to the rough set, statistical and machine learning methodologies in various forms (cf. [4,7]).

Definition 5. Let $\mathbb{A} = (U, A)$ and $X \subseteq A$ be given. By entropy of X we mean

$$H_\mathbb{A}(X) = -\sum_{w_X \in V_X^U} P_\mathbb{A}(w_X) \log_2 P_\mathbb{A}(w_X) \tag{6}$$

By entropy of X conditioned by Y we mean

$$H_\mathbb{A}(X/Y) = \begin{cases} H_\mathbb{A}(X \cup Y) - H_\mathbb{A}(Y) & \text{iff } Y \neq \emptyset \\ H_\mathbb{A}(X) & \text{otherwise} \end{cases} \tag{7}$$

Proposition 1. Let $\mathbb{A} = (U, A \cup \{d\})$ and $B \subseteq A$ be given. We have equalities

$$H_\mathbb{A}(B) = -\log_2 G_\mathbb{A}(B) \qquad H_\mathbb{A}(d/B) = -\log_2 G_\mathbb{A}(d/B) \tag{8}$$

Given the above interpretation of $H_\mathbb{A}$, let us focus on the following way of approximate preserving of accuracy under the conditional attribute reduction.

Definition 6. Let $\varepsilon \in [0, 1)$, $\mathbb{A} = (U, A \cup \{d\})$ and $B \subseteq A$ be given. We say that B ε-approximately μ-preserves d iff $G_\mathbb{A}(d/B) \geq (1 - \varepsilon) G_\mathbb{A}(d/A)$, i.e., iff

$$H_\mathbb{A}(d/B) + \log_2(1 - \varepsilon) \leq H_\mathbb{A}(d/A) \tag{9}$$

We say that B is an ε-approximate μ-decision reduct (ε-approximate Markov boundary) iff it satisfies (9) and none of its proper subsets does it.

Definition 7. Let $\varepsilon \in [0, 1)$, $\mathbb{A} = (U, A)$ and $X, Y, Z \subseteq A$ be given. We say that Y makes X conditionally ε-approximately independent from Z iff

$$H_\mathbb{A}(X/Y) + \log_2(1 - \varepsilon) \leq H_\mathbb{A}(X/Y \cup Z) \tag{10}$$

Such a criterion of *approximate* probabilistic conditional independence is more robust to possible fluctuations in real life data. Moreover, we have equivalence of the notions of independence and 0-approximate independence.

5 Bayesian Networks

Bayesian network (BN) has the structure of a directed acyclic graph (DAG) $\mathcal{D} = (A, \vec{E})$, where $\vec{E} \subseteq A \times A$. The objective of BN is to encode conditional independence statements involving groups of probabilistic variables corresponding to elements of A, in terms of the following graph-theoretic notion [6]:

Definition 8. *Let DAG $\mathcal{D} = (A, \vec{E})$ and $X, Y, Z \subseteq A$ be given. We say that Y d-separates X from Z iff any path between any $x \in X \setminus Y$ and any $z \in Z \setminus Y$ comes through: (1) a serial or diverging connection covered by some $y \in Y$,[1] or (2) a converging connection not covered by Y, having no descendant in Y.*[2]

Let us formulate the notion of BN in terms of data analysis:

Definition 9. *Let $\mathbb{A} = (U, A)$ and DAG $\mathcal{D} = (A, \vec{E})$ be given. We say that $\mathcal{D}$ is a bayesian network for $\mathbb{A}$ iff for any $X, Y, Z \subseteq A$, if Y d-separates X from Z, then Y makes X conditionally independent from Z.*

Theorem 1. *([6]) Let $\mathbb{A} = (U, A)$, $A = \langle a_1, \ldots, a_n \rangle$, be given. Let us assume that for each table $\mathbb{A}_i = (U, \{a_1, \ldots, a_{i-1}\} \cup \{a_i\})$, $i > 1$, a μ-decision reduct B_i is provided. Then we obtain a bayesian network $\mathcal{D} = (A, \vec{E})$ defined by*

$$\vec{E} = \bigcup_{i=1}^{n} \{\langle b, a_i \rangle : b \in B_i\} \tag{11}$$

In [7] the following approach to approximation of the notion of BN was proposed:

Definition 10. *Let $\varepsilon \in [0, 1)$, $\mathbb{A} = (U, A)$ and DAG $\mathcal{D} = (A, \vec{E})$ be given. We say that $\mathcal{D}$ is ε-approximately consistent with $\mathbb{A}$ iff*

$$H_\mathbb{A}(\mathcal{D}) + \log(1 - \varepsilon) \leq H_\mathbb{A}(A) \tag{12}$$

where $H_\mathbb{A}(\mathcal{D}) = \sum_{a \in A} H_\mathbb{A}(a/\{b \in A : \langle b, a \rangle \in \vec{E}\})$.

Condition (12) keeps the aggregate information induced by $\mathcal{D}$-based local conditional distributions *close* to that encoded within the whole of $P_\mathbb{A}(A)$.

Definition 11. *Let $\varepsilon \in [0, 1)$, $\mathbb{A} = (U, A)$, $\mathcal{D} = (A, \vec{E})$ be given. We say that $\mathcal{D}$ is an ε-approximate bayesian network (ε-BN) iff for any $X, Y, Z \subseteq A$, if Y d-separates X from Z, then Y makes X ε-approximately independent from Z.*

The following result generalizes Theorem 1. In particular, any DAG $\mathcal{D}$ built on the basis of μ-decision reducts is 0-approximately consistent with a given $\mathbb{A}$, as well as any 0-approximate bayesian network is a bayesian network.

Theorem 2. *[7] Let $\varepsilon \in [0, 1)$ and $\mathbb{A} = (U, A)$ be given. Each DAG which is ε-approximately consistent with $\mathbb{A}$ is an ε-approximate BN for $\mathbb{A}$.*

---

[1] Descriptions '*serial*', '*diverging*' and '*converging*' correspond to directions of arrows meeting within a given path, in a given node

[2] We say that b is a *descendant* of a iff there is a directed path from a towards b in $\mathcal{D}$

6 BN-Based Classification

Bayesian decision models are related to the analysis of approximations of distribution $P_\mathbb{A}(A(u)/v_d)$. One can let $u \in U$ be classified as having decision value

$$v = \arg\max_{v_d \in V_d}[prior(v_d) P_\mathbb{A}(A(u)/v_d)] \qquad (13)$$

for $prior : V_d \to [0,1]$. Let us set up an arbitrary ordering $A = \langle a_1, \ldots, a_n \rangle$ and denote by V_i the set of all values of a_i. We decompose $P_\mathbb{A}(A/d)$ by noting that for any supported combination of values $v_d \in V_d$, $v_i \in V_i$, $i = 1, \ldots, n$, one has

$$P_\mathbb{A}(v_1, \ldots, v_n/v_d) = \prod_{i=1}^{n} P_\mathbb{A}(v_i/v_d, v_1, \ldots, v_{i-1}) \qquad (14)$$

Proposition 2. *[7] Let $\mathbb{A} = (U, A \cup \{d\})$, $A = \langle a_1, \ldots, a_n \rangle$, be given. Assume that for each table $\mathbb{A}_i = (U, \{d, a_1, \ldots, a_{i-1}\} \cup \{a_i\})$, $i = 1, \ldots, n$, a μ-decision reduct B_i has been found. For any $u \in U$, decision obtained by (13) equals to*

$$v = \arg\max_{v_d \in V_d} prior(v_d) \prod_{i:\, d \in B_i} P_\mathbb{A}(a_i(u)/v_d, (B_i \setminus \{d\})(u)) \qquad (15)$$

The way of classifying objects in Proposition 2 corresponds to the DAG construction in Theorem 1, if applied to $\mathbb{A} = (U, A \cup \{d\})$, for d at the first position of the ordering over $A \cup \{d\}$. We obtain a scheme of the bayesian classification, where conditional probabilities are propagated along the DAG structure, beginning with decision as the root. In particular, we obtain an interpretation of the *Naive Bayes* approach (cf. [2]), formulated in terms of the following principle:

$$v = \arg\max_{v_d \in V_d} prior(v_d) \prod_{a \in A} P_\mathbb{A}(a(u)/v_d) \qquad (16)$$

$\mathcal{D}_0 = (A \cup \{d\}, \vec{E}_0)$ corresponding to (16) is given by the following set of edges:

$$\vec{E}_0 = \bigcup_{a \in A} \{\langle d, a \rangle\} \qquad (17)$$

If $\mathcal{D}_0$ is BN for $\mathbb{A} = (U, A \cup \{d\})$, then the performance of (16) is the same as in case of (13) and (15). This is because in $\mathcal{D}_0$ any pair $a, b \in A$ is d-separated by d, so – according to Definition 9 – d makes them independent from each other.

7 Related Optimization Problems

BN can be regarded as optimal in terms of the law of encoding of PCI-statements and/or performance of DAG-based classification scheme (15). In both cases ε-approximately consistent $\mathcal{D} = (A \cup \{d\}, \vec{E})$, which minimize quantity of $Q_1(\mathcal{D}) = |\vec{E}|$, are worth finding. Let us consider the following exemplary measures as well:

$$Q_2(\mathcal{D}) = \sum_{a \in A} |V_{\pi(a)}^U| \quad Q_2^d(\mathcal{D}) = \frac{\sum_{a \in \delta(d)} |V_{\pi(a)}^U|}{|\delta(d)|} \quad Q_3(\mathcal{D}) = \sum_{a \in A} H_\mathbb{A}(\pi(a)) \qquad (18)$$

where $\pi(a) = \{b \in A \cup \{d\} : \langle b, a \rangle \in \vec{E}\}$ and $\delta(a) = \{b \in A \cup \{d\} : \langle a, b \rangle \in \vec{E}\}$ denote, respectively, the sets of parents and children of node $a \in A \cup \{d\}$ in $\mathcal{D}$.

Q_2 counts all distinct premises of inexact decision rules, which may occur while using classification scheme (15). Q_2^d takes into account only these rules, which directly participate to the classification process. Q_3 is partially correlated with Q_2 but it is more flexible with respect to the rule supports.[3]

To search for classical BNs, one can begin with extracting initial (partial) ordering and then search for locally optimal Markov boundaries [3]. One can also search for (approximate) BNs over the space of DAGs or, as proposed in [8], apply order-based genetic algorithm to work on permutations of nodes. The following result explains, how one can construct ε-BNs by basing on orderings.

Proposition 3. *Let* $\varepsilon \in [0,1)$, $\mathbb{A} = (U, A)$, $A = \langle a_1, \ldots, a_n \rangle$ *and* $\vec{E} = \{\langle a_i, a_j \rangle : 1 \leq i < j \leq n\}$ *be given. Set up an ordering over* $\vec{E}$. *Consider the following steps:* (i) *Take the first* $e \in \vec{E}$, (ii) *Check whether* $\mathcal{D} = (A, \vec{E} \setminus \{e\})$ *is* ε-*approximately consistent with* $\mathbb{A}$, (iii) *If it is, remove* e *from* $\vec{E}$, (iv) *Repeat* (i)-(iii) *for foregoing elements of* $\vec{E}$. *DAG obtained at the end is an irreducible* ε-*BN for* $\mathbb{A}$.

Let us skip discussion about complexity of searching for BNs [4] and focus on simulations showing what should be optimized to get the most efficient classifiers.

8 Experimental Results

We analyzed several known benchmark data tables available at [1]. Experiments were performed on relatively large data sets, all of them equipped with the testing table and, in general, discrete values of attributes (DNA splices data set was considered in its preprocessed version[5]). For a given $\varepsilon \in [0,1)$, ε-BNs were created by using a method described in Proposition 3. The obtained networks were then applied to classify the testing table, by using techniques described in Section 6. The aim of our experiments was to learn how to choose the most suitable optimization measures and the best levels of ε.

For each considered $\varepsilon \in [0,1)$ we generated randomly 50 DAGs with decision as a root. Then we collected the classification rates for the testing table. Average classification rates of 10 DAGs being the best with respect to each optimization measure were calculated.[6] During initial calculations the most interesting results were obtained for the approximation thresholds near to that corresponding to the DAG-based interpretation of Naive Bayes, i.e.:[7]

$$\varepsilon_0 = 1 - 2^{H_\mathbb{A}(A/d) - \sum_{a \in A} H_\mathbb{A}(a/d)} \tag{19}$$

Let us parameterize interval $[0,1)$ as follows:

$$[0,1) = \{\varepsilon_\alpha, \alpha \in \mathbb{R}\} \quad \text{where} \quad \varepsilon_\alpha = 1 - (1 - \varepsilon_0)^{(1-\alpha)} \tag{20}$$

---

[3] One could consider Q_3^d, defined analogously to Q_2^d, as well as other measures.
[4] We would like to refer the reader to [7] and [8] for further details.
[5] It consists of 20 out of original 60 conditional attributes, each of them with 4 values.
[6] Besides functions defined by (18), we considered also other possibilities.
[7] Indeed, $\varepsilon_0 \in [0,1)$ defined by (19) is the minimal approximation threshold, for which DAG $\mathcal{D}_0 = (A \cup \{d\}, \vec{E}_0)$, defined by (17), is ε_0-approximately consistent with $\mathbb{A}$.

Results for ε_α-BNs with various levels of $\alpha \in \mathbb{R}$ are shown in Table 1. In majority of cases either Q_2^d or Q_3 turn out to be the best choice.

Table 1. Average rates of the proper classification. Left: letter. Right: DNA splices.

α	Q_1	Q_2	Q_2^d	Q_3	α	Q_1	Q_2	Q_2^d	Q_3
0.0025	76.15%	76.28%	76.30%	76.28%	0.0008	95.54%	95.50%	95.66%	95.54%
0.04	76.32%	77.26%	76.65%	76.27%	0.0027	95.65%	95.43%	95.43%	95.67%
0.09	74.99%	75.42%	75.03%	75.56%	0.0064	94.32%	94.69%	95.07%	94.09%

Fig. 1 shows correlation between values of these functions (calculated on the training data) and final results of correct classification of the test objects.

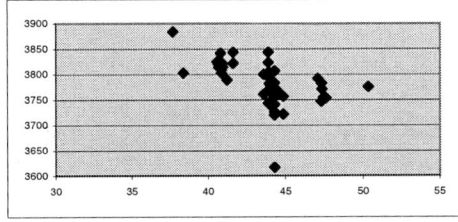
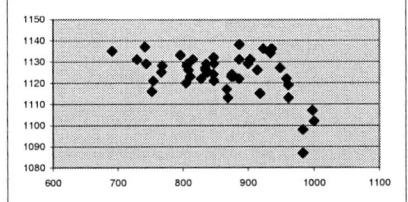

Fig. 1. Values of quality measure (horizontal) and classification results (vertical) for letter (left, measure Q_3) and DNA splices (right, measure Q_2^d) databases.

Fig. 2 shows that ε-BNs being optimized by using Q_2^d and Q_3 are significantly more efficient than the average.

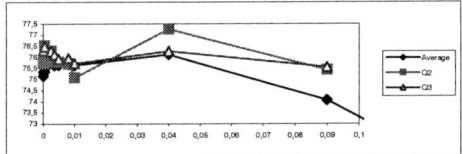
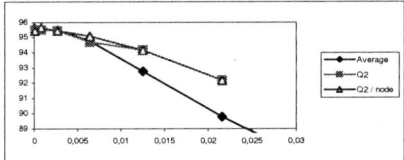

Fig. 2. Classification results on letter (left) and DNA splices (right) databases for different α values (horizontal): average and for minima of measures Q_3, Q_2^d.

Some regularities repeat for all tables we have worked on: By setting $\alpha = 0$ we obtain fair ε_α-BNs, similar to ε_0-BN related to Naive Bayes. The most efficient α values are usually between 0.0005 and 0.005. After reaching some threshold (depending on data) the average performance decreases but its diversification increases. It may lead to obtaining very good ε_α-BNs for suboptimal $\alpha \in \mathbb{R}$.

In Fig. 3 the best results found in our experiments are collected. The classification rate of Naive Bayes method is significantly exceeded, not only for optimal, but often even for average (random-ordered) case. Classification result for DNA splices is one of the best ever obtained. It is also interesting to observe that relatively small change of ε_0-BN may dramatically improve classification rate. Fig. 4 illustrates the case of improvement from 74.8% to 80.2%.

Table	obj.×attr. (test ob.)	Naive	Best BN
letter	15000 × 17 (5000)	74.8%	80.2%
DNA spl.	2000 × 21 (1186)	95.6%	96.2%
optdigits	3823 × 65 (1797)	82.0%	82.2%
soybean	307 × 36 (376)	64.0%	78.9%

Fig. 3. The best classification results obtained during experiments.

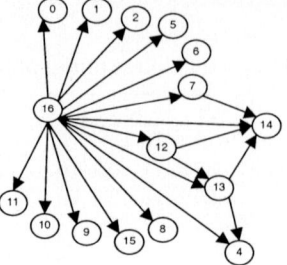

Fig. 4. The best network found for letter data (classification rate: 80.2%). Attributes are numbered starting with 0; attribute 16 is a decision.

9 Conclusions

We considered approximate BNs, almost keeping entropy of a decision table. Experiments confirmed potential efficiency of classifiers based on such BNs, depending on the choice of the approximation parameter and the strategy of searching for optimal graphs. We extracted optimal DAGs from data in a very basic way, just to provide a material for simulations. Development of more sophisticated methods is a direction for further research. Some algorithms for learning approximate BNs are proposed in [8]. Various other approaches to extraction of classical BNs (cf. [3]) are worth generalizing onto the approximate case as well.

Acknowledgements. Supported by Polish National Committee for Scientific Research (KBN) grant No. $8T11C02519$.

References

1. Bay, S.D.: The UCI Machine Learning Repository, http://www.ics.uci.edu/ml
2. Box, G.E.P., Tiao, G.C.: Bayesian Inference in Statistical Analysis. Wiley (1992).
3. Buntine, W.: A guide to the literature on learning probabilistic networks from data. IEEE Transactions on Knowledge and Data Engineering (1996).
4. Kapur, J.N., Kesavan, H.K.: Entropy Optimization Principles with Applications. Academic Press (1992).
5. Pawlak, Z.: Rough sets – Theoretical aspects of reasoning about data. Kluwer Academic Publishers (1991).
6. Pearl, J.: Probabilistic Reasoning in Intelligent Systems: Networks of Plausible Inference. Morgan Kaufmann (1988).
7. Ślęzak, D.: Approximate Bayesian networks. In: B. Bouchon-Meunier, J. Gutierrez-Rios, L. Magdalena, R.R. Yager (eds), Technologies for Contructing Intelligent Systems 2: Tools. Springer-Verlag (2002) pp. 313–326.
8. Ślęzak, D., Wróblewski, J.: Order-based genetic algorithms for extraction of approximate bayesian networks from data. In: Proc. of IPMU'2002. France (2002).

Accuracy and Coverage in Rough Set Rule Induction

Shusaku Tsumoto

Department of Medicine Informatics,
Shimane Medical University, School of Medicine,
Enya-cho Izumo City, Shimane 693-8501 Japan
tsumoto@computer.org

Abstract. Rough set based rule induction methods have been applied to knowledge discovery in databases, whose empirical results obtained show that they are very powerful and that some important knowledge has been extracted from datasets. For rule induction, lower/upper approximations and reducts play important roles and the approximations can be extended to variable precision model, using accuracy and coverage. However, the formal characteristics of accuracy and coverage for rule induction have never been discussed. In this paper, several following characteristics of accuracy and coverage are discussed: (1) accuracy and coverage measure the degree of sufficiency an necessity, respectively. Also, they measure that of lower approximation and upper approximation. (2) Coverage can be viewed as likelihood. (3) These two measures are related with statistical independence. (4) These two indices have trade-off relations. (5) When we focus on the conjunction of attribute-value pairs, coverage decreases more than accuracy.

1 Introduction

Rough set based rule induction methods have been applied to knowledge discovery in databases[2,3,7,8,9]. The empirical results obtained show that they are very powerful and that some important knowledge has been extracted from datasets. Furthermore, Tsumoto discusses that the core ideas of rough sets to the reasoning style of medical experts, which makes the results obtained easier for physicians to understand and to discover useful knowledge from those results[8, 9].

For rule induction, lower/upper approximations and reducts play important roles and the approximations can be extended to variable precision model, using accuracy and coverage. However, the formal characteristics of accuracy and coverage for rule induction have never been discussed. In this paper, several following characteristics of accuracy and coverage are discussed: (1) accuracy and coverage measure the degree of sufficiency an necessity, respectively. Also, they measure that of lower approximation and upper approximation. (2) Coverage can be viewed as likelihood. (3) These two measures are related with statistical independence. (4) These two indices have trade-off relations. (5) When we focus on the conjunction of attribute-value pairs, coverage decreases more than accuracy.

2 Accuracy and Coverage

2.1 Definition of Accuracy and Coverage

In the subsequent sections, we adopt the following notations, which is introduced by Skowron and Grzymala-Busse[6]. Let U denote a nonempty, finite set called the universe and A denote a nonempty, finite set of attributes, i.e., $a : U \rightarrow V_a$ for $a \in A$, where V_a is called the domain of a, respectively. Then, a decision table is defined as an information system, $A = (U, A \cup \{d\})$. The atomic formulas over $B \subseteq A \cup \{d\}$ and V are expressions of the form $[a = v]$, called descriptors over B, where $a \in B$ and $v \in V_a$. The set $F(B,V)$ of formulas over B is the least set containing all atomic formulas over B and closed with respect to disjunction, conjunction and negation. For each $f \in F(B,V)$, f_A denote the meaning of f in A, i.e., the set of all objects in U with property f, defined inductively as follows.

(1) If f is of the form $[a = v]$ then, $f_A = \{s \in U | a(s) = v\}$
(2) $(f \wedge g)_A = f_A \cap g_A$; $(f \vee g)_A = f_A \vee g_A$; $(\neg f)_A = U - f_a$

By the use of this framework, classification accuracy and coverage is defined as follows.

Definition 1.
Let R and D denote a formula in $F(B,V)$ and a set of objects which belong to a decision d. Classification accuracy and coverage(true positive rate) for $R \rightarrow d$ is defined as:

$$\alpha_R(D) = \frac{|R_A \cap D|}{|R_A|} (= P(D|R)), \text{ and } \kappa_R(D) = \frac{|R_A \cap D|}{|D|} (= P(R|D)),$$

where $|A|$ denotes the cardinality of a set A, $\alpha_R(D)$ denotes a classification accuracy of R as to classification of D, and $\kappa_R(D)$ denotes a coverage, or a true positive rate of R to D, respectively.

2.2 Fundamental Characteristics of Accuracy and Coverage

As measures of necessity and sufficiency. One of the most important features of accuracy and coverage for rule induction is that they can be viewed as measures for sufficiency and necessity. The values of these indices provides the degree of these conditions, which can be interpreted as the power of a given proposition.

Theorem 1.
$\alpha_R(D)$ *measures the degree of the sufficiency of a proposition, $R \rightarrow d$ and $\kappa_R(D)$ measures the degree of its necessity. Thus, if both measures are 1.0, then $R \leftrightarrow d$ ($R_A = D$).*

Proof.
If $\alpha_R(D)$ is equal to 1.0, then $|R_A \cap D| = |R_A|$. Thus, $R_A \subseteq D$. This means R_A is a subset of D and $R \to d$ is true. On the other hand, if $\kappa_R(D)$ is equal to 1.0, then $|R_A \cap D| = |D|$. Thus, $d \subseteq R_A$. This means D is a subset of R_A and $d \to R$ is true. □

Rough Set Approximation. As discussed in the last subsection, $\alpha_R(D) = 1.0$ is equivalent to $R_A \subseteq D$ and $\kappa_R(D) = 1.0$ is equivalent to $D \subseteq R_A$. Thus,

Corollary 1 (Rough Set Approximation). $\alpha_R(D)$ *and* $\kappa_R(D)$ *measures the degree of the lower and upper approximation. In other words, both approximations can be characterized by these two indices.*

$$\text{Lower Approximation} \cup R_A \text{ s.t. } \alpha_R(D) = 1.0$$
$$\text{Upper Approximation} \cup R_A \text{ s.t. } \kappa_R(D) = 1.0$$

3 Coverage as Likelihood

3.1 Intuitive Interpretation

Since accuracy and coverage are interpreted as conditional probabilities, it is easy to show that they have a strong relation with others by using Bayes formula. Again, from the definition of accuracy,

$$\alpha_R(D) = \frac{|R_A \cap D|}{|R_A|} = \frac{P(R \cap D)}{P(R)} = \frac{P(R, D)}{P(R)} = \frac{P(D)}{P(R)} \kappa_R(D),$$

which is equal to Bayes formula: $P(D|R)P(R) = P(R|D)P(D)$.

In Bayesian computation, likelihood function is a key concept for parameter estimation. That is, when we consider a list of parameters $\{\theta_i\}$, $P(D|\{\theta_i\})$ corresponds to the posterior probability and $P(\{\theta_i\}|D)$ corresponds to the likelihood function. Since a formula R can be viewed as a list of parameters ($\{\theta_i\}$), accuracy and coverage corresponds to posterior probability and likelihood, respectively.(It is notable that P(D) corresponds to a prior probability.)

Thus, when induction of rules with maximum accuracy is preferred, it can be said that a criteria of rule induction is maximum posteriors. On the other hand, when induction of rules with maximum coverage is preferred, these rules can be viewed as maximum likelihood estimators.

3.2 Semi-formal Interpretation

Likelihood. A statistical model based on likelihood is defined as a model with statistical density functions for observed data. If we assume that observed data (random variables) $y_i (i = 1, \cdots, n)$ are independent and a statistical distribution $f(y_i; \boldsymbol{\theta})$ is given as $f(x_i; \boldsymbol{\theta})$, then a statistical model is defined as:

$$\prod_{i=1}^{n} f(y_i; \boldsymbol{\theta}),$$

which is a function of $\boldsymbol{\theta}$.

If we fixed the observation data $\mathbf{y} = (y_1, \cdots, y_n)$ and consider each parameter as a function of $\mathbf{y}$, then we call this function $f(\boldsymbol{\theta}; \mathbf{y})$ as a likelihood function. From the formula of the statistical model, the likelihood function for the statistical model is given as:

$$L(\boldsymbol{\theta}) = \prod_{i=1}^{n} f(\boldsymbol{\theta}; y_i).$$

Let us consider these concepts in the context of rule induction. It is easily observed that the observation data corresponds to the target concept, a set of D and the parameters corresponds to a set of attributes, a set of R ($\mathcal{A}$). From these observations, $p(R|D)$ is equivalent to $f(\boldsymbol{\theta}; y_i)$.

Readers may argue that parameters are not fixed in the context of rule induction. However, this problem can be avoided in the following way: when we consider $[b = 0]$ as a parameter, we assume that $[b = 0]$ is equivalent to $[a = any] \wedge [b = 0] \wedge [c = any] \wedge [d = any] \wedge [e = any]$, where *any* means that any values in its domain are allowable.

Thus, we can summarize this discussion in the following way.

Theorem 2. *Let $\mathcal{R}$ and $\mathcal{D}$ denote a list of parameters of rule induction (attributes) and a list of observed data (target concepts; label), respectively. Then, for each formula $R \in (\mathcal{R})$ and each label $D \in (\mathcal{D})$, a likelihood function of the rule $R \to D$ is defined as $p(R|D)$, that is:*

$$L(R) = p(R|D).$$

Thus, concerning the classification of D, the relation R which gives the maximum value of coverage gives a maximum likelihood estimator.

3.3 Statistical Dependence

Let $P(R)$ and $P(D)$ be defined as:

$$P(R) = \frac{|R_A|}{|U|} \quad \text{and} \quad P(D) = \frac{|D|}{|U|},$$

where U denotes the total samples. Then, a index for statistical dependence ς_c is defined as:

$$\varsigma_R(D) = \frac{|R_A \cap D|}{|R_A||D|} = \frac{P(R, D)}{P(R)P(D)},$$

where $P(R, D)$ denotes a joint probability of R and D ($P(R, D) = |R_A \cap D|/|U|$). Since the formula $P(R, D) = P(R)P(D)$ is the definition of statistical independence, $\varsigma_R(D)$ measures the degree of statistical dependence. That is,

$$\varsigma_R(D) = \begin{cases} > 1.0 \ Dependent \\ = 1.0 \ Statistical\ Independent \\ < 1.0 \ Independent \end{cases}$$

From the definition of $\varsigma_R(D)$,

$$\varsigma_R(D) = \frac{\alpha_R(D)}{P(D)} = \frac{\kappa_R(D)}{P(R)} \tag{1}$$

This formula gives several interesting results.

Theorem 3. *Lower approximation and upper approximation gives (strong) statistical dependent relations.*
Proof. Since $\alpha_R(D) = 1.0$ for the lower approximation, $\varsigma_R(D) = \frac{1}{P(D)} > 1.0$ In the same way, for the upper approximation, $\varsigma_R(D) = \frac{1}{P(R)} > 1.0$ □

Definition 2 (A Sequence of Conjunctive Formula). Let U be described by n attributes. A conjunctive formula $R(i)$ is defined as:

$$R(i) = \bigwedge_{k=1}^{i} [a_i = v_i],$$

where index i is sorted by a given criteria, such as the value of accuracy. Then, the sequence of a conjunction is given as:

$$R(i+1) = R(i) \wedge [a_{i+1} = v_{j+1}]$$

Since $R(i+1)_A = R(i)_A \cap [a_{i+1} = v_{i+1}]_A$, for this sequence, the following proposition will hold.

Proposition 1.

$$R(i+1)_A \subseteq R(i)_A$$

Thus, the following theorem is obtained.

Theorem 4. *When we consider a sequence of conjunctive formula such that the value of accuracy should be increased, the statistical dependence will increase.*
Proof.

$$\varsigma_{R(i+1)}(D) = \frac{\alpha_{R(i+1)}(D)}{P(D)} \geq \frac{\alpha_{R(i)}(D)}{P(D)} = \varsigma_{R(i)}(D)$$

□

The measure of statistical dependence gives a nice interpretaion of the thresholds for accuracy and coverage[8]. When we would like to induce probabilistic rules such as:

$$R \to D \quad \text{s.t.} \ \alpha_R(D) \geq \delta_\alpha \ \text{and} \ \kappa_R(D) \geq \delta_\kappa,$$

we need to set the thresholds. If the thresholds for accuracy and coverage are set to high values, the meaning of the conditional part of probabilistic rules corresponds the highly overlapped region. From the definition of $\varsigma_R(D)$, the following theorem is obtained.

Theorem 5. *Let $\varsigma_R(D)$ be equal to 1.0. To induce probabilistic rules, the threshold should be set to:*

$$\delta_\alpha \leq P(D) \quad \text{and} \quad \delta_\kappa \leq P(R)$$

Proof. Since $\alpha_R(D) \geq \delta_\alpha$, from the equation (1),

$$\varsigma_R(D) = \frac{\alpha_R(D)}{P(D)} = 1.0 \geq \frac{\delta_\alpha}{P(D)}.$$

Therefore,

$$\delta_\alpha \leq P(D)$$

□

4 Tradeoff between Accuracy and Coverage

One of the important characteristics of the relation between classification accuracy and coverage is a trade-off relation on description length. This relation can be viewed as one variant of MDL principle(Minimum Description Length principle)[5] which is easy to be proved from the definitions of these measures. First, we show that coverage decreases its value when a sequence of conjunction of R is considered.

Theorem 6 (Monotonicity of Coverage). *Let a sequence of conjunctive formula $R(i)$ given with n attributes. Then,*

$$\kappa_{R(i+1)}(D) \leq \kappa_{R(i)}(D).$$

Proof.
Since $R(i+1)_A \subseteq R(i)_A$ holds, $\kappa_{R(i+1)}(D) = \frac{|R(i+1)_A \cap D|}{|D|} \leq \frac{|R(i)_A \cap D|}{|D|} = \kappa_{R(i)}(D)$.
□

Then, since accuracy and coverage has the following relation:

$$\frac{\kappa_R(D)}{\alpha_R(D)} = \frac{P(R)}{P(D)}$$

Since from the above proposition, $P(R)$ will decrease with the sequence of conjunction, the following theorem is obtained.

Theorem 7. *Even if a sequence of conjunction for R is selected such that the value of accuracy increases monotonically, $\kappa_R(D)$ will decrease. That is, the decrease of $\kappa_R(D)$ is larger than the effect of the increase of $\alpha_R(D)$.* □

This effect actually come from $P(R)$. It is easy to see from the equation (1).

4.1 MDL Principle

Let us define the description length of a rule as:

$$L = -\log_2 \alpha_R(D) - \log_2 \kappa_R(D),$$

which represents the length of a bit strings to describe all the information about classification of accuracy and coverage. In this definition, the length of coverage corresponds to the cost of "theory" in MDL principle because of the following theorem on coverage. Thus, the following theorem is obtained.

Theorem 8. *the following inequality holds unless $\alpha_R(D)$ or $\kappa_R(D)$ is equal to 1.0.* [1]

$$L \geq -\log_2 \frac{P(R)}{P(D)}.$$

Proof.

$$\begin{aligned} L &= -\log_2 \alpha_R(D) - \log_2 \kappa_R(D) \\ &= -\log_2 \frac{P(R \cap D)}{P(R)} - \log_2 \frac{P(R \cap D)}{P(D)} \\ &= -\log_2 \frac{(P(R \cap D)P(R \cap D)}{P(D)P(R)} \\ &\geq -\log_2 \frac{P(R)}{P(D)}. \end{aligned}$$

□

When we add an attribute-value pair to the conditional part of a rule, R_A will decrease and equivalently, the value of $P(R)$ will be smaller. Thus, $\log_2 P(R)$ will approach to $-\infty$ as a result.

Thus, if we want to get a rule of high accuracy, the coverage of this rule will be very small, which causes the high cost of the description of rules. On the other hand, if we want to get a rule of high coverage, the accuracy of this rule will be very small, which also causes the high cost of the description of rules.

It also means that a rule of high accuracy should be described with additional information about positive examples which do not support the rule, or that a rule of high coverage should be described with additional information about negative examples which support the rule.

---
[1] Since MDL principle do not consider the concept of coverage, it is difficult to incorporate the meaning of coverage in an explicit way. However, as discussed in the section on negative rules, the situation when the coverage is equal to 1.0 has a special meaning to express the information about negative reasoning. It will be our future work to study the meaning when the coverage is equal to 1.0. in the context of the description length of "theory".

5 Conclusion

In this paper, several following characteristics of accuracy and coverage are discussed: (1) accuracy and coverage measure the degree of sufficiency an necessity, respectively. Also, they measure that of lower approximation and upper approximation. (2) Coverage can be viewed as likelihood. (3) These two measures are related with statistical independence. (4) These two indices have trade-off relations. (5) When we focus on the conjunction of attribute-value pairs, coverage decreases more than accuracy. This paper is a preliminary formal study on accuracy and coverage. More formal analysis will appear in the future work.

Acknowledgments. This work was supported by the Grant-in-Aid for Scientific Research (13131208) on Priority Areas (No.759) "Implementation of Active Mining in the Era of Information Flood" by the Ministry of Education, Science, Culture, Sports, Science and Technology of Japan.

References

1. Darst, R. B. *Introduction to Linear Programming*, Marcel and Dekker, 1990.
2. Polkowski, L. and Skowron, A.(Eds.) *Rough Sets and Knowledge Discovery 1*, Physica Verlag, Heidelberg, 1998.
3. Polkowski, L. and Skowron, A.(Eds.) *Rough Sets and Knowledge Discovery 2*, Physica Verlag, Heidelberg, 1998.
4. Pawlak, Z., *Rough Sets*. Kluwer Academic Publishers, Dordrecht, 1991.
5. Rissanen J: *Stochastic Complexity in Statistical Inquiry*. World Scientific, Singapore, 1989.
6. Skowron, A. and Grzymala-Busse, J. From rough set theory to evidence theory. In: Yager, R., Fedrizzi, M. and Kacprzyk, J.(eds.) *Advances in the Dempster-Shafer Theory of Evidence*, pp. 193–236, John Wiley & Sons, New York, 1994.
7. Tsumoto, S. Extraction of Experts' Decision Rules from Clinical Databases using Rough Set Model Journal of Intelligent Data Analysis, 2(3), 1998.
8. Tsumoto, S. Knowledge discovery in clinical databases and evaluation of discovered knowledge in outpatient clinic. *Information Sciences*, **124**, 125–137, 2000.
9. Tsumoto, S. Automated Discovery of Positive and Negative Knowledge in Clinical Databases based on Rough Set Model., *IEEE EMB Magazine*, 56–62, 2000.
10. Tsumoto, S. Statistical Extension of Rough Set Rule Induction *Proceedings of SPIE: Data Mining and Knowledge Discovery: Theory, Tools, and Technology III*, 2001.
11. Yao, Y.Y. and Wong, S.K.M., A decision theoretic framework for approximating concepts, *International Journal of Man-machine Studies*, **37**, 793–809, 1992.
12. Yao, Y.Y. and Zhong, N., An analysis of quantitative measures associated with rules, N. Zhong and L. Zhou (Eds.), *Methodologies for Knowledge Discovery and Data Mining, Proceedings of the Third Pacific-Asia Conference on Knowledge Discovery and Data Mining*, LNAI **1574**, Springer, Berlin, pp. 479–488, 1999.
13. Ziarko, W., Variable Precision Rough Set Model. *Journal of Computer and System Sciences*, 46, 39–59, 1993.

Statistical Test for Rough Set Approximation Based on Fisher's Exact Test

Shusaku Tsumoto

Department of Medicine Informatics,
Shimane Medical University, School of Medicine,
Enya-cho Izumo City, Shimane 693-8501 Japan
tsumoto@computer.org

Abstract. Rough set based rule induction methods have been applied to knowledge discovery in databases, whose empirical results obtained show that they are very powerful and that some important knowledge has been extracted from datasets. However, quantitative evaluation of lower and upper approximation are based not on statistical evidence but on rather naive indices, such as conditional probabilities and functions of conditional probabilities. In this paper, we introduce a new approach to induced lower and upper approximation of original and variable precision rough set model for quantitative evaluation, which can be viewed as a statistical test for rough set methods. For this extension, chi-square distribution, F-test and likelihood ratio test play an important role in statistical evaluation. Chi-square test statistic measures statistical information about an information table and F-test statistic and likelihood ratio statistic are used to measure the difference between two tables.

1 Introduction

Rough set based rule induction methods have been applied to knowledge discovery in databases[3,6,7]. The empirical results obtained show that they are very powerful and that some important knowledge has been extracted from datasets. Furthermore, Tsumoto discusses that the core ideas of rough sets to the reasoning style of medical experts, which makes the results obtained easier for physicians to discover useful knowledge from those results[6,7].

However, rough sets have several disadvantages. First, the original rough set model only generates deterministic rules, solved by Ziarko's variable precision rough set model[11]. Second, the original rough set model has difficulties in dealing with missing data, which is extended by Kryszkiewicz and Rybinski[2]. The third one is that quantitative evaluation of induced rules are based not on statistical evidence but on rather naive indices, such as conditional probabilities and functions of conditional probabilities, pointed out by Zytkow[12]. In order to solve this problem, Tsumoto introduce a new approach to statistical evaluation of classification of a target concept with a given attribute, from the viewpoint of lower and upper approximation, using F-test[8].

In this paper, another type of statistical test is introduced. For this extension, Fisher's Exact test and likelihood estimation play an important role in statistical evaluation.

2 From Information Systems to Contingency Tables

2.1 Accuracy and Coverage

In the subsequent sections, we adopt the following notations, which is introduced by Skowron and Grzymala-Busse[5]. Let U denote a nonempty, finite set called the universe and A denote a nonempty, finite set of attributes, i.e., $a : U \to V_a$ for $a \in A$, where V_a is called the domain of a, respectively. Then, a decision table is defined as an information system, $A = (U, A \cup \{d\})$. The atomic formulas over $B \subseteq A \cup \{d\}$ and V are expressions of the form $[a = v]$, called descriptors over B, where $a \in B$ and $v \in V_a$. The set $F(B, V)$ of formulas over B is the least set containing all atomic formulas over B and closed with respect to disjunction, conjunction and negation. For each $f \in F(B, V)$, f_A denote the meaning of f in A, i.e., the set of all objects in U with property f, defined inductively as follows.

(1) If f is of the form $[a = v]$ then, $f_A = \{s \in U | a(s) = v\}$
(2) $(f \wedge g)_A = f_A \cap g_A$; $(f \vee g)_A = f_A \vee g_A$; $(\neg f)_A = U - f_a$

By the use of this framework, classification accuracy and coverage is defined as follows.

Definition 1.
Let R and D denote a formula in $F(B, V)$ and a set of objects which belong to a decision d. Classification accuracy and coverage(true positive rate) for $R \to d$ is defined as:

$$\alpha_R(D) = \frac{|R_A \cap D|}{|R_A|} (= P(D|R)), \text{ and } \kappa_R(D) = \frac{|R_A \cap D|}{|D|} (= P(R|D)),$$

where $|A|$ denotes the cardinality of a set A, $\alpha_R(D)$ denotes a classification accuracy of R as to classification of D, and $\kappa_R(D)$ denotes a coverage, or a true positive rate of R to D, respectively.

2.2 Contingency Tables

From the viewpoint of information systems, contingency tables summarizes the relation between attributes with respect to frequencies. These viewpoints have already been discussed by Yao.[9,10] However, in this study, we focus on more statistical interpretation of this table. Let R_1 and R_2 denote a formula in $F(B, V)$. A contingency tables is a table of a set of the meaning of the following formulas: $|[R_1 = 0]_A|, |[R_1 = 1]_A|, |[R_2 = 0]_A|, |[R_1 = 1]_A|, |[R_1 = 0 \wedge R_2 = 0]_A|, |[R_1 = 0 \wedge R_2 = 1]_A|, |[R_1 = 1 \wedge R_2 = 0]_A|, |[R_1 = 1 \wedge R_2 = 1]_A|, |[R_1 = 0 \vee R_1 = 1]_A|(= |U|)$. This table is arranged into the form shown in Table 1. From this table, accuracy and coverage for $[R_1 = 0] \to [R_2 = 0]$ are defined as:

Table 1. Two way Contingency Table

	$R_1 = 0$	$R_1 = 1$	
$R_2 = 0$	a	b	a + b
$R_2 = 1$	c	d	c + d
	a + c	b + d	a+b+c+d
			$(= \|U\| = N)$

$$\alpha_{[R_1=0]}([R_2 = 0]) = \frac{a}{a+c}, \quad \text{and} \quad \kappa_{[R_1=0]}([R_2 = 0]) = \frac{a}{a+b}.$$

For example, let us consider an information table shown in Table 2.

Table 2. A Small Dataset

a	b	c	d	e
0	0	0	0	1
1	0	1	1	1
0	1	1	1	0
1	1	1	1	1
0	0	1	0	0

Table 3. Corresponding Contingency Table

	b=0	b=1	
e=0	1	1	2
e=1	2	1	3
	3	2	5

When we examine the relationship between b and e via a contingency table, first we count the frequencies of four elementary relations, called *marginal distributions*: $[b = 0]$, $[b = 1]$, $[e = 0]$, and $[e = 1]$. Then, we count the frequencies of four kinds of conjunction: $[b = 0] \wedge [e = 0]$, $[b = 0] \wedge [e = 1]$, $[b = 1] \wedge [e = 0]$, and $[b = 1] \wedge [e = 1]$. Then, we obtain the following contingency table (Table 3). From this table, accuracy and coverage for $[b = 0] \rightarrow [e = 0]$ are obtained as $1/(1+2) = 1/3$ and $1/(1+1) = 1/2$. From the definition of accuracy and coverage, the contingency tables for lower and upper approximation of $[R_2 = 0]$ are obtained if c is set to 0 (Table 4) and if b is set to 0 (Table 5), respectively.

3 Fisher's Exact Test

In [8], chi-square test is applied to measure the quality of a given contingency table. The problem with chi-square test is that the approximation of chi-square distribution is not good and loses its reliability when the frequency of each cell is low. In other words, when many cells includes 0 or a very small number, compared with the number of margin, the reliability of this test is very low.

In these cases, one of the solutions is to calculate the *p*-value directly, which is called Fisher exact test [1]. This test also assumes that the marginal frequencies are given. Let us illustrate this test by using a contingency table shown in

Table 4. Contingency Table for Lower Approximation

	$R_1 = 0$	$R_1 = 1$	
$R_2 = 0$	a	b	$a+b$
$R_2 = 1$	0	d	d
	a	$b+d$	N

Table 5. Contingency Table for Upper Approximation

	$R_1 = 0$	$R_1 = 1$	
$R_2 = 0$	a	0	a
$R_2 = 1$	c	d	$c+d$
	$a+c$	d	N

Table 6. Contingency Table

	A_1	A_2	$\cdots$	A_n	Sum
B_1	x_{11}	x_{12}	$\cdots$	x_{1n}	b_1
B_2	x_{21}	x_{22}	$\cdots$	x_{2n}	b_2
$\cdots$	$\cdots$	$\cdots$	$\cdots$	$\cdots$	$\cdots$
B_m	x_{m1}	x_{m2}	$\cdots$	x_{mn}	b_m
Sum	a_1	a_2	$\cdots$	a_n	N

Table 6. Marginal frequencies are $a_1, a_2, \cdots, a_n$ and $b_1, b_2, \cdots, b_n$. Assuming this condition, the conditional probability $p(x_{11}, x_{12}, \cdots, x_{mn}|a_1, \cdots, a_n, b_1, \cdots, b_n)$ is given as:

$$p(x_{11}, x_{12}, \cdots, x_{mn}|a_1, \cdots, a_n, b_1, \cdots, b_n) = \frac{\prod_i^{m-1} \prod_j^n {}_{a_{ij}}C_{x_{ij}}}{\prod_i^{m-1} {}_NC_{b_i}}, \quad (1)$$

which follows a hypergemertic distribution. Since a hypergemertic distribution converges to a multinominal distribution when n grows large, its distribution can be approximated by normal distribution eventually. In the case of two-way table, this formula is simplified as:

$$p(x_{11}, x_{12}, x_{21}, x_{22}|a_1, a_2, b_1, b_2) = \frac{{}_{a_1}C_{x_{11}} \times {}_{a_2}C_{x_{12}}}{{}_NC_{b_1}}$$

For example, the p-value of Table 3 is calculated as:

$$p(1,1,2,1|3,2,2,3) = \frac{{}_3C_1 \times {}_2C_1}{{}_5C_2} = \frac{3 \times 2}{\frac{5 \times 4}{2}} = \frac{6}{10} = 0.6$$

It is notable that the conditional probability of Fisher's exact test can be viewed as the likelihood of marginal frequencies, which implicitly shows that the log-likehood ratio test can be applied to comparison between two tables.

3.1 Log-Likelihood Ratio Test for Rough Set Approximation

Fisher's exact test for lower approximation. As discussed in 4.1.2, the contingency table for lower approximation is obtained if c is set to 0. That is, the following contingency table corresponds to the lower approximation of $R_2 = 0$ in Two-way table. Thus, the test statistic is simplified into:

$$p(x_{11}, x_{12}, x_{21} = 0, x_{22}|a_1, a_2, b_1, b_2) = \frac{{}_{a_1}C_{x_{11}} \times {}_{a_2}C_{x_{12}}}{{}_{N}C_{b_1}} = \frac{{}_{b+d}C_b}{{}_{N}C_{a+b}} \quad (2)$$

Fisher's exact test for upper approximation. From the definition of coverage shown in Section 2, the contingency table for lower approximation is obtained if c is set to 0. That is, the following contingency table corresponds to the lower approximation of $R_2 = 0$. In this case, the test statistic is simplified into:

$$p(x_{11}, x_{12} = 0, x_{21}, x_{22}|a_1, a_2, b_1, b_2) = \frac{{}_{a_1}C_{x_{11}} \times {}_{a_2}C_0}{{}_{N}C_{b_1}} = \frac{{}_{a_1}C_{x_{11}}}{{}_{N}C_{b_1}} = \frac{{}_{a+c}C_a}{{}_{N}C_a} \quad (3)$$

Exact test based Distance from Two Approximations. From the representation of conditional probabilities of Fisher's exact test, the p-value can be viewed as the likelihood of given marginal frequencies. One of the approached to measure the distance between likelihood functions is also to take the ratio between likelihood. Then, the logarithm of a likelihood ratio test statistic follows the chi-squre distribution with the freedom of one. That is,

Theorem 1. Let x_{T_1} and x_{T_2} denote a list of the value of all the cells in information tables T_1 and T_2, respectively. If the four marginal distributions of an information table T_1 is equal to those of the other table T_2, then the test-statistic

$$l(T_1, T_2) = -2 \log \frac{p(x_{T_1}|M)}{p(x_{T_2}|M)}$$

follows χ^2-distribution with the freedom of one, where M denotes the shared marginal distribution.

3.2 How to Make a New Table for Comparison

The next step for table comparison is to make tables corresponding to lower and upper approximation from a original table. In this step, the assumption that the marginal distribution should be the same is the most important constraints. That is,

Lower Approximation. Let us consider the two-way contingency table shown in Table 1. If we consider the case of lower approximation, c should be changed to 0. Thus, since the marginal distribution of $R_1 = 0$ is equal to $(a + c)/N$, so a is substituted to $a + c$. Then, since the marginal distribution of $R_2 = 0$ is equal to $(a + b)/N$, so b is substituted to $b - c$. Also, since the marginal distribution of $R_1 = 1$ is equal to $(b + d)/N$ and the marginal distribution of $R_2 = 1$ is equal to $(c + d)/N$, so d is substituted to $d + c$. From these constraint propagation, the final table of upper approximation is obtained as shown in Table 7

Upper Approximation. Let us consider the two-way contingency table shown in Table 1. If we consider the case of upper approximation, b should be changed to 0. Thus, since the marginal distribution of $R_2 = 0$ is equal to $(a+b)/N$, so a is substituted to $a+b$. Then, since the marginal distribution of $R_1 = 0$ is equal to $(a+c)/N$, so c is substituted to $a+c-b$. Also, since the marginal distribution of $R_1 = 1$ is equal to $(b+d)/N$ and the marginal distribution of $R_2 = 1$ is equal to $(c+d)/N$, so d is substituted to $b+d$. From these constraint propagation, the final table of upper approximation is obtained as shown in Table 8.

Table 7. Table of Lower Approximation obtained from Table 1

	$R_1 = 0$	$R_1 = 1$	
$R_2 = 0$	$a+c$	$b-c$	$a+b$
$R_2 = 1$	0	$d+c$	$c+d$
	$a+c$	$b+d$	$(=|U|=N)$

Table 8. Table of Upper Approximation obtained from Table 1

	$R_1 = 0$	$R_1 = 1$	
$R_2 = 0$	$a+b$	0	$a+b$
$R_2 = 1$	$c-b$	$b+d$	$c+d$
	$a+c$	$b+d$	$(=|U|=N)$

4 Example

From the above tables, let us calculate the similarity between Table 3 and a table for upper approximation shown in Table 9.

From the above tables, let us calculate the similarity between Table 3 and a table for lower approximation shown in Table 10. It is notable that if we want to preserve the marginal distribution, then we have to allow a negative value for $[b=1]\&[e=0]$. Although negative values are not allowed in statistical analysis, this meaning have a very good intuitive meaning: this combination of attribute-value pairs is strongly negated if the original table is reliable.

In the same way, log-likelihood ratio can be applied to the same example. The p-value is calculated as:

$$p(1,1,2,1|3,2,2,3) = \frac{{}_3C_1 \times {}_2C_1}{{}_5C_2} = \frac{3 \times 2}{\frac{5 \times 4}{2}} = \frac{6}{10} = 0.6$$

Thus, this table can be frequently observed in the given marginal distribution.

In the case of Table 9 (upper approximation), p-value is calculated as:

$$p(2,0,1,2|3,2,2,3) = \frac{{}_3C_2 \times {}_2C_0}{{}_5C_2} = \frac{3 \times 1}{\frac{5 \times 4}{2}} = \frac{3}{10} = 0.3$$

Thus, log-likelihood ratio is equal to:

$$l(x_{Table3}, x_{Table13}) = -2\log\frac{0.3}{0.6} = -2\log 2 = 1.38629$$

Table 9. Table Corresponding to Upper Approximation

	b=0	b=1	
e=0	2	0	2
e=1	1	2	3
	3	2	5

Table 10. Table Corresponding to Lower Approximation

	b=0	b=1	
e=0	3	-1	2
e=1	0	3	3
	3	2	5

The p-value of this ratio statistic is 0.239. Thus, the probability that these two tables are different from each other is equal to 0.239. On the other hand, p-value for lower approximation is calculated as:

$$p(3,-1,0,3|3,2,2,3) = \frac{{}_3C_3 \times {}_2C_{-1}}{{}_5C_2} = \frac{3 \times 0}{\frac{5 \times 4}{2}} = \frac{0}{10} = 0$$

Thus, Table 3 cannot be similar to the upper approximation if marginal distributions are fixed.

5 Discussion: Negative Values in Cells

As shown in the above example, negative values may be observed in constructed tables for lower approximation or upper approximations. Since negative values are not allowed for a contingency table in principle, these observations suggest that lower or upper approximation may not exist in some given marginal distribution. In Table 8, the relation between $a + c$ and $a + b$ is important: if $a + c$ is smaller than $a + b$, then we cannot construct a table of upper approximation from the original table without negative values. (That is, the relation between b and c is important.) On the other hand, in Table 9, if $a + b$ is smaller than $a + c$, then we cannot construct a table of lower approximation from the original table.

Thus, in two-way tables (binary classification), it is easy to check the existence of lower and upper approximation in a given marginal distribution. Since N-way contingency tables may have a larger freedom, the situations become more complicated. For example, in the case of three-way tables shown in Table 11, we have to check the relation between $a + b + c$ and $a + d + e$. However, they are not the only candidates for upper approximations. It is our future work to develop the way to check whether lower or upper approximations exists in a given marginal distribution.

6 Conclusion

In this paper, we introduce a new approach to induced lower and upper approximation of original and variable precision rough set model for quantitative evaluation, which can be viewed as a statistical test for rough set methods. For this extension, chi-square distribution, F-distribution and likelihood ration test play an important role in statistical evaluation. Chi-square test statistic measures statistical information about an information table and F-test statistic and likelihood ratio test statistic are used to measure the difference between two tables. This paper is a preliminary study on a statistical evaluation of information tables, and the discussions are very intuitive, not mathematically rigor. Also, for simplicity of discussion, we assume that all conditional attributes and decision attributes in information tables are binary. More formal analysis will appear in the future work.

Acknowledgements. This work was supported by the Grant-in-Aid for Scientific Research (13131208) on Priority Areas (No.759) "Implementation of Active Mining in the Era of Information Flood" by the Ministry of Education, Science, Culture, Sports, Science and Technology of Japan.

References

1. Fisher, R.A. *Statistical Methods for Research Workers* (5th Ed.), Oliver&Boyd, Edinburgh, 1934.
2. Kryszkiewicz, M.and Rybinski, H. Incompleteness Aspects in Rough Set Approach. *Proceedings of Sixth International Workshop on Rough Sets, Data Mining and Granular Computing*, Duke, N.C., 1998.
3. Polkowski, L. and Skowron, A.(Eds.) *Rough Sets and Knowledge Discovery 1 and 2*, Physica Verlag, Heidelberg, 1998.
4. Pawlak, Z., *Rough Sets*. Kluwer Academic Publishers, Dordrecht, 1991.
5. Skowron, A. and Grzymala-Busse, J. From rough set theory to evidence theory. In: Yager, R., Fedrizzi, M. and Kacprzyk, J.(eds.) *Advances in the Dempster-Shafer Theory of Evidence*, pp.193-236, John Wiley & Sons, New York, 1994.
6. Tsumoto, S. Knowledge discovery in clinical databases and evaluation of discovered knowledge in outpatient clinic. *Information Sciences*, **124**, 125–137, 2000.
7. Tsumoto, S. Automated Discovery of Positive and Negative Knowledge in Clinical Databases based on Rough Set Model., *IEEE EMB Magazine*, 56-62, 2000.
8. Tsumoto, S. Statistical Extension of Rough Set Rule Induction *Proceedings of SPIE: Data Mining and Knowledge Discovery: Theory, Tools, and Technology III*, 2001.
9. Yao, Y.Y. and Wong, S.K.M., A decision theoretic framework for approximating concepts, *International Journal of Man-machine Studies*, **37**, 793–809, 1992.
10. Yao, Y.Y. and Zhong, N., An analysis of quantitative measures associated with rules, N. Zhong and L. Zhou (Eds.), *Methodologies for Knowledge Discovery and Data Mining, Proceedings of the Third Pacific-Asia Conference on Knowledge Discovery and Data Mining*, LNAI **1574**, Springer, Berlin, pp. 479–488, 1999.
11. Ziarko, W., Variable Precision Rough Set Model. *Journal of Computer and System Sciences*, 46, 39–59, 1993.
12. Zytkow, J. M. Granularity refined by knowledge: contingency tables and rough sets as tools of discovery *Proceedings of SPIE: Data Mining and Knowledge Discovery: Theory, Tools and Technology II* p. 82–91, 2000.

Triangulation of Bayesian Networks: A Relational Database Perspective

S.K.M. Wong, D. Wu, and C.J. Butz

Department of Computer Science
University of Regina
Regina, Saskatchewan, Canada, S4S 0A2
{wong,danwu,butz}@cs.uregina.ca

Abstract. In this paper, we study the problem of triangulation of Bayesian networks from a relational database perspective. We show that the problem of triangulating a Bayesian network is equivalent to the problem of identifying a maximal subset of conflict free conditional independencies. Several interesting theoretical results regarding triangulating Bayesian networks are obtained from this perspective.

1 Introduction

The Bayesian network model [5] has been well established as an effective and efficient tool for managing uncertain information. A *Bayesian network* (BN) consists of (i) a qualitative component, namely, *directed acyclic graph* (DAG), which encodes *conditional independence* (CI) information existing in a problem domain, and (ii) a quantitative component, namely, a set of *conditional probability distributions* (CPDs) whose product defines a *joint probability distribution* (jpd). A BN is normally transformed into a (decomposable) Markov network for probabilistic inference. This transformation consists of two separate and sequential graphical operations, namely, *moralization* and *triangulation*. The moralization of a given BN is unique, while there may exist multiple choices of triangulation. The particular choice of triangulation is important since efficiency of probabilistic reasoning is affected by the chosen triangulated graph [3].

On the other hand, the relational database model [4] has been established for designing data management systems. Historically, the relational database model was proposed for processing data consisting of records (or tuples); it was not designed as a reasoning tool. In our recent research, it has been emphasized that there exists an intriguing relationship between the relational database model and the Bayesian network model [6,7,8,9].

In this paper, we provide an analytical study of the triangulation problem from a relational database perspective. In particular, we show that this problem is equivalent to that of identifying a maximal subset of conflict free conditional independencies. This new perspective is not only consistent with those graphical methods developed for triangulation, but also enables us to immediately obtain several interesting theoretical results regarding the triangulation of BNs.

The paper is organized as follows. We review triangulation of BNs in Section 2. In Section 3, constructing acyclic database schemes is discussed. Section 4 investigates the relationship between triangulation in BNs and the construction of acyclic database schemes. The conclusion is given in Section 5.

2 Triangulation in Bayesian Networks

A BN is usually transformed into a (decomposable) Markov network [5] for inference. During this transformation, two graphical operations are performed on the DAG of a BN, namely, moralization and triangulation.

Given a BN, we use $\mathcal{D} = (U, E)$ to denote its associated DAG, where U represents the nodes in $\mathcal{D}$, and $E \subseteq U \times U$ represents the set of directed edge of $\mathcal{D}$. Moralizing a DAG simply means for each node of $\mathcal{D}$, adding undirected edges between every pair of its parents if they are not connected in $\mathcal{D}$, and then dropping the directionality of all directed edges of $\mathcal{D}$. We use $\mathcal{M}^{\mathcal{D}}$ to denote the moralized graph of $\mathcal{D}$, and omit the superscript when it is understood from context. The moralized graph $\mathcal{M}$ of $\mathcal{D}$, by definition, is undirected.

A *cycle* in a undirected graph G means a sequence of nodes $x_1, x_2, \ldots, x_m$ such that x_j, $j = 2, \ldots, m-1$, are distinct, $x_1 = x_m$ and (x_i, x_{i+1}), $i = 1, \ldots, m-1$, is an edge in G. The *length* of this cycle is m. A undirected graph G is said to be *complete* if every pair of its nodes are connected by an edge. A subset S of nodes in G is said to be complete if there are edges between every pair of nodes in S. A subset S of nodes in G is said to be a *maximal clique* if S is complete and there does not exist another subset S' of nodes which is complete and $S \subset S'$.

The moralized DAG is transformed into a triangulated graph. A graph is *triangulated* if and only if every cycle of length four or greater contains an edge between two nonadjacent nodes in the cycle. If a graph is not triangulated, one can make it triangulated by adding some edges, called *fill-in* edges. It is noted that one may have many choices of adding fill-in edges to make a graph triangulated. We will use $\mathcal{T}^{\mathcal{D}}$ to represent a triangulated graph from a DAG $\mathcal{D}$ and omit its superscript if no confusion arises.

Example 1. Consider the DAG $\mathcal{D}$ shown in Fig 1 (i). Its unique moralized graph $\mathcal{M}$ is shown in Fig 1 (ii). $\mathcal{M}$ is not triangulated since there is a cycle, i.e., A, B, D, E, C, A. We may have multiple choices to triangulate this moralized graph, including, for instance, we may add fill-in edges, (B, C), (C, D) as shown in Fig 1 (iii), or (B, C), (B, E) as shown in Fig 1 (iv), or (A, D), (A, E) as shown in Fig 1 (v). The graphs in Fig 1 (iii), (iv), (v) are triangulated.

3 Construction of Acyclic Database Schemes

In this section, we divert our discussion to the construction of acyclic database schemes in the relational database model [4]. We first briefly introduce some pertinent notions.

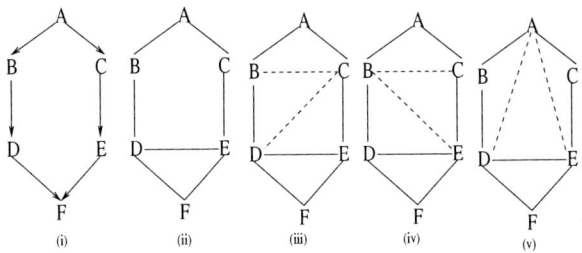

Fig. 1. A DAG $\mathcal{D}$ in (i) and its moralized graph $\mathcal{M}$ in (ii). Three possible triangulations are in (iii), (iv) and (v), where fill-in edges are indicated as dotted lines.

Let $\mathcal{N}$ be a finite set of symbols, called *attributes*. We define a *database scheme* $\mathbf{R} = \{R_1, R_2, \ldots, R_n\}$ to be a set of subsets of $\mathcal{N}$. By XY, we mean $X \cup Y$. For each i, the set R_i is called a *relation scheme*. If $r_1, r_2, \ldots, r_n$ are relations, where r_i is a relation over the scheme R_i, $1 \leq i \leq n$, then we call $r = \{r_1, r_2, \ldots, r_n\}$ a *database* over $\mathbf{R}$. We also use $r_i[R_i]$ to explicitly indicate that the relation r_i is over the scheme R_i. A relation $r[R]$ is said to satisfy the (full) *multivalued dependency* (MVD) [4] $Y \twoheadrightarrow X|Z$, if $r[R] = r[XY] \bowtie r[YZ]$, where $R = XYZ$, $r[XY]$ and $r[YZ]$ are projections [4] of $r[R]$ onto schemes XY and YZ, respectively, and Y is called the *key* of this MVD. A MVD $Y \twoheadrightarrow X|Z$ is said to *split* a set W of attributes if $W \cap X \neq \emptyset$, and $W \cap Z \neq \emptyset$. Given a set M of MVDs, the left hand sides of the MVDs in M are called the *keys* of M. A set M of MVDs are said to be *conflict free* [2] if (i) the keys of M are not split by any MVD in M, and (ii) M satisfies the *intersection property* [2].

A database scheme can be conveniently represented by a hypergraph [2]. A hypergraph is a pair $(\mathcal{N}, \mathbf{S})$, where $\mathcal{N}$ is a finite set of nodes (attributes) and $\mathbf{S}$ is a set of edges (hyperedges) which are arbitrary subsets of $\mathcal{N}$. If the nodes are understood, we will use $\mathbf{S}$ to denote the hypergraph. A hypergraph $\mathbf{S}$ is *acyclic* (or a *hypertree*) if its elements can be ordered, say $S_1, S_2, \ldots, S_N$, such that $(S_i \cap \bigcup_{k=1}^{i-1} S_k) \subseteq S_j$, where $1 \leq j \leq i - 1$, $i = 2, \ldots, N$. We call any such ordering a *tree (hypertree) construction ordering* for $\mathbf{S}$.

There is a one to one correspondence between a hypergraph and a relational database scheme. For a database scheme $\mathbf{R} = \{R_1, R_2, \ldots, R_n\}$, its corresponding hypergraph representation has as its set of nodes those attributes that appear in one or more of the R_i's, and as its set $\mathbf{R} = \{R_1, R_2, \ldots, R_n\}$ of hyperedges. In other words, we treat $\mathbf{R}$ as a hypergraph, each of hyperedge is one of the relation schemes in $\mathbf{R}$. On the other hand, for a hypergraph, we can treat each of its hyperedge as a relation scheme and all the hyperedges compose a database scheme. For instance, given a database scheme $\mathbf{R} = \{R_1 = \{A, B, C\}, R_2 = \{B, C, E\}, R_3 = \{B, D, E\}, R_4 = \{D, E, F\}\}$, we can represent it as a hypergraph as shown in Fig 2, and vice versa. A database scheme $\mathbf{R}$ is called *acyclic* if its corresponding hypergraph is acyclic [2]. Therefore, we will use the terms acyclic database scheme and acyclic hypergraph interchangeably.

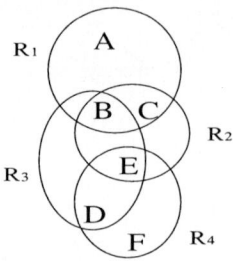

Fig. 2. A hypergraph example.

Relational database scheme design has been extensively studied [4]. A culminating result [2] is the desirability of an *acyclic database scheme*, since acyclic schemes possess a number of desirable properties. One of the properties that is relevant to our discussion is that an acyclic hypergraph is equivalent to a set of conflict free MVDs. Furthermore, an efficient algorithm [2] was developed to construct an acyclic hypergraph from a set of conflict free MVDs. A graphical method [2] was also developed to identify all the MVDs implied by an acyclic hypergraph.

4 Triangulation from a Relational Database Perspective

In this section, we first review the relationship between a triangulated graph and an acyclic hypergraph. We then study the triangulation problem from the relational database perspective.

In [2], many equivalent definitions of acyclic database scheme were suggested.

Theorem 1. [2] *There is a one-to-one correspondence between triangulated graphs and acyclic hypergraphs.*

That is, for each triangulated undirected graph, denoted $\mathcal{G}$, there is a corresponding equivalent acyclic hypergraph, denoted $\mathcal{H}$, where each hyperedge is a *maximal* clique of $\mathcal{G}$; and for each acyclic hypergraph $\mathcal{H}$, there is a corresponding undirected $\mathcal{G}$, which has the same nodes as $\mathcal{H}$ and an edge between every pair of nodes that are in the same hyperedge of $\mathcal{H}$.

Example 2. Consider the triangulated undirected graph $\mathcal{G}$ in Fig 3 (i) and its corresponding acyclic hypergraph $\mathcal{H}$ shown in Fig 3 (ii). The maximal cliques of $\mathcal{G}$, i.e., ABC, BCE, BDE, and DEF, are exactly the four hyperedges of $\mathcal{H}$. On the other hand, if we draw edges between every pair of nodes that are contained by the same hyperedge of $\mathcal{H}$, we will obtain the triangulated undirected graph $\mathcal{G}$.

It immediately follows from theorem 1 that we can consider the problem of triangulating a Bayesian network as the equivalent problem of constructing an acyclic hypergraph. This connection also makes it possible to apply approaches

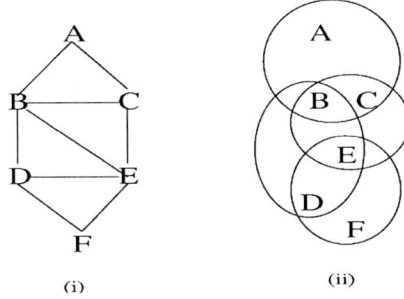

Fig. 3. A triangulated undirected graph $\mathcal{G}$ in (i) and its corresponding acyclic hypergraph $\mathcal{H}$ in (ii).

that were originally developed in relational databases model for constructing an acyclic hypergraph to the problem of triangulation in Bayesian networks.

In relational database theory, an algorithm was developed to construct an acyclic hypergraph from a set of MVDs which satisfies the condition of *conflict free* [2]. Moreover, the acyclic hypergraph constructed is equivalent to this input set of conflict free MVDs. In [8], the relationship between the notion of MVD in relational database model and the notion of CI in Bayesian network model has been thoroughly studied. Given a BN over set $U = \{X_1, \ldots, X_n\}$ of variables, we say X is *conditional independent* (CI) of Z given Y, denoted $I(X, Y, Z)$, if $p(X|YZ) = p(X|Y)$, where X, Y, Z are disjoint subsets of U. A CI $I(X, Y, Z)$ is *full* if $XYZ = U$, and Y is the *key* of this CI. In this paper, we are only concerned with full CIs and we will use the term CI to refer to full CI unless otherwise explicitly mentioned. Since the logical implication for MVD and CI coincides [8], algorithms and notions developed for one can be safely applied to the other. For instance, the notion of a conflict free set of MVDs can be applied as the notion of a conflict free set of CIs [8]. Furthermore, in [7], we can construct an acyclic hypergraph from an input set of conflict free CIs.

Theorem 2. [7] *There is a one-to-one correspondence between acyclic hypergraphs and conflict free CIs.*

The algorithm in [7] suggests that for a given Bayesian network, if we can obtain a set of conflict free CIs, then we can construct an acyclic hypergraph. By theorem 1, constructing an acyclic hypergraph from an input set of conflict free CIs is equivalent to constructing a triangulated graph. By theorem 2, the problem of triangulation in Bayesian networks now turns out to be the problem of how to obtain a set of conflict free CIs from a Bayesian network. It is worth mentioning that the set of conflict free CIs obtained from a Bayesian network should be *maximal*, otherwise, although the triangulated graph of the Bayesian network obtained from a (not necessarily maximal) set of conflict free CIs is indeed triangulated, it will contain superfluous [3] fill-in edges in the triangulation.

All CIs holding in a DAG, denoted $\mathcal{C}$, can be identified using the d-separation method [5]. By using the method developed in [10], we can remove any redundant

CIs in $\mathcal{C}$ to obtain a *reduced* cover, denoted $\mathcal{C}'$. The problem of triangulation in BNs now turns out to be the problem of obtaining a maximal conflict free subset of $\mathcal{C}'$. A subset S of $\mathcal{C}'$ is a *maximal conflict free* subset if (i) S is conflict free; and (ii) no other subset S' is also conflict free, where $S \subset S' \subseteq \mathcal{C}'$. For a reduced cover $\mathcal{C}'$, we may have multiple maximal conflict free subsets. Since the intersection property is always satisfied by any CIs that hold in a DAG [5], therefore, to form a maximal conflict free subset S, we only need to check whether the CIs in S split its keys.

Based on the above discussion, we have the following theorem.

Theorem 3. Let $\mathcal{D}$ be a DAG of a BN and $\mathcal{C}'$ be the reduced cover of all CIs $\mathcal{C}$ holding in $\mathcal{D}$. There is a one-to-one correspondence between the triangulations of $\mathcal{D}$ and the maximal conflict free subsets of $\mathcal{C}'$.

Theorem 3 indicates that for each maximal conflict free subset of $\mathcal{C}'$, there is a corresponding triangulation of $\mathcal{D}$, and vice versa.

Example 3. Consider the DAG $\mathcal{D}$ shown in Fig 1 (i). The reduced cover of all CIs holding in $\mathcal{D}$ is

$$\mathcal{C}' = \{c_1 = I(A, BC, DEF), c_2 = I(AC, BE, DF), c_3 = I(AB, CD, EF),$$
$$c_4 = I(B, AD, CEF), c_5 = I(C, AE, BDF), c_6 = I(F, DE, ABC)\}.$$

It can be verified that $S_1 = \{c_6, c_3, c_1\}$ is a maximal conflict free subset of $\mathcal{C}'$, from which the acyclic hypergraph $\mathcal{H}_1$ in Fig 4 (i) can be constructed. Similarly, it can be verified that $S_2 = \{c_6, c_2, c_1\}$ is a maximal conflict free subset of $\mathcal{C}'$, from which the acyclic hypergraph $\mathcal{H}_2$ in Fig 4 (ii) can be constructed. Similarly, it can also be verified that $S_3 = \{c_6, c_4, c_5\}$ is a maximal conflict free subset of $\mathcal{C}'$ as well, from which the acyclic hypergraph $\mathcal{H}_3$ in Fig 4 (iii) can be constructed. The corresponding triangulated undirected graphs for $\mathcal{H}_1$, $\mathcal{H}_2$, and $\mathcal{H}_3$ are shown in Fig 1 (iii), (iv), and (v), respectively.

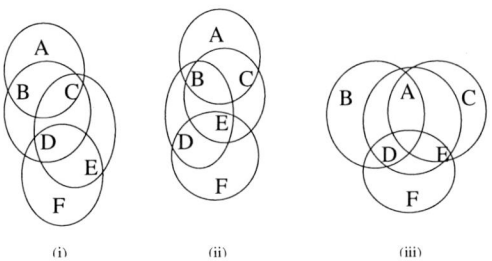

Fig. 4. Acyclic hypergraphs $\mathcal{H}_1$, $\mathcal{H}_2$ and $\mathcal{H}_3$ corresponding to maximal conflict free subsets S_1, S_2 and S_3.

It is noted that in the above example, in all three maximal conflict free subsets, namely, S_1, S_2 and S_3, the CI $c_6 = I(F, DE, ABC)$ appears in all of them and this is not an coincidence. Another interesting result that is revealed by the new perspective of triangulation is as follows.

Theorem 4. Let $\mathcal{D}$ be a DAG of a BN, $\mathcal{C}'$ be the set of reduced cover of all CIs $\mathcal{C}$ implied by $\mathcal{D}$. Let $\mathcal{M}^\mathcal{D}$ be the moralized graph of $\mathcal{D}$, and $S_1, S_2, \ldots, S_n$ be all maximal conflict free subsets of $\mathcal{C}'$. If $I(X, Y, Z) \in \mathcal{C}'$ and Y is a subset of a maximal clique in $\mathcal{M}^\mathcal{D}$, then $I(X, Y, Z) \in \bigcap_{i=1}^{n} S_i$.

Proof. We prove this theorem by contradiction. Assume $I(X, Y, Z)$ is not in at least one of $S_1, S_2, \ldots, S_n$. Without loss of generality, suppose $I(X, Y, Z) \notin S_j$, where $1 \leq j \leq n$. Since S_j is a maximal conflict free set of CIs and all the CIs in $\mathcal{C}'$ satisfy the intersection property, the only reason for $I(X, Y, Z)$ not being in S_j is that the key Y of $I(X, Y, Z)$ is split by some CI in S_j. However, since Y is a subset of a maximal clique in $\mathcal{M}^\mathcal{D}$, Y can not be split by any CI in S_j. A contradiction.

Theorem 4 states that any CI $I(X, Y, Z)$ in $\mathcal{C}'$ whose key Y is contained by a maximal clique of the moralized graph of a DAG will appear in all maximal conflict free subsets of $\mathcal{C}'$.

Theorem 3 shows that the triangulation problem of Bayesian networks can be solved by choosing a maximal conflict free subset of the reduced cover $\mathcal{C}'$. This analytical view suggests that we can use the techniques developed for solving constraint satisfaction problem to help us choose a maximal conflict free subset. Theorem 4 shows that in the course of choosing a maximal conflict free subset, certain CIs must always be chosen.

5 Conclusion

In this paper, we have studied the problem of triangulation of Bayesian networks from a relational database perspective. This new perspective views the graphical problem of triangulation as an analytical one by utilizing the notion of maximal conflict free subset of CIs. Two interesting theoretical results have been presented and they show the potential of treating the problem of triangulation as a constraint satisfaction problem.

References

[1] Roman Bartak. Constraint programming: In pursuit of the holy grail. In *Proceedings of the Week of Doctoral Students (WDS)*, Czech Republic, 1999. Prague.
[2] C. Beeri, R. Fagin, D. Maier, and M. Yannakakis. On the desirability of acyclic database schemes. *Journal of the ACM*, 30(3):479–513, July 1983.
[3] U. Kjaerulff. Triangulation of graphs—algorithms giving small total state space. Technical report, JUDEX, Aalborg, Denmark, 1990.
[4] D. Maier. *The Theory of Relational Databases*. Principles of Computer Science. Computer Science Press, Rockville, Maryland, 1983.
[5] J. Pearl. *Probabilistic Reasoning in Intelligent Systems: Networks of Plausible Inference*. Morgan Kaufmann Publishers, San Francisco, California, 1988.

[6] S.K.M. Wong. An extended relational data model for probabilistic reasoning. *Journal of Intelligent Information Systems*, 9:181–202, 1997.
[7] S.K.M. Wong and C.J. Butz. Constructing the dependency structure of a multi-agent probabilistic network. *IEEE Transactions on Knowledge and Data Engineering*, 13(3):395–415, 2001.
[8] S.K.M. Wong, C.J. Butz, and D. Wu. On the implication problem for probabilistic conditional independency. *IEEE Transactions on System, Man, Cybernetics, Part A: Systems and Humans*, 30(6):785–805, 2000.
[9] S.K.M. Wong, Tao Lin, and Dan Wu. Construction of a bayesian dag from conditional independencies. In *The Seventh International Symposium on Artificial Intelligence and Mathematics*. Accepted, 2002.
[10] S.K.M. Wong, Tao Lin, and Dan Wu. Construction of a non-redundant cover for conditional independencies. In *The Fifteenth Canadian Conference on Artificial Intelligence*. Accepted, 2002.

A New Version of Rough Set Exploration System

Jan G. Bazan[1], Marcin S. Szczuka[2], and Jakub Wróblewski[3]

[1] Institute of Mathematics, University of Rzeszów
Rejtana 16A, 35-959 Rzeszów, Poland
bazan@univ.rzeszow.pl
[2] Institute of Mathematics, Warsaw University
Banacha 2, 02-097, Warsaw, Poland
szczuka@mimuw.edu.pl
[3] Polish-Japanese Institute of Information Technology
Koszykowa 86, 02-008, Warsaw, Poland
jakubw@mimuw.edu.pl

Abstract. We introduce a new version of the Rough Set Exploration System – a software tool featuring a library of methods and a graphical user interface supporting variety of rough-set-based computations. Methods, features and abilities of the implemented software are discussed and illustrated with a case study in data analysis.

1 Introduction

Research in decision support systems, classification algorithms in particular those concerned with application of rough sets requires experimental verification. To be able to make thorough, multi-directional practical investigations one have to possess an inventory of software tools that automatise basic operations, so it is possible to focus on the most essential matters. Several such software systems have been constructed by various researchers, see e.g. [10, vol. 2]. That was also the idea behind creation of Rough Set Exploration System (**RSES**).

First version of RSES and the library RSESlib was released several years ago. After several modifications, improvements and removal of detected bugs it was used in many applications. Comparison with other classification systems (see [9, 2]) proves its value. The RSESlib was also used in construction of computational kernel of ROSETTA — an advanced system for data analysis (see [15]).

The first version of Rough Set Exploration System (RSES v. 1.0) in its current incarnation was introduced approximately two years ago (see [4]). Present version (2.0) introduces several changes, improvements as well as new algorithms - the result of selected, recent research developments in the area of rough-set-based data analysis.

The RSES software and its computational kernel maintains all advantages of previous version. The algorithms from the previous version have been remastered to provide better flexibility and extended functionality. New algorithms added to the library follow the current state of our research. Improved construction of the system allows further extensions and supports augmentation of RSES methods into different data analysis tools.

Another important change in terms of technical development is the re-implementation of the RSES core classes in Java^{TM} 2. Most of the computational procedures are now written in Java using its object-oriented paradigms. The migration to Java simplifies some development operations and, ultimately, leads to improved flexibility of the product permitting future migration of RSES software to operating systems other than Windows.

2 Basic Notions

The structure of data that is central point of our work is represented in the form of *information system* or, more precisely, the special case of information system called *decision table*.

Information system is a pair of the form $\mathbf{A} = (U, A)$ where U is a *universe* of *objects* and $A = \{a_1, ..., a_m\}$ is a set of *attributes* i.e. mappings of the form $a_i : U \to V_a$, where V_a is called *value set* of the attribute a_i. The decision table is also a pair of the form $\mathbf{A} = (U, A \cup \{d\})$ with distinguished attribute d. In case of decision table the attributes belonging to A are called *conditional attributes* or simply *conditions* while d is called *decision*. We will further assume that the set of decision values is finite. The i-th *decision class* is a set of objects $C_i = \{o \in U : d(o) = d_i\}$, where d_i is the i-th decision value taken from decision value set $V_d = \{d_1, ..., d_{|V_d|}\}$

For any subset of attributes $B \subset A$ *indiscernibility relation* $IND(B)$ for $x, y \in U$ is defined as follows:

$$x\,IND(B)\,y \iff \forall_{a \in B}\, a(x) = a(y). \tag{1}$$

Having indiscernibility relation we may define the notion of reduct. $B \subset A$ is a *reduct* of information system if $IND(B) = IND(A)$ and no proper subset of B has this property. In case of decision tables *decision reduct* is a set $B \subset A$ of attributes such that it cannot be further reduced and $IND(B) \subset IND(d)$.

Decision rule is a formula of the form $(a_{i_1} = v_1) \wedge ... \wedge (a_{i_k} = v_k) \Rightarrow d = v_d$, where $1 \le i_1 < ... < i_k \le m$, $v_i \in V_{a_i}$. Atomic subformulas $(a_{i_1} = v_1)$ are called *conditions*. We say that rule r is *applicable* to object, or alternatively, the object *matches* rule, if its attribute values satisfy the premise of the rule. With the rule we can connect some numerical characteristics such as *matching* and *support* (see [2,3]).

By *cut* for an attribute $a_i \in A$, such that V_{a_i} is an ordered set we will denote a value $c \in V_{a_i}$. With the use of cut we may replace original attribute a_i with new, binary attribute which tells as whether actual attribute value for an object is greater or lower than c (more in [7]).

Template of $\mathbf{A}$ is a propositional formula $\bigwedge(a_i = v_i)$ where $a_i \in A$ and $v_i \in V_{a_i}$. A generalised template is the formula of the form $\bigwedge(a_i \in T_i)$ where $T_i \subset V_{a_i}$. An object *satisfies* (matches) a template if for every attribute a_i

occurring in the template the value of this attribute on considered object is equal to v_i (belongs to T_i in case of generalised template). The template induces in natural way the split of original information system into two distinct subtables. One of those subtables contains objects that satisfy the template, the other those that do not. Decomposition tree is a binary tree, whose every internal node is labelled by some template and external node (leaf) is associated with a set of objects matching all templates in a path from the root to a given leaf (see [7]).

3 Contents of RSES v. 2.0

3.1 Input/Output Formats

During operation certain functions belonging to RSES may read and write information to/from files. Most of these files are regular ASCII files.

The major change from the previous RSES versions is the format used for representing the basic data entity i.e. the decision table. There is no longer limitation on the type of attribute values. The new file format permits attributes to be represented with use of integer, floating point number or symbolic (text) value. There is also a possibility of using the "virtual", calculated during operation of the system. There may be for example derived as a linear combinations of other attributes as discussed further in the article. The file format used to store decision tables includes header where the user specifies size of the table, name and type of attributes. The effect of such a specification is visible to the user, as attribute names are used for displaying data tables in the RSES GUI.

The user is also given an option of saving the whole workspace (project) in a single file. The project layout together with underlying data structures is stored using dedicated, optimised binary file format.

3.2 The Algorithms

The algorithms that have been implemented in the RSES fall into two general categories.

First category gathers the algorithms aimed at management and edition of data structures. Functions allowing upload and download of data as well as derived structures, procedures for adding/removing objects, setting decision attributes, calculating statistical information about data and others are provided.

The algorithms for performing Rough Set theory based operations on data constitute the second, most essential kind of tools implemented inside RSES. Most important of them are:

Reduction algorithms i.e. algorithms allowing calculation of the collections of reducts for a given information system (decision table). The exhaustive algorithm for calculation of all reducts is present along with implementations of approximate and heuristic solutions such as genetic, covering and Johnson algorithms (see [12,5]).

Rule induction algorithms. Based on the calculated reduct it is possible to calculate decision rules (see [3]). Procedures for rule calculation allow user to determine some crucial constraints for the set of decision rules such as required accuracy, coverage and so on. Rules received are accompanied with several coefficients that are further used while the rules are being applied to the set of objects (see [2]).

Discretisation algorithms. Discretisation permits discovery cuts for attributes. By this process initial decision table is converted to one described with simplified, symbolic attributes; one that is less complex and contains the same information w.r.t. discernibility of objects. More in [7,2].

Algorithms for generation of new attributes – Recently added and discussed in detail further in the paper.

Template generation algorithms provide means for calculation of templates and generalised templates. Placed side by side with template generation are the procedures for inducing table decomposition trees. Details in [8].

Classification algorithms used determine decision value for objects with use of decision rules and/or templates. Discussion in [8,3,2].

3.3 The RSES GUI

To simplify the use of RSES algorithms and make it more intuitive a graphical user interface was constructed. It is directed towards ease of use and visual representation of workflow. Project interface window (see Fig. 1) consists of two parts. The visible part is the project workspace where icons representing objects occurring during our computation are presented. Behind the project window there is history window dedicated to messages, status reports, errors and warnings produced during operations. The history window is reachable via tab on the bottom part of the interface window.

It was designers intention to simplify the operations on data within project. Therefore, the entities appearing in the process of rough set based computation are represented in the form of icons placed in the upper part of workplace. Such an icon is created every time the data (table, reducts, rules,...) is loaded from the file. User can also place an empty object in the workplace and further fill it with results of operation performed on other objects. The objects that may exist in the workplace are: decision table, collection of reducts, set of rules, decomposition tree, set of cuts, set of new attributes and collection of results. Every object appearing in the project have a set of actions connected with it. By right-clicking on the object the user invokes a context menu for that object. It is also possible to call the necessary action from general pull-down program menu in the main window. Menu choices allow to view and edit objects as well as make them input to some computation. In many cases choice of some option from context menu will cause a new dialog box to open. In this dialog box user can set values of coefficients used in desired calculation. If the operation performed on the object leads to creation of new object or modification of existing one then such a new object is connected with edge originating in object(s) which contributed to its current state. Setting of arrows connecting icons in the workspace changes dynamically as new operations are being performed.

There is also a possibility of working with multiple projects at the same time. In such a case all project windows are placed in the GUI and accessible via tabs in the upper part of main window.

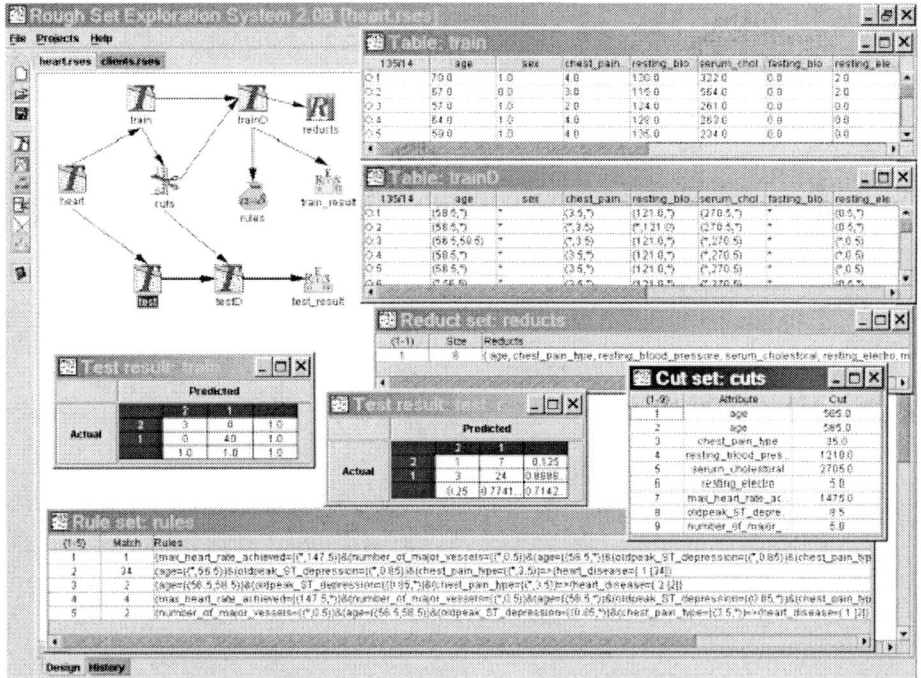

Fig. 1. The project interface window

3.4 New Features

In the current version several new methods have been added or extended. The entirely new feature is the possibility for generating new attributes as linear combinations of existing ones (Fig. 2) as discussed in the section 4.1. Another significant addition is the incorporation of the decision rule generation algorithm LEM2 based on the original concept formulated by J. Grzymała-Busse in [6].

The new features are also directly visible to the user when it comes to interaction with RSES GUI. As already mentioned, the central data structure - decision table have been re-designed. Visible result is that the attribute names in the column headers are displayed (see Fig. 1). Other significant new features are:

- Presentation of results in the form of confusion matrix.
- Presentation of decision rules using original names of attributes, which improves readability. Also, each rule is accompanied with the number of objects from different decision classes that are matched by the rule.
- Classification of new (previously unseen) cases. The program can either compare its predictions to the desired values or add one more decision column containing the predicted decision values.

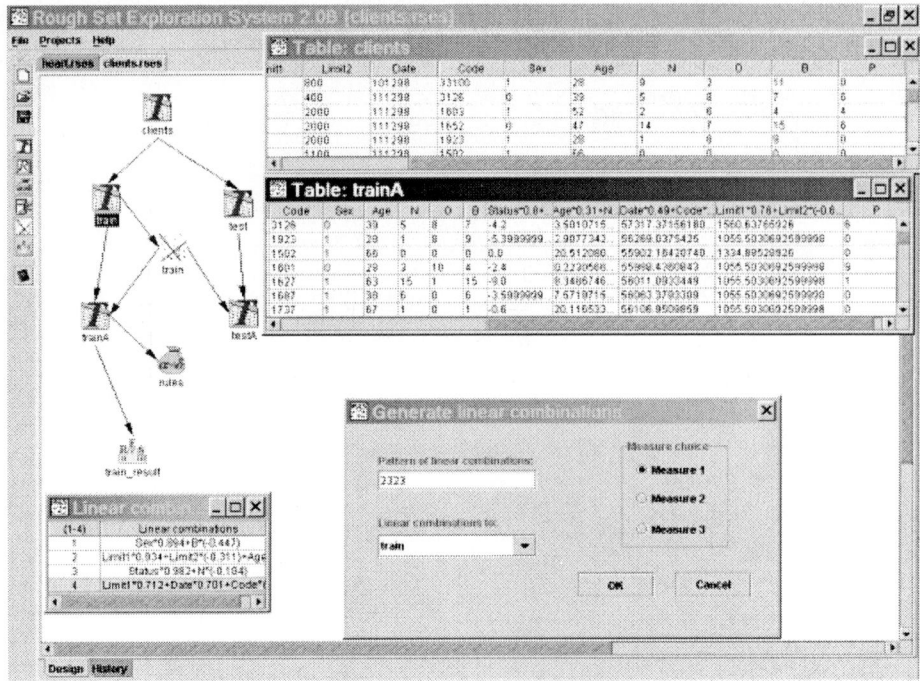

Fig. 2. New attribute generation - controls

4 Case Study

4.1 Generation of New Attributes

In our approach the original data set is extended by a number of new attributes defined as a linear combination of existing ones. Let $B = b_1, ..., b_m \subseteq A$ be a subset of numerical attributes, $|B| = m$, and let $\alpha = (\alpha_1, ..., \alpha_m) \in \mathbb{R}^m$ be a vector of coefficients. Let $h : U \to \mathbb{R}$ be a function defined as $h(u) = \alpha_1 b_1(u) + ... + \alpha_m b_m(u)$.

Usefulness of new attribute defined as $\overline{a}(u) = h(u)$ depends on proper selection of parameters B and α. The new attribute $\overline{a}$ is useful, when the model of data (e.g. decision rules) based on discretised values of $\overline{a}$ becomes more general (without loss of accuracy). Evolution strategy algorithm optimises $\overline{a}$ using quality functions described below. Three such quality measures are implemented in the current version of RSES. Detailed description can be found in [11,13]. Let L be a straight line in $\mathbb{R}^m$ defined by given linear combination h.

The *distance measure* is average (normalised) distance of objects from different decision classes in terms of $\overline{a}$ (i.e. projected onto L).

The *discernibility measure* takes into account two components: distance (as above) and average discernibility, defined as a sum of squares of cardinalities of decision-uniform intervals defined on L.

The *predictive measure* is an estimate of expected classifier's prediction quality when using only $\bar{a}$. It is constructed with use of some probabilistic methods for approximating the expected values of coverage and sensibility (ability to assign the objects to proper classes; cf. [13]).

4.2 Experimental Results

Two databases from repository [16] were used for experiments: sat_image database (4435 training and 2000 test objects, 36 attributes) and letter_recognition database (15000 training and 5000 test objects, 16 attributes). Four new attributes were generated for each table: two of them as a linear combination of two selected attributes, two other was created basing on three selected attributes (experiments show, that considering more than three attributes hardly improves results, while the computation time grows dramatically). Both the training and test table were extended by four new attributes; only the training tables, however, were used to choose the linear combinations.

Then, the newly created data sets were analysed using two data mining methods: k-NN (for k from 1 to 10; distances on all dimensions were normalised) and a rough set based analyser using local reducts (see [12]) which is implemented as part of RSES. Table 1 presents results of classification of test tables of the databases extended by new attributes as well as containing only these new ones. In the case of local-reduct-based method there is a number of decision rules presented in the last column.

Results show that in case of both k-NN and rough sets based method a table extended with four additional attributes can be analysed more accurately (see Table 1). Moreover, even if only four additional attributes are taken into account, a classification can be done with a pretty good efficiency (e.g. 70.8% of correct answers in case of letter_recognition – this is good result if one recalls that there are 26 possible answers). Note that in these cases we have 4 attributes instead of 36 or 16 – this is a significant compression of information.

The best results obtained in case of both sat_image and letter_recognition database are better than the best results in [9]. However, the result on sat_image is worse than one obtained using k-NN on feature subsets (91.5%, see [1]).

Table 1. Classification efficiency on the test data

Table name	Result (k-NN)	Result (local reducts)	No. of rules
sat_image	90.60%	81.30%	5156
extended	**91.05%**	82.40%	1867
new attributes	84.30%	76.60%	475
letter_recognition	95.64%	79.64%	21410
extended	**95.90%**	79.74%	15506
new attributes	67.80%	70.84%	4569

5 Perspective

The RSES toolkit will further grow as new methods and algorithms emerge. More procedures are still coming from current state-of-the-art research. The article reflect the state of software tools at the moment of writing, i.e. beginning of April. For information on most recent developments visit the Website [14].

Acknowledgement. In the first place the special tribute should be paid to Professor Andrzej Skowron who, for many years, overlooks the pursuit of research that led to the creation of RSES. Development of our software is supported by Polish grant KBN 8T11C02519. M. Szczuka is also supported by the WITAS project of the Wallenberg Foundation.

References

1. Bay, S.D.: Combining Nearest Neighbor Classifiers Through Multiple Feature Subsets. In: Proc. of 15 ICML, Morgan Kaufmann, Madison, 1998
2. Bazan J., A Comparison of Dynamic and non-Dynamic Rough Set Methods for Extracting Laws from Decision Tables, In [10], vol. 1, pp. 321–365
3. Bazan, J.G., Nguyen, H.S., Nguyen, S.H, Synak, P., Wróblewski, J.: Rough Set Algorithms in Classification Problem. In: Polkowski, L., Tsumoto, S., Lin, T.Y. (eds), Rough Set Methods and Applications, Physica-Verlag, 2000 pp. 49–88.
4. Bazan J., Szczuka M. RSES and RSESlib – A Collection of Tools for Rough Set Computations, Proc. of RSCTC'2000, LNAI 2005, Springer Verlag, Berlin, 2001
5. Garey M., Johnson D., Computers and Intarctability: A Guide to the Theory of NP-completness, W.H. Freeman&Co., San Francisco, 1998, (twentieth print)
6. Grzymała-Busse J., A New Version of the Rule Induction System LERS Fundamenta Informaticae, Vol. 31(1), 1997, pp. 27–39
7. Nguyen Sinh Hoa, Nguyen Hung Son, Discretization Methods in Data Mining, In [10] vol.1, pp. 451–482
8. Hoa S. Nguyen, A. Skowron and P. Synak, Discovery of Data Patterns with Applications to Decomposition and Classfification Problems. In [10] vol.2, pp. 55–97.
9. Michie D., Spiegelhalter D. J., Taylor C. C., Machine Learning, Neural and Statistical Classification, Ellis Horwood, London, 1994
10. Skowron A., Polkowski L.(ed.), Rough Sets in Knowledge Discovery vol. 1 and 2, Physica Verlag, Heidelberg, 1998
11. Ślęzak D., Wróblewski J., Classification Algorithms Based on Linear Combinations of Features. In: Proc. of PKDD'99. LNAI 1704, Springer Verlag, Berlin, 1999, pp. 548–553.
12. Wróblewski J., Covering with Reducts – A Fast Algorithm for Rule Generation, Proceeding of RSCTC'98, LNAI 1424, Springer Verlag, Berlin, 1998, pp. 402–407
13. Wróblewski J.: Ensembles of classifiers based on approximate reducts, Fundamenta Informaticae **47** (3,4), IOS Press (2001) 351–360.
14. Bazan J., Szczuka M., The RSES Homepage, http://alfa.mimuw.edu.pl/~rses
15. Ørn A., The ROSETTA Homepage, http://www.idi.ntnu.no/~aleks/rosetta
16. Blake C.L., Merz C.J., UCI Repository of machine learning databases, Irvine, CA: University of California, 1998, http://www.ics.uci.edu/~mlearn

Local Attribute Value Grouping for Lazy Rule Induction

Grzegorz Góra and Arkadiusz Wojna

Institute of Informatics, Warsaw University
ul. Banacha 2, 02-097 Warszawa, Poland
{ggora,wojna}@mimuw.edu.pl

Abstract. We present an extension of the lazy rule induction algorithm from [1]. We extended it to deal with real-value attributes and generalised its conditions for symbolic non-ordered attributes. The conditions for symbolic attributes are defined by means of a metric over attribute domain. We show that commonly used rules are a special case of the proposed rules with a specific metric. We also relate the proposed algorithm to the discretisation problem. We illustrate that lazy approach can omit the discretisation time complexity.

1 Introduction

One of the main goals of machine learning, knowledge discovery and data mining is to induce the description of a target concept from its instances. The instances can be represented, e.g., in the form of a decision table. Objects from a decision table are represented by values of some features, also called attributes.

In order to obtain an approximation of a concept with good quality, searching for relevant primitive concepts is required. Feature extraction is a problem of searching for relevant primitive concepts. Two important cases of a feature extraction problem are those of presence of real value attributes and symbolic (nominal) value attributes with large cardinality of domain. In these cases we look for new features like $age \in [30, 50]$ and $color \in \{green, yellow, blue\}$ respectively.

A well known approach in machine learning is the lazy learning (see e.g. [4], [1]). We base our research on the lazy rule induction algorithm presented in [1]. It classifies objects equivalently to the algorithm considering all minimal decision rules, i.e., the most general rules consistent with training examples. We propose extension of this algorithm to deal with real-value attributes and generalisation for symbolic non-ordered attributes. In the latter case we propose descriptors for symbolic attributes grouping the values of the attribute domain. For both kinds of attributes the partition of attribute domains is made locally for a tested object.

Our algorithm is related to the problem of discretisation of the numerical attributes and the methods for grouping attribute values (see e.g. [8], [9]). Our approach does not require a previous discretisation. A similar approach for numerical attributes was presented in [6]. However, in our approach discretisation is done during classification locally for a test example. Also our approach is parameterised by the choice of a metric on non-ordered attributes.

The paper is organised as follows. Section 2 outlines the basics of rule induction and discretisation. In Section 2.3 the algorithm for lazy rule induction is introduced. Our modification of this algorithm is presented in Section 3. Section 4 concludes the paper with a discussion of possible directions for future research.

2 Preliminaries

Let $\mathbf{A} = (U, A \cup \{d\})$ be a decision table, where U is a finite set of examples. Each example is described by a finite set of attributes (features) $A \cup \{d\}$, i.e. $a : U \to V_a$ for $a \in A \cup \{d\}$, where $d \notin A$ denotes the decision attribute and V_a is the value domain of an attribute a. The domain of a symbolic (discrete-value) attribute is a finite set, while the domain of a numerical (real-value) attribute is an interval. We denote by $Class(v)$ a subset of training examples with a decision v. We also assume that $V_d = \{1, ..., m\}$, where $m = |V_d|$ is finite.

2.1 Minimal Rule Induction

Rule induction algorithms induce decision rules from a training set. A decision rule consists of a conjunction of attribute conditions and a consequent. The commonly used conditions for symbolic attributes are equations *attribute = value*, while for numerical attributes are specified by interval inclusions, e.g.:

$$IF\ (a_1 = 2 \wedge a_3 \in [3;7] \wedge a_6 = 5)\ THEN\ (d = 1)$$

A rule is said to cover an example, and vice versa the example is said to match it, if all the conditions in the rule are true for the example. The consequent $(d = v)$ denotes a decision value that is assigned to an object if it matches the rule.

From the knowledge discovery perspective, an important problem is to compute a complete set of consistent and minimal decision rules denoted by *MinRules* (see e.g. [10]), i.e. all rules (matched at least by one training example) that are maximally general and consistent with the training set. In order to discover $MinRules$, rough set methods could be used (see e.g. [10]).

The rules induced from training examples are then used to classify objects. For a given test object the subset of rules matched by the object is selected. If the object matches only rules with the same decision, then the decision predicted by those rules is assigned to the example. If the test object matches rules corresponding to different decisions, the conflict has to be resolved (see e.g. [2]). A common approach is to use a measure for conflict resolving. Then the decision with the highest measure value is chosen. In this paper we focus on a commonly used measure, i.e.:

$$Strength(tst, v) = \left| \bigcup_{r \in MatchRules(tst,v)} supportSet(r) \right|, \qquad (1)$$

where v denotes the v-th decision ($v = 1, ..., |V_d|$), tst is a test example, $supportSet(r)$ is the set of training examples matching the rule r, $MatchRules(tst, v)$ is the subset of minimal rules $MinRules$, such that the premise is satisfied by tst and the consequent is a decision v. For each decision $Strength$ measure counts the number of training examples that are covered by the minimal rules with the decision matching a test example tst.

The minimal rule induction classifier based on the $Strength$ measure predicts the decision that is most frequent in the set of training examples covered by the rules matched by a test example, i.e.:

$$decision_{MinRules}(tst) = \arg\max_{v \in V_d} Strength(tst, v).$$

Algorithms for computing all minimal rules ($MinRules$) are very time consuming, especially when the number of training objects or attributes is large. This is due to the fact that the size of the $MinRules$ set can be exponential with respect to the size of the training set. There are also other approaches to induce a set of rules, which cover the input examples using e.g. smallest number of rules (see e.g. [5], [2]). However, we focus in this paper on the $MinRules$ set.

2.2 Discretisation and Value Partitioning

When data are described with real-value attributes, they must undergo a process called discretisation (or quantisation), which divides the range of attribute values into intervals. Such intervals form new values for the attribute and, in consequence, allow to reduce the size of the attribute value set.

Let a be a real-value attribute. A cut is defined as a pair (a, c), where $c \in V_a$. A set of cuts over attribute a defines a partition on V_a into sub-intervals. Any set of cuts transforms $\mathbf{A} = (U, A \cup d)$ into a new decision table $\mathbf{A^P} = (U, A^P \cup \{d\})$, where $A^P = \{a^P : a \in A\}$ and $a^P(x) = i \Leftrightarrow a(x) \in [c_i^a, c_{i+1}^a)$ for any $x \in U$ and $i \in \{0, ..., k_a\}$, where k_a is the number of cuts over the attribute a. A set of cuts is said to be consistent with $\mathbf{A}$ if and only if the generalised decisions of $\mathbf{A}$ and $\mathbf{A^P}$ are identical. For more details on discretisation the reader is referred to [8]. Our attention in the paper is focused on the following theorem (see e.g. [8]):

Theorem 1. *The problem of searching for a consistent partition with the minimal number of cuts is NP-hard.*

It shows that the problem of discretisation from the global point of view is a complex task. We will show in the Subsection 3.2 that it is in a sense possible to overcome this problem if one focuses on a local area instead of the whole universe. This is the case with the presented lazy rule induction algorithm.

Sometimes it is also desired to partition not only real-value attributes, but also symbolic non-ordered attributes. Formally the partition over an attribute a is any function $P_a : V_a \to \{1, ..., m_a\}$. There is a similar theorem to the presented above (see e.g. [9]):

Theorem 2. *The problem of searching for a consistent family of partitions with the minimal $\sum_{a \in A} m_a$ is NP-hard.*

2.3 Lazy Rule Induction

In the previous section we have discussed an approach based on calculating *MinRules*. Another approach can be based on construction of algorithms that do not require calculation of the decision rule set in advance. These are memory based (lazy concept induction) algorithms. An example of such an algorithm is presented in [1]. Below we briefly describe this algorithm.

Definition 1. *For objects tst, trn we denote by $rule_{tst}^H(trn)$ the local rule with decision $d(trn)$ and the following conditions t_i for each symbolic attribute a_i:*

$$t_i = \begin{cases} a_i = a_i(trn) & \text{if } a_i(tst) = a_i(trn) \\ a_i = * & \text{if } a_i(tst) \neq a_i(trn) \end{cases}$$

*where * denotes any value (such a condition is always true).*

The conditions are chosen in such a way that both the training and the test example satisfy the rule and the rule is maximally specific. Please note that it is formed differently then minimal rules that are minimally specific. But, the important thing is that if only such local rule is consistent with the training data then it can be extended to a minimal rule. Thus, we have the following relation between *MinRules* and local rules (see e.g. [1]):

Proposition 1. *Premise of the $rule_{tst}^H(trn)$ implies a premise of a rule from the set MinRules if and only if $rule_{tst}^H(trn)$ is consistent with a training set.*

This proposition shows that instead of computing the support sets for rules contained in *MinRules* and covering a new test case, it is sufficient to generate the local rules formed by the test case with all the training examples and then check their consistency against the training set. It is done by the lazy rule induction algorithm (RIA^H) presented below. The function $isConsistent(r, verifySet)$ checks if a local rule r is consistent with a $verifySet$.

Algorithm 3 $RIA^H(tst)$

> **for** each decision $v \in V_d$
> $supportSet(v) = \emptyset$
>   **for** each $trn \in U$ with $d(trn) = v$
>   **if** $isConsistent(rule_{tst}^H(trn), U)$ **then**
> $supportSet(v) = supportSet(v) \cup \{trn\}$
> $RIA^H = \arg\max_{v \in V_d} |supportSet(v)|$

From Proposition 1 it can be concluded that the algorithm RIA^H computes the measure *Strength* and therefore the results of the mentioned algorithm are equivalent to the results of the algorithm based on calculating *MinRules* and using the *Strength* measure as a strategy for conflict resolving (see [1]).

Corollary 1. *For any test object tst, $RIA^H(tst) = decision_{MinRules}(tst)$.*

The time complexity of the RIA^H algorithm for a single test object is $O(n^2)$, where n is the number of objects in training data. For more details related to this algorithm the reader is referred to [1].

3 Lazy Rule Induction with Attribute Value Grouping

Here we present the extension of the algorithm presented in the previous section. The idea is that we want to use more specific conditions forming a local rule instead of the "star" condition in case when attribute values of the examples differ. In a sense star represents the group of all values from the domain of an attribute. Our idea bases on the observation that it is possible to find smaller groups of attribute values that can be more relevant for the classification.

We divide attributes into two groups according to whether domains of the attributes are linearly ordered or not. In the first group there are numerical attributes and some of linearly ordered symbolic attributes. For such attributes we form the condition requiring the attribute to lay between the values of the examples forming a local rule.

Non-ordered attributes are treated differently. For each such attribute we require a metric to be defined (see example in Subsection 3.1). Such a metric should measure the distance between two values belonging to the domain of the attribute. Then we consider the group of values which are described as balls $B_a(c, R) = \{v \in V_a : \delta_a(c, v) \leq R\}$, where $a \in A$ is an attribute, δ_a is a metric related to this attribute, $c \in V_a$ is a center of the ball and R is a radius of the ball. Then one can measure the distance between values of examples and create condition allowing only these attribute values that are close to a test example in terms of the measured distance. Hence, we propose the following generalisation of Definition 1.

Definition 2. *For objects tst, trn we denote by $rule^{\delta}_{tst}(trn)$ the local rule with decision $d(trn)$ and the following conditions t_i for each attribute a_i:*

$$t_i = \begin{cases} min \leq a_i \leq max & \text{when } a_i \text{ is linearly ordered} \\ a_i \in B\left(a_i(tst), R_{a_i}\right) & \text{otherwise} \end{cases}$$

where $min = min(a_i(tst), a_i(trn))$, $max = max(a_i(tst), a_i(trn))$, $R_{a_i} = \delta_{a_i}(a_i(tst), a_i(trn))$ and δ_{a_i} is a measure of attribute value similarity.

For both kinds of attributes the conditions are chosen in such a way that both the training and the test example satisfy a rule and the conditions are maximally specific. Using this definition one can use Algorithm 3 with local rules $rule^{\delta}_{tst}(trn)$ from Definition 2 instead of $rule_{tst}(trn)$ from Definition 1. This algorithm groups attribute values during the classification and we denote it by RIA^{δ}.

The advantage of the algorithm for lazy rule induction is that it does not require generating rules in advance. Here we have another advantage, i.e. the algorithm deals with numerical attributes without need of discretisation and it groups symbolic attributes without prior searching for global partition.

3.1 Metrics for Attribute Value Grouping and Example

In this section we discuss the variety of the proposed local rules while changing a metric. First, let us consider the case when all attributes are symbolic and when we use Kronecker delta as a metric for all attributes ($\delta_a^H(v_1, v_2) = 1$ if $v_1 \neq v_2$ and 0 otherwise). This case relates to the Hamming distance between attribute vector values (counting the number of attributes for which examples differ). Please note that in case when $a_i(trn) \neq a_i(tst)$ then $B(a_i(tst), R_{a_i}) = V_{a_i}$ and in case when $a_i(trn) = a_i(tst)$, we get $B(a_i(tst), R_{a_i}) = \{a_i(tst)\}$. Thus, the conditions from Definition 2 are equivalent to the conditions from the Definition 1 when Kronecker metric is used.

But the proposed generalisation of local rules opens a variety of possibilities for grouping the attributes. Let us now present more informative alternative of a metric than Hamming distance, i.e. Simple Value Difference Metric (SVDM):

$$\delta_a^{SVDM}(v_1, v_2) = \sum_{v \in V_d} |P(Class(v)|a = v_1) - P(Class(v)|a = v_2)|^q,$$

where $v_1, v_1 \in V_a$, $a \in A$ and q is a natural-value parameter ($q = 1, 2, 3, ...$). SVDM considers two symbolic values to be similar if they have similar decision distribution, i.e. if they correlate similarly with the decision. Different variants of this metric have been successfully used previously (see e.g. [3]).

As an example let us consider the following training set and the test example:

Object	Age	Weight	Gender	BloodGroup	Diagn	Object	Age	Weight	Gender	BloodGroup	Diagn
trn_1	35	90	M	A	Sick	trn_5	45	75	M	B	Sick
trn_2	40	65	F	AB	Sick	trn_6	35	70	F	B	Healthy
trn_3	45	68	F	AB	Healthy	trn_7	45	70	M	O	Healthy
trn_4	40	70	M	AB	Healthy	tst	50	72	F	A	?

Age and Weight are numerical while Gender and BloodGroup (BG) are symbolic non-ordered attributes. Let us take SVDM metric for attributes BG and $Gender$. We have $\delta_{BG}^{SVDM}(A, AB) = |1 - \frac{1}{3}| + |0 - \frac{2}{3}| = \frac{4}{3}$, $\delta_{BG}^{SVDM}(A, B) = 1$, $\delta_{BG}^{SVDM}(A, O) = 2$. Let us consider $rule_{tst}^{SVDM}(trn_1)$ and $rule_{tst}^{SVDM}(trn_2)$:

if $(A \in [35; 50] \wedge W \in [72; 90] \wedge BG \in \{A\})$ then $Diagn = Sick$

if $(A \in [40; 50] \wedge W \in [65; 72] \wedge Gen = F \wedge BG \in \{A, AB, B\})$ then $Diagn = Sick$

The former rule is consistent just because no other object from the training set satisfy the premise of this rule. The latter rule is inconsistent because the object trn_3 satisfies the premise of the rule and has a different decision.

3.2 Relation to Discretisation

In this section we are going to relate the proposed algorithm to the local discretisation (in the area of a tested object). First, we will introduce definitions analogous to the presented in Section 2. Let us consider a decision table with all real-value attributes. We will say that a set of cuts is locally consistent with $\mathbf{A}$ for a case u if $\mathbf{A^P}$ preserves the generalised decision of an object u. The set of cuts is locally irreducible if any proper subset of cuts is not locally consistent.

For each training object we consider all possible consistent and irreducible sets of local cuts. Please note that there are many possible local cuts for a single example and different sets of local cuts are possible for different examples. Every set of local cuts defines a rule. The set of all such rules over the training objects is denoted by $MinRules_{LC}$. This is analogous to the construction of $MinRules$, where each rule is created locally.

We have the following relation between $MinRules_{LC}$ and local rules:

Proposition 2. *For decision tables with real-value attributes the premise of the $rule_{tst}^{\delta}(trn)$ implies premise of a rule from the set $MinRules_{LC}$ if and only if $rule_{tst}^{\delta}(trn)$ is consistent with a training set.*

Proof. If $rule_{tst}^{\delta}(trn)$ is inconsistent then no rule from $MinRules_{LC}$ could be implied by this rule. In other case the local cuts would not preserve the consistency. If $rule_{tst}^{\delta}(trn)$ is consistent then let us maximally lengthen each interval so that consistency is preserved. Such extended rule is contained in the set $MinRules_{LC}$ (from the definition of $MinRules_{LC}$).

This is the proposition analogous to Proposition 1. It shows that instead of computing the support sets for rules contained in $MinRules_{LC}$ and covering a new test case, it is sufficient to generate the local rules $rule^{\delta}$ for all training examples and then check their consistency against the training set. We have also the analogy to the Corollary 1:

Corollary 2. *For any test object tst, $RIA^{\delta}(tst) = decision_{MinRules_{LC}}(tst)$.*

Again it can be concluded that the results of the algorithm RIA^{δ} are equivalent to the results of the algorithm based on calculating $MinRules_{LC}$ and using the *Strength* measure as a strategy for conflict resolving. It shows that in a sense one can overcome the complexity of discretisation problem by using lazy discretisation with lazy rule induction. Finally, let us note that the presented results hold true for a decision table with mixed real-value and symbolic non-ordered attributes with Kronecker delta as a measure of attribute value similarity. In such case the proof of Proposition 2 would be analogous to the presented one.

4 Conclusions and Further Research

We considered lazy rule induction algorithm. We presented local rules that can deal with all types of attributes without prediscretisation of numerical attributes. Moreover, the presented rules group values of symbolic attributes. The kind of grouping depends on the metric used. For the special kind of a metric, i.e. Kronecker delta metric, the proposed local rules coincide with the commonly used rules.

The value grouping of the attributes is made locally, i.e. for each test example different grouping is possible. It is parameterised by a metric used, thus it opens many possibilities of forming rules and opens the field for a range of experiments. Practical verification of the possible classifiers needs further research.

As a good starting step we propose SVDM metric, which gave good results in many applications.

We also showed interpretation of the lazy rule induction algorithm for real-value attributes. We showed analogous proposition known for symbolic attributes.

Further research requires explanation whether a specific distribution of training examples in domain space and the related position of a classified object may influence performance of the created classifier. Also it is interesting how noise in data may influence final results.

Acknowledgements. The authors are grateful to prof. Andrzej Skowron and dr Marcin Szczuka for their useful remarks. This work was supported by grants 8 T11C 009 19 and 8 T11C 025 19 from the Polish National Committee for Scientific Research.

References

1. Bazan, J.G. (1998). *Discovery of decision rules by matching new objects against data tables.* In: L. Polkowski, A. Skowron (eds.), Proceedings of the First International Conference on Rough Sets and Current Trends in Computing (RSCTC-98), Warsaw, Poland, pp. 521–528.
2. Bazan, J.G., Szczuka, M. (2000). *RSES and RSESlib - A Collection of Tools for Rough Set Computations.* In: W. Ziarko, Y. Yao (eds.), Proceedings of the Second International Conference on Rough Sets and Current Trends in Computing (RSCTC-2000), Banf, Canada, pp. 106–113.
3. Biberman, Y. (1994). *A context similarity measure.* Proceedings of the Ninth European Conference on Machine Learning, pp. 49–63, Catania, Italy: Springer-Verlag.
4. Friedman, J.H., Kohavi, R., Yun, Y. (1996). *Lazy Decision Trees.* Proceedings of the Thirteenth National Conference on Artificial Intelligence, Cambridge, pp. 717–724, MA: MIT Press.
5. Grzymala-Busse, J.W. (1992). *LERS – A system for learning from examples based on rough sets.* In: R. Slowinski (Ed.) Intelligent Decision Support. Handbook of Applications and Advances of the Rough Sets Theory. Kluwer Academic Publishers, Dordrecht, Boston, London, pp. 3–18.
6. Grzymala-Busse, J.W., Stefanowski, J. (1997). *Discretization of numerical attributes by direct use of the LEM2 induction algorithm with interval extension.* Proceedings of the VI Int. Symp. on Intelligent Information Systems, Zakopane, IPI PAN Press, pp. 149–158.
7. Michalski, R.S. (1983). *A theory and methodology of inductive learning.* Artificial Intelligence, 20, pp. 111–161.
8. Nguyen, H. Son and Nguyen, S. Hoa. (1998). *Discretization Methods in Data Mining* In: Polkowski, L., Skowron A. (eds.) Rough sets in knowledge discovery 1 - methodology and applications, Physica-Verlag, Heidelberg, pp. 451–482.
9. Nguyen, S. Hoa (1999). *Regularity analysis and its applications in data mining* Ph.D Dissertation, Warsaw University.
10. Skowron, A. and Rauszer, C. (1992). *The Discernibility Matrices and Functions in Information Systems.* R. Słowiński (ed.), Intelligent Decision Support. Handbook of Applications and Advances of the Rough Set Theory, pp. 331–362, Dordrecht: Kluwer.

Incomplete Data Decomposition for Classification

Rafał Latkowski

Institute of Computer Science, Warsaw University
ul. Banacha 2, 02–097 Warsaw, Poland
rlatkows@mimuw.edu.pl

Abstract. In this paper we present a method of data decomposition to avoid the necessity of reasoning on data with missing attribute values. The original incomplete data is decomposed into data subsets without missing values. Next, methods for classifier induction are applied to such sets. Finally, a conflict resolving method is used to combine partial answers from classifiers to obtain final classification. We provide an empirical evaluation of the decomposition method with use of various decomposition criteria.

1 Introduction

In recent years a great research effort has been made to develop methods inducing classifiers for data with missing attribute values. Some approaches making possible to handle missing attribute values have been developed within the roughsets framework [7,14]. In those approaches a modification of indiscernibility relation is considered to handle missing attribute values. The other approach presented in *LEM1* and *LEM2* methods [4,5] is to modify an algorithm that search for covering set of decision rules. In this paper we present a method of data decomposition to avoid the necessity of reasoning on data with missing attribute values and without modification of the inductive learning algorithm itself.

The decomposition method was developed to meet certain assumptions. The primary aim was to find a possibility to adapt many existing, well known classification methods that are initially not able to handle missing attribute values to the case of incomplete data. The secondary aim was to cope with the problem of incomplete information systems without making an additional assumption on independent random distribution of missing values and without using data imputation methods [3,4]. Many real world applications have showed that appearance of missing values is governed by very complicated dependencies and the application of arbitrary method for data imputation can increase error rate of the classifier.

The decomposition method tries to avoid the necessity of reasoning on data with missing attribute values. The original incomplete data is decomposed into data subsets without missing values. Next, methods for classifier induction are applied to such sets. Finally, a conflict resolving method is used to combine partial answers from classifiers to obtain final classification. In this paper we are focused on the selecting the efficient decomposition criteria for classification. We provide an empirical evaluation of the decomposition method in comparison to the Quinlan's C4.5 method [11,12].

2 Preliminaries

In searching for concept approximation we are considering a special type of information systems — decision tables $\mathbb{A} = (U, A \cup \{d\})$, where $d : U \to V_d$ is a decision attribute. In a presence of missing data we may consider the attributes $a_i \in A$ as a functions $a_i : U \to V_i^*$, where $V_i^* = V_i \cup \{*\}$ and $* \notin V_i$. The special symbol "$*$" denotes absence of regular attribute value and if $a_i(x) = *$ we say that a_i is not defined on x. We can interpret $a_i : U \to V_i^*$ as a *partial* function in contrast to $a_i : U \to V_i$ interpreted as a *total* function.

In such tables we can search for patterns of regularities in order to discover knowledge hidden in data. We would like to focus here on searching for regularities that are based on the presence of missing attribute values. A standard tool for describing a data regularities are *templates* [10,9]. The concept of template require some modification to be applicable to the problem of incomplete information table decomposition.

Definition 1. *Let $\mathbb{A} = (U, A \cup \{d\})$ be a decision table and let $a_i \in V_i$ be a total descriptor. An object $u \in U$ satisfies a total descriptor $a_i \in V_i$, if the value of the attribute $a_i \in A$ for this object u is not missing in $\mathbb{A}$, otherwise the object u does not satisfy total descriptor.*

Definition 2. *Let $\mathbb{A} = (U, A \cup \{d\})$ be a decision table. Any conjunction of total descriptors $(a_{k_1} \in V_{k_1}) \wedge \ldots \wedge (a_{k_n} \in V_{k_n})$ is called a total template. An object $u \in U$ satisfies total template $(a_{k_1} \in V_{k_1}) \wedge \ldots \wedge (a_{k_n} \in V_{k_n})$ if values of attributes $a_{k_1}, \ldots, a_{k_n} \in A$ for the object u are not missing in $\mathbb{A}$.*

Total templates are used to discover regular areas in data that contain no missing values. Once we have a total template, we can identify it with a subtable of original data table. Such a subtable consists of attributes that are elements of total template and contains all objects that satisfy this template. With such a unique assignment of total templates and complete subtables of original data we can think of the data decomposition as a set of total templates.

3 Method Description

The decomposition method consist of two phases. In the first step the data decomposition is done. In the second step classifiers are induced and combined with a help of a conflict resolving method.

In the data decomposition phase original decision table with missing attribute values is partitioned to a number of decision subtables with complete

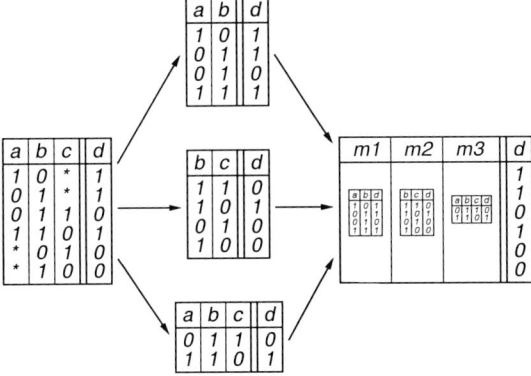

Fig. 1. The incomplete data is decomposed into complete subtables. Then, a conflict resolving method is applied.

object descriptions. Such a data decomposition should be done in accordance to regularities in real-world interest domain. We expect that the decomposition could reveal patterns of missing attribute values with a similar meaning for investigated real-world problem. Ideally the complete subtables that are result of the decomposition should correspond to natural subproblems of the whole problem domain.

The considered decomposition itself becomes the problem of covering data table with templates, as investigated in [10,9]. A standard approach to cover data table with templates is to iteratively generate the best template for objects that remains uncovered. The algorithm starts from the full set of objects. Than the (sub)optimal template is generated according to chosen criterion. In our experiments we used a dedicated, effective genetic algorithm to generate a suboptimal template. All objects that satisfy the generated template are removed and the process is continued until the set of uncovered objects becomes empty. The set of templates generated by this algorithm covers all objects from original decision table. We can treat covering set of total templates as the result of decomposition.

Subsets of original decision table must meet some requirements in order to achieve good quality of inductive reasoning as well as to be applicable in case of methods that cannot deal with missing attribute values. We expect the decision subtables corresponding to templates are exhaustively covering the input table. They should contain no missing attribute values. It is obvious that the quality of inductive reasoning depends on a particular partition and some partitions are better than others. We should construct the template evaluation criteria for templates defining decision subtables relevant to the approximated concept.

Once we have data decomposed into complete decision subtables we should merge partial classifiers to one global classifier. This is the second step of the decomposition method. Answer of classifiers induced from decision subtables are combined by a conflict resolving method. In presented experiments a Quinlan's *C4.5* method was used to induce classifiers from the decision subtables. This method was chosen to be able to compare missing attribute values handling built in C4.5 with the decomposition method that does not relay on any other missing attribute values handling. The empirical evaluation provided by Grzymała-Busse in [4] and by Quinlan in [11] suggest that C4.5 has very effective mechanism for missing attribute values handling. The initial experiments showed that application of voting conflict resolving for the decomposition method is not enough to achieve good results. Partially this is a consequence of possible *positive region* [6,13] reduction in subtables of original data. Objects that are covered by small number of total templates and contain many missing values were often incorrectly classified. In experiments we use an inductive learning method to resolve conflicts. The expressiveness of regular classifier makes it possible to combine partial answers induced from inconsistent decision subtables in much more sophisticated way. To be consequent also here the C4.5 method was used for conflict resolving.

Briefly we can summarize the decomposition method as follows:
1. Create a temporary set $\mathbb{T}$ of objects being a copy of the original decision table and repeat 2-3 until the temporary set $\mathbb{T}$ is empty;
2. Generate the best total template according to chosen criterion;
3. Remove objects from the temporary set $\mathbb{T}$ that are covered by generated template;
4. Create complete decision subtables that correspond to generated set of templates;
5. Induce classifiers over complete decision subtables;
6. Induce, from answers of the classifiers based on subtables, the top classifier used as a conflict resolving method.

4 Decomposition Criteria

Common approach to measure adequateness of a template for decomposition of a particular data set is to define a function q which describes overall quality of the investigated template. Then, the best template is understood as a template with the best value of such a quality function [9]. To achieve good results we should select quality function q very carefully and in accordance to nature of the optimized problem.

A standard approach to measure template quality is to define a quality function using *width* and *height* of a template [10,9]. The *template height* is the number of objects that satisfy a template and the *template width* is the number of attributes that are elements of a template. To obtain a quality function q of a template we have to combine width and height to get one value. A usual formula that combines these two factors is

$$q = w \cdot h. \tag{1}$$

We can also add a simple mechanism to control the importance of each factor

$$q = w^\alpha \cdot h, \tag{2}$$

where $\alpha > 0$. If we apply $\alpha > 1$ the importance of the width, thus importance of the size of available object description, increases and the number of necessary templates to cover original decision table is higher. The empirical results showed, however, that α does not have significant impact on overall classification quality.

The quality function based only on width and height is not always enough to classify objects better than the C4.5 method with native missing attribute values handling. The empirical evaluation demonstrated that in data exist many templates with similar width and height, but with different potential for the data decomposition.

We can estimate the template quality by measuring *homogeneous degree* of indiscernibility classes [9]. Such a measure corresponds to the quality of the classification by prime implicants [6]. We measure the homogeneous degree within the indiscernibility classes

$$G = \frac{\sum_{i=1}^{K} max_{c \in V_d} card(\{y \in [x^i]_{IND} : d(y) = c\})}{K^2}, \quad (3)$$

where K is the number of indiscernibility classes $[x^1]_{IND}, \ldots, [x^K]_{IND}$. We can easily incorporate the G factor into the quality function

$$q = w \cdot h \cdot G^\alpha, \quad (4)$$

where α controls influence of the G factor to the whole quality value.

The second measure is similar to the *wrapper* approach in the feature selection [1]. Instead estimating the template quality we can use the predictive accuracy of the data subset. The classifier itself is executed on decision subtable determined by the total template and the number of correct answers is counted.

$$P = \frac{number\ of\ correct\ answers}{number\ of\ objects}. \quad (5)$$

Also this factor can be easily incorporated into the quality function

$$q = w \cdot h \cdot P^\alpha. \quad (6)$$

The predictive accuracy turned out to be applicable to the template evaluation even without width and height i.e.

$$q = P. \quad (7)$$

5 Empirical Evaluation

There were carried out some experiments in order to evaluate the decomposition method with various template evaluation functions. A genetic algorithm was used for generation of the best template with respect to the selected decomposition criterion. Results were obtained from the average of classification quality from 100 times repeated five-fold Cross-Validation (CV5) evaluation. This testing method was introduced to assure preciseness in measuring the classification

Table 1. Comparison of the decomposition method that use various template evaluation criteria with the C4.5 method.

	C4.5	$w \cdot h$	$w \cdot h \cdot G$	$w \cdot h \cdot G^8$	$w \cdot h \cdot P$	$w \cdot h \cdot P^8$	P
att	52.55 ±0.12	54.94 ±0.14	59.48 ±0.13	59.28 ±0.12	55.77 ±0.13	61.94 ±0.09	63.33 ±0.09
ban	62.14 ±0.25	65.82 ±0.15	65.57 ±0.16	65.34 ±0.17	68.51 ±0.15	74.91 ±0.14	76.30 ±0.15
cmc2	45.72 ±0.10	44.92 ±0.11	42.23 ±0.10	42.37 ±0.10	47.28 ±0.09	51.33 ±0.09	51.41 ±0.10
dna2	86.84 ±0.06	80.73 ±0.09	80.48 ±0.07	80.43 ±0.08	86.20 ±0.08	88.39 ±0.08	89.07 ±0.06
hab2	71.54 ±0.14	68.07 ±0.15	74.40 ±0.16	74.45 ±0.15	69.14 ±0.13	74.67 ±0.10	75.98 ±0.10
hep	80.12 ±0.22	75.88 ±0.27	77.14 ±0.25	77.94 ±0.25	79.53 ±0.16	85.29 ±0.16	86.59 ±0.15
hin	70.47 ±0.09	69.96 ±0.09	66.54 ±0.10	68.63 ±0.12	70.16 ±0.10	71.10 ±0.08	70.53 ±0.10
hyp	95.82 ±0.01	96.72 ±0.02	95.23 ±0.01	95.23 ±0.02	96.76 ±0.01	96.81 ±0.01	97.09 ±0.01
pid2	60.81 ±0.12	61.98 ±0.13	61.73 ±0.12	62.14 ±0.10	62.19 ±0.13	67.11 ±0.09	68.29 ±0.08
smo2	60.75 ±0.07	56.14 ±0.07	69.52 ±0.11	69.53 ±0.15	57.92 ±0.10	68.95 ±0.03	69.66 ±0.02
$\sum$		-11.6%	+5.56%	+8.58%	+6.7%	+53.74%	+61.49%

quality as well as the number of generated templates. The *C4.5* method was used as a classifier and tests were performed with different decomposition approaches as well as without using decomposition method at all. The *WEKA* software system [2], which contains re-implementation of Quinlan's C4.5 Release 8 algorithm in Java, was utilized in experiments. Data sets from *StatLib* [8] were used for evaluation of the decomposition method. Data sets contain missing values in the range from 14.1% to 89.4% of all values in data.

Table 1 presents the results of the decomposition method. In the first column there are the results of the C4.5 method. In the following columns the results of the decomposition method are presented with various template quality function described in the header of each column. The big numbers represents the average accuracy of a classification method while the small numbers represents the standard deviation of results. The sum at the bottom row corresponds to a difference of the classification accuracy in comparison to the C4.5 method.

The decomposition method performs better than the C4.5 method, especially when the predictive quality is included in the template quality function. We should consider that evaluation of the predictive quality is very time-consuming, even in spite of partial result caching and other optimizations. The homogeneous degree is much more easier to compute, however, the results not always overcome the C4.5 method.

Table 2 presents the average number of generated templates with its standard deviation. The number of templates corresponds to the number of subclassifiers being result of the data decomposition. As we can see there are no strong general correlation between the number of templates and classifier accuracy. For some data sets the better classification is related to the increase of the number of templates while for the other data sets better accuracy is achieved without any increase of the number of templates.

Table 2. Comparison of the number of subtables (templates) used in the decomposition method.

	$w \cdot h$	$w \cdot h \cdot G$	$w \cdot h \cdot G^s$	$w \cdot h \cdot P$	$w \cdot h \cdot P^s$	P
att	3.96 ±0.02	4.18 ±0.02	9.23 ±0.05	3.97 ±0.03	3.88 ±0.03	4.97 ±0.07
ban	8.92 ±0.24	7.20 ±0.05	5.67 ±0.05	8.18 ±0.05	10.62 ±0.08	23.10 ±0.18
cmc2	2.00 ±0.00	4.97 ±0.01	5.93 ±0.02	2.15 ±0.02	4.11 ±0.04	5.25 ±0.05
dna2	1.06 ±0.01	1.01 ±0.01	1.01 ±0.00	2.54 ±0.02	3.55 ±0.04	7.08 ±0.04
hab2	3.65 ±0.02	5.00 ±0.00	4.73 ±0.02	3.67 ±0.02	3.08 ±0.03	2.33 ±0.04
hep	4.02 ±0.03	3.89 ±0.02	3.61 ±0.03	4.15 ±0.02	5.50 ±0.05	8.77 ±0.10
hin	3.83 ±0.03	13.72 ±0.06	21.66 ±0.08	4.91 ±0.04	8.77 ±0.07	13.22 ±0.11
hyp	2.00 ±0.00	5.95 ±0.01	5.82 ±0.02	2.02 ±0.01	2.14 ±0.02	7.53 ±0.08
pid2	2.98 ±0.01	2.99 ±0.01	2.00 ±0.00	2.98 ±0.01	3.26 ±0.03	4.81 ±0.05
smo2	2.00 ±0.00	2.20 ±0.02	1.59 ±0.03	1.26 ±0.02	1.26 ±0.02	2.06 ±0.04

6 Conclusions

The decomposition method turned out to be an efficient tool for adapting existing methods to deal with missing attribute values in decision tables. It can be applied to various algorithms for classifier induction to enrich them with capabilities of incomplete information systems processing. The time-consuming predictive quality evaluation can be replaced now with easier to compute measures of the template quality. The further research will focus on application of rule-based inductive learning with uniform conflict resolving method at the subtables and the whole system level. We believe that decomposition done in accordance to the natural structure of analyzed data can result in classifier close to the common sense reasoning.

Acknowledgments. I wish to thank professor Andrzej Skowron for a great support while writing this paper. This work was partially supported by the Polish State Committee for Scientific Research grant No. 8T11C02519.

References

1. M. Dash and H. Liu. Feature selection for classification. *Intelligent Data Analysis*, 1(3), 1997.
2. E. Frank, L. Trigg, and M. Hall. *Weka 3.3.2, Waikato Environment for Knowledge Analysis.* http://www.cs.waikato.ac.nz/ml/weka, The University of Waikato, Hamilton, New Zealand, 2002.
3. Y. Fujikawa and T. B. Ho. Scalable algorithms for dealing with missing values. 2001.
4. J. W. Grzymała-Busse and M. Hu. A comparison of several approaches to missing attribute values in data mining. In W. Ziarko and Y. Y. Yao, editors, *Proceedings of 2nd International Conference on Rough Sets and Current Trends in Computing, RSCTC-2000*, volume 2005 of *LNAI*, pages 180–187. Springer, 2000.

5. J. W. Grzymała-Busse and A. Y. Wang. Modified algorithms LEM1 and LEM2 for rule induction from data with missing attribute values. In *Proceedings of 5th Workshop on Rough Sets and Soft Computing (RSSC'97) at the 3rd Joint Conference on Information Sciences*, pages 69–72, Research Triangle Park (NC, USA), 1997.
6. J. Komorowski, Z. Pawlak, L. Polkowski, and A. Skowron. Rough sets: A tutorial. In S. K. Pal and A. Skowron, editors, *Rough Fuzzy Hybridization. A New Trend in Decision Making*, pages 3–98, Singapore, 1999. Springer.
7. M. Kryszkiewicz. Properties of incomplete information systems in the framework of rough sets. In L. Polkowski and A. Skowron, editors, *Rough Sets in Knowledge Discovery 1: Methodology and Applications*, pages 422–450. Physica-Verlag, 1998.
8. M. Meyer and P. Vlachos. *StatLib — Data, Software and News from the Statistics Community*. http://lib.stat.cmu.edu/, Carnegie Mellon University, Pittsburgh, PA, 1998.
9. S. H. Nguyen. *Regularity Analysis and its Application in Data Mining*. PhD thesis, Warsaw University, Faculty of Mathematics, Computer Science and Mechanics, 1999.
10. S. H. Nguyen, A. Skowron, and P. Synak. Discovery of data patterns with applications to decomposition and classification problems. In L. Polkowski and A. Skowron, editors, *Rough Sets in Knowledge Discovery*, volume 2, pages 55–97, Heidelberg, 1998. Physica-Verlag.
11. J. R. Quinlan. Unknown attribute values in induction. In A. M. Segre, editor, *Proceedings of the Sixth International Machine Learning Workshop*, pages 31–37. Morgan Kaufmann, 1989.
12. J. R. Quinlan. *C4.5: Programs for Machine Learning*. Morgan Kaufman, San Mateo, 1993.
13. A. Skowron and C. Rauszer. The discernibility matrices and functions in information systems. In R. Słowiński, editor, *Intelligent Decision Support. Handbook of Applications and Advances in Rough Sets Theory*, pages 331–362, Dordrecht, 1992. Kluwer.
14. J. Stefanowski and A. Tsoukiàs. Incomplete information tables and rough classification. *International Journal of Computational Intelligence*, 17(3):545–566, August 2001.

Extension of Relational Management Systems with Data Mining Capabilities

Juan F. Martinez[1], Anita Wasilewska[2], Michael Hadjimichael[3], Covadonga Fernandez[1], and Ernestina Menasalvas*[1]

[1] Facultad de Informatica, U.P.M., Madrid, Spain
juanfran@pegaso.ls.fi.upm.es; {cfbaizan,emenasalvas}@fi.upm.es
[2] Computer Science Department, Stony Brook University, NY
anita@cs.sunysb.edu;
[3] Naval Research Laboratory, Monterey, CA
hadjimic@nrlmry.navy.mil

Abstract. The relational model provides simple methods for data analysis, such as query and reporting tools. Data mining systems also provide data analysis capabilities. However, there is no uniform model which handles the representation and mining of data in such a way as to provide a standardization of inputs, outputs, and processing. In this paper we present a model of a data mining operator and a data mining structure that can be implemented over a relational database management system in the same way that multidimensional structures have been implemented.

1 Introduction

Organizations need to analyze large amounts of data that is being collected and stored on a daily basis. Sophisticated analysis requires extended capabilities (structures and operations) that relational technology does not support. As a consequence two major approaches have been developed: a multidimensional model using new structures and a multidimensional model over a relational technology. For example, major commercial database systems have extended their relational engines to handle multidimensional structures. However, there is no unifying model for data mining operations. Thus, intermediate or final results of one data mining system cannot be used by any other data mining system. This is a handicap for organizations using different systems for different areas and departments. The main goal of our paper is to present a mathematical model of knowledge representation for data mining supporting this kind of integration.

The remainder of the paper is organized as follows. In Sec. 2 we present an extention of Pawlak's definition of an information system [Pawlak81]. We call such an extension a knowledge system. In Sec. 3 we use the notion of knowledge system to define the data analysis operator as the most general case of data

---

* This project has been partially supported thanks to Universidad Politecnica de Madrid

mining operators and as the first step towards our goal of building the unifying model for data mining operations. Section 4 presents the main conclusions and discussion of the presented research.

2 Knowledge System

The *knowledge system* is a generalization of the notion of an information system. In the data analysis processes, although the information begins as relational tables, the meaning of the intermediate and final results are considered to be of a higher level of generalization. We represent those levels of generalization by a grouping of objects of a given (data mining) universe [Hadjimichael98, Wasilewska98]. This provides a granular view of the data mining. We define a knowledge system as follows:

Definition: A *knowledge system* is a system $K = (O, A, E, V_A, V_E, f, g)$ where

- O is a finite set of objects and $O \neq \emptyset$.
- A is a finite set of attributes $A \neq \emptyset$.
- E is a finite set of *group attributes*. $A \cap E = \emptyset$
- V_A is a finite set of values of attributes from A $V_A \neq \emptyset$.
- V_E is a finite set of values of group attributes.
- f is the *information function* defined as $f : O \times A \longrightarrow V_A$
- g is the group information function. g is a partial function defined as: $g : \mathcal{P}(\mathcal{P}(O)) \times E \longrightarrow V_E$.

Fact: Pawlak information system [Pawlak81] is a knowledge system.
Proof: Take $E = \emptyset$, $V_E = \emptyset$ (so $g = \emptyset$ as well).
Definition: $I = (O, A, V_A, f)$ is called *Object Information System*.
Definition: Given $E \neq \emptyset$, $V_E \neq \emptyset$ and $g : \mathcal{P}(\mathcal{P}(O)) \times E \longrightarrow V_E$, any set $S \in \mathcal{P}(\mathcal{P}(O))$ i.e. $S \subseteq \mathcal{P}(O)$ is called a *group*, and $e \in E$, $v \in V_E$ are called group S attribute and group S value of attribute, respectively, where $g(S, e) = v$.
Definition: $V_S \subseteq V_E$, $V_S = \{v : \exists e \in E\ g(S, e) = v\}$ are called *values of attributes* for a group S.
Definition: $E_S = \{e \in E : g(S, e) = v\}$ are called group attributes of the group S.
Definition: The set $U = \{S \in \mathcal{P}(\mathcal{P}(O)) : \exists e \in E\ (S, e) \in DOMAIN(g)\}$ is called a *group universe* of K.
Definition: A system $K_U = (U, E, V_e, g)$ where $g : U \times E \longrightarrow V_E$ and U, E, V_E defined above, is called a *group attribute system*.
Definition: Given $K_U = (U, E, V_E, g)$ and any group $S \in U$, define a partial function $f_S : \bigcup S \times A \longrightarrow V_A$ such that for any $(o, a) \in DOMAIN(f_S)$, $f_S(o, a) = f(o, a)$ where f is the information function of K. f_s is called a *restricted information* function, as it is f restricted to the domain defined by $\bigcup S \times A$.
Definition: With each group $S \in U$ we associate a *group information* system $I_S = (\bigcup S, A_S, V_{A_S}, f_S)$, where $A_S = \{a \in A : (o, a) \in DOMAIN(f_S)\}$ is called

a set of *attributes* of S and $V_{A_S} = \{v \in V_A : f_S(o,a) = v\}$ is called a set of values of attributes of A_S.

Observe: For any group $S \in U$, and restricted information function f_S, the group information system $I_S = (\cup S, A_S, V_{A_S}, f_S)$ represents a *portion* of our object information system I, that contains all *object* information about the group S.

Observe: Given a knowledge system K with group universe U and object universe O, the set $I_U = \{I_S : S \in U\}$ contains full information about objects in all groups in K.

The system $K_U = (U, E, V_E, g)$ contains full information about *groups* (as a whole) in K. When the systems K_U, I_U are defined we can equivalently represent knowledge system K as $K = (O, U, K_U, I_U)$ where

- O - set of objects of K
- U - universe of K (which is defined by *data mining* operators)
- K_U - represents information about all *groups* in K
- I_U - represents full information about structures inside the groups (objects of the groups)

3 Definition of Operator

If we recognize that high-level knowledge is represented in the knowledge system by its groupings of objects in its universe, then it is clear that a data analysis operator must function by modifying those groupings.

Definition: A *Data Analysis Operator* (G) is defined as a function, possibly partial, that is applied to a given knowledge system, reorganizes its groupings, and returns a new knowledge system. Where $K_1 = (O, A, E, V_A, V_{E_1}, f, g_1)$ and $K_2 = (O, A, E, V_A, V_{E_2}, f, g_2)$, $G(K_1) = K_2$, and thus as group attribute systems, $K_1 = (O, U_1, K_{U_1}, I_{U_1})$, and $K_2 = (O, U_2, K_{U_2}, I_{U_2})$. For a data analysis operator to be useful, the new universe (U_2) will group the objects in a way which reveals new and interesting information about the O.

Clearly, by imposing restrictions on the relationship between K_1 and K_2 we can define specific classes of data analysis operators.

4 Conclusions

In this paper we presented a first step towards building an unifying model for data mining process. The basic structure of the model is a grouping of objects. Hence it has a higher semantic meaning than the relational table. It is known that in general the data mining algorithms cannot be expressed only in terms of relational operators.

The model we have presented is the first step towards defining new operators characteristic to the data mining process with capacities that can not be expressed in terms of standard relational operators. We are currently working on the implementation of this model under a relational system in order to find the total integration.

References

[Fayyad96] Fayyad U., Piatetsky-Shapiro G., Smyth P. *Advances in Knowledge Discovery and Data Mining*, ISBN 0-262-56097-6 1996

[Fernandez99] Fernandez C., Peña J., Martinez J., Delgado O., Lopez I., Luna M., Pardo J. *DAMISYS: An overview*, Proceedings of DAWAK'99, Florencia, Italy pag. 224–230, 1999

[Hadjimichael98] M. Hadjimichael, A. Wasilewska. A Hierarchical Model for Information Generalization. Proceedings, The Sixth International Workshop on Rough Sets, Data Mining and Granular Computing, Research Triangle Park, NC, October 23–28, 1998, vol.II, 306–309.

[Johnson2000] Johnson T., Lakshmanan L., Ng R. *The 3W Model and Algebra for Unified Data Mining*. Proceedings of the 26th VLDB Conference, Cairo, Egypt, 2000

[Meo96] Meo R., Psaila G., Ceri S. *A New SQL-like Operator for Mining Association Rules*, Proceedings of the 22nd VLDB Conference Mumbai (Bombay) India 1996

[Pawlak81] Pawlak, Z. *Information systems – theoretical foundations*. Information systems, 6 (1981), pag. 205–218

[Skowron93] Skowron, A. *Data Filtration: A Rough Set Approach*. Proceedings de Rough Sets, Fuzzy Sets and Knowledge Discovery. (1993). Pag. 108–118

[Wasilewska98] A. Wasilewska, Ernestina Menasalvas Ruiz, María C. Modelization of rough set functions in the KDD frame. Fernández-Baizán). 1st International Conference on Rough Sets and Current Trends in Computing (RSCTC'98) June 22–26 1998, Warsaw, Poland.

[Williams96] Williams G., Huang Z. *Modelling de KDD Process*. Data Mining Portfolio – TR DM 96013 CSIRO Division of Information Technology, Graham.Williams@cbr.dit.csiro.au

Reducing Number of Decision Rules by Joining

Michał Mikołajczyk

Institute of Mathematics, Warsaw University
ul. Banacha 2, 02-097 Warsaw, Poland
M.Mikolajczyk@mimuw.edu.pl

Abstract. Sets of decision rules induced from data can often be very large. Such sets of rules cannot be processed efficiently. Moreover, too many rules may lead to overfitting. The number of rules can be reduced by methods like Quality-Based Filtering [1,10] returning a subset of all rules. However, such methods may produce decision models unable to match many new objects. In this paper we present a solution for reducing the number of rules by joining rules from some clusters. This leads to a smaller number of more general rules.

1 Introduction

Classical decision models based on decision rules induced from data often consist of huge amount of decision rules. However, such large sets of rules cannot be effectively processed, e.g., in matching of new objects. Moreover, too many rules may lead to overfitting. Reducing the number of decision rules is also important for experts analyzing the induced rules. There is a growing research interest in searching for clustering methods or reduction methods of induced from data decision or association rule sets (see, e.g., [1,3,6,7,8,15]).

There is a need to develop methods for inducing set of rules of feasible sizes or methods for decision rule pruning without decreasing the classification quality.

The number of rules can be reduced by methods like Quality-based Filtering returning a subset of all rules. Such methods, however, may produce decision models unable to recognize many new objects.

We present a method for reduction of the number of rules by joining rules from some clusters. This leads to a smaller number of more universal decision rules. We also present experimental results showing that it is possible to induce sets of rules of a feasible size without decreasing the classification quality.

Let us assume data are represented in decision tables [11] of the form presented below.

-	a_1 ... a_N	d
x_1		d_1
⋮		⋮
x_k		d_k

where in rows are described objects $x_i \in \mathbb{X}$ by means of attributes $a_1, \ldots, a_N$, and d denotes the decision attribute with values d_i corresponding to decision classes. From such data table one can generate all (minimal) decision rules [11]. Calculated rules have the form of conjunction, for example: $r : (a_1 = 1 \wedge a_3 = 4 \wedge a_7 = 2) \Rightarrow d^r$. If the conjunction is satisfied by the object x, then the rule classifies x to the decision class d^r ($r(x) = d^r$). If the conjunction is not satisfied by x, then the rule for x is not applicable what is expressed by the answer $d^?$ ($r(x) = d^?$).

One can represent decision rules by means of sequences

$$\{r^A(i)\}_{i=1}^N \text{ or by } r : (a_1 = r^A(1) \wedge \cdots \wedge a_N = r^A(N)) \Rightarrow d$$

where: $r^A(i) = $ *attribute value* or "$\star$" if an attribute value can be arbitrary.

New objects can be classified by means of voting strategies [5] using decisions returned by rules matching the objects. Rules can have assigned weights describing their importance in voting. A very important question is how to rate the quality of the rules and how to calculate the weights for voting. There are some partial solutions for these problems [2].

One can induce all (minimal) rules from decision table [11]. Unfortunately, we can get too many rules and then new objects can not be classified efficiently. The other important reason why we want to have fewer rules is their readability [13]. If a large set of rules is generated then we are unable to understand what they describe. Small number of rules is easier to analyze and understand by experts. This is very important when we want to explore an unknown phenomenon from data.

One can reduce the number of rules by selecting a subset of the set of all rules (see, e.g., Quality-Based Filtering [1,10]). In this way one can obtain a small number of rules. However, it is necessary to take care about the quality of classification of new objects [14]. After pruning of many rules from a given set it is highly probable that many new objects will not be recognized because they do not match any decision rule.

One can group (cluster) rules and then use hierarchical classification. This makes possible to reduce the time needed for classification, but it can be still hard to analyze such clusters by human being. Moreover, the process of rule's grouping is also a very difficult problem. The results of clustering give us extra information about the set of rules and dependencies between them. Unfortunately, no universal solution for such task is known.

2 System of Representatives

We would like to propose another solution based on joining the rules from some clusters. By joining we can produce a smaller set of more general rules. Such rules are able to recognize every object that was classified by the source rules. They can also recognize many more unseen objects. It is important to note that the joining should be performed on rules with similar logical structure. Therefore, first we will group the rules into clusters using some similarity measures and next we join the clusters to more general rules. System of Representatives consists of the set of induced generalized decision rules. Figure 1 presents all stages necessary to build the System of Representatives.

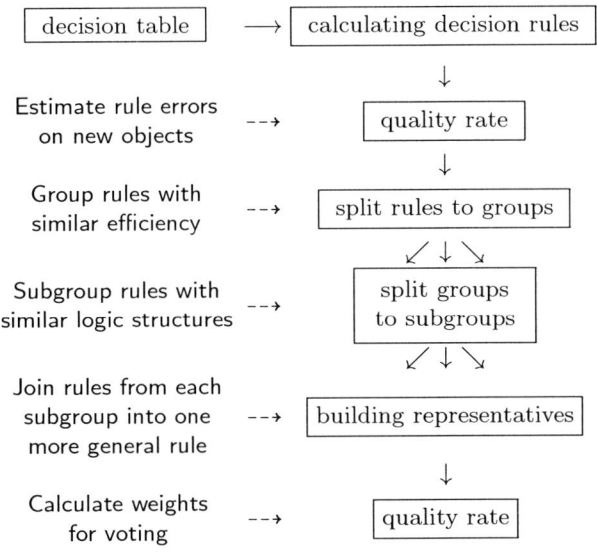

Fig. 1. System of Representatives construction

2.1 Rule Induction

We do not have to use the whole decision table for rule induction. A part of the table can be used for rule generation and the remaining part makes possible to estimate the quality of generated rules.

Decision rules, which are too detailed, are difficult to join. One can overcome this drawback by shortening rules (from generated rules we try to drop some conjuncts from the left part of the rule; see, e.g., [5]).

2.2 Splitting the Set of Decision Rules into Groups

Splitting a given set of decision rules into clusters should guarantee that rules joined (into a generalized rule) from the same cluster are of similar quality. It is very important, because a rule of high quality joined with a rule of low quality can give a weak rule, i.e., rule making many mistakes during the classification of objects. Hence we should try to join high quality rules with high quality rules and low quality ones with low quality rules. First we split rules into classes of rules with the same decision. Next, each class is split into clusters using some clustering methods like the standard k-means algorithm [4]. Below we present an exemplary set of the parameters used for splitting of a given set of rules $\mathbb{R} = \{r_1, \ldots, r_n\}$ into groups:

- a function which determines a weight for any rule [2,14], for example:

$$Q(r) = \text{card}\left(\{x \in \mathbb{X} : r(x) = d^r \text{ and the proper decision on } x \text{ is } d^r\}\right) - \text{card}\left(\{x \in \mathbb{X} : r(x) = d^? \text{ and the proper decision on } x \text{ is } d^r\}\right)$$

- a distance function between rules, for example: $d(r_1, r_2) = |Q(r_1) - Q(r_2)|$.

Similarly to splitting into groups, one can split groups into subgroups using the standard k-means algorithm [4], where the distance function used in our experiments is the following one:

$$d_L(r_1, r_2) = N \cdot |s_\star(r_1) - s_\star(r_2)| + \sum_{i=1}^{N} d_{L0}(r_1^A(i), r_2^A(i))$$

where: $s_\star(r) = \text{card}\left(\{i : r^A(i) = \star\}\right)$ and:

$$d_{L0}(a, b) = \begin{cases} 0 & \text{if } a = b \\ 1 & \text{if } a \neq b \land a \neq \star \land b \neq \star \\ 2 & \text{if } a \neq b \land (a = \star \lor b = \star) \end{cases}$$

Observe that $s_\star(r)$ is equal to the number of free attributes in rule r, and $\sum_{i=1}^{N} d_{L0}(r_1^A(i), r_2^A(i))$ expresses the degree of similarity of logical structures of r_1 and r_2.

Using the above distance function we guarantee that rules with similar logical structures are joined into the same clusters. The joining of rules with different logical structures into one more general rule could cause many errors in classification of new objects.

2.3 Joining Rules

After joining rules from any constructed cluster we obtain one rule called a *representative*:

$$R: R^A(1) \ R^A(2) \ R^A(3) \ \ldots \ R^A(N) \Rightarrow d$$

where $R^A(i) = \{r_1^A(i), \cdots, r_n^A(i)\}$ for $i = 1, \cdots, N$, N is the number of attributes, and $r_1, \ldots, r_n$ are joined rules from a given cluster.

We use one more parameter for the representative R, i.e., the maximal number W_{max}^R of free attributes $(s_\star(r))$ in joined rules: $W_{max}^R = \max_{i=1,\ldots,n}\{s_\star(r_i)\}$. This number is used in the matching of objects by generalized rules. Without this parameter the rules are too general, which decreases the quality of classification by such rules.

Matching Objects by Representatives - R(x)

1. Let $W_A := W_{max}^R$.
2. Let $i = 1$.
3. If $a_i(x) \in R^A(i)$ then go to Step 5.
4. If $\star \in R^A(i)$ then $W_A := W_A - 1$,
   otherwise STOP and return $R(x) = d^?$.
5. If $i < N$ then $i := i + 1$ and go back to Step 3.
6. STOP and return $R(x) = \begin{cases} d^R & \text{if } W_A \geqslant 0 \\ d^? & \text{if } W_A < 0 \end{cases}$.

Let us consider an example. Rules to be joined are the following ones:

$$r_1: 1\ 3 \star 1 \star \star 2 \Rightarrow d \qquad r_2: 2\ 3 \star \star 1 \star 2 \Rightarrow d \qquad r_3: 5\ 3 \star 1\ 1 \star 4 \Rightarrow d$$

After joining we obtain a representative:

$$R: \{1,2,5\}\ 3 \star \{1,\star\}\ \{\star,1\} \star \{2,4\} \Rightarrow d \ ; \ W_{max}^R = 3$$

Now let us take some objects:

x_1: 1 3 3 1 2 3 2 x_5: 6 3 4 1 5 3 2
x_2: 2 3 1 2 1 5 2 x_6: 5 3 4 1 5 3 3
x_3: 2 3 6 1 1 3 4 x_7: 5 1 4 1 5 3 2
x_4: 5 3 4 1 5 3 2 x_8: 5 3 9 9 9 9 2

Objects x_1, x_2, x_3, x_4 are classified by representative R to the decision class corresponding to d^R. Objects x_5, x_6, x_7, x_8 are not recognized by R and the representative R will return for them the answer $d^?$.

By bounding to W_{max}^R the maximal number of free attributes we do not make the rules too general. This makes possible to obtain the high classification quality of the induced representatives.

2.4 Algorithm Parameters and Complexity

The following parameters are used in tuning of the System of Representatives: (i) a parameter describing a fraction of the number of objects from training set used for inducing rules to the number of those used for the estimation of classification quality of induced rules, (ii) a parameter describing the acceptable error in shortening rules, (iii) all parameters used for splitting into groups, (iv) all parameters used for splitting into subgroups.

Experiments have shown that the System of Representatives can be tuned for any tested data.

Observe that the computational complexity of the k-means algorithm is quadratic. However, the System of Representatives is built only once and next it can be used many times.

Table 1. Decision tables used in all experiments

Decision table name	examples	Number of conditional attributes	Number of possible decisions	Average number of attributes value
Austra0	690	14	2	83.4
Austra1	345	14	2	55.0
Austra2	345	14	2	56.8
Diab0	768	8	2	156.4
Diab1	384	8	2	111.9
Diab2	384	8	2	111.5
Heart0	270	13	2	29.5
Heart1	135	13	2	22.6
Heart2	135	13	2	22.8
Irys	120	4	3	29.0
Kan 1	84	16	17	8.1
Kan 12	84	17	15	8.0
Kan 2	84	16	14	7.5
Kan 21	84	17	15	8.1
Lymn0	148	18	4	3.3
Lymn1	74	18	4	3.2
Lymn2	74	18	4	3.3
Monk1dat	124	6	2	2.8
Monk1tes	432	6	2	2.8
Monk2dat	169	6	2	2.8
Monk2tes	432	6	2	2.8
Monk3dat	122	6	2	2.8
Monk3tes	432	6	2	2.8
Tttt	615	8	2	140.1

3 Results of Experiments

3.1 Tested Data

In this section we present the results of experiments. All tests were made using the CV5 (Cross Validation) method [9]. In experiments we used twenty-four decision tables presented in Table 1. Most of the data tables are from UCI Machine Learning Repository [9] http://www.ics.uci.edu/ mlearn/MLRepository.html.

3.2 System of Representatives

Now we are ready to present the results of experiments obtained using our parameterized System of Representatives. For each table all parameters have been tuned experimentally. The results are summarized in Table 2.

3.3 The Discussion of the Results

Let us look at the averaged results presented in Table 3. From Table 3 one can observe that the strategy shortening of rules improves classification quality and reduces the number of rules. Therefore, we used this strategy in the System of Representatives. Additional experiments showed that this improves significantly the results.

Table 2. Results obtained by means of the proposed System of Representatives

Decision table	Objects identified correctly	wrongly	not recognized	Number of rules	Average time of classification
Austra0	85.51%	14.49%	0.00%	24.80	0.01 s
Austra1	80.00%	20.00%	0.00%	30.60	< 0.01 s
Austra2	87.25%	12.75%	0.00%	26.40	< 0.01 s
Diab0	66.02%	33.98%	0.00%	146.60	< 0.01 s
Diab1	62.76%	37.24%	0.00%	90.40	< 0.01 s
Diab2	67.45%	32.55%	0.00%	77.80	0.02 s
Heart0	83.70%	16.30%	0.00%	13.40	< 0.01 s
Heart1	80.00%	20.00%	0.00%	15.40	< 0.01 s
Heart2	75.56%	24.44%	0.00%	11.00	< 0.01 s
Irys	92.50%	7.50%	0.00%	24.80	0.07 s
Kan 1	14.29%	83.33%	2.38%	150.00	< 0.01 s
Kan 12	39.29%	60.71%	0.00%	116.60	0.01 s
Kan 2	40.48%	59.52%	0.00%	100.00	< 0.01 s
Kan 21	33.33%	66.67%	0.00%	127.40	< 0.01 s
Lymn0	81.76%	18.24%	0.00%	49.40	0.16 s
Lymn1	81.08%	18.92%	0.00%	44.00	< 0.01 s
Lymn2	83.78%	16.22%	0.00%	30.00	0.06 s
Monk1dat	90.32%	9.68%	0.00%	59.00	< 0.01 s
Monk1tes	100.00%	0.00%	0.00%	49.40	0.01 s
Monk2dat	68.64%	28.40%	2.96%	67.20	< 0.01 s
Monk2tes	66.20%	33.80%	0.00%	22.60	< 0.01 s
Monk3dat	93.44%	6.56%	0.00%	27.60	< 0.01 s
Monk3tes	97.22%	2.78%	0.00%	13.20	< 0.01 s
Tttt	65.69%	34.31%	0.00%	45.40	< 0.01 s
Average	72.34%	27.43%	0.22%	56.79	0.02 s

Table 3. Averaged results of presented systems calculated on twenty-four tables, where: kNN – k Nearest Neighbour system with $k = 1$, *Classical std.* – classical rule system [12], *Classical ext.* – classical rule system with rule shortening [12] , *QbF std.* – Quality-based Filtering system, *QbF ext.* – Quality-based Filtering system with rule shortening, *Rep. System* – proposed System of Representatives

Decision table	Objects identified correctly	wrongly	not recognized	Number of rules	Average time of classification
kNN	70.04%	29.86%	0.10%	0.00	0.06 s
Classical std.	69.56%	30.36%	0.08%	2772.55	0.06 s
Classical ext.	71.08%	28.91%	0.01%	2135.53	0.05 s
QbF std.	60.16%	17.38%	22.47%	347.37	0.10 s
QbF ext.	64.08%	18.33%	17.58%	23.51	0.08 s
Rep. System	72.34%	27.43%	0.22%	56.79	0.02 s

System of Representatives, like classical rule systems [12], makes more mistakes classifying objects than Quality-based Filtering systems. However, it recognizes correctly more objects. System of Representatives leads to better classification quality than classical systems and to smaller number of decision rules. Time needed for the classification of new objects is very short.

4 Conclusions

The results presented in the paper show that it is possible to reduce the number of decision rules without decreasing the classification quality. Moreover, we obtain less, more general rules. Hence, the time needed for classification of new objects is very short.

Unfortunately, it takes time to build and tune the System of Representatives. However, by tuning of parameters the high quality System of Representatives can be induced for various data. Once tuned and trained, the system exhibits excellent efficiency and the very good classification quality.

System of Representatives consists of relatively small number of rules and in consequence the size of decision model built using such rules is substantially smaller that in case of not generalized rules. Hence, using the Minimal Description Length Principle [13] one can expect that such models will be characterized by higher quality of classification than the traditional decision models.

Acknowledgments. I would like to thank professor Andrzej Skowron for his support while writing this paper. This work was partially supported by the Polish State Committee for Scientific Research grant No. 8T11C02519.

References

1. T. Ågotnes, Filtering large propositional rule sets while retaining classifier performance. Department of Computer and Information Science, Norwegian University of Science and Technology, 1999
2. I. Bruha, Quality of decision rules. Machine Learning and Statistics. The Interface, chapter 5, 1997
3. P. Gago, C. Bento, A metric for selection of the most promising rules. In PKDD, pages 19–27, 1998
4. A. K. Jain and R. C. Dubes, Algorithms for Clustering Data. Englewood Cliffs, New Jersey: Prentice Hall, 1988
5. Jan Komorowski and Zdzisław Pawlak and Lech Polkowski and Andrzej Skowron, Rough Fuzzy Hybridization. A New Trend in Decision Making. Springer-Verlag, pages 3–98, 1999
6. B. Lent, A. N. Swami, J. Widom, Clustering association rules, In ICDE, pages 220–231, 1997
7. B. Liu, W. Hsu, Y. Ma, Prunig and summarization of discovered associations, In SIGKDD, pages 125–134, 1999
8. B. Liu, M. Hu, W. Hsu, Multi-level organization and summarization of discovered rules, In SIGKDD, pages 208–217, 2000
9. Michell T.M.: Machine Learning. Mc Graw-Hill, Portland, 1997.
10. A. Øhrn, L. Ohno-Machado, T. Rowland, Building manageable rough set classifiers. AMIA Annual Fall Symposium, pages 543–547, Orlando, USA, 1998
11. Z. Pawlak, Rough sets – Theoretical aspects of reasoning about data. Kluwer Academic Publishers, Dordrecht, 1991
12. RSES system: alfa.mimuw.edu.pl
13. J. Rissanen, Modeling by the shortest data description. Authomatica 14, pages 465–471, 1978
14. J. A. Swets, Measuring the accuracy of diagnostic systems. Science, 240: 1285–1293, 1988
15. H. Toivonen, M. Klementinen, P. Ronkainen, K. Hätönen, H. Manila, Pruning and grouping discovered association rules. In ML Net Familiarization Workshop on Statistics, Ml and KDD, pages 47–52, 1995

Scalable Classification Method Based on Rough Sets

Hung Son Nguyen

Institute of Mathematics,
Warsaw University, Banacha 2, Warsaw 02095, Poland
son@mimuw.edu.pl

Abstract. The existing rough set based methods are not applicable for large data set because of the high time and space complexity and the lack of scalability. We present a classification method, which is equivalent to rough set based classification methods, but is scalable and applicable for large data sets. The proposed method is based on lazy learning idea [2] and Apriori algorithm for *sequent item-set approaches* [1]. In this method the set of decision rules matching the new object is generated directly from training set. Accept classification task, this method can be used for adaptive rule generation system where data is growing up in time.

Keywords: Data mining, Scalability, Rough set, Lazy learning.

1 Introduction

Classification of new unseen objects is a most important task in data mining. There are many classification approaches likes "nearest neighbors", "naive Bayes", "decision tree", "decision rule set", "neural networks" and many others. Almost all methods based on rough sets use the rule set classification approach (see e.g., [3,10,11,12]), which consists of two steps: generalization and specification. In generalization step, some decision rule set is constructed from data as a knowledge base. In specialization step the set of such rules, that match a new object (to be classified) is selected and a conflict resolving mechanism will be employed to make decision for the new object.

Unfortunately, there are opinions that rough set based methods can be used for small data set only. The main reproach is related to their lack of scalability (more precisely: there is a lack of proof showing that they can be scalable). The biggest troubles stick in the rule induction step. As we know, the potential number of all rules is exponential. All heuristics for rule induction algorithms have at least $O(n^2)$ time complexity, where n is the number of objects in the data set and require multiple data scanning. In this paper we propose to adopt lazy learning idea to make rough set based methods more scalable. The proposed method does not consist of the generalization step. The main effort is shifted in to rule matching step. We show that the set of such rules, that match a new object (to be classified) can be selected by modification of *Apriori algorithm* proposed in [1] for sequent item set generation from data bases.

2 Preliminaries

An *information system* [7] is a pair $\mathbb{A} = (U, A)$, where U is a non-empty, finite set of *objects* and $A = \{a_1, ..., a_k\}$ is a non-empty finite set of *attributes* (or *features*), i.e. $a_i : U \to V_{a_i}$ for $i = 1, ..., k$, where V_{a_i} is called *the domain of* a_i. Let $B = \{a_{i_1}, ..., a_{i_j}\}$, where $1 \leq i_1 < ... < i_j \leq k$, be a subset of A, the set $INF_B = V_{a_{i_1}} \times V_{a_{i_2}} \times ... \times V_{a_{i_j}}$ is called *information space defined by* B. Function $inf_B : U \to INF_B$ defined by $inf_B(u) = \langle a_{i_1}(u), ..., a_{i_j}(u) \rangle$ is called "B-information map". The function inf_B defines a projection of objects from U into information space INF_B (or a view of U on features from B).

Using information map one can define the relation $IND(B) = \{(x, y) : inf_B(x) = inf_B(y)\}$ called *indiscernibility relation* (if $(x, y) \in IND(B)$ then we say that they are *indiscernible* by attributes from B. It is easy to show that $IND(B)$ is equivalent relation (see [9]). For any $u \in U$, the set $[u]_B = \{x \in U : (x, u) \in IND(B)\}$ is called equivalent class of u in B. Equivalent classes can be treated as building block to define basic notions of rough set theory.

The main subject of rough set theory is concept description. Let $X \subset U$ be a concept to be describe and $B \subset A$ is a set of accessible attributes. The set X can be described by attributes form B by $(\underline{B}X, \overline{B}X)$ where $\underline{B}X = \{u \in U : [u]_B \subset X\}$ and $\overline{B}X = \{u \in U : [u]_B \cap X \neq \emptyset\}$.

2.1 Classification Problem

Any information system of the form $\mathbb{A} = (U, A \cup \{dec\})$ with a distinguished attribute dec is called *decision table*. The attribute $dec \notin A$ is called *decision attribute*. In this paper we are dealing with the decision rule based approach, which is preferred by many Rough Set based classification methods [3,10,11,12].

Let $\mathbb{A} = (U, A \cup \{dec\})$ be a decision table. Without loss of generality we assume that $V_{dec} = \{1, ..., d\}$. Then the set $DEC_k = \{x \in U : dec(x) = k\}$ will be called the kth *decision class of* $\mathbb{A}$ for $1 \leq k \leq d$. Any implication of form

$$(a_{i_1} = v_1) \wedge ... \wedge (a_{i_m} = v_m) \Rightarrow (dec = k) \tag{1}$$

where $a_{i_j} \in A$ and $v_j \in V_{a_{i_j}}$, is called *decision rule* for k^{th} decision class. Let $\mathbf{r}$ be an arbitrary decision rule of the form (1), then $\mathbf{r}$ can be characterized by:

$length(\mathbf{r})$ = the number of descriptor on the assumption of $\mathbf{r}$ (i.e. the left hand side of implication)

$[\mathbf{r}]$ = the carrier of $\mathbf{r}$, i.e. the set of objects from U satisfying the assumption of $\mathbf{r}$

$support(\mathbf{r})$ = the number of objects satisfying the assumption of $\mathbf{r}$: $support(\mathbf{r}) = card([\mathbf{r}])$

$confidence(\mathbf{r})$ = the confidence of $\mathbf{r}$: $confidence(\mathbf{r}) = \frac{|[\mathbf{r}] \cap DEC_k|}{|[\mathbf{r}]|}$

The decision rule $\mathbf{r}$ is called *consistent* with $\mathbb{A}$ if $confidence(\mathbf{r}) = 1$.

In data mining philosophy, we are interested on *short, strong* decision rules with *high confidence*. The linguistic features like "short", "strong" or "high confidence" of decision rules can be formulated by term of their length, support and confidence. Such rules can be treated as interesting, valuable and useful patterns in data. Any rule based classification method works in three phases (Figure 1):

1. Learning phase: generates a set of decision rules $RULES(\mathbb{A})$ (satisfying some predefined conditions) from a given decision table $\mathbb{A}$.
2. Rule selection phase: selects from $RULES(\mathbb{A})$ the set of such rules that can be supported by x. We denote this set by $MatchRules(\mathbb{A}, x)$.
3. Post-processing phase: makes a decision for x using some voting algorithm for decision rules from $MatchRules(\mathbb{A}, x)$

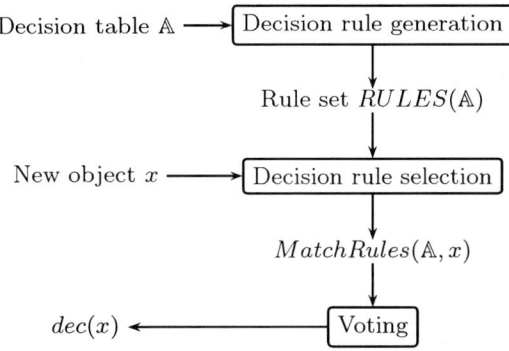

Fig. 1. The Rule base classification system

2.2 Rough Sets and Classification Problems

Unfortunately, the number of all decision rules can be exponential with regard to the size of the given decision table [3,4,9,11]. In practice, we apply some heuristics to generate a subset of "interesting" decision rules. Many decision rule generation methods have been developed by using Rough set theory. One of the most interesting approaches is related to *minimal consistent decision rules*. Given a decision table $\mathbb{A} = (U, A \cup \{dec\})$, the decision rule:

$$\mathbf{r} =_{def} (a_{i_1} = v_1) \wedge ... \wedge (a_{i_m} = v_m) \Rightarrow (dec = k)$$

is called minimal consistent decision rule if it is consistent with $\mathbb{A}$ and any decision rule $\mathbf{r}'$ created from $\mathbf{r}$ by removing one of descriptors from left hand side of $\mathbf{r}$ is not consistent with $\mathbb{A}$. The set of all minimal consistent decision rules for a given decision table $\mathbb{A}$, denoted by $MinConsRules(\mathbb{A})$, can be found by computing *object oriented reducts* (or local reducts) [4,3,11]. In practice, instead of $MinConsRules(\mathbb{A})$, we can use the set of short, strong, and high accuracy decision rules defined by:

$$MinRules(\mathbb{A}, \lambda_{\max}, \sigma_{\min}, \alpha_{\min}) = \left\{ \begin{array}{l} \mathbf{r}: \mathbf{r} \text{ is minimal} \wedge length(\mathbf{r}) \leq \lambda_{\max} \wedge \\ support(\mathbf{r}) \geq \sigma_{\min} \wedge confidence(\mathbf{r}) \geq \alpha_{\min} \end{array} \right\}$$

All heuristics for object oriented reducts can be modified to extract decision rules from $MinRules(\mathbb{A}, \lambda_{\max}, \sigma_{\min}, \alpha_{\min})$.

2.3 Lazy Learning

The classification methods based on learning schema presented in Figure 1 are called *eager (or laborious) methods*. In *lazy learning* methods new objects are classified without generalization step.

Lazy learning methods need more time complexity for the classification step, i.e., the answer time for the question about decision of a new object is longer than in eager classification methods. But lazy classification methods are *well scalable*, i.e. it can be realized for larger decision table using distributed computer system [5,8]. The scalability property is also very advisable in data mining. Unfortunately, the eager classification methods are weakly scalable. As we recall before, the time and memory complexity of existing algorithms does not make possible to apply rule base classification methods for very large decision table[1].

3 Lazy Learning for Rough Sets Methods

The most often reproach, which is placed for Rough set based methods, relates to the lack of scalability. In this paper we try to defend rough set methods again such reproaches. We show that some classification methods based on rough set theory can be modified by using lazy learning algorithms that make them more scalable. The lazy rule-based classification diagram is presented in Figure 2

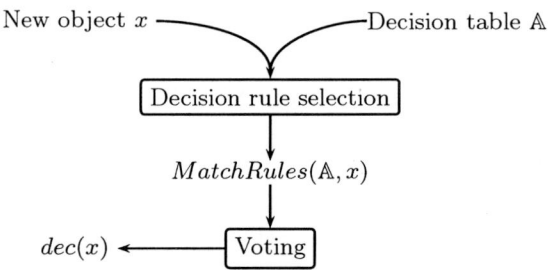

Fig. 2. The lazy rule-based classification system

In other words, we will try to extract the set of decision rules that match object x directly from data without learning process. The large decision table must be held in a data base system and the main problem is to minimize the number SQL queries used in the algorithm. We show that this diagram can work for the classification method described in Section 2.3 using the set $MinRules(\mathbb{A}, \lambda_{\max}, \sigma_{\min}, \alpha_{\min})$ of decision rules. The problem is formulated as follows: *given a decision table $\mathbb{A} = (U, A \cup \{dec\})$ and a new object x, find all (or almost all) decision rules of the set*

$$MatchRules(\mathbb{A}, x) = \{\mathbf{r} \in MinRules(\mathbb{A}, \lambda_{\max}, \sigma_{\min}, \alpha_{\min}) : x \text{ satisfies } \mathbf{r}\}$$

---
[1] i.e., such tables containing more than 10^6 objects and 10^2 attributes.

Let $Desc(x) = \{d_1, d_2, ...d_k\}$, where $d_i \equiv (a_i = a_i(x))$, be a set of all descriptors derived from x. Let $\mathbf{P}_i = \{S \subset Desc(x) : |S| = i\}$ and let $\mathbf{P} = \bigcup_{i=1}^{k} \mathbf{P}_i$. One can see that every decision rule $\mathbf{r} \in MatchRules(\mathbb{A}, x)$ has a form $[\bigwedge S \Rightarrow (dec = k)]$ for some $S \in \mathbf{P}$. Hence the problem of searching for $MatchRules(\mathbb{A}, x)$ is equivalent to the problem of searching for corresponding families of subsets from $\mathbf{P}$ using minimal number of I/O operations to the database. We will show that the set $MatchRules(\mathbb{A}, x)$ can be found by modifying Apriori algorithm (see [1]).

Let $S \in \mathbf{P}$ be an arbitrary set of descriptors from $Desc(x)$. The support of S can be defined by $support(S) = |\{u \in U : u \text{ satisfies } \bigwedge S\}|$. Let $s_i = |\{u \in U : (u \in DEC_i) \wedge (u \text{ satisfies } \bigwedge S)\}|$, then the vector $(s_1, ..., s_d)$ is called *class distribution of S*. Obviously $support(S) = s_1 + ... + s_d$. We assume that the function $GetClassDistribution(S)$ returns the class distribution of S. One can see that this function can be computed by using simple SQL query of form "SELECT COUNT FROM ... WHERE ... GROUP BY ...".

ALGORITHM: Rule selection

Input: The object x, the maximal length $\lambda_{\max}$, the minimal support $\sigma_{\min}$, and the minimal confidence $\alpha_{\min}$.
Output: The set $MatchRules(\mathbb{A}, x)$ of decision rules from $MinRules(\mathbb{A}, \lambda_{\max}, \sigma_{\min}, \alpha_{\min})$ matching x.
BEGIN
    $\mathbf{C}_1 := \mathbf{P}_1$; $i := 1$;
    WHILE $(i \leq \lambda_{\max})$ AND ($\mathbf{C}_i$ IS NOT EMPTY)) DO
        $\mathbf{F}_i := \emptyset$; $\mathbf{R}_i := \emptyset$;
        FOR $C \in \mathbf{C}_i$ DO
            $(s_1, ..., s_d) := GetClassDistribution(C)$;
            $support = s_1 + ... + s_d$;
            IF $support \geq \sigma_{\min}$ THEN
                IF $(\max\{s_1, ..., s_d\} \geq \alpha_{\min} * support)$ THEN
                    $\mathbf{R}_i := \mathbf{R}_i \cup \{C\}$;
                ELSE
                    $\mathbf{F}_i := \mathbf{F}_i \cup \{C\}$;
        ENDFOR
        $\mathbf{C}_{i+1} := AprGen(\mathbf{F}_i)$; $i := i + 1$;
    ENDWHILE
    RETURN $\bigcup_i \mathbf{R}_i$
END

Fig. 3. The rule selection method based on Apriori algorithm

The algorithm consists of a number of iterations. In the ith iteration all decision rules containing i descriptors (length $= i$) are extracted. For this purpose we compute three families $\mathbf{C}_i$, $\mathbf{R}_i$ and $\mathbf{F}_i$ of subsets of descriptors in the ith iteration:

- The family $\mathbf{C}_i \subset \mathbf{P}_i$ consists of "candidate sets" of descriptors and it can be generated without any database operation.
- The family $\mathbf{R}_i \subset \mathbf{C}_i$ consists of such candidates which contains descriptors (from left hand side) of some decision rules from $MatchRules(\mathbb{A}, x)$.
- The family $\mathbf{F}_i \subset \mathbf{C}_i$ consists of such candidates which are supported by more than $\sigma_{\min}$ (frequent subsets).

In the algorithm, we apply the function $AprGen(\mathbf{F}_i)$ to generate the family $\mathbf{C}_{i+1}$ of candidate sets from $\mathbf{F}_i$ (see [1]) using following observations:

1. Let $S \in \mathbf{P}_{i+1}$ and let $S_1, S_2, ..., S_{i+1}$ be subsets formed by removing from S one descriptor, we have $support(S) \leq \min\{support(S_j)\}$, for any $j = 1, ..., j+1$. This means that if $S \in \mathbf{R}_{i+1}$ then $S_j \in \mathbf{F}_i$ for $j = 1, ..., i+1$. Hence if $S_j \in \mathbf{F}_i$ for $j = 1, ..., i+1$, then S can be inserted to $\mathbf{C}_{i+1}$;
2. Let $s_1^{(j)}, ..., s_d^{(j)}$ be the class distribution of S_j and let $s_1, ..., s_d$ be the class distribution of S, we have $s_k \leq \min\{s_k^{(1)}, ..., s_k^{(i+1)}\}$, for $k = 1, ..., d$. This means that if $\max_k\{\min\{s(1)_k, ..., s(i+1)_k\}\} \leq \alpha_{\min} * \sigma_{\min}$, then we can remove S from $\mathbf{C}_{i+1}$;

4 Example

In Figure 4, we illustrate the *weather* decision table and in Figure 5 we present the set $MinConsRules(\mathbb{A})$ generated by system ROSETTA [6].

$\mathbb{A}$	a_1	a_2	a_3	a_4	dec
ID	outlook	temperature	humidity	windy	play
1	sunny	hot	high	FALSE	no
2	sunny	hot	high	TRUE	no
3	overcast	hot	high	FALSE	yes
4	rainy	mild	high	FALSE	yes
5	rainy	cool	normal	FALSE	yes
6	rainy	cool	normal	TRUE	no
7	overcast	cool	normal	TRUE	yes
8	sunny	mild	high	FALSE	no
9	sunny	cool	normal	FALSE	yes
10	rainy	mild	normal	FALSE	yes
11	sunny	mild	normal	TRUE	yes
12	overcast	mild	high	TRUE	yes
13	overcast	hot	normal	FALSE	yes
14	rainy	mild	high	TRUE	no
x	sunny	mild	high	TRUE	?

Fig. 4. A decision table $\mathbb{A}$, and new object x

One can see that $MatchRules(\mathbb{A}, x)$ consists of two rules:

rules	support
outlook(overcast)⇒play(yes)	4
humidity(normal) AND windy(FALSE)⇒play(yes)	4
outlook(sunny) AND humidity(high)⇒play(no)	3
outlook(rainy) AND windy(FALSE)⇒play(yes)	3
outlook(sunny) AND temperature(hot)⇒play(no)	2
outlook(rainy) AND windy(TRUE)⇒play(no)	2
outlook(sunny) AND humidity(normal)⇒play(yes)	2
temperature(cool) AND windy(FALSE)⇒play(yes)	2
temperature(mild) AND humidity(normal)⇒play(yes)	2
temperature(hot) AND windy(TRUE)⇒play(no)	1
outlook(sunny) AND temperature(mild) AND windy(FALSE)⇒play(no)	1
outlook(sunny) AND temperature(cool)⇒play(yes)	1
outlook(sunny) AND temperature(mild) AND windy(TRUE)⇒play(yes)	1
temperature(hot) AND humidity(normal)⇒play(yes)	1

Fig. 5. The set of all minimal decision rules generated by ROSETTA

(outlook = sunny) AND (humidity = high) ⇒ $play = no$ (rule nr 3)
(outlook = sunny) AND (temperature = mild) AND (windy = TRUE) ⇒ $play = yes$ (rule nr 13)

Figure 6 shows that this set can be found using our algorithm.

$i=1$				$i=2$				$i=3$			
C_1	check	R_1	F_1	C_2	check	R_2	F_2	C_3	check	R_3	F_3
$\{d_1\}$	(3,2)		$\{d_1\}$	$\{d_1,d_2\}$	(1,1)		$\{d_1,d_2\}$	$\{d_1,d_3,d_4\}$	(0,1)		$\{d_1,d_3,d_4\}$
$\{d_2\}$	(4,2)		$\{d_2\}$	$\{d_1,d_3\}$	(3,0)	$\{d_1,d_3\}$		$\{d_2,d_3,d_4\}$	(1,1)		$\{d_2,d_3,d_4\}$
$\{d_3\}$	(4,3)		$\{d_3\}$	$\{d_1,d_4\}$	(1,1)		$\{d_1,d_4\}$				
$\{d_4\}$	(3,3)		$\{d_4\}$	$\{d_2,d_3\}$	(2,2)		$\{d_2,d_3\}$				
				$\{d_2,d_4\}$	(1,1)		$\{d_2,d_4\}$				
				$\{d_3,d_4\}$	(2,1)		$\{d_3,d_4\}$				

$MatchRules(\mathbb{A},x) = R_2 \cup R_3$:
(outlook = sunny) AND (humidity = high) ⇒ $play = no$
(outlook = sunny) AND (temperature = mild) AND (windy = TRUE) ⇒ $play = yes$

Fig. 6. The illustration of algorithm for $\lambda_{max}=3; \sigma_{min}=1; \alpha_{min}=1$.

5 Concluding Remarks

We presented the rough set based classification method which is scalable for large data set. The method is based on lazy learning idea and Apriori algorithm.

One can see that if $x \in U$ then the presented algorithm can generate the object oriented reducts for x. Hence the proposed method can be applied also for eager learning. This method can be used for adaptive rule generation system where data is growing up in time. In the next paper we will describe more details about this observation.

Acknowledgement. This paper has been partially supported by Polish State Committee of Research (KBN) grant No 8T11C02519 and grant of the Wallenberg Foundation.

References

1. Agrawal R., Mannila H., Srikant R., Toivonen H., Verkamo A.I.: Fast discovery of assocation rules. In V.M. Fayad, G.Piatetsky Shapiro, P. Smyth, R. Uthurusamy (eds): *Advanced in Knowledge Discovery and Data Mining*, AAAI/MIT Press, 1996, pp. 307–328.
2. Aha D.W. (Editorial): "Special Issue on Lazy Learning", Artificial Intelligence Review, 11(1-5), 1997, pp. 1–6.
3. Bazan J.: A comparison of dynamic non-dynamic rough set methods for extracting laws from decision tables. In: L. Polkowski and A. Skowron (Eds.), *Rough Sets in Knowledge Discovery* **1**, Physica-Verlag, Heidelberg, 1998, pp. 321–365.
4. Komorowski J., Pawlak Z., Polkowski L. and Skowron A.: Rough sets: A tutorial. In: S.K. Pal and A. Skowron (eds.), Rough-fuzzy hybridization: A new trend in decision making, Springer-Verlag, Singapore, 1999, pp. 3–98.
5. Manish Mehta, Rakesh Agrawal, and Jorma Rissanen. SLIQ: A fast scalable classifier for data mining. In Proc. of the Fifth Int'l Conference on Extending Database Technology (EDBT), Avignon, France, March 1996. pp. 18–32
6. Ohrn A., Komorowski J., Skowron A., Synak P.: The ROSETTA Software System.In Polkowski, L., Skowron, A. (Eds.): *Rough Sets in Knowledge Discovery* **Vol. 1,2**, Springer Physica-Verlag, Heidelberg, 1998, pp. 572–576.
7. Pawlak Z.: *Rough sets: Theoretical aspects of reasoning about data*, Kluwer Dordrecht, 1991.
8. J. Shafer, R. Agrawal, and M. Mehta. SPRINT: A scalable parallel classifier for data mining. In Proc. 1996 Int. Conf. Very Large Data Bases, Bombay, India, Sept. 1996, pp. 544–555.
9. Skowron, A., Rauszer, C.: The discernibility matrices and functions in information systems. In. R. Słowiński (ed.). Intelligent Decision Support – Handbook of Applications and Advances of the Rough Sets Theory, Kluwer Academic Publishers, Dordrecht, 1992, pp. 311–362
10. Stefanowski J.: On rough set based approaches to induction of decision rules. In: A. Skowron, L. Polkowski (red.), Rough Sets in Knowledge Discovery Vol 1, Physica Verlag, Heidelberg, 1998, 500–529.
11. Wróblewski J., 1998. Covering with reducts – a fast algorithm for rule generation. In L. Polkowski and A. Skowron (Eds.): Proc. of RSCTC'98, Warsaw, Poland. Springer-Verlag, Berlin Heidelberg, pp. 402–407.
12. Ziarko, W.: Rough set as a methodology in Data Mining. In Polkowski, L., Skowron, A. (Eds.): *Rough Sets in Knowledge Discovery* **Vol. 1,2**, Springer Physica-Verlag, Heidelberg, 1998, pp. 554–576.

Parallel Data Mining Experimentation Using Flexible Configurations

José M. Peña[1]*, F. Javier Crespo[2], Ernestina Menasalvas[1], and Victor Robles[1]

[1] Universidad Politécnica de Madrid, Madrid, Spain
[2] Universidad Carlos III de Madrid, Madrid, Spain

Abstract. When data mining first appeared, several disciplines related to data analysis, like statistics or artificial intelligence were combined toward a new topic: extracting significant patterns from data. The original data sources were small datasets and, therefore, traditional machine learning techniques were the most common tools for this tasks. As the volume of data grows these traditional methods were reviewed and extended with the knowledge from experts working on the field of data management and databases. Today problems are even bigger than before and, once again, a new discipline allows the researchers to scale up to these data. This new discipline is distributed and parallel processing. In order to use parallel processing techniques, specific factors about the mining algorithms and the data should be considered. Nowadays, there are several new parallel algorithms, that in most of the cases are extensions of a traditional centralized algorithm. Many of these algorithms have common core parts and only differ on distribution schema, parallel coordination or load/task balancing methods. We call these groups *algorithm families*. On this paper we introduce a methodology to implement *algorithm families*. This methodology is founded on the MOIRAE distributed control architecture. In this work we will show how this architecture allows researchers to design parallel processing components that can change, dynamically, their behavior according to some control policies.

1 Introduction

Distributed data mining (DDM) deals with retrieval, analysis and further usage of data in a non-centralized scenario. The way this distribution is performed depends on two different factors: (i) Whether the data are not stored in a single site and the data sources are disperse and (ii) Whether data analysis process requires high performance computation techniques (like parallel processing). If any of these two factors is present traditional data mining has deep problems to achieve the expected results. Collective data mining [4] deals with distributed data source mining and parallel data mining tackles the second problem.
Modern data mining tools are complex systems in which extensiveness (new

---

* This research project is funded under the Universidad Politécnica de Madrid grant program

algorithms) and performance (mining time) are key factors. If new problems require these systems to be distributed, their complexity will also increase. The new parallel algorithms are also more complex than the original version they come from. Parameters like, network bandwidth, memory and processor usage or data access schemas are considered when these algorithms are designed. Our proposal presents a new method to design algorithms. Using this method, core algorithm components are developed once, as efficient and compact elements, and then they are combined and configured in many different ways. This method not only allows the researchers to combine algorithm components in different schemas, but also provides the mechanisms to change component behavior and performance dynamically.

On this contribution we propose MOIRAE architecture as a tool to implement flexible algorithms in a distributed computation environment.

2 Distributed Data Mining Systems and Algorithms

During the last two years, the first distributed and parallel data mining systems were developed. These systems can be divided into two different groups: (i) **Specific parallel/distributed algorithm implementations**, like, JAM [13], PADMA [5], BODHI [4] or Papyrus [2]. These systems implement only one algorithm or a very restricted set of algorithms/techniques. The system architecture has been designed to deal with this specific technique and algorithm. (ii) **General purpose systems**, for example Kensington [6], PaDDMAS [11] or DMTools [1]. Provost [10] analyzed two main parallel and distributed schemas (fine-grain and coarse-grain) and their application to distributed data mining problems. Krishnaswamy defined cost models for distributed data mining [7]. Joshi et al. [3] provided an overview of different parallel algorithms for both association and classification rules. Zaki also provides a very interesting analysis in [14].

2.1 Flexible Optimization Environment

Much effort has been addressed on the development of efficient distributed algorithms for data mining, nevertheless this is not the only way to outperform existing data mining solutions. Although the specific distributed implementation of a rule extraction algorithm plays an important role, distribution schema, task scheduling and resource management are also key factors.

We propose the capability to plug-in and update control strategies and decisions during the system run-time. As a consequence, we might have two or more sets of system configurations and behavior decisions. If the system state changes or if a different functional operation is expected the appropriate strategies is applied to the system. Based on this idea a new architecture is proposed as the foundation of the elementary parts of a system with these features. To develop this idea the first stage is to present how the M/P paradigm is used.

Our contribution presents how MOIRAE generic architecture [8,9] can be used to implement *algorithm families*. These families are groups of algorithms based on the same core process. Many algorithm variants share the same basic operations and they only differ in terms of small features.

3 MOIRAE Architecture

MOIRAE architecture is a generic architecture that uses the Mechanism/Policy (M/P) paradigm to design flexible systems. System tasks are divided into two different levels:

- Operational level: Features provided by the system. This level contains all the actions (operations) performed by the system as well as the functions used to monitor its status and the environment.
- Control level: Decisions that rule the system. This second level defines the control issues applicable to the operational level functions. These rules describe when and how the operations are performed.

This M/P paradigm is quite common under design phases of complex applications like operating systems (OS). MOIRAE architecture is one step ahead. This architecture presents a run-time engine to manage control level decisions while the system is running. This technique allows the user not only to change control policies during execution time during the system design/implementation phases. The option to configure complex systems without any re-design has two main profits: (i) Research on new algorithms and techniques can easily test many different variations of the algorithm only defining new control policies, (ii) Complete systems may be configured for specific installations and user requirements customizing their control policies. As a drawback this control schema may include additional overhead because of the separation of responsibilities into control and operational elements. The effect of both benefits and drawbacks will be studied in the next sections.

3.1 MOIRAE Components

The design of the MOIRAE architecture is founded on the concept of *component*, as each of the software pieces of the distributed system. According to the division of operational and control tasks, each component is also divided in two planes:

- **Operational Plane**: That provides all the functions required to achieve the work performed by the component. The functions, their design/implementation and the exact elements included in the plane depend on the task performed by the component. The responsibilities of this plane heavily depend on the functions of the component.
- **Control Plane**: This plane interacts either with the control plane from other components or with the operational part of their own component. The control plane solves complex situations called *conflicts*, sending orders to the operational plane. Inside of this component there exists *Policy Engine*, that

manages the decisions taken by the control plane. When the control plane is summoned the *policy engine* is activated. Inside of this element, there is a *Policy Database* or p-DB. This database stores all the information applicable to conflict solving and all possible control actions. The *Policy Engine* queries p-DB to decide the control plans.

3.2 MOIRAE Architecture Model

The architecture model describes how multiple components are combined and interconnected to deal with the tasks performed by any specific system. The network of interconnected components is called *interaction graph*. This *graph* defines the components and their relationships. For any system, there are two different *graphs*: *operational graph* and *control graph*. The *operational graph* shows the relations used by the operational planes of the components. This *graph* depends on the task performed by the components and the services provided by the system. MOIRAE does not define any specification on this *graph*. *Control graphs* represent the control relationships among the components. This Model provides a generic schema of this *graph*. Control interactions are based on a hierarchical organization. This organization describes two types of components: (i) Control-oriented components and (ii) Operational-oriented components. The first group has few operational functions and the most important part of the component is its control part. Operational-oriented components provide important operational functions and have very basic control features. The hierarchical structure places operational-oriented components at the lower levels of the *graph*. These components performs simple control tasks. Global control decisions and complex configuration/optimization issues are managed in the upper levels by the control-oriented components. *Control* and *operational graphs* are completely independent. A component can have relations with different components on the control and on the operational plane.

3.3 MOIRAE Control Model

MOIRAE control model shows how control decisions are taken either locally or as a contribution of different control planes. When the control plane is activated, for example when a conflict is detected by the *event sensor*, the *policy engine* evaluates the alternatives to solve the problem. As a result, the control plane returns a sequence of actions to be performed to solve the conflict. For complex problems the control plane would be unable to achieve an appropriate solution by itself. Control Model specifies three different control actions that rule the cooperative solution of complex problems:

- ❒ **Control Propagation**: When a control plane is unable to solve a problem it submits the problem description (e.g.: the conflict) and any additional information to the control plane immediately superior in the hierarchy.
- ❒ **Control Delegation**: After receiving a control propagation from a lower element, the upper element may take three different alternatives:

① If it is also unable to solve the problem it propagates up the conflict as well.
② If it can solve the problem, it may reply to the original component with the sequence of actions necessary to solve the problem. This original component executes these actions.
③ In the last situation it is also possible that the component, instead of replying with the sequence of actions the component may provide the p-DB information necessary to solve the problem in the lower component. This information could be used also in any future situation. This alternative is called *Control Delegation*.

❐ **Control Revoke**: This action is the opposite to the *control delegation* one. Using this control action any upper component in the hierarchy may delete information from the p-DB of any lower element. This action may be executed anytime and not only as a response of a *control propagation*.

4 Association Rules: Distributed Generalized Calculation

Association rule extraction describes patterns present in OLTP databases. A variant of this problem is what is called generalized associations. These association patterns is related to a conceptual hierarchy. This hierarchy generalizes the possible values of a transaction from less to more generic concepts in a tree graph.

Shintani and Kitsuregawa [12] define different algorithms to extract generalized associations from a transaction database using a cluster of workstations. The basic steps in any association calculation are: (i) Candidate itemsets generation, (ii) Counting and (iii) Large itemsets selection. For real world data many possible items may appear in the transaction base. This makes it impossible to handle candidate itemsets in memory. Many distributed association strategies follow an approach based on itemset space partitioning. The authors describe five different association algorithms to deal with partitioned itemsets:

① **H–HPGM (hash)** (Hierarchical Hash Partitioned Generalized association rule Mining).
② **H–HPGM (stat)** (H–HPGM with stats).
③ **H–HPGM–TGD (stat+)** (H–HPGM with Tree Grain Duplication).
④ **H–HPGM–PGD (stat+)** (H–HPGM with Path Grain Duplication).
⑤ **H–HPGM–FGD (stat+)** (H–HPGM with Fine Grain Duplication).

Shintani and Kitsuregawa's paper [12] has a complete description of these algorithms and their comparative performance.

4.1 Algorithm Family Implementation

In our contribution we focus at how the five variants of the same algorithm (and future versions) could be implemented in the component schema mentioned above. The M/P paradigm could be used at many different points of this problem, but itemset partitioning is the key problem of these algorithms. The partitioning strategy is defined by the coordination node that gathers all the itemsets at the end of each iteration. This node computes the most frequent itemsets and then it distributes the next iteration candidates among the computational nodes. The nodes also have the necessary information to locate the appropriate node when a non-local itemset is counted.

- ❒ *Data Partitioning*: When candidate itemsets had to be distributed a control decision should be taken. The control plane defines a partitioning schema depending on which algorithm is selected.
- ❒ *Itemset Counting*: When the process component scans every transaction it updates local itemset counters if they are present in the transaction. If an itemset is not present a conflict event happened. This event is handled by the control plane to select which component should be notified for this itemset. The mechanism used to solve this conflict is previously unknown by the component and when the first conflict arises a control propagation–delegation is performed. At the beginning of each iteration this mapping information is deleted (control revoke) because a different partitioning schema may be selected.

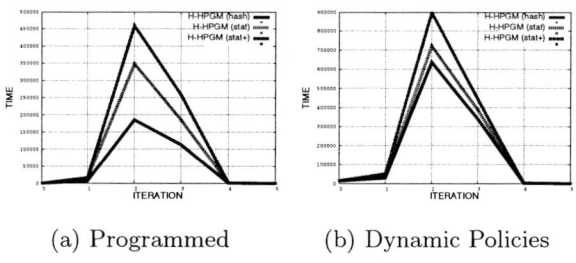

(a) Programmed   (b) Dynamic Policies

Fig. 1. Candidate distribution time

4.2 Experimental Results

The plots 1.a and 1.b show candidate distribution time spent by the coordination node. This measure represents only decision time, not the time necessary for candidate sets re-transmission. In both cases, standard programmed solution and dynamic policy solution kept a similar ratio. If the different algorithm implementations (programmed vs. dynamic) are compared, different performance rations can be observed. **H–HPGM (hash)** implementation (figure 2.a) is 240% slower. In **H–HPGM (stat)** (figure 2.b) the performance difference is 107%. And in **H–HPGM (stat+)** (figure 2.c) is only a 95% slower. This candidate distribution time is less representative, in terms of algorithm overall performance,

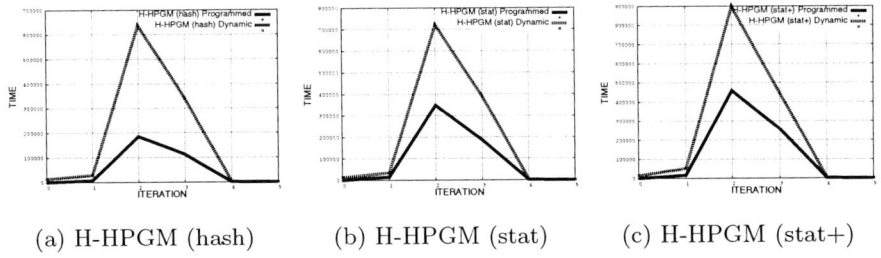

(a) H-HPGM (hash) (b) H-HPGM (stat) (c) H-HPGM (stat+)

Fig. 2. Candidate distribution time: Programmed vs. Dynamic

than the time spent in each of the database scans. Once the candidate itemsets are distributed, each node processes its partition of the database. For each of the records read from the database the itemsets counters are updated. If the itemset is stored locally it is updated immediately, otherwise the changes are queued in a buffer. When this buffer is full it is broadcasted to all the nodes.

Table 1. Average control time: Programmed vs. Dynamic Reactive Policies

Phase	Programmed	Dynamic	% Increment
First itemset location failure	12.11ms	198.12ms	1536.0033%
Next location failures	12.17ms	12.98ms	6.6557%

In this case, the control decisions performed by the operational plane have been programmed as reactive control agents. These agents cannot handle complex control decisions but their performance is much better. Table 1 presents the average time of component operations[1], comparing standard programmed implementations and dynamic reactive policies.

5 Conclusions

We have presented an alternative for programming distributed data mining algorithms. This alternative fills the lack of the flexibility of a traditional programmed solution allowing the user to manipulate algorithm behaviour in a very configurable way. As a drawback, dynamic control represents an overhead in terms of performance form the standard programmed implementations, but this performance is minimal ($\sim 6\%$) in record-by-record management and it is only important between two iteration phases. If we take into account that each iteration takes several minutes to be completed this performance loss is insignificant if it is compared with the new flexibility opportunities offered.

---

[1] first itemset location failure requires control propagation–delegation management

References

1. Peter Christen, Ole M. Nielsen, and Markus Hegland. DMtools – open source software for database mining. *In PKDD'2001*, 2001.
2. Robert L. Grossman, Stuart M. Bailey, Harinath Sivakumar, and Andrei L. Turinsky. Papyrus: A system for data mining over local and wide-area clusters and super-clusters. In ACM, editor, *SC'99*. ACM Press and IEEE Computer Society Press, 1999.
3. Mahesh V. Joshi, Eui-Hong (Sam) Han, George Karypis, and Vipin Kumar. *CRPC Parallel Computing Handbook, chapter Parallel Algorithms for Data Mining*. Morgan Kaufmann, 2000.
4. H. Kargupta, B. Park, D. Hershbereger, and E. Johnson. *Advanced in Distributed and Parallel Knowledge Discovery*, chapter Collective Data Mining: A new perspective towards distributed data mining. AAAI Press / MIT Press, 2000.
5. Hillol Kargupta, Ilker Hamzaoglu, and Brian Stafford. Scalable, distributed data mining – an agent architecture. page 211.
6. Kensingston, Enterprise Data Mining. Kensington: New generation enterprise data mining. White Paper, 1999. Parallel Computing Research Centre, Department of Computing Imperial College, (Contact Martin Khler).
7. S. Krishnaswamy, S. W. Loke, and A. Zaslavsky. Cost models for distributed data mining. Technical Report 2000/59, School of Computer Science and Software Engineering, Monash University, Australia 3168, February 2000.
8. José M. Peña. *Distributed Control Architecture for Data Mining Systems*. PhD thesis, DATSI, FI, Universidad Politécnica de Madrid, Spain, June 2001. Spanish title: "Arquitectura Distribuida de Control para Sistemas con Capacidades de Data Mining".
9. José M. Peña and Ernestina Menasalvas. Towards flexibility in a distributed data mining framework. In *Proceedings of ACM-SIGMOD/PODS 2001*, pages 58–61, 2001.
10. Foster Provost. *Advances in Distributed and Parallel Knowledge Discovery*, chapter Distributed Data Mining: Scaling Up and Beyond, pages 3–28. AAAI Press/MIT Press, 2000.
11. O.F. Rana, D.W. Walker, M. Li, S. Lynden, and M. Ward. PaDDMAS: Parallel and distributed data mining application suite. In *Proceedings of the Fourteenth International Parallel and Distributed Processing Symposium*, 2000.
12. T. Shintani and M. Kitsuregawa. Parallel algorithms for mining association rule mining on large scale PC cluster. In Mohammed J. Zaki and Ching-Tien Ho, editors, *Workshop on Large-Scale Parallel KDD Systems*, San Diego, CA, USA, August 1999. ACM. in conjunction with ACM SIGKDD International Conference on Knowledge Discovery and Data Mining (KDD99).
13. S. Stolfo, W. Fan, W. Lee, A. Prodromidis, and P. Chan. Cost-based modeling for fraud and instrusion detection: Results from the JAM project. In *DARPA Information Survivability Conference and Exposition*, pages 130–144. IEEE Computer Press, 2000.
14. M. Zaki. *Large-Scale Parallel Data Mining*, volume 1759 of *Springer Lecture Note in Artificial Intelligence*, chapter Parallel and Distributed Data Mining: An Introduction. Springer Verlag, 1999.

An Optimization of Apriori Algorithm through the Usage of Parallel I/O and Hints

María S. Pérez[1], Ramón A. Pons[1], Félix García[2], Jesús Carretero[2], and María L. Córdoba[1]

[1] DATSI. FI. Universidad Politécnica de Madrid. Spain
[2] Departamento de Informática. Universidad Carlos III de Madrid. Spain

Abstract. Association rules are very useful and interesting patterns in many data mining scenarios. Apriori algorithm is the best-known association rule algorithm. This algorithm interacts with a storage system in order to access input data and output the results. This paper shows how to optimize this algorithm adapting the underlying storage system to this problem through the usage of hints and parallel features.

1 Introduction

Association rules are very useful and interesting patterns in many data mining scenarios. These patterns represent features that "happen together" in event-recording logs. Their very best known application is what is known as "basket analysis", a generic problem that deals with the identification of the products a client gets in the same purchase. The "basket analysis" defines a clear pattern-recognition task, which is applicable to many other problems such as network failure prediction, genome analysis or medical treatments, to name a few.

An association rule is an implication of the form $A \to B$, where A and B are sets of data features called "items". These itemsets have no common elements ($A \bigcap B = \emptyset$) and they are non-empty sets ($A \neq \emptyset \land B \neq \emptyset$). The rule $A \to B$ is read as "if an instance has the feature A then it also has the feature B".

Apriori algorithm [4] is the best-known association rule algorithm. It has two differents phases: (i) frequent itemsets calculation and (ii) rule extraction using these frequent itemsets. The first of these two phases becomes a performance "bottleneck" in all the Apriori algorithms. In the first phase it is necessary to access to the storage system for getting a huge amount of data which must be processed. I/O system access is slow and traditional systems do not increase I/O operations performance. Parallel I/O was developed in an attempt to face up to this problem, aggregating logically multiple storage devices into a high-performance storage system. Parallel I/O allows applications to access in parallel to the data, providing better performance in the operations of the file system.

This work presents an optimization of Apriori algorithm, making use of MAPFS (Multi-Agent Parallel File System) [2], a high-performance parallel file system, which distributes the data and provides parallel access to files data, what reduces the bottleneck that constitutes the accesses to conventional servers.

Apriori algorithm is lightly modified in order to use the MAPFS interface. The storage system provides parallel access and makes decisions about the frequent itemsets calculation, reducing the candidates in the first phase of the algorithm.

This paper is organized into four sections. Section 2 describes our proposed solution. Section 3 shows the solution evaluation. Finally, section 4 summarizes our conclusions and outlines the future work.

2 Association Rules Calculation Using Parallel I/O

In [3] the relation between Data Mining applications and the underlying storage system is shown, proposing MAPFS system as a suitable framework. This paper shows how to use MAPFS in order to increase Apriori algorithm efficiency.

2.1 Problem Scenario

Data mining processes require multiple scans over databases. An important characteristic is that these scans are not always complete. Induction tree construction or itemset calculation (in an association extraction algorithm) eliminates records on early stages of the algorithm that are not required in following iterations.

If the behaviour of a data mining algorithm is known, I/O requirements could be achieved in advance before the algorithm actually needs the data. An optimal usage of computational resources, like I/O operations or disk caches is also a key factor for high-performance algorithms.

Other kind of algorithms start with the complete set of attributes and during the multiple iterations this set is reduced by several elements. If these attributes are marked as removed, an interesting strategy could be skip this positions on further readings. This is the technique used by our proposal. The storage system is responsible for discarding data blocks whose items are not suitable candidates for the following steps in the algorithm.

2.2 I/O Model

This section describes the I/O model we propose. This I/O model is based on the MAPFS (Multi-Agent Parallel File System) I/O model [2], but adapted to the problem described previously.

Although MAPFS is a general purpose file system, it is very flexible and it can be configured in order to adjust to different I/O access patterns. The main configuration parameters of the MAPFS file system are the following: (i) **I/O Caching and Prefetching**, data items from secondary storage are "cached" in memory for faster access time. This approach allows to increase the performance of the I/O operations. (ii) **Hints**, the previous tasks can be made in a more efficient way using hints on future access patterns. Storage systems using hints provide greater performance because they use this information in order to decrease the cache faults and prefetch the most probable used data in the next executions. Analogously, the hints can be used for increasing the performance of file processing because additional information related to data is stored, what can help in making decisions about them. This is the way in which we have to use the hints for increasing Apriori algorithm performance.

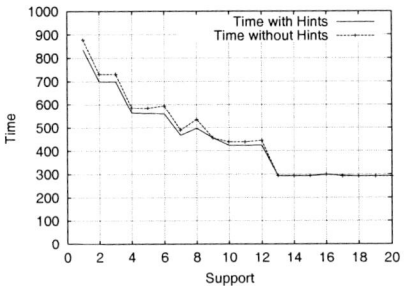

Fig. 1. Performance Comparison with the usage of hints in the parallel version

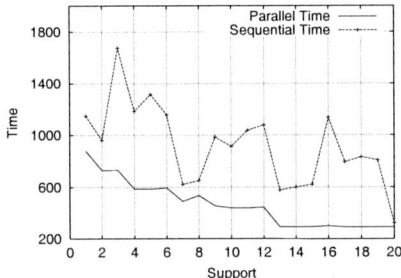

Fig. 2. Performance Comparison of the Parallel Version versus Sequential Version

2.3 Apriori Algorithm: A Case of Hints Optimization

Apriori algoritmh is used in order to build significant association rules between items in databases.

For optimizing Apriori algorithm, we have used the Christian Borgelt's implementation that uses a prefix tree to organize the counters for the item sets [1]. This implementation uses flat-file as input data and output files containing rules together with the confidence and support of the association rule.

Our optimization is made at file system level. The storage system discards for the iteration i those data blocks that are not members of the candidates in the level $i-1$.

Christian Borgelt's implementation reads all the input file lines in every iteration. In order to increase this implementation performance, the chosen block is one line per input file. The storage system uses hints that define if a block (a line) must be evaluated in the next iterarion or not. The blocks are marked as removed if they are not selected in the previous iteration. If a block is marked as removed, the file system skip this block and the input data is reduced.

We have modified Christian Borgelt's implementation in two aspects: (i) the new implementation uses MAPFS I/O operations; (ii) also, it has to interact with MAPFS in order to communicate the storage system that an itemset belongs to candidates. If the storage system is not said that any itemset belongs to candidates during a line processing, this block is marked as removed.

3 Apriori Algorithm Evaluation

This section shows the evaluation of our proposal, which consists of the optimization of two aspects: (i) parallel access to the data; (ii) usage of hints for discarding data blocks.

In order to evaluate our optimization, two parameters have been analysed: (i) time for the algorithm conclusion with the usage of hints and (iii) comparison between the parallel version and sequential version. We have calculated these parameters varying the data support.

For making the evaluation, we have used an input file with size 1000 MB. and the results have been calculated as the average value of five executions, in order to avoid noise. The figures 1 and 2 represent these evaluations.

As it is shown in the graphics, the usage of hints and parallel features increases the algorithm performance.

4 Conclusions and Future Work

Apriori algorithm interacts with a storage system in order to access input data and output the results. This paper evaluates our Apriori algorithm optimization, in which the underlying storage system makes decisions about the input data. This proposal improves the Apriori algorithm global time by means of both parallel access and hints usage, taking into account that the selected implementation of such algorithm is very optimized.

As future work, this technique could be applied to other algorithms with the same structure, that is, which need to filter some of their input data. Furthermore, it would be desirable to build a generic framework for adapting this I/O model to different algorithms.

References

1. Christian Borgelt's Homepage *http://fuzzy.cs.uni-magdeburg.de/borgelt*.
2. Maria S. Perez et al. A New MultiAgent Based Architecture for High Performance I/O in clusters. In *Proceedings of the 2nd International Workshop on MSA'01*, 2001.
3. Maria S. Perez et al. A Proposal for I/O Access Profiles in Parallel Data Mining Algorithms. In *3rd ACIS International Conference on SNPD'02*, June 2002.
4. Rakesh Agrawal et al. Mining Association Rules between Sets of Items in Large Databases. In *The ACM SIGMOD International Conference on Management of Data*, 1993.

Patterns in Information Maps

Andrzej Skowron[1] and Piotr Synak[2]

[1] Institute of Mathematics
Warsaw University
Banacha 2, 02-097 Warsaw, Poland
[2] Cognitron Technology Inc.
87 McCaul Str.
Toronto, ONT, M5T 2W7 Canada

Abstract. We discuss information maps and patterns defined over such maps. Any map is defined by some transition relation on states. Each state is a pair consisting of a label and information related to the label. We present several examples of information maps and patterns in such maps. In particular, temporal patterns investigated in data mining are special cases of such patterns in information maps. We also introduce association rules over information maps. Patterns over such maps can be represented by means of formulas of temporal logics. We discuss examples of problems of extracting such patterns from data.

1 Introduction

Patterns discussed in data mining [1], [5], [11] are special cases of patterns defined over information maps. Any such map consists of a relation on states, i.e., pairs $(label, information(label))$. Exemplary information maps can be extracted from decision systems [10], [7]. In this case one can take attribute value vectors as labels. The information corresponding to any label is a subsystem of a given decision system consisting of all objects consistent with the label. Patterns over information maps describe sets of states and can be expressed by means of temporal formulas [3], [2], [6]. For example, one can look for minimal (with respect to the length) labels with the following property: any state reachable (by means of a given transition relation) from the state s with such label consists of a subsystem of a given decision system with a required property (e.g., expressing that the entropy is not changing significantly in transition to any state reachable from the given state s comparing the entropy of the subsystem corresponding to s). In the paper we present several examples of information maps showing how they can be constructed from data represented, e.g., by information systems, decision tables, or ordered sequences of feature value vectors. Examples of patterns and generalized association rules over such maps are also presented. We discuss searching problems for optimal (in a given information map) association rules. Such rules can be obtained by tuning parameters of parameterized temporal formulas expressing the structure of association rules. Finally, we outline classification problems for states embedded in neighborhoods defined by information maps.

2 Preliminaries

We use in the paper standard notation of rough set theory (see, e.g., [7]). In particular by $\mathbb{A}$ we denote information system [10] with the universe U and the attribute set A. Decision systems are denoted by $\mathbb{A} = (U, A, d)$ where d is the decision attribute.

Temporal formulas can be used for expressing properties of states in information maps. We recall an example of temporal logic syntax and semantics [3], [2]. We begin from syntax of formulas. Let Var be a set of propositional variables. One can distinguish two kinds of formulas: state and path, and we define the set F of all formulas inductively:

S1. Every propositional variable from Var is a state formula,
S2. if α and β are state formulas, so are $\neg \alpha$ and $\alpha \wedge \beta$,
S3. $\mathsf{A}\alpha$ is a state formula, if α is a path formula,
P1. any state formula is also a path formula,
P2. if α and β are path formulas, so are $\neg \alpha$ and $\alpha \wedge \beta$,
P3. if α and β are path formulas, so is $\mathsf{U}(\alpha, \beta)$.

Both A and U are modal operators, where the former denotes "all paths" and the latter "until".

The semantics of temporal formulas is defined as follows. Assume S is a given set of *states* and let $R \subseteq S \times S$ be a *transition relation*. The pair (S, R) is called a *model*. Let Val be a *valuation function* $Val : Var \rightarrow 2^S$. Satisfaction of state formula $\alpha \in F$ in state $s \in S$ we denote by $s \models \alpha$ and define by

S1. $s \models \alpha$ iff $s \in Val(\alpha)$ for $\alpha \in Var$,
S2. $s \models (\neg \alpha)$ iff not $s \models \alpha$, $s \models \alpha \wedge \beta$ iff $s \models \alpha$ and $s \models \beta$,
S3. $s \models \mathsf{A}\alpha$ iff $\pi \models \alpha$ for every path π starting at s,

Let $\pi = s_0 s_1 s_2 \ldots$ be a path and let π_i denote the suffix $s_i s_{i+1} s_{i+2} \ldots$ of π. Satisfaction of path formula $\alpha \in F$ in path π we denote by $\pi \models \alpha$ and define by

P1. $\pi \models \alpha$ iff $s_0 \models \alpha$ for any state formula α,
P2. $\pi \models (\neg \alpha)$ iff not $\pi \models \alpha$, $\pi \models \alpha \wedge \beta$ iff $\pi \models \alpha$ and $\pi \models \beta$,
P3. $\pi \models \mathsf{U}(\alpha, \beta)$ iff $\pi_i \models \alpha$ and $\pi_j \models \beta$ for some $j \geq 0$ and all $0 \leq i < j$.

The semantics $\|\alpha\|_M$ (or $\|\alpha\|$, for short) of formula α in the model M is a set $\{s : s \models \alpha\}$ of all states in M in which α is satisfied.

There are numerous other temporal logic studied in literature [2], [6]. They are characterized by temporal operators defined on the basis of the introduced above operators or some new ones. Let us consider such exemplary past operator H_k^l (where $l \leq k$) with the following intended meaning: $s \models H_k^l \alpha$ if and only if for any path $\pi = s_1 \ldots s_m$ where $m \leq k$ and $s_m = s$ any l-window of π (i.e., subsequence $s_i s_{i+1} \ldots s_{i+l}$ of π) satisfies α. Analogously, one can define operator G_k^l related to the states reachable from s.

One can apply temporal formulas, like those defined above, to describe patterns expressing properties of states in information maps. Problems discussed in the paper are different from typical model checking problems. We consider

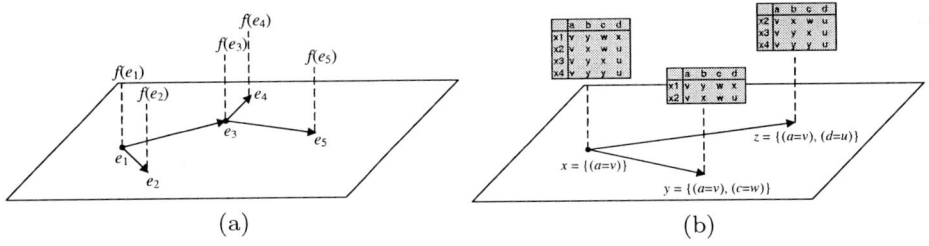

Fig. 1. (a) Information map, (b) Information map of information system

problems assuming that a model (represented by means of information map) is given. Such models are generated from given information sources. The problems we consider are related to searching for patterns (which can be expressed by means of temporal formulas from a given set) having *required properties in a given model*. Examples presented in the following sections are explaining what we mean by the phrase *required properties in a given model*.

3 Information Maps

In this section we introduce the notion of an information map. Such maps are usually generated from experimental data, like information systems or decision tables, and are defined by means of some binary (transition) relations on set of states. Any state consists of *information label* and *information* extracted from a given data set corresponding to the information label. Presented examples explain the meaning of information labels, information related to such labels and transition relations (in many cases partial orders) on states. We show that such structures are basic models over which one can search for relevant patterns for many data mining problems.

An *information map* $\mathcal{A}$ is a quadruple $(E, \leq, I, f)$, where E is a finite set of *information labels*, *transition relation* $\leq \subseteq E \times E$ is a binary relation on information labels, I is an *information set* and $f : E \rightarrow I$ is an *information function* associating the corresponding information to any information label.

In Figure 1a we present an example of information map, where $E = \{e_1, e_2, e_3, e_4, e_5\}$, $I = \{f(e_1), f(e_2), f(e_3), f(e_4), f(e_5)\}$ and the transition relation $\leq$ is a partial order on E.

A *state* is any pair $(e, f(e))$ where $e \in E$. The set $\{(e, f(e)) : e \in E\}$ of all states of $\mathcal{A}$ is denoted by $S_\mathcal{A}$. The transition relation on information labels is extended to relation on states: $(e_1, i_1) \leq (e_2, i_2)$ iff $e_1 \leq e_2$. A *path* in $\mathcal{A}$ is any sequence $s_0 s_1 s_2 \ldots$ of states, such that for every $i \geq 0$: (1) $s_i \leq s_{i+1}$; (2) if $s_i \leq s \leq s_{i+1}$ then $s = s_i$ or $s = s_{i+1}$.

A *property* of $\mathcal{A}$ is any subset of $S_\mathcal{A}$. Let F be a set of temporal formulas. We say that property φ is *expressible* in F if and only if $\varphi = \|\alpha\|$ for some $\alpha \in F$.

Any information system $\mathbb{A} = (U, A)$ defines its information map as a graph consisting of nodes being elementary patterns generated by $\mathbb{A}$, where an *elemen-*

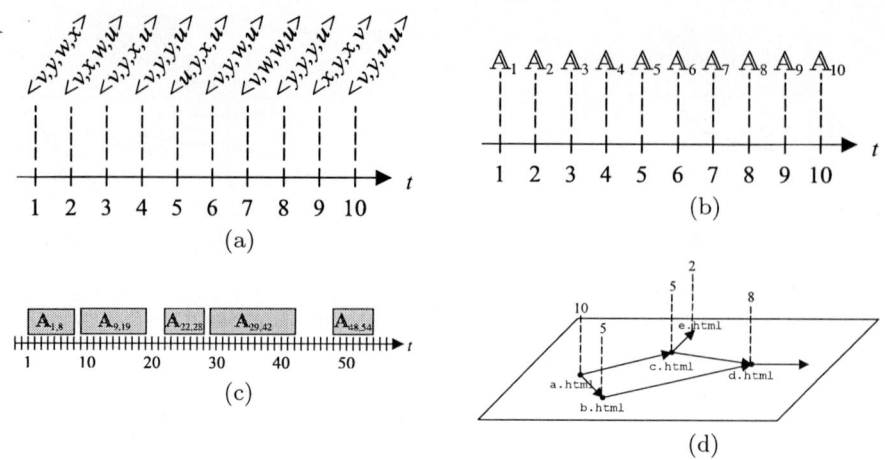

Fig. 2. Information map of (a) temporal information system, (b) information systems changing in time, (c) temporal patterns of temporal information system, (d) web pages

tary pattern $Inf_B(x)$ is a set $\{(a, a(x)) : a \in B\}$ of attribute-value pairs over $B \subseteq A$ consistent with a given object $x \in U$. Thus, the set of labels E is equal to the set $INF(A) = \{Inf_B(x) : x \in U, B \subseteq A\}$ of all elementary patterns of $\mathbb{A}$. The relation $\leq$ is then defined in a straightforward way, i.e. for $u, v \in INF(A)$ $u \leq v$ iff $u \subseteq v$. Hence, relation $\leq$ is a partial order on E. Finally, the information set I is equal to $\{\mathbb{A}_v : v \in INF(A)\}$ where $\mathbb{A}_v$ is a sub-system of $\mathbb{A}$ with the universe U_v equal to the set $\{x \in U : \forall (a,t) \in v \text{ we have } a(x) = t\}$. Attributes in $\mathbb{A}_v$ are attributes from $\mathbb{A}$ restricted to U_v. The information function f mapping $INF(A)$ into I is defined by $f(v) = \mathbb{A}_v$ for any $v \in INF(A)$. An example is presented in Figure 1b where three information vectors $x = \{(a,v)\}$, $y = \{(a,v),(c,w)\}$ and $z = \{(a,v),(d,u)\}$ are shown such that $x \leq y$, $x \leq z$.

One can investigate several properties of such system, e.g. related to distribution of values of some attribute. Let α_v be a formula, such that $(e, \mathbb{A}_e) \models \alpha_v$ has the following intended meaning: "at least 75% of objects of system $\mathbb{A}_e$ has value v on attribute d". In our example $\|\alpha\|_\mathbb{A} = \{(x, \mathbb{A}_x), (z, \mathbb{A}_z)\}$.

A *temporal information system* [13] is a system $\mathbb{A} = (\{x_t\}_{t \in E \subseteq \mathbb{N}}, A)$ with linearly ordered universe by $x_t \leq x_{t'}$ iff $t \leq t'$. Patterns in such systems are widely studied in data mining (see, e.g., [8], [11]).

Any temporal information system $\mathbb{A}$ defines in a natural way its information map. Let the information label set E be the set of all possible time units and let the relation $\leq$ be the natural order on $\mathbb{N}$ restricted to E. The information function f maps any given unit of time t into information corresponding to object of U related to t, i.e. $f(t) = Inf_A(x_t)$. In this case the map reflects temporal order of attribute value vectors ordered in time. An example of such information map is presented in Figure 2a.

Let $\mathcal{F} = \{\mathbb{A}_t\}_{t \in E \subseteq \mathbb{N}}$ be a family of decision systems ordered in time. Assume $\mathbb{A}_t = (U_t, A_t, d_t)$, $A_t = \{a_1^{(t)}, \ldots, a_k^{(t)}\}$, and $U_t \subseteq U_{t'}$ for $t \leq t'$. Moreover, let $a_i^{(t)}(u) = a_i^{(t')}(u)$ and $d_t(u) = d_{t'}(u)$ for $i = 1, \ldots, k$, $t \leq t'$ and $u \in U_t$.

Such a family of decision systems defines the following $\mathcal{F}$-information map. E is the set of time stamps and each $\mathbb{A}_t$ corresponds to state of information system (knowledge) at a given time stamp. The transition relation $\leq$ is naturally derived from the order on $\mathbb{N}$ and the function f is a map from E onto $\mathcal{F}$. An example is presented in Figure 2b. For properties of such systems see [15].

One can consider properties of such information map invariant in time. Let us recall the decomposition problem of information systems changing in time [14]. Then the *time stability* property of a given cut c in $\mathcal{F}$-information map can be expressed by the following state expression: "c is the *optimal* cut for $\mathbb{A}_t$" for any $t \leq t_o$ where t_o is a given time threshold. A cut c on a given attribute is optimal for $\mathbb{A}_t$ if and only if it discerns the maximal number object pairs from different decision classes in $\mathbb{A}_t$.

Let $\mathbb{A} = (\{x_t\}_{t \in E \subseteq \mathbb{N}}, A)$ be a temporal information system. Let $\mathcal{F}_\tau$ be a family $\{\mathbb{A}_{t_i, t_i + \Delta_i}\}_{i=1,\ldots,k}$ of information systems ordered in time, such that $\mathbb{A}_{t_i, t_i + \Delta_i} = (\{x_{t_i}, x_{t_i+1}, \ldots, x_{t_i+\Delta_i}\}, A)$. Moreover, assume for any i a generalized template (see e.g. [9]) T_i of the quality at least τ occurs in the table $\mathbb{A}_{t_i, t_i + \Delta_i}$. Let $\leq$ be the natural order on $\mathbb{N}$ restricted to E. Finally, function f maps E onto $I = \mathcal{F}_\tau \cup \{\emptyset\}$ and is defined by (see Figure 2c):

$$f(t) = \begin{cases} \mathbb{A}_{t_i, t_i + \Delta_i} & \text{if exists } i \text{ such that } t_i \leq t \leq t_i + \Delta_i \\ \emptyset & \text{otherwise} \end{cases}$$

Any template in each of the systems $\mathbb{A}_{t_i, t_i + \Delta_i}$ is a pattern that has its occurrence time and the validity period. One can consider a collection of templates and characterize their relative occurrence in time by higher order patterns. For example, relative occurrence of templates T_1, T_2 can be of the form "the pattern T_1 is always followed by the pattern T_2" in a given information map [13].

4 Exemplary Problems

The notion of information map looks quite abstract, however, using maps one can formulate numerous problems relevant for data mining. In this section we formulate some examples. In general, solution of a given problem is based on searching for *good* patterns in relevant (temporal) language. Such patterns express (temporal) properties of given information system.

Let $\mathcal{A} = (E, \leq, I, f)$ be na information map of a given information system (or decision table). Let us observe that states in $\mathcal{A}$ consist of subtables defined by labels (elementary patterns) from a given information system. Hence, patterns (temporal formulas) describe properties of sets of subtables pointed by elementary patterns. Let us consider an example.

Problem 1. For information map $\mathcal{A}$ of a given decision table, find minimal, with respect to the partial order $\leq$, element e of E such that the set of subtables $S(e) = \{f(e') : e \leq e'\}$ satisfies given constraints (expressible in a fixed temporal logic).

One can choose such constraints in the following way. We are looking for such states that the set of states reachable from them is sufficiently large and has the following property: any two states $s_1 = (e_1, f(e_1))$, $s_2 = (e_2, f(e_2))$ reachable from state $s = (e, f(e))$ (i.e. $s \leq s_1$ and $s \leq s_2$) consist of decision subtables $f(e_1), f(e_2)$ with *close* relative positive regions [7]. The closeness of relative positive regions can be defined by means of closeness measures of sets. Other possible choices can be made using entropy or association rules parameterized by some values of thresholds (support and confidence) [1] instead of positive regions.

In the new setting one can consider a generalization of association rules [1] by considering implications of the form $\alpha \Rightarrow \beta$ where α, β are some temporal formulas from a fixed (fragment of) temporal logic interpreted in an information map. The support and confidence can be defined in an analogous way as in the case of the standard association rules taking into account the specificity of states in information maps. Let us consider an example of searching problem assuming an information map is given. The goal is to search for such pattern α of subtables that if a state s is satisfying α then with certainty defined by the confidence coefficient this state has also property β (e.g., any path starting from such state s consists of a subtable with sufficiently small entropy). At the same time the set of states satisfying α and β should be sufficiently large to a degree defined by the support coefficient. The temporal structure of association rules depends on the application (see below).

One can generalize a prediction problem considered for linear orders in data mining [5], [11]. The following example is included to illustrate this point of view.

Problem 2. Let $\mathcal{A} = (E, \leq, I, f)$ be an information map. Assume the relation $\leq$ is a partial order. Let us consider a searching problem for association rules of the form $H_k^l \alpha \Longrightarrow \circ \beta$ where $\circ$ is the next operator [2], β is a fixed formula and α is from a given set of formulas.

The intended meaning of such formula is the following: $s \models H_k^l \alpha \Longrightarrow \circ \beta$ if and only if any immediate successor of s has property β if the neighborhood of s defined by the operator H_k^l has property specified by α. Let us observe that the space of formulas from which we would like to extract relevant association rules is parameterized by non-negative integers k, l satisfying $l \leq k$ as well as α from a fixed set of temporal formulas.

For a given state s in an information map two neighborhoods are defined. The first called the *past neighborhood* $P(s)$ of s consists of some states from which s is reachable (by the transition relation of information map). The second one, the *future neighborhood* $F(s)$, consists of some states reachable from s. Let γ be a given formula representing a specified property of $F(s)$. For example, it can be of the form $G_n^2 \delta$ where δ is expressing that in any 2-window of states from $F(s)$ changes are not significant. Moreover, let L be a set of formulas expressing properties of 2-windows in $P(s)$. L can be chosen as a set of formulas specifying trends of changes of attribute values in labels of 2-windows.

Problem 3. For given δ, L, n and information map $\mathcal{A}$ find k and formula $\beta \in L$ such that $H_k^2 \beta \Longrightarrow G_n^2 \delta$ is an association rule of the required quality specified by the support and confidence coefficients.

An interesting task is to search for so called labels of changes. The 2-windows in past neighborhoods of states with such labels are showing significant changes while 2-windows in future neighborhoods are not showing significant changes of information.

One can consider more general structures than neighborhoods, for representing trends of pattern changes. We use terminology from granular computing (see, e.g., [12]).

An interesting class of rules (see also [4]) is defined by the following scheme of association rules:

$$\alpha(G) \land R(F_1(G), F_2(G)) \land \beta(F_1(G)) \Longrightarrow \gamma(F_2(G))$$

where $G, F_1(G), F_2(G)$ are information granules; $F_1(G), F_2(G)$ are parts of G; α, β, γ are given properties of granules and R is a binary constraint relation on granules.

Such rules have the following intended meaning. If the granule G has property α and its parts $F_1(G), F_2(G)$ are satisfying a given constraint R and $F_1(G)$ has property described by β then $F_2(G)$ satisfies γ.

Let us consider an example. Assume G is a sequence of information granules $(g_1, \ldots, g_k)$ being a sequence of states $((e_1, f(e_1)), \ldots, (e_k, f(e_k)))$, respectively in a map $\mathcal{A}$ of information system $\mathbb{A}$. Moreover, let $F_1(G), F_2(G)$ be granules $(e_1, \ldots, e_k), (f(e_1), \ldots, f(e_k))$, respectively. The intended meaning of formulas α, β, γ, R are as follows:

- $\alpha(G)$ holds iff $\{g_1, \ldots, g_k\}$ is an anti-chain in $(E, \leq)$ in which all states are reachable from some state;
- $R(G, G')$ iff (G, G') is a state in $\mathcal{A}$;
- $\beta \in L$ where L is a set of formulas making possible to check if attribute values in $(e_1, \ldots, e_k)$ have some trends of changes, e.g., they are increasing, decreasing, changing significantly;
- $\gamma(f(e_1), \ldots, f(e_k))$ holds iff the cardinalities of relative positive regions of decision tables from $(f(e_1), \ldots, f(e_k))$ create a decreasing sequence.

Certainly, one can consider other semantics of the above formulas, for example, the following intended meaning of the formula γ: $\gamma(f(e_1), \ldots, f(e_k))$ if and only if a sequence of the most probable decision values of decision tables from $(f(e_1), \ldots, f(e_k))$ is increasing.

Finally, we obtain the following searching problem.

Problem 4. Assume $\mathcal{A}$ be an information map and consider the set of anti-chains each of them reachable from one state in $\mathcal{A}$. Find, for a given formula γ and a set of temporal formulas L, a formula $\beta \in L$ predicting trends of changing in $(f(e_1), \ldots, f(e_k))$ expressible by γ by means of trends of changes of attribute values in $(e_1, \ldots, e_k)$ expressible by β. The quality of extracted association rules can be measured by the required support and confidence coefficients.

5 Conclusions

We have introduced a class of patterns in information maps. Presented examples show that searching for such patterns can be important for data mining

problems. In the future we plan to develop heuristics searching for solutions of
the discussed problems and we would like to apply them to real-life problems.
Boolean reasoning methods [7] can be used for extracting at least some of considered patterns. The details of methods based on Boolean reasoning for the
temporal pattern extraction will be included in one of our next papers.

Acknowledgements. The research has been supported by the KBN research
grant 8 T11C 025 19. The research of Andrzej Skowron has been also supported
by the Wallenberg Foundation grant.

References

1. Agrawal, R., Mannila, H., Srikant, R., Toivonen, H., Verkamo, I.: Fast Discovery of Association Rules. *Proc. of the Advances in Knowledge Discovery and Data Mining.* AAAI Press/The MIT Press, CA (1996) 307–328
2. Bolc, L., Szałas, A. (Eds.): Time and logic. UCL Press, London (1995)
3. Clark, E.M., Emerson, E.A., Sistla, A.P.: Automatic verification of finite state concurrent systems using temporal logic specifications: A practical approach. *ACM Transactions on Programming Languages and Systems* **8**(2), (1986) 244–263
4. Dubois, D., Prade, H., Ughetto, L.: A new perspective on reasoning with fuzzy rules. In: Pal, N.R., Sugeno, M.: Lecture Notes in Artificial Intelligence **2275**, Springer-Verlag, Berlin (2002) 1–11
5. Fayyad, U.M., Piatetsky-Shapiro, G., Smyth, P., Uthurusamy, R. (Eds.): *Advances in knowledge discovery and data mining.* AAAI/MIT Press (1996)
6. Gabbay, D.M., Hogger, C.J., Robinson, J.A. (eds.): *Handbook of logic in artificial intelligence and logic programming, Epistemic and temporal reasoning.* (vol. 4), Oxford University Press, Oxford (1995)
7. Komorowski, J., Pawlak, Z., Polkowski, L., Skowron, A.: Rough sets: A tutorial. In: Pal, S.K., Skowron, A. (eds.): *Rough fuzzy hybridization: A new trend in decision–making.* Springer-Verlag, Singapore (1999) 3–98
8. Mannila, H., Toivonen, H.,Verkamo, A.I.: Discovery of frequent episodes in event sequences. *Report C-1997-15*, University of Helsinki, Finland (1997)
9. Nguyen S.H.: Regularity Analysis And Its Applications In Data Mining. PhD Dissertation, Warsaw University, Poland (2000)
10. Pawlak, Z.: *Rough sets – Theoretical aspects of reasoning about data*, Kluwer Academic Publishers, Dordrecht (1991)
11. Roddick, J.F., Hornsby, K., Spiliopoulou, M.: An updated bibliography of temporal, spatial and spatio–temporal data mining research. Lecture Notes in Artificial Intelligence **2007**, Springer-Verlag, Berlin (2001) 147–163
12. Skowron, A.: Toward intelligent systems: Calculi of information granules. *Bulletin of the International Rough Set Society* **5**(1–2) (2001) 9–30
13. Synak, P.: Temporal templates and analysis of time related data. In: Ziarko, W. , Yao, Y.Y. (eds): Proc. of The Second International Conference on Rough Sets & Current Trends in Computing (RSCTC'00), Banff Kanada (2000)
14. Synak, P.: Decomposition of large databases growing in time. Proc. of Eigth International Conference on Information Processing and Management of Uncertainty on Knowledge Based Systems (IPMU'2000), Madrid Spain (2000) 234–239
15. Wakulicz-Deja, A.: Clasification of time-varying information systems. *Information Systems* (1991)

Discernibility Matrix Approach to Exception Analysis

Min Zhao and Jue Wang

Institution of Automation, Chinese Academy of Sciences,
P.O.Box 2728, Beijing 100080, P. R. China
{m.zhao,jue.wang}@mail.ia.ac.cn

Abstract. Exception plays an important role in Knowledge Discovery in Databases (KDD). As far as data description is concerned, exception could serve as the complement to rule to form concise representation about data set. More importantly, exception may provide more information than rule for people to understand the data set. This paper defines text as the description of data set and considers some special objects as exceptions to complement text. An approach based on the distribution of core in discernibility matrix of text is presented to identify exceptions, and the exceptions selected by this way do bear some interesting properties.

1 Introduction

There are two goals in KDD: prediction and description [1]. Exception plays important role in both of them. For prediction, exception could serve as the complement to rule to further classification and reasoning [2] [6]; for description, by selecting exceptions from data set the concise representation may be obtained [7]. Most importantly, exception may provide more information than rule for people to understand data set. For example, supposing we get a rule — "the bird can fly" — and an exception — "the penguin is bird but can not fly" from a data set, obviously, the rule is the general knowledge for most people but the exception is novel for many people. Therefore, in some fields of KDD the identification of exceptions is more important than rule induction, a typical example is fraud detection.

In this paper we consider exception as the necessary component for data description. Many patterns can be found from a data set by machine learning approaches. Although they can help people understand the data, most of them just summarize the data set but do not provide "new" knowledge. On the other hand, exceptions are often interesting and novel for people.

In the sequel, we first define text as the description of data set and give its measurement. We find the text based on reduct in rough set theory could describe the data set succinctly. From the discernibility matrix of the text, some special objects (called exceptions) could be identified. Removing these exceptions from original data set we can obtain more concise text, and from these exceptions we may learn some interesting information. In this paper the data set is also called the information system.

2   Text and Text Measurement

Let $\langle U, C \cup D \rangle$ be an information system, where U is the set of objects, C is the set of condition attribute and D is the set of decision attributes. Supposing $\emptyset \neq H \subseteq U$ and $\emptyset \neq B \subseteq C$, then $\langle H, B \cup D \rangle$ is a sort of description of the information system. If all the objects in H are consistent, that is, there do not exist objects taking same values on attributes of B and different values on attributes of D in H, we call $\langle H, B \cup D \rangle$ a *text* of $\langle U, C \cup D \rangle$.

By rough set theory [3], let $\underline{B}X = \{x \in U : [x]_B \subseteq X\}$ be the *B-lower approximation* of X in U, and $POS_B(D) = \cup_{X \in U/D} \underline{B}X$ be the *positive region* of condition attributes B for decision attributes D, then $\langle POS_B(D), B \cup D \rangle$ is a *text* of $\langle U, C \cup D \rangle$.

We use two criteria to measure the fitness of a text: *coverage* and *complexity*, defined by

$$coverage = \frac{Card(H)}{Card(U)}, \quad complexity = \frac{Card(B)}{Card(C)}$$

Clearly, for users the text with maximal *coverage* and minimal *complexity* is the best, but it is impossible to satisfy the two conditions simultaneity for most data sets. Many methods summarize data set into the text bearing some tradeoff between *coverage* and *complexity*. In rough set theory, such text can be obtained by computing reduct.

For given information system $\langle U, C \cup D \rangle$, the set R of condition attributes is called the *reduct relative to C* (or *reduct* in short) if $POS_R(D) = POS_C(D)$ and $\forall r \in R, POS_{R-\{r\}}(D) \neq POS_R(D)$. We may construct text $\langle POS_R(D), R \cup D \rangle$ by R, obviously, it has the same *coverage* with text $\langle POS_C(D), C \cup D \rangle$ and lower *complexity* than that. We give an example to illustrate it.

Example 1. The information system described by Table 1 contains 20 kinds of vertebrates and takes "*bird*" as decision attribute, whose range is {Y, N}. The set of condition attributes is {*gregarious* (*greg* in short), *egg, milk, fly, swim, lung, warm blood* (*warm* in short), *food*}. The range of "*food*" is {0: herbivorous, 1: carnivorous, 2: omnivorous}.

By rough sets, one of its reducts is $R = \{greg, fly, egg, lung\}$. Since the information system is consistent, that is, $POS_C(D) = U$, we can get a text $\langle U, R \cup D = \{bird\} \rangle$, as shown in Table 2. For text $\langle U, R \cup D \rangle$, $coverage = 1$, and $complexity = 4/9$.

3   Discernibility Matrix and Core

The core is the most important subset of condition attributes because it is included in every reduct, and hence reducts are confined by core. If we want to get different texts by computing reduct we have to break away from the confinement of core. First, let us recall the notion of the core.

Table 1. The vertebrate world — an original information system

Object[a]	greg	fly	egg	milk	swim	lung	warm	food	bird	Animal
1(1)	N	Y	Y	N	N	Y	Y	1	Y	Vulture(Vu)
2(1)	N	Y	Y	N	N	Y	Y	2	Y	Pheasant(Ph)
3(1)	Y	Y	Y	N	N	Y	Y	1	Y	Egret(Eg)
4(1)	Y	Y	Y	N	Y	Y	Y	0	Y	Latham(La)
5(1)	Y	Y	Y	N	Y	Y	Y	1	Y	Scoter(Sc)
6(1)	Y	N	Y	N	Y	Y	Y	1	Y	Penguin(Pe)
7(1)	Y	N	Y	N	N	Y	Y	2	Y	Ostrich(Os)
8(1)	Y	Y	Y	N	Y	Y	Y	2	Y	Shelduck(Sh)
9(1)	Y	Y	Y	N	N	Y	Y	2	Y	Sparrow(Sp)
10(1)	N	N	N	Y	N	Y	Y	1	N	Opossum(Op)
11(1)	N	N	N	Y	Y	Y	Y	1	N	Mink(Mi)
12(1)	N	N	Y	N	Y	Y	N	1	N	Toad(To)
13(1)	N	N	Y	Y	Y	Y	Y	1	N	Platypus(Pl)
14(1)	N	N	Y	N	N	Y	N	1	N	Viper(Vi)
15(1)	N	N	Y	N	Y	N	N	1	N	Dogfish(Do)
16(1)	N	N	Y	N	Y	Y	N	2	N	Turtle(Tu)
17(1)	Y	N	N	Y	N	Y	Y	0	N	Reindeer(Re)
18(1)	Y	N	N	Y	Y	Y	Y	1	N	Seal(Se)
19(1)	Y	N	Y	N	Y	N	N	1	N	Hairtail(Ha)
20(1)	Y	Y	N	Y	N	Y	Y	0	N	Fruit bat(Fr)

[a] The number in the parentheses of the first column is the number of animals covered by this object, the same with other tables.

Table 2. Text based on reduct R

O	greg	fly	egg	lung	bird	Animal
1(2)	N	Y	Y	Y	Y	Vu,Ph
2(5)	Y	Y	Y	Y	Y	Eg,La,Sc,Sh,Sp
3(2)	Y	N	Y	Y	Y	Pe,Os
4(2)	N	N	N	Y	N	Op,Mi
5(4)	N	N	Y	Y	N	To,Pl,Vi,Tu
6(1)	N	N	Y	N	N	Do
7(2)	Y	N	N	Y	N	Re,Se
8(1)	Y	N	Y	N	N	Ha
9(1)	Y	Y	N	Y	N	Fr

Table 3. Distribution of core attributes in discernibility matrix of Table 2

O	1(2)	2(5)	3(2)
4(2)			
5(4)	fly		greg
6(1)			
7(2)			egg
8(1)			lung
9(1)	egg		

In rough set theory [3], for information system $\langle U, C \cup D \rangle$, the *core of C relative to D* (*core* in short) is the set of all indispensable attributes in C relative to D. We call the attribute belonging to core the *core attribute*.

By discernibility matrix principle [4], discernibility matrix $M(C)$ of $\langle U, C \cup D \rangle$ is defined by

$$c_{ij} = \{a \in C : a(x_i) \neq a(x_j), x_i, x_j \in U\} \text{ for } i, j = 1, \ldots, n.$$

Condition attribute $c \in C$ is a core attribute if and only if $\exists c_{ij} = \{c\}$, for some i, j, where c_{ij} is the discernibility element between object x_i and object x_j.

From the definition of the core it can be seen that if two objects x_i and x_j belong to different decision classes, i.e., $D(x_i) \neq D(x_j)$, and can be partitioned by unique condition attribute, that is, $\exists c_r \in C$ such that $c_r(x_i) \neq c_r(x_j)$ and $\forall c \in C - \{c_r\}, c(x_i) = c(x_j)$, then c_r is a core attribute. In other words, if c_r is removed, the two objects will be inconsistent for decision attributes. On the other hand, if we delete x_i or x_j from U, then discernibility element $c_{ij} = \{c\}$ does no longer exist, and c is no longer a core attribute. Therefore, the objects that produce core attribute may be the most special objects in U. We may select exceptions from such objects.

It should be noted that the core do not occur in every information system. Then the question arises that if there is no core in the information system, how we can get exceptions? We have the following relation between reduct and core:

If R is a reduct of $\langle U, C \cup D \rangle$, R is the core of $\langle U, R \cup D \rangle$.

Since R is a reduct of $\langle U, C \cup D \rangle$, by definition of reduct, $POS_R(D) = POS_C(D)$ and $\forall r \in R, POS_{R-\{r\}}(D) \neq POS_R(D)$. Then $\forall r \in R$, there exist at least two objects x_i and x_j such that $r(x_i) \neq r(x_j)$ and $\forall c \in R - \{r\}, c(x_i) = c(x_j)$, that is, their discernibility element in M is $\{r\}$, so r is a core attribute of $\langle U, R \cup D \rangle$. Therefore, we could select exceptions by the distribution of core attributes in discernibility matrix of $\langle U, R \cup D \rangle$.

Example 1 in section 2 could illustrate the relation. $R = \{greg, fly, egg, lung\}$ is a reduct of the information system in Table 1, and it is also the core of information system in Table 2.

4 Exception Analysis

We still use the information system of Example 1 to study exception.

Example 2. Table 3 describes the distribution of core attributes in discernibility matrix of information system shown in Table 2. Since $U/D=\{\{1,2,3\}, \{4,5,6,7,8,9\}\}$, the discernibility matrix can be reduced as shown in Table 3, and the discernibility elements including more than one attributes have been omitted.

From the discernibility matrix, it can be seen that object 3 is most special because it produces core attributes "*greg*", "*egg*" and "*lung*" with object 5, 7 and 8, respectively, and other objects do not produce "*greg*" and "*lung*". Removing the two animals covered by object 3 — *Penguin* and *Ostrich* — from U and making reduct, a new text $\langle U - \{Penguin, Ostrich\}, \{fly, egg\} \cup \{bird\}\rangle$ is obtained, as shown in Table 4. For this text, *coverage* = 18/20, and *complexity* = 2/9.

Table 4. Text with *Penguin* and *Ostrich* as exceptions

O	fly	egg	bird	Animal
1(7)	Y	Y	Y	Vu,Ph,Eg,La,Sc,Sh,Sp
2(4)	N	N	N	Op,Mi,Re,Se
3(6)	N	Y	N	To,Pl,Vi,Tu,Do,Ha
4(1)	Y	N	N	Fr

Table 5. Distribution of core attributes in discernibility matrix of Table 4

O	1(7)
2(4)	
3(6)	fly
4(1)	egg

Table 6. Text with *Penguin*, *Ostrich* and *Fruit bat* as exceptions

O	fly	bird	Animal
1(7)	Y	Y	Vu,Ph,Eg,La,Sc,Sh,Sp
2(10)	N	N	Op,Mi,Re,Se,To,Pl,Vi,Do,Tu,Ha

Similar to Table 3, we can compute the distribution of core attributes in Table 4, as shown in Table 5. From this discernibility matrix, it can be seen that objects 1, 3 and 4 produce core attributes. Object 1 covers seven animals, 3 covers six animals and 4 covers only one animal, so we may regard 4 as the exception. Removing the animal covered by object 4 —*Fruit bat* — from U and making further reduct, a new text $\langle U-\{Penguin, Ostrich, Fruitbat\}, \{fly\} \cup \{bird\}\rangle$ can be obtained, as shown in Table 6. Its $coverage = 17/20$ and $complexity = 1/9$.

From these texts it is seen that concise descriptions about data set can be obtained by removing exceptions. For information system shown in Table 1, removing three exceptions we get a text description with higher *coverage* and lowest *complexity* — "the vertebrates that can fly are birds, and the vertebrates that cannot fly are not birds ". The text generalizes the information system in a concise but inexact manner. We may say it accords with the common sense for most people, but provides little "new" knowledge.

Considering the three exceptions *Penguin*, *Ostrich* and *Fruit bat* again, we find *Penguin* and *Ostrich* cannot fly but are birds, and *Fruit bat* can fly but is not bird. The information provided by these exceptions may be novel for many people.

This example shows exceptions could not only help to form concise summarization of data set, but also provide valuable information.

As far as data description is concerned, we hope to get text with larger *coverage* and lower *complexity*. To make *coverage* as larger as possible, we expect the number of exceptions as fewer as possible. Thus, we can conclude the strategy of selecting exceptions:

- Select exceptions that can reduce *complexity* of text mostly.
- Select exceptions that make least change to *coverage* of text.

5 Conclusion

Exception is the necessary component for data description. By removing exceptions we can summarize data set more concisely. Furthermore, exceptions may provide us more information than rules. There are many methods for identifying exceptions, such as statistics. In this paper we just discuss the identification of exceptions on the distribution of core in discernibility matrix, because the exception selected by this method usually has certain meanings. In addition, it can be seen that exception is different from noise. If exception is treated as noise, valuable information may be lost.

On the other hand, the exception space in a data set is rather complex. Any object has some possibility to become exception if we choose different methods or strategies. Additionally, different users may have different opinions with the same object: some may treat it as a rule, and others may treat it as an exception. Therefore, it is necessary to study the exception space under certain definition or certain approach. We have discussed detailedly the exception space based on the distribution of core in discernibility matrix and gave formal description of it in [5]. In future work, we will discuss exception in other form and seek more effective strategies.

Acknowledgements. This work is partially supported by the National Key Project for Basic Research (G1998030500).

References

1. Fayyad, U.M., Piatetsky-Shapiro, G., Smyth, P.: From Data Mining to Knowledge Discovery: an Overview. In: Fayyad, U., Piatetsky-Shapiro, G., Smyth, P., Uthurusamy, R. (eds.): Advances in Knowledge Discovery and Data Mining. AAAI Press (1996) 1–30
2. Gaines, B.R., Compton, P.: Induction of Ripple-down Rules Applied to Modeling Large Database. Journal of Intelligent Information Systems 5(3) (1995) 211–228
3. Pawlak, Z.: Rough Set — Theoretical Aspects of Reasoning about Data. Kluwer Academic Publishers, Dordrecht (1991)
4. Skowron, A., Rauszer, C.: The Discernibility Matrices and Functions in Information Systems. In: Slowinski, R. (ed.): Intelligent Decision Support — Handbook of Applications and Advances of the Rough Set Theory. Kluwer Academic Publishers, Dordrecht (1992) 331–362
5. Wang, J., Zhao, M., Zhao, K., Han, S.: Multilevel Data Summarization from Information System: a "Rule + Exception" Approach . Technical Report AI-Group-2002-2, Institution of Automation, Chinese Academy of Sciences.
6. Zhang, J., Michalski, R.S.: An Integration of Rule Induction and Examplar-based Learning for Graded Concepts. Machine Learning 21(3) (1995) 235–267.
7. Zhou, Y., Jue Wang: Rule+Exception Modeling Based on Rough Set Theory. In: Polkowski, L., Skowron, A. (eds.): Rough Sets and Current Trends in Computing. Lecture Notes in Artificial Intelligence 1424. Springer (1998) 529–536

Gastric Cancer Data Mining with Ordered Information

Ning Zhong[1], Ju-Zhen Dong[1], Y.Y. Yao[2], and Setsuo Ohsuga[3]

[1] Dept. of Information Eng., Maebashi Institute of Technology
[2] Dept. of Computer Science, University of Regina
[3] Dept. of Information and Computer Science, Waseda University

Abstract. *Ordered information* is a kind of useful background knowledge to guide a discovery process toward finding different types of novel rules and improving their quality for many real world data mining tasks. In the paper, we investigate ways of using ordered information for gastric cancer data mining, based on rough set theory and granular computing. With respect to the notion of ordered information tables, we describe how to mine *ordering rules* and how to form granules of values of attributes in a pre/post-processing step for improving the quality of the mined classification rules. Experimental results in gastric cancer data mining show the usefulness and effectiveness of our approaches.

1 Introduction

The motivation of the work is based on two observations for the real world problems.

Firstly, in real world situations, we may be faced with many problems that are not simply classification [1,9]. One such type of problems is the ordering of objects. Consider the example of ranking consumer products. Attributes may be the price, warranty, and other information. The values of a particular attribute, say the price, naturally induce an ordering of objects. The overall ranking of products may be produced by their market shares of different manufacturers. The orderings of objects by attribute values may not necessarily be the same as the overall ordering of objects. In this setting, a number of important issues arise. It would be interesting to know which attributes play more important roles in determining the overall ordering, and which attributes do not contribute at all to the overall ordering. Another real world example is a gastric cancer dataset collected at Japan National Cancer Center. There are about 27 attributes of patients such as type of cancer, serosal invasion, peritoneal metastasis, liver metnastasis, maximal diameter, pre-operative complication etc. A purpose of analysis is to find the major reasons why patients died within 90 days after operated.

In order to deal with this type of problems, we use *ordered information* that is a kind of data semantics for mining interesting *ordering rules*. An ordering rules may state that "if the value of an object x on an attribute a is ordered ahead of the value of another object y on the same attribute, then x is ordered ahead of y". For mining ordering rules, we first transform an ordered information table into a binary information, and then apply our GDT-RS rule mining system [17].

Secondly, we observed that many real world data are unbalanced ones and the coverage of classification rules mined from such data is usually very low. The problem of unbalanced data can be formalized as follows. A data set D contains n objects, m attributes, and k classes. Focusing on the class $C_i (1 \le i \le k)$ is of interest (positive class $C+$) and others are considered as negative class ($C-$). Thus, $|C+| \ll |C-|$ and many objects in $C+$ and $C-$ are indiscernible. Standard data mining techniques cannot produce rules with high coverage and accuracy from such data sets. The gastric cancer dataset mentioned above is a typical unbalanced one. Let objects with respect with that patients died within 90 days after operated be C+, $|C+| = 207 \ll |C-| = 5963$. Hence, how to improve the quality of the mined rules is a key issue for such unbalanced data. Our idea is to use *granular computing with ordered information* in a pre/post-processing step of a knowledge discovery process for improving the quality of the mined classification rules.

The emerging theory of *Granular Computing (GrC)* grasps the essential concept – granules, and makes use of them in general problem solving [14,15]. An underlying idea of GrC uses of groups, classes, or clusters of elements called granules. In some situations, although detailed information may be available, it may be sufficient to use granules in order to have an efficient and practical solution. Very precise solutions may in fact not be required for many practical problems in data mining and knowledge discovery [11].

In the paper, we investigate ways of gastric cancer data mining with ordered information, based on rough set theory and granular computing. Section 2 defines ordered information tables as a preparation. Sections 3 and 4 describe how to mine *ordering rules* in gastric cancer data, and how to form granules of values of attributes in a pre/post-processing step for improving the quality of the mined classification rules, respectively. Experimental results in gastric cancer data mining are also discussed in the sections. Finally, Section 5 gives conclusions.

2 Ordered Information Tables

In many information processing systems, objects are typically represented by their values on a finite set of attributes. Such information may be conveniently described in a tabular form [8]. The rows of the table correspond to objects of the universe, the columns correspond to a set of attributes, and each cell gives the value of an object with respect to an attribute.

Definition 1. *An information table is a quadruple:*

$$IT = (U, At, \{V_a \mid a \in At\}, \{I_a \mid a \in At\}),$$

where U is a finite nonempty set of objects, At is a finite nonempty set of attributes, V_a is a nonempty set of values for $a \in At$ $I_a : U \to V_a$ is an information function.

For simplicity, we have considered only information tables characterized by a finite set of objects and a finite set of attributes. Each information function I_a is a total function that maps an object of U to exactly one value in V_a. An information table represents all available information and knowledge about the objects under consideration. Objects are only perceived, observed, or measured by using a finite number of properties.

An information table does not consider any semantic relationships between distinct values of a particular attribute. By incorporating semantics information, we may obtain different generalizations of information tables [3,4,12]. Generalized information tables may be viewed as information tables with added semantics.

Definition 2. *Let U be a nonempty set and $\succ$ be a binary relation on U. The relation $\succ$ is a weak order if it satisfies the two properties:*

$$\text{Asymmetry} : x \succ y \implies \neg(y \succ x),$$
$$\text{Negative transitivity} : (\neg(x \succ y), \neg(y \succ z)) \implies \neg(x \succ z).$$

An important implication of a weak order is that the following relation,

$$x \sim y \iff (\neg(x \succ y), \neg(y \succ x)), \tag{1}$$

is an equivalence relation. For two elements, if $x \sim y$ we say x and y are indiscernible by $\succ$. The equivalence relation $\sim$ induces a partition $U/\sim$ on U, and an order relation $\succ^*$ on $U/\sim$ can be defined by:

$$[x]_\sim \succ^* [y]_\sim \iff x \succ y, \tag{2}$$

where $[x]_\sim$ is the equivalence class containing x. Moreover, $\succ^*$ is a linear order. Any two distinct equivalence classes of $U/\sim$ can be compared. It is therefore possible to arrange the objects into levels, with each level consisting of indiscernible elements defined by $\succ$. For a weak order, $\neg(x \succ y)$ can be written as $y \succeq x$ or $x \preceq y$, which means $y \succ x$ or $y \sim x$. For any two elements x and y, we have either $x \succ y$ or $y \succeq x$, but not both.

Definition 3. *An ordered information table is a pair:*

$$OIT = (IT, \{\succ_a | a \in At\}),$$

where IT is a standard information table and $\succ_a$ is a weak order on V_a.

An ordering of values of a particular attribute a naturally induces an ordering of objects, namely, for $x, y \in U$:

$$x \succ_{\{a\}} y \iff I_a(x) \succ_a I_a(y), \tag{3}$$

where $\succ_{\{a\}}$ denotes an order relation on U induced by the attribute a. An object x is ranked ahead of another object y if and only if the value of x on the attribute

a is ranked ahead of the value of y on a. The relation $\succ_{\{a\}}$ has exactly the same properties as that of $\succ_a$. For a subset of attributes $A \subseteq At$, we define

$$x \succ_A y \iff \forall a \in A[I_a(x) \succ_a I_a(y)]$$
$$\iff \bigwedge_{a \in A} I_a(x) \succ_a I_a(y) \iff \bigcap_{a \in A} \succ_{\{a\}}. \quad (4)$$

That is, x is ranked ahead of y if and only if x is ranked ahead of y according to all attributes in A. The above definition is a straightforward generalization of the standard definition of equivalence relations in rough set theory, where the equality relation $=$ is used [8].

For many real world applications, we also need a special attribute, called the decision attribute. The ordering of objects by the decision attribute is denoted by $\succ_{\{o\}}$ and is called the overall ordering of objects.

Table 1. An ordered information table

	a	b	c	d	o
p_1	middle	3 years	$200	heavy	1
p_2	large	3 years	$300	very heavy	3
p_3	small	3 years	$300	light	3
p_4	small	3 years	$250	very light	2
p_5	small	2 years	$200	very light	3

$\succ_a$: small $\succ_a$ middle $\succ_a$ large,
$\succ_b$: 3 years $\succ_b$ 2 years,
$\succ_c$: \$200 $\succ_c$ \$250 $\succ_c$ \$300,
$\succ_d$: very light $\succ_d$ light $\succ_d$ heavy $\succ_d$ very heavy,
$\succ_o$: 1 $\succ_o$ 2 $\succ_o$ 3.

Example 1. Suppose we have an ordered information table of a group of products produced by five manufacturers as shown in Table 1. In this table, a, b, c, d, and o stand for size, warranty, price, weight, and overall ordering on a set of products, respectively. Based on orderings of attribute values, we obtain the following orderings of products:

$$\succ^*_{\{a\}} : [p_3, p_4, p_5] \succ^*_{\{a\}} [p_1] \succ^*_{\{a\}} [p_2],$$
$$\succ^*_{\{b\}} : [p_1, p_2, p_3, p_4] \succ^*_{\{b\}} [p_5],$$
$$\succ^*_{\{c\}} : [p_1, p_5] \succ^*_{\{c\}} [p_4] \succ^*_{\{c\}} [p_2, p_3],$$
$$\succ^*_{\{d\}} : [p_4, p_5] \succ^*_{\{d\}} [p_3] \succ^*_{\{d\}} [p_1] \succ^*_{\{d\}} [p_2],$$
$$\succ^*_{\{o\}} : [p_1] \succ^*_{\{o\}} [p_4] \succ^*_{\{o\}} [p_2, p_3, p_5].$$

For subsets $\{a,b\}$ and $\{c,d\}$, we have

$$\succ_{\{a,b\}} : \emptyset,$$
$$\succ_{\{c,d\}} : p_1 \succ_{\{c,d\}} p_2, \quad p_4 \succ_{\{c,d\}} p_2, \quad p_5 \succ_{\{c,d\}} p_2,$$
$$p_4 \succ_{\{c,d\}} p_3, \quad p_5 \succ_{\{c,d\}} p_3.$$

By combining attributes a and b, all objects are put into the same class. It is interesting to note that $\succ_{\{c,d\}}$ is not a weak order. That is, the intersection of two weak orders may not produce a weak order. This suggests that rules using simple condition $\bigwedge_{a \in A} I_a(x) \succ_a I_a(y)$ might not be very useful.

With respect to the notion of (ordered) information table, there are extensive studies on the relationships between values of different attributes and relationships between values of the same attribute, i.e., the horizontal analysis and the vertical analysis of an (ordered) information table [10]. Furthermore, the horizontal analysis can be divided into two levels:

- global relationships: all combinations of values on one set of attributes determine the values on another set of attributes. *Ordering rules* mined from the ordered information table are a typical example of global relationships. For instance, the following is an ordering rule mined from a group of products shown in Table 1.

  $r_1 : b(\preceq) \wedge c(\preceq) \rightarrow o(\preceq).$

  This rule shows that *warranty* and *price* are the most important features for the products ranking. Section 3 will give further discussion on ordering rule mining in gastric cancer data.

- local relationships: one specific combination of values on one set of attributes determines the values on another set of attributes. Finding local relationships (e.g. *classification rules*) is one of the main tasks of data mining. Our main contribution is that our method can mine interesting classification rules from unbalanced real world data by using granular computing with ordered information. The following is an example of such rule mined from a gastric cancer data set.

  $r_2 : peritoneal\_meta(\geq 1) \wedge spec\_histologi(A, U)$
  $\wedge ln\_metastasis(\geq 1) \rightarrow d90.$

  This example will be further discussed in Section 4.

Before the discussion on our approaches in detail, it is necessary that giving here main attributes of the gastric cancer data collected at Japan National Cancer Center and their values with ordered information (see Table 2).

3 Mining Ordering Rules in Gastric Cancer Data

In order to mine ordering rules from an ordered information table, we transform an ordered information table into a binary information. Thus, our GDT-RS rule mining system can be applied immediately.

GDT-RS is a soft hybrid rule mining system for discovering classification rules from databases with uncertain and incomplete data [17]. The system is based on a hybridization of *Generalization Distribution Table (GDT)* and the *Rough Set* methodology. The GDT-RS system can generate, from uncertain and incomplete

Table 2. Gastric Cancer Data with Ordered Information

Attributes	Meaning	Values with Ordered Information
multilesions	Multiple lesions	"." $\succ$ 0 $\succ$ 1 $\succ$ 2 $\succ$ 3
typeofcancer	Type of cancer	A $\succ$ L $\succ$ M $\succ$ O $\succ$ P $\succ$ T $\succ$ U 0 = EC (early cancer) 1 = B1, 2 = B2, 3 = {B3, B5}, 4 = B4
serosal_inva	Serosal invasion	"." $\succ$ 0 $\succ$ 1 $\succ$ 2 $\succ$ 3
peritoneal_meta	Peritoneal metastasis	"." $\succ$ 0 $\succ$ 1 $\succ$ 2 $\succ$ 3
liver_meta	Liver metastasis	"." $\succ$ 0 $\succ$ 1 $\succ$ 2 $\succ$ 3
maximal_diam	Maximal diameter	"< 50" $\succ$ "$\geq$ 50"
pre_oper_compA	Pre-operative complication = A	0 = no $\succ$ 1 = yes
pre_oper_compB	Pre-operative complication = B	same as above
pre_oper_compC	Pre-operative complication = C	same as above
pre_oper_compD	Pre-operative complication = D	same as above
pre_oper_compE	Pre-operative complication = E	same as above
pre_oper_compH	Pre-operative complication = H	same as above
pre_oper_compI	Pre-operative complication = I	same as above
pre_oper_compL	Pre-operative complication = L	same as above
pre_oper_compP	Pre-operative complication = P	same as above
pre_oper_compR	Pre-operative complication = R	same as above
pre_oper_compS	Pre-operative complication = S	same as above
histological	Histological type	0 = {PAP, WEL, MOD} $\succ$ 1 = {POR, SIG, MUC, ADM, SCM, OTH}
spec_histologi	Special histological type	"." $\succ$ A $\succ$ S $\succ$ C $\succ$ U
stromal_type	Stromal type	"." $\succ$ M $\succ$ S
cellular_atyp	Cellular atypism	"." $\succ$ 1 $\succ$ 2 $\succ$ 3
structural_atyp	Structural atypism	"." $\succ$ 1 $\succ$ 2 $\succ$ 3
growth_pattern	Growth pattern	"." $\succ$ 1 $\succ$ 2 $\succ$ 3
depth	Depth of invasion	".." $\succ$ MM $\succ$ SM $\succ$ PM $\succ$ SS $\succ$ S1 $\succ$ S2 $\succ$ S3
lymphatic_inva	Lymphatic invasion	"." $\succ$ 1 $\succ$ 2 $\succ$ 3
vascular_inva	Vascular invasion	"." $\succ$ 1 $\succ$ 2 $\succ$ 3
ln_metastasis	LN metastasis (macroscopic)	"." $\succ$ 1 $\succ$ 2 $\succ$ 3 $\succ$ 4

training data, a set of rules with the minimal (semi-minimal) description length, having large strength, and covering of all instances.

In our GDT-RS system, the quality of the mined rules can be evaluated from several aspects including accuracy and coverage. The accuracy is given by:

$$accuracy(P \rightarrow Q) = \frac{card([P]_{IT)} \cap [Q]_{IT})}{card([P]_{IT})} \qquad (5)$$

It shows the quality of a rule measured by the number of instances satisfying the rule's antecedent P which are classified into the rule's consequent Q. The user can specify an allowed accuracy level as a threshold value. For our the application, the threshold value is 0.6.

On the other hand, the coverage simply denotes how many instances in all positive and negative ones are contained in a rule.

In the binary information table, we consider object pairs $(x, y) \in (U \times U)^+$. The information function is defined by:

$$I_a(x, y) = \begin{cases} 1, & x \succ_{\{a\}} y \\ 0, & x \preceq_{\{a\}} y. \end{cases} \quad (6)$$

Statements in an ordered information table can be translated into equivalent statements in the binary information table. For example, $x \succ_{\{a\}} y$ can be translated into $I_a(x, y) = 1$. In the translation process, we will not consider object pairs of the form (x, x), as we are not interested in them.

From the results shown in Table 3, we can see that in the 22 rules, 17 of them are with attribute: *live_meta*, and 11 with attribute: *peritoneal − mate* (5 of them are independent with *live_meta*). The results show that liver metastasis and/or peritoneal metastasis are the major reasons why patients died within 90 days after operated. The results have been evaluated by experts at Japan National Cancer Center. According to their opinion, the discovered ordering rules are reasonable and interesting.

4 Granular Computing with Ordered Information

In general, informed knowledge discovery uses background knowledge about a domain to guide a discovery process toward finding interesting and novel rules hidden in data. Background knowledge may be of several forms including rules already found, taxonomic relationships, causal preconditions, and semantic categories.

This section discusses how to use ordered information as background knowledge to change data granules so that the quality of the classification rules mined from unbalanced gastric cancer data is improved.

4.1 Forming Granules of Condition Attributes in Post-processing

Each rule candidate generated by the GDT-RS rule mining system is evaluated by checking gastric cancer data again and using ordered information as a step of post-processing.

Based on ordered information for values of each attribute, we use heuristics to analyse how the accuracy and coverage of classification increase or decrease as values of each condition attribute increase or decrease.

 - If the positive coverage of classification increases and the accuracy is greater than the threshold as values of each condition attribute increase or decrease, the corresponding values of the rule candidate are adjusted to form a granule.
 - If the accuracy and positive coverage of classification decrease as values of each condition attribute increase and decrease, the rule candidate is uninteresting.

Table 3. Analysis 1: the reasons why patients died within 90 days

No.	reasons	accuracy
1	**liver_meta**($\succ$) ∧ pre_oper_compI($\succ$)	95%
2	**peritoneal_meta**($\succ$) ∧ pre_oper_compI($\succ$)	71%
3	**peritoneal_meta**($\succ$) ∧ spec_histologi($\succ$)	64%
4	**peritoneal_meta**($\succ$) ∧ pre_oper_compH($\succ$) ∧ pre_oper_compP($\succ$)	96%
5	**liver_meta**($\succ$) ∧ pre_oper_compB($\succ$) ∧ pre_oper_compH($\succ$)	95%
6	**liver_meta**($\succ$) ∧ spec_histologi($\succ$) ∧ stromal_type($\succ$)	95
7	**liver_meta**($\succ$) ∧ pre_oper_compC($\succ$) ∧ pre_oper_compP($\succ$)	68%
8	**liver_meta**($\succ$) ∧ pre_oper_compB($\succ$) ∧ pre_oper_compP($\succ$) ∧ histological($\succ$)	97%
9	multilesions($\succ$) ∧ **peritoneal_meta**($\succ$) ∧ **liver_meta**($\succ$) ∧ pre_oper_compP($\succ$)	97%
10	**peritoneal_meta**($\succ$) ∧ **liver_meta**($\succ$) ∧ pre_oper_compD($\succ$) ∧ pre_oper_compH($\succ$)	96%
11	multilesions($\succ$) ∧ **peritoneal_meta**($\succ$) ∧ **liver_meta**($\succ$) ∧ pre_oper_compH($\succ$)	96%
12	**peritoneal_meta**($\succ$) ∧ **liver_meta**($\succ$) ∧ pre_oper_compC($\succ$) ∧ pre_oper_compH($\succ$)	96%
13	**peritoneal_meta**($\succ$) ∧ pre_oper_compP($\succ$) ∧ pre_oper_compR($\succ$) ∧ cellular_atyp($\succ$)	96%
14	**liver_meta**($\succ$) ∧ pre_oper_compA($\succ$) ∧ pre_oper_compD($\succ$) ∧ pre_oper_compP($\succ$)	96%
15	**liver_meta**($\succ$) ∧ maximal_diam_disc($\prec$) ∧ pre_oper_compR($\succ$) ∧ stromal_type($\prec$)	91%
16	**peritoneal_meta**($\prec$) ∧ **liver_meta**($\succ$) ∧ pre_oper_compH($\succ$) ∧ spec_histologi($\succ$)	89%
17	**peritoneal_meta**($\prec$) ∧ **liver_meta**($\succ$) ∧ spec_histologi($\succ$) ∧ growth_pattern($\succ$)	89%
18	**liver_meta**($\succ$) ∧ pre_oper_compA($\succ$) ∧ pre_oper_compH($\succ$) ∧ stromal_type($\succ$)	79%
19	**peritoneal_meta**($\succ$) ∧ pre_oper_compB($\prec$) ∧ pre_oper_compP($\succ$) ∧ pre_oper_compR($\succ$)	73%
20	**liver_meta**($\succ$) ∧ pre_oper_compB($\succ$) ∧ histological($\succ$) ∧ growth_pattern($\succ$)	71%
21	**liver_meta**($\succ$) ∧ pre_oper_compB($\succ$) ∧ pre_oper_compC($\succ$) ∧ stromal_type($\prec$)	66%
22	**liver_meta**($\succ$) ∧ spec_histologi($\succ$) ∧ cellular_atyp($\succ$) ∧ lymphatic_inva($\succ$)	69%

Example 2. Let us consider the following rule candidate mined from the gastric cancer dataset.

$r_3 : peritoneal\_meta(3) \land spec\_histologi(U) \land ln\_metastasis(4) \to d90$
    with coverage = {2, 0}, accuracy = 100%.

We can see that the coverage of the rule is very low. In order to increase the coverage, we check again the following gastric cancer data with respect to the rule:

peritoneal_meta	spec_histologi	ln_metastasis	+coverage	-coverage	accuracy
1	C	3	0	1	0%
1	A	3	1	1	50%
2	A	3	1	0	100%
3	A	1	1	0	100%
1	U	2	0	1	0%
1	U	3	1	0	100%
1	U	4	1	0	100%
2	U	1	1	0	100%
3	U	3	0	1	0%
3	U	4	2	0	100%

and use the heuristics stated above to form granules:

$peritoneal\_meta \geq 1$ from $peritoneal\_meta = 3$,
$spec\_histologi = \{A, U\}$ from $spec\_histologi = U$,
$ln\_metastasis \geq 1$ from $ln\_metastasis = 4$.

Thus, the following rule with larger coverage is formed to replace r_3.

$r_{3'}$: $peritoneal\_meta(\geq 1) \wedge spec\_histologi(A, U) \wedge ln\_metastasis(\geq 1) \rightarrow d90$
with coverage = $\{8, 3\}$, accuracy = 73%.

Example 3. By checking the following data with respect to r_4 :

depth	lymphatic_inva	ln_metastasis	+coverage	-coverage	accuracy
ss	2	2	2	19	10%
ss	2	3	2	0	100%
ss	3	2	0	21	0%
ss	others	others	0	≥ 1	0%

we can see that the accuracy and positive coverage of the rule decrease as values of attributes *lymphatic_inva* and *ln_metastasis* increase or decrease. Hence, the rule candidate is uninteresting.

r_4 : $depth(ss) \wedge lymphatic\_inva(2) \wedge ln\_metastasis(3) \rightarrow d90$
with coverage = $\{2, 0\}$, accuracy = 100%.

Table 4 shows the results of mining in gastric cancer data. The results have been evaluated by experts at Japan National Cancer Center based on acceptability and novelty of each rule. According to their opinion, most of rules are acceptable and some of them is novel.

Table 4. Analysis 2: the reasons why patients died within 90 days (1 is the lowest and 5 is the highest evaluation for acceptability (*accept*) and novelty of each rule)

No.	reasons	accuracy	accept	novelty
1	liver_meta(3) ∧ structural_atyp(≥ 1) ∧ ln_metastasis(3)	7/11=64%	4	2
2	liver_meta(3) ∧ lymphatic_inva(3) ∧ ln_metastasis(3)	4/5=80%	5	1
3	typeofcancer(B2) ∧ liver_meta(3) ∧ lymphatic_inva(3)	4/5=80%	4	4
4	typeofcancer(B4) ∧ serosal_inva(≤ 2) ∧ peritoneal_meta(3) ∧ ln_metastasis(4)	6/7=86%	4	3
5	typeofcancer(EC,B1,B2) ∧ peritoneal_meta(≥ 2) ∧ stromal_type(.) ∧ ln_metastasis(4)	7/11=64%	4	4
6	pre_oper_compP(1) ∧ pre_oper_compR(1) ∧ ln_metastasis(4)	3/4=75%	3	1
7	typeofcancer(B4) ∧ peritoneal_meta(3) ∧ maximal_diam_disc(≥ 50) ∧ pre_oper_compP(1)	3/4=75%	5	1
8	liver_meta(3) ∧ stromal_type(M) ∧ growth_pattern(3)	7/11=64%	3	2
9	serosal_inva(3) ∧ liver_meta(3) ∧ growth_pattern(3)	10/17=59%	3	1
10	pre_oper_compA(1) ∧ pre_oper_compS(1) ∧ vascular_inva(3)	2/2=100%	5	1
11	typeofcancer(B4) ∧ peritoneal_meta(3) ∧ pre_oper_compI(1)	2/2=100%	5	1
12	peritoneal_meta(≥ 1) ∧ spec_histologi(A,U) ∧ ln_metastasis(≥ 1)	8/11=73%	5	4
13	peritoneal_meta(3) ∧ pre_oper_compS(1) ∧ vascular_inva(3)	2/2=100%	5	1
14	pre_oper_compA(1) ∧ pre_oper_compP(1) ∧ depth(S3) ∧ ln_metastasis(4)	2/2=100%	4	1
15	liver_meta(≥ 2) ∧ pre_oper_compC(1) ∧ ln_metastasis(4)	6/7=86%	4	2
16	typeofcancer(EC) ∧ peritoneal_meta(≥ 2)	3/5=60%	1	5
17	spec_histologi(A) ∧ vascular_inva(3)	1/1=100%	3	3
18	pre_oper_compP(1) ∧ spec_histologi(U) ∧ ln_metastasis(4)	1/1=100%	4	1
19	serosal_inva(3) ∧ spec_histologi(S,U) ∧ cellular_atyp(≤ 2)	2/2=100%	3	2

4.2 Forming Granules of Symbolic Data in Pre-processing

We know that discretization of continuous valued attributes is an important pre-processing step in the process for rule discovery in the databases with mixed type of data including continuous valued attributes. The results of discretization affect directly the quality of the discovered rules.

In order to solve the discretization issues, we have developed a discretization system called RSBR that is based on hybridization of rough sets and Boolean reasoning proposed in [6,7,18]. RSBR combines discretization of continuous valued attributes and classification together. Thus, in the process of the discretization of continuous valued attributes, we also take into account the effect of the discretization on the performance of our rule mining system GDT-RS.

Furthermore, we observed that the discretization of continuous valued attributes is a solution to form granules not only from continuous values, but symbolic data with ordered information. In other words, symbolic data with ordered information can be regarded as continuous values. For instance, attribute *depth* (depth of invasion) with ordered information, in the gastric cancer data shown in Table 2,

$$".." \succ MM \succ SM \succ PM \succ SS \succ S1 \succ S2 \succ S3,$$

can be regarded as a data set with continuous values such as

$$\{0, 1, 2, 3, 4, 5, 6, 7\}.$$

Thus, our RSBR can be immediately applied to form granules of symbolic data in a pre-processing step.

5 Conclusions

Ordering of objects is a fundamental issue in human decision making and may play a significant role in the design of intelligent information systems. This problem is considered from the perspective of knowledge discovery and data mining. The main contribution of the paper is to show the usefulness and effectiveness of *ordered information* in many aspects of real world applications of data mining. We proposed novel ideas on using ordered information in a pre/post processing step of a discovery process for improving the quality of the mined rules.

Acknowledgements. The authors would like to thank Dr. Naohito Yamaguchi from National Cancer Center Research Institute, Dr. Hitoshi Katai, Keiichi Maruyama, Takeshi Sano, Mitsuru Sasako from National Cancer Center Hospital, for providing the gastric cancer dataset, background knowledge, and evaluating the experimental results.

References

1. Cohen W.W., Schapire R.E., and Singer Y. "Learning to Order Things", *Advances in Neural Information Processing Systems*, Vol 10 (1998).
2. Dougherty, J, Kohavi, R., and Sahami, M. "Supervised and Unsupervised Discretization of Continuous Features", *Proc. 12th Inter. Conf. on Machine Learning* (1995) 194–202.

3. Greco S., Matarazzo B., and Slowinski R. "Rough Approximation of a Preference Relation by Dominance Relations", *European Journal of Operational Research* Vol. 117 (1999) 63–83.
4. Iwinski T.B. "Ordinal Information System", *Bulletin of the Polish Academy of Sciences, Mathematics*, Vol. 36 (1998) 467–475.
5. Lin, T.Y. and Cercone, N. (ed.) *Rough Sets and Data Mining: Analysis of Imprecise Data*, Kluwer (1997).
6. Nguyen, H. Son, Skowron, A. "Boolean Reasoning for Feature Extraction Problems", Z.W. Ras, A. Skowron (eds.), *Foundations of Intelligent Systems*, LNAI 1325, Springer (1997) 117–126.
7. Nguyen H. Son and Nguyen S. Hoa "Discretization Methods in Data Mining", L. Polkowski, A. Skowron (eds.) *Rough Sets in Knowledge Discovery*, Physica-Verlag (1998) 451–482.
8. Pawlak, Z. *Rough Sets, Theoretical Aspects of Reasoning about Data*, Kluwer (1991).
9. Pawlak Z. and Slowinski R. "Rough set approach to multi-attribute decision analysis". *European Journal of Operational Research*, Vol. 72 (1994) 443–359.
10. Sai, Y., Yao, Y.Y., and Zhong, N. "Data Analysis and Mining in Ordered Information Tables", *Proc. 2001 IEEE International Conference on Data Mining (IEEE ICDM'01)*, IEEE Computer Society Press (2001) 497–504.
11. Yao, Y.Y. and Zhong, N. "Potential Applications of Granular Computing in Knowledge Discovery and Data Mining", *Proc. 5th Inter. Conf. on Information Systems Analysis and Synthesis (IASA'99)* (1999) 573–580.
12. Yao, Y.Y. "Information Tables with Neighborhood Semantics", *Data Mining and Knowledge Discovery: Theory, Tools, and Technology II*, Dasarathy, B.V. (Ed.), Society for Optical Engineering, Bellingham, Washington (2000) 108-116.
13. Yao, Y.Y. and Sai, Y. "Mining Ordering Rules Using Rough Set Theory", *Bulletin of International Rough Set Society*, Vol. 5 (2001) 99–106.
14. Zadeh, L.A. "Fuzzy Sets and Information Granularity", Gupta, N., Ragade, R., and Yager, R. (Eds.) *Advances in Fuzzy Set Theory and Applications*, North-Holland (1979) 3–18.
15. Zadeh, L. A. "Toward a Theory of Fuzzy Information Granulation and Its Centrality in Human Reasoning and Fuzzy Logic", *Fuzzy Sets and Systems*, Elsevier, Vol 90 (1997) 111–127.
16. Zhong, N., Dong, J.Z., and Ohsuga, S. "Using Background Knowledge as a Bias to Control the Rule Discovery Process", Djamel A. Zighed, Jan Komorowski, and J. Zytkow (eds.) *Principles of Data Mining and Knowledge Discovery*. LNAI 1910, Springer (2000) 691–698.
17. Zhong, N., Dong, J.Z., and Ohsuga, S. "Rule Discovery by Soft Induction Techniques", *Neurocomputing, An International Journal*, Vol. 36 (1-4) Elsevier (2001) 171–204.
18. Zhong, N. and Skowron, A. "A Rough Sets Based Knowledge Discovery Process", *International Journal of Applied Mathematics and Computer Science*, Vol. 11, No. 3, Technical University Press, Poland (2001) 101–117.

A Granular Approach for Analyzing the Degree of Affability of a Web Site

Esther Hochsztain[1], Socorro Millán[2], and Ernestina Menasalvas[*,3]

[1] Universidad ORT UDELAR. Uruguay, `esthoc@adinet.com.uy`
[2] Universidad del Valle. Cali Colombia, `millan@eisc.univalle.edu.co`;
[3] Facultad de Informática, U.P.M., Madrid, Spain, `emenasalvas@fi.upm.es`

Abstract. Due to the competitive environment in which we are moving, web sites need to be very attractive for visitors. In this paper we propose an approach to analyze and determine the level of affability of a web site that tends to secure user's satisfaction, based on both the kind of page and the kind of user. We propose a granular approach based on the idea that a page can be considered as a set of features or factors. In fact, each of them can be perceived at different granularity levels. The proposed approach makes it possible to estimate a measure of affinity of a user for each level of each particular factor. On any particular page, each factor takes a certain level or value. The global measure of affinity for a certain page will be calculated jointly considering the levels or values that the attributes of this particular page have for each design factor.

Keywords: Data mining, web mining, granular approach, design factors, page utility

1 Introduction

The number of web sites has increased considerably, as they have become the communication channel on many activities for millions of users all over the world. For any kind of activity in mind there are lots of choices offered by different web sites. The web has become such a competitive environment that the owners of sites need to make pages eye-catching to its visitors. In particular, e-commerce has been growing so rapidly that companies have seen the need to introduce data mining, personalization and e-CRM solutions to be able to survive [PM01]. It has become necessary for them to customize their web sites according to it's user's behavioral patterns [AGJ00, Ga01].

In order to solve this particular problem several approaches, based on navigational analysis, have been proposed. Proposals to explore web usage mining have been developed to improve web site structure. Both include models, algorithms systems and techniques to analyze web server mainly based on data mining techniques, statistics and data warehousing.

---

[*] This project has been partially supported thanks to Universidad Politecnica of Madrid

A framework for web mining is proposed in [MJHS97] in which data and transactions models for association rules and sequential patterns are presented together with a web mining system called WEBMINER, based upon the proposed framework. The Association Rules Model is also used in [LAR00] as an underlying technique for collaborative recommendation systems. In [GS00] a new algorithm of A priori type is proposed to mine all generalized subsequences of user navigation paths. In [MMP+02] user sessions are studied in order to find subsessions or subsequences of clicks that are semantically related and reflect a particular behavior of the user even within the same session. A model usable for both anonymous and online analysis is proposed in [SFKFF01]. According to the authors, it is flexible, tunable, and adaptable.

A statistical model to capture user behavior when browsing the web is proposed in [BM00]. In [KNY00] techniques to help web site publishers find ineffective pages on web sites are proposed. The techniques are useful to find the gaps between web site publisher expectations and user behavior. Based on data warehousing techniques Andersen et al. [AGJ00] model clickstream data. The subsession fact table they propose can be used for capturing explicit sequences of clicks and for performing new kinds of analyses useful for the company web site.

In [SFBF00], a path clustering technique based on the similarity of the history of user navigation is presented. Although a lot of approaches have been proposed, getting to know most frequent users' paths is not enough; it is necessary to integrate web mining and the organization site goals in order to make more competitive sites. Intelligent Web mining can harness the huge potential of clickstream data and supply business critical decisions together with personalized Web interactions [MJHS97]. However, data have to be enhanced with information about the business. According to [PM01], today, unless you can demonstrate profits, you are not likely to make it or survive. In order to offer an alternative solution to that problem in [HM02], an algorithm to improve the traditional web analysis is proposed. It focuses on business and its goals, integrates server logs analysis with both the background from the business goals and business area available knowledge in order to determine a user's session value.

In order to design attractive pages, different aspects can be taken into consideration and one of the main challenges is to find the most relevant features that will make pages eye-catching. Once this problem is solved, the second challenge is to find a model to quantify any of the concepts identified as relevant. The problem would probably be solved with a model that considers both the features and their quantification, and accounts for both different user profiles and different kinds of pages. Considering that different domains (i.e. educational, business, administration, government) can be distinguished in the web, the proposed methodology will include aspects common to any web domain.

The web site designer will have to act depending on the working domain. Thus, there are design decisions that cannot be defined in a generic way. In this sense, we will have to distinguish types of pages (i.e. e-commerce, information) and user profiles and features (i.e. ability to use computers, performing arts education). Regardless of the working domain, the main purpose of the present work is to provide site administrators with a methodology to establish the degree of affability of a web site, which in the long run, might help them design attractive pages and web sites. An answer to the question " Which pages attract users' attention most?" will facilitate adaptive web sites construction and predict the behavior of site visitors according to their profiles and the visited pages in a session. It will make it possible to attach pages design to web site business targets.

To identify features that increase pages affability will certainly include features usually taken into consideration in web sites design. Aspects never used or considered irrelevant before will be included. The latter will certainly help improve sites quality considering that different users have different tastes, likes and dislikes, page affability can be associated with user profiles (i.e. education, sex, age, hobbies, religion). Thus the proposed methodology needs to consider target users in order to adapt new feature findings to user's profiles. Web usage patterns analysis can be relevant in order to identify features that attract users. Assume for instance that users visit more frequently those pages that attract them either because of their design or because of its information contents. Our task is to discover the value a user assigns to a web site and/or to a page.

We are proposing a granular approach to discover the value a user assigns to a page, quantifying each of the involved design options using a decomposition approach of the value. The main idea that underlies the proposed methodology is as follows: a visitor evaluates the value of a page combining separate values that unconsciously assigns to certain features of the page. Web page utility from the user's viewpoint is a subjective judgment. It represents a global preference for the web page. This user's preference is the conceptual framework for measuring a web page value.

In our proposal, we assume that the value (utility) of a page is based on the individual values assigned to each design factor, that can be taken into account in page design. Thus, by adding individual values we will obtain the joint utility of the page. Those pages with higher utility values will be considered more attractive and we will assume they will have higher probability to be chosen.

The rest of the paper is organized as follows. Section 2 presents the methodology to calculate web pages utility. Section 3 shows how the methodology can be used. Section 4 presents the conclusions and future research lines.

2 Methodology to Calculate Web Pages Utility

We propose a methodological approach based on estimating the utility that a page has for a certain user. Our proposal uses multivariate joint analysis [HA+98] [GC+89] for the construction of the model and for estimating its parameters but several adjustments have to be made as we are dealing with a non experimental design.

A model to explain user's behavior will be designed. The dependent variable (y) is the time a user stays on a page. We assume that there is a direct relationship between this time and the affability of the page, that is to say that the longer the user stays on a page the more he likes it.

We will also consider that the permanence time is dependent both on the design alternatives and the contents of the page. We want to discover how to design pages so that permanence time increases.

We consider design factors those elements that can be modified while designing the page. Each factor can be studied using different values or levels. Among the factors that could be taken into account we can consider:

- The kind of images the page contains: static (level 1), dynamic (level 2)
- Background color: smooth (level 1), strong (level 2)
- The kind of language used: technical (level 1), colloquial (level2)
- Font size: big (level 1), small (level 2)

Note that although only two levels for each factor have been suggested many more could be considered. What is required is that only one level at a time is assigned to a page for a given factor. We will build a model that explains the permanence time taking into account the design factors.

The average value (μ) of the permanence time can increase or decrease depending on the levels considered for each factor (β_{ab}). Thus, the parameters β have 2 sub-indexes: the first one identifies the factor and the second one the level of such a factor. An error rate (ε) is also considered. Considering three design factors the model would look like: $y_{ijk} = \mu + \beta_{1i} + \beta_{2j} + \beta_{3k} + \varepsilon_{ijk}$

In order to calculate the permanence time, the parameters of the model μ, β_{1i}, β_{2j} and β_{3k} are estimated with $\hat{\mu}$, $\hat{\beta}_{1i}$, $\hat{\beta}_{2j}$, $\hat{\beta}_{3k}$ respectively. Where i, j and k range from 1 to the number of levels of the factors 1, 2 and 3 respectively. The values of $\hat{\beta}_{1i}$, $\hat{\beta}_{2j}$, $\hat{\beta}_{3k}$ for each level are used to estimate if the permanence time increases or decreases depending on the design alternatives used on a page.

The estimation procedure can be metric or non metric depending on whether the method used to transform the dependent variable is lineal or monotonic. Depending on the specified model the parameters estimation may require iterations. The utility of a page will be calculated based on the value of each of the possible factors that influence its design (levels of attributes). A function that determines the utility of a page based on different combinations of attributes will be proposed. Thus, pages with higher utility values are more attractive and consequently will be more probably chosen.

Data gathering

Analyzing site visitors behavior, particularly their decisions while visiting a page, information concerning the relevance of each page design factor can be obtained. Thus, each page can be evaluated taking into consideration different attributes that take different values (levels) in its design. The traditional methodology of joint analysis [HA+98] is based on experimental design in which different options are presented to a person. These options are combinations of attributes each having different levels. The user reveals a global preference for each of the individual options. Our proposal is based on this methodology but, in our case, instead of designing an experiment to consult the user, the web server logs are analyzed.

Due to the fact that in our proposal neither independent variables are used nor there is an entity (person) controlling the users, a non experimental design has been considered. In fact, our design is an "expost facto" design (after the facts have occurred) because primarily, the result will be observed and secondly, the presumptively causal factor of the effect is calculated.

Attribute identification

The following methods can be used to identify relevant attributes in a web page:
1. Expert advice to choose the relevant features.
2. Qualitative methods, generally based on a small number of interviewed persons. These methods can be based on focus groups or personal interviews.
3. Experimental identification. The latter is used for our purposes. First, we use the proposed technique considering all the possible design factors of a web page in order to identify the most relevant ones. Secondly, only the most relevant attributes will be taken into consideration. To apply this method we require a particular web site containing pages with different design criteria. This procedure can be described as follows:

Independent variables:
1. Identify design factors.
2. Describe values for each design factor.
3. Describe web pages in function of these levels.

Each page will be then characterized as a list of value pairs of the form:
(factor1-level$_{1x}$, factor2-level$_{2y}$, ... , , factork-level$_{ky}$)

Dependent Variable

Obtain measurements of the response variable on that page. We should be able to analyze the permanence time on that page, the number of clicks, etc.

Estimation process

User's utility for each factor level is estimated. These partial estimations of individual factor levels will be used to calculate global utility estimation of the page. Preliminary concepts considered in the experiment are:
- Target population: user of given pages
- Experimental unit: the user's visit to the site
- Parameters: features of the page (kind of page, main goal, abilities required)
- Response variables (dependent variables): the utility of a page.
- Factors (independent variables): features that affect dependent variables. A factor is a design attribute (i.e. type of images on a page, font size). We are interested in identifying factor impact, defined as design attribute's utility. Alternatives for identifying factors have been already mentioned.
- Levels: different values an independent variable can take (i.e. images on a page can be static or dynamic, font size can be bigger or smaller).

3 Example

The following is an example of parameters estimation using the method of joint metric analysis. The results will be analyzed too. Page design factors (independent variables of the model) and their corresponding levels are the ones in table 1.

Table 1. Sample factors and levels

FACTOR		Level 1	Level 2
β_1	Images kind	β_{11} =static	β_{12} = dynamic
β_2	Font size	β_{21} =big	β_{22} = small
β_3.	Background color	β_{31} =smooth	β_{32} = strong

Assuming the following data related to the utility a user has assigned to different combinations of the three design factors.

Table 2. Sample Data

Image Kind	Font Size	Background Color	Time
Static	big	smooth	15
Static	big	strong	12
Static	small	smooth	12
Static	small	strong	8
Dynamic	big	smooth	18
Dynamic	Big	strong	16
Dynamic	Small	smooth	18
Dynamic	Small	strong	14

The parameters of $y_{ijk} = \mu + \beta_{1i} + \beta_{2j} + \beta_{3k} + \varepsilon_{ijk}$ are estimated considering the following restrictions $\beta_{11} + \beta_{12} = \beta_{21} + \beta_{22} = \beta_{31} + \beta_{32} = 0$. The error term is ε_{ijk}. Utilities sum zero within each attribute. The metric conjoint analysis creates a main-effect design matrix from the specified variables.

The ANOVA table provides a rough indication of the fit of the conjoint model. Its results are, at best, approximate since the normality and independence assumptions are violated. In this example, R^2= 0.94436 and Adjusted R^2 = 0.9026.

The obtained output is each factor's estimated relevance as well as that of each of the corresponding levels. The next table represents each attribute's estimated relevance.

Table 3. Factor importance estimates

FACTOR		IMPORTANCE
β_1	Images Kind	46.342%
β_2	Font Size	21.951 %
β_3.	Background Color	31.707%

The utility pattern shows the most preferred attribute levels. Levels with positive utility are preferred over those with negative utility. In Table 3, we can see that the kind of predominant image is the most relevant feature, the next relevant feature is the background color and the last one, font size. The estimate of the intercept $\hat{\mu}$ is 14.250. Estimation of the utility of each factor levels is presented in table 4.

Table 4. Factor levels estimates

FACTOR		Level 1	Utility Estimate	Level 2	Utility Estimate
β_1	Images Kind	β_{11}static	$\hat{\beta}_{11} = -2.375$	β_{12}dynamic	$\hat{\beta}_{12} = +2.375$
β_2	Font Size	β_{21}big	$\hat{\beta}_{21} = +1.125$	β_{22}small	$\hat{\beta}_{22} = -1.125$
β_3	Background Color	β_{31}smooth	$\hat{\beta}_{31} = +1.625$	β_{32}strong	$\hat{\beta}_{11} = -1.625$

The positive value $\hat{\beta}_{12} = +2.375$ in a dynamic image shows the preference for this kind of images in contrast to the negative value $\hat{\beta}_{11} = -2.375$ for static images. Proceeding similarly with the rest of attributes we can say that the preferred values are dynamic images, big size and smooth background. For the most preferred Images Kind/Font Size/Background Color combination, estimated utility and actual preference values are 14,125 + 2,375 + 1,125 + 1,625 = 19,25 = $\hat{y} \approx y = 18$. For the least preferred combination, utility and actual preference values are 14,125+ -2,375+ -1,125 + -1,625 = 9 25 = $\hat{y} \approx y = 8$. Utility can be considered as regression predicted values. The squared correlation between the utility for each combination and the actual time is R^2. The importance value is computed from the utility range for each factor (attribute). Each range is divided by the sum of all ranges and multiplied by 100. Factors with the largest utility ranges are the most important in determining time estimates.

4 Conclusions

We have presented a methodology to estimate page utility based on combinations of page design factors. We have shown that it is possible to estimate the utility of different design alternatives of a web page. It is assumed that users will stay longer on those pages they find to be more interesting.

The main result of our approach is that web pages can be parameterized taking into account different design factors and can be dynamically designed to adapt to user's preferences (estimated along the session of a user). Thus, the proposed approach enables web page designers to make decisions concerning the best layout as they become aware of the relative contributions of each page attribute to the affability of such a page. The designer can estimate the best combination of attributes for a particular page.

The approach also considers information on user profiles related to preference for certain kind of pages. This allows for the design of pages for groups of users if designers know in advance the segments of users that will be highly potential visitors of the page. Thus, users preference for a page can be taken into account in adaptive web mining algorithms.

The proposed methodology is the first approach to the problem. We are currently experimenting with more design factors in order to improve the methodology.

References

[AGJ00] Andersen J., Giversen A., Jensen A. Larse R., Bach T., Skyt J. Analysing clickstreams using subsessions. Proc. DOLAP-OO, pp. 25–32, 2000.

[BM00] Borges J., Levene M. A fine grained heuristic to capture web navigation patterns. SIGKDD Exploration, 2(1) pp 40–50, 2000.

[CY00] Chang Wei-Lun, Yuan Soe-Tsyr. A synthesized Learning Approach for Web-Based CRM. Working Notes of Workshop on Web Mining for E-commerce: Challenges and Opportunities. August 20, 2002 Boston USA pp. 43–59

[GS00] G. Wolfang, Schmidt-Thieme Lars. Mining web navigation path fragments. Workshop on Web Mining for E-Commerce – Challenges and Opportunities. Working notes pp. 105–110. Kdd-2000, August 20,2000, Boston, MA.

[Ga01] J. Gajan Rajakulendran. Personalised Electronic Customer Relationships: Improving The Quality of Data Within Web Clickstreams - Individual Project (MSc) – Newcastle University (UK) & Universidad Politecnica Madrid. Supervisor: E. Menasalvas (UPM)

[GA96] I. Grande, E. Abascal - Fundamentos y Técnicas de Investigación Comercial - ESIC - España 1996

[GC+89] Paul E. Green, Frank J. Carmone, JR. Scott M. Smith. Multidimensional Scaling Concepts and applications – Allyn and Bacon – A Division of Simon & Schuster, USA 1989.

[HK01] Han J., Kamber M. Data Mining: Concepts nad Techniques. Acadc. Press, USA 2001

[HA+98] Joseph F. Hair, Jr, Rolph E. Anderson, Ronald L. Tathan, William C. Black. Multivariate Data Analysis. Prentice Hall USA 1988

[HM02] Hochztain E., Menasalvas E. Sessions value as measure of web site goal achievement. In Procc. SNPD'02. June 2002-Madrid

[KNY00] Kato H., Nakayama T., Yamane Y. Navigation Analysis Tool based on the Correlation between Contents Distribution and Access Patterns. Workshop on Web Mining for E-Commerce – Challenges and Opportunities Kdd-2000, August 2000, Boston, MA

[LAR00] L. Weiyang, Alvarez S., Ruiz C.. Collaborative Recommendation via Adaptative Association Rule Mining. Working Notes of Workshop on Web Mining for E-commerce: Challenges and Opportunities. 2002 Boston USA pp. 35–41

[MB+97] Salvador Miquel, E. Bigné, J.P. Lévy, A. C. Cuenca, Mª José Miguel. Investigación de Mercados-Mc Graw-Hill /Interamericana de España, 1997

[MJHS97] Mobasher B., Jain N., Han, E-H., Srivastava J. Web Mining: Pattern Discovery from World Wide Web Transactions. In International Conference on Tools with Artificial Intelligence, pp. 558–567, New Port 1997

[MMP+02] Menasalvas E., Millán S., Peña J., Hadjimichael M., Marbán O. Subsessions: a granular approach to click path analysis. In Proc. WICI'02

[PM01] Gregory Piatetsky-Shapiro 2001: Interview with Jesus Mena, (WebMiner)

[SFBF00] Shahabi C., Faisal A., Banaei F., Faruque J. INSITE: A tool for real-time knowledge Discovery from users web navigation. Proc. VLDB-2000, 2000.

[SFKFF01] Shahabi C., F. Banaiei-Kashaani, J. Faruque, A. Faisal. Feature Matrices: A model for e-Ecient and anonymous web usage mining. Proc. of EC-Web 2001.

Comparison of Classification Methods for Customer Attrition Analysis

Xiaohua Hu

DMW Software, 504 E. Hillsdale Ct., San Mateo, CA 94403, USA
xiaohua_hu@acm.org

Abstract. In this paper, we present a data mining approach for analyzing retailing bank customer attrition. We discuss the challenging issues such as highly skewed data, time series data unrolling, leaker field detection etc, and the procedure of a data mining project for the attrition analysis for retailing bank. We explain the advantages of lift as a proper measure for attrition analysis and compare the lift of data mining models of decision tree, boosted naïve Bayesian network, selective Bayesian network, neural network and the ensemble of classifiers of the above methods. Some interesting findings are reported. Our research work demonstrates the effectiveness and efficiency of data mining in attrition analysis for retailing bank.

1 Introduction

In this paper we discuss on applying data mining techniques to help retailing banks for the attrition analysis. The goal of attrition analysis is to identify a group of customers who have a high probability to attrite, and then the company can conduct marketing campaigns to change the behavior in the desired direction (change their behavior, reduce the attrition rate). If the data mining model is good enough and target criteria are well defined, the company can contact a much small group of people with a high concentration of potential attriters [7]. The paper is organized as follow: we first define the problem and formulation of business problems in the area of customer retention, data review and initial, then data gathering, cataloging and formatting, data unfolding and time-sensitive variable definition. Then we discuss sensitivity analysis, feature selection and leaker detection. Next we describe data modeling via decision trees, neural networks, Bayesian networks, selective Bayesian network and an ensemble of classifier with the above four methods. Finally we conclude with our findings and next steps.

2 Business Problem

Our client is one of the leading retailing banks in the US. It offers many type of financial retail products to various customers. The product we discussed in this paper belongs to certain type of loan service. Over 750,000 customers currently use this service with $1.5 billion in outstanding, the product has had significant losses. Revenue is constantly challenged by a high attrition rate: every month, the call centers receive over 4500 calls from customers wishing to close their accounts. This, in addition to approximately 1,200 write-ins, "slow" attriters (no balance shown over 12 consecutive months) and pirated accounts constitutes a serious challenge to the profitability of the product, which totals about 5,700/month mostly due to rate, credit line, and fees. In addition to that, many customers will use the product as long as the introductory or "teaser" rate (currently at 4.9%) is in effect and lapse thereafter. There are different types of attriters in the product line:

- Slow attriters: Customers who slowly pay down their outstanding balance until they become inactive. Attrition here is understood comprehensively, where voluntary attrition can show more than one behavior.
- Fast attriters: Customers who quickly pay down their balance and either lapse it or close it via phone call or write in.

The focus of the modeling process, and subsequent campaigns, will revolve around the resolution of retention of Existing Customers. The problem requires the stratification of customer segments by leveraging current segmentation model in order to:

- Develop models that predict the customers who are likely to attrite within 30 to 60 days on an ongoing basis.
- Identify the characteristics of the most profitable/desirable customer segments in order to develop policies to ensure their continued support, to grow the group, and to acquire more customers with similar characteristics.

2.1 Data Preprocessing Goals

The data preprocessing state consists of the series of activities necessary to create a compacted file that:

- Reflects data changes over time.
- Recognizes and removes statistically insignificant fields
- Defines and introduces the "target" field
- Allows for second stage preprocessing and statistical analysis.

This was accomplished through three steps, detailed in the sections below:

- Time series "unrolling"
- Target value definition

Time Series "Unrolling" and Target Field Definition

In our application, historical customers records are used to group customers into two classes – those who are attriters and those who are not. In order to save space, every month a query checks every field against the previous month. If there is no change, no rows are added and the value of Effective Start Date (EFF_START_DT) remains as that during which a change was last recorded (which is the same as "a new row was inserted"). If any attribute changes, a whole new row is added with the corresponding EFF_START_DT updated. The data format used required for the implicit data to be made explicit and the time periods to be itemized into individual fields. To accomplish this, the time sensitive variables were assigned a time prefix. So, for example, the variable *CURRENT_BALANCE* for the period of December 2001 to March 2002 is redefined as:

Table 1. Naming Convention for Time Sensitive DDS Data for the 4 months Period

Period	Nomenclature
Current Month (March 2002)	T0_BALANCE
One Month Back (Feb 2002)	T1_BALANCE
Two Month Back (Jan 2002)	T2_BALANCE
Three Month Back (Dec 2001)	T3_BALANCE

Like many real data mining applications, normally there is no data mining target field defined directly in the data warehouse. It is part of the data mining procedure to define the proper target field based on the business objective for the data mining analysis. With the help of the business domain experts, we define the target value in terms of existing data and, with these, define the value of the target variable, i.e., the variable that determines the voluntary attriters, hereby defined as **VA_ACCTS**. It is defined in terms of:
1. Status_code (*CRD_ST_CD*)
2. Status_change_date *(CRD_STATUS_CHANGE_DATE)*
3. Closed_reason_code (*CRD_CLS_REA_CD*)

According to this definition, the average attrition rate for the section of the data received is 2.2% of all customers for 4 months time period

First stage statistical analysis

The statistical analysis, the first in a series, is done in order to obtain an initial understanding of the data quality: number of unknown fields, relative frequency, early indicators, averages and target data distribution. As an initial field discrimination step, the fields where a single value appeared in more than 99.8% of all records was deemed statistically insignificant and removed from the set of attributes. These fields are removed from both the data and metadata files to ensure their removal from the modeling process, thus reducing the computing time required.

2.2 Data Premodeling

The data premodeling stage is the next critical step in the generation of the files used for modeling. This stage consists of three main steps, namely: (1) field sensitivity analysis to filter fields with low correlation to target the field and detect data *"leakers"*, (2) field reduction to create a compacted file with highly relevant fields, (3) file set generation of all balanced and unbalanced sets required for training, testing and iterative verification of results and model refinement. The field sensitivity analysis is used to determine each attribute's "contribution" to the modeling process. Using a customized program, each field can be used to predict the target value in order to determine its impact on the predicted value. When the relative value is low, the field can conceivably be removed from the set. On the other hand, a field whose accuracy is very high, it is considered to be a potential *leaker*. Leakers are fields that "leak" information on the target. For example, a field with a value representing account closure could leak information on attrition, and would confound modeling efforts.

While some leakers are readily explained, many times they are included in business rules whose relation to the target is not apparent. In this case, the best way to determine if a field is indeed a leaker is to discuss the findings with those familiar with the data schema and the business problem. In many circumstances, field names and values are not always representative of their function, and need clarification. One the other hand, fields that are suspected but turn out *not* to be leakers constitute potential predictors in the model. Using our homegrown feature selection component, results from the field sensitivity analysis can be used to discard fields that provide very little contribution to the prediction of the target field. Contribution is defined by the accuracy of the single field prediction. A threshold accuracy of 45% was used to discard fields (i.e.: fields with a predicted error rate greater than 45% were discarded). In some cases, the values for a field are constant (i.e.: have a standard deviation of zero) and thus have no predictive value. These fields should be removed in order to improve data mining processing speed and to generate better models. For example, through this effort, the initial set of 309 attributes in the data set was reduced to 242 after processing. Our sample file comprises of 45814 records, based on the historical data of the recent 4 months, the attrition rate is around 2.2%. In order to build a good model from this highly skewed data set, we need to build a more balanced representation of attriters and non-attriters in the training data set. The reason is that in the original data file, we have high non-attriters percentage (98%) vs. a very low attriter rate (2%); a learning model can achieve high accuracy by always predicting every customer to be a non-attriters. Obviously, such a high accurate model is useless for our attrition analysis. We created a random sample file where we include about 938 attriters and then we add enough non-attriters into it to make it a dataset with 50-50 percentage of each class category (attriters vs non-attriters), then file was divided into *balanced, train* and *test* files as well as *raw* (i.e., unbalanced) *test* and *held aside* files for verification purpose. The *balanced train file* consisted of 50% of the records containing target values, i.e., for whom VA_ACCTs=1. The *balanced test, raw test*, and *raw held aside files* consisted of approximately 1/6 of the targets each. As defined earlier in Section 2.3.2, targets in the raw files represent 2% of the total number of records for the files being reviewed. These files were handed over to the data mining component for further statistical analysis, data mining and clustering work.

3 Model Development Process

As pointed in [5,6,7], prediction accuracy, which was used to evaluate the machine learning algorithm, cannot be used as a suitable evaluation criterion for the data mining application such as attrition analysis. The main reason is that classification errors (false negative, false positive) must be dealt with differently. So it is required that learning algorithms need to classify with a confidence measurement, such as a probability estimation factor or certainty factor (also called scores in attrition analysis). The scores will allow us to rank customers for promotion or targeting marketing. Lift instead of the predictive accuracy is used as an evaluation criterion. As pointed in [5], if the data mining model is good enough, we should find a high concentration of attriters at the top of the list and this higher proportion of attriters can be measured in terms of "lift" to see how much better than random the model-based targeting is. Generally, lift can be calculated by looking at the cumulative targets captured up to p% as a percentage of all targets and dividing by p% [6]. For example, the top 10% of the sorted list may contain 35% of likely attriters, then the model has a lift of 35/10=3.5. A lift reflects the redistribution of responders in the testing set after the testing examples are ranked. After the learning algorithm ranks all testing examples from most likely responders to least likely responders, we divide the ranked list into some deciles, and see how the original responders distributed in these deciles. We need to use learning algorithms that can produce scores in order to rank the testing examples. Algorithms such as Naïve Bayesian, decision tree, neural network satisfy our requirement. We performed several data mining analyses using four different data mining algorithms and an ensemble of classifiers. These are:

1. Boosted Naïve Bayesian (BNB)
2. NeuralWare Predict (a commercial neural network from NeuralWare Inc)
3. Decision Tree (based on C4.5 with some modification)
4. Selective Naïve Bayesian (SNB).

Pct	Cases	Hits Boosted BN	Lift	Hits decision tree	Lift	Hits No model
1	70	3	1.9	6	3.9	1.5
5	354	33	4.2	25	4.0	7.8
10	709	62	4.0	47	3.8	15.6
15	1063	71	3.0	56	4.0	23.4
20	1418	78	2.5	60	3.8	31.2
30	2127	100	2.1	95	3.0	46.8

PCT	Cases	Hits Neural Net	Lift	Hits SelectiveBN	Lift	Hits No model
1	70	9	5.8	5	3.2	1.5
5	354	41	5.3	34	4.4	7.8
10	709	53	3.4	69	4.4	15.6
15	1063	73	3.1	83	3.5	23.4
20	1418	86	2.8	92	2.9	31.2
30	2127	116	2.5	112	2.4	46.8

4 Conclusion

In this paper, we present a data mining approach for retailing bank customer attrition analysis. We discuss the challenging issues such as highly skewed data, time series data unrolling, leaker field detection etc, and procedure of a data mining task for the attrition analysis for retailing bank. We discuss the use of lift as a proper measure for attrition analysis and compare the lift of data mining model of decision tree, boosted naïve Bayesian network, selective Bayesian network, neural network and the ensemble of class of the above methods. Our initial findings show some interesting results. Next step, based on above results and new source files available on segmentation, we will review the voluntary attrition trends on a segment-by-segment basis. A thorough clustering study is planned for the data to review the natural grouping of the data and how it lines up with the segmentation in terms of incidence, variables and number of groups.

References

1. Bhattacharya S., "Direct Marketing Response Models Using Genetic Algorithms", Proc. of the 4th International Conference on Knowledge Discovery and Data Mining, pp144–148
2. Elkan, C. Boosted and Naïve Bayesian Learning. Technical Report No. CS97-557, September 1997, UCSD.
3. Hughes, A. M., The Complete database marketer: second-generation strategies and techniques for tapping the power of your customer database. Chicago, IL: Irwin Professional
4. Ling C, Li C, "Data Mining for Direct Marketing: Problem and Solutions", Proc. Of the 4th International Conference on Knowledge Discovery & Data Mining,
5. Masand B., Piatetsky-Shapiro G., "A Comparison of Approaches for Maximizing Business Payoff of Prediction Models", Proc. Of the 2nd International Conference on Knowledge Discovery and Data Mining
6. Piatetsky-Shapiro G. , Masand B., "Estimating Campaign Benefits and Modeling Lift", Proc. Of the 5th SIGKDD International Conference on Knowledge Discovery and Data Mining, pp185–193
7. Provost, F., and Fawcett T., "Analysis and Visualization of Classifiers Performance: Comparison Under Imprecise Class and Cost Distribution", Proc. Of the 3rd International Conference on Knowledge Discovery and Data Mining, pp 43–48

User Profile Model: A View from Artificial Intelligence

Yuefeng Li[1] and Y.Y. Yao[2]

[1] School of Software Engineering and Data Communications
Queensland University of Technology, Brisbane QLD 4001 Australia
y2.li@qut.edu.au
[2] Department of Computer Science
University of Regina Regina, Saskatchewan S4S 0A2 Canada
yyao@cs.uregina.ca

Abstract. The goal of this paper is to develop a user profile model for agent-based information filtering. We try to formalize the whole process of information filtering from an Artificial Intelligence point view. This research is related to develop novel techniques for interactive information gathering with the application of Artificial Intelligence, and Information Retrieval technologies. In this paper, we present a dynamical model to represent user profiles. We describe the user profiles as random sets on a concept space (taxonomy). We also present a rough set based qualitative decision model for the task of information filtering.

1 Introduction

One of the very important and difficult problems for information filtering is the representation of user profiles [3]. This research area currently receives strong attention from both communities of Information Retrieval (IR) and Artificial Intelligence (AI). Traditional information retrieval has been developed to overcome these problems [1]. Some AI techniques have been used in the case of uncertainty or vague information in the queries. The information filtering now is an important track of TREC (Text REtrieval Conference). The basic idea of filtering model in TREC is to use a big set of feedback documents (or called "training set") which include some relevant or irrelevant documents that have been decided by users. The filtering models observe the score on the training set and decide a threshold to group the documents into two categories: relevant and irrelevant.

The advantage of IR-based information filtering systems is that they can quickly search in specified collections to respond to users' queries. They do not pay more attention about the semantic parts of the filtering models. The earlier attempt of AI based techniques for information filtering systems was based on rule-based system. Later, machine-learning techniques are used to generate user profiles.

To decrease the burden of on-line learning, a decomposing model is presented in [3]. This method first classifies the incoming document into some groups, then selects top documents in each groups. This method uses the technique of clustering. The semantics of groups in this method is not clear for applications. For this reason, a rough set based model is presented in [2]. In this model, the user information need is viewed as a rough set on the document space, and the classification is made on a concept space that is used by the user. The precondition of this model is that the users should provide structures for their information need.

In this paper, we try to formalize the whole process of information filtering from an AI point view. We will discuss the semantics aspect of the problem of information filtering. For this purpose, we present a dynamical model to represent user profiles in the case of different importance, which uses both user feedback and activities. We also view the task filtering is a problem of qualitative decisions.

2 Formalization of User Profiles

It is probably best to let the users describe his/her profiles on a concept space. However, often the user does not have the requisite technical knowledge to describe her/his profiles, or simply the user often prefers not to have to do so. Therefore, learning user profiles from their activities and feedback is the preferred and more practical approach.

Let $FB = \{f_1, f_2, ..., f_m\}$ be a set of documents which are the feedback of a user or a group of users. Each document supplies an individual opinion that specifies which class (category) is relevant to the user information need. The feedback documents may have different importance according the user's activities. The more times access, the more important.

Suppose that feedback document f_i ($i = 1, ..., m$) supplies the opinion that the user information need is relevant to the lexical category (class, or concept) X on a taxonomy (or a concept space). We assume there is a Keywords-list, K, over the taxonomy. The opinion of feedback document f_i can be described by the following set-valued mapping:

$$\Gamma: FB \to 2^K - \{\emptyset\};$$
$$\Gamma(f_i) = \begin{cases} X \text{ if } f_i \text{ indexed the user information need using } X \\ K \text{ otherwise} \end{cases}$$

The purpose of we using the mapping Γ is to describe the user feedback information, where, the lexical category means this concept is relevant to the user information need. If a document cannot be indexed as a concept on the Keywords-list, we simply assume that only K, the Keywords-list, is relevant. In fact, the Keywords-list should be expanded in case of non-indexed documents existing. It, however, is beyond the scope of this research.

Given feedback documents, the knowledge encoded by mapping Γ is fixed for the given K. However the degrees of importance of feedback documents will change when the user changes her/his interests. So, the only thing that we cannot describe clearly at this moment is the degrees of importance.

To aggregate the user's activities, we should discuss the problem of finding suitable weights for the feedback documents. To clarify the idea let us consider a set Ω containing k "activities" each of which is equally important, where an activity is opening a feedback document. So there is a point-wise project mapping $\theta : \Omega \to FB$. If we imagine these activities voting on some motion, then the weight of some "party" $Y \in \Omega$ is given by $|Y|$. So selecting activities $\omega \in \Omega$ randomly would yield, in a long run, members of Y in ($\frac{1}{k}|Y| \cdot 100$)% of all cases. Thus we can consider $P(Y) = \frac{1}{k}|Y|$ to be the probability of Y. Thus the weight of each $f \in FB$ is given by the probability of the set of $\{\omega \in \Omega \mid \theta(\omega) = f\}$. That is we can interpret the importance weights of feedback documents as probabilities. So we assume that there is a probability function Pr on FB, which describes the degrees of importance of feedback documents. This probability can be used to decide the membership of feedback documents in FB.

Based on the above analysis, we can use a random set (Γ, Pr) as the basic represent model for user profiles. The next step is finding an efficient computational procedure (a filtering model) to find the relevant documents according to what (a random set) we have known.

3 Decision Model

Based on the above assumptions, we can define a function m_R to replace the random set (Γ, Pr) when we build a filtering model:

$$m_R : 2^K \to [0, 1];$$
$$m_R(A) = \begin{cases} 0, & \text{if } A = \emptyset; \\ Pr(\{b \mid b \in FB, \Gamma(b) = A\}), & \text{otherwise} \end{cases}$$

It is easy to prove m_R is a Dempster-Shafer mass function.

In [2] the user information need is a rough set on the document space. So it is a nature way to classify the incoming documents into three groups. We call the first group is the positive region, in which every document is treated as relevant documents. The second group is called the boundary region, in which each document is possible relevant. The last group is called negative region, in which every document is non-relevant.

In the terms of the decision models, we use a set of actions $A_d = \{a_1, a_2, a_3\}$ to represent the three decision actions:

$$a_1 = \text{deciding } d \in POS(X_R)$$
$$a_2 = \text{deciding } d \in BND(X_R)$$
$$a_3 = \text{deciding } d \in NEG(X_R)$$

where, d is the current document under consideration, X_R is the user information need, $POS(X_R)$ is the positive region, $BND(X_R)$ is the boundary region, and $NEG(X_R)$ is the negative.

By using the mass function m_R, we can define the positive, boundary, and negative regions as follows:

$POS(X_R) = \{d | \exists b \in FB \text{ such that } LIB(C_d) \supseteq LIB(\Gamma(b))\}$
$BND(X_R) = \{d | \exists b \in FB \text{ such that } LIB(C_d) \cap VOL(\Gamma(b)) \neq \emptyset\} - POS(X_R)$
$NEG(X_R) = \{d | \forall b \in FB \text{ such that } LIB(C_d) \cap VOL(\Gamma(b)) = \emptyset\}$

where, C_d is a class on the taxonomy - the document d's representation on the taxonomy, $LIB(X)$, the library rooted at X, contains all the descendants of X, including X itself, and $VOL(X)$, the volumes of X, contains of $LIB(X)$ as well as all the predecessors of terms in $LIB(X)$. If we believe all the classes on a the taxonomy are subsets of K, then we have:

$POS(X_R) = \{d | \exists b \in FB \text{ such that } C_d \supseteq \Gamma(b)\}$
$BND(X_R) = \{d | \exists b \in FB \text{ such that } C_d \cap \Gamma(b) \neq \emptyset\} - POS(X_R)$
$NEG(X_R) = \{d | \forall b \in FB \text{ such that } C_d \cap \Gamma(b) = \emptyset\}$

where, C_d is a subset of K - the document d's representation on the Keywords-list. We can simplify the above equations to obtain the following set of decision rules:

(R_P) $bel_{m_R}(C_d) > 0 \Rightarrow a_1$
(R_B) $bel_{m_R}(C_d) = 0$, and $pl_{m_R}(C_d) > 0 \Rightarrow a_2$
(R_N) $bel_{m_R}(C_d) = 0 \Rightarrow a_2$

where, bel_{m_R} is the belief function of m_R, and pl_{m_R} is the plausibility function of m_R.

4 Summary

This research uses the techniques of AI and IR to develop a qualitative decision model for information filtering agents. This research discovers the general relationship between users' information need and their feedback and activities. From theoretical, we believe the positive region is fine, but the boundary probably is large. We, however, could use pignistic decision model (a quantitative decision method) for the boundary region. Because we do not think this problem is real probability problem, so we do not use rough set based decision model [4] in this paper. The related method has been used in [2].

References

[1] R. Baeza-Yates and B. Ribeiro-Neto, *Modern Information Retrieval*, Addison Wesley, 1999.
[2] Y. Li, C. Zhang, and J. R. Swan, An information filtering model on the Web and its application in JobAgent, *Knowledge-based Systems*, 2000, **13(5)**: 285–296.
[3] J. Mostafa, W. Lam and M. Palakal, A multilevel approach to intelligent information filtering: model, system, and evaluation, *ACM Transactions on Information Systems*, 1997, **15(4)**: 368–399.
[4] Y. Y. Yao and S. K. M. Wong, A decision theoretic framework for approximating concepts, *International Journal of Man-machine Studies*, 1992, **37**: 793–809.

Mining the Client's Life Cycle Behaviour in the Web

Oscar Marban[1], Javier Segovia[2], Juan J. Cuadrado[1], and Cesar Montes[2]

[1] Computer Science Department, Universidad Carlos III de Madrid
Leganés (Madrid), Spain
omarban@inf.uc3m.es
[2] Facultad de Informática, U.P.M.
Madrid, Spain
{cmontes, fsegovia}@fi.upm.es

Abstract. This paper analyses e-CRM and the problems that we may find trying to achieve an effective and two-way relationship between customer and vendor. Most of these problems relate to the fact that there is not direct contact between these actors because the web is the buying channel. This paper focus on understanding those problems, their effects on effective commercial relations and finally explains how to achieve a better understanding of the clients making Life Cycle Behavioural Models by means of mining the client's purchasing behaviour in a web site.

1 Introduction

The web is increasingly becoming a retailing channel of choice for million of users. However, the traditional conception of web-based commerce systems fails to achieve many of the features that enable small businesses to develop a warm human relationship with customers. This must not be understood as if those features cannot be translated onto the web for thereby improving the shopping experience in Internet. The inability of e-business applications to establish good customer relationship by developing a mature understanding of their customers is the central motivating-force behind this paper. The wider recognition and valuation that data mining companies are experimenting are indicative of the current failure of e-Commerce in delivering eCRM or Personalisation, and the importance of both issues for e-Commerce.

The absence of physical contact minimises the personalised experience of shopping, and thus directly strikes at the heart of establishing a good one-to-one relationship. To the prior we should add to the fact that there is very little experience in creating fluent relationships with customers using e-commerce. Both aspects contribute to the lack of a close one-to-one relationship, which is a major drawback to shopping on the Internet. However, the advantages of convenience, 'relative' speed and the cheapness of the products offered on the Web offset these disadvantages.

Most of the problems of the web as a buying channel may be solved by developing a mature understanding of the customers, applying intelligent methods to data about them collected either from the web (web logs, questionnaires, ...) or from external sources (postal code data bases, statistics, ...). This paper will focus on understanding those problems, their effects on effective commercial relations and how to achieve a better understanding of and, therefore, relation with any user by means analysing its needs with a softcomputing method like a Neural Network.

2 Related Work

Many approaches have focused on applying intelligent techniques to provide personal advice and interaction. Collaborative filtering is one of the key techniques for providing customisation for e-commerce. Collaborative filtering is based on the assumption that finding similar users and examining their usage patterns leads to useful recommendations being made [1]. The most common collaborative filtering algorithms are nearest neighbour-based algorithms where a subset of users that are as similar as possible to an active user is chosen and a weighted average of their scores is used to estimate preferences of the active user on other items [2], [3]. In contrast, model based algorithms first develop a description model from a database and use it to make predictions for a user. Systems of this type include Bayesian networks [1] and classification-based algorithms [4]. In [5] an alternative regression-based approach to collaborative filtering is proposed, which searches for relationships among items instead of looking for similarities among users and builds a collection of experts in the form of simple linear models that are combined to provide preference predictions. In [6], the authors examine a richer model that makes it possible to reason about many different relations between the objects. The authors also show how probabilistic relational models PRM can be applied to the task of collaborative filtering. They also focus on model-based methods and review the two-side clustering model for collaborative filtering [7].

3 CRM in E-commerce

CRM is interchangeable with the idea of 'fostering a mature one-to-one relationship' between business and its customers. This kind of close relations are data intensive in both directions. Companies need enough good quality data to perform them. But it is also true that the closer the relationship is, bigger is the amount of data available, therefore enabling better-informed decisions. Other general advantages are obtained by including good CRM methods: the discovery of potential new customers, the discovery of market niches, combating unseen commoditisation (the convergence in product identity), or overcoming the limitations of traditional marketing approaches (reduce money on ineffective an unfocused marketing) are just some of them. Moreover, appropriate CRM practices help to deal successfully with short life cycle products, which are typical in Internet-based commerce. Having a good knowledge about customers allows early identification of new or potential products. In the other hand, but not less important, knowing the needs of potential clients helps to choose better the products to include in the catalogue and the stock size for each of them. This ends in powerful defence against competitors, profit increase and better service, not to mention the increase of the loyalty of the customer to the e-business, which is a key aim of CRM.

3.1 Reasons Why E-commerce Has Failed to Establish Effective CRM

It is clear that users are not very confident about e-commerce, so many don't use it at all, or if they do, they prefer to remain anonymous, not even providing basic data about them. This has a dramatic consequence on e-business. Not knowing about the customer means being unable to improve the relation and, therefore, the service provided. Then again, the visitor will not get enough satisfaction and the confidence will continue decreasing. The problem is that there are very few e-businesses with good and sufficient data concerning customers. Moreover, using these data when available normally needs the identity or some personal facts of the visitors, who, as commented before, are very reticent to provide them. So now we know that we are dealing with unconfident customers and that we really know very little about them, but still we have to understand them so as to provide a better service. The only source of information left and the only moment in which we have direct contact, electronic but direct, with them is the session itself. So it seems clear that e-commerce has to learn to extract as much knowledge as possible about user's needs during it's visit, and to achieve so in an almost anonymous way, identifying users and user behaviours in terms of typologies. However, any solution is limited by the kind and the amount of information available about customers-business interactions. Until now, very little information concerning the behaviour of each single customer in a site was stored. Web-logs frequently consist on just the set of pages visited in a session, or not even that when pages contain applets or plug-ins. Even more, security issues and privacy laws also affect the kind and quality of the information stored about each visit to the site. Taking all the prior into account, three major consequences can be derived:

– Any kind of e-business that wants to improve its relations with potential customers needs to know what kinds of behaviours can be expected, and which of them are profitable and which are not.
– In order to use that knowledge, a major concern must be to identify on the fly the kind of user that is visiting the site in a precise moment.
– Data Mining techniques are a must in all this decision-making process, and any available source of data must be considered.

3.2 Data Sources for E-CRM

The data generated from a website is only the starting point in the data mining process as its value increases when merged with datawarehouse and third party information. There are various optimal methods and sources for gathering information rather than asking for it directly. Asking too many questions can lead to intentionally incorrect information from visitors. Several external sources of information can be linked to a web site for additional insight into the identity, lifestyle and behaviour of your visitor. Web logs hold data such as the domain name/IP address of the client, the time in which the request reached the server or information about the pages visited in a session to name a few. Nevertheless, there is a lack of quality information on web logs. We must not forget that they were conceived as a help for system administrators, not as a vital tool for marketing. Therefore, analysts had to add other tools for collecting data, such as applications logs, cookies, beacons or bugs functions embedded in web pages and the more conventional sources of user data: user registration forms, email responses, Web purchase data and data from external sources.

The last four, identified by [15], are conventional sources, which require either voluntary responses or actions whereas the former four are more automated and are simply transparent for the user. Consequently the first four sources are more accurate and require no extra effort from the user. The most important sets of data are acquired from the session, application and click event levels [15].

The primary objectives of extended customer intelligence services are to decrease the elapsed time between the business and technical processes that use information in the data warehouse, to provide insight into customers' past behaviour as well as to guess likely future behaviours and to tailor interaction and dialogs so that they are likely to be more productive and profitable.

In the following sections we introduce an approach that makes possible to perform CRM in an on-line e-Commerce environment, accomplishing a good CRM strategy: targeting the right offer to the right customer at the right time for the right price. Using a neural network and taking as inputs the clickstream and purchase transactions collected at a web server of a virtual shop, we will produce a model of the clients. It will be based on their past behaviour and on their social and economic description, which will describe their tendency of purchasing different products during his/her life cycle. This model can be used to guide the interaction (including its content) with potential customers that visit the virtual shop.

4 A Client's Life Cycle Model Based on a Neural Network

4.1 Data Description

Clients' Clickstreams and purchase transactions were collected at a web server of a virtual shop, which sells legware and legcare products [18]. The web server logs customer transactions and clickstreams, assigning unique ids to sessions through the use of *jsp* pages. The logged information was enriched adding demographic external data. The amount of available information was really vast. In order to keep our experiments small in size and easily manageable, we only worked with a small subset of the clients' attributes. This decision conditions the quality of the resulting models because the more complete description of the client is, the more accurate the models will be. However, the positive reading is that if we are able to obtain useful models with a small set of descriptors then we will assure the quality of the outputs when using the whole set. The attributes that have been used are code (session value), age of the client, gender, occupation, income and brad of four different products.

4.2 The Client Model

The objective is to obtain a model of the Client's tendency of purchasing a particular brand of legware based on the available description of the client. The used description depends on 4 variables: gender, age, occupation and income of the client, and the purchased brand is described with a binary YES/NO variable. Neural Networks such as a Multilayer Perceptron [16], have been extensively used to build categorizating models in which the inputs are descriptions of the category and the output indicates whether the description belongs or not to a category. Multilayer perceptrons implement a mathematical function f in the form of: $O = f(x)$ where the components of the vector x are the description of the category and o is the output, indicating the category. The descriptors x_i are real numbers, so binary, integer or qualified data should be adapted to a desired continuous range, lets say $[-1, +1]$. In the case of qualified data, such as Occupation which has 17 values, the data must be expanded to the same number of binary inputs, each of them indicating if the current input record has that value or not. For example, Occupation must be expanded to 17 binary inputs, the first of them indicating whether the value is "Sales/service", the second whether it is "professional/technical", and so on. For a given input record, only one of the 17 binary inputs should be on. For instance, let's consider that the current record belongs to a Professional. The first binary input is then off, the second is on, the third off, and so on. Once we have all binary inputs, all of them are normalised to the continuous range, $[-1, +1]$, with -1 indicating that the input is off, and $+1$ that is on. Ordered qualified data, such as Income, can be translated to a continuous range if the distances between values can be calculated somehow. In the case of the variable Income, that distances can be calculated translating each value in various ways. One way is adopting the value of the arithmetic mean of each qualified range. For example, the value $20,000 - $29,999 can be translated to 25000. Other way is to use one of the extremes, 20000 or 29999. In our experiments we adopted the later approach, selecting the upper extreme. For the problematic last value, $125,000 OR MORE, we used a compromised value of 175000. In the case of the output, the process is reversed. The output is the result of the application of the function f to the input data. This function is a mathematical composition of functions called Activation Functions [16] which should be increasing, continuous and derivable functions in a specified range, such as $[-1, +1]$, so the output o will stay within that range. Training the neural network consists on finding the right values for a set of constants that are used within the function f, so that the output o is producing $+1$ when the input data belongs to the category and -1 when it doesn't for all the training input set.

But training a neural network is not a perfect process, and the outputs are few times $+1$ or -1 but rather a real number within $(-1,+1)$. It is then needed a process for binarising the output. To decide if a input record belongs or not to the category, the output o is binarised using the simple method of assigning a "yes" if the output is in the range of $[0,+1]$ or "not" if it is within the range $[-1,0)$. That is the usual way of doing it, with some variations such as including an intermediate range like $[-0.5,+0-5]$ to indicate "unknown" answers. In our approach we decided not to interrupted the reversing process of binarise the output and just keep its continuous value, which can be interpreted as a "tendency" of belonging to a category. Summarising all the processing applied to the data, we have 1 input data for age, 1 for gender, 17 for occupation and 1 for income, making a total of 20 input variables within the range of [-1, +1]. In the case of the outputs, we treated separately each brand creating one different neural network model for each of them. All Multiplayer Perceptron used as brand models have the same architecture [16]: 20 inputs, 8 hidden nodes and one output, and were trained with all the data set using the backpropagation learning procedure [16].

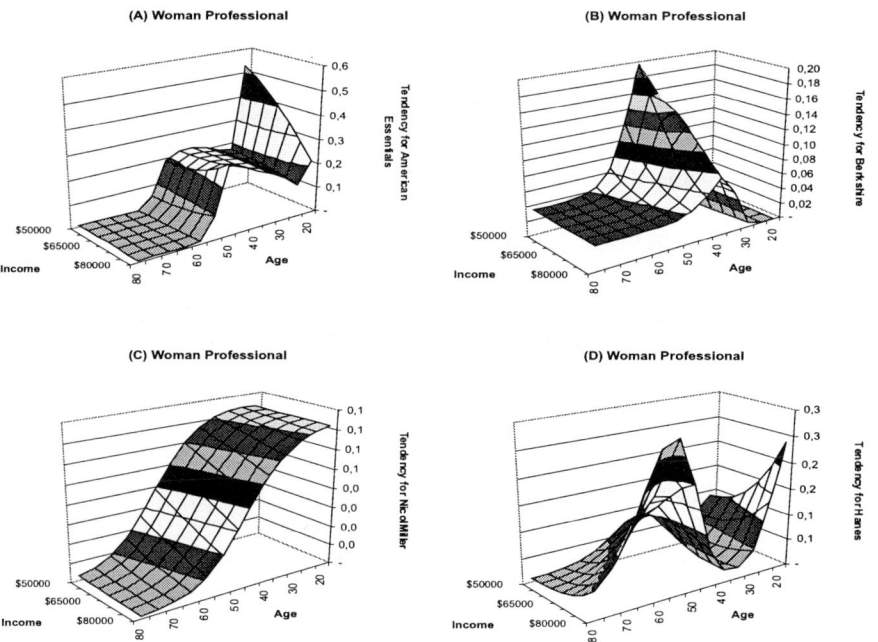

Fig. 1. 4 different Life Cycle models for 4 different brands of a woman professional

4.3 Exploiting the Life Cycle Model

The models made in the previous section on clients' tendencies can be exploited taking into account that the concept "client" is evolutionary; descriptors such as age or income change in time. How? Each of the developed models is able to react to any input in the range of the training data. For instance, all the models produce outputs for any value of the input variable age within [20, 80], provided that all other variables remain within their appropriate range. The key point here is to observe the outputs of the models while varying input variables which may describe the Life Cycle of the client. Such variables can be age and income[1]. Figure 1 shows four of those experiments, for a woman with the same professional profile. The four graphs show how the woman varies her purchase tendency to four distinct brands. These differences depend not only on the selected brand but, what is more relevant for this paper, on her life status. While tendencies in figures 1.A and 1.C only seem to vary significantly on the age of the woman, 1.B and 1.D show how the income is also affecting the tendencies. This fact can be used to be aware to the next tendency of the on-line shopping's clients and improve the recommending systems, being proactive in its marketing campaigns and solving some of the problems exposed in section 3.1.

The past of the client is also important when analysing the tendencies. Figure 2 shows the tendencies for a professional woman of about $65000 constant income. In the range of 35 and 55 years old, there is a marked tendency for the brand 'American Essentials', while at the age of 40 and the age of 50 'Berkshire' and 'Hanes' respectively experiment a peak in their tendencies. Despite that 'American Essentials' is the most favoured by the models, the other two brands should be taken into account around the age of their peaks. This is strongly important if there is evidence of a past history of 'American Essentials' purchases for this woman, because novelty may increase the tendencies of the other two brands, and lower the main one.

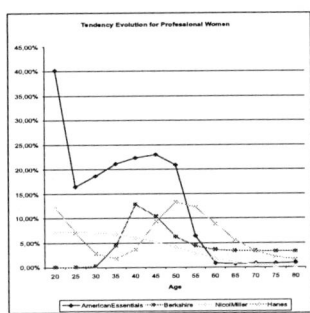

Fig. 2. Tendency evolution for professional women

---

[1] More attributes may and must be used, but in order to simplify the explanations and figures for the paper we just selected age, income, sex and profession

5 Conclusions

There is a theory that says that the web is only a good channel for those services that meet the couple Wyni Wyli (What you need is what you get, What you like is what you get) [24]. So any successful e-business must take this into account. How can then e-commerce improve to meet any of the previous? Shopping is an obvious need, but people don't like shopping in those impersonal e-shops where no help can be found and everybody is treated just in the same tedious way. Personalisation is the key concept, to offer the right thing in the right moment to the right customer. Personalisation needs on-line detection plus prediction. Detection can be performed in any of the ways described in previous sections, whilst Life Cycle models can be used to anticipate to the behaviour and reactions of the clients during his/her life, therefore predicting their needs or tastes. Using models such as those shown in figures 1 or 2, the CRM manager is able to identify current or future trends in the purchasing tendencies of each individual client, being then ready to launch the appropriated marketing campaign or the personalised treatment. Life Cycle models can be automated. When a tendency of a client is clearly dependent on a identified feature such as age or income, changes in that features can be detected automatically and an alert may be sent to the customer contact person while the personalised presentation of the virtual shop is adapted to the new client likeness.

References

1. J. S. Breese, D. Heckerman, C. Kadie. (1998) Empirical analysis of predictive algorithms for collaborative filtering. Proceedings of the UAI-98, p.p. 43–52
2. J.A. Konstan et al. (1997) GroupLens: Applying collaborative filtering to Usenet news. Communications of the ACM, 40(3):77–87, March.
3. U. Shardanand, P. Maes. (1995) Social information filtering: Algorithms for automating word of mouth. In Proceedings of ACM CHI'95, vol. 1, p.p. 210–217.
4. D. Billsus, M.J. Pazzani. (1998) Learning collaborative information filters. In Proc. 15th Int. Conf. on Machine Learning, pages 46–54.
5. S. Vucetic et al. (2000) A regression based approach for scaling-up personalized recommeder systems in e-commerce. In the 6th ACM SIGKDD Int. Conf. on KDD
6. L. Getoor, M. Sahami. Using probabilistic models for collaborative filtering.
7. T. Hofmann, J, Puzicha. (1999) Latent class models for collaborative filtering. Proceedings of the IJCAI-99, p.p. 688-693, S.F., July 31–August 6.
8. http://www.netmining.com/page.jsp?PadeID=152
9. Microsoft, Great Plains e-Enterprise (2001). "Fully Integrated Customer Relationship Management Solutions." Microsoft Corporation
10. http://www.acius.net/pdf/pdf_cID-24.pdf
11. Han J, & Kamber M, (2001). "Data Mining Concepts and Techniques." Morgan Kaufmann Publishers. ISBN 1-55860-489-8
12. J. Andersen et al. (2000). "Analysing Clickstreams Using Subsessions." ACM
13. Theusinger C, Huber KP, (2000). "Analysing the footsteps of your customers- A case study by ASK—net and SAS Institute GmbH." SAS Institute GmbH
14. http://www.appiancorp.com/consulting/expertise/clickstreamanalysis.asp

15. Rudd O.P, (2001). "Data Mining Cookbook: Modelling Data for Marketing, Risk, and Customer Relationship Management." Wiley Computer Publishing.
16. J. Hertz et al.(1991). "Introduction to the theory of Neural Computation"
17. Avatars Virtual Technologies (2001). "Strategies in Internet". White Paper.
18. R. Kohavi, C. Brodley, B. Frasca, L. Mason, Z. Zheng. KDD-Cup 2000 organizers' report: Peeling the onion. SIGKDD Explorations, 2(2):86–98, 2000.

PagePrompter: An Intelligent Web Agent Created Using Data Mining Techniques

Y.Y. Yao, H.J. Hamilton, and Xuewei Wang

Department of Computer Science, University of Regina
Regina, Saskatchewan, Canada S4S 0A2
{yyao,hamilton}@cs.uregina.ca

Abstract. Some challenges for Website designers are to provide correct and useful information to individual users with different backgrounds and interests, as well as to increase user satisfaction. Intelligent Web agents offer a potential solution to meet such challenges. A Web agent collects information, discovers knowledge through Web mining and users' behavior analysis, and applies the discovered knowledge to give dynamically recommendations to Website users, to update Web pages, and to provide suggestions to Website designers. The basic functionalities and components of an intelligent Web agent are discussed. A prototype system, called PagePrompter, is described. The knowledge of the system is extracted based on a combination of Web usage mining and machine learning.

1 Introduction

With the fast growth of information available on the World Wide Web, finding and retrieving useful information has become a very important issue. Web search engines offer a popular solution to this problem. Typically, a search engine returns a list of Web pages ranked according to their relevance to a user query. Little information is provided about the structure and access frequency of the Websites containing the suggested Web pages. A user needs to use the list for navigating the Web and finding relevant pages. Once a user arrives at a particular Website, it becomes crucial that the user finds the needed information quickly. At the same time, the Website may promote itself and increase user satisfaction by providing easy navigation, more and better services and additional relevant information.

Conceptually, a Website may be interpreted as a graph, in which each page is a node of the graph and each link is an edge of the graph connecting two pages. The graph representation provides a good way of viewing relationships among Web pages, but it is a physical view of the Website. It is not necessarily a good description of the semantic relationships among Web pages. For effective and efficient retrieval, different logical views of the Website may be created by Web users and Website designers. A Web user may create a logical view of the Website based on his/her information needs. For example, a user may create bookmark files and personalized link pages, which reflect the user's personal interests. A

Website designer can create different logical views of a Website for individual users or distinct groups of users.

Intelligent agent techniques can be combined with data mining and machine learning techniques to support Website designers in creating logical views. An intelligent Web agent acts likes a tour guide to promote a Website by assisting a visitor in navigating the Website. It can help the visitors find information quickly and effectively by offering different logical views of the Website and providing additional information not available on the Web pages. With the assistance of the Web agent, a user can fully exploit the Website. Such an agent may improve the performance of a Website and has great potential in E-commence.

An intelligent Web agent should have at least three functionalities, namely, data and information collection, knowledge discovery, and visitor support. The agent builds its databases by collecting information from Web users, Website designers, Web log files, and Web structures. From the collected data, machine learning and data mining techniques can be used to discover useful knowledge to build its knowledge base. A Website designer may directly access the knowledge base of the agent by performing operations such as adding, deleting, and updating. The visitor support activities of the agent are based on its knowledge.

We have implemented a prototype Web agent, called PagePrompter, to evaluate the effectiveness of the agent idea. PagePrompter combines research results from intelligent agents and data mining. PagePrompter's knowledge is obtained from Website designers, user behavior analysis, and Web mining. In particular, we propose a new method for knowledge base construction by combining date mining and machine techniques, which takes into consideration Website structures.

In this paper, we only present a brief conceptual description of the PagePrompter agent. The implementation details, many screen shots of the system, and some initial evaluations can be found in a technical report [13] and a M.Sc. thesis [11].

2 Background and Related Research

A key issue for the design and implementation of an effective Web agent is the construction of a knowledge base that supports agent activities. Results from statistical analysis of a Website and Web mining can be used for such a purpose.

Software packages, such as Analog (http://www.analog.cx/) and WUSAGE (http://www.boutell.com/wusage), have been used by many Web servers for Web log analysis. Results of the analysis typically include a summary report, a list of the most requested URLs, and a list of the browsers used. Such statistical information provides the basic factual knowledge of the Web agent.

Data mining is a step in the Knowledge Discovery in Databases (KDD) process consisting of applying data analysis and discovery algorithms that, within acceptable computational efficiency constraints, produce a particular enumeration of patterns over the data [2]. Web mining is the application of data mining techniques to large Web data repositories [7]. Three major Web mining methods are Web content mining, Web structure mining and Web usage mining [6]. Web content mining is the application of data mining techniques to unstructured data residing in Web documents. Web structure mining aims to generate structural summaries about Websites and Web pages. Web usage mining is the application of data mining techniques to discover usage patterns from Web data. All three types of Web mining can produce high level knowledge for a Web agent. We will focus mainly on the Web log mining with consideration of Web structures.

A Web access pattern is a recurring sequential pattern among the entries in Web log files. For example, if many users repeatedly access the same series of pages, a corresponding series of log entries will appear in the Web log file, and this series can be considered a Web access pattern. Sequential pattern mining and clustering have been applied to discover Web access patterns from log files [3,12]. The problem of finding pages visited together is similar to finding associations among itemsets in transaction databases [1]. Many Web usage mining techniques search for association rules [7].

Web usage mining research can be classified into personalization, system improvement, site modification, business intelligence, and usage characterization [10]. We will focus on two tasks of a Web agent, namely, recommendation and adaptive page generation. Making a dynamic recommendation to a Web user, based on the user profile in addition to usage behavior, is also called personalization. WebWatcher [5] and SiteHelper [8] provide personalization for Website users. Adaptive Web page generation deals with automatic modification of a Website's contents and organization using results of Web usage mining.

Based on the above mentioned studies of Web statistical analysis, Web mining and machine learning, we discuss the basic ideas of intelligent Web agents through a prototype system called PagePrompter.

3 The PagePrompter System

The goal of PagePrompter is to generate an effective and flexible intelligent Web agent to help a user navigating a Website. In particular, PagePrompter uses data mining and machine learning techniques to build its knowledge base by discovering knowledge from Web log files and Web structures. The visitor support activities of the PagePrompter include supplying information, recommendation, and adaptive Web page generation.

The main functionalities and features of PagePrompter are summarized below. The first two deal with data collection and knowledge base construction, and the last two deal with Web visitor support.

- **Data and information collection**. PagePrompter collects various types of data and information that can be used to build its knowledge base.
  - The major source of information is Web log files. Web servers commonly record an entry in a Web log file for every access. Log files contain the most accessible information about Website usage and visitor behaviors.

    - PagePrompter regularly traverses the entire Website to collect data concerning Web page updates, Website structure changes, and related information.
    - PagePrompter collects user feedback from visitors of the Website.
- **Data analysis, knowledge discovery and data mining**. PagePrompter analyzes the collected data by using statistical and data mining techniques to extract useful facts and knowledge. A knowledge base is constructed that contains both factual knowledge and discovered high level knowledge. The following issues are considered.
    - The raw Web log file contains many entries that are irrelevant or redundant for tasks of data mining and user behavior analysis. PagePrompter cleans the raw data to remove unneeded entries. After cleaning the data, PagePrompter identifies user sessions.
    - PagePrompter can extract simple facts, including 1) visitor statistics: the number of accesses, the number of hits, the number of visitors, and the number of hosts for a given time period; 2) visitor information: visitor IP addresses and visitors' browser and operating system platforms; and 3) Website statistics: the hottest pages and the most recently updated pages.
    - PagePrompter can extract useful knowledge, including associations of Web pages, commonly visited sequences of Web pages, and clusters of Web pages.
- **Dynamic recommendation**. Recommendation is one of the basic functions of PagePrompter. By using the collected data and mined knowledge, the PagePrompter agent can give users assistance in Web navigation. When a visitor reaches any page in the Website, his/her action is captured by PagePrompter and sent to the PagePrompter server. The server connects to a database and queries the database for any relevant recommendations for the current page. If PagePrompter finds any relevant information, it pops up a small window, which contains the following useful information and recommendations:
    - the hottest pages: obtained from statistical information collected by the agent;
    - recently created or modified pages: obtained from the regular traversal of the Website by the agent;
    - user feedback: obtained from current or previous users by the agent;
    - the next choice (pages usually visited by other users after the current page): obtained from mining sequential patterns;
    - groups of related pages (clusters of pages related to the current page or usually visited by other users together): obtained from a combination of page association mining, clustering, and machine learning from Website structures.

The agent provides additional information about the Website that is not directly available from Web pages and thus may increase user satisfaction. For example, a user looking for updated information on the Website can simply read recently created or modified pages. A new visitor at the Website may read other users' comments to gain a better understanding of the Website.

- **Personalized recommendation.** For advanced users, PagePrompter provides an interface that allows a user to query PagePrompter's database and to control the process of data mining. By doing so, PagePrompter can extract only relevant and useful rules for the particular user, which in turn leads to personalized recommendation.
- **Adaptive Web page generation.** Based on the mined knowledge, PagePrompter can adaptively change the Website by generating new Web pages.
  - The site usage report page provides Website designers with simple statistical information, a general description of visitors, and knowledge represented by association rules, clusters, and decision trees.
  - A *fresh page* is a Web page that is automatically created either for each visitor or periodically, such as once a day, based on Web usage mining. The fresh pages form the main interface for the adaptive Website. They include three types of pages: *jump pages, access paths,* and *frequently accessed Web pages*. A fresh page may become the favorite starting point of site visitors. The fresh pages are available to a Website visitor whenever he/she visits the Website.
  - A jump page lists the URLs of other pages, grouped under textual headings. Each group contains Web pages on a common subject that have been frequently visited together. The jump pages are formed by the LCSA algorithm (discussed in detail in Section 4). The jump pages are the most common type of adaptive Web pages.
  - An access path is a sequence of URLs such that the probability that a visitor will visit each successive URL, given that he/she has visited the previous one, exceeds a support threshold. Access paths reveal relationships between the Web pages that users access.
  - Frequently accessed Web pages are Web pages that are most frequently visited by users. They indicate the hottest pages in the Website.

We have carried out initial evaluations of PagePrompter by explicitly interviewing users and observing user behavior. The preliminary results are very encouraging and clearly suggest that PagePrompter is effective [11].

4 Knowledge Discovery from Web Log and Web Structures

A crucial issue in the design and implementation of an intelligent Web agent is construction of its knowledge base. We address this issue from the viewpoint of machine learning and data mining. In particular, we use association mining method to find associated Web pages, and propose a new algorithm LCSA for Web page clustering.

4.1 Association Rules

Association rule mining was originally introduced and studied in the context of transaction databases [1]. It deals with the problem of finding the subsets of items called itemsets that are frequently bought together by customers. The well known algorithm for finding association rules is the Apriori algorithm [1]. This algorithm finds association rules in two steps. The first step finds all frequent itemsets, i.e., all combinations of items having transaction support above a support threshold. The support is defined as the ratio of the number of transactions containing the itemset to the total number of transactions. The second step generates the association rules from the frequent itemsets.

Once the user sessions have been identified, we search for association rules to find relationships between Web pages. The set of pages visited by each visitor can be viewed as a transaction, and each page as an item. The frequent itemsets mined by using the Apriori algorithm are combinations of pages that are often accessed together. PagePrompter uses the discovered associations between Web pages to provide recommendation to Website designers and visitors.

Associations discovered from Web log data summarize the visitor behavior at a Website. Since a visitor may not have enough information about the Website, the discovered associations may not be sufficient and accurate. In order to avoid such problems, alternative methods need to be exploited.

4.2 Web Page Clustering Based on Website Structure

Usually, Website designers arrange Web pages using certain logical structures. For example, the physical tree structure layout of Web pages in a Website reveals the inherent connections between Web pages from the Web designers' point of view. Such structures may be used to refine the associations discovered from Web log files, or to generate different clusterings of Web pages.

We propose an algorithm called LCSA (Leader clustering algorithm [4], C4.5 machine learning algorithm [9], and Web Structure for Adaptive Website) to generate useful knowledge for an intelligent Web agent. Figure 1 gives a schematic description of Algorithm LCSA. The structure tree T is basically the physical tree structure of Web page files. It is assumed that a Website designer put pages of similar nature under the same subdirectory. The description D provides additional semantic information for each Web page. It is assumed that D is provided by a Website designer. The LCSA algorithm first constructs page clusters based on Web log data by using the Leader clustering algorithm, and then filters out the uninteresting clusters by considering semantic information provided by T and D. The rules for describing clusters are generated using the C4.5 algorithm. A similar approach has been used to discover conditional association rules [14]. The results of LCSA are semantically related clusters of Web pages that can be used to build an adaptive Website.

Clustering seeks to identify a finite set of categories or clusters to describe the data. It divides a data set so that records with similar content are in the same group, and groups are as different as possible from each other. The Leader algorithm for clustering is used because the number of entries in a Web log file is large and efficiency is a major concern. We adapted the Analog software package [12], which uses the Leader algorithm, to create page clusters. We choose to cluster Web pages based on user navigation patterns, whereby pages visited

Input: log file L, Web structure tree T, and description D for nodes of T.
Output: Semantically related clusters of Web pages.
1. Clean L to generate cleaned data CD.
2. Identify user sessions in CD to produce the set of sessions S.
3. Run Leader algorithm on S to generate a set C of clusters.
4. Create input for the C4.5 algorithm from clusters of the Leader algorithm:
    for each cluster c in C
        for each page P in c
            Derive the complete set P' of prefixes
                from the pathname of page P;
            Use k shortest prefixes in P' as
                condition attributes for a C4.5 training instance;
            Use the name of c as the decision attribute
                for the C4.5 training instance.
5. Run the C4.5 algorithm to generate a decision tree DT.
6. Combine decision tree DT, description D, and Web structure tree T to derive semantically related clusters of Web pages.

Fig. 1. LCSA Algorithm

together are grouped in the same cluster. Although we can use the clusters from a clustering algorithm to generate adaptive Web pages, preliminary experiments showed that the quality of the resulting pages was poor. A typical cluster of pages often had little in common. To give the users high quality suggestions, the clusters of pages should be related by content or location in the Website's structure. PagePrompter thus combines the clustering of pages with information about the contents and the Website structure to generate an adaptive Website.

Given page clusters produced by the Leader algorithm, we use the cluster id as the decision attribute for C4.5. The condition attributes are described from the Website's structure, i.e., its arrangement in a series of directories/folders of files. The resulting decision tree contains access patterns and Web structure information. We combine it with Website description D to produce adaptive Web pages called jump pages.

5 Conclusion

We argued that intelligent Web agents can be used to promote a Website. With an agent, a Website can actively provide useful and valuable information to a visitor and increase its effectiveness at satisfying users. We illustrated the basic ideas through a prototype system called PagePrompter. PagePrompter collects data, user information, and Website information, obtains knowledge directly from Website designers and indirectly from Web log files and Web structures through data mining and machine learning, dynamically gives recommendations to the Website's visitors, and generates adaptive Web pages. Knowledge obtained by the agent may also be used to improve the design of the Website. The initial evaluation of PagePrompter has shown its effectiveness.

As future research, we will add more functionalities to intelligent Web agents. Knowledge obtained using Web structure mining and Web content mining will be added to the knowledge base. We will also investigate the interaction between many agents on different Websites. The long term goal is to make Websites dynamic and active, instead of static and passive, through the use of intelligent agent technology.

References

1. Agrawal, R., Imielinski, T. and Swami, A. Mining association rules between sets of items in large databases, *Proceedings of SIGMOD*, 207–216. 1993.
2. Fayyad, U.M., Piatetsky-Shapiro, G., Smyth, P. and Uthurusamy, R. *Advances in Knowledge Discovery and Data Mining*, AAAI/MIT Press, 1996.
3. Florescu, D., Levy, A.Y. and Mendelzon, A.O. Database techniques for the World-Wide Web: a survey, *SIGMOD Record*, **27**, 59–74, 1998.
4. Hartigan, J. *Clustering Algorithms*, John Wiley, New York, 1975.
5. Joachims, T., Freitag, D. and Mitchell, T.M. WebWatcher: a tour guide for the World Wide Web, *Proceedings of the 15th International Joint Conference on Artificial Intelligence*, 770–777, 1997.
6. Madria, S.K., Bhowmick, S.S., Ng, W.K. and Lim, E. Research issues in Web data mining, *Proceedings of the First International Conference on Data Warehousing and Knowledge Discovery*, 303–312, 1999.
7. Mobasher, B., Jain, N., Han, J. and Srivastava, J. Web mining: pattern discovery from World Wide Web transactions, *Proceedings of International Conference on Tools with Artificial Intelligence*, 558–567, 1997.
8. Ngu, D.S.W. and Wu, X. SiteHelper: a localized agent that helps incremental exploration of the World Wide Web, *Proceedings of 6th International World Wide Web Conference*, 1249–1255, 1997.
9. Quinlan, J.R. *C4.5: Programs for Machine Learning*, Morgan Kaufmann. San Mateo, 1993.
10. Srivastava, J., Cooley, R., Deshpande, M. and Tan, P.N. Web usage mining: discovery and applications of usage patterns from Web data, *SIGKDD Explorations*, **1**, 12–23, 2000.
11. Wang, X.W. *PagePrompter: An Intelligent Agent for Web Navigation Created Using Data Mining Techniques*, M.Sc. Thesis, Department of Computer Science, University of Regina, 2001.
12. Yan, T.W., Jacobsen, M., Garcia-Molina, H. and Dayal, U. From user access patterns to dynamic hypertext linking, *Proceedings of the 5th International World Wide Web Conference*, 1007–1014, 1996.
13. Yao, Y.Y., Hamilton, H.J. and Wang, X.W. *PagePrompter: An Intelligent Agent for Web Navigation by Using Data Mining Techniques*, Technical Report, TR 2000-08, 2000, http://www.cs.uregina.ca/Research/2000-08.doc.
14. Yao, Y.Y., Zhao, Y. and Maguire, R.B. Explanation oriented association mining by combining unsupervised and supervised learning algorithms, Manuscript, 2002.

VPRSM Approach to WEB Searching

Wojciech Ziarko and Xue Fei

Computer Science Department
University of Regina
Regina, SK S4S 0A2 Canada

Abstract. An information retrieval methodology based on variable precision rough set model (VPRSM) is proposed. In the methodology, both queries and documents are represented as rough sets. The documents are relevance-ranked using rough set theory algebraic operators. The results of preliminary tests with the system WebRank for retrieving Web pages are also reported.

1 Introduction

The basic problems faced today by the Web search systems builders are essentially the same as identified by information retrieval researchers over 30 years ago [4-7]. They come down to two major questions: how to maximize the recall, that is the percentage of all relevant documents being retrieved and how to maximize the precision, that is the percentage of relevant documents in the retrieved set of documents. These problems have never been solved satisfactorily despite years of research. This lack of success indicates that the problems are fundamentally difficult, similar to some pattern recognition problems, such as speech recognition, which cannot be dealt with effectively with simple pattern matching techniques.

Among the information retrieval techniques developed in the past and applicable to Web searches, the rough set-based, non-pattern matching approach proposed by Das Gupta [1] deserves particular attention and further investigation. In this approach, the search strategies for document ranking are based on the notions of rough equality, rough inclusion and rough overlap of rough set theory [3]. The approach seems to be particularly appealing since it explicitly recognizes and models limitations of document meaning and search query representation in terms of keywords. The theoretical basis for Gupta's approach is developed around the original rough set theory as proposed by Pawlak [3]. According to Gupta, both the document and the query are perceived as rough sets in the common approximation space [3]. The rank of a document with respect to a query is then determined by comparing the query and the document rough sets using rough equality, rough inclusion and rough overlap operators [3]. The main difficulty with this ranking procedure is that it ranks documents into very few rank levels thus making it impossible to determine the differences in relevance status between many documents belonging to the same rank level. It appears that finer ranking and consequently more accurate relevance judgments can be produced by applying the extension of the Pawlak's rough set model, the variable precision rough set model (VPRSM) [8,9] in the Gupta's approach. The paper reports our research results in that respect. In particular, the extension of the Gupta's approach in the context of VPRSM is presented. Related work on applying rough set theory to information retrieval was reported in [2,7].

2 Document and Query Representation

In the proposed approach, each document and a query are represented as collections of higher order, composite semantic indexes each of which reflects some information about the meaning of the document or the query. In other words, the semantic indexes are trying to capture the notion of what the document is about. Each composite semantic index by itself is a set of defining index terms. Semantic indexes can be perceived as aggregations of semantically close index terms. For example the composite index reflecting the meaning of the word *car* can be defined by using terms such as: *car, wheels, engine, piston, valve, transmission*. In this representation, any document whose index terms obtained via standard process of manual or automatic indexing [5] has sufficient degree of overlap with the defining indexes for the notion of *car* will be considered to be about cars.

Any collection of semantic indexes corresponds to a family of sets of respective defining index terms. It can be assumed, without loss of generality, that all these sets are disjoint as otherwise more basic semantic indexes corresponding to atoms of the algebra of sets can be used for document and query representation. With this assumption, one can define the structure of approximation space $A = (U, R)$ [3] on the universe U of index terms used for defining semantic indexes and for indexing documents. The equivalence relation R represents the partition of U into disjoint sets corresponding to semantic indexes. In rough set theory terminology, each semantic index is an elementary set in A whereas each document D or query Q is a rough set [3] in A.

In more detail, the document D can be perceived as a set of index terms, that is $D \subseteq U$. In general, D is not definable in the rough set sense [3] in terms of equivalence classes (semantic indexes) of R. This means that the document D cannot be precisely represented by the semantic indexes. Instead, it can be represented by a pair of its rough approximations [3], the lower approximation $\underline{RD}$ and the upper approximation $\overline{RD}$ constructed with the semantic indexes. The document is considered to be *with certainty* about subjects corresponding to semantic indexes included in the lower approximation of the document. It is *possibly* about subjects corresponding to semantic indexes included in the upper approximation of the document.

Similarly, a query Q initially expressed as a set of index terms is a rough set in the same approximation space A. What it means is that the original query, the subset of index terms, can be represented by standard semantic indexes as defined in the approximation space A. In this representation, the query is perceived as a pair $(\underline{RQ}, \overline{RQ})$ of rough approximations of the original set of index terms forming the query. The query is considered to be *with certainty* about subjects corresponding to semantic indexes included in the lower approximation of the query terms and it is *possibly* about subjects corresponding to semantic indexes included in the upper approximation of the query terms. In particular, the query can be expressed by specifying some semantic indexes rather than index terms. In such case, the query is a precise set in the approximation space A and it is *with certainty* about subjects corresponding to semantic indexes contained in the query definition.

3 Rough Set-Based Document Ranking

Since both the document and the query are rough sets, the ranking of documents with respect to the degree of match with the query is based on rough set theory relations and operations. Das Gupta suggested using relations of rough equality, rough inclusion and the operation of rough overlap for the preliminary, first iteration document ranking [1]. According to his approach, more precise ranking would be obtained by applying a rough set theory-based query-document similarity measure in the second iteration ranking of documents with the same first iteration rank. In what follows we briefly summarize this ranking procedure, starting with the introduction of the relations of rough equality, rough inclusion and of the operation of rough overlap.

3.1 Rough Relations

In the approximation space $A = (U, R)$ two rough sets X and Y can be compared with respect to *rough equality* relation [3], based on the comparisons of their lower or upper approximations as follows:

X and Y are roughly bottom equal, i. e., $X \underset{\sim}{\sim} Y$ if $\underline{RX} = \underline{RY}$

X and Y are roughly top equal, i. e., $X \simeq Y$ if $\overline{RX} = \overline{RY}$.

X and Y are roughly equal, i. e., $X \approx Y$ if $\underline{RX} = \underline{RY}$ and $\overline{RX} = \overline{RY}$.

The above rough equality definitions can also be re-expressed as follows:

When X and Y are roughly bottom equal, it means that the positive regions of sets X and Y are the same. Similarly, when X and Y are roughly top equal, it means that the negative regions of sets X and Y are the same and, if X and Y are roughly equal, then both the positive and the negative regions of sets X and Y are equal to each other respectively.

Another basic concept of rough set theory used for document ranking is the *rough inclusion* relation [3] that is applicable to any two rough sets X and Y. The formal definition of rough inclusion is as follows:

X is roughly bottom included in Y, i. e. $X \sqsubseteq Y$ if $\underline{RX} \subseteq \underline{RY}$.

X is roughly top included in Y, i. e. $X \sqsubset Y$ if $\overline{RX} \subseteq \overline{RY}$.

X is roughly included in Y, i. e. $X \sqsubseteq Y$ if $\underline{RX} \subseteq \underline{RY}$ and $\overline{RX} \subseteq \overline{RY}$.

The above rough inclusion definitions can also be stated less formally:

When X is roughly bottom included in Y, it means that the lower approximation of X is included in the lower approximation of Y. Similarly, when X

is roughly top included in Y, it means that the upper approximation of X is included in the upper approximation of Y and, if X is roughly included in Y, then both the lower approximation of X is included in the lower approximation of Y and the upper approximation of X is included in the upper approximation of Y.

When further investigating the relationships between two rough sets it is quite common that two rough sets overlap while not satisfying the rough equality and rough inclusion relations. As other operations in the domain of rough sets, the *rough overlap* [3] is defined in terms of the overlaps of set approximations as follows.

X is roughly bottom overlapped with Y, i. e., $X \underline{\cap} Y$
if $\underline{RX} \cap \underline{RY} \neq \phi$ and $\overline{RX} \cap \overline{RY} = \phi$.
X is roughly top overlapped with Y, i. e., $X \overline{\cap} Y$
if $\underline{RX} \cap \underline{RY} = \phi$ and $\overline{RX} \cap \overline{RY} \neq \phi$.
X is roughly overlapped with Y, i. e., $X \overline{\underline{\cap}} Y$
if $\underline{RX} \cap \underline{RY} \neq \phi$ and $\overline{RX} \cap \overline{RY} \neq \phi$.

One may notice that the rough overlap represents a much weaker relationship than rough equality and rough inclusion.

3.2 Approximate Document Ranking

Because all documents and queries are represented as rough sets, one can rank documents with respect to the strength of the relationships between document rough sets D_i and the query rough set Q, using strategies $S_1 - S_{13}$, as specified below:

(S_1) $Q = D_i$, (S_2) $Q \approx D_i$, (S_3) $Q \underline{\approx} D_i$, (S_4) $Q \simeq D_i$, (S_5) $Q \underline{\sqsubseteq} D_i$

(S_6) $Q \sqsubseteq D_i$, (S_7) $Q \overline{\sqsubseteq} D_i$, (S_8) $D_i \underline{\sqsubseteq} Q$, (S_9) $D_i \sqsubseteq Q$, (S_{10}) $D_i \overline{\sqsubseteq} Q$

(S_{11}) $Q \overline{\underline{\cap}} D_i$, (S_{12}) $Q \underline{\cap} D_i$, (S_{13}) $Q \overline{\cap} D_i$.

According to these strategies, the top ranked documents S_1 will have the same index terms as the query. The documents in the next group S_2, will all be roughly equal to the query rough set, and so on. The least rank will be assigned to documents satifying strategy S_{13} which are roughly top, overlapped with the query rough set. Note that these strategies will not produce meaningful results if query or document lower approximations are empty, or if query or document upper approximations are equal to the universe of index terms U.

The following similarity measure $SIM(Q, D_i)$ between query Q and a document D_i, introduced by Das-Gupta [1], can be applied to differentiate between documents belonging to the same rank groups. $SIM(Q, D_i) = \overline{SIM}(Q, D_i) + \underline{SIM}(Q, D_i)$ where $\underline{SIM}(Q, D_i) = \frac{|\underline{RQ} \cap \underline{RD_i}|}{|\underline{RQ} \cup \underline{RD_i}|}$ and $\overline{SIM}(Q, D_i) = \frac{|\overline{RQ} \cap \overline{RD_i}|}{|\overline{RQ} \cup \overline{RD_i}|}$.

The higher value of the similarity leads to a higher rank for the corresponding fetched document. These similarity measures can be used only after the retrieved documents have been ranked by the search strategies S_1 through S_{13}. Note that $\underline{SIM}(Q, D_i)$ is undefined if both lower approximations of Q and D are empty. The natural fix of this problem is to declare $\underline{SIM}(Q, D_i) = 0$ if both lower approximations of Q and D are empty. This extension however, will not help in the ranking process. In addition, if only one of the lower approximations is empty, the resulting value of the similarity function will also be zero.

4 VPRSM-Based Document Ranking

It appears that the ranking results obtained with using the rough set-based strategy described above can be made finer if the definitions of lower approximations are softened by allowing partial inclusion of a lower approximation elementary set in the target set X, as opposed to total inclusion required by the original rough set model [3]. Replacing total inclusion relation with partial inclusion in the lower approximation definition would reduce the possibility of having empty document or query lower approximation, thus increasing the "resolution" of the document ranking process. This can be achieved by adopting the variable precision rough set model (VPRSM) as a basic framework in the rough set-based document ranking. In what follows the basics of the VPRSM are briefly summarized and its adaptation to document ranking is explained.

4.1 Basic Definitions

Let $X \subseteq U$ be a subset of the universe U and let R be an equivalence relation on U with the equivalence classes (elementary sets) $E_1, E_2, \ldots, E_n$. We will assume that all sets under consideration are finite and non-empty. Each elementary set E can be assigned a measure of overlap with the set X by the function $P(X|E) = \frac{|X \cap E|}{|E|}$, referred here as conditional probability function. Based on the values of the function P and of two criteria parameters l and u such that $0 \leq l < u \leq 1$, the basic definitions of the original rough set model can be generalized as follows.

The first parameter, referred to as lower limit l, represents the highest acceptable degree of the conditional probability $P(X|E_i)$ to include the elementary set E_i in the negative region of the set X. The $l-$*negative region* of the set X is defined as

$NEG_l(X) = \cup \{E_i : P(X|E_i) \leq l\}$.

The second parameter, referred to as the upper limit u defines the u-*positive region* or the u-*lower approximation* of the set X. The u-positive region of the set X is defined as

$POS_u(X) = \cup \{E_i : P(X|E_i) \geq u\}$.

The objects which do not belong to the u-positive region and to the l-negative region belong to the (l,u)-*boundary* region of the set X, denoted as

$BNR_{l,u}(X) = \cup \{E_i : l < P(X|E_i) < u\}$.

As in the original rough set model, the $l-$*upper approximation* of the set X is a union of lower approximation and of the boundary region, that is,

$UPP_l(X) = \cup\{E_i : l < P(X|E_i)\}$.

The approximation regions defined above are generalizations of the corresponding notions appearing in Pawlak's rough sets. They preserve almost all algebraic properties of the original rough sets. In particular, the operations of rough equality, rough inclusion and the operation of rough overlap directly extend to rough sets defined in the VPRSM framework. This allows for application of VPRSM-based rough sets operators to document ranking using strategies presented in section 3.2.

4.2 Adapting VPRSM to Document Indexing

In the context of query or document representation using VPRSM rather than the original rough set model, the value of the parameter u represents the minimum acceptable degree of overlap between document index terms and the semantic index defining terms to consider the document as being with high certainty about the subject represented by the semantic index. Any semantic index satisfying that requirement is included in u-lower approximation of the document.

The value of the parameter l is a minimum degree of overlap between document index terms and the semantic index defining terms to consider the document as possibly being about the subject corresponding to the semantic index. In this case the semantic index is a part of the l−upper approximation of the document.

If the degree of overlap between documents index terms and the semantic index is equal or below the value l then the document is considered to be unlikely about subject corresponding to the semantic index. In case like that, the semantic index is contained in the l−negative region of the document.

An open question remains how to set the values of the parameters l and u. At the moment, it appears that experimentation with various data collections and queries is the only answer. In the experiments conducted for this project, the value of the parameter u was set arbitrarily to 0.5 and the value of l was 0. With these settings, the original definition of upper approximation was preserved whereas the lower approximation included all elementary sets (semantic indexes) which contained no less than 50% of its defining terms in common with the document or query index terms. The following example illustrates the main ideas presented in this section.

Example 1.
Given index terms $U = \{a_1, a_2, a_3, a_4, a_5, a_6, a_7, a_8, a_9, a_{10}, a_{11}\}$, documents $D_1 = \{a_1, a_2, a_4, a_5, a_7, a_{10}\}$, $D_2 = \{a_3, a_4, a_6, a_7, a_8, a_9\}$, $D_3 = \{a_1, a_5, a_7, a_{10}, a_{11}\}$, $D_4 = \{a_5, a_8, a_{11}\}$ and a query $Q = \{a_1, a_2, a_4, a_5, a_9\}$, all expressed as sets of index terms. The equivalence relation R partitions U into classes of index terms corresponding to semantic indexes as follows: $E_1 = \{a_1, a_2, a_3\}$, $E_2 = \{a_4, a_5\}$, $E_3 = \{a_6, a_7, a_8\}$, $E_4 = \{a_9, a_{10}\}$, $E_5 = \{a_{11}\}$. The attribute indexing of each document is summarized in the Table 1. A binary value 1 indicates that a document index term a_i appears in an attribute class E_j, otherwise a binary value 0 is used.

Table 1. Document Indexing

Doc	E_1			E_2		E_3			E_4		E_5
D_i	a_1	a_2	a_3	a_4	a_5	a_6	a_7	a_8	a_9	a_{10}	a_{11}
D_1	1	1	0	1	1	0	1	0	0	1	0
D_2	0	0	1	1	0	1	1	1	1	0	0
D_3	1	0	0	0	1	0	1	0	0	1	1
D_4	0	0	0	0	1	0	0	1	0	0	1
D_5	1	1	0	1	0	0	0	0	1	0	0

The values of the conditional probability function $P(D_1|E_i) = \frac{|D_1 \cap E_i|}{|E_i|}$, ($i = 1..5$) for the document D_1 are $P(D_1|E_1) = \frac{2}{3}$, $P(D_1|E_2) = 1$, $P(D_1|E_3) = \frac{1}{3}$, $P(D_1|E_4) = \frac{1}{2}$, $P(D_1|E_5) = 0$.

Based on the values of the conditional probability function, the lower and upper VPRSM approximations for document D_1 are:
$\underline{AD_1} = \cup\{E_1, E_2, E_4\}$ and $\overline{AD_1} = \cup\{E_1, E_2, E_3, E_4\}$.

Following the same procedure, the lower and the upper approximations of all the other documents and the query Q can also be found as summarized in the Table 2.

Table 2. Query and Document Representation

Doc	Lower Approximation $\underline{AD_i}$	Upper Approximation $\overline{AD_i}$
D_1	$\cup\{E_1, E_2, E_4\}$	$\cup\{E_1, E_2, E_3, E_4\}$
D_2	$\cup\{E_2, E_3, E_4\}$	$\cup\{E_1, E_2, E_3, E_4\}$
D_3	$\cup\{E_2, E_4, E_5\}$	$\cup\{E_1, E_2, E_3, E_4, E_5\}$
D_4	$\cup\{E_2, E_5\}$	$\cup\{E_2, E_3, E_5\}$
Q	$\cup\{E_1, E_2, E_4\}$	$\cup\{E_1, E_2, E_4\}$

5 Final Remarks

System WebRank [10] is a Java implementation of the document retrieval strategy based on the VPRSM model as described in previous section. WebRank treats each Web page as a document. The vector space model [5] is used as an experimental benchmark to compare it with the rough set approach for Web page ranking. The user can issue queries through the Web browser from the Java Applet GUI front-end that is embedded on the client side of a Web page. In the experiments, queries on the subject of databases and transportation engineering were used. In total 42 sample pages were used with 22 relevant ones. The relevant Web pages were judged manually in relation to the query Web page. The average precision improvement of rough set query is 11.1% over the vector space approach in this case. Based on the experiments we noted the following:

Firstly, the rough set ranked query results demonstrate better recall-precision performance than the vector space model-ranked query.

Secondly, when the number of retrieved Web pages is small, the recall-precision curves are identical for the rough set and vector space approaches. As the number of retrieved Web pages increase, the rough set queries produce better results than the vector space queries since the rough set method has a much higher precision value than the vector space method for a fixed recall value. The precision improvements range from 5% to 33% for the sample query.

Thirdly, in both approaches, the precision values of the recall-precision curves tend to stabilize in a certain range as the recall value increases. This feature distinguishes WenRank from the conventional information retrieval systems where precision value keeps decreasing as the recall value increases [5].

In summary, the results of tests are not conclusive although they indicated better performance of the rough set-based method over vector space model in our experiments. It appears that more extensive testing is required for full evaluation of the proposed methodology.

Acknowledgement. The research reported in this article was supported by the research grant awarded by the Natural Sciences and Engineering Research Council of Canada.

References

1. P. Das-Gupta. "Rough Sets and Information Retrieval". *Proc. of 11th Conference on R&D in Information Retrieval*, ACM SIGIR, Grenoble, pp. 567–581, 1988.
2. T. B. Ho, and K. Furakoshi. "Information Retrieval Using Rough Sets". *Journal of Japanese Society for AI*, Vol. 23, No. 102, 1990.
3. Z. Pawlak. *Rough Set: Theoretical Aspects of Reasoning about Data*, Kluwer Academic Publishers, 1991.
4. J. Van. Rijsbergen. *Information Retrieval*, London: Butterworth, 1979.
5. G. Salton and M. J. McGill. *Introduction to Modern Information Retrieval*, McGraw-Hill Book Company, 1983.
6. G. Salton. *Dynamic Information and Library Processing*, Prentice-Hall Inc., Englewood Cliffs, New Jersey, 1975.
7. S. K. M. Wong and W. Ziarko. "A Machine Learning Approach to Information Retrieval". *Proceeding of 1986 ACM SIGIR Conference*, Italy, pp. 228–233, 1986.
8. W. Ziarko. "Variable Precision Rough Sets Model", Journal of Computer and Systems Sciences, Vol. 46. No. 1, pp. 39–59, 1993.
9. J. Katzberg and W. Ziarko. "Variable Precision Rough Sets with Asymmetric Bounds", in *Rough Sets, Fuzzy Sets and Knowledge Discovery*, Springer Verlag, pp. 167–177, 1994.
10. X. Fei. "WebRank: A Web Ranked Query System Based on Rough Sets". M.Sc. thesis, University of Regina, 2001.

Rough Set Approach to the Survival Analysis

Jan Bazan[1], Antoni Osmólski[2], Andrzej Skowron[3],
Dominik Ślęzak[4], Marcin Szczuka[3], and Jakub Wróblewski[4]

[1] Institute of Mathematics, University of Rzeszów
Rejtana 16A, 35-959 Rzeszów, Poland
[2] Medical Center of Postgraduate Education
Marymoncka 99, 01-813 Warsaw, Poland
[3] Institute of Mathematics, Warsaw University
Banacha 2, 02-097 Warsaw, Poland
[4] Polish-Japanese Institute of Information Technology
Koszykowa 86, 02-008 Warsaw, Poland

Abstract. Application of rough set based tools to the post-surgery survival analysis is discussed. Decision problem is defined over data related to the head and neck cancer cases, for two types of medical surgeries. The task is to express the differences between expected results of these surgeries and to search for rules discerning different survival tendencies. The rough set framework is combined with the Kaplan-Meier product estimation and the Cox's proportional hazard modeling.

1 Introduction

Analysis of medical data requires decision models well understandable by medical experts. The theory of rough sets [4] provides knowledge representation which is well understandable for the medical experts. A number of valuable rough set based applications to medical domain is known from the literature [1,2].

We analyze data about medical treatment of patients with various kinds of the head and neck cancer cases. The data, collected for years by Medical Center of Postgraduate Education in Warsaw, consists of 557 patient records described by 29 attributes, reduced – after consultation with medical experts – to 7 columns. Except the dates, important conditional attributes are well-defined symbolic attributes. On the other hand, decision problems are defined over especially designed attributes, which are of a complex structure. It enables focusing in the foregoing analysis on the complex decision semantics, having a clear interpretation of the conditional part of decision rules. Thus, this data set seems to be perfect for learning how complex decision semantics can influence the algorithmic framework and results of its performance.

The main topics of the paper are the following: *(i)* Given statistical methods used in the medical survival analysis, like the Kaplan-Meier's product-limit estimate and the Cox's proportional hazard model [3], find descriptions of patient groups with different survival estimates. *(ii)* Given information about the type of surgery applied to each particular patient, describe patient groups with different comparative statistics of survivals versus the surgery type chosen.

2 Rough Set Framework

In the rough set theory [4] the sample of data takes the form of an information system $\mathbb{A} = (U, A)$, where each attribute $a \in A$ is a function $a : U \to V_a$ into the set of all possible values on a. Given arbitrary $a \in A$ and $v_a \in V_a$, we say that object $u \in U$ *supports descriptor* $a = v_a$ iff $a(u) = v_a$.

One can regard descriptors as *boolean variables* and use them to construct logical formulas as their boolean combinations. The sets of objects supporting such combinations are obtained by using standard semantics of logical operators. The domain of the rough set theory is to *approximate concepts* $X \subseteq U$ by means of supports of boolean formulas constructed over $\mathbb{A} = (U, A)$ [4,7].

One often specifies a distinguished decision d to be predicted under the rest of attributes A. Let us consider *decision table* $\mathbb{A} = (U, A \cup \{d\})$, $d \notin A$. Concepts to be approximated are *decision classes* of objects supporting descriptors $d = v_d$, $v_d \in V_d$. The most widely applied formulas are conjunctions of *conditional descriptors* $a = v_a$, $a \in A$, $v_a \in V_a$. They correspond to *decision rules*

$$\bigwedge_{a \in B}(a = v_a) \Rightarrow (d = v_d) \tag{1}$$

where (*almost*) all objects, which support $a = v_a$, $a \in B$, should support $d = v_d$.

In case of many real-life decision problems, in particular the one we are dealing with, there is an issue of data inconsistency, where construction of the above decision rules is difficult or impossible. In the rough set theory this problem is addressed by introducing *the set approximations* [4], *generalized decision functions* and, e.g., *rough membership functions* [5]. In some applications decision can be expressed as a continuous value, function plot or a compound decision scheme (like, e.g., *rough membership distribution* – probabilistic distribution spanned over the set of original decision values [9]). Then there is a need for measuring how close two values of decision are. Such measures may be devised in a manner supporting the particular goal we want to achieve.

Regardless of the decision value semantics, the rough set principle of searching for approximations of decision concepts remains the same. It corresponds to the problem of extraction of the optimal set of (*approximate*) decision rules from data; In other words – the problem of construction of an *approximation space* [7, 10], within which the classes of objects with similar decision behavior will be well described by conditional boolean formulas. Given decision table $\mathbb{A} = (U, A \cup \{d\})$, we would thus like to search for such *indiscernibility classes*

$$[u]_B = \{u' \in U : \forall_{a \in B}(a(u) = a(u'))\} \tag{2}$$

that objects $u' \in [u]_B$ have decision values (sets, vectors, distributions, function plots, estimates, etc.) similar to $d(u)$, and objects $u' \notin [u]_B$ have decision values being far from $d(u)$, according to specified decision distance semantics. Moreover, we would like to optimize and simplify the structure of such classes (clusters, neighborhoods), to obtain possibly general description of approximate conditions→decision dependencies (cf. [7,9,10]).

3 Medical Data

We consider the data table gathering 557 patients, labeled with values over the columns described in Fig. 1, selected by the medical experts as of special importance while analyzing the surgery results:

Operation (O)	Radical (r), Modified (m)
Treatment (T)	Operation Only (oo)
	With Radiotherapy (wr)
	Unsuccessful Radiotherapy (ur)
Ext. Spread (E)	1 iff extracapsullar spread is observed, 0 otherwise
Stage (S)	Pathological stages, denoted by 0,1,2
Localization (L)	Integer codes of the cancer localization
Time Interval (I)	Measured between the date of operation and the date of the last notification
Notification (N)	Dead (d), Alive (a), No information (n)

Fig. 1. The selected attributes of medical data

The size of data, understood in terms of the number of objects and attributes, is relatively small and thus, any – even exhaustive – approach to searching for appropriate solutions could be applied. A question is, however, not about complexity of the search but about the definition of the problem itself.

The main task is to show, whether the risk of modified operation is not greater than in case of radical operation. It is an important factor, since modified operation is less invasive and giving less side effects. According to the experts' knowledge, a person who survives more than 5 years after surgery is regarded as a positively supporting case, even if the same type of cancer repeats after. We have three classes of patients: ***Success***: those who survived more than 5 years after surgery, ***Defeat***: those who died because of the same cancer as that previously treated, ***Unknown***: those who died within 5 years but because of the other reasons and those with no data about the last notification provided.

Let us consider a new decision attribute with three values, corresponding to the above classes. Technically, this attribute can be created by basing on *Time Interval* and *Notification* columns. Searching for rules pointing at the *Success* and *Defeat* decision values may provide the wanted results.

Such decision table is very inconsistent: all conditional indiscernibility classes contain objects with all three decision values. Hence, a kind of probabilistic analysis should be applied (cf. [1,2,9]). While analyzing probabilistic decision distributions we should, however, remember that the only thing we know for sure is that objects from *Success* and *Defeat* classes should be discerned. What about the *Unknown* class? How to relate it to the others? How to adjust the discernibility criteria in order to get well-founded results? – We try to answer to these questions by handling decision values having a compound type, partially symbolic (for the *Success* class), partially numeric (since one may be interested e.g. in averages over the survival periods in the *Defeat* class), and partially undefined (unknown), needing perhaps a kind of indirect estimation.

4 Survival Analysis

4.1 The Kaplan-Meier Product-Limit Estimate

In the studies concerned with survival analysis, especially in medical domain, we consider two types of observations (patient records) – *complete* and *censored*. The observation is complete if it has lasted for the period of 5 years and in that time a repeating cancer was recorded. Otherwise, the observation is censored – In our case the set of censored objects coincides with the sum of the *Success* and *Unknown* classes of patients.

The Kaplan-Meier product-limit estimate (cf. [3]) is a method providing the means for construction of so called *survival function* (or *survivorship*) $S(t)$, given the complete and censored observations ordered in time. It returns the cumulative proportion of cases surviving up to the time t:

$$S(t) = \prod_{j=1}^{t} \left(\frac{N-j}{N-j+1}\right)^{\delta(j)} \tag{3}$$

where N denotes the total number of patients and $\delta(j) = 0$ if the j-th case is censored, and 1 otherwise (complete case). The advantage of this method is that it does not depend on grouping of cases into intervals.

In Fig. 2 we present the plot of Kaplan-Meier product-limit estimate for our data set (a) and estimates for groups corresponding to two considered types of surgery (b). One can see that operations (Radical/Modified) form the groups of patients with different survival characteristics. However, we need an automated method of searching for decision rules pointing at possibly more distinguishable characteristics. According to discussion at the end of Section 2, we need an algorithm which is able to search for minimal conjunctions of descriptors enabling to discern objects with local Kaplan-Meier curves that are *far enough* one to the others. Since it's difficult to design an appropriate decision attribute enabling such a performance, we follow a well known statistical method for approximating such curves, described in the next subsection.

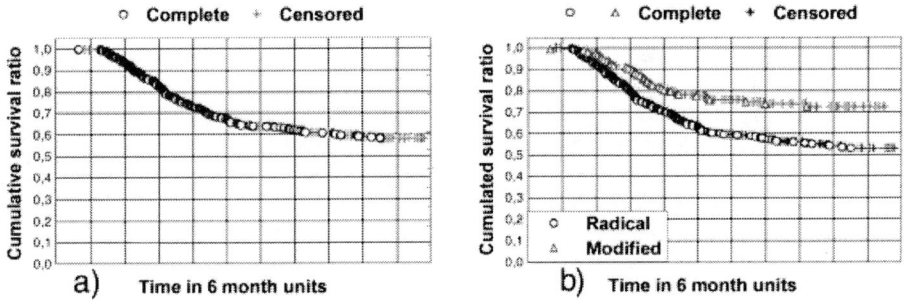

Fig. 2. Kaplan-Meier estimate: a) global b) with respect to the surgery type.

4.2 The Cox's Proportional Hazard Model

This is a semi-parametric method essentially based on assumption that the survival time distribution is exponential (cf. [6]). It attempts to estimate the instantaneous risk of death (hazard) of each particular patient $u \in U$ at time t, by using formula:

$$h(t, a_1(u), \ldots, a_n(u)) = h_0(t) e^{\beta_1 a_1(u) + \cdots + \beta_n a_n(u)} \quad (4)$$

where $a_1, \ldots, a_n$ are attributes (called *indicator variables*), $\beta_1, \ldots, \beta_n$ are *regression coefficients*, and function $h_0(t)$ is so called *baseline hazard*. This model can be linearized by considering a new attribute:

$$\mathsf{PI}(u) = \ln \frac{h(t, a_1(u), \ldots, a_n(u))}{h_0(t)} = \beta_1 a_1(u) + \cdots + \beta_m a_n(u) \quad (5)$$

Prognostic Index PI is a linear combination of existing attributes. Coefficients $\beta_1, \ldots, \beta_n$ are retrieved by using linear regression with the goal of reflecting the actual survival pattern present in the data (expressed as, e.g., Kaplan-Meier estimate) as closely as possible. The task is to find a collection of time-independent variables (attributes) that, at the same time, have clear clinical interpretation and allow the PI to be applied efficiently to making prognosis. In our experiments we used 5 variables (attributes) to form PI – The first 5 listed in Fig. 1. The choice of attributes was suggested by medical experts. By comparing the prediction from the Cox's model with Kaplan-Meier estimate in Fig. 2a, we noticed that the choice of attributes is proper as those two plots were very close (practically indistinguishable at a picture).

If the choice of attributes is proper, one can identify the intervals of values of PI, which correspond to the patient groups with different survivorship patterns. By dividing the data set into three groups with respect to the values of PI we obtain a significant diversification of survivorship patterns, as shown in Fig. 3a. We follow [6], where this method is considered for other type of medical data.

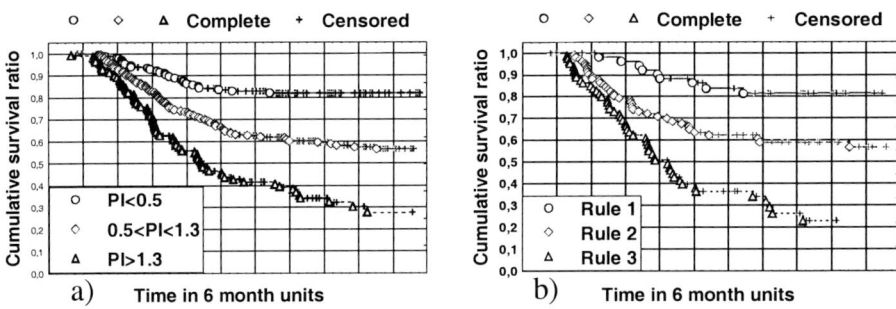

Fig. 3. Application of results from the Cox's proportional hazard model: a) Kaplan-Meier estimate for three groups of patients, defined with respect to the values of PI; b) Kaplan-Meier estimate for objects matching decision rules targeting these intervals.

4.3 Prognostic Rules

Given PI-based patterns shown in Fig. 3a, we can describe efficiently particular tendencies. We define a new decision table, where conditional attributes are, as before, the first 5 in Fig. 1, and values of decision correspond to the above found intervals of values of PI. By searching for decision rules within this table, we can construct approximations of different survival tendencies. We show just three exemplary decision rules (abbreviations are consistent with Fig. 1):

$$\begin{aligned}\text{Rule 1:} & \quad O = m \wedge E = 0 \wedge S = 1 \wedge L = 1 \Rightarrow PI < 0.5 \\ \text{Rule 2:} & \quad O = r \wedge T = ur \wedge S = 1 \Rightarrow PI \in [0.5, 1.3) \\ \text{Rule 3:} & \quad O = r \wedge T = ur \wedge E = 1 \wedge S = 2 \wedge L = 1 \Rightarrow PI \geq 1.3\end{aligned} \quad (6)$$

The above rules are exact, with matching at the level of 54, 106 and 82 objects, respectively.[1] The right sides can be recalculated in terms of Kaplan-Meier curves corresponding to subsets of objects (patients) defined by the left sides. We illustrate them in Fig. 3b. It leads to the following *prognostic rules*:

$$\begin{aligned}& O = m \wedge E = 0 \wedge S = 1 \wedge L = 1 \Rightarrow \textit{Upper tendency in Fig. 3b} \\ & O = r \wedge T = ur \wedge S = 1 \Rightarrow \textit{Middle tendency in Fig. 3b} \\ & O = r \wedge T = ur \wedge E = 1 \wedge S = 2 \wedge L = 1 \Rightarrow \textit{Lower tendency in Fig. 3b}\end{aligned} \quad (7)$$

The proposed method is a two-step process, providing rules related to the complex, Kaplan-Meier-related decision. In the first step we encode the actual decision in terms of PI. Then we recalculate the actual survivorship estimates.

5 Cross-Decision Rules

The task is to compare the risk of modified and radical operations. Descriptions of groups of patients who should be treated with the particular kind of operation are especially worth finding. According to Fig. 2, modified operations seem to provide better results. However, this type is generally not applied to more serious cases. We should search for groups of patients treated with both types and compare survival characteristics between such obtained subgroups. If we are able to find description of a set of patients, which splits onto reasonably large subsets in terms of type of operation applied, then knowledge resulting from the differences in survival characteristics can be informative for medical experts.

A solution would be to search for pairs of subsets with Kaplan-Meier estimates as distant to each other as possible. Such estimates are difficult to compare in a direct manner. Hence, one may consider approximations of their behavior, like, e.g., probabilistic distributions over the values of Prognostic Index. Another approach is to focus on percentages of successful operations. Let us explain it by basing on an exemplary rule derived from data:

$$T = wr \wedge E = 0 \wedge S = 1 \Rightarrow \left| \begin{array}{l} P(\text{success after } \textit{radical}) = 0.36 \\ P(\text{success after } \textit{modified}) = 0.626 \end{array} \right. \quad (8)$$

---

[1] Obviously, one can search also for inexact PI-related rules, which are regarded as better fitting medical phenomena than exact ones (cf. [1,2]). However, the resulting rules are not exact by means of application to survival analysis anyway.

It means that within the set of patients with surgeries performed after unsuccessful radiotherapy, without extracapsullar spread observed and with the middle level of pathological stage, only 36% patients treated with radical operation survives successfully while modified operation provides success in 62.6%. Let us call this kind of knowledge representation a *cross-decision rule*. It describes two-dimensional statistics related to a pair of features – the type of operation and successful patient's survival – similarly as in case of contingency tables [11].

The question is how to express the criteria enabling automatic extraction of descriptors discerning between different behaviors of such two-dimensional statistics. We propose to extend the distance-based approach to approximate discernibility between probabilistic distributions [9]. For a given $u \in U$, let us consider probabilities of success of radical and modified operations over its A-indiscernibility class $[u]_A$, where $A = \{T, E, S, L\}$. They take the following form:

$$R(u) = \frac{|\{u' \in [u]_A : O(u') = r \wedge Suc(u')\}|}{|\{u' \in [u]_A : O(u') = r\}|} \quad M(u) = \frac{|\{u' \in [u]_A : O(u') = m \wedge Suc(u')\}|}{|\{u' \in [u]_A : O(u') = m\}|} \quad (9)$$

where $Suc(u)$ denotes that surgery turned out to be successful for a given $u \in U$. Let us consider the difference $D(u) = R(u) - M(u)$ and approximation threshold $\varepsilon \in [0, 1)$. We regard objects $u_1, u_2 \in U$ as necessary to be discerned, iff

$$DD(u_1, u_2) = |D(u_1) - D(u_2)| > \varepsilon \quad (10)$$

Otherwise, we allow putting objects together, as matching the same rule. It provides a method for searching for object-based rules by keeping only these descriptors $a = a(u)$, which are necessary for discerning pairs satisfying (10).

Fig. 4 provides characteristics of groups of patients in terms of decision rules. It relates these rules to each other, as being generalizations for higher and counterexamples for lower approximation thresholds. This way of visualization remains analogous to methodology based on *information maps* [8]. We show only these combinations of descriptors, which are irreducible at the level at most $\varepsilon = 0.2$ and – moreover – such that the subsets of objects supporting each of both types of surgeries are at least of cardinality 10. There are 11 rules satisfying such requirements. Each rule is labeled with: description of its premise, number of patients treated with two considered surgery types within the set of objects matching the rule, and probabilities of success of these surgeries, conditioned by the premise. Rules are connected with arrows, leading to more specified descriptions, irreducible in terms of (10) for some thresholds $\varepsilon > 0.2$.

6 Conclusions

Application of rough set based tools to the post-surgery survival analysis of cancer data was discussed. The task was to express the differences between expected results of applications of two types of medical operations and to discover rules, which discern different tendencies in survival statistics. To cope with it, the rough set framework for generating optimal decision rules was combined with the Kaplan-Meier product estimation and the Cox's proportional hazard modeling. Moreover, we proposed how to search for and visualize so-called cross-decision rules, helpful while comparing the considered surgeries in terms of their results.

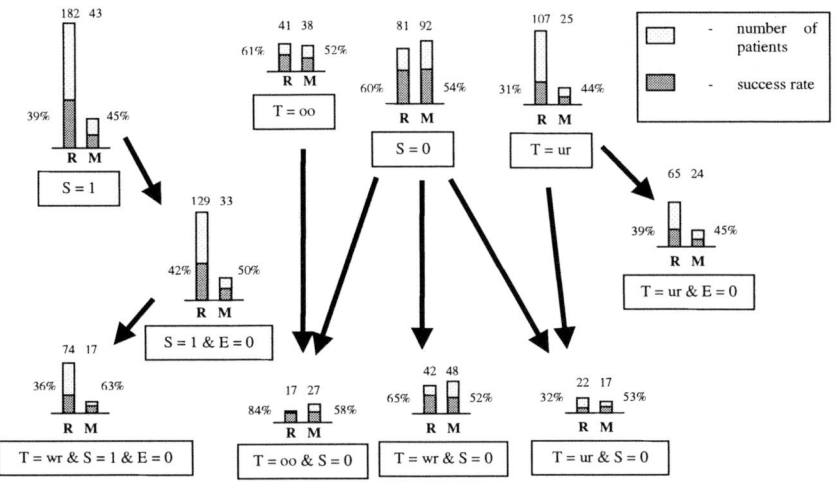

Fig. 4. Visualization of cross-decision rules.

Acknowledgements. Supported by Polish National Committee for Scientific Research (KBN) grant No. 8T11C02519. Special thanks to Medical Center of Postgraduate Education.

References

1. Cios K.J., Kacprzyk J. (eds): Medical Data Mining and Knowledge Discovery. Studies in Fuzziness and Soft Computing 60, Physica Verlag, Heidelberg (2001).
2. Grzymala-Busse J.P., Grzymala-Busse J.W., Hippe Z.S.: Prediction of melanoma using rule induction based on rough sets. In: Proc. of SCI'01 (2001) 7, pp. 523–527.
3. Hosmer D.W. Jr., Lemeshow S.: Applied Survival Analysis: Regression Modeling of Time to Event Data. John Wiley & Sons, Chichester (1999).
4. Pawlak Z.: Rough sets – Theoretical aspects of reasoning about data. Kluwer Academic Publishers (1991).
5. Pawlak Z., Skowron A.: Rough membership functions. In: R.R. Yaeger, M. Fedrizzi, J. Kacprzyk (eds), Advances in the Dempster Shafer Theory of Evidence. Wiley (1994) pp. 251–271.
6. Schlichting P. et al.: Prognostic Factors in Cirrhosis Identified by Cox's Regression Model. Hepatology, 3(6) (1983) pp. 889–895.
7. Skowron A., Pawlak Z., Komorowski J., Polkowski L.: A rough set perspective on data and knowledge. In: W. Kloesgen, J. Żytkow (eds), Handbook of KDD. Oxford University Press (2002) pp. 134–149.
8. Skowron A., Synak P.: Patterns in Information Maps. In Proc. of RSCTC'02 (2002).
9. Ślęzak D.: Approximate decision reducts (in Polish). Ph.D. thesis, Institute of Mathematics, Warsaw University (2001).
10. Wróblewski, J.: Adaptive methods of object classification (in Polish). Ph.D. thesis, Institute of Mathematics, Warsaw University (2001).
11. Zytkow J.M, Zembowicz R.: Contingency Tables as the Foundation for Concepts, Concept Hierarchies, and Rules: The 49er System Approach. Fundamenta Informaticae 30, IOS Press (1997) pp. 383–399

The Identification of Low-Paying Workplaces: An Analysis Using the Variable Precision Rough Sets Model

Malcolm J. Beynon

Cardiff Business School, Cardiff University, Colum Drive,
CF10 3EU, Wales, UK
BeynonMJ@Cardiff.ac.uk

Abstract. The identification of workplaces (establishments) most likely to pay low wages is an essential component of effectively monitoring a minimum wage. The main method utilised in this paper is the Variable Precision Rough Sets (VPRS) model, which constructs a set of decision 'if ... then ...' rules. These rules are easily readable by non-specialists and predict the proportion of low paid employees in an establishment. Through a 'leave n out' approach a standard error on the predictive accuracy of the sets of rules is calculated, also the importance of the descriptive characteristics is exposited based on their use. To gauge the effectiveness of the VPRS analysis, comparisons are made to a series of decision tree analyses.

1 Introduction

Britain introduced its National Minimum Wage (NMW) in April 1999. The aim was to prohibit the payment of low hourly wage-rates in the British economy. An adult minimum wage of £3.60 per hour was set. A major problem faced by those implementing the minimum wage was monitoring its operation. This has involved the use of targeted inspections by the Inland Revenue, the body charged with the responsibility for monitoring the NMW [4]. These are based on 'a model aimed at identifying those sectors and geographical areas where non-compliance is likely to be most prevalent, as well as those types of workers most at risk of non-payment'. The details of this model have not, however, been disclosed.

In this paper the Variable Precision Rough Sets (VPRS) model [9, 3] is used to identify establishments potentially paying low wages. The results of a VPRS analysis are a set of decision 'if ... then ...' rules. An ordered criteria is introduced which enables the automated selection of a β-reduct (from VPRS). Through a 'leave n out' approach further measures are obtained, including a standard error of the predictive accuracy and the importance (frequency of use) of characteristics utilised to classify establishments. Comparisons are made with a series of 'leave n out' decision tree analyses.

2 Discussion of Problem and Data

The analysis outlined in this paper uses the British Workplace Employee Relations Survey, immediately prior to the NMW's introduction. Questions were explicitly asked about low pay, and the one used in this paper asked managers most responsible for personnel matters the number of employees at the establishment earning less than £3.50 per hour. This figure (£3.50) when augmented to allow for inflation in the period up to April 1999, is close to the rate of £3.60 set for the adult national minimum wage. The eight condition attributes used in this analysis are described in Table 1.

Table 1. Description of Condition attribute

Attribute	Description
emps	Establishment size (number of employees)
age	Age (years)
%yng	Percentage young (under 20 years old)
%fem	Percentage female
union	Recognised union in establishment (1 – yes, 0 – no)
Single	Single establishment (1 – yes, 0 – no)
Foreign	Foreign owned establishment (1 – yes, 0 – no)
Public	Public owned establishment (1 – yes, 0 – no)

These condition attributes are a subset of the variables considered in [5]. As discussed earlier, the decision attribute in this paper is the proportion of low paid employees in an establishment, here proxies on different levels of pay are considered, i.e. three intervals of low pay are defined, see Table 2.

Table 2. Description of Decision attribute

Attribute	Description
%pay	Proportions of employees paid less than £3.50, partitioned into 3 intervals; 'Z' - 0%, 'L' - between 0% and 10% and 'H' above 10%.

3 Criteria in 'Leave n Out' VPRS Analysis

A VPRS analysis of a randomly selected set of 100 establishments is undertaken. This analysis is based on a 'leave n out' approach, based on the generation of 1000 random information systems (runs) each made up of 85 establishments (in-sample), leaving 15 as the out-of-sample. There are various stages of VPRS analysis [9], i.e. in each run the following considerations have to be performed; *i*) Construction and selection of an acceptable reduct, *ii*) Construction of minimum set of rules and *ii*) Classification and Prediction of in-sample and out-of-sample establishments.

Before the VPRS analysis can be undertaken, in this problem four of the condition attributes (see Table 1) are continuous in nature. Since the descriptor values in VPRS are required to be in categorical form, there is the need for continuous value discretisation (CVD). In this paper the FUSINTER method of CVD is used (see [10]). FUSINTER is a supervised CVD technique, the actual value (Z, L and H) of the decision attribute (%pay), is employed to enable the CVD of each of the four condition attributes to take place, see Table 3. From Table 3 the four (continuous) condition attributes are each partitioned into two or three intervals. Also shown in Table 3 is the number of objects within each of the constructed intervals.

Table 3. Condition attribute intervals from FUSINTER discretisation

Attribute	Interval '0'	Interval '1'	Interval '2'
emps	[12, 83.5), 45	[83.5, 2585], 55	
age	[0, 7.5), 15	[7.5, 665], 85	
%yng	[0, 0.075), 67	[0.075, 0.78], 33	
%fem	[0.03, 0.50), 35	[0.50, 0.575), 9	[0.575, 1], 56

VPRS is without a formal historical background of empirical evidence to support any particular method of β-reduct selection. Recently, [2, 3] considered the problem of β-reduct selection specifically in VPRS. They considered the interval domain of permissible β associated with a β-reduct as a measure to be used when selecting a β-reduct. To automate the process of β-reduct selection, the following ordered criteria is used to select the acceptable β-reduct from the available β-reducts.

i) The highest quality of classification possible.
ii) The highest β value from those satisfying i).
iii) Least number of attributes in the β-reduct from those satisfying ii).
iv) The largest interval domain of β from those satisfying iii).

In the case of more than one β-reduct identified using this ordered criteria, a β-reduct is then randomly chosen from them. This ordered criteria includes previous methods of reduct selection in RST etc. To construct the minimal set of rules the method in [1] is used. Finally in each run a method of predicting the decision values of the out-of-sample establishments was employed, the method used [6, 7] calculates a measure of the distance between each classifying rule and each new object (using $p = 2$ and $k_t = 1$).

4 Results of VPRS Analysis

In this section, the results of the VPRS analysis are reported, from the 1000 'leave n out' runs undertaken. The first aspect concerns the set of ordered criteria for reduct selection described in section 3. It was found, from the 1000 runs, on 989 occasions a single β-reduct was identified, with 11 occasions finding two β-reducts. In Table 4 five descriptive statistics are shown resulting from the 1000 runs.

Table 4. Descriptive statistics for VPRS analysis based on 1000 runs

Variable	Min	Max	Mean	Median	Mode
Prediction Accuracy	20%	93.3%	60.8%	60.0%	60.0%
Number of Attributes	2	7	4.976	5	5
Number of Rules	2	30	11.126	10	5
Quality of Classification	74.1%	97.6%	74.5%	75.0%	75.0%
Correct classification	41.1%	92.8%	76.8%	77.3%	78.7%

First reported in Table 4 is the predictive accuracy (standard error), perhaps the most important statistic, which shows the mean accuracy was 60.8%, i.e. just over 9 out of the 15 out-of-sample establishments were given the correct %pay classification. Secondly, the number of attributes used (within each β-reduct) ranges from 2 to 7, with mean value near 5. This is further exposited in Fig. 1 where a more detailed spread of the number of attributes in each β-reduct used in the 1000 runs is given.

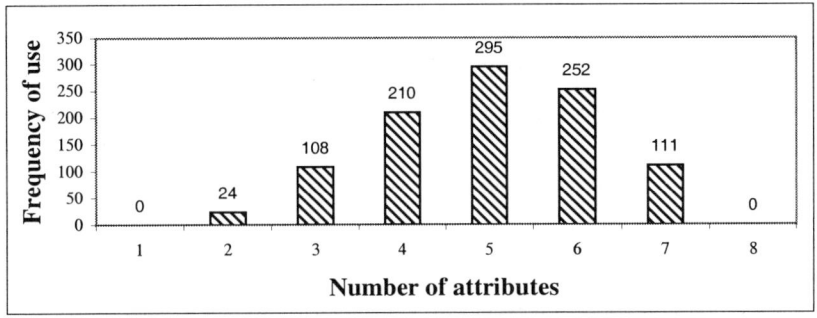

Fig. 1. Frequency of reduct size (number of attributes)

From Fig. 1, the number of attributes approximately follows a normal distribution around a mean value of five attributes. The next statistic in Table 4 is the (minimal) number of rules which were constructed from the identified β-reduct in each of the 1000 runs, these ranged from 2 to 30, with a mean of just above 11, see Fig. 2.

In Fig. 2, a positive skewness on the spread of the number of rules is clearly shown. The last two (VPRS specific) descriptive statistics; quality of classification, refers to the percentage of (in-sample) establishments given a classification, here the mean is near 75% (64 establishments out of 85). The correct classification statistic refers to the number of establishments correctly classified (of those given a classification), here the mean is near 77%. One further aspect to exposit is the frequency of use (importance) of the individual attributes within the VPRS analysis, see Fig. 3.

From Fig. 3, the %yng (and public) attribute is clearly the most (and least) used attribute, appearing in 896 (and 406) β-reducts out of the 1000 runs undertaken. The importance of these attributes in predicting the incidence of low pay is unsurprising

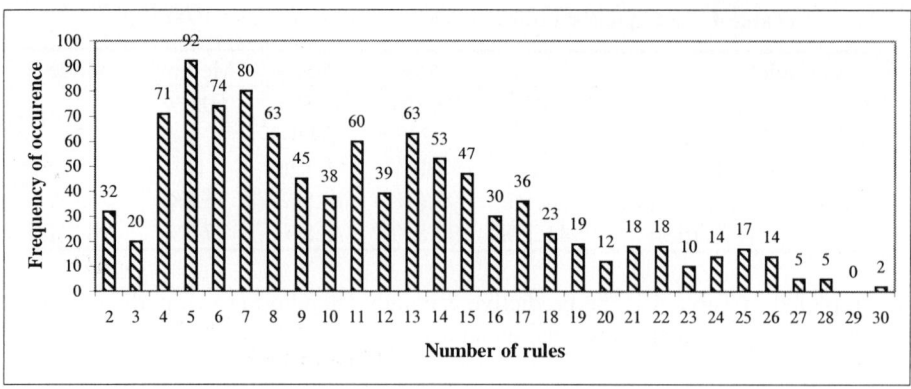

Fig. 2. Frequency of number of rules

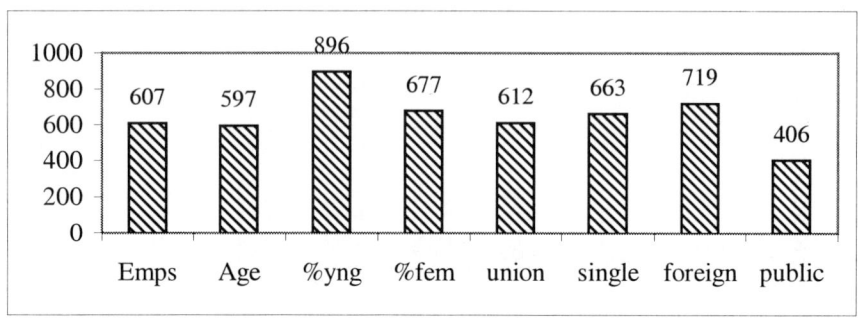

Fig. 3. Frequency of attribute use (importance)

and accords well with the results of other studies [5]. To further illustrate the results of a VPRS analysis, the rules constructed from one of the runs are given below. For each rule their set of criteria are shown, also their strength value (out of 85) and confidence in correct classification.

Rule 1 : (%yng < 7.5%) ∧ (%fem ≥ 57.5%) $\xrightarrow{34/85 \quad 22/34 \quad 64.7\%}$ Z

Rule 2 : (%yng < 7.5%) ∧ (foreign = 0) $\xrightarrow{20/85 \quad 12/20 \quad 60.0\%}$ Z

Rule 3 : (%yng ≥ 7.5%) ∧ (%fem < 50%) ∧ (foreign = 0) $\xrightarrow{4/85 \quad 3/4 \quad 75.0\%}$ L

Rule 4 : (%yng < 7.5%) ∧ (%fem < 50%) ∧ (foreign = 1) $\xrightarrow{3/85 \quad 2/3 \quad 66.7\%}$ L

Rule 5 : (50% ≤ %fem < 57.5%) $\xrightarrow{6/85 \quad 5/6 \quad 83.3\%}$ L

Rule 6 : (%yng ≥ 7.5%) ∧ (foreign = 1) $\xrightarrow{6/85 \quad 6/6 \quad 100.0\%}$ H

Rule 7 : (%yng ≥ 7.5%) ∧ (%fem ≥ 57.5%) $\xrightarrow{10/85 \quad 8/10 \quad 80.0\%}$ H

5 Comparison with Other Methods

In this section a series of analyses using the non-parametric ID3 decision tree method is considered. Each of these analyses follow a similar 'leave n out' approach as for the VPRS analysis. ID3 [8] is one of the most widely used decision tree methods, it is an iterative process, which creates a tree structure with nodes and branches, where each path to a terminal node is analogous to a single rule.

ID3 uses an entropy measure to determine which attribute to branch at each step (node). Necessary within this method is a stopping criterion to end the stepwise determination of nodes. Here a method of construction pruning is utilised, i.e. a node is deemed a terminal node based simply on when an acceptable (majority) proportion of the objects at the node classify to the same decision category. Four separate decision tree sets of runs are performed, for when this acceptable proportion takes the values 100%, 90%, 80% and 70%. No further (lower) acceptable proportions were considered since 70% is the first below the mean confidence in correct classification values in the VPRS analysis (i.e. 76.8%). Fig. 4 gives a series of sets of box plots expositing three descriptive statistics of the decision tree analyses, namely predictive accuracy (Fig. 4a), number of attributes (Fig. 4b) and number of rules (Fig. 4c).

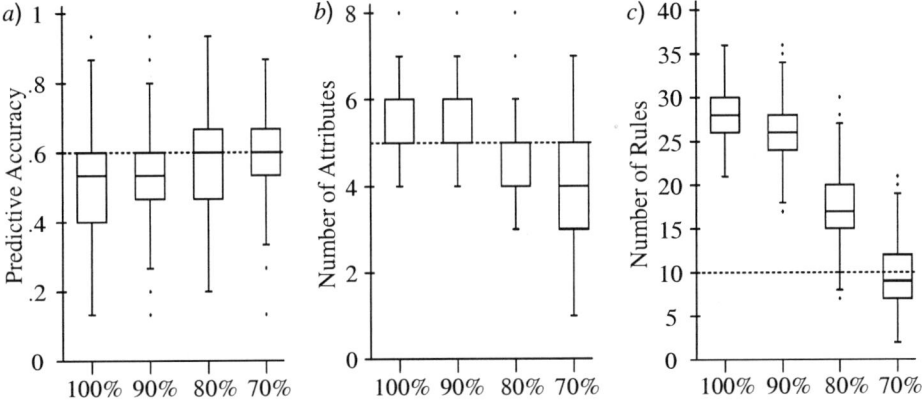

Fig. 4. Box plots from decision tree descriptive statistics

Also included in each set of box plots is a horizontal dashed line, which gives the respective median value found from the VPRS analysis, to enable quick comparison. In Fig. 4a) as the acceptable proportion decreases so predictive accuracy increases (at a rate which is overall decreasing). For acceptable proportions 100% to 70% the mean predictive accuracy values were 51.3%, 52.5%, 56.4% and 60.1% respectively (compared to 60.8% in the VPRS analysis). In Fig. 4b) understandably the number of attributes decreases as the majority proportion threshold goes down. In Fig. 4c) the movement of the number of rules also decreases as the proportion value decreases.

One further disclosure from the decision tree analysis is that of the frequency of use of attributes used in the study. Fig. 5 gives the frequency of use of the condition attributes over each of the four different decision tree 'leave n out' approaches.

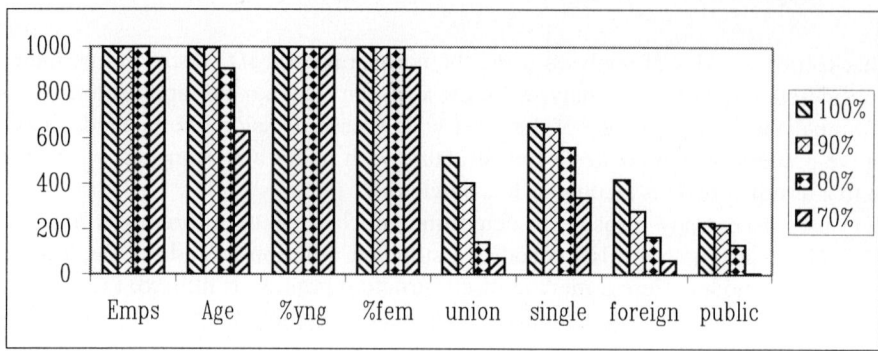

Fig. 5. Frequency of attribute use within decision tree simulations

From Fig. 5, as the acceptable proportion decreases from 100% down to 70% so the usage of attributes within the decision tree runs also decrease. Of note is the high proportion of usage of the first four attributes, the reason being that they are continuous hence within ID3 they would partition the objects with more granularity than the other nominal condition attributes. A comparison with the results from the VPRS analysis shows the %yng attribute to be continually the most used attribute and public the least used attribute over all four decision tree sets of runs.

6 Conclusion

The effective monitoring of a minimum wage requires that some model is used to predict those workplaces (establishments) most likely to be paid low wages. This allows those monitoring the wages to target establishments at which breaches of the regulations are most probable. The analysis used was Variable Precision Rough Sets (VPRS) model, which constructs a set of readable rules to perform the classification. Through the definition of an ordered criteria for reduct selection, a 'leave n out' approach is undertaken in the analysis.

Comparisons on predictive accuracy with the results from ID3 decision tree analyses (with construction pruning) show the VPRS results to be favourable. In the case of the ID3 analyses, further comparisons on attribute usage and number of rules is also given. Indeed the use of a 'leave n out' approach allows the investigation of the importance of attributes.

References

1. An, A., Shan, N., Chan, C., Cercone, N., Ziarko, W.: Discovering rules for water demand prediction: An enhanced rough-set approach. Engineering Application and Artificial Intelligence 9 (1996) 645–653.

2. Beynon, M.: An Investigation of β-reduct Selection within the Variable Precision Rough Sets Model. In: The Second International Conference on Rough Sets and Current Trends in Computing, Lecture Notes in Artificial Intelligence Series, Springer-Verlag (2000) 114–122
3. Beynon, M.: Reducts within the Variable Precision Rough Set Model. A Further Investigation. European Journal of Operational Research 134 (2001) 592–605.
4. Low Pay Commission: The National Minimum Wage: The Story So Far: Second Report of the Low Pay Commission. Cm 4571, London: HMSO (2000).
5. McNabb, R., Whitfield, K.: 'Worth So Appallingly Little': A Workplace-level of Low pay. British Journal of Industrial Relations 38 (2000) 585–609.
6. Slowinski, R., Stefanowski, J.: RoughDAS and RoughClass software implementations of the rough sets approach. in *Intelligent Decision Support, Applications and Advances of the Rough Sets Theory*, ed. R. Slowinski, Kluwer, Academic Publishers, London (1992).
7. Stefanowski, J.: Classification support based on the rough set theory. Proc. IIASA Workshop on User-Oriented Methodlogy and Techniques of Decision Analysis and Support, Serock (1992).
8. Quinlan, J.R.: Introduction of Decision trees. Machine Learning 1 (1986) 81–106.
9. Ziarko, W.: Variable precision rough set model. Journal of Computer and System Sciences 46 (1993) 39–59.
10. Zighed, D.A., Rabaseda, S., Rakotomala, S.: FUSINTER: A method for discretisation of continuous attributes, International Journal of Uncertainty. Fuzziness and Knowledge-Based Systems 6 (1998) 307–326.

A Search for the Best Data Mining Method to Predict Melanoma

Jerzy W. Grzymała-Busse[1] and Zdzisław S. Hippe[2]

[1] Department of Electrical Engineering and Computer Science, University of Kansas, Lawrence, KS 66045, USA
Jerzy@eecs.ku.edu
http://lightning.eecs.ku.edu/index.html
[2] Department of Expert Systems and Artificial Intelligence, University of Information technology and Management, 35-225 Rzeszow, Poland
ZHippe@wenus.wsiz.rzeszow.pl

Abstract. Our main objective was to decrease the error rate of diagnosis of melanoma, a very dangerous skin cancer. Since diagnosticians routinely use the so-called ABCD formula for melanoma prediction, our main concern was to improve the ABCD formula. In our search for the best coefficients of the ABCD formula we used two different discretization methods, agglomerative and divisive, both based on cluster analysis. In our experiments we used the data mining system LERS (Learning from Examples based on Rough Sets). As a result of more than 30,000 experiments, two optimal ABCD formulas were found, one with the use of the agglomerative method, the other one with divisive. These formulas were evaluated using statistical methods. Our final conclusion is that it is more important to use an appropriate discretization method than to modify the ABCD formula. Also, the divisive method of discretization is better than agglomerative. Finally, diagnosis of melanoma without taking into account results of the ABCD formula is much worse, i.e., the error rate is significantly greater, comparing with any form of the ABCD formula.

Keywords. Rough set theory, data mining, melanoma prediction, ABCD formula, discretization.

1 Introduction

In this paper we present out latest research results that are a continuation of our previous attempts [5] to find the optimal ABCD formula. The ABCD formula is routinely used in melanoma diagnosis [4], [15]. The result of the ABCD formula is called TDS (Total Dermatoscopic Score). The data mining system LERS (Learning from Examples based on Rough Sets) [6], [7], [12], [13] was used for our experiments aimed at improving diagnosis of melanoma, a very dangerous skin cancer.

In previous research [5] we used a smaller data set, consisting of 276 cases, while our current data set consists of 410 cases and it is a superset of the previous data set. In both cases data were collected by the Dermatology Center in Rzeszow, Poland [9]. In addition, in the past [5] we used only one approach to discretization, based on an agglomerative method of cluster analysis. Our recent research [1] showed that another method of discretization, based on a divisive method of cluster analysis, produces much better results. Consequently, we present results obtained using both approaches to discretization, based on agglomerative and divisive methods of cluster analysis.

Our main objective was to find the optimal ABCD formula, using the two discretization methods, agglomerative and divisive. To accomplish this objective we performed two phases of experiments. In the first phase more than 30,000 experiments of ten-fold cross validation were performed, searching through the space of different ABCD formulas. First, we conducted about 10,000 experiments of ten- fold cross validation using the agglomerative discretization method, then another 20,000 experiments of ten-fold cross validation using the divisive discretization method. In both cases, the optimal formula was found using the criterion of the smallest error rate.

The second phase of experiments was used for evaluation of formulas obtained in the first phase. Three ABCD formulas: the original one, used by diagnosticians of melanoma and given in [15] and the two new ABCD formulas, obtained in the first phase of our experiments were compared using 30 experiments of ten-fold cross validation for each method. Additionally, two series of 30 experiments were used to the original data with deleted attribute TDS, to validate the claim from [11] that TDS is not useful for melanoma diagnosis.

2 Melanoma Data

TDS is computed on the basis of the ABCD formula, where four variables are used: *Asymmetry, Border, Color* and *Diversity*. The variable *Asymmetry* has three different values: *symmetric spot, one axial symmetry*, and *two axial symmetry*. *Border* is a numerical attribute, with values from 0 to 8. *Asymmetry* and *Border* are single-value attributes. The remaining two attributes, *Color* and *Diversity*, are many-value attributes. *Color* has six possible values: *black, blue, dark brown, light brown, red* and *white*. Similarly, *Diversity* has five values: *pigment dots, pigment globules, pigment network, structureless areas* and *branched stricks*. We introduced six single-valued variables describing color: *Color_black, Color_blue, Color_dark_brown, Color_light_brown, Color_red* and *Color_white* and five single-valued variables describing diversity: *Diversity_pigment_dots, Diversity_pigment_globules, Diversity_pigment_network, Diversity_structureless_areas* and *Diversity_branched_stricks*. In all of these 11 attributes the values are 0 or 1, 0 meaning lack of the corresponding property and 1 meaning the occurrence of the property. Thus, every case was characterized by the values of 13 attributes. On the basis of those 13 attributes the TDS was computed using the following formula (known as the ABCD formula):

$TDS = 1.3 * Asymmetry + 0.1 * Border + 0.5 * \Sigma Colors + \Sigma Diversities,$

where for *Asymmetry* the value *symmetric spot* counts as 0, *one axial symmetry* counts as 1, and *two axial symmetry* counts as 2, $\Sigma Colors$ represents the sum of all values of the six color attributes and $\Sigma Diversities$ represents the sum of all values of the five diversity attributes.

3 Discretization, Rule Induction, Validation

The melanoma data set contained three numerical attributes: Asymmetry, Border and TDS. The numerical attributes should be discretized before rule induction. The data mining system LERS uses for discretization a number of discretization algorithms. In our experiments we used two methods of cluster analysis: agglomerative (bottom-up) [3] and divisive (top-down) [14]. In both methods, during the first step of discretization, *cluster formation*, cases that exhibit the most similarity are fused into clusters. Once this process is completed, clusters are projected on all attributes to determine initial intervals on the domains of the numerical attributes. During the second step (*merging*) adjacent intervals are merged together. In the sequel, the former method will be called the agglomerative discretization method, the latter will be called the divisive discretization method.

In our experiments rules were induced by the algorithm LEM2 (Learning from Examples Module, version 2). LEM2 is a part of the system LERS [6], [7]. The classification system of LERS [7], to classify unseen cases, is a modification of the *bucket brigade algorithm* [2], [10].

The most important performance criterion for methods of data mining is the error rate. For evaluation of an error rate we used the ten- fold cross validation: all cases were randomly re-ordered, and then the set of all cases is divided into ten mutually disjoint subsets of approximately equal size. For each subset, all remaining cases are used for training, i.e., for rule induction, while the subset is used for testing. Thus, each case is used nine times for training and once for testing. Note that using different re-orderings causes slightly different error rates. LERS may use *constant ten-fold cross validation* by using the same way of re-ordering for all experiments. Also, LERS may perform ten-fold cross validation using different re-orderings for every experiment, called *variable ten-fold cross validation*.

4 Experiments

We assumed that the modified ABCD formula for a new TDS should have the same form of a linear equation as the old one:

$$new\_TDS = c_1 * Asymmetry + c_2 * Border + c_3 * Color\_black +$$
$$c_4 * Color\_blue + c_5 * Color\_dark\_brown + c_6 * Color\_light\_brown +$$
$$c_7 * Color\_red + c_8 * Color\_white + c_9 * Diversity\_pigment\_dots +$$
$$c_{10} * Diversity\_pigment\_globules + c_{11} * Diversity\_pigment\_network +$$
$$c_{12} * Diversity\_structureless\_areas + c_{13} * Diversity\_branched\_stricks.$$

The problem is what are optimal values for coefficients $c_1, c_2,..., c_{13}$. The criterion of optimality was the smallest total number errors for constant tenfold cross validation for data with 13 old, unchanged attributes and with a new fourteenth attribute, new_TDS, that replaced the original TDS attribute.

Table 1. Coefficient ranges for the agglomerative discretization method

Attribute	Tested range	Optimal coefficient
Asymmetry	0.1 – 2.0	0.9
Border	0.01 – 0.2	0.14
Color_black	0.4 – 0.6	0.5
Color_blue	0.4 – 0.6	0.5
Color_dark_brown	0.2 – 0.6	0.3
Color_light_brown	0.3 – 0.6	0.4
Color_red	0.4 – 0.6	0.5
Color_white	0.4 – 0.6	0.5
Diversity_pigment_dots	0.4 – 0.6	0.5
Diversity_pigment_globules	0.4 – 0.6	0.5
Diversity_pigment_network	0.4 – 0.6	0.5
Diversity_structureless_areas	0.4 – 0.6	0.5
Diversity_branched_stricks	0.4 – 0.5	0.5

In the first phase two series of experiments were performed. In the first series we performed about 10,000 experiments, for different vectors $(c_1, c_2,..., c_{13})$, applying the same agglomerative discretization method. For each vector $(c_1, c_2,..., c_{13})$ the corresponding new_TDS was computed and then the constant ten-fold cross validation was used for the evaluation of the number of errors. The smallest error (13 cases) indicated the optimal choice of (c1, c2,..., c13), see Table 1. In the sequel, such a data set, with TDS computed on the basis of the optimal $(c_1, c_2,..., c_{13})$ and with all remaining 13 attributes unchanged, will be called a data set obtained by the agglomerative method. In a similar way, about 20,000 experiments were conducted for the divisive discretization method. The optimal choice for $(c_1, c_2,..., c_{13})$ was associated with 11 errors, see Table 2. Similarly, the resulting new data set will be called a data set obtained by the divisive method.

A special script was created to compute the new TDS given ranges for all 13 coefficients $(c_1, c_2,..., c_{13})$. Due to computational complexity, not all combinations of coefficients that are implied by Tables 1 and 2 were tested. Experiments were conducted in sets of a few thousand at a time. Some overlapping occurred between such sets of experiments.

In phase 2 of our experiments, four different data sets were used: a data set with TDS computed according to the original formula; another data set, with a deleted TDS attribute; and the data sets obtained by the agglomerative and divisive methods. For each of these data sets two discretization methods were applied: agglomerative and divisive. Thus eight different methods were

Table 2. Coefficient ranges for the divisive discretization method

Attribute	Tested range	Optimal coefficient
Asymmetry	0.1 – 1.9	1.3
Border	0.1 – 0.13	0.11
Color_black	0.4 – 0.6	0.5
Color_blue	0.3 – 0.6	0.4
Color_dark_brown	0.3 – 0.6	0.4
Color_light_brown	0.4 – 0.6	0.5
Color_red	0.4 – 0.6	0.5
Color_white	0.3 – 0.6	0.4
Diversity_pigment_dots	0.3 – 0.6	0.4
Diversity_pigment_globules	0.4 – 0.6	0.5
Diversity_pigment_network	0.4 – 0.6	0.5
Diversity_structureless_areas	0.4 – 0.6	0.5
Diversity_branched_stricks	0.3 – 0.6	0.4

Table 3. Number of intervals for numerical attributes

Method	Number of intervals		
	Asymmetry	Border	TDS
1	2	4	3
2	2	3	3
3	3	5	–
4	3	5	–
5	3	3	3
6	3	3	3
7	3	5	2
8	2	3	3

tested using 30 experiments of variable ten-fold cross validation for each method. Results of these experiments are presented in Tables 3–5, where the following codes were used for the different methods:

1. The original data set was discretized using the agglomerative discretization method,

2. The original data set was discretized using the divisive cluster analysis algorithm,

3. From the original data the attribute TDS was deleted and then the agglomerative discretization method was used,

4. From the original data the attribute TDS was deleted and then the divisive discretization method was used,

5. For the data set obtained by the agglomerative method the agglomerative discretization method was used,

6. For the data set obtained by the agglomerative method the divisive discretization method was used,

7. For the data set obtained by the divisive method the agglomerative discretization method was used,

8. For the data set obtained by the divisive method the divisive discretization method was used.

In order to compare the overall performance of all eight methods, the standard statistical two tailed test about the difference between two means was used, with the level of significance 5%. All eight methods were compared and ordered, from the best to the worst. The best methods are 2 and 8 (methods 2 and 8 are not significantly different). The next best methods are 1, 5, and 6 (again, methods 1, 5, and 6 are not significantly different). Then comes method 7. The worst methods are 3 and 4 (methods 3 and 4 are not significantly different).

Table 4. Number of rules and total number of conditions

Method	Number of rules	Total number of conditions
1	31	118
2	23	84
3	71	349
4	76	367
5	31	124
6	29	110
7	62	291
8	27	108

Table 5. 95 % confidence intervals for the error mean

Method	Confidence interval
1	17.97 ± 1.09
2	14.33 ± 1.09
3	56.67 ± 1.59
4	55.30 ± 1.55
5	18.50 ± 1.14
6	18.37 ± 0.99
7	42.17 ± 1.60
8	14.87 ± 0.72

5 Conclusions

First of all, our current results differ from previously reported [5], even though one of our discretization methods, agglomerative, was used in our research before and now. The difference is caused by the size of the input data set. Before, the data set contained 276 cases, in our current data set 134 additional cases were included. Thus our current data set is more representative. Before we observed significant difference in performance between the original ABCD formula and the optimal ABCD formula (the error rate dropped from 10.21% for the original ABCD formula to 6.04% for the optimal ABCD formula). By the way, for our current best method (the original data set was discretized using the divisive cluster analysis algorithm), the error rate is 3.50%. More importantly, there is not significant difference in performance between the original and optimal ABCD formulas.

Also, there is no significant difference in performance in applying the divisive method of discretization to the data set with TDS computed using the original ABCD formula or using the optimal ABCD formula, obtained by using the divisive method, and then divisive method of discretization. The same is true, with corresponding changes, for our second method of discretization, agglomerative. However, the divisive method of discretization is significantly better than the agglomerative method of discretization. Thus, the choice of the discretization method is more important than the choice of the best ABCD formula.

Another interesting observation is that if the optimal ABCD formula, obtained by the agglomerative method was used later for discretization using the divisive method of discretization, results were good (the same quality as using the agglomerative method for both: search for the best ABCD formula and for discretization). But the agglomerative method of discretization, used for the optimal formula obtained using the divisive method of discretization, was significantly worse. It reinforces the issue that the choice for the final discretization is more important than the choice of the ABCD formula.

Surprisingly, the worst methods (3, 4, and 7) are characterized by the largest number (five) intervals of the attribute Border, see Table 3. Also, the two methods (2 and 8) producing the smallest number of rules (Table 4) are also performing the best in the terms of the smallest error number, see Table 4. It reaffirms the principle that the simplest description is the best.

The worst results were associated with ignoring attribute TDS altogether. The same result was reported in our previous research [5]. Therefore, the claim by [11] that the ABCD formula is not helpful is not true.

In this paper we restricted our attention to the two methods of discretization mostly because corresponding experiments are very time consuming. In the future we plan to extend our research to other methods of discretization.

Acknowledgment. This research has been partially supported by the State Committee for Research (KBN) of the Republic of Poland under the grant 7 T11E 030 21.

References

1. Bajcar, S., Grzymala-Busse, J. W., and Hippe. Z. S.: A comparison of six discretization algorithms used for prediction of melanoma. Accepted for the Eleventh International Symposium on Intelligent Information Systems, Poland, June 3–6, 2002.

2. Booker, L. B., Goldberg, D. E., and Holland J. F.: Classifier systems and genetic algorithms. In Machine Learning. Paradigms and Methods. Carbonell, J. G. (Ed.), The MIT Press, Boston, MA, 1990, 235–282.
3. Chmielewski, M. R. and Grzymala-Busse, J. W.: Global discretization of continuous attributes as preprocessing for machine learning. Int. Journal of Approximate Reasoning 15, 1996, 319–331.
4. Friedman, R. J., Rigel, D. S., and Kopf, A. W.: Early detection of malignant melanoma: the role of physician examination and self-examination of the skin. CA Cancer J. Clin. 35, 1985, 130–151.
5. Grzymala-Busse, J. P., Grzymala-Busse, J. W., and Hippe Z. S.: Melanoma prediction using data mining system LERS. Proceeding of the 25th Anniversary Annual International Computer Software and Applications Conference COMPSAC 2001, October 8–12, 2001, Chicago, IL, 615–620.
6. Grzymala-Busse, J. W.: LERS—A system for learning from examples based on rough sets. In Intelligent Decision Support. Handbook of Applications and Advances of the Rough Sets Theory. Slowinski, R. (ed.), Kluwer Academic Publishers, Dordrecht, Boston, London, 1992, 3–18.
7. Grzymala-Busse J. W.: A new version of the rule induction system LERS. Fundamenta Informaticae 31 (1997), 27–39.
8. Grzymala-Busse J. W. and Hippe Z. S.: Postprocessing of rule sets induced from a melanoma data set. Accepted for the COMPSAC 2002, 26th Annual International Conference on Computer Software and Applications, Oxford, England, August 26–29, 2002.
9. Hippe, Z. S.: Computer database NEVI on endargement by melanoma. Task Quarterly 4, 1999, 483–488.
10. Holland, J. H., Holyoak, K. J., and Nisbett, R. E.: Induction. Processes of Inference, Learning, and Discovery. The MIT Press, Boston, MA, 1986.
11. Lorentzen, H. Weismann, K. Secher, L. Peterson, C. S. Larsen, F. G.: The dermatoscopic ABCD rule does not improve diagnostic accuracy of malignant melanoma. Acta Derm. Venereol. 79, 1999, 469–472.
12. Pawlak, Z.: Rough Sets. International Journal of Computer and Information Sciences, 11, 1982, 341–356.
13. Pawlak, Z.: Rough Sets. Theoretical Aspects of Reasoning about Data. Kluwer Academic Publishers, Dordrecht, Boston, London, 1991.
14. Peterson, N.: Discretization using divisive cluster analysis and selected postprocessing techniques. Department of Computer Science, University of Kansas, internal report, 1993.
15. Stolz, W., Braun-Falco, O., Bilek, P., Landthaler, A. B., Cogneta, A. B.: Color Atlas of Dermatology, Blackwell Science Inc., Cambridge, MA, 1993.

Towards the Classification of Musical Works: A Rough Set Approach

Monika P. Hippe

Institute of Music, University of Rzeszów
2 Dekerta St., 35-030 Rzeszów, Poland

Abstract. This paper suggests an approach to classifying musical works using a rough set approach. Base on a review of available literature devoted to applications of programming tools in studying mechanisms of music perception, the paper focuses on discovering hidden regularities in pieces of various types of music. This work is motivated by an interest in determining the influences of one composer on other composers. A brief overview of rough set methods underlying this study is presented. We also report a variety of different experiments that have been performed on some sample data extracted from musical compositions. The contribution of this paper is the identification of a set of attributes that can be used to classify musical works with a considerable accuracy.

Keywords: Attributes of music, attribute reduction, classify, decomposition tree, discretization, inference rules, rough sets.

1 Introduction

Application of computers to uncover mechanisms of perception of music and its influence on human beings has been for a long time an objective of a broad-based, extensive research effort. For example, particular attention has been devoted to cognitive psychology of music [1] and algorithmic representation of compositions [2]. Recently, new research directions like simulation and computer improvisation in music [3] and the use of machine learning and rough sets in understanding of personal style differences between individual artists [4], [8] have been reported. But the available literature does not supply any information about machine learning methods applied (in broader sense) in advanced classification of music works. The form of classification of musical works we have in mind is based on the inspection of standard music notations. Development of methodology for such classification could show how machine learning would profitably be applied to study various problems in the field of tonal music. Moreover, elaborated classifiers can be broadly applied in modern teaching of musicology. The classification methodology described in this paper can be useful in discovering characteristic features of the investigated musical compositions, and in identifying characteristic features of the production of a given composer.

The scope of this article limited to a study of selected polonaises of F. Chopin [g-moll from 1817, B-dur from 1817, As-dur from 1821, A-dur op. 40 no. 1, es-moll op. 26 no. 2, d-moll op. 71 no.1), and polonaises of other Polish composers ('*Polonez staropolski*' [5], '*Polonez*' by Chmielowski, from 1738, '*Pożegnanie Ojczyzny*' (a-moll) by Ogiński, '*Polonez Miechodmucha*' by Kurpiński, and polonaise '*Kto z mych dziewek serce której*' by Moniuszko [6]). Classification begins with the identification of some descriptive attributes (features) that provide a basis for a representation of musical knowledge on investigated objects (pieces of music) and their mutual interrelations in a rule-based system. A basic, limited set of attributes useful in classifying such musical works are presented. Other attributes besides those given in this paper are possible (see, e.g., [15]). The contribution of this paper is the presentation of a methodology based on rough sets that can be used to classify musical works.

This paper has the following organization. A brief explanation of the attributes of musical compositions considered in this study is presented in Section 2. An overview of rough set methods is given in Section 3. A rough set approach to musical classification is presented in Section 4, and experimental results are reported in Section 5.

2 Attributes of Selected Music Works

The following attributes (and their logical values, see Table 1) were chosen: *beat_characteristic, structure, figuration, harmony, imitation, melody, motif, repeating_of_ motif, succession_of_harmony, succession_of_melody, repeating_of_ succession,* and *rhythm_disorder*. Thus, all pieces of music (both Chopin's and not_Chopin's) have been analyzed to find characteristic attributes (features) mentioned in Table 1. In this way the inherent musical content of a given composition has been represented in the form of a vector, containing 12 elements (12 descriptive attributes), and one binary decisive attribute (<Chopin>, <not_Chopin>). Simultaneously, names of the attributes displayed in Table 1, labeled columns of the **decision table** (not shown here), used later – according to current needs – for the development of decision trees and/or production rules. This approach was substantiated by a very low suitability, in our investigations, of typical database architecture and computer programs for searching data. Namely, using a standard query tool, the user probably always assumes that regarded feature is affected by a relation, known to him/her. For example, rising a question "*what is the fraction of music compositions with progression of melody for etudes, and what is for ballades?*"), the user certainly assumes that progression of melody is influenced by the type of music composition.

On the other hand, machine learning methods (and directly connected with them data mining procedures) tackle a broader underlying goal, namely, determining the most significant factors that affect hidden features of music pieces. In this way machine learning (and data mining, too) methods try to discover relationships and hidden patterns that may not always be obvious. Taking into account specificity of the research performed, the condition attributes (features)

Table 1. Condition Attributes Used to Classify Musical Works

index	Condition Attribute	Logical Value
0	Beat_characteristic	[mixed] [bichronic] [trichronic] [tetrachronic] [pentachronic]
1	Structure	[homophonic] [polyphonous]
2	Figuration	[absent] [is_8] [is_16] [is_32] [is_64]
3	Harmony	[absent] [dur_moll] [modal]
4	Imitation	[absent] [present]
5	Melody	[wavy] [figurative] [cantillate] [falling] [raising] [ornamental]
6	Motif	[absent] [wavy] [arched] [falling] [raising]
7	Repeating_of_motif	[absent] [literal] [spread out] [abridged] [variant]
8	Succession_of_harmony	[absent] [mod_falling] [mod_raising] [not_mod_falling] [not_mod_raising]
9	Succession_of_melody	[absent] [falling] [raising]
10	Repeating_of_succession	[absent] [twofold] [threefold] [fourfold] [fivefold]
11	Rhythm_disorder	[absent] [present]

in Table 1 are intended to represent musical knowledge of pieces of music and their mutual interrelations.

3 Rough Set Methods

This section gives a brief overview of some fundamental concepts and features of rough set theory that are important to an understanding of music work classification methods described in this article. Rough set theory provides a suite of methodologies useful in the numerical characterization of imprecise data [9]. For computational reasons, a syntactic representation of knowledge is provided by rough sets in the form of data tables. Informally, a data table is represented as a collection of rows each labeled with some form of input, and each column is labeled with the name of an attribute that computes a value using the row input. Consider, for example, a small table reflecting evaluaton of two polonaises w1 and w2 using beat_characteristic, structure, and figuration. If a decision column is added to the table, then the data table is called a decision table (see Fig. 1).

input \ A	beat_characteristic	structure	figuration	composer
w1	4_chronic	homophonic	is_32	Chopin
w2	5_chronic	homophonic	is_32	Chopin

Fig. 1. Partial Sample Decision Table

In Fig. 1, for example, polonaise w1 is tetrachronic, homophonic, and its figuration attribute value equals 'is_32'. In this sample partial decision table, the composer of w1 is asserted to be Chopin. In effect, this table encodes knowledge about two musical works w1 and w2. Formally, a data (information) table is represented by a pair (U, A), where U is a non-empty, finite set of objects and A is a non-empty, finite set of attributes, where $a : U \to V_a$ for every $a \in A$.

4 Music Classification Methods

A brief description of two methods that can be used to set up a musical work classification system is given in this section. The input to such an algorithm is a condition vector without information about a decision value. The two change prediction methods are distinguished by the reduct-derivation method used. The simplest of the two methods does not use discretization of real-valued condition attributes (i.e., partition of the value set of each attribute into subintervals). The second of the two prediction methods relies on discretization of real-valued attributes. Because condition attributes are associated with subintervals of reals, the resulting rules using the discretization method of software change prediction are more general. A straightforward way for software managers to build such a software change prediction system is to use an existing rough set based toolset that has been extensively tested. More than a dozen such toolsets are currently available. The results reported in this article are based on a music composition prediction system using the Rough Set Exploration System (RSES) described in [12].

4.1 Decision Tree Classification Method

The decomposition tree method has been used to classify the music data. Many different splits of the music data were used for the training and testing sets. It was found that a 60/40 split of a musical composition decision table yielded the best classification results reported in this paper, namely, 100% accuracy in classifying non-Chopin compositions, and approximately 70% accuracy in classifying Chopin polonaises.

4.2 Non-discretization Rule-Based Classification Method

The non-discretization rule-based musical composition prediction method is based on matching condition attribute values in an input vector of musical composition attribute values (i.e., condition attribute values) with exact values associated with each of the condition attributes of a derived rule. In the case where musical compositions are similar, the non-discretization method has some chance of success. That is, for similar musical compositions, it is more likely that a composer prediction rule can be found where the exact values of the attributes in the premise of the rule match composition attribute values for a new composition. The RSES toolset constructs training (TRNtable) and testing (TSTtable) tables randomly. The following algorithm is a high-level description of a very detailed algorithm for non-discretized decision rule generation.

Algorithm 1.
[Non-Discretization-Based Musical Composition Prediction]

Input	Table T (set of real-valued condition vectors plus corresponding decisions)
Output	Set of reducts, set of decision rules, and classification results
Step 1	Split T into training table (TRN) and testing table (TST)
Step 2	Derive Reducts from TRN from Step 1
Step 3	Derive decision rules from TRN (Step 1) and reducts (Step 2)
Step 4	Based on condition vectors in TST and rules (Step 3), predict decision values
Step 5	Stop

The rules obtained using Algorithm 1 can be used to predict a musical composer decision based on the input of the condition vector containing musical composition attribute values where the corresponding composer decision is unknown. It is important to notice that the ith condition attribute a_i with value v_{ai} in a non-discretized rule has the form ($a_i=v_{ai}$). This means non-discretized rules lack generality (a rule only applies if condition attributes values in a test case exactly match the condition attribute values in a rule). For this reason, a more general musical composer prediction system results from the derivation of a set of discretized rules.

4.3 Musical Composition Prediction Algorithm with Discretization

A musical composition prediction algorithm with discretization is given in this section. Let A be a set of attributes (e.g., software complexity metrics) and let a $\in$ A be defined by a mapping a: X $\rightarrow$ V, where X, V are the domain and range of attribute a, respectively. In discretization of attribute, attributes are real-valued and it is also assumed that $V_a = [l_a, r_a] \subset \Re$ for any a $\in$ A where $\Re$ is a set of real numbers. Discretization leads to a partition of V_a into (a, c), where a $\in$ A and c $\in$ $\Re$. The Algorithm 2 is a high-level description of a very detailed algorithm for decision rule generation in [12].

The rules obtained using Algorithm 2 can be used to predict a software change decision based on the input of the condition vector containing discretized software metric values where the corresponding change decision is unknown. All of the experimental results reported in this article use the order-based genetic algorithm [12]. A 70/30 split of a musical composition data table gave 100% accuracy in classifying non-Chopin compositions and 50% accuracy in classifying Chopin compositions. This is a marked improvement over the non-discretized experiment and still is not as good as the decomposition tree experimental results.

Algorithm 2.
[Discretization-Based Musical Composition Prediction]
Input Table T(set of real-valued condition vectors plus corresponding dec.)
Output Set of cuts, set of reducts, set of dec. rules, and classification results
Step 1 Split T into training table (TRN) and testing table (TST)
Step 2 Derive set of cuts for each attribute in TRN
Step 3 Discretize TRN using the cuts from (2)
Step 4 Derive Reducts from discretized TRN from (3)
Step 5 Derive discretized decision rules from TRN (3) and reducts (4)
Step 6 Discretize TST using cuts from (2) to obtain discretized test table
Step 7 Based on condition vectors in TST and rules (5) predict dec. values
Step 8 Stop

5 Experimental Results

Classification of polonaises reported in this paper has been carried in an earlier study [13]-[14] using a number of toolsets 1stClass [7], LERS [10], GTS [10], and VVT [10]. The results reported in this paper are limited to what has been found using the Rough Sets Exploration System (RSES), version 1.1 [12]. A total of 11 musical compositions are represented in the sample decision table used in this study. A summary of the classification results found in this study is given in Table 2.

Table 2. Summary of Classification Results

Case	Split (train/test)	Error Train	Test	# of Rules	Reduct Set
ND		Non-Discretized Attributes (original table)			
ND1	60/40 tree	0.0	0.0 (d1) 0.3 (d2)	none	All attributes
ND2	90/10	0.0	1.0 (d1) 0.0 (d2)	21	0,1,2,3,4,6,7 (beat_char, structure, figuration, harmony, melody, motif)
D		Discretized Attributes (original table)			
D2	70/30	0.0	1.0 (d1) 0.5 (d2)	4	0, 1, 2 (beat_char, structure, figuration)
ND		Non-Discretized Attributes (reduced table)			
ND1	60/40 tree	0.0	1.0 (d1) 0.0 (d2)	None	All attributes
ND2	50/50	0.0	0.0 (d1) 1.0 (d2)	12	1,2,3,6,7 (structure, figuration, harmony, melody, motif)
D		Discretized Attributes (reduced table)			
D1	50/50	0.0	0.4 (d1) 0.0 (d2)	2	9 (succession_of_melody)
D2	70/30	0.0	0.0 (d1) 0.5 (d2)	4	0, 1, 2 (beat_char, structure, figuration)

Four types of experiments are represented in Table 2: non-discretization and discretization for two different decision tables (original table with 11 cases, and reduced table with 9 cases). It was found in an earlier study that cases 5 and 10 were inconsistent and led to incorrect classification [13]. Hence both the original table and classification results with the reduced table were compared. Notice that discretization of the reduced table led to a case where succession_of_melody was sufficient to classify the compositions in a 50/50 split of the table. In all of the experimental results except one, structure and figuration were part of the reducts used to derive classification rules. This partly corroborates the earlier study of this data.

6 Concluding Remarks

A rough set approach to classifying musical works has been presented in this paper. This work complements earlier work using machine learning methods to classify musical works. Based on a review of available literature devoted to applications of programming tools in studying mechanisms of music perception, this paper points how one might discover hidden regularities in pieces of various types of music using rough set methods. Chief among these methods is attribute reduction, where rough set methods facilitate the search for minimal sets of attributes (reducts) needed to classify musical works. We report a variety of different experiments that have been performed on some sample data extracted from musical compositions. In the continuation of this research, larger data sets extracted from musical works will be considered. It is also possible to consider adding to the set of attributes, especially real-valued attributes of musical works, used in constructing decision tables.

Acknowledgements. Research of this type would not have been possible without substantial contribution to the application of RSES program in analyzing my data and was generously done by Prof. Dr. James F. Peters from the University of Manitoba, Canada. I acknowledge gratefully his valuable support and comments.

References

1. Sloboda J.: The Musical Mind: The Cognitive Psychology of Music. Clarendan Press, Oxford 1985.
2. Desain P.: *A (de)composable Theory of Rythm Perception.* Computers in Music Res. 9(1992,4)439–454.
3. Risset J.C.: *ACROE Programme.* Proc.13th Intern. Joint Conference on Artificial Intelligence, Chambery 28.08-3.09.1993, pp. 26–27.
4. Widmer G.: *Application of Machine Learning to Music Research: Empirical Investigation into the Phenomenon of Musical Expression.* In: Michalski R.S., Bratko I., Kubat M. (Eds.) Machine Learning and Data Mining. Methods and Applications. J. Wiley & Sons, Ltd., New York 1998, pp. 269–295.

5. Hławiczka K. (Ed.): *From Polish Polonaises*. Vol. 1, PWM, Cracow 1975. (in Polish).
6. Lachowska S. (Ed.): *From Polish Polonaises*. Vol. 2, PWM, Cracow1975. (in Polish).
7. Hapgood W.: *1stClass Instruction Manual*. Programs in Motion Inc., Wayland (MA) 1989.
8. Kostek B.: Computer-Based Recognition of Musical Phrases Using the Rough-Set Approach. J. Information Sciences, vol. 104, 15–30, 1998.
9. Pawlak Z.: *Knowledge and Rough Sets*. In: Traczyk W. (Ed.) *Problems of Artificial Intelligence*. Wiedza i ycie Publishers, Warsaw 1995, pp. 9–21.(in Polish).
10. Hippe Z.S.: *New Method of Expert Systems Design: Concept and Implementation*. In: Bubnicki Z, Grzech A. (Eds.) *Knowledge Engineering and Expert Systems*. Editorial Office Wrocław University of Technology, Wrocław 1997, pp. 13–20.(in Polish).
11. Mazur M.: *Virtual Visualization Tool.* In: *New Algorithms and Methods of Domain-oriented Knowledge Representation and Processing.* State Committee for Scientific Research, Res. Reprot No. 8 T11C 004 09, Rzeszów 1999. (in Polish).
12. RSES 2002, http://logic.mimuw.edu.pl/~rses/
13. M.P. Hippe, Computer-Assisted Searching for Hidden Regularities in Selected Music Works. In: N. Schuler (Ed.), Computer Application in Music Research: Concepts, Methods, Results. P. Lang Publ., Frankfurt/Main 2002, 135–143.
14. M.P. Hippe, Informational Database on Selected Music Works, TASK QUARTERLY, vol. 4 (1) 2000, 83–90.
15. N. Schuler, D. Uhrlandt, Musana 1.0 – Ein Musikanalyse-Programm. Germany: Verlag & Vertrieb Axel Dietrich, 1994.

Segmentation of Medical Images Based on Approximations in Rough Set Theory

Shoji Hirano and Shusaku Tsumoto

Department of Medical Informatics, Shimane Medical University, School of Medicine
89-1 Enya-cho, Izumo, Shimane 693-8501, Japan
hirano@ieee.org; tsumoto@computer.org

Abstract. This paper presents an image segmentation method based on rough set theory. The focus of this paper is to discuss how to approximate a region of interest (ROI) when we are given multiple types of expert knowledge. The method contains three steps including preprocessing. First, we derive discretized attribute values that describe the characteristics of a ROI. Secondly, using all attributes, we build up the basic regions (namely categories) in the image so that each region contains voxels that are indiscernible on all attributes. Finally, according to the given knowledge about the ROI, we construct an ideal shape of the ROI and approximate it by the basic categories. Then the image is split into three regions: a set of voxels that are – (1) certainly included in the ROI (Positive region), (2) certainly excluded from the ROI (Negative region), (3) possibly included in the ROI (Boundary region). The ROI is consequently represented by the positive region associated with some boundary regions. In the experiments we show the result of implementing a rough image segmentation system.

1 Introduction

With rapid prevalence of high-speed computers and high-resolution medical scanners such as X-ray computed tomography (CT) and magnetic resonance imaging (MRI), computer-based medical image analysis has received wide recognition as an indispensable technique for efficient and accurate diagnosis. Over the past two decades, a number of tools for segmenting regions of interests (ROIs) have been developed to facilitate the use of volumetric images that enable us to reveal abnormality of the ROI by means of three-dimensional visual inspection and volumetry [1,2,3].

Due to anatomical complexity of the ROIs, most of the medical image segmentation systems use domain knowledge of experts to determine boundary of the ROIs. One of the widely used technique is rule-based segmentation, in which domain knowledge is represented as an anatomical model [4] or a set of rules in the expert system [5]. Arata *et al.* [6] presented a method for constructing an anatomical model of the brain from actual MR images and a segmentation method of cerebral ventricles using the constructed anatomical model. Li *et* al. [7] proposed a knowledge-based method for labeling brain tissue and finding abnormality in brain MR images. Brown et al. [8] proposed an automated, knowledge-based expert system for segmenting chest CT images. Generally, in such rule-based segmentation systems, domain knowledge is considered to be stable, and rarely modified during the routine operation. However, due to unexpected factors in image acquisition, for example superposition of noise and distortion of the images, the employed knowledge may not provide sufficient information to determine the boundary of the ROI. In such a case, we should consider the way to represent inconsistency between the expected boundary of the ROI derived using the expert knowledge and actual boundary of the ROI obtained using local image features.

This paper presents a knowledge-based image segmentation method based on rough set theory [9]. The main advantage of this method is its ability to represent inconsistency between the expected and actual shapes of the ROI using approximations. The method contains three steps including preprocessing. First, we derive discretized attribute values that describe the characteristics of a ROI. Secondly, using all attributes, we build up the basic regions (namely categories) in the image so that each region contains voxels that are indiscernible on all attributes. Finally, according to the given knowledge about the ROI, we construct an ideal shape of the ROI and approximate it by the basic categories. Then the image is split into three regions: (1) a set of voxels that are certainly included in the ROI (Positive region), (2) a set of voxels that are certainly excluded from the ROI (Negative region), (3) a set of voxels that are possibly included in the ROI (Boundary region). The ROI is consequently represented by the positive region associated with some boundary regions. In the experiments we show the result of implementing a rough image segmentation system.

2 Preliminary

Let $U \neq \phi$ be a universe of discourse and X be a subset of U. An equivalence relation, R, classifies U into a set of subsets $U/R = \{X_1, X_2, ...X_n\}$ in which the following conditions are satisfied: (1) $X_i \subseteq U, X_i \neq \phi$ for any i, (2) $X_i \cap X_j = \phi$ for any i, j, (3) $\cup_{i=1,2,...n} X_i = U$. Any subset X_i, called a category, represents an equivalence class of R. A category in R containing an object $x \in U$ is denoted by $[x]_R$. An indiscernibility relation $IND(R)$ is defined as follows.

$$xIND(R)y = \{(x,y) \in U^2 \mid (x,y) \in P, P \in U/R\}.$$

Approximation is used to represent roughness of the knowledge. Suppose we are given an equivalence relation R and a set of objects $X \in U$. The R-lower and R-upper approximations of X are defined as

$$\underline{R}X = \cup\{Y \in U/R \mid Y \subseteq X\},$$

$$\overline{R}X = \cup\{Y \in U/R \mid Y \cap X \neq \phi\}.$$

The lower approximation $\underline{R}X$ contains sets that are certainly included in X, and the upper approximation $\overline{R}X$ contains sets that are possibly included in X. R-positive, R-negative and R-boundary regions of X are respectively defined as follows.

$$POS_R(X) = \underline{R}X,$$
$$NEG_R(X) = U - \overline{R}X,$$
$$BN_R(X) = \overline{R}X - \underline{R}X.$$

3 Rough Representation of a ROI

3.1 Single Knowledge

Usually, the constant variables defined in the prior knowledge, for example some threshold values, do not meet the exact boundary of images due to inter-image variances of the intensity. Our approach tries to roughly represent the shape of the ROI by approximating the given shapes of the ROI by the primitive regions derived from feature of the image itself.

Let us assume the simplest case where we have only information about intensity range of the ROI. In this case intensity thresholding is a conventional approach to obtain the voxels that fall into the given range. Let us denote the lower and upper thresholds by Th_L and Th_H, respectively. Then the ROI can be represented by

$$ROI = \{x(p) \mid Th_L \leq I(x(p)) \leq Th_H\}$$

where $x(p)$ denotes a voxel at location p and $I(x(p))$ denotes intensity of voxel $x(p)$. For the sake of simplicity we denote $I(x(p))$ by $I(p)$ in the following sections.

Generally, this simple approach involves a major problem. A voxel whose intensity is outside the range is excluded from the ROI regardless of the degree of deviation of intensity and geometric distance from the ROI. Although the edge-based approaches, for example combination of edge detection filters and the region growing technique may produce better results, discontinuity of edge often leads to failure in controlling the growing process. One of the promising approaches that overcomes this problem is clustering. It gathers up a set of voxels by minimizing intra-cluster deviations and maximizing inter-cluster deviations. Therefore the boundary is determined based on the separability of the regions, not on the difference of each pixel. This produces reasonable boundary, however, there are no means of knowing how well the boundary overlaps the given knowledge. For example, suppose that a cluster (namely region) C_i contains voxels whose intensity is ranged from 100 to 120, and that Th_L is given as 110. In this case, we have no enough information that can be used for making a decision whether or not we should include C_i to the ROI. For practical use, one may make a decision based on intensity distribution of C_i. Let us denote $d(C_i)$ an evaluation function for C_i that returns $d(C_i) = 1$ when it is reasonable to include C_i to the ROI. Such a $d(C_i)$ can be defined as

$$d(C_i) = \begin{cases} 1, \text{ if } \frac{1}{N_i}\sum_{j=1}^{N_i} I(j) \geq Th_L, \\ 0, \text{ otherwise.} \end{cases}$$

where N_i denote the number voxels in C_i. Another function is also definable.

$$d(C_i)' = \begin{cases} 1, \text{ if } \frac{|Pi_L|}{|Pi_H|} \leq 1, \\ 0, \text{ otherwise.} \end{cases}$$

where $Pi_L = \{x(p) \in C_i | I(p) < Th_L\}$ and $Pi_H = \{x(p) \in C_i | I(p) \geq Th_L\}$. The function C_i uses average intensity of the region and C_i' uses ratio of the number of voxels that have lower/higher intensity than Th_L. By employing one of these functions, one can determine the crisp boundary of the ROI. However, the outer boundary of C_i may not exactly match the boundary that the prior knowledge provides. Namely, with respect to the knowledge that $Th_L = 110$, the 'True' boundary lies on somewhere in the boundary clusters. Therefore, we should say that the boundary cluster is possibly included in the ROI.

We use rough sets, especially the concept of approximations, to represent such an uncertain boundary region. On a volumetric image, a category X is built up as a set of contiguous voxels that have indistinguishable attribute values, for example the same intensity or same location. Discretization tools such as clustering methods and classifiers can be used to build up the elementary categories with proper level of granularity. In other words, the elemental categories are formed according to homogeneity of the low-level characteristics of the image itself. Note that we regard the two non-contiguous sets of voxels as different categories even if they have indistinguishable attribute values. This is because contiguity is the essential properties of a region and thus should be preserved in the resultant ROI.

After building the elementary categories, we determine the upper and lower approximations of the ROI given by the prior knowledge. The knowledge about intensity described previously defines an ideal shape of the ROI containing voxels that satisfy the threshold condition. However, such a ROI may not exactly be represented by the elementary sets of the image. In other words, boundary of the ROI may not fit to low-level feature of the image. In order to represent this inconsistency, we split the image into the following three regions:

Positive region: voxels that are certainly included in the ROI,
Negative region: voxels that are certainly excluded from the ROI
Boundary region: voxels that are possibly included in the ROI

Let us denote elementary categories by $U/IND(R) = \{C_1, C_2, \ldots, C_N\}$. Also let us denote a set of voxels that belong to the ideal ROI by $X_{ROI'}$. Then the above three region can be represented respectively as

$$POS_R(X_{ROI'}) = \underline{R}X_{ROI'},$$
$$NEG_R(X_{ROI'}) = U - \overline{R}X_{ROI'},$$
$$BN_R(X_{ROI'}) = \overline{R}X_{ROI'} - \underline{R}X_{ROI'}.$$

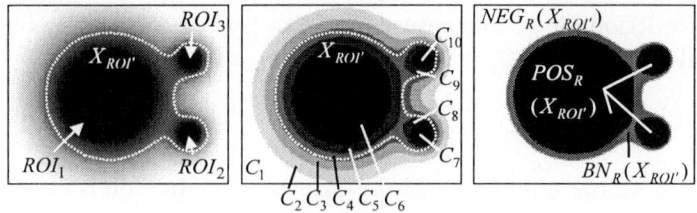

Fig. 1. A simple example of rough ROI representation. Left: an original image. Middle: elementary categories $C_1 - C_9$. Right: roughly segmented ROI. ROI=$POS_R(X_{ROI'})+BN_R(X_{ROI'})$.

The ROI in the image can be roughly represented by

$$ROI = POS_R(X_{ROI'}) + BN_R(X_{ROI'}).$$

Figure 1 illustrates the concept of rough ROI representation. The left image is an original grayscale image. Suppose that the ROIs are three black circular regions: ROI_1, ROI_2, and ROI_3. Also suppose that we are given a prior knowledge about the ROIs, that is, the lower threshold value Th_L of the ROIs, derived from some knowledge base. With this knowledge we can segment an ideal ROI $X_{ROI'}$:

$$X_{ROI'} = \{x(p) \mid Th_L \leq I(p)\}$$

However, $X_{ROI'}$ does not correctly match the expected ROIs. This is because Th_L was too small to separate the ROIs. Th_L is a global threshold determined on the other sets, therefore, it should not be directly applied to this image.

Then we represent the possible boundary of the ROIs according to the low-level feature of this image. First, we discretize intensity of the image into several levels. In this case, we obtained 10 regions $C_1 - C_{10}$ as shown in the center image of Figure 1. According to the previous definition, Positive, Negative, and Boundary regions can be obtained as follows.

$$POS_R(X_{ROI'}) = \underline{R}X_{ROI'} = \{C_5, C_6, C_7, C_8, C_9, C_{10}\},$$
$$NEG_R(X_{ROI'}) = U - \overline{R}X_{ROI'} = \{C_1, C_2, C_3\},$$
$$BN_R(X_{ROI'}) = \overline{R}X_{ROI'} - \underline{R}X_{ROI'} = \{C_4\}.$$

Then we obtain

$$ROI = POS_R(X_{ROI'}) + BN_R(X_{ROI'}) = \{C_4, C_5, C_6, C_7, C_8, C_9, C_{10}\}.$$

Consequently, we conclude that 'with respect to the given knowledge and image characteristics, the ROI is union of regions $C_5 - C_{10}$, along with possible boundary of C_4.

3.2 Multiple Knowledge

Medical image segmentation essentially involves the use of various types of expert knowledge due to anatomical complexity of the ROI. Such knowledge may be represented without referring to intensity information. For example, knowledge about proximity of organs can be defined using location of the voxels. It provides useful information in distinguishing the ROI and other regions connected homogeneously because location of organs are usually fixed in the human body. This section extends the concept of rough ROI representation so that it can handle multiple types of knowledge.

Let us assume that we have N types of prior knowledge about a ROI. Also let us assume that each of the knowledge is independent and associated with certain image attribute; for example, knowledge about intensity is represented using intensity of a voxel and knowledge about location is represented using position of a voxel in the Cartesian coordinate system. First, we discretize these attribute values and build basic categories for each of them as follows.

$$U/IND(R_1) = \{C_{11}, C_{12}, \ldots, C_{M_1}\},$$
$$U/IND(R_2) = \{C_{21}, C_{22}, \ldots, C_{M_2}\},$$
$$\vdots$$
$$U/IND(R_N) = \{C_{N1}, C_{N2}, \ldots, C_{M_N}\},$$

where $R_i (1 \leq i \leq N)$ denotes knowledge concerning attribute i, $C_{ij} (1 \leq j \leq M_i)$ denote an R_i-basic category containing voxels that are indiscernible on attribute i. Taking set theoretical intersections of all the elementary category, we can obtain the finest partition of voxels as follows.

$$U/IND(\mathbf{R}) = \bigcap_{1 \leq i \leq N} U/IND(R_i) = \{D_1, D_2, \ldots, D_M\}.$$

The set $\{D_1, D_2, \ldots, D_M\}$ represents the finest image-driven partition of the image.

Each of the prior knowledge can be used to define the expected shape of the ROI. For example, in the previous case of single knowledge about intensity, we represented the shape by $X_{ROI'}$. $X_{ROI'}$ was determined as a set of voxels that have higher intensity than Th_L. Now we extend it so that the shape of the expected ROI can be derived with respect to all of the given knowledge. We redefine $X_{ROI'}$ as an intersection of all of the expected shapes of the ROI:

$$X_{ROI'} = \bigcap_{1 \leq i \leq N} X_{ROI'_i},$$

where $X_{ROI'_i}$ represents an expected shape of the ROI derived with respect to the i-th knowledge. Using $U/IND(\mathbf{R})$ and $X_{ROI'}$, we then redefine the Positive, Negative and Boundary regions as follows.

$$POS_\mathbf{R}(X_{ROI'}) = \underline{\mathbf{R}} X_{ROI'},$$

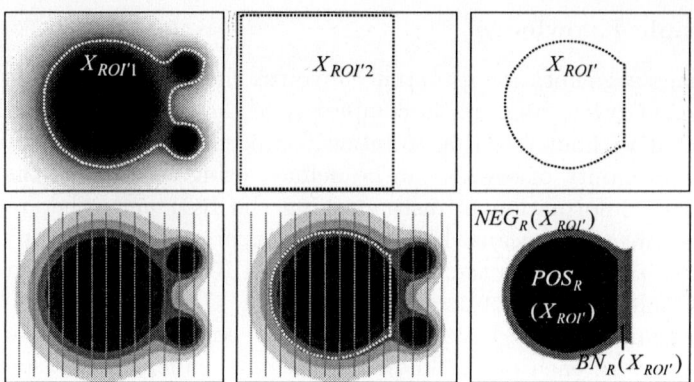

Fig. 2. An example of rough ROI representation with two types of knowledge. Upper Left: $X_{ROI'_1}$ with intensity knowledge. Upper Middle: $X_{ROI'_2}$ with location knowledge. Upper Right: $X_{ROI'}$ with both types of knowledge. Lower Left: $U/IND(\mathbf{R})$. A vertical line represents boundary of discretized horizontal location. Lower Middle: $X_{ROI'_2}$ over the discretized space. Lower Right: roughly segmented ROI. ROI=$POS_R(X_{ROI'})$ + $BN_R(X_{ROI'})$.

$$NEG_{\mathbf{R}}(X_{ROI'}) = U - \overline{\mathbf{R}}X_{ROI'},$$
$$BN_{\mathbf{R}}(X_{ROI'}) = \overline{\mathbf{R}}X_{ROI'} - \underline{\mathbf{R}}X_{ROI'}.$$

Also the ROI can be redefined as follows.

$$ROI = POS_{\mathbf{R}}(X_{ROI'}) + BN_{\mathbf{R}}(X_{ROI'}).$$

Figure 2 an shows example of rough ROI representation with two types of knowledge about intensity and location. Here we use simple knowledge description given below.

$$X_{ROI'_1} = \{x(p) \mid Th_{L_1} \leq I(p)\} \text{ (Intensity)},$$

$$X_{ROI'_2} = \{x(p) \mid Th_{L_2} \leq h(p)\} \text{ (Location)},$$

where Th_{L_1} and Th_{L_2} denote lower thresholds of intensity and location respectively, and h(p) denotes horizontal location of voxel $x(p)$. h(p) is assumed to be small if $x(p)$ is located on the right.

With proper threshold values, $X_{ROI'_1}$ and $X_{ROI'_2}$ define expected shapes of the ROI as shown in Figure 2 (upper left and middle respectively). Then they are integrated into $X_{ROI'}$ that represents the expected shape of the ROI with respect to both types of knowledge:

$$X_{ROI'} = X_{ROI'_1} \cap X_{ROI'_2}.$$

Figure 2 (upper right) shows $X_{ROI'}$.

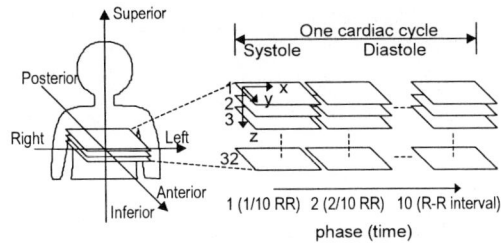
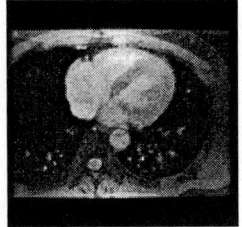

Fig. 3. The coordinate system.   **Fig. 4.** A raw MR image.

Then we check low-level feature of the image and construct the finest building blocks $U/IND(\mathbf{R})$. Assume that a discretization process yields 10 regions from intensity feature and 15 regions from location feature. The former regions correspond to $U/IND(R_1)$, and are represented as the gray-colored regions in Figure 2 (lower left). The latter regions correspond to $U/IND(R_2)$, and are represented by bands separated by laddered vertical lines. In the image, $U/IND(\mathbf{R})$ can be represented as a set of small regions where each region contains indiscernible voxels in terms of both intensity and location.

The final step is analogous to the case of single knowledge. In the same way, we obtain approximation of $X_{ROI'}$ by the regions in $U/IND(\mathbf{R})$. Consequently, we obtain the Positive, Negative and Boundary regions of $X_{ROI'}$ as shown in Figure 2 (lower right).

4 Implementation of Rough ROI Representation on Medical Images

This section describes an example of implementing rough ROI representation in medical images. The ROI was set to the heart on cardiovascular magnetic resonance (MR) images. The images were acquired using a 1.5T MR Scanner (Signa CV/i, GE Medical Systems). The scanning sequence was breath-hold two-dimensional FastCard FastCine (TE/TR = 4.3ms/R-R interval; FOV 260×260mm; matrix 256×256; thickness 3mm) without contrast agent. 33 coronal scans were performed to cover the entire heart. Each scan was performed in a single 15-heartbeat breath-hold, and 10 images (phases) were acquired per breath-hold. This produced a four-dimensional data consists of 256×256×33×10 voxels, in which a voxel is referred by $\alpha(p), p = \{x, y, z, t\}$. Figures 3 and 4 show the coordinate system and an example of raw MR image, respectively.

We employed three types of prior knowledge related to the characteristics of the heart in the images: myocardial motion, location and intensity.

1. Myocardial Motion
Under a breath-hold condition, movement of the diaphragm is suspended and the heart becomes the only organ moving spatially. This means that only voxels in and around the heart have intensity variance during one cardiac cycle. Therefore

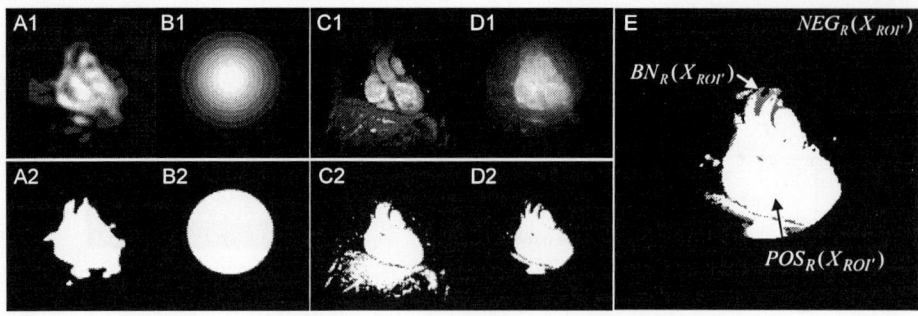

Fig. 5. An experimental result. A1: $U/IND(R_{mot})$, A2: $X_{ROI'_{mot}}$, B1: $U/IND(R_{loc})$, B2: $X_{ROI'_{loc}}$, C1: $U/IND(R_{int})$, C2: $X_{ROI'_{int}}$, D1: $U/IND(\mathbf{R})$, D2: $X_{ROI'}$, E: ROI=$POS_R(X_{ROI'}) + BN_R(X_{ROI'})$.

we designed an image filter, $\mu_{mot}(\alpha)$, that translates variance of intensity of voxel α during one cardiac cycle into the degree of being the heart, $X_{ROI'_{mot}}$, as follows.

$$X_{ROI'_{mot}} = \{\alpha(p) \mid Th_{L_{mot}} \leq \mu_m(\alpha(p))\}$$

2. Location

The heart has spherical shape and occupies center area in the image. This feature can be parameterized by using the Euclidean distance $\epsilon(\alpha)$ of voxel α to the center voxel in the data. The knowledge is then described as

$$X_{ROI'_{loc}} = \{\alpha(p) \mid \epsilon(\alpha(p)) \leq Th_{L_{loc}}\}.$$

3. Signal Intensity

Surface of the heart is mostly adjacent to the lung, which occupies lowest intensity range in the histogram. Since intensity ranges of the ventricles, atria, vessels and myocardia have little overlap with that of the lung, signal intensity can serve as a measure to distinguish the heart and the lung. Thus we simply employed intensity of a voxel, I, and represented knowledge about intensity as

$$X_{ROI'_{int}} = \{\alpha(p) \mid Th_{L_{int}} \leq I(\alpha(p))\}.$$

Figure 5 shows an experimental result. The lower thresholds for obtaining $X_{ROI'}$ were set as follows: $Th_{L_{mot}}$=87, $Th_{L_{loc}} = 80$, $Th_{L_{int}} = 61$. $U/IND(R_{mot})$ (A1), $U/IND(R_{loc})$(B1), $U/IND(R_{int})$(C1) were obtained by discretizing corresponding attributes into 10 levels. From Figure 5 E, We can visually confirm that the shape of the ROI could be roughly represented by approximating the ideal shape of the ROI (D2) by the finest, image-driven categories of the image (D1).

5 Conclusions

This paper has presented the concept of rough ROI representation associated with multiple types of expert knowledge. In it we represented an 'approximated'

ROI using two types of regions: Positive and Boundary regions. The former corresponds to the region that can certainly be defined as the ROI with respect both to the given knowledge and the actual feature of the image. The latter corresponds to the region that has partial insistence between them. It remains as a future work to include weight for each knowledge.

Acknowledgments. This work was partly supported by the Grant-in-Aid for Scientific Research (No. 14780289) by the Ministry of Education, Culture, Science and Technology of Japan.

References

1. J. C. Russ, *The IMAGE PROCESSING Handbook Second Edition*, CRC Press Inc., 1995.
2. E. Gose, R. Johnsonbaugh and S. Jost, *Pattern Recognition and Image Analysis*, Prentice Hall, Inc., 1996.
3. G. Lohmann, *Volumetric Image Analysis*, John Wiley & Sons Ltd and B. G. Teubner, 1998.
4. T. McInerney and D. Terzopoulos, "Deformable Models in Medical Image Analysis," in *Proc. the IEEE Workshop on Mathematical Methods in Biomedical Image Analysis*, pp. 171–180, 1996.
5. A. Kandel, *Fuzzy Expert Systems*, CRC Press Inc., 1992.
6. L. K. Arata, A. P. Dhawan, J. P. Broderick, M. F. Gaskil-Shipley, A. V. Levy and N. D. Volkow, "Three-dimensional Anatomical Model-Based Segmentation of MR Brain Images Through Principal Axes Registration," *IEEE Trans. Biomed. Eng.*, vol. 42, no. 11, pp. 1069–78, 1995.
7. C. Li, D. B. Goldgof and L. O. Hall, "Knowledge-based Classification and Tissue Labeling of MR Images of Human Brain," *IEEE Trans. Med. Imaging*, vol. 12, no. 4, pp. 740–750, 1993.
8. M. S. Brown, M. F. McNitt-Gray, N. J. Mankovich, J. G. Goldin, J. Hiller, L. S. Wilson and D. R. Aberie, "Method for Segmenting Chest CT Image Data Using an Anatomical Model: Preliminary Results," *IEEE Trans. Med. Imaging*, vol. 16, no. 6, pp. 828–939, 1997.
9. Z. Pawlak, *Rough Sets, Theoretical Aspects of Reasoning About Data*, Kluwer Academic Publishers, Dordrecht, 1991.

Adaptive Robust Estimation for Filtering Motion Vectors

Seok-Woo Jang[1], Essam A. El-Kwae[1], and Hyung-Il Choi[2]

[1] Computer Science, University of North Carolina at Charlotte, USA
{jseokwoo,eelkwae}@uncc.edu
[2] School of Media, Soongsil University, Seoul, South Korea
hic@computing.soongsil.ac.kr

Abstract. We propose an adaptive robust estimation algorithm for filtering motion vectors. We first extract motion vectors from consecutive images by using size-variable block matching and then apply the extracted motion vectors to adaptive robust estimation to filter them. The proposed robust estimation defines a sigmoid weight function, and eliminates outliers by gradually tuning the sigmoid function to the hard limit as the error between model parameters and input data is minimized.

1 Introduction

The robust estimation method is well-known for a good statistical estimator that is insensitive to small departures from the idealized assumptions for which the estimation is optimized [1]. It requires a merit function that measures the agreement between the data and the model with a particular choice of parameters. The parameters of the model are then adjusted to achieve a minimum in the merit function. The adjustment process is thus a problem in minimization of the residual error with respect to model parameters in many dimensions.

A common approach to multi-dimensional minimization problems is Levenberg-Marquardt method [2]. This method works well in practice and has become the standard of nonlinear least-squares data fitting. However, Levenberg-Marquardt method does not improve global convergence capabilities if it is not controlled effectively [3]. We also noticed that the robust estimation method uses a binary weight function called a threshold even in the initial steps of the minimization process. In those steps, it is very difficult to separate outliers from non-outliers since model parameters have not been fitted yet.

In this paper, to deal with these limitations, we propose an adaptive robust estimation method for filtering motion vectors. We first extract motion vectors from consecutive images by using size-variable block matching and then apply the extracted motion vectors to adaptive robust estimation to filter them.

2 Extraction of Motion Vectors

Block matching techniques have been extensively used for motion vector estimation [4]. However, most of them are concerned on how to define a search area where a candidate block is looked for. On the other hand, the proper selection of block size is another important criterion that determines the quality of the resulting motion vectors. Generally, larger blocks are suitable for rough but robust estimation. While smaller blocks are suitable for localizing the estimation, they are susceptive to noises.

We introduce size-variable block matching which dynamically determines the size of a block. Our size-variable block matching algorithm employs the evaluation function that examines matching degrees of candidate blocks to determine the appropriateness of the size of a block. This function is designed with the following considerations. First, we consider the distinctiveness of the best match. If the degree of the best match is close to those of its neighbor candidates, it may reflect that candidate blocks are within somewhat large area of a homogeneous region. We then suspect the inappropriateness of the size of a block and try to expand it. The second consideration is when to stop expanding the size. We take a simple criterion such that expanding stops when the distinctiveness of the best match does not improve any further even if we expand the size.

In order to formalize the above idea in the form of equation, we define the evaluation function $\Phi(i,j;n)$ as in Eq. (2). In Eq. (1), $(i^*,j^*;n)$ is the position where the best match occurs for the block at (i,j) of the size of n. We denote as $DT(i,j;n)$ the distinctiveness of the best match, which is the minimal difference between matching degrees of the best match and its neighbor candidates. $GD(i,j;n)$ denotes the gradient of the distinctiveness with respect to size, which is computed by subtracting the distinctiveness evaluated at size of n-1 from the distinctiveness evaluated at size of n. T_{pk}, e_1, and e_2 are constants that control the speed of convergence.

$$\Phi(i,j;n) = \max \begin{bmatrix} e_1 + TH(i,j;n) \\ e_2 + GD(i,j;n) \end{bmatrix} \times \frac{e_1 + TH(i,j;n)}{e_2 + GD(i,j;n)} \quad (1)$$

$$TH(i,j;n) = T_{PK} - DT(i,j;n)$$

$$GD(i,j;n) = DT(i,j;n) - DT(i,j;n-1)$$

$$DT(i,j;n) = \min_{-1 \leq l,m \leq 1}[DBS(i^*,j^*;n) - DBS(i+l,j+m;n)]$$

The evaluation function $\Phi(i,j;n)$ is so constructed that it has a positive value only when the distinctiveness is not greater than the threshold of T_{pk} and the gradient of the distinctiveness is positive.

3 Filtering of Motion Vectors

The proposed adaptive robust estimation is based on detection of outliers [1]. The outliers are mainly due to local moving objects or unsatisfactory correspondence between some feature points of image sequences. Outliers are independent of accurate motion vectors and degrade the estimation accuracy. Thus, they should be properly eliminated for a good estimation.

Adaptive robust estimation uses a continuous sigmoid weight function to effectively define the degree of membership between outliers and non-outliers.

Eq. (2) shows our weight function. In Eq. (2), W^k denotes the weight vector used in the k-th iteration, and w_j^k denotes the weight of the j-th input data that has values from 0 to 1. In the sigmoid function $sig^k(x; a^k, c^k)$, x denotes the input variable, c^k denotes the bias, and a^k denotes the gradient of the position where x equals to c.

$$W^k = \left(w_1^k, w_2^k, ..., w_j^k, ..., w_N^k\right) \qquad (2)$$
$$w_j^k = \alpha \cdot w_j^{k-1} + \beta \cdot (1 - sig^k(x = j; a^k, c^k))$$
$$sig^k(x; a^k, c^k) = \frac{1}{1 + e^{-a^k(x - c^k)}}$$
$$where\ 0 \leq \alpha, \beta \leq 1,\ \alpha + \beta = 1$$

Adaptive robust estimation separates outliers from non-outliers by gradually tuning the sigmoid weight function to the hard limit as the error between model parameters and input data is minimized. For this purpose, we tune the parameters c^k and a^k of the sigmoid weight function. We perform the tuning of the parameter c^k by using the x coordinate that corresponds to the steepest position in the graph of an accumulated residual error. In order to formalize the above idea in the form of equation, we define the parameter c^k as in Eq. (3).

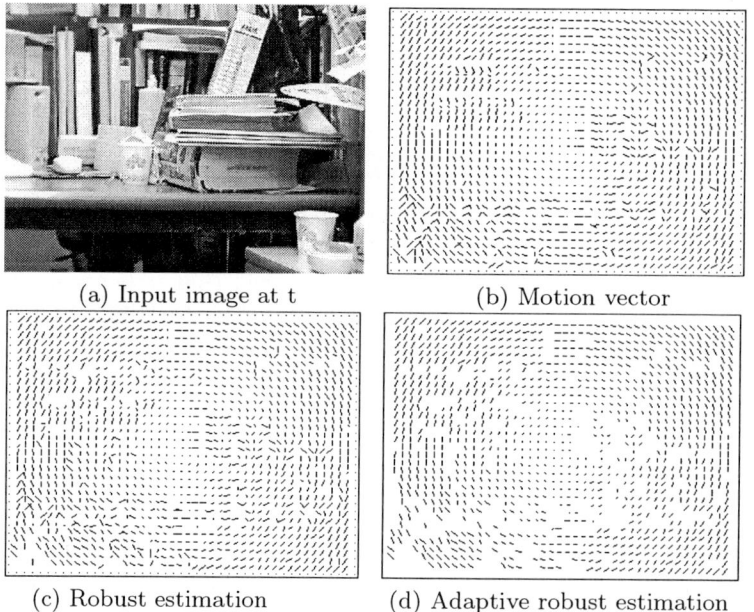

(a) Input image at t (b) Motion vector

(c) Robust estimation (d) Adaptive robust estimation

Fig. 1. Motion vector filtering

$$c^k = \alpha \cdot c^{k-1} + \beta \cdot \arg\max_{j} \max_{1 \leq j \leq N} \{D_j\} \qquad (3)$$

$$D_j = \frac{\left| \frac{E^k(N) - E^k(1)}{N-1} \cdot j - E^k(j) + \frac{N \cdot E^k(1) - 1 \cdot E^k(N)}{N-1} \right|}{\sqrt{\left(\frac{E^k(N) - E^k(1)}{N-1}\right)^2 + (-1)^2}}$$

$$E^k(j) = \sum_{l=1}^{j} w_l^{k-1} \| r_l^k \|$$

In Eq. (3), $E^k(j)$ denotes an accumulated residual error, and D_j denotes the distance between the accumulated residual error and the line which connects $E_k(0)$ and $E_k(N)$. We perform the tuning of the parameter a^k by using the ratio of the distance between $E^k(c)$ and $E^k(N)$. The value of $E^k(c)$ is decreased as the iteration of adaptive robust estimation proceeds since the error between model parameters and input data is gradually minimized. That is, the distance between $E^k(c)$ and $E^k(N)$ increases gradually as the iteration proceeds. In order to formalize the above idea in the form of equation, we define the parameter a^k as in Eq. (4).

$$a^k = a^{k-1} \times \frac{\frac{E^{k-1}(c)}{E^{k-1}(N)}}{\frac{E^k(c)}{E^k(N)}} \qquad (4)$$

4 Experimental Results and Discussions

Fig. 1 (a) shows an input frame in a sequence of test images. In this sequence, frames are captured with such camera operations as the rotation by two degrees per frame in a clockwise direction per frame. We extract motion vectors from the input images as in Fig. 1 (b). Ideally, the motion vectors should rotate in a form of a circle whose origin is the center of the image. We then apply the extracted motion vectors to adaptive robust estimation. During the robust estimation process, motion vectors corresponding to outliers are eliminated. Fig. 1 (c) and (d) shows the resulting outlier-filtered motion vectors.

Acknowledgement. This work was supported by the KOSEF through the AITrc.

References

1. J. I. Park and C. W. Lee: Robust Estimation of Camera Parameters from Image Sequence for Video Composition. Signal Processing, Vol. 9, No. 1 (1996) 43–53
2. W. H. Press, S. A. Teukolsky, W. T. Vetterling, and B. P. Flannery: Numerical Recipes in C : The Art of Scientific Computing. Cambridge University Press (1992)
3. S. Sclaroff and J. Isidoro: Active Blobs. Proc. of ICCV (1998) 1146–1153
4. S. W. Jang, K. J. Kim, and H. I. Choi: Accurate Estimation of Motion Vectors Using Active Block Matching. Proc. of RSCTC (2000) 527–531

Rough Set Feature Selection and Diagnostic Rule Generation for Industrial Applications

Seungkoo Lee, Nicholas Propes, Guangfan Zhang, Yongshen Zhao, and George Vachtsevanos

Georgia Institute of Technology
Electrical & Computer Engineering
Atlanta, GA 30332-0250
{sl145,gte813f,gte516x}@prism.gatech.edu; zhaoyongsheng01@hotmail.com;
gjv@ece.gatech.edu
http://icsl.marc.gatech.edu

Abstract. *Diagnosis* or *Fault Detection and Identification* is a crucial part of industrial process maintenance systems. In this paper, a methodology is proposed for fault feature selection that includes (1) feature preparation to obtain potential features from raw data, (2) multi-dimensional feature selection based on rough set theory, and (3) diagnostic rule generation to identify impending failures of an industrial system and to provide the causal relationships between the input conditions and related abnormalities.

1 Introduction

Modern industry is interested in extending the lifetime of its critical processes and maintaining them only when required. Emphasis has been placed recently on the development of reliable diagnostic systems for various industrial applications including aircraft [5], gas turbine engines [1], and shipboard machinery [4].

A generic and systematic framework to select relevant input features and to reveal the relationships among them for diagnosis is required. In this paper, a methodology based on rough set data-mining is suggested to select useful features from pre-selected feature candidates and to generate appropriate diagnostic rules. The proposed methods are applied to a navy chiller system in order to detect and identify critical fault conditions.

2 Feature Selection and Rule Generation for Industrial Diagnostic Systems

The proposed methodology consists of feature preparation, feature selection, and diagnostic rule generation. After raw data is accumulated in a suitable database, the data is transformed into candidate features. Next, multi-dimensional feature selection based on rough set methods is performed to derive those features that are relevant to a given fault mode. A rule generation task builds a diagnostic rulebase using rough set. Finally, the resulting rules are utilized to detect and identify the impending failures.

2.1 Feature Pre-processing and Pre-selection

Features are pre-processed first to remove artifacts, reduce noise and convert them to a discrete version by applying Kerber's ChiMerge algorithm with χ^2-threshold values for stopping conditions [6].

Feature pre-selection removes unreasonable features with narrow intervals or the existence of serious inconsistencies in the intervals. Each feature is evaluated using the following interval factor, IF,

$$IF = \sqrt[M/C_I]{\prod_{i=1}^{M} \frac{L_i}{L_t} max\{\frac{n_{ij}}{N_i}, j \in \{1,2,\ldots,O\}\}} \quad (1)$$

where L_i is the length of the ith interval, L_t, $|L_t| < \infty$, is the total length of the intervals, M is the number of intervals, C_I, $C_I \geq 1$, is the scaling factor, O is the number of output classes, n_{ij} is the objects of jth output class in the ith interval, and N_i is the total number of objects in the ith interval. The value of IF reflects the narrow intervals caused by noisy objects. By choosing a proper threshold, features with lower IF values are eliminated from the candidate set.

2.2 Rough Set Feature Selection and Rule Generation

Rough set methods in [2] and [3] are utilized for feature selection and rule generation. Rough set reduction is performed for feature selection using a discernibility matrix. For a subset of attributes $B \subseteq A$, the matrix is defined by

$$M_D(B) = \{m_D(i,j)\}_{n \times n}, \text{ for } i,j \in \{1,2,\ldots,n\} \quad (2)$$

where the entry $m_D(i,j)$, $m_D(i,j) = \{a \in B | a(E_i) \neq a(E_j)\}$, is the set of attributes from B that discerns object classes $E_i, E_j \in U/B$, $n = |U/B|$, and $|U/B|$ is the cardinality of U/B.

As a result of the reduction process, multiple reducts with the same degree of information may be obtained. However, features of the reducts may have different importance with respect to a certain fault mode. Thus, post-selection is performed to choose the best reduct. If the number of *complete* equivalence classes of the jth feature of a reduct is M_j, and the number of objects in the ith complete equivalence class is denoted by CE_{ij}, then the degree of separability of the feature, d_{sj}, is defined by

$$ds_j = \frac{1}{N} \sum_{i=1}^{M_j} CE_{ij} \quad (3)$$

where N is the number of objects in the set. Now, the degree of total separability of a reduct, Tds, is expressed by

$$Tds = \frac{1}{R} \sum_{j=1}^{R} ds_j \quad (4)$$

where, R is the number of features in a reduct. The elements of the feature vector are utilized for on-line feature extraction of the fault mode.

Once a feature vector is chosen for a certain fault mode, diagnostic rules are generated. A relative discernibility function, $f(E_i, B)$, was suggested to compute the minimal sets of attributes required to discern a given class E_i from the others, and the function of an object class E_i and attributes $B \subseteq A$ is defined by

$$f(E_i, B) = \wedge_{i,j \in \{1,2,\ldots,n\}, i \neq j} \vee \bar{m}_D(E_i, E_j) \tag{5}$$

where $n = |U/B|$, and $\vee \bar{m}_D(E_i, E_j)$ is recognized as the disjunction taken over the set of Boolean variables corresponding to the discernibility matrix $m_D(i,j)$. The following modified relative discernibility function is suggested to reduce redundant discriminations between the equivalence classes with the same output class. Let O_i be an output class of the ith equivalence class, where $i \in \{1, 2, \ldots, n\}$ and $n = |U/B|$. Then, the modified relative discernibility function is defined by

$$f(E_i, B) = \wedge_{i,j \in \{1,2,\ldots,n\}, i \neq j, O_i \neq O_j} \vee \bar{m}_D(E_i, E_j) \tag{6}$$

Minimal covering approach is considered for diagnostic rule generation.

3 Industrial Chiller Application

A chiller is a major component in an industrial cooling plant such as a shipboard air-conditioning process, as shown in Fig. 1. Abnormal conditions may degrade

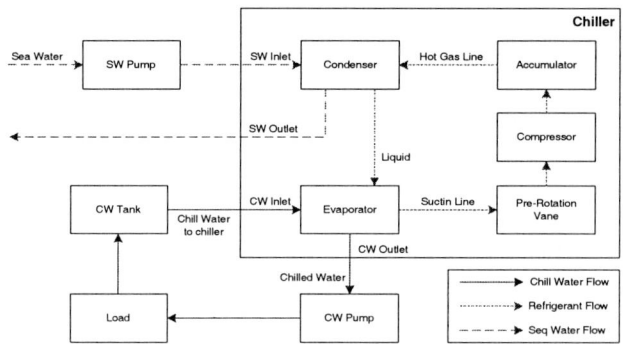

Fig. 1. Configuration of an air-conditioning plant in a navy carrier.

chiller performance or result in serious system failures. It is important, therefore, that relationships be discovered between the operating conditions and the corresponding system anomalies. Table 1 illustrates two typical fault modes in a navy chiller system. For feature selection and rule generation, feature candidates are

Table 1. Features and diagnostic rules for diagnosis of a navy chiller system.

Fault Mode	Number of Feature Candidates	Selected Features	Diagnostic Rules
Decreased sea water flow	11	Condenser sea water flow (CSWF), Condensor PD Pressur (CPDP)	If CSWF $\leq$ 750, then Sea water flow is decreased. Or If CPDP $\leq$ 1.9, then Sea water flow is decreased.
Decreased chilled water flow	8	Evaporator chill water flow (ECWF)	If ECWF $\leq$ 650, then Chilled water flow is decreased.

chosen based on experimental results and the system experts' experience. Features are discretized and pre-selected using the χ^2-statistic method. Then, the discernibility matrix is called upon to determine the features for each fault mode, as shown in the third column of the table. Finally, the diagnostic rules are induced using the modified relative discernibility functions, as shown in the last column of the table.

4 Conclusions

This paper introduces a conceptual framework for the selection of relevant features and the generation of diagnostic rules for industrial applications of a CBM architecture. Relevant features are selected from the feature candidates, and a rule generation module provides diagnostic relationships between input features and the resultant fault mode.

References

1. M. J. Roemer and G. J. Kacprzynski, "Advanced Diagnostics and Prognostics for Gas Turbine Engine Risk Assessment," In *Proceedings of IEEE Aerospace Conference*, 2000, pp. 345–353.
2. Z. Pawlak, *Rough Sets: Theoretical Aspects of Reasoning about Data*, Kluwer Academic Publishers, 1991.
3. J. Stepaniuk, "Rough set data mining of diabetes data," In *Proceeding of ISMIS'99: 11th International Symposium on Methodologies for Intelligent Systems*, 1999, pp. 457–65.
4. G. Hadden, G. Vachtsevanos, B. Bennett, and J. Van Dyke, "Shipboard Machinery Diagnostics and Prognostics/Condition Based Maintenance: A Progress Report," In *2000 IEEE Aerospace Conference*, 2000, vol. 6, pp. 277–292.
5. R. Heider, "Troubleshooting CFM 56-3 engines for the Boeing 737 using CBR and data-mining," In *Aneural Fuzzy Systems*, Prentice Hall P T R, Upper Saddle River, NJ, 1996.
6. R. Kerber, "Feature selection via discretization," In *Proceedings of Tenth National Conference on Artificial Intelligence*, 1992, pp. 123–128.

λ-Connected Approximations for Rough Sets

Li Chen

University of The District of Columbia, Washington, DC 20008, USA,
lchen@udc.edu

Abstract. Rough sets was first studied by Pawlak to describe the approximation of a set X by using its lower bound $L(X)$ and upper bound $U(X)$. λ-connectedness was originally proposed as a technique to search layers in 2D or 3D digital seismic data. This note introduces λ-connected components to represent lower and upper approximations for rough sets. According to Pawlak's definition of the boundary of X, $BN(X) = U(X) - L(X)$, $U(X)$ contains two "layers:" $L(X)$ and $BN(X)$. Representing the "layer" of $BN(X)$ is one of the key problems in rough set theory. This note shows when the boundary of X contains the property of gradual variations, $BN(X)$ can be represented by a partition of λ-connectedness which is a generalization of α-cut representation.

1 Introduction

In order to describe an unknown subset of a universal set, Pawlak proposed two crisp sets called lower and upper approximations, also known as rough sets [8][9][10][11]. These two approximations indicate the boundary of the uncertainty. Similar to fuzzy set theory, where a set is defined by a membership function, rough set theory also deals with the problem of imperfect knowledge. However, their philosophical differences are clear–Rough sets use crisp sets whereas fuzzy sets use non-crisp sets. On the other hand, the λ-connectedness method was developed for searching layers in 2D or 3D seismic data [2][4][5]. λ-connectedness can also be used to segment an image, find an object, or fit numerical surfaces/functions.

Previously, Pawlak indicated that the gradual variation, a special case of λ-connectedness, is directly related to rough continuous functions [10] and Rosenfeld's "continuous" digital functions [12]. In this aspect, an important theorem for the necessary and sufficient condition for filling a gradually varied surface/function, was proven in [3]. Adjei and Chen et al attempted to use λ-connectedness to represent special cases of rough sets in the applications of image processing [1].

Representing the boundary of a subset X is one of the key problems in rough set theory. A general consideration of the approximation of the boundary was studied by Skowron and Stepaniuk [13]. This note introduces λ-connected approximations to represent lower and upper approximations for general rough sets. This technique especially fit the case that the boundary contains the property of gradual variations. Since the λ-connected approximation is based on λ-connectedness which is a generalized fuzzy measure for fuzzy relations on graphs, we can use many existing graph-theoretic methods and algorithms to rough sets applications. For example, a maximum λ-connected spanning tree [6] can represent the structural information of the rough membership function of rough sets.

2   Basic Concept of Rough Sets and λ-Connectedness

Mathematically, given an equivalence relation R on the base set U, U can be partitioned by R into disjoint components, $P_1, ..., P_k$. Let X be a subset of U. The lower approximation $L_R(X)$ and upper approximation $U_R(X)$ are defined below:

$$L_R(X) = \cup_j \{P_j | P_j \subset X\} \text{ and } U_R(X) = \cup_j \{P_j | P_j \cap X \neq \emptyset\}.$$

In other words, $L_R(X)$ is the union of interior equivalence classes of X and $U_R(X)$ is the closure of X with respect to R. Thus,

$$L_R(X) \subset X \subset U_R(X). \tag{1}$$

On the other hand, computer science always concerns with discrete objects. The objects often have some kinds of relationship among them. Sometimes, the relationship is strong and sometime it is weak. The measure for such cases is called partial relation, fuzzy relation, or random relation. Chen [2] and Chen et al. [5][4] proposed λ-connectedness to describe the phenomenon that geophysical and geological parameters and properties exhibit gradual or progressive changes in a layer as well as sudden changes frequently occur between two layers.

λ-connectedness can be defined on an undirected graph $G = (V, E)$ with an associated (potential) function $\rho : V \to R^m$, where R^m is the m-dimensional real space. Given a measure $\alpha_\rho(x, y)$ on each pair of adjacent points x, y based on the values $\rho(x), \rho(y)$, we define

$$\alpha_\rho(x, y) = \begin{cases} \mu(\rho(x), \rho(y)) & \text{if } x \text{ and } y \text{ are adjacent} \\ 0 & \text{otherwise} \end{cases} \tag{2}$$

where $\mu : R^m \times R^m \to [0, 1]$ with $\mu(u, v) = \mu(v, u)$ and $\mu(u, u) = 1$. Note that one can define $\mu(u, u) = c$ and $\mu(u, v) \leq c$ where $c \in [0, 1]$ for all u. α_ρ is used to measure "neighbor-connectivity." The next is to develop path-connectivity so that λ-connectedness on $<G, \rho>$ can be defined in a general way.

In graph theory, a finite sequence $x_1, x_2, ..., x_n$ is called a path, if $(x_i, x_{i+1}) \in E$. A path is called a simple path if $x_i \neq x_j$, $i \neq j$ excepting $x_1 = x_n$. The path $x_1, x_2, ..., x_{n-1}, x_n = x_1$ is called a cycle. The path-connectivity β of a path $\pi = \pi(x_1, x_n) = \{x_1, x_2, ..., x_n\}$ is defined as

$$\beta_\rho(\pi(x_1, x_n)) = \min\{\alpha_\rho(x_i, x_{i+1}) | i = 1, ..., n-1\} \tag{3}$$

or

$$\beta_\rho(\pi(x_1, x_n)) = \prod\{\alpha_\rho(x_i, x_{i+1}) | i = 1, ..., n-1\} \tag{4}$$

Finally, the degree of connectedness (connectivity) of two vertices x, y with respect to ρ is defined as:

$$C_\rho(x,y) = \max\{\beta(\pi(x,y))|\pi \text{ is a (simple) path.}\} \quad (5)$$

For a given $\lambda \in [0,1]$, point $p = (x, \rho(x))$ and $q = (y, \rho(y))$ are said to be λ-connected if $C_\rho(x,y) \geq \lambda$. In image processing, $\rho(x)$ is the intensity of a point x and $p = (x, \rho(x))$ defines a pixel.

If $<G, \rho>$ is an image, then this equivalence relation can be used for segmentation meaning to partition the image into different objects. On the other hand, if a potential function f is partially defined on G, then one can fit f to be ρ such that $<G, \rho>$ is λ-connected on G. The generalized λ-connectedness on directed graphs is studied in [4].

3 λ-Connected Representation for General Rough Sets

Skowron and Stepaniuk proposed a method that uses a rough membership function to represent rough sets [13]. This section attempts to use λ-connectedness to express rough sets and to determine the "lower approximation" and the "upper approximation" by finding two special λ-connected sets.

3.1 λ-Connected Approximations

Assume that U is the base set (or the universal set) and R is an equivalence relation. Let R partition U into k components $P_1,...,P_k$, and an arbitrary set $X \subset U$. We need to create a graph $G = (V, E)$ and a potential function ρ.

Let $V = \{P_1, ..., P_k\}$, and $E = \{(P_i, P_j)|i \neq j; i, j = 1, ..., k\}$. and

$$f(P_i) = \frac{|P_i \cap X|}{|P_i|}.$$

is called the rough membership function [9][10]. Thus, $B_*(X) = L_R(X) = \cup\{P_i|f(P_i) = 1\}$, and $B^*(X) = U_R(X) = \cup\{P_i|f(P_i) > 0\}$. An α-cut bound of X, $\alpha \in (0,1]$ can be defined as $B_\alpha(X) = \{P_i|f(P_i) \geq \alpha\}$. Therefore, $B_1(X) = B_*(X)$ and $B_{0+}(X) = B^*(X)$.

It seems like that $B_\alpha(X)$ provides a total information of X with respect to R. However, if one asks that which value of α should be chosen so that B_α is the best approximation of X. The answer should be "it depends on how big is the boundary $BN(X) = B_{0+}(X) - B_1(X)$." If $BN(X)$ is relatively small, then $B_{1/2}(X)$ could be a good approximation [13]. If $BN(X)$ is big or even contains some structures, the answer will not be easy.

Two of the most popular structures are: (1) there is distinct line to separate the boundary $BN(X)$, and (2) the boundary $BN(X)$ changes gradually in terms of its rough membership function which offen appears in image processing [7]. For structure (1), the statistical method and typical fuzzy method can be used to solve the problem. For example the fuzzy c-mean is suitable to find such a distinct line. For structure (2), λ-connected approximation will be appropriate even through it can be forced to fit any other situation.

Lemma 1. *Since G is a complete graph (in the case above), for any kind of C_ρ, $L_R(X)$ can be searched by assigning $\lambda = 1$ and starting at a P_i with $f(P_i) = 1$. $U_R(X)$ can be searched by letting $\lambda > 0$ and starting at P_i with $f(P_i) = 1$ or the largest value.*

Furthermore, λ-connected search can also acquire more detailed information by assigning different values of λ. In other words, λ-connectedness not only can represent a rough set, but also get a complete hierarchy information for the rough set with respect to the value of λ. In Section 4, we will use maximum connectivity spanning tree to solve the problem of the λ value selection.

After $<G, \rho>$ is defined, given a value of λ, a λ-(connected) approximation of X is a λ-connected set starting at P_i with $f(P_i) = 1$ or the largest value. A λ-approximation is not necessarily an α-approximation. The relationship between them is under investigation.

3.2 Normal λ-Connected Sets and Rough Sets

A normal λ-connected set is that every pair of adjacent nodes (with its potential function values) are λ-adjacent [5]. So, it is a subset of the general λ-connected component. Normal λ-connected sets are a strict representation while the general λ-connected component is a relax representation. This philosophy is similar to rough set theory. For λ-connectedness, any subset of U, X, can be represented by the "lower" segmentation containing X (approximation) which is the union of all normal λ-connected components each of which has a point in X, and "upper" segmentation (approximation) which is the union of all λ-connected components each of which has a point in X. When U is a symbolic space, λ-connectedness is still applicable depending on the specific situation. Ziarko's variable precision rough set model has some similar considerations [14].

3.3 Rough Sets in the Real World

In the above two subsections, we used a complete graph to be a based graph. In fact, in many applications, the based graph is not a complete graph. In most of cases, U is a set of m-dimensional vectors such as the points in a multi-dimensional space or a relational database with multi-dimensional attributes. An equivalence relation partitioning such a space turns to be a segmentation that includes the physical location of a partition. Therefore, the base graph is no longer a complete graph. λ-connectedness will be more efficient.

4 Maximum Connectivity Spanning Tree and Rough Sets

The value of λ determines the number of partitions in vertex set of $<G, \rho>$. In this section, the maximum connectivity spanning tree is introduced to provide the total information for what value of λ should be selected.

A spanning tree of a graph G is a tree which contains all vertices of G [6]. A graph G has a spanning tree if and only if G is connected. A famous problem in graph theory is to find a minimal spanning tree (with the minimal total weights) for a weighted graph. The maximum connectivity spanning tree is the one in which there is a path in the tree that has the maximum connectivity for every pair of points.

Kruskal's algorithm can be used to find such a tree. The tree T initially contains all vertices but no edges. It then starts an iterative process: to add an edge to T under the condition that the edge has the minimum weight; however, it does not complete a cycle in T. When T has $|G| - 1$ edges, the process stops.

In order to find the Maximum Connectivity Spanning Tree, it is necessary to first calculate all neighbor-connectivities for each adjacent pair in $< G, \rho >$ to form a weighted graph.

Algorithm A. Modified Kruskal's algorithm can be used to find a Maximum Connectivity Spanning Tree, where $G = (V, E)$ is the original graph.

Step 1: Let $T = V$.
Step 2: Repeat step 3-4 until T has $|V| - 1$ edges.
Step 3: Find an edge e with the maximum connectivity value.
Step 4: If $T \cup e$ has no a cycle, $T \leftarrow T \cup e$ and
delete e from G; otherwise, delete e from G. Go to Step 3.

One advantage of using the maximum connectivity spanning tree is that it gives the complete information for the λ-connectivity. With this tree, one can easily get a refinement of λ-connected classification. One can also find which value of λ should be selected for a particular segmentation. For example, the number of segments that is desired is controllable. However, a disadvantage is that Algorithm A takes $O(n^3)$ time in terms of computational complexity and an extra space to store the tree. It is very slow when a large set of points/edges is considered.

After the maximum connectivity spanning tree is generated, one can easily find the all connected components for each λ. In addition, this tree gives a complete description of a rough sets not only the lower and upper approximation, but also the detailed information for all λ-approximations.

So, we can also say that the rough set of X is the the maximum connectivity spanning tree of X with the potential function values.

Notes and Comments. λ-connectedness can be a very useful tool for understanding rough sets. There are a great deal of relationships between them. In an email, Professor Pawlak wrote " From the philosophical point of view it seems to me that idea of continuity, or in other words the concept of a real number, is not understood fully yet and the example of rough continuity (or gradual variation confirm this. There is kind of contradiction between how we think (real numbers) and how we measure and compute (rational numbers). We cannot measure or compute with real numbers. Thus it seems that there is a gap between how we think and how we compute or measure.

Of course the applications of gradual variation for image processing, control, measurement is of great importance, but I guess that the philosophical problems here is also important. "

It should be noticed that even through a rough set can be completely represented by λ-connected sets in computation, rough sets has its own simplicity and philosophical beauty. Again, the λ-connected representation of rough sets provides the more detailed information but it needs more memory space for the representation.

Acknowledgment. The author wishes to express thanks to Professor Pawlak for his comments on gradual variation, a special case of λ-connectedness. The comments attracted the author to study the relationship between rough set theory and fuzzy connectedness especially λ-connectedness.

References

1. Adjei, O., Chen, L., Cheng, H.D., Cooley, D., Cheng, R., Twombly, X.: A fuzzy search method for rough sets and data mining. Proceedings of IFSA/NAFIPS Conference (2001) 980–985
2. Chen, L.: Three-dimensional fuzzy digital topology and its applications(I). Geophysical Prospecting for Petroleum 24 (1985) 86–89
3. Chen, L.: The necessary and sufficient condition and the efficient algorithms for gradually varied fill. Chinese Science Bulletin 35(1990) 870–873 (Its Chinese version was published in 1989.)
4. Chen, L, Adjei, O., Cooley, D.H.: λ-connectedness: method and application. Proceedings of IEEE Conference on System, Man, and Cybernetics (2000) 1157–1562
5. Chen, L., Cheng, H.D., Zhang, J.: Fuzzy subfiber and its application to seismic lithology classification. Information Science: Applications 1 (1994) 77–95
6. Cormen, T.H., Leiserson, C.E., Rivest, R.L.: Introduction to Algorithms. MIT Press (1993)
7. Gonzalez, R.C., Wood, R.: Digital Image Processing. Addison-Wesley, Reading, MA (1993)
8. Pal, S., Skowron, A. (eds): Rough Fuzzy Hybridization. Springer-Verlag (1999)
9. Pawlak, Z.: Rough set theory. In: Wang, P. P.(ed): Advances in Machine Intelligence and Soft-computing. Duke University (1997) 34–54
10. Pawlak, Z.: Rough sets, rough functions and rough calculus. In: Pal, S., Skowron, A. (eds): Rough Fuzzy Hybridization. Springer-Verlag (1999) 99–109
11. Polkowski, L., Skowron, A.(eds): Rough Sets in Knowledge Discovery, Physica Verlag, Heidelberg (1998)
12. Rosenfeld, A.: "Continuous" functions on digital pictures. Pattern Recognition Letters 4(1986) 177–184
13. Skowron, A., Stepaniuk, J.: Tolerance approximation spaces, Fundamenta Informaticae 27(1996) 245–253
14. Ziarko, W.: Variable precision rough set model. Journal of Computer and System Sciences 46(1993) 39–59

Adaptive Classifier Construction: An Approach to Handwritten Digit Recognition

Tuan Trung Nguyen

Polish-Japanese Institute of Information Technology
ul. Koszykowa 86, 02-008 Warsaw, Poland
nttrung@pjwstk.edu.pl

Abstract. Optical Character Recognition (OCR) is a classic example of decision making problem where class identities of image objects are to be determined. This concerns essentially of finding a decision function that returns the correct classification of input objects. This paper proposes a method of constructing such functions using an adaptive learning framework, which comprises of a multilevel classifier synthesis schema. The schema's structure and the way classifiers on a higher level are synthesized from those on lower levels are subject to an adaptive iterative process that allows to learn from the input training data. Detailed algorithms and classifiers based on similarity and dissimilarity measures are presented. Also, results of computer experiments using described techniques on a large handwritten digit database are included as an illustration of the application of proposed methods.

Keywords: Pattern recognition, handwritten digit recognition,clustering, decision support systems, machine learning

1 Introduction

Pattern Recognition algorithms can be grouped within two major approaches: statistical (or decision theoretic), which assumes an underlying and quantifiable statistical basis for the generation of a set of characteristic measurements from the input data that can be used to assign objects to one of n classes, and syntactic (or structural), which favors the interrelationships or interconnections of features that yield important structural description of the objects concerned. While both approaches seem to be widely used in Pattern Recognition in general, in the particular field of Optical Character Recognition the structural approach, especially methods based on trees an attributed graphs appear to be gaining popularity [7].

Typically, a structural-based OCR system attempts to develop a descriptive language that can be used to reflect the structural characteristics of the input image objects. Once such a language has been established, it is used to describe the characteristic features of the target recognition classes so that new images could be assigned to one of them when checked against those features [2]. Most existing systems employ some kind of hierarchical descriptions of complex patterns built from *primitives*, elemental blocks that can be extracted directly from input data. (See, e.g., [5],[2]).

Based on the assumption that the construction of a recognition system itself needs to reflect the underlying nature of the input data, we propose a new framework in which the extraction of *primitives*, the development of the descriptive language and the hierarchy of description patterns are all dynamically constructed and improved by an iterative adaptive process driven by the recognition performance achieved on the input data. The framework is essentially based on the granular computing model, in which representational primitives equipped with similar measures play part of information granules, whereas the pattern hierarchy implements the idea of the granular infrastructure comprising interdependencies among information blocks (For a more comprehensive description of granular computing see [6]). This allows for a great flexibility of the system in response to the input data and as a consequence, a gradual improvement of the system's suitability to the underlying object domain.

We later show that the same framework can also be used effectively to generate class dissimilarity functions that can be combined with similarity measures in the final recognition phase of the system, which makes our approach distinct from majority of existing systems, usually employing only class similarity when classifying new, unseen images.

Finally, we present results of experiments on the large NIST 3 handwritten digit database which confirm the effectiveness of the proposed methods.

2 Structural OCR Basics

While both statistical and structural approaches proved to be equally effective in PR in general, the graphical nature of the input data in OCR intuitively favors employing structural methods. A major structural approach is the *relational graph* method, where the image objects from the training data set are first converted to graphs, where specific image features are encoded in *nodes* and relations between them are represented by *edges*. Then, for each target class, a set (library) of protopypical graphs is developed, most often by means of some similarity measures. These prototypes, also called *skeleton* graphs are considered to contain characteristic traits for each target class and, in a way, represent images of that class. Now, given a new image object, a representation graph is extracted and compared with the skeleton graphs from each set. The final class assignment can vary depending on the chosen classification strategy [7].

It is obvious that the successful recognition depends on the choice of:

- the graph model for the image data,
- similarity measures used to build skeleton graphs,
- the distance functions and classification strategy in the final recognition phase

In this paper, we shall show that all three components can be dynamically constructed by an adaptive process based extensively on the actual input image domain.

3   Relational Graph Model for Handwritten Digits

For the researches in this paper we have chosen the Enhanced Loci coding scheme, which assigns to every image's pixel a code reflecting the topology of its neighborhood. The Enhanced Loci algorithm, though simple, has proved to be very successful in digit recognition. For a detailed description of the Loci coding scheme, see [4].

Once the Loci coding is done, the digit image is segmented into regions consisting of pixels with the same code value. These regions then serve as *primitives* to build the graph representation of the image.

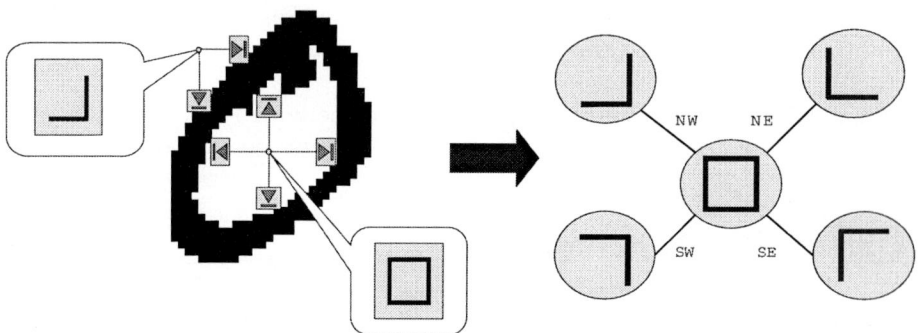

Fig. 1. Graph Model based on Loci Encoding.

Suppose that an image I has been segmented into coded regions $R_1, R_2, ..., R_k$. The graph representation of the image is an attributed labeled graph denoted as:

$$G_I = \{N, P, E\}$$

where $N = \{n_1, n_2, ..., n_k\}$ is a set of *nodes* representing $R_1, R_2, ..., R_k$, P is a set of *properties* of the nodes, containing, among other things, the Loci code, the number of pixels, and the gravity center of the corresponding regions, E is a set of directed labeled edges between pairs of nodes, describing the relative direction between corresponding regions.

One can observe that such a graph G_I will contain local information about black strokes in nodes and non-local features about the shapes of the digit as edges (See also [4]).

3.1 Base Skeleton Graph Construction

Definition 1. *A base segment $S_b = \{N_b, P, E_b\}$ is any 2-node segment of any digit representation graph, i.e. $|N_b| = 2$ and $|E_b| = 1$. We shall say that a base segment S_b matches a graph G_I, or $match(S_b, G_I)$ if S_b is isomorphic to a subgraph of G_I.*

Definition 2. *Given a set of base segments with common node and edge sets $S_1 = \{N, P_1, E\}, S_2 = \{N, P_2, E\}, ..., S_k = \{N, P_k, E\}$, a base skeleton segment is defined as:*

$$S_{bs} = \{N, P_{bs}, E\}$$

where P_{bs} is a combined set of properties:

$$P_{bs} = \{(L_1, f_1), (L_2, f_2), ..., (L_k, f_k)\}$$

with Loci code $L_i \in P_i$, and the frequency of occurrence of L_i:

$$f_i = \frac{|\{G_m : match(S_i, G_m)\}|}{|\{G_m : \exists 1 \leq j \leq k : match(S_j, G_m)\}|}$$

We shall say that a base skeleton segment $S_{bs} = \{N, \{(L_1, f_1), (L_2, f_2), ..., (L_k, f_k)\}, E\}$ matches a graph G_I, or $match(S_{bs}, G_I)$ if $\exists 1 \leq j \leq k : match(\{N, L_k, E\}, G_I)$

Having constructed base skeleton segments, we can build *base skeleton graphs*:

Definition 3. *A base skeleton graph (BSG) is any set of base skeleton segments.*

One can look at BSGs as "soft" or "blurred" prototypical graphs that may be used to represent class of digits. By fine-tuning various parameters of the model, e.g. the set of properties or connection labels or by imposing various cut-off thresholds, we can dynamically control the primitives extraction process.

3.2 Graph Similarity Measures

Given a BSG S and a digit representation graph G, the similarity $\tau(S, G)$ is established as follows:

Definition 4. *Suppose that for each node $n \in S, P(n) = \{(L_1, f_1), (L_2, f_2), ..., (L_{k_n}, f_{k_n})\}$ is the set of $(code, frequency)$ pairs at n. Then*
 if $match(S, G)$ then for each $n \in S$

$$\tau_n(S, G) = \sum_{i=1}^{k_n} f_i \tau_C(L_i, L^n(G))$$

where $L^n(G)$ is the Loci code found at the node matching n in G, and τ_C is a code-defined similarity function that returns the similarity between two given Loci codes.

$$\tau(S,G) = \sum_{n \in S} w_n \tau_n(S,G)$$

where w_n are connection-defined weight coefficients.

else

$$\tau(S,G) = 0.$$

This definition provides a tolerant matching scheme between representation graphs and skeleton graphs, which allows us to concentrate on the specific aspects of the graph description concepts at each given stage of the learning process. By fine-tuning code-defined and connection-defined weight coefficients, we can achieve a significant flexibility in information granules' construction.

Now let $S = \{S_1, S_2, ..., S_k\}$ be an BSG. The similarity $\tau(S,G)$ can be defined as:

$$\tau(S,G) = \mathbb{F}(\tau_1(S_1,G), \tau_2(S_2,G), ..., \tau_k(S_k,G))$$

where τ_i are single node-defined similarity measures and $\mathbb{F}$ is a synthesis operator. The choice of $\mathbb{F}$ is greatly influenced by the actual structure of the granules' hierarchy, which can either be the interconnections between local patterns in skeleton graphs, or be derived from an interaction with a domain expert. It is noteworthy here that while the expert's domain knowledge can be used to construct the hierarchical infrastructure, we may not rely on the expert's choice of the descriptive language for the primitives. In that way, knowledge passed by the expert will not be blindly used in a stiff manner, but it will rather be refined and combined with other tools on the lower level that we deem more adequate to the problem.

Definition 5. *A distance function between two graphs G_1, G_2 with regard to a skeleton graph S is defined as:*

$$d_S(G_1, G_2) = |\tau_S(G_1) - \tau_S(G_1)|$$

Suppose that for a digit class k, a set (library) of prototypical graphs PG_k has been established. We then can consider different distance functions with regard to that class using various synthesis operators, e.g.

- $d_k(G_1, G_2) = \max_{S \in PG_k} d_S(G_1, G_2)$
- $d_k(G_1, G_2) = \sum_{S \in PG_k} w_S d_S(G_1, G_2)$

where w_S are weight coefficients.

4 Adaptive Construction of Distance Functions

Based on the relational graph, similarity measure and distance function models defined in previous sections, we can construct an iterative process that searches for a optimal classification model as follows:

Algorithm

Step 1 – Initial Skeleton Graph Set

for each digit class k, a set of initial BSGs are constructed based on::

- Heuristic construction of representational BSGs based on class discrimination performance.
- Frequency and histogram analysis.
- Adjustment of connection-defined weights using a **greedy clustering scheme** with recognition rate as quality criteria.
- Manual selection of a number of core initial EBSGs using some domain knowledge.

Step 2 – Distance Function Evaluation

With the established sets of skeleton graphs for each digit class, develop graph similarity measures and distance functions as described in Section 3.3. and perform a k-NN clustering on the input training data collection to obtain class separation.

Evaluate the recognition rate based on developed clusters.

Step 3 – Adjustment of Parameters

Using a **greedy strategy** with regard to the recognition rate, make adjustments to single code similarity function, code-based and connection-based similarity weights and BSG-based distance function weight.

Reconstruct the skeleton graph set as needed. Repeat steps 2-3 until quality criteria are met.

End Algorithm

It can be observed that this is an adaptive iterative process with a two-layered k-NN clustering scheme, aimed at the optimization of three components crucial to the recognition process:

- Primitives extraction process, implemented by Loci coding scheme, code-defined and connection-defined similarity measures.
- Similarity measures model, represented by base skeleton graphs.
- Class distance functions (discriminants), synthesized over extended skeleton graphs.

5 Dissimilarity Measures

So far, similarity measures are used to construct libraries of prototypes so that future input data may be checked against them. Thus, the recognition process relies on how a new object resembles those that had been learnt. However, sometimes it could really help if we knew whether an object u *does not* belong to a class c.

In our relational graph model, dissimilarity to a skeleton graph is defined as similarity to its complementary graph.

Based on the same framework described in Section 4, we can construct complementary skeleton sets for each digit target class or several target classes and use them as discriminants in the recognition process to improve the classification quality.

6 Results of Experiments

In order to verify the developed methods, extensive testing has been conducted. We have chosen the U.S. National Institute of Standards and Technology (NIST) Handwritten Segmented Character Special Database 3, a major reference base within the handwritten character recognition community, as the main data collection. The base contains 223,125 128 × 128 normalized binary images with isolated handwritten digits from 2,100 different people.(For details see [3])

As a reference experiment's data collection, we have chosen a random portion of the whole base that contained:

- 44,000 digits as a training table, of which 4,000 have been separated for tests during the learning process.
- 4,000 digits for final test table

Table 1. Recognition results with dissimilarity improvement.

Class	No. of skeleton graphs	No. of digits	Misclassified	Reject
0	8	439	0.46 %	0 %
1	7	328	0.61 %	0 %
2	12	417	0.72 %	0 %
3	11	375	2.67 %	0 %
4	14	421	2.85 %	0 %
5	9	389	3.34 %	0 %
6	11	397	1.26 %	0 %
7	8	366	0.00 %	0 %
8	13	432	1.16 %	0 %
9	9	436	0.69 %	0 %
	Total	4000	**1.38 %**	0 %

The results obtained qualify our system close to the leading recognition packages tested at NIST, of which the average zero-rejection error rates were 1.70 percent. (See [3])

7 Conclusion

We presented a uniformed framework for the automatic construction of classifiers based on an adaptive scheme. A model for the synthesis of similarity measures from the input data primitives through higher level features has been proposed. The method allows for a flexible learning from the input training data during the construction phase and proved to be effective. The same framework can be used to develop dissimilarity measures that are highly useful in the improvement of the classification quality. Experiments conducted on a large handwritten digit database showed that the method can be applied to practical problems with encouraging results. The framework can easily be adapted to the recognition of other structured objects such as handwritten characters, fingerprints, iris images or human faces.

Acknowledgment. This work has been supported by Grant 8 -T11C02519 from the State Committee for Scientific Researches of the Republic of Poland (KBN).

References

1. Michael R. Anderberg. *Cluster Analysis for Applications*. Academic Press, Inc., 1973.
2. Jan Bazan, Hung Son Nguyen, Tuan Trung Nguyen, Jaroslaw Stepaniuk, and Andrzej Skowron. Application of modal logics and rough sets for classifying objects. In Michel De Glas and Zdzislaw Pawlak, editors, *Proceedings of the Second World Conference on the Fundamentals of Artificial Intelligence*, pages 15–26, Paris, France, 1995. Ankor.
3. J. Geist, R. A. Wilkinson, S. Janet, P. J. Grother, B. Hammond, N. W. Larsen, R. M. Klear, C. J. C. Burges, R. Creecy, J. J. Hull, T. P. Vogl, and C. L. Wilson. The second census optical character recognition systems conference. *NIST Technical Report NISTIR 5452*, pages 1–261, 1994.
4. K. Komori, T. Kawatani, K. Ishii, and Y. Iida. A feature concentrated method for character recognition. *IFIP Proceedings*, pages 29–34, 1977.
5. Z.C. Li, C.Y. Suen, and J. Guo. Hierarchical models for analysis and recognition of handwritten characters. *Annals of Mathematics and Artificial Intelligence*, pages 149–174, 1994.
6. L. Polkowski and A. Skowron. Towards adaptive calculus of granules. In L.A. Zadeh and J. Kacprzyk, editors, *Computing with Words in Information/Intelligent Systems*, pages 201–227, Heidelberg, 1999. Physica-Verlag.
7. Robert J. Schalkoff. *Pattern Recognition: Statistical, Structural and Neural Approaches*. John Wiley & Sons, Inc., 1992.
8. Kodratoff Y. and Michalski R. *Machine Learning: An Artificial Intelligence Approach*, volume 3. Morgan Kaufmann, 1990.

The Application of Support Diagnose in Mitochondrial Encephalomyopathies

Piotr Paszek and Alicja Wakulicz-Deja

Institute of Computer Science, University of Silesia,
ul. Zeromskiego 3, 41–200 Sosnowiec, Poland

Abstract. The work contains an example of applying the rough sets theory to application of support decision making - diagnose Mitochondrial Encephalomyopathies (MEM) in a child. The resulting decision support system in MEM should maximally limiting the indications for invasive diagnostic methods that finally decide about diagnosis. Moreover he has to shorten the time necessary to making diagnosis. System has arisen using induction (machine learning from examples) – one of the methods artificial intelligence.

1 Introduction

In the last years the progressive encephalopathy (PE) became an important problem in neurology. It is a progressive loss of psychomotor and neuromuscular functions occurring in the infancy or in older children. The causes of PE are metabolic diseases. In the work we have paid attention to encephalopathy in which respiratory enzymes of the cell located in mitochondria's are impaired. Mitochondrial encephalomyopathies (MEM) occur with elevated levels of lactic and pyruvic acid in the blood serum and the cerebrospinal fluid (CSF). The main diseases in this group of disorders are: Leigh syndrome, Kearn–Sayre syndrome, Alpers syndrome, Menkes syndrome, MELAS and MERRF [4].

The disease is grave and life threatening [7]. The disease detection requires a series of tests, of which some are typically invasive ones and they are not indifferent to a child's health. It is important to have a preliminary classification after the non-invasive tests, such that only that group of children is identical in whom the disease threat is not fully confirmed and further tests are needed. The invasive tests are divided into two groups here: testing levels of pyruvic and lactic acids in the blood serum, and cerebrospinal fluid and the examinations of a nerve or muscle segment to determine the enzyme levels, which are the final tests confirming the disease. As they are most threatening to a child's health, they are made as the last resort for a small group of children.

In such a way we create a three stages classification where a set of objects (patients) on each classification level is smaller. The most important problem is to create an appropriate classification system of patients on each level. This consists of an appropriate choice of attributes for the classification process and the generation of a set of rules, a base to make decisions in new cases. Rough sets theory provides the appropriate methods which form to solve this problem.

2 Aim of the Work

The MEM etiology is not clear for all disease entities. In majority of cases, it has the genetic background [4]. An early diagnosis is very essential for all metabolic and degenerative diseases, because in some of them a specific therapy is possible and additionally the genetic counseling depends on the proper diagnosis. In connection with this, it is equally important to shorten time of making the final diagnosis and to include prenatal diagnostics, which should prevent a birth of a next child with that disease in the same family.

The final diagnosis is obtained as a result of the performed invasive tests. It is not only essential to diagnose this disease early but to limit the patients subjected to invasive and health threatening tests to a maximum.

Aim of the work is to designing and developing a decision support system in MEM. The resulting decision support system in Mitochondrial Encephalomyopathies should maximally limiting the indications for invasive diagnostic methods (puncture, muscle and/or nerve specimens) that finally decide about diagnosis and shorten time necessary to make the final diagnosis. The system must respect three stages of diagnosing corresponding to multistage medical diagnostic.

3 Selection of an Information Method for Support Diagnose in MEM

A detailed analysis of the medical problem results in creating a three-staged diagnostic process, which allows to classify children into suffering from mitochondrial encephalomyopathy and ones suffering from other diseases [9].

Data on which the decisions were based, like any real data, contained errors. Incomplete information was one of them. It resulted from the fact that some examinations or observations were not possible to be made for all patients. Inconsistency of information was another problem. Inconsistency occurred because there were patients who were differently diagnosed at the same values of the parameters analyzed.

Additionally developing a supporting decision system in diagnosing MEM was connected with reducing of knowledge, generating decision rules and with a suitable classification of new information.

In such a system a knowledge base formed on the basis of earlier diagnosed patients were to be created (training data). Classification of new patients should be made on its basis. It is a schema appearing in machine learning (learning from examples). In our case training data set consisted of patients suspected of mitochondrial encephalopathies, who had been already diagnosed. Patients suspected of MEM, requiring diagnosing were data, which were later classified (unseen data).

Such problems are solved, among other things, by machine learning using the rough sets theory.

An analysis of the problems presented here leads to a natural application of the rough sets theory in the conducted decision making process.

The rough sets theory method was used both in diagnostic processes and during creating decision making system. The proposed system is a multistage decision making system reflecting the multistage medical diagnosis.

4 The Project of the Application of Support Decision Making

To accelerate the diagnosing process it was necessary to create the application of support decision making. The selection of the appropriate set of attributes taken into account during the classification at each stage of the MEM diagnosis is required for the system to be created and it is necessary to determine the values which those attributes can reach. Next the knowledge base should be created – a set of rules, which would describe the MEM diagnosing process at each of the stages in the most complete way.

4.1 Machine Learning

The knowledge base formation is possible with use of the knowledge induction so called machine learning [1]. In most cases the rule sets, induced from machine learning system from training data, are used for classification of new example, unseen before by the learning system. Because input data (training, unseen) are - in general - imperfect, a data preprocessing is required.

For the MEM diagnosis support the training set consisted of patients suspected of mitochondrial encephalopathies. New data (unseen set), subjected to classification on the basis of the knowledge base obtained from the training set, are new patients suspected of MEM, which require diagnosing.

In the literature there are a lot of applications generating knowledge bases on the basis of examples. In view of medical application and using the rough sets theory to create the knowledge base, the LERS system was chosen to select decision rules at each stage of diagnosing. LERS (Learning from Examples based on Rough Sets) [3] is a program generating rules on the basis of the knowledge base (decision tables). A decision table can be inconsistent. In the LERS system there are two algorithms for the rules generating – LEM1 and LEM2.

4.2 Classification under Uncertainty

While classifying new object we can say about complete and partial matching. In complete matching all attribute-value pairs of a rule must match all values of the corresponding attributes for the example. In partial matching some attribute-value pairs of a rule match the values of the corresponding attributes.

There are many schemes for classification of new objects. For example C4.5 [6] or AQ15 [5]. In LERS another approach was used. For every example LERS first attempts complete matching. When complete matching is impossible partially matching are considered. For every concept, using strength, specificity of rules and matching factor support is computed. The concept with the largest support wins the contest.

In this work for classification new data we used rule strength. We started for complete matching. The rule with the largest strength classified new example. When complete matching is impossible partially matching are considered. For every rule R, strength factor is computed, as the product strength and matching factor. The rule with the largest strength factor classified new example.

4.3 The Selection of the Set of Attributes

In order to created the system it is necessary to determine the set of appropriate attributes and its values on each stage of diagnosis MEM.

Stage I. Classification based on the clinical symptoms. In the first stage diagnostics of children suspected of mitochondrial encephalopathies is based on clinical symptoms.

Table 1. Attribute in the first stage of diagnosing MEM

Number	Attribute
1 –	development retardation;
2 –	hypotony;
3 –	spasticity;
4 –	epileptic seizures;
5 –	ophthalmologic changes;
6 –	episodic vomitus;
7 –	brain system dysfunction;
8 –	circulatory system disturbance;
9 –	liver dysfunction;
10 –	disturbed dynamics of heat circumference;
11 –	ataxia;
12 –	acute hemiplegia.

The clinical symptoms associated with mitochondrial encephalopathies can be different for different disease entities of the MEM group (so called polymorphism clinical symptoms). Additionally their intensification can be different and have variable character [4]. Therefore, it ought to be established, which clinical symptoms are considered in the preliminary classification of patients.

On the basis of the data obtained from II Clinic Department of Pediatrics of the Silesian Academy of Medicine, and reviewing the literature dealing with diagnosis of inborn metabolic diseases it has been established that in diagnosing MEM at the first stage 27 features – attributes should be used.

After further analysis and observation of medical diagnosis a number of attributes was reduced by combining features describing similar symptoms – so called „group" attributes were created. The number of attributes was reduced to 12. Majority of new attributed was formed by combining some attributes describing similar features. A few of them were unchanged. Table 1 presents the description of those attributes.

The attributes before combining had values from -1 to 2. New values for the group attributes should be determined. For example attribute *hypotony* was created from joining other three attributes : *hypotony, peripheral neuropathy* and *myopathy*. It was given a value 2 – if three symptoms from which it was formed ,occurred. If one or two symptoms were present it was given value 1, -1 in the other case.

Stage II. Classification on the basis of biochemical data. At the beginning to classify patients in the second stage four parameters were used. They described levels of lactic and formic acids in the blood serum and cerebrospinal fluid.

However, there were cases (patients) where levels of those four attributes were normal but the proportions between those acids lost balance. Therefore, two new attributes were introduced considering this information. The preliminary set of attributes included 6 parameters. Table 2 presents the description of those attributes.

Table 2. Attribute in the second stage of diagnosing MEM

Number	Attribute
1 –	lactate level in blood;
2 –	pyruvate level in blood;
3 –	ratio of lactate to pyruvate level in blood;
4 –	lactate level in CSF;
5 –	pyruvate level in CSF;
6 –	ratio of lactate to pyruvate level in blood;.
7 –	changes in the level of lactic and pyruvic acid in the serum and cerebrospinal fluid.

Attributes used in the second stage of diagnosing determined levels of acids and ratios of those acids in the blood serum and cerebrospinal fluid. Thus, values of those attributes are real numbers (continuous values). For such attributes discretization of values should be made [2].

For discretization of those attributes the limit values given in the literature should be used. There are, however, divergences among physicians – experts - as far as limit values (norms) for those parameters are concerned. For Karczmarewicz abnormal level of lactate is above 1.8 mmol/l, for Nelson above 2,0 mmol/l, for Clark above 2,1 mmol/l, for physicians – neurologists (experts with whom we co-operated) the laboratory norm was 2,5 mmol/l [4].

In work [8] we check quality of classification rules, which were obtained using different discretization methods of the attributes obtained in the second stage of diagnosing MEM. Results obtained in this work suggest explicitly that the method based on evaluation of norms on basis of a control group leads to the best results (smallest error rate). Using the calculated boundary values of norms for acids discretization of data was made. Because some patients had some attributes measured several times and values of the same attributes were different in successive tests, another attribute was added which were to reflect changes in levels of acids (table 2 - attribute #7).

After that a set of the decision attribute values should be enlarged to include this case. After comprehensive analysis of different cases and consultations with a group of neurologists rules were determined which were the basis of calculating the decision making attribute values. For example one of them is:
If in the fluid the level of any acid (or a ratio of acids) is higher than the maximum value $\rightarrow$ decision: classify for further tests.

With such treatment of the attribute value in the second stage of diagnosing and introducing a new attribute, the fact that tests of measurement of the level of acids were repeated for the same patient. On the basis of the modified set of attributes rules classifying patients for the third stage were made.

5 Quality of System Classification

In the system to generate the rules LEM1 and LEM2 algorithms from the LERS program were used. During classification of new cases complete and partial matching were used. Besides at the selection of a rule classifying a new case, two schemes of classification of new objects were used: strength of the rule and support of a decision class (LERS).

It should be decided which one gives the best results – rules, which classify new cases the best (rules for which quality of classification is the best).

In order to do it, two methods evaluating classification quality of new cases on the basis of rules obtained from the decision table were used: a schema of machine learning (method with a teaching and unseen set) and 10-fold cross validation test of rules.

Results of the first stage of diagnosing. Quality of classification obtained in the first stage of diagnosing presents table 3.

Table 3. Error rates in first stage of diagnosis

Classification scheme	rule strength				concept support			
matching	complete		partial		complete		partial	
algorithm	LEM1	LEM2	LEM1	LEM2	LEM1	LEM2	LEM1	LEM2
Machine learning								
Training set:	114				cases			
Unseen set:	72				cases			
Correctly classified	68	66	68	66	68	66	68	66
Incorrectly classified	4	6	4	6	4	6	4	6
Unclassified	0	0	0	0	0	0	0	0
error rate	0.06	0.08	0.06	0.08	0.06	0.08	0.06	0.08
10-fold cross validation								
Training set:	186				cases			
correctly classified	175	174	175	174	175	173	175	173
incorrectly classified	11	12	11	12	11	13	11	13
Unclassified	0	0	0	0	0	0	0	0
error rate	0.06	0.06	0.06	0.06	0.06	0.07	0.06	0.07

Results obtained by use of two different methods of quality evaluation of rules do not differ significantly.

The lowest classification error – 11 cases out of 186 (5.91%) – was obtained in the 10-fold cross validation of rules, with the LEM1 algorithm, classification: strength of rules or concept support. It should be noticed that for both methods it was enough to use the complete match of objects with the rules.

The lowest classification error both in machine learning and 10-fold cross validation of rules occurred for the LEM1 algorithm and classification based on strength of rules. Therefore in the MEM diagnosis support program in the first stage of diagnosis, the LEM1 algorithm was used to generate rules, whereas during classification strength of rules was used while selecting rules.

Results of the second stage of diagnosing. Quality of classification obtained in the second stage of diagnosing presents table 4.

Table 4. Error rates in second stage of diagnosis

Classification scheme	rule strength				concept support			
matching	complete		partial		complete		partial	
algorithm	LEM1	LEM2	LEM1	LEM2	LEM1	LEM2	LEM1	LEM2
Machine learning								
Training set: 114 cases								
Unseen set: 92 cases								
correctly classified	57	57	86	86	55	56	84	85
incorrectly classified	6	6	6	6	8	7	8	7
unclassified	29	29	0	0	29	29	0	0
error rate	0.38	0.38	0.07	0.07	0.40	0.39	0.09	0.08
10-fold cross validation								
Training set: 206 cases								
Correctly classified	188	186	189	187	185	187	186	188
Incorrectly classified	17	19	17	19	20	18	20	18
Unclassified	1	1	0	0	1	1	0	0
error rate	0.09	0.10	0.08	0.09	0.10	0.09	0.10	0.09

Comparing the results obtained in the 10-fold cross validation of rules with ones obtained in the machine learning, great difference in the classification errors can be noticed. There was also a great difference in the number of non-classified cases for those two methods. Such great differences result from incomplete data (missing values of attributes). In the machine learning from examples method patients with incomplete data were only in the testing set. In the 10-fold validation of rules the patients with incomplete data were mixed (they were in learning and testing set). While using the partial match in the machine learning non-classified patients were correctly classified (all cases).

The lowest classification error was for the machine learning method with the partial match of an object with a rule, with the classification on the basis of strength of rules, for rules generated by the LEM1 algorithm and it was 6.52% (6 cases out of 92). For the 10-fold cross validation of rules at the partial match of an object with a rule, with the classification based on strength of rules, for rules generated by the LEM1 algorithm, it was 8.27% (17 out of 206).

For that reason in the second stage of diagnosis, in the MEM diagnosis support program, the LEM1 algorithm was used to generate rules, and during classification of new cases a scheme based on the partial match of an object with a rule on the basis of strength of a rule.

6 Conclusion

The work presents a medical problem, an application of rough sets theory in the MEM diagnosing process, a project and implementation of the support diagnostic process (decision making) system. The solved problems have clearly applied aspects after verification on the real data.

The resulting system maximally limiting the indications for invasive diagnostic methods that finally decides about diagnosis. Moreover systems shorten the time necessary to making diagnosis.

References

1. Carbonell, J.: Machine learning Paradigm and Methods. Cambridge, MA, MIT Press (1989)
2. Chmielewski, M.R., Grzymala–Busse, J.W.: Global discretization of continuous attributes as preprocessing for machine learning. In T.Y. Lin and A.M. Wilderberger (eds.), Soft Computing (1995) 294–297
3. Grzymala–Busse, J.: LERS – a system for learning from examples based on Rough Sets. In Slowinski R. (ed.). In intelligent decision support. Handbook of Applications and Advances of the Rough Sets Theory. Kluwer Academic Publishers (1992) 3–18
4. Marszal, E. (ed.): Leukodystrofie i inne choroby osrodkowego ukladu nerwowego z uszkodzeniem istoty bialej u dzieci i mlodziezy. Slaska Akademia Medyczna (1998)
5. Michalski, R., Mozetic, I., Hong, J., Lavrac, N.: The multi–purpose incremental learning system AQ 15 and testing application to three medial domains. The 5th nat. Conf. on AI. USA (1986) 1041–1045
6. Quinlan, R.: C4.5: Programs for machine Learning. Morgan Kaufmann Publishers (1993)
7. Tulinius, M.H., Holme, E., Kristianson, B., Larsson, N., Oldfors, A.: Mitochondrial encephalomyopathies in childhood: 1. Biochemical and morphologic investigations. J. Pediatrics **119** (1991) 242–250
8. Wakulicz–Deja, A., Boryczka, M., Paszek, P.: Discretization of continuous attributes on Decision System in Mitochondrial Encephalomyopathies. Lecture Notes in Computer Science **1424** (1998) 483–490
9. Wakulicz–Deja, A., Paszek, P.: Diagnose Progressive Encephalopathy Applying the Rough Set Theory. International Journal of Medical Informatics **46** (1997) 119–127

Obstacle Classification by a Line-Crawling Robot: A Rough Neurocomputing Approach

James F. Peters[1], T.C. Ahn[2], and Maciej Borkowski[1]

[1] Department of Electrical and Computer Engineering, University of Manitoba
Winnipeg, Manitoba R3T 5V6 Canada
jfpeters@ee.umanitoba.ca
[2] Intelligent Information Control & System Lab,
School of Electrical & Electronic Engineering, Won-Kwang University
344-2 Shinyong-Dong, Iksan, Chon-Buk, 570-749, Korea

Abstract. This article considers a rough neurocomputing approach to the design of the classify layer of a Brooks architecture for a robot control system. In the case of the line-crawling robot (LCR) described in this article, rough neurocomputing is used to classify sometimes noisy signals from sensors. The LCR is a robot designed to crawl along high-voltage transmission lines where noisy sensor signals are common because of the electromagnetic field surrounding conductors. In rough neurocomputing, training a network of neurons is defined by algorithms for adjusting parameters in the approximation space of each neuron. Learning in a rough neural network is defined relative to local parameter adjustments. Input to a sensor signal classifier is in the form of clusters of similar sensor signal values. This article gives a very brief description of a LCR that has been developed over the past three years as part of a Manitoba Hydro research project. This robot is useful in solving maintenance problems in power systems. A description of the basic features of the LCR control system and basic architecture of a rough neurocomputing system for robot navigation are given. A sample LCR sensor signal classification experiment is also given.

1 Introduction

Various forms of rough neural networks work quite well in solving the problem of classifying noisy sensor signals. This problem is intense in the case of a line-crawling robot (LCR) designed to navigate along high-voltage power lines because of the electromagnetic field surrounding the conductors. The set approximation paradigm from rough set theory [1] and parameterized approximation spaces [8] provide a basis for the design of rough neural networks (RNNs) [2]-[4]. This article gives a brief overview the neural network used by the LCR to classify power line objects. The LCR control system is patterned after the Brooks' subsumption architecture for a robot control system [9]. This architecture is organized into separate layers, each with its own control function and with the ability to subsume the control functions of lower layers. This article focuses on the use of a RNN in the design of the classify layer of the LCR as a step towards the solution of the LCR navigation problem. This article is organized as follows. An overview of the LCR navigation problem and LCR control system architecture are presented in Section 2. A brief presentation of rough set methods underlying the design of a rough neural network for the LCR is given in Section 3. The architecture of the rough neural network built into the classify layer of the LCR is described in Section 4. Experimental results using a rough neural network to classify sample LCR proximity sensor values are also presented in Section 4.

2 Basic Features of Line-Crawling Robot

A brief introduction to two features of one form of line-crawling robot is given in this section, namely, architecture of control system and method of locomotion of robot designed to navigate along transmission lines for a power system. In this description, we do not deal with such issues as types of servos and micros or shielding required to permit operation of the robot in the presence of a high electromagnetic field associated with high-voltage (e.g., 350 KV) lines carrying up high current (e.g., 1200 amps of current). This robot has been designed to operate on transmission lines with many types of obstacles (e.g., insulators, commutators) like the ones used by Manitoba Hydro.

2.1 LCR Navigation Problem

A principal task of the LCR control system is to guide the movements of the robot so that it maintains a safe distance from overhead conductors and any objects such as insulators attached to conductor wires or towers used to hold conductors above the ground (see Fig. 1).

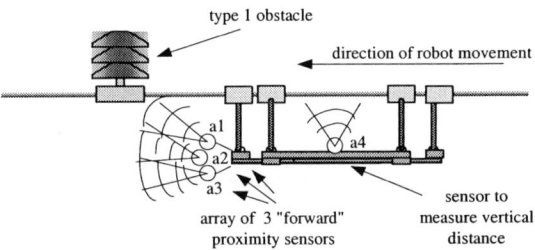

Fig. 1. Power towers   **Fig. 2.** Sample proximity Sensors of LCR

To move along a conductor, the LCR must continuously measure distances between itself and other objects around it, detect and maneuver to avoid collision with obstacles. Only two types of obstacles are considered in the description of the navigation problem in this section: (1) obstacles that are attached to the wire and protrude above the wire (e.g., insulators), and (2) obstacles that are attached to the wire and hang down from the wire (see Fig. 1). In both cases, the robot must "crawl" around these obstacles, and continue its forward or backward movement along the wire.

The LCR body is equipped with 6 proximity sensor arrays, each containing 3 sensors for a total of 18 proximity sensors. Each LCR leg is equipped with an array of 4 proximity sensors (a total of 16 sensors on the legs) because legs slide independently along a track in the robot base and must avoid collision with each other as well as with obstacles in the neighborhood of the robot. Hence, LCR navigation decisions are based on the evaluation of signals from a total of 34 sensors. For simplicity, we consider only 4 of these sensors (see Fig. 2). Let a1, a2, a3, a4 denote proximity sensors (e.g., ultrasonic sensors). The following assumptions are made about the movements and sensors (see Fig. 2) on a line-crawling robot.

- The robot moves only in one direction ("forward"). The end of the robot that moves in the forward direction is called the "front" of the robot.
- A single proximity sensor (namely, a4) is positioned in the center of the robot to measure the distance between the robot and wire or the bottom of an obstacle. Sensor a4 measures objects in the [0.1, 1] meter range. If a4<0.4 m, then the robot lowers the robot to obtain better overhead clearance for the robot body.
- An array of three proximity sensors (namely, a1, a2, a3) is connected to the front of the robot (see Fig. 2). Each sensor detects objects in the [0.1, 3] meter range:
  - a1 is positioned to detect objects connected to and projecting above the wire. If a1<0.5 m, the robot executes a small obstacle avoidance routine.
  - a2 is positioned to detect objects in front of the robot. If a2<0.5 m, the robot executes a small obstacle avoidance routine.
  - a3 is positioned to detect objects connected to and hanging down from the wire. If a3<0.5 m, the robot executes a large obstacle avoidance routine.

We want to train a neural network so that the LCR can make a decision about which type of movement it can safely make based on readings from its sensors. Sensor measurements are separated in collections (a form of sensor fusion) used to construct convex sets. Each convex set contains sensor measurements (often with some noise) either close to a preset threshold or significantly greater than {less than} the threshold. In effect, this form of convex set represents what is known as an upper approximation in rough set theory. In addition, each convex set is associated with a LCR navigation decision that initiates a set of many movements robot parts to carry a LCR maneuver. Because of noisy signals (a high-voltage power transmission line is a hostile environment with a severe electromagnetic field surround the conductor), it is not possible to use simple if-then statements to make navigation decisions. Let d denote a decision class. Table 1 gives some sample navigation decisions based on aggregate information from fusion of various sensors.

Table 1. Sample Decision classes for Robot

convex set of measurements	decision	explanation of decision
{a1, a2, a3}	d = 1	avoid small obstacle protruding down from conductor, maintain leg extension, slide legs under obstacle
{a2, a3, a4}	d = 2	avoid large obstacle protruding down from conductor, increase leg extension, slide legs under obstacle
{a1, a2, a3, a4}	d = 3	avoid small obstacle protruding down from conductor, increase leg extension, slide legs under obstacle
{a1, a2, a3, a4}	d = 4	avoid large obstacle protruding down from conductor, maintain leg extension, slide legs under obstacle
{a1, a2, a3, a4}	d = 5	move forward (normal state)

3 LCR Neural Classification System

Because of the complexity of information and high number of inputs from LCR sensors, a neural computing approach to object classification offers a fairly straightforward solution to the LCR navigation problem. In this section, a particular form of neural classification based on rough sets is briefly presented. It is assumed that the reader is familiar with the basic rough set methods described in [1]. Let $IS = (U, A)$ be an infinite information system where U is a non-empty subset of the reals $\Re$ and A is a non-empty, finite set of attributes, where $a : U \to V_a$ for every $a \in A$. The notation $\lfloor a(x)/\delta \rfloor$ denotes the greatest integer less than or equal to $a(x)/\delta$, where for $\delta > 0$. Reals within the same subinterval bounded by $k\delta$ and $(k+1)\delta$ are considered indistinguishable. Let $B \subseteq A$ and define an equivalence relation $\text{Ing}_{A,\delta}(B)$ introduced in [4]: $\text{Ing}_{A,\delta}(B) = \{(x, x') \in \Re^2 \mid \forall a \in B. \lfloor a(x)/\delta \rfloor = \lfloor a(x')/\delta \rfloor\}$. The notation $[x]_B^\delta$ denotes equivalence classes of $\text{Ing}_{A,\delta}(B)$, and the partition $U/\text{Ing}_{A,\delta}(B)$ denotes the family of all equivalence classes of relation $\text{Ing}_{A,\delta}(B)$ on U. For $X \subseteq U$, the set X can be approximated only from information contained in B by constructing a B-lower and a B-upper approximation denoted by $\underline{B}X$ and $\overline{B}X$, respectively, where $\underline{B}X = \{x \mid [x]_B^\delta \subseteq X\}$ and $\overline{B}X = \{x \mid [x]_B^\delta \cap X \neq \emptyset\}$. Also notice that $\text{Ing}_{A,\delta}(B)$ is an equivalence relation.

3.1 Rough Inclusion

In this section, a set function form of the traditional rough membership function is presented. The rough membership set function was introduced in [5].

Definition 1. Let $IS = (U, A)$ be an information system with non-empty set U and non-empty set of attributes A. Further, let $B \subseteq A$ and let $[y]_B^\delta$ be an equivalence class of any sensor reading $y \in \Re$. Let ρ be a measure of a set $X \in \wp(U)$, where $\wp(U)$ is a class (set of all subsets of U). Then for any $X \in \wp(U)$ the *rough membership set function (rmf)* $\mu_y^{B,\delta} : \wp(U) \to [0,1]$ is defined in (1).

$$\mu_y^{B,\delta}(X) = \frac{\rho\left(X \cap [y]_B^\delta\right)}{\rho\left([y]_B^\delta\right)} \qquad (1)$$

If $\rho([y]_B^\delta) = 0$, then of course $\rho(X \cap [y]_B^\delta) = 0$ and in this situation we consider symbol $\frac{0}{0}$ to be equal to 0.

Example 1. The rmf in (1) can be written as in (1).

$$\mu_y^{B,\delta}(X) = \frac{\rho\left(X \cap [y]_B^\delta\right)}{\rho\left([y]_B^\delta\right)} = \frac{\int_{X \cap [y]_B^\delta} 1 \, dx}{\int_{[y]_B^\delta} 1 \, dx} \qquad (2)$$

where ρ in (1) can be interpreted as $\int_{Y \subseteq U} 1 \, dx$.

It has been shown that $\mu_y^{B,\delta}(X)$ is a measure of X.

3.2 Discrete Rough Integral

The discrete rough integral was introduced in [5] and applied in [6]. In the earlier study of rough integrals, only rough measures define relative to finite sets were considered. In this paper, the discrete rough integral is defined relative to a measure of uncountable sets.

Definition 2. Discrete Rough Integral. Let ρ_y for $y = a(x)$ and $x \in U$ be a *rough measure* on the δ-indistinguishability space $(X, \wp(X), U/\text{Ing}_{A,\delta}(B))$ relative to $U/\text{Ing}_{A,\delta}(B)$ and y, and let $f : X \to \Re^+$ be a real-valued function such that $f(x_{(1)}) \leqslant ... \leqslant f(x_{(n)})$ (monotonic non-decreasing), $X_{(i)} := \{x_{(i)}, ..., x_{(n)}\}$, and $f(x_{(0)}) = 0$, where $\bullet_{(i)}$ is a permuted index. Then the discrete rough integral of f with respect to rough measure ρ_y is defined in the following way.

$$\int_X f \, d\rho = \sum_{i=1}^n \left[(f(x_{(i)}) - f(x_{(i-1)})) \rho_u(X_{(i)})\right]$$

It has been shown that the discrete rough integral computes an ordered weighted average [8]. This integral value can be useful in evaluating the relevance of sensors, if we enforce the criterion that the integral of a sensor must have a value greater than (or less than) some pre-set threshold.

3.3 Convex Sets

Ideally all decision classes should have Gaussian distribution to facilitate neural classification. Unfortunately, they are usually not distributed normally. One solution to the problem of distinguishing these values is to construct convex sets that "enclose" as many of these values as possible. This also means that the entire data set needs to be partitioned into the least number of convex sets.

Definition 3. *Convex Set.* A set A is said to be convex if the straight line segment joining any two points in A lies entirely within A.

Definition 4. *Convex Hull.* The convex hull H of an arbitrary set S is the smallest convex set covering S.

4 Rough Neurocomputing by Robot

The study of various forms of rough neurons is part of a growing number of papers on neural networks based on rough sets.

4.1 Basic Architecture of RNN

The basic architecture of a rough neural network for classifying sensor signals using convex sets is shown in Fig. 3. For each cluster, the neural network maintains decision class information that is used to make a classification decision after calibration.

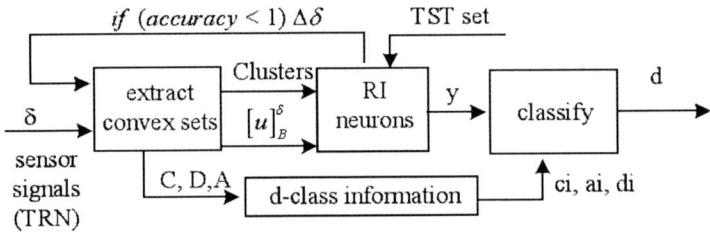

Fig. 3. Basic RNN Architecture

The rough neural network (RNN) in Fig. 3 calibrates δ to obtain a training set that matches target information about LCR decision classes. The RNN itself consists of a single layer of neurons. Each neuron constructs a table of rough integral values relative to a single decision class.

4.2 Experimental Results

The rough neural network used in classifying power line obstacles has been implemented in a toolset (called MBnet) called MB in Visual C++. The MBnet toolset computes a closeness measure which is the root mean square of all the differences between training and testing tables over all epochs up to the current epoch. MBnet measures the accuracy of the classification which equals the % of correctly classified test data in the current epoch. In each epoch after the first epoch, an adjusted δ to construct convex sets from the sample data until the computation is halted by a user or when 100% of the test table entries are correctly classified. To verify the design of classify layer of the LCR control system, a set of 7000 values output by three proximity sensors relative to 6 decision classes was a source of training and testing sets. A classification accuracy of 51.2% is achieved after 501 epochs. After 1841 epochs, the classification accuracy between training and testing tables is 95.6% (see Fig. 4).

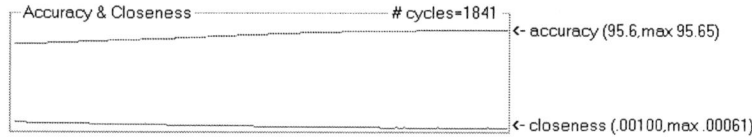

Fig. 4. Sample Classification Accuracy

5 Concluding Remarks

This article has focused on an approach to designing the classify layer of the LCR control system. The classify layer is part of a layered architecture for robot control systems introduced by Brooks. It has been verified that rough neural networks work quite well in classifying noisy sensor signals commonly produced by sensors on a line-crawling robot. Navigation by a robot crawling along a high-voltage transmission line is a complex task because of the many operations that must be performed by the robot in working its way between, round and underneath various obstacles such insulators and girders on towers. Because noisy sensor signals are common in an LCR, it is better to make navigation decisions based on approximation methods commonly used in rough set theory. Inputs to a classifier neural network are in the form of convex sets. Such sets provide input to neurons that compute ordered weighted averages for each robot sensor relative to particular navigation decision class. It has been shown that proposed approach results in high classification accuracy.

Acknowledgements. The research of James Peters has been supported by the Natural Sciences and Engineering Research Council of Canada (NSERC) research grant 185986, a grant from Manitoba Hydro, research support from the

University of Information Technology, Rzeszów, Poland. The research of Maciej Borkowski has been supported by a research grant from Manitoba Hydro.

References

1. Z. Pawlak, Rough Sets: Theoretical Aspects of Reasoning About Data. Boston, MA, Kluwer Academic Publishers, 1991.
2. S.K. Pal, L. Polkowski, A. Skowron (Eds.), Rough-Neuro Computing: Techniques for Computing with Words. Berlin: Springer-Verlag, 2002.
3. S.K. Pal, J.F. Peters, L. Polkowski, A. Skowron (Eds.), Rough-Neuro Computing: An Introduction. In: [2], 16–43.
4. J.F. Peters, S. Ramanna, Z. Suraj, M. Borkowski, Rough neurons: Petri net models and Applications. In: [2], 472–491.
5. Z. Pawlak, J.F. Peters, A. Skowron, Z. Suraj, S. Ramanna, M. Borkowski, Rough measures: Theory and Applications. In: S. Hirano, M. Inuiguchi, S. Tsumoto (Eds.), Rough Set Theory and Granular Computing, Bulletin of the International Rough Set Society, vol. 5, no. 1 / 2, 2001, 177–184.
6. J.F. Peters, S. Ramanna, M. Borkowski, A. Skowron: Approximate sensor fusion in a navigation agent, in: N. Zhong, J. Liu, S. Ohsuga and J. Bradshaw (Eds.), Intelligent agent technology: Research and development. Singapore: World Scientific Publishing, 2001, 500–504.
7. Z. Pawlak, J.F. Peters, A. Skowron, Z. Suraj, S. Ramanna, M. Borkowski, Rough measures, rough integrals, and sensor fusion. In: S. Hirano, M. Inuiguchi, S. Tsumoto (Eds.), *Rough Sets and Granular Computing*. Berlin: Physica Verlag [to appear].
8. A. Skowron, Toward intelligent systems: Calculi of information granules. In: S. Hirano, M. Inuiguchi, S. Tsumoto (Eds.), Bulletin of the International Rough Set Society, vol. 5, no. 1 / 2, 2001, 9–30.
9. R.A. Brooks, A robust layered control system for a mobile robot, vol. RA-2, no. 1, March 1986, 14–23.

Rough Neural Network for Software Change Prediction

Sheela Ramanna

Department of Business Computing, University of Winnipeg
Winnipeg, Manitoba, Canada R3B 2E9
s.ramanna@uwinnipeg.ca

Abstract. This paper focuses on calibrating a rough neural network based on software complexity measurements and the corresponding number of changes required to bring a software product (either during development or during post-deployment) into compliance with project standards. A good predictive model for software maintenance that can estimate the number of changes that will allow the early identification of modules that are most likely to require extensive modifications. The results reported in this paper are limited to assessing prediction accuracy based on software engineering data obtained during product development. The Rough Set Exploration System (RSES) is used to derive training and testing sets that are used both by RSES and by a rough neural network toolset named MBnet to predict the number of software module changes needed to bring a module intro compliance with project standards. A comparison between MBnet and RSES in predicting the number of changes for a particular software module is also given.

Keywords: Neural network, preprocessing, rough sets, software change prediction, software quality.

1 Introduction

Considerable work has been done in studying methods of software quality assessment using statistics [2], neural networks [3], and rough set methods [12],[13]. This paper presents a new rough neurocomputing approach to software change prediction as a means of identifying modules requiring considerable effort. Developing a large-scale software system requires the use of quantitative models to provide insight about software quality based on historical data from similar projects[1]. Decisions concerning the extent (i.e., number of changes) that software requires improvement are based on measurements of software quality. It has been pointed out that the availability of regression models for software change prediction will lead to more efficient allocation of project resources to program modules that are likely to require modification.

Quality of software is identified with the degree to which software satisfies specified requirements. The measurement of software is performed relative to attributes such as size, entropy, maintainability and so on. Each software attribute provides information about a characteristic of software. In particular, measuring the extent to which various *internal* software attributes such as size, complexity, control-flow structures, information flow attributes are present in a software product, will affect the accuracy of predictions about the external "quality" of software without actually running it. Previous studies with software complexity measures based predictive modeling of software quality have traditionally used statistical estimation techniques such as least squares and least absolute value technique [2]. It has also been shown that classical statistical techniques are not always well suited to software engineering data [1].

In this paper, two common rough set methods are used in setting a neurocomputing model for software change prediction, namely, attribute reduction during preprocessing of tables of software complexity measurements and the use of rough measure inclusion of information granules. During preprocessing, the Rough Set Exploration System (RSES) [14] is used to find reducts (reduced sets of attributes) and to derive training and testing sets that are used both by RSES and by a rough neural network toolset named MBnet to predict the number of software module changes needed to bring a module intro compliance with project standards. The predictive quality of both RSES and MBnet are compared. The contribution of this article is a new rough neurocomputing approach to software change prediction. A comparison between MBnet and RSES in predicting the number of changes for a particular software module is also given.

This paper is organized as follows. A brief overview of rough set-based set approximation is given in Section 2. A software quality approximation space is introduced in Section 3. The architecture of an approximation neural network is presented in Section 4. A summary of the results of experiments with sample quality metrics data is given in Section 5.

2 Rough Set Preliminaries

It is assumed that the reader is familiar with the basic rough set methods described in [5]. Let $IS = (U, A)$ be an infinite information system where U is a non-empty subset of the reals $\Re$ and A is a non-empty, finite set of attributes, where $a : U \to V_a$ for every $a \in A$. The notation $\lfloor a(x)/\delta \rfloor$ denotes the greatest integer less than or equal to $a(x)/\delta$, where for $\delta > 0$. Reals within the same subinterval bounded by $k\delta$ and $(k+1)\delta$ are considered indistinguishable. Let $B \subseteq A$ and define an equivalence relation $\text{Ing}_{A,\delta}(B)$ introduced in [11]: $\text{Ing}_{A,\delta}(B) = \{(x, x') \in \Re^2 \mid \forall a \in B. \lfloor a(x)/\delta \rfloor = \lfloor a(x')/\delta \rfloor\}$. The notation $[x]_B^\delta$ denotes equivalence classes of $\text{Ing}_{A,\delta}(B)$, and the partition $U/\text{Ing}_{A,\delta}(B)$ denotes the family of all equivalence classes of relation $\text{Ing}_{A,\delta}(B)$ on U. For $X \subseteq U$, the set X can be approximated only from information contained in B by constructing a B-lower and a B-upper approximation denoted by $\underline{B}X$ and $\overline{B}X$, respectively, where $\underline{B}X = \{x \mid [x]_{B \cup Id}^\delta \subseteq X\}$ and $\overline{B}X = \{x \mid [x]_{B \cup Id}^\delta \cap X \neq \emptyset\}$. Also notice that $\text{Ing}_{A,\delta}(B)$ is an equivalence relation.

2.1 Rough Inclusion

In this section, a set function form of the traditional rough membership function is presented

Definition 1. Let $IS = (U, A)$ be an information system with non-empty set U and non-empty set of attributes A. Further, let $B \subseteq A$ and let $[y]_B^\delta$ be an equivalence class of any sensor reading $y \in \Re$. Let ρ be a measure of a set $X \in \wp(U)$, where $\wp(U)$ is a class (set of all subsets of U). Then for any $X \in \wp(U)$ the *rough membership set function (rmf)* $\mu_y^{B,\delta} : \wp(U) \to [0,1]$ is defined in (1).

$$\mu_y^{B,\delta}(X) = \frac{\rho\left(X \cap [y]_B^\delta\right)}{\rho\left([y]_B^\delta\right)} \quad (1)$$

If $\rho([y]_B^\delta)=0$, then of course $\rho(X \cap [y]_B^\delta) = 0$ and in this situation we consider symbol $\frac{0}{0}$ to be equal to 0.

Example 1. The rmf in (1) can be written as in (2).

$$\mu_y^{B,\delta}(X) = \frac{\rho\left(X \cap [y]_B^\delta\right)}{\rho\left([y]_B^\delta\right)} = \frac{\int_{X \cap [y]_B^\delta} 1\, dx}{\int_{[y]_B^\delta} 1\, dx} \quad (2)$$

where ρ in (1) can be interpreted as $\int_{Y \subseteq U} 1\, dx$.

It has been shown that $\mu_y^{B,\delta}(X)$ is a measure of X.

2.2 Discrete Rough Integral

The discrete rough integral was introduced in [7], and elaborated in [8]. In the earlier study of rough integrals, only rough measures define relative to finite sets were considered. In this paper, the discrete rough integral is defined relative to a measure of uncountable sets.

Definition 2. Discrete Rough Integral. Let ρ_y for $y = a(x)$ and $x \in U$ be a *rough measure* on the δ-indistinguishability space $(X, \wp(X), U/\mathrm{Ing}_{A,\delta}(B))$ relative to $U/\mathrm{Ing}_{A,\delta}(B)$ and y, and let $f: X \to \Re^+$ be a real-valued function such that $f(x_{(1)}) \leqslant ... \leqslant f(x_{(n)})$ (monotonic non-decreasing), $X_{(i)} := \{x_{(i)}, ..., x_{(n)}\}$, and $f(x_{(0)}) = 0$, where $\bullet_{(i)}$ is a permuted index. Then the discrete rough integral of f with respect to rough measure ρ_y is defined in the following way.

$$\int_X f\, d\rho = \sum_{i=1}^n \left[(f(x_{(i)}) - f(x_{(i-1)}))\rho_u(X_{(i)})\right]$$

It has been shown that the discrete rough integral computes an ordered weighted average [8]. This integral value can be useful in evaluating the relevance of sensors, if we enforce the criterion that the integral of a sensor must have a value greater than (or less than) some pre-set threshold.

2.3 Convex Sets

When software quality metric values from different modules/projects are close to each other, it becomes difficult to make accurate decisions. Ideally all decision classes should have Gaussian distribution to facilitate neural classification. Unfortunately, software quality metric values are usually not distributed normally. One solution to the problem of distinguishing these values is to construct convex sets that "enclose" as many of these values as possible. This also means that the entire data set needs to be partitioned into the least number of convex sets.

Definition 3. *Convex Set*. A set A is said to be convex if the straight line segment joining any two points in A lies entirely within A.

Definition 4. *Convex Hull*. The convex hull H of an arbitrary set S is the smallest convex set covering S.

3 Rough Neural Network

The study of various forms of rough neurons is part of a growing number of papers on neural networks based on rough sets [5], [11]. In what follows, we give a brief description of the basic architecture of the rough neural network used in the design of the software change prediction system. The basic architecture of a rough neural network for classifying condition vectors of software metric values using convex sets is shown in Fig. 1. For each cluster, the neural network maintains decision class information that is used to make a classification decision after calibration.

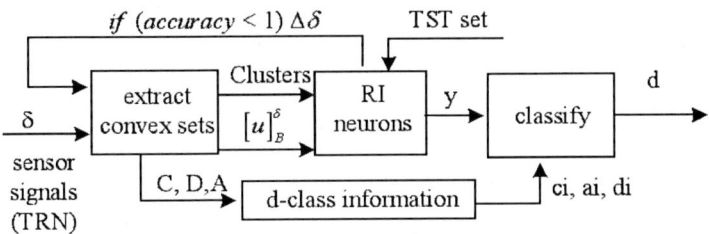

Fig. 1. Basic RNN Architecture

For each cluster, the neural network maintains decision class information that is used to make a classification decision after calibration. The rough neural network (RNN) in Fig. 1 calibrates δ to obtain a training set that matches target information about software change decision classes. The RNN itself consists of a single layer of neurons. Each neuron constructs a vector of rough integral values relative to a single decision class.

Definition 5. Given a sensor-based information system $IS = (U, A)$, define a function $f_u : \wp(U) \to \Re^k$ for each k-dimensional Rough Neuron $\mathcal{N}_k$ where $[u]_B^\delta \in \wp(U)$ and $p_i \in \Re^k$ is an element of the vector computed by f_U such that

$$\forall_{1 \leqslant i \leqslant k} \; p_i = \int_U a_i \, d\mu_{[u]_B^\delta}^{a_i} \quad \text{where } a_i \in A.$$

Input to a rough neuron is a cluster extracted from a convex set $[u]_B^\delta$, and an output is a k-dimensional vector of rough integral values p. The input $[u]_B^\delta$ is defined relative to a δ-indistinguishability relation over a point set containing software metric values. The set U denotes the universe (point set defining a region of the Euclidean plane containing possible sensor values), and the set C denotes a cluster extracted from a convex set. Each $[u]_B^\delta$ represents a partition of U. The output of a single rough neuron is a pattern vector $[p_1 \; p_2 \; ... \; p_k]$ that is associated with a row in a software change decision table. This vector defines a pattern that should be as close as possible to a known pattern (target vector) $[t_1 \; t_2 \; ... \; t_k]$ associated with a particular decision. Adjustments are made to δ (and $[u]_B^\delta$) during training to make $[p_1 \; p_2 \; ... \; p_k]$ as close as possible to $[t_1 t_2 ... t_k]$.

4 Software Change Prediction

In this section, a brief summary of the results of the experiments using RSES and the RNN Tool (called MBnet) for one sample software change study is given. To facilitate comparison of the rough set approach to software change prediction reported in this article, one set of complexity measurement data reported in a number of other software engineering studies is used in this study: International Computers Ltd. (ICL) mainframe operating system called Virtual Machine Environment (VME) [4]. The sample software metrics data and the corresponding number of changes made to 27 modules during program development of a VME subsystem used in this study was reported by [4] and analyzed by [2].

4.1 Preprocessing VME Metric Data

Metrics used to collect data about VME software include the following: Machine code instructions (Bytes), Lines of code, Modules called (calls), Data items (Ditems), Parameters (params), η_1(# of distinct operators), η_2(# of distinct operands), N_1(total # of distinct operators), N_2(total # of distinct operators), and McCabe's cyclomatic complexity V(G), After removing the outlier changes from Subsystem 1, it was found that attribute η_1 had the highest frequency-of-occurrence in the reducts obtained from a 90% (training), 10% (testing) split of the data in the non-discretized case using RSES 1.1. This suggests that η_1 is the most important metric in predicting the number of changes to a program module during software development. In our experiments, metric data with many different splits (e.g., 50/50, 60/40, 70/30, 80/20 and 90/10) were considered in random selection of training and testing sets using

Table 1. Experiments with the Kitchenham Dataset

rough NN Experiment	NN accuracy	RSES accuracy
Fig. 2 90/10 Experiment	90/10 split 100% (training) 66.7% (testing)	90/10 split 100% (training) 66.7% (testing)
Fig. 3 80/20 split	80/20 split 77.8% (training) 20% (testing)	80/20 split 100% (training) 40 % (testing)
Fig. 4 70/30 split	70/30 split 81.3% (training) 57% (testing)	70/30 split 100% (training) 14 % (testing)
Fig. 5 60/40 split	60/40 split 100% (training) 50% (testing)	60/40 split 100% (training) 50 % (testing)

RSES 1.1. Only the non-discretized case with seven decisions classes (1, 2, 3, 4, 5, 7, and 9 program changes) were included in the study. The best classification accuracy of 66.67% for the testing set was obtained using the 90/10 split with the genetic algorithm method for reducts/rules. The classification accuracy for the training set was 100%.

4.2 Neural Prediction Experiments

The rough neural network (called MBnet) described in [10] is used in classifying quality metrics. The MBnet toolset computes a closeness measure which is the root mean square of all the differences between training and testing tables over all epochs up to the current epoch. MBnet measures the accuracy of the classification equals the % of correctly classified test data in the current epoch. In each epoch after the first epoch, an adjusted δ to construct convex sets from the sample data until the computation is halted by a user or when 100% of the test table entries are correctly classified. A classification accuracy of 66.67% is achieved after 1,428 epochs which compares well with results from RSES 1.1 (see Fig. 2 in Table 1).

After experimenting with many other splits of the reduced Kitchenham dataset, it was found that only a 70/30 split into training and testing tables had prediction accuracy approaching the accuracy of a 90/10 split (see Table 1). The testing accuracy after an 80/20 split is 20% (see Fig. 3), while the testing accuracy after a 70/30 split is 57% (see Fig. 4). The testing accuracy after a 60/40 split is 50% (see Fig. 5), while the testing accuracy after a 50/50 split is 40%. Notice that in two of the cases (namely, 70/30 and 50/50) the accuracy of the neural network is higher that achieved using RSES, which RSES does better with a 80/20 split. The results of this study are inconclusive because we have only reported experiments with one, small VME dataset. However, it has been demonstrated that the predictive capability of the rough neural network is comparable with RSES.

5 Conclusion

The design of the neural network used to predict software changes that incorporates recent results concerning rough measures of sets and rough integrals has been given in this paper. Experiments with this network (MBnet toolset) have been limited to change predictions for one set of software development reported by Kitchenham for the VME system. The accuracy of the neural network is compared with the accuracy of RSES in predicting the required number of changes for a software module. Future work will include applications of rough measures as well as further work with convex hulls and rough integrals in identifying clusters of metric data useful in making change predictions both during software development and during post-deployment of a software system.

Acknowledgements. This research has been supported by the Natural Sciences and Engineering Research Council of Canada (NSERC) research grant 194376. The author also gratefully acknowledges the tremendous help and support of Dr. James F. Peters, University of Manitoba, Canada. This research benefited form the use of the MBnet toolset developed by Maciej Borkowski, University of Manitoba.

References

1. L.C. Briand, V.R. Basili, W.M. Thomas, A pattern recognition approach to software engineering data analysis, IEEE Trans. on Software Engineering, 18(11), Nov. 1992, 931–942.
2. T.M. Khoshgoftaar, J.C. Munson, B.B. Bhattacharya and G.D. Richardson, Predictive Modeling Techniques of Software Quality from Software Measures, IEEE Trans. on Software Engineering, 18(11), Nov. 1992, 979–986.
3. T.M. Khoshgoftaar, E.B. Allen, Neural networks for software quality prediction. In: W. Pedrycz, J.F. Peters (Eds.), Computational Intelligence in Software Engineering. Singapore, World Scientific, 1998, 33–63.
4. B. Kitchenham, L. Pickard, Towards a constructive quality model, I and II, Software Engineering Journal, 1987, 105–126.
5. S.K. Pal, J.F. Peters, L. Polkowski, A. Skowron (Eds.), Rough-Neuro Computing: An Introduction. In S. Pal, L. Polkowski, A. Skowron (Eds.), Rough-Neuro Computing. Berlin: Physica-Verlag, 2002, 16–43
6. Z. Pawlak, Rough Sets: Theoretical Aspects of Reasoning About Data. Boston, MA, Kluwer Academic Publishers, 1991.
7. Z. Pawlak, J.F. Peters, A. Skowron, Z. Suraj, S. Ramanna, M. Borkowski, Rough measures: Theory and Applications. In: S. Hirano, M. Inuiguchi, S. Tsumoto (Eds.), Rough Set Theory and Granular Computing, Bulletin of the International Rough Set Society, vol. 5, no. 1 / 2, 2001, 177–184.
8. Z. Pawlak, J.F. Peters, A. Skowron, Z. Suraj, S. Ramanna, M. Borkowski, Rough measures and Integrals. In: S. Hirano, M. Inuiguchi, S. Tsumoto (Eds.), *Lecture Notes in Computer Science*, 2002 [to appear].
9. W. Pedrycz, L. Han, J.F. Peters, S. Ramanna, R. Zhai, Calibration of software quality: Fuzzy neural and rough neural approaches. *Neurocomputing*, vol. 36, 2001, 149–170.
10. J.F. Peters, T.C. Ahn, M. Borkowski, V. Degtyaryov, S. Ramanna, Line Crawling Robot Navigation: A Rough Neuro-Computing Approach. In: C.Zhou, D. Maravall, D.Ruan(Eds.), Fusion of Soft Computing and Hard Computing Techniques for Autonomous Robotic Systems. Berlin: Physica-Verlag, 2002 [to appear].
11. J.F. Peters, S. Ramanna, Z. Suraj, M. Borkowski, Rough neurons: Petri net models and applications. In In S. Pal, L. Polkowski, A. Skowron (Eds.), Rough-Neuro Computing. Berlin: Physica-Verlag, 2002, 474–493.
12. J.F. Peters, S. Ramanna, A rough sets approach to assessing software quality: Concepts and rough Petri net models. In: S.K. Pal and A. Skowron (Eds.), *Rough-Fuzzy Hybridization: New Trends in Decision Making*. Berlin: Springer-Verlag, 1999, 349–380.
13. S. Ramanna, Approximation Methods in a Software Quality Measurement Framework. In: *Proc. of Canadian Conference on Electrical and Computer Engineering* 2002, Winnipeg, Manitoba, CA, May 2002 [to appear].
14. RSES 2002, http://logic.mimuw.edu.pl/~rses/

Handling Spatial Uncertainty in Binary Images: A Rough Set Based Approach

D. Sinha[1] and P. Laplante[2]

[1] Medical Imaging Division, Eastman Kodak Co.,
1 Pearl Court, Annendale, NJ, 07401,
[2] Penn State University, Great Valley School of Graduate Professional Studies, 30 East Swedesford Road, Malvern, PA 19355,
`dsinha@kodak.com; plaplante@psu.edu`

Abstract. In this paper we consider the problem of detecting binary objects. We present a method for constructing a gray-scaled (or, fuzzy) template for use in correlation-based matching of Boolean images, using rough sets. First, we represent the binary images in the morphological sense – that is – as sets. Next, we assume a cause for spatial uncertainty that is quite common in machine vision applications and present a methodology for modeling it indirectly in the construction of the template. Then we show how rough sets can be used to determine the matching probabilities constructively, rather than through trial and error, as is usually the case. Our technique is computationally efficient and is superior to correlation-based techniques, which can be easily fooled and automates the hand-selection of structuring elements for the hit-or-miss transform technique, both of which are usually used to solve this problem.

1 Introduction

Most binary image detection algorithms are based on either a variant of Peterson's correlation coefficient [1] or Morphological hit-or-miss transform [2]. In both cases, pattern-matching is achieved by overlaying a template image and then using an algorithm to generate a number which judges the closeness of the image (or image segment) with the template. With correlation coefficients one defines a number (less than 1) above which the match is considered exact. This approach – though good in many situations – leads to an algorithm that often fails to detect the dissimilarity between two objects. For example, when the image is binary, the template is usually binary as well, in which case the algorithm easy to deceive. If the template is gray-scale – even for binary images, then we contend that the algorithm is not so easy to fool.

On the other hand, the hit-or-miss transform can use gray-scale templates, even in the binary case. However, this techniques requires "hand-selection" of the gray-scale values for the templates (called "probes" or "structuring elements"). Hence, the problem, for both correlation-based matching and the hit-or-miss transform, is how does one derive the gray-scale template other than trial-and-error? We know of no algorithmic approach to choosing the gray-scale (or fuzzy) values for the template. Our contribution is to provide such a technique.

Furthermore, handling spatial uncertainty has always been problematic in both approaches. Consider a machine vision application where an object is imaged by a camera system after it has been placed at the viewing station. The mechanism that moves the object has a positioning error that is non-zero and more importantly, may be appreciable enough not to be ignored – especially in high accuracy applications. If the camera is attached to a stage, then it too has associated positioning errors.

The effect of the positioning errors is seen in the discretization of the object's image. If positioning errors are very small compared to the pixel size, the effect is barely noticeable. However, when they are comparable, depending upon the objects location vis-à-vis the camera's location, the image could look quite different. In Fig. 1, for example, depending upon the position of the object (triangle) vis-à-vis the camera's coordinate system, the image will be different. The discretization process usually considers the intensity at each square and then maps it to 0 or 1 depending upon certain threshold. Boundary pixels usually are partially covered squares and are thus affected by the exact positioning of the object.

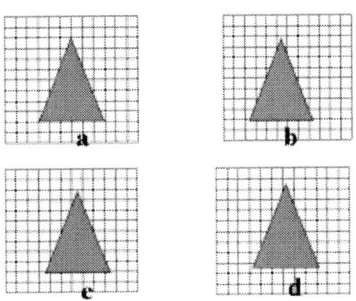

Fig. 1. Spatial error induced by camera positioning.

The effect is, of course, on the boundary pixels. and in certain applications, boundary pixels may need to be modeled extremely carefully. For example, irrespective of the underlying special uncertainty model, a correlation-based algorithm will conclude that the first five objects of Fig. 2 a- e will match equally well to the square (Fig. 2f).

In some applications (such as semiconductor manufacturing) certain types of boundary pixel drop offs may be tolerable, but others not. For example, Fig. 3 represents a cross-sectional image of electrical lines on a substrate. Here the

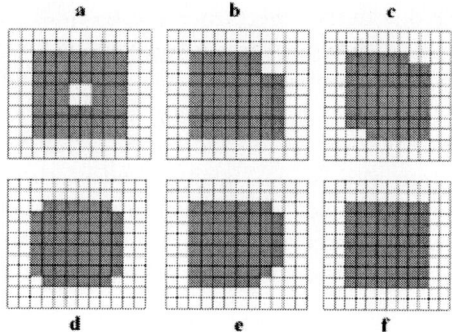

Fig. 2. Six images whose correlation-based matching scores may be equal.

first line (a) may be acceptable as it meets the minimum thickness requirement; the second line (b) may not meet the requirements. As previously described, a correlation-based technique is not well suited for this task.

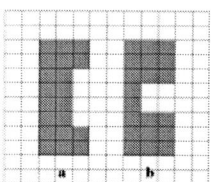

Fig. 3. Electrical connection lines.

In the case of morphological hit-or-miss transform, one must design the hit and miss structuring elements "by hand" so as to take into consideration the spatial uncertainty [2]. If this process were to be automated, we contend that it will look very similar to the one we present using rough sets.

2 Rough Sets on Image Spaces

The object space is modeled as a finite subset of the Euclidean space. Once the object's image is captured via an imaging system, the model of underlying space is a finite subset of the Cartesian coordinates. For example, if a 1K × 1K camera is used to capture the image, the image space is assumed to be $\{<i,j>: \quad i,j = 0, 1, \cdots, 1023\}$ and each $<i,j>$ is called a pixel. If the pixel size is $p \times q$ units, then each pixel $<i,j>$ in the image space denotes an area (of $p \times q$ units)

$$\aleph_{\alpha,\beta,p,q}(i,j) = \left[\alpha + i - \frac{p}{2}, \alpha + i + \frac{p}{2}\right) \times \left[\beta + j - \frac{q}{2}, \beta + j + \frac{q}{2}\right)$$

in the object space. $\langle \alpha, \beta \rangle$ is the coordinate of origin of the image space in the object space's coordinate space. In case of the binary images, the camera looks at the intensity coming from the area $\aleph_{\alpha,\beta,p,q}(i,j)$ and if it is above a certain threshold, the corresponding pixel $< i, j >$ is assumed to be present; otherwise it is assumed to be absent. For non-visual imaging systems an analogous procedure is applied.

Relating back to our earlier discussions, positioning errors will modify the value of $\langle \alpha, \beta \rangle$ and hence change the set $\aleph_{\alpha,\beta,p,q}(i,j)$. The positioning errors will, in general, result in different binary image representation of the object.

We wish to look into how the rough sets can be used to help in bounding the sets $\aleph_{\alpha,\beta,p,q}(i,j)$ and thus providing a mechanism to model the spatial uncertainty in the object's image. The Rough set is a mathematical formulation of the concept of approximate (rough) equality of sets in a given approximation space Ω [3]. Rather than go into the Rough Set theory, we will provide an intuitive introduction in the context of our application. A thorough mathematical treatment of rough sets can be found in [3] and [4]. The theory of Rough Sets introduces the notion of an approximation of a set by a pair of sets called the *upper approximation*, **U**, and the *lower approximation*, **L**. Consider any set X in the original space and define

$$\mathbf{L}(X) = \bigcup \{Y \subset \Omega | Y \subseteq X\}. \tag{1}$$

The lower approximation is the union of all subsets (in the approximate universe Ω) of X. Similarly,

$$\mathbf{U}(X) = \bigcap \{Y \subset \Omega | Y \cap X \neq \phi\} \tag{2}$$

is the intersection of all sets Y (in the approximate universe Ω) that intersect with X [5].

Let the approximation space, Ω, be the Cartesian coordinates. Then by inspecting Fig. 4, it is easy to see how the upper and lower approximations are derived for image, X.

Although the Rough Set framework seems well suited for dealing with images, surprisingly, there has been little previous work published in this regard. Wojcik used rough sets derived from an equivalence relation that could "take noise X apart from image I" to do edge enhancement [6]. The problem here is that finding such an equivalence relation seems to obviate the need for any further processing to do the edge detection. Wojcik and Wojcik demonstrate how rough sets are more accurately used in context based image processing than statistical means, and they present a neural network to uncover "casual relationships [between images] using a rough sets approach" [7]. In essence they show how through the empirical algorithms based on rough sets, are superior to those based on statistics (guessing). Mohabey and Ray use rough sets to segment colored images [5]. Beaubouef and Petry introduce the idea of using rough sets to deal with

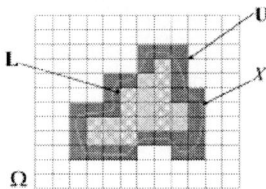

Fig. 4. An arbitrary image $X \subset \Omega$ and its upper approximation **U** and lower approximation **L**.

spatial uncertainty, but only in terms of classifying the different kinds of spatial uncertainty – not to solve any problems using it [8]. Wu introduces the notion of using "rough neural nets" for image classification, but the result is a traditional neural net, using rough sets to provide training data [9]. Therefore, another contribution of this work is that it provides a framework for utilizing the rich theory of Rough Sets for a very practical imaging application.

3 A Framework for Using Rough Sets in Handling Spatial Uncertainty

Let **A** be an object and let $x \in \mathbf{A}$ be a pixel point. Let us assume that the range of image positioning error is $\pm \Delta$. The error range can be zero, less than one pixel, or one or more pixels.

For each positioning error $\delta \in [-\Delta, \Delta]$, one can determine the upper and lower approximations of the object **A**. This collection of all upper and lower approximations will be finite[1] and let us denote them as (for some $n \geq 1$)

$$\{\langle \mathbf{L}_i, \mathbf{U}_i \rangle : i = 1, 2, \cdots, n\}.$$

Why do we wish to consider such a collection? Intuitively speaking, the pixels in the set $\bigcap_{i=1}^{n} \mathbf{L}_i$ are almost definitely going to be present in the image no matter what the positioning error. Similarly, pixels that do not belong to the set $\bigcup_{i=1}^{n} \mathbf{U}_i$ are not going to be present in the image. For all other pixels we need to determine a likelihood that they will appear in the image. We will do this by inspecting all the lower and upper approximations.

Define the following sets:

---

[1] The collection will be finite so long as Δ is finite. Very few positioning errors will lead to unique pairs of upper and lower sets. See Fig. 6 and the worked example at the end of the paper.

$$\mathbf{X}_1 = \bigcap_{i=1}^{n} \mathbf{L}_i, \quad \mathbf{X}_2 = \bigcup_{i=1}^{n} \bigcap_{\substack{j=1 \\ i \neq j}}^{n} \mathbf{L}_j, \quad \mathbf{X}_3 = \bigcup_{i=1}^{n} \bigcup_{\substack{j=1 \\ j \neq i}}^{n} \bigcap_{\substack{k=1 \\ k \neq i \\ k \neq j}}^{n} \mathbf{L}_k, \quad \ldots\ldots,$$

$$\mathbf{X}_n = \bigcup_{i=1}^{n} \mathbf{L}_i,$$

$$\mathbf{Y}_1 = \bigcap_{i=1}^{n} \mathbf{U}_i, \quad \mathbf{Y}_2 = \bigcup_{i=1}^{n} \bigcap_{\substack{j=1 \\ i \neq j}}^{n} \mathbf{U}_j, \quad \mathbf{Y}_3 = \bigcup_{i=1}^{n} \bigcup_{\substack{j=1 \\ j \neq i}}^{n} \bigcap_{\substack{k=1 \\ k \neq i \\ k \neq j}}^{n} \mathbf{U}_k, \quad \ldots\ldots,$$

$$\mathbf{Y}_n = \bigcup_{i=1}^{n} \mathbf{U}_i. \quad (3)$$

In words, $\mathbf{X}_1$ is the collection of pixels found in any of the lower approximations and $\mathbf{Y}_1$ is the collection of pixels found in all upper approximations. $\mathbf{X}_2$ is the collection of pixels found in all but one of lower approximations and $\mathbf{Y}_2$ is the collection of pixels found in all but one of the upper approximations. $\mathbf{X}_3$ is the collection of pixels found in all but two of the lower approximations and $\mathbf{Y}_3$ is the collection of pixels found in all but two of upper approximations. In general, $\mathbf{X}_k$ is the collection of pixels found in all but $k-1$ of the lower approximations and $\mathbf{Y}_k$ is the collection of pixels found in all but $k-1$ of the upper approximations. Clearly, $\mathbf{X}_n$ and $\mathbf{Y}_n$ contain pixels found in all lower and upper approximations, respectively. In a sense, the $\langle \mathbf{X}_i, \mathbf{Y}_i \rangle$ pairs provide a set of sorted weightings of pixels located in the image.

Only the following relationships can be stated for these $2n$ sets:

$$\mathbf{X}_1 \subseteq \mathbf{X}_2 \subseteq \mathbf{X}_3 \subseteq \cdots \subseteq \mathbf{X}_n,$$
$$\mathbf{Y}_1 \subseteq \mathbf{Y}_2 \subseteq \mathbf{Y}_3 \subseteq \cdots \subseteq \mathbf{Y}_n,$$
$$\mathbf{X}_1 \subseteq \mathbf{Y}_1,$$
$$\mathbf{X}_2 \subseteq \mathbf{Y}_2,$$
$$\cdots$$
$$\mathbf{X}_n \subseteq \mathbf{Y}_n.$$

These follow trivially from the construction of the sets.

In general, the set

$$\Theta \equiv \{\mathbf{X}_1, \mathbf{X}_2, \cdots, \mathbf{X}_n, \mathbf{Y}_1, \mathbf{Y}_2, \cdots, \mathbf{Y}_n\}$$

is a lattice. We can write the multi-set Θ using the standard multi-set terminology as

$$\Theta = \{ \mathbf{P}_1|_{\lambda_1}, \mathbf{P}_2|_{\lambda_2}, \cdots, \mathbf{P}_m|_{\lambda_m} \} \tag{4}$$

with $\lambda_i \geq 1$ and $\lambda_1 + \lambda_2 + \cdots + \lambda_m = 2n$ and

$$\mathbf{P}_i \neq \mathbf{P}_j \text{ for } i \neq j. \tag{5}$$

λ_i denotes the number of times set $\mathbf{P}_i$ appears in the multi-set Θ. We also let $\mathbf{P}_1 = \mathbf{X}_1$ and $\mathbf{P}_m = \mathbf{Y}_n$ - the lattice zero and one, respectively.

4 Deriving a Matching Template

Consider finding a matching template, $\mathbf{T}$, for object $\mathbf{A}$ based on a series of image samples represented by the upper and lower approximations, $\langle \mathbf{U}_i, \mathbf{L}_i \rangle$ defined by equations (1) and (2) and the $\langle \mathbf{X}_i, \mathbf{Y}_i \rangle$ defined as in equation set (3). To find $\mathbf{T}$, apply the following construction. First, find the corresponding $\mathbf{P}_i$ by forming Θ as in equation (4) and computing the λ_i as in equation (5). Next, apply the following for each $x \in \mathbf{A}$,
Case 1: if $x \notin \mathbf{P}_m$. Let $\mathbf{T}(x) = 0$.
Case 2: if $x \in \mathbf{P}_m$. Define a subset of Θ as follows:

$$\Theta_x = \{ \mathbf{P}_i|_{\lambda_i} : x \in \mathbf{P}_i \text{ and } i = 1, 2, \cdots, m \}$$

and denote the set of minimal elements of Θ_x as Γ_x. Γ_x is not necessarily a singleton. Now we can define the value of $\mathbf{T}(x)$ as

$$\mathbf{T}(x) = 1 - \frac{\sum_{\mathbf{P}_i \subset \mathbf{Q} \in \Gamma_x} \lambda_i}{2n}. \tag{6}$$

Note that the proper set containment, $\mathbf{P}_i \subset \mathbf{Q}$, does not allow for $\mathbf{P}_i = \mathbf{Q}$. The expression $\mathbf{P}_i \subset \mathbf{Q} \in \Gamma_x$ in Equation (6) in words is "Consider every proper subset $\mathbf{P}_i$ of all elements $\mathbf{Q}$ of Γ_x." In particular,

$$\Gamma_x = \mathbf{P}_1 \Rightarrow \mathbf{T}(x) = 1$$
$$\Gamma_x = \mathbf{P}_m \Rightarrow \mathbf{T}(x) = \frac{\lambda_m}{2n}.$$

This template represents the likelihood that a pixel belongs to the image in the presence of special noise caused by the positioning error. Pixels belonging to the innermost core get assigned higher likelihood values that those at the boundary. In fact, the likelihood decreases as one travels towards the boundary in any direction. In essence, $\mathbf{T}$ counts the number of times a pixel appears at the same "level" in the lattice and assigns a probability to it accordingly. The following statement captures this more formally:

$$\forall \mathbf{P} \in \Theta, \; \forall \mathbf{Q} \subset \mathbf{P}, \; \forall x \in \mathbf{Q}, \; \forall y \in \mathbf{P} - \mathbf{Q}, \quad \mathbf{T}(x) > \mathbf{T}(y). \tag{7}$$

As an example of finding **T**, suppose we processed an image, and yielded a set of upper and lower approximations, and derived Θ as follows:

$$\Theta = \{\{<0,0>\}|_1, \{<0,0>,<0,1>\}|_1, \{<0,0>,<1,0>\}|_1,$$
$$\{<0,0>,<0,1>,<1,0>,<1,1>\}|_1\}$$

Then, $\mathbf{T}(<i,j>) = 0$ for all $i, j \notin \{0, 1\}$,

$$\Gamma_{<0,0>} = \{\{<0,0>\}|_1\},$$
$$\Gamma_{<0,1>} = \{\{<0,0>,<0,1>\}|_1\},$$
$$\Gamma_{<1,0>} = \{\{<0,0>,<1,0>\}|_1\},$$
$$\Gamma_{<1,1>} = \{\{<0,0>,<0,1>,<1,0>,<1,1>\}|_1\}.$$

Graphically, the lattice structure can be visualized as in Fig. 5.

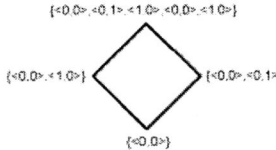

Fig. 5. Lattice Structure for example template calculation.

In any case, we have,

$$\mathbf{T}(<0,0>) = 1 - \frac{0}{4} = 1,$$
$$\mathbf{T}(<0,1>) = 1 - \frac{1}{4} = \frac{3}{4},$$
$$\mathbf{T}(<1,0>) = 1 - \frac{1}{4} = \frac{3}{4},$$
$$\mathbf{T}(<1,1>) = 1 - \frac{1+1+1}{4} = \frac{1}{4}.$$

As can be seen the statement (6) holds.

5   A Simple Application

To demonstrate the algorithm, consider a rather trivial example of a rectangular image that is 1 pixel by 2 pixels. Suppose that $0 < \Delta < 1$ pixel. We will have positioning errors in both x- and y- directions. Depending on these errors, nine different discretizations are possible – see Fig. 6. We obtain

$$\mathbf{L}_1 = \{<0,0>,<1,0>\} \quad \mathbf{U}_1 = \{<0,0>,<1,0>\}$$

$$L_2 = \{<0,0>\} \quad U_2 = \{<-1,0>,<0,0>,<1,0>\}$$
$$L_3 = \{<1,0>\} \quad U_3 = \{<0,0>,<1,0>,<2,0>\}$$
$$L_4 = \{\} \quad U_4 = \{<0,-1>,<0,0>,<1,-1>,<1,0>\}$$
$$L_5 = \{\} \quad U_5 = \{<-1,-1>,<-1,0>,<0,-1>,<0,0>,<1,-1>,<1,0>\}$$
$$L_6 = \{\} \quad U_6 = \{<0,-1>,<0,0>,<1,-1>,<1,0>,<2,-1>,<2,0>\}$$
$$L_7 = \{\} \quad U_7 = \{<0,0>,<0,1>,<1,0>,<1,1>\}$$
$$L_8 = \{\}$$
$$U_8 = \{<-1,0>,<-1,1>,<0,0>,<0,1>,<1,0>,<1,1>\}$$
$$L_9 = \{\} \quad U_9 = \{<0,0>,<0,1>,<1,0>,<1,1>,<2,0>,<2,1>\}$$

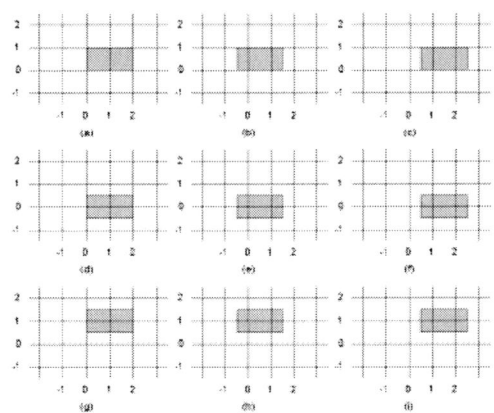

Fig. 6. Various discretizations of a 1x2 rectangle. (a) $\delta_x = \delta_y = 0$; (b) $\delta_x < 0, \delta_y = 0$; (c) $\delta_x > 0, \delta_y = 0$; (d) $\delta_x = 0, \delta_y < 0$; (e) $\delta_x < 0, \delta_y < 0$; (f) $\delta_x > 0, \delta_y < 0$; (g) $\delta_x = 0, \delta_y > 0$; (h) $\delta_x < 0, \delta_y > 0$; and (i) $\delta_x > 0, \delta_y > 0$.

Referring to Fig. 6, it is easy to see that the upper and lower approximation pair $\langle \mathbf{U}_1, \mathbf{L}_1 \rangle$ corresponds to image (a), $\langle \mathbf{U}_2, \mathbf{L}_2 \rangle$ corresponds to image (b) and so on with $\langle \mathbf{U}_9, \mathbf{L}_9 \rangle$ corresponding to image (i). In any case we find:

$$\mathbf{X}_1 = \mathbf{X}_2 = \mathbf{X}_3 = \mathbf{X}_4 = \mathbf{X}_5 = \mathbf{X}_6 = \mathbf{X}_7 = \{\} \quad \equiv \mathbf{P}_1,$$
$$\mathbf{X}_8 = \mathbf{X}_9 = \mathbf{Y}_1 = \mathbf{Y}_2 = \mathbf{Y}_3 = \mathbf{Y}_4 = \mathbf{Y}_5 = \mathbf{Y}_6 = \{<0,0>,<1,0>\} \quad \equiv \mathbf{P}_2,$$

$$\mathbf{Y}_7 = \mathbf{Y}_8 = \{<-1,0>,<0,-1>,<0,0>,<0,1>,<1,-1>,$$
$$<1,0>,<1,1>,<2,0>\} \quad \equiv \mathbf{P}_3, \text{ and}$$

$$\mathbf{Y}_9 = \{<-1,-1>,<-1,0>,<-1,1>,<0,-1>,<0,0>,<0,1>,<1,-1>,$$
$$<1,0>,<1,1>,<2,-1>,<2,0>,<2,1>\} \quad \equiv \mathbf{P}_4.$$

We can now write

$$\Theta = \{\mathbf{P}_1|_7, \mathbf{P}_2|_8, \mathbf{P}_3|_2, \mathbf{P}_4|_1\} \ .$$

Note that Θ is a chain: $\mathbf{P}_1 \subset \mathbf{P}_2 \subset \mathbf{P}_3 \subset \mathbf{P}_4$ - see Fig. 7.

$$x \in \mathbf{P}_2 \ \Rightarrow \ \mathbf{T}(x) = 1 - \frac{7}{18} = \frac{11}{18},$$
$$x \in \mathbf{P}_3 - \mathbf{P}_2 \ \Rightarrow \ \mathbf{T}(x) = 1 - \frac{7+8}{18} = \frac{1}{6},$$
$$x \in \mathbf{P}_4 - \mathbf{P}_3 \ \Rightarrow \ \mathbf{T}(x) = 1 - \frac{7+8+2}{18} = \frac{1}{18}.$$

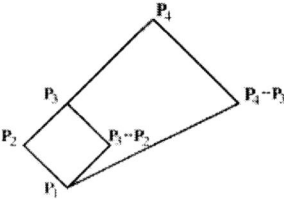

Fig. 7. Lattice structure of Θ in the worked example.

Thus, the template for matching our 1 by 2 rectangle will be:

$$\mathbf{T} \approx \begin{pmatrix} 0.055 & 0.167 & 0.167 & 0.055 \\ 0.167 & \underline{0.611} & 0.611 & 0.167 \\ 0.055 & 0.167 & 0.167 & 0.055 \end{pmatrix} .$$

The underlined pixel is at origin. As we can see the assigned weights are intuitively pleasing.

The weight at pixels $\langle 0, 0 \rangle$ and $\langle 1, 0 \rangle$ are not 1. The reason being that there is some non-zero probability that the image may not contain either of these two pixels. In this example, this probability is the relative frequency of set $\mathbf{P}_1$, that is, $\frac{7}{18} \approx 0.389$. Other weights can be similarly reasoned in an intuitive manner. Note that the expression (7) again holds here.

6 Conclusions

In this paper an algorithm is presented for determining the template needed for template based pattern-matching algorithms using rough sets. The algorithm automates the construction of templates for correlation-based matching and for hit-or-miss transform-based matching. In most machine vision applications, the task of selecting an appropriate template is the most time consuming one. Moreover, once selected, the template is used many times over. Our scheme is part of the up front analysis that one needs to perform either mentally or heuristically.

The proposed algorithm is also superior to other techniques in that the error can be controlled to any precision through the selection of additional image samples that yield additional upper and lower approximations. And the construction is algorithmic, not heuristic. Our proposed technique can be applied when the source of spatial uncertainty is due to other factors such as vibration, light diffraction and parallax.

We have introduced a powerful technique for building pattern matching systems with a wide range of applications. Future work needs to be done in applying the algorithm to real inspection systems and to gray valued and fuzzy images, and those images that have uncertainty not due to fuzzification [10].

References

1. M. J. Narasimha and A. M Peterson, "On the computation of the discrete cosine transform," IEEE Transaction on Communications, COM-26(6):934-936, June 1978.
2. E. R. Dougherty and C. R. Giardina, Morphological Methods in Image and Signal Processing, Prentice Hall, 1988.
3. Z. Pawlak, Rough Sets: Theoretical Aspects of Reasoning about Data, Boston, MA, Kluwer Academic Publishers, 1991.
4. J. Komorowski, Z. Pawlak, L. Polkowski, A. Skowron, Rough Sets: A Tutorial, In: S. K. Pal, A. Skowron (Eds.), Rough Fuzzy Hypbridization:A New Trend in Decision-Making, Springer-Verlag, Berlin, 1999, pp. 3-98.
5. A. Mohabey and A. K. Ray, "Rough Set Theory Based Segmentation of Color Images, Proceedings of the 19th International Conference on NAFIPS, Fuzzy Information Processing Society, 2000, 338-342.
6. Z. M Wojcik, "Application of Rough Sets for Edge Enhancing Image Filters," Proceedings of the IEEE International Conference on Image Processing, Volume 2, 1994, 525-529.
7. Z. M. Wojcik and B. E. Wojcik, "Structural Modeling Using Rough Sets," Proceedings of the Fifth IEEE International Conference on Fuzzy Systems, 1996, 761-766.
8. T. Beaubouef and F. Petry, "Vagueness in Spatial Data: Rough Set and Egg-Yolk Approaches," Lecture Notes in Computer Science, Vol. 2070, 2001, . 367-373.
9. Z. Wu, "Research on Remote Sensing Image Classification Using Neural network Based on Rough Sets," Proceedings of the Info-tech and Info-net International Conferences, Volume 1, 2001, 279-284.
10. P. A. Laplante and D. Sinha, "Handling Uncertain Data in Imaging Systems," IEEE Transactions on Systems, Man and Cybernetics, Volume 26, No. 1, February 1996, 21-28.

Evolutionary Algorithms and Rough Sets-Based Hybrid Approach to Classificatory Decomposition of Cortical Evoked Potentials

Tomasz G. Smolinski[1], Grzegorz M. Boratyn[1], Mariofanna Milanova[2], Jacek M. Zurada[1], and Andrzej Wrobel[3]

[1] Computational Intelligence Laboratory,
Department of Electrical and Computer Engineering, University of Louisville,
Louisville, KY 40292, USA
{tomasz.smolinski,grzegorz.boratyn,jacek.zurada}@louisville.edu

[2] Department of Computer Science, University of Arkansas at Little Rock,
Little Rock, AR 72204, USA
mgmilanova@ualr.edu

[3] Laboratory of Visual System,
Department of Neurophysiology, Nencki Institute of Experimental Biology,
3 Pasteur Street, 02-093 Warsaw, Poland
wrobel@nencki.gov.pl

Abstract. This paper presents a novel approach to decomposition and classification of rat's cortical evoked potentials (EPs). The decomposition is based on learning of a sparse set of basis functions using Evolutionary Algorithms (EAs). The basis functions are generated in a potentially overcomplete dictionary of the EP components according to a probabilistic model of the data. Compared to the traditional, statistical signal decomposition techniques, this allows for a number of basis functions greater than the dimensionality of the input signals, which can be of a great advantage. However, there arises an issue of selecting the most significant components from the possibly overcomplete collection. This is especially important in classification problems performed on the decomposed representation of the data, where only those components that provide a substantial discernibility between EPs of different groups are relevant. In this paper, we propose an approach based on the Rough Set theory's (RS) feature selection mechanisms to deal with this problem. We design an EA and RS-based hybrid system capable of signal decomposition and, based on a reduced component set, signal classification.

1 Introduction

Signal decomposition plays a very important role in the analysis of Evoked Potentials (EPs) [1]. Among the most popular methods for EP decomposition, one will find Principal Component Analysis (PCA) [2], Independent Component Analysis (ICA) [3], [4] or wavelet-based analysis [5]. In general, a common way to represent real-valued EPs can be based upon a linear superposition of some basis functions (i.e. components). Bases such as wavelets can provide a very useful representation of some signals, however, they have serious limitations in terms of the number as well as the characteristics of the basis functions they employ [5], [6].

An alternative and more general method of signal representation via transformation uses Sparse Coding with Overcomplete Bases (SCOB) [7], [8]. This methodology is based on the assumption that data can be represented by a set of statistically independent events (i.e. basis functions). An additional conjecture requires the probability distributions of those events to be sparse, meaning that the data can be usually described in terms of a relatively small number of those events. At the same time, an overcomplete representation allows for a greater number of basis functions than the dimensionality of the input signals, which provides much greater flexibility in terms of capturing structures hidden in data [9], [10], [11]. The SCOB methodology, due to the employment of an overcomplete representation, provides a powerful mechanism for a detailed data modeling. However, even if the sparseness of the basis functions is accounted for and preserved, the issue of selecting the most significant components from the possibly overcomplete collection is still crucial. This is especially important for some signal classification applications that can use SCOB as a data preprocessing/transformation tool. In such applications, only those components that provide the best discernibility between signals that belong to different groups or classes, are relevant.

While a similar idea of dimensionality reduction via a two-stage feature selection has already been proposed by Swiniarski in the hybridization of PCA and Rough Sets (RS) [12], it appears that the application of this approach to sparse coding with overcomplete bases is quite unique. Subsequently, we propose an algorithm for learning a potentially overcomplete basis of the EP components by viewing it as a probabilistic model of the observed data. From this model, we derive a simple and robust learning algorithm by maximizing the data likelihood over the basis.

2 Bayesian Motivated Model

The primary step in measuring the form of EPs is to decompose them into parts (i.e. components). Components can be expressed by some basis functions weighted by coefficients. Therefore, we assume that each data vector $\mathbf{x}$ can be described by a set of basis functions $\mathbf{M}$ and coefficients $\mathbf{a}$, plus some additive noise ε:

$$\mathbf{x} = \mathbf{M}\mathbf{a} + \varepsilon. \qquad (1)$$

The unknown parameters to be estimated are $\mathbf{a}$ and $\mathbf{M}$. Developing efficient algorithms to solve this equation is an active research area. A given data point can have many possible representations. Nevertheless, this ambiguity can be removed by a proper choice of the prior probability of the basis coefficients, $P(\mathbf{a})$, which specifies the probability of the alternative representations. Standard approaches to signal representation do not specify the prior for the coefficients. A more general approach is to use the information theory and the probabilistic formulation of the problem [13], [14]. Rather than making prior assumption about the shape or form of the basis functions, those functions are adapted to the data using an algorithm that maximizes the log-probability of the data under the model.

The coefficients **a** from (1) can be inferred from **x** by maximizing the conditional probability of **a**, given **x** and **M**, which can be expressed via Bayes' rule as:

$$\mathbf{a} = \arg\max_{\mathbf{a}} P(\mathbf{a}|\mathbf{x},\mathbf{M}) \propto \arg\max_{\mathbf{a}} P(\mathbf{x}|\mathbf{a},\mathbf{M})P(\mathbf{a}). \tag{2}$$

The first term of the right hand side of the proportion specifies the likelihood of the signal under the model for a given state of the coefficients:

$$P(\mathbf{x}|\mathbf{a},\mathbf{M}) \propto \exp\left(-\frac{\lambda}{Z_{\sigma N}}|\mathbf{x}-\mathbf{Ma}|^2\right), \tag{3}$$

where $Z_{\sigma N}$ is normalizing constant, $\lambda = 1/\sigma^2$, and σ is the standard deviation of the additive noise. The second term specifies the prior probability distribution over the basis coefficients, where:

$$P(\mathbf{a}) = \prod_j \exp\left(-S(a_j)\right), \tag{4}$$

where a_j is the coefficient of the j-th basis function and $S(a_j)$ is a sparseness term given by $\beta\log(1+(a_j/\gamma)^2)$, where β and γ are scaling factors. This sparse coding constraint encourages the model to use relatively few basis functions to represent the input signal. This leads to approximate redundancy reduction [15].

Thus, the maximization of the log-probability in (2) becomes:

$$\mathbf{a} = \arg\min_{\mathbf{a}} \left(\frac{\lambda_N}{2}|\mathbf{x}-\mathbf{Ma}|^2 + \sum_j S(a_j)\right). \tag{5}$$

3 Evolutionary Algorithm for Proposed Sparse Coding

From the model presented in Sect. 2, we derive a simple and robust learning algorithm by maximizing the data likelihood over the basis functions.

Some research has been previously done in applying Genetic Algorithms (GAs) to the blind source separation (BSS) and ICA [16]. In our work, an Evolutionary Algorithm (EA) is used to solve the problem of finding the best representation of a given signal in terms of basis functions and coefficients. The EA searches for an optimum by iteratively changing a population of temporary solutions encoded into chromosomes [17]. Each chromosome represents the matrix of basis functions **M** and the matrix of coefficients **a**. Fitness function, minimized in our case, is based on (5) and consists of two parts: 1) the error of the reconstructed signals and 2) the sparse cost of the values of the coefficients:

$$f = \sum_i \left(\sum_t \left| x_i(t) - \sum_j a_{ij} M_j(t) \right| + \sum_j S(a_{ij}) \right), \quad (6)$$

where $x_i(t)$ is the value of the i-th input signal at time t, $M_j(t)$ is the value of the j-th basis function at time t, and a_{ij} is the value of the coefficient for the j-th basis function for the i-th input signal.

4 Rough Sets-Based Selection of Classification-Relevant Components from a Potentially Overcomplete Set of Basis Functions

The SCOB methodology provides a very efficient mechanism for data transformation. The fact that the collection of basis functions is potentially overcomplete allows for a very detailed and accurate modeling. On the other hand, this can cause a given problem to become more difficult to analyze, due to the increase of the conceptual dimensionality of the task. In traditional techniques, such as PCA, feature extraction is based upon minimization of the reconstruction error and the "most expressive" components are selected according to some statistical criteria [18]. Sometimes, however, the reconstruction error is not important, while the feature reduction task is crucial. This is especially true for any classification problem performed on the new representation of the data (i.e. coefficients for a given set of basis functions), in which one is looking for the smallest possible set of components that explain all the variations between different classes (i.e. groups) of objects. In terms of evoked potentials, for instance, traditional approaches do not guarantee that selected components, as a feature vector in the new representation, will be competent for classification.

One possibility for dealing with this problem, is to apply the theory of rough sets [19], [20]. In this case, especially useful will be the concept of reducts, inherently embedded in the theory. Intuitively, an application of the SCOB methodology will yield an adequate and detailed model of the input data, whilst the RS-based search for reducts will determine the most significant components in that model, in terms of data classification.

Obviously, since the RS theory operates on integer-valued data by principle, the real values of coefficients representing the signals need to be first discretized (i.e. divided into intervals that will be assigned ordered, integer values) [21], [22].

5 Experiments and Results

5.1 Data

In the neuro-physiological experiments underlying our project, a piezoelectric stimulator was attached to a vibrissa of a rat. An electrical impulse of 5 V amplitude and 1 ms duration was applied to the stimulator causing the vibrissa deflection. Evoked Potentials were then registered – each of them related to a single stimulus. Based on same previous work, a hypothesis about a relation between two components of the registered evoked potentials and particular brain structures (i.e. supra- and infra-granular pyramidal cells) was stated. In order to verify the hypothesis, a series of additional stimuli was applied to the surface of the cortex – cooling events allowing to temporarily "switch off" some structures of the brain. The main goal of these experiments was to investigate those stimuli in the sense of their impact on the brain activity represented by the registered EPs (for a detailed description of the study, see [23], [24]).

A single, four-level electrode positioned in the cortex of a rat, collected the data. The electrode registered brain activity in a form of evoked potentials on four depths (i.e. channels) simultaneously. Each EP was then sampled and is represented in the database by 100 values. The complete database consists of four separate data sets for each of the four channels with 882 records in each data set.

Because of the fact that the third channel's electrode was acknowledged as the most "representative" perspective at the activity of the cortex, it was usually chosen as the input to our experiments.

5.2 Analysis

A sequence of experiments was performed in order to verify and analyze the performance of the proposed approach. The overall effectiveness of the algorithm, in the light of previous findings, was considered. The most important issue was to investigate if the system was capable of determining components similar to the ones obtained in previous work by PCA [24] and ICA [6]. Furthermore, it was crucial to explore the ability of the system to automatically select the components that really mattered in terms of the discrimination between the registered EPs. Those components, were assumed to explain most of the differences between EPs in the database, especially between *normal* and *cooled* potentials.

In all the experiments described in this section, an evolutionary algorithm implemented by the authors of this article was used for the signal decomposition (see also [6]). Additionally, the Rosetta system [25] along with some authors' implementations of rough sets were employed for the RS-based value discretization and feature selection/reduction.

The complete set of 882 evoked potentials, registered on the 3rd channel, was used as the input to the evolutionary algorithm. Based on the conclusions derived from some preliminary work on the same data (i.e. having too many basis functions, some of them appeared to be completely insignificant – see [6]) the goal of the algorithm was to determine a set of 10 basis functions (note: not really overcomplete in this case). A graphical representation of the discovered basis functions is shown in Fig. 1.

It is important to point out that the "polarization" of the basis functions is not really relevant, since the coefficients can also take negative values.

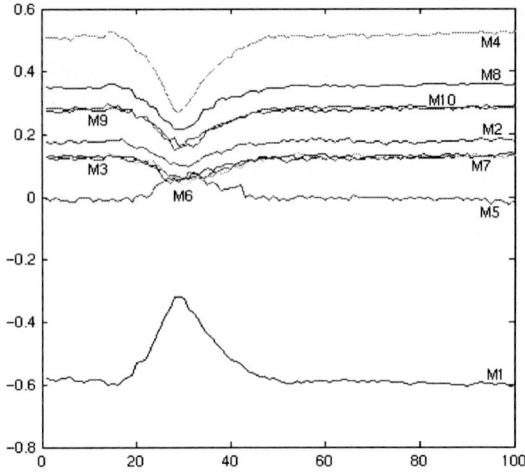

Fig. 1. 10 basis functions computed from the complete data set (Mx denotes the x-th basis function).

Based on this new representation of the input data (i.e. coefficients for the basis functions), RS-driven search for reducts was applied – after the prior discretization, the Johnson's reduction algorithm [25] was launched.

Various configurations of the discretization and/or reduction algorithms were investigated. The most interesting results are shown in Fig. 2, where the averaged selected components of the signals registered on the 3rd channel (i.e. basis functions weighted by the coefficients of the signals) are shown.

Since the decision attribute (i.e. cooling event) was only approximately defined in our database, it was impossible to directly determine the classification accuracy based on the discretized and reduced data. However, the most important part of this project was to verify the coherency of the results obtained with our approach with the results produced by other methods and, based on this, improve and extend the process of EP analysis by providing an automatic methodology for signal decomposition and selection of significant components. This goal was successfully achieved since the characteristics of two basis functions determined by the evolutionary algorithm, were extremely similar to the first two components received with both, PCA and ICA (see [24], [6]), and those two basis functions were always selected by the reduction algorithms. Additionally, as it can be clearly seen in Fig. 2, the system, after the signal decomposition, pointed out several other important components that provide an ability to discern between the EPs in the database (guaranteed by the reduction algorithm – indiscernibility relation holds). Additionally, the algorithm determined some clear differences between two main classes of the analyzed evoked potentials – *normal* vs. *cooled*, which was the main goal of the neuro-physiological experiments underlying our project.

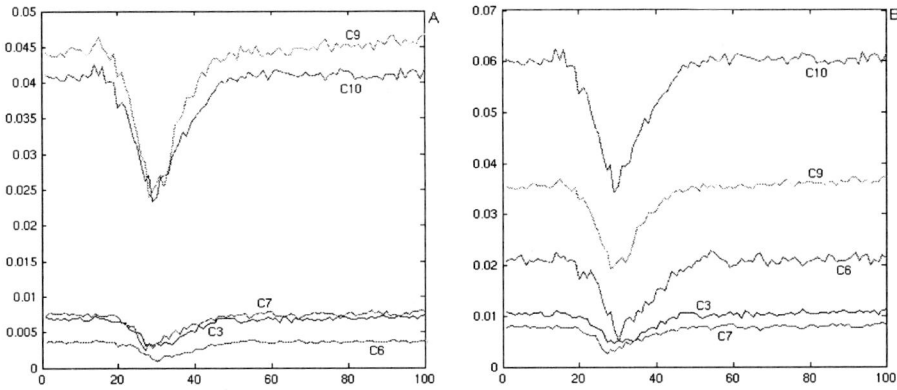

Fig. 2. Comparison of the reduced averaged components between *normal* (A) and *cooled* (B) 3rd channel (Cx denotes the averaged x-th component). Discretization method: *Equal Frequency Bin*. Reduction method: *Johnson's Algorithm* (reduct: *[C3, C6, C7, C9, C10]*).

6 Conclusions

On the basis of the experiments described above, we can conclude that the proposed EA and RS-based hybrid system provides a useful and effective tool in terms of EP decomposition and classification. Our results, obtained via the SCOB methodology, were coherent with previous work in terms of the signal's main components, which suggests that this approach delivers comparable capabilities in terms of signal decomposition. On the other hand, the system provides a significant extension to the traditional approaches thanks to the potentially overcomplete representation of the input data as well as the mechanisms for an automatic determination of relevant components, in terms of signal classification.

References

1. Freeman, W. J.: Measurement of Cortical Evoked Potentials by Decomposition of their Wave Forms. J. of Cybernetics and Information Science, **2-4** (1979) 22–56
2. Chapman, R.M. and McCrary, J.W.: EP Component Identification and Measurement by Principal Components Analysis. Brain and Cognition. **27** (1995) 288–301
3. Makeig, S., Bell, A. J., Jung, T.-P., and Sejnowski, T. J.: Independent Component Analysis of Electroencephalographic Data. Advances in Neural Information Processing Systems **8** (1996) 145–151
4. Makeig, S., Jung, T.-P., Bell, A. J., Ghahremani, D., and Sejnowski, T. J.: Blind Separation of Auditory Event-related Brain Responses into Independent Components. Proc. Natl. Acad. Sci. USA **94** (1997) 10979–10984
5. Raz, J., Dickerson, L., and Turetsky, B.: A Wavelet Packet Model of Evoked Potentials. Brain and Language **66** (1999) 61–88

6. Milanova, M., Smolinski, T. G., Boratyn, G. M., Zurada, J. M., and Wrobel, A.: Sparse Correlation Kernel Analysis and Evolutionary Algorithm-based Modeling of the Sensory Activity within the Rat's Barrel Cortex. Proc. of the International Workshop on Pattern Recognition with Support Vector Machines (SVM2002), Niagara Falls, Canada, August 10 (2002)
7. Olshausen, B. and Field, D. J.: Sparse Coding with an Overcomplete Basis Set: A Strategy Employed by V1? Vision Research **37(23)** (1997) 3311–3325
8. Olshausen, B.: Sparse Codes and Spikes. In: Rao, R. P. N., Olshausen, B. A., Lewicki, M. S. (eds.): Probabilistic Models of Perception and Brain Function. MIT Press, Cambridge, MA (2001) 245–260
9. Chen, S., Donoho, D. L., and Saunders, M. A.: Atomic Decomposition by Basis Pursuit. Technical report, Dept. Stat., Stanford University (1996)
10. Mallat, S. G. and Zhang, Z.: Matching Pursuits with Time-Frequency Dictionaries. IEEE Trans. on Signal Processing **41(12)** (1993) 3397–3415
11. Lewicki, M. and Sejnowski, T.: Learning Overcomplete Representations. Neural Computation **12** (2000) 337–365
12. Swiniarski, R.: Rough Sets and Principal Component Analysis and Their Applications in Data Model Building and Classification. In: Pal, S. K. and Skowron, A. (eds.): Rough Fuzzy Hybridization: A New Trend in Decision-Making. Springer-Verlag, Singapore (1999) 275–300
13. Vapnik, V.: The Nature of Statistical Learning Theory. Springer-Verlag, New York (1995)
14. Lewicki, M. S. and Olshausen, B. A.: Probabilistic Framework for Adaptation and Comparison of Image Codes. J. Opt. Soc. of Am., **16** (1999) 1587–1600
15. Field, D. J.: What is the Goal of Sensory Coding? Neural Computation **6** (1994) 559–601
16. Yoshioka, M. and Omatu, S.: Independent Component Analysis Using Time Delayed Sampling. IEEE International Joint Conference on Neural Networks, Como, Italy, July 24–27 (2000)
17. Michalewicz, Z.: Genetic Algorithms + Data Structures = Evolution Programs. Springer-Verlag, New York (1996)
18. Jolliffe, I. T.: Principal Component Analysis. Springer-Verlag, New York (1986)
19. Pawlak, Z.: Rough Sets. International J. of Computer and Information Sciences **11** (1982) 341–356
20. Marek, W. and Pawlak, Z.: Rough Sets and Information Systems. Fundamenta Matematicae **17** (1984) 105–115
21. Nguyen, S. H. and Nguyen, H. S.: Discretization Methods in Data Mining. In: Polkowski, L. and Skowron A. (eds.): Rough Sets in Knowledge Discovery. Physica-Verlag, Heidelberg (1998) 451–482
22. Nguyen, S. H.: Discretization Problems for Rough Set Methods. Proc. of the First International Conference on Rough Sets and Current Trend in Computing (RSCTC'98), June 1998, Warsaw, Poland (1998) 545–552.
23. Wrobel, A., Kublik, E., and Musial, P.: Gating of the Sensory Activity within Barrel Cortex of the Awake Rat. Exp. Brain Res. **123** (1998) 117–123
24. Kublik, E., Musial, P., and Wrobel, A.: Identification of Principal Components in Cortical Evoked Potentials by Brief Surface Cooling. Clinical Neurophysiology **112** (2001) 1720–1725
25. ROSETTA: A Rough Set Toolkit for Analysis of Data. Available: http://www.idi.ntnu.no/~aleks/rosetta/

Rough Mereological Localization and Navigation

Adam Szmigielski

Polish-Japanese Institute of Information Technology
Koszykowa 86, 02-008 Warsaw, Poland
Institute of Control and Computation Engineering, Warsaw University of Technology
Nowowiejska 15/19, 00-665 Warsaw, Poland
aszmigie@pjwstk.edu.pl

Abstract. In this paper we present localization and navigation method based on rough mereology introduced by Polkowski and Skowron [8], which can make the bridges between linguistic and quantity spatial descriptions. Localization can be described as functional relations between localizing object and reference objects. If we define these relations within theory of rough mereology we have semantical description of object localization and by the numerical determination we obtain quantitative models. We also present simulation results of mobile robot localization and navigation.

1 Introduction

Spatial models should be effective in the sense of numerical complexity, but also they should be enough expressive in the sense of human understanding. While standard, quantitative models, are very well developed and powerful, cannot itself illuminate expression like "near", "front off" or express intentions of robot movement - like "moved further away from" or "go near ". One of the possible ways to express linguistic knowledge is to view the spatial relation as a fuzzy class, defined on the continuum set. Coventry [3] considered spatial expression as the functional relation between reference object and located object. This treatment of spatial localization shifted to satisfy a relation in some degree. Continuum measure can be also obtained by considering the degree of overlap of different regions. Relations between nonempty regions like *'connected'*, *'to be in contact'*, *'convex'* and *'to be a part'* could be efficient for describing spatial relations and could be the base for constructing geometry system [7], [10], [11], [12]. In our work we adopted geometry system proposed by Polkowski and Skowron and based on rough mereology [7].

2 Leśniewski's Systems – Ontology and Mereology

There are different formal systems dealing with natural language. One of them is the *theory of semantical categories*, which is the key to determinacy of Leśniewski's languages. The mereology was the first system developed by

Leśniewski, ontology came next and protothetics followed. The logical order of these system is inverse - the most elementary is prothotethics, which can be used to determine ontology. Mereology is based on these both systems.

2.1 Ontology

Ontology was intended by Stanisław Leśniewski as a formulation of names calculus, where all names (whether empty, singular or general) are grouped into one *semantical category*. All logical expressions, included semantical categories and different then them are called *functors*. Every functor in Leśniewski's systems together with its arguments constitutes the category of *propositions* or *names*. The general functor of Leśniewski ontology is denoted with the symbol ϵ and defined as follow:

$$X \epsilon Y \iff (\exists_Z Z \epsilon X) \land (\forall_{U,W} U \epsilon X \land W \epsilon X \Rightarrow U \epsilon W) \land (\forall_Z Z \epsilon X \Rightarrow Z \epsilon Y) \quad (1)$$

The meaning of primitive therm of ontology ϵ ("being") stands nearest the symbol $\in$ (when symbol $\in$ is used to describe the relation of membership between set and an element). Similarly, symbol ϵ describes including relation related to *semantical categories*, even if our object are different logical type.

For spatial, semantical categories we can say that $X \epsilon Y$ (region X *is* Y) iff the following conditions are satisfied:

1. $\exists_Z Z \epsilon X$ - this asserts the existence of region Z which is X, so X is nonempty region.
2. $\forall_{U,W} U \epsilon X \land W \epsilon X \Rightarrow U \epsilon W$ - this asserts that any two regions which are X are each other.
3. $\forall_Z Z \epsilon X \Rightarrow Z \epsilon Y$ - this asserts that every region which is X is also region Y as well. It also mean that region X is contained in region Y.

2.2 Mereology

Mereology is the theory of collective classes i.e. individual entities representing general name as opposed to Ontology which is a theory of distributive classes i.e. general names. The distinction between a distributive class and its collective class counterpart is like the distinction between a family of sets and its union being a set. Mereology may be based on each of few notions like those of *part*, an *element*, a *class* a *connection*, a *contact* or *convex*. Historically it has been conceived by Stanisław Leśniewski [4] as a theory of the relation *part*. Names of mereological constructs of predicate *part pt* could be formed by means of ontological rules as follow:

- **M1** $X \epsilon pt(Y) \Rightarrow X \epsilon X \land Y \epsilon Y$ - this mean that predicate *pt* is defined for nonempty regions.
- **M2** $X \epsilon pt(Y) \land Y \epsilon pt(Z) \Rightarrow X \epsilon pt(Z)$ - this mean that predicate *pt* is transitive.
- **M3** $\neg(X \epsilon pt(X))$ - this mean that predicate *pt* is non-reflexive and defines proper part.

The notion of element can be defined as $X \epsilon el(Y) \iff X \epsilon pt(Y) \lor X = Y$.

3 Rough Mereology

Leśniewski's mereology can be extended by the predicate of *being in a part in a degree*. This predicate is rendered as a family μ_r parameterized by a real parameter $r \in [0,1]$ with the intent that $X\epsilon\mu_r(Y)$ reads *"X is a part of Y in degree r"*. We recall the set of axioms introduced by Polkowski and Skowron [8].

- **RM1** $X\epsilon\mu_1(Y) \Leftrightarrow X\epsilon el(Y)$ - this means that being a part in degree 1 is equivalent to being an element. It also means that region X is included in region Y or both regions are equal.
- **RM2** $X\epsilon\mu_1(Y) \Rightarrow \forall_Z (Z\epsilon\mu_r(X) \Rightarrow Z\epsilon\mu_r(Y))$ - meaning the monotonicity property: any region Z is a part of region Y in degree not smaller than that of being a part in X whenever X is an element of Y.
- **RM3** $(X = Y \wedge X\epsilon\mu_r(Z)) \Rightarrow Y\epsilon\mu_r(Z)$ - this means that the identity of individual is a congruence with respect to μ
- **RM4** $(X\epsilon\mu_r(Y) \wedge s \leq r) \Rightarrow X\epsilon\mu_s(Y)$ - establish the meaning "a part in degree at least r" It means that if some region is a part in some degree is also a part in smaller degree.

Rough mereology can make the bridges between the qualitative and quantitative spatial description by the numericall determination of region-based relations. We recall Pawlak and Skowron [6] idea of rough membership function. For given two non-empty regions X, Y we have

$$\mu_X(Y) = \frac{|X \cap Y|}{|Y|}, \qquad (2)$$

where $|X \cap Y|$ and $|Y|$ are areas of adequate regions. Thus $\mu_X(Y)$ measures degree of partial containing region Y into region X. The value r of rough membership function (2) is numerically equivalent to the degree which region X is a part of region Y.

$$r = \frac{|X \cap Y|}{|Y|}. \qquad (3)$$

3.1 Spatial Description Based on Rough Mereology

The foundations of rough-mereology geometry system can be found in [7]. Predicates μ_r may be regarded as weak metrics also in the context of geometry. From that point of view we may apply μ in order to define basic notions of rough mereological geometry. We recall [7] a notion of distance κ_r in rough mereological universe by

$$\kappa_r(X,Y) \Longleftrightarrow r = \min\{u, w : X\epsilon\mu_u(Y) \wedge Y\epsilon\mu_w(X)\}. \qquad (4)$$

Rough mereological distance, or shorter *mero-distance*, is defined in an opposite way - the smaller r, the greater distance. Using formula (4) we can define other spatial relations like *nearness*, *between* etc.

3.2 From Linguistic to Quantity Spatial Description by Rough Mereology

Localization can be based on functional relations between localizing and reference objects [3]. However the major difficulty is to distinguish the set of spatial relations useful for specific task, which formalized some spatial intuitions. If we define spatial relations within mereology we can also treat them in semantical categories. It causes complementary interpretations of defined relations. From one point of view we can understand them as sematical (psychological) from other one as an description of physical space. Rough mereology can deal with real world data to numerically specify defined relations. This duality can make the bridges between quality and quantity spatial description.

4 Rough Mereology in Mobile Robot Localization and Navigation – Examples

To illustrate our idea let us give a few examples. Our goal is to define rough mereological relations to express natural language spatial understanding and apply them to mobile robot localization and navigation.

4.1 System Description

Our navigation system consists of one, omni-directional transmiter, located on the robot and set of receivers placed in the robot environment to describe topology of building - walls, corridors, corners etc. The navigation system can measure distances from robot to receivers and also distance to the nearest obstacle. The set of measurements is the base to define some regions. One of them is associated with the non-collision robot movement area and others are receiver regions. The configuration of non-collision region with one receiver region is shown in Fig. 1.

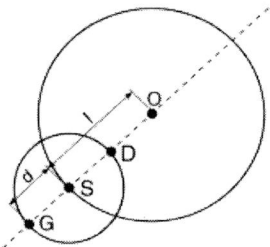

Fig. 1. Omni-directional transmitter is located at the point S and receiver at the point O. Non-collision region is the disk with the center S and the radius d. Receiver region is the disk with the center O and radius l. In our configuration point S is always located on the boundary circle of receiver region.

Both regions shown in Fig. 1 have always non-empty intersection region. It means, that we can calculate the mereo-distance κ_{SO} of these two regions using formulas (4) and (3)

$$\kappa_{SO} = \min\{\frac{|R_S \cap R_O|}{|R_O|}, \frac{|R_S \cap R_O|}{|R_S|}\}, \tag{5}$$

where R_S is as non-collision region and R_O is receiver region. It is easy to show, that mereo-distance is smallest when both radii are equal $d = l$. Movement control is limited to two control parameters - rotation angle α and the length of movement.

4.2 Tasks of Localization and Navigation

Coming Close to the Receiver. In robot navigation we may want robot to come closer to receiver. That requirements can be formulated in mereological language by definition functor *Closeness Cl*

$$X \epsilon Cl(Y) \Longleftrightarrow \kappa(X, Y) = max \tag{6}$$

Regions in Fig. 1 are close iff radius of non-collision region is equal radius of receiver region.
According to *Closeness* definition non-collision region in Fig. 2 specified with dotted line is not close to receiver region. Region, which is close to receiver is included in non-collision region and we can tread it as also non-collision region. In that situation we can recognize, that robot is close to receiver. The idea of closeness depends not only absolute distance, but also on environment.

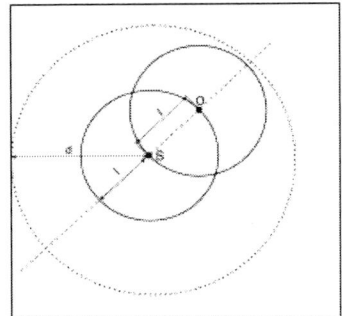

Fig. 2. Distance from point S (transmitter) to point O (receiver) is equal to l, but mereo-distance of non-collision and receiver regions depends on external limitations

The changing radius of non-collision region sometimes cannot satisfy closeness relation. In that case we have to move robot to receiver. In Fig. 1 the best trajectory of movement is marked with dotted line. To follow that trajectory robot should obtain correct direction. It can be done by dynamically changing robot orientation for bettering direction. For the constant value of radius d, we can calculate mereo-distances between transmitter regions and receiver regions when the transmitter is located in points G, S and D (see Fig. 1). Denoting by κ_{GO}, κ_{SO} and κ_{DO} adequate mereo-distances following inequality is satisfied $\kappa_{GO} < \kappa_{SO} < \kappa_{DO}$. For simplicity we assume that length of movement is maximal and equal to d. Table below presents relation between mereo-distances of receiver and non-collision regions, distances between receiver and transmitter and rotate angle in the most characteristic cases.

	mereo-distance	distance of centers	rotate angle
the best case	κ_{DO}	1 - d	$0°$
the same	κ_{SO}	1	$\frac{\pi}{2}$
the worst case	κ_{GO}	1+d	π

Taking into consideration intermediary values of distances we propose to calculate the angle of rotation as the function of next mereo-distance of both regions κ_{XO} as follows

$$\alpha = \arctan(\gamma \cdot \frac{\kappa_{SO} - \kappa_{XO}}{(\kappa_{XO} - \kappa_{GO})(\kappa_{DO} - \kappa_{XO})}) + \frac{\pi}{2}, \quad (7)$$

where $\gamma = \kappa_{DO} - \kappa_{GO}$ is normalizing coefficient. The mereo-distances κ_{DO}, κ_{SO} and κ_{GO} have to be calculated before movement in every movement step. The control rules can be described as follow:

1. If the value of calculated angle is bigger then value of previous angle then change the direction of rotation.
2. If the area of receiver region is bigger then non-collision move robot to receiver, otherwise robot is close to receiver.

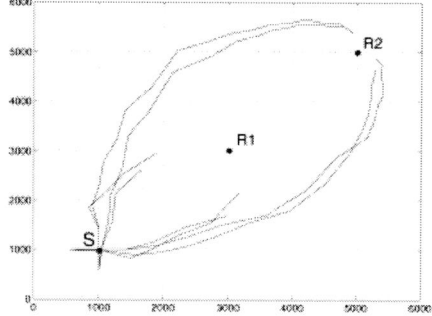

Fig. 3. Two Sets of trajectories - four trajectories from point $S(1000, 1000)$ close to point $R_1(3000, 3000)$ and four trajectories close to point $R_2(5000, 5000)$. Robot moves in the rectangular room with the corners in the points $(0, 0)$ and $(6000, 6000)$ with different starting orientation $0°$, $90°$, $180°$ and $270°$.

Driving robot in straight line. Another movement intention is requirement robot to move in the straight line. It could be done with by defining *Nearness* N and *Equidistance* E_q functors

$$Z \epsilon N(X, Y) \iff Z \epsilon Z \wedge (\kappa_r(Z, X) \wedge \kappa_s(Z, Y) \Rightarrow s < r). \quad (8)$$

Nearness means, that region Z is close to region X that Y. If neither region X is closer then region Y nor region Y is not closer then region X both region are in the same mereo-distance to region Z.

$$Z \epsilon E_q(X,Y) \Leftrightarrow Z \epsilon Z \wedge (\neg(X \epsilon N(Z,Y)) \wedge \neg(Y \epsilon N(Z,X))). \tag{9}$$

In our case equidistance is the straight line ortogonal to line liking two receivers and intersecting it. If O_1 and O_2 are receiver regions then the function

$$g(\kappa_{O_1}S, \kappa_{O_2}S) = | \frac{\kappa_{O_1}S - \kappa_{O_2}S}{\kappa_{O_1}S + \kappa_{O_2}S} | \tag{10}$$

is equal to zero in equidistance and positive otherwise. The robot orientation is proper iff during movement the value of function (10) is equal to zero and does not change. The proposed method minimizes the value of function (10) by applying following rules:

1. If present value of function (10) is smaller then previous (or equal to zero) do not change direction,
2. otherwise change direction via the formula

$$\alpha = \tau \cdot \frac{\kappa_{O_1}S - \kappa_{O_2}S}{\kappa_{O_1}S + \kappa_{O_2}S} \cdot \pi, \tag{11}$$

where τ is coefficient $\tau \in \{-1, 1\}$, which distinguishes the left and right side of equidistance.

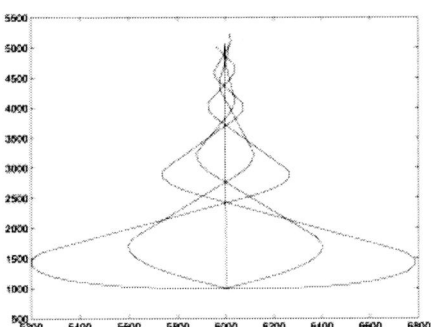

Fig. 4. The set of trajectories for robot moving along the line $x = 6000$. Starting point is $(6000, 1000)$ with orientations $0°$, $45°$, $90°$, $-45°$ and $-90°$. The receivers are located in the point $O_1 = (5000, 5000)$ i $O_2 = (7000, 5000)$.

Turning the robot. If our intention is to turn robot we can use the same functors like in the case moving straight line. If we can navigate robot in straight line we can also build more complicated trajectory by composing trajectory with the segments of straight lines. As a typical example we can consider the task of turning robot. It could be done in three stages

1. to go straight,
2. to reach the point of changing the navigated pair of receivers,
3. to go following the new navigating points.

The first and third stages are tasks of 'going the straight line'. The moment of switching the pair of receivers can be identified according to function (10). Obtained results are presented in Fig. 5.

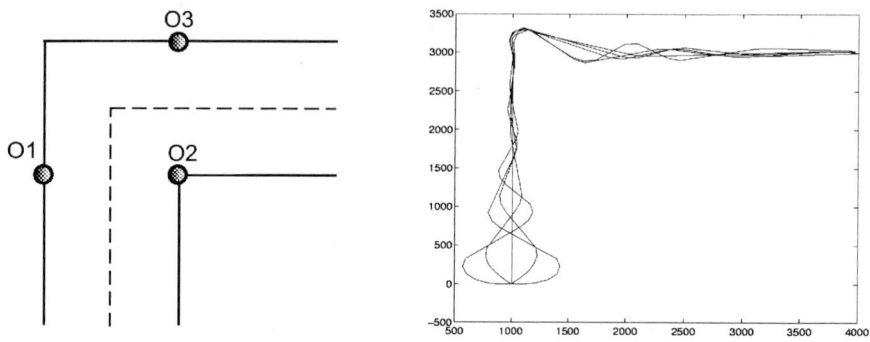

Fig. 5. Started point is $(0, 1000)$ with different orientations $0°$, $45°$, $90°$, $-45°$ i $-90°$. Coordinates of receivers are $O_1 = (0, 2000)$, $O_2 = (2000, 2000)$ and $O_3 = (2000, 4000)$

Acknowledgment. This work was supported by the grant of The State Committee for Scientific Research of Republic of Poland (KBN) number 8T11C02417.

References

1. van Benthem: "The logic of time", Reidel, Dortrecht, 1983
2. T. Bittner, J.G. Stell: "Rough sets in approximate spatial reasoning", RSCTC'2000, Springer Verlag 2000
3. Coventry, Kenny R.: "Spatial preposition, functional relation and lexical specification" in Representation and Processing of Spatial Expression, eds. P. Olivier and K. Gapp, Lawrence Erlbaum Associates, 1996
4. J.T.J. Srzednicki, V.F. Rickey: "Lesniewski's Systems Ontology and Mereology", Ossolineum, 1984
5. Amitabha Mukerjee: "Neat vs Scruffy: A survey of Computationa Models for Spatial Expresion" in Representation and Processing of Spatial Expression, eds. P. Olivier and K. Gapp, Lawrence Erlbaum Associates, 1997
6. Z. Pawlak, A. Skowron: "Rough membership function" in R.R. Yager, M. Fedrizzi, J. Kacprzyk (eds.), Advanced in Dempster-Schafer Theory of Evidence, John Wiley and Sons, New York 1994, pp. 251–271.
7. L. Polkowski, A. Skowron: "Rough Mereology in Information System with Application to Qualitative Spatial Reasoning", Fundamenta Informaticae 43 (2000) 291–320 IOS Press

8. L. Polkowski, A. Skowron: "Rough mereology: a new paradigm for approximate reasoning, International Journal of Approximate Reasoning 15(4), 1997, pp. 333–365
9. I. Pratt-Hartmann: "Empiricism and Rationalism in Region-based Theories of Space", Fundamenta Informaticae 34 (2000) 1–31, IOS Press
10. I. Pratt O. Lemon: "Ontologies for Plane, Polygonal Mereotopology", Technical raport issued by the Department of Computer Science, Manchester University, January 1997
11. I. Pratt D. Schoop: "Expressivity in Polygonal, Plane Mereotopology", Technical raport issued by the Department of Computer Science, Manchester University, May 1998
12. Alfred Tarski: "Foundations of the geometry of solids", Logic, Semantics, Metamathematics. Oxford: Claredon Press, 1956

Author Index

Ahn, T.C. 594
Alpigini, James J. 183, 289

Bazan, Jan 307, 522
Beynon, Malcolm J. 61, 530
Boratyn, Grzegorz M. 621
Borkowski, Maciej 218, 300, 594
Butz, C.J. 339, 344, 349, 389

Carretero, Jesús 449
Cattaneo, Gianpiero 69, 77
Chen, Li 572
Chiang, Yi-Ting 226
Chiang, Yu-Cheng 226
Choi, Hyung-Il 564
Ciucci, Davide 69, 77
Córdoba, María L. 449
Crespo, F. Javier 441
Cuadrado, Juan J. 497

Dardzińska, Agnieszka 189
Dong, Ju-Zhen 467
Dubois, Vincent 239

El-Kwae, Essam A. 564
Engel, Paulo Martins 234

Fei, Xue 514
Fernandez, Covadonga 421
Filho, Homero Chaib 234

García, Félix 449
Giove, Silvio 247
Góra, Grzegorz 405
Greco, Salvatore 44, 85, 93, 247, 255
Grzymała-Busse, Jerzy W. 538

Hadjimichael, Michael 421
Hamilton, H.J. 506
Hippe, Monika P. 546
Hippe, Zdzisław S. 538
Hirano, Shoji 554
Hochsztain, Esther 479
Hsu, Tsan-sheng 226
Hu, Xiaohua 487

Intan, Rolly 357
Inuiguchi, Masahiro 85, 105

Järvinen, Jouni 123
Jang, Seok-Woo 564
Janicki, Ryszard 113
Jiang, S.L. 139

Katarzyniak, Radoslaw 131
Komorowski, Jan 13, 144

Laplante, P. 610
Latkowski, Rafał 413
Lee, Seungkoo 568
Li, Yuefeng 493
Liau, Churn-Jung 226
Lin, Tsau Young 14, 296
Lingras, Pawan 263
Liu, Qing 139

Małuszyński, Jan 205
Marban, Oscar 497
Martinez, Juan F. 421
Matarazzo, Benedetto 44, 247, 255
Mateescu, Gabriel 279
Menasalvas, Ernestina 421, 441, 479
Midelfart, Herman 144
Mikołajczyk, Michał 425
Milanova, Mariofanna 621
Millán, Socorro 479
Montes, Cesar 497
Moshkov, Mikhail 156
Mukaidono, Masao 357
Murai, Tetsuya 161

Nakata, Michinori 161
Nguyen, Hung Son 433
Nguyen, Ngoc Thanh 131
Nguyen, Tuan Trung 578

Ohsuga, Setsuo 467
Osmólski, Antoni 522

Paszek, Piotr 586
Pawlak, Zdzisław 1, 93
Peña, José M. 441
Pérez, María S. 449

Peters, James F.   300, 308, 316, 594
Polkowski, Lech   167
Pomykała, J.A.   175
Pons, Ramón A.   449
Prado, Hércules Antonio do   234
Propes, Nicholas   568

Quafafou, Mohamed   239

Raś, Zbigniew W.   189
Ramanna, Sheela   602
Ramsey, Frederick V.   183
Robles, Victor   441
Russell, David W.   33
Rząsa, Wojciech   197, 300

Sanscartier, M.J.   339, 344, 349
Segovia, Javier   497
Sinha, D.   610
Skowron, Andrzej   300, 316, 453, 522
Ślęzak, Dominik   365, 522
Słowiński, Roman   44, 85, 93, 247, 255
Smolinski, Tomasz G.   621
Stefanowski, Jerzy   255, 271
Stepaniuk, Jarosław   316
Suraj, Zbigniew   197, 300
Synak, Piotr   453
Szczuka, Marcin S.   308, 397, 522
Szmigielski, Adam   629

Tanino, Tetsuzo   105

Tsoukiàs, Alexis   271
Tsumoto, Shusaku   373, 381, 554
Türksen, I.B.   60

Vachtsevanos, George   568
Valdés, Julio J.   279
Vitória, Aida   205

Wakulicz-Deja, Alicja   586
Wang, Da-Wei   226
Wang, G.Y.   213
Wang, Jue   461
Wang, Xuewei   506
Wasilewska, Anita   421
Wojna, Arkadiusz   405
Wong, S.K.M.   389
Wrobel, Andrzej   621
Wróblewski, Jakub   365, 397, 522
Wu, D.   389

Yager, Ronald R.   324
Yao, J.T.   331
Yao, Y.Y.   263, 331, 467, 493, 506

Zadeh, Lotfi A.   10
Zhang, Guangfan   568
Zhao, Min   461
Zhao, Yongshen   568
Zhong, Ning   467
Ziarko, Wojciech   514
Zurada, Jacek M.   621

Lecture Notes in Artificial Intelligence (LNAI)

Vol. 2333: J.-J.Ch. Meyer, M. Tambe (Eds.), Intelligent Agents VIII. Revised Papers, 2001. XI, 461 pages. 2001.

Vol. 2336: M.-S. Chen, P.S. Yu, B. Liu (Eds.), Advances in Knowledge Discovery and Data Mining. Proceedings, 2002. XIII, 568 pages. 2002.

Vol. 2338: R. Cohen, B. Spencer (Eds.), Advances in Artificial Intelligence. Proceedings, 2002. XII, 373 pages. 2002.

Vol. 2356: R. Kohavi, B.M. Masand, M. Spiliopoulou, J. Srivastava (Eds.), WEBKDD 2002 – Mining Web Log Data Across All Customers Touch Points. Proceedings, 2002. XI, 167 pages. 2002.

Vol. 2358: T. Hendtlass, M. Ali (Eds.), Developments in Applied Artificial Intelligence. Proceedings, 2002 XIII, 833 pages. 2002.

Vol. 2366: M.-S. Hacid, Z.W. Raś, D.A. Zighed, Y. Kodratoff (Eds.), Foundations of Intelligent Systems. Proceedings, 2002. XII, 614 pages. 2002.

Vol. 2371: S. Koenig, R.C. Holte (Eds.), Abstraction, Reformulation, and Approximation. Proceedings, 2002. XI, 349 pages. 2002.

Vol. 2375: J. Kivinen, R.H. Sloan (Eds.), Computational Learning Theory. Proceedings, 2002. XI, 397 pages. 2002.

Vol. 2377: A. Birk, S. Coradeschi, T. Satoshi (Eds.), RoboCup 2001: Robot Soccer World Cup V. XIX, 763 pages. 2002.

Vol. 2381: U. Egly, C.G. Fermüller (Eds.), Automated Reasoning with Analytic Tableaux and Related Methods. Proceedings, 2002. X, 341 pages. 2002 .

Vol. 2385: J. Calmet, B. Benhamou, O. Caprotti, L. Henocque, V. Sorge (Eds.), Artificial Intelligence, Automated Reasoning, and Symbolic Computation. Proceedings, 2002. XI, 343 pages. 2002.

Vol. 2389: E. Ranchhod, N.J. Mamede (Eds.), Advances in Natural Language Processing. Proceedings, 2002. XII, 275 pages. 2002.

Vol. 2392: A. Voronkov (Ed.), Automated Deduction – CADE-18. Proceedings, 2002. XII, 534 pages. 2002.

Vol. 2393: U. Priss, D. Corbett, G. Angelova (Eds.), Conceptual Structures: Integration and Interfaces. Proceedings, 2002. XI, 397 pages. 2002.

Vol. 2394: P. Perner (Ed.), Advances in Data Mining. VII, 109 pages. 2002.

Vol. 2403: Mark d'Inverno, M. Luck, M. Fisher, C. Preist (Eds.), Foundations and Applications of Multi-Agent Systems. Proceedings, 1996-2000. X, 261 pages. 2002.

Vol. 2407: A.C. Kakas, F. Sadri (Eds.), Computational Logic: Logic Programming and Beyond. Part I. XII, 678 pages. 2002.

Vol. 2408: A.C. Kakas, F. Sadri (Eds.), Computational Logic: Logic Programming and Beyond. Part II. XII, 628 pages. 2002.

Vol. 2413: K. Kuwabara, J. Lee (Eds.), Intelligent Agents and Multi-Agent Systems. Proceedings, 2002. X, 221 pages. 2002.

Vol. 2416: S. Craw, A. Preece (Eds.), Advances in Case-Based Reasoning. Proceedings, 2002. XII, 656 pages. 2002.

Vol. 2417: M. Ishizuka, A. Sattar (Eds.), PRICAI 2002: Trends in Artificial Intelligence. Proceedings, 2002. XX, 623 pages. 2002.

Vol. 2424: S. Flesca, G. Ianni (Eds.), Logics in Artificial Intelligence. Proceedings, 2002. XIII, 572 pages. 2002.

Vol. 2430: T. Elomaa, H. Mannila, H. Toivonen (Eds.), Machine Learning: ECML 2002. Proceedings, 2002. XIII, 532 pages. 2002.

Vol. 2431: T. Elomaa, H. Mannila, H. Toivonen (Eds.), Principles of Data Mining and Knowledge Discovery. Proceedings, 2002. XIV, 514 pages. 2002.

Vol. 2443: D. Scott (Ed.), Artificial Intelligence: Methodology, Systems, and Applications. Proceedings, 2002. X, 279 pages. 2002.

Vol. 2445: C. Anagnostopoulou, M. Ferrand, A. Smaill (Eds.), Music and Artificial Intelligence. Proceedings, 2002. VIII, 207 pages. 2002.

Vol. 2446: M. Klusch, S. Ossowski, O. Shehory (Eds.), Cooperative Information Agents VI. Proceedings, 2002. XI, 321 pages. 2002.

Vol. 2447: D.J. Hand, N.M. Adams, R.J. Bolton (Eds.), Pattern Detection and Discovery. Proceedings, 2002. XII, 227 pages. 2002.

Vol. 2448: P. Sojka, I. Kopeček, K. Pala (Eds.), Text, Speech and Dialogue. Proceedings, 2002. XII, 481 pages. 2002.

Vol. 2464: M. O'Neill, R.F.E. Sutcliffe, C. Ryan, M. Eaton, N. Griffith (Eds.), Artificial Intelligence and Cognitive Science. Proceedings, 2002. XI, 247 pages. 2002.

Vol. 2475: J.J. Alpigini, J.F. Peters, A. Skowron, N. Zhong (Eds.), Rough Sets and Current Trends in Computing. Proceedings, 2002. XV, 640 pages. 2002.

Vol. 2479: M. Jarke, J. Koehler, G. Lakemeyer (Eds.), KI 2002: Advances in Artificial Intelligence. Proceedings, 2002. XIII, 327 pages.

Vol. 2484: P. Adriaans, H. Fernau, M. van Zaanen (Eds.), Grammatical Inference: Algorithms and Applications. Proceedings, 2002. IX, 315 pages. 2002.

Lecture Notes in Computer Science

Vol. 2445: C. Anagnostopoulou, M. Ferrand, A. Smaill (Eds.), Music and Artificial Intelligence. Proceedings, 2002. VIII, 207 pages. 2002. (Subseries LNAI).

Vol. 2446: M. Klusch, S. Ossowski, O. Shehory (Eds.), Cooperative Information Agents VI. Proceedings, 2002. XI, 321 pages. 2002. (Subseries LNAI).

Vol. 2447: D.J. Hand, N.M. Adams, R.J. Bolton (Eds.), Pattern Detection and Discovery. Proceedings, 2002. XII, 227 pages. 2002. (Subseries LNAI).

Vol. 2448: P. Sojka, I. Kopeček, K. Pala (Eds.), Text, Speech and Dialogue. Proceedings, 2002. XII, 481 pages. 2002. (Subseries LNAI).

Vol. 2449: L. Van Gool (Ed.), Pattern Recognotion. Proceedings, 2002. XVI, 628 pages. 2002.

Vol. 2451: B. Hochet, A.J. Acosta, M.J. Bellido (Eds.), Integrated Circuit Design. Proceedings, 2002. XVI, 496 pages. 2002.

Vol. 2452: R. Guigó, D. Gusfield (Eds.), Algorithms in Bioinformatics. Proceedings, 2002. X, 554 pages. 2002.

Vol. 2453: A. Hameurlain, R. Cicchetti, R. Traunmüller (Eds.), Database and Expert Systems Applications. Proceedings, 2002. XVIII, 954 pages. 2002.

Vol. 2454: Y. Kambayashi, W. Winiwarter, M. Arikawa (Eds.), Data Warehousing and Knowledge Discovery. Proceedings, 2002. XIII, 339 pages. 2002.

Vol. 2455: K. Bauknecht, A M. Tjoa, G. Quirchmayr (Eds.), E-Commerce and Web Technologies. Proceedings, 2002. XIV, 414 pages. 2002.

Vol. 2456: R. Traunmüller, K. Lenk (Eds.), Electronic Government. Proceedings, 2002. XIII, 486 pages. 2002.

Vol. 2458: M. Agosti, C. Thanos (Eds.), Research and Advanced Technology for Digital Libraries. Proceedings, 2002. XVI, 664 pages. 2002.

Vol. 2459: M.C. Calzarossa, S. Tucci (Eds.), Performance Evaluation of Complex Systems: Techniques and Tools. Proceedings, 2002. VIII, 501 pages. 2002.

Vol. 2460: J.-M. Jézéquel, H. Hussmann, S. Cook (Eds.), «UML» 2002 – The Unified Modeling Language. Proceedings, 2002. XII, 449 pages. 2002.

Vol. 2461: R. Möhring, R. Raman (Eds.), Algorithms – ESA 2002. Proceedings, 2002. XIV, 917 pages. 2002.

Vol. 2462: K. Jansen, S. Leonardi, V. Vazirani (Eds.), Approximation Algorithms for Combinatorial Optimization. Proceedings, 2002. VIII, 271 pages. 2002.

Vol. 2463: M. Dorigo, G. Di Caro, M. Sampels (Eds.), Ant Algorithms. Proceedings, 2002. XIII, 305 pages. 2002.

Vol. 2464: M. O'Neill, R.F.E. Sutcliffe, C. Ryan, M. Eaton, N. Griffith (Eds.), Artificial Intelligence and Cognitive Science. Proceedings, 2002. XI, 247 pages. 2002. (Subseries LNAI).

Vol. 2465: H. Arisawa, Y. Kambayashi (Eds.), Conceptual Modeling for New Information Systems Technologies. Proceedings, 2001. XVII, 500 pages. 2002.

Vol. 2469: W. Damm, E.-R. Olderog (Eds.), Formal Techniques in Real-Time and Fault-Tolerant Systems. Proceedings, 2002. X, 455 pages. 2002.

Vol. 2470: P. Van Hentenryck (Ed.), Principles and Practice of Constraint Programming – CP 2002. Proceedings, 2002. XVI, 794 pages. 2002.

Vol. 2471: J. Bradfield (Ed.), Computer Science Logic. Proceedings, 2002. XII, 613 pages. 2002.

Vol. 2475: J.J. Alpigini, J.F. Peters, A. Skowron, N. Zhong (Eds.), Rough Sets and Current Trends in Computing. Proceedings, 2002. XV, 640 pages. 2002. (Subseries LNAI).

Vol. 2476: A.H.F. Laender, A.L. Oliveira (Eds.), String Processing and Information Retrieval. Proceedings, 2002. XI, 337 pages. 2002.

Vol. 2477: M.V. Hermenegildo, G. Puebla (Eds.), Static Analysis. Proceedings, 2002. XI, 527 pages. 2002.

Vol. 2478: M.J. Egenhofer, D.M. Mark (Eds.), Geographic Information Science. Proceedings, 2002. X, 363 pages. 2002.

Vol. 2479: M. Jarke, J. Koehler, G. Lakemeyer (Eds.), KI 2002: Advances in Artificial Intelligence. Proceedings, 2002. XIII, 327 pages. (Subseries LNAI).

Vol. 2480: Y. Han, S. Tai, D. Wikarski (Eds.), Engineering and Deployment of Cooperative Information Systems. Proceedings, 2002. XIII, 564 pages. 2002.

Vol. 2483: J.D.P. Rolim, S. Vadhan (Eds.), Randomization and Approximation Techniques in Computer Science. Proceedings, 2002. VIII, 275 pages. 2002.

Vol. 2484: P. Adriaans, H. Fernau, M. van Zaanen (Eds.), Grammatical Inference: Algorithms and Applications. Proceedings, 2002. IX, 315 pages. 2002. (Subseries LNAI).

Vol. 2488: T. Dohi, R. Kikinis (Eds), Medical Image Computing and Computer-Assisted Intervention – MICCAI 2002. Proceedings, Part I. XXIX, 807 pages. 2002.

Vol. 2489: T. Dohi, R. Kikinis (Eds), Medical Image Computing and Computer-Assisted Intervention – MICCAI 2002. Proceedings, Part II. XXIX, 693 pages. 2002.

Vol. 2496: K.C. Almeroth, M. Hasan (Eds.), Management of Multimedia in the Internet. Proceedings, 2002. XI, 355 pages. 2002.

Vol. 2498: G. Borriello, L.E. Holmquist (Eds.), UbiComp 2002: Ubiquitous Computing. Proceedings, 2002. XV, 380 pages. 2002.